Study Guide and T...

David W. Findlay
Colby College

Farrokh R. Zandi
York University

MACROECONOMICS

Second Canadian Edition

Olivier Blanchard
Massachusetts Institute of Technology

David Johnson
Wilfrid Laurier University

Angelo Melino
University of Toronto

Toronto

© 2003 Pearson Education Canada Inc., Toronto, Ontario.
Original U.S. edition published by Prentice-Hall, Inc., a division of Pearson Education, Upper Saddle River, NJ 07458. Copyright © 2000. This edition is authorized for sale in Canada only.

All rights reserved. This publication is protected by copyright, and permission should be obtained from the publisher prior to any prohibited reproduction, storage in a retrieval system, or transmission in any form or by any means, electronic, mechanical, photocopying, recording, or likewise. For information regarding permission, write to the Permissions Department.

0-13-120020-8

Acquisitions Editor: Gary Bennett
Senior Developmental Editor: Madhu Ranadive
Production Editor: Cheryl Jackson
Production Coordinator: Deborah Starks

5 WC 06 05

Printed and bound in Canada.

TABLE OF CONTENTS

Preface		v
Chapter 1	A Tour of the World	1
Chapter 2	A Tour of the Book	6
Appendix	National Income and Product Accounts	18
Chapter 3	The Goods Market	23
Chapter 4	Financial Markets	40
Chapter 5	Goods and Financial Markets: The *IS-LM* Model	56
Chapter 6	Openness in Goods and Financial Markets	72
Chapter 7	The Goods Market in an Open Economy	85
Chapter 8	Output, the Interest Rate, and the Exchange Rate	95
Chapter 9	The Labour Market	108
Chapter 10	Putting All Markets Together: The *AS-AD* Model	119
Chapter 11	The Phillips Curve	130
Chapter 12	Inflation, Activity and Money Growth	139
Chapter 13	Exchange Rates in the Medium Run: Adjustments, Crises, and Regimes	149
Chapter 14	The Facts of Growth	161
Chapter 15	Saving, Capital Accumulation, and Output	170
Chapter 16	Technological Progress and Growth	182
Chapter 17	Economic Growth in the Open Economy	196
Chapter 18	Expectations: The Basic Tools	202
Chapter 19	Financial Markets and Expectations	219
Chapter 20	Expectations, Consumption, and Investment	235
Chapter 21	Expectations, Output, and Policy	246
Chapter 22	Pathologies I: High Unemployment	259
Chapter 23	Pathologies II: High Inflation	270
Chapter 24	Pathologies III: Transition in Eastern Europe and the Asian Crisis	279
Chapter 25	Should Policy Makers Be Restrained?	288
Chapter 26	Monetary Policy: A Summing Up	295
Chapter 27	Fiscal Policy: A Summing Up	304
Chapter 28	Epilogue: The Story of Macroeconomics	314

SOLUTIONS TO REVIEW PROBLEMS AND ANSWERS TO
MULTIPLE CHOICE QUESTIONS   323

Preface

This study guide has been developed to accompany *Macroeconomics,* Second Canadian Edition, by Olivier Blanchard, David Johnson, and Angelo Melino. Our primary objectives in the Study Guide and Tutorial are to help you learn the concepts that are presented in the textbook and help you obtain a strong understanding of macroeconomics.

Success in your course depends on your ability to explain and apply the concepts presented in class. Specifically, you <u>must</u> be able to explain intuitively the underlying factors that determine the economic relationships included in the models. Simply memorizing the material is most likely an inefficient allocation of your time. You should, therefore, read the material carefully (several times!), constantly review your lecture notes, and work through the material included in the Study Guide and Tutorial.

We have developed a study guide that gives you an opportunity to work through problems, reinforce the concepts, and apply the concepts. The questions have been constructed in such a way as to take you step by step through the models and their applications. The Study Guide and Tutorial includes approximately 500 self-test questions, over 400 review problems (many of which include multiple parts), and approximately 600 multiple choice questions. While time constraints may prevent you from completing all of the questions, you should complete as many as possible.

Description of Contents

Each chapter of the Study Guide and Tutorial is divided into five sections.

- **Objectives, Review, and Tutorial**

This section includes a list of the objectives for each chapter. You might want to review this list prior to and/or after reading the chapters in the textbook. The objectives are followed by a summary of the key concepts in each chapter. These discussions will help reinforce the material presented. These sections also include highlighted "Learning Tips." We have used the Learning Tips: (1) to emphasize particularly important concepts, (2) to offer an alternative presentation of a concept, and (3) to offer advice about how to study, learn, and apply the material.

- **Self-Test Questions**

This section includes questions about the basic concepts presented in each chapter. The answers to these questions are found on the corresponding page numbers included at the end of each question.

- **Review Problems**

These problems provide opportunities to practice the skills presented in each chapter. We have included a significant number of numerical problems to give you an opportunity to reinforce (and test) your understanding of the material presented in the textbook. We have also included questions that require you to use the graphs presented in the textbook. It is crucial that you become comfortable with the graphical presentation of the material. These questions will help you achieve this goal.

- **Multiple Choice Questions**

The multiple choice questions range in level of difficulty. Like the review problems, these questions require numerical and graphical analysis.

- **Solutions and Answers**

This section (located at the end of the Study Guide and Tutorial) includes the solutions to all problems and answers to all multiple choice questions.

Using the Study Guide and Tutorial

There are many ways to study in this course and to use this Study Guide and Tutorial. You should use the one that works best for you. Having noted that, let us offer you one possible approach.

1. After reading the chapter in the textbook and attending class (there are NO perfect substitutes for these activities!), you can review the list of objectives included in the Study Guide and Tutorial. Make sure you completely understand each of them.

2. If, after reviewing your lecture notes, you still are not comfortable with a particular topic, read through the relevant section of the Objectives, Review, and Tutorial section.

3. Now that you are familiar with the material, you can quickly test your understanding of the concepts by answering the self-test questions. We recommend that you jot down your answers to these questions on a separate piece of paper. Check your answers by referring to the relevant textbook pages (included, for your convenience, at the end of each question). If you cannot answer these questions, you should review the textbook material as soon as possible.

4. The best way to learn and reinforce your understanding of the concepts is to work through the review problems. We have included a mix of problems that give you an opportunity to apply the material. After you complete a problem, check your solution with that found in the Solution section. Once again, if you have difficulty with the problem, you should review: (1) the relevant section of the Study Guide and Tutorial, (2) your lecture notes, and (3) the chapter in the textbook.

5. In addition to the review problems, you should work through the multiple choice questions. However, be careful! While several of these questions are relatively easy (asking you, for example, to determine the components of the money supply), other questions will ask you to apply the concepts and conduct your own analysis of an example.

Final Thoughts and Advice

We have several final suggestions for you. First, when examples are presented in class, make sure you can explain the opposite example (e.g., the output effects of a reduction versus increase in the money supply). Second, you should constantly ask yourself the following types of questions during the course: What does this curve (or equation) represent? Why does it have its particular shape? What causes the curve to shift? What causes the curve's shape/slope to change? If you can answer all of these questions, you will not only completely understand the mechanics of the model, but will also be able to examine the implications of the model.

In short, you should constantly practise your new skills. The more actively you participate in the learning process, the better will be your understanding of the important and exciting material presented in the textbook.

CHAPTER 1. A TOUR OF THE WORLD

OBJECTIVES, REVIEW AND TUTORIAL

After working through the chapter and the material found below, you should be able to:

(1) Know the distinction between macroeconomics and microeconomics.

(2) Recognize the need for simplifying assumptions and the use of models in macroeconomics.

(3) Understand why macroeconomists sometimes disagree.

(4) Know the variables economists focus on when examining an economy.

(5) Know the main issues concerning the Canadian economy.

(6) Know the two main issues concerning the U.S. economy.

(7) Know the two main issues concerning the European Union.

(8) Know the two main issues concerning the Japanese economy.

1. DISTINCTION BETWEEN MACROECONOMICS AND MICROECONOMICS

• <u>Macroeconomics</u> is the study of aggregate economic variables. Examples of aggregate economic variables are:
  (1) aggregate production (aggregate output);
  (2) the average price of all goods and services (the aggregate price level); and
  (3) the unemployment rate.

• <u>Microeconomics</u> is the study of production and prices in specific markets.

2. THE SIMPLIFICATION OF MACROECONOMICS

The goal of macroeconomics is to explain the behaviour of aggregate variables. To do so, macroeconomists:

(1) make assumptions to simplify the analysis; and
(2) construct simple structures (called models) to examine an d interpret the economy.

Learning Tip

As you read through the text, pay particular attention to the assumptions (i.e., simplifications). Make sure you can explain how changes in assumptions can alter the ability of a model to illustrate economic behaviour.

---

3. WHY MACROECONOMISTS DISAGREE

You should be aware that macroeconomists sometimes disagree. This can occur for two reasons.

(1) Different Objectives

Economists will place different weights on different objectives. These different objectives (or goals) include:
- (1) to reduce wage inequality;
- (2) to maintain (or increase) economic activity;
- (3) to reduce the inflation rate; and
- (4) to reduce the unemployment rate.

(2) Absence of controlled experiments

Actual economies are highly complex, consisting of many individuals, firms and markets. Because of this, it is difficult for macroeconomists to conduct controlled experiments. These controlled experiments could be used to study, for example, the effects of monetary policy on the economy. As a result, different macroeconomists can look at the same event and reach different conclusions.

4. FOCUS OF MACROECONOMICS

Macroeconomists focus on three measures of an economy:

- <u>Aggregate output</u> and its rate of growth.

- The <u>unemployment rate</u>: the proportion of the labour force that is unemployed.

- The <u>inflation rate</u>: the rate of change in the aggregate price level.

Learning Tip

The above variables can be used to describe several states of the economy.
- The economy is said to be in a <u>recession</u> when aggregate output falls (a decline in output that generally lasts at least two consecutive quarters [i.e., six months]).
- A period of <u>stagflation</u> occurs when the inflation rate and the unemployment rate are both high.

---

5. THE MAIN ISSUES CONFRONTING POLICY MAKERS IN CANADA

<u>Inflation and Growth</u>

- Canada's macroeconomic performance with respect to inflation and growth is comparable with those in the U.S. in 2001– see next section. Both countries grew slowly, 1.2% in the US and 1.5% in Canada. Both countries experienced inflation between 2 and 3 percent. However, during the 1990s, Canada's inflation was substantially below that in the U.S.

Unemployment

- As for unemployment, Canada's performance has been worse than the U.S. The average unemployment rate between 1992-1996 in Canada was 10.4% as opposed to 6.3% in the U.S., while during 1997-2001 period, Canada's unemployment was 7.8% versus 4.5% in the U.S.

Budget Balance

- Canada's recent performance on the budget front is superior to that in the U.S. After seeing large deficits dating back to mid-1970s, the Canada's federal government achieves its budget surplus in 1997 fiscal year, a year ahead of the U.S. While in Canada the upward trend in the budget surplus has continued to this date, the situation has been reversed in the U.S. Since 2001, the US government budget surplus has been replaced by a deficit.

6. **FOUR ISSUES CONFRONTING UNITED STATES POLICY MAKERS**

- Unemployment. Some economists are concerned that the unemployment rate in the United States might be too low. As we will discuss in later chapters, reductions in the unemployment can result in increases in inflation. Others, however, believe that the reductions in the unemployment rate will not cause increases in inflation.

- The stock market. Some believe that increases in stock prices merely reflect strong fundamentals in the economy. Others believe that recent increases in stock prices reflect excessive optimism. In this case, a sudden drop in stock prices could cause a drop in economic activity.

- Slowdown in growth. The average rate of growth in output has declined since 1973. As the rate of growth in output declines, the rate at which per capita income rises may also decline.

- Increasing wage inequality. One measure of wage inequality is represented by the gap between wages of skilled and unskilled workers.

7. **TWO ISSUES CONFRONTING POLICY MAKERS IN THE EUROPEAN UNION**

- High unemployment. The relatively high unemployment in Europe has a number of possible explanations ranging from labor market rigidities (e.g. high levels of worker protection) to misguided macroeconomic policy.

- European integration. The European Union has eliminated many of the barriers to trade in goods among its members. The European Union also:

  (1) plans to further reduce barriers to people (labour) and capital; and
  (2) has created a common currency with the adoption of the Euro for the eleven European countries.

8. **TWO ISSUES CONFRONTING POLICY MAKERS IN JAPAN AND ASIA**

- Current slowdown in growth in output. Between 1960 and 1997, output grew approximately 6% per year in Japan. Between 1997 and 1999, output grew by less than 1% per year. The concern is whether Japan can return to the high growth rate of this earlier period.

- <u>The Asian crisis in 1997.</u> Prior to 1997, countries in Asia experienced significant growth. The 1997 Asian crisis that began in Thailand brought an end to this growth.

    (1) Investors observed a number of problems in these countries and, therefore, pulled funds out of these markets; and
    (2) These markets were affected by a number of "speculative" attacks on the domestic currencies.

Learning Tip

The issues confronting Canada, the U.S., the European Union and Japan have a number of possible explanations. Not surprisingly, macroeconomists and policy makers differ on what policies should be implemented to address each issue. As you read through the text, think about these issues (and other issues) and about the policies that could be implemented. By thinking about such issues, you will apply the concepts learned in your course and will, therefore, assume a more active role in the learning process. As a result, you will increase your understanding of macroeconomics and of macroeconomic policy.

REVIEW PROBLEMS

1. Define macroeconomics.

2. Define microeconomics.

3. Provide a list of six variables you think would be studied in a <u>macroeconomics</u> course.

4. Briefly explain why it is difficult for macroeconomists to conduct controlled experiments.

5. Know the main issues concerning the economy of Canada?

6. Know the two main issues concerning the economy of the United States?

7. Know the two main issues concerning the economy of the European Union?

8. Know the two main issues concerning the economy of Japan?

MULTIPLE CHOICE QUESTIONS

1. Which of the following economic variables would most likely be studied in <u>microeconomics</u>?

a. the unemployment rate
b. automobile production
c. aggregate output
d. the aggregate price level

2. Which of the following economic variables would most likely be studied in <u>macroeconomics</u>?

a. the price of personal computers
b. the production of macroeconomic textbooks
c. aggregate output
d. the price of college tuition

3. Based on your understanding of the chapter, macroeconomists sometimes disagree because:

a. they dislike each other
b. they assign different weights to different objectives
c. they cannot conduct controlled experiments
d. both b and c
e. none of the above

4. The average (annual) output growth rate in Canada between 1997 and 2001 was:

a. higher than the average output growth rate in Canada between 1992 and 1996
b. lower than the average output growth rate in Canada between 1992 and 1996
c. the same as the average output growth rate in Canada between 1970 and 1991
d. none of the above

5. A comparison of the unemployment rates in Canada and in the U.S. in this decade suggests that:

a. they are generally the same
b. the U.S. unemployment rate has been consistently lower
c. only between 1997 and 2001, the unemployment rate in the U.S. was lower
d. the unemployment rate in Canada since 1992 has been lower than the unemployment rate in the U.S.

6. Stagflation is a situation that occurs when:

a. the unemployment rate is high and the inflation rate is low
b. the unemployment rate and the inflation rate are both high
c. the unemployment rate and the inflation rate are both low
d. the unemployment rate is low and the inflation rate is high
e. aggregate output declines for two consecutive quarters

7. Which of the following is viewed as a possible cause of the 1997 Asian crisis?

a. high stock prices in the United States.
b. high unemployment in Europe.
c. speculative attacks against domestic currencies.
d. all of the above

8. Wage inequality in the United States has increased since the late 1970s. Which of the following is viewed as a possible cause of this increase in wage inequality?
a. international trade
b. technological progress
c. budget deficits in the United States
d. all of the above
e. both a and b

CHAPTER 2. A TOUR OF THE BOOK

OBJECTIVES, REVIEW AND TUTORIAL

After working through the chapter and the material found below, you should be able to:

(1) Define Gross Domestic Product (GDP).

(2) Understand the three different approaches to measuring GDP.

(3) Know the distinction between nominal GDP and real GDP.

(4) Understand what role hedonic pricing plays in the construction of estimates of real GDP.

(5) Know the definition and construction of the unemployment rate (u).

(6) Explain the definition and construction of the GDP deflator and the Consumer Price Index.

(7) Discuss why economists care about the unemployment rate and the inflation rate.

(8) Explain and interpret Okun's law.

(9) Explain what the Phillips curve represents.

(10) Reorganize what role demand and supply factor play in affecting output in the: (1) short run; (2) medium run; and (3) long run.

(11) Recognize what role demand and supply factors play in affecting output in the: (1) short run; (2) medium run; and (3) long run.

1. DEFINITION AND MEASUREMENT OF GROSS DOMESTIC PRODUCT (GDP)

GDP is the value of the final goods and services produced in the economy during a given period. There are three approaches to measuring GDP. You should understand that all three will yield the <u>same</u> value of GDP.

• <u>Approach 1</u>: GDP is the sum of the value of the final goods and services produced in a given period. In the example found in Chapter 2, cars represented the only final good or service. The $210 of revenues from car sales represents GDP.

• <u>Approach 2</u>: GDP is the sum of value added in the economy. The value added of a certain stage of the production of a good is defined as the value of its product minus the value of the intermediate inputs (excluding labour) used in the production process.

• <u>Approach 3</u>: GDP is equal to the sum of incomes in the economy during a given period. To see why this is so, you must understand that the value of a firm's production and the value of its intermediate inputs must go towards:
    (1) workers as income
    (2) the firm as profit
    (3) to the government in the form of indirect taxes (e.g., sales taxes).
In the example in Chapter 2, there are no indirect taxes; therefore, GDP is equal to the sum of labour income and firm profits.

> **Learning Tip**
>
> If we simply added the value of <u>all</u> goods and services (both intermediate and final) exchanged in an economy during a given period, we would over-estimate the value of GDP for two reasons:
>
> (1) Some of the transactions that occur in year t represent the value of intermediate goods. If we added, for example, both the value of a new 2003 Ford Taurus sedan <u>and</u> the value of the Good Year tires Ford purchased from Good Year, we would "<u>double count</u>" the value of the tires; and
>
> (2) Some final goods sold in 2003 were produced in a previous period and, therefore, were already included in the previous period's measure of GDP (e.g., the sale of a used car, used personal computer, etc.).

2. NOMINAL AND REAL GDP

(1) Nominal GDP

<u>Nominal GDP</u> in year t ($\$Y_t$) is the sum of the quantities of final goods and services produced in year t times their <u>current</u> prices. $\$Y_t$ measures the value of GDP in year t at year t prices. Nominal GDP is also called GDP in current dollars and dollar GDP.

> **Learning Tip**
>
> Be careful when interpreting changes in nominal GDP (or changes in the value of any variable measured in nominal terms — that is, measured in current dollars). Suppose $\$Y_t$ increases by 6% in 2002 (above its 2001 level). This increase in $\$Y_t$ can occur for two reasons:
>
> (1) The actual amount of final goods and services produced can increase; and/or
> (2) The prices of these final goods and services can increase.

(2) Real GDP

<u>Real GDP</u> in year t (Y_t) is the sum of the quantities of goods and services produced in year t times the prices of the same goods and services in some particular year. This "particular year" is called the <u>base year</u>. To calculate Y_t, we must first choose a base year. Once chosen (say 1997), real GDP in any year is the value of that year's final goods and services measured at 1992 prices. Real GDP is also called GDP in terms of goods, GDP in constant dollars, GDP adjusted for inflation, and GDP in 1997 dollars.

> **Learning Tip**
>
> Economists focus on real GDP since it eliminates the effects of changing prices on the measure of output. For example, if real GDP in 2002 (measured at 1997 prices) increased by 2% over the level of real GDP in 2001, we know that total output increased. When we receive information about nominal GDP, we do not know whether nominal GDP is changing because of changes in the amount of goods and services produced or because of changes in prices.

Economists use real GDP (Y_t) to calculate GDP growth in year t.

- GDP growth in year t is defined as $(Y_t - Y_{t-1}) / Y_{t-1}$. This measures the percent change in real GDP between years t and t-1.

- Expansions are periods of positive GDP growth.

- Recessions are periods of two or more consecutive quarters of negative GDP growth.

3. TECHNOLOGICAL PROGRESS AND HEDONIC PRICING

Two developments in an economy complicate the calculation of GDP:

(1) the emergence of new goods; and
(2) goods (e.g., personal computers) whose characteristics change from year to year.

When the characteristics of a good change from year to year, the price of that good might change to reflect these changes in characteristics. Economists will use an approach (called hedonic pricing) to adjust actual prices to changes in the product's characteristics.

Learning Tip

- You should review the discussion of hedonic pricing in this Chapter.
- Review problem #7 will also focus on hedonic pricing.

---

4. DEFINITION AND CONSTRUCTION OF THE UNEMPLOYMENT RATE (u_t)

The unemployment rate represents the percent of the labour force that is unemployed. Specifically, $u_t = U/L$ where
- U is the number of individuals unemployed;
- L is the number of individuals in the labour force;
- L is equal to the number of individuals unemployed plus the number of individuals employed (N); and
- Therefore, $L = U + N$.

To be counted as unemployed, an individual:
(1) must not have a job; AND
(2) must have been looking for work in the past four weeks.

Learning Tip

You must understand that to be part of the labour force, an individual must either be: (1) employed; or (2) unemployed and actively searching for a job. Unemployed individuals who stop searching will no longer be counted as part of the labour force. These individuals are called discouraged workers. The exit or entry of discouraged labour workers from or into the labour force can cause the unemployment rate to change without any change in the number of employed workers. Review problem #8 will focus on this.

The participation rate is defined as the ratio of the labour force to the working age population. A high unemployment rate is typically associated with a low participation rate. Why?

Because a larger number of unemployed individuals will drop out of the labour force (i.e., become discouraged workers) when the unemployment rate is high.

5. PRICE INDEXES: THE GDP DEFLATOR AND THE CONSUMER PRICE INDEX (CPI)

The GDP deflator in year t (P_t) is defined as the ratio of nominal GDP to real GDP in year t: $P_t = \$Y_t/Y_t$. The GDP deflator gives the average price of all goods and services included in GDP.

Learning Tip

- $P_t = 1$ in the base year. Why? In the base year, say 1997, $\$Y_{97} = Y_{97}$. In other words, in the base year, the real and nominal value of GDP will be the same since, when obtaining real GDP, we will use the current prices to calculate this inflation-adjusted measure of output. Review problems #1 and #2 will allow you to verify this.
- How do you interpret the size of P_t? Suppose $P_t = 1.37$. This suggests that the average price of goods and services in year t is 37% higher than in the base year.
- We can rearrange the definition of P_t to illustrate why changes in nominal GDP can occur for two reasons. Multiply both sides by Y_t so that $\$Y_t = P_t Y_t$. An increase in P_t and/or an increase in Y_t will cause increases in $\$Y_t$.

The <u>Consumer Price Index</u> (CPI) measures the price of a given "basket" of goods and services consumed by households. Until 2000, the basket of goods and services was based on 1992 spending behaviour; therefore, 1992 represented the base year. In 2000, the base year was changed to 1997, reflecting a new spending behaviour.

Learning Tip

- Suppose the CPI in 2002 equals 107.6. This suggests that the average price of goods and services in 2002 is 7.6% higher than the average price of the same basket of goods and services in the base period (i.e., 1997).
- Be aware that, while both the GDP deflator and the CPI are price indexes and generally move together over time, there can be periods when the change in the CPI is different from the change in the GDP deflator. This is because:
 (1) The CPI includes the price of some goods NOT included in GDP and, therefore, not taken into account in the GDP deflator (e.g., the price of imported goods).
 (2) The GDP deflator includes the price of all final goods and services produced in the economy. Some of these goods are NOT consumed by households and, therefore, not included in the CPI (e.g., some expenditures by the government and by firms).

The GDP deflator and the CPI can be used to calculate the inflation rate. The inflation rate between year t and t-1 (using the GDP deflator) equals $(P_t - P_{t-1})/P_{t-1}$.

Learning Tip

Be careful when interpreting price indexes and the rate of inflation. If the CPI in 2002 equals 107.6, this does NOT mean that there has been a 7.6% ANNUAL rate of inflation between the 1997 and 2002 periods. This number DOES indicate that the average price of the basket of goods and services has increased 7.6% over the ENTIRE period. The inflation rate almost always is calculated on an annual basis indicating, for example, the percent change in the average price level from one year to the next.

6. WHY DO WE STUDY INFLATION AND UNEMPLOYMENT?

We study the unemployment rate because:

(1) The unemployment rate tells us something about the current state of the economy relative to some normal level (when the unemployment rate increases, GDP growth tends to fall); and
(2) The unemployment rate tells us something about the possible effects on the well-being of the unemployed.

We study inflation because:

(1) Inflation can affect the distribution of income (e.g. an increase in inflation can cause a reduction in the real value of the income of individuals who receive fixed, nominal incomes);
(2) Inflation can cause changes in relative prices and, therefore, cause distortions;
(3) If tax brackets are not adjusted for inflation, inflation can cause distortions by moving individuals into higher tax brackets; and
(4) As a result of (2) and (3), inflation can cause uncertainty. This increased uncertainty can have negative effects on economic activity.

7. UNEMPLOYMENT AND ECONOMIC ACTIVITY: OKUN'S LAW

High GDP growth is often associated with a reduction in the unemployment rate. This relationship between changes in the unemployment and GDP growth is known as <u>Okun's Law</u>. This relationship has two implications:

(1) If u_t is too high, an increase in GDP growth will be needed to reduce u_t; and
(2) If u_t is too low, a reduction in GDP growth will be needed to increase u_t.

Learning Tip

The relationship between the unemployment rate and GDP growth has intuitive appeal. For example, suppose that GDP growth is relatively high. What will firms be doing to cause GDP growth to increase at a relatively fast pace? They will most likely hire more workers. As employment rises, the unemployment rate will generally fall. The opposite is also true.

8. INFLATION AND UNEMPLOYMENT: THE PHILLIPS CURVE

The <u>Phillips curve</u> represents the relationship between the unemployment rate and the <u>change</u> in the inflation rate. While this relationship can change over time and may be different for different countries, we tend to observe the following:

(1) When the unemployment rate is low, the inflation rate tends to increase; and
(2) When the unemployment rate is high, the inflation rate tends to fall.

The Phillips curve can be illustrated graphically with the change in the inflation rate on one axis and the unemployment rate on the other axis.

Learning Tip

The message is NOT that accumulating debt is bad. To the contrary, if a government or country borrows to finance investment that leads to higher GDP growth in the future, one can easily justify this type of borrowing. However, if the borrowing occurs to finance current consumption, there may be costs to such borrowing.

9. DETERMINANTS OF CHANGES IN OUTPUT

- Over short periods of time (i.e., the <u>short run</u>), changes in output depend primarily on changes in the demand for goods and services.

- Over long periods of time (i.e., the <u>long run</u>), changes in output depend on supply factors such as the capital stock, the labour force and technology.

- For periods of time in between the short run and long run (i.e., the <u>medium run</u>), both demand and supply factors cause changes in output.

10. CONSTRUCTION OF REAL GDP AND CHAIN-TYPE INDEXES

The construction of real GDP described above uses the same set of prices for a particular year; this year is called the base year. There are several concerns associated with using such an approach to calculating read GDP:

(1) the choice of a particular base year fixes the weights (i.e., prices) associated with each good (and service), we know that relative prices change over time;
(2) because relative prices change over time, the calculated rates of growth of real GDP will depend on the base year chosen; and
(3) when the base year is changed, the calculated rates of growth of real GDP will change.

To avoid these problems, economists now use chain-type indexes to calculate rates of growth in real GDP. This involves several steps:

- The rate of growth of real GDP between 2002 and 2001 is based on using the average of prices in 2001 and 2002. The rate of growth of real GDP between 2001 and 2000 would be based on using the average prices in 2001 and 2000.
- An index of real GDP is obtained by linking/chaining the calculated rates of change for each year.
- The index is set equal to one in some arbitrary year (1997).
- By multiplying this index by nominal GDP in 1997 (the year in which the index equals 1), we can obtain a measure of real GDP in chained, 1997 dollars.

Learning Tip

Some instructors will emphasize the material contained in Appendix 1 of the text. I have included a short review of the material in Appendix 1 in the next section. This review contains a summary of this material and some questions. You should look at this material and work through the problems if you cover this in your course.

SELF-TEST QUESTIONS

1. Define Gross Domestic Product (p. 23).

2. Explain the difference between nominal GDP and real GDP (p. 25).

3. Why is hedonic pricing used when calculating GDP? Explain (p. 27).

4. What does the unemployment rate measure? Briefly explain how it is calculated (p. 27).

5. What is the GDP deflator and how is it calculated (p. 30)?

6. What is the Consumer Price Index (CPI) and how is it calculated (p. 31)?

7. Why should we be concerned about an <u>increase</u> in the unemployment rate? Briefly explain (p. 30).

8. Increases in the rate of inflation can have a number of negative effects on the economy. Briefly explain two (2) of them (p. 32).

9. What is meant by Okun's law (p. 28)?

10. What does the Phillips curve represent (p. 32)?

REVIEW PROBLEMS

1. Consider an imaginary economy that produces only three goods: steaks, eggs and wine. Information on the quantities and prices of each good sold for two years is given below.

	1997	2002
Output		
Steak (kgs)	10	7
Eggs (dozens)	10	13
Wine (bottles)	8	11
Price		
Steak (per kg)	$9.10	$11.50
Eggs (per dozen)	$1.10	$ 1.30
Wine (per bottle)	$6.00	$ 6.50

For this hypothetical economy, calculate each of the following for both years:

a. Nominal GDP in both years
b. Real GDP in constant 1997 dollars (i.e., 1997 is the base year)
c. GDP deflator
d. The percentage change in real GDP and the GDP deflator between 1997 and 2002.

2. Based on your analysis in #1, was nominal GDP in 1997 greater than, less than or equal to real GDP in 1997? If the values for nominal and real GDP in 1997 are different, explain why this is so.

3. Suppose you are provided with the following information about an economy that consists of just three firms.

STEEL COMPANY
    Revenues from sales $400
    Expenses (wages) $340
    Profits $60

LOBSTER COMPANY
    Revenues from sales $200
    Expenses (wages) $160
    Profits $40

CAR COMPANY
    Revenues from sales $1000
    Expenses
        wages $500
        steel purchases $400
    Profits   100

a. Using the final goods approach, what is GDP?
b. Calculate the value added for each of the three firms. Based on your calculations, what is GDP using the value added approach?
c. What are the total wages (i.e., labour income) in this economy? What are total profits in this economy? Given your calculations and using the incomes approach, what is GDP?
d. Compare the levels of GDP obtained in parts (a), (b) and (c). Which of these approaches yields the highest and smallest level of GDP? Explain.
e. Based on your analysis, what percentage of GDP is allocated to: (1) labour income; and (2) profits?

4. Suppose nominal GDP in 2002 increased by 7% (over its level in 2001). Based on this information, what happened to the rate of inflation (as measured by the GDP deflator) and real GDP growth between 2001and 2002? Explain.

5. Use the information provided below to answer the following questions.

Year	Nominal GDP (millions of dollars)	GDP Deflator (1997 = 1.0)	Real GDP (in 1997 dollars)
1997	855,103	1.0	-
1998	914,973	-	918,910
1999	-	1.013	968,541
2000	1,064,995	1.052	-
2001	1,092,246	1.063	-
2002	1,142,123	1.075	-

Source: CANSIM, April, 2003.

a. What was nominal GDP in 1999? What was the GDP deflator in 1998?
b. Using the GDP deflator (where 1997 = 1.0), calculate real GDP for the remaining years.
c. Based on your calculations in part (b), compare the levels of real GDP with the levels of nominal GDP for each year. What does this comparison suggest about prices (in that year relative to 1997)?
d. Explain why economists focus on real rather than nominal GDP when analyzing the level of economic activity.

6. Briefly explain how nominal GDP can increase and real GDP can decrease during the same period.

7. Suppose an economy only produces three goods: potatoes, automobiles and personal computers. Further suppose that over the past 10 years, the actual price of potatoes increased by 20%, the actual price of automobiles increased by 50% and the actual price of personal computers did not change. If a hedonic price index were calculated for each of the three goods over this period, how would the hedonic pricing affect the change in the good's price during the period (when compared to the change in the actual price—would it be higher, lower or the same)? Explain.

8. Suppose you are provided with the following information about an economy. There are 100 million working-age individuals in the economy. Of these 100 million, 50 million are currently working, 10 million are looking for work, 10 million stopped looking for work two months ago, and the remaining 30 million do not want to work.
a. Calculate the number of unemployed individuals, the size of the labour force, the unemployment rate, and the participation rate.
b. Now suppose that of the 10 million individuals looking for work, 5 million stop looking for work. Given this change, calculate what will happen to the size of the labour force, the unemployment rate and the participation rate. Did the unemployment rate and participation rate move in the same direction? Explain.
c. Use the original numbers to answer part c. Suppose firms experience an increase in the demand for their products and they respond by increasing employment. Specifically, two million of the previously unemployed individuals now have jobs. Given this change, calculate what will happen to the size of the labour force, the unemployment rate and the participation rate.
d. If discouraged workers were officially counted as unemployed, explain what would happen to: (1) the size of the labour force; (2) the number of employed individuals; (3) the number of unemployed individuals; (4) the unemployment rate; and (5) the participation rate.

MULTIPLE CHOICE QUESTIONS

1. Suppose nominal GDP decreased during a given year. Based on this information, it is always true that:

a. real GDP fell during the year
b. the GDP deflator fell during the year
c. real GDP and/or the GDP deflator fell during the year
d. both real GDP and the GDP deflator fell during the year

2. Suppose <u>nominal</u> GDP increased by 5% in 2002 (over its previous level in 2001). Given this information, we know with certainty that:

a. the aggregate price level (i.e., the GDP deflator) increased in 2002
b. real GDP increased in 2002
c. both the aggregate price level and real GDP increased in 2002
d. more information is needed to answer this question

3. Suppose nominal GDP in 2002 was <u>less</u> than real GDP in 2002. Given this information, we know with certainty that:

a. the price level (i.e., the GDP deflator) in 2002 was greater than the price level in the base year
b. the price level in 2002 was less than the price level in the base year
c. real GDP in 2002 was less than real GDP in the base year
d. real GDP in 2002 was greater than real GDP in the base year

Use the information provided below to answer questions 4, 5 and 6. Suppose this economy consists of just three firms.

STEEL COMPANY
    Revenues from sales $600
    Expenses (wages) $440
    Profits $160

POTATO COMPANY
    Revenues from sales $400
    Expenses (wages) $260
    Profits $140

CAR COMPANY
    Revenues from sales $2000
    Expenses
      wages $1200
      steel purchases $600
    Profits $200

4. The value added created by the car company is:

a. $1400
b. $200
c. $800
d. $1200

5. The value added created by the potato company is:

a. $140
b. $260
c. $400
d. $120

6. GDP for this economy is:

a. $3000
b. $500
c. $2400
d. $2000

7. Hedonic pricing is used:

a. to convert nominal values to real values
b. to calculate the difference between nominal GDP and real GDP
c. to measure the rate of change in the GDP deflator
d. to adjust the price of goods for changes in their characteristics

Use the information provided below to answer questions 8 – 11. Suppose you are provided with the following information about an economy. There are 200 million working-age individuals in the economy. Of these 200 million, 100 million are currently working, 20 million are looking for work, 20 million stopped looking for work 1 month ago, and the remaining 60 million do not want to work.

8. The size of the labour force for this economy is:

a. 200 million individuals
b. 100 million individuals
c. 120 million individuals
d. 140 million individuals

9. Given the current definitions used to classify the labour force in Canada, the number of unemployed individuals in this economy is:

a. 20 million individuals
b. 40 million individuals
c. 60 million individuals
d. 100 million individuals

10. Given the current definitions used to classify the labour force in Canada, the unemployment rate is:

a. 10%
b. 16.7%
c. 20%
d. 14.3%

11. Given the current definitions used to classify the labour force in Canada, the labour force participation rate in this economy is:

a. 86%
b. 83%
c. 70%
d. 60%

12. Suppose a recent report indicates that the number of individuals who fall into the "discouraged worker" category has increased. Based on the definitions used to determine the size and composition of the labour force and assuming that all other factors are constant, this report would indicate that:

a. the number of employed individuals has fallen
b. the unemployment rate has decreased
c. the percent of the labour force that is unemployed has increased
d. the number of unemployed individuals has increased

13. Given the current definitions used to classify the labour force in Canada, which of the following individuals would be considered to be unemployed:

a. an individual who does not have a job and stopped searching for work 6 weeks ago

b. an individual who does not have a job and stopped searching for work 5 weeks ago
c. an individual who has a job but is working less than 40 hours a week (i.e., part-time)
d. an individual who does not have a job and is currently searching for work
e. an individual who does not have a job and never searches for a job

14. Suppose the GDP deflator in year t equals 1.2 and equals 1.35 in year t+1. The rate of inflation between year t and year t+1 is:

a. 0.15%
b. 15%
c. 12.5%
d. 1.125%

15. Prices for which of the following are included in the GDP deflator, but not included in the Consumer Price Index?

a. intermediate goods and services
b. firms' purchases of new plants and machinery
c. imports
d. consumption goods and services

16. The Phillips curve illustrates the relationship between:

a. changes in the inflation rate and the unemployment rate
b. the unemployment rate and GDP growth
c. the unemployment rate and the labour force participation rate
d. the rate of change in the GDP deflator and the Consumer Price Index

17. Okun's law illustrates the relationship between:

a. the unemployment rate and the labour force participation rate
b. changes in the unemployment rate and GDP growth
c. the inflation rate and the unemployment rate
d. the rate of change in the GDP deflator and the Consumer Price Index

18. In the medium run, changes in GDP are caused by changes in:

a. demand factors
b. supply factors
c. demand and supply factors
d. only monetary policy

19. The calculated rate of growth of real GDP between the years 2001 and 2002 will be based on which of the following years using the current methodology (i.e., chain-type indexes)?

a. the average of prices in 2001 and 2002
b. the prices in the base year, 1997
c. the average prices in 2002 and 2003
d. prices in 2002

APPENDIX 1. NATIONAL INCOME AND PRODUCT ACCOUNTS

OBJECTIVES, REVIEW AND TUTORIAL

Some instructors spend a considerable amount of time on the material included in this appendix. If your instructor emphasizes this material, you should review the material included below (even if this material is not emphasized, you should review it!). After working through this appendix (and taking notes!) and the material found below, you should be able to:

(1) Recognize that there is an income side and product side to the National Income and Product Accounts.

(2) Know the distinction between Gross Domestic Product (GDP) and Gross National Product (GNP).

(3) Understand the components of national income.

(4) Understand the relation among national income, personal income and disposable personal income.

(5) Know the components of Gross Domestic Product based on the product side of the national accounts.

(6) Recognize that we need to be careful when interpreting Gross Domestic Product as a measure of economic activity and when examining the components of Gross Domestic Product.

1. THE INCOME AND PRODUCT ACCOUNTS

• The income side of the national accounts illustrates the relationship among GDP, GNP, national income, personal income and personal disposable income.

• The product side of the national accounts focuses on the goods and services bought by households, firms and governments (at all levels). The product side shows that GDP equals the sum of consumption, government purchases, investment, net exports and changes in business inventories.

2. THE RELATIONSHIP BETWEEN GDP AND GNP

• <u>GDP</u> is the market value of all final goods and services produced by factors of production (i.e., labour, capital) <u>located</u> within Canada.

• <u>GNP</u> is the market value of all final goods and services produced by factors of production <u>supplied</u> by Canadian residents.

• Receipts of factor income from the rest of the world represent income from Canadian capital or Canadian residents abroad.

• Payments of factor income to the rest of the world represent income received by foreign capital or foreign labour in Canada.

> **Learning Tip**
>
> To understand the difference between GDP and GNP, recall that GDP is the value of the final goods and services produced by labour and other inputs located in Canada. Some of the labour and other inputs located in Canada is supplied by foreign residents. At the same time, some of the labour and capital outside Canada is supplied by Canadian residents. To obtain GNP, we:
> (1) first add to GDP receipts of factor income from the rest of the world; and then
> (2) subtract from GDP payments of factor income to the rest of the world.
> This leaves us with GNP.

3. COMPONENTS OF NATIONAL INCOME

National income equals the sum of the following types of income:

- <u>Compensation of employees</u>: wages, salaries and other adjustments

- <u>Corporate profits</u>

- <u>Net interest</u>: net interest paid by firms and net interest paid by the rest of the world

- <u>Proprietors' income</u>: income of individuals who are self-employed

- <u>Rental income</u>: actual rents <u>plus</u> imputed rents on homes and apartments that are owner occupied

4. NATIONAL INCOME, PERSONAL INCOME AND PERSONAL DISPOSABLE INCOME

Not all of national income goes to households. To go from national income to <u>personal income</u>, we must:

- subtract corporate profits
- add back that portion of corporate profits that individuals receive as personal dividend income
- subtract all net interest payments by firms
- add back the net interest payments by firms that households receive
- add transfers.

Personal income is income actually received by households. To obtain personal <u>disposable</u> income, we must:

- subtract from personal income personal taxes and non-tax payments.

<u>Personal disposable income</u> represents income that is available to households after taxes.

5. THE PRODUCT SIDE VIEW OF GDP

To understand this view of GDP, simply think about the <u>final</u> goods and services bought by households, government and firms.

- <u>Personal consumption expenditures</u> (consumption) equals the sum of goods and services bought by persons resident in Canada and includes the purchase of:

    (1) durable goods;
    (2) nondurable goods; and
    (3) services.

- <u>Gross private domestic fixed investment</u> (investment) is the sum of nonresidential investment (new plants, equipment and machinery) and residential investment (the purchase of new homes or apartments by persons).

- <u>Government purchases</u> equal (at the federal, provincial and local levels) the purchase of goods and services by governments <u>plus</u> the compensation of government employees.

Learning Tip

- Why include compensation of government employees? You should view the employees as selling their labour services to the government.
- Government purchases do NOT include transfer payments or interest payments on the debt.

- <u>Net exports</u> (the trade balance) equals exports minus imports where:

    (1) Exports equal the foreign purchase of Canadian goods; and
    (2) Imports equal Canadian residents' purchase of foreign goods.

- <u>Changes in business inventories</u> equal the change in the physical volume of inventories held by businesses. It also equals production minus sales and, therefore, can be positive, negative or zero.

6. WARNINGS

- GDP and GNP are not perfect measures of aggregate economic activity. Why? Some economic activity (e.g. household chores done in the home by the homeowner) occurs outside formal markets and, therefore, is excluded from both GDP and GNP.

- The classification of some expenditures seems inconsistent. For example,

    (1) The purchase of new machinery by firms (which will produce goods in the future) is investment while the purchase of education (which will allow the individual to produce goods and services in the future) is viewed as consumption; and

    (2) The purchase of a new home or apartment is investment while housing services are included in consumption.

REVIEW PROBLEMS

1. Define Gross National Product (GNP).

2. Based on the product side view of the national income accounts, what are the components of GDP?

3. Give two reasons why national income does not equal personal income.

4. Why is personal disposable income less than personal income?

5. What are the two components of gross private domestic investment?

6. What are the three components of consumption?

7. Can net exports be negative? If so, briefly explain.

8. a. In a given year, is it possible for a country's GNP to be greater than the country's GDP? If so, briefly explain.
    b. In a given year, is it possible for a country's GNP to be less than the country's GDP? If so, briefly explain.

MULTIPLE CHOICE QUESTIONS

1. If GNP exceeds GDP, we know with certainty that:

a. a budget deficit exists
b. a trade deficit exists
c. receipts of factor income from the rest of the world exceed payments of factor income to the rest of the world
d. receipts of factor income from the rest of the world are less than payments of factor income to the rest of the world

2. Net national product (NNP) is equal to:

a. GDP minus consumption of fixed capital
b. GNP minus consumption of fixed capital
c. personal disposable income plus net interest payments
d. personal income plus net interest payments

3. Which of the following is NOT a component of national income?

a. wages and salaries
b. corporate profits
c. rental income
d. indirect taxes

4. Which of the following is NOT a component of consumption?

a. purchase of a new home
b. durable goods
c. housing services
d. education services

5. Which of the following activities would NOT be included in the official measure of GDP?

a. the purchase of a new home
b. a firm's purchase of a new plant
c. a firm's purchase of a new machine
d. wages and salaries received by government employees
e. government purchases at the provincial and local level
f. the purchase of intermediate goods

6. Changes in business inventories will be positive when:

a. production exceeds sales
b. production is less than sales
c. production is equal to sales
d. a budget deficit exists
e. a trade deficit exists

7. Which of the following is NOT a component of investment?

a. education expenses
b. a firm's purchase of a new plant
c. a firm's purchase of a new machine
d. the purchase of a new home

8. If imports exceed exports, we know with certainty that:

a. GNP exceeds GDP
b. GDP exceeds GNP
c. a budget deficit exists
d. a trade deficit exists

CHAPTER 3. THE GOODS MARKET

OBJECTIVES, REVIEW AND TUTORIAL

After working through the chapter and the material found below, you should be able to:

(1) Understand the interaction among demand, aggregate production, and income.

(2) Become familiar with the composition of GDP and with the relative size of each of its components.

(3) Know the distinction between endogenous and exogenous variables.

(4) Understand the characteristics of the consumption function.

(5) Discuss and explain what is meant by equilibrium output.

(6) Know the difference between autonomous spending and the other components of spending that depend on income.

(7) Recognize that models have three equations: (1) behavioural equations; (2) equilibrium conditions; and (3) identities.

(8) Graphically illustrate and explain the effects of changes in autonomous spending on demand and on equilibrium output.

(9) Discuss and explain the multiplier.

(10) Explain the relationship between investment and the sum of private and public saving.

(11) Explain what is meant by the paradox of saving.

12) Understand that the adjustment of output in reality is not instantaneous but rather slow.

13) Recognize that firms and consumers may not immediately adjust their production and consumption.

1. INTERACTION AMONG AGGREGATE PRODUCTION, INCOME, AND DEMAND

To understand the interaction among aggregate production, income and demand, think about the following scenario: suppose the economy is in equilibrium (i.e., a situation where there is no pressure for output to change). Now assume that some event occurs that causes an increase in the demand for goods at each level of output (e.g., an increase in government spending).
• Firms respond to this increase in demand by increasing production. As we observed in Chapter 2, income equals production.
• This increase in income will cause a second increase in demand as households increase their purchase of goods and services (i.e., as consumption increases).
• Firms will respond to this second increase in demand by producing even more goods and services.
• This process continues until a new equilibrium output level is achieved.

2. COMPONENTS OF GDP

Three different agents exist in the economy: households (both domestic and foreign), firms, and governments (at all levels). To understand the components of GDP, think about the expenditures of these three groups.

- Consumption (C)

Households buy goods and services. The purchase of these goods by households represents consumption (C). Consumption also happens to represent the largest component of GDP. Note: some of the goods and services bought by households represent foreign goods.

- Investment (I)

Investment represents the purchase of new plants and equipment by firms (nonresidential investment) and the purchase of new homes and apartments by households (residential investment). The sum of residential and nonresidential investment is called fixed investment (I).

Learning Tip

Be careful when referring to investment. From this point on, investment will refer to the sum of residential and nonresidential investment. Investment does **not** refer to the purchase of stocks or bonds or to the amount of funds a student has in his or her savings account, for example.

- Government spending (G)

Government spending (G) represents the purchase of goods and services by governments at the federal, provincial and local levels.

Learning Tip

G does **not** include transfer payments such as social assistance payments or employment insurance benefits.

- Net Exports (X - Q)

Some of the goods and services bought by households, firms and governments may be foreign goods. These purchases of foreign goods and services represent imports (Q). Some of the goods and services produced in the country are sold to foreign households, firms and governments (can you think of relevant examples?). The sale of domestically produced goods and services to foreign agents represents exports (X). The difference between X and Q represents net exports; net exports are also often called the trade balance. If $X > Q$, a trade surplus exists. If $Q > X$, a trade deficit exists.

- Inventory Investment (I_S)

Inventory investment (I_S) is the difference between production and sales. I_S, therefore, can be positive, negative or zero. For example, if production exceeds sales, I_S is positive and firms' inventories of goods must be rising. While these goods are not purchased during the current period, they have obviously been produced and, therefore, should be included in our measure of economic activity (i.e., GDP).

3. DISTINCTION BETWEEN EXOGENOUS AND ENDOGENOUS VARIABLES

An endogenous variable is a variable that is determined within (or by) the model. In Chapter 3, output (Y) is an endogenous variable. An exogenous variable is a variable we take as given (i.e., determined outside the model). Changes in exogenous variables (e.g., changes in consumer confidence) will cause changes in endogenous variables (e.g., C and Y). Changes in endogenous variables, however, will not cause changes in exogenous variables.

4a. THE CONSUMPTION FUNCTION

We assume that consumption is an increasing function of disposable income (Y_D). That is, increases in disposable income will cause increases in consumption. C is represented by the following behavioural equation:

$C = c_0 + c_1 Y_D$ where c_0 and c_1 are both parameters.

c_1 represents the effect of a given change in disposable income on consumption. For example, if $c_1 = 0.85$, a \$1 increase in disposable income will cause an 85-cent increase in consumption [Question: What happens to the remaining 15-cent increase in disposable income? We answer this below in part 4b]. c_1 is referred to as the <u>marginal propensity to consume</u> and equals $\Delta C / \Delta Y_D$ where ΔC and ΔY_D represent the change in consumption and the change in disposable income (Δ is read as "change in"). Since $Y_D = C + S$, any change in disposable income is divided between consumption and saving. Hence, c_1 will be greater than 0 and less than 1.

c_0 represents the level of consumption that occurs when $Y_D = 0$. How can there be positive consumption when $Y_D = 0$? This will occur via dissaving (individuals will either draw down their assets or borrow). c_0 can also be referred to as autonomous consumption—that portion of consumption that is independent of income.

Graphically, we have:

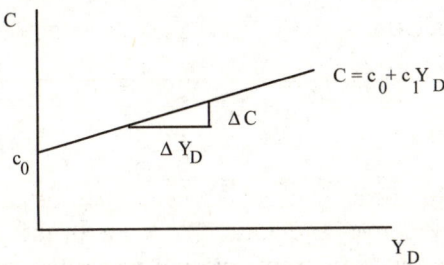

Learning Tip

• If c_0 increases (due to, for example, an increase in consumer confidence), the consumption function will shift up by the change in c_0 (note: the slope does not change when c_0 changes).
• If c_1 increases, the consumption function becomes steeper. What is the intuition behind this result? Any given increase in Y_D now would cause an even greater increase in consumption - this is represented by a steeper consumption function.
• Any change in Y_D will cause movements along the consumption function. Y_D (i.e., $Y_D = Y - T$) will increase when total income (Y) increases and/or taxes (T) fall.
• Given the definition for disposable income, the consumption function can be rewritten as $C = c_0 + c_1[Y - T]$.

4b. THE SAVING FUNCTION

The saving and consumption functions are closely related since $Y_D = C + S$. Furthermore, any increase in disposable income will cause an increase in consumption and an increase in saving. The extent to which consumption and saving will increase depends on the marginal propensity to consume. As we saw in the text, the saving function is given by the following:

$$S = -c_0 + (1 - c_1)[Y - T].$$

If we set $Y_D = 0$ (i.e., $Y - T = 0$), we see that $S = -c_0$. As we discussed above, $C = c_0$ if $Y_D = 0$.

Learning Tip

- How can consumption occur when $Y_D = 0$? Individuals must either be drawing down their assets or borrowing. Either situation represents dissaving—a situation where $S < 0$.
- What does the expression $(1 - c_1)$ represent? Let $c_1 = 0.85$. If Y_D increases by \$1, consumption will increase by 85 cents. What happens to the remaining 15 cents of additional disposable income? It must be used to increase saving. The expression $(1 - c_1)$, therefore, represents the marginal propensity to save. The marginal propensity to save measures the extent to which saving changes for a given change in disposable income.

Graphically, we have:

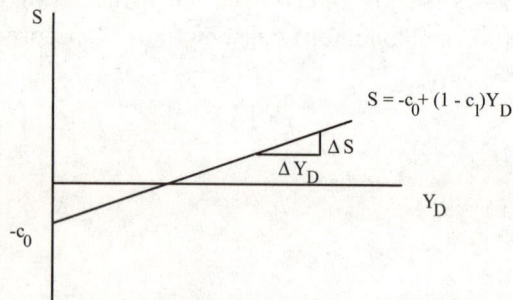

Learning Tip

- Any <u>increase</u> in c_0 (i.e., an increase in autonomous consumption) will cause the saving function to shift <u>down</u> by the amount of the change in c_0.
- Any increase in c_1 will cause the saving function to become flatter (the slope of the saving function decreases).
- Changes in Y_D will cause movements along the saving relationship.

5. MODEL ASSUMPTIONS AND DEMAND (Z)

In this chapter, it is assumed that:

a. firms do not hold inventories;
b. the economy is closed (i.e., $X = Q = 0$);
c. firms produce the same good—we can then look at the market for this one good; and
d. firms are willing to supply any amount of the good at a given price.

For this economy, the demand for goods (Z) is defined as $Z = C + I + G$. After substituting the consumption function for C, we have:

$Z = c_0 + c_1[Y - T] + I + G.$

Learning Tip

Recall that both I and G (and, for that matter, T) are exogenous. Furthermore, c_0, T, I and G will be referred to as <u>autonomous</u> expenditures. Autonomous expenditures are those expenditures that are independent of income. You should note that total consumption (C) is not autonomous because it does depend on income.

Equilibrium in the goods market will occur when production (Y) equals demand (Z). This equilibrium condition (i.e., $Y = Z$) helps explain the interaction among aggregate production, income, and demand. Any event that causes an increase in autonomous expenditures will cause an increase in income. As Y increases, Z will increase as a result of the income-induced increase in consumption. There is, however, only one level of output (for given values of c_0, c_1, T, I and G) that will satisfy the equilibrium condition.

6. EQUILIBRIUM OUTPUT

The equilibrium condition indicates that firms will set production so that it equals demand. As we saw in the text, the equilibrium level of output is represented by the following:

$Y = [1/(1 - c_1)][c_0 - c_1T + I + G].$

Learning Tip

If you have trouble following the steps described in the text, think back to the algebra course you completed in high school. We have one equation (i.e., $Y = Z$) and one unknown variable (i.e., Y).

The above equation represents the equilibrium level of output given the parameters (c_0 and c_1) and the exogenous variables in the model (T, I and G). You should understand that if any of these parameters or exogenous variables changes, the equilibrium level of output will also change.

Learning Tip

- The expression in brackets, $c_0 - c_1 T + I + G$, has a simple interpretation. This represents the level of demand that would occur if Y were zero. It also represents the level of demand that does not depend on income; hence, it represents autonomous spending.
- The other term, $1/(1 - c_1)$, will be some number greater than one since $c_1 < 1$. For example, if $c_1 = 0.8$, the term equals 5. This term "multiplies" the effect of autonomous spending and is, therefore, called the <u>multiplier</u>. You should also understand that as c_1 increases, the multiplier will increase. To verify this, calculate the multiplier if c_1 increases to 0.9.

Equilibrium output can also be illustrated graphically. To do this, we will first plot the demand function Z in Z–Y space (i.e., a graph with Z on the vertical axis and Y on the horizontal axis)—this is represented by the line ZZ in the figure below:

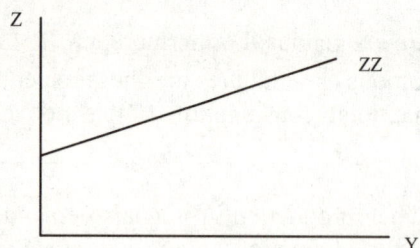

Learning Tip

- The vertical intercept is simply autonomous spending (i.e., if $Y = 0$, $Z = c_0 - c_1 T + I + G$).
- This line is upward sloping because as Y increases households increase consumption. This increase in consumption causes an increase in demand. The slope of ZZ is, therefore, equal to the marginal propensity to consume (c_1).
- Any change in autonomous spending will cause ZZ to shift. A change in c_1 will cause the slope of ZZ to change.

To determine equilibrium output, we will now include in the figure a 45 degree line which has a slope of 1. This 45-degree line illustrates the relationship between production and income. Since production and income are the same, a 1-unit increase in income will equal, by definition, a 1 unit increase in production.

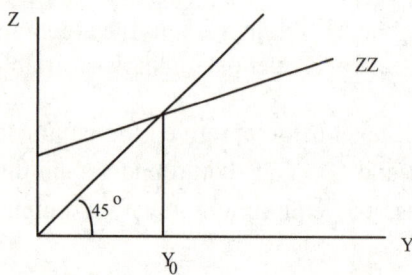

As we can see graphically, there is only one level of output that yields a level of demand (Z) that is equal to income; this occurs at Y_0. For any other level of output, Z will not equal Y. If output exceeds Y_0, then $Y > Z$. If output is less than Y_0, $Z > Y$. Review problem #9 will help reinforce this concept.

7. THE MULTIPLIER

What happens to output if autonomous spending changes? We will examine this both graphically and algebraically. Suppose government spending <u>falls</u> by 100. Further, assume that the marginal propensity to consume is 0.8. Algebraically, the change in output caused by this reduction in G equals 1/(1-0.8)(-100) = -500. That is, every one dollar change in G causes a $5 change in equilibrium output. Graphically, we observe that the reduction in G causes a dollar-for-dollar reduction in autonomous spending. This decline in G, therefore, causes the demand relation, ZZ, to shift down by 100.

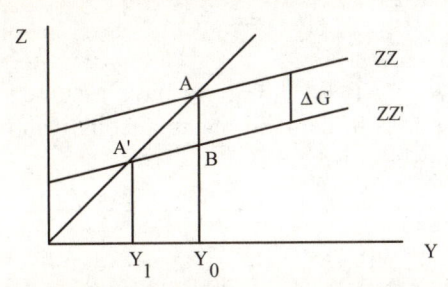

This initial decline in G causes a decrease in demand to point B. As demand falls, production changes by 100. As income falls, demand falls again as we move along the new ZZ line. Production changes again and the process continues until the economy is at point A' where Y = Z at the lower level of output. Both graphically and intuitively, we observe that this one-time, permanent reduction in G causes the drop in Y to exceed the initial drop in autonomous spending. The multiplier indicates the extent to which Y will change for a given change in autonomous spending. In this case, the multiplier is 5.

8. SAVING, INVESTMENT AND THE PARADOX OF SAVING

Equilibrium output can be obtained using the Y = Z equilibrium condition. Equilibrium output can also be illustrated using an approach which focuses on the relationship between investment and saving. As we saw in Chapter 3, S = I + G - T when the economy is in equilibrium. Rearranging this equation yields I = S + (T - G). This equation allows us to obtain an alternative interpretation of equilibrium output:

- S represents private saving by households.
- T - G represents public saving.
- The sum of private and public saving represents national saving.
- In short, the economy is also in equilibrium when investment equals national saving.

A basic understanding of this investment-saving relationship combined with an understanding of the model presented above will shed light on the paradox of saving. In particular, what are the effects of an increase in saving? Any autonomous increase in saving will be represented by an equal reduction in autonomous consumption ($\Delta c_0 < 0$).

Learning Tip

If you understand the link between consumption and saving, the answer to the above question is obvious.
- A decline in c_0 (increase in autonomous saving) will cause an equal reduction in demand at each level of output.
- This reduction in demand will cause a decline in production equal to the change in c_0 times the multiplier.

What happens to saving? Since I, G and T are all autonomous, they do not change as income falls. This implies, given the alternative interpretation of equilibrium (S = I + [G - T]), that the level of saving will remain unaffected by the initial change in saving. Any attempt to increase saving will cause: (1) a reduction in output; and (2) no permanent change in the level of saving. These two results are referred to as the paradox of saving. Review problem #12 will allow you to work through a numerical problem to illustrate these two results.

9. DYNAMICS OF ADJUSTMENT

In writing the equilibrium condition, $Y = [1/(1-c_1)] \{c_0 - c_1 T + I + G\}$, we have assumed that production is always equal demand, i.e. production responds to demand instantaneously and that consumption responds to disposable income instantaneously.

Learning Tip

Firms in reality do not respond instantaneously to a change in demand. Therefore, if purchases exceed production, firms draw down inventories to satisfy purchases. If purchases are lower than production, firms accumulate inventories.

SELF-TEST QUESTIONS

1. What is the largest component of GDP (p. 43)?

2. Explain the difference among exogenous, endogenous and autonomous variables (p. 46).

3. What is the difference between fixed investment and inventory investment (p. 43)?

4. Can inventory investment take on negative (positive) values? If so, explain (p. 44).

5. Explain what the marginal propensity to consume is (p. 45).

6. What effect, if any, will an increase in consumer confidence have on: (1) the consumption function; and (2) the demand line (ZZ) (pp. 50)?

7. What variables determine the vertical intercept and slope of the ZZ line (p. 49)?

8. Why is the demand line (ZZ) upward sloping (p. 49)?

9. Give two examples of an economic event that would cause demand (Z) to fall and, therefore, cause the demand line (ZZ) to fall (pp. 50 and 55).

10. Explain what is meant by the multiplier (p. 50).

11. What cause the adjustment of output to take place over time rather than instantaneously? (p. 51)?

12. What factors determine the length of this adjustment? (p. 52)?

REVIEW PROBLEMS

1. The table below includes information about real GDP (measured in billions of 1997 dollars) for Canada in 2001 and 2002.

	2000	2001
Consumption (C)	565.5	580.0
Investment (I)	182.4	183.2
Nonresidential	45.8	48.0
Residential	136.7	135.2
Government Spending (G)	208.0	215.8
Exports (X)	451.7	434.5
Imports (Q)	405.8	382.3

a. Calculate the level of GDP for 2000 and 2001. Then calculate the rate of GDP growth between 2000 and 2001. Based on your calculations, briefly explain what happened to economic activity between 2000 and 2001.

b. Calculate the rate of growth/decline in each of the components of GDP between 2000 and 2001. Which of the components of GDP grew the fastest and slowest between these two periods? Calculate each component's share of GDP in 2000 and 2001. Did any of the components of GDP experience any changes in their size relative to total output? Briefly comment.

c. Based on the information in these two tables, what happened, if anything, to the size of Canada's trade deficit between these two years? If the deficit did change, did it occur primarily because of changes in exports or imports? Explain.

2. The definition of GDP includes (or, equivalently, takes into account) the value of changes in inventories (i.e., inventory investment). Suppose we developed an alternative measure of GDP that ignored inventory investment. First, describe and explain a situation in which the exclusion of inventory investment would cause the value of this alternative (and, by the way, incorrect!) measure of GDP to be <u>greater</u> than the value of output obtained using the current definition's measure of GDP. Second, describe and explain a situation in which the exclusion of inventory investment would cause the value of this alternative measure of GDP to be <u>less</u> than the value of output obtained using the current definition's measure of GDP. Finally, given your analysis, <u>briefly</u> discuss why it is important to include inventory investment when measuring the value of current output.

3. The definition of GDP includes (or, equivalently, takes into account) the value of net exports (X - Q). Suppose we developed an alternative measure of GDP that ignored net exports. First, describe and explain a situation in which the exclusion of net exports would cause the value of this alternative (and, by the way, incorrect!) measure of GDP to be <u>greater</u> than the value of output obtained using the current definition's measure of GDP. Second, describe and explain a situation in which the exclusion of net exports would cause the value of this alternative measure of GDP to be <u>less</u> than the value of output obtained using the current definition's measure of GDP. Finally, given your analysis, <u>briefly</u> discuss why it is important to include net exports when measuring the value of current output.

4. Suppose consumption in Canada is represented by the following equation:

$C = 200 + 0.5Y_D$ where $Y_D = Y - T$ and $T = 200$.

a. What is the level of consumption in this economy if $Y_D = 0$? Briefly explain how individuals "pay for" this consumption when $Y_D = 0$.
b. Given the above parameters, calculate the level of consumption if $Y = 1200$. Suppose Y increases to 1300. What happens to the level of Y_D as Y increases to 1300 (i.e., calculate the change in Y_D)? What happens to the level of consumption when Y rises to 1300? Based on this analysis, what is the marginal propensity to consume for this economy?
c. Write out the saving function for this economy. What is the level of saving (S) when $Y_D = 0$? Explain how and why this occurs. What is the marginal propensity to save for this economy? How do you know?

5. Suppose the following information represents current economic conditions and behaviour in some economy:

$C = 400 + 0.75Y_D$ where $Y_D = Y - T$, $T = 400$ and $Y = 2000$.

a. First, graphically depict the above consumption function in C - Y_D space (with C on the vertical axis and Y_D on the horizontal axis). What does the vertical intercept represent? Explain. What is the slope of this consumption function? Explain. With $Y = 2000$, what is the level of consumption for this economy?

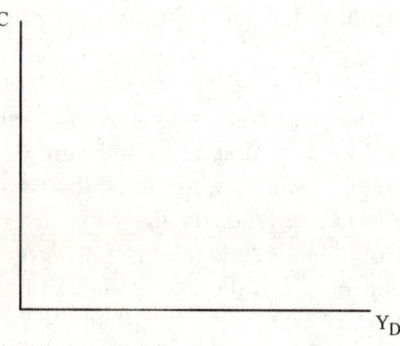

b. Assuming that Y does not change, graphically illustrate (in the above graph) and explain the effects of a reduction in the marginal propensity to consume to 0.5. Calculate what happens to the level of consumption.

6. Suppose the Canadian economy is represented by the following equations:

$Z = C + I + G$ $C = 400 + 0.5Y_D$ $T = 400$ $I = 200$
$Y_D = Y - T$ $G = 600$

a. What is the marginal propensity to consume for this economy? What is the marginal propensity to save?
b. Write out the equation that indicates how demand (Z) is a function of income (Y) and the remaining autonomous expenditures. What will be the level of demand if $Y = 0$? What does this level of demand represent? Furthermore, given your equation, what will happen to the level of demand (Z) as Y increases by $1? What does this number represent?

c. Based on your answer in part (b), calculate the level of demand (Z) for the following levels of income: Y = 1600, Y = 1800, Y = 2000, Y = 2200 and Y = 2400. Now compare the level of demand that you calculated at each level of income with the corresponding level of income. Is the economy in equilibrium at any of these levels of income? Explain.

d. Use your calculations in part (c) to answer this question. When Y = 1600, compare the levels of income and demand. How will firms respond to this situation? Briefly explain. When Y = 2400, compare the levels of income and demand. How will firms respond to this situation? Briefly explain.

7. Suppose the Canadian economy is represented by the following equations:

$Z = C + I + G$ $C = 300 + 0.5Y_D$ $T = 400$ $I = 200$
$Y_D = Y - T$ $G = 1000$

a. Given the above variables, calculate the equilibrium level of output. Hint: First specify (using the above numbers) the demand equation (Z) for this economy. Second, using the equilibrium condition, equate this expression with Y. Once you have done this, solve for the equilibrium level of output. Using the ZZ–Y graph (i.e., a graph that includes the ZZ line and 45 degree line with Z on the vertical axis, and Y on the horizontal axis), illustrate the equilibrium level of output for this economy.

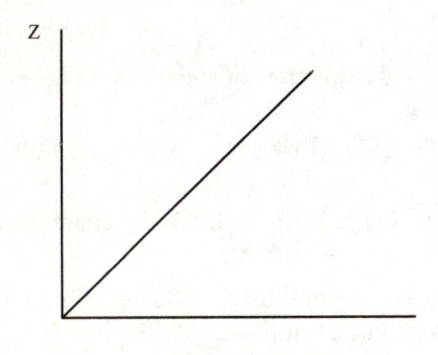

b. Now, assume that consumer confidence increases causing an increase in autonomous consumption (c_0) from 300 to 400. What is the new equilibrium level of output? How much does income change as a result of this event? What is the multiplier for this economy?

c. Graphically illustrate (in the above graph) the effects of this change in autonomous consumption on the demand line (ZZ) and Y. Clearly indicate in your graph the initial and final equilibrium levels of output.

d. Briefly explain why this increase in output is greater than the initial increase in autonomous consumption.

8. Repeat the analysis in question 7, parts (a) to (c). This time, however, assume that the marginal propensity to consume is 0.8.

a. See #7, part (a).
b. See #7, part (b).
c. What happened to the slope of the ZZ line as a result of the increase in the marginal propensity to consume? Explain.
d. What happened to the changes in output and, therefore, the size of the multiplier as a result of the increase in c_1? Explain.
e. Graphically illustrate using the ZZ–Y graph the effects of an increase in c_1 on equilibrium output.

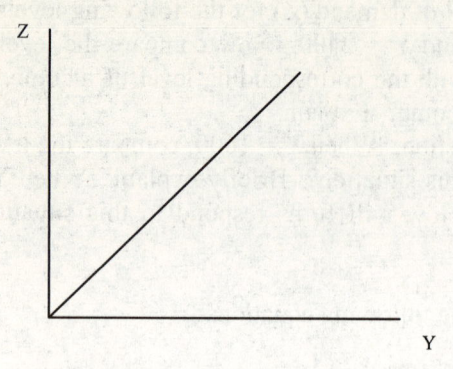

9. Use the ZZ–Y graph found below to answer the following questions:

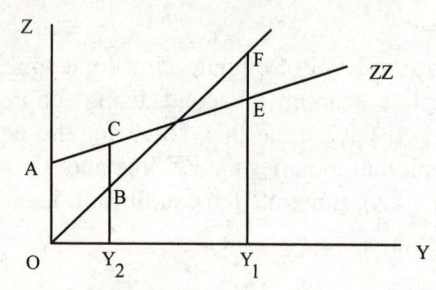

a. What does the distance OA represent? Briefly discuss and explain what events could occur in this model that would cause the distance OA to decrease.
b. Briefly explain what the following distances represent: OY_1, Y_1E, Y_1F. Is the economy in equilibrium when output equals Y_1? Explain.
c. Briefly explain what the following distances represent: OY_2, Y_2B, Y_2C. Is the economy in equilibrium when output equals Y_2? Explain.
d. Given your analysis in parts (b) and (c), what is the level of equilibrium output? What must occur for the economy to be in equilibrium? Illustrate this condition in the above graph.

10. a. Calculate the multiplier for each of the following values of the marginal propensity to consume: $c_1 = 0.4$, $c_1 = 0.5$, $c_1 = 0.6$, $c_1 = 0.8$ and $c_1 = 0.9$. Briefly explain what happens to the multiplier as the marginal propensity to consume increases.
b. Explain what happens, if anything, to the demand line (ZZ) as the marginal propensity to consume takes on the following values: $c_1 = 0.4$, $c_1 = 0.5$, $c_1 = 0.6$, $c_1 = 0.8$ and $c_1 = 0.9$. Briefly explain what happens to equilibrium output as the marginal propensity to consume increases.
c. Suppose policy makers want to increase equilibrium output by 1000. For each of the following values of the marginal propensity to consume, calculate the required change in government spending that would yield the desired change in equilibrium output: $c_1 = 0.4$, $c_1 = 0.5$, $c_1 = 0.6$, $c_1 = 0.8$ and $c_1 = 0.9$.

11. Suppose there are two different economies, both represented by the model presented in Chapter 3. Further assume that the equilibrium level of output is the same in both countries. For simplicity, we can illustrate the equilibrium for both economies in the same graph. The demand line for economy A (B) is represented by ZZ_A (ZZ_B). This situation is depicted in the following graph.

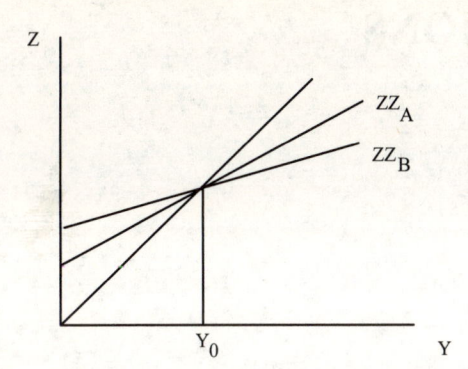

a. First, briefly discuss the different characteristics of the demand lines for these two economies.
b. Now, suppose policy makers in both countries decide to increase government spending by the same amount (e.g., G will increase by, say, $100 billion). First, briefly explain what will happen to the level of autonomous expenditures in each economy. Second, graphically illustrate (in the above graph) what will happen to the demand lines as a result of this identical increase in G.
c. Will the effects of this $100 billion increase in government spending on equilibrium output be the same in the two economies? Explain.

12. Suppose the Canadian economy is represented by the following equations:

$Z = C + I + G$ $C = 300 + 0.9Y_D$ $T = 1000$ $I = 200$
$Y_D = Y - T$ $G = 2000$

a. Calculate the equilibrium level of output.
b. After you have calculated equilibrium income, calculate the level of consumption at this level of output. Hint: Since you know the level of taxes and income, you can easily obtain the level of disposable income to calculate consumption.
c. Write out the saving function for this economy. Then, calculate the level of saving that occurs at the equilibrium level of output.
d. Now, suppose households decide to increase their autonomous saving by 100. Equivalently, households have decided to cut their autonomous consumption by 100. Calculate the new equilibrium level of output which occurs as a result of the decrease in autonomous consumption of 100. Has this increased desire to save had a positive or negative effect on economic activity? Explain.
e. Based on your analysis in part (d), calculate the level of saving that occurs at this new equilibrium level of output. Compare this level of saving with the level of saving obtained in part (c). What has happened to the level of saving in this economy as a result of the increased desire to save? Explain.

13. For each of the following events, explain what effect each event has on: (1) autonomous expenditures; (2) equilibrium output; (3) the slope of ZZ; and (4) the multiplier.

a. decrease in business confidence that results in a reduction in nonresidential investment
b. increase in consumer confidence that results in an increase in residential investment
c. the Parliament passes a budget that calls for a reduction in government spending
d. an increase in the marginal propensity to consume
e. an increase in the marginal propensity to save

MULTIPLE CHOICE QUESTIONS

1. A reduction in government spending (G) can occur if:

a. government spending at the provincial level declines
b. government spending at the local level declines
c. government spending at the federal level declines
d. all of the above

2. Assume that the Canadian economy is an open economy. Given this information, we would expect that:

a. exports (X) exceed imports (Q)
b. $X < Q$
c. $X = Q = 0$
d. Canadian households (in addition to the government and business sectors) trade goods and services with individuals/firms from other countries

3. In this chapter, we studied the difference between endogenous and exogenous variables. Which of the following is (are) an endogenous variable(s) in our model of the goods market?

a. consumption and saving
b. government spending and consumption
c. investment and saving
d. taxes
e. all of the above
f. none of the above

4. Which of the following is (are) an exogenous variable(s) in our model of the goods market?

a. saving and investment
b. government spending and taxes
c. disposable income and taxes
d. demand for goods (Z)
e. all of the above
f. none of the above

5. Which of the following variables is (are) an endogenous variable(s) in our model of the goods market?

a. autonomous consumption and the marginal propensity to consume
b. government spending
c. taxes
d. consumption

Answer the following four questions (i.e., questions 6 – 9) using the information included in the following behavioural equation:

$C = 200 + 0.75Y_D$

a. 150
b. 200
c. less than 150
d. more than 200

7. If $Y_D = 0$, we know that:

a. saving equals 0
b. saving equals 200
c. saving equals -200
d. saving and consumption are both equal to 0

8. The saving function for the above economy would be:

a. $S = 200 + 0.25Y_D$
b. $S = 0.75Y_D$
c. $S = 200 + 0.25Y_D$
d. $S = -200 + 0.25Y_D$

9. The multiplier for this economy is equal to:

a. 0.75
b. 0.25
c. 4
d. 1.33
e. 1

10. When the economy is in equilibrium, we know with certainty that:

a. private saving equals investment
b. public saving equals investment
c. the federal budget is balanced (i.e., G = T)
d. income equals demand
e. consumption equals private saving

11. An increase in the marginal propensity to save will tend to cause:

a. an increase in the multiplier and a given change in government expenditures to have a smaller effect on equilibrium output
b. an increase in the multiplier and a given change in government expenditures to have a greater effect on equilibrium output
c. a reduction in the multiplier and a given change in government expenditures to have a smaller effect on equilibrium output
d. a reduction in the multiplier and a given change in government expenditures to have a greater effect on equilibrium output

12. An increase in the marginal propensity to consume will tend to cause:

a. an increase in the multiplier and a given change in government expenditures to have a smaller effect on equilibrium output
b. an increase in the multiplier and a given change in government expenditures to have a greater effect on equilibrium output
c. a reduction in the multiplier and a given change in government expenditures to have a smaller effect on equilibrium output
d. a reduction in the multiplier and a given change in government expenditures to have a greater effect on equilibrium output

Answer the following five questions (i.e., 13 – 17) using the following information. Suppose the Canadian economy is represented by the following behavioural equations:

$Z = C + I + G$ $C = 300 + 0.5 Y_D$ $T = 1600$ $I = 200$
$Y_D = Y - T$ $G = 2000$

13. The endogenous variables in this economy are:

a. government expenditures (G)
b. taxes (T)
c. fixed investment (I)
d. consumption and saving (C and S)

14. Given the above variables, the equilibrium level of output for this economy is:

a. 900
b. 1800
c. 1700
d. 2500
e. 3400

15. The multiplier for the above economy is:

a. 0.5
b. 1
c. 2
d. 4

16. Suppose fiscal policy makers implemented a policy that causes government spending to increase by 200 (i.e., the new level of government spending would be 2200). Based on our understanding of the above economy, we would expect that equilibrium output will:

a. increase by 200
b. increase by less than 200
c. increase by 400
d. increase by 100

17. In addition to using disposable income for consumption, households also will use a portion of disposable income for saving. The saving function for the above economy that summarizes the behaviour of households is given by:

a. $S = 300 + 0.5Y_D$
b. $S = -300 - 0.5Y_D$
c. $S = -300 + 0.5Y_D$
d. $S = 300 + 0.5Y$
e. $S = -300 + 0.5Y$

18. Assume that households experience a reduction in confidence. Further assume that this reduction in confidence causes a reduction in autonomous consumption (c_0). This reduction in c_0 will cause

a. no change in output and no change in the final level of consumption
b. a reduction in output and a reduction in the level of saving
c. no change in output if the level of saving does not change
d. no change in the level of saving

19. An increase in the marginal propensity to consume will cause:

a. an increase in output and an increase in the multiplier
b. a reduction in output and a reduction in the multiplier
c. an increase in output and a reduction in the multiplier
d. a reduction in output and an increase in the marginal propensity to save

20. An increase in fixed investment (I) will cause:

a. a reduction in output and a reduction in the multiplier
b. an increase in output and an increase in the multiplier
c. an increase in output and no change in the multiplier
d. no change in the multiplier and, therefore, no change in output

21. The slow adjustment of output is due to:

a. a reduction in consumption spending not matched by an increase in investment spending
b. people being kept uninformed about the market by policy makers
c. production responding slowly to a change in demand
d. economy's weak conditions

CHAPTER 4. FINANCIAL MARKETS

OBJECTIVES, REVIEW AND TUTORIAL

After working through the chapter and the material found below, you should be able to:

(1) Know the distinction between money and bonds.

(2) Recognize the difference among saving, savings, wealth, income and investment.

(3) Understand the difference between stock and flow variables.

(4) Explain the determinants of money demand.

(5) Explain the determinants of bond demand.

(6) Explain what is meant by velocity and explain how changes in the interest rate affect velocity.

(7) Explain the determinants of the interest rate and be familiar with the LM relation.

(8) Discuss the balance sheet of banks and the balance sheet of the central bank.

(9) Understand the components and determinants of the money supply.

(10) Explain the dynamic effects of open market operations on the money supply.

11) Explain the dynamic efforts of open market operations on the money supply.

12) Understand the relationship between the interest rate and the price of the bond.

13) Explain the determinants of demand and supply of reserves (central bank money)

14) Discuss the determinants of money supply in relation to the supply of reserves.

15) Understand the concepts of overnight interest rate and the Bank Rate.

1. DISTINCTION BETWEEN MONEY AND BONDS

In this chapter, we assume that there are only two financial assets: money and bonds.

(1) Money

Money is a financial asset which can be used for transactions and pays no interest. There are several definitions of money (i.e., M1, M2). M1 which will be used here consists of:
   (1) currency (CU): coins and bills issued by the central bank; and
   (2) chequable deposits: deposits (at banks) on which one can write a cheque.

(2) Bonds

Bonds are financial assets that pay an interest rate (i) but cannot be used for transactions. You must be careful not to confuse money and bonds with the following variables:

- saving: that part of disposable income not consumed
- wealth ($Wealth): value of financial assets minus value of financial liabilities

- income: payments one receives for working, rental income, and interest and dividends
- investment: the purchase of new plants and machinery by firms and the purchase of new homes and apartments by homeowners

> **Learning Tip**
>
> It is easy to confuse the above variables because they are often used interchangeably (and incorrectly!). For example, think about what is wrong with the following statements. How would we correct them?
> (1) "I expect to earn a lot of money after graduation."
> (2) "She has a lot of investment in the stock market."

(3) Stock versus flow variables

We can use the above variables to distinguish between flow and stock variables.

- A <u>flow</u> variable is a variable that must be expressed per unit of time. Examples: income per year; saving per quarter; and budget deficits per year.

- A <u>stock</u> variable can be measured at a given point in time. Wealth and money are stock variables since they can be measured at a given moment in time.

2. THE CHOICE BETWEEN HOLDING MONEY AND BONDS

Individuals decide how to allocate their wealth between money and bonds. Two extreme cases will illustrate the factors that affect this decision.

- <u>Case 1</u>. Suppose all of your wealth will be held in bonds. This portfolio allocation will:
(1) maximize interest income; but also
(2) maximize the costs (transaction fees) associated with converting bonds to money when you want to buy something.

- <u>Case 2</u>. Suppose all of your $Wealth were held in money. This allocation would:
(1) minimize the costs (in fact, they would be zero) associated with converting bonds into money; but also
(2) minimize the interest income received on your wealth (interest income would be zero).

Individuals will, therefore, hold both money and bonds.

3. THE DETERMINANTS OF MONEY DEMAND (M^d)

Money demand (M^d) depends on:

(1) <u>Level of transactions</u>: As the level of transactions increases, individuals will allocate a greater proportion of their portfolio to money. We include nominal income ($Y) in place of the level of transactions. Why? Unlike the level of transactions, $Y can be measured. As $Y increases, the level of transactions rises causing M^d to increase as well.

(2) <u>The interest rate on bonds</u> (i): As i increases, individuals are willing to accept the additional costs of converting bonds into money in order to benefit from the higher interest rate on bonds. As i increases, M^d falls.

M^d is, therefore, an increasing function of $Y and a decreasing function of i.

M^d is written as: $M^d = \$YL(i)$. How do we interpret this?

(1) M^d is proportional to $Y. If your nominal income rises by 5%, your demand for money will increase by 5%.
(2) Increases in the interest rate cause a reduction in money demand. This effect is captured by the function, L(i).

M^d is shown graphically in Figure 4-1. You must know the following about M^d:

(1) Each money demand curve is drawn for a given level of $Y;
(2) Money demand is downward sloping because as i increases, individuals increase their bond holdings and reduce their money holdings (the curve does NOT shift!); and
(3) Changes in $Y will cause changes in money demand and, therefore, cause <u>shifts</u> in the money demand curve.

4. THE DETERMINANTS OF BOND DEMAND (B^d)

Given that the sum of money holdings and bond holdings must equal $Wealth, we know that bond demand (B^d) is given by:

$B^d = \$Wealth - \$YL(i)$.

B^d is a function of three variables: (1) $Wealth; (2) the interest rate; and (3) nominal income.

• <u>$Wealth</u>: Increases in $Wealth cause a one-for-one increase in bond demand. Since money demand is only a function of i and $Y, increases in $Wealth go completely to increasing bond demand.
• <u>Interest rate</u>: As i increases, bonds are more attractive, causing individuals to reduce their money holdings and, therefore, increase their bond holdings.
• <u>Nominal income</u>: An increase in $Y, <u>given</u> $Wealth, causes a reduction in B^d. Why? The higher income leads to higher transactions. With $Wealth fixed at any point in time, the only way the individual can increase money holdings is by reducing bond holdings.

5. MONEY DEMAND, THE INTEREST RATE AND VELOCITY

Two characteristics can be seen in figures 4-2 and 4-3:

(1) Increases in i cause reductions in (M^d/$Y) M/$Y, which is consistent with the assumption that money demand is a decreasing function of the interest rate.
(2) The ratio of M to $Y, after taking into account the interest rate, has decreased over time.

The <u>velocity</u> of money is the ratio of $Y to M (i.e., velocity = $Y/M). Velocity will increase when:

(1) the interest rate rises. A higher interest rate causes a reduction in money demand and, for a given $Y, an increase in $Y/M; and
(2) innovations occur that allow individuals to reduce the average amount of money held. Examples of such innovations are: (1) the increased use of credit cards; and (2) the increased availability and use of automated teller machines (ATMs).

Learning Tip

Credit cards do NOT represent money. Credit cards allow you to combine the payments of goods and services on one day each month. Individuals decrease the average amount of money held and velocity increases.

6. INTEREST RATE DETERMINATION: THE MONEY MARKET APPROACH

(1) Introduction

Financial markets are in equilibrium when the supply of money (M) equals money demand: M = $YL(i). This equilibrium condition is called the <u>LM relation</u>. What does this LM relation mean? For equilibrium to occur, the interest rate must be at a level that causes individuals to hold an amount of money (M^d) equal to the existing stock of money (i.e., M = M^d). Figure 4-4 illustrates this.

Learning Tip

If M = M^d, we also know that the supply of bonds (B) equals bond demand. Why?
- Assume the stocks of money and bonds are given.
- $M^d + B^d$ = $Wealth
- We also know that M + B = $Wealth.
- Therefore, $M^d + B^d$ = M + B.
- If M^d = M, B^d must equal B.

Make sure you can explain why the money supply curve is vertical. Answer: Changes in the interest rate do not cause changes in the supply of money. Changes in the money supply WILL cause shifts in the money supply curve.

(2) Changes in i

The interest rate will change when $Y or the money supply changes.

- <u>Changes in $Y</u>. An increase in $Y causes an increase in M^d. At the initial interest rate, M^d exceeds the supply of money (M^d > M). i must increase to reduce the amount of money individuals want to hold. This occurs at i' in figure 4-5. At the higher i, M once again equals money demand.

Learning Tip

Note: The increase in $Y causes a <u>shift</u> in the money demand curve. The increase in the interest rate causes a <u>movement along</u> the now higher money demand curve.

- <u>Changes in the money supply</u>. An increase in the money supply causes a rightward shift in the money supply curve. At the initial interest rate i, the money supply now exceeds money demand. i must fall to induce individuals to hold more money. This occurs at i' in figure 4-6. At the lower i', M once again equals money demand.

7. MONETARY POLICY, OPEN MARKET OPERATIONS AND THE BOND MARKET

(1) The bond market

In the bond market:

- Individuals who sell bonds (in exchange for money) want to increase the proportion of money in their portfolio;
- Individuals who buy bonds want to reduce the proportion of money in their portfolios; and
- In equilibrium, the interest rate is such that $B = B^d$ (or, as we saw earlier, $M = M^d$).

(2) The central bank and the bond market

The central bank can change the stock of money by buying and selling bonds in the bond market (i.e., open market operations).

- <u>Increase the money supply</u>: The central bank <u>buys</u> bonds and pays for the bonds by creating money. This has two effects on the central bank's balance sheet:
    (1) the increased bond holdings represent an increase in the central bank's assets; and
    (2) the increased money in circulation represents an increase in the central bank's liabilities.

- <u>Decrease the money supply</u>: The central bank <u>sells</u> bonds and receives money as payment for these bonds. This has two effects on the central bank's balance sheet:
    (1) the reduced bond holdings represent a reduction in the central bank's assets; and
    (2) the reduced money in circulation represents a reduction in the central bank's liabilities.

Learning Tip

You should understand the relationship between the price of a bond ($\$P_B$) and the interest rate. On a one-year bond that promises a fixed, nominal payment of $100 in one year, the interest rate is defined as:

$i = (\$100 - \$P_B)/\$P_B$.

This definition indicates that the higher is $\$P_B$, the lower will be the interest rate. The lower is $\$P_B$, the higher will be the interest rate. This makes sense because, for example, as $\$P_B$ falls, the numerator (your gain), $\$100 - \$P_B$, gets larger AND the denominator, $\$P_B$, gets smaller. i, therefore, rises. Alternatively, the return per dollar allocated to bonds rises as the price of the bond falls.

---

(3) Policy

- <u>Expansionary open market operations</u>. This central bank <u>purchase</u> of bonds will increase the demand for bonds, raise the price of bonds, reduce the interest rate and increase the supply of money

- <u>Contractionary open market operations</u>. This central bank <u>sale</u> of bonds will increase the supply of bonds, reduce the price of bonds, raise the interest rate and reduce the supply of money.

8. DETERMINATION OF INTEREST RATES: MARKETS FOR CENTRAL BANK MONEY

1) In the presence of banks, whose chequable deposits are held by the public, the central bank does not directly control the money supply. But it does control the supply of central bank money, H, which is partly in the form of currency and partly in the form of banks reserves. Money supply in turn is determined by an interaction between the central bank, commercial banks and the public. Banks are financial institutions. They receive funds by offering chequable deposits (D) and use these funds to buy bonds, issue loans and hold reserves (R). The deposits are the <u>bank's liabilities</u> (the public's assets). The bonds, loans and reserves are the <u>bank's assets</u> (the liabilities of the insurer of bonds, the borrowers and the central bank, respectively.

2) Demand for central bank money

There are two components of the demand for central bank money: the demand for currency and the demand for reserves.

- Currency demand: CU^d. This is given by: $CU^d = cM^d$.
- c is a parameter representing the proportion of money demand, M^d, that individuals wish to hold as CU.
- Demand for reserves: R^d. This is given by: $R^d = \theta D = \theta(1-c)M^d$.
- θ is the reserve ratio (the proportion of deposits bank wish to hold as reserves).

Therefore:

- $H^d = CU^d + R^d = cM^d + \theta(1-c)M^d = [c + \theta(1-c)]M^d$ and,
- $H^d = [c + \theta(1-c)]\$YL(i)$

3) Supply of Central Bank Money (H)

The Bank of Canada has complete control over the supply of central bank money (H). The central bank can change the amount of H through open market operations (buying or selling bonds).

Learning Tip

Note that parameter c is <u>not</u> the currency deposit ratio that you might have seen in previous courses. Here, c represents the proportion of money (the sum of currency and chequable deposits), that individuals wish to hold as money.

---

4) The determination of the interest rate

The interaction between the supply and demand for central bank money can also be used to examine the determinants of the interest rate. That is, the interest rate will adjust to equate the supply of central bank money with the demand for central bank money: $H = H^d$ or, $H = [c + \theta(1-c)]\$YL(i)$. This is shown graphically in Figure 4-10.

> **Learning Tip**
>
> There are several characteristics of the market for central bank money that you must know.
>
> - The quantity of central bank money, H (not M), is measured along the horizontal axis.
> - The Bank of Canada controls the supply of H using open market operations.
> - The demand for central bank money is a decreasing function of the interest rate because as i increases, (a) the demand for currency goes down, and (b) the demand for chequable deposits also goes down.
> - The demand for central bank money is drawn for a given level of income. If income changes, money demand, and, therefore, currency demand and reserve demand will change.

Therefore, this model can be used to examine what would cause a change in the equilibrium interest rate.

- <u>Open market operations</u>. The Bank of Canada's purchase or sale of bonds will cause a change in the supply of central bank money and, therefore, a new equilibrium interest rate.

- <u>Changes in $Y</u>. Any change in income will cause a change in money demand, a change in currency and reserve demand, and, therefore, a change in the demand for central bank money. For example, an increase in the demand for central bank money will cause an increase in the interest rate.

9. INTEREST RATE DETERMINATION: ALTERNATIVE WAYS

1) Introduction

There are two other was of viewing equilibrium: while they are equivalent, each provides a different way of thinking about the equilibrium:

a) Through supply and demand of reserves; and
b) Through supply and demand of money.

2) The demand and supply of reserves (Overnight Funds market and the overnight interest rate).

i) The market for reserves in Canada is called the market for overnight funds.

ii) The interest rate that reconciles the demand and supply reserves is referred to the overnight (interest) rate. In Canada, the overnight lending rate ranges within .5%. The upper boundary of this range is called the Bank Rate.
- The supply of reserves = H – [demand for currency by public (CU^d)]
- The demand for reserves = R^d
- In equilibrium = H - CU^d = R^d

3) The Demand and Supply of Money

The overall supply and demand for money is also obtained from the equilibrium condition for central bank money, equation 4-10:

$$H = [c + \theta(1-c)]\$YL(i)$$

In equilibrium money supply equals money demand, $M = \$YL(i)$. By substituting for $\$YL(i)$ we obtain:

$$M = H/[c + \theta(1-c)]$$

The expression, $1/[c + \theta(1-c)]$, is the money multiplier.

a) Case 1: $c > 0$
Suppose $c = .6$ and $\theta = .2$ the money multiplier is 1.47. A $1 change in H will cause a $1.47 change in the money supply.

b) Case 2: $c = 0$
When $c = 0$, then $CU^d = 0$, $H = R^d$ and $M = D$. The amount of chequable deposits is given by $D = (1/\theta)R$. If $\theta = .2$ and $R = \$100$ million, the supply of chequable deposits will be $500 million. Why? When $\theta = .2$, banks hold $20 of reserves for every $100 dollars of chequable deposits. If $R = \$100$ million, banks can issue $500 million of chequable deposits.

Since $M = D$, we know that

$$M = (1/\theta)R.$$

The money supply equals the money multiplier, $(1/\theta)$, times the monetary base, R.

c) Case 3: $c = 1$
Another special case of $CU^d > 0$ is the case of $CU^d = M^d$. In this, people only hold currency: $c = 1$. This reduces the money supply/high powered relationship, above, into: $H = M$, and banks play no role in the money supply.

SELF-TEST QUESTIONS

1. Compare the characteristics of money and bonds (p. 60).

2. Define each of the following: wealth and saving (p. 60).

3. Explain the difference between a stock and flow variable (p. 60).

4. What effect will an increase in the interest rate (i) have on the demand for money and on the demand for bonds? Briefly explain (pp. 61-62).

5. What effect will an increase in nominal income ($Y) have on the demand for money and on the demand for bonds? Briefly explain (P.61)?

6. Discuss what is meant by "velocity" (p. 63).

7. What effect will an increase in the money supply have on the interest rate? Show this graphically (p. 66).

8. What effect will a contractionary open market operation have on the price of bonds, the interest rate and the money supply (p. 67)?

9. Define central bank money. How does the market for central bank money work (pp. 70-71)?

10. What is the market for reserves (p. 73)?

11. What are the two ways of looking at the equilibrium of the interest rate (p. 73)?

12. Define the overnight interest rate (p. 73).

13. What is the relationship between the Bank Rate and the over night rate (p. 73)?

14. What is the money multiplier (p. 73)?

15. In the presence of currency the money supply is determined by three valuable parameters. What are they (pp. 70-71)?

REVIEW PROBLEMS

1. The purpose of this question is to make sure that you understand the definitions of several variables discussed in this chapter.
a. Is it possible for someone to have zero income and a large amount of wealth? Briefly explain.
b. Is it possible for someone to have zero saving and positive wealth? Briefly explain.
c. Can wealth ever be negative for an individual? Explain.

2. The following is a list of variables you have now studied: wealth, saving, investment, business inventories, the money supply, capital, and income.
a. Which of the above variables are flow variables?
b. Which of the above variables are stock variables?

3. What effect will a reduction in nominal income have on money demand? Explain.

4. Briefly explain what happens to money demand, bond demand and the money supply as a result of each of the following events:

a. a 10% increase in $Y
b. a 4% reduction in $Wealth
c. a reduction in i
d. expansionary open market operation

5. Use the information and space provided below to answer the following questions.

Year	$Y	M	i	$Wealth	Velocity
1980	315,245	33,037	12.681	1,611,962	
1990	679,921	89,439	12.805	2,829,053	
2000	1,064,995	209,517	5.479	3,906,637	

$Y is nominal GDP measured in millions; M is M1B measured in millions; $Wealth is nominal wealth in millions; and i is the interest rate on 91-day Treasury Bills.
Source: Statistics Canada: CANSIM Database.

a. Calculate velocity for the above three years. Briefly comment on what has happened, if anything, to velocity during the above period.
b. Assume that the above changes in the interest rate represent the only change in financial markets. Are the changes in velocity that you calculated consistent with what you would expect given our assumption about money demand? Explain.
c. Based on the model of money demand presented in this chapter, what effect did the above changes in $Wealth have on velocity? Briefly explain.

6. Use the graph provided below to answer the following question.

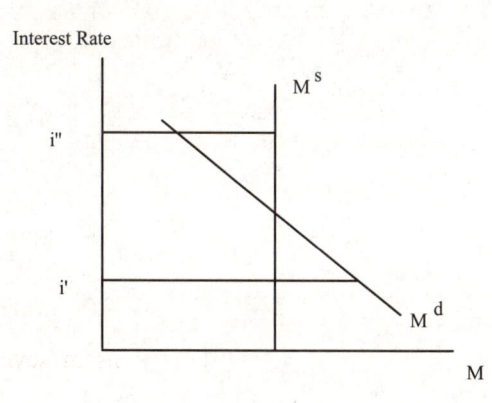

a. Given money demand and money supply, explain what type of situation exists when the interest rate equals i". At this interest rate, how much money do individuals want to hold? At this interest rate, how much money actually exists?
b. Based on your analysis in part (a), what must happen to the interest rate for financial market equilibrium to occur? What happens to money demand and money supply as i changes?
c. Given money demand and money supply, explain what type of situation exists when the interest rate equals i'. At this interest rate, how much money do individuals want to hold? At this interest rate, how much money actually exists?
d. Based on your analysis in part (c), what must happen to the interest rate for financial market equilibrium to occur? What happens to money demand and money supply as i changes?

7. Use the graph provided below to answer the following questions.

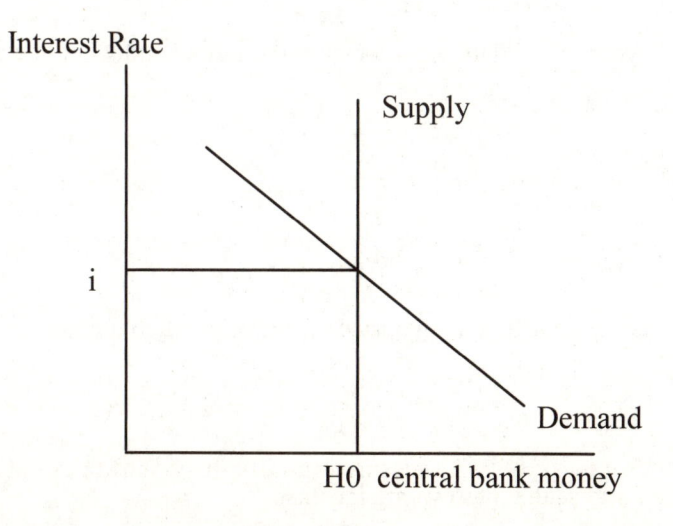

a. How much central bank money is held at the initial interest rate (i)? Show this in the graph.
b. Suppose there is a reduction in $Y. What effect will this have on demand for central bank money and on the interest rate? Why? Show this graphically.
c. At the initial interest rate of i, what has happened to demand for central bank money?
d. What must happen to the interest rate to restore equilibrium?
e. As i changes, what happens to demand?
f. How much money currency and reserves are held at this new interest rate?

8. Use the space provided below to answer this question.

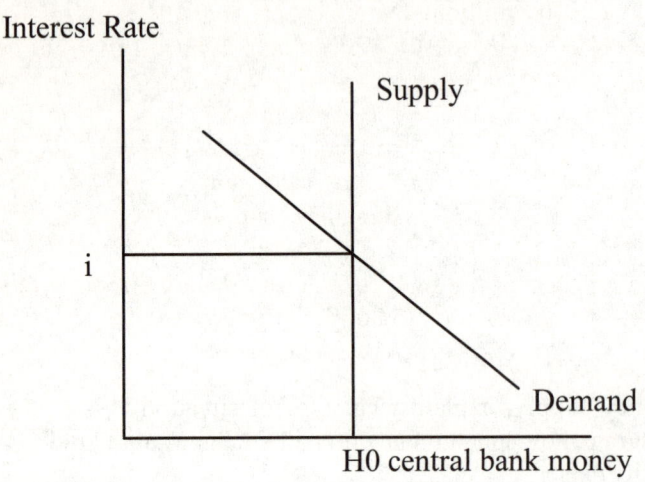

Interest Rate

Supply

i

Demand

H0 central bank money

a. How much central bank money is held at the initial interest rate (i)? Show this in the graph.
b. Suppose there is a reduction in the supply of central bank money. What effect will this have on the supply curve and on the interest rate? Show this graphically.
c. At the initial interest rate of i, what has happened to the actual quantity of central bank money?
d. What must happen to the interest rate to restore equilibrium?
e. As i changes, what happens to demand?
f. How much central bank money is held at this new interest rate? Compare your answer here with your answer to part (a).

9. Suppose a bond pays $200 in one year. Calculate the interest rate on this bond when the price of the bond (P_B) is:
a. $150
b. $160
c. $180
d. $195
e. What happens to the interest rate as the price of the bond falls?

10. Suppose a bond pays $1000 in one year. Calculate the price of the bond when the interest rate is:
a. 5% (.05)
b. 10% (.10)
c. 15% (.15)
d. What happens to the price of the bond as the interest rate increases?

11. For this question, assume that all money is held in the form of currency. Assume that central bank money is initially equal to $100 million. Now suppose that the Bank of Canada pursues an expansionary open market operation equal to $10 million. Given this information, explain what effect this has on:
a. the amount of the Bank's assets
b. the amount of the Bank's liabilities
c. bond demand, bond supply and the price of bonds
d. the interest rate
e. the money demand curve
f. central bank money
g. the money supply curve

12. For this question, assume that all money is held in the form of currency. Again, assume that central bank money is initially equal to $100 million. Now suppose that the Bank of Canada pursues a contractionary open market operation equal to $20 million. Given this information, explain what effect this has on:
a. the amount of the Bank's assets
b. the amount of the Bank's liabilities
c. bond demand, bond supply and the price of bonds
d. the interest rate
e. the money demand curve
f. central bank money
g. the money supply curve

13. For this question, assume that individuals do not hold currency and that the reserve ratio (θ) is 0.2. Also assume that the monetary base equals $500 million. Given this information, calculate:
a. the amount of reserves
b. the amount of chequable deposits
c. the money supply
d. the money multiplier

14. Based on your analysis in #13, calculate what happens to the following variables if the Bank of Canada buys $50 million of bonds:
a. the monetary base
b. the amount of reserves
c. the overnight rate
d. the money supply

15. Based on your analysis in #13 (and using the original numbers), calculate what happens to the following variables if the Bank of Canada sells $10 million of bonds:
a. the monetary base
b. the amount of reserves
c. the overnight rate
d. the money supply

16. The expression, $(1/\theta)$, represents the money multiplier when $CU^d = 0$.
a. Calculate the money multiplier for of the following values of θ: 0.1, 0.2, 0.3, 0.4, and 0.5.
b. What happens to the size of the money multiplier when θ increases?
c. Provide a brief, intuitive explanation of the effects of an increase in θ on the money multiplier.

17. Use the information provided below to answer the following questions:

$R^d = 50$ $CU^d = 250$ $D = 500$

a. Calculate the reserve ratio.
b. Calculate the value of the parameter c.
c. Calculate the size of the monetary base.
d. Calculate the size of the money supply.
e. Calculate the money multiplier.
f. In the space below, fill in the information about the banks' and central bank's balance sheets. Specifically, what is the dollar value of the bonds held by banks? What is the dollar value of the bonds held by the central bank?

Central Bank's Balance Sheet		Banks' Balance Sheet	
Assets	Liabilities	Assets	Liabilities

18. Use your calculations in #17 to answer these questions.
a.   Suppose the Bank of Canada wishes to increase the money supply by $100 million. What type of open market operation should it pursue? What should the dollar amount of the Bank's purchase or sale of bonds be in order for M to increase by $100 million?
b.   What effect will this Bank action have on the price of bonds? Explain.
c.   Suppose the Bank wants to reduce the money supply by $40 million. What type of open market operation should it pursue? What should the dollar amount of the Bank's purchase or sale of bonds be in order for M to fall by $40 million?
d.   What effect will this Bank action have on the price of bonds? Explain.

19. a.   Suppose $c = 0.2$. Calculate the money multiplier for each of the following values of the reserve ratio (θ): 0.1, 0.2, and 0.5.
b.   What happens to the money multiplier when the reserve ratio increases?
c.   Provide an intuitive explanation of the effects of an increase in the reserve ratio on the money multiplier.

20. a.   Suppose $\theta = 0.1$. Calculate the money multiplier for each of the following values of c: 0.1, 0.2, and 0.5.
b.   What happens to the money multiplier when the parameter c increases?
c.   Provide an intuitive explanation of the effects of an increase in c on the money multiplier.

21. Can the Bank of Canada influence the currency/money supply ratio (c)?

22. In what way can the Canada Deposit Insurance Corporation affect the money multiplier?

MULTIPLE CHOICE QUESTIONS

1. Which of the following variables is NOT a stock variable?

a.   the money supply
b. $Wealth
c.   investment
d.   the monetary base

2. An increase in nominal income ($Y) will cause:

a.   an increase in money demand
b.   an increase in bond demand
c.   an increase in the monetary base
d.   an increase in the money supply

3. A reduction in $Wealth will cause:

a. a reduction in money demand
b. an increase in money demand
c. an increase in bond demand
d. a reduction in bond demand

4. An increase in the interest rate (i) will cause:

a. a rightward shift in money demand
b. a leftward shift in money demand
c. an increase in the money supply
d. a reduction in money demand in the form of a movement along the curve

5. Which of the following events will cause a reduction in the interest rate?

a. a Bank of Canada sale of bonds
b. a reduction in the money supply
c. a reduction in $Y
d. an increase in $Y

6. Which of the following variables is an asset on a bank's balance sheet?

a. reserves
b. chequable deposits
c. the monetary base
d. gold

7. Which of the following variables is a liability on a bank's balance sheet?

a. currency
b. chequable deposits
c. bonds
d. reserves

8. Which of the following variables is a liability on the Bank of Canada's balance sheet?

a. chequable deposits
b. bonds
c. currency
d. loans

9. A central bank purchase of bonds will cause which of the following to occur?

a. a reduction in the monetary base
b. an increase in the monetary base
c. a reduction in the price of bonds
d. an increase in the interest rate

10. An expansionary open market operation will tend to cause:

a. an increase in bond prices (P_B) and an increase in the interest rate (i)
b. an increase in P_B and a reduction in i
c. a reduction in P_B and a reduction in i
d. a reduction in P_B and an increase in i

11. A contractionary open market operation will cause:

a. a reduction in the money supply
b. an increase in the money supply
c. an increase in the monetary base
d. the interest rate to fall

12. Which of the following will occur when the interest rate increases?

a. the price of bonds will fall
b. the money demand curve shifts to the left
c. the money demand curve shifts to the right
d. the money supply curve shifts to the right

13. Suppose a bond pays $1000 in one year. If the price of the bond is $750, we know that the interest rate on this bond is:

a. 7.5%
b. 15%
c. 25%
d. 33%

14. Suppose demand for central bank money is greater than supply of central bank money at the current interest rate. Given this information, we know that:

a. the interest rate (i) must fall to restore equilibrium
b. i must increase to restore equilibrium
c. the bond market is in equilibrium at the current interest rate
d. none of the above

15. Suppose individuals do not hold currency and that the banks' reserve ratio is 0.25. The money multiplier is:

a. 1/(1-0.25) = 1.33
b. 2.5
c. 4
d. 5

16. Suppose the ratio of currency to chequable deposits is 0.5 and the reserve ratio (θ) is 0.25. The money multiplier is:

a. 1/0.75 = 1.33
b. 2
c. 1/(1-0.75) = 4
d. 5

17. Which of the following events will cause an increase in the money multiplier?

a. an increase in the reserve ratio
b. an increase in the parameter c
c. a reduction in the reserve ratio
d. an increase in the monetary base

18. Which of the following events will cause an increase in the supply of reserves?

a. an increase in the interest rate
b. an increase in $Wealth
c. a Bank of Canada's purchase of bonds
d. an increase in the parameter c

19. The overnight interest rate is

a) the rate of interest banks charge their best customers.
b) the rate of interest paid to holders of treasury bills.
c) the rate of interest that equilibrates the market for reserves.
d) the interest rate that is determined by the demand and supply of chequable deposits.

20. The supply of reserves is

a) the difference between high powered money and demand for currency.
b) the sum of currency and chequable deposits.
c) determined by chartered banks that wish to cover their reserves short fall.
d) the high powered money times by the money multiplier.

21. The interest rate can be determined within

a) the market for central bank money.
b) the money market.
c) the market for overnight funds.
d) all of the above.

22. The demand by banks for reserves

a) increases with an increase in chequable deposits.
b) decreases with an increase in chequable deposits.
c) increases with an increase in the federal deposit insurance.
d) is positively related to the currency deposit ratio.

CHAPTER 5. GOODS AND FINANCIAL MARKETS: THE *IS-LM* MODEL

OBJECTIVES, REVIEW AND TUTORIAL

After working through the chapter and the material found below, you should be able to:

(1) Understand the determinants of investment.

(2) Interpret and explain the IS relation.

(3) Understand how the IS curve is derived; explain its shape; and explain what factors cause it to shift.

(4) Explain the relationship between the real money supply and real money demand.

(5) Understand how the LM curve is derived; explain its shape; and explain what factors cause it to shift.

(6) Understand what is meant by equilibrium in the IS-LM model.

(7) Examine the effects of fiscal policy in the IS-LM model.

(8) Examine the effects of monetary policy in the IS-LM model.

(9) Discuss what is meant by the "policy mix."

(10) Explain how factors other than monetary and fiscal policy can affect the IS-LM model.

(11) Re-examine the implications of the IS-LM model when dynamics are introduced.

1. THE DETERMINANTS OF INVESTMENT

Investment is now assumed to be:

(1) an increasing function of sales; and
(2) a decreasing function of the interest rate.

• <u>Sales</u>. As sales rise, firms will increase their purchase of equipment and will build new plants. As sales decrease, firms will cut back on investment.

Learning Tip
In this chapter, we assume that output always equals sales. Therefore, investment is an increasing function of output.

• <u>The interest rate</u>. As i increases, the cost of borrowing rises. As the cost of borrowing increases, some firms will not purchase new equipment since the now higher cost of borrowing is greater than the additional profits from the new equipment.

2. THE IS RELATION AND THE IS CURVE

(1) Introduction

The equilibrium condition in the goods market is represented by the <u>IS relation</u>:
$Y = C(Y-T) + I(Y,i) + G$.
We use the IS relation to derive the IS curve.

- <u>The IS curve</u> represents the relationship between the interest rate and the equilibrium level of output in the goods market.

(2) Slope of the IS curve

- A reduction in the interest rate causes an increase in investment.
- The increase in I causes an increase in demand (Z).
- The increase in Z causes an increase in equilibrium output through the multiplier effect.
- A lower i, therefore, leads to an increase in equilibrium output in the goods market.

This gives rise to a downward sloping IS curve.

Learning Tip

The IS curve is derived by examining the effects of changes in i on I and on Y. Changes in i and Y do NOT cause shifts in the IS curve, only movements along the IS curve.

---

(3) Shifts in the IS curve

Any factor, other than a change in i, that causes a change in Y in figure 5-1 (i.e., the ZZ–45º line graph) will cause a shift in the IS curve.
- The IS curve shifts to the right when government purchases (G) increase, taxes (T) fall, consumer confidence increases, etc.
- The IS curve shifts to the left when G falls, T increases, consumer confidence falls, etc.

Learning Tip

To understand shifts, consider the following example. Suppose G falls by 100. Let's also keep i arbitrarily fixed. The drop in G causes Y to fall by an amount equal to the change in G times the multiplier. At the same i, equilibrium output is now lower. We now need a new IS curve to reflect this. The IS curve then shifts left with the horizontal distance equal to the change in G times the multiplier.

---

3. FINANCIAL MARKETS AND THE LM RELATION

(1) Introduction

The financial markets equilibrium condition is now expressed in real terms. That is, equilibrium occurs when the interest rate equates the real supply of money with real money demand. This is represented by the following <u>LM relation</u>:

$M/P = YL(i)$.

> **Learning Tip**
>
> - M/P is the real supply of money.
> - YL(i) is real money demand and Y is real income.
> - The relationship between real income and real money demand is specified here as a one for one relationship such that a 5% increase in Y causes a 5% increase in Y.L (i).
> - In contrast, the inverse relationship between the interest rate (i) and real money demand, L(i) is stated in a general qualitative functional form. That is, while the an increase in the interest rate causes a reduction in real money demand, the magnitude of the change in the latter cannot be detected from this general functional form.

- <u>The LM curve</u> represents the relationship between income (Y) and the equilibrium interest rate in the financial markets.

(2) Slope of the LM curve

- An increase in income causes an increase in real money demand.
- At the initial interest rate, money demand now is greater than the supply of money.
- i must rise to restore equilibrium in the financial markets.
- A higher Y, therefore, requires an increase in the interest rate to maintain financial markets equilibrium giving rise to an upward sloping LM curve.

(3) Shifts in the LM curve

The LM curve will shift whenever the financial markets equilibrium interest rate changes because of factors other than a change in Y.
- The LM curve is drawn for a given value of the real money supply (M/P).
- A change in M/P causes a change in the equilibrium interest rate at every level of output.
- The LM curve shifts down and to the right when M/P increases because a lower i (or a higher Y) is needed to maintain equilibrium in the financial markets.
- The LM curve shifts up to the left when M/P decreases because a higher i (or a lower Y is needed to maintain equilibrium in the financial markets.
- Also, the LM curve is drawn for a given money demand function, L. A change in L for reasons <u>not</u> associated with Y or i shifts the LM curve. The Lm curve shifts down and to the right when L decreases, say, due to an increased use of debit cards, and vice versa.

> **Learning Tip**
>
> - M/P can increase when M increases or when P falls.
> - Changes in M (or P) will, therefore, cause shifts in the LM curve.
> - A change in Y (or a change in i) does NOT cause shifts in the LM curve, only movements along the curve.
> - If you do not understand how changes in M/P cause shifts in the LM curve, return to figure 5-4.
>   - For a given level of Y, change M/P.
>   - This change in M/P causes a change in i.
>   - This change in i determines the extent to which the LM curve shifts up or down.

4. EQUILIBRIUM IN THE IS-LM MODEL

- The IS curve represents the relationship between the interest rate and the level of output, which maintains equilibrium in the goods market.
- The LM curve represents the relationship between the interest rate and the level of output, which maintains equilibrium in the financial markets.
- Refer to figure 5-7. There is only one i and one level of output which simultaneously maintain equilibrium in BOTH the goods and financial markets. This equilibrium is called the <u>overall equilibrium</u>.
- Since the economy is operating on both the IS and LM curves, we know that the goods and financial markets are in equilibrium.

Learning Tip

Recall that:
(1) The IS curve can shift when, for example, G, T or consumer confidence changes. Any shift in the IS curve will yield a new overall equilibrium;
(2) The LM curve can shift when the real money supply changes. Any shift in the LM curve will yield a new overall equilibrium;
(3) As the IS and LM curves shift, the interest rate, the level of output, and the composition of output may also change.

---

5. FISCAL POLICY

- A <u>fiscal expansion</u> occurs when government purchases (G) increase or when taxes are cut.
- A <u>fiscal contraction</u> occurs when government purchases are cut or when taxes are increased.

Consider the effects of a reduction in G in the IS-LM model; the graphical analysis is identical to that found in figure 5-8.
- The cut in G causes the IS curve to shift left. The size of the horizontal shift equals the change in G times the multiplier.
- The leftward shift in the IS curve yields a new equilibrium at the intersection of the new IS curve and the original LM curve.
- This cut in G causes a reduction in Y and a reduction in i.

Learning Tip

You must be able to explain intuitively these shifts and the economy's response to these shifts.
- The decrease in G causes a reduction in demand (Z).
- The decrease in demand causes firms to cut production.
- As Y falls, individuals reduce their demand for money.
- As money demand falls, the interest rate must fall to restore equilibrium in the financial markets.
- At the lower i, money demand once again equals the money supply.
- Question: Why does Y fall to Y' (A') and not to the level associated with point D (in figure 5-8)? Answer: as i falls, some of the drop in Y is offset by the positive effects of the lower i on investment.

To summarize, a fiscal contraction will cause:
- a reduction in Y
- a lower i
- a reduction in consumption and saving via the reduction in disposable income
- ambiguous effects on investment
  - the lower i causes an increase in I
  - the lower Y causes a reduction in I

Learning Tip

• Make sure you can explain the effects of a fiscal expansion. Review problem #9, below, which examines this.
• The above analysis applies to any leftward shift in the IS curve (e.g. increases in taxes, reductions in consumer confidence).

---

6. MONETARY POLICY

- A <u>monetary expansion</u> occurs when the money supply increases.
- A <u>monetary contraction</u> occurs when the money supply falls.

A Bank of Canada <u>purchase</u> of bonds (i.e., a monetary expansion) will cause:
- an increase in the money supply and a rightward shift in the money supply curve
- the increase in the money supply requires a reduction in the interest rate to induce individuals to hold the larger quantity of money
- the drop in i causes the LM curve to shift down
- the shift down in the LM curve yields a new equilibrium with a lower i and higher Y

Other results/explanations of a monetary expansion:
- Why does Y increase? The lower i causes an increase in investment, which has a positive, multiplier effect on Y.
- Consumption and saving both increase via the increase in disposable income.
- Investment increases for two reasons. Both the reduction in i and increase in Y cause I to increase.

Learning Tip

• Does the increase in the money supply or the reduction in the interest rate cause the IS curve to shift? NO! We move along the IS curve.
• Make sure you can explain the opposite example (a monetary contraction).
• You must understand that changes in the reserve ratio (θ) and the parameter c (the proportion of money held in currency) will also cause changes in the money supply and, therefore, cause the LM curve to shift.
• A shift in money demand caused by factors other than changes in Y will also cause the LM curve to shift. Review problem #8 will allow you to examine this.

---

7. THE MONETARY AND FISCAL POLICY MIX

- The combination of monetary policy and fiscal policy is called the monetary-fiscal policy mix.
- The policy mix refers to situations where both the LM and IS curves shift.

- There are four possible cases of the policy mix:
  - <u>Case 1</u>: Expansionary monetary policy and expansionary fiscal policy (LM shifts right and the IS shifts right).
  - <u>Case 2</u>: Expansionary monetary policy and contractionary fiscal policy (LM shifts right and the IS shifts left).
  - <u>Case 3</u>: Contractionary monetary policy and contractionary fiscal policy (LM shifts left and the IS shifts left).
  - <u>Case 4</u>: Contractionary monetary policy and expansionary fiscal policy (LM shifts left and the IS shifts right).

Learning Tip

- In each case, the effects of the policy mix on one of the endogenous variables (Y or i) will always be ambiguous (unless we know the exact magnitude of the policy changes).
- The effect on the other endogenous variable will be known. For example:
- For Case 2, i unambiguously falls with the change in Y depending on the size of the shifts in the IS and LM curves.
- In the figure associated with the German Unification example (Case 4), i unambiguously increases and the change in Y again depends on the size of the shifts.
- Make sure you can explain the effects of each combination of monetary and fiscal policy.
- Also make sure you can explain the effects of the policy mix on consumption, saving and investment.

8. INTRODUCTION OF DYNAMICS TO THE IS-LM MODEL

When the IS curve shifts, Y will not immediately adjust to its new equilibrium level for three reasons:
(1) Y will respond with a lag to changes in demand
(2) C will respond with a lag to change in disposable income
(3) Investment may respond with a lag to changes in sales

In figure 5-10 (a),

- A rightward shift in the IS curve will cause a slow movement of Y from Y_B to Y'_A.
- A leftward shift in the IS curve will cause a slow movement of Y from Y'_A to Y_B.

Financial markets will, however, adjust rapidly to changes in supply and demand. We can assume that the economy is always on the LM curve.

In figure 5-10 (b),

- An upward shift in the LM curve, say due to a monetary contraction, will cause an instantaneous (and a sharp) increase in the interest rate from i_A to i_B so that the economy is always on the LM curve. The increase in the interest rate leads over time to a decline in output.

Learning Tip

- The assumption about rapid adjustment in the financial markets is not unrealistic. Think about how quickly the bond market responds to any change in supply or demand conditions.
- Review the discussion regarding figure 5-11.
- Make sure you can repeat this analysis for a situation where the money supply declines.

The dynamic effects of an increase in government purchases are shown in the graph below:

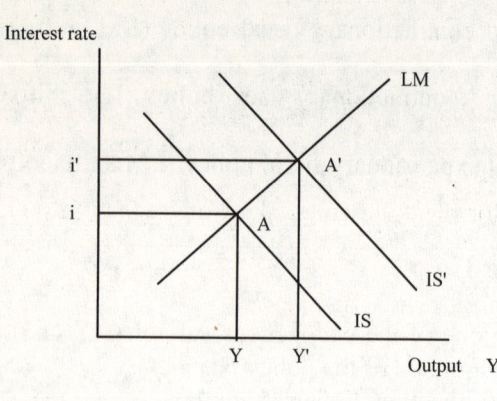

- The increase in G causes an increase in demand (Z).
- Firms respond by slowly increasing Y.
- As soon as Y begins to increase, money demand rises and i rises to maintain financial markets equilibrium.
- Therefore, as Y increases, the economy <u>moves along</u> the LM curve. Y continues to increase (and i rises) until the new equilibrium is reached at A'.

SELF-TEST QUESTIONS

1. What are the two determinants of investment (p. 79)?

2. What does the IS curve represent (p. 82)?

3. Why is the IS curve downward sloping (p. 81)?

4. Changes in what variables cause the IS curve to shift (p. 82)?

5. What does the LM curve represent (pp. 83-84)?

6. Why is the LM curve upward sloping (p. 84)?

7. Changes in what variables cause the LM curve to shift (pp. 84-85)?

8. What is meant by overall equilibrium in the IS-LM model (p. 89)?

9. Why are the effects of fiscal policy on investment ambiguous (p. 89)?

10. What effect will a monetary expansion have on Y and i (p. 90)?

11. What is meant by the policy mix (p. 92)?

12. In the IS-LM model which incorporates dynamics, which market (goods or financial) will respond more quickly to a change in the money supply (p. 94)?

REVIEW PROBLEMS

1. Suppose investment is represented by the following expression:

$I = 200 - 20i + .1Y$.

a. Let Y = 5000. Calculate the level of investment for the following values of i: 5%, 10% and 15%. Let i = 5 when the interest rate is 5% and so on. What happens to investment as i increases?
b. Let i = 5. Calculate the level of investment for the following values of Y: 5500, 6000 and 6500. What happens to I as Y increases?

2. Suppose the goods market is represented by the following equations:

$C = 180 + 0.7Y_D$ $Y_D = Y - T$ $T = 400$
$I = 100 - 18i + 0.1Y$ $G = 400$
$Y = C + I + G$

a. Solve for the equilibrium level of output. That is, obtain an equation with Y on the left hand side and all other variables on the right hand side.
b. Calculate the level of output that occurs when the interest rate is: 5%, 10%, 15% and 20% (i.e., i = 5, and so on). On a separate piece of paper, plot these 4 combinations of i and Y. What does this curve represent?
c. As the goods market adjusts to these increases in i, what happens to consumption, saving and investment? Briefly explain why each variable changes.
d. Calculate the equilibrium level of output when i = 8% (let i = 8). Where is this point on your graph? Assume that i continues to be 8%. Calculate the equilibrium level of output when G increases by 100 (to 500). What is the size of the multiplier?
e. What does your analysis in part (d) suggest happens to the IS curve depicted in your graph? Briefly explain.

3. Assume the goods market is represented by the equations provided in question #2. Note: no calculations are needed here, just provide brief explanations. Briefly explain what would happen to the IS curve as a result of each of the following events:
a. reduction in the interest rate
b. increase in the interest rate
c. a reduction in c_0 from 180 to 100
d. an increase in taxes

4. Assume that money is represented only by coins and bills held by individuals (i.e., there are no chequable deposits). Suppose an individual, given her current income, always wants to hold enough currency to buy three bottles of her favourite beverage each day.
a. Suppose a can of this beverage costs $1. How much currency will this individual hold? This is her nominal money demand.
b. Now suppose that the price of the beverage increases to $1.20. What happens to her nominal money demand? How much currency (in nominal terms) will she now hold? Explain.
c. For simplicity, assume that the GDP deflator increases from 1 to 1.2 during this same period. What happened to the individual's real money demand? Briefly explain.
d. Now suppose that her real income increases. Briefly explain what will happen to her consumption (including her consumption of this beverage). What do you think will happen to her real demand for money? Briefly explain.

5. Use the graphs provided below to answer the following questions.

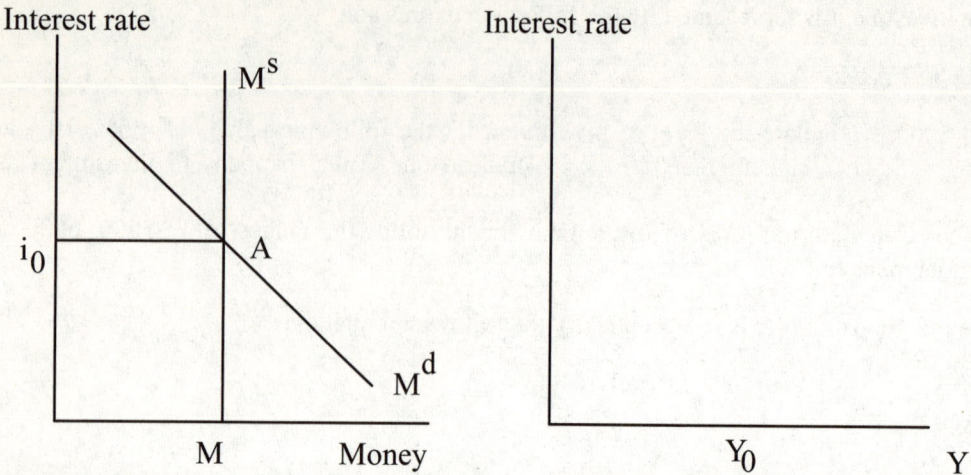

[Graphs: Left graph shows money market with M^s vertical, M^d downward sloping, equilibrium at point A with interest rate i_0 and money M. Right graph has axes Interest rate vs Y, with Y_0 marked.]

a. Initially let $i = i_0$ and $Y = Y_0$. Suppose Y falls to Y_1. Illustrate what happens to money demand as a result of this drop in Y. At the initial interest rate, what type of situation exists? Briefly explain.

b. What must happen to i as a result of this drop in Y? Briefly explain. Label this new equilibrium A'. In the graph to the right, plot the points A and A'.

c. Repeat the analysis in (a) and (b) assuming that Y falls even further to Y_2. Label this point A" and plot it in the graph to the right.

d. What does this plot of points in the above graph represent? Explain.

6. Use the graphs provided below to answer the following questions. Assume price (P) is constant.

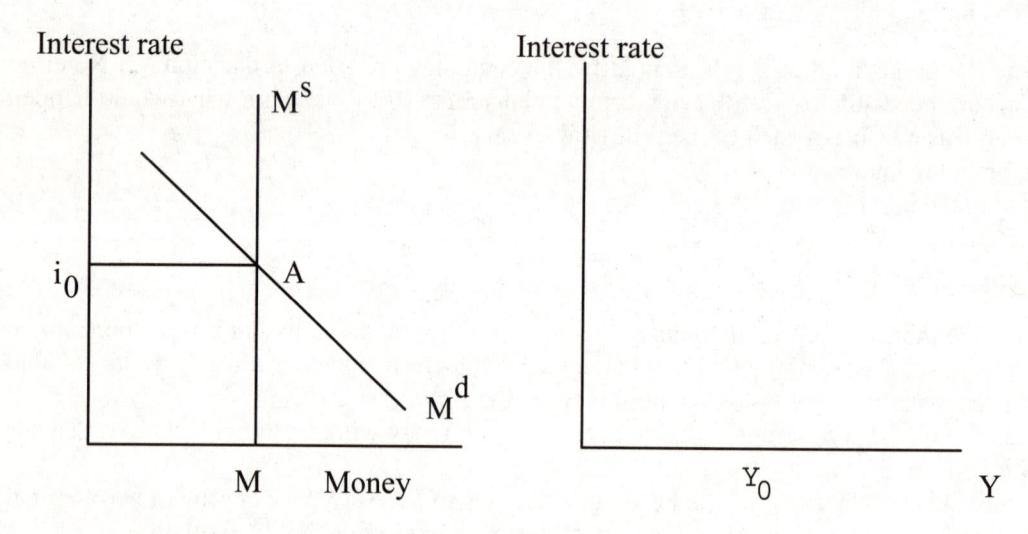

[Graphs: Left graph shows money market with M^s vertical, M^d downward sloping, equilibrium at point A with interest rate i_0. Right graph has axes Interest rate vs Y, with Y_0 marked.]

a. Initially let $i = i_0$ and $Y = Y_0$. Suppose the real money supply falls to M'^s. Illustrate what happens to the money supply curve as a result of this drop in M. At the initial interest rate, what type of situation exists? Briefly explain.

b. What must happen to i as a result of this drop in the money supply? Briefly explain. Label this new equilibrium A'.

c. What effect does this drop in the money supply have on the position of the LM curve? Illustrate this in the above graph.

7. Suppose real money supply and real money demand are represented by the following equations, and price is fixed and set equal to one:

$M^d = 6Y - 120i$ $M^s = 5400$

a. Equate the above expressions for real money demand and money supply and solve for i. That is, i should appear on the left-hand side with all other variables on the right-hand side.
b. Calculate i when Y equals: 1000, 1100 and 1200. On a separate piece of paper, plot these combinations of i and Y. What does this curve represent?
c. Calculate i when Y = 1400. Where is this point on the curve? Assume that Y remains at 1400. Suppose the money supply falls to 5000. Calculate the new equilibrium i when M falls by 400. How much does i change?
d. What does your analysis in part (c) suggest happens to the LM curve? Briefly explain.

8. Use the graph provided below to answer this question. Suppose the financial markets are in equilibrium and that Y does not change.

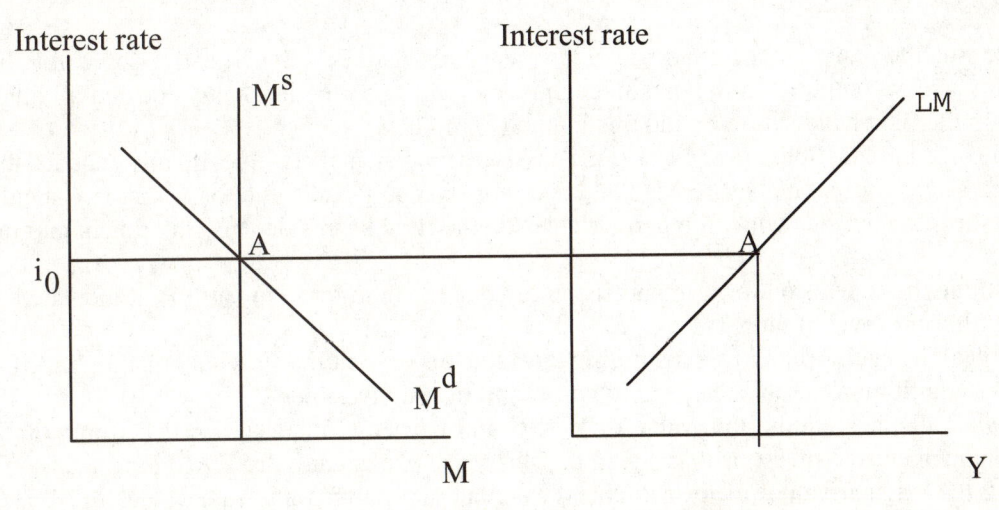

a. What effect has the increased use and availability of credit cards had on money demand? Briefly explain.
b. Illustrate the effects of this on money demand in the above graph. Briefly explain what must happen to i to restore equilibrium.
c. What does your analysis suggest happens to the position of the LM curve <u>given</u> that income (Y) has not changed?
d. During holiday periods, individuals will often increase their holdings of money even though the interest rate and their incomes have not changed. What effect would this behaviour have on the LM curve? Briefly explain.

9. Use the IS-LM model to answer this question.
a. Suppose government purchases (G) increase. What effect will this have on the IS curve and on the LM curve?
b. What effect will this increase in G have on i and Y?
c. What effect will this increase in G have on consumption and saving? Briefly explain.
d. What effect will this increase in G have on investment?
Note: Make sure you can illustrate graphically the effects of this change in G.

10. Use the IS-LM model to answer this question.
a. Suppose the money supply decreases. What effect will this have on the IS curve and on the LM curve?
b. What effect will this decrease in M have on i and Y?
c. What effect will this decrease in M have on consumption and saving? Briefly explain.
d. What effect will this decrease in M have on investment?
Note: Make sure you can illustrate graphically the effects of this change in M.

11. The effects of a fiscal expansion on investment are ambiguous.
a. Why is this so?
b. Is it possible for investment to increase when government purchases increase? Explain.
c. Is it possible for investment to increase when G falls? Explain.

12. Suppose the economy is represented by the following equations (these are identical to those included in questions #2 and #7).

$M^d = 6Y - 120i$ $M^s = 5400$ $T = 400$
$C = 180 + .07Y_D$ $Y_D = Y - T$ $G = 400$
$I = 100 - 18i + 0.1Y$ $P = 1$
$Y = C + I + G$

a. Write out the equation for equilibrium in the goods market. Specifically, solve for the equilibrium level of output. That is, obtain an equation with Y on the left hand side and all other variables on the right hand side. You did this in part (a) of #2.
b. Write out the equation for equilibrium i in the financial market. Specifically, equate the above expressions for real money demand and real money supply and solve for i. That is, i should appear on the left hand side with all other variables on the right hand side. You did this in part (a) of #7.
c. Substitute the expression for i (in part [b]) into your equation for Y in part (a). Calculate the overall equilibrium level of output.
d. Calculate the equilibrium i by substituting the value of Y from (c) into your equation in (b).
e. At this equilibrium, what is the level of consumption and investment?
f. Calculate the new equilibrium value of Y, i, C and I when G increases by 10 (from 400 to 410). What happened to investment as a result of this fiscal expansion? Briefly comment.
g. Using the original values of the variables, calculate the new equilibrium values of Y, i, C and I when M increases by 200 (from 5400 to 5600). What happened to investment as a result of this monetary expansion?

13. Use the graph provided below to answer the following questions. Suppose the economy is initially at point A in the graph. Assume that government spending increases.

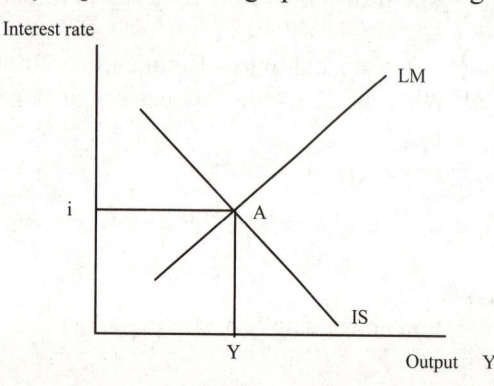

a. What effect will this increase in G have on the IS curve?
b. Suppose the Bank of Canada wants to maintain i at the initial level. What type of policy must the Bank pursue (i.e., contractionary or expansionary) to maintain the interest rate at its initial level? What effect will this Bank policy have on the LM curve? Illustrate the effects of the higher G and Bank response on the IS and LM curves. In your graph, clearly label the new equilibrium.
c. What happens to consumption, saving and investment as a result of this policy mix? Briefly explain.

14. Use the graph provided below to answer the following questions. Suppose the economy is initially at point A in the graph. Assume that taxes are reduced.

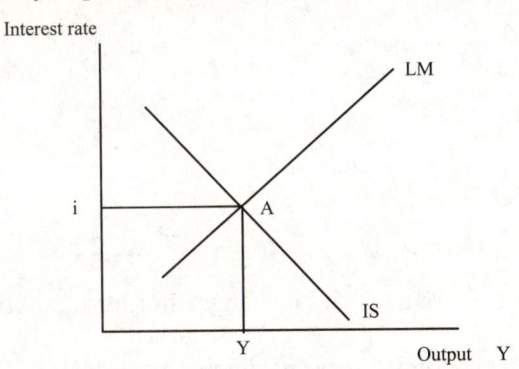

a. What effect will this cut in T have on the IS curve?
b. Suppose the Bank of Canada wants to maintain Y at the initial level. What type of policy must the Bank pursue (i.e., contractionary or expansionary) to maintain output at its initial level? What effect will this policy have on the LM curve? Illustrate the effects of the lower T and the Bank response on the IS and LM curves. In your graph, clearly label the new equilibrium.
c. What happens to consumption, saving and investment as a result of this policy mix? Briefly explain.

15. Briefly discuss what effect each of the following events will have on the IS curve, the LM curve, output, the interest rate, consumption, and investment.
a. an increase in consumer confidence
b. a reduction in consumer confidence
c. an increase in the use of credit cards

16. Assume that Y responds slowly to changes in demand (i.e., take into account dynamics). Assume that there is an increase in taxes.
a. What effect will this have on the IS curve? Briefly explain.
b. Use the graph provided below to answer this question. In your IS-LM graph, trace out the path the economy takes in response to this increase in taxes. What will be the final equilibrium? Show this in your graph.

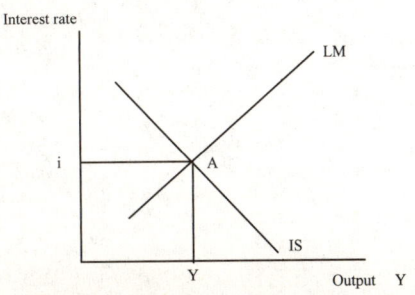

c. What happens to consumption, the interest rate and investment during this adjustment?

17. Assume that Y responds slowly to changes in demand (i.e., take into account dynamics). Assume that there is an increase in the money supply.
a. What effect will this have on the LM curve? Briefly explain.
b. Use the graph provided below to answer this question. In your IS-LM graph, trace out the path the economy takes in response to this increase in the money supply. What will be the final equilibrium? Show this in your graph.
c. What happens to consumption, the interest rate and investment during this adjustment?

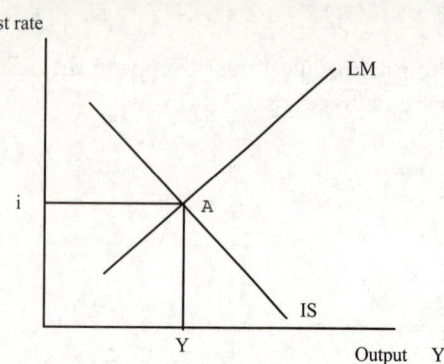

18. Suppose investment is independent of the interest rate. That is, changes in i have no effect on I.
a. What would the IS curve look like for such an economy? Briefly explain.
b. In such an economy, to what extent would changes in the money supply affect output? Explain.
c. In such an economy, to what extent would changes in G (or taxes) affect output? Explain.

MULTIPLE CHOICE QUESTIONS

1. In the IS-LM model, an increase in income (Y), all else fixed, will cause:

a. an increase in consumption
b. an increase in money demand
c an increase in investment
d. all of the above

2. In the IS-LM model, an increase in the interest rate, all else fixed, will cause:

a. an increase in the money supply
b. a reduction in investment
c. an increase in investment
d. none of the above

3. A tax cut will cause:

a. the IS curve to shift to the right
b. the IS curve to shift to the left
c. the LM curve to shift to the right
d. the LM curve to shift to the left

4. A reduction in government purchases will cause:

a. the IS curve to shift to the right
b. the IS curve to shift to the left
c. the LM curve to shift to the right
d. the LM curve to shift to the left

5. An increase in consumer confidence will cause:

a. the IS curve to shift to the right
b. the IS curve to shift to the left
c. the LM curve to shift to the right
d. the LM curve to shift to the left

6. A reduction in the money supply will cause:

a. the IS curve to shift to the right
b. the IS curve to shift to the left
c. the LM curve to shift to the right
d. the LM curve to shift to the left

7. An increase in money demand caused by factors other than a change in income (or the interest rate) will cause:

a. the IS curve to shift to the right
b. the IS curve to shift to the left
c. the LM curve to shift down to the right
d. the LM curve to shift up to the left

8. The IS curve is downward sloping because:

a. an increase in government purchases causes an increase in income
b. an increase in the money supply causes an increase in income
c. a reduction in the interest rate causes an increase in investment and income
d. an increase in the interest rate causes a reduction in money demand

9. The LM curve is upward sloping because:

a. an increase in Y causes an increase in money demand and an increase in the interest rate
b. an increase in the money supply causes a reduction in the interest rate
c. a reduction in the money supply causes an increase in the interest rate
d. all of the above

10. A Bank of Canada purchase of bonds will cause:

a. the LM curve to shift up
b. the LM curve to shift down
c. a lower interest rate, an increase in investment and a rightward shift in the IS curve
d. a higher interest rate, a reduction in investment and a leftward shift in the IS curve

11. In the IS-LM model presented in this chapter, we know <u>with certainty</u> that a fiscal expansion will cause:

a. an increase in the interest rate and an upward shift in the LM curve
b. an increase in the interest rate and an increase in output
c. an increase in the interest rate and a reduction in investment
d. an increase in output and an increase in investment

12. A monetary contraction will cause:

a. an increase in the interest rate and a reduction in investment
b. an increase in i, a reduction in I and a leftward shift in the IS curve
c. the LM curve to shift down
d. a reduction in Y, a reduction in money demand and a reduction in the interest rate

13. A monetary expansion combined with a fiscal expansion will cause:

a. an increase in Y with ambiguous effects on i
b. a reduction in Y with ambiguous effects on i
c. an increase in i with ambiguous effects on Y
d. a reduction in i with ambiguous effects on Y

14. A monetary expansion combined with a fiscal contraction will cause:

a. an increase in Y with ambiguous effects on i
b. a reduction in Y with ambiguous effects on i
c. an increase in i with ambiguous effects on Y
d. a reduction in i with ambiguous effects on Y

15. A monetary contraction combined with a fiscal expansion will cause:

a. an increase in Y with ambiguous effects on i
b. a reduction in Y with ambiguous effects on i
c. an increase in i with ambiguous effects on Y
d. a reduction in i with ambiguous effects on Y

16. A monetary contraction combined with a fiscal contraction will cause:

a. an increase in Y with ambiguous effects on i
b. a reduction in Y with ambiguous effects on i
c. an increase in i with ambiguous effects on Y
d. a reduction in i with ambiguous effects on Y

17. In the IS-LM model which incorporates the dynamic adjustment of the goods market, we know that a change in the money supply will cause:

a. an immediate change in the interest rate with no change in output
b. an immediate change in both the interest rate and output
c. shifts in both the IS and LM curves
d. none of the above

18. In the IS-LM model which incorporates the dynamic adjustment of the goods market, we know that a reduction in the money supply will cause:

a. the interest rate to adjust immediately to the final, overall equilibrium level
b. the interest rate to initially rise above its final, overall equilibrium level
c. output to adjust immediately
d. none of the above

19. In the IS-LM model which incorporates the dynamic adjustment of the goods market, we know that a fiscal expansion will cause:

a. the interest rate to adjust immediately to the final, overall equilibrium level
b. the interest rate to initially rise above its final, overall equilibrium level
c. output and, therefore, the interest rate to adjust slowly over time
d. an increase in the interest rate and a leftward shift in the IS curve

CHAPTER 6. OPENNESS IN GOODS AND FINANCIAL MARKETS

OBJECTIVES, REVIEW AND TUTORIAL

After working through the chapter and the material found below, you should be able to:

1. List and explain the three distinct notions of openness.

2. Define the nominal exchange rate and explain what is meant by a depreciation and appreciation of the domestic currency.

3. Define the real exchange rate and explain the determinants of the real exchange rate.

4. Explain what the balance of payments, current account and capital account measure.

5. Know the distinction between GDP and GNP.

6. Explain what factors influence an individual's decision to hold domestic versus foreign bonds.

7. Explain what is meant by the uncovered interest parity condition.

1. THE THREE DISTINCT NOTIONS OF OPENNESS

(1) Openness in goods markets

Consumers and firms can choose between domestic and foreign goods. To restrict these choices, countries can impose <u>tariffs</u> (a tax on imported goods) or <u>quotas</u> (a restriction on the quantity of imported goods).

(2) Openness in financial markets

Financial investors can choose between domestic and foreign assets. Individuals will, therefore, compare the expected returns on Canadian and U.S. bonds. Countries can impose capital controls which restrict the flow of financial assets between countries.

(3) Openness in factor markets

This represents the opportunity of firms to choose their location and of workers to choose where they work and immigrate.

Learning Tip

You should recognize that recent developments (e.g. free trade agreements) have made economies increasingly more open in all three markets.

---

2. THE NOMINAL EXCHANGE RATE (E)

• The nominal exchange rate (E) equals the number of units of the domestic currency you obtain with one unit of the foreign currency.
• The nominal exchange rate also represents the price of foreign currency in terms of the domestic currency.

Learning Tip

• The nominal exchange rate is the relative price of currencies.
• Let E be the number of Canadian dollars, (C$), one can obtain with one U.S. dollar, (U.S.$), (E = C$/U.S.$). Suppose E = 1.50. How do we interpret this?
  • One U.S.$ can "buy" 1.50 C$.
  • Equivalently, it takes C$1.50 to buy one U.S.$.

An increase in E represents a nominal <u>depreciation</u>. Suppose E increases from 1.50 to 1.55.
  • This increase in E indicates that one U.S.$ now obtains more (1.55 to be exact) C$.
  • As E increases, U.S.$ is now "worth" more.
  • The increase in E also indicates that it takes more C$ to buy one U.S.$.
  • The value of C$ (in terms of U.S.$) drops as E increases.

A reduction in E represents an <u>appreciation</u> and has the exact opposite effects as those just described (i.e., C$ is worth more, etc.).

Learning Tip

You must understand that an increase in E is a C$ depreciation while a reduction in E is a C$ appreciation. To understand this, recall the definition of E, E = C$/U.S.$.
   • When E increases, <u>more</u> dollars are needed to obtain one unit of foreign currency. The value of our dollar decreases and our dollar depreciates.
   • When E decreases, <u>fewer</u> dollars are needed to obtain one unit of foreign currency. The value of our dollar increases and our dollar appreciates.

---

3. THE REAL EXCHANGE RATE (ε)

(1) Introduction

The real exchange rate (ε) is the price of foreign goods in terms of domestic goods. The real exchange rate is, therefore, equal to the ratio of the Canadian dollar price of U.S. goods to the Canadian dollar price of Canadian goods: $\varepsilon = EP^*/P$ where
   • P^* is the U.S. price of U.S. goods.
   • If we multiply P^* by E, we obtain the Canadian price of U.S. goods.
   • P is the Canadian dollar price of Canadian goods.
   • The ratio of EP^* to P represents the price of foreign goods in terms of Canadian goods.

(2) Real depreciation

• An increase in ε indicates that C$ price of foreign goods relative to C$ price of U.S. goods has increased.
• This indicates that foreign goods have become more expensive than domestic goods.
• An increase in ε is called a real depreciation.

(3) Real appreciation

• A reduction in ε indicates that C$ price of foreign goods relative to C$ price of U.S. goods has decreased.
• This indicates that foreign goods have become less expensive than domestic goods.
• A reduction in ε is called a real appreciation.

Learning Tip

• You must understand what effect changes in P, P* and E have on ε.
  • An increase in E (nominal depreciation) causes an increase in ε and a real depreciation.
  • An increase in P* causes an increase in ε and a real depreciation.
  • An increase in P causes a reduction in ε and a real appreciation.
• You must also understand that changes in ε (not E) reflect changes in the relative price of foreign and domestic goods. Why? The effects of a nominal depreciation on ε could be completely offset by a change in P and/or P* leaving ε unchanged.
• IF P and P* tend to move together, changes in E will cause similar changes in ε.

---

(4) Other measures of the real exchange rate

You should also understand the differences between bilateral and multilateral real exchange rates.
• The <u>bilateral real exchange rate</u> measures the real exchange rate between two countries.
• The <u>real multilateral Canadian exchange rate</u> (or effective real exchange rate) measures the average price of Canadian goods relative to those of its trading partners. The effective real exchange rate is a weighted average of bilateral real exchange rates. The weights used are based on import or export shares for each trading partner.

4. THE BALANCE OF PAYMENTS, THE CURRENT ACCOUNT AND THE CAPITAL ACCOUNT

(1) Balance of payments

The balance of payments measures a country's transactions with the rest of the world.

(2) Current account

Transactions "above the line" in the balance of payments are called current account transactions. These transactions include:
• the trade balance (exports - imports)
• net investment income
• net transfers received

The sum of these components represents the current account.
• A current account deficit implies that Canada needs to borrow from the rest of the world.
• A current account surplus implies the opposite.

(3) Capital account

Transactions "below the line" are called capital account transactions. These transactions include:
• Net increase in foreign holdings of Canadian assets (net capital flows to Canada)

- The net increase in foreign holdings of Canadian assets equals [increase in foreign holdings of Canadian assets] – [increase in Canadian holdings of foreign assets]
- Statistical discrepancy

Learning Tip

- When the increase in foreign holdings of Canadian assets exceeds the increase in Canadian holdings of foreign assets, a capital account surplus exists.
- This capital account surplus reflects:
    - a net increase in Canadian foreign indebtedness
    - net capital flows to Canada
    - the borrowing required to finance the capital account deficit.

---

5. DISTINCTION BETWEEN GDP AND GNP

GDP is the value added domestically (within a country).
GNP is the value added by domestically owned factors of production.
GNP = GDP plus net factor payments from the rest of the world.

Learning Tip

- For most countries, the difference between GNP and GDP is small.
- For some countries like Kuwait, however, the difference can be significant.

---

6. THE DECISION TO HOLD DOMESTIC VERSUS FOREIGN FINANCIAL ASSETS

Openness in financial markets indicates that individuals have a choice of holding domestic or foreign bonds.

(1) Returns form holding one-year Canadian bonds

For every dollar you put in a one-year Canadian bond, you receive $(1 + i_t)$ C$ in one year.

(2) Expected returns from holding one-year U.S. bonds

For every C$ dollar you put in a one-year U.S. bond, you expect to receive $(1/E_t)(1 + i^*_t)E^e_{t+1}$ dollars in one year. There are several steps required to illustrate this.
- To buy a U.S. bond, you must first obtain U.S.$.
- Every C$ buys $1/E_t$ U.S.$.
- For example, if $E_t = 1.50$, one U.S. dollar "costs" one dollar and fifty cents Canadian.
- One Canadian dollar, therefore, obtains 67 cents American.
- You take the $1/E_t$ U.S. dollar and buy American bonds. At the end of one year, you will have $(1/E_t)(1 + i^*_t)$ U.S.$.

- Let E^e_{t+1} be the nominal exchange rate you expect to occur in one year. To convert the $(1/E_t)(1 + i^*_t)$ U.S.$ back into C$, simply multiply $(1/E_t)(1 + i^*_t)$ by E^e_{t+1}.

(3) The interest parity condition

When we assume that financial investors only want to hold the asset with the highest rate of return, the following arbitrage relation must hold:

$(1 + i_t) = (1/E_t)(1 + i^*_t)E^e_{t+1}$.

This relation is called the uncovered interest parity or interest parity condition.

Learning Tip

• Two factors suggest that the assumption that individuals hold only the asset with the highest return is too strong:
    (1) the existence of transaction costs of buying and selling U.S. dollars and buying American bonds are ignored; and
    (2) the uncertainty (risk) about the future nominal exchange rate is ignored.

• For simplicity, we can ignore the decision to hold domestic versus foreign money. Why? Individuals hold money to engage in transactions. For individuals and firms in Canada, their transactions are mostly, but not entirely, in Canadian dollars.

---

7. A CLOSER LOOK AT THE INTEREST PARITY RELATION

An approximation of the arbitrage relation is:

$i_t = i^*_t + (E^e_{t+1} - E_t)/E_t$.

This indicates that the decision to hold domestic versus foreign bonds depends not only on a comparison of the interest rates, but also on an assessment of what will happen to the exchange rate over the next year.
• When you buy an American bond, you receive interest income (i^*) plus, if C$ is expected to depreciate, you will receive U.S.$ in one year that will be worth more in terms of C$.
• The term $(E^e_{t+1} - E_t)/E_t$ represents this exchange gain or loss from an expected depreciation or appreciation of the C$.

Learning Tip

• Will you always buy Canadian bonds when $i > i^*$? Not necessarily. If the expected rate of depreciation of the Canadian dollar exceeds the interest rate differential, the return from holding American bonds will be greater.
• Will you always buy American bonds when $i^* > i$? Not necessarily. If the expected rate of appreciation of the Canadian dollar is greater than the interest rate differential, the expected rate of return on Canadian bonds will be greater.

SELF-TEST QUESTIONS

(1) What are the three notions of openness (p. 101)?

(2) Briefly discuss what tariffs, quotas and capital controls are (p. 101).

(3) Explain how exports can exceed GDP (p. 103).

(4) Define the nominal exchange rate, E (p. 104).

(5) What effect does an increase in E have on the value of the dollar (p. 105)?

(6) When the dollar depreciates, what happens to E (p. 105)?

(7) Define the real exchange rate (pp. 105–106).

(8) What happens to the price of American goods in terms of Canadian goods when the real exchange rate increases (p. 107)?

(9) Does an increase in ε correspond to a real appreciation or real depreciation of the domestic currency (p. 107)?

(10) What does the balance of payments measure (p. 110)?

(11) How is the real multilateral Canadian exchange rate constructed (p. 109)?

(12) What are the different types of transactions included in the current account (p. 110)?

(13) What are the different types of transactions included in the capital account (p. 111)?

(14) Suppose the current nominal exchange rate between our dollar and the U.S.$ is E_t. How many U.S.$ can you obtain with one C$ (p. 113)?

(15) What does the expression E^e_{t+1} represent (p. 113)?

(16) Suppose you have one C$ to invest in American bonds. What is the expression that represents the expected return on American bonds measured in C$ (p. 113)?

(17) What does the expression $(E^e_{t+1} - E_t)/E_t$ represent (p. 114)?

(18) Suppose the one-year nominal interest rate in Canada is 6% and 4% in the U.S.. Further assume that the arbitrage relation holds. Given this information, is our dollar expected to appreciate or depreciate over the coming year? How much (p. 114)?

REVIEW PROBLEMS

1. Suppose the C$/U.S.$ exchange rate on Monday is 1.50 and on the following Friday is 1.55.
a. Briefly discuss what has happened to the price of the foreign currency in terms of the domestic currency?
b. How many C$ can 1 U.S.$ buy on Monday? How many on Friday?
c. Has the value of our dollar increased or decreased during the week? Briefly explain.
d. Has our dollar appreciated or depreciated during the week?
e. What happened to E during the week?

2. Suppose the C$/U.S.$ exchange rate on Monday is 1.50 and on the following Friday is 1.40.
a. Briefly discuss what has happened to the price of the foreign currency in terms of the domestic currency?
b. How many C$ can 1 U.S. buy on Monday? How many on Friday?
c. Has the value of our dollar increased or decreased during the week? Briefly explain.
d. Has our dollar appreciated or depreciated during the week?
e. What happened to E during the week?

3. Suppose the nominal exchange rate, E (as defined in the chapter), decreases.
a. What does the drop in E suggest about the price of the foreign currency in terms of our dollars?
b. Has the value of our dollar increased or decreased?
c. Has our dollar appreciated or depreciated?

4. Suppose the C$/U.S.$ nominal exchange rate one week ago was 1.50.
a. If our dollar has depreciated by 10% during the past week, what is the current C$/U.S.$ exchange rate?
b. If our dollar has depreciated by 20% during the past week, what is the current C$/U.S.$ exchange rate?
c. If our dollar has appreciated by 10% during the past week, what is the current C$/U.S.$ exchange rate?
d. If our dollar has appreciated by 20% during the past week, what is the current C$/U.S.$ exchange rate?

5. Suppose a German bottle of wine costs 30 euros (€)
a. Calculate the Canadian dollar price of the German bottle of wine for each of the following C$/ € exchange rates: 0.4, 0.5, 0.6, and 0.7.
b. What happens to the price of the German bottle of wine measured in dollars as E increases?
c. What does your analysis suggest happens to the price of foreign goods measured in dollars as E increases?
d. What does your analysis suggest happens to the price of foreign goods measured in dollars as E decreases?

6. Suppose a bottle of domestic (Canadian) wine is $10 and suppose a German bottle of wine costs 30 euros.
a. For each of the following C$/ € exchange rates, calculate the ratio of the price of a bottle of German wine to the price of a bottle of Canadian wine: 0.4, 0.5, 0.6, and 0.7.
b. Based on your analysis, what happens to the price of a German good (bottle of wine) in terms of a Canadian good (bottle of wine) as E increases?
c. Based on your analysis, what happens to the price of a German good (bottle of wine) in terms of a Canadian good (bottle of wine) as E decreases?

7. Let P be the GDP deflator in Canada and P* be the GDP deflator in the U.S. Suppose P = 1.6 and P * = 1.1.
a. Calculate the real exchange rate for each of the following C$/U.S.$ nominal exchange rates: 1.30, 1.35, 1.40, 1.50.
b. What happens to the real exchange rate as E increases?
c. What happens to the price of American goods in terms of Canadian goods as E increases? Briefly explain.
d. Does an increase in E cause a real appreciation or depreciation of the dollar?

8. Use the following information to answer this question.

	E	P	P*
2001	0.65	1.5	1.2
2002	0.60	1.45	1.25

Note: E is the C$/ € nominal exchange rate.

a. Calculate the real exchange rate in 2001 and 2002.
b. What was the percentage change in the real exchange rate between 2001 and 2002? Does this change in the real exchange rate represent a real appreciation or depreciation?
c. Calculate the percentage change in the nominal exchange rate between the two years. Does this change represent a nominal appreciation or depreciation of our dollar?
d. Calculate the percentage change in P and P*.
e. Was the nominal appreciation (or depreciation) greater than, less than or equal to the real appreciation (or depreciation)? Explain.

9. Suppose P and P* are both increasing. Now suppose that our dollar experiences a 5% nominal depreciation.
a. Which country (domestic or foreign) is experiencing the higher rate of inflation if the domestic currency experiences a real appreciation? Briefly explain.
b. Which country (domestic or foreign) is experiencing the higher rate of inflation if the domestic currency experiences a real depreciation? Briefly explain.
c. Compare the changes in P and P* if the real exchange rate does not change.

10. Suppose you have one C$ and wish to obtain U.S.$.
a. Calculate how many U.S.$ you will obtain for each of the following nominal exchange rates: 1.30, 1.40, 1.50, 1.60.
b. As E increases, what happens to the number of U.S.$ you can obtain with one C$? Briefly explain.

11. Let i^*_t be the one-year interest rate on American bonds. Let $i^*_t = 0.10$ (10%). Suppose you have one C$ and wish to obtain American bonds. Based on your analysis in #10, calculate how many U.S.$ you will have at the end of one year when 1.30, 1.40, 1.50, 1.60.

12. Based on your analysis in #11, calculate the number of C$ you receive for every C$ invested if you expect the nominal exchange rate next year to be 1.0.

13. Use the following information and equation (6.4) in the chapter to answer this question: $i^* = 0.10$; $E_t = 1.50$; and $E^e_{t+1} = 1.55$.
a. Based on the above information, what must the domestic interest rate be for the arbitrage relation to hold?
b. Is $i = i^*$? If i does not equal i^*, which bond has the highest expected return (measured in our dollars)? Explain.

14. Use the following information and equation (6.4) to answer this question: $i^* = 0.06$; and $E_t = 1.50$.
a. Suppose $E^e_{t+1} = 1.45$. Do individuals expect our dollar to appreciate or depreciate? Calculate the expected rate of appreciation or depreciation. Based on your analysis, what must the domestic interest rate be to satisfy the arbitrage relation?

b. Now, suppose $E^e_{t+1} = 1.46$. Do individuals expect our dollar to appreciate or depreciate? Calculate the expected rate of appreciation or depreciation. Based on your analysis, what must the domestic interest rate be to satisfy the arbitrage relation?

c. Now, suppose $E^e_{t+1} = 1.52$. Do individuals expect our dollar to appreciate or depreciate? Calculate the expected rate of appreciation or depreciation. Based on your analysis, what must the domestic interest rate be to satisfy the arbitrage relation?

15. Suppose our dollar is expected to depreciate during the next year. Does the arbitrage relation indicate that the Canadian interest rate is greater than, less than or equal to the foreign interest rate? Briefly explain.

16. Suppose our dollar is expected to appreciate during the next year. Does the arbitrage relation indicate that the Canadian interest rate is greater than, less than or equal to the foreign interest rate? Briefly explain.

17. For each of the following cases, determine whether an individual should buy Canadian bonds or foreign bonds.
a. $i = 4\%$, $i^* = 6\%$, expected depreciation of our dollar of 3%
b. $i = 4\%$, $i^* = 6\%$, expected depreciation of our dollar of 1%
c. $i = 4\%$, $i^* = 6\%$, expected depreciation of our dollar of 2%
d. $i = 6\%$, $i^* = 5\%$, expected depreciation of our dollar of 3%
e. $i = 6\%$, $i^* = 5\%$, expected depreciation of our dollar of 1%
f. $i = 6\%$, $i^* = 5\%$, expected depreciation of our dollar of 2%
g. $i = 5\%$, $i^* = 5\%$, expected depreciation of our dollar of 3%
h. $i = 5\%$, $i^* = 5\%$, expected appreciation of our dollar of 1%
i. $i = 5\%$, $i^* = 5\%$, expected appreciation of our dollar of 2%
j. $i = 5\%$, $i^* = 5\%$, expected depreciation of our dollar of 0%

MULTIPLE CHOICE QUESTIONS

1. The nominal exchange rate is:

a. the number of units of domestic currency you can obtain with one unit of foreign currency
b. the price of foreign currency in terms of domestic currency
c. the number of units of foreign goods you can get with one unit of domestic currency
d. both a and b
e. both b and c

2. The real exchange rate defined in the text (ε) is:

a. EP/P^*
b. price of foreign goods in terms of domestic goods
c. price of domestic goods in terms of foreign goods
d. both a and b

3. An increase in E represents a:

a. real appreciation
b. real depreciation

c. nominal appreciation
d. nominal depreciation

4. When the value of our dollar (in terms of U.S.$) increases, we know that:

a. E increases
b. E decreases
c. our dollar has depreciated
d. none of the above

5. A depreciation of the Canadian dollar indicates that:

a. E has decreased
b. it takes more domestic currency to purchase one unit of foreign currency
c. E has increased
d. both b and c

6. When the dollar appreciates, we know that:

a. the dollar price of foreign currency has increased
b. the dollar price of foreign currency has decreased
c. E has increased
d. none of the above

7. Which of the following expressions represents the real exchange rate as defined in the text?

a. EP^*/P
b. EP/P^*
c. P^*/EP
d. P/EP^*

8. An increase in the real exchange rate indicates that:

a. foreign goods are now relatively more expensive compared to domestic goods
b. domestic goods are now relatively more expensive compared to foreign goods
c. a real depreciation of the domestic currency has occurred
d. both a and c

9. A reduction in the real exchange rate indicates:

a. foreign goods are now relatively more expensive compared to domestic goods
b. domestic goods are now relatively more expensive compared to foreign goods
c. a real depreciation of the domestic currency has occurred
d. a real appreciation of the domestic currency has occurred
e. both b and d

10. Which of the following events would cause a real depreciation of the domestic currency?

a. reduction in E
b. increase in E
c. reduction in P^*
d. increase in P

11. Which of the following events would cause a real appreciation of the domestic currency?

   a. reduction in E
   b. reduction in P*
   c. increase in P
   d. all of the above
   e. none of the above

12. Which of the following transactions is included in the current accounts?

   a. statistical discrepancy
   b. net investment income
   c. increase in foreign holdings of Canadian assets
   d. increase in Canadian holdings of foreign assets

13. Which of the following transactions is included in the capital account?

   a. trade balance
   b. net investment income
   c. increase in foreign holdings of Canadian assets
   d. all of the above
   e. both b and c

14. Suppose a country has a current account deficit. Given this information, we know that:

   a. this country's exports exceed its imports
   b. this country lends to the rest of the world
   c. a capital account deficit exists
   d. a capital account surplus exists

15. Based on the definition of GDP and GNP, we know that:

   a. GNP = GDP + net factor payments from the rest of the world
   b. GDP = GNP + net factor payments from the rest of the world
   c. GNP = GDP + the balance of payments
   d. GNP = GDP + net investment income
   e. GNP = GDP + net capital flows from the rest of the world

16. Which of the following expressions represents the expected return (in C$) from holding an American bond:

   a. i^*
   b. $(1 + i)E^e_{t+1}$
   c. $(1/E^e_{t+1})(1 + i^*)E_t$
   d. $(1/E_t)(1 + i^*)E^e_{t+1}$

17. Assume the interest parity condition holds. If i = 5% and i* = 7%, we know with certainty that:

   a. individuals will only hold domestic bonds
   b. individuals will only hold foreign bonds

c. the dollar is expected to appreciate by 2%
d. the dollar is expected to depreciate by 2%

18. Assume the interest parity condition holds. If i = 10% and i* = 8%, we with certainty know that:

a. the expected return on Canadian bonds is greater than the expected return on American bonds
b. the expected return on Canadian bonds is less than the expected return on American bonds
c. our dollar is expected to appreciate by 2%
d. our dollar is expected to depreciate by 2%

19. Assume the interest parity condition holds and that individuals expect our dollar to appreciate by 4% during the next year. Given this information, we know that:

a. $i > i^*$
b. $i < i^*$
c. $i = i^*$
d. individuals will only hold Canadian bonds

20. Assume the interest parity condition holds. Suppose i* = 10% and that Canadian dollar is expected to depreciate by 2% during the next year. For every dollar an individual invests in a foreign bond, she can expect to receive how many dollars in one year?

a. 1.02
b. 1.08
c. 1.10
d. 1.12

21. Assume the interest parity condition holds. Suppose i* = 10% and that Canadian dollar is expected to appreciate by 3% during the next year. For every dollar an individual invests in a foreign bond, she can expect to receive how many dollars in one year?

a. 1.03
b. 1.07
c. 1.10
d. 1.13

22. Suppose i = 10%, i* = 8% and our dollar is expected to depreciate by 3% during the next year. Given this information, we know that:

a. individuals will prefer to hold Canadian bonds
b. individuals will prefer to hold American bonds
c. the expected return from holding an American bond (measured in Canadian dollars) will equal 5%
d. the expected return from holding an American bond (measured in Canadian dollars) will equal 11%
e. both a and c
f. both b and d

23. Suppose i = 10%, i* = 8% and our dollar is expected to appreciate by 3% during the next year. Given this information, we know that:

a. individuals will prefer to hold domestic bonds
b. individuals will prefer to hold foreign bonds
c. the expected return from holding a foreign bond (measured in dollars) will equal 5%
d. the expected return from holding a foreign bond (measured in dollars) will equal 11%
e. both a and c
f. both b and d

CHAPTER 7. THE GOODS MARKET IN AN OPEN ECONOMY

OBJECTIVES, REVIEW AND TUTORIAL

After working through the chapter and the material found below, you should be able to:

1. Know the distinction between domestic demand for goods and the demand for domestic goods.

2. Understand the determinants of imports and exports.

3. Explain the determinants of equilibrium output and the trade balance.

4. Examine the effects of changes in domestic demand on output and net exports.

5. Examine and graphically illustrate the effects of foreign demand on output and net exports.

6. Understand that the multiplier is smaller in an open economy.

7. Explain the effects of a real depreciation on output, imports and net exports.

8. Examine the combined effects of changes in the exchange rate and fiscal policy on output and the trade balance.

9. Discuss what is meant by the Marshall-Lerner condition and the J-curve.

10. Understand the relationship among saving, investment, and the trade deficit.

1. DOMESTIC DEMAND AND THE DEMAND FOR DOMESTIC GOODS

(1) Domestic demand for goods

This represents the demand for goods by individuals, governments, and firms residing in the country. It, therefore, equals: $C + I + G$.

(2) Demand for domestic goods

Two adjustments must be made to obtain the demand for domestic goods: (1) add exports; and (2) subtract imports. It, therefore, equals: $C + I + G + X - \varepsilon Q$.

Learning Tip

- Why add exports? X represents the demand for domestic goods that comes from abroad.
- Why subtract imports? Some of the goods bought by domestic residents, firms and governments may include foreign goods.
- Why do we multiply Q by the real exchange rate, ε? Q is the quantity of imports. To express this quantity of imports in terms of domestic goods, multiply Q by the relative price of foreign goods in terms of domestic goods.

---

2. DETERMINANTS OF EXPORTS AND IMPORTS

(1) Imports (Q)

• As domestic income (Y) rises, C and I both increase. Some of this increase in C and I will include foreign goods. Hence, Q increases as Y increases.
• An increase in ε, the real exchange rate, represents a real depreciation of the domestic currency.
• An increase in ε also indicates that foreign goods are now relatively more expensive. An increase in the relative price of foreign goods will cause a reduction in Q.

(2) Exports (X)

• As foreign income (Y*) rises, foreign C and foreign I both increase. Some of this increase in foreign C and foreign I will include Canadian goods. Hence, X increases as Y* increases.
• A real depreciation (an increase in ε) corresponds to a decrease in the relative price of Canadian goods. The Canadian goods become more attractive, and X increases.

3. EQUILIBRIUM, THE TRADE BALANCE AND THE MULTIPLIER

(1) Equilibrium output

Equilibrium output occurs when output equals the demand for domestic goods (Y = Z):

$Y = C + I + G + X - \varepsilon Q$.

(2) The trade balance

The trade balance (net exports, NX) is the difference between exports and imports: $NX = X(Y^*, \varepsilon) - \varepsilon Q(Y, \varepsilon)$. NX is shown graphically in figure 7-1. The NX line is downward sloping because an increase in Y will cause an increase in Q. The higher Q, given X, causes NX to decline (a trade surplus will shrink, or a trade deficit will grow).

Learning Tip

There are several features of the NX line that you must understand.
• For a given value of ε and Y*, the equilibrium level of Y will determine the trade balance. Equilibrium output occurs when Y = Z.
• Equilibrium Y does NOT occur when NX = 0!
• An increase in Y* will cause an increase in X and cause the NX line to shift up by the change in X.
• An increase in ε will cause X to increase and Q to fall and NX will increase (assuming the Marshall-Lerner condition holds) at each level of Y. The NX line will shift up.
• A change in Y does NOT cause a shift of the NX line, only a movement along it.

---

(3) The multiplier

An increase in Y causes an increase in demand (the ZZ line is upward sloping).
• In a closed economy, all of the increase in Y falls on domestic goods (DD line in figure 7-1(a, b)).
• In an open economy, some of the increase in Y falls on foreign goods (Q). The ZZ line is, therefore, flatter than DD.
• The flatter ZZ line corresponds to a smaller multiplier.

4. CHANGES IN DEMAND AND THEIR EFFECTS ON Y AND NX

(1) Changes in demand

Changes in demand represent changes in C, I and/or G that fall entirely on domestic goods.
• Any change of this type will cause the ZZ line to shift.
• The size of the shift equals the initial change in demand.
• Equilibrium will occur at the point where Y = Z.
• As Y changes, Q will change as we move along the NX line; therefore, NX will change.
• For example, a decrease in ZZ will cause lower Y, lower Q and an increase in NX (either a trade surplus increases or a trade deficit falls).

Learning Tip

• You must understand that changes in domestic demand do not cause shifts in the NX line.
• Changes in Y cause movements along the NX line and cause the trade balance to change.
• Along the NX line, exports do not change since Y* and ε are given.
• The multiplier is smaller here (compared to a closed economy) because some of the change in demand now also goes to foreign goods.

---

(2) Changes in foreign demand (ΔY*)

Changes in foreign demand represent changes in X. [I will review the effects of changes in the real exchange rate in the next section]. An increase in Y* will cause an increase in exports (X). The increase in X has two effects: (1) ZZ shifts up by the change in X; and (2) the NX line shifts up by the change in X.

• The effects of the change in X are the same as those described above.
• The new equilibrium again occurs where Y = Z.
• The change in Y equals the change in X times the multiplier.
• As Y increases, Q will rise.
• The increase in Q is, however, smaller than the increase in X.
• NX, therefore, increase as X increases (the trade balance improves).

Learning Tip

Make sure you understand the discussion which accompanies Figure 7-4.
• Any increase in X will cause Y and Q to increase. The trade balance will improve.
• Any reduction in X will cause Y and Q to fall. The trade balance will deteriorate.

---

5. THE REAL EXCHANGE RATE, NET EXPORTS AND OUTPUT

The real exchange rate, ε, is the relative price of foreign goods in terms of domestic goods. An increase in ε (a real depreciation) will cause:
(1) an increase in X as domestic goods are relatively cheaper;
(2) a reduction in the quantity of imports (Q) as foreign goods are relatively more expensive; and
(3) an increase in the price of imports and, therefore, an increase in the import bill. The same quantity of imports now costs more to buy.

For a depreciation to cause an increase in NX, the combined effects of (1) and (2) must exceed the effects of (3). The condition for which a depreciation causes NX to increase is called the <u>Marshall-Lerner condition</u>.

> **Learning Tip**
>
> If the Marshall-Lerner condition does NOT hold, a depreciation would cause NX to fall. Why? The effects of (3) would dominate the combined effects of (1) and (2).

Assuming the Marshall-Lerner condition holds, an increase in the real exchange rate will cause an increase in X, a decrease in Q and an increase in NX. As NX increases, the ZZ line shifts up by the change in NX and the NX line shifts up by the change in NX.

The effects of an increase in the real exchange rate on Y and on the trade balance are the same as the effects of a an increase in Y*:
- Y increases
- as Y increases, Q increases but not enough to offset the initial increase in NX
- the trade balance improves

6. EXCHANGE RATE POLICY AND FISCAL POLICY

By now, you should recognize the following:

(1) increases in G cause Y to increase and NX to fall
(2) reductions in G cause Y to fall and NX to increase
(3) increases in ε (depreciations) cause Y to increase and NX to increase
(4) reductions in ε (appreciations) cause Y to fall and NX to fall

Therefore,

- To raise Y, governments can: (1) increase G; and/or (2) increase ε.
- To improve the trade balance, governments can: (1) reduce G; and/or (2) increase ε.

> **Learning Tip**
>
> • Different situations can exist causing governments to pursue a variety of combinations of exchange rate and fiscal policies.
> • You should review Table 7-1.

7. THE J-CURVE

(1) Introduction and review

First, you should review the material in #5. If the Marshall-Lerner condition does NOT hold, a depreciation (increase in ε) will cause NX to fall. For example, suppose the real exchange rate increases by 8%. This 8% depreciation causes the price of imports to increase by 8%. Further assume that the quantity of exports increases by 2% and that the quantity of imports falls by 3%.
• In this case, the depreciation has a relatively greater effect on the price of imports than on the quantities of X and Q.
• This depreciation will also cause a deterioration of the trade balance (NX falls).

(2) Graphical depiction of this adjustment

- Over time, the quantities of X and Q will respond to the change in the real exchange rate.
- Eventually, this depreciation will cause the trade balance to improve.
- The graphical representation of this adjustment is called the J-curve.

> **Learning Tip**
>
> • If the Marshall-Lerner condition does NOT initially hold, a depreciation will cause NX to fall and have a negative effect on domestic output.
> • The existence of the J-curve effect can also explain the lagged response of Canada net exports to real depreciations and appreciations during the 1990s.

SELF-TEST QUESTIONS

(1) What are the components of domestic demand for goods (p. 120)?

(2) What are the components of demand for domestic goods (p. 120)?

(3) Why must we multiply Q by ε to obtain the value of imports (p. 121)?

(4) What are the two determinants of imports? Briefly explain how an increase in each affects imports (p. 121).

(5) What are the two determinants of exports? Briefly explain how an increase in each affects exports (p. 121)?

(6) Why is the NX line downward sloping (p. 123)?

(7) What happens to the size of the multiplier after introducing net exports (p. 124)??

(8) What effect does an increase in G have on demand, the ZZ line, imports, exports and net exports (pp. 124–125)?

(9) An increase in Y* causes an increase in exports, an increase in income (Y) and an increase in imports (as Y increases). Given that both exports and imports increase, what happens to the trade balance as Y* increases (p. 125)?

(10) What effect will an increase in ε have on the quantities of imports and exports (p. 130)?

(11) What effect will an increase in ε have on the cost of imports (p. 130)?

(12) Briefly explain what is meant by the Marshall-Lerner condition (p. 130)?

(13) If the Marshall-Lerner condition holds, what effect will an increase in ε have on the NX relation (p. 130)?

(14) Suppose policy makers want to reduce a trade deficit while leaving Y unchanged. What type of exchange rate and/or fiscal policy can they pursue (p. 131)?

(15) Suppose the Marshall-Lerner condition does NOT hold. A 12% depreciation will have what effect on the quantities of imports, exports and on the trade balance (pp. 131-133)?

(16) What does the J-curve represent (p. 133)?

REVIEW PROBLEMS

1. Suppose you are given the following information about an economy: C = 1200; I = 300; G = 500; X = 450; and Q = 400. Further assume that all variables are expressed in terms of domestic goods.
a. Calculate the level of "domestic demand for goods", the level of "demand for domestic goods" and net exports. What is the difference between the demand for domestic goods and the domestic demand for goods? Compare this with the trade balance.
b. Repeat the analysis in part (a). This time, however, assume Q = 500 and that all other variables are the same.
c. Repeat the analysis in a. This time, however, assume that X = 400. Use the original values of the variables.
d. Based on your analysis in parts a, b and c, under what condition will the demand for domestic goods be greater than, less than or equal to the domestic demand for goods?

2. Suppose the goods market is represented by the following behavioural equations.

$C = 500 + 0.5Y_D$ $I = 500 - 2000r + 0.1Y$ $G = 500$
$X = 0.1Y^* + 100\varepsilon$ $Q = 0.1Y - 100\varepsilon$ $T = 400$
$Y^* = 1000$ $r = 0.05 \; (5\%)$ $\varepsilon = 1$
$Z = C + I + G + X - \varepsilon Q$ $Y = Z$ in equilibrium

a. Calculate equilibrium GDP (Y).
b. Given your answer in a, calculate C, I, X and Q.
c. At this level of output, is the economy experiencing a trade surplus or deficit?
d. Suppose G increases by 100 (to 600). Calculate the new equilibrium level of output. What is the size of the multiplier?
e. Based on your answer to d, calculate the new level of Q. Calculate the change in net exports caused by this increase in G.

3. Repeat the analysis in #2 (parts [a] to [d]). This time, however, assume that the marginal propensity to import is 0.2. That is, $Q = 0.2Y - 100\varepsilon$. Assume all other variables are the same.

4. This question refers to your analysis in #2 and #3. Compare the changes in Y caused by the increase in G in #2 and #3. What happened to the size of the multiplier as the marginal propensity to import increases?

5. For each of the following events, assume that the goods market is initially in equilibrium and that a trade surplus exists (NX > 0) at the initial level of output. Explain what effect each event will have on the demand for domestic goods, the ZZ line, equilibrium output, exports, imports, the trade balance and the NX line.
a. Tax cut
b. Reduction in G
c. Decrease in Y^*
d. Reduction in ε
e. a simultaneous increase in ε and increase in G

6. Suppose the domestic economy is initially experiencing a trade deficit. Further assume that government officials would like to eliminate the trade deficit.

a. What type of (domestic) policy could be pursued to eliminate the trade deficit? What effect would this policy have on output? Explain.
b. What type of exchange rate policy could be pursued to eliminate the trade deficit? What effect would this policy have on output? Explain.
c. Suppose domestic policy makers can put pressure on foreign policy makers to alter their fiscal policy. What type of foreign fiscal policy could be implemented to eliminate the trade deficit? What effect would this policy have on domestic and foreign output? Explain.

7. Assume that trade is balanced (NX = 0) at the initial level of output. Further assume that the government wants to increase Y while leaving trade in balance. Discuss and explain what type of policies could be implemented to achieve this goal.

8. Assume that NX < 0 and that the government wants to increase Y and simultaneously eliminate the trade deficit at the new equilibrium level of output. Discuss and explain what type of policies could be implemented to achieve this goal.

9. Assume that Y is too high and that NX > 0. Further assume that the government wants to reduce Y without changing the trade surplus. Discuss and explain what type of policies could be implemented to achieve this goal.

10. For this question, assume the Marshall-Lerner condition does NOT hold. Further assume that there is a trade deficit at the initial level of output. Now suppose that a real depreciation occurs.
a. Discuss and explain what effect this depreciation will have on X, Q, NX, the NX line, the ZZ line and domestic output. In the graph below, illustrate the effects of this depreciation. Clearly illustrate in the graph, the new equilibrium.

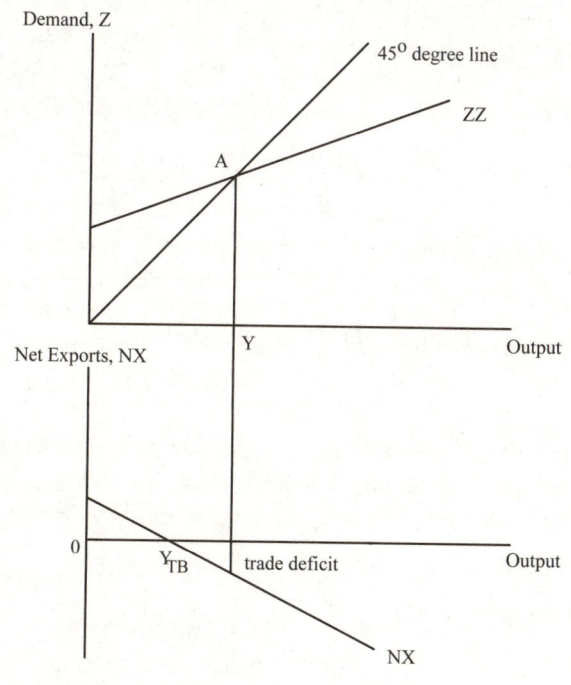

b. Based on your analysis in a, what type of exchange rate policy should be pursued in the short-run (when the Marshall-Lerner condition does not hold) to increase economic activity? Explain.

11. Suppose the real exchange rate depreciates by 12%. For each of the following cases, briefly explain whether the Marshall-Lerner condition holds, and explain what effect the 12% real depreciation will have on NX and Y.
a. X increases by 4%, Q falls by 6%
b. X increases by 7%, Q falls by 4%
c. X increases by 7%, Q falls by 6%
d. X increases by 6%, Q falls by 7%
e. X increases by 5%, Q falls by 9%

MULTIPLE CHOICE QUESTIONS

NOTE: Unless specified otherwise, assume the Marshall-Lerner condition holds.

Use the information provided below to answer questions 1 and 2. Assume the domestic economy is in equilibrium and that:

C = 1000   I = 200   G = 400   Exports = 300   Imports = 350

All of the above variables are measured in terms of domestic goods.

1. The level of "demand for domestic goods" is:

a. 1550
b. 1600
c. 1900
d. 2250

2. The level of "domestic demand for goods" is:

a. 1550
b. 1600
c. 1900
d. 2250

3. Which of the following expressions represents the "demand for domestic goods"?

a. $C + I + G$
b. $C + I + G + X$
c. $C + I + G + \varepsilon X - Q$
d. all of the above
e. none of the above

4. Which of the following expressions represents net exports (NX)?

a. $X - Q$
b. $Q - X$
c. $Q - \varepsilon X$
d. $X - \varepsilon Q$

5. Which of the following events would cause a reduction in exports?

a. increase in ε
b. increase in Y
c. reduction in Y*
d. all of the above

6. Which of the following events would cause a reduction in imports?

a. increase in Y*
b. decrease in Y*
c. increase in ε
d. increase in Y

7. The net export line is downward sloping because of the effects of:

a. Y on Q
b. Y* on X
c. ε on X
d. ε on Q

8. In the model presented in this chapter, a reduction in G will cause:

a. both the ZZ line and NX line to shift down by the change in G
b. a reduction in Y and a reduction in imports
c. an increase in exports and an increase in net exports
d. an increase in net exports and the net export line to shift up

9. Which of the following events will cause both Y and NX to increase?

a. increase in ε
b. reduction in Y*
c. increase in G
d. reduction in T

10. An increase in the marginal propensity to import will cause:

a. the ZZ line to become flatter and a given change in G to have a smaller effect on output
b. the ZZ line to become flatter and a given change in G to have a larger effect on output
c. the ZZ line to become steeper and a given change in G to have a smaller effect on output
d. the ZZ line to become steeper and a given change in G to have a larger effect on output

11. Assume the Marshall-Lerner condition holds. A real appreciation will cause:

a. the NX line to shift up
b. a reduction in NX
c. an increase in Y
d. all of the above

12. A reduction in Y* will tend to cause:

a. the ZZ line to shift down
b. the NX line to shift down
c. a reduction in Y
d. a reduction in NX
e. all of the above
f. none of the above

13. Suppose a government wishes to increase Y and leave NX unchanged. The government, therefore, should:

a. increase G
b. reduce T
c. increase G and increase ε
d. increase ε

14. Suppose a government wishes to reduce Y and increase NX. Which of the following policies would most likely achieve this?

a. increase ε
b. reduce G
c. increase G and increase ε
d. reduce ε

15. Suppose the Marshall-Lerner condition does NOT hold. A real depreciation will tend to cause:

a. a reduction in NX and a reduction in Y
b. an increase in NX and a reduction in Y
c. an increase in NX and an increase in Y
d. a reduction in NX and an increase in Y

16. The J-curve illustrates the effects of:

a. Y on NX
b. Y* on exports
c. a real depreciation on NX
d. Y on imports

17. The goods market is in equilibrium when:

a. NX = 0
b. Y equals the demand for domestic goods
c. Y equals domestic demand for goods
d. domestic demand equals demand for domestic goods

CHAPTER 8. OUTPUT, THE INTEREST RATE, AND THE EXCHANGE RATE

OBJECTIVES, REVIEW AND TUTORIAL

After working through the chapter and the material found below, you should be able to:

1. Understand what is meant by equilibrium in the goods and financial markets (review).

2. Understand the interest parity condition and what it implies about the relation between the interest rate and the exchange rate.

3. Understand the Mundell-Fleming model: the open economy version of the IS/LM model.

4. Explain the effects of fiscal and monetary policy in the open economy under flexible exchange rates.

5. Understand the concept of fixed exchange rates, pegs, crawling pegs and bands.

6. Discuss the concepts of the EMS and the euro.

7. Discuss the role of monetary policy and fiscal policy under fixed exchange rates.

8. Understand how changes in capital mobility alter the ability of monetary policy to affect domestic output under fixed exchange rates.

1. A REVIEW OF THE GOODS AND FINANCIAL MARKETS EQUILIBRIUM

(1) Assumptions

In this chapter, we assume:
- The Marshall-Lerner condition holds.
- The aggregate price level (both domestic and foreign) is constant.
- The expected future exchange rate (E^e) is given (i.e., does not change).

Learning Tip
• The first assumption implies that an increase in the real exchange rate depreciation) will cause an increase in NX.
• The second assumption implies that inflation is zero and, therefore, that $i = r$.
• The second assumption also implies that $\varepsilon = E$.

(2) Goods market

The goods market is in equilibrium when output equals demand. This condition is represented graphically by the IS relation. You should understand that:
• An increase in the interest rate (i) will cause a reduction in I, a reduction in demand (expenditure) and a reduction in output.

- An increase in E (depreciation) will cause an increase in NX, an increase in demand and an increase in output.

(3) Financial market (money versus bonds)

Financial market equilibrium occurs when the supply of money equals the demand for money. This condition is represented graphically by the LM relation.

Learning Tip

- The demand for domestic money is assumed to be determined solely by domestic residents. That is, we assume that Americans do not hold Canadian dollars.
- An increase in Y causes an increase in money demand and an increase in i.
- An increase in the money supply causes a reduction in i.

---

2. THE INTEREST PARITY CONDITION AND THE DETERMINANTS OF THE EXCHANGE RATE

The interest parity condition indicates that the domestic interest rate must equal the foreign interest rate plus the expected rate of depreciation of the domestic currency. The interest parity condition can be rearranged to obtain the following:

$$E = \overline{E}^e/(1 + i - i^*).$$

This implies a negative relation between E and i. Why? Suppose the interest parity condition holds and that i increases.
- The increase in i makes domestic bonds relatively more attractive.
- Financial investors will switch out of foreign bonds and into domestic bonds.
- To buy domestic bonds, investors must first obtain C$. This causes an increase in the demand for C$.
- The increase in the demand for C$ causes an increase in the price of C$. Our dollar appreciates (E falls).
- Hence, an increase in i causes an appreciation (a reduction) in E.
- The interest parity (IP) relation illustrates this negative relation between i and E (given i* and $\overline{E}^e$).

Learning Tip

You must understand the above discussion which implies that E is a decreasing function of i.
- An increase in i causes an appreciation and a reduction in E.
- A reduction in i causes depreciation and an increase in E.

You must also understand how much E must change given $\overline{E}^e$. Suppose i increases by 2%.
- This will cause our dollar to <u>appreciate</u> by 2% <u>today</u>.
- With $\overline{E}^e$ unchanged, our dollar is now <u>expected to depreciate</u> by 2% <u>over the coming year</u>.
- This expected 2% depreciation of C$ corresponds to a 2% appreciation of U.S.$.
- In fact, U.S.$ must be expected to appreciate by 2% to compensate for the 2% increase in i.

3. THE OPEN ECONOMY VERSION OF THE IS-LM MODEL

Y, i and E will be determined simultaneously given the IS, LM and IP relations.

(1) The IS relation

Output depends on i, E and the other factors (i.e., T, G, Y*, i* and $\overline{E}^e$) included in the equilibrium condition. An increase in i now has two effects on Y:
- I falls, demand falls, and output falls
- Given the IP relation, the increase in i causes an appreciation, a reduction in NX, a reduction in demand and a reduction in output.

These changes in I and NX will have a multiplier effect on Y.

(2) The LM relation

It is the same as before.

(3) The IP relation

It is the same as above.

Learning Tip

Make sure you can explain why the IP relation is downward sloping.

You may also be required to understand how change in i* and $\overline{E}^e$ affect the position of the IP curve.

(1) The foreign interest rate (i*):
- An increase in the foreign interest rate will make foreign bonds more attractive.
- The demand for the foreign currency will increase, and the demand for the domestic currency will decrease.
- Therefore, the domestic currency will depreciate (E increases).
- This increase in i* and subsequent increase in E is represented as a rightward shift in the IP curve.
- How much does E increase? Enough to cause an expected appreciation of the domestic currency to offset the rise in i*.

(2) The expected exchange rate ($\overline{E}^e$):
- An increase in the expected future exchange rate will cause individuals to expect a depreciation of the domestic currency.
- The expected rate of return on foreign bonds is now higher.
- The demand for the foreign currency bonds is now higher.
- The demand for the foreign currency will increase and the demand for the domestic currency will decrease.
- Therefore, the domestic currency will depreciate (E increases).

This increase in $\overline{E}^e$ and subsequent increase in E is represented as a rightward shift in the IP curve.

(3) Warning
- Changes in either i* or $\overline{E}^e$ will cause shifts in the IP curve AND will cause changes in the exchange rate.
- These changes in the exchange rate will also cause changes in net exports and cause SHIFTS of the IS curve.
•

(4) Equilibrium

The IS and LM curves determine Y and i. The equilibrium value of E is found by looking at the IP relation given i.

Learning Tip

(1) A shift in the IS and LM curve for any reason other than changes in $\overline{E}^e$ and/or R*, brings about a movement along (not a shift in) the IP relation.

(2) A shift in the IS and the LM curve due to a change in $\overline{E}^e$ and/or R* also entails a shift in the IP relation.

4. FISCAL AND MONETARY POLICY UNDER FLEXIBLE EXCHANGE RATES

Learning Tip

This is a good place to check your understanding of what has been discussed in class and in the text. Make sure you understand what the IS, LM and IP relations represent.
- Can you define them?
- Can you explain why each has its particular shape?
- Can you explain what causes the IS and LM curves to shift?

(1) Fiscal policy

An increase in G will cause:
- An increase in demand and a rightward shift in the IS curve.
- As output increases, transactions increase and, therefore, money demand increases.
- To maintain equilibrium in the financial markets, i must rise (we move along the LM curve).
- As i rises, Canadian. Bonds are more attractive.
- Financial investors switch from foreign bonds to Canadian bonds.
- This switch corresponds to an increase in the demand for C$ and an appreciation of C$ (E falls as we move along the IP relation).
- The higher i causes a reduction in I and a reduction in NX.
- FINAL RESULT: Y increases, i increases, and E falls.

Learning Tip

- The fiscal expansion causes a deterioration of the trade balance for two reasons: (1) as Y increases, imports rise; and (2) the appreciation also reduces NX.
- An increase in G will cause an increase in both the budget deficit and trade deficit (twin deficits).
- The effects on I are still ambiguous since Y and i both increase.

(2) Monetary policy

A reduction in the money supply will cause:
• An increase in i to maintain financial market equilibrium causing the LM curve to shift up.
• The higher i has two negative effects on demand: (1) investment falls; and (2) the appreciation of the dollar (Canadian bonds are more attractive) causes NX to fall.
• The drop in I and NX has a multiplier effect on Y.
• FINAL RESULT: Y falls, i increases and E falls.

Learning Tip

Make sure you can discuss and explain the effects of an increase in the money supply and the effects of a reduction in government spending.

---

5. FIXED EXCHANGE RATES (PEGS, CRAWLING PEGS, BANDS)

(1) Introduction

There are many types of exchange rate arrangements. They range from fully flexible exchange rates to crawling pegs, pegs, to fixed exchange rates, etc. Countries that operate under a pegged rate system, peg their respective currency to the US dollar or other currencies. Countries that operate under a crawling peg choose a predetermined rate of depreciation or appreciation against the currency they have pegged their currency. The crawl means a slow movement of the currency against, say, the dollar. Another currency arrangement is for a group of countries to maintain their bilateral exchange rates (between each pair of countries) within some bands.

The most prominent example of currency bands is the European Monetary System (EMS) – 1978-1998, where countries agreed their exchange rate vis-à-vis other currencies within narrow bands.

The euro, the common currency of twelve members of the European Union – known as euro zone – was adopted in a full fledged manner in 2002.

In a pegged rate system, the central bank: (1) chooses to peg the exchange rate at some level $\bar{E}$; and (2) takes actions (i.e., changes the money supply) while trying to keep E pegged at $\bar{E}$. It is assumed that financial and foreign exchange markets believe that the exchange rate will remain pegged at $\bar{E}$.

Learning Tip

There are several important implications of the above assumptions:
• First, given that the expected exchange rate equals $\bar{E}$, $i = i^*$.
• Second, financial market equilibrium can be represented as $M/P = YL(i^*)$.
• Third, the central bank must change the money supply to keep $i = i^*$.
• And finally, the central bank gives up monetary policy as a policy instrument to maintain the pegged exchange rate.

6. FISCAL AND MONETARY POLICY UNDER FIXED EXCHAMNGE RATES

(1) Fiscal policy

An increase in G causes:
• An increase in demand and an increase in Y.
• As Y increases, money demand increases and i tends to increase.
• The increase in i will tend to cause an appreciation of the dollar.
• The central bank, given its commitment to a pegged exchange rate, will prevent the appreciation by maintaining $i = i^*$.
• To keep $i = i^*$, the central bank "accommodates" the increase in money demand by increasing the money supply.
• As the IS curve shifts to the right, the LM curve shifts down to keep $i = i^*$.
• FINAL RESULT: Y increases, i and E do not change.

Learning Tip

• Make sure you can explain the opposite of this example.
• Make sure you can explain why fiscal policy is more powerful under fixed exchange rates.
• You should review the reasons why countries choose to fix their exchange rates.

---

(2) Monetary policy

Suppose $i = i^*$ and that the central bank reduces M so that $i > i^*$.
• In a closed economy, the higher i causes a reduction in I and reduction in Y.
• In the open economy, the increase in i will cause the dollar to appreciate.
• FINAL RESULT: i returns to i^*, M returns to its original level (to keep $i = i^*$ and to prevent the change in E) and Y does not change. Hence, monetary policy cannot be used to change output under fixed exchange rates.

7. CAPITAL MOBILITY AND FIXED EXCHANGE RATES

Recall that the monetary base represents the central bank's liabilities. The central bank has two assets: (1) bonds; and (2) foreign exchange reserves. I will review an increase in the central bank's purchase of bonds in two situations.

(1) Perfect capital mobility

• The central bank purchase of bonds ($\Delta B > 0$) causes an increase in the money supply.
• This increase in M causes i to fall below i^*.
• With no intervention, E increases and a depreciation occurs.
• Given its commitment to peg E, the central must intervene and buy dollars with its holdings of foreign exchange reserves. This causes i to increase.
• The central bank keeps buying the domestic currency (and loses foreign exchange reserves) until $i = i^*$.
• With perfect capital mobility, the above events happen very quickly.
• In sum, the central bank cannot permanently affect i.

(2) Imperfect capital mobility

With imperfect capital mobility, it takes time for investors to shift between domestic and foreign bonds.
- The central bank again buys bonds ($\Delta B > 0$), M increases and i falls below i*.
- With imperfect capital mobility, only some investors move into foreign bonds and, therefore, sell domestic currency.
- The central bank will again intervene by buying domestic currency with its foreign exchange reserves.
- This time, however, the intervention will be small, only partially offsetting the initial bond purchase.
- In short, the central bank will lose some foreign exchange reserves; however, i may remain below i* for a sufficient amount of time for Y to increase as I increases.

> **Learning Tip**
>
> As capital becomes increasingly mobile, the ability of a central bank to use open-market operations (purchase and sale of bonds) to affect Y will diminish. Why? When $i < i^*$, a more rapid response by investors will require a larger central bank intervention and a greater loss of foreign exchange reserves.

SELF-TEST QUESTIONS

(1) What are the determinants of consumption (p. 138)?

(2) What are the determinants of investment (p. 138)?

(3) What are the determinants of net exports (p. 138)?

(4) Briefly discuss the interest parity condition (pp. 139-140).

(5) What effect on the exchange rate will an increase in the interest rate have on the exchange rate (p. 140)?

(6) Briefly explain the relation between i and E (p. 141).

(7) Suppose $i < i^*$ and that the interest parity condition holds. What is expected to happen to the value of the domestic and foreign currencies over the next year (p. 141)?

(8) In the goods market, changes in the interest rate now have two effects on output. What are they (p. 142)?

(9) What effect does an increase in G have on Y, i, E, and NX under flexible exchange rates (pp. 143–144)?

(10) What effect does a reduction in M have on Y, i, E, and NX under flexible exchange rates (pp. 144-145)?

(11) Briefly discuss the difference between fixed exchange rates and a crawling peg (p. 146).

(12) Briefly discuss the difference between a devaluation and a revaluation (p. 146).

(13) Under fixed exchange rates with perfect capital mobility, the central bank must do what to peg the currency (pp. 147)?

(14) Under fixed exchange rates, an increase in government spending will have what effect on Y, i and E (pp. 147-148)?

(15) How does the central bank respond to the increase in G in #14 (pp. 147-148)?

(16) Briefly discuss some of the reasons why countries choose fixed exchange rates (p. 148).

(17) What are the two assets central banks hold (p. 152)?

(18) Under fixed exchange rates with perfect capital mobility, what happens to the central bank's balance sheet if the central bank attempts to increase the money supply (pp. 152-153)?

REVIEW PROBLEMS

1. Suppose the expected exchange rate between C$ and U.S.$ in one year is 1.40 (C$1.40 buys one U.S.$). Now suppose that the Canadian one-year interest rate is 5% (i = 0.05) and is 7% in the U.S. (i* = 0.07). Assume that interest parity holds.
a. Calculate the current exchange rate given the above information.
b. Calculate the current exchange rate if i increases to 6%.
c. Calculate the current exchange rate if i increases to 7%.
d. Calculate the current exchange rate if i increases to 8%.
e. Based on your analysis in (a) to (d), what happens to E as i increases? Does our dollar appreciate or depreciate as i increases?
f. What happens to the value of US$ as i increases?

2. Assume the interest parity condition holds.
a. What happens to the expected rate of depreciation or appreciation of our dollar as i increases? Explain.
b. What happens to the expected rate of return on American bonds as i increases.

3. For given values of $\overline{E}^e$ and i*, why is the interest parity relation downward sloping?

4. Assume interest parity holds and that i = 6%, i* = 6% and $\overline{E}^e$ = 0.9.
a. What is the current exchange rate?
b. What is the expected rate of appreciation or depreciation?
c. What is the expected rate of return on American bonds?
d. Based on your analysis, if i = i*, what do financial and foreign exchange markets expect will happen to the exchange rate during the next year? Explain.

5. Suppose an economy is initially closed. Now assume the country becomes "open" under flexible exchange rates. What happens to the slope of the IS curve as the economy becomes open under flexible exchange rates? Explain.

6. a. In the graph provided below, illustrate the effects of a reduction in G under flexible exchange rates. Initially assume that NX = 0.

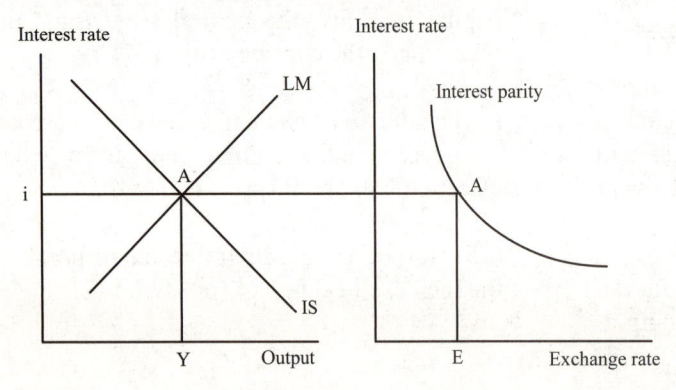

b. Explain what effect the decrease in G has on i, Y and E.
c. Explain what happens to C, I, and NX.

7. Based on your analysis in #6, what do you think would happen to Canada's trade deficit if G were reduced (or T increased) to cut the budget deficit? Explain.

8. The text includes an example where M falls under flexible exchange rates. Suppose NX was initially zero prior to the decrease in M.
a. Discuss what effect this decrease in M has on C and I.
b. What effect does this decrease in M have on E and Y? Why does E change?
c. What effect does this decrease in M have on NX? Explain.

9. a. In the graph provided below, illustrate the effects of an increase in M under flexible exchange rates. Initially assume that NX = 0.

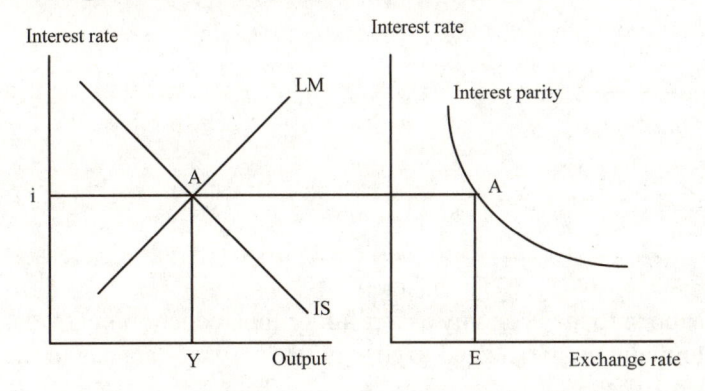

b. Explain what effect the increase in M will have on i, Y and E.
c. Why does E change?
d. What happens to the expected rate of return on foreign bonds as a result of the increase in M? What happens to i*?
e. What happens to C and I as a result of the increase in M?
f. Explain what happens to NX as a result of the increase in M.

10. Use the graph provided below to answer this question. Assume the economy is initially operating at the level of output Y_0, NX = 0 and the exchange rate is fixed.

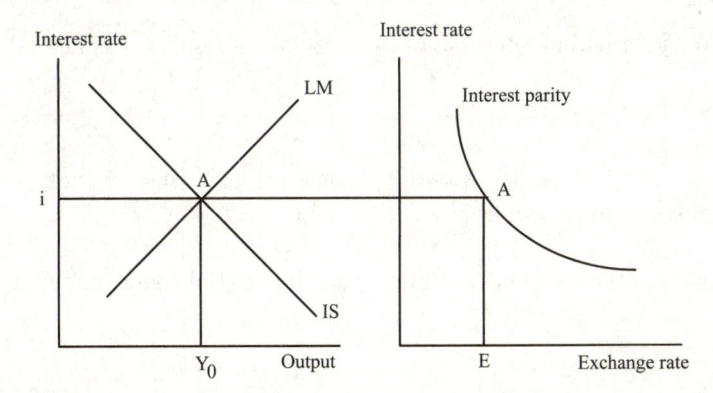

a. Suppose G increases. Further assume that the central bank wants to maintain output at the initial level of output. What type of policy must the central bank pursue to keep Y at the original level? Explain and show this in your graph.

b. What happens to i and E as a result of this combined monetary and fiscal policy?
c. Discuss what happens to the components of demand as a result of this combined policy action.

11. The chapter includes an example where G increases under fixed exchange rates.
a. What happens to C and I in this example?
b. What happens to the exchange rate in this example?
c. What happens to net exports in this example (assume the NX was initially negative – a trade deficit exists)?

12. Use the IS-LM graph provided below to answer this question. Suppose government spending decreases under fixed exchange rates.

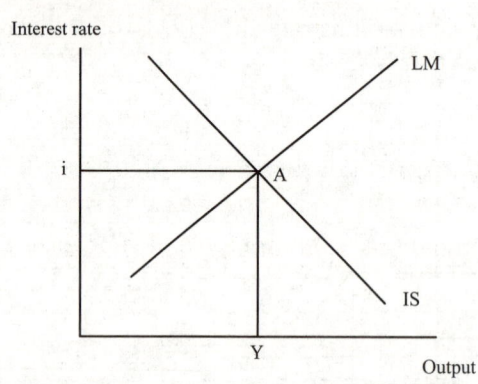

a. Graphically illustrate what will happen to the economy as a result of this reduction in G.
b. What must the central bank do to maintain the pegged exchange rate? What happens to the money supply?
c. What happens to C and I?
d What happens to net exports? Initially assume that NX < 0.

13. Suppose there are two countries (A and B) that are <u>identical</u> in every way with the following exception: A operates under fixed exchange rates and B operates under flexible exchange rates. Suppose G falls by the same amount in both countries.
a. In which of the two countries will the change in Y be the greatest? Explain.
b. Based on your analysis in part (a), what effect will the choice of fixed versus flexible exchange rates have on the output effects of fiscal policy? Explain.

14. Under fixed exchange rates, what effect will an increase in i* have on the model? Explain.

15. How do the exchange rate bands work?

16. Under fixed exchange rates with perfect capital mobility, what effect will a monetary contraction have on Y, i and the composition of the central bank's balance sheet?

17. Under fixed exchange rates with imperfect capital mobility, can the central bank pursue a policy to reduce Y? Explain.

MULTIPLE CHOICE QUESTIONS

Unless specified otherwise, assume that the Marshall-Lerner condition holds.

1. Investment does NOT depend on which of the following variables?

a. Y
b. r
c. r*
d. all of the above

2. Which of the following events will cause an increase in net exports?

a. increase in Y
b. decrease in Y
c. decrease in Y*
d. reduction in E

3. If both the domestic and foreign price levels are fixed (do not change), we know that:

a. $Y = Y^*$
b. $r = I$, and $r^* = i^*$
c. $NX = 0$
d. $E > 1$

4. The interest parity condition indicates that the exchange rate (E) is a function of which set of variables?

a. $\overline{E}^e, i, i^*$
b. i, i^*, Y
c. i, i^*, Y^*
d. none of the above

5. Assume the interest parity condition holds and that $i = 8\%$ and $i^* = 6\%$. This implies that:

a. the dollar is expected to appreciate by 2%
b. the dollar is expected to depreciate by 2%
c. the foreign currency is expected to depreciate by 2%
d. the expected return (measured in dollars) on foreign bonds is less than the expected return on Canadian bonds

6. Assume the interest parity condition holds. An increase in i will cause:

a. an increase in E
b. a reduction in E
c. an increase in i*
d. a reduction in i*

7. Assume the interest parity condition holds. A reduction in i will cause:

a. the dollar to be expected to appreciate over the next year
b. the dollar to be expected to depreciate over the next year
c. a reduction in E
d. a reduction in i*

8. In the open economy model, the IS relation indicates that an increase in i now has effects on which components of demand?

a. I and NX
b. C and NX
c. NX and G
d. only I

9. An increase in G under flexible exchange rates will cause:

a. a reduction in E
b. a depreciation of the domestic currency
c. an increase in Y and an increase in NX
d. all of the above

10. A reduction in G under flexible exchange rates will cause:

a. an increase in NX
b. an increase in E
c. a reduction in Y
d. all of the above

11. A monetary expansion under flexible exchange rates will cause:

a. a reduction in i, reduction in E, and increase in Y
b. an increase in E and an increase in Y
c. ambiguous effects on I since i falls and Y increases
d. a reduction in i* and reduction in E

12. A monetary contraction under flexible exchange rates will cause:

a. a reduction in I and a reduction in Y
b. an increase in E
c. an increase in i and a leftward shift in the IS curve
d. a depreciation of the domestic currency and a reduction in Y

13. Suppose there is a simultaneous reduction in G and increase in M under flexible exchange rates. Given this information, we know with certainty that:

a.   E increases
b.   E decreases
c.   Y increases
d.   Y decreases

14. In a fixed exchange rate regime, we know that:

a. $i = i^*$
b. $i > i^*$
c. $i < i^*$
d. $E = 1$

15. Under fixed exchange rates, the central bank must act to keep:

a. $Y = Y^*$
b. $NX = 0$
c. $i = i^*$
d. the money supply constant

16. Under a fixed exchange rate regime, an increase in G will cause:

a. an increase in Y
b. an increase in M
c. no change in the domestic interest rate
d. all of the above

17. An increase in G will tend to have the greatest effect on Y in which of the following cases?

a. fixed exchange rates, all else fixed
b. flexible exchange rates, all else fixed
c. flexible exchange rates in which the central bank simultaneously reduces the money supply
d. flexible exchange rates in which the central bank does not accommodate the increase in G

18. With fixed exchange rates and imperfect capital mobility, a central bank's attempt to increase output will result in:

a. an increase in foreign exchange holdings
b. a reduction in foreign exchange holdings
c. a reduction in bond holdings
d. an increase in i

CHAPTER 9. THE LABOUR MARKET
OBJECTIVES, REVIEW AND TUTORIAL

After working through the chapter and the material found below, you should be able to:

1. Understand the difference among the participation rate, unemployment rate and the non-employment rate.

2. Be familiar with the three characteristics of the large flow of workers.

3. Explain the effects of movements in the unemployment rate on individual behaviour.

4. Explain how bargaining power, labour market conditions, and efficiency wage considerations affect wages.

5. Explain the relationship among output, employment, wages and prices.

6. Understand both the WS and PS relations.

7. Explain what is meant by the equilibrium real wage and the natural rate of unemployment.

8. Explain what the natural level of employment and the natural level of output represent.

1. A REVIEW OF LABOUR MARKET STATISTICS

You should be familiar with the following definitions:

- labour force = unemployed + employed
- participation rate = (labour force)/(noninstitutional civilian population)
- unemployment rate = unemployed/labour force
- non-employment rate = (population - employment)/population

2. THREE CHARACTERISTICS OF THE LARGE FLOWS OF WORKERS

(1) Employment

- Flows into employment come from: (1) unemployment; and (2) out of the labour force.
- Flows out of employment go: (1) to unemployment; and (2) out of the labour force.

(2) Unemployment

- Flows out of unemployment: (1) go to employment; and (2) leave the labour force.
- Flows into unemployment come from: (1) layoffs; (2) out of the labour force.

(3) Labour force

• These flows include retirees, those who finish school and those who enter the labour force for the first time.
• These flows also include those who switch between participation and non-participation.

3. EFFECTS OF MOVEMENTS IN THE UNEMPLOYMENT RATE

Firms can reduce employment by:

(1) hiring fewer workers; and
(2) laying off existing workers.

(1) Decreased hires

A reduction in hires causes:

• a reduction in the chances that an unemployed worker gets a job
• fewer job openings
• a higher unemployment rate and more applicants; and
• an increase in the duration of unemployment.

(2) Decreased hires and more layoffs

This will cause an increase in unemployment. This increase in unemployment implies:

• a reduction in the chances that an unemployed worker gets a job; and
• a higher chance that employed workers will lose their jobs.

Learning Tip

• The proportion of unemployed finding a job each month tends to decrease when the unemployment rate rises.
• The separation rate tends to increase when the unemployment rate rises.
• You should be aware that these changes occur differently for different groups.

---

4. WAGE DETERMINATION

Learning Tip

You should understand that:
(1) Workers are typically paid a wage that exceeds their reservation wage; and
(2) Wages depend on labor market conditions.

---

(1) Bargaining power

Many employed workers have bargaining power. When unemployment is low, their bargaining power increases.

(2) Efficiency wages

Firms may want to pay workers above their reservation wages:
- to increase the chances that productive workers will stay with the firm; and
- to increase the cost of workers losing their jobs if they are found shirking.

> **Learning Tip**
>
> Labour market conditions will also affect the firms' decisions to change wages. When unemployment decreases, firms may increase wages:
> (1) to reduce the probability that workers will quit; and
> (2) to deter shirking (with low unemployment, the cost of losing a job is lower).

You must also be able to interpret the following wage equation: $W = P^e F(u, z)$; where W is the nominal wage, P^e is the expected price level, u is the unemployment rate, and z is a catch-all variable.

(3) Expected price level

Both workers and firms care about the real wage (W/P). Since P is not known when W is set, the nominal wage depends on P^e. An increase in P^e will cause a proportionate increase in W.

(4) Unemployment

When u increases, bargaining power falls and workers are forced to accept lower wages.

(5) Other factors

Employment Insurance (or benefits), structural change, and changes in minimum-wage legislation will also affect W.

5. RELATION AMONG OUTPUT, EMPLOYMENT, W AND P

The production function, $Y = N$, implies that:
(1) an increase in employment will cause an equal increase in output; and
(2) the cost of producing one more unit of output equals the cost of employing one more worker.

Firms set their price according to:

$P = (1 + \mu)W$ where W is the cost of labour and μ is the markup of price over cost.

> **Learning Tip**
>
> - With perfect competition, firms set price equal to cost so $\mu = 0$.
> - When $\mu = 0$, P must equal W.
> - Since many goods markets are not perfectly competitive, some firms can set P above W.
> - Note: as markets become more competitive, μ decreases and P is closer to W.

6. THE WAGE-SETTING AND PRICE-SETTING RELATIONS

(1) The WS relation

Assume that nominal wages depend on the actual price level (P). The <u>WS relation</u> is represented by the following:

$W/P = F(u, z)$.

This equation indicates that there is a negative relation between the real wage and unemployment. As u increases, workers have less bargaining power and W/P is lower. This is represented by the WS relation in figure 9-4.

(2) The PS relation

The <u>PS relation</u> is given by:

$W/P = 1/(1 + \mu)$.

Price-setting decisions determine the real wage paid by firms. An increase in the markup, μ, causes firms to increase P, given W. The real wage, therefore, falls when μ increases. The PS relation in figure 9-4 is a horizontal line. Why? Changes in u have no effect on μ and, therefore, no effect on the real wage implied by price-setting behaviour.

Learning Tip

- Make sure you can explain the shape of the WS and PS relations.
- The WS relation will shift up if the catch-all variable increases (e.g. if employment insurance benefits increase, or the minimum wage increases).
- The PS relation will shift up if μ falls.
---

7. EQUILIBRIUM REAL WAGE, EMPLOYMENT AND UNEMPLOYMENT

Equilibrium in the labour market requires that the real wage implied by the WS relation be equal to the real wage implied by the PS relation:

$F(u, z) = 1/(1 + \mu)$.

This is represented by the point in the following graph where the two relations intersect:

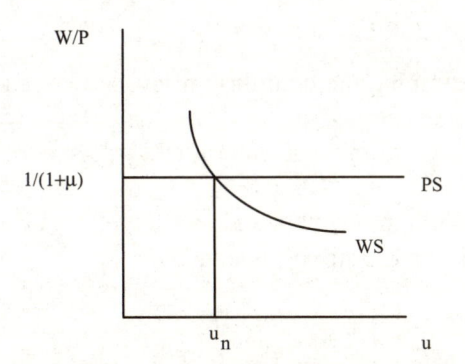

The unemployment rate consistent with equilibrium is the natural rate of unemployment (u_n).

> **Learning Tip**
>
> - Shifts in the WS and PS relations will cause a changes in u_n. However, shifts in PS also cause changes in the real wage.
> - For example, changes in μ, unemployment compensation, minimum wages, etc. will yield to new equilibria.
> - Make sure you can explain intuitively the slope of the WS and PS relations.
> - Make sure you can explain intuitively what factors cause shifts in the WS and PS relations. Since $u = (L - N)/L$, $u = 1 - (N/L)$. Given u_n, there are corresponding natural levels of employment (N_n) and output (Y_n). Specifically, $Y_n = N_n = L(1 - u_n)$.

8. THE WS, PS, LABOUR DEMAND, AND LABOUR SUPPLY RELATIONS

In previous economics courses, you might have examined the labour market using supply and demand curves for labour. In this labor demand/labour supply framework, the market for labour determines both the equilibrium real wage and equilibrium level of employment. The model presented in this chapter can be modified so that it resembles what you might have seen previously.

(1) The WS curve when N is on the horizontal axis.

- An increase in employment will cause a reduction in the unemployment rate.
- A reduction in u will cause an increase in bargaining power.
- The increase in bargaining power will cause an increase in the nominal wage.
- Given the aggregate price level, the rise in W will cause an increase in W/P.
- The WS curve, with N on the horizontal axis, is upward sloping.
- The WS curve appears similar to the labour supply curve.

(2) The PS curve when N is on the horizontal axis.

- An increase in N will cause a reduction in u.
- A reduction in u has no effect on the markup.
- Because P does not change, the real wage does not change either when N changes.
- Hence, the PS curve (with N on the horizontal axis) is horizontal.

(3) Determination of equilibrium u, N, and W/P

- The interaction of the WS and PS relations will determine the equilibrium levels of N and W/P.
- There is only one level of N that equates the real wage from wage-setting and price-setting behavior.
- These levels of N and W/P are the equilibrium levels of employment and real wage.
- Changes in z and the markup will have similar effects on the curves, u, and W/P.

> **Learning Tip**
>
> - The horizontal PS curve is similar to a labour demand curve when the marginal product of labour is constant.
> - With Y = N (the production function), the marginal product of labour is constant.
> - If labour exhibited diminishing marginal returns (i.e., the marginal product of labour falls as N increases), the PS curve in Figure 9-4 would be upward sloping. The PS curve in the figure associated with the Focus material would then be downward sloping.
> - While these curves appear similar to labour supply and labour demand curves, there are several important differences. You should review that section of the Focus that discusses these issues.

SELF-TEST QUESTIONS

(1) What are the two components of the labour force (p. 157)?

(2) What is the difference between the participation rate and the unemployment rate (p. 157)?

(3) What are "separations" and what are the two reasons they occur (pp. 157-158)?

(4) What is the employment rate (p. 159)?

(5) Monthly separation rates tend to be high for which groups (p. 160)?

(6) What is the relation between the proportion of unemployed workers finding a job each month and the unemployment rate (p. 161)?

(7) What does the reservation wage represent (p. 163)?

(8) How does bargaining power affect wage determination (p. 163)?

(9) What is meant by "efficiency wages" (p. 163)?

(10) Why do firms and workers care about real wages (p. 289)?

(11) Why do nominal wages depend on the expected price level (p. 289)?

(12) An increase in the unemployment rate will have what effect on wages (p. 289)?

(13) When the production function is given by Y = N, what is the marginal cost of production (p. 165)?

(14) Why is the wage-setting relation downward sloping (p. 167)?

(15) Why is the price-setting relation a horizontal line (p. 168)?

(16) What is the natural rate of unemployment (p. 168)?

(17) What effect will an increase in employment benefits have on the real wage and on the natural rate of unemployment (p. 169)?

(18) What might cause the PS relation to shift down (p. 169)?

(19) What might cause the WS relation to shift (p.169)?

20. What is the relationship between labour demand and real wage (p. 169-170)?

21. What is the relationship between labour supply and real wage (p. 170)?

REVIEW PROBLEMS

1. Use the information provided below to answer the following questions.

Civilian noninstitutional population	25
Employed	15
Unemployed	1

a. What is the size of the labour force?
b. How many individuals are "out of the labour force"?
c. Calculate the participation rate.
d. Calculate the unemployment rate.
e. Calculate the employment rate.

2. Based on your understanding of the efficiency wage theory, explain what effect an increase in the wage would have on the following: (a) quits; (b) productivity.

3. Explain what must occur for the average duration of unemployment to increase.

4. Explain what must occur for the separation rate to increase.

5. What are the basic differences between the primary and secondary labour markets?

6. Using the wage equation (equation [9.1]), briefly explain how each of the following events will affect the nominal wage.
a. reduction in P^e
b. reduction in the unemployment rate
c. a reduction in employment benefits

7. Briefly explain how each of the following events will affect the price set by firms.
a. increased merger activity causes markets to become less competitive
b. enforcement of competition law
c. a reduction in the nominal wage

8. This question focuses on the wage setting (WS) relation.
a. Briefly explain what effect a reduction in the unemployment rate will have on the real wage.
b. Why is the WS relation downward sloping?
c. What effect will a reduction in unemployment benefits have on the WS curve?
d. What effect will an increase in the rate of structural change have on the WS curve?
e. What effect will an increase in the price level have on the WS relation?

9. For the following values of μ, calculate the real wage.
a. $\mu = 0.1, 0.2, 0.3,$ and 0.4.
b. What happens to the real wage as μ increases?
c. Explain why the real wage changes as μ increases.

10. Suppose all markets are perfectly competitive.
a. What is the value of μ when perfect competition exists?
b. What will be the real wage paid by firms when all markets are perfectly competitive?

11. Use the WS and PS relations to examine the effects of the following events on the natural rate of unemployment and on the real wage. Be sure to explain the effects of the event on the WS and PS relations.
a. reduction in employment insurance
b. increase in the rate of structural change in the labour market
c. less stringent competition law
d. increase in the minimum wage

12. Based on your analysis in #11, explain what effect each event will have on the level of employment and output.

13. Explain why the PS curve is similar to a labour demand curve and the WS similar to a labour supply curve.

MULTIPLE CHOICE QUESTIONS

Use the information provided below to answer questions 1 to 4.

Civilian noninstitutional population   200 million
Employed   100 million
Unemployed   6 million

1. The labour force for this economy is:

a. 100 million
b. 106 million
c. 194 million
d. 200 million

2. The unemployment rate for this economy is:

a. 6/100 = 6%
b. 6/106 = 5.7%
c. 6/194 = 3.1%
d. 6/200 = 3%

3. The labour force participation rate is:

a. 100/200 = 50%
b. 94/200 = 47%
c. 94/100 = 94%
d. 106/200 = 53%

4. The employment rate for this economy is:

a. 100/200 = 50%
b. 106/200 = 53%
c. 100/106 = 94.3%
d. 194/200 = 97%

5. Suppose the average monthly flows out of unemployment is 3 million. Further assume that the average number of individuals who are unemployed in any month is 6 million. The average duration of unemployment will be:

a. 2 months
b. 3 months
c. 6 months
d. one half of a month

6. Which of the following variables would be included in separations?

a. quits
b. layoffs
c. new hires
d. all of the above
e. both a and b

7. Between 1976 and 1991, which of the following groups of workers had the lowest average monthly separation rate?

a. Young (15-24 years old)
b. Older (25+)
c. males
d. female

8. Suppose firms decide to hire fewer workers. This will tend to:

a. increase the chances of losing a job if currently employed
b. decrease the chances of an unemployed worker finding a job
c. all of the above
d. none of the above

9. An increase in the unemployment rate will tend to be associated with:

a. an increase in the proportion of unemployed workers finding a job
b. a reduction in the proportion of unemployed workers finding a job
c. an increase in wages
d. an increase in bargaining power

10. A reduction in the unemployment rate will tend to be associated with:

a. a reduction in the separation rate
b. an increase in the separation rate
c. a reduction in wages
d. a reduction in bargaining power

11. If an individual is offered a wage <u>below</u> her/his reservation wage, we would expect:

a. the individual will prefer to work at that wage
b. the individual will prefer not to work at that wage
c. is indifferent to working or being employed (at the offered wage)
d. none of the above

12. Suppose workers and firms expect P to increase by 5%. Given this information, we would expect that:

a. the nominal wage will increase by more than 5%
b. the nominal wage will increase by less than 5%
c. the nominal wage will increase by exactly 5%
d. the real wage will increase by 5%

13. In a graph with the real wage on the vertical axis and the unemployment rate on the horizontal axis, which of the following statements is true?

a. the PS relation is downward sloping
b. the PS relation is upward sloping
c. the WS relation is horizontal
d. none of the above

14. A reduction in employment insurance will cause:

a. the PS relation to shift up
b. the PS relation to shift down
c. the WS relation to shift up
d. the WS relation to shift down

15. As markets become more competitive, we know that:

a. the PS relation will shift up
b. the PS relation will shift down
c. the WS relation will shift up
d. the WS relation will shift down

16. An increase in the markup of price over cost will cause:

a. the PS relation to shift up
b. the PS relation to shift down
c. the WS relation to shift up
d. the WS relation to shift down

17. If the markup over cost is zero ($\mu = 0$), we know that:

a. the real wage is 1
b. the real wage is greater than 1
c. the real wage is less than one
d. the PS relation is upward sloping

18. Less stringent competition law will tend to cause:

a. an increase in u_n and an increase in W/P
b. an increase in u_n and a reduction in W/P
c. a reduction in u_n and a reduction in W/P
d. a reduction in u_n and an increase in W/P

19. An increase in u_n will be associated with:

a. an increase in N
b. an increase in Y
c. a reduction in N
d. none of the above

20. In a graph with the real wages on the vertical axis and the employment rate on the horizontal axis, which of the following statement is true?
a. the PS relation is upward sloping.
b. the WS relation is horizontal.
c. the WS relation is upward sloping.
d. none of the above.

21. If the marginal product of labour, A, is subject to diminishing returns, then
a. the PS relation will be downward sloping.
b. the PS relation will be horizontal.
c. the WS relation is horizontal.
d. all of the above.

CHAPTER 10. PUTTING ALL MARKETS TOGETHER: The *AS-AD* Model

OBJECTIVES, REVIEW AND TUTORIAL

After working through the chapter and the material found below, you should be able to:

1. Understand what is meant by general equilibrium.

2. Understand the derivation and interpretation of the AS relation.

3. Understand the derivation and interpretation of the AD relation.

4. Be able to explain why output returns to the natural level of output in the long run.

5. Explain the short-run and long-run effects of a change in monetary policy.

6. Explain the short-run and long-run effects of a change in fiscal policy.

7. Explain the short-run and long-run effects of a change in oil prices.

1. A REVIEW OF THE AS RELATION AND THE AS CURVE

The AS relation is represented by the following:

$P = P^e(1 + \mu)F(1 - (Y/L), z)$.

You need to understand two key characteristics of the AS relation.

(1) An increase in the expected price level causes a proportionate increase in the actual price level.

Learning Tip
• If P^e increases by 5%, the nominal wage will increase by 5% and firms will raise prices by 5%. • If P^e falls, the opposite occurs. • In this chapter, $P^e_t = P_{t-1}$. • When the AS curve shifts, it shifts along the vertical line where $Y=Y_n$.

(2) An increase in Y causes an increase in P.

Learning Tip
• The positive relation between Y and P is represented by the upward sloping AS curve. • Why is the AS curve upward sloping? 　• As output increases, employment (N) increases. 　• As N increases, u falls. 　• Reductions in u cause increases in bargaining power and an increase in nominal wages. 　• As nominal wages increase, firms raise prices. 　• Therefore, an increase in Y is associated with higher prices.

You also need to understand the relation among P, P^e, Y_n and the AS curve. These characteristics are:

(1) Each AS curve is drawn for a given P^e.
(2) If $P = P^e$, Y must equal Y_n.
(3) When $Y > Y_n$, P exceeds P^e. (Tighter labour markets cause W to increase. The increase in W causes P to increase above P^e.)
(4) When $Y < Y_n$, P is less than P^e (for the opposite reasons).

> **Learning Tip**
>
> • If you draw a vertical line at Y_n, each AS curve intersects this vertical line at the point where $P = P^e$.
> • If P^e changes, the AS curve shifts by the amount of the change in P^e.

2. A REVIEW OF THE AD RELATION AND THE AD CURVE

The AD curve captures the effects of P on Y given equilibrium in the goods and financial markets. You must understand two characteristics of the AD curve: (1) why it is downward sloping; and (2) what causes it to shift.

(1) Slope

- A drop in P will cause the LM curve to shift down.
- This shift in the LM curve causes i to fall.
- As i falls, Y increases to maintain equilibrium in the two markets.
- A drop in P, therefore, causes Y to increase and the AD curve is downward sloping.

> **Learning Tip**
>
> You can also explain the slope of the AD curve in the following way:
> • A lower P causes a decline in nominal money demand.
> • As money demand drops, i must fall to maintain equilibrium in the financial markets.
> • The lower i causes an increase in the demand for goods and an increase in Y.

(2) Shifts

Any event, other than a change in P, which shifts the IS or LM curves will cause a shift in the AD curve.
• Increases in G, M, consumer confidence and reductions in T will cause Y to increase and, therefore, cause the AD curve to shift right.
• The opposite of these changes will cause the AD curve to shift to the left.

> **Learning Tip**
>
> • Make sure you understand that a change in P only causes a movement along the AD curve.
> • Other shifts in the IS or LM curves cause the AD curve to shift.

3. ADJUSTMENT TO Y_n

To understand the adjustment of Y, you must understand that:
(1) the AS curve this year depends on the expected price level for this year (P^e_t);
(2) $P^e_t = P_{t-1}$; and, therefore,
(3) the position of this year's AS curve depends on last year's price level.

The adjustment when Y is above Y_n:

• For Y to exceed Y_n, $P > P^e$.
• At the end of this year, the expected price level will increase causing the AS curve to shift up.
• This shift in the AS curve causes P to increase and Y to fall.
• As long as $Y > Y_n$ [and, therefore, $P > P^e$], prices continue to increase as the AS curve shifts up.
• P will no longer increase when $Y = Y_n$.

> **Learning Tip**
>
> • Make sure you can explain what happens when $Y < Y_n$.
> • Recall that next year's AS curve depends on this year's price level.
> • As P changes, we move along the AD curve; the AD curve does NOT shift.
> • In the short run, Y can deviate from Y_n.
> • In the medium run, $Y = Y_n$.

4. THE EFFECTS OF MONETARY EXPANSIONS AND CONTRACTIONS

Assume Y initially equals Y_n.

• An increase in the nominal money supply causes an increase in aggregate demand and an increase in Y.
• The increase in Y causes an increase in P (above P^e).
• As expectations of P adjust, nominal wages and the price level increase as the AS curve shifts up.
• As long as $Y > Y_n$, expectations adjust and the AS curve shifts up.
• The shifts in AS will cause P to increase and Y to fall.
• The adjustment stops when $Y = Y_n$.

> **Learning Tip**
>
> • The change in M has no effect on Y and the real interest rate in the medium run.
> • M is said to be "neutral" in the medium run.
> • For example, a 10% increase in M will eventually lead to a 10% increase in P.
> • The LM curve also returns to its original position leaving the interest rate unchanged.
> • In the short run, the interest rate does fall. In the medium run, however, as P increases, the real money stock returns to its original level.
> • The short-run effects of a change in M on Y will depend on the slope of the AS curve.
> • Make sure you can explain the short-run and medium-run effects of a reduction in M.

5. THE EFFECTS OF A FISCAL EXPANSION AND CONTRACTION

Changes in G or T will cause changes in aggregate demand. These changes in aggregate demand will affect the level of Y and P in the same way that changes in M did:

(1) An increase in G will cause Y to increase in the short run.
(2) Eventually, Y returns to Y_n at a higher price.

Learning Tip

• The short-run effects of a reduction in G on Y and P are similar to the short-run effects of a drop in M: Y decreases and P decreases.
• The medium-run effects of a reduction in G on Y and P are similar to the medium-run effects of a drop in M: Y returns to Y_n and P is permanently lower.

While M is neutral in the medium run, changes in G, T or consumer confidence are not.

• A decrease in G causes a leftward shift in the IS curve and a drop in i.
• As P continues to fall, the real money stock increases and the LM curve shifts down, further depressing i.
• We know that P decreases until Y returns to Y_n.
• This implies that all of the drop in G will be offset by an equal increase in I in the medium run (via the drop in i).

Learning Tip

• Changes in G, T and consumer confidence will have no medium run effects on the level of output.
• Changes in these variables will, however, affect i and the composition of output.

---

6. THE EFFECTS OF CHANGES IN THE PRICE OF OIL

(1) Medium-run effects

Firms produce goods with labour and other inputs (e.g. oil). When the price of oil increases, we know that:
• the firms' non-labour costs increase
• given wages, firms respond by increasing prices
• this increase in P represents an increase in the markup (μ).

An increase in μ causes:
• a lower real wage implied by price setting behaviour (the PS relation shifts down)
• a reduction in the equilibrium real wage
• an increase in u_n
• As u_n falls, Y_n falls. This increase in the price of oil, therefore, causes a reduction in Y_n.
• An increase in μ causes an increase in P at each level of output. The AS curve, therefore, shifts up.

> **Learning Tip**
>
> You must understand the shift in the AS curve.
> - The new AS curve goes through the point where output equals the new Y_n at a price level of P_{t-1}.
> - The horizontal distance between the first two AS curves represents the change in Y_n.

(2) Short-run effects

An increase in the price of oil causes the following:
- the AS curve shifts up, Y falls and P increases
- Y initially remains above the now lower Y_n
- as expectations adjust, the AS curve will continue to shift until $Y = Y_n'$
- an increase in the price of oil, therefore, causes an increase in P and a permanent reduction in Y
- the increase in the price of oil also causes an increase in u_n and a reduction in W/P

> **Learning Tip**
>
> - It is assumed that changes in the price of oil do not cause changes in the AD curve.
> - Make sure you can explain the effects of a reduction in the price of oil.

SELF-TEST QUESTIONS

(1) What is meant by general equilibrium (p. 175)?

(2) What does the AS relation represent and how is it derived (p. 176)?

(3) Why does an increase in output cause an increase in the price level (p. 177)?

(4) Based on the AS relation, what effect does a 4% increase in the expected price level have on the actual price level (pp. 176-177)?

(5) What does the AD relation represent, and how is it derived (p. 178)?

(6) Suppose $Y > Y_n$. Compare u with u_n and P with P^e (pp. 182-183).

(7) If $P = P^e$, compare Y and Y_n (p. 177).

(8) Money is believed to be neutral in the medium run. What does that mean (pp. 185-186)?

(9) In the medium run, what effect will a decrease in G have on Y, I, and i (pp. 188–190)?

(10) What effect does an increase in the price of oil have on μ (p. 191)?

(11) What effect does an increase in the price of oil have on W/P, u_n, Y_n and the AS curve (p. 191)?

(12) What are the medium-run effects of an increase in the price of oil on P and Y (p. 192)?

(13) What is meant by stagflation (p. 193)?

(14) What is meant by propagation mechanisms (pp. 195-196)?

(15) Approximately how long does it take for the output effects of a change in the money supply to disappear (pp. 186-187)?

REVIEW PROBLEMS

1. Using the AS relation, <u>explain</u> how each of the following events will affect the price level.

   a. 5% increase in P^e
   b. 2% reduction in P^e
   c. increase in μ
   d. decrease in μ
   e. increase in Y
   f. decrease in Y

2. Concisely explain why the AS relation is upward sloping.

3. In the graph below, illustrate the effects of a reduction in the price level on output. Explain what effect the drop in P has on M, M/P, nominal money demand, i and I.

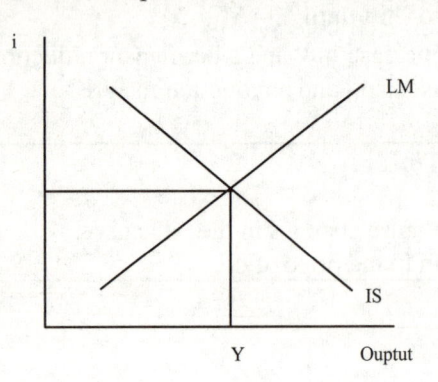

4. Concisely explain why the AD relation is downward sloping.

5. Explain what effect each of the following events has on the IS curve, the LM curve, and the AD curve.
   a. increase in G
   b. decrease in G
   c. increase in M
   d. decrease in M
   e. rise in consumer confidence
   f. drop in consumer confidence
   g. increase in T
   h. decrease in T
   i. increase in P
   j. decrease in P

6. Suppose $Y > Y_n$.
   a. In this case, compare u with u_n, N with N_n and P with P^e.
   b. What will happen to the expected price level for next year?
   c. What will happen to the nominal wage for next year?
   d. What happens to the AS curve for next year?

7. Suppose $Y < Y_n$.
   a. In this case, compare u with u_n, N with N_n and P with P^e.
   b. What will happen to the expected price level for next year?
   c. What will happen to the nominal wage for next year?
   d. What happens to the AS curve for next year?

8. a. In #6, as the AS shifts, what happens to M, M/P, i, I and Y?
b. In #7, as the AS shifts, what happens to M, M/P, i, I and Y?

9. Suppose the economy is initially operating at Y_n. Now suppose the Bank of Canada conducts a monetary contraction where the nominal money supply falls.

a. Use the graph below to illustrate the initial equilibrium, dynamic adjustment and medium-run equilibrium. In your graph, illustrate the equilibrium for the next two periods (in addition to the medium-run equilibrium).

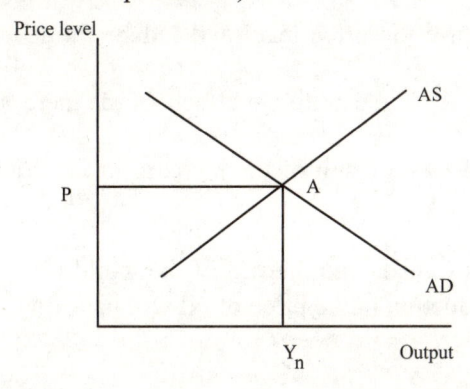

b. What are the initial effects of the drop in M on P, M/P, i, I and Y?
c. What happens to u and Y relative to their natural levels during: the short run, the dynamic adjustment and the medium run?
d. When Y is less than Y_n, what happens to the AS curve for the next year? Explain.
e. As the AS curve shifts, what happens to P, M/P, i, I and Y?
f. What are the medium-run effects of the drop in M on P, M/P, i, I and Y?
g. Does Y return to Y_n? If so, what does this suggest about P and P^e in the medium run?

10. The following questions are based on your analysis in #9. Suppose M fell by 6% in #9.
a. How much did P and P^e fall in the medium run?
b. Did the drop in M have any medium-run effects on real variables (i, Y, I, .. etc.)?
c. What are the medium-run effects on the nominal and real wages?

11. Suppose the economy is initially operating at Y_n. Now suppose G increases.

a. Use the graph below to illustrate the initial equilibrium, dynamic adjustment and medium-run equilibrium. In your graph, illustrate the equilibrium for the next two periods (in addition to the medium-run equilibrium).

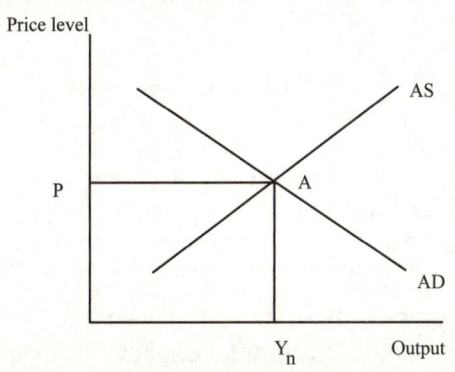

b. What are the initial effects of the increase in G on P, M/P, i, I and Y?

c. What happens to u and Y relative to their natural levels during: the short run, the dynamic adjustment and the medium run?
d. When Y is greater than Y_n, what happens to the AS curve for the next year? Explain.
e. As the AS curve shifts, what happens to P, M/P, i, I and Y?
f. What are the medium-run effects of the increase in G on P, M/P, i, I and Y?
g. Does Y return to Y_n? If so, what does this suggest about P and P^e in the medium run?

12. Did the increase in G in #11 have any effects on real variables in the medium run? Explain.

13. An increase in the price of oil was found to raise the price level and reduce the level of output.
a. Use the IS-LM graph, on a separate piece of paper, to illustrate the effects of the increase in the price of oil on the interest rate.
b. Based on your analysis, what happens to C and I as a result of the increase in the price of oil?

14. Between year 2001 and 2003, the price of oil in Canada and the rest of the world increased fell. Using the graph below, explain what effect a reduction in the price of oil will have on μ, the real wage and u_n.

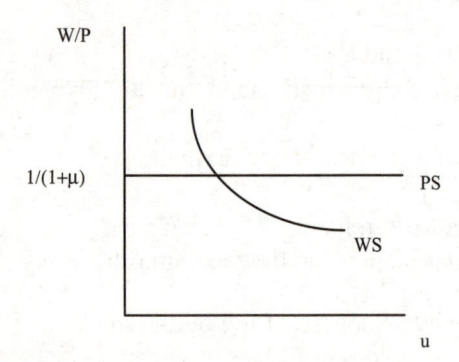

15. Using the AS and AD graph and the IS-LM graph, illustrate and explain the short-run and medium-run effects of a reduction in the price of oil. Explain what happens to P, Y, i, W/P, I and u.

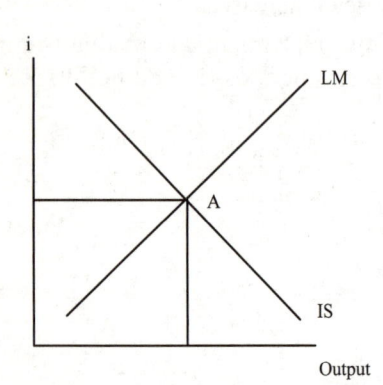

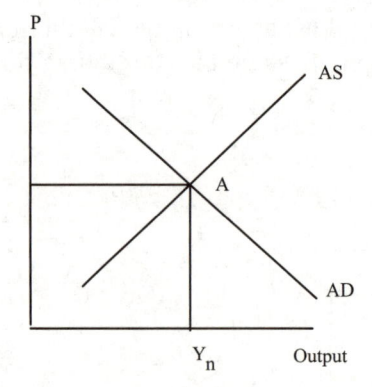

16. Using the AS and AD, WS and PS, and IS-LM graphs, illustrate and explain the short-run and medium-run effects of a reduction in employment insurance benefits. Explain what happens to P, Y, i, W/P, I and u. Use a separate piece of paper to show your graphs.

MULTIPLE CHOICE QUESTIONS

1. Based on the AS relation, an increase in which of the following variables will cause an increase in the price level (P)?

a. P^e
b. μ
c. output
d. all of the above

2. Based on the AS relation, a 4% increase in P^e in the medium run will cause:

a. P to increase by more than 4%
b. P to increase by less than 4%
c. P to increase by exactly 4%
d. no change in P

3. We have assumed that wage setters expect the price level for period t to be equal to:

a. the actual P in period t
b. the actual P in period t-1
c. the expected P in period t-1
d. the medium-term price level

4. When $Y = Y_n$, we know that:

a. $P > P^e$
b. $P < P^e$
c. $P = P^e$
d. none of the above

5. When $Y < Y_n$, we know that:

a. $P > P^e$
b. $P < P^e$
c. $P = P^e$
d. none of the above

6. The AD curve is downward sloping because of the effects of:

a. G on the IS curve
b. the nominal money supply on the LM curve
c. P on M/P
d. G on i

7. Which of the following events will cause a rightward shift in the AD curve?

a. increase in P
b. decrease in P
c. increase in T
d. increase in M

8. An increase in the money supply will cause which of the following to occur in the short run?

a. i will increase
b. $P > P^e$
c. $u > u_n$
d. a decrease in i and a rightward shift in the IS curve

9. A increase in M will cause which of the following to occur in the medium run?

a. no change in the real wage
b. no change in the composition of output
c. a higher nominal wage
d. all of the above

10. A reduction in M will cause:

a. a proportionate drop in P in the medium run
b. a reduction in i in the short run
c. an increase in I in the medium run
d. a reduction in W/P in the medium run

11. Money is said to be "neutral" because it has no effect on:

a. nominal variables in the medium run
b. real variables in the medium run
c. nominal variables in the short run
d. real variables in the short run

12. A reduction in G will have which of the following effects in the short run?

a. increase in P
b. increase in i
c. $P > P^e$
d. $P < P^e$

13. A reduction in G will have which of the following effects in the medium run?

a. no change in i
b. an increase in I
c. a reduction in P
d. all of the above
e. both b and c

14. A tax cut will have which of the following effects in the short run?

a. a lower i
b. a higher i
c. a leftward shift in the AD curve
d. $P < P^e$

15 A $100 (real) billion increase in G will have which of the following effects in the medium run?

a. no change in I or Y
b. drop in I equal to $100 billion
c. drop in I greater than $100 billion
d. drop in I less than $100 billion

16. An increase in the price of oil will tend to cause which of the following in the short run?

a. decrease in Y and decrease in P
b. increase in P and a leftward shift in the AD curve
c. decrease in Y and an increase in P
d. increase in the real wage

17. An increase in the price of oil will tend to cause which of the following in the medium run?

a. increase in i
b. decrease in W/P
c. decrease in Y and an increase in P
d. all of the above

18. A reduction in the price of oil will tend to cause which of the following in the medium run?

a. increase in Y and an increase in P
b. increase in Y and a drop in P
c. lower i
d. both a and b
e. both b and c

19. When $P > P^e$, we know that:

a. $Y > Y_n$
b. $u > u_n$
c. $N < N_n$
d. all of the above

CHAPTER 11. THE PHILLIPS CURVE

OBJECTIVES, REVIEW AND TUTORIAL

After working through the chapter and the material found below, you should be able to:

1. Explain what the original Phillips curve illustrates.

2. Based on the aggregate supply relation, explain what factors determine inflation.

3. Be familiar with the Phillips curve when expected inflation is zero.

4. Understand what two factors caused the original Phillips curve to vanish.

5. Understand the Phillips curve when expected inflation depends on last period's inflation rate.

6. Define the natural rate of unemployment (u_n) and explain the determinants of u_n.

7. Know what effect wage indexation has on the Phillips curve.

8. Recognize that u_n varies across countries and over time.

1. INFLATION, EXPECTED INFLATION AND UNEMPLOYMENT

The aggregate supply relation indicates that π_t can be represented as:

$$\pi_t = \pi^e_t + (\mu + z) - \alpha u_t.$$

There are three factors that affect inflation.

- Expected inflation (π^e_t). Higher expected inflation causes an increase in nominal wages which causes an increase in the rate at which P increases.
- ($\mu + z$). An increase in the markup (μ) or an increase in factors which determine wages (z) will increase inflation.
- Unemployment (u). As u increases, wages decreases and inflation will decrease.

2. THE ORIGINAL PHILLIPS CURVE

The relation between unemployment and inflation first discovered by Phillips, Solow and Samuelson is represented by:

$$\pi_t = (\mu + z) - \alpha u_t.$$

- This equation indicates a negative relation between the <u>level</u> of inflation and the <u>level</u> of the unemployment rate.
- The equation is based on the assumption that expected inflation is zero.
- A high unemployment rate leads to lower wages and lower inflation.
- A lower unemployment rate leads to higher wages and higher inflation.

> **Learning Tip**
>
> • The parameter α indicates how responsive inflation is to a given (in this case) level of unemployment.
> • You must understand that the original Phillips curve is a relation between the unemployment rate and the rate of inflation.
>   • A low u will cause a high (but constant) rate of inflation.
>   • A high u will cause a low (but constant) rate of inflation.
> • This original Phillips curve vanished because of: (1) high oil prices in the 1970s; and (2) firms and workers changed the way they formed expectations.

3. THE (MODIFIED) PHILLIPS CURVE

As inflation became persistent, rather than expect this year's price level to be equal to last year's price level ($P^e_t = P_{t-1}$), workers and firms formed expectations about inflation using the following: $\pi_t = \theta \pi_{t-1}$.

> **Learning Tip**
>
> • When $\pi > 0$, individuals would always <u>under predict</u> this period's price level if they used the following relation to form expectations: $P^e_t = P_{t-1}$.
> • As inflation became more persistent, θ became larger and approached 1.

When $\theta > 0$, π_t will depend on π_{t-1}. Why? Because the nominal wage will change based on expected inflation. If prices increased 5% last year, workers will expect prices to increase by some fraction of 5% this year. Nominal wages increase by some percentage causing prices to increase this period as well.

> **Learning Tip**
>
> • When $\theta = 0$, we obtain the original Phillips curve.
> • We will assume that $\theta = 1$.

When $\theta = 1$, the AS relation becomes:

$\pi_t = \pi_{t-1} + (\mu + z) - \alpha u_t$; or

$\pi_t - \pi_{t-1} = (\mu + z) - \alpha u_t$.

> **Learning Tip**
>
> This relation implies that π_t is a function of π^e_t, $(\mu + z)$ and u_t. In particular, when π_{t-1} increases (i.e., when expected inflation increases), inflation this period will increase by the same amount.

The natural rate of unemployment, u_n, is the unemployment rate such that actual inflation (π_t) equals expected inflation (π^e_t). As explained in the text, $u_n = (\mu + z)/\alpha$.

The AS relation becomes:

$$\pi_t - \pi_{t-1} = -\alpha(u_t - u_n).$$

There are several features of the AS relation you must understand:

(1) When $u_t < u_n$, the rate of inflation will increase;
(2) When $u_t > u_n$, the rate of inflation will decrease; and
(3) When $u_t = u_n$, the rate of inflation is constant (i.e., $\pi_t = \pi_{t-1}$).

Learning Tip

- If u were kept below the natural rate, inflation would increase each year (above the previous year's rate).
- Inflation will only be constant when $u_t = u_n$. It is for this reason that u_n is also called the non-accelerating inflation unemployment rate.
- To reduce inflation, u, therefore, must exceed the natural rate.

---

4. OTHER ISSUES

You should also understand: (1) the effects of wage indexation on inflation; and (2) the determinants of u_n.

(1) Wage indexation

As the proportion (λ) of labour contracts that are indexed increases, changes in unemployment will have a greater effect on inflation. Why?

- When u falls, wages increase.
- As wages increase, prices increase.
- With wage indexation, some wages will increase within the same period as prices rise.
- This indexation-induced increase in wages causes a second increase in prices within the same period.
- Therefore, the same drop in u causes a greater increase in π.

(2) Differences in u_n across countries

$u_n = (\mu + z)/\alpha$. Differences in μ, z and/or α will cause u_n to vary across countries.

Learning Tip

The higher Canadian natural unemployment rate, relative to that in the U.S., can be explained by Canada's relatively generous employment insurance program that has been translated into longer duration of unemployment; 1.5 times the U.S. level in the 1990s. Relatively higher minimum wages is another reason for the apparent difference in the natural unemployment rate between the two countries.

(3) Differences in u_n over time

The natural rate of unemployment in Canada appears to have increased by 3% to 4% since the 1960s. One possible explanation is Canada's relatively generous employment insurance program. However, the government of Canada has recently taken initiatives to make these benefits less accessible and more difficult to qualify for. Another explanation that seems to be common to both Canada and the U.S. is the decrease in the relative wage of unskilled labour. As the relative wage of unskilled labour declines, the unemployment rate for this group increases.

SELF-TEST QUESTIONS

(1) What are the determinants of inflation (pp. 200-201)?

(2) Given the original Phillips curve, why is there a negative relation between inflation and the unemployment rate (p. 201)?

(3) What is meant by the "wage-price spiral" (p. 201)?

(4) Give the two reasons why the original Phillips curve vanished (p. 202).

(5) How does the original Phillips curve differ from the modified Phillips curve (pp. 202-204)?

(6) What happens to inflation when the unemployment rate is low (p. 204)?

(7) Define the natural rate of unemployment (p 205).

(8) List the determinants of u_n (p. 205).

(9) What happens to inflation when $u > u_n$? What happens to inflation when $u < u_n$ (p. 206)?

(10) What is the level of u_n today in Canada (p. 205)?

(11) What does wage indexation represent (p. 207)?

(12) What effect does an increase in wage indexation have on the relation between the unemployment rate and changes in inflation (p. 207)?

(13) Compare the level of u_n and the flows of workers in the Canadian and U.S. economies (p. 209).

(14) What has happened to u_n in Canada since the 1960s (p. 208)?

REVIEW PROBLEMS

1. For each of the following variables explain how a <u>reduction</u> in the variable affects the inflation rate: (a) π^e_t; (b) μ; and (c) z.

2. Use the original Phillips curve to answer the following questions.
a. Suppose policy makers wish to reduce the unemployment rate. What must happen to π? Explain.
b. Suppose policy makers wish to reduce π. What must happen to u? Explain.

3. Let $\pi^e_t = \theta \pi_{t-1}$. Suppose $\pi_{t-1} = 10\%$.
a. For each of the following values of θ, calculate π^e_t: $\theta = 0.4, 0.6, 0.8$ and 1.0.
b. What happens to π^e_t as θ increases? Explain.

4. Suppose the Phillips curve is represented by the following:

$\pi_t = \pi^e_t + 0.10 - 2u_t$ where $\pi^e_t = \theta \pi_{t-1}$.

a. Assume $\theta = 0.25$. Calculate u_n.
b. Now assume $\theta = 1$. Calculate u_n.
c. What happens to u_n as θ changes? Briefly explain.

5. Suppose the Phillips curve is represented by the following:

$\pi_t = \pi^e_t + 0.20 - 2u_t$ where $\pi^e_t = \theta \pi_{t-1}$.

a. Assume $\theta = 0.5$, $\pi_{t-1} = 0.06$ (6%) and $u_t = 0.08$ (8%). Calculate π_t.
b. Suppose u_t increases to 10%. Calculate what happens to π_t. How much does π_t change? Briefly explain why inflation in t changes as u_t changes.
c. What happens to π^e_t as u_t increases? Briefly explain.

6. Assume $\pi^e_t = \pi_{t-1}$ and that the Phillips curve for Canada is given by the following: $\pi_t - \pi_{t-1} = -1.5(u_t - u_n)$. Suppose $u_t = 0.06$, $u_n = 0.05$ and $\pi_{t-1} = 0.04$.
a. Calculate π_t. Is π_t greater than, less than or equal to π_{t-1}?
b. Calculate π_t for each of the following values of u_t: 0.07, 0.08, and 0.09.
c. What happens to the change in inflation in t for each 1% increase in u_t?
d. As u_t increases, is inflation in period t increasing or decreasing?

7. Assume $\pi^e_t = \pi_{t-1}$ and that the Phillips curve for Canada is given by the following: $\pi_t - \pi_{t-1} = -1.5(u_t - u_n)$. Suppose $u_t = 0.07$, $u_n = 0.08$ and $\pi_{t-1} = 0.04$.
a. Calculate π_t. Is π_t greater than, less than or equal to π_{t-1}?
b. Calculate π_t for each of the following values of u_t: 0.06, 0.05, and 0.04.
c. What happens to the change in inflation in t for each 1% reduction in u_t?
d. As u_t falls, is inflation in period t increasing or decreasing?

8. Assume $\pi^e_t = \pi_{t-1}$ and that the Phillips curve for Canada is given by the following: $\pi_t - \pi_{t-1} = -1.5(u_t - u_n)$. Suppose $u_t = 0.06$, $u_n = 0.06$ and $\pi_{t-1} = 0.04$.
a. Calculate π_t. Is π_t greater than, less than or equal to π_{t-1}?
b. Calculate π_t for each of the following values of π_{t-1}: 0.03 and 0.06.
c. Given your analysis in b, compare π_t with π_{t-1} when $u_t = u_n$.

9. Use your analysis in questions 6, 7, and 8 to answer the following questions.
a. Suppose inflation is increasing in a country. Given this information, is u_t greater than, less than or equal to u_n? Explain.
b. Suppose inflation is decreasing in a country. Given this information, is u_t greater than, less than or equal to u_n? Explain.
c. Suppose inflation is constant in a country. Given this information, is u_t greater than, less than or equal to u_n? Explain.

10. Suppose there are two economies: A and B where $u^A_t = 6\%$ and $u^B_t = 5\%$.

a. Given this information, what can you say, if anything, about the change in inflation in these two economies? Specifically, what happened to π_t (relative to π_{t-1}) in these two economies? Briefly explain.

b. Suppose $\pi^A_t < \pi^A_{t-1}$. Given this information, where is u^A_t relative to the natural rate of unemployment?

c. Suppose $\pi^B_t > \pi^B_{t-1}$. Given this information, where is u^B_t relative to the natural rate of unemployment?

11. a. Suppose policy makers keep u less than u_n. What will happen to inflation over time?
b. Suppose policy makers keep u above than u_n. What will happen to inflation over time?

12. Suppose the proportion of contracts that are indexed in Canada declines. Will a given reduction in unemployment now have a greater or smaller effect on inflation? Explain.

13. Suppose the proportion of skilled workers in the labour force increases. What effect will this have on u_n? Explain.

MULTIPLE CHOICE QUESTIONS

1. An increase in which of the following variables will cause an increase in π_t?

a. μ
b. z
c. π^e_t
d. all of the above

2. An increase in which of the following variables will cause a reduction in π_t?

a. Phillips curve
b. z
c. u_t
d. none of the above

3. The original Phillips curve represented a relation between:

a. changes in inflation and changes in unemployment
b. inflation and unemployment
c. changes in inflation and unemployment
d. inflation and changes in unemployment

4. Which of the following equations represents the (modified) Phillips curve?
a. $\pi_t = \pi^e_t + (\mu + z) - \alpha u_t$
b. $\pi_t - \pi_{t-1} = \mu + z - \alpha u_t$
c. all of the above
d. none of the above

5. Suppose the Phillips curve is represented by the following equation:

$\pi_t - \pi_{t-1} = 12 - 2u_t$.

The natural rate of unemployment in this economy is:

a. 12%
b. 6%
c. the unemployment which occurs when inflation is rising
d. 5.5%

6. The natural rate of unemployment is represented by the following expression:

a. $\alpha/(\mu + z)$
b. $\mu/(z + \alpha)$
c. $z/(\mu + \alpha)$
d. $(\mu + z)/\alpha$

7. An increase in which of the following variables will cause a reduction in u_n?

a. μ
b. z
c. α
d. π^e

8. Which of the following equations represents the Phillips curve?

a. $\pi_t = \pi^e_t - \alpha(u_n - u_t)$
b. $\pi^e_t = \pi_t - \alpha(u_t - u_n)$
c. $\pi_t = \pi^e_t - \alpha(u_t - u_n)$
d. none of the above

9. The natural rate of unemployment in Canada is believed to be:

a. around 10%
b. around 8%
c. around 7.5%
d. around 4%

10. Suppose $u_n = 7\%$ and that $\pi_{t-1} = 4\%$. If $u_t = 8\%$, we know that:

a. inflation in time t will be less than 4%
b. inflation in t will equal 4%
c. inflation in t will be greater than 4%
d. more information is needed to answer this question

11. Suppose $u_n = 7\%$ and that $\pi_{t-1} = 4\%$. If $u_t = 6\%$, we know that:

a. inflation in time will be less than 4%
b. inflation in t will equal 4%
c. inflation in t will be greater than 4%
d. more information is needed to answer this question

12. Suppose $u_n = 7\%$ and that $\pi_{t-1} = 4\%$. If $u_t = 7\%$, we know that:

a. inflation in t will be less than 4%
b. inflation in t will equal 4%
c. inflation in t will be greater than 4%
d. more information is needed to answer this question

13. Which of the following helps explain why the original Phillips curve vanished?

a. wage indexation
b. higher oil prices
c. low-wage jobs
d. all of the above
e. none of the above

14. As the proportion of indexed contracts decreases, we would expect that a reduction in the unemployment rate will cause:

a. a larger increase in inflation
b. a smaller increase in inflation
c. a larger reduction in inflation
d. a smaller reduction in inflation

15. As the proportion of indexed contracts gets closer to 1, we would expect:

a. small changes in unemployment will cause large changes in inflation
b. expected inflation will have no effect on actual inflation
c. small changes in unemployment will cause small changes in inflation
d. none of the above

16. Which of the following explains why Canadian u_n is higher than the U.S. u_n?

a. relatively more generous employment benefits in the United States
b. relatively more generous employment benefits in Canada
c. higher inflation in Canada
d. larger budget deficits in Canada

17. Which of the following is believed to be the common explanation for the increase in u_n in Canada and the United States?

a. the relatively lower wages of unskilled workers
b. a reduction in the proportion of indexed contracts
c. an increase in inflation
d. all of the above
e. none of the above

18. If the unemployment rate in Canada is 8.9 and the rate of inflation is decreasing, then we know that the natural unemployment rate:

a. is greater than 8.9%
b. equals 8.9%
c. is less than 8.9%
d. cannot be determined

CHAPTER 12. INFLATION, ACTIVITY, AND MONEY GROWTH

OBJECTIVES, REVIEW AND TUTORIAL

After working through the chapter and the material found below, you should be able to:

(1) Understand and interpret the Okun's Law relation.

(2) Understand and interpret the aggregate demand relation.

(3) Understand the relation among inflation, unemployment, output growth and nominal money growth in the long run.

(4) Explain what is meant by disinflation policy, point-years of excess unemployment and the sacrifice ratio.

(5) Explain how the economy adjusts to a reduction in nominal money growth (i.e., a disinflation).

(6) Discuss how expectations and credibility (i.e., the Lucas critique) can alter how the economy adjusts to a reduction in nominal money growth.

(7) Discuss how nominal rigidities and contracts can alter the effects of a disinflation policy.

(8) Be familiar with the 1988–1993 Canadian disinflation.

1. OKUN'S LAW

Okun's law summarizes the relation between output growth and the change in unemployment:

$u_t - u_{t-1} = -0.33(g_{yt} - 3.7\%)$.

There are three features of Okun's law that you should know.

(1) <u>Inverse relation</u>. Increases in output growth will cause reductions in u. Why? To increase output, firms must increase employment. As employment increases, u will fall.

(2) <u>Okun's coefficient</u>. A 1% increase in the growth rate will cause u to fall by less than 1% (.33%). Why? First, labour hoarding occurs. Second, labour force participation changes as employment changes.

(3) <u>Normal growth rate</u> ($\bar{g_y}$). Actual output growth must exceed $\bar{g_y}$, (3.7%) for u to fall. Alternatively, g_{yt} must equal $\bar{g_y}$ for u to remain constant. Why? First, employment must grow at the same rate as the labour force. Second, labour productivity is growing each year.

2. THE AGGREGATE DEMAND RELATION

Aggregate demand is an increasing function of the real money stock. The growth rate of output is given by the following:

$g_{yt} = g_{mt} - \pi_t$.

> **Learning Tip**
>
> - When $g_{mt} > \pi_t$, we know that $g_{yt} > 0$.
> - When $g_{mt} < \pi_t$, we know that $g_{yt} < 0$.
> - When $g_{mt} = \pi_t$, we know that $g_{yt} = 0$.

3. INFLATION, UNEMPLOYMENT AND THE GROWTH RATE IN THE MEDIUM RUN

Suppose $\bar{g}_m = 6\%$. What are the values of π, y and g_{yt} in the medium run?

- Since u will return to some constant level, from Okun's law we know that $g_{yt} = \bar{g}_y = 3.7\%$.
- If $g_{yt} = \bar{g}_y$, from the AD relation, we know that $\pi = \bar{g}_m - \bar{g}_y = 6\% - 3.7\% = 2.3\%$. Recall that adjusted money growth is $g_m - g_y$
- Since π does not change, from the Phillips curve we know that $u = u_n = 8.6\%$.
- In the medium run, $u = u_n$, $g_y = \bar{g}_y$, and $\pi = \bar{g}_m - \bar{g}_y$.

What are the medium run effects of a change in money growth? Changes in g_m will only affect inflation in the medium run. In fact, there is a one-for-one relation between changes in g_m and π.

> **Learning Tip**
>
> - For example, a 3% decrease in g_m will cause inflation to fall by 3%. u and g_y will not be affected in the medium run.
> - Once again, we see that money (in this case, a change in nominal money growth) is neutral in the medium run.

4. INTRODUCTION TO DISINFLATION POLICY

You must understand three concepts.

(1) <u>Disinflation</u> refers to a decrease in inflation. This can only occur when $(u_t - u_n) > 0$. That is, u must rise above u_n for inflation to decrease.

(2) A <u>point-year of excess of unemployment</u> is a difference between u and u_n of one percentage point for one year. The number of point-years of excess unemployment is given by (the number of years that u is above u_n) times $(u-u_n)$.

> **Learning Tip**
>
> - Assume $\alpha = 1$ and that the central bank wants to reduce inflation by 8%.
> - From the Phillips curve we have $\Delta\pi = -1(u - u_n)$.
> - Since $\Delta\pi = -8$, $u - u_n = 8$.
> - The number of point-years of excess unemployment is 8.
> - Any combination of years and $u - u_n$ which yields 8 will achieve the 8% drop in inflation.
> - The central bank CAN choose the distribution of excess unemployment over time.
> - The central bank CANNOT change the total amount of point-years of excess unemployment.

(3) The <u>sacrifice ratio</u> is the number of point-years of excess unemployment needed to reduce inflation by 1%.

- The change in inflation equals -1.
- Specifically, $-1 = -\alpha(u - u_n)$.
- The sacrifice ratio is, therefore, $1/\alpha$ (which equals $u - u_n$).

5. DISINFLATION: THE TRADITIONAL APPROACH

Learning Tip

- The best way to learn this is to work through the material in the chapter step by step.
- It is crucial that you understand the material corresponding to Table 12-1.
- Review problem #15 will allow you to practice this.

There are three periods associated with a disinflation: (1) the pre-period; (2) the disinflation; and (3) the post-period.

To complete a table similar to 12-1, simply follow these steps:

(1) Determine the target path of inflation.
(2) Given (1), use the Phillips curve relation to calculate the required path of u (for each year).
(3) Given the required path of u, use the Okun's law relation to calculate the required growth rate of output.
(4) Now that you have the target path of inflation and the growth rate of output for each year, use the AD relation to calculate the required nominal money growth for each year.

Learning Tip

There are several features of the traditional approach you need to understand.
- u must first rise above u_n to begin a period in which π falls.
- Once π is at its desired level, u can return to u_n.
- g_{yt} must first decrease to cause the increase in u. g_{yt} returns to normal as long as u does not have to change. g_{yt} then increases above normal to cause u to fall to u_n.
- g_{mt} must first drop to cause the drop in g_{yt}. g_{mt} will then change to keep g_{yt} at 3.7%. Consequently, as π falls, g_{mt} falls as well. At the end, g_{mt} must increase to push u back to u_n.
---

6. THE LUCAS CRITIQUE, NOMINAL RIGIDITIES AND CONTRACTS

(1) The Lucas Critique

Lucas argued that wage setters' expectations would incorporate the effects of policy changes. A Bank of Canada policy to reduce inflation (IF credible) could reduce inflation without any increase in unemployment. Wage setters would adjust expectations causing wages and, therefore, prices to change. Note that credibility is the key ingredient to a disinflation without a recession.

(2) Nominal Rigidities and Contracts

The fact that wages and prices are set in nominal terms suggests that a decrease in money growth (even if credible) would cause an increase in unemployment.

The <u>staggering of wage decisions</u> would also cause a rapid decrease in money growth to result in an increase in u.

(3) Conclusion

- Announce in advance the disinflation policy.
- Reduce money growth slowly at first to allow those few contracts that are negotiated to take this policy into account.
- Over time, money growth can be reduced more quickly.

7. THE CANADIAN DISINFLATION OF 1988–1993

Learning Tip

- You should become familiar with this example.
- You should also read this section in the chapter for an earlier period.
- Two issues stand out:
    - The Bank of Canada's disinflation (1988-1993) was not credible.
    - The sacrifice ratio by 1988 and 1993 was higher than that observed in the traditional approach (i.e., this disinflation caused a substantial increase in unemployment).

SELF-TEST QUESTIONS

1. What relation does Okun's Law represent (p. 216)?

2. What relation does aggregate demand represent (p. 219)?

3. To keep the unemployment rate constant, annual output growth has to be at least 3.7. (p. 217)?

4. What is meant by the "normal growth rate" of output (p. 216)?

5. Output growth of 1% in excess of the normal growth rate causes unemployment to decline by less than 1%. Why is this so (p. 218)?

6. The AD relation indicates that the growth rate of output is equal to what (p. 219)?

7. Output must grow at what rate in the medium run (pp. 219-220)?

8. What determines inflation in the medium run (p. 220)?

9. Define "adjusted nominal money growth" (p. 220).

10. What will unemployment be in the medium run (p. 221)?

11. What effect does a reduction in nominal money growth have on u, output growth and inflation in the medium run (p. 221)?

12. What must happen to the unemployment rate in the short run for the inflation rate to fall (p. 222)?

13. Explain what is meant by a "point-year of excess unemployment" (p. 222).

14. What is meant by the sacrifice ratio (p. 222)?

15. Briefly discuss the Lucas critique (pp. 225-226).

16. What is meant by the "credibility of monetary policy" (p. 226)?

17. What are nominal rigidities (p. 226)?

18. What does the staggering of wage decisions represent (p. 227)?

19. How did the Bank of Canada's behaviour in the 1980s affect the credibility of the Bank (pp. 228-229)?

20. Research by Laurence Ball indicates that faster disinflations have what effect on the sacrifice ratio (p. 230)?

REVIEW PROBLEMS

1. a. Suppose labour productivity is growing 2% a year. Given this, calculate, for each of the following rates of growth in the labour force, what output growth must be to keep u constant: 0, 1%, 2% and 3%.
b. Briefly explain what happens to the normal growth rate as the rate of growth in the labour force increases.
c. Suppose the labour force is growing at 1% per year. Given this, calculate, for each of the following rates of growth in labour productivity, what output growth must be to keep u constant: 0, 1%, 2% and 3%.
d. Briefly explain what happens to the normal growth rate as labour productivity increases.

2. Use the following Okun's law relation to answer these questions:

$u_t - u_{t-1} = -0.4(g_{yt} - 3\%)$. Assume $u_{t-1} = 6\%$.

a. Calculate the change in u ($u_t - u_{t-1}$) for each of the following values of g_{yt}: 4%, 5% and 6%. What happens to the change in unemployment for each 1% increase in output growth?
b. Calculate the change in u ($u_t - u_{t-1}$) for each of the following values of g_{yt}: 2%, 1% and 0. What happens to the change in unemployment for each 1% decrease in output growth?
c. Calculate the change in u ($u_t - u_{t-1}$) when output growth is 3%. What must the growth rate of output be to keep u_t from changing?

3. Suppose the normal growth rate is 2% and that output growth is currently 1%. Explain why this output growth of 1% below normal leads to an increase in u of less than 1%.

4. The Okun's law coefficient has increased for a number of countries. Does this increase cause u to be more or less sensitive to deviations of output growth from normal? Briefly explain.

5. Use the AD relation to answer this question.
a. Assume $\pi_t = 3\%$. Calculate output growth for each of the following values of nominal money growth: 7%, 5%, 3% and 1%. What happens to g_{yt} as money growth falls?
b. Assume nominal money growth is 6%. Calculate output growth for each of the following values of inflation: 6%, 4%, and 2%. What happens to g_{yt} as the inflation rate falls?

6. This question focuses on the medium run. Suppose $\bar{g}_m = 7\%$, $u_n = 8\%$ and $\bar{g}_y = 2\%$.
a. What will g_{yt} and u_t be in the medium run? Briefly explain.
b. Calculate what the rate of inflation and adjusted nominal money growth will be in the medium run.

7. Suppose the central bank decides to reduce $\bar{g}_m$ from 7% to 3%. Using the original numbers in question 6, answer the following questions.
a. What happens to g_{yt} and u_t in the medium run as a result of the decrease in money growth?
b. What happens to the rate of inflation and to adjusted nominal money growth in the medium run as a result of the reduction in money growth?

8. Suppose a central bank decides to increase $\bar{g}_m$ by 3%. What will be the medium-run effects of this on g_{yt}, u_t and π_t?

9. Suppose $u_n = 6\%$ and that $u_t = 8\%$. Calculate the point-years of excess unemployment for each of the following number of years assuming that u_t remains at 8%: 1, 2, 3, 4 and 5. What happens to the point-years of excess unemployment as the number of years for which $u = 8\%$ increases?

10. Suppose the central bank wishes to reduce inflation by 8%.
a. Calculate the point-years of excess unemployment needed to reduce inflation by 8% for each of the following values of α: 1.5, 1.4, 1.15 and 1.
b. What happens to the point-years of excess unemployment as α decreases in size. Briefly explain.

11. Suppose the central bank would like to reduce inflation by 9%.
a. If $\alpha = 1.15$, what is the number of point-years of excess unemployment?
b. Given the goal of reducing inflation by 9%, can the central bank affect the number of point-years of excess unemployment calculated in a? Briefly explain.
c. Can the central bank choose the distribution of excess unemployment over time? If so, give three examples.

12. Let $\beta = 0.5$, $\bar{g}_y = 2\%$ and $u_{t-1} = 6\%$.
a. To reduce u_t by 2%, what must g_{yt} be?
b. To increase u_t by 3%, what must g_{yt} be?

13. a. Define the sacrifice ratio.
b. Calcuate the sacrifice ratio for each of the following values of α: 1.5, 1.3, 1.15, 1, and 0.9.
c. What happens to the size of the sacrifice ratio as α declines? Explain.

14. Assume $\beta = 0.5$, $\alpha = 1$, $\bar{g}_y = 3\%$, $u_n = 8\%$ and $u_{t-1} = 8\%$. Suppose the central bank wants to reduce inflation by 8% and wants this to occur in one year.
a. Calculate what u_t must be to achieve the 8% decline in inflation.
b. Given Okun's law and your answer to part a, calculate output growth in t needed to reduce inflation by 8%.

15. Suppose $\pi = 18\%$, $u_n = 6\%$, $\alpha = 1$, $\bar{g}_y = 3\%$, $\beta = 0.5$. Assume in year 0 that $u = 6\%$ and that the central bank decides that it wants to begin a disinflation in year 1 to reduce inflation to 3%. Assume that the desired path of inflation is: inflation starts at 18% in year 0 (before the change in monetary policy) and decreases 3% a year until it reaches 3%.
a. Given this information, construct a table similar to table 12-1 in the text. Include in your table for years 0 - 8 the values of inflation, unemployment, output growth and money growth.
b. Briefly explain the path of each variable in your table. Specifically, why do they change as they do?

16. Given the Lucas critique, do you think the central bank should announce in advance a policy to reduce inflation? Explain.

17. Are the sacrifice ratios for 1991, 1992 and 1993 (included in table 12-2) consistent with the sacrifice ratios of: (1) the traditional approach; and (2) the Lucas critique? Explain.

MULTIPLE CHOICE QUESTIONS

1. Which of the following equations represents the Phillips curve relation?

a. $g_{yt} = g_{mt} - \pi_t$
b. $u_t - u_{t-1} = -\beta(g_{yt} - \bar{g}_{yt})$
c. $\pi_t - \pi_{t-1} = -\alpha(u_t - u_n)$
d. none of the above

2. Which of the following equations represents the Okun's law relation?

a. $u_t - u_{t-1} = -\beta(g_{yt} - \bar{g}_{yt})$
b. $u_t - u_{t-1} = -\beta(\bar{g}_{yt} - g_{yt})$
c. $\pi_t - \pi_{t-1} = -\alpha(u_t - u_n)$
d. $g_{yt} = g_{mt} - \pi_t$

3. Which of the following represents the AD relation?

a. $\pi_t - \pi_{t-1} = -\alpha(u_t - u_n)$
b. $g_{yt} = g_{mt} - \pi_t$
c. $u_t - u_{t-1} = -\beta(g_{yt} - \bar{g}_{yt})$
d. $u_t - u_{t-1} = -g_{yt}$

4. Which of the following expressions represents adjusted nominal money growth?

a. M/P
b. $g_{mt} - \pi_t$
c. g_{mt}
d. $g_{\bar{m}}$
e. $\bar{g}_m - \bar{g}_y$

5. Which of the following does NOT explain why output growth of 1% in excess of normal growth leads to a 0.33% reduction in unemployment?

a. labour hoarding
b. changes in labour force participation
c. the parameter α does not equal 1
d. some workers are needed no matter what the level of output is

6. The normal rate of growth of the economy in Canada is approximately:

a. 3.7%
b. 1.15%
c. 3%
d. 6%
e. 0.4%

7. Let nominal money growth be 10% and the inflation rate be 3%. Given this information, we know that the growth rate of output is:

a. 4%
b. 3%
c. 6%
d. 7%
e. 9%

8. Given a certain rate of nominal money growth, an increase in inflation will cause output growth to:

a. increase
b. decrease
c. remain constant
d. more information is needed to answer this question

9. Which of the following events will cause an increase in the size of the sacrifice ratio?

a. an increase in β
b. a reduction in β
c. an increase in α
d. a reduction in α

10. Which of the following events will cause an increase in adjusted nominal money growth?

a. a reduction in $\bar{\pi}$
b. an increase in $\bar{g_y}$
c. a reduction in $\bar{g_y}$
d. a reduction in $\bar{g_m}$

11. Which of the following variables will be affected in the medium run by a change in $\bar{g}_m$?

a. u
b. u_n
c. g_y
d. π

12. In the medium run, which of the following expressions determines the rate of inflation?

a. $\bar{g}_m - \bar{g}_y$
b. $\bar{g}_y - \bar{g}_m$
c. $u - u_n$
d. $g_y - \bar{g}_y$

13. Suppose the central bank wants to reduce inflation by 12%, u_n = 6%, and α = 1.2. How many point-years of excess unemployment will be needed to reduce inflation by 12%?

a. 10
b. 12
c. 6
d. 10.8

14. If α = 1.5, the sacrifice ratio is approximately:

a. 0.5
b. 0.67
c. 2
d. 3

15. Suppose unemployment must increase by 5% to reduce inflation by 5%. Assume u_n = 6%, β = 0.4, $\bar{g}_y$ = 3% and u_{t-1} = 6%. Output growth must be equal to what rate for one year to increase u by 5% (in year t)?

a. -9.5%
b. -15.5%
c. -2%
d. -11%

16. The Lucas critique suggests that an announced disinflation policy will:

a. have no effect on u
b. have no effect on g_{yt}
c. yield a sacrifice ratio of 0
d. all of the above
e. none of the above

17. The traditional approach to disinflation requires which of the following conditions to reduce inflation?

a. $u_t > u_n$
b. $\alpha > 1$
c. $u_t < u_n$
d. none of the above

18. Research by John Taylor on the staggering of wage decisions indicates which of the following actions by the central bank should be taken to reduce inflation?

a. a rapid, unannounced reduction in g_m
b. a slow, unannounced reduction in g_m
c. a rapid, announced reduction in g_m
d. a slow (but gradually faster), announced reduction in g_m

19. Nominal rigidities refer to which of the following?

a. disinflation policy
b. the fact that many wages and prices are set in nominal terms
c. the fact that changes in nominal money growth cause changes in inflation
d. contracts which index wages to inflation

CHAPTER 13. EXCHANGE RATES IN THE MEDIUM RUN: Adjustments, Crises, and Regimes

OBJECTIVES, REVIEW AND TUTORIAL

1. Name the determinants of aggregate demand and aggregate supply in a flexible exchange rate system.

2. Understand the relationship between inflation and the exchange rate changes.

3. Explain in detail the exchange rate movements under flexible exchange rates.

4. Re-examine the effects of monetary policy on interest rates and exchange rates, and understand the importance of expectations

5. Understand the determinants of aggregate demand and aggregate supply in a fixed exchange rate system.

6. Explain the short-run and medium-run effects of a devaluation on P, Y, the real exchange rage, and net exports.

7. Explain what is meant by an "overvaluation" or "revaluation" and explain under what circumstances a devaluation can eliminate an overvaluation.

8. Discuss the arguments for and against devaluations.

9. Understand that the expected return on domestic and foreign bonds must be equal.

10. Explain the advantages and disadvantages of fixed and flexible exchange rate regimes?

11. Understand the difference among a hard peg, a currency board, and a dollarization.

12. Understand what role expectations play under fixed exchange rates, and explain how exchange rate crises can occur

1. FLEXIBLE EXCHANGE RATES, AD AND AS

(1) AD in a flexible exchange rate system

Aggregate demand consists of three elements.

(i) Goods market equilibrium, which occurs when Y = C + I + G + NX,
where NX depends on domestic (Y) and foreign income (Y*), and the real exchange rate $\left(\varepsilon = \dfrac{EP^*}{P} \right)$

- An increase in P will cause a real appreciation, a reduction in net exports, and a reduction in output. The AD is therefore downward sloping.
- Increases (decreases) in E, P*, Y*, and G and reductions in T will cause rightward shift in the AD curve.

(ii) Money market equilibrium, $\frac{M}{P}$ = Y. L(i) is the second element of aggregate demand.

(iii) Uncovered parity is the last element of the AD curve, $i = i^* + \frac{E^e - E}{E}$

- Increases in i* and E^e will cause E and hence ε to rise (real depreciation), which in turn will result in rightward shifts in the AD curve.

(2) AS
- The AS curve is essentially the same as previously presented.
- All other properties of the model are the same. In the medium run, (1) Y will return to Y_n, and (2) P will change, and the AS curve will shift when Y does not equal Y_n.

Learning Tip

In a world of flexible exchange rates and flexible prices, the real exchange rate $\varepsilon = \frac{EP^*}{P}$ can change due to any combination of movements in E, P and P*.

---

2. FLEXIBLE EXCHANGE RATES WITH FULL EMPLOYMENT

- In the medium run, the actual and expected price (inflation) are equal (chapters 6, 7, 8). Therefore, in an AD/AS diagram, as P^e (and hence P) changes, both curves, the AD and the AS, shift in the same direction and the same proportion.

- An increase P (and hence P^e) of a certain percentage causes the AS curve to shift up by the same percentage.

- An increase in P also causes a nominal exchange rate depreciation $(E \uparrow)$ such that the real exchange rate remains unchanged. Therefore, there will be no change in demand for domestic good. Exports and imports remain unchanged. All that happens is that the AD curve will shift up vertically by the same percentage change as P.

- The outcome of these two shifts is a higher price and no change in output $Y = Y_n$.

3. FIXED EXCHANGE RATES, AD, AND AS

(1) Review

Under fixed exchange rates:

- the government fixes the price of foreign currency (in terms of the domestic currency) at some rate, $\overline{E}$.
- $E = E^e = \overline{E}$, so i = i*.
- Since i = i*, the central bank no longer can choose the money supply.

Learning Tip

- An increase in $\overline{E}$ is called a devaluation.
- A reduction in $\overline{E}$ is called revaluation.
- An increase in the real exchange rate (a real depreciation) causes an increase in net exports.
- A reduction in the real exchange rate has the opposite effects.

---

(2) AD under fixed exchange rate.

AD is essentially the same as in the case of flexible exchange rates. The AD curve is downward sloping for the same reason as before, and shifts due to changes in the same determining variables such as G, T, P*, Y*, etc.

Learning Tip

- Be warned that under fixed exchange rates, unlike flexible rates, domestic interest rate (i) is pinned to the foreign rate (i*). Hence, an increase in i* instead of causing a depreciation (as in the flexible rates system) and thereby a rightward shift in the AD, and an increase in output, causes, in the fixed exchange rate case, an equal increase in i and hence a drop in output.
- Increase in $\overline{E}$, see below, will cause a rightward shift in the AD curve.

---

(3) AS and equilibrium

- The AS curve is essentially the same as previously presented.
- All other properties of the model are the same: (1) Y will return to Y_n; and (2) P will change, and the AS curve will shift when Y does not equal Y_n.

4. DEVALUATIONS

(1) Short-run analysis

A devaluation (increase in $\overline{E}$) will cause:
- a real depreciation, increase in net exports, an increase in Y, and a rightward shift in the AD curve.
- as Y increases above Y_n, P will increase but not enough to offset the increase in $\overline{E}$.

(2) The dynamics and medium-run analysis

- With Y above Y_n, the AS keeps shifting and P increasing until $Y = Y_n$.
- As P increases, the effects of the devaluation on the real exchange rate disappear.
- In the medium run, $Y = Y_n$, and P is higher.
- The increase in P completely offsets the initial devaluation, leaving the real exchange rate unchanged.
- In the medium run, the level of $\overline{E}$ is neutral; it has no real effect on the real exchange rate, net exports, and Y.

Learning Tip

Make sure you can explain the effects of a revaluation.

5. OVERVALUATIONS (REVALUATIONS)

An overvalued real exchange rate makes a country's goods too expensive and will cause a trade deficit. There are two cases to consider.

(1) Overvaluation with a recession

With Y less than Y_n, the economy will adjust by itself. AS shifts down and P falls. As P falls (we move along the AD curve).

- a real depreciation occurs and net exports increase
- as net exports increase, Y returns to Y_n
- this adjustment, however, will take time

A devaluation can solve this problem. An increase in $\overline{E}$ will cause a real depreciation. This real depreciation will cause an increase in net exports and an increase in AD. The increase in AD will cause Y to return to Y_n.

Learning Tip

In theory, the devaluation is preferred because the adjustment most likely occurs more quickly (when compared to the case where the economy adjusts by itself). The other approach will require more time as AS shifts down over time.

(2) Overvaluation without a recession

A devaluation cannot permanently affect the real exchange rate when $Y = Y_n$. To permanently change net exports, the government must increase public or private saving or reduce investment.

For example, a reduction in government spending will, in the medium run, leave Y unchanged. The lower P, however, will cause a real depreciation and an increase in net exports. Specifically, the drop in government spending will be completely offset by an equal increase in net exports. You should note that Y will fall in the short run.

To prevent the recession, the government could combine a cut in G with a devaluation leaving AD unchanged. The drop in G will be exactly offset by the devaluation-induced increase in net exports.

Learning Tip

You might want to examine the effects (both short-run and medium-run) of other events in the economy (e.g. increase in G, a change in P*, etc.).

---

6. EXCHANGE RATE CRISES

Under the fixed exchange rates, i = i* since $\overline{E} = E^e$. (An exchange rate crisis can occur if financial market participants, for whatever reason, expect a devaluation (i.e., an increase in $\overline{E}$).

(1) An Example

Suppose individuals are certain there will be 5% devaluation during the coming month. What are the effects?
- The expected devaluation of the domestic currency causes foreign bonds to be more attractive and cause capital outflows.
- The demand for the domestic currency will drop, and there will be pressure for the currency to depreciate.
- To prevent the depreciation, the central bank can buy its domestic currency with foreign exchange reserves. However, it will quickly lose its reserves.

(2) Other Possible Responses

- Raise interest rates. The increase in the interest rate must be enough to offset the expected devaluation. In the above example, the monthly rate would have to increase by 5% (60% higher at an annual rate).
- Devalue. Unless the central bank wants to accept the higher interest rate (which would have negative effects on demand), it will eventually have to devalue.

Learning Tip

- The belief that a devaluation will occur can cause a devaluation to occur.
- Review the EMS example in the chapter. This event was triggered by the increase in interest rates in Germany.

---

(3) Arguments for devaluations

- They can be used to correct over valuations and avoid recessions.
- The cost of not devaluing (an exchange rate crisis, high domestic interest rates, etc.) may be too high.

(2) Arguments against devaluations

- Without devaluations, the economy will adjust by itself to a simultaneous overvaluation and recession.
- They defeat the purpose of fixed exchange rates and, by changing the exchange rate, reintroduce risk.
- Frequent devaluations may lead to expectations of future devaluations and, therefore, cause exchange rate crises.

(3) Effects of expected devaluations (exchange rate crises)

As long as $E = E^e = \overline{E}$, $i = i^*$. If, however, foreign exchange markets expect a devaluation, they expect E to increase in the future. To maintain interest parity, one of two events will occur:

- i must rise to offset the effects of the expected devaluation
- the government will be forced to devalue

If the domestic interest rate rises, demand for domestic goods will fall, and aggregate demand will drop.

7. THE CHOICE OF FIXED VS. FLEXIBLE EXCHANGE RATE REGIMES

The choice between these two regimes is based on a comparison of the following:

(1) In a fixed exchange rate regime, one gives up the ability to manipulate the interest rate and nominal exchange rate.

(2) In a fixed exchange rate regime, exchange rate crises can occur forcing a devaluation.

(3) In a flexible exchange rate regime, the exchange rate might experience significant volatility.

8. HARD PEGS, CURRENCY BOARDS, AND DOLLARIZATIONS

It is important for you to know the differences among hard pegs, currency boards, and dollarizations. Therefore, review this material in the chapter.

It is also important for you to understand the requirements for a common currency.

- Countries must experience similar shocks.
- If countries experience different shocks, there must be a high degree of factor mobility.

SELF-TEST QUESTIONS

1. Discuss the determinants of AD and AS in a flexible exchange rate system (pp. 237-238).

9. What are the medium-run effects of a devaluation on the real exchange rate, net exports, aggregate demand, the price level and output (P.247)?

2. Explain what effect an increase in the price level (P) has on the real exchange rate, net exports, demand and output (p. 238).

3. Explain how the nominal exchange rate adjusts under flexible exchange rates (p. 239).

4. Explain what happens to the real exchange rate in the medium run (p. 239).

5. Discuss how an economy under flexible exchange rates can choose a different inflation rate from the inflation rate in the rest of the world (p. 240).

6. Discuss what happens to the nominal exchange rate when a devaluation and revaluation occur (p. 247).

7. What does the interest parity condition suggest occurs when exchange rates are fixed (p. 247)?

8. What are the short-run effects of a devaluation on the real exchange rate, net exports, aggregate demand, the price level and output (p. 247)?

10. Suppose $Y = Y_n$ and that a trade deficit exists. Can a devaluation by itself eliminate this trade deficit? Explain (p. 247-248).

11. Suppose foreign exchange markets expect a devaluation. What must happen to the domestic interest rate to maintain the interest parity condition (p. 250)?

12. What are the advantages of a fixed exchange rate regime (p. 254)?

13. What are the advantages of a flexible exchange rate regime (pp. 252-253)?

14. What are the conditions for an optional currency area (p. 253)?

15. What is a currency board (p. 255)?

16. What is a hard peg (p. 255)?

17. What is dollarization and why will one occur (p. 255)?

REVIEW PROBLEMS

1. a. Briefly explain what effect a reduction in P will have on the real exchange rate, net exports, demand, and output.

   b. Based on (a), does a reduction in P cause the AD curve to shift? Explain.

2. How does a change in E^e and i* affect aggregate demand and output?

3. Discuss how the medium run equilibrium is sustained under flexible exchange rates.

4. Initially assume $Y = Y_n$ Briefly discuss the medium run effect of a 10% inflation per year on the real exchange rate, E, net exports, and Y.

5. In the open economy version of the aggregate supply and aggregate demand model, why is the AD curve downward sloping? Explain.

6. a. Briefly discuss what effect a revaluation has on $\overline{E}$, the real exchange rate, and net exports.
   b. Based on (a), what effect does a revaluation have on the AD curve? Breifly explain.

7. Initially assume that $Y = Y_n$.
a. Briefly discuss the medium-run effect of a 5% devaluation on the real exchange rate, P and Y.
b. Given (a), what are the medium-run effects of a 5% devaluation on net exports? Briefly explain.
c. Devaluations are said to be neutral in the medium run. Explain.

8. Suppose the economy is initially operating at the natural level of output. Now suppose the government revalues the domestic currency by 10%. Discuss and explain the short-run and medium-run effects of this revaluation on the real exchange rate, P, net exports, and output. Use the graph below to illustrate the dynamic effects of revaluation.

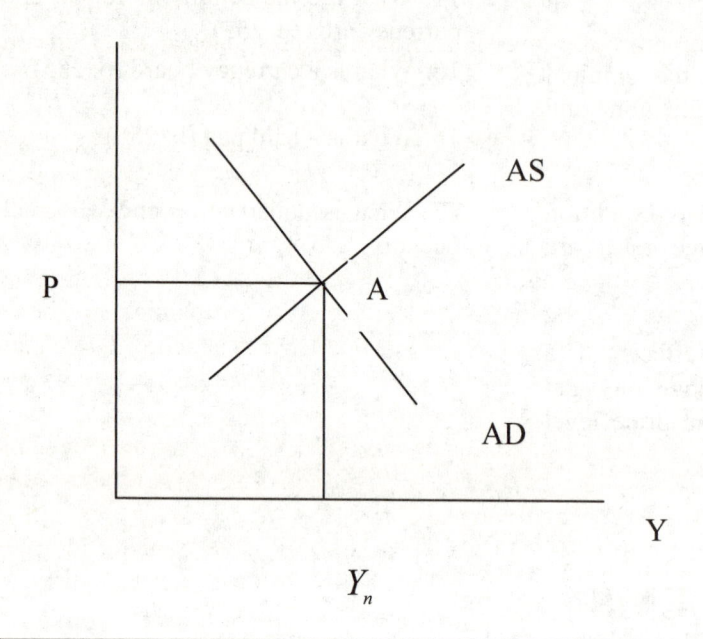

9. Suppose the economy is initially operating at the natural level of output. Now suppose the government increases government spending. Discuss and explain the short-run and medium-run effects of this increase in G on the real exchange rate, P, net exports and output. On a separate piece of paper, illustrate the dynamic effects of the revaluation.

10. Suppose $Y > Y_n$.

a. If the government allows the economy to adjust to this situation by itself, discuss what will happen to the price level (P), the real exchange rate, net exports and output.
b. If the government wants to change $\overline{E}$ to reach Y_n (when $Y > Y_n$), what should the government do? Briefly explain.

11. Suppose the economy is initially operating at the natural level of output. Now suppose the government reduces government spending.
   a. Discuss and explain the short-run and medium-run effects of this decrease in G on the real exchange rate, P, net exports and output.
   b. Does this decrease in G have a permanent effect on the trade deficit? Briefly explain.
   c. To prevent any short-run change in output when G is reduced, should the government increase $\overline{E}$, decrease $\overline{E}$, or leave $\overline{E}$ fixed at its current level? Explian.

12. Assume (initially) that E = E^e = $\overline{E}$, and that i = i* = 5%. Let i and i* be the interest rate on one-year (domestic and foreign) bonds.
   a. Suppose foreign exchange markets expect a 5% devaluation over the next year. Calculate what must happen to i to maintain the interest parity condition.
   b. Based on your answer in (a), what will happen to aggregate demand and output? Explain.
   c. To prevent the change in i, what must the government do in response to this expected devaluation? Explain.

13. What are the choices confronting the government and the central bank when the market expects that a devaluation?

14. Suppose the Dollar-Mexican peso exchange rate is fixed and that financial market participants suddenly expect a devaluation of the peso. Assume that there is now believed to be a 50% chance of a 10% devaluation over the next month and a 50% chance of no devaluation.
   a. How much must the Mexican central bank raise the monthly interest rate to maintain interest parity? How much does the interest rate increase when expressed at an annual rate?
   b. Repeat the analysis in (a). This time, however, assume that the expected devaluation is 20%. What happens to the required increase in i as the size of the expected devaluation increases? Briefly explain.
   c. Repeat the analysis in (a). This time, however, assume that the chance of a devaluation is greater and is now equal to 75%. What happens to the required increase in i as the chance of the expected devaluation increases? Briefly explain.
   d. As the interest rate changes in (a), (b), and (c), what happens to the demand for goods in Mexico? Briefly explain.

15. a. When financial market participants expect a devaluation and the central bank does not raise the interest rate, what happens to the relative attractiveness of domestic bonds? Briefly explain.
    b. What will the central bank have to do to maintain the current exchange rate if it does not raise the interest rate? How long will this last?

16. Why is an increase in the interest rate in response to an expected devaluation viewed as an unpleasant option?

MULTIPLE CHOICE QUESTIONS

1. The open economy version of the AD curve is downward sloping because:

a. a decrease in P causes an increase in M/P, a drop in r and an increase in investment
b. an increase in $\overline{E}$ causes an increase in net exports
c. an increase in P causes a real appreciation and a decrease in the demand for domestic goods.
d. an increase in Y causes an increase in nominal wages and an increase in P

2. Which of the following events will NOT cause a real depreciation of the domestic currency?

a. a decrease in P
b. an increase in E
c. an increase in P*
d. none of the above

3. Which of the following events will NOT cause a rightward shift in the AD curve?

a. a decrease in P
b. an increase in E
c. an increase in P*
d. a reduction in T

4. In the medium run with the economy under flexible exchange rate an increase in P

a. is matched by an equal increase in E leaving ε unchanged
b. causes Y to exceed Y_n
c. leave Y unchanged at Y_n
d. both a and c

5. Under flexible exchange rate

a. domestic inflation can differ from foreign inflation rate.
b. domestic inflation must be equal to the foreign inflation rate.
c. Y cannot be different from Y_n at any time.
d. the real exchange rate follows changes in the nominal exchange rate.

6. A devaluation represents:

a. an increase in $\overline{E}$
b. a reduction in $\overline{E}$
c. an increase in P
d. a reduction in the real exchange rate

7. A revaluation represents:

a. an increase in $\overline{E}$
b. a reduction in P
c. an increase in P*
d. none of the above

8. Under the fixed exchange rates, we would expect:

a. net exports to be zero
b. i = i*
c. i > i*
d. net exports to be negative (i.e., a trade deficit)

9. A 5% devaluation:

a. represents a 5% increase in $\overline{E}$
b. will cause P to increase by 5% in the medium run
c. will cause no change in the real exchange rate in the long run
d. all of the above
e. none of the above

10. In the short run, a 10% devaluation will cause:

a. an increase in net exports
b. P to increase by less than 10%
c. a real depreciation
d. all of the above
e. none of the above

11. Initially assume that Y = Y_n. In the medium run, a devaluation will have:

a. no effect on Y
b. no effect on P
c. no effect on net exports
d. all of the above
e. both a and c

12. Suppose the country has an overvalued real exchange rate and that Y < Y_n. In this situation, we would expect that:

a. P will increase over time until Y = Y_n
b. as the economy adjusts by itself, net exports will increase as a real depreciation occurs
c. a decrease in $\overline{E}$ will cause a rightward shift in the AD curve and an increase in output
d. domestic goods will become less competitive as the economy adjusts itself

13. Suppose the country has an overvalued real exchange rate and that $Y = Y_n$. Which of the following events will cause a permanent increase in net exports?

a. an increase in $\overline{E}$
b. a reduction in $\overline{E}$
c. an increase in government spending
d. a reduction in government spending

14. Suppose the country has an overvalued real exchange rate and that $Y = Y_n$. Which of the following combination of policies will most likely reduce a trade deficit without causing a change in output?

a. an increase in government spending (G) and an increase in $\overline{E}$
b. an increase in G and a reduction in $\overline{E}$
c. a reduction in G and an increase in $\overline{E}$
d. a reduction in G and a reduction in $\overline{E}$

15. Initially assume that $Y = Y_n$. A 5% revaluation will cause:

a. a 5% increase in P in the medium run
b. a 5% reduction in P in the medium run
c. a permanent increase in net exports
d. a permanent reduction in net exports

16. Suppose the financial market participants expect a devaluation. Which of the following might occur as a result of the government's or central bank's actions (in response to the expected devaluation)>

a. increase in interest rates
b. loss of foreign exchange reserves
c. devaluation
d. all of the above

17. Suppose the financial market participants expect a devaluation. Further assume that the government and central bank do not want to implement a policy which might result in a loss of output. Given this information, which of the following actins will most likely to be taken?

a. increase in interest rates
b. devaluation
c. revaluaion
d. none of the above

CHAPTER 14. THE FACTS OF GROWTH

OBJECTIVES, REVIEW AND TUTORIAL

After working through the chapter and the material found below, you should be able to:

1. Make the distinction between fluctuations and growth.

2. Understand the three main conclusions about growth in rich countries.

3. Understand the three main conclusions about growth across time and about growth across a larger number of countries.

4. Explain the characteristics of the aggregate production function.

5. Discuss the two sources of growth.

1. SUMMARY OF CONCLUSIONS

(1) Rich countries since 1950

There are three conclusions you should understand about the level of output per capita and about growth in output per capita for these countries.

- Growth has been strong (i.e., there have been significant increases in the standard of living).
- Growth has slowed since the mid-1970s.
- The levels of output per capita have converged over time.

Learning Tip

- You should understand how the use of exchange rates to obtain measures of GDP can exaggerate differences in the standard of living across countries.
- To eliminate these problems, economists use purchasing power parity numbers in order to obtain measures of GDP across countries.
- You should review the discussion of purchasing power parity in the text. Review problem # 6 will allow you to work on this.

---

(2) A broader look at growth

This section of the chapter examines growth over longer periods of time and for a larger number of countries. There are three main conclusions you should understand.

- Growth has not always occurred.
- The observed convergence of OECD countries to the United States may be a prelude to "leapfrogging."
- What may be most puzzling is not the growth slowdown after 1973, but the relatively fast growth that occurred in the period prior to 1973.

> **Learning Tip**
>
> - Convergence indicates that there will be a negative relation between initial levels of output per capita and the rate of growth in output per capita.
> - Convergence has occurred for Asian countries.
> - Convergence is not the rule in Africa.
> - Growth did not occur in Europe prior to 1500.
> - More recently, growth has been negative for some countries in Africa.

2. THE AGGREGATE PRODUCTION FUNCTION

There are several characteristics of the aggregate production function ($Y = F(K,N)$) that you <u>must</u> understand.

(1) Constant returns to scale

This implies that if the quantities of all inputs (N and K), for example, double in size, output will also double. Alternatively, if N and K both <u>fall</u> by 5%, Y will drop by exactly 5%.

(2) Decreasing returns to capital and decreasing returns to labour

An increase in K will cause Y to increase. An increase in N will cause Y to increase. Decreasing returns to capital and labour imply that:

- equal increases in K, given N, will lead to smaller and smaller increases in Y
- equal increases in N, given K, will lead to smaller and smaller increases in Y.

> **Learning Tip**
>
> - For example, a 5% increase in K, given N, will cause Y to increase but by <u>less than</u> 5%.
> - The <u>state of technology</u> indicates how much output is produced given N and K.
> - Improvements in the state of technology are called <u>technological progress</u>.

(3) Output per worker (Y/N) and capital per worker (K/N)

- Constant returns to scale allow us to obtain the following relation between Y/N and K/N: $Y/N = F(K/N, 1)$.
- Increases in K/N cause Y/N to increase.
- Because of decreasing returns to capital, equal increases in K/N will cause smaller and smaller increases in Y/N.

3. SOURCES OF GROWTH

(1) Capital accumulation

Capital accumulation <u>cannot</u> sustain increases in growth forever. Why?

- Steady increases in Y/N would require larger and larger increases in K/N.
- To increase capital, the <u>saving rate</u> (the proportion of income that is saved) must rise.
- The saving rate cannot rise forever.
- Therefore, capital accumulation cannot be the source of growth forever.

Learning Tip
• Increases in the saving rate will have no long-run effect on the growth of output per capita.
• Increases in the saving rate WILL cause increases in the level of output per capita.

(2) Technological progress

Technological progress will cause sustained increases in growth. This is shown in figure 14-6. When measured in log scale, the slope of the line represents the rate of growth in the variable on the vertical axis (in this case, the rate of growth in output per capita).

Learning Tip
• The faster is technological progress, the steeper the line.
• An increase in the saving rate will cause the line to shift (with NO change in the slope).
• Questions you should think about:
• If the growth rate were zero, what would the line look like?
• If the growth rate were negative, what would the line look like?

SELF-TEST QUESTIONS

(1) What is meant by "growth" (p. 260)?

(2) Define output per capita (p. 261).

(3) What are the two main reasons for focusing on output per capita rather than the level of output (pp. 261-262)?

(4) What happens to the difference between output per capita in the United States and India after adjusting GDP using the purchasing power parity numbers (p. 262)?

(5) What are the three main conclusions about growth for the seven rich countries discussed in this chapter (p. 264)?

(6) What is convergence (p. 265)?

(7) What is the relation between the initial level of output per capita and the rate of growth for OECD countries (p. 265)?

(8) Prior to the year 1500, what was the rate of growth of output per capita in Europe (p. 267)?

(9) For which group of countries does convergence tend not to occur (pp. 267-268)?

(10) Write down the aggregate production function. What are the two determinants of aggregate output (p. 269)?

(11) What is meant by the state of technology (p. 270)?

(12) Explain what is meant by constant returns to scale (p. 270).

(13) Explain what is meant by decreasing returns to capital and decreasing returns to labour (p. 270).

(14) Output per worker is determined by changes in what variable (pp. 270-271)?

(15) What are the two sources of growth (p. 271)?

(16) Define technological progress (pp. 271-272).

(17) Define what is meant by an economy's saving rate (p. 272).

(18) Will capital accumulation and/or technological progress sustain output growth forever (p. 272)?

REVIEW PROBLEMS

1. Suppose you receive $1000 at the age of 20.
a. Calculate what this $1000 will yield in 40 years if invested at the following interest rates: 2.2% (0.022), 1.7% (0.017), 1.2% (0.012), and 0.7% (0.007).
b. What happens in a as the interest rate falls?

2. Between 1950 and 1973, output per capita grew 2.7% per year in Canada. Between 1973 and 1992, it grew by 1.7% per year. In 1992, real per capita output was $16,362.
a. Assuming this lower rate of growth remains constant over the next 40 years, calculate what real output per capita will be in 40 years.
b. Now assume that real output per capita grows by the higher rate of 2.7% per year over the next 40 years. Calculate what real output per capita will be in 40 years.
c. Compare your answers in a and b. What does your analysis suggest happens to the standard of living as the growth rate in per capita output declines?

3. Look at table 14-1. List the three main conclusions about the growth of per capita output for these countries.

4. Suppose convergence occurs. Based on the 1992 levels of per capita output included in table 22-1, which of these countries should experience the highest rate of growth in per capita output in the future? Which of these countries should experience the lowest rate of growth in per capita output in the future? Explain.

5. Suppose Canada's growth rate of per capita output had not decreased between 1973 and 1992. Instead, assume it had grown at the same rate as Japan's per capita output during the same period (i.e., at 3%).
a. Calculate what Canada's output per capita would have been in 1992 if this had occurred.
b. How much larger is the measure of output calculated in a than the actual level that occurred in 1992?

6. Assume the typical consumer in Canada and in Mexico buys only two types of goods: (1) food; and (2) durable goods. Use the information provided below to answer the following questions.

	Price of food	Quantity of food consumed	Price of durables	Quantity of durables consumed
Canada	$2	4000	$4	8000
Mexico	2 pesos	2000	20 pesos	1000

a. Calculate Canada's consumption per capita in dollars ($).
b. Calculate Mexican consumption per capita in pesos.
c. Assume the exchange rate is 0.10 (i.e., $0.10 per peso). Using the exchange rate method, calculate Mexican consumption per capita in dollars. What is the relative consumption per capita in Mexico compared to that in Canada?
d. Use the purchasing power parity method to calculate Mexican per capita consumption in dollars. Using this method, what is the relative consumption per capita in Mexico compared to that in Canada?
e. To what extent does the relative standard of living (or, in this case, consumption) between these two countries depend on the method used to obtain measures of Mexican consumption?

7. Suppose the aggregate production function is given by the following: $Y = (K^{1/2})(N^{1/2})$ where $K^{1/2}$ and $N^{1/2}$ are the square roots of K and N.

a. Calculate Y when K = 200 and N = 100.
b. Calculate Y when K = 400 and N = 200. What is the percentage increase in N, K and Y?
c. Calculate Y when K = 220 and N = 110. What is the percentage increase (compared to the calculations in a) in N, K and Y?
d. Does the above aggregate production function represent constant returns to scale? Explain.
e. Given the above aggregate production function, if N and K both increase by 2.7%, what will be the percentage increase in Y? Briefly explain.

8. Suppose the aggregate production function is given by the following: $Y = (K^{1/2})(N^{1/2})$ where $K^{1/2}$ and $N^{1/2}$ are the square roots of K and N.
a. Divide both Y and the right hand side of the equation by N. [Hint: Let X be some positive number. $(X^{1/2})/X = (X^{1/2})(X^{-1}) = X^{-1/2} = 1/X^{1/2}$.] What does your answer suggest determines the level of output per capita?
b. Let K = 200 and N = 100. Calculate output per worker and capital per worker.
c. Calculate output per worker for each of the following levels of capital per worker: 2, 3 and 4. What happens to output per worker as capital per worker increases? Does it increase at an increasing, decreasing or constant rate?
d. What does the relation between Y/N and K/N look like? Draw it in the graph below.

Output per worker, Y/N

Capital per worker, K/N

9. Use the graph provided below to answer this question.

Output per capita (log scale)

Country B

Time

a. The curve for country B is upward sloping. What does this suggest is occurring over time in country B?
b. What would cause this curve to shift up? Briefly explain.
c. What would cause this curve to shift down? Briefly explain.
d. What does the slope of the line represent?
e. What would cause the slope of this line to increase?
f. What would the above curve look like for Europe prior to the year 1500?

10. Use the graph provided below to answer the following questions.

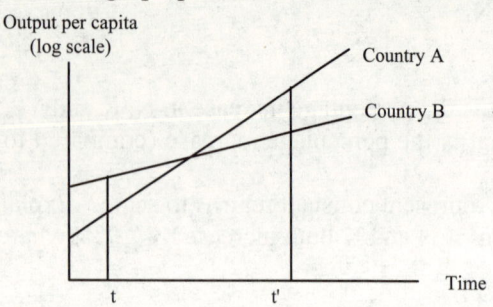

a. At time t, which country has the highest level of output per capita?
b. At time t, which country has highest rate of growth in output per capita?
c. At time t', which country has the highest level of output per capita?
d. At time t', which country has highest rate of growth in output per capita?

MULTIPLE CHOICE QUESTIONS

1. Which of the following variables provides the best measure of the standard of living?

a. level of real output
b. nominal output per capita
c. capital per worker
d. real output per capita

2. A comparison of output per capita for the seven rich countries included in the chapter reveals that:

a. there has been strong growth in all countries
b. the levels of output per capita have converged
c. growth has declined since the mid-1970s
d. all of the above

3. When calculating and comparing GDP across countries, economists generally use:

a. per capita measures of real output
b. exchange rates to measure real output
c. purchasing power parity numbers to measure real output
d. all of the above
e. both a and c

4. After adjusting Canada and Indian GDP figures using the purchasing power parity numbers, we see that:

a. the difference in the two countries GDP per capita is greater
b. the difference in the two countries GDP per capita is smaller
c. the difference in the two countries GDP per capita is about the same
d. the difference in the two countries GDP per capita disappears

5. When comparing the initial level of output per capita in 1950 with the rate of growth since 1950 for OECD countries, we observe:

a. a negative relation
b. a positive relation
c. no relation
d. no evidence of convergence

6. Purchasing power parity numbers:

a. use exchange rates to calculate GDP
b. use a common set of prices to calculate GDP across countries
c. provide relatively less accurate information about GDP
d. overstate, for example, U.S. output per capita

7. An analysis of GDP growth over long periods of time and across many countries indicates which of the following (circle all that apply)?

a. growth in output per capita has not always occurred
b. convergence does occur for all countries
c. some countries tend to "leapfrog" one another in terms of growth
d. growth was greatest after 1973 for OECD countries

8. For which of the following groups of countries has convergence NOT occurred?

a. the seven richest countries
b. OECD countries
c. African countries
d. Asian countries
e. none of the above

9. Which of the following events will cause an increase in aggregate output?

a. an increase in N
b. an increase in K
c. technological progress
d. all of the above

10. Constant returns to scale suggest that if K and N both increase by 5%, we know that:

a. Y will increase by more than 5%
b. Y will increase by exactly 5%
c. K/N increases by exactly 5%
d. K/N will decrease

11. Decreasing returns to capital indicate that a 10% increase in K will cause:

a. a reduction in K/N
b. a reduction in Y/N
c. Y to increase by exactly 10%
d. Y to increase by less than 10%

12. Which of the following events will cause an increase output per worker (Y/N)?

a. a reduction in K
b. an increase in K
c. a reduction in K/N
d. all of the above

13. Based on the aggregate production function presented in the chapter, equal increases in capital per worker (K/N) over time will cause:

a. no change in Y/N
b. equal increases in Y/N
c. smaller and smaller increases in Y/N
d. reductions in Y/N over time

14. Which of the following events most likely explains sustained output growth forever?

a. capital accumulation
b. an increase in the saving rate
c. technological progress
d. all of the above

15. An increase in the saving rate will tend to cause:

a. an increase in the level of output per capita
b. no change in the level of output per capita
c. a permanently higher growth rate of output per capita
d. a permanently lower growth rate of output per capita

Use the following graph to answer questions 16 and 17.

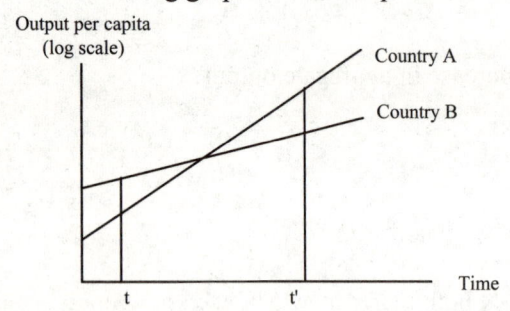

16. At time t,

a. country B has a relatively faster rate of growth in output per capita
b. country B has a relatively lower level of output per capita
c. country A has a relatively faster rate of growth in output per capita
d. country A has a relatively higher level of output per capita

17. By time t', which of the following events, given the current situation shown in the above graph, would cause the level of output per capita in country A to drop below output per capita in B?

a. a reduction in the saving rate in B
b. an increase in technological progress in A
c. a reduction in technological progress in B
d. a reduction in the saving rate in A

CHAPTER 15. SAVING, CAPITAL ACCUMULATION, AND OUTPUT

OBJECTIVES, REVIEW AND TUTORIAL

After working through the chapter and the material found below, you should be able to:

1. Understand the relation among capital, output, saving, investment and changes in the capital stock.

2. Understand the graphical representation of output per worker, saving per worker and depreciation per worker.

3. Discuss the dynamics of capital and output.

4. Explain what is meant by the "steady state of the economy" and the steady-state values of output and capital.

5. Explain the effects of changes in the saving rate on the level of output, the growth of output in the short run, and the growth of output in the long run.

6. Discuss what is meant by the golden rule level of capital.

7. Explain what effect changes in human capital have on output per worker.

1. OVERVIEW OF THE MODEL

The model can be summarized by the following equations:

- Output (per worker): $Y_t/N = f(K_t/N)$
- Saving/Investment (per worker): $I_t/N = s(Y_t/N)$
- Capital Accumulation (per worker): $(K_{t+1}/N) - (K_t/N) = s(Y_t/N) - \delta(K_t/N)$

Learning Tip

- S = I when the budget deficit is zero AND the economy is closed.
- Capital stock per worker increases when I > depreciation.
- Capital stock per worker decreases when I < depreciation.
- Capital stock per worker is constant when I = depreciation.

---

2. THE DYNAMICS OF CAPITAL AND OUTPUT

(1) The graph

Make sure you completely understand all aspects of the graph found below:

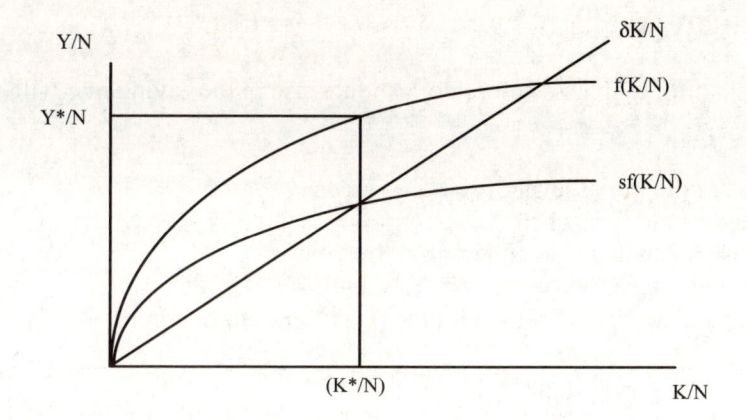

- The production function [f(K/N)]. Output per worker increases at a decreasing rate as K/N increases. Why? Answer: We assume decreasing returns to capital.
- Investment per worker [sf(K/N)]. Since saving is a proportion of income and since S = I, the investment per worker line has the same shape as the production function.
- Depreciation per worker [δ(K/N)]. Since depreciation increases in proportion to capital per worker, the line is upward sloping with a slope equal to δ.

(2) The adjustment to the steady state when $K_t/N < K^*/N$

- As you can see in the above graph, investment exceeds depreciation at all levels of capital per worker when $K_t/N < K^*/N$.
- When investment exceeds depreciation, K/N will increase.
- As K/N increases, Y/N also increases.
- K/N and Y/N will continue to increase until K/N = K*/N and Y/N = Y*/N.
- At K*/N, investment equals depreciation and K/N (and Y/N) is constant.

(3) The adjustment to the steady state when $K_t/N > K^*/N$

- As you can see in the above graph, investment is less than depreciation at all levels of capital per worker when $K_t/N > K^*/N$.
- When investment is less than depreciation, K/N will decrease.
- As K/N decreases, Y/N also decreases.
- K/N and Y/N will continue to decrease until K/N = K*/N and Y/N = Y*/N.
- At K*/N, investment equals depreciation and K/N (and Y/N) is constant.

3. THE STEADY STATE

- The <u>steady state</u> occurs when K/N is constant.
- The steady state, therefore, occurs at K*/N where investment equals depreciation.
- Since K/N is constant in the steady state, Y/N will also be constant in the steady state.
- If investment does not equal depreciation, the capital stock per worker will change until steady state is reached.

4. THE SAVING RATE AND GROWTH

Assume the economy is in steady state for a given saving rate. An increase in the saving rate will cause:

- investment to exceed depreciation at the initial level of K/N.
- K/N will increase until a new steady state is reached.
- During the adjustment, the increase in s will cause higher growth in output.
- In the long run, the higher saving rate causes an increase in Y/N and K/N.
- In the long run, the increase in the saving has **NO** effect on the rate of growth in output.

Learning Tip

- In this model, once a steady state is reached, the rate of growth in output (Y) is zero.
- Make sure you understand the effects of changes in the saving rate.
- You should also be able to examine the effects of a reduction in the saving rate.
- You should understand that there are two parameters in the model: s and δ (the saving rate and rate of depreciation).

Learning Tip

- Changes in δ and s will cause a new steady state to occur.
- Make sure you can explain the effects of changes in the rate of depreciation as well.
- Some instructors might emphasize this issue; therefore, you need to understand it.
- Changes in δ will cause the slope of the depreciation line to change.
- At the initial K/N, investment and depreciation will not be equal.
- K/N will then change until a new steady state is reached.
- To understand this concept, you should examine graphically and explain the effects of a reduction in δ

---

5. THE GOLDEN RULE

The golden rule level of capital is the level of capital at which consumption is maximized in the long run. There exists a corresponding saving rate consistent with the golden rule level of capital. There are two cases to consider.

(1) K/N below the golden rule level of K/N

Here, s must increase. As s increases, consumption will increase at the new steady state (i.e., consumption will increase in the long run). In the short run, however, since K and Y do not immediately change in response to the increase in s, an increase in the saving rate will cause a reduction in consumption.

(2) K/N above the golden rule level of K/N

Here, the saving rate must fall. As s falls, consumption will increase at the new steady state. In the short run, consumption will also increase since s is now lower.

(3) Graphical analysis of the golden rule

Figure 15-6 illustrates (for a given value of δ and for a given aggregate production function) all possible levels of steady state per capita consumption. There are several features of this figure that you must understand.

- If $s = 0$, steady state consumption is zero. Why? If $s = 0$, there will be no investment, no capital, no output, and, therefore, no consumption.
- If $s = 1$, steady state consumption is zero. Why? If $s = 1$, all income is saved. If all income is saved, consumption is zero.
- There is a unique value of s that maximizes consumption in the steady state. This is represented by s_G.
- The figure indicates that an increase in the saving rate will cause an increase in C/N if s is initially less than s_G.
- Increase in the saving rate above s_G, however, will cause reduction in C/N.
- It is, therefore, possible to save "too much."

Learning Tip

• Canada (like most economies) is most likely below the golden rule level of capital.
• To increase consumption, these countries must increase the saving rate. This policy, however, will reduce consumption in the short run.
• Because individuals care about consumption (rather than output), such a policy which reduces consumption (in the short run) may not be preferred.
• You should review the numerical example in the chapter.

6. HUMAN CAPITAL AND GROWTH

• Human capital is the set of skills possessed by workers.
• Aggregate output can be represented by $Y = F(K, N, H)$ where H is human capital.
• Constant returns to scale allow us to obtain the following: $Y/N = F(K/N, H/N)$.
• Increases in H/N (like increases in K/N caused by an increase in the saving rate) will cause an increase in output per worker.
• Increases in H/N occur via education and on-the-job training.

Learning Tip

• You should review the short discussion of models of endogenous growth.
• In these models, growth DOES depend on the saving rate and on spending on education in the long run.

SELF-TEST QUESTIONS

(1) What effect does an increase in K/N have on Y/N (p. 277)?

(2) Equal increases in K/N have what effect on Y/N (p. 277)?

(3) The saving rate (s) can take on what values (p. 278)?

(4) When the budget deficit is zero and the economy is closed, what does saving equal (p. 278)?

(5) The amount capital in period t + 1 is determined by what variables and represented by what equation (p. 279)?

(6) What determines the change in the capital stock per worker (p. 279)?

(7) Why is the depreciation per worker line upward sloping in figure 15-2 (p. 280)?

(8) Discuss what happens to K/N when depreciation is less than investment (pp. 280-281).

(9) Discuss what happens to K/N when depreciation is greater than investment (p. 280).

(10) What is the "steady state" of the economy (p. 281)?

(11) What happens to K/N and Y/N when the economy is in the steady state (p. 281)?

(12) What effect does an increase in s have on the growth rate of Y/N in the long run (p. 282)?

(13) What effect does an increase in s have on the level of Y/N in the long run (pp. 283)?

(14) What effect does an increase in s have on the growth rate of Y/N in the short run (pp. 283-284)?

(15) What can the government do to increase the saving rate (p. 285)?

(16) When s = 0, what is the level of K/N, Y/N and consumption per worker (p. 285)?

(17) When s = 1, what is the level of K/N, Y/N and consumption per worker (p. 285)?

(18) What is meant by the "golden rule" level of capital (p. 285)?

(19) On which side of the golden rule is Canada (p. 291)?

(20) What is human capital (p. 291)?

(21) What determines human capital accumulation (p. 292)?

(22) What is meant by "endogenous growth" (pp. 293-294)?

REVIEW PROBLEMS

1. In period t, suppose Y/N = 2 and K/N = 4.
a. Calculate K/N in period t+1 when s = 0.4 and δ = 0.1.
b. Now assume that s = 0.6 and δ = 0.1. Calculate K/N in period t+1. What happens to capital accumulation as s increases? Briefly explain.
c. Now assume that s = 0.4 and δ = 0.2. Calculate K/N in period t+1. What happens to capital accumulation as δ increases? Briefly explain.

2. "When $I_t > 0$, we know that the capital stock will increase between period t and t+1 ($K_{t+1} > K_t$)." Is this statement true, false or uncertain? Explain.

3. Saving per worker and depreciation (per worker) determine capital accumulation.
a. Compare saving per worker and depreciation when the change in the capital stock is positive.
b. Compare saving per worker and depreciation when the change in the capital stock is negative.
c. Compare saving per worker and depreciation when there is no change in the capital stock.

4. Assume δ = 0.1.
a. Calculate depreciation (per worker) for the following values of K/N: 2, 3, 4, and 5.
b. What happens to deprecation (per worker) as K/N increases? Does it change at an increasing, decreasing or constant rate?

5. Use the graph provided below to answer the following question.

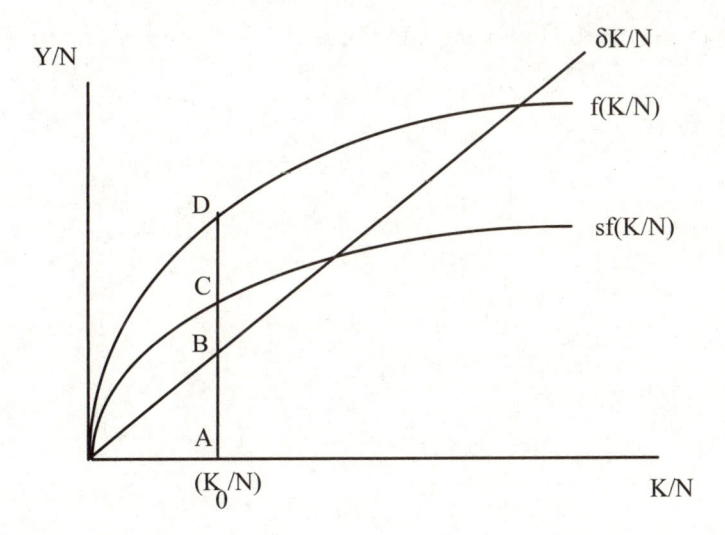

a. What do the distances AB, AC, AD, BC and CD represent?
b. What will happen to K/N and Y/N over time? Explain.
c. Is the economy in steady state at K_0/N?
d. What will be the final levels of K/N and Y/N?

6. Use the graph provided below to answer the following questions.

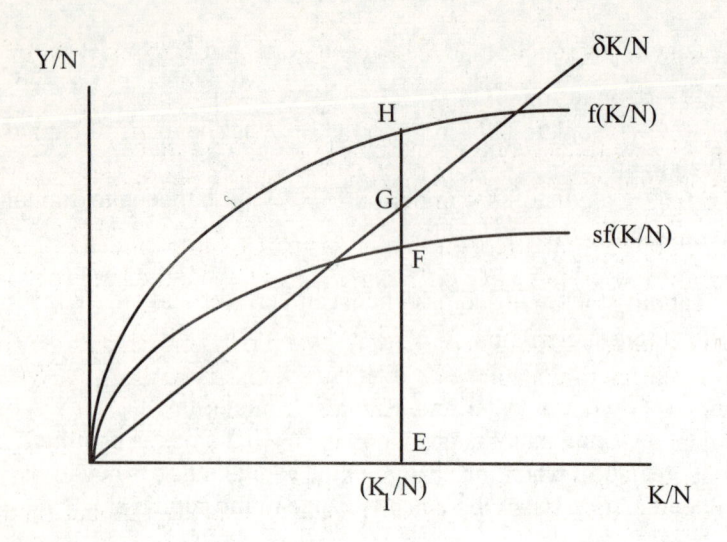

a. What do the distances EF, EG, EH, FG and FH represent?
b. What will happen to K/N and Y/N over time? Explain.
c. Is the economy in steady state at K_1/N?
d. What will be the final levels of K/N and Y/N?

7. Use the graph provided below to answer the following questions.

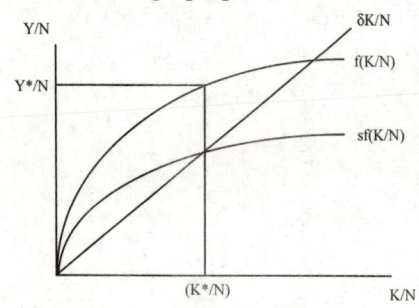

a. Graphically illustrate the effects of a reduction in the saving rate in period t.
b. In period t, what happens to K/N, Y/N, S/N and C/N as a result of the reduction in the saving rate?
c. Explain what happens to K/N and Y/N over time.
d. What are the short-run effects of this reduction in s on the growth rate of Y/N?
e. What are the long-run effects of this reduction in s on the growth rate of Y/N?
f. What are the long-run effects of this reduction in s on the level of Y/N?

8. a. Explain what effect a reduction in the rate of depreciation (δ) will have on the depreciation per worker line.
b. Based on part (a), what effects will a reduction in δ have on K/N and Y/N over time? Briefly explain.

9. a. To achieve the highest level of output per worker, what must the saving rate be?
b. Do you see any disadvantages of a policy that seeks to maximize output per worker?

10. a. An increase in s in period t will have what effect on K/N, Y/N and C/N in period t?
b. What effect will this increase in the saving rate have on Y/N, K/N and C/N in the long run?

11. a. A reduction in s in period t will have what effect on K/N, Y/N and C/N in period t?
b. What effect will this reduction in the saving rate have on Y/N, K/N and C/N in the long run?

12. Assume that $Y/N = (K/N)^{1/2}$; Y/N equals the square root of K/N.
a. Calculate Y/N for the following values of K/N: 1, 2, 3, 4, and 5.
b. Does Y/N increase at an increasing, decreasing or constant rate for each additional (and equal) increase in K/N?
c. Does this production function exhibit constant returns to scale?

13. Assume that $Y/N = (K/N)^{1/2}$ and let $\delta = 0.05$.
a. For each of the following saving rates, calculate the steady-state levels of K/N and Y/N: s = 0.1, 0.3, 0.5, 0.7, and 0.9.
b. Given a, calculate the steady-state levels of C/N for each value of s.
c. What happens to the steady-state level of C/N as s increases from 0.1 to 0.5?
d. What happens to the steady-state level of C/N as s increases from 0.5 to 0.9?
e. What are the golden rule levels of K/N, C/N and s?

14. Suppose the current saving rate is 0.2 and that the golden rule saving rate is 0.5.
a. What can the government do to achieve the golden rule level of K/N?
b. What effect will this policy have on C/N in the short run?
c. What effect will this policy have on C/N in the long run?

15. Let $Y/N = (K/N)^{1/2}(H/N)^{1/2}$ where H/N is human capital per worker.
a. Calculate Y/N when K = 400, N = 100 and H = 400.
b. Does this production function exhibit constant returns to scale?
c. Does this production function exhibit decreasing returns to physical capital?
d. Does this production function exhibit decreasing returns to human capital?

16. Let $Y/N = (K/N)^{1/2}(H/N)^{1/2}$.
a. Given N, what are the two determinants of Y/N? Briefly explain.
b. What must occur for the steady state level of K/N to increase?
c. What must occur for H/N to increase?

MULTIPLE CHOICE QUESTIONS

1. Suppose K/N increases from 2 to 3. We know that this increase in K/N will cause:

a. Y/N to fall
b. Y/N to remain constant
c. Y/N to increase
d. output to diminish

2. When the budget deficit is zero and the economy is closed, we know that:

a. S = I
b. S > I
c. S < I
d. the economy is in the steady state

3. An <u>increase</u> in which of the following will cause K_{t+1} to <u>fall</u>?

a. δ
b. I_t
c. K_t
d. all of the above

4. If the capital stock per worker does not change, we know that:

a. Y/N = I/N
b. the economy is NOT in steady state
c. $S/N = \delta(K/N)$
d. none of the above

5. If $K_{t+1} > K_t$, we know that:

a. saving per worker equals depreciation per worker
b. saving per worker is less than depreciation per worker
c. saving per worker is greater than depreciation per worker
d. the saving rate fell in period t

6. The change in the capital stock equals:

a. consumption - depreciation
b. output - depreciation
c. investment - saving
d. investment - depreciation

7. When the economy is in steady state, we always know that:

a. saving per worker equals depreciation (per worker)
b. $s = \delta$
c. consumption per worker is at its highest level
d. the capital stock per worker is increasing

Use the graph provided below to answer questions 8 - 11.

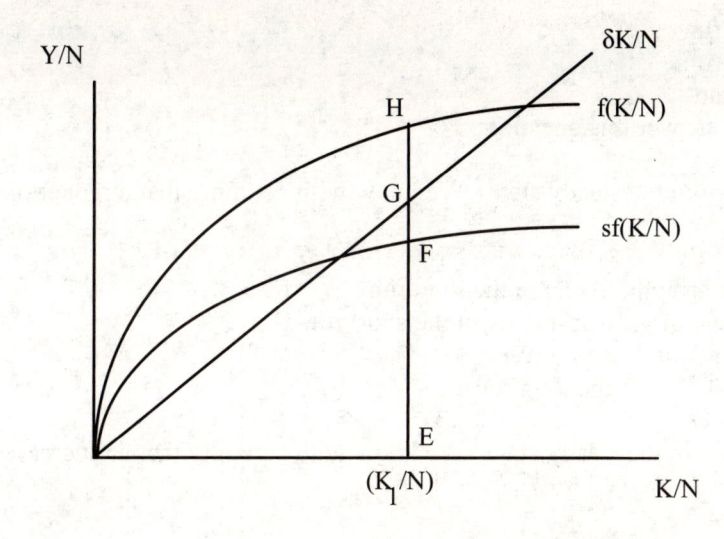

8. The distance EF is:

a. C/N
b. S/N
c. Y/N
d. the change in the capital stock

9. The distance FG is:

a. S/N
b. C/N
c. I/N
d. the change in the capital stock

10. The distance FH is:

a. S/N
b. C/N
c. I/N
d. the change in the capital stock

11. Given the situation at K_1/N, which of the following will tend to occur over time?

a. S/N will decrease
b. K/N will decrease
c. Y/N will decrease
d. all of the above

12. Assume the economy is initially in the steady state. We know with certainty that a reduction in the saving rate will cause:

a. an increase in C/N in the long run
b. a reduction in C/N in the long run
c. no change in C/N in the long run
d. more information is needed to answer this question

13. Assume the economy is initially in the steady state. We know with certainty that a reduction in the saving rate will:

a. cause a reduction in the rate of growth in Y/N in the long run
b. have a negative effect on the rate of growth in Y/N in the short run
c. have no effect on the level of Y/N in the long run
d. cause an increase in the level of Y/N in the long run

14. Assume the economy is initially in the steady state. We know with certainty that an increase in the saving rate will cause:

a. an increase in C/N in the long run
b. a reduction in C/N in the long run
c. no change in C/N in the long run
d. ambiguous effects on C/N in the long run

15. Which of the following represents the effects in period t of an increase in the saving rate in period t?

a. a reduction in consumption
b. no change in Y/N
c. no change in K/N
d. all of the above

16. Which of the following represents the effects in period t of a reduction in the saving rate in period t?

a. output will fall
b. investment will be less than depreciation
c. consumption will fall
d. all of the above

17. The golden rule level of capital is the level of capital which:

a. maximizes output per worker
b. maximizes saving per worker
c. maximizes consumption per worker
d. yields a constant level of capital per worker

18. Assume that the economy is in the steady state and that the current level of capital per worker does not equal the golden rule level of capital. Which of the following actions should be taken to achieve the golden rule level of capital?

a. increase the saving rate
b. reduce the saving rate
c. the economy will achieve the golden rule level of capital by itself
d. more information is needed to answer this question

19. Assume that the economy is in the steady state and that the current level of capital per worker is greater than the golden rule level of capital. Which of the following actions should be taken to achieve the golden rule level of capital?

a. increase the saving rate
b. reduce the saving rate
c. the economy will achieve the golden rule level of capital by itself
d. more information is needed to answer this question

20. Which of the following will cause an increase in Y/N?

a. increase in education
b. increase in on-the-job training
c. increase in the saving rate
d. all of the above

21. Human capital represents:

a. the set of skills of skilled workers
b. the set of skills of unskilled workers
c. all of the above
d. none of the above

22. Models of endogenous growth suggest that growth depends in the long run on:

a. the saving rate
b. the rate of spending on education
c. all of the above
d. none of the above

CHAPTER 16. TECHNOLOGICAL PROGRESS AND GROWTH

OBJECTIVES, REVIEW AND TUTORIAL

After working through the chapter and the material found below, you should be able to:

1. Understand what determines the level of research and development and the rate of technological progress.

2. Explain how technological progress (the state of technology) is included in the production function.

3. Understand the relation between output per effective worker and capital per effective worker.

4. Explain the dynamics of capital and output (per effective worker).

5. Discuss what happens to Y/NA, K/NA, the growth rate of output, output per worker, and the capital stock when the economy is in steady state (balanced growth).

6. Examine the effects of changes in the saving rate on Y/NA, K/NA, the growth rate of output, output per worker, and the capital stock.

7. Explain whether changes in growth are caused by capital accumulation or technological progress.

8. Discuss and understand the facts of growth.

1. SUMMARY OF RESEARCH AND DEVELOPMENT (R&D) AND TECHNOLOGICAL PROGRESS

• Technological progress is the result of R&D spending.
• Increases in R&D spending increase the probability a firm will develop a new product or method to produce a product.
• Patent laws give a firm the right to exclude other firms from producing a newly developed product.
• The fertility of research tells us how R&D spending translates into new ideas and products.
• The appropriability of research results captures the extent to which a firm benefits from the results of R&D.

Learning Tip

• If research is very fertile, R&D spending will increase; the opposite is also true.
• If appropriability is high, firms will increase R&D spending; the opposite is also true.

---

2. OVERVIEW OF THE MODEL

(1) A review of the variables

• The state of technology: A
• The amount of effective labour: NA

- Aggregate output: $Y = F(K,N,A)$
- Capital per effective worker: K/NA
- Output per effective worker: $Y/NA = f(K/NA)$
- Saving/investment per effective worker: $I/NA = sf(K/NA)$
- Required investment per effective worker: $(\delta + g_N + g_A)K/NA$
- Output per worker: Y/N
- Capital per worker: K/N

Learning Tip

- The amount of effective labour increases for two reasons:
    (1) The number of workers (N) grows at rate g_N.
    (2) Technological progress grows at rate g_A.
- To maintain a constant level of capital per effective worker, investment per effective worker must take into account:
    (1) the depreciation of capital (δ);
    (2) the fact that N grows at rate g_N; and
    (3) the fact that technological progress grows at rate g_A.
- Effective labour grows at rate $(g_N + g_A)$.
- To keep K/NA constant, K must increase at the same rate as NA $(g_N + g_A)$.
- An increase in δ, g_N, or g_A will increase the amount of required investment.
- The slope of the required investment line is $(\delta + g_N + g_A)$.

---

(2) The graph

Make sure you completely understand all aspects of the following graph.

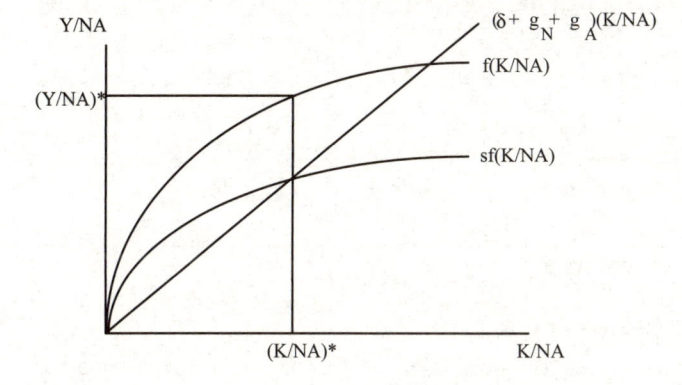

Note:
- The production function continues to exhibit constant returns to scale.
- The production function also continues to exhibit decreasing returns to K, N and A.

(3) The adjustment to the steady state when $K/NA < (K/NA)^*$

- In this case, investment exceeds required investment and K/NA will increase.
- As K/NA increases, Y/NA will also increase.
- K/NA and Y/NA will rise until K/NA = (K/NA)* and Y/NA = (Y/NA)*.
- At (K/NA)*, Y/NA and K/NA are constant.

(4) The adjustment to the steady state when K/NA > (K/NA)*

- In this case, investment is less than required investment and K/NA will fall.
- As K/NA decreases, Y/NA will also decrease.
- K/NA and Y/NA will fall until K/NA = (K/NA)* and Y/NA = (Y/NA)*.
- At (K/NA)*, Y/NA and K/NA are constant.

3. SUMMARY OF THE STEADY STATE: BALANCED GROWTH

> **Learning Tip**
>
> You must understand the following two characteristics of the steady state to understand the characteristics of the balanced growth path:
>
> (1) once the steady state is reached, we know that Y/NA and K/NA are constant; and
> (2) N grows at rate g_N and technological progress grows at rate g_A; NA, therefore, grows at rate $(g_N + g_A)$.

Suppose g_A = 2% and g_N = 4%. On the balanced growth path:

(1) The rate of growth of output per effective worker is zero since Y/NA is constant.
(2) The rate of growth of capital per effective worker is zero since K/NA is constant.
(3) When Y/NA is constant, the level of output (Y) grows at the same rate as NA which equals 6% $(g_N + g_A)$.
(4) When K/NA is constant, the capital stock (K) grows at the same rate as NA which equals 6% $(g_N + g_A)$.
(5) Since Y grows at 6% and N grows at 2%, output per worker (Y/N) grows at 4% (g_A).
(6) Since K grows at 6% and N grows at 2%, capital per worker (K/N) grows at 4% (g_A).

> **Learning Tip**
>
> - What is constant in the steady state is Y/NA and K/NA.
> - Since Y/NA and K/NA are constant in the steady state (i.e., on the balanced growth path), we know that Y, K and NA all grow at the same rate which is $(g_N + g_A)$.

4. THE EFFECTS OF CHANGES IN THE SAVING RATE

Assume the economy is initially in steady state. An increase in the saving rate will have the following effects:

(1) Investment will exceed required investment so K/NA will increase.
(2) K/NA and Y/NA will increase until the new steady state is reached.
(3) As K/NA and Y/NA increase, Y and K grow faster than $(g_N + g_A)$.
(4) As K/NA and Y/NA increase, Y per worker and K per worker grow faster than g_A.

(5) Once the steady state is reached, Y and K grow at $(g_N + g_A)$ and Y per worker and K per worker grow at g_A.
(6) Changes in the saving rate have no long-run effect on growth rates (of any of the variables).
(7) An increase in s WILL cause a permanent change in the levels of Y/NA and K/NA.

Learning Tip

Make sure you can explain the effects of a reduction in the saving rate.

---

5. OTHER ISSUES

(1) Causes of high growth

• When growth is caused by technological progress, we expect output per worker (Y/N) to grow at g_A (i.e., balanced growth).
• When growth is caused by increases in capital accumulation (caused by, for example, an increase in s), we would expect output per worker to grow at a rate that exceeds g_A.

Learning Tip

• So, if growth in Y/N > g_A, growth is from capital accumulation.
• If growth in Y/N = g_A, growth is from technological progress.

---

(2) Facts of growth

The period of high growth (1950-73), the growth slowdown (since 1973), and the convergence of Y/N all appear to be caused by technological progress, NOT from changes in capital accumulation.

(3) The Solow residual

The Solow residual is given by the following:

residual = $g_Y - [\alpha g_N + (1 - \alpha)g_K]$

The Solow residual can be used to obtain estimates of the rate of technological progress:

g_A = residual/α.

6. FINAL ADVICE

Depending on your instructor, you might be asked to examine the effects of changes in □, g_N, and g_A in the model.

• Increases in δ, g_N, and g_A cause the required investment line to become steeper and cause Y/NA and K/NA to fall.
• In the cases of changes in g_N and g_A, changes in the rate of growth at the new steady state will also occur.

> **Learning Tip**
>
> - Make sure you understand the graph, the dynamic adjustment to steady state and the characteristics of the steady state (balanced growth).
> - As suggested above, you might want to examine and discuss the effects of an increase (or decrease) in each of the following variables: δ, g_N, and g_A.
> - Changes in these three parameters will cause changes in the slope of the required investment line and, therefore, changes in the steady state levels of K/NA and Y/NA.
> - Changes in the depreciation rate and rate of growth of the population will not cause permanent changes in the rate of growth in Y/N.
> - As discussed above, changes in the rate of technological progress will cause permanent changes in the rate of growth of Y/N.
> - To test your understanding of this material, you might want to examine graphically and then explain changes in each of these parameters.

SELF-TEST QUESTIONS

(1) Technological progress is primarily the result of what activity (p. 304)?

(2) What is the difference between the purchase of a machine and spending on R&D (p. 307)?

(3) What are patents (p. 307)?

(4) What is meant by the fertility of research (p. 305)?

(5) What is meant by the appropriability of research results (p. 306)?

(6) What are the different dimensions of technological progress (p. 298)?

(7) Given the production function, what are the three determinants of output (p. 298)?

(8) What determines "effective labour" (p. 299)?

(9) What determines the level of output per effective worker (p. 299)?

(10) What determines the level of investment per effective worker (p. 300)?

(11) What is the expression which indicates how much investment is needed to maintain a given level of capital per effective worker (p. 301)?

(12) What happens to output per effective worker and capital per effective worker in the steady state (p. 302)?

(13) What happens to Y and K in the steady state? If they are changing, at what rate do they change in the steady state (p. 302)?

(14) What happens to output per worker in the steady state (p. 302)?

(15) What is meant by "balanced growth" (p. 302)?

(16) In steady state, what determines the rate of growth in output (p. 302)?

(17) What effect does an increase in the saving rate have on Y/NA and K/NA in the long run (p. 303)?

(18) What are the short-run and long-run effects of an increase in the saving rate on the growth rate of output and capital (pp. 303- 304)?

(19) Compare the rate of growth of output per worker with the rate of technological progress if growth reflects high balanced growth (p. 307).

(20) Compare the rate of growth of output per worker with the rate of technological progress if growth reflects capital accumulation (p. 307).

(21) The period of high growth (between 1950 and 1973) was caused by what (p. 308)?

(22) The slowdown in growth since 1973 was caused by what (p. 309)?

(23) Convergence of output per capita has come from what (p. 309)?

(24) List the three hypotheses that attempt to explain the reduction in the rate of technological progress (pp. 309-311).

(25) What is industrial policy (p. 311)?

(26) What is the technology gap (p. 313)?

REVIEW PROBLEMS

1. To what extent do patents affect: (1) the fertility of research; and (2) the appropriability of research results? Explain.

2. Briefly explain why relatively poor patent protection might affect spending on R&D and technological progress.

3. Suppose N = 100.
a. Calculate the amount of effective labour (NA) for the following values of A (the state of technology): 1, 1.1, 1.2, 1.3, 1.5.
b. What happens to the amount of effective labour as A increases? Why?

4. Suppose $Y = (K)^{1/2}(NA)^{1/2}$.
a. Calculate Y when K = 100 and NA = 100.
b. Calculate Y when K = 200 and NA = 200. When K and NA both increase by a factor of 2, what happens to Y? Does this production function exhibit constant returns to scale?
c. Assume NA = 100 and does not change. Calculate Y for each of the following values of K: 100, 150 and 200. Does this production function exhibit decreasing returns to K?
d. Assume K = 100 and does not change. Calculate Y for each of the following values of NA: 100, 140 and 180. Does this production function exhibit decreasing returns to NA?

5. Using equation (16.1), discuss what factors determine the level of output.

6. Assume $\delta = 0.10$, $g_N = 0.03$ and $g_A = 0.02$.
a. Calculate the level of investment needed to maintain the level of capital at each of the following values of K: 100, 110, 120 and 130.
b. What happens to this level of investment for each 10 unit increase in K? Does it increase at an increasing, decreasing or constant rate?

7. Assume $\delta = 0.10$, $g_N = 0.05$ and $g_A = 0.05$.
a. Calculate the amount of "required investment" (per effective worker) for each of the following levels of K/NA: 10, 20, 30 and 40.
b. What happens to required investment for each 10-unit increase in K/NA? Does it increase at an increasing, decreasing or constant rate?

8. Briefly explain how an increase in each of the following variables will affect required investment:
a. g_N
b. g_A
c. δ

9. Assume $\delta = 0.10$, $g_N = 0.03$, $g_A = 0.02$ and K/NA = 10.
a. Given this information, calculate "required investment."
b. Suppose the current I/NA = 2. Given your answer in a, what will happen, if anything, to K/NA? Briefly explain.
c. Suppose the current I/NA = 1. Given your answer in a, what will happen, if anything, to K/NA? Briefly explain.
d. What must I/NA be to maintain K/NA at 10?

10. Use the graph provided below to answer the following questions.

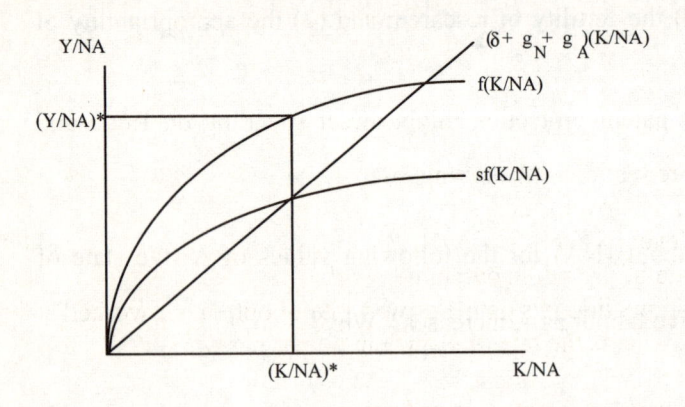

a. If K/NA < (K/NA)*, explain what happens to K/NA and Y/NA over time.
b. If K/NA > (K/NA)*, explain what happens to K/NA and Y/NA over time.
c. Is (K/NA)* the steady state level of K/NA? Briefly explain.

11. Assume $\delta = 0.10$, $g_N = 0.03$, $g_A = 0.02$ and K/NA = 10. Assume the economy is in steady state.
a. What is the rate of growth in Y/NA and K/NA in steady state?
b. What is the rate of growth in Y and K in steady state?
c. What is the rate of growth in N in steady state?
d. What is the rate of growth in capital per worker in steady state?
e. What is the rate of growth in output per worker in steady state?

12. a. What can cause the rate of growth in output (Y) to increase in the steady state?
b. What can cause the rate of growth in the output per worker to increase in the steady state?

13. Use the graph provided below to answer the following questions.

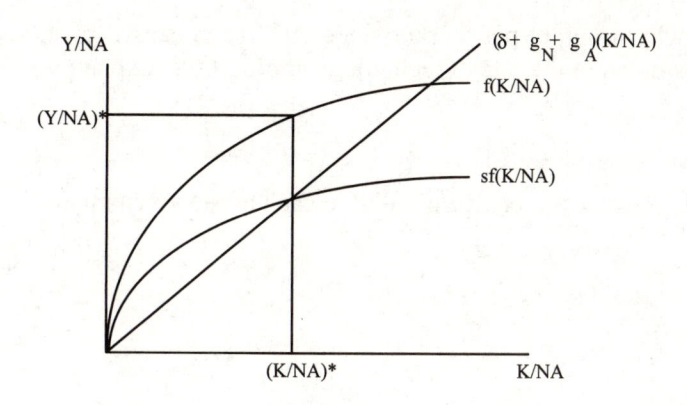

a. Graphically illustrate the effects of a reduction in the saving rate.
b. Explain what happens to K/NA and Y/NA over time.
c. What are the long run effects on the level of Y/NA and K/NA?
d. Prior to the drop in s, what was the rate of growth in output per worker?
e. What are the short run-effects of this reduction in s on the growth rate of output per worker?
f. Once the new steady state is reached, what is the rate of growth in output per worker?

14. "A reduction in the saving rate will cause a permanent reduction in the rate of growth of output per worker." Is this statement true, false, or uncertain? Explain.

15. In the steady state, what determines the rate of growth of Y, K, output per worker and capital per worker?

16. Discuss the long run effects of an increase in the rate of technological progress on the rate of growth of output per worker.

17. Discuss the short run and long run effects of an increase in the saving rate on K/NA and on the rate of growth in output per worker.

18. Suppose output per worker is growing at 6% and $g_A = 2\%$.
a. Is the economy in steady state? Why or why not?
b. What is causing this relatively high rate of growth in output per worker?

19. Suppose output per worker is growing at 2% and $g_A = 4\%$.
a. Is the economy in steady state? Why or why not?
b. What is causing this relatively low rate of growth in output per worker?

20. Suppose output per worker is growing at 2% and $g_A = 2\%$.
a. Is the economy in steady state? Why or why not?
b. What is causing this rate of growth in output per worker?

21. Has the slowdown in the rate of growth in output per worker since 1973 been caused by a slowdown in capital accumulation or a slowdown in the rate of technological progress? Explain.

MULTIPLE CHOICE QUESTIONS

1. Industrial R&D expenditures account for what percentage of GDP in each of the seven major rich countries?

a. 1.7–3%
b. 10%
c. 15%
d. 25–26%

2. Patent laws will:

a. increase the fertility of research
b. increase the appropriability of research results
c. all of the above
d. none of the above

3. The fertility of research tells us:

a. how R&D spending translate into new ideas
b. how R&D spending translate into new products
c. the extent to which firms benefit from the results of their R&D
d. both a and b
e. none of the above

4. The appropriability of research results tells us:

a. how R&D spending translate into new ideas
b. how R&D spending translate into new products

c. the extent to which firms benefit from the results of their R&D
d. both a and b
e. none of the above

5. Which of the following represents the dimensions of technological progress?

a. larger quantities of output given N and K
b. better products
c. new products
d. all of the above

6. An increase in which of the following variables will cause an increase in output (Y)?

a. N
b. K
c. A
d. all of the above

7. Which of the following expressions represents the amount of effective labour?

a. N
b. NA
c. N/A
d. A/N

8. Output per effective worker is equal to:

a. Y/N
b. Y/A
c. Y/NA
d. none of the above

9. Suppose A increases by 50% and N decreases by 50%. Given this information, we would expect that:

a. Y will increase
b. Y will decrease
c. Y will not change
d. the amount of effective labour will increase

10. If K and NA both increase by 10%, we know that:

a. Y will increase by exactly 10%
b. Y will increase by less than 10%
c. Y will increase by more than 10%
d. there will be no change in Y

11. Which of the following expressions represents required investment per effective worker?

a. $(\delta + g_N + g_A)K/NA$
b. $(\delta + g_N + g_A)Y/NA$
c. $(g_N + g_A)K/NA$
d. $(\delta + g_N)K/NA$

Use the information provided below to answer questions 12-19:

$\delta = 0.10$ (10% per year) $g_N = 0.03$ (3% per year) $g_A = 0.02$ (2% per year).

12. Effective labour grows at what rate?

a. 2%
b. 3%
c. 5%
d. 10%
e. 15%

13. The number of workers is growing at what rate?

a. 1%
b. 2%
c. 3%
d. 5%

14. The level of investment per effective worker needed to maintain a constant level of capital per effective worker (K/NA) is:

a. 0.02(K/NA)
b. 0.03(K/NA)
c. 0.05(K/NA)
d. 0.10(K/NA)
e. 0.15(K/NA)

15. The steady state rate of growth of Y/NA is:

a. 0
b. 2%
c. 3%
d. 5%
e. 10%
f. 15%

16. The steady state rate of growth of output per worker is:

a. 0
b. 2%
c. 3%
d. 5%
e. 10%

17. The steady state rate of growth of output (Y) is:

a. 0
b. 2%
c. 3%
d. 5%
e. 10%

18. The steady state rate of growth of capital per effective worker (K/NA) is:

a. 0
b. 2%
c. 3%
d. 5%
e. 10%

19. The steady state rate of growth of capital (K) is:

a. 0
b. 2%
c. 3%
d. 5%
e. 10%

20. An increase in the saving rate will cause:

a. a permanent increase in Y/NA
b. a permanent increase in K/NA
c. a temporary increase in the rate of growth in output per worker
d. all of the above

21. A reduction in the saving rate will cause:

a. a permanent reduction in the rate of growth of output per worker
b. no change in K/NA
c. a permanent reduction in the rate of growth of output (Y)
d. all of the above
e. none of the above

22. Which of the following will cause a permanent increase in the rate of growth of output per worker?

a. increase in g_A
b. increase in s
c. reduction in s
d. none of the above

23. Which of the following will cause a permanent reduction in the rate of growth of output per worker?

a. increase in s
b. reduction in s
c. reduction in g_A
d. none of the above

24. In the model presented in this chapter, balanced growth occurs when:

a. Y and K are constant
b. output per worker is constant
c. output per effective worker is increasing
d. the number of workers, output and capital grow at the same rate

25. If the growth rate of output per worker is greater than the rate of technological progress, we know that:

a. the high growth is caused by high balanced growth
b. the high growth is caused by capital accumulation
c. the economy is in steady state
d. none of the above

26. If the growth rate of output per worker is equal to the rate of technological progress, we know that:

a. the high growth is caused by high balanced growth
b. the high growth is caused by capital accumulation
c. the economy is NOT in steady state
d. none of the above

27. The slowdown in growth since the mid-1970s appears to be caused by:

a. a reduction in the saving rate
b. a reduction in g_A
c. a reduction in capital accumulation
d. none of the above

28. Which of the following are hypotheses used to explain the technological slowdown since 1973? NOTE: CIRCLE ALL THAT APPLY.

a. reduction in the saving rate
b. measurement error
c. the rise of the service sector
d. reductions in R&D spending

29. Which of the following is true about the cause of growth in Singapore and Hong Kong from 1970 to 1990?

a. capital accumulation in Singapore, balanced growth in Hong Kong
b. capital accumulation in Singapore, capital accumulation in Hong Kong
c. balanced growth in Singapore, balanced growth in Hong Kong
d. balanced growth in Singapore, capital accumulation in Hong Kong

CHAPTER 17. ECONOMIC GROWTH IN THE OPEN ECONOMY

OBJECTIVES, REVIEW AND TUTORIAL

After working through the chapter and the following material, you should be able to:

1. Explain the trend in employment-to population ratio for males and females since 1976.

2. Explain what the Labour Force Survey.

3. Discuss the components of population growth in Canada since mid 1950s.

4. Discuss the concepts of brain drain and brain gain.

5. Explain how consumption and investment choices are difficult in an open economy as opposed to a closed economy.

6. Discuss the role of foreign direct investment.

7. Explain how international debt could be useful.

8. Discuss the policy implications of the transfer of technology.

9. Explain the concept of the optimal amount of foreign borrowing.

1. SUMMARY OF CONCLUSIONS

- In contrast with a domestic economy, growth in output in an open economy arises from both domestic and international sources.
- The labour input has grown mainly due to net immigration population growth in Canada and in the last decade has been dominated by net immigration.
- The capital input in Canada also has benefited tremendously from international capital inflow.
- Canada has made substantial use of international technology and knowledge inflow.

2. A MEASURE OF LABOUR INPUTS

- A useful measure of labour inputs is best captured by total hours of work.

Total hours = Average hours of work x number of work employees.

- Growth of the labour input into the production process in Canada is primarily due to growth of population.
- Population growth in Canada primarily due to net immigration.
- Population change = number of births – number of deaths + (net immigration = immigration – emigration).

3. CAPITAL-LABOUR RATIO IN AN OPEN ECONOMY

- In contrast to the closed economy case, in which equipping workers with more capital requires a reduction (sacrifice) in consumption, in an open economy a country can increase its capital and hence its growth if its net exports become more negative: I = Y – C – NX.
- In order for I to exceed S (Y - C), NX must be negative.
- A negative NX (more imports than exports) also implies net foreign borrowing. Therefore, a nation can invest (in future capital) more than it saves by borrowing.
- Borrowing from abroad, however, gives rise to foreign debt accumulation which requires servicing.

Learning Tip

- The difference between national income and spending is best captured by GNP (not GDP). If a nation's GNP exceeds its spending, including spending on capital, then it is able to lend internationally. If GNP falls short of expenditures, then the nation must borrow from abroad.

---

4. INTERNATIONAL DEBT AND THE CURRENT ACCOUNT BALANCE

- The current account balance equals GNP minus (C + I). When GNP is less than the sum of C and I, the current account is in a deficit situation and vice versa.
- The flip side of a deficit in the current account is net foreign borrwing: Δ debt = GNP – (C + I).
- If a nation wants to increase its stock physical capital for the purpose of future growth without sacrificing its consumption, it can do so by increasing its international debt (Δ debt > 0).
- As the debt grows, the cost of servicing it (paying interest) increases. This can only be justified as long as the new capital installed is productive enough to pay the interest on the debt.

5. TECHNOLOGY TRANSFERS

- Like inputs of labour and capital that can be imported through immigration or international capital inflow (borrowing), technology can be imported too.
- Imports of technology is either in the form of buying a new foreign product through the arm (subsidiary) of a foreign company, or through renting a patented foreign technology.

SELF-TEST QUESTIONS

1. What is the employment-to-population ratio (p. 320)?

2. What is the employment-to-population trend for males and females in Canada (p. 320)?

3. What is the national population growth (p. 321)?

4. What are the two macroeconomic questions that arise from the dominant role of immigration (p. 323)?

5. What is brain drain (p. 324)?

6. What is investment constrained by in an open economy in contrast to a closed economy (p. 325)?

7. What determines the change in the capital stock per worker (p. 325)?

8. What are the sources of investment in an open economy (pp. 326-328)?

9. What is Canada's current international portfolio made up (p. 328)?

10. Under what circumstances borrowing from abroad may or may not pose a problem (p. 329)?

11. How can the current account deficit trigger economic growth (pp. 326-327)?

REVIEW PROBLEMS

1. What is the role of international patents registration in economic growth?

2. "When I > S, we know that the economy has to borrow from abroad." Is this statement true, false? Explain.

3. What is the "steady state" of output in an open economy?

4. Suppose the following information for a given year in a hypothetical economy:
   population   30 million
   employment – population ratio   60%
   average number of hours
   per week per employed   38 hours
   a) Calculate the total hours that citizens of this country worked during that year.

   b) If population is expected to grow by 1% per year in the future, whereas the average hours of work is expected to drop by 0.5% per year, what is your expectation of the total hours rate of change assuming that employment-population ratio remains unchanged.

5. Between 1997 and 2001 the following demographic changes took place in Canada:

   (In thousands)
   Births rose by 1,708
   Deaths rose by 1,103

Immigration rose by 1,050
Emigration rose by 290

a) Calculate the population change.
b) Calculate the natural population change.
c) How much is the net immigration?

6. Suppose Y = 500 billion, C = 400 billion, and I = 200
   a) What is the level of domestic saving?
   b) What is the gap between S and I?
   c) How is this nation able to sustain the existing gap between saving and investment?

7. Suppose X = 100, Q = 70, B^f = 1000, r = 5%, C = 500, I = 200.
   a) Determine gross domestic product (GDP) for this economy.
   b) Determine the gross national product (GNP) for this economy.
   c) What is the level of international debt accumulation (net borrowing or lending)?

8. In Yorktonia, international investment position is as follows:

   (millions of Yorktonian dollars)

Foreign Assets of Yorktonians	---------
Direct investment abroad	340,366
Portfolio foreign assets (stocks)	215,328
All other assets	263,421
Official international reserves	47,801
Foreign liabilities of Yorktonians	1,021,593
Foreign direct investment in Yorktonia	----------
Portfolio foreign liabilities (stocks)	485,215
All other liabilities	234,079

   a) Calculate foreign direct investment in Yorktonia.
   b) What is this Yorktonia's net international investment position?

MULTIPLE CHOICE QUESTIONS

1. If in a hypothetical nation population is 20 million, the employment-to-population ratio is 70%, and average hours per employee per week is 35
   a. 14 million hours
   b. 490 million hours
   c. 25.480 billion hours
   d. 700 million hours

2. Population change equals

   a. number of births − number of deaths + emigration − emigration
   b. number of births − number of deaths − emigration
   c. natural population growth + net immigration
   d. both a and c

3. All but one of the following is true about Canada's recent immigrants. Which is the odd one?

   a. recent immigrants are more educated than native-born Canadians
   b. immigrants are as productive as native-born Canadians
   c. immigrants cause unemployment
   d. immigrants use EI and other forms of social assistance less than native-born Canadians

4. When the economy is open and the budget deficit is zero, we know that:
   a. S can be equal to I
   b. S can be larger than I
   c. S can be smaller than I
   d. S and I cannot be determined

5. In an open economy with zero budget deficit, when $Y < C + I$, we know
   a. $NX > 0$
   b. $NX < 0$
   c. $NX = 0$
   d. ??????

6. In an open economy with zero budget deficit, when $Y < C + T$, we know
   a. This country can increase its investment without sacrificing its consumption
   b. This country cannot increase its investment without sacrificing its consumption
   c. This country must accumulate foreign debt.
   d. both a and c.

7. The net foreign debts relationship is captured by
   a. $Y - (C + I) - rB^f$
   b. $rB^f + Y - (C + I)$
   c. $rB^f + GNP$
   d. $rB^f - NX$

8. The net foreign debts relationship is equal to
   a. the current account balance
   b. trade account balance
   c. GNP – GDP
   d. none of the above

9. A nation's net international investment position equals
   a. its foreign assets minus its foreign liabilities
   b. its direct investment abroad minus foreign direct investment in the nation
   c. its portfolio foreign stocks plus direct investment abroad
   d. none of the above

10. Borrowing from the rest of the world is not a problem as long as
    a. the new capital installed financed by borrowing is less productive than the interest paid on the loan
    b. the new capital installed is more productive than the interest paid on the loan.
    c. GNP exceeds GDP
    d. the current account is balanced

11. When the current account balance is positive
    a. the net foreign debt is increasing
    b. the net foreign debt is decreasing (or negative)
    c. net exports plus the interest paid on net debts is negative
    d. net exports is positive

12. When Canadians make payments to non-residents for the rental of their technology they are
    a. exporting ideas
    b. importing capital
    c. importing products
    d. importing technology

13. The "technology balance of payments" is
    a. is the same as the current account
    b. is the same as the "international balance of payments"
    c. is the difference between receipts from exports of technology and payments for imports of technology
    d. none of the above

14. Without international borrowing or lending
    a. consumption in each year can be higher than production in that year
    b. the sum of consumption and investment in each year must equal production in that year
    c. foreign debt is always zero
    d. both b and c

15. We can increase both consumption and investment simultaneously
    a. if we are willing to lend to the rest of the world
    b. if we are willing to borrow from the rest of the world
    c. by forcing the current account into a surplus situation
    d. none of the above

CHAPTER 18. EXPECTATIONS: THE BASIC TOOLS

OBJECTIVES, REVIEW AND TUTORIAL

After working through the chapter and the material found below, you should be able to:

(1) Understand the difference between nominal and real interest rates.

(2) Explain how the real interest rate is calculated.

(3) Understand the concept of expected present discounted value (i.e., present value).

(4) Explain what factors influence the present value of a sequence of payments.

(5) Become familiar with the equations used to calculate present value.

(6) Recognize that the real interest rate affects investment and, therefore, that the real interest rate belongs in the IS relation.

(7) Explain why the nominal interest rate, not the real interest rate, influences the individual's decision to hold money and bonds.

(8) Understand that the LM relation depends on the nominal interest rate.

(9) Explain the effects of changes in expected inflation in the IS-LM model.

Learning Tip

• To best understand the material in this chapter, you should carefully read the appendix to the chapter and the first few pages of Appendix 2 ("A Math Refresher").
• When reading this material, take notes and work through the equations. It is important that you become comfortable with the equations.

---

1. DISTINCTION BETWEEN NOMINAL AND REAL INTEREST RATES

• The <u>nominal interest rate</u> (i_t) indicates how many dollars ($1 + i_t$) one repays in the future in exchange for one dollar today. Alternatively, one dollar today is worth $1 + i_t$ dollars in the future.

• The <u>real interest rate</u> (r_t) indicates how many goods ($1 + r_t$) one repays next year in exchange for one good today.

2. CALCULATION OF THE REAL INTEREST RATE

You must understand why $1 + r_t$ is expressed as follows:

$1 + r_t = (1 + i_t)/(1 + \pi^e_t)$.

> **Learning Tip**
>
> Let P_t be the price of a basket of goods (similar to the Consumer Price Index).
> - To buy a basket of goods today, you borrow P_t.
> - Next year, you must repay $(1 + i_t)P_t$ dollars (i.e., P_t, the amount borrowed, plus $i_t P_t$ the nominal interest payment).
> - To convert $(1 + i_t)P_t$ dollars to baskets of goods, simply divide by the price of the basket you expect to occur next year (P^e_{t+1}).
> - This yields: $(1 + i_t)P_t/P^e_{t+1}$.
> - This expression represents the amount of goods you must pay next year in exchange for one basket today.
>
> How do you go from $(1 + i_t)P_t/P^e_{t+1}$ to $(1 + i_t)/(1 + \pi^e_t)$?
>
> - $\pi^e_t = (P^e_{t+1} - P_t)/P_t$.
> - Add 1 to both sides:
> $1 + \pi^e_t = ((P^e_{t+1} - P_t)/P_t) + P_t/P_t$ ($P_t/P_t = 1$)
> - The right-hand side simplifies to P^e_{t+1}/P_t
> - Therefore, $1 + \pi^e_t = P^e_{t+1}/P_t$ and $P_t/P^e_{t+1} = 1/(1 + \pi^e_t)$.
> - Replace this expression for P_t/P^e_{t+1} above and you have $(1 + i_t)/(1 + \pi^e_t)$.
> - So, $1 + r_t = (1 + i_t)/(1 + \pi^e_t)$

The exact definition of the real interest rate (r_t) is given by:

$r_t = (1 + i_t)/(1 + \pi^e_t) - 1$.

A close approximation of the real interest rate is given by:

$r_t = i - \pi^e_t$.

> **Learning Tip**
>
> - $i = r$ only when $\pi^e = 0$.
> - Since π^e is generally greater than zero, i is generally greater than r.
> - If $i = \pi^e$, $r = 0$. For example, if $i = 20\%$ and $\pi^e = 20\%$, a dollar today yields 1.20 dollars in one year. One dollar in a year, however, is worth 20% less in terms of goods. The real cost of borrowing and the real return from lending are zero.

3. INTRODUCTION TO EXPECTED PRESENT DISCOUNTED VALUE (PV): ONE AND TWO PERIOD CASES

The expected present discounted value is the value today of a sequence of payments. You can examine two examples.

(1) The one period example

If you lend one dollar today, you receive $1 + i_t$ dollars in one year (i.e., the one dollar (1) plus interest on the dollar (i_t)). If you borrow one dollar today, you will repay $1 + i_t$ dollars in one

year. One dollar today is, therefore, worth $1 + i_t$ dollars next year. And, $1 + i_t$ dollars next year are worth one dollar today.
- One dollar next year is worth $1/(1 + i_t)$ dollars today.
    - If you lend $1/(1 + i_t)$ dollars today, you receive one dollar in a year [to prove this, simply multiply this expression by $(1 + i_t)$].
    - $1/(1 + i_t)$ is called the <u>discount factor</u>.

Learning Tip

- If $i_t = 20\%$, 1 dollar today is worth 1.20 dollars in a year.
- One dollar next year is worth 83 cents today.
    - When $i_t > 0$, having a dollar next year is worth less than having a dollar today.
    - As i_t increases, a dollar next year is worth less today. That is, an increase in the interest rate reduces the present value of a future dollar.

---

(2) The two period example

If you lend one dollar for two years, you receive $(1 + i_t)(1 + i_{t+1})$ dollars in two years. Why?
- In one year, the one dollar is worth $(1 + i_t)$ dollars.
- If you lend the $1 + i_t$ dollars for one more year, you receive the $1 + i_t$ <u>plus</u> interest (at a rate of i_{t+1}) on the $1 + i_t$ dollars (i.e., $i_{t+1}(1 + i_t)$) in two years.
- Therefore, you receive $1 + i_t + i_{t+1}(1 + i_t)$ in two years.
- Factor out $(1 + i_t)$ and you have $(1 + i_t)(1 + i_{t+1})$.

Learning Tip

- Let $i_t = i_{t+1} = 5\%$.
- The PV of a dollar received one year from now is 95 cents.
- The PV of a dollar received two years from now is 91 cents.
- As i_t and/or i_{t+1} increases, the PV of a future payment decreases.
- Having a dollar two years from now is worth less than having a dollar one year from now, which is worth less than having one dollar today.
- The PV of one dollar received in one year is: $1/(1 + i_t)$.
- $1/(1 + i_t)$ is the relevant discount factor for a payment received in one year.
- The PV of one dollar received in two years is: $1/(1 + i_t)(1 + i_{t+1})$.
- $1/(1 + i_t)(1 + i_{t+1})$ is the relevant discount factor for a payment received in two years.

---

4. EXPECTED PRESENT DISCOUNTED VALUE: OTHER CASES

Individuals will not always know with certainty: (1) future interest rates; and/or (2) future payments. Individuals, therefore, must form expectations of future interest rate (i^e_{t+2}) and of future payments ($\$z^e_{t+2}$). The general formula for expected present discounted value of a sequence of payments is given by:

$$\$V_t = \$z_t + (1/(1 + i_t))\$z^e_{t+1} + (1/(1 + i_t)(1 + i^e_{t+1}))\$z^e_{t+2} + ...$$

Each expected payment (the z^e variables) is adjusted by the appropriate discount factor. There are several implications of this equation that you must know.

$V will decline:
- the higher the interest rate(s)
- the more distant the payment—that is, $1000 ten years from now is worth less than $1000 five years from now
- the lower the expected payment $$z^e$

Learning Tip

- If you understand this equation and understand the material presented in the appendices, you will understand all of the applications of PV analysis.
- If we know the future payments with certainty, replace $$z^e$ with $$z$.
- If we know the future interest rates with certainty, replace i^e with i
- If i and $$z^e$ are constant, the above expression simplifies to the expression found in the text.
- To calculate real PV, simply replace i with r and $$z$ with z. This yields V_t.

There are two final cases to consider.

- <u>Case 1: Consol bond</u>. A consol bond is a bond that promises to make some payment ($$z$) each year forever. Such a bond never matures.
    - The PV of an infinite series of fixed payments to begin next period is given by $$V_t = z/i.
    - The PV of a consol increases when:
        (1) i falls; and/or
        (2) $$z$ increases.

- <u>Case 2: Zero interest rates</u>. When the interest rate is zero, all of the discount factors equal 1. That is, the PV of a sequence of payments simply equals the sum of the payments.

5. NOMINAL INTEREST RATES, THE REAL INTEREST RATE AND THE IS-LM MODEL

You must understand that: (1) investment, the IS relation, and the IS curve depend on the real interest rate; and (2) individuals' portfolio decisions (money versus bonds) depend on the nominal interest rate.

(1) Investment, the real interest rate and the IS curve

When firms borrow to finance an investment project, they care about how much they will repay in terms of goods. The real interest rate (NOT the nominal interest rate) determines investment.

> **Learning Tip**
>
> There are several key issues that you must understand.
>
> (1) Changes in r cause changes in investment.
>
> (2) When the real interest rate (r) is on the vertical axis:
>
> - A change in r causes a movement along the IS curve.
> - A change in the nominal interest rate (i) will have no effect on investment and the IS curve.
>
> (3) When the nominal interest rate (i) is on the vertical axis:
> - A change in i, given expected inflation, will cause a movement along the IS curve.
> - A change in expected inflation, given i, will cause a change in r and a shift of the IS curve.
> - In particular, the IS curve is drawn for a given expected rate of inflation.

(2) Money, bonds, the nominal interest rate and expected inflation

Recall that: (1) bonds pay a nominal interest rate (i); and (2) money pays a zero nominal interest rate. Changes in i, therefore, affect money demand and bond demand.

- When i increases, the opportunity cost of holding money increases and money demand falls (and bond demand increases).
- When i falls, the opportunity cost of holding money falls and money demand increases (bond demand falls).
- In general, it is the difference between the rate of return on bonds and the rate of return on money which determines money demand. This difference in returns equals i (i - 0 = i).

> **Learning Tip**
>
> Changes in expected inflation (π^e) have no effect on money demand. Why? Changes in π^e do not affect the opportunity cost (measured in nominal or real terms) of holding money. Let i = 10% and $\pi^e = 0$.
> - The opportunity cost of holding money in nominal terms is 10%.
> - The real rate of return on bonds is 10% and the real rate of return on money is 0.
> - The opportunity cost of holding money is still 10%.
>
> Suppose π^e increases to 5% and i remains fixed at 10%.
> - The opportunity cost of holding money (in nominal terms) is still 10%.
> - The real rate of return on bonds is now 5% and the real rate of return on money is now -5% (0 - 5% = -5%).
> - The opportunity cost of holding money in real terms, despite the increase in π^e, is still 10% (5% - (-5%) = 10%).

You should now realize that:
- Changes in expected inflation have no effect on money demand.
- Money demand is a function of i (NOT the real interest rate).
- The LM relation, therefore, is also a function of i (NOT r).
- i (NOT r) will adjust to maintain financial market equilibrium: M/P = YL(i).

6. MONEY GROWTH, INFLATION, OUTPUT, AND INTEREST RATES

(1) Short-run effects

In the short run, an increase in money growth will cause:
- a reduction in the nominal interest rate (see Figure 18-5);
- a reduction in the real interest rate for a given expected rate of inflation; and
- an increase in output.

(2) Medium-run effects

In the medium run, an increase in money growth will cause:
- no change in output (Y returns to the natural level of output)
- no change in the real interest rate (r returns to the natural real interest rate)
- an equal increase in inflation
- an equal increase in the nominal interest rate (i.e., the Fisher effect)
- the Fisher effect summarizes the medium-run effects of a change in inflation on the nominal interest rate.

Learning Tip

There are several issues that you <u>must</u> understand in this section.

(1) Determinants of inflation.
- $\pi = g_m - g_Y$. If $g_Y = 0$, we have $\pi = g_m$.

(2) The natural real interest rate: r_n.
- r_n is the real interest rate that occurs, for given G and T, when $Y = Y_n$.
- To determine r_n, simply determine the position of the IS curve. Then, determine Y_n. r_n is the real rate that occurs at this level of output.
- Note: r_n will change as G and T (and Y_n) change.

(3) The nominal interest rate
- In general, $i = r + \pi^e$.
- In the medium run, $r = r_n$ and $\pi = \pi^e = g_m$ (assuming $g_Y = 0$).
- Therefore, in the medium run, $i = r_n + g_m$.

(3) From the short run to the medium: the adjustment process

An increase in money growth will cause:
- a reduction in both i and r in the short run; and
- no change in r and an increase in i in the medium run.

During the adjustment process, the increase in money growth causes:
- Y to rise initially above Y_n.
- expected inflation to rise with $Y > Y_n$
- with $Y > Y_n$, eventually inflation will exceed money growth
- with real money growth negative, i must increase
- for given π^e, r must also rise as I rises (see Figure 18-6)
- eventually, r returns to r_n and i is permanently higher (i.e., medium-run effects).

Learning Tip

How do we know that inflation will eventually exceed money growth during the adjustment process? There are two ways to explain this.

(a) If we use the IS-LM model with r on the vertical axis, the analysis is easy. The initial increase in money growth causes a reduction in r. Given previous analysis, we know that money is neutral in the medium run. In other words, the LM curve will shift up as the price level (and inflation increases). For the LM curve to shift up, inflation must exceed money growth so that the real supply of money falls.

(b) Recall that $\pi = g_m - g_Y$. In the short run, output growth is positive. As expectations adjust, however, Y will return to the natural level causing g_Y to be negative. If $g_Y < 0$, the above equation implies that $\pi > g_m$.

---

7. EXPECTED INFLATION AND THE IS-LM MODEL

(1) Review

When $\pi^e = 0$, the nominal and real interest rates are the same (i.e., a change in i represents an equal change in r) and the IS-LM model is unchanged.
- Reductions in i (or r) cause increases in investment and movements along the IS curve.
- Increases in income cause increases in money demand, increases in the interest rate and movements along the LM curve.

When $\pi^e > 0$, we need to do two things. First, we need to determine which interest rate (i or r) belongs on the vertical axis in the IS-LM model. Second, we need to examine the effects of changes in expected inflation on the IS-LM model.

Learning Tip

The IS-LM model can be presented with either the nominal interest rate (i) or the real interest rate (r) on the vertical axis. The following discussion includes i on the vertical axis. You might want to think carefully about how this analysis differs if the real interest rate is on the vertical axis.

(2) Which interest rate?

We will measure the nominal interest rate (i) on the vertical axis. Changes in i cause only movements along the LM curve and, for a given rate of expected inflation (π^e), movements along the IS curve.

(3) Changes in π^e and the IS curve.

The IS curve shifts when expected inflation changes. For a given i, an increase in expected inflation causes a (measured in absolute terms) reduction in the real interest rate. As the real interest rate falls, I increases and the equilibrium level of output in the goods market at a given i is higher. This is represented as a rightward shift in the IS curve.

(4) Changes in π^e and the LM curve.

Suppose i = 10%. An increase in π^e from 0 to 5% will not affect money demand. The nominal interest rate, therefore, does not change initially since financial markets remain in equilibrium. The LM curve does not shift as a result of a change in expected inflation.

(5) The macroeconomic effects of an increase in expected inflation.
   An increase in π^e will cause:
- an initial reduction in r equal to the change in π^e
- a rightward shift in the IS curve
- an increase in investment as r falls
- the increase in investment causes an increase in output and an increase in money demand
- as money demand increases, i will rise (a movement along the LM curve)
- output continues to increase until equilibrium is reached.

Here is a summary of the final effects of the change in expected inflation:

- expected inflation is higher
- the real interest rate falls
- the nominal interest rate rises (but by less than the change in π^e)
- investment and output increase

> **Learning Tip**
>
> • Make sure you can graphically illustrate and explain the effects of a reduction in expected inflation on the IS-LM model.
> • Note the difference between the effects of changes in the price level (P) and changes in expected inflation (π^e).
>   • An increase in P causes a reduction in the real supply of money, an increase in the nominal interest rate and an upward shift in the LM curve.
>   • An increase in expected inflation causes, as described above, a rightward shift in the IS curve. Changes in expected inflation do not reflect changes in the current price level; consequently, changes in expected inflation do not cause changes in the real supply of money.

> **Advice/Warning**
>
> Some instructors will want you to understand the concept of present value. Others might require you to use many of the formulas found in this chapter. In the latter case, students must work through these calculations. You should, therefore, carefully work through each step in the derivation of the equations. The only way to become comfortable with these expressions is to work through them yourself.

SELF-TEST QUESTIONS

1. Define the nominal interest rate (p. 345).

2. Define the real interest rate (p. 345).

3. Can the real interest rate equal the nominal interest rate? Explain (p. 347).

4. If the real interest rate is 3% and the expected inflation rate is 7%, what is the nominal interest rate (p. 347)?

5. What does "expected present discounted value" measure? Explain (p. 348).

6. What effect does an increase in the interest rate (i) have on the present value of a dollar you receive next year (p. 349)?

7. Suppose you are offered $1000 at the end of two years. How would you calculate the present value of the $1000 (p. 349)?

8. The present value of a sequence of payments is a weighted sum of current and expected future payments. What happens to the size of the weights through time (p. 349)?

9. What type of bond is a consol (p. 351)?

10. How does one calculate the <u>real</u> present value of future payments (p. 352)?

11. Which interest rate (nominal or real) affects investment (p. 352)?

12. Which interest rate (nominal or real) affects money demand (p. 352)?

13. What initial effect will an increase in expected inflation have on money demand (p. 353)?

14. What effect will a reduction in expected inflation have on the IS curve and on the LM curve (p. 353)?

REVIEW PROBLEMS

1. Use the information provided below to answer the following questions. Assume the nominal interest rate is 10% ($i_t = 0.10$) and that the average price of goods (as measured by the Consumer Price Index) equals 1.0 ($P_t = 1.0$). Using the definition of expected inflation (π^e) and the exact definition of the real interest rate (r), calculate expected inflation and r for each of the following price levels which are expected to prevail in the next period (P^e_{t+1}).
   a. 1.0
   b. 1.03
   c. 1.05
   d. 1.07
   e. 1.10
   f. In which of these cases is i = r? Explain.
   g. In which of these cases is i > r? Explain.
   h. In which of these cases is r = 0? Explain.

2. Repeat the analysis in #1 for parts a - e; ignore parts f, g and h. This time, however, use the approximate definition of the real interest rate (see equation 18.4 in the chapter). Are any of your calculations of r different from those obtained in #1? Briefly explain.

3. a. For each of the following pairs of expected inflation and the nominal interest rate, calculate the real interest rate using: (1) the exact definition (call this r^I); and (2) the "approximate" definition of the real interest rate (call this r^{II} – see equation 18-4). Use the space below to write down your answers.

i	π^e	r^I	r^{II}
2%	0		
5%	3%		
10%	8%		
15%	13%		
20%	18%		
50%	48%		
100%	98%		

b. What happens to the ability of the approximate definition (r^{II}) to measure accurately the actual real interest rate (r^I) as i and π^e increase? Briefly explain.

4. Based on the definition of the real interest rate, the real interest rate can increase for two reasons. What are they? Briefly explain.

5. Is it possible for the nominal interest rate to fall and the real interest rate to increase during the same period? Explain.

6. Suppose you will receive $100,000 each year for the next two years, beginning in one year. Calculate the present value of this sequence of payments when the interest rate is:
a. 0%
b. 4%
c. 8%
d. What happens to the present value of this sequence of payments as the interest rate increases? Explain.

7. Suppose individual A will receive $50,000 each year for the next three years beginning one year from now. Suppose individual B also receives three annual payments of $50,000. She, however, receives the first $50,000 today, the second $50,000 payment a year from now and the final $50,000 payment two years from now.
a. Suppose the nominal interest rate is expected to be constant for the next three years. Which of these two individuals will receive the larger present value given these two sequences of payments? Explain.
b. Under what condition, if any, would the present value of these two sequences of payments be equal? Explain.

8. Suppose a friend of yours wins the lottery and must choose among three different payment options:

option 1: receive $100,000 in one year
option 2: receive $100,000 in two years
option 3: receive $100,000 in three years

Your friend asks you to determine which option is best. Suppose the nominal interest rate is expected to remain constant at 10% for each of the next three years.
a. Calculate the present value of option 1.
b. Calculate the present value of option 2.
c. Calculate the present value of option 3.
d. Discuss what happens to the present value as the same payment occurs further into the future.

9. Suppose a college introduces a payment plan in which incoming first-year students can: (1) make a one-time payment on the first day of classes in their first year; or (2) pay $20,000 on the first day of classes in their first year, pay $22,000 at the beginning of their second year, pay $25,000 at the beginning of their third year and pay $28,000 at the beginning of their fourth year. Assume that the interest rate is to remain constant at 10% over the next four years.
a. Suppose it is the first day of classes of the first year. Calculate (separately) the present value of each of the four yearly payments.
b. Based on your analysis in part a, what is the maximum one-time payment you would recommend that this student make if he chooses the one-time payment plan? Explain.

10. Suppose you have $100,000 and want to calculate what it will be worth at the end of three years given the following three different interest rate scenarios:

	i_t	i_{t+1}	i_{t+2}
Case 1:	0%	0%	0%
Case 2:	10%	12%	14%
Case 3:	10%	8%	6%

a. Calculate what the $100,000 will be worth at the end of three years in each of the above three cases.
b. Which of these three cases would be preferred if you wish to maximize what the $100,000 will be worth in three years? Explain.

11. Suppose bonds pay a nominal interest rate of 9% and that expected inflation is initially 0. Recall that money pays a zero nominal interest rate.
a. What is the opportunity cost of holding money?
b. When $\pi^e = 0$, what is the real interest rate on bonds? What is the real interest rate on money?
c. For each of the following values of expected inflation, calculate the real rates of return on bonds and on money: 1%, 3%, 7% and 9%.
d. As expected inflation increases, what happens to the opportunity cost (measured in nominal terms) of holding money? Briefly explain.
e. Given the nominal interest rate of 9%, what happens to the opportunity cost of holding money (measured in nominal terms) when expected inflation increases? Briefly explain.
f. Given your analysis in c, d and e, what does your analysis suggest happens to money demand when expected inflation or the real interest rate change? Explain.

12. Use the graph provided below to answer the following questions. Initially assume that the nominal interest rate which maintains financial market equilibrium is 10% and that expected inflation is 0. Since $\pi^e = 0$, the nominal interest rate is initially equal to the real interest rate.

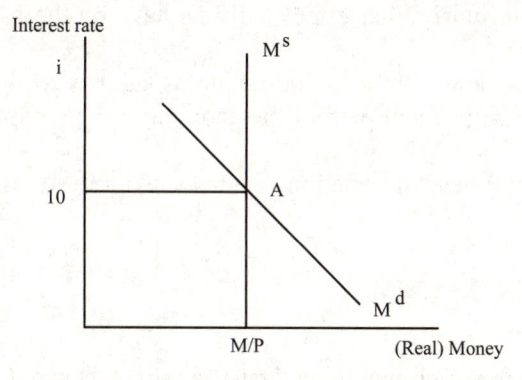

a. If expected inflation is 0, what must the real interest rate be to maintain financial market equilibrium?
b. Suppose expected inflation increases from 0 to 2%. Given your analysis in #11, what effect does this have on money demand and on the nominal interest rate? What is the real interest rate consistent with financial market equilibrium when $\pi^e = 2\%$?
c. Repeat the analysis in part (b) with expected inflation now equal to 5%.

13. Explain the short-run and medium-run effects of a reduction in money supply growth on output, inflation, the nominal interest rate and the real interest rate.

14. Discuss what effect each of the following events will have on the natural real rate (r_n):
a. a reduction in government spending
b. a reduction in taxes
c. a reduction in the price of oil

15. Suppose the goods and financial markets are in equilibrium and that the initial equilibrium nominal interest rate in the financial markets is 8% and that expected inflation is 6%. Also assume that financial markets are always in equilibrium (i.e., the economy is always on the LM curve).
a. Given the above information, what is the initial equilibrium real interest rate? That is, what is the real interest rate that maintains equilibrium in the goods market and is consistent with equilibrium in the financial markets?
b. Use the graph provided below to answer the following questions.

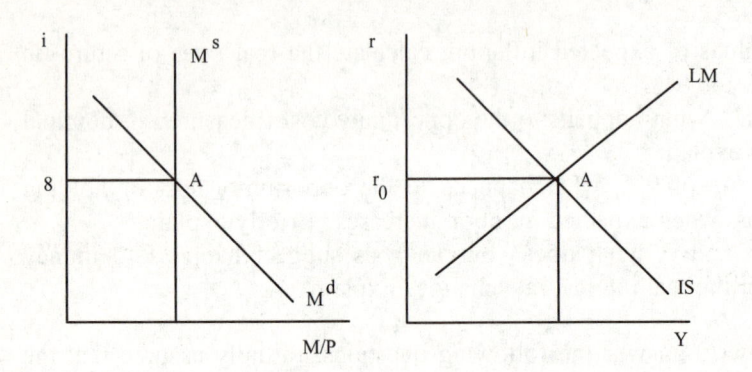

Suppose expected inflation falls to 3%. What will this drop in expected inflation do to the real interest rate consistent with financial market equilibrium? What effect will this have on the LM curve and, therefore, on the real interest rate?
c. What happens to r, i, investment, consumption and output as the economy adjusts to this reduction in expected inflation? Explain. Show the adjustment path of the economy in the graph. Where is the final equilibrium? Label this point A'.
d. What are the total effects of this reduction in expected inflation on the real interest rate? Explain.

MULTIPLE CHOICE QUESTIONS

1. The nominal interest rate:
a. measures the cost of borrowing in terms of goods
b. is approximately equal to the real interest rate minus the expected rate of inflation
c. measures the cost of borrowing one dollar today in terms of how many dollars one repays in the next year
d. measures the rate of return on money

2. Which of the following expressions represents the exact definition of the real interest rate?
a. $i - \pi^e$
b. $i + \pi^e$
c. $(1 + i)/(1 + \pi^e)$
d. $[(1 + i)/(1 + \pi^e)] - 1$

3. Suppose the nominal interest rate is fixed. An increase in expected inflation will cause:
a. an increase in the real interest rate
b. a reduction in the real interest rate
c. no change in the real interest rate since the nominal interest rate is fixed
d. none of the above

4. If $\pi^e = 0$, we know that:

a. $r > i$
b. $r < i$
c. $r = i$
d. $i > 0$ and $r = 0$

5. Suppose $\pi^e = 5\%$ and does not change. We know with certainty that:

a. $r > i$
b. $r < i$
c. $r = i$
d. $r < 5\%$
e. $i > 5\%$

6 Suppose the real interest rate does not change while the nominal interest rate falls during a given period. This would suggest that:

a. π^e increased
b. the change in $\pi^e >$ the change in i
c. the change in $\pi^e =$ the change in i
d. the change in $\pi^e <$ the change in i

7. Suppose you will receive $100 one year from now and that i = 10%. The present value (PV) of this $100 is:

a. $110
b. $100
c. $90.91
d. $90

8. Suppose you borrow $1000 today and will repay the $1000 in one year. If the nominal interest rate is 15%, what will you repay in one year?

a. $1150
b. $1015
c. $869.56
d. $850

9. Assume the nominal interest rate equals 5% and does not change. The PV of $1000 to be received at the end of two years is:

a. $1102.50
b. $952.38
c. $907.03
d. $900

10. Suppose you are to receive a sequence of future payments. The PV of this sequence of payments will increase as:

a. the nominal interest rate increases
b. the nominal interest rate falls
c. the higher the value of the future payments
d. both b and c

11. Suppose you are to receive a sequence of future payments. The PV of this sequence of payments will be lower:

a. the higher the nominal interest rate
b. the lower the nominal interest rate
c. the later you receive the payment
d. both a and c

12. Suppose you are to receive a one-time payment of $1000 at the end of ten years. Also assume that the nominal and real interest are zero and expected to remain at this level for the next 10 years. We know that:

a. the PV of this payment is greater than $1000
b. the PV of this payment is less than $1000
c. the PV of this payment is equal to $1000
d. none of the above

13. Suppose you hold a consol which promises to pay you $100 each year, forever, starting next year. If the nominal interest rate is 10% and not expected to change, the PV of this consol is:

a. $110
b. $900
c. $1000
d. will increase as the nominal interest rate increases

14. Suppose expected inflation is greater than zero. Which of the following statements is correct about the IS-LM model?

a. the nominal interest rate belongs in the IS relation
b. the nominal interest rate belongs in the LM relation
c. the real interest rate belongs in the LM relation
d. none of the above

15. Suppose the nominal interest rate is fixed. An increase in expected inflation will cause:

a. the IS curve to shift to the right
b. the IS curve to shift to the left
c. an increase in investment and an increase in output
d. a decrease in investment and a reduction in output
e. a reduction in the real interest rate and a rightward shift in the IS curve

16. In the financial market (that is, in the money supply and money demand graph), an increase in expected inflation will cause:

a. an immediate drop in i
b. an immediate increase in i
c. a reduction in the real interest rate associated with financial market equilibrium
d. an increase in the real interest rate associated with financial market equilibrium

17. A reduction in expected inflation will cause:

a. the LM curve to shift down
b. the LM curve to shift up
c. the IS curve to shift to the right
d. the IS curve to shift to the left

18. Which of the following statements is correct concerning the decision individuals make about how much money and bonds to hold?

a. an increase in expected inflation will cause an individual to hold more bonds and less money
b. an increase in the nominal interest rate will cause an increase in the opportunity cost of holding money
c. a reduction in expected inflation will cause an individual to hold more money and fewer bonds
d. both a and c

19. An increase in expected inflation will cause:

a. the LM curve to shift down, a reduction in r and an increase in investment
b. the LM curve to shift up, an increase in r and a reduction in investment
c. the IS curve to shift to the right, an increase in r and an increase in output
d. the IS curve to shift left, a reduction in r and a reduction in output

Use the IS-LM model to answer the next three questions.

20. An increase in expected inflation will result in:

a. a lower r and higher i
b. a lower r and lower i
c. a higher r and higher i
d. a higher r and lower i

21. A reduction in expected inflation will cause:

a. the LM curve to shift down, a reduction in r and an increase in investment
b. the LM curve to shift up, an increase in r and a reduction in investment
c. the IS curve to shift to the right, an increase in r and an increase in output
d. the IS curve to shift left, a reduction in r and a reduction in output

22. A reduction in expected inflation will cause:
a. a lower r and higher i
b. a lower r and lower i
c. a higher r and higher i
d. a higher r and lower i

23. An increase in government spending will cause:
a. the natural real interest rate to increase
b. the natural real interest rate to decrease
c. no change in the natural real interest rate
d. ambiguous effects on the natural real interest rate

24. An increase in taxes will cause:
a. the natural real interest rate to increase
b. the natural real interest rate to decrease
c. no change in the natural real interest rate
d. ambiguous effects on the natural real interest rate

25. In the short run, an increase in money growth will cause:
a. an increase in i and an increase in r
b. an increase in i and a reduction in r
c. a reduction in i and a reduction in r
d. a reduction in i and an increase in r

26. In the medium run, an increase in money growth will cause:
a. an increase in i and an increase in r
b. an increase in i and a reduction in r
c. a reduction in i and a reduction in r
d. a reduction in i and an increase in r
e. none of the above

CHAPTER 19. FINANCIAL MARKETS AND EXPECTATIONS

OBJECTIVES, REVIEW AND TUTORIAL

After working through the chapter and the material found below, you should be able to:

(1) Understand that the price of a bond is equal to the present value of the payments on the bond.

(2) Explain how arbitrage is used to examine the relationship between the expected returns on two assets.

(3) Explain the relationship between current long-term interest rates, current short-term interest rates and future expected short-term interest rates.

(4) Explain what is meant by yield to maturity and the yield curve.

(5) Explain what upward sloping and downward sloping yield curves suggest about expected future short-term interest rates.

(6) Use the IS-LM model to make predictions about future short-term interest rates and, therefore, make predictions about the shape of the yield curve.

(7) Explain the determinants of current stock prices.

(8) Explain how anticipated and unanticipated changes in both economic activity and fiscal and monetary policy affect stock prices.

(9) Explain what is meant by the fundamental value of a stock price.

(10) Understand the difference between rational speculative bubbles and fads.

(11) Understand how the real interest rate and the real exchange rate are related.

(12) Understand the real interest rate parity relationship.

(13) Explain the exchange rate overshooting phenomenon.

1. BOND MARKET VOCABULARY

• <u>Risk premium</u>. Bonds with a higher probability of default generally have a higher interest rate. The difference between the interest rate on a relatively risky bond and the interest rate on a bond with a relatively low probability of default is the <u>risk premium</u>.

• <u>Junk bonds</u>. These are bonds with a relatively high probability of default and, therefore, a relatively high risk premium.

• <u>Coupon bond</u>. These are bonds that promise multiple payments prior to maturity, and one payment (the face value) at maturity. These payments are called coupon payments.

• <u>Coupon rate</u>. The coupon rate is the ratio of the coupon payments to the face value.

• <u>Current yield</u>. The current yield is the ratio of the coupon payment to the current price of the bond.

• <u>Indexed bonds</u>. These are bonds that promise payments adjusted for inflation.

> **Learning Tip**
>
> There are several other terms you might want to review in this chapter. Depending on the preferences of your instructor, you might be expected to know, for example, the differences among short-term, medium-term and long-term bonds. It would be worthwhile to quickly review these and other terms and definitions.

2. BOND PRICES AND PRESENT VALUE

Assume that all bonds promise to pay $100 upon maturity.

- One-year bond. The price of a one-year bond (P_{1t}) is given by:

    $\$P_{1t} = \$100/(1 + i_{1t})$ where i_{1t} is the nominal one-year interest rate.

- Two-year bond. The price of a two-year bond (P_{2t}) is given by:

    $\$P_{2t} = \$100/[(1 + i_{1t})(1 + i^e_{1t})]$.

3. ARBITRAGE AND EXPECTED RETURNS

(1) <u>Returns from one-year bond held for one year</u>.

• For every dollar you put in a one-year bond, you receive $1 + i_t$ dollars in one year.

(2) <u>Returns from two-year bond held for one year</u>.

• For every dollar you put in a two-year bond, you receive $1/\$P_{2t}$ two-year bonds today.
• When you sell your two-year bond in one year, the bond will become a one-year bond since it has just one more year until maturity.
• Your proceeds from selling $1/\$P_{2t}$ two-year bonds in one year at an expected price for one-year bonds are $\$P^e_{1t} / \$P_{2t}$.

(3) <u>Arbitrage relation</u>.

The market for one- and two-year bonds will only be in equilibrium when the above returns are equal:

$1 + i_{1t} = \$P^e_{1t} / \$P_{2t}$.

> **Learning Tip**
>
> • If the returns from holding the one-year bond are greater than the returns from holding the two-year bond, no one would hold two-year bonds.
> • If the returns from holding the two-year bond are greater than the returns from holding the one-year bond, no one would hold one-year bonds.
> • Therefore, the two bonds must offer the same expected returns.

As shown in the text, the above arbitrage relation can be rearranged to yield:

$$\$P_{2t} = \$100/[(1 + i_{1t})(1 + i^e_{1t})]$$

Arbitrage between these two bonds implies that the price of the two-year bond is the present value of the $100 payment using i_{1t} and i^e_{1t+1}.

4. YIELD TO MATURITY AND THE YIELD CURVE

• The <u>yield to maturity</u> on an n-period bond (i.e., the n-year interest rate) is the interest rate which makes the price of the bond equal to the present value of the future payments of the bond (using the n-year interest rate). For example, i_{2t} and i_{3t} are the yields to maturity (as defined below) on two-year and three-year bonds:

$$\$P_{2t} = \$100/(1 + i_{2t})^2$$

$$\$P_{3t} = \$100/(1 + i_{3t})^3$$

• The <u>yield curve</u> (or term structure of interest rates) plots the relation between yields and maturity.

Learning Tip

• Don't be confused by the definition of the yield curve. The yield curve is simply a graph with time (maturity) on the horizontal axis and the yield to maturity on the vertical axis.
• The yield curve shows what rates are on the one-year, 3-year, etc. bonds.
• The yield curve is generally (though not always) upward sloping.

Does the yield curve provide any information about future interest rates? Yes!! The arbitrage relation between one-year and two-year bonds indicates that the price of a two-year bond is:

$$\$P_{2t} = \$100/[(1 + i_{1t})(1 + i^e_{1t+1})].$$

The definition of the yield to maturity on a two-year bond indicates that:

$$\$P_{2t} = \$100/(1 + i_{2t})^2.$$

Equating these two expressions for $\$P_{2t}$ and rearranging yields:

$$(1 + i_{2t})^2 = (1 + i_{1t})(1 + i^e_{1t+1}).$$

An approximation of this relation is:

$$i_{2t} = (i_{1t} + i^e_{1t+1})/2.$$

> **Learning Tip**
>
> How do we get the approximate relation. If you expand both sides of the above equation, you obtain:
>
> $$1 + 2i_{2t} + (i_{2t})^2 = 1 + i_{1t} + i^e_{1t+1} + (i_{1t})(i^e_{1t+1}).$$
>
> - Subtract one from both sides.
> - As shown in the "Math Refresher" appendix, the terms $(i_{2t})^2$ and $(i_{1t})(i^e_{1t+1})$ will be small so we can ignore them.
> - That leaves us with $2i_{2t} = i_{1t} + i^e_{1t+1}$.
> - Divide by 2 and we have the above approximation.

The above equation has a very simple interpretation:

- i_{2t} is (approximately) an average of the current one-year rate and the one-year rate expected to occur next year.
- More generally, the n-year rate is the average of the current one-year rate and expected future one-year rates over the next n-1 periods.

The above equation can also be used:
(1) to explain the slope of the yield curve; and
(2) to provide information about what financial markets expect the future one-year rate to be.

- <u>Upward sloping yield curve</u>.

  - The yield curve is upward sloping when $i_{2t} > i_{1t}$.
  - If $i_{2t} > i_{1t}$, financial markets expect the one-year rate to increase in the future (above its current level).

- <u>Downward sloping yield curve</u>.

  - The yield curve is downward sloping when $i_{1t} > i_{2t}$.
  - If $i_{1t} > i_{2t}$, financial markets expect the one-year rate to decrease in the future (above its current level).

> **Learning Tip**
>
> What will i^e_{t+1} be?
> - After rearranging the above equation, we obtain: $i^e_{t+1} = 2i_{2t} - i_{1t}$.
> - Given i_{1t} and i_{2t}, we can infer what financial markets expect the future one-year rate to be.

5. EXPECTATIONS, THE YIELD CURVE AND THE IS-LM MODEL

Assume: (1) expected inflation is 0; and (2) the one-year rate is on the vertical axis of the IS-LM graph. Given these assumptions, what determines i^e_{t+1} and, therefore, the slope of the yield curve? The answer is relatively easy.

The positions of the IS and LM curves that financial markets expect to occur in one-year determine the equilibrium interest rate in one year (this happens to be i^e_{t+1}). There are at least four types of events that can occur which will cause i^e_{t+1} and the slope of the yield curve to change. Assume that in all four cases the yield curve is initially upward sloping.

Case 1: An expected monetary contraction. This expected future reduction in the money supply will cause the LM curve to shift up, the future one-year rate to increase and the yield curve to become steeper.

Case 2: An expected monetary expansion. This expected future increase in the money supply will cause the LM curve to shift down, the future one-year rate to decrease and the yield curve to become flatter.

Case 3: An expectation that consumer confidence and, therefore, consumption will increase (or, equivalently, an expected increase in G or expected reduction in T). This expected future increase in spending will cause the IS curve to shift to the right, the future one-year rate to increase and the yield curve to become steeper.

Case 4: An expectation that consumer confidence and, therefore, consumption will decrease (or, equivalently, an expected reduction in G or expected increase in T). This expected future reduction in spending will cause the IS curve to shift to the left, the future one-year rate to decrease and the yield curve to become flatter.

In general, any expectation of a future shift in the IS or LM curves will cause a change in i^e_{t+1}.

Learning Tip

How does the current long-term rate respond to a given change in the current short-term rate?
 • An increase in i_{1t} will cause an increase in i_{2t} since i_{2t} is an average of i_{1t} and i^e_{t+1}.
 • The change in i_{2t} is generally smaller than the change in i_{1t} because some of the change in i_{1t} is not expected to last (i.e., $\Delta i_{1t} > \Delta i^e_{t+1}$).

---

6. DETERMINANTS OF STOCK PRICES

Stocks pay dividends. <u>Dividends</u>: (1) are paid from profits; and (2) generally increase when profits increase.

Learning Tip

Firms' profits increase when sales increase. Increases in income cause increases in sales.
 • Therefore, increases in Y generally will cause increases in dividends.
 • Increases in expected future income will cause increases in expected future profits and, therefore, increases in expected future dividends.

The current price of stock ($\$Q_t$) is given by the present value of the expected future dividends using the current one-year rate and expected future one-year rates. This is also called the <u>fundamental value</u> of the stock price.

The nominal stock price (Q_t) will increase when:

(1) Expected future nominal dividends increase; and/or
(2) The current and expected future nominal one-year rates decrease.

The real stock price (Q_t) will increase when:

(1) Expected future real dividends increase; and/or
(2) The current and expected future real one-year rates decrease.

Learning Tip

Make sure you understand the material presented in the appendix to this chapter. In particular, you should understand how the arbitrage relation between stocks and bonds is used to show that the price of stock is the present value of future dividends.

---

7. ECONOMIC ACTIVITY, MACROECONOMIC POLICY AND STOCK PRICES

You must recognize that: (1) major movements in stock prices cannot be predicted; and (2) fully anticipated changes in interest rates and economic activity will have no effect on stock prices.

(1) Why anticipated events do not matter

Suppose the Bank of Canada decreases the money supply causing the one-year rate to increase and income to fall. If this policy were fully anticipated, the current stock price would already reflect:
- the expectation of the increase in the interest rate; and
- the expectation of the reduction in output and the reduction in expected dividends.

Hence, the stock price does not change in response to this anticipated reduction in the money supply because the latter is already reflected in the former.

Learning Tip

• Conclusion #1. For the current stock price to change in response to a change in the current one-year interest rate or to a change in current output, at least some of the change must be unanticipated.
• Conclusion #2. Changes in expected future interest rates and in expected future output (and, therefore, expected future dividends) will cause changes in stock prices.

You must also understand that:

- unanticipated changes in monetary policy cause unambiguous changes in stock prices; and
- unanticipated shifts in the IS curve have ambiguous effects on stock prices.

(2) Unexpected changes in monetary policy

An increase in the money supply that is at least partially unexpected causes financial markets to expect:

- a reduction in the expected future one-year interest rate. The lower expected future one-year rate causes, via the definition of the stock price, an increase in $\$Q_t$; and
- an increase in income, an increase in sales, an increase in profits and, therefore, an increase in $\$Q_t$.

Both of these effects will cause $\$Q_t$ to increase.

(3) Unexpected shifts in the IS curve

An unexpected increase in consumption (or an unexpected increase in G or cut in T) will cause the IS curve to shift to the right. The effects on stock prices are ambiguous for two reasons.

- <u>Reason 1</u>: The higher Y causes an increase in profits and dividends; therefore, stock prices will tend to increase. The higher Y, however, causes the one-year interest rate to rise as money demand increases. The higher interest rates will cause stock prices to fall. If the interest rate effects are large enough, stock prices could actually fall.

- <u>Reason 2</u>: The Bank of Canada's response to this unexpected shift in the IS curve can also influence how stock prices respond. Three cases can occur.

<u>Case 1</u>: The Bank does nothing. In this case, the analysis is the same as that described in Reason 1. The effects on $\$Q_t$ are still ambiguous.

<u>Case 2</u>: If the Bank wishes to accommodate the shift in the IS curve to keep the one-year interest rate from rising (i.e., the LM shifts down), stock prices will rise as dividends increase. Since i does not change, there is no offsetting effect of higher interest rates here.

<u>Case 3</u>: If the Bank contracts to keep output constant (i.e., the LM curve shifts up), stock prices fall as the one-year rate increases.

Learning Tip

The Bank of Canada does not have to respond to this shift in the IS curve for the above effects to occur. The <u>expectation</u> of a Bank response will affect expectations of future interest rates or future output (and, therefore, dividends). Changes in expected interest rates and expected output will affect current stock prices.

---

(4) The slope of the LM curve

The slope of the LM curve can influence what effect unexpected shocks to the IS curve have on stock prices. Suppose there is an unexpected increase in demand that causes the IS curve to shift to the right. There are two cases to consider.

- <u>Case 1</u>: Relatively flat LM curve
  - We will observe a relatively small increase in the interest rate.
  - We will also observe a relatively large increase in output.
  - Stock prices are more likely to rise in this case (the output effects are more likely to dominate the interest rate effects.

- Case 2: Relatively steep LM curve
- We will observe a relatively large increase in the interest rate.
- We will also observe a relatively small increase in output.
- Stock prices are more likely to fall in this case (the interest rate effects are more likely to dominate the output effects).

8. BUBBLES AND FADS

- The <u>fundamental value</u> of a stock price is the present value of expected future dividends.
- Stocks can be overpriced or underpriced for two reasons: bubbles and fads.
- <u>Rational speculative bubbles</u>. This occurs when investors buy stock today expecting the price to be higher in the future. The expectation of increased stock prices causes stock prices to increase today. Such an episode is called a "bubble."

Result: The stock price can differ (above or below) its fundamental value.

- <u>Fads</u>. Sometimes stock prices increase for no other reason than stock prices have increased in the past. In this case, the change in the stock price is called a fad.

Result: The stock price can differ (above or below) its fundamental value.

9. THE REAL INTEREST RATE PARITY RELATION

(1) An approximation of the real interest rate arbitrage relation for one-year bonds is:

$$r_t = r_t^* + \frac{\left(\varepsilon_{t+1}^e - \varepsilon_t\right)}{\varepsilon_t}$$

This relationship looks like the nominal interest parity condition from which it is derived, but explains differences in real interest rates between Canada and the US by expected movements in the C$/$ real exchange rate. This relationship also helps us to explain the determinants of the real exchange rate.

Learning Tip

- The real exchange rate today depends both on the long-run real exchange rate and on the difference between domestic and foreign long-term real interest rates.
- An increase in the domestic long-term real interest rate over the corresponding foreign interest rate leads to a real appreciation, a decrease in a real depreciation.

---

(2) In practice, movements in Canadian interest rates relative to the US interest rates explain some of the movements in the Canadian real exchange rates in the 1990s (Figure 19-11).

(3) When exchange rate expectations are taken into account, changes in monetary policy may result in large variations in the exchange rate. An increase in interest rates leads to a large appreciation, followed by a slow depreciation. This large initial movement of the exchange rate is known as overshooting.

SELF-TEST QUESTIONS

1. What is an indexed bond (p. 366)?

2. What is the expression for the present value of a one-year bond which pays $100 in one year (p. 366)?

3. What is the expression for the present value of a two-year bond which pays $100 in two years (p. 367)?

4. What does the arbitrage relation suggest about the expected return on two assets (pp. 367-368)?

5. Define what is meant by the yield to maturity on an n-period bond (p. 368)?

6. What does the yield curve represent (p. 369)?

7. A reduction in the expected one-year interest rate, all else fixed, will have what effect on the current two-year rate (p. 369)?

8. What does an upward sloping yield curve suggest about the financial market's expectation of future short-term interest rates (p. 369)?

9. If individuals expect consumer confidence and consumption to decline over the next year, what will happen to the shape of the yield curve (p. 370)?

10. A drop in current short-term interest rates of 1% will generally cause a drop in long-term rates of less than 1%. Why (p. 371)?

11. What is the difference between debt finance and equity finance (p. 372)?

12. List the determinants of the price of stock (p. 373).

13. Why does fully anticipated monetary (or fiscal) policy have no effect on current stock prices (p. 375)?

14. Why are the effects on stock prices of an unanticipated change in consumer spending ambiguous (p. 375)?

15. What is the fundamental value of a stock price (p. 377)?

16. Explain the two causes of deviations of stock prices from their fundamental values (pp. 377-378).

17. Suppose you have enough dollars to invest in one US good. What is the expression which represents the expected return on the US good measured in terms of one Canadian good (p. 381)?

18. What are the determinants of the real exchange rate? (pp. 382 – 383)?

19. What does the expression $(\varepsilon^e - \varepsilon)/\varepsilon$ represent (p. 382)?

20. What factors explain the movement of the movement of the Canadian dollar (pp. 383-384)?

21. What is the exchange rate overshooting phenomenon (p. 385)?

REVIEW PROBLEMS

1. Suppose a coupon bond promises $100 coupon payments and has a face value of $1000. Assume that the current price of the bond is $900.
a. What is the coupon rate for this bond?
b. What is the current yield for this bond?

2. Moody's Investors Service rates bonds. As the rating of a bond increases, its interest rate generally falls. Explain why this is so.

3. In late 1995 and early 1996, the failure of budget negotiations in the United States, some believe, raised the probability that the U.S. government would default on its bonds. What effect, if any, would this have on the interest rates on bonds issued by the U.S. government? Explain.

4. Use the information provided below to answer the following questions about one-year and two-year bonds that make a $1000 payment upon maturity: $i_{1t} = 10\%$; $i^e_{1t+1} = 8\%$; let $i_{1t} = 0.10$ when $i_{1t} = 10\%$ and let $i^e_{1t+1} = 0.08$ when $= 8\%$.
   a. What is the price of the one-year bond today?
   b. What is the price of the two-year bond today?
   c. What is the price of the two-year bond in one year?

5. Repeat the analysis in #4. This time, however, assume that $i_{1t} = 8\%$ and $i^e_{1t+1} = 6\%$. After you have completed parts a-c, what effect do the lower interest rates have on each of the prices you calculated (when compared to your answers in #4).

6. Suppose the current one-year interest rate is 6%. For each of the following values of the one-year interest rate that financial markets expect to occur next year, calculate the current two-year rate and briefly explain the shape of the yield curve.
   a. $i^e_{t+1} = 8\%$
   b. $i^e_{t+1} = 5\%$
   c. $i^e_{t+1} = 6\%$

7. Repeat parts a and b in #6. This time, however, assume that:
a. $i^e_{t+1} = 9\%$. What happens to the two-year rate as i^e_{t+1} increases (from 8% to 9%)? What happens to the shape of the yield curve? Explain.
b. $i^e_{t+1} = 4\%$. What happens to the two-year rate as i^e_{t+1} decreases (from 5% to 4%)? What happens to the shape of the yield curve? Explain.

8. Suppose the one-year rate is 5% and that $i^e_{t+1} = 7\%$.
a. Calculate the current two-year interest rate. What is the shape of the yield curve?
b. Now, suppose the i_{1t} increases to 6% (assume that i^e_{t+1} does not change). Calculate what happens to the two-year rate. Did i_{2t} change by more or less than the change in the one-year rate? Explain.
c. Use the original values to answer this question. Suppose i_{1t} increases to 6% and i^e_{t+1} increases to 7.5%. Calculate what happens to the two-year rate. Did i_{2t} change by more or less than the change in the one-year rate? Explain.
d. Use the original values to answer this question. Suppose i_{1t} increases to 6% and i^e_{t+1} increases to 8%. Calculate what happens to the two-year rate. Did i_{2t} change by more or less than the change in the one-year rate? Explain.
e. In parts b, c and d, you examined the effects of changes in the one-year interest rate on the two-year interest rate. In which case, if any, did the two-year rate increase by the same amount as the change in the one-year rate? Based on your analysis, what must occur for this to happen?

9. Suppose the yield curve is initially upward sloping. Briefly explain what must occur to cause each of the following events:
a. the yield curve becomes steeper
b. the yield curve becomes flat (i.e., horizontal)
c. the yield curve becomes downward sloping

10. Suppose the yield curve is initially upward sloping. Use your knowledge of the IS-LM model and the yield curve to explain what effect each of the following events will have on the shape of the yield curve.
a. financial markets expect a future reduction in consumer confidence which results in a reduction in consumer spending
b. financial markets expect a future Bank of Canada monetary expansion
c. financial markets expect a future reduction in government spending which is accompanied by a Bank of Canada monetary expansion
d. financial markets expect a future tax cut

11. Briefly explain how each of the following events will affect current stock prices.
a. financial markets expect a future monetary expansion will reduce future interest rates
b. financial markets expect a prolonged reduction in economic activity

12. a. Suppose an economic report indicates that output will increase by 5% for each of the next ten years. If financial markets already expect that this increase in Y will occur, what effect will this report have on current stock prices? Explain in detail.
b. Suppose the Bank of Canada announces that it will pursue a monetary contraction for the next two years. If financial markets already expect that this monetary contraction will occur, what effect will this announcement have on current stock prices? Explain in detail.

13. Explain how and why each of the following unanticipated events will affect current stock prices:
a. a monetary contraction
b. an increase in taxes
c. an increase in consumer confidence and spending that is accompanied by a monetary expansion (which leaves the interest rate unchanged)

14. a. Explain why unanticipated changes in monetary policy have unambiguous effects on stock prices.
b. Explain why unanticipated changes in fiscal policy have ambiguous effects on stock prices.

15. Use the graph provided below to answer the following questions. Assume that the economy is initially operating at point A. Now suppose there is an unexpected reduction in spending which causes the leftward shift in the IS curve.

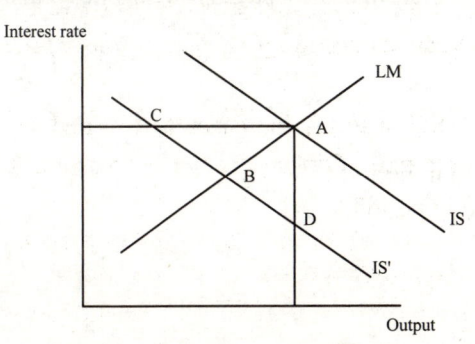

a. Explain what effect this unexpected reduction in spending will have on stock prices if the economy moves to point B.
b. Explain what type of a policy response by the Bank of Canada financial markets expect if the economy is to move to point C.
c. Explain what type of a policy response by the Bank of Canada financial markets expect if the economy is to move to point D.
d. Suppose the economy does move to point C (from point A). What effect will this event have on stock prices? Explain.
e. Suppose the economy does move to point D (from point A). What effect will this event have on stock prices? Explain.

16. Suppose the expected real exchange rate between the Canadian dollar and euro in one year is 1.40 (C$1.40 equals 1 €). Now suppose that the Canadian one-year real interest rate is 4% (r = 0.04) and is 5% in the euro zone (r* = 0.05). Assume that real interest parity holds.
a. Calculate the current real exchange rate given the above information.
b. Calculate the current real exchange rate if r increases to 6%.

17. Assume that the real interest parity holds and that r = 5%, r* = 5% and ϵ_{10}^e = 1.0. (Note that interest rates are one year rates).
a. What is the current real exchange rate?
b. What is the expected real rate of appreciation or depreciation?

18. Suppose the dollar is expected to appreciate in real terms during the current year. Does the arbitrage relation indicate that the real interest rate in Canada is greater than, less than, or equal to the foreign real interest rate? Explain.

19. Suppose that the real interest parity holds, and that r_{10} (domestic ten-year bond) is 5%, r_{10}^* (foreign ten-year bond) is 3%, and ϵ_{10}^e (expected ten-year rate of exchange) = 1.4.
a. What is the real interest differential?
b. What is the current real exchange rate?

20. How would the following change affect domestic currency's real exchange rate in terms of foreign currencies?

Domestic residents decide to spend more of their income on domestic goods and less on foreign country's exports.

MULTIPLE CHOICE QUESTIONS

1. An increase in the price of a one-year bond (which promises to pay $100 in one year) in period t will cause:

a. i_{1t} to increase
b. i_{1t} to decrease
c. a reduction in the present value of the one-year bond in period t
d. no change in the present value of the one-year bond in period t

2. Which of the following events will cause the price of a two-year bond in period t to decrease?

a. an increase in i_{1t}
b. an increase in i^e_{1t}
c. a reduction in i_{1t}
d. both a and b

3. The arbitrage relation between one-year and two-year bonds indicates that:

a. $\$P_{1t} = \$P_{2t}$
b. $i_{1t} = i_{2t}$
c. the expected return from holding a one-year bond is equal to the expected return from holding a two-year bond
d. the yield to maturity on a one-year bond is equal to the yield to maturity on a two-year bond

4. An increase in the yield to maturity on a two-year bond will cause:

a. a reduction in $\$P_{2t}$
b. an increase in $\$P_{2t}$
c. the maturity on the two-year bond to increase
d. none of the above

5. The yield curve represents:

a. the yield to maturity on a particular bond over time
b. the relation between yield to maturity and maturity
c. the risk premium on a particular bond over time
d. the relation between the price of a bond and the interest rate on that bond

6. An upward sloping yield curve suggests that:

a. financial markets expect long-term rates to increase
b. financial markets expect long-term rates to fall
c. $i_{1t} > i^e_{1t}$
d. $i_{1t} < i^e_{1t}$

7. A downward sloping yield curve suggests that:

a. financial markets expect long-term rates to increase
b. financial markets expect long-term rates to fall
c. $i_{1t} > i^e_{1t}$
d. $i_{1t} < i^e_{1t}$

8. Suppose $i_{1t} = 4\%$ and $i_{2t} = 5\%$. This suggests that the one-year rate expected to occur one year from now is:

a. 1%
b. 6%
c. 5%
d. 9%

9. Suppose i_{1t} is 6% and financial markets expect the one-year rate in one year to be 4%. Given this information, the interest rate on the two-year bond is:

a. 2%
b. 4%
c. 5%
d. 10%

10. Suppose the yield curve is initially upward sloping. Suppose the current one-year interest rate increases by 2% while the expected future one-year interest rate does not change. This event will tend to cause:

a. i_{2t} to increase by less than 2%
b. i_{2t} to increase by 2%
c. i_{2t} to fall by less than 2%
d. i_{2t} to fall by 2%

11. Assume that the one-year interest rate is on the vertical axis in the IS-LM model and that the yield curve is initially upward sloping. If financial markets now expect a monetary contraction in one year, we would expect that:

a. the yield curve will become steeper
b. the yield curve will become flatter
c. the yield curve will become horizontal (i.e., flat)
d. the yield curve will become downward sloping

12. Assume that the one-year interest rate is on the vertical axis in the IS-LM model and that the yield curve is initially upward sloping. If financial markets now expect an increase in taxes in one year, we would expect that:

a. the yield curve will become steeper
b. i_{2t} will decrease
c. i_{2t} will increase
d. none of the above

13. Which of the following events will cause an increase in stock prices in period t?

a. an increase in expected future dividends
b. a reduction in the current one-year interest rate
c. a reduction in the expected future one-year interest rate
d. all of the above

14. Suppose IBM announces that its profits for the next three years will drop. If this drop in profits were already expected by financial markets, we would expect that:

a. price of IBM stock will increase as a result of this announcement
b. the price of IBM stock will decrease as a result of this announcement
c. the price of IBM stock will not change as a result of this announcement
d. the present value of expected future dividends will increase

15. A fully anticipated increase in consumer spending will cause the IS curve to shift right and:

a. current stock prices to increase
b. current stock prices to decrease
c. no change in current stock prices
d. have ambiguous effects on current stock prices

16. A fully anticipated reduction in the money supply will cause:

a. current stock prices to increase
b. current stock prices to decrease
c. no change in current stock prices
d. ambiguous effects on current stock prices

17. A partially unexpected increase in the money supply will cause:

a. current stock prices to increase
b. current stock prices to decrease
c. no change in current stock prices
d. ambiguous effects on current stock prices

18. Suppose the Bank of Canada is not expected to respond to the following event. A partially unexpected reduction in spending will cause:

a. current stock prices to increase
b. current stock prices to decrease
c. no change in current stock prices
d. ambiguous effects on current stock prices

19. Suppose the Bank of Canada is expected to respond to the following event by keeping the interest rate constant (i.e., equal to its initial level). An unexpected increase in spending will cause:

a. current stock prices to increase
b. current stock prices to decrease
c. no change in current stock prices
d. ambiguous effects on current stock prices

20. A real appreciation of the dollar indicates that:
a. ε has increased.
b. ε has decreased.
c. the dollar price of foreign goods has increased.
d. both a and c.

21. Which of the following expression represents the real interest differential?
a. $(i - i^*)$
b. $(r - i)$
c. $(r - \pi^e)$
d. $(r - r^*)$

22. Which of the following expressions represent the expected real rate of depreciation or appreciation?
   a. $(\varepsilon^e - \varepsilon)/\varepsilon$
   b. $(E^e - E)/E$
   c. E^e
   d. ε^e

23. Which of the following events may cause a real depreciation of the domestic currency?
   a. reduction in domestic real interest rate relative to the foreign rate.
   b. an increase in domestic real interest rate relative to the foreign rate.
   c. an increase in the expected future real exchange rate.
   d. both a and c.

24. Assume the interest parity condition holds and that individuals expect the dollar to appreciate by 5% in real terms during the next year. Given this information, we know that:
   a. $r > r^*$
   b. $r < r^*$
   c. $r = i$
   d. $r = r^*$

25. When account is taken of expectations, changes in monetary policy
   a. may lead to large variations in the exchange rate.
   b. may stabilize the exchange rate.
   c. may cause a deviation in the current exchange rate from its long term value.
   d. both a and c.

26. The overshooting phenomenon occurs when
   a. inflation in the short run overshoots its long term target level.
   b. the exchange rate in the short run overshoots its long term target level.
   c. governments impose capital control.
   d. exchange rates are completely fixed.

CHAPTER 20. EXPECTATIONS, CONSUMPTION, AND INVESTMENT

OBJECTIVES, REVIEW AND TUTORIAL

After working through the chapter and the material found below, you should be able to:

(1) Know the components of total wealth.

(2) Explain what factors influence consumption.

(3) Explain the effects of permanent and transitory changes in income on consumption.

(4) Understand how a firm decides to buy, for example, a new machine (i.e., invest).

(5) Explain what effect changes in expected profits have on investment.

(6) Explain what is meant by the "user cost of capital."

(7) Understand why both expected profits and current profits affect investment.

(8) Explain the determinants of profits.

(9) Understand why investment is more volatile than consumption.

1. COMPONENTS AND CALCULATION OF TOTAL WEALTH

There are two types of wealth: (1) nonhuman wealth; and (2) human wealth.

(1) Nonhuman wealth

Nonhuman wealth is the sum of financial wealth and housing wealth.

• <u>Financial wealth</u> is the total value of an individual's stock and bond holdings, savings accounts, chequing accounts, etc. MINUS any liabilities (e.g. personal loans and any outstanding balances on credit cards).
• <u>Housing wealth</u> is the value of one's house (minus the mortgage still due) plus the value of other goods one owns (e.g. cars, art, etc.).

(2) Human wealth

Human wealth is the expected present value of the individual's after-tax labour income: $V(Y^e_{Lt} - T^e_t)$ where Y^e_{Lt} is expected labour income and T^e_t is expected taxes.

• <u>Total wealth</u> = Nonhuman wealth + Human wealth.

2. THE DETERMINANTS OF CONSUMPTION

There are two cases to consider:

(1) Case 1: The very foresighted consumer
To determine her consumption, this individual would: (1) determine her total wealth; and then (2) consume a proportion of total wealth so that consumption per year is approximately the same for the rest of her life. What are the implications of this?
• Consumption is an increasing function of total wealth.
• If this constant level of consumption exceeds current (disposable) income, she borrows the difference.
• If this constant level of consumption is less than current (disposable) income, she saves the difference.

(2) Case 2: The more realistic scenario

There are four reasons why the individual might not act like the above very foresighted individual:

• Individuals might prefer to defer consumption to later periods;
• Individuals might act in a simpler, less forward-looking fashion;
• There is uncertainty about future wealth; and
• Banks are not likely to lend the amount the individual wishes to borrow to achieve this constant level of consumption.

These four reasons suggest that consumption is an increasing function of total wealth AND current disposable income

---

Learning Tip

Think about all of the variables that determine total wealth and current disposable income. Specifically, think about how changes in these variables may affect consumption. For example, what effect would a reduction in housing prices (i.e., housing wealth) have on consumption?

There are two implications of this consumption relation:

(1) An increase in current income will likely cause a less than one-for-one increase in consumption. Why?
• A permanent change in income may cause a one-for-one change in consumption.
• A perceived temporary (transitory) change in income will cause a less than one-for-one change in consumption.

(2) Consumption may change even if current income does not change. These changes in consumption would be caused by changes in total wealth.

Learning Tip

In an economic expansion, income rises and consumption will rise. However, some of the change in income may be viewed as temporary. Therefore, C changes less than one-for-one.
• Permanent changes in current income cause relatively larger changes in consumption.
• Transitory changes in current income cause relatively smaller changes in consumption.

You should now understand that consumption is a function of:
- current disposable income
- financial wealth
- housing wealth
- human wealth
- human wealth is affected by changes in expectations of future income and future taxes.

3. THE FIRM'S DECISION TO INVEST

When a firm decides whether to purchase a new machine (or build a new factory) it must:

(1) determine how long the machine will last;
(2) compute the present value of expected profits; and
(3) compare the PV of the expected profits with the price of the machine.

• <u>Life of the machine</u>: Machines (capital) lose their usefulness (i.e., depreciate) at a rate of δ per year. δ is the <u>depreciation rate</u>.

• <u>Present value of expected profits</u>: Π represents profit per machine in real terms. The PV of expected profits is represented by the expression $V(\Pi^e_t)$ found in the text.

Learning Tip

- Machines bought in year t become operational in year $t + 1$.
- $V(\Pi^e_t)$ increases when:
  (1) expected future profits increase;
  (2) the depreciation rate falls; and
  (3) the current and/or expected future real interest rate falls.

• <u>Decision to buy the machine</u>: Profit maximizing firms will purchase a machine if $V(\Pi^e_t)$ is greater than the price of the machine. Firms will NOT buy the machine if $V(\Pi^e_t)$ is less than the price of the machine. The analysis suggests that investment is an increasing function of the PV of expected future profits.

Learning Tip

The ratio of the PV of expected profits to the price of the machine is referred to as Tobin's Q where Q is the ratio.

4. THE USER COST OF CAPITAL

Assume that the real interest rate is constant and that future expected profits are also constant. In this case,

$V(\Pi^e_t) = \Pi_t/(r_t + \delta)$ and, therefore, $I_t = I(\Pi_t/[r_t + \delta])$.

• <u>User cost of capital</u>. The expression $r + \delta$ represents the user cost of capital. An increase in r or an increase in δ will cause the user cost (or rental cost) of capital to increase.

> **Learning Tip**
>
> Consider the example discussed in the chapter. If a firm rents its machines (rather than purchases them), the rental agency would have to charge at least the real interest rate (r) plus the rate of depreciation. Why? Rather than rent the machine, the rental agency could hold bonds and receive r. Furthermore, given that the rental agency rents the machines, it will charge for the loss of usefulness (δ) which occurs each period.

Investment depends on the ratio of profit to the user cost of capital. Investment will increase when:
(1) profit increases;
(2) the real interest rate falls; and
(3) the rate of depreciation falls.

5. PROFIT, EXPECTATIONS AND INVESTMENT

In addition to the PV of expected profit, investment strongly responds to changes in current profit. Current profit may affect investment for two reasons.

(1) Even if expectations of future expected profits are high, firms may be reluctant to borrow. The only way firms will invest is by using some of their retained earnings (profits) to finance this investment.

(2) Firms may be unable to borrow from banks. Firms would only be able to use current profits to finance investment.

Investment is, therefore, an increasing function of: (1) the PV of expected future profit; and (2) current profit.

> **Learning Tip**
>
> - Current profits are called <u>cash flow</u>.
> - The PV of expected future profits is called <u>profitability</u>.
> - An increase in cash flow or profitability will cause an increase in investment.

6. DETERMINANTS OF PROFIT

Profit per unit of capital is determined by:

(1) <u>The level of sales</u>: as sales increase, profit increases; and

(2) <u>The existing capital stock</u>: if the capital stock is already high, profit per unit of capital is likely to be low.

If we assume that output equals sales, profit per unit of capital can be expressed as:

$\Pi_t = \Pi(Y_t/K_t)$.

There are several implications of this:

- In a recession, output and sales decrease causing a reduction in profit. As profit falls, investment falls.
- In an expansion, output and sales increase causing an increase in profit. As profit increases, investment rises.
- The link between Y_t and Π_t indicates that there is a link between expected output (expected sales) and expected profit. The expectation of a long expansion causes an increase in expected profit and an increase in current investment.

7. VOLATILITY OF CONSUMPTION AND INVESTMENT

(1) Response of consumption to changes in income

- A permanent increase in income will cause consumption to increase, at most, by the increase in Y.
- A transitory increase in Y will cause a smaller increase in consumption.
- Consumption, therefore, generally responds less than one-for-one to changes in income.

Learning Tip

If consumption increases by more than the change in income, consumption would have to be cut at some point in the future. Individuals are unlikely to act this way.

---

(2) Response of investment to changes in income

There is no reason why firms cannot increase investment by an amount greater than the change in income (sales). Suppose a firm has a ratio of capital to annual sales of 3 (K/Sales = 3). A permanent increase in sales of $5 million will require that the firm spend $15 million on additional capital. If the firm responds immediately, the change in investment equals $15 million and, therefore, exceeds the change in Y.

We can conclude that investment responds more than consumption to the same change in income.

Learning Tip

An alternative view: The (Y/K, Π, I) link.

An increase in income will cause:
- an increase in Y/K.
- As Y/K increases, profit per unit of capital increases.
- As profit per unit of capital increases, investment will increase.
- As investment increases, the capital stock will eventually increase.
- The higher K will cause Y/K to return to normal.
- As Y/K returns to normal, so do profit per unit of capital and investment.

SELF-TEST QUESTIONS

1. What are panel data sets (p. 394)?

2. What are the two components of nonhuman wealth (p. 395)?

3. What are of the components of total wealth (p. 395)?

4. What are the determinants of consumption (p. 398)?

5. Give four reasons why individuals might not act like the "very foresighted" individual described in the chapter (pp. 396-398).

6. Compare the effects of permanent and temporary changes in income on consumption (p. 399).

7. What does the depreciation rate measure (p. 400)?

8. For a firm to buy a new machine, what must be the relationship between the present value of expected profits and the price of the machine (p. 400)?

9. What two factors determine the user cost of capital (p. 401)?

10. Why does current profit affect investment (pp. 403)?

11. What is meant by "profitability" and "cash flow" (p. 404)?

12. What are the two determinants of profits (p. 405)?

13. What effect will an increase in the existing capital stock have on profit per unit of capital (p. 405)?

14. What effect will an increase in expected future output have on investment (p. 405)?

15. This chapter examines both consumption and investment. Which of these two variables represents the larger share of output (p. 406)? Which of these two variables is more volatile (pp. 406-407)?

REVIEW PROBLEMS

1. Use the information provided below to answer the following questions.

Financial wealth = $50,000
Housing wealth = 0
Present value of human wealth = $1,550,000

a. Calculate the individual's total wealth.
b. Suppose the individual will live for 40 more years. If he wants to maintain the same level of consumption for each of the next 40 years, how much will the individual consume in each year?
c. Suppose the individual's current (disposable) income equals $25,000. In order to achieve the level of consumption in the current period (a level of consumption you calculated in part [b]), what will the individual have to do? Briefly explain.
d. Suppose the individual receives a one-time bonus of $10,000 in the current period. What effect will this bonus have on the individual's total wealth? What effect will this bonus have on the individual's consumption in the current period and in the future? Explain.
e. Now suppose the individual receives a permanent pay raise of $10,000; assume that he will receive this for the next 40 years. What effect will this have on the individual's total wealth? What effect will this permanent increase in income have on current and future consumption? Compare your analysis here with your analysis in part (d).

2. Explain how each of the following events will affect the components of total wealth and/or current (disposable) income.
   a. a reduction in the demand for houses causes a reduction in the average price of homes
   b. the 1987 stock market crash in which stock prices, on average, fell by 20%
   c. a federal budget is passed which calls for a permanent increase in taxes
   d. an increase in expected future nominal interest rates

3. Use the information provided below to answer the following questions.

$\delta = 10\%$ $\Pi^e_{t+1} = \$10,000$ $\Pi^e_{t+2} = \$12,000$ $r_t = 5\%$
$r^e_{t+1} = 7\%$

Let $r = 0.05$ when $r = 5\%$ and $\delta = 0.10$ when $\delta = 10\%$.

a. Suppose a machine is purchased in period t and is expected to yield the above levels of profits (measured in real terms). Calculate the present value, in year t, of the expected profits of this machine in year t+1.
b. Calculate the present value, in year t, of the expected profits of this machine in year t+2.
c. If this machine is only used in periods t+1 and t+2, what is the present value of the expected profits of this machine?
d. Suppose r_t and r_{t+1} both increase by 1% (to 6% and 8%). Calculate what happens (compared to your analysis in part [c[) to the present value of expected profits.
e. Use the original values to answer this question. Suppose the firm's expectations of profits in t+1 and t+2 increase by $1000 (to $11,000 and $13,000). Calculate what happens (compared to your analysis in part [c]) to the present value of expected profits.
f. Again, use the original values to answer this question. Suppose the depreciation rate falls to 8%. Calculate what happens (compared to your analysis in part [c]) to the present value of expected profits.
g. What is the maximum price the firm will be willing to pay for this machine in parts (c), (d), (e) and (f)? Briefly explain.
h. What does your analysis suggest happens to the present value of expected profits of a machine as:
   (1) r increases;
   (2) firms revise upwards their expectations of future profits; and
   (3) the depreciation rate falls.

4 Suppose firms expect both future profits (per unit of capital) and future interest rates to remain constant at the same level as today's levels where $r_t = 5\%$ and $\Pi_t = \$10,000$. Assume that $\delta = 10\%$. Note: when calculating PV, let $r = 0.05$ when $r = 5\%$ and $\delta = 0.10$ when $\delta = 10\%$.
a. Given this information, calculate the PV of expected profits. What is the highest price the firm would be willing to pay for this machine? What is the user cost of capital?
b. Repeat the analysis in part (a). This time, however, assume that $r_t = 4\%$. What happens to the user cost of capital as the real interest rate falls?
c. Repeat the analysis in part (a). This time, however, assume that $\delta = 12\%$. What happens to the user cost of capital as a result of this change in the depreciation rate?
d. Repeat the analysis in part (a). This time, however, assume that $\Pi_t = \$9,000$. What happens to the user cost of capital?
e. Based on your analysis, what would tend to happen to investment in parts (b), (c) and (d) as a result of these changes?

5. Intuitively explain how an increase in the user cost of capital affects the level of investment.

6. Suppose there are two firms. Firm A only produces steel. The second firm, B, has two parts (i.e., operations). The first is in steel production, and the second is in oil exploration. Suppose there is a sharp increase in the price of oil resulting in increased profits in oil exploration.
a. Suppose that only cash flows determine investment. Explain what effect this increase in the price of oil will have on investment for firm A, on investment in firm B's steel production operation, and on investment in firm B's oil exploration operation.
b. Suppose that only profitability determines investment. Explain what effect this increase in the price of oil will have on investment for firm A, on investment in firm B's steel production operation, and on investment in firm B's oil exploration operation.

7. Briefly explain how each of the following events will affect profit per unit of capital and, therefore, investment.
a. a permanent decrease in sales
b. an increase in output
c. a decline in the capital stock

8. For this question, assume that firms seek to maintain their current ratio of capital to annual sales of 4. Any deviation of the actual ratio from 4 will cause an immediate change in investment to achieve the desired ratio.
a. Suppose there is a permanent increase in sales (and, therefore, output) of $20 million in period t. Discuss what effect this increase in sales (and output) will have on investment and consumption. Which of these two variables, if either, will be most affected by this change in sales? Briefly explain.
b. In part (a), what effect will this increase in sales eventually have on the capital stock? Explain.
c. As the capital stock changes, what happens to profit per unit of capital? Briefly explain.

9. In 1990, the Canadian economy entered a recession. Based on your understanding of the material presented in this chapter, what effect do you think this recession had on: (1) sales; (2) profit per unit of capital; (3) investment; and (4) the capital stock. Briefly explain.

MULTIPLE CHOICE QUESTIONS

1. Which of the following is included in nonhuman wealth?

a. financial wealth
b. housing wealth
c. expected future taxes
d. both a and b

2. Which of the following events would cause an increase in human wealth?

a. an increase in the amount in one's savings account
b. a reduction in expected taxes
c. an increase in the value of one's house
d. an increase in the expected future real interest rate

3. Which of the following statements is true about the very foresighted consumer?

a. she will consume a proportion of total wealth so that consumption per year is approximately the same for the rest of her life
b. consumption is an increasing function of total wealth
c. if the constant level of consumption (described in [a]) is less than current (disposable) income, she saves the difference
d. all of the above

4. Which of the following explains why individuals' consumption is (in addition to total wealth) an increasing function of current income?

a. individuals might prefer to defer consumption to later periods
b. individuals might act in a simpler, less forward-looking fashion
c. banks are not likely to lend the amount the individual wishes to borrow to achieve a constant level of consumption
d. all of the above

5. For this question, assume that current income does not change. With fixed current income, current consumption will fall if:

a. future expected taxes decrease
b. total wealth falls
c. expected future income increases
d. none of the above

6. Which of the following events would tend to cause the greatest reduction in current consumption?

a. a one-time tax increase of $1000
b. a temporary decline in current income of $1000
c. a permanent decrease in your annual salary of $1000
d. both a and b

7. An increase in which of the following variables will cause an increase in current consumption?

a. in current disposable income
b. in financial wealth
c. in housing wealth
d. in human wealth
e. all of the above

8. When a firm makes the decision to buy a new machine, it will buy the machine if the present value of expected profit from the machine:

a. is greater than zero
b. is greater than the rate of depreciation
c. is greater than the real interest rate
d. is greater than the price of the machine

9. An increased in the rate of depreciation will cause the present value of expected profits to:

a. increase
b. decrease
c. remain unchanged if the real interest rate increases by the same amount of the increase in the rate of depreciation
d. none of the above

10. A reduction in the current and expected future real interest rates will cause:

a. the present value of expected profit to increase
b. the present value of expected profit to decrease
c. a reduction in investment
d. a reduction in the rate of depreciation

11. The rental cost of capital will decrease if:

a. the rate of depreciation increases
b. the real interest rate falls
c. the firm's expectation of future profits decrease
d. none of the above

12. Suppose firms' expect future profits and future real interest rates to remain constant at their current levels. Given this information, we know that investment will decrease if:

a. the real interest rate falls
b. the rate of depreciation falls
c. current profit falls
d. the user cost of capital decreases

13. An increase in "profitability" suggests that:

a. firms have increased their expectations of future profits
b. the real interest rate has decreased
c. the rate of depreciation has decreased
d. current profits have increased

14. A reduction in "cash flow" suggests that:

a. the real interest rate has increased
b. the rate of depreciation has decreased
c. the user cost of capital has increased
d. current profits have decreased

15. Which of the following statements is true?

a. sales and profits are positively related
b. income and profit are negatively related
c. expected income and expected profits are negatively related
d. the user cost of capital and investment are positively related

16. Which of the following events would cause an increase in profit per unit of capital?

a. an increase in income
b. an increase in sales
c. a reduction in the capital stock
d. all of the above

17. In a recession, we would expect that:

a. profit increases
b. investment increases
c. income and sales would decrease
d. both a and b

18. A temporary $100 million increase in output will tend to cause:

a. an equal change in consumption and investment
b. the change in consumption to be greater than the change in investment
c. the change in investment to be greater than the change in consumption
d. a reduction in profit and a reduction in investment

CHAPTER 21. EXPECTATIONS, OUTPUT, AND POLICY

OBJECTIVES, REVIEW AND TUTORIAL

After working through the chapter and the material found below, you should be able to:

(1) Explain what is meant by aggregate private spending.

(2) Explain what effect changes in current and expected future income, real interest rates and taxes have on the components of private aggregate spending and on the IS curve.

(3) Explain why the IS curve is relatively steeper when we take into account the effects of expectations.

(4) Recognize that the LM relation is NOT affected by changes in expected future income and real interest rates.

(5) Discuss how changes in monetary policy in the current period can affect expected future real interest rates.

(6) Re-examine the effects of monetary policy and explain why the IS curve can shift as a result of a monetary expansion or contraction.

(7) Explain what is meant by rational expectations and discuss how it differs from animal spirits and adaptive expectations.

(8) Re-examine the effects of fiscal policy and explain why the effects of, for example, deficit reduction on current output are ambiguous.

(9) Become familiar with the effects of the federal government deficit reduction program starting in 1996.

1. THE IS RELATION AND EXPECTATIONS

(1) Review of the IS relation

The IS relation is now represented by the following equation:

$$Y = A(Y, T, r, Y'^e, T'^e, r'^e) + G$$

where $A(Y, T, r, Y'^e, T'^e, r'^e)$ is aggregate private spending (i.e., consumption plus investment).

Learning Tip
• Recall that we are assuming that there are only two periods: (1) the current period; and (2) the future period. • The future period represents all future years lumped together.

(2) Slope of the IS curve

A reduction in the current real interest rate causes an increase in spending and has a multiplier effect on output. Recall that changes in current output and the current real interest rate do not cause shifts in the IS curve (they represent movements along the curve).

(3) Shifts in the IS curve

• <u>Current taxes</u> (T): An increase in T causes a reduction in current consumption and a leftward shift in the IS curve.

• <u>Expected future output</u> (Y'^e): An increase in Y'^e will cause: (1) an increase in current consumption as the present value of human wealth increases; and (2) an increase in investment as firms expect future profits to rise. The IS curve, therefore, will shift to the right.

• <u>Expected future r</u> (r'^e): An increase in r'^e will cause: (1) a reduction in consumption as the present value of human wealth decreases; and (2) a reduction in investment as the present value of future profits falls. The IS curve, therefore, shifts to the left.

• <u>Expected future taxes</u> (T'^e): An increase in T'^e will cause a reduction in the present value of human wealth and a reduction in consumption. The IS curve, therefore, shifts to the left.

• <u>Government spending</u> (G): An increase in G will cause an increase in spending and a rightward shift in the IS curve.

Learning Tip
• In general, if firms and households become less confident of the future, investment and consumption will fall as expectations of future profits and income fall.
• Make sure you can explain how an increase or decrease in each of the variables in the IS relation affects the IS curve in the current period.

---

2. THE STEEPER SLOPE OF THE IS CURVE

When compared to the slope of the IS curve in the basic model, the slope of the IS curve is now most likely <u>steeper</u> for two reasons:

(1) A reduction in the current real interest rate, with future expected real interest rates unchanged, will not have much of an effect on the present value of future profits and future income; and

(2) The multiplier is likely to be smaller. The multiplier depends on how much current spending changes as a result of a given change in current income. A temporary increase in income will have a smaller effect on consumption and investment.

3. THE LM RELATION AND EXPECTATIONS

Money demand is an increasing function of current income and a decreasing function of the current nominal interest rate.

• Current money demand depends on your current level of transactions. Therefore, expected future income will have no effect on money demand and, therefore, no effect on the LM relation.

• Current money demand depends on the current opportunity cost of holding money (i.e., the nominal interest rate). What you expect the interest rate to be in one year does not affect the current opportunity cost of holding money. Therefore, future expected interest rates have no effect on current money demand and no effect on the current LM curve.

4. MONETARY POLICY, EXPECTATIONS AND THE IS-LM MODEL

To understand the effects of monetary policy on output, you must recognize the distinction between:

(1) nominal and real interest rates; and
(2) current and expected future real interest rates.

When the Bank of Canada increases the money supply, the current nominal interest rates fall and the LM curve shifts down. The effects of the change in the current nominal interest rate on current and future expected real interest rates depend on:

(1) whether the lower nominal interest rate causes financial markets to revise their expectations of future nominal interest rates; and
(2) whether the lower nominal interest rate causes financial markets to revise their expectations of current and future inflation.

Learning Tip

- Assume that current and expected future inflation are equal to zero.
- We can, therefore, ignore the second effect described above.
- Since expected inflation is zero, we know that $i = r$.

There are two cases to consider.

Case 1: Financial markets do NOT adjust expectations of future interest rates.

The increase in the money supply causes the LM curve to shift down and the interest rate (both nominal and real since they are the same) to fall. As the current real interest rate falls, there is some increase in spending and output. The steeper IS curve, however, implies that the change in Y is small.

Case 2: Financial markets revise expectations of future interest rates.

- An increase in the money supply again causes the LM curve to shift down and the current interest rate to fall.
- Financial markets expect lower future interest rates.
- The lower future interest rates are expected to cause an increase in future output.
- A reduction in future expected interest rates will cause an increase in spending (both consumption and investment).
- The increase in future expected income will cause an increase in spending (both consumption and investment).
- The increased spending caused by the change in expected future interest rates and future income will cause the IS curve to shift to the right.

Learning Tip

- Monetary policy's initial effects on the economy are on the current nominal interest rate and LM curve.
- Changes in monetary policy can have significant effects on expectations of future interest rates and future income.
- These changes in expected future interest rates and future income will cause shifts in the IS curve and changes in current economic activity.

5. RATIONAL EXPECTATIONS, ANIMAL SPIRITS AND ADAPTIVE EXPECTATIONS

How do individuals form expectations? Three approaches are presented in this chapter.

• <u>Animal spirits</u>. In this case, changes in expectations are taken as unexplained (or random).

• <u>Adaptive expectations</u>. This approach assumes that individuals base their expectations on past movements in variables. This backward-looking approach might assume, for example, that expected inflation this year will be equal to the average of actual inflation during the past two years.

• <u>Rational expectations</u>. This approach assumes that individuals form expectations by assessing the impact of future expected policy and then determining the implications of that policy on, for example, interest rates and income. This forward-looking approach assumes that individuals look to the future and do the best job they can in predicting it.

Learning Tip

• We assume in this chapter that firms, households and investors have rational expectations.
• You must recognize that rational expectations do not imply that individuals know the future. It does, however, assume that individuals use information as best as they can to predict future variables.

---

6. FISCAL POLICY, EXPECTATIONS AND THE IS-LM MODEL

The effects of a fiscal contraction also depend on expectations. Let's review the deficit reduction example in which T and T' increase. There are two cases to consider.

<u>Case 1</u>: No response expected from the Bank of Canada.

• The higher T causes a reduction in consumption and a leftward shift in the IS curve.
• The higher T' will cause the IS curve (in the future) to shift left. Individuals, therefore, expect future income and the future real interest rate to fall.
• The lower Y'^e will cause a further reduction in consumption (the present value of human wealth falls). The IS curve shifts to the left.
• The lower Y'^e also causes a reduction in investment as firms revise down their expectations of future profits. The IS curve shifts to the left.
• The lower r'^e will, however, cause an increase in both consumption and investment. This effect causes the IS curve to shift to the right.

Without knowing the magnitude of the above shifts in the IS curves, the effects of the increase in T and T' on current output are ambiguous. The ambiguity arises because the net effect depends on three opposing factors:
  • The increase in T causes Y to decrease (the IS shifts left).
  • The increase in T' has two effects. One, it decreases Y since it lowers the expected future income (the IS shifts to left). Two, it increases Y since it also lowers expected future real interest rates (the IS shifts to right).

> **Learning Tip**
>
> How do you determine the effects of future events and future policy on r'^e and Y'^e? Actually, this is easy to do. Simply use the IS-LM model to evaluate the effects of the expected event on the IS and LM curves.
>
> - If the IS curve is expected to shift to the right, Y'^e and r'^e will increase.
> - If the IS curve is expected to shift to the left, Y'^e and r'^e will fall.
> - If the LM curve is expected to shift down, Y'^e will increase and r'^e will fall.
> - If the LM curve is expected to shift up, Y'^e will fall and r'^e will increase.
>
> Often, several events might be expected to occur simultaneously in the future. It might be the case that the effects on future output will be ambiguous while the effects on r'^e will be unambiguous. Or, vice versa.

<u>Case 2</u>: The Bank of Canada expected to accommodate both the current and future increase in taxes and assume that individuals consider only the short-term effects of changes in expected future macroeconomic variables.

The analysis is similar to that of Case 1 with several exceptions.

- As the IS curve shifts left as a result of the increase in T, the Bank increases the money supply to keep current output from falling.
- Individuals expect a similar response in the future. So, the future increase in T does not cause a reduction in Y'^e, only a reduction in r'^e.
- The lower T and T' cause current spending to decrease and the current IS curve to shift left.
- The lower r'^e, however, causes consumption and investment to increase and the IS curve to shift right.

NOTE: It is possible that current output could increase as a result of a deficit reduction package. For this to occur, the future interest rate effects must offset all other effects.

<u>Case 3</u>: Individuals use their understanding of the medium-run effects of a change in future taxes when forming expectations of future output and future interest rates.

- The higher T and T'^e again cause the IS curve to shift left as current consumption falls.
- The higher T'^e will cause the future real interest rate to be lower. This reduction in r'^e will cause current consumption and investment to increase, causing the IS curve to shift right in the current period.
- The higher T'^e has no effect on future expected output, however.
- The final position of the current IS curve is ambiguous. The direct effects of the higher T and T'^e on current consumption cause it to shift left. The lower r'^e will cause the IS curve to shift to the right.

Case 4: Individuals use their understanding of the medium-run effects of a change in future taxes when forming expectations of future output and future interest rates.

- The higher T and T'^e again cause the IS curve to shift left as current consumption falls.
- The higher T'^e will cause the future real interest rate of be lower. This reduction in r'^e will cause current consumption and investment to increase, causing the IS curve to shift right in the current period.
- The higher T'^e will also cause future investment and the future capital stock to be higher. Expected future output will, therefore, also be higher. This increase in future expected output will cause current consumption and current investment to rise. The IS curve will shift right in the current period as a result of this.
- The final position of the current IS curve is ambiguous. The direct effects of the higher T and T'^e on current consumption cause it to shift left. The lower r'^e will cause the IS curve to shift to the right. The higher Y'^e will also cause the IS curve to shift to the right.

Learning Tip

• The less the Bank of Canada is expected to accommodate the increase in taxes, the greater will be the negative effect on current spending of the expected drop in future income.
• The deficit reduction program could be backloaded. That is, most of the tax increase could occur in the future.
• If individuals do not respond much to changes in expected future taxes, the increase in T and T' will have little effect on current spending.
• Make sure you can explain the effects of a fiscal expansion.
• To summarize, depending on expectations, fiscal policy can have ambiguous effects on current output.

---

7. QUICK REVIEW OF THE FEDERAL GOVERNMENT BUDGET OF 1996

(1) Features of the program

• The federal government reported its first budget surplus in 1999, the first in almost 30 years in Canada. The budget surplus has remained to be the prevailing feature of the federal budget to this date.
• An immediate tax relief and a promise of a continued relief for the majority of taxpayers.
• Expectations that the period of government spending cuts was over (no renewed fiscal contraction).

• The announcement that the Bank of Canada would stay the course of price stability within the current inflation target range of 1–3%.

(2) Effects of deficit reductions

• The long-term interest rates continued their fall that started in 1996. This has been due to a gradual disappearance of the interest rate risk premium on Canada's government bonds.

• The deficit was eliminated ahead of its schedule primarily due to a stronger economy and lower interest rates than expected, with the former generating a greater tax revenue and the latter giving rise to a reduced cost of debt servicing.

SELF-TEST QUESTIONS

1. What are the components of aggregate private spending (pp. 420-421)?

2. Explain what effect increases in current (and expected future) income, taxes and real interest rates have on aggregate private spending (p. 421).

3. There are two reasons why the IS curve is now likely steeper than the IS curve in the basic model. What are they (pp. 421-422)?

4. What effect will an increase in expected future output have on the IS curve in the current period (p. 422)?

5. What effect will an increase in the expected future real interest rate have on the IS curve in the current period (p. 422)?

6. What effect will an increase in expected future taxes have on the IS curve in the current period (p. 422)?

7. What effect does an increase in expected future income have on the LM curve in the current period (p. 423)?

8. What effect does a reduction in the expected future real interest rate have on the LM curve in the current period (p. 423)?

9. The extent to which the Bank of Canada (by changing the nominal interest rate) can affect current and expected future real interest rates depends on two factors. What are they (p. 423)?

10. Why might a monetary expansion cause a rightward shift in the IS curve (pp. 424-425)?

11. What is meant by rational expectations (p. 425)?

12. What are the effects of an expected future tax increase on future output and future real interest rates (pp. 426-427)?

13. What are the effects of an expected future monetary expansion on future output and future real interest rates (p. 425)?

14. The deficit reduction program (described in the chapter) and subsequent, expected Bank of Canada's response resulted in four factors shifting the IS curve. What are they (pp. 427-428)?

15. What is meant by a "backloaded" tax package (p. 429)?

REVIEW PROBLEMS

1. Briefly note how each of the following events affects: (1) each of the components of current spending; (2) the position of the IS curve in the current period; and (3) the position of the LM curve in the current period.

a. reduction in expected future real dividends
b. increase in expected future real after-tax profits
c. reduction in expected future taxes
d. reduction in current cash flow
e. increase in the real money supply in the current period
f. reduction in expected future real interest rates
g. reduction in expected future income
h. increase in government spending in the current period

2. Discuss briefly how each of the following expected future events affects: (1) the position of the future IS and LM curves; and, therefore, (2) expected future income and the expected future real interest rate.

a. an expected future reduction in the money supply
b. an expected future increase in government spending
c. an expected future increase in consumer confidence which results in an increase in spending

3. a. What determines the size of the multiplier?
b. Why is the multiplier likely to be smaller in this chapter?

4. a. Why does an increase in the current real interest rate cause a reduction in spending?
b. Why is the effect of an increase in the current real interest rate, all else constant, more likely to be smaller in this chapter?

5. Briefly explain what your analysis in questions #3 and #4 suggests about the slopes of the: (a) IS curve; and (b) LM curve.

6. For each of the following events, graphically illustrate and explain the effects on: (1) the components of current spending; (2) the current IS and LM curves; and (3) the current real interest rate and income.
a. a reduction in r'^e
b. an increase in r'^e
c. an increase in Y'^e
d. a reduction in Y'^e

7. For each of the following events, graphically illustrate and explain the effects on: (1) the components of current spending; (2) the current IS and LM curves; and (3) the current real interest rate and income. NOTE: If the effects of the event on any of the current variables are ambiguous, briefly explain why this occurs.
a. an increase in the expected future money supply
b. an increase in expected future government spending
c. an increase in expected future taxes

8. Suppose that government spending is expected to increase in the future and that the Bank of Canada is expected to change the money supply to leave the future real interest rate unchanged.
a. Briefly discuss what effect this increase in future government spending and the Bank of Canada's response will have on r'^e and Y'^e.
b Based on your analysis in part (a), what effect will this increase in future government spending and the Bank of Canada's response have on: (1) the components of current spending; (2) the position of the IS and LM curves in the current period; and (3) the current real interest rate and current output?

9. Suppose that government spending is expected to increase in the future and that the Bank of Canada is expected to change the money supply to leave future output unchanged.
a. Briefly discuss what effect this increase in future government spending and the Bank response will have on r'^e and Y'^e.
b. Based on your analysis in part (a), what effect will this increase in future government spending and the Bank's response have on: (1) the components of current spending; (2) the position of the IS and LM curves in the current period; and (3) the current real interest rate and current output?

10. Suppose that government spending is expected to increase in the future and that the Bank of Canada is not expected to respond to this change in government spending.
a. Briefly discuss what effect this increase in future government spending and the Bank's response will have on r'^e and Y'^e.
b. Based on your analysis in part (a), what effect will this increase in future government spending (with no response from the Bank) have on: (1) the components of current spending; (2) the position of the IS and LM curves in the current period; and (3) the current real interest rate and current output?

11. You evaluated the effects of changes in expected future government spending on current output in questions 8–10.
a. In which of these three cases did current output change the most? Explain.
b. Briefly discuss how the expected Central Bank response (or non-response) to a change in expected future G can affect the current output effects of this expected fiscal policy action.

12. Suppose a budget is passed that calls for an increase in future taxes. Further assume that the Bank of Canada is not expected to alter the money supply in response to this future tax increase.
a. What effect will this expected future tax increase have on the yield curve in the current period? Explain.
b. What effect will this expected future tax increase have on future output? Explain.
c. Under what conditions will this increase in future taxes have NO effect on current output? Explain.
d. Under what conditions will this increase in future taxes cause current output to increase? Explain.
e. Under what conditions will this increase in future taxes cause current output to decrease? Explain.

13. Suppose a budget is passed that calls for an increase in current and future taxes and assume that the Bank of Canada is not expected to alter the money supply in response to this future tax increase.
a. What effect will this budget have on current output?
b. Discuss how your analysis in part (a) would differ IF financial markets and other individuals (i.e., firms and households) do not believe that taxes will increase in the future. Specifically, does current output change more or less as a result of this lack of credibility in the future tax increase? Explain.

14. Assume that individuals consider only the long-run effects of changes in expected future macroeconomic variables. Suppose there is an increase in current government spending. Also assume that individuals expect future government spending will increase.
a. What do individuals expect will happen to future output and the future interest rate? Explain.
b. Based on your analysis in part (a), what effect will this increase in current government spending and increase in expected future government spending have on current output? Explain.
c. Based on your analysis in part (b), is it possible that a budget deficit increase can lead to a recession? Explain.

15. Briefly explain how the analysis in #14 is different if we assume that individuals consider only the medium-run effects of changes in expected future macroeconomic variables.

MULTIPLE CHOICE QUESTIONS

1. Aggregate private spending (A) is equal to:

a. consumption plus government spending
b. investment plus government spending
c. consumption plus investment
d. consumption plus investment and government spending

2. An increase in expected future output will cause in the current period:

a. an increase in aggregate private spending (A) and a rightward shift in the IS curve
b. a reduction in aggregate private spending (A) and a leftward shift in the IS curve
c. a shift up in the LM curve
d. a shift down in the LM curve

3. A reduction in the expected future real interest rate will cause in the current period:

a. an increase in aggregate private spending (A) and a rightward shift in the IS curve
b. a reduction in aggregate private spending (A) and a leftward shift in the IS curve
c. a shift up in the LM curve
d. a shift down in the LM curve

4. An increase in expected future taxes (all else constant) will cause in the current period:

a. an increase in aggregate private spending (A) and a rightward shift in the IS curve
b. a reduction in aggregate private spending (A) and a leftward shift in the IS curve
c. a shift up in the LM curve
d. a shift down in the LM curve

5. A reduction in the current real interest rate is now likely to have a relatively smaller effect on current output because:

a. a change in current income, given unchanged expectations of future income, is unlikely to have much of an effect on spending
b. the LM relation depends on the nominal interest rate
c. a reduction in the current real interest rate, given unchanged expectations of future real interest rates, does not have much of an effect on spending
d. both a and c

6. An increase in future expected income will cause:

a. the LM curve to shift up in the current period
b. the LM curve to shift down in the current period
c. the LM curve in the current period to become flatter
d. have no effect on the LM curve in the current period

7. A reduction in the expected future real interest rate will cause:

a. the LM curve to shift up in the current period
b. the LM curve to shift down in the current period
c. the LM curve in the current period to become flatter
d. no effect on the LM curve in the current period

8. An increase in current income will cause:

a. an increase in the interest rate and a movement along the LM curve in the current period
b. the LM curve to shift up in the current period
c. the LM curve to shift down in the current period
d. the LM curve in the current period to become flatter

9. The effects of a monetary expansion in the current period on economic activity in the current period depend on:

a. whether financial markets alter their expectations of future nominal interest rates
b. whether financial markets alter their expectations of current and future expected inflation
c. both a and b
d. none of the above

10. A reduction in expected future income will tend to cause:

a. a reduction in consumption and a leftward shift in the IS curve in the current period
b. a reduction in investment and a leftward shift in the IS curve in the current period
c. both a and b
d. a shift down in the LM curve in the current period

11. An increase in the expected future real interest rate will tend to cause:

a. a reduction in consumption and a leftward shift in the IS curve in the current period
b. a reduction in investment and a leftward shift in the IS curve in the current period
c. both a and b
d. a shift down in the LM curve in the current period

12. Suppose the Bank of Canada reduces the money supply in the current period. Further assume that individuals now expect the future real interest rate to be higher and future income to be lower. Given this information, we would expect:

a. the LM curve to shift up and the IS curve to shift left in the current period
b. the LM curve to shift down and the IS curve to shift left in the current period
c. the LM curve to shift up and the IS curve to shift right in the current period
b. the LM curve to shift down and the IS curve to shift right in the current period

13. Suppose the Bank of Canada increases the money supply in the current period. Further assume that individuals now expect the future real interest rate to be lower and future income to be higher. Given this information, we know with certainty that:

a. current income will increase
b. current real interest rate will decrease
c. current real interest rate will increase
d. current income will remain unchanged

14. Which of the following statements represents rational expectations?

a. individuals use the information they have to make predictions about the future
b. individuals know with certainty the future value of income, the interest rate, etc.
c. expectations are forward-looking
d. both a and b
e. both a and c

15. If expectations are based on animal spirits, we know that:

a. changes in expectations are random events
b. expectations are determined by backward-looking behaviour
c. individuals know with certainty the future value of income, the interest rate, etc.
d. both a and b

16. If expectations are "adaptive," we know that:

a. changes in expectations are random events
b. expectations are determined by backward-looking behaviour
c. individuals know with certainty the future value of income, the interest rate, etc.
d. both a and b

17. Assume that individuals consider only the short run effects of changes in expected future macroeconomic variables. Suppose individuals expect that future government spending will increase and expect that the Bank of Canada will not respond to this. Individuals will, therefore, expect:

a. future income to increase
b. future interest rates to increase
c. the IS curve to shift to the right in the future
d. all of the above

18. Assume that individuals consider only the short-run effects of changes in expected future macroeconomic variables. Suppose individuals expect a reduction in future taxes. Further assume that the Bank of Canada is not expected to respond to this reduction in future taxes. The expected reduction in future taxes will:

a. cause an increase in current income and an increase in the current real interest rate
b. cause an increase in current income and a reduction in the current real interest rate
c. cause the LM curve to shift up in the current period
d. have an ambiguous effect on the current IS curve

19. Assume that individuals consider only the short-run effects of changes in expected future macroeconomic variables. Suppose a budget is passed which calls for an increase in current and future government spending. Further assume that the Bank of Canada is not expected to respond to these changes in G. This increase in current and future G will:

a. cause an increase in current income
b. cause an increase in the current real interest rate
c. have an ambiguous effect on current income
d. both a and b

20. Assume that individuals consider only the short-run effects of changes in expected future macroeconomic variables. Suppose a budget is passed which calls for an increase in current and future government spending. Further assume that the Bank of Canada is expected to offset any effects of the changes in current and future G on current and future real interest rates. This increase in current and future G will tend to cause:

a. an increase in current income
b. an ambiguous effect on current income
c. an increase in the current real interest rate
d. a reduction in current income

21. Assume that individuals consider only the medium-run effects of changes in expected future macroeconomic variables. Suppose individuals expect that future government spending will increase and expect that the Bank of Canada will not respond to this: Individuals will, therefore, expect:

a. future income to increase
b. future interest rates to increase
c. future investment to increase
d. all of the above

22. Assume that individuals consider only the medium-run effects of changes in expected future macroeconomic variables. Suppose individuals expect that future government spending will increase and expect that the Bank of Canada will not respond to this. Given this information, we know with certainty that:

a. the IS curve in the current period will shift to the right
b. the IS curve in the current period will shift to the left
c. the IS curve in the current period will not shift
d. the effects on the position of the IS curve in the current period are ambiguous

23. Assume that individuals consider only the long-run effects of changes in expected future macroeconomic variables. Suppose individuals expect that future government spending will increase and expect that the Bank of Canada will not respond to this. Individuals will, therefore, expect:

a. future income to decrease
b. future income will not change
c. future investment to increase
d. all of the above

CHAPTER 22. PATHOLOGIES I: HIGH UNEMPLOYMENT

OBJECTIVES, REVIEW AND TUTORIAL

After working through the chapter and the material found below, you should be able to:

(1) Understand the causes of the Great Depression.

(2) Understand the factors which contributed to the recovery from the Great Depression.

(3) Discuss the possible effects of labour market rigidities on European unemployment.

(4) Explain the hysteresis view of European unemployment.

1. FACTORS CONTRIBUTING TO THE U.S. GREAT DEPRESSION

(1) The fall in spending

The stock market crash caused a decline in consumer wealth and an increase in uncertainty.

• The decline in wealth and increase in uncertainty caused a decrease in consumption.
• The increase in uncertainty also caused firms to reduce investment.
• The drop in consumption and investment caused the IS curve to shift left and, all else fixed, caused Y and r to fall.

Learning Tip

• Recall that the crash occurred <u>after</u> the Great Depression had begun.
• The crash was most likely the result of the end of a speculative bubble - not caused by news about the Great Depression.

---

(2) The drop in the nominal money supply

The bank failures between 1929 and 1933 caused individuals to increase their currency holdings.

• The increase in the ratio of currency to deposits caused a reduction in the money multiplier and a reduction in the nominal money supply.
• The decline in M was not caused by a reduction in the monetary base (H); H actually increased during the period.
• The drop in M was largely offset by an equal drop in P.
• Since M/P did not change, the LM curve did not shift down with the drop in P.

(3) Deflation

You should recall that changes in expected inflation cause the LM curve to shift. Given i,
• an increase in expected inflation causes r to fall and the LM curve to shift down by the change in π.

- A reduction in π has the opposite effects.
- An increase in expected deflation (π becomes more negative) will cause r to increase and the LM curve to shift up.

The expected deflation in the early 1930s caused the LM curve to shift up, r to increase and Y to fall even further.

2. THE U.S. RECOVERY

The recovery was caused by:

(1) an increase in nominal money growth (LM shifts down);
(2) the end of deflation (the LM shifts down); and
(3) possibly as a result of programs included in the New Deal.

Learning Tip

- You should review the features of the New Deal discussed in the text.
- The simultaneous high unemployment and high output growth can be easily explained by Okun's law. A long period of high growth was needed to reduce the high unemployment.

---

3. FACTORS CONTRIBUTING TO THE GREAT DEPRESSION IN CANADA

(1) The commodity price shock: the fall in the price of natural resources and agricultural products, especially wheat, which by 1930 had experienced a 50 percent drop, had a profound effect on Canada's export revenue.

(2) The weakness in the U.S. economy and the reduced domestic spending in Canada.

- In 1928, 38% of Canada's exports went to the U.S. The sharp drop in income in the U.S. was, therefore, transmitted into Canada. Remember that Canada, the U.S., and a large part of the prosperous world operated under the fixed exchange rates rule inherited from the Gold Standard. Fixed exchange rates are efficient conduits in transmitting business cycles, typically from the larger to the smaller economy.
- The large external debt and high foreign ownership of Canadian firms were also responsible for the reduced spending activity in Canada. Given that most of Canada's external debt was held by Americans, the investment environment in Canada deteriorated along with that in the U.S.

Learning Tip

- You should compare and contrast monetary and fiscal conditions in Canada and the U.S. during the Great Depression.
- You should review the features of the New Deal discussed in the text.
- The simultaneous high unemployment and high output growth can be easily explained by Okun's law. A long period of high growth was needed to reduce the high unemployment.

4. LABOUR MARKET RIGIDITIES AND EUROPEAN UNEMPLOYMENT: EUROSCLEROSIS

Labour market rigidities imposed on firms:

- prevent firms from adjusting to changes in the economy
- make the cost of doing business too high.

These labour market rigidities, therefore, may cause u to increase. The following is a list of labour market rigidities:

- non-wage labour costs (e.g. social security)
- severance payments
- unions
- unemployment benefits
- minimum wages.

Changes in labour market rigidities can affect the WS and PS relations and, therefore, cause changes in u. For example, a <u>reduction</u> in the minimum wage will cause:

- a drop in z
- the drop in z causes the WS relation to shift down
- the shift in the WS relation causes u to fall.

Different levels of the above labour market rigidities can, in theory, be used to explain differences in unemployment rates across countries.

> **Learning Tip**
>
> - Make sure you understand the determinants of the natural rate of unemployment (i.e., the graph that includes the WS and PS relations).
> - Make sure you can explain how an increase in each of the above labour market rigidities affects u_n.
> - Recognize that these labour market rigidities have become less important over time in Europe.

5. HYSTERESIS

(1) Introduction

- This alternative explanation of changes in the unemployment rate argues that the natural rate of unemployment is NOT independent of actual unemployment.
- The hysteresis view argues that u_n depends on the history of actual u.
- In particular, a long period of high u leads to an increase in u_n.
- As u_n increases, there will be less and less downward pressure on inflation.

(2) The effects of u on u_n

Persistently high unemployment may cause increases in <u>employment benefits</u>. As the government increases employment benefits,

- the WS relation shifts up
- as the WS relation shifts up, the natural rate of unemployment increases.

Persistently high unemployment will cause an increase in <u>long-term unemployment</u>. As long-term unemployment increases,

- the long-term unemployed become unemployable
- the currently employed no longer compete with these unemployable workers
- bargaining power, therefore, increases causing the WS relation to shift up
- as the WS relation shifts up, u_n increases.

(3) Implications

- There may be room to decrease unemployment in Europe by implementing a policy which increases aggregate demand. As AD increases u falls and the hysteresis mechanism can work in reverse!
- Disinflation may have greater costs than earlier presented. Specifically, the increase in u may cause u_n to increase.

Learning Tip

You should review the discussion about unemployment in Spain.

SELF-TEST QUESTIONS

1. What is a depression (p. 435)?

2. Did the stock market crash occur before the beginning of the Great Depression (p. 436)?

3. What was the primary cause of the US stock market crash (p. 436)?

4. List the two effects of the crash on individuals. (p. 436).

5. What effect did the crash have on the IS curve (p. 436)?

6. Why did M1 fall in the US between 1929 and 1933 (p. 437)?

7. What happened to M/P between 1929 and 1933 (pp. 437–438)?

8. What effect did deflation have on r and on the LM curve (p. 439)?

9. What effect did the <u>end</u> of deflation have on r and on the LM curve (pp. 439–440)?

10. What was the "New Deal" (p. 440)?

11. Why was the decline in the money supply in Canada not as dramatic as in the U.S. (p. 441)?

12. How was the depreciation in the U.S. transmitted into Canada (pp. 440-441)?

13. What is meant by Eurosclerosis and by labour market rigidities (p. 444)?

14. List several of the labour market rigidities which exist in Europe (p. 444).

15. What effect does an increase in z have on the WS relation, W/P, and u_n (p. 445)?

16. What effect does an increase in μ have on the WS relation, W/P, and u_n (p. 445)?

17. Have the rigidities become more or less important over time (pp. 445–446)?

18. What should happen to the dispersion of the rates of change in employment if "structural change" increases (p. 446)?

19. What has happened to the demand for unskilled workers in Europe and to their real wage (p. 446)?

20. Define hysteresis (p. 447).

21. How do increases in unemployment benefits increase u_n? (p. 444)

22. How might the emergence of long-term unemployment increase u_n (p. 448)?

23. List the two important implications of hysteresis (p. 449).

24. Does the high unemployment in Spain reflect large deviations of u from u_n or a high u_n (p. 450)?

REVIEW PROBLEMS

1. Explain what effect each of the following events will have on the IS curve, LM curve, real interest rate, and output.
a. reduction in consumer wealth
b. increase in uncertainty (i.e., reduction in confidence) of consumers
c. increase in uncertainty (i.e., reduction in confidence) of firms
d. a reduction in the nominal supply of money

2. When expected inflation is negative (i.e., $\pi^e < 0$), what do individuals expect will happen to the price level over time? Briefly explain.

3. Suppose the nominal interest rate (i) is 5%.
a. Calculate the real interest rate for each of the following rates of expected inflation (or deflation): 3%, 2%, 1%, 0, -1% and -3%.
b. As expected inflation falls from 3% to 0, what happens to r?
c. As expected inflation goes from 0 to -3% (i.e., an expected deflation), what happens to r?

4. Use the IS and LM model to answer this question. Suppose expected inflation is 3%.
a. Now suppose expected inflation falls to 0. What effect will this have on the position of the IS and LM curves? Briefly explain. What effect will this have on Y and r? Briefly explain.
b. Now suppose individuals expect a deflation of 3% (i.e., $\pi^e = -3\%$). What effect will this expected deflation have on the position of the IS and LM curves? Briefly explain. What effect will this expected deflation have on Y and r? Briefly explain.

5. Use the IS and LM model (and graph found below) to answer this question. Assume individuals currently expect a deflation of 3% (i.e., $\pi^e = -3\%$). Now suppose that individuals no longer expect the price level to fall so that $\pi^e = 0$. What effect will the end of the deflation on the position of the IS and LM curves? Briefly explain. What effect will then end of the expected deflation have on r and Y? Briefly explain.

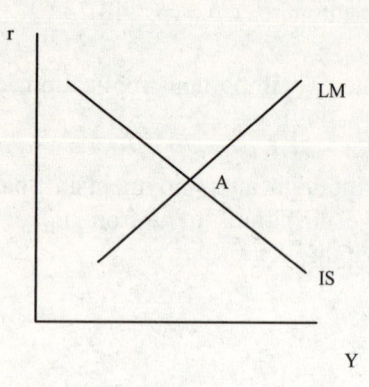

[Graph: IS-LM diagram with axes r (vertical) and Y (horizontal), showing upward-sloping LM curve and downward-sloping IS curve intersecting at point A.]

6. Explain the effects of an increase in the ratio of currency to deposits on the following variables: the monetary base, the money multiplier, the nominal money supply, and the LM curve.

7. Between 1929 and 1933, the nominal money supply in the U.S. fell by 27%, whereas the real money supply remained approximately the same during this period. Given this information, what must have happened to leave the real money supply unchanged? Briefly explain.

8. Between 1929 and 1933, three <u>simultaneous</u> events occurred in the U.S.: (1) consumer wealth fell; (2) uncertainty increased; and (3) deflation. Use the graph provided below (where A represents the initial equilibrium) to explain how these three simultaneous shocks could cause the real interest rate (r) to: (1) increase; (2) decrease; or (3) remain constant.

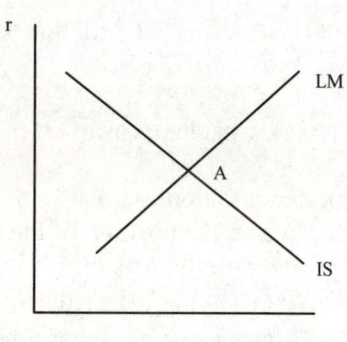

[Graph: IS-LM diagram with axes r (vertical) and Y (horizontal), showing upward-sloping LM curve and downward-sloping IS curve intersecting at point A.]

9. a. Based on your understanding of the IS-LM model, what type of fiscal policy do think could have been implemented in the early 1930s to help offset the effects of the Great Depression on output in Canada and the U.S.? Briefly explain.
b. Based on your understanding of the IS-LM model, what type of monetary policy do you think could have been implemented in the early 1930s to help offset the effects of the Great Depression on output in either country? Briefly explain.

10. Between 1933 and 1941, both the average growth rate (of output) and unemployment rate were high. Are these facts inconsistent with Okun's law? Briefly explain.

11. How did the deflation contribute to the Great Depression? Briefly explain.

Note: Use the graph found below to help answer questions 12–15.

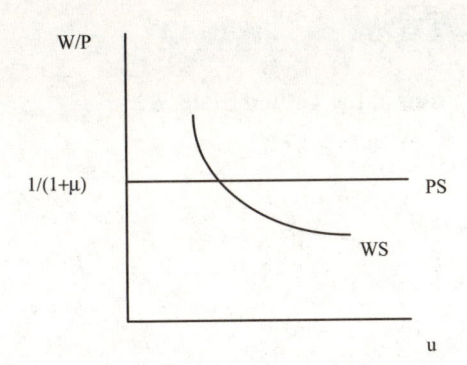

[Graph: vertical axis W/P, horizontal axis u. Horizontal line at $1/(1+\mu)$ labeled PS. Downward-sloping curve labeled WS.]

12. Explain what effect an increase in severance payments will have on z, μ, the WS relation, the PS relation, the real wage, and u_n.

13. Explain what effect an increase in unions will have on z, μ, the WS relation, the PS relation, the real wage, and u_n.

14. Explain what effect an increase in employment insurance benefits will have on z, μ, the WS relation, the PS relation, the real wage, and u_n.

15. Explain what effect an increase in the minimum wage will have on z, μ, the WS relation, the PS relation, the real wage, and u_n.

16. Labour market rigidities have decreased in Europe since the early 1980s.
a. Based on your analysis in questions 12–15, what effect will this reduction in labour market rigidities have on unemployment in Europe? Briefly explain.
b. Is your conclusion consistent with the actual change in the unemployment rate in Europe during the 1980s? Explain.

17. How can unemployment in Europe be high today with stable inflation? Briefly explain.

18. Suppose persistently low unemployment causes a government to reduce employment insurance benefits. What effect will this persistently low unemployment have on the PS relation, the WS relation, W/P, and u_n? Briefly explain.

19. Suppose policies caused the elimination of long-term unemployment. What effect will the elimination of long-term unemployment have on bargaining power of workers, the PS relation, the WS relation, W/P, and u_n? Briefly explain.

20. Suppose the increase in employment insurance benefits and emergence of long-term unemployment are the cause of the high unemployment rate in Europe. What type of aggregate demand policy should policy makers pursue to reduce unemployment? Briefly explain.

21. Suppose the hysteresis view of the unemployment problem in Europe also applied to Canada between 1989 and 1996. In this case, what effect would the Bank of Canada's disinflation have had on u and u_n in this period? Briefly explain.

MULTIPLE CHOICE QUESTIONS

1. Between 1929 and 1932, which of the following occurred in the United States?

a. the average annual growth rate was negative
b. the price level fell
c. the nominal money supply fell
d. all of the above
e. both a and b

2. The stock market crash in 1929 occurred:

a. before the beginning of the Great Depression
b. after the start of the Great Depression
c. at the same time that the Great Depression began
d. as a result of news about the Great Depression

3. The stock market crash had which of the following effects?

a. a reduction in consumer wealth
b. a reduction in the purchase of durable goods
c. a reduction in the purchase of investment goods
d. all of the above

4. Based on the IS-LM model, the stock market crash caused:

a. a leftward shift in the IS curve
b. a lower interest rate (r) and a rightward shift in the IS curve
c. a shift down in the LM curve
d. a reduction in Y and an increase in r

5. The decrease in the nominal money supply in the U.S. between 1929 and 1933 was caused by:

a. a reduction in the money multiplier
b. a reduction in the monetary base
c. a reduction in the price level
d. an increase in the price level

6. Between 1929 and 1933, the fall in the nominal money supply in the U.S.:

a. was significantly greater than the drop in the price level (P)
b. was significantly smaller than the drop in P
c. was approximately equal to the drop in P
d. caused the LM curve to shift down

7. During the Great Depression, which of the following did NOT occur in Canada?

a. a wide spread bank failure
b. the general price level dropped
c. unemployment increased
d. all of the above

8. The depression in the U.S. was transmitted into Canada via

a. the federal government commitment to parity with the U.S.
b. the flexibility of the exchange rates
c. decreases in U.S. money supply
d. prevailing fixed exchange rates

9. Canada's own version of "New Deal"

a. helped Canada to come out of the depression quickly
b. proved inadequate in dealing with the massive impact of the depression
c. was never implemented
d. was the cause of depression in Canada

10. An increase in the rate of deflation will cause:

a. an increase in the real interest rate (r)
b. a reduction in r
c. no change in r
d. the IS curve to shift down

11. If the rate of <u>deflation</u> goes from 3% to 10%, we know that the IS curve will shift:

a. down by 7%
b. down by 10%
c. up by 7%
d. up by 10%

12. An increase in the rate of expected deflation will cause:

a. an increase in r and a decrease in Y
b. a reduction in r and an increase in Y
c. an increase in Y and an increase in r
d. a reduction in Y and a reduction in r

13. Prior to 1970, the unemployment rate in Canada:

a. was greater than unemployment in Europe
b. was less than unemployment in Europe
c. was equal to unemployment in Europe
d. was greater than unemployment in the U.S.

14. The increase in unemployment in Europe during the 1970s was most likely caused by:

a. supply shocks
b. demand shocks
c. a reduction in the natural rate of unemployment
d. all of the above

15. Which of the following represents a labour market rigidity in Europe?

a. powerful unions
b. large severance payments
c. high minimum wages
d. high unemployment benefits
e. all of the above
f. both c and d

16. Unions tend to decrease firms' flexibility and increase workers' bargaining power. Unions, therefore, have the following effects:

a. the WS relation shifts up and the PS relation shifts up
b. the WS relation shifts up and the PS relation shifts down
c. the WS relation shifts down and the PS relation shifts up
d. the WS relation shifts down and the PS relation shifts down

17. An increase in the minimum wage in Europe will cause:

a. the WS relation to shift up and unemployment (u) to increase
b. the WS relation to shift down and u to increase
c. the PS relation to shift up and u to increase
d. the PS relation to shift down and u to increase

18. Which of the following most likely explains the increase in unemployment in Europe since the early 1980?

a. the Eurosclerosis view
b. increased labour market rigidities
c. increased union density
d. hysteresis

19. Which of the following has occurred in the market for unskilled workers in Europe?

a. increase in demand and an increase in their real wage
b. decrease in demand and a reduction in their real wage
c. decrease in demand and no change in their real wage
d. increase in demand an no change in their real wage

20. The hysteresis view of unemployment suggests that an increase in actual unemployment will tend to:

a. cause an increase in u_n
b. have no effect on u_n
c. be temporary
d. cause an increase in inflation

21. Past unemployment could affect the natural rate of unemployment as a result of:

a. increases in employment benefits
b. the emergence of long-term unemployment
c. all of the above
d. none of the above

22. The hysteresis view of unemployment suggests that disinflation:

a. will have no long-term effects on u_n
b. may cause u_n to fall
c. may cause u_n to increase
d. will not cause a reduction in inflation

CHAPTER 23. PATHOLOGIES II: HIGH INFLATION

OBJECTIVES, REVIEW AND TUTORIAL

After working through the chapter and the material found below, you should be able to:

(1) Understand the relation between budget deficits and money creation.

(2) Define seignorage and explain the determinants of seignorage.

(3) Explain the effects of inflation on real money balances.

(4) Explain the relation among budget deficits, seignorage, and inflation when money growth is constant.

(5) Explain the relation among budget deficits, seignorage, and inflation when money growth is not constant.

(6) Discuss both orthodox and heterodox stabilization programs and explain how they can be used to end hyperinflations.

1. INTRODUCTION TO HYPERINFLATION

There are several concepts that you must understand.

(1) Ingredients of a hyperinflation

- High inflation is associated with high money growth.
- Money growth is high because the budget deficit is high.
- The budget deficit is high because of a major shock (economic or political) which affects spending or taxes.

(2) Financing of deficits

The government can finance a budget deficit by:

- borrowing (issuing bonds)
- creating money (debt monetization)

Learning Tip

In both instances, the government issues bonds.
- With debt monetization, the central bank buys the bonds causing an increase in the monetary base and money supply.
- In the first case, the bonds are NOT bought by the central bank. M does not change in this case.

---

(3) Seignorage

- When the deficit is financed entirely by money creation we observe that $\Delta M = \$Deficit$ (all measured in nominal terms and on a monthly basis).
- Seignorage is the revenues (in real terms) from money creation: $\Delta M/P$.
- Rearranging, we observe that seignorage = $\Delta M/P = (\Delta M/M)(M/P)$.

Seignorage is greater:

- the higher is money growth, for given real money balances
- the higher are real money balances, for a given rate of money growth.

Learning Tip

- Be careful with the above interpretation. Faster money growth, for given real money balances, will increase seignorage. However, M/P will not remain constant when money growth changes (see below).
- Make sure you understand how equation 23.2 is obtained.
---

(4) Inflation and real money balances

Real money balances are given by:

$$M/P = YL(i) = YL(r + \pi^e).$$

As expected inflation increases, i increases and the opportunity cost of holding money increases.
- People reduce their real money balances.
- With hyperinflation, two other effects occur that cause individuals to reduce their real money balances: (1) barter; and (2) dollarization.

2. THE RELATION AMONG DEFICITS, SEIGNORAGE AND INFLATION

There are two cases to consider.

(1) Case 1: Constant money growth

In the medium run, we can assume that:

- Y and r are constant
- $\Delta M/M = \pi = \pi^e$
- Therefore, seignorage = $(\Delta M/M)[\overline{Y} L(\overline{r} + \Delta M/M)]$.

An increase in money growth has an ambiguous effect on seignorage. Why?

- As money growth increases, the first term increases causing seignorage to increase.
- As money growth increases, however, real money balances (the second term) decline, causing seignorage to fall.
- The effects of money growth on seignorage are, therefore, ambiguous.
- Empirical evidence indicates the following relation between money growth and seignorage:

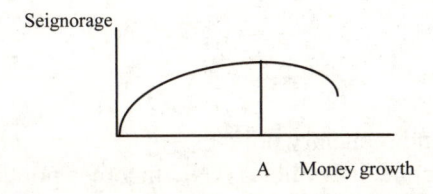

> **Learning Tip**
>
> - There is a seignorage-maximizing rate of money growth (see A).
> - If to the right of A, increases in money growth will cause reductions in seignorage.
> - If to the left of A, increases in money growth will cause increases in seignorage.
> - This analysis indicates that, in the medium run, there is a maximum level of seignorage; this occurs at A.

(2) Case 2: Dynamics

In the short run, increases in money growth lead to little change in real money balances. Why?

- It may take time for π and π^e to adjust to the change in money growth.
- Increases in money growth, with real money balances relatively constant in the short run, can yield increases in seignorage above the level shown in the above graph.
- As expected inflation adjusts and M/P falls, the government will have to continue to increase the rate of money growth to achieve these temporarily high levels of seignorage.
- Result: we will observe continually increasing rates of money growth and inflation.

3. RELATED ISSUES

(1) Inflation tax

The inflation tax = $\pi(M/P)$

Seignorage = $(\Delta M/M)(M/P)$

The inflation tax will equal seignorage only when $\pi = \Delta M/M$.

(2) Hyperinflation and economic activity

In the short run, a hyperinflation may increase economic activity.

In the medium run, a hyperinflation will reduce economic activity. Why?
- The exchange system is less efficient.
- Price signals are less useful.
- Borrowing at a nominal interest rate is more of a gamble causing investment to fall.

4. END OF HYPERINFLATIONS: STABILIZATION PROGRAMS

(1) Elements of a stabilization program

- fiscal reform and credible reductions in the budget deficit
- a credible central bank commitment to refrain from debt monetization
- incomes policies (e.g. wage and price controls)

(2) Types of stabilization programs

- <u>Orthodox</u> stabilization programs rely only on fiscal and monetary policies.
- <u>Heterodox</u> stabilization programs rely on fiscal and monetary policies AND incomes policies.

> **Learning Tip**
>
> You should review the discussion about the Bolivian hyperinflation.

SELF-TEST QUESTIONS

1. Define hyperinflation (p. 456).

2. What are the two ways a government can finance a budget deficit (p. 456)?

3. What is meant by debt monetization (p. 457)?

4. How does one interpret the following equation: ΔM = $Deficit (p. 458)?

5. Define seignorage (p. 458).

6. Seignorage is equal to the product of what two variables (p. 458)?

7. What are the three determinants of real money balances (p. 459)?

8. An increase in inflation has what effect on real money balances (p. 459)?

9. Define barter (p. 460).

10. Define dollarization (p. 460).

11. When nominal money growth is constant forever, what is the relation between actual inflation and expected inflation (p. 461)?

12. What does the relation between seignorage and money growth look like (p. 461)?

13. What is the expression for the inflation tax (p. 463)?

14. What must happen to money growth for seignorage to continue to increase in the short run (pp. 463–464)?

15. What does the Tanzi-Olivera effect represent (p. 464)?

16. What effect does hyperinflation have on economic activity in the short run and in the long run (p. 464)?

17. What are the three possible elements of a stabilization program (p. 465)?

18. What is the difference between orthodox and heterodox stabilization programs (p. 466)?

19. What were the three main features of the (successful) September, 1985 Bolivian stabilization program (p. 467)?

REVIEW PROBLEMS

1. For each of the following (constant) monthly rates of inflation, calculate the percentage rise in the price level over 12 months. Assume that the price level is 1 at the beginning of the period. Hint: refer to footnote 2 in the chapter.
a. 0.1% b. 0.2% c. 1% d. 9% e. 20% f. 40%

2. Suppose government spending increases by $200 billion which results in a $200 billion increase in the deficit. This government has two options to finance this deficit: (1) borrowing; or (2) debt monetization.

a. Briefly discuss what effect this increase in G has on the IS and LM curves when the government pursues option 1.
b. Briefly discuss what effect this increase in G has on the IS and LM curves when the government pursues option 2.

3. In 1997, the real money supply in Canada (measured at 1992 dollars) was 378 billion; M2 = 404 billion and the CPI for 1997 was 107.6. For this question, assume that real money balances remain constant.
a. Calculate seignorage for each of the following rates of money growth: 1% (0.01), 5% (0.05) and 10% (0.10).
b. What happens to seignorage as money growth increases?
c. Realistically, will real money balances remain constant as money growth increases? Explain.

4. Suppose money growth is 5% (0.05).
a. Calculate seignorage for each of the following levels of real money balances (measured in billions): 800, 600 and 400.
b. What happens to seignorage as real money balances decrease? Explain.

5. Explain what effect an increase in each of the following variables will have on real money balances (Note: make sure you explain why real money balances change):
a. Y
b. π^e

6. For this question, assume that r and Y are constant.
a. Given M/P, what happens to seignorage as money growth increases? Briefly explain.
b. What happens to π^e in the medium run when money growth increases? Briefly explain.
c. What happens to real money balances when π^e increases? Briefly explain.
d. Based on your answers to parts a – c, what will happen to seignorage in the medium run when money growth increases to some permanently higher level? Briefly explain.

7. Suppose the rate of money growth which maximizes seignorage in the long run is 10%.
a. If money growth is now 5%, what happens to seignorage in the medium run if the government increases money growth? Explain.
b. If money growth is now 15%, what happens to seignorage in the medium run if the government increases money growth? Explain.

8. Suppose π = 10% and that real money balances (M/P) are 500.
a. Calculate the inflation tax.
b. Given π and M/P, under what conditions will the inflation tax be equal to seignorage?
c. Given π and M/P, under what conditions will the inflation tax be greater than seignorage?
d. Given π and M/P, under what conditions will the inflation tax be less than seignorage?

9. Assume that the demand for real balances is represented by the following: $M/P = Y[0.5 - (r + \pi^e)]$, where Y = 2000 and r = 0.05 (5%). Initially assume that π^e = 0.10 (10%) and does not change in the short run.
a. Given the above information, calculate seignorage for the following rates of money growth: 0.01 (1%), 0.10 (10%), 0.25 (25%) and 0.30 (30%).
b. What happens to seignorage in part a as money growth increases?

c. Now assume that π^e equals the rate of money growth in the medium run. Calculate seignorage that occurs in the medium run for each of the following rates of money growth: 0.01 (1%), 0.10 (10%), 0.25 (25%) and 0.30 (30%).
d. In c, as money growth increases from 0.01 to 0.25, what happens to seignorage?
e. In c, as money growth increases from 0.25 to 0.30, what happens to seignorage? Can you explain why this occurs?
f. Why does seignorage always increase in part a but not always increase in part c?

10. Which of the following policies would be included in a: (1) orthodox stabilization program; and (2) heterodox stabilization program?
a. monetary contraction
b. the adoption of fixed exchange rates
c. decrease in G
d. rules which limit the extent to which wages can increase
e. restrictions of firms' pricing policies

11. Briefly explain what effect a hyperinflation can have on economic activity in the short run and in the medium run.

MULTIPLE CHOICE

1. Suppose the monthly rate of inflation is 0.05 (5%). What is the annual rate of inflation assuming this monthly rate of inflation does not change:

a. 5%
b. 50%
c. 60%
d. 79.6%

2. Which of the following is generally associated with hyperinflation?

a. money growth is high
b. the budget deficit is high
c. the economy is affected by a major shock
d. all of the above

3. When the government finances its deficit through debt monetization, we know that:

a. M increases
b. M decreases
c. there is no change in M
d. none of the above

4. When the government finances its budget deficit entirely by money creation, the <u>real</u> budget deficit equals:

a. M/P
b. $\Delta M/M$
c. $\Delta M/P$
d. $\Delta M/\Delta P$

5. Seignorage represents:

a. revenues from money creation
b. the Tanzi-Olivera effect
c. real money balances
d. none of the above

6. Which of the following expressions represents seignorage?

a. $(\Delta M/M)(M/P)$
b. $\Delta M/M$
c. $YL(i)/P$
d. none of the above

7. Which of the following events will cause an <u>increase</u> in the real money balances that people want to hold?

a. decrease in Y
b. increase in r
c. increase in π
d. none of the above

8. Assume real money balances are constant. Seignorage will increase when:

a. money growth decreases
b. money growth increases
c. an increase in money growth can have a positive or negative effect on seignorage in this case
d. none of the above

9. Assume money growth is constant. A reduction in real money balances will:

a. cause seignorage to increase
b. cause seignorage to fall
c. have no effect on seignorage
d. have uncertain effects on seignorage

10. During a hyperinflation, we might expect:

a. barter to occur
b. dollarization to occur
c. debt monetization to occur
d. all of the above

11. In the medium run, an increase in inflation will tend to cause:

a. real money balances to increase
b. real money balances to decrease
c. no effect on real money balances
d. a decrease in the opportunity cost of holding money

12. Assume output growth is zero. If money growth is constant forever, which of the following will occur?

a. $\pi = \pi^e$
b. $\Delta M/M = \pi$
c. $\Delta M/M = \pi^e$
d. all of the above

13. Suppose money growth increases to some permanently higher rate. In the medium run, we know that:

a. seignorage will increase
b. seignorage will fall
c. seignorage will not change
d. the effects on seignorage are ambiguous

14. The inflation tax will be greater than seignorage when:

a. $\pi > \Delta M/M$
b. $\pi = \Delta M/M$
c. $\pi < \Delta M/M$
d. the inflation tax can never be greater than seignorage

15. At low rates of money growth, an increase in money growth will most likely:

a. increase seignorage
b. decrease seignorage
c. leave seignorage unchanged
d. cause real money balances to increase

16. In the short run, a sufficiently large increase in money growth will:

a. leave seignorage unchanged
b. decrease seignorage
c. increase seignorage
d. none of the above

17. The Tanzi-Olivera effect represents:

a. the effects of money growth on seignorage
b. the effects of money growth on inflation
c. the effects of higher inflation on budget deficits
d. the inflation tax

18. In a hyperinflation, which of the following will occur?

a. the exchange system will be less efficient
b. price signals are less useful
c. borrowing at a given nominal interest rate becomes more of a gamble
d. barter will occur
e. all of the above

19. Which of the following would NOT be included in an orthodox stabilization program?

   a. a monetary contraction
   b. a fiscal contraction
   c. wage and price controls
   d. none of the above

20. Which of the following would be included in a heterodox stabilization program?

   a. a monetary contraction
   b. a fiscal contraction
   c. wage and price controls
   d. all of the above

21. Which of the following might cause a stabilization program to fail?

   a. lack of credibility
   b. the anticipation of failure
   c. a monetary contraction
   d. all of the above
   e. both a and b

CHAPTER 24. PATHOLOGIES III: TRANSITION IN EASTERN EUROPE AND THE ASIAN CRISIS

OBJECTIVES, REVIEW AND TUTORIAL

After working through the chapter and the material found below, you should be able to:

1. Understand the dimensions of transition.

2. Explain the characteristics of economic growth under central planning for the Soviet Union.

3. Discuss and explain the decline in output during the transition.

4. Discuss and explain the changes in employment in the state sector and private sector during the transition.

5. Understand the causes of the Asian crisis and the lessons learned from it.

1. DIMENSIONS OF TRANSITION

(1) Price liberalization: The extent to which prices are decontrolled and allowed to clear markets.

(2) Privatization: The transfer of state-owned firms to private owners.

(3) Macroeconomic control: Firms cannot systematically expect to receive transfers from the state if the firms have losses.

Learning Tip
The transfers from the government can lead to: • larger budget deficits • higher money growth (to finance the budget deficits) • higher inflation

2. ECONOMIC GROWTH UNDER CENTRAL PLANNING: THE CASE OF THE SOVIET UNION

There are several facts you should know:

• Soviet growth of output per worker (3%) compared favourably to growth of Western economies between 1928 and 1987.
• Between 1928 and 1987, the growth rate of capital per worker exceeded the growth rate of output per worker.
• The previous fact indicates that the growth rate of Y/N was caused by increases in capital accumulation.
• The rate of technological progress declined during the period.

Learning Tip
• To sustain the growth of Y/N, the saving rate must have increased.
• This increase in the saving rate, at some point, most likely pushed capital beyond the golden rule level of capital and, therefore, caused a reduction in consumption.

3. PROBLEMS WITH THE SOVIET UNION'S OFFICIAL STATISTICS

There were several reasons why Soviet growth data were unreliable:
• Firms had incentives to overstate production.
• Firms had incentives to overstate quality improvements (upon which price increases were based).
• The Soviet Union as a country had an incentive to overstate its growth rate (to impress its competitors!).
• The Soviet Union's measure of total output, Net Material Product, was different from that used in West.

4. THE DECLINE IN OUTPUT

There are three reasons for the drop in output.

(1) Measurement issues

Under central planning, some goods were virtually useless yet included in measures of output. In a market economy, the price and quantity of those goods will go to zero. The conventional measure of GDP ignores these useless goods; goods previously included (under central planning) are no longer counted.

(2) Large informal economy

A large informal economy has emerged in which unexpected economic activity occurs.

(3) Structural change

Transition has introduced sharp changes in relative demand. This has caused reductions in employment and output. See the next section.

5. STRUCTURAL CHANGE, RELATIVE DEMAND AND EMPLOYMENT

You should become familiar with the following graph.

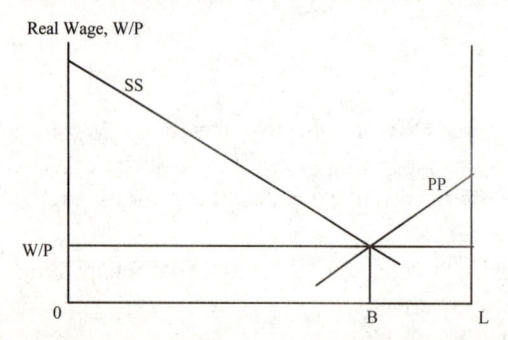

(1) The pre-transition

- The demand curves for labour in both sectors are downward sloping.
- The downward sloping demand curves reflect decreasing returns to labour; higher employment requires a reduction in the real wage.
- The real wage is assumed constant (and is the same in both sectors).
- Prior to transition, unemployment was zero; all of the labour force (the distance 0L) was employed in the two sectors.

(2) The transition

- The transition caused a sharp decline in the demand for goods produced in the state sector.
- This caused the demand for labour in the state sector (SS) to decrease and employment in the state sector to decrease.
- Demand for products and, therefore, the demand for labour in the private sector (PP) increased. The increase in PP also caused an increase in employment in the private sector.
- The increase in demand for labour in the private sector, however, was not enough to offset the drop in SS.
- RESULT: Total employment fell and unemployment occurred.

Learning Tip

- Why didn't the private sector grow fast enough and, therefore, PP increase enough to prevent the unemployment? There are several causes:
  - the lack of capital
  - the lack of expertise
  - the lack of credit (loans)

- As the transition continues, we should observe (if all goes well):
  - increases in SS
  - increases in PP
  - RESULT: increase in total employment and reductions in unemployment

---

6. THE ASIAN CRISIS

(1) Overview

- From 1970 to 1996, many Asian countries experienced relatively high rates of growth (i.e., the Asian miracle).
- These relatively high rates of growth appear to have been caused by levels of investment.
- This period of fast growth ended in 1997 when Thailand was hit by the first crisis (i.e., the Asian crisis).

(2) Cause of the Asian crisis: fundamentals

- Each of the four countries included in the chapter had large trade deficits and large current account deficits.
- The cause of the high trade deficits was high investment.
- In 1997, foreign investors realized that the high growth rates could not last forever, pulling funds out of Thailand (this effect later spread to other countries).

> **Learning Tip**
>
> Make sure you understand the following expression:
>
> NX = S + (T − G) − I
>
> This suggests that a trade deficit can be caused by:
> - low private saving (S)
> - budget deficits (T − G < O)
> - high investment

(3) Causes of the Asian crisis: self-fulfilling expectations

Some economists dispute the argument that growth in these countries was caused primarily by high investment; they note that technological progress was also high.
These economists note that:
- foreign lending was largely short-term; and
- foreign lending was primarily made to banks (not firms and governments in Asia).

Because of this, when foreign investors panicked, two runs occurred:
- runs on Asian banks (banks could not pay back all short-term debt); and
- runs on these currencies.

(4) Effects of crisis

Regardless of the cause (fundamentals versus self-fulfilling expectations), we observed a banking crisis and exchange rate crisis. We also observed reductions in output. However, why did output fall when these countries experienced such significant depreciations of their domestic currencies?

Output fell because:
- Governments initially responded to the crisis by raising interest rates. The high interest rates had a negative effect on demand; and
- The lingering financial crisis had a negative effect on bank lending, the availability of credit, and, therefore, the ability of domestic firms to expand production.

(5) Lessons learned from the Asian crisis

There are two general lessons learned from the Asian crisis:

- The advantage and disadvantage of capital controls
- The role of the International Monetary Fund (IMF)

> **FINAL ADVICE/WARNING**
>
> There are many facts presented in this chapter. Depending on your instructor, you might be expected to know them. In this case, you should become familiar with the examples and observations presented.

SELF-TEST QUESTIONS

(1) To what does the economic big bang refer (pp. 509–510)?

(2) Of those countries that were centrally planned in the 1980's, which two have resisted transition (p. 510)?

(3) What is meant by price liberalization (p. 511)?

(4) What is meant by privatization (p. 511)?

(5) Why and by how much has output declined in the former centrally planned countries since the transition (pp. 474-475)?

6. What happened to the demand of some goods under price liberalization (p. 474)?

7. Why are the demand curves for labour in Figure 24-2 downward sloping (p. 475)?

8. Prior to transition, employment was greatest in which sector of the Soviet economy (p. 475)?

9. Prior to transition, unemployment was officially equal to what (p. 476)?

10. The initial effects of transition had the greatest effect on demand for labour in which sector (p. 476)?

11. List several factors which prevented growth in the private sector(pp.476-477).

12. Why aren't central European countries growing faster (p. 478)?

13. What is the soft budget constraint (p. 479)?

14. What country was first hit by the Asian crisis (p. 481)?

15. There are two general explanations for the Asian crisis. What are they (p. 482)?

16. The Asian crisis caused two types of 'runs' for these countries. What were they (p. 484)?

17. How did the bank run in Asia differ from the Standard bank run (p. 486)?

18. What were some of the criticisms of the IMF's policies toward these Asian countries (p. 486)?

REVIEW PROBLEMS

1. Briefly discuss how transfers from the state to firms that make losses will affect: (a) firms' incentives; (b) budget deficits; (c) money growth; and (d) inflation.

2. List the reasons why the output numbers provided by the Soviet Union could not be "trusted."

3. "The existence of goods that were virtually useless in the pre-transition period contributed to the decline in measured output during the transition." Explain.

4. Use the graph provided below to answer the following questions. Assume that the real wage does not change.

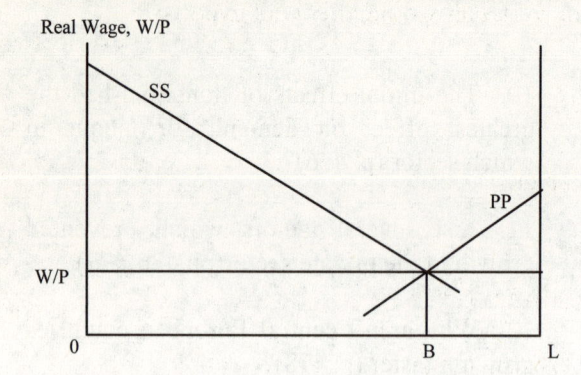

[Graph: Real Wage W/P on vertical axis, L on horizontal axis. SS curve slopes downward from upper left; PP curve slopes upward to the right. A horizontal W/P line intersects both curves at point B.]

a. How many workers are employed in the state and private sectors?
b. What is the unemployment rate in this economy? How do you know?
c. Suppose there is a reduction in the demand for labour in the state sector with no change in the private sector. Discuss what happens to employment in the state sector, total employment and the unemployment rate.
d. Briefly discuss what happens to employment in the private sector, total employment and unemployment as PP increases.

5. In the above graph, why are PP and SS downward sloping?

6. Use the graph provided below to answer this question. Assume that the real wage does not change.

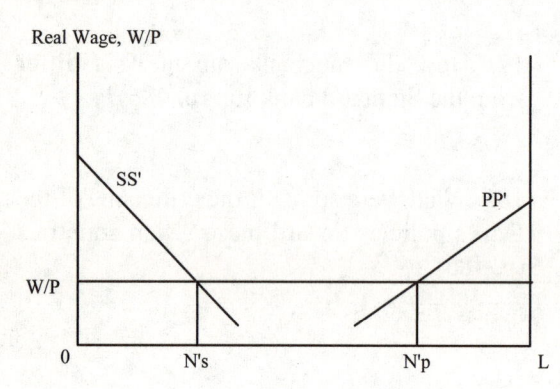

[Graph: Real Wage W/P on vertical axis, L on horizontal axis. SS' curve on the left, PP' curve on the right, with horizontal W/P line. Points N's and N'p marked on horizontal axis.]

If all goes well during the transition, what will the final situation look like? Explain.

7. List the factors which have prevented fast growth in the private sector during the transition.

8. Define foreign direct investment.

9. As the "budget constraint" becomes harder, what will happen to: (a) firms' incentives; (b) budget deficits; (c) money growth; and (d) inflation.

10. Briefly discuss what policy makers can do in response to a crisis like the one experienced in Asia

11. Discuss how a change in each of the following variables would affect net exports.
   a. budget deficit
   b. private saving
   c. investment

12. Briefly discuss the possible causes of the Asian crisis.

MULTIPLE CHOICE QUESTIONS

1. Which of the following countries has resisted transition?

a. Poland
b. Hungary
c. Cuba
d. Vietnam

2. The economic "big bang" refers to:

a. the 1987 stock market crash
b. the removal of controls in Poland in January 1990
c. the introduction of reforms in Hungary in the 1970s
d. the elimination of the soft budget constraint in Russia

3. Which of the following represents dimensions of transition?

a. price liberalization
b. privatization
c. macroeconomic control
d. all of the above
e. both a and b

4. Transitions tend to have what effect on measured output in the short run?

a. measured output increases
b. measured output decreases
c. measured output does not change

5. The Soviet Union's measure of output <u>overstated</u> GDP because:

a. firms overstated production
b. firms overstated quality adjustments
c. prices did not reflect market prices
d. all of the above

6. When price liberalization is introduced, we would expect:

a. the price of some goods to fall
b. the quantities of some goods to fall
c. the conventional measure of GDP to overstate the true decline in GDP

d. all of the above
e. both a and b

Use the graph provided below to answer questions 10 through 14.

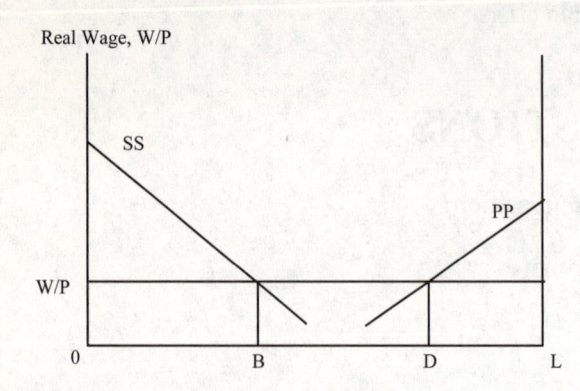

7. Employment in the state sector is represented by the distance:

a. 0B
b. BD
c. BL
d. DL

8. Employment is the private sector is represented by the distance:

a. 0B
b. BD
c. BL
d. none of the above

9. Unemployment in this economy is represented by the distance:

a. 0B
b. BD
c. BL
d. 0L minus 0B

10. Total employment in this economy is represented by the distance:

a. 0L
b. BD
c. 0B plus DL
d. none of the above

11. If transition in this economy goes well, we would expect:

a. SS and PP both to increase
b. SS to decrease and PP to increase
c. SS to decrease and PP to decrease
d. SS to increase and PP to decrease

12. Which of the following helps explain why the private sector could not grow fast enough during the transition?

a. insufficient quantities of capital
b. little expertise
c. difficulties in obtaining credit (i.e., loans)
d. all of the above

13. Foreign direct investment represents:

a. the purchase of existing firms by foreign firms
b. the development of new plants by foreign firms
c. the export of goods and services
d. all of the above
e. both a and b

14. Restructuring has been slow because restructuring:

a. involves large amounts of capital
b. involves an initial further decline in employment
c. is complex and requires incentives and authority within firms
d. all of the above

15. The existence of the soft budget constraint can cause:

a. increases in budget deficits
b. increases in money growth
c. increase in inflation
d. all of the above

16. In which of the following countries did the Asian crisis start?

a. Japan
b. Indonesia
c. Korea
d. none of the above.

17. Which of the following represents a condition common to Indonesia, Malaysia, Korea, and Thailand prior to the Asian crisis?

a. high inflation
b. high investment
c. large budget deficits
d. trade surpluses

18. Which of the following expressions represent net exports (NX)?

a. $NX = S + (T - G) - I$
b. $NX = S + (G - T) - I$
c. $NX = I + (T - G) - S$
d. $NX = I + G - T) - S$

CHAPTER 25. SHOULD POLICY MAKERS BE RESTRAINED?

OBJECTIVES, REVIEW AND TUTORIAL

After working through the chapter and the material found below, you should be able to:

1. Explain why the effects of policy on output are uncertain.

2. Recognize that this uncertainty should lead policy makers to be more cautious.

3. Understand how game theory can be used to examine policy.

4. Discuss what is meant by the time inconsistency of optimal policy and its implications for restraints on policy makers.

5. Discuss the games between policy makers and voters and the games between policy makers.

6. Explain the cases for and against the Balanced-Budget Amendment.

1. UNCERTAINTY OF MACRO POLICY

(1) Explanation of uncertainty

The effects of changes in the money supply are uncertain because we do not know:
• how much short-term and long-term interest rates will change
• how much stock prices will change
• how long it will take for changes in the above variables to affect investment and consumption
• how long it will take for the J-curve effects to disappear (i.e., for NX to increase in response to a depreciation).

There is also uncertainty because:
• the policy may affect the economy after it is needed (e.g. after the recession is over)
• an increase in unemployment may reflect either a deviation from u_n or an increase in u_n.

(2) Implications of uncertainty

The uncertainty of policy (caused by, for example, a range of possible values of Okun's coefficient or the parameter α in the Phillips curve relation) leads policy makers to be more cautious. Why?
• The more active is policy (both monetary and fiscal), the wider the range of possible outcomes (the more uncertain the effects).
• For example, an increase in money growth could push Y well above Y_n and cause an increase in inflation.

2. GAME THEORY AND THE TIME INCONSISTENCY OF OPTIMAL POLICY

(1) Game theory

Economists use game theory to explain the implementation and effects of macro policy. This explains the strategic interactions between the policy makers and people and firms (the players).
• The effects of policy depend on the expectations of people and firms.
• Policy makers determine policy based on how the economy is doing (as determined by people and firms).

(2) Time inconsistency of optimal policy

This occurs when incentives exist to cause policy makers to deviate from announced policies.
• In terms of the central bank, the central bank has an incentive to deviate from a stated policy of zero inflation once people and firms have responded to this announced policy. Why?
• Once people and firms respond to the stated policy, an increase in money growth will cause an increase in output above Y_n AND an increase in inflation (above zero).

Learning Tip

You should review the hijacking discussion to understand the time inconsistency problem.

---

3. ESTABLISHING CENTRAL BANK CREDIBILITY

To establish central bank credibility, the central bank can give up some (or all!) of its policy making power.

(1) Suggested changes to deal with time inconsistency
• make the central bank independent
• choose conservative central bankers

(2) Restraints on policy makers

Tight restraints on macro policy (e.g. fixed-money-growth rules) will deal with time inconsistency. However, they also may have large costs.

Learning Tip

Think about the following example. Suppose there is a large drop in output below Y_n.
• What type of monetary and fiscal policy do you think should be implemented?
• If tight rules were imposed on policy makers, could your policies be implemented?
• If these policies cannot be implemented, what happens to the economy?

---

4. THE GAMES PEOPLE (POLICY MAKERS) PLAY

(1) Policy makers and voters

To please voters and get re-elected, policy makers might pursue expansionary macro policy prior to elections; this would cause political business cycles. There is little evidence of this.

(2) Policy makers and policy makers

- Deficit reduction: In Canada, the Liberals and the NDP have traditionally been more open to tax increases, while the Tories have traditionally preferred cuts in spending. However, the experience of the last 15 years at the federal scene proves the opposite.
- Preferences about inflation and unemployment: The Liberals and the NDP have allegedly been more concerned about unemployment, whereas the Tories and now the newly emerged Reform Party, the champions of the free market system, have been said to favour control of inflation over unemployment. In reality, however, the more recent policy of price stability of the Bank of Canada has been independent of the ruling party's preferences.

5. THE BALANCED-BUDGET AMENDMENT IN THE U.S.

(1) The case against

- It eliminates the use of fiscal policy as a policy instrument.

(2) The case for

- Deficits during recessions may have negative effects on the economy.
- Existence of lags limits the effectiveness of fiscal policy.
- The amendment is the only way to reduce the deficit.

Learning Tip

A balanced-budget amendment may also make the economy more unstable. See review problem #13.

SELF-TEST QUESTIONS

(1) Arguments for restraints on policy makers fall into what two categories (p. 494)?

(2) List some of the questions which indicate why the effects of changes in the money supply on output are uncertain (p. 493).

(3) What is meant by the baseline case (p. 491)?

(4) Does uncertainty about the effects of macro policy suggest that policy makers should be more or less active (p. 494)?

(5) Explain what is meant by fine tuning (p. 494).

(6) What is the "optimal control" approach to macro policy (p. 494)?

(7) What is game theory (p. 494)?

(8) Who are the "players" in the context of macro policy (p. 494)?

(9) Briefly explain what is meant by the time inconsistency of optimal policy (p. 495).

(10) What would be a government's best policy toward hijackings (p. 495)?

(11) Describe an "independent central bank" (p. 497).

(12) What is the relation between central bank independence and inflation (p. 497)?

(13) Would you characterize Alan Blinder as a conservative central banker (pp. 496–497)?

(14) Explain what the political business cycle suggests will happen to the growth of output (p. 498).

(15) Does the evaluation of the ratio of Canada's debt to GDP support the existence of political business cycles (p. 498-499)?

(16) How do "wars of attrition" help explain the debate about deficit reduction (p. 500)?

(17) What is the primary argument against a balanced-budget amendment (p. 501)?

(18) Why do some economists support a balanced-budget amendment (p. 502)?

REVIEW PROBLEMS

1. List the reasons why a given change in the money supply will have uncertain effects on output.

2. When the economy is operating at the baseline case, what is unemployment and the rate of growth of output?

3. Refer to figure 25-1.
a. By end of year one, which model predicted the largest increase in output?
b. By end of year one, which model predicted the smallest increase in output?
c. By end of year Six, which model predicted the largest increase in output?
d. By end of year six, which model predicted the smallest increase in output?

4. Explain the difference between self restraints by policy makers and restraints on policy makers.

5. Given the uncertainty about the effects of macro policy, what are the advantages and disadvantages of a policy that tries to achieve constant unemployment?

6. Briefly comment on how effective each of the following policies/strategies would be in dealing with hijacking:
a. Stated policy of NO negotiations. If a hijacking occurs, the government does negotiate.
b. Stated policy of NO negotiations. If a hijacking occurs, the government does NOT negotiate.
c. Stated policy of negotiations. If a hijacking occurs, the government does negotiate.
d. Stated policy of negotiations. If a hijacking occurs, the government does NOT negotiate.

7. Suppose the Bank of Canada increases the money supply by, say, 10%.
a. Discuss what happens to the effect on unemployment as the range of possible values of Okun's coefficient increases.
b. For a given value of Okun's coefficient, discuss what happens to the effects on inflation as the range of possible values of the parameter α increases.
c. Discuss what happens to the effects on inflation as the range of possible values of the parameter α increases AND the range of possible values of Okun's coefficient simultaneously increases.

8. Suppose the Bank of Canada announces a policy of zero inflation. Further assume that individuals and firms believe the Bank is credible.
a. Why is there an incentive for the Bank to deviate from the above stated policy?
b. Would its actions, if the Bank were to deviate, be consistent with the goals of the policy?
c. What would happen over time to the central bank's credibility?
d. To what extent does your analysis in parts a, b and c illustrate the time inconsistency of optimal policy?

9. What are the problems associated with a constant-money-growth rule?

10. What type of relation do you think exists between central bank independence and average money growth? Explain.

11. a. Assuming that political business cycles exist, discuss what most likely happens to each of the following variables during the periods prior to an election: government spending, taxes, unemployment, and the growth of output.
b. Is the average rate of growth of output during the years of the Liberals and the Conservatives administrations consistent with political business cycles? Explain.

12. Given preferences about inflation and unemployment, what do you think a comparison of the average money growth during the Liberals and the Conservatives administrations would reveal? Explain.

13. Taxes are affected by the level of economic activity: When output increases, tax revenues typically increase—when output falls, tax revenues fall. Suppose a balanced-budget amendment is passed which requires that the budget always be in balance (i.e., G must always equal T). Further assume that the economy is initially operating at the natural level of output and that the budget is currently in balance.
a. Suppose consumer confidence suddenly drops. What effect will this have on the IS curve, the AD curve, output, tax revenues and on the budget?
b. Given the existence of the balanced-budget amendment, what will policy makers have to do in this situation?
c. Based on a and b, what effect does the existence of a balanced-budget amendment have on the output effects of any shock to aggregate demand?
d. Based on your analysis in c, what happens to the fluctuations in output caused by shocks to aggregate demand in the presence of a balanced-budget amendment?

MULTIPLE CHOICE QUESTIONS

1. The effects of changes in the money supply on output are uncertain because policy makers do not know how much:

a. short-term interest rates will change
b. long-term interest rates will change
c. stock prices will change
d. all of the above

2. The baseline case refers to the situation where:

a. inflation is zero
b. unemployment is equal to the natural rate of unemployment rate
c. output growth is zero
d. all of the above

3. The 12 models discussed in the chapter illustrate that changes in money growth will have:

a. identical output effects in all 12 models
b. no effect on output after three years in all 12 models
c. different effect on output depending on the model
d. none of the above

4. Uncertainty about the effects of policy on output should cause policy makers to use:

a. more active policies
b. less active policies
c. fine tuning
d. both a and c

5. Which of the following policies toward hijackings would you recommend to a government?

a. State policy of NO negotiations. If a hijacking occurs, the government does negotiate.
b. State policy of NO negotiations. If a hijacking occurs, the government does NOT negotiate.
c. State policy of negotiations. If a hijacking occurs, the government does negotiate.
d. State policy of negotiations. If a hijacking occurs, the government does NOT negotiate.

6. The time inconsistency of optimal policy refers to:

a. fine tuning
b. optimal control theory
c. a situation where there is an incentive for policy makers to deviate from an announced policy
d. wars of attrition

7. Which of the following actions do you think would better deal with time inconsistency? Circle all that apply.

a. appoint central bankers for longer terms
b. choose conservative central bankers
c. appoint central bankers for shorter terms
d. choose liberal central bankers

8. Alan Blinder's statement that the Fed in the United States had a responsibility to use monetary policy to help the economy from a recession had which of the following effects?

a. bond prices increased
b. interest rates fell
c. interest rates increased
d. none of the above

9. The more independent the central bank, we would expect:

a. higher inflation
b. lower inflation
c. higher money growth
d. both a and c

10. If a political business cycle exists, we would expect increases in growth of output:

a. in the first year of an administration
b. in the second year of an administration
c. just after an election
d. just prior to an election

11. Between the end of World War II and the end of the 1970s, the ratio of Canada's debt to GDP:

a. increased
b. decreased
c. remained constant
d. supports the existence of a political business cycle

12. Which of the following helps explain why some economists favour a balanced-budget amendment?

a. deficits during recessions may have negative effects on the economy
b. because of lags in the legislative process
c. because of skepticism of any rules the parliament imposes on itself
d. all of the above

CHAPTER 26. MONETARY POLICY: A SUMMING UP

OBJECTIVES, REVIEW AND TUTORIAL

After working through the chapter and the material found below, you should be able to:

1. Summarize what we have learned about monetary policy.

2. Understand the costs and benefits of inflation.

3. Briefly discuss the current debate about the optimal inflation rate.

4. Distinguish between money and other liquid assets.

5. Discuss the effects of and proper response of the Bank of Canada to changes in the demand for M1.

6. Become familiar with the organization and instruments of the Bank of Canada.

7. Discuss the practice of monetary policy.

1. THE COSTS OF INFLATION

There are four types of costs of inflation.

(1) Shoe-leather costs

• Increases in inflation cause increases in the nominal interest rate.
• As i increases, individuals reduce their holdings of real money balances.
• Individuals, therefore, make more trips to the bank.
• These "trips" reduce leisure and/or time spent working.

(2) Tax distortions

• Increases in inflation can increase the effective tax rate on capital gains (even though the real value of the asset did not change).
• Increases in inflation, since the early 1990s, pushed individuals into higher income tax brackets as their nominal income increased (bracket creep). This would occur even if their real income did not change.

(3) Money illusion

• Certain computations become more difficult when there is inflation.
• Evidence exists which indicates that some people make incorrect decisions as a result of money illusion.

(4) Inflation variability

• Inflation generally becomes more variable as inflation increases.
• Bonds, therefore, become riskier.

2. THE BENEFITS OF INFLATION

(1) Seignorage

- The ultimate source of inflation is money creation.
- The money creation can finance some government spending which allows for less borrowing or lower taxes.

(2) Option of negative real interest rate

- The nominal interest rate cannot be negative.
- A positive rate of inflation, therefore, can cause a negative real interest rate.
- This negative real interest rate can make investment very attractive.
- If inflation were zero, the real interest rate would always be positive.

(3) Money illusion

- The existence of money illusion can make it easier for individuals to accept reductions in the real wage.
- Suppose a reduction in the real wage is needed. Individuals are more likely to accept a fixed nominal wage when inflation occurs rather than accept a reduction in the nominal wage when there is no inflation.

3. THE OPTIMAL RATE OF INFLATION

- One's views about the optimal rate of inflation depend on one's views of the costs and benefits of inflation.
- Those who argue for some inflation note that going from a low rate of inflation (say 4%) to 0% is likely to increase the unemployment rate for some time.
- This would result in "transition" costs not discussed above.

4. M1, M1B and M2

> **Learning Tip**
>
> - Make sure you understand the components of M1, M1B and M2.
> - Also make sure you understand the difference among the components of M1, M1B and M2.

5. CHANGES IN THE DEMAND FOR M1 AND THE IMPLICATIONS FOR MONETARY POLICY

- The demand for M1 depends on how attractive the components of M1 are in comparison to other liquid assets.
- If other liquid assets become more attractive, the demand for M1 will fall.
- This decrease in the demand for M1 will cause the LM curve to shift down, i to fall and Y to increase.

> **Learning Tip**
>
> • If the Bank of Canada keeps M1 constant, these shifts in the demand for M1 can cause changes in output (via the effects on i).
> • To prevent any change in output, the Bank of Canada should:
>   • increase the supply of M1 when the demand for M1 increases
>   • reduce the supply of M1 when the demand for M1 falls
>   • these responses keep the LM curve from shifting and i from changing
> • These shifts in the demand for M1 can also cause the price level to change (via the effects on the aggregate demand curve).
> • This last result can explain why there is not a perfect relation between the monetary aggregates and inflation.

6. THE TAYLOR RULE

The Taylor rule is given by the following: $i = i^* + a(\pi - \pi^*) - b(u - u_n)$ where:

- i^* is the target nominal interest rate = the nominal interest rate associated with the target rate of inflation in the medium run (i.e., $i^* = r_n + \pi^*$ where rn is the natural real interest rate);
- π^* is the target rate of inflation;
- u_n is the natural unemployment rate; and
- a and b are parameters.

The rule indicates the following actions to be taken by the central bank:

(1) if inflation is greater than π^*, the central bank should raise the nominal interest rate; and

(2) if $u > u_n$, the central bank should reduce the nominal interest rate.

The parameters a and b indicate the extent to which the central bank will raise (or lower) the nominal interest rate when inflation and unemployment deviate from target.

7. ORGANIZATION AND INSTRUMENTS OF THE BANK OF CANADA

(1) Mandate

You should become familiar with:
• the Bank of Canada's mandate as defined in its original Act
• the current focus of the Bank

(2) Instruments

The Bank of Canada has three policy instruments:
• deposit switching which changes settlement balances
• open market operations
• the Bank rate and the overnight rate.

> **Learning Tip**
>
> • Changes in "settlement balances" affect the supply of cash reserves and hence the money supply.
> • Open market operations are generally regarded as a supplementary tool to fine-tune the quantity of reserves.
> • The Bank rate and the overnight rate are the summing indicators of these operations.

8. PRACTICE OF POLICY

(1) The Bank of Canada explicitly targets the rate of inflation and in so doing, it pre-announces its target range. This is:
• to serve as a signal to the public of the Bank's intentions
• to help the Bank to create and maintain credibility with the public

(2) The Bank also sets target ranges for the overnight rate and monitors the economy by closely tracing an important indicator known as the *Monetary Conditions Index (MCI)*.

SELF-TEST QUESTIONS

(1) What is the optimal rate of inflation (p. 508)?

(2) What happens to the nominal interest rate, opportunity cost of holding money and real money balances when inflation increases (p. 508)?

(3) What are shoe-leather costs (p. 508)?

(4) Describe bracket creep (p. 508).

(5) What tends to happen to inflation variability as inflation increases (p. 509)?

(6) Do bonds become more or less risky as inflation increases (p. 509)?

(7) What is an indexed bond (p. 509)?

(8) List the three benefits of inflation (pp. 510–511).

(9) Can the real or nominal interest rate be negative (p. 511)?

(10) What are the components of M1, M1B, M2, M2+ and M3 (pp. 14-516)?

(11) What are money market mutual funds (p. 515)?

(12) What is broad money (p. 554)?

(13) What is narrow money (p. 516)?

(14) What happened to the demand for M1 when money market mutual funds were introduced (p. 515)?

(15) Which monetary aggregate has the stronger relation with inflation, M1B or M2 (p. 516)?

(16) What are the three target variables included in the Taylor's rule (p. 517)?

(17) Briefly discuss the original mandate of the Bank of Canada and compare it with the Bank's current objectives (p. 518)?

(18) List the two instruments of monetary policy (pp. 518-519).

(19) What is the Bank rate (p. 519)?

(20) What is the overnight rate (p. 519)?

(21) What are SPRA and SRA (p. 519)?

(22) What is the target range for inflation and what is its role (p. 520)?

REVIEW PROBLEMS

1. Suppose an individual bought a house for $100,000 in 2001 and sold it five years later. For simplicity, assume that: (1) the value of the house increases by the rate of inflation during each year; and (2) the capital gains tax is 25%.
a. Calculate the effective tax rate on the sale of the house for each of the following rates of inflation: 0%, 3%, 6%. Assume that the rate of inflation is constant at that rate for each of the five years.
b. What happens to the real value of the house over the five years for each of the rates of inflation?
c. When inflation is zero, how much tax is owed? Briefly explain.
d. What happens to the effective tax rate as the rate of inflation increases?

2. List the costs of inflation.

3. a. List the benefits of inflation.
b. What determines the optimal rate of inflation?

4. Can the nominal interest rate on a bond be negative? Explain.

5. Suppose the nominal interest rate is 1%.
a. Calculate the real interest rate when inflation equals: -2%, -1%, 0%, 1%, 2%, 3% and 5%.
b. What happens to the real interest rate as inflation increases?
c. What do you think happens to investment in this example as inflation increases?
d. Why might policy makers want a negative real interest rate?

6. Is M1B larger than M2? Explain.

7. a. List the components of M1B.
b. List the components of M2.
c. List the components of M2+.

8. Use the graph provided below to answer this question.
a. In the late 1970s, what effect did the introduction of money market funds have on the demand for M1B?

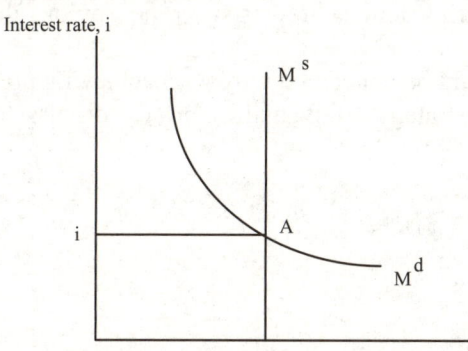

b. Discuss what effect this event had on the interest rate.

9. Use the graph provided below to answer this question.

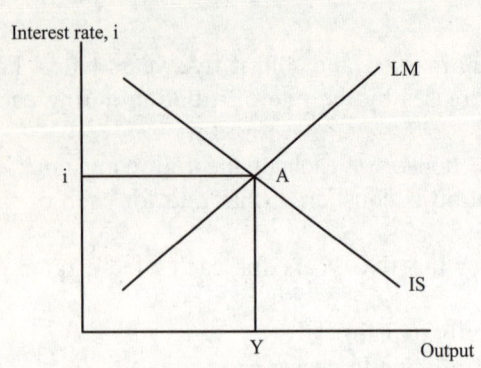

[Graph: IS-LM diagram with Interest rate i on vertical axis, Output Y on horizontal axis, curves LM and IS intersecting at point A, with i and Y marked on axes]

a. In the late 1970s, what effect did the introduction of money market funds have on the LM curve, i, and output (Y)?
b. Based on your analysis in a, what happened to aggregate demand and the price level?
c. Did this change in the price level occur as a result of a change in the quantity of M1?

10. Assume that output is initially at the natural level of output. Now suppose that individuals decide to switch their assets holdings from M1B to money market mutual funds.
a. What effect will this have on the demand for M1B and M2?
b. What effect will this have on aggregate demand and on the price level?
c. If the Bank of Canada is concerned about increases in the price level, should it keep the supply of M1B fixed? Explain.

11. What does your analysis in #9 and #10 suggest about the relation between the monetary aggregates and inflation?

12. When was the Bank of Canada formed and what has become the focus of the Bank since 1989?

13. a. List the two instruments of monetary policy.
b. Briefly describe how each of the two instruments can be used to increase the money supply.

14. Why does the Bank of Canada announce ranges for its inflation target?

15. Assume the central bank follows the Taylor rule discussed in the chapter.
a. Suppose a central bank is confronted with the following situation: $\pi > \pi^*$ and $u > u_n$. In such a situation, what should the central bank do, given that its actions are based on the Taylor rule? Explain.
b. Some economists believe that the central bank should be concerned only with achieving price stability. Suppose the central bank adopted such a strategy. Given this, briefly discuss the relative magnitude of the parameters a and b.

MULTIPLE CHOICE QUESTIONS

1. Which of the following is a function of money?

a. store of value
b. unit of account
c. medium of exchange
d. all of the above

2. An increase in inflation has which of the following effects?

a. increase in the nominal interest rate
b. increase in the opportunity cost of holding money
c. reduction in real money balances
d. all of the above
e. both a and b

3. As inflation increases, the effective tax rate on capital gains:

a. increases
b. decreases
c. becomes negative
d. remains constant if the real value of the asset does not change

4. Which of the following is a cost of inflation?

a. tax distortions
b. inflation variability
c. money illusion
d. all of the above

5. Bracket creep refers to:

a. the effects of inflation on the effective tax on capital gains
b. money illusion
c. the fact that inflation could push individuals into higher income tax brackets
d. none of the above

6. Higher inflation generally causes:

a. inflation variability to increase
b. inflation variability to decrease
c. no effect on inflation variability
d. an increase in individuals' demand for real money balances

7. Which of the following is a benefit of inflation? Circle all that apply.

a. seignorage
b. the possibility of negative real interest rates
c. money illusion and real wage adjustments
d. tax distortions

8. Which of the following cannot occur?

a. $r = 0$
b. $r < 0$
c. $i < 0$
d. $i > r$

9. Which of the following is a component of M1B?

a. travellers' cheques
b. currency inside banks
c. time deposits
d. demand deposits

10. Which of the following is a component of M2 but not a component of M1B?

a. float
b. notice deposits
c. currency outside banks
d. demand deposits

11. Which of the following is the least liquid monetary aggregate?

a. demand deposits
b. M1B
c. M2
d. M2+

12. Narrow money refers to:

a. the monetary base
b. M1B
c. M2
d. M3

13. Broad money refers to:

a. the monetary base
b. M1B
c. M2
d. M3 as well as M2

14. Reduced restrictions on cheque writing on money market mutual funds would have which of the following effects?

a. demand for M1B falls
b. the LM curve shifts down
c. the interest rate decreases
d. all of the above
e. none of the above

15. The introduction of money market funds in the late 1970s most likely caused (all else fixed):

a. i to increase
b. Y to fall
c. the LM curve to shift down
d. an increase in the demand for M1B

16. Suppose the Bank of Canada wishes to keep Y constant. Now, assume that individuals switch some of their assets from M1 to money market funds. Which of the following actions should the Bank take to achieve its goal?

a. increase the supply of M1B
b. decrease the supply of M1B
c. leave M1B constant
d. buy bonds

17. Which of the following monetary aggregates has the strongest relation with inflation?

a. M1B
b. M2
c. the currency outside banks
d. none of the above

18. An increase in the reserve ratio has which of the following effects?

a. reduces the money multiplier
b. increases the money multiplier
c. decreases H (the monetary base)
d. increases the money supply

19. An increase in the Bank rate is viewed as a signal that:

a the Bank of Canada is going to follow an expansionary policy
b the Bank of Canada is going to follow a contractionary policy
c. the Bank of Canada is going to increase its purchase of bonds
d. the Bank of Canada is going to reduce the reserve requirements

20. Which of the following explains why the Bank of Canada announces target ranges for the inflation rate? Circle all that apply.

a. so it can miss them
b. to serve as a signal of the Bank policy
c. to serve as a benchmark for its behaviour
d. to help gain credibility

21. In Taylor's rule the coefficient a should be
a. greater than zero.
b. greater than one.
c. less than one.
d. unrelated to the inflation gap.

CHAPTER 27. FISCAL POLICY: A SUMMING UP

OBJECTIVES, REVIEW AND TUTORIAL

After working through the chapter and the material found below, you should be able to:

1. Understand the government budget constraint.

2. Understand the relation between the change in debt, the initial level of debt and current government spending and taxes.

3. Know the implications of tax cuts on the path of debt and future taxes.

4. Explain the determinants of changes in the debt-to-GDP ratio.

5. Understand the Ricardian equivalence proposition.

6. Discuss the other three fiscal policy issues (i.e., stabilization, wars, and the dangers of high debt).

7. Understand the dangers of high debt.

8. Discuss the phenomenon of the twin deficits.

9. Discuss the Federal fiscal policy between 1993 – 2002.

1. THE GOVERNMENT BUDGET CONSTRAINT

There are several issues you need to understand.

(1) Deficit measures

The correct measure of the deficit (all variables in real terms) is:

Deficit = $rB_{t-1} + G_t - T_t$ where

- rB_{t-1} are the interest payments on the debt
- $G_t - T_t$ is the primary deficit.

The official measure of the deficit is:

Official deficit = $iB_{t-1} + G_t - T_t$.

Learning Tip

- The correct measure is also called the inflation-adjusted deficit.
- The official measure overstates the correct measure by πB_{t-1}.
- A primary surplus occurs if $T_t > G_t$.

---

(2) The government budget constraint

This simply states that the change in government debt during t equals the deficit in t.

$B_t - B_{t-1}$ = Deficit = $rB_{t-1} + G_t - T_t$.

Or, $B_t = (1 + r)B_{t-1} + G_t - T_t$.

Learning Tip

Increases in B_{t-1}, r and G_t and reductions in T_t cause B_t to increase.

---

2. IMPLICATIONS OF TAX CUTS ON THE PATH OF DEBT AND ON FUTURE TAXES

There are two cases to consider.

(1) Full repayment in year 1

Prior to year 0, assume the government has balanced its budget (G = T = 500) and that $B_0 = 0$. Also assume that G does not change. Suppose the government cuts T by 100 in year 0 and decides to repay the debt in year 1.

Implications:
• Debt at the end of 0 is now 100.
• Debt at the end of 1 is $B_1 = (1 + r)100 + G_1 - T_1 = (1 + r)100 + 500 - T_1$.
• $B_1 = 0$ since the government repays the debt.
• To repay the debt, the government must raise T_1 and run a primary surplus. What is T_1?
• Set $B_1 = 0$ and solve for T_1. $0 = (1 + r)100 + 500 - T_1$; $T_1 - 500 = (1 + r)100$.
• The government must run a primary surplus equal to $(1 + r)100$. Equivalently, T_1 must increase by $(1 + r)100$ above G_1.
• This tax increase will pay off the debt and interest payments.

(2) Full repayment in year t

Assume the same initial situation as described above.

Implications:
• Prior to the repayment of the debt, the primary deficit is zero for each year.
• Since G = T, the debt increases each year by the size of the interest payments (they accumulate over time).
• By year t-1, $B_{t-1} = 100(1 + r)^{t-1}$.
• Since $B_t = 0$, we see that $0 = 100(1 + r)(1 + r)^{t-1} + G_t - T_t$.
• So, $T_t - G_t = 100(1 + r)^t$.

> **Learning Tip**
>
> - The future tax increase to repay the debt is larger:
>   - the larger the initial tax cut
>   - the higher is r
>   - the longer the government waits to repay the debt
> - If the primary deficit is 0, the debt increases each year by the size of the interest payments.
> - To keep the debt constant, a primary surplus equal to the interest payments must occur each year.

3. THE DEBT-TO-GDP RATIO

The change in the debt ratio is given by the following:

$(B_t/Y_t) - (B_{t-1}/Y_{t-1}) = (r - g)(B_{t-1}/Y_{t-1}) + (G_t - T_t)/Y_t$.

There are two cases to consider.

(1) <u>Case 1</u>: primary deficit is 0

The debt ratio increases if $r > g$; it decreases if $r < g$; and it remains constant if $r = g$. For example, suppose $r > g > 0$. Here, Y is growing over time. However, the effects of the interest payments on the debt dominate ($r > g$) causing the ratio to increase.

(2) <u>Case 2</u>: $r = g$

Here, the debt ratio increases or decreases depending on the ratio of the primary deficit to GDP. If $G > T$, the debt ratio will increase over time. If $G < T$, the debt ratio will shrink.

> **Learning Tip**
>
> - Make sure you understand how the above ratio was obtained.
> - Assuming $G = T$, the relative size of r and g will determine whether the debt ratio increases.

4. THE RICARDIAN EQUIVALENCE PROPOSITION

The Ricardian proposition works as follows:
- Suppose the government cuts T by 100 in t announcing it will increase T in t+1 to repay the debt.
- Taxes will increase by $100(1 + r)$ in t+1.
- The present value of the future tax increase is $100(1 + r)/(1 + r) = 100$.
- Summary: Taxes are cut by 100 today, and the present value of the future tax increase is 100.
- The present value of after-tax income is, therefore, constant.
- Individuals do not change consumption when taxes are cut today because human wealth does not change.

Implications:
(1) The tax cut does not change consumption; the IS curve does not shift to the right; Y and r do not change.
(2) What do people do with the tax cut? They save it!
(3) Private saving increases one for one with the deficit.

> **Learning Tip**
>
> The evidence suggests that increases in deficits are not met with an equal increase in private saving.

5. OTHER FISCAL POLICY ISSUES

(1) The cyclically adjusted deficit

This measure of the deficit is what the deficit would be, given existing tax (T) and spending (G) rules, if $Y = Y_n$.

> **Learning Tip**
>
> - Changes in G, T and, by the way, Y_n will cause changes in the cyclically adjusted deficit.
> - Changes in Y caused by other factors (e.g. consumer confidence) have no effect on the cyclically adjusted deficit.

(2) Wars and deficits

Governments may use deficits to finance wars in order to: (1) pass on the burden of the debt; and (2) smooth taxes.

> **Learning Tip**
>
> - IF governments did not rely on deficits, the current generation would be solely responsible for "financing" (via a tax increase) the increase in G.
> - Tax rates would change over time to "pay for" the changes in G.
> - These changes in tax rates would affect worker-leisure decisions, untaxed activities, .. etc.

(3) Dangers of high debt

If financial market participants require a risk premium to hold domestic bonds, r will increase. This increase in r will have two effects:
- the debt ratio increases faster (assuming $r > g$)
- Y could fall as r increases (this would cause g to fall).

What can high debt ratio countries do?
- They could reduce debt ratios by pursuing policies that increase g and/or construct budgets that call for primary surpluses.
- They could also use debt repudiation; this is an extreme action that would make it very difficult to borrow in the future.
- The link between the current account deficit and the government deficit and the government deficit is referred to as the twin deficits.

6. A decade of Canadian Federal Fiscal Policy

(1) The first Liberal budget, 1994.
(2) The second Liberal budget, 1995.
(3) The Fourth Liberal budget, 1997.

> **Learning Tip**
>
> • You should review this section of the chapter.
> • Make sure you understand the differences between the government budget numbers and the NIPA numbers.

SELF-TEST QUESTIONS

(1) What equation represents the budget deficit in year t (p. 525)?

(2) What is the inflation-adjusted deficit (p. 526)?

(3) The change in the government debt in period t is determined by what (pp. 526)?

(4) The change in the government debt can be decomposed into two parts. What are they (p. 526)?

(5) What is the primary deficit/surplus (p. 526)?

(6) What is the expression which represents the official measure of the deficit in year t (p. 526)?

(7) Official measures of the deficit overstate the correct measure by what amount (p. 526)?

(8) Suppose the debt is now positive and that the primary deficit is zero and will remain so in the future. What will happen, if anything, to the debt over time (pp. 528-530)?

(9) To keep the debt from changing, what must happen to the primary deficit (p. 530)?

(10) What determines whether the debt/GDP ratio increases or decreases over time (p. 530)?

(11) What is the Ricardian equivalence proposition (p. 532)?

(12) What is the cyclically adjusted deficit (p. 533)?

(13) The deficit can serve as an automatic stabilizer. Explain (p. 534)?

(14) What are the two reasons for relying on deficits to finance wars (pp.534-535)?

(15) What is meant by tax smoothing (p. 536)?

(16) What is meant by debt repudiation (p. 537)?

REVIEW PROBLEMS

1. Use the information provided below to answer this question. Assume that B, G and T are measured in real terms (and in billions of dollars).

$B_{t-1} = 900$ $G_t = 200$ $T_t = 190$ $i_t = .10$ $\pi_t = 0.05$

a. Calculate the official measure of the deficit in year t.
b. Calculate the correct (i.e., inflation-adjusted) measure of the deficit in year t.
c. Calculate the primary deficit in year t.

d. Discuss what happens to the primary deficit in year t if the nominal interest rate in year t increases to 15%.
e. To what extent does the official measure of the deficit overstate the correct measure?
f. Given the above information, what will happen to the level of the debt between years t-1 and t? Explain.

2. Use the information provided in #1 to answer this question.
a. What must happen to taxes in year t for the primary deficit to be zero?
b. What must happen to taxes in year t for the debt to remain constant between t-1 and t?
c. What must happen to taxes in year t for the debt to be fully repaid in t?

3. Use the information provided in #1 to answer this question.
a. Calculate the official measure of the deficit for each of the following rates of inflation (assume that all other variables are the same): 0.02, 0.04, 0.06 and 0.10.
b. Calculate the correct measure of the deficit for the following rates of inflation: 0.02, 0.04, 0.06 and 0.10.
c. To what extent does the official measure of the deficit overstate the correct measure for each of the following rates of inflation: 0.02, 0.04, 0.06 and 0.10?
d. What happens to the difference between the two measures of the deficit as inflation becomes higher? Explain.

4. Use the information provided below to answer this question: $B_{t-1} = 0$; $G_{t-1} = 400$; $T_{t-1} = 400$; and $r = 0.05$ Assume in year t that the government cuts taxes by 50 (for one year). Assume r and G do not change.
a. Calculate the debt at the end of t.
b. Suppose the government decides to repay the debt fully in year t + 1. What will the debt be at the end of t + 1? What must happen to taxes in period t + 1 to repay the debt fully in year t + 1? How much must they change?

5. Use the information provided in #4 to answer this question. Assume in year t that the government cuts taxes by 50 (for one year). Assume r and G do not change. Suppose the government decides to repay fully the debt in year t + 3. What is the level of the debt at the end of t + 3? What must happen to taxes in period t + 3 to repay fully the debt? How much must they change?

6. If spending is unchanged, a reduction in taxes must eventually be offset by an increase in taxes in the future.
a. What will happen to the size of the future tax increase as the government waits longer to increase taxes? Explain.
b. What will happen to the size of the future tax increase as r increases? Explain.

7. To keep the debt from increasing over time, what must happen to the primary deficit? To keep the debt from increasing over time, what must happen to the inflation-adjusted deficit? Explain.

8. Use the information provided below to answer this question; B, G and T are all measured in real terms; $G_t = 500$; $T_t = 400$; $Y_t = 2000$; $B_{t-1} = 1000$; $Y_{t-1} = 2000$; $r = 0.05$; and $g = 0$.
a. Calculate the debt ratio at the end of years t-1 and t.
b. Did the debt ratio increase, decrease or remain constant? Explain why any change might have occurred.

9. Suppose r = 0.04 and that the primary deficit is zero. Discuss what will happen to the debt ratio for each of the following values of g: 0, 0.02, 0.04, 0.06.

10. Suppose g = 0.02 and that the primary deficit is zero. Discuss what will happen to the debt ratio for each of the following values of r: 0.01, 0.02, 0.03, 0.04.

11. Discuss what factors could cause the debt ratio to decrease over time.

12. Assume the Ricardian equivalence proposition holds. Suppose the government cuts taxes by $100 billion in period t and announces it will increase taxes in period t+1 to repay the debt.
a. How much will taxes increase in period t+1?
b. Explain what effect this tax cut in period t will have on consumption, private saving, total saving, the IS curve, the interest rate, investment and output in period t?
c. In this case, to what extent did this tax cut increase output?

13. Discuss what effect each of the following events will have on the cyclically adjusted deficit.
a. increase in consumer confidence, which causes an increase in consumption
b. reduction in taxes
c. reduction in government spending
d. reduction in business confidence which causes a reduction in investment

14. What are the two reasons why governments rely on deficits to finance wars?

15. a. Discuss what effect a reduction in r will have on the debt ratio?
b. Discuss what effect a reduction in g will have on the debt ratio.
c. To keep the debt ratio from changing in (a) and (b), what would have to happen to the primary deficit? What effect would this change in the primary deficit have on output growth (g) in the short run? Explain.

16. Do you see any long-run consequences of debt repudiation? Explain.

17. What are the salient features of the Liberal budgets of 1994, 1995, and 1997?

MULTIPLE CHOICE QUESTIONS

1. Which of the following represents the correct measure of the deficit in year t (in real terms)?

a. $G_t - T_t$
b. $rB_{t-1} + G_t - T_t$
c. $G_t - T_t - \pi_t B_{t-1}$
d. $rB_t + G_t - T_t$

2. The government budget constraint is represented by:

a. $B_t - B_{t-1}$ = Deficit
b. $B_t - B_{t-1} = rB_{t-1} + G_t - T_t$
c. all of the above
d. none of the above

3. The official measure of the deficit overstates the correct measure by:

a. iB_{-1}
b. rB_{-1}
c. πB_{-1}
d. $(i - \pi)B_{-1}$

4. An increase in which of the following variables will cause an increase in the level of debt in period t (B_t)?

a. r
b. G_t
c. B_{t-1}
d. all of the above

5. The primary deficit is represented by what?

a. $G_t - T_t$
b. $(1 + r)B_{t-1} + G_t - T_t$
c. $rB_{t-1} + G_t - T_t$
d. $iB_{t-1} + G_t - T_t$

6. Which of the following events would cause the official measure of the deficit to be more inaccurate? Circle all that apply.

a. an increase in inflation
b. an increase in G
c. an increase in r
d. an increase in the level of the debt

7. To keep the debt level constant, which of the following must occur?

a. primary deficit must equal zero
b. the official deficit must equal zero
c. the primary surplus must equal zero
d. the primary surplus must equal the interest payments

8. Assume r = 0.05. Suppose the government cuts taxes by $100 billion in period t and will repay the debt in full in year t + 1. How much must taxes increase in year t + 1?

a. $5 billion
b. $100 billion
c. $105 billion
d. none of the above

9. Assume r = 0.05 and that B_t = 500. What must occur in the next period to repay the debt in full?

a. a primary surplus of $25 billion
b. a primary surplus of $500 billion
c. a primary surplus of $525 billion
d. a primary surplus of zero

10. Assume government spending does not change. Suppose the government cuts taxes in year t. The future tax increase to repay this debt will be higher:

a. the longer the government waits to raise taxes
b. the higher is the interest rate (r)
c. the lower is the interest rate (r)
d. both a and b

11. Which of the following conditions will cause a reduction in the level of debt over time?

a. primary surplus > real interest payments on the debt
b. primary surplus < real interest payments on the debt
c. primary deficit > real interest payments on the debt
d. primary deficit < real interest payments on the debt

12. Which of the following events will cause the debt ratio to increase?

a. reduction in r
b. reduction in g
c. a reduction in the primary deficit
d. all of the above

13. Which of the following events will cause the debt ratio to decrease?

a. an increase in r
b. an increase in the primary deficit
c. an increase in g
d. all of the above
e. none of the above

14. During the 1970s, debt ratios in OECD countries:

a. increased as r increased
b. increased as g fell
c. decreased as r fell
d. none of the above

15. During the 1980s, debt ratios in OECD countries:

a. increased as r increased
b. decreased as g increased
c. decreased as r decreased
d. did not change

16. Suppose the government cuts taxes in period t and announces it will increase taxes in t + 1. According to the Ricardian equivalence proposition, this tax cut in year t will have which of the following effects in year t?

a. no change in consumption
b. an equal increase in private saving
c. no change in investment
d. no change in output
e. all of the above

17. According to the Ricardian equivalence proposition,

a. private saving increases one-for-one with the deficit
b. total saving increases as the deficit increases
c. total saving decreases as the deficit increases
d. investment increases one-for-one with the deficit

18. The recent federal government's success in turning a budget deficit into a surplus can be attributed to:

a. lower interest rates
b. drastic cuts in government spending
c. a strong economy
d. all of the above

19. Which of the following will cause an increase in the cyclically adjusted deficit?

a. increase in G
b. reduction in taxes
c. a reduction in consumer confidence which causes a recession
d. all of the above
e. both a and b

20. Countries tend to rely on deficits to finance wars in order to:

a. pass on the burden of the debt
b. use the deficit as an automatic stabilizer
c. smooth taxes
d. all of the above
e. both a and c

21. Debt repudiation occurs when:

a. the government runs a primary deficit
b. the primary deficit is zero
c. the government repays the debt in full
d. the government cancels its debt

22. The federal budget has been in surplus since
a. Year 2000
b. Year 1997
c. Year 1993
d. Year 1999

CHAPTER 28. EPILOGUE: THE STORY OF MACROECONOMICS

OBJECTIVES, REVIEW AND TUTORIAL

After working through the chapter and the material found below, you should be able to:

1. Discuss the building blocks of modern macroeconomics introduced by Keynes.

2. Discuss the progress made on the neoclassical synthesis.

3. Understand the debate about monetary versus fiscal policy.

4. Understand the debate about the Phillips curve.

5. Discuss the three implications of rational expectations.

6. Become familiar with the integration of rational expectations and its implications.

7. Know the current developments in macroeconomics.

8. Understand the basic propositions of the core of macroeconomics.

1. BUILDING BLOCKS OF MODERN MACROECONOMICS INTRODUCED BY KEYNES

Keynes argued that changes in effective demand (what we now call aggregate demand) determined output in the short run. In developing effective demand, Keynes introduced:

- the multiplier
- the notion of liquidity preference (demand for money)
- the importance of expectations in affecting consumption and investment
- the idea that expectations can cause changes in demand and output

2. PROGRESS MADE DURING THE NEOCLASSICAL SYNTHESIS

Much progress was made during this period. For example,

- The IS-LM model was developed.
- The theories of consumption, investment, and money demand were developed.
- Macroeconometric models were constructed to make predictions about economic activity.

Learning Tip
You might want to review which economists were responsible for which developments.

3. EARLY AREAS OF DEBATE

There were several areas of debate during this period.

(1) Monetary versus fiscal policy
• Keynes emphasized fiscal rather than monetary policy.
• Later, others argued that the IS curve was relatively steep making fiscal policy the more effective policy tool.
• Friedman and Schwartz challenged this by arguing that the Great Depression was caused by a reduction in the money supply.

(2) The Phillips curve

• In the 1960s, many Keynesian economists believed that there was a trade-off between inflation and unemployment in the long run.
• Friedman and Phelps, however, argued that there was no long-run trade-off.

(3) Role of policy

• Some argued for the use of fine tuning, while others (e.g. Friedman) argued that policy makers should use simple rules.

4. IMPLICATIONS OF RATIONAL EXPECTATIONS

Lucas and Sargent argued that Keynesian economics ignored the full implications of expectations on behaviour. Rational expectations had three implications.

(1) Lucas critique

Since individuals' expectations and, therefore, behaviour would adjust to policy changes, macroeconometric models would not predict well what would occur as a result of policy changes.
• The macroeconometric models were based on backward-looking behaviour and expectations.
• Under rational expectations, however, behavioural equations would change as policy changes; the models did not take this into account.

(2) The Phillips curve

• When rational expectations were introduced in Keynesian models, deviations in output from the natural level were short-lived.
• Anticipated changes in the money supply, under rational expectations, had no effects on output even in the short run.
• Unanticipated changes in the money supply, under rational expectations, would cause changes in output.

(3) Policy

The theory of policy now needed to take into account the strategic interactions among the players (policy makers, firms and people): game theory (rather than optimal control theory).

Learning Tip

You should review the discussion in the text about:
- the random walk of consumption
- the staggering of wage and price decisions
---

5. CURRENT DEVELOPMENTS

There are three groups of current research.

(1) New Classicals

- These economists generally assume competitive markets and flexible wages and prices.
- Early work focused on real business cycle models where output always equals the natural level of output, and changes in output are caused by changes in technological progress (or regress).

(2) New Keynesians

These economists have focused on:
- efficiency wages
- nominal rigidities
- menu costs

(3) New Growth Theory

These economists, led by Romer and Lucas, have explored:
- the determinants of technological progress
- the possibility of increasing returns to scale

6. THE CORE (COMMON BELIEFS)

Learning Tip

You should simply review this short section of the chapter.

SELF-TEST QUESTIONS

(1) What was business cycle theory (p. 548)?

(2) What is meant by effective demand (p. 548)?

(3) What does liquidity preference represent (p. 548)?

(4) What are "animal" spirits (p. 548)?

(5) The neoclassical synthesis refers to what (p. 548)?

(6) Who developed the IS-LM model (p. 549)?

(7) Which economist helped develop the theory of investment AND money demand (p. 549)?

(8) What type of policy did Keynes argue should be used to fight recessions (p. 549)?

(9) Friedman and Schwartz concluded that the Great Depression was caused by what (p. 550)?

(10) In the 1960s, most economists believed what about the relation between unemployment and inflation in the long run (p. 550)?

(11) What is stagflation (pp. 551)?

(12) What was Lucas and Sargent's main argument about Keynesian economics (p. 552)?

(13) What does the Lucas critique represent (p. 552)?

(14) Rational expectations suggests that anticipated changes in the money supply will have what effect on output (pp. 553)?

(15) Does rational expectations suggest that policy should be based on optimal control theory or on game theory (p. 553)?

(16) What is meant by the random walk of consumption (p. 553)?

(17) Who developed the overshooting model of exchange rates, and what does this model predict (p. 553)?

(18) What does the staggering of wage and price decisions represent (p. 553)?

(19) In real business cycle models, output always equals what (p. 554)?

(20) Prescott argued that fluctuations in output in real business cycle models were caused by what (p. 554)?

(21) What is meant by new Keynesians (p. 555)?

(22) Describe menu cost (p. 555).

(23) What is new growth theory (p. 555)?

REVIEW PROBLEMS

In addition to the following problems, make sure you can answer the questions included in the Self-test section.

1. List the building blocks of modern macroeconomics introduced by Keynes.

2. List the economists responsible for each of the following developments/theories:
a. IS-LM model
b. consumption
c. investment
d. money demand
e. growth theory
f. rational expectations
g. real business cycle
h. new growth theory

3. As the IS curve becomes steeper, what happens to the output effects of a given change in the money supply? Explain.

4. Suppose the Bank of Canada wishes to reduce aggregate prices and assume that output initially equals the natural level of output. Based on rational expectations, should the Bank announce its policy in advance of the policy's implementation? Explain.

5. Assume: (1) individuals have rational expectations; (2) individuals believe the Bank will increase the money supply by 4%; and (3) the economy is initially operating at the natural level of output. Given this information, explain what happens to output for the following cases: (a) the money supply increases by 6%; (b) the money supply increases by 4%; and (c) the money supply increases by 2%.

6. Can output slowly return to the natural level with rational expectations? Briefly explain.

7. What are the characteristics of markets in rational expectations and real business cycle models?

8. In the real business cycle model developed by Prescott, what must happen for output to change (i.e., increase and decrease)? Explain.

9. List the areas of research in New Keynesian economics.

10. Briefly describe the basic set of propositions which represent the core of macroeconomics.

MULTIPLE CHOICE QUESTIONS

1. Which of the following is a building block of modern macroeconomics introduced by Keynes? Circle all that apply.

a. the multiplier
b. liquidity preference
c. rational expectations
d. technological regress

2. Liquidity preference refers to the theory of what?

a. consumption
b. investment
c. money demand
d. exchange rates

3. Who wrote *The General Theory*?

a. Solow
b. Keynes
c. Friedman
d. Lucas

4. By which decade had the neoclassical synthesis occurred?

a. 1930s
b. 1940s
c. 1950s
c. 1960s

5. Which of the following economists was (were) responsible for the theory of consumption? Circle all that apply.

a. Keynes
b. Modigliani
c. Friedman
d. Tobin

e. Lucas
f. Solow

6. Which of the following economists was (were) responsible for the theory of investment? Circle all that apply.

a. Keynes
b. Modigliani
c. Friedman
d. Tobin
e. Lucas
f. Solow

7. Which of the following economists was (were) responsible for the theory of money demand? Circle all that apply.

a. Keynes
b. Modigliani
c. Friedman
d. Tobin
e. Lucas
f. Solow

8. Which of the following economists was (were) responsible for the theory of growth? Circle all that apply.

a. Keynes
b. Modigliani
c. Friedman
d. Tobin
e. Lucas
f. Solow

9. When the IS curve is steep:

a. changes in the interest rate will have a greater effect on demand and output
b. monetary policy will work very well
c. fiscal policy can affect output faster and more reliably than monetary policy
d. fiscal policy will NOT work very well

10. The work by Friedman and Phelps indicates that:

a. there is a long-run trade-off between inflation and unemployment
b. there is NO long-run trade-off between inflation and unemployment
c. there is NO short-run trade-off between inflation and unemployment
d. none of the above

11. The Lucas critique refers to:

a. the debate about monetary and fiscal policy
b. the criticism of the use of macroeconometric models
c. stagflation
d. technological regress

12. Lucas' work on rational expectations suggests that:

a. only unanticipated changes in the money supply affect output
b. only anticipated changes in the money supply affect output
c. both anticipated and unanticipated changes in the money supply affect output
d. neither anticipated nor unanticipated changes in the money supply will affect output

13. Rational expectations suggests that policy should be based on:

a. game theory
b. optimal control theory
c. business cycle theory
d. backward-looking expectations

14. Which of the following statements is true about real business cycle theory?

a. Y is always above the natural level
b. Y is always below the natural level
c. Y always equals the natural level
d. Y is sometimes above, below or equal to the natural level

15. The work by Robert Hall suggests that the best forecast of consumption next year:

a. is last year's consumption
b. is this year's consumption
c. equals last year's level of disposable income
d. equals this year's level of disposable income

16. Which of the following is a characteristic of the New Classical model?

a. menu costs
b. efficiency wages
c. nominal rigidities
d. competitive markets with flexible wages and prices

17. Imperfections in credit markets indicate that:

a. individuals can borrow freely at the quoted interest rate
b. firms can borrow freely at the quoted interest rate
c. banks turn down potential customers at the quoted interest rate
d. both a and b

18. Which of the following is an area of research in New Keynesian economics? Circle all that apply.

a. menu costs
b. efficiency wages
c. the determination of technological progress
d. nominal rigidities

19. Which of the following is NOT one of the basic propositions of the core of macroeconomics?

a. changes in aggregate demand affect output in the short run
b. monetary policy affects output in the short run and medium run
c. output always equals the natural level
d. fiscal policy affects output in both the short run and long run

20. Those economists who believe that the economy adjusts slowly over time believe that:

a. there is a need for active stabilization policy
b. Y never returns to the natural level
c. tight rules should be imposed on monetary and fiscal policy
d. Y always equals the

SOLUTIONS

TO REVIEW PROBLEMS

AND

ANSWERS

TO MULTIPLE CHOICE

QUESTIONS

CHAPTER 1

REVIEW PROBLEMS

1. Macroeconomics is the study of aggregate economic variables (e.g. aggregate output, inflation, and the unemployment rate).

2. Microeconomics is the study of production and prices in specific markets.

3. This list could vary: inflation, employment, unemployment, output, interest rates, the budget deficit and money growth.

4. Actual economies are highly complex, consisting of many individuals, firms and markets. Because of this, it is difficult for economists to conduct controlled experiments.

5. Canada's macroeconomic performance of the Canadian economy between 1998-2000 has been exemplary. The only issue of concern has been low productivity relative to that in the US.

6. Between 1999-2003, the US economy has gone through difficult time with respect to growth unemployment and more recently the budget deficit.

7. Labour market rigidities (minimum wage, employment insurance benefits, worker protection) might have caused the high unemployment in the 1990s. More recently, deflation, recession, and low growth appear to be dominating the macroeconomic scene in the EU.

8. High unemployment, sluggish economic activity, deflation, and the structural problems within the economy.

MULTIPLE CHOICE QUESTIONS

1. B 2. C 3. D 4. A 5. B 6. B 7. C 8. E

CHAPTER 2

REVIEW PROBLEMS

1. a. $Y in 1997 is $9.10 (10) + $1.10 (10) + $6.00 (8) = $150.00.
$Y in 2002 = $11.50 (7) + $1.30 (13) + 6.50 (11) = $168.90.
b. Y in 1997 equals $Y in 1997 since 1997 is the base year: $150.
Y in 2002 is $9.10 (7) + $1.1 (13) + $6.00 (11) = $144.
c. The GDP deflator in 1997 = ($Y in 1997/Y in 1997) = $150/$150 = 1.
The GDP deflator in 2002 = ($Y in 2002/Y in 1997) = $168.9/$144 = 1.17.
d. The percentage change in Y is -4%. The percentage change in the GDP deflator is 17%.

2. Nominal GDP and real GDP in 1997 are the same since we use the same prices to calculate both figures. The prices in 1997 are the same prices used to obtain real GDP since 1992 is the base year.

3. a. The final product of steel is 0 since steel is not a final good. The final product of the lobster company is $200, and the final product of the car company is $1000. GDP = $200 + $1000 = $1200.
b. Value added for steel is $400. Value added for the lobster company is $200. Value added for the car company is $1000 - $400 = $600. GDP is $400 + $200 + $600 = $1200.
c. Total wages are $1000. Total profits are $200. GDP is (again!) $1200.
d. As discussed in the chapter, all three approaches to GDP yield the SAME value of total output.
e. Labour's share is 83%; profit's share is 17%.

4. Without more information, we can say nothing about inflation and real GDP. Nominal GDP can increase because of changes in the price level and/or changes in real output.

5. a. $Y in 1999 = 1.013 ($968,541) = $980,524. The GDP deflator in 1998 = ($914,973/$918,910) = 0.995.
b. To obtain real GDP we simply divide nominal GDP by the GDP deflator to obtain $855,103, $1,012,352.7 $1,027,512.7, $1,062,440 respectively for year 2000, 2001 and 2002.
c. Since the starting year in this exercise coincides with the base year and since prices have been continually rising since that year, nominal GDP figures should be greater than real GDP figures.
d. Nominal GDP can change because of changes in the price level as well as changes in physical output. If economists are concerned about economic growth, they should focus on real GDP that abstracts from inflation.

6. If the increase in the price level is greater (in a proportionate sense) than the reduction in real output, nominal GDP will increase.

7. The price of potatoes would not change since their quality is most likely the same. Cars now offer more services/characteristics (e.g. air bags). The increase in the price of cars would be reduced to reflect the fact that some of the increase in the price is due to improvements in the quality of cars. Personal computers also now offer greater characteristics (more memory, more features, .. etc.). Hedonic pricing would indicate that the price of computers actually fell.

8. a. Number unemployed = 10; number employed = 50; therefore, the labour force = 60. u = 10/60 = 16.7%. The participation rate = 60/100 = 60%.
b. The labour force drops to 55. u = 5/55 = 9.1%. The participation rate falls to 55/100 = 55%. Both rates fell. As fewer people search, the number of unemployed (and u) falls and the participation rate falls.
c. The number of employed = 52; the number of unemployed = 8; therefore, the labour force remains constant at 60. u falls to 8/60 = 13.3%. The participation rate does not change.
d. The size of the labour force would increase (to 70). The number of employed individuals would not change. The number of unemployed individuals would increase (to 20). The unemployment rate would increase to 28.6% and the participation rate would increase to 70%.

MULTIPLE CHOICE QUESTIONS

1. C 2. D 3. B 4. A 5. C 6. C 7. D 8. C 9. A 10. B 11. D 12. B 13. D 14. C 15. B 16. A 17. B 18. C 19. A

CHAPTER 3

REVIEW PROBLEMS

1. a. Y in 2000: 1001.8. Y in 2001: 1031.2. Rate of growth: 2.93%. The level of economic activity increased; that is, real aggregate output increased.
b. Rates of growth: C (2.56), I (.44%), G (3.75%), X (-3.80%), Q (-5.79%). Fastest: government spending. Slowest: the fastest negative growth belonged to imports (which fell by 5.79%)! Components shares in 2000: C (56.5%), I (18.2%), G (20.7%), X (45.1%), Q (40.4%). Components shares in 2001: C (56.2%), I (17.8%), G (21%), X (42.1%), Q (37%). X's and Q's share fell, while C's, I's share, and G's share remained virtually unchanged.
c. The trade surplus (X-Q) rose from 4.58% to 5.6%. Both X and Q decreased between the two years.

2. Call the alternative measure which excludes inventory investment Yalt. Yalt > Y when I_S is negative. When inventories fall, firms have sold goods that were produced in a previous period. Y adjusts C, I, G and X for any sales that come from inventory. Yalt < Y when I_S is positive. Here, firms have increased inventories during the period. These goods represent production. If we excluded them from the output numbers, we would obtain a measure that understates the "true" level of aggregate output. It is important to include I_S since some goods are produced and not sold in a year (I_S>), and in other cases some goods that are purchased were produced in a previous period ($I_S < 0$).

3. Call the alternative measure which excludes net exports (NX) Yalt. Yalt > Y when NX is negative (a trade deficit). Yalt does not take into account the fact that some goods are sold abroad (X) and some goods purchased by domestic residents (firms and governments) were produced abroad (Q). Yalt < Y when NX is positive. In this case, Yalt understates the level of output since it ignores the fact that the country is selling more goods to foreigners than it is importing. The correct measure of Y should adjust purchases by recognizing that some of C, I, and G are imports and that some goods produced at home are sold abroad.

4. a. 200. They draw down their savings accounts or borrow.
b. C = 800. C increases by 50 to 850. Disposable income increased by 100, and C increased by 50; the marginal propensity to consume (mpc) is .5.
c. S = -200 + .5Y_D. S = -200. This represents the dissaving that would occur to pay for the consumption that occurs when disposable income is 0. The marginal propensity to save is .5; it is 1 -mpc.

5. a. The vertical intercept is 400, autonomous consumption. The slope is .75, the mpc. C = 1600.
b. A reduction in the mpc will cause C to fall and the consumption function to become flatter. C falls to 1200.

6. a. The mpc is .5. The marginal propensity to save is 1 - .5 = .5.
b. Z = 1200 + .5(Y - 400) = 1000 + .5Y. Z is 1000 when Y is 0. This is the level of autonomous expenditures. If Y increases by 1, Z rises by .5. This is the mpc.
c. When Y is 1600, Z is 1800; when Y is 1800, Z is 1900; when Y is 2000, Z is 2000; when Y is 2200, Z is 2100; when Y is 2400, Z is 2200. Equilibrium occurs when Y is 2000 since Y = Z at that level of Y.
d. When Y is 1600, Z > Y. Firms set production equal to demand. Since demand exceeds Y, firms will increase Y over time. When Y is 2400, Y > Z. Production exceeds demand, and firms will cut back on production.

7. a. $Y = 1500 + .5(Y - 400) = 1300 + .5Y$. Solve for Y: $Y = 1300/.5 = 2600$.
b. Plug in the numbers and you get: $Y = 1400 + .5Y$; $Y = 2800$. Output increases by 200. The multiplier is 2 (every one dollar change in C causes a 2 dollar change in Y).
c. See graph.
d. As demand increases by 100, firms respond by increasing production. The higher production also represents higher income. As income rises, consumption rises again, causing firms to increases Y yet again. This is the multiplier process at work.

8. a. $Y = 1500 + .8(Y - 800) = 1500 - 320 + .8Y$; $Y = 1180/.8 = 5900$.
b. $Y = 1280 + .8Y$; $Y = 1280/.8 = 6400$. Y rises 500 given the increase in C of 100; the multiplier is 5.
c. The ZZ line became steeper, the slope is greater. A change in Y now has a greater effect on Z (via C).
d. The change in output and the multiplier both increased. Any change in Y now causes an even greater increase in C and a greater subsequent increase in Y.
e. ZZ becomes steeper (see ZZ').

9. a. OA is autonomous spending. OA will decrease when G, I or autonomous consumption decrease, or when T increases.
b. OY_1 is production, Y_1E is demand, Y_1F is production. The economy is not in equilibrium since production is greater than demand.
c. OY_2 is production, Y_2B is production, Y_2C is demand. No, the economy is not in equilibrium since demand is greater than production.
d. Equilibrium output occurs at the level of Y where $Y = Z$. This occurs at the point where ZZ crosses the 45 degree line.

10. a. The multiplier will be $(1/1-c_1)$: 1.7, 2, 2.5, 5, and 10. The multiplier increases as the mpc increases.
b. As the mpc increases, the ZZ line becomes steeper causing a higher level of equilibrium output.
c. How much should G increase to achieve this change in Y? The required change in G = 1000/(the multiplier). Plug in the numbers and you get: 588, 500, 400, 200 and 100.

11. a. Autonomous expenditures are greater in B, while the mpc is greater in A.
b. The level of autonomous expenditures in both countries will increase the SAME amount (100). Both curves will shift up by the exact same amount.
c. Output will increase more in A than in B, even though G increased by the same amount. Why? The multiplier is greater in A than in B.

12. a. $Y = 300 + .9(Y - 1000) + 200 + 2000 = 1600 + .9Y$; $Y = 16000$.
b. $C = 300 + .9(16000 - 1000) = 13890$.
c. $S = -300 + .1(Y - T)$. Plug in the numbers: $S = 1210$.
d. $Y = 1500 + .9Y$; $Y = 15000$. Y falls as individuals increase their desire to save. This increased desire to save reflects a reduction in C and a reduction in demand. The drop in demand causes a drop in Y.
e. Be careful here! $S = -200 + .1(15000 - 1000) = 1210$. When the new equilibrium is reached, S returns to its original level. This represents the paradox of thrift.

13. a. autonomous expenditures and Y both fall; the slope of ZZ and the multiplier do not change
b. autonomous expenditures and Y both increase; the slope of ZZ and the multiplier do not change
c. autonomous expenditures and Y both fall; the slope of ZZ and the multiplier do not change

d. autonomous expenditures do not change, Y increases, the slope of ZZ and the multiplier also increase.
e. autonomous expenditures do not change, Y decreases, the slope of ZZ and the multiplier also decrease.

MULTIPLE CHOICE QUESTIONS

1. D 2. D 3. A 4. B 5. D 6. A 7. C 8. D 9. C 10. D 11. C 12. B 13. D 14. E 15. C 16. C 17. C 18. D 19. A 20. C 21. C

CHAPTER 4

REVIEW PROBLEMS

1. a. Yes. Recall that wealth represents assets minus liabilities. An individual could have saved in earlier periods and accumulated a large quantity of wealth. Even though their income today could be low (or even 0), they could have a sizable quantity of wealth.
b. Yes. The answer is similar to a. If the individual saved in earlier periods, she will have accumulated assets. Even if saving is 0 today, the individual can still have wealth.
c. Yes. This can occur if one's liabilities exceed one's assets.

2. a. Flow variables: saving, investment, income
b. Stock variables; wealth, business inventories, the money supply and capital. Note: the <u>change</u> in business inventories is a flow variable.

3. As nominal income falls, transactions fall. As transactions fall, the individual will reduce her nominal money demand.

4. a. Nominal money demand increases by 10%, a reduction in bond demand (given wealth), and no change in the money supply.
b. Bond demand falls, and there is no change in money demand and money supply.
c. Nominal money demand increases, bond demand falls, and there is no change in the money supply.
d. Bond demand increases (via the actions of the central bank), the money supply increases, and there is no change in money demand.

5. a. Velocity = $Y/M. Therefore, 1980: 9.54; 1990: 7.6; 2000: 5.08. M1B velocity has steadily declined between 1980 and 2000.
b. Yes, they are over the entire period, as well as the period between 1980 and 2000. As i dropped, individuals, as expected, increased their money holdings for a given level of income. This caused the velocity to fall.
c. Changes in wealth should have no effect on money demand. There might be an indirect effect, however, through its effects on bond demand. As wealth increases, bond demand increases, causing bond prices to increase and i to fall.

6. a. See the graph included below. At i", individuals demand M" while the supply of money equals M; there is an excess supply of money. M represents the amount of money that actually exists.
b. i must fall to restore equilibrium. As i falls, the supply of money does NOT change. As i falls, however, the demand for money increases.
c. At i', money demand exceeds money supply. Individuals want to hold M' while only M exists.
d. i must increase to restore equilibrium. As I increases, money supply does not change while money demand falls.

7. a. See the graph below. The public holdings of the central bank is found at the intersection between the two curves, H_0.
b. The reduction in $Y will cause a reduction in demand for central bank money $H^{d'}$. i will fall to i'.
c. At i, demand is lower, therefore supply exceeds money.
d. i must fall.
e. As i falls, demand increases.
f. At i', the public now holds the same level of central bank money again, H_0. This is the same quantity that was held in part a.

8. a. See the graph. They hold H_0 at the initial interest rate.
b. This will cause the supply curve to shift to the left. i will rise.
c. The actual supply of high powered, H, has decreased.
d. i must increase to restore equilibrium (to reduce demand so that supply and demand are again equal).
e. As i increases, H^d falls.
f. They now hold less than H_0.

9. Use the following equation to answer these questions: i = ($200 - $P_B)/$P_B. Simply plug in the numbers.

a. 33.3%
b. 25%
c. 11.1%
d. 2.6%
e. As expected, i falls as the price of the bond increases.

10. Use the following formula to calculate the price of the bond: $P_B = $1000(1 + i). Simply plug in the numbers.

a. $952.38
b. $909.09
c. $869.75
d. The price of the bond falls.

11. a. The Bank of Canada's holding of bonds (assets) increases by $10 million.
b. The Bank of Canada's liabilities (currency) increase by the same amount.
c. Bond demand increases, bond supply does not change, and bond prices increase.
d. The interest rate will fall.
e. The money demand curve does NOT shift.
f. Central bank money increases by $10 million.
g. The money supply also increases by $10 million.

12. a. The Bank of Canada's holding of bonds (assets) decreases by $20 million.
b. The Bank of Canada's liabilities (currency) fall by the same amount.
c. Bond supply increases, bond demand does not change, and bond prices fall.
d. The interest rate will increase.
e. The money demand curve does NOT shift.
f. Central bank money falls by $20 million.
g. The money supply also decreases by $20 million.

13. When CU = 0, M = D, H = R, and the money multiplier is 1/θ. All numbers are in millions of dollars.
a. The monetary base, H, will equal 500.
b. Given the reserve ratio, every $1 of reserves can support $5 of deposits, so D = 2500 (5 x 500).
c. The money supply is given by M = CU + D = 0 + 2500 = 2500.
d. The money multiplier is 1/θ = 1/.2 = 5.

14. a. The monetary base increases by 50 to 550.
b. Since no currency is held, reserves also increase by 50 to 550.
c. The overnight rate falls.
d. The money supply will also increase by 250.

15. a. The monetary base decreases by 10.
b. The amount of reserves will fall by 10.
c. The overnight rate rises.
d. The money supply will also fall by 50.

16. a. Plugging in the numbers, we get: 10, 5, 3.33, 2.5, and 2.
b. It decreases.
c. We can illustrate this relation using a simple example. Suppose a bank has 100 additional reserves (from a new deposit of 100). When the reserve ratio is .1, the bank can increase loans by 90 (or increase bond holdings by 90); 10 must be held as reserves. If the reserve ratio were .5, the bank could only increase loans by 50 (or increase bond holdings by 50); it must hold 50 as reserves. The higher reserve ratio limits the extent to which banks can create money. Alternatively, when the ratio is .1, the 100 of new reserves can support 1000 of new deposits. When the ratio is 5, the 100 of new reserves can support "only" 200 of new deposits.

17. a. 50/500 = .10
b. c = CU/M = 250/750 = .33.
c. H = CU + R = 50 + 250 = 300.
d. M = D + CU = 250 + 500 = 750.
e. There are two ways to do this: (1) M/H = 750/300 = 2.5; (2) 1/[c + θ(1 − c)] = 2.5.
f.

Central Bank's Balance Sheet   Banks' Balance Sheet

Assets	Liabilities		Assets	Liabilities
Bond holdings 300	D 500 R 50		R 50 Bond holdings 450	D 500

18. All numbers in millions.
a. It should buy bonds. Given that the multiplier is 2.5, the Bank of Canada should buy $40 worth of bonds (100/2.5 = 40).
b. The increase in bond demand will increase the price of bonds.
c. It should sell bonds. It should sell $16 worth of bonds (-40/2.5 = -16).
d. The increase in supply will cause bond prices to fall.

19. The money multiplier is $1/[c + \theta(1 - c)]$.
a. Plugging in the numbers yields 3.57, 2.78, and 1.61.
b. It decreases.
c. See the answer to part c of #16.

20. a. Plugging in the numbers, we get: 5.27, 3.57, and 1.82.
b. It falls.
c. As c increases, a greater portion of the monetary base is held in the form of currency. CU is a "leakage" from the banking system. The more currency is held, banks cannot use this portion of H to create money. Hence, the money supply is smaller.

21. The Bank of Canada can influence the currency/money supply ratio by first influencing the demand for currency. This can be done by changing the cost of holding currency, i.e. interest rates.

22. Deposit insurance increases security of depositing money with banks in the eyes of the public. This decreases the currency/deposit ratio and hence increases the money multiplier.

MULTIPLE CHOICE QUESTIONS

1. C 2. A 3. D 4. D 5. C 6. A 7. B 8. C 9. B 10. B 11. A 12. A 13. D 14. B 15. C
16. B 17. C 18. C 19. C 20. A

CHAPTER 5

REVIEW PROBLEMS

1. a. Plugging in the numbers, we get: I = 600 when i = 5; I = 500 when i = 10; and I = 400 when i = 15. As expected, I falls when i increases.
b. Plugging in the numbers, we get: 650, 700 and 750. Again, as expected, I increases as Y increases.

2. a. Y = 180 + .7(Y - 400) + 100 - 18i + .1Y + 400. This yields: Y = 400 + .8Y - 18i. Subtract .8Y from both sides and then divide by .2. This gives us the following: Y = 2000 - 90i. This is the IS equation.
c. The lower i causes an increase in investment which causes an increase in demand and output. The higher output/income causes an increase in both consumption and saving.
d. Y = 2000 - 18(8) = 1280. WARNING: Y does not just increase by 100; there is a multiplier effect here. Replace G with 500 and we get: Y = 500 + .8Y - 18i. Solving for Y and letting i = 8 yields: Y = 2500 - 90(8) = 1780. The 100 increase in G causes Y to increase by 500. The multiplier must be 5.
e. An increase in G causes the IS curve to shift to the right by 500 (i.e., the size of the shift equals the increase in G times the multiplier).

3. a. A lower interest rate causes an increase in I and an increase in Y; this explains the slope of the IS curve and represents a movement along the IS curve. The IS curve does NOT shift as i falls.
b. The exact opposite of a. This will cause a movement along the IS curve (no shift).
c. This reduction in consumption will cause the IS curve to shift to the left; the equilibrium level of output is now lower (at each i) because of this drop in demand.
d. This will cause a reduction in consumption and a leftward shift in the IS curve.

4. a. 3 x $1 = $3. Her (daily) nominal money demand is $3.
b. 3 x $1.20 = $3.60. As the price of the good increases, the individual will increase her nominal money demand so that she can continue to purchase the same real quantity of goods and services (in this case, her favourite beverage).
c. To convert hr nominal money demand to real money demand, we simply divide her nominal money demand by the price deflator. Her initial real money demand was: $3/1 = $3. Her final real money demand is $3.60/1.2 = $3. Her real money demand did NOT change. She simply increase her nominal money demand proportionately as the price of the good increased.
d. As income increases, the demand for goods and, therefore, transactions increase. She probably will increase her consumption of her favourite beverage. To purchase these goods, she will increase her nominal money demand and, since P is assumed to be constant, real money demand.

5. a. The drop in Y will cause a drop in transactions and, therefore, a drop in money demand. Money demands falls to $M^{d'}$. At the initial interest rate, there is now an excess supply money. Individuals hold more money than they would like.
b. For the financial market to be in equilibrium, i must fall to restore equilibrium. The new equilibrium is given by point A'. See the graph.

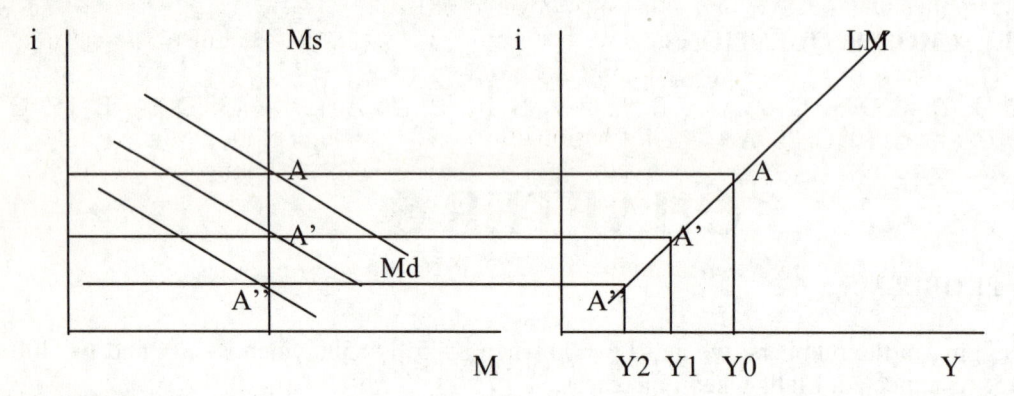

c. See the graph.
d. The combinations of i and Y which maintain equilibrium in the financial market is the LM curve.

6. a. See the graph. At the initial i, money demand exceeds money supply.

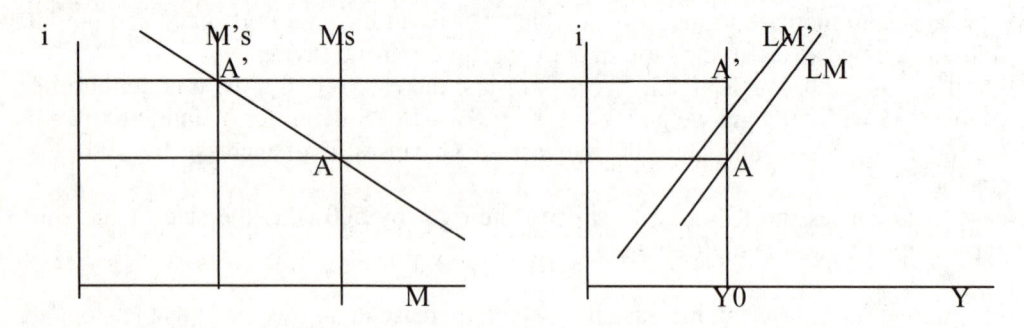

b. i must increase to i'. As i increases, money demand falls resulting in a new equilibrium at point A'.
c. The LM curve must shift up to reflect the higher interest rate which is required to maintain equilibrium in the financial market. The LM curve shifts up to LM'.

7. a. 5400 = 6Y - 120I. So, 120i = 6Y - 5400. Dividing by 120 yields: i = .05Y - 45. This is the LM relation.
b. Plugging in the numbers yields: 5%, 10% and 15%. Plotting the i - Y combinations should (?!) yield an upward sloping line. This is the LM curve.
c. i = .05(1400) - 45 = 25%. Return to the original equation included in a. Replace 5400 with 5000 and solve for i when Y = 1400. Plugging in the numbers yields: i = 28.33%. i increases by 3.33%.
d. The LM curve must shift up (by 3.33%) to reflect this higher interest rate. i must be higher at each level of Y to maintain equilibrium when the money supply falls.

8. a. The increased use of credit cards has caused a reduction in money demand. This causes the money demand curve to shift to the left. People can consolidate their payments each month; hence, they can hold/demand less money.
b. See the graph. The money demand curve shifts to Md'. At the original interest rate, money supply now exceeds money demand. i must fall to restore equilibrium (as i fall, money demand increases). The new equilibrium is at A'.
c. The interest rate must now be lower (at each Y) to maintain equilibrium in the financial market. This implies that the LM curve must shift down to LM'.
d. This is the exact opposite of the example we just examined. Money demand increases causing an increase in i. The LM curve would shift up in this case.

9. a. The IS curve will shift to the right; this has no effect on the position of the LM curve.
b. Y will increase as the demand for goods increases. As Y increases, money demand will increase causing the equilibrium interest rate to increase; i increases.
c. Both C and S increase because Y increases.
d. The effects on I are ambiguous. The higher Y will tend to increase I. The higher i, however, will tend to cause I to fall.

10. a. This has no effect on the IS curve. The LM curve will shift up.
b. The reduction in the money supply will cause i to increase. As i increases, I will fall. The reduction in I causes a reduction in demand, and firms respond by reducing output.
c. The lower Y causes both C and S to fall.
d. I unambiguously falls because Y is lower and i is higher; both of these events cause I to fall.

11. a. A fiscal expansion will cause the IS curve to shift to the right and cause Y and i to increase. The higher Y will cause I to increase. The higher i will cause I to fall. Without knowing the exact magnitudes of these effects, we do not know whether I will increase or decrease.
b. Yes. The output effects must dominate the interest effects.
c. Yes. The effects of the lower i on I must dominate the effects of the lower Y on I.

12. a. Y = C + I + G. Substitute in the equations for C and I and we have: Y = 180 + .7(Y - 400) + 100 - 18i + .1Y + 400. Collecting terms yields: Y = .8Y + 400 - 18i. Solve for Y: .2Y = 400 - 18i. Divide both sides by .2 and we get the IS equation: Y = 2000 = 90i.
b. 5400 = 6Y - 120i. Solving for i yields: 120i = 6Y - 5400. Dividing both sides by 120 yields the LM equation: i = .05Y - 45.
c. Y = 2000 - 90[.05Y - 45] = 2000 - 4.5Y + 4050. Adding 4.5Y to both sides yields: 5.5Y = 6050. Dividing by 5.5 gives us the overall equilibrium level of Y: Y = 6050/5.5 = 1100.
d. i = .05(1100) - 45 = 55 - 45 = 10 (10%).
e. C = 180 + .7(1100 - 400) = 670. I = 100 - 18(10) + .1(1100) = 30.
f. Be careful here. You must change G in the original equation included in a. Y = .8Y + 410 - 18i. So, .2Y = 410 - 18i. Y = 2050 - 90I
Calculation of Y: Y = 2050 - 90(.05Y - 45). Solving for Y, we get Y = 1109.1.

Calculation of i: i = .05(1109.1) - 45 = 55.46 - 45 = 10.46(10.46%).
Calculation of C: C = 180 + .7(1109.1 - 400) = 676.4.
Calculation of I: I = 100 - 18(10.46) + .1(1109.1) = 22.6 (I fell). The negative effects of the higher i must have offset the positive effects of the higher Y.
g. Return to the original LM equation and replace 5400 with 5600. 5600 = 6Y - 120i. Solving for i yields i = .05Y - 46.67. Substituting this into the original IS equation, we get: Y = 2000 - 90[.05Y - 46.67] = 2000 - 4.5Y + 4200.3. Solving for Y: Y = 1127.3.
Calculation of i: i = .05(1127.3) - 46.67 = 9.7(9.7%).
Calculation of C: C = 180 + .7(1127.3 - 400) = 689.1.
Calculation of I: I = 100 - 18(9.7) + .1(1127.3) = 38.1.
I increases as M increases for two reasons: (I) i is lower; and (2) Y is higher.

13. a. The IS curve shifts to the right.
b. To keep i at the initial level, the Bank of Canada must increase the money supply as money demand increases. This will shift the LM curve down; see the graph. The final equilibrium is at point A'.
c. C and S both increase because Y increase. I also increases because Y increases (there is no offsetting effect of higher i here).

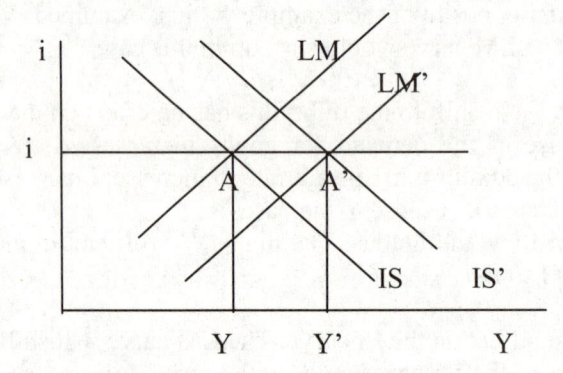

14. a. The IS curve shifts to the right.
b. To keep Y constant, the Bank of Canada will have to pursue contractionary monetary policy and reduce the money supply. This will cause the LM curve to shift up. The final equilibrium will be point A'. See the graph.

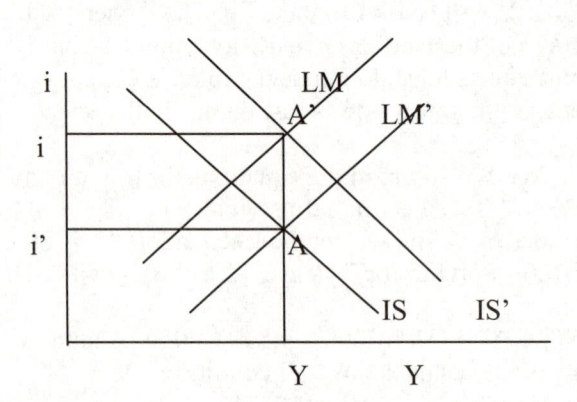

c. The effects on C and S are a bit subtle here. Y does not change. However, T is lower. So, at A', disposable income is higher; therefore, C and S are higher. In fact, it is the tax cut that stimulates C which causes the IS curve to shift to the right. Investment falls because of the higher i (there is no change in Y to offset this). In fact, the drop in I completely offsets the increase in C.

15. a. IS to right, move along the LM curve, Y increases, i increases, consumption increases, ambiguous effects on I (Y is higher, i is higher).
b. The exact opposite of a.
c. LM shifts down, move along the IS curve, i is lower, Y is higher, I is higher and so is C.

16. a. The IS curve shifts to the left. The increase in T causes a reduction in disposable income. This causes a reduction in C and a reduction in demand.
b. See the graph. IS shifts to the left. As Y falls, money demand falls causing i to fall. The economy moves from point A along the LM curve to point A'.

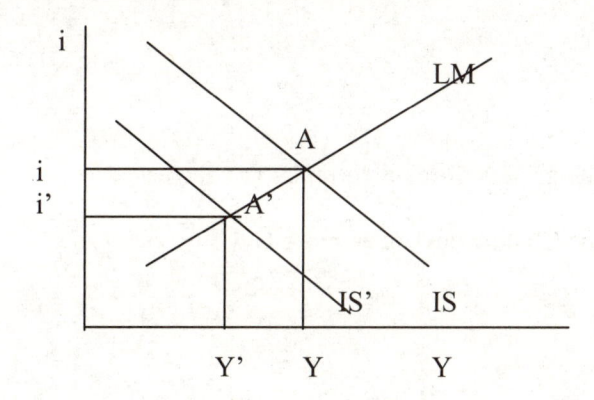

c. Consumption falls as Y falls. i falls as money demand falls. The effects on investment are ambiguous since i falls and Y falls.

17. a. The LM curve shifts down to LM'.
b. See the graph. The financial market is always assumed to be in equilibrium so the economy moves from point A to point B on the LM curve. The lower i causes an increase in I. As demand increases, Y increases. As Y increases, money demand increases causing I to increase, and the economy moves along the LM curve until it reaches the new overall equilibrium at point A'.
c. C increases during the adjustment as Y increases. The interest rate initially falls to the point indicated by point B. As money demand increases, however, we move from B to A' and the interest rate rises to its final (lower) level. I increases because of the increase in Y and drop in i.

18. a. A lower i would have no effect on demand. Therefore, equilibrium output in the goods market would be independent of the interest rate. In this case, the IS curve would be vertical.
b. An increase in M would cause a lower i. The lower i, however, would have no effect on I and on demand. Y would not increase.
c. Increases in G would cause Y to increase. In this case, Y would increase even further. The higher i would have no negative effect on I. None of the increase in G would be offset by an increase in i.

MULTIPLE CHOICE QUESTIONS

1. D 2. B 3. A 4. B 5. A 6. D 7. D 8. C 9. A 10. B 11. B 12. A 13. A 14. D 15. C 16. B 17. A 18. B 19. C

CHAPTER 6

REVIEW PROBLEMS

1. a. It now costs C$1.55 to buy one U.S.$. The price of foreign currency has, therefore, increased.
b. On Monday, C$1.50. On Friday, C$1.55.
c. The value of our dollar has decreased. By Friday, one C$ now buys fewer U.S.$ (or, it takes more C$ to buy one U.S.$).
d. Depreciated.
e. E increased.

2. This is the opposite of #1.
a. It now costs C$1.40 to buy one U.S.$. The price of foreign currency has decreased.
b. On Monday, 1.50. On Friday, 1.40.
c. The value of our dollar has increased. One C$ now buys even more U.S.$.
d. Appreciated.
e. E fell.

3. a. It declines.
b. The value of our dollar has increased.
c. An appreciation.

4. E = 11.50 one week ago. If the currency depreciates, E increases. If the currency appreciates, E falls.
a. E increased by 10% to 1.65.
b. E increased by 20% to 1.80.
c. E fell by 10% to 1.35.
d. E fell by 20% to 1.20.

5. Use the following expression to calculate C$ cost of a German good (in this case wine): EP*.
a. Plugging in the numbers, we get: $12, $15, $18, $21.
b. Increases.
c. The price of foreign goods increases, they become more expensive.
d. The price of foreign goods will decrease; they become less expensive.

6. Use the answers from #5 and the equation $\varepsilon = EP^*/P$ to calculate the ratio.
a. Plugging in the numbers, we get: 1.2, 1.5, 1.8, 2.1.
b. It increases.
c. It will decrease.

7. Use the definition of the real exchange rate included in the answer to #6 here.
a. Plugging in the numbers, we get:.89, .92, .96 and 1.03.
b. It increases. Given P and P*, as our dollar depreciates (E increases), it takes more C$ to obtain the same number of U.S.$. With P* constant, C$ cost of American goods will be relatively higher.
c. It increases.
d. Real depreciation (all else fixed).

8. a. The real exchange rate is 2001 is $.65(1.2)/1.5 = .52$. The real exchange rate in 2002 is $.60(1.25)/1.45 = .51$.
b. $(.51 - .52)/.52 = -1.9\%$. The real exchange rate decreased: a real appreciation.
c. The percentage change in E is -7.7%. A nominal appreciation.
d. The percentage change in P was 3.3%. The percentage change in P* was 4.2%.
e. The nominal appreciation was greater than the real appreciation. P increased less than P*.

9. E increases by 5% and P and P* are both increasing.
a. If the real exchange rate appreciates (falls) while the nominal exchange rate depreciates (increases), this implies that P must be increasing at a rate at least 5% above the rate of increase in P*. The more than 5% higher rate of inflation in the domestic economy more than offsets the nominal depreciation.
b. Not clear. There are two cases. Case 1: Foreign country is experiencing the higher rate of inflation. This would cause the real depreciation to be even greater. Case 2: Inflation in the domestic economy is greater than in the foreign country; however, the differential must be less than 5% to prevent a real appreciation.
c. The nominal depreciation of 5% would cause, all else fixed, a 5% real depreciation; however, both P and P* are increasing AND the real exchange rate does not change. What is happening? The rate of inflation in the domestic economy must be exactly 5% higher than in the foreign country to offset the increase in P* AND the nominal depreciation.

10. We know that one C$ will obtain 1/E U.S.$.
a. Plugging in the numbers, we get: .77, .71, .67 and .62.
b. It decreases. The price of foreign currency increases as E increases. This means that one C$ will be fewer U.S.$ as E increases.

11. Use the following expression to answer this: $(1 + i^*)(1/E)$. Plugging in the numbers, we get: $.77(1.1) = .85$; $.71(1.1) = .78$; $.67(1.1) = .74$; $.62(1.1) = .68$.

12. This is a pretty easy question. At the end of the year, you can convert the U.S.$ back into C$ one-for-one. So, you get: $.85, $.78, $.74, $.68.

13. Use the following equation: $i = i^* + (E^e - E)/E$.
a. $i = .10 + (1.55 - 1.50)/1.50 = 13.3\%$.
b. No, $i > i^*$. Despite this, the bonds offer the same expected return. When you buy American bonds, you will receive U.S.$ that will appreciate over the course of the year. The expected depreciation of our dollar (appreciation of U.S.$) offsets the interest rate differential.

14. Use the equation included in the answer to #13.
a. They expect an appreciation. The expected appreciation is 3.3% (E is expected to fall by 3.3%). i must be $.06 - .033 = 2.7\%$.
b. Appreciate. The expected appreciation is 2.67% (E will fall by 2.67%). i must be $.06 - 0.267 = 3.3\%$.
c. They expect a depreciation. The expected depreciation is 11.3%. i must be $.06 + .013 = 7.3\%$.

15. i is greater than i*. The expected depreciation of our dollar (appreciation of U.S.$) offsets the interest rate differential to satisfy the arbitrage relation.

16. i is less than i*. The expected appreciation of C$ (depreciation of U.S.$) offsets the interest rate differential to satisfy the arbitrage relation.

17. a. foreign b. foreign c. foreign d. foreign e. they both offer the same expected returns f. foreign g. foreign h. domestic I. domestic j. they both offer the same expected returns

MULTIPLE CHOICE QUESTIONS

1. D 2. B 3. D 4. B 5. D 6. B 7. A 8. D 9. E 10. B 11. D 12. B 13. C 14. D 15. A 16. D 17. C 18. D 19. B 20. D 21. B 22. F 23. E

CHAPTER 7

REVIEW PROBLEMS

1. a. domestic demands = C + I + G = 2000; demand for domestic goods = C + I + G + (X - Q) = 2050. The difference is 50. X - Q = 50. They are the same.
b. Domestic demand does not change: 2000; demand for domestic goods = 1950. The difference is -50. X - Q = -50. They are the same.
c. Domestic demand does not change: 2000; demand for domestic goods = 2000. There is no difference. X - Q = 0.
d. The demand for domestic goods is greater than domestic demand when X > Q (a trade surplus). The demand for domestic goods is less than domestic demand when X < Q (a trade deficit). The demand for domestic goods equals domestic demand when X = Q (a trade balance).

2. Simply plug in the numbers (given the equilibrium condition) and solve.
a. Y = Z = 500 + .5Y - 200 + 500 - 100 + .1Y + 500 + 100 + 100 - .1Y + 100 = 1500 + .5Y. Y = 1500/.5 = 3000.
b. C = 500 + .5(3000 - 400) = 1800
I = 500 - 100 + .1(3000) = 700
X = 200
Q = .1(3000) - 100 = 200
c. X = Q = 200; a trade balance
d. Jumping some steps, we have Y = 1600 + .5Y; Y = 1600/.5 = 3200. Y increases by 200 given the 100 increase in G; so, the multiplier is 2.
e. Q = .1(3200) - 100 = 220. X does not change; therefore, there is now a trade deficit of 20.

3. a. Again, jumping some steps, we have: Y = 1500 + .5Y + .1Y - .2Y. So, Y = 1500 + .4Y; Y = 1500/.6 = 2500.
b. C = 500 + .5(2500 - 400) = 1550
I = 500 - 100 + .1(2500) = 650
X = 200
Q = .2(2500) - 100 = 400
c. A trade deficit of 200 now exists (Q - X = 200).
d. Y = 1600 + .4Y; Y = 1600/.6 = 2666.7. The increase in G causes Y to increase by 166.7. Every one dollar increase in G causes Y to increase by 1.667.

4. The change in Y is smaller in #3 because the marginal propensity to import is higher. As the marginal propensity to import increases, a greater portion of any given change in Y will fall on foreign goods, thus reducing the effects on Y.

5. a. Demand for domestic goods rises; ZZ shifts up, Y increases, X does not change; Q increases; NX falls; we move along the NX line (no shift).
b. Demand for domestic goods falls; ZZ shifts down; Y falls, X does not change; Q falls; NX increases, we move along the NX line (no shift).
c. X falls so the demand for domestic goods falls; ZZ shifts down; Y falls; X falls; Q falls with Y; NX falls; NX line shifts down.
d. X increases and Q falls so the demand for domestic goods increases; ZZ shifts up; Y increases; NX increases; the NX line shifts up.
e. The increase in the real exchange rate causes an increase in NX. The increase in NX combined with the increase in G causes the demand for domestic goods to increase; ZZ shifts up; Y increases; the depreciation causes the NX line to shift up; X increases because of the depreciation; Q increases because of the depreciation (all else fixed); the final effects on NX are ambiguous since the depreciation and increase in G have competing effects.

6. a. A reduction in G or increase in T will cause Y to fall and Q will fall. This will reduce the trade deficit.
b. A depreciation will make domestic goods relatively cheaper. NX will increase and the trade deficit will shrink. Y will increase.
c. Expansionary fiscal policy. For example, if foreign governments were to increase G or cut T, Y* would increase. As Y* increases, X increases. Y will increase.

7. An increase in G by itself will increase Y. However, Q will increase causing a trade deficit. A depreciation by itself will raise output but cause a trade surplus. So, the government will have to combine a fiscal expansion with a depreciation.

8. Depreciate the currency. This stimulates Y AND increases NX. If the depreciation cannot be used to achieve the exact level of output with trade balance, a depreciation combined with a change in fiscal policy will be needed.

9. An appreciation will cause the drop in Y but it will reduce the trade surplus. A cut in G will cause Y to fall but it will cause the trade surplus to increase (as Q falls). So, a combination of the two will be needed: contractionary fiscal policy and appreciation of the currency.

10. a. See the graph. The economy moves from point A to B. Since the Marshall-Lerner condition does NOT hold, a depreciation will cause NX to fall, the NX line to shift down and the ZZ line to shift down (the size of the shifts in ZZ and NX will be the same). Such a policy will cause Y to fall to Y'. At the new level of output, the trade deficit has increased.
b. An appreciation would cause an increase in Y. Even though the quantities of X and Q would fall, the price effects would dominate causing an increase in NX and, therefore, an increase in ZZ and Y.

11. a. No. The price effect dominates the quantity effect.
b. No. The price effect dominates the quantity effect.
c. Yes. The quantity effect dominates the price effect.
d. Yes. The quantity effect dominates the price effect.
e. Yes. The quantity effect dominates the price effect.

MULTIPLE CHOICE QUESTIONS

1. A 2. B 3. E 4. D 5. C 6. C 7. A 8. B 9. A 10. A 11. B 12. E 13. C 14. B 15. A 16. C 17. B

CHAPTER 8

REVIEW PROBLEMS

1. Use the following interest parity condition to answer this: $i = i^* + (E^e - E)/E$.
a. Plug in the numbers and we get: $-.02 = (1.4 - E)/E$. Solve for E and we get: $E = 1.428$.
b. Repeat the analysis in a: $-.01 = (1.4 - E)/E$. Solve for E and we get: $E = 1.414$.
c. This should (?!) be easy. If $i = i^*$, we know that $E = E^e = 1.40$.
d. Repeat the analysis in a: $0.1 = (1.4 - E)/E$. Solve for E and we get: 1.272.
e. As i increases, E will fall (appreciate).
f. The lower E reflects an appreciation of our dollar; our dollar's value has increased. The U.S.$'s value, therefore, decreases as i increases.

2. a. Suppose $i < i^*$. Our dollar is expected to appreciate. If i increases, E falls today and, therefore, does not have to fall as far given E^e. Therefore, the size of the expected appreciation decreases as i increases.
b. It increases.

3. Assume interest parity initially holds. A reduction in i makes domestic bonds less attractive. The demand for the dollar decreases causing a reduction in the price of the dollar. The dollar, therefore, depreciates and E increases. Hence, the IP relation is downward sloping. The dollar is now expected to appreciate (which maintains the interest parity condition given E^e).

4. Easy question!
a. .9
b. 0
c. 6%
d. Nothing. Since $i = i^*$, the expected rate of depreciation must be zero to maintain the interest parity condition (equate the expected returns on the two bonds).

5. The IS curve becomes flatter since there are now two effects of a change in i on the demand for goods. In the closed economy, the lower i stimulated investment which had a multiplier effect on Y. In an open economy the lower i still causes an increase in investment. There is now a second, additional effect on the demand for goods. As i falls, the dollar will depreciate causing net exports to increase. Thus, a lower i causes I and NX to increase. The effects of the lower i on Y will, therefore, be greater in an open economy.

6. a. The economy moves from point A to B.

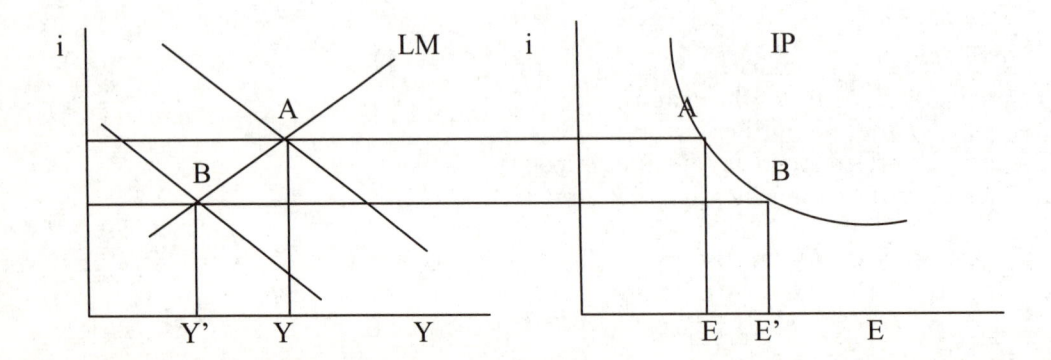

b. The IS curve shifts to IS' and I falls to i'. The decrease in G causes a reduction in Y. The lower i causes, via the IP relation, an increase in E; the currency depreciates.
c. C will fall as Y is lower. The effects on I are ambiguous since i is lower but Y is lower, too. NX increases for two reasons: (1) Y is lower causing Q to fall; and (2) the depreciation causes NX to increase.

7. A reduction in the budget deficit (caused by either a reduction in G or an increase in T) as shown in #6 will cause lower Y and, most importantly, an increase in E; NX will increase. Therefore, a reduction in the budget deficit will cause (if NX is initially negative) a reduction in the trade deficit. This is the twin deficit issue.

8. a. The decrease in M causes an increase in i and lower Y. C will fall as Y falls. I also falls since Y is lower and i is higher.
b. Y falls. E will decrease as i increases (the currency appreciates). E must fall to maintain the interest parity condition. In particular, as i increases, domestic bonds are more attractive which causes an increase in the demand for the dollar. This causes an increase in the price of the dollar (E falls).
c. Ambiguous! The lower Y (brought about by the effects of i on I) will cause Q to fall and NX to increase. The reduction in E (the appreciation) will cause NX to fall. These two effects compete with one another! This is an issue not discussed in the text.

9. a. See the graph. The economy moves from point A to B.

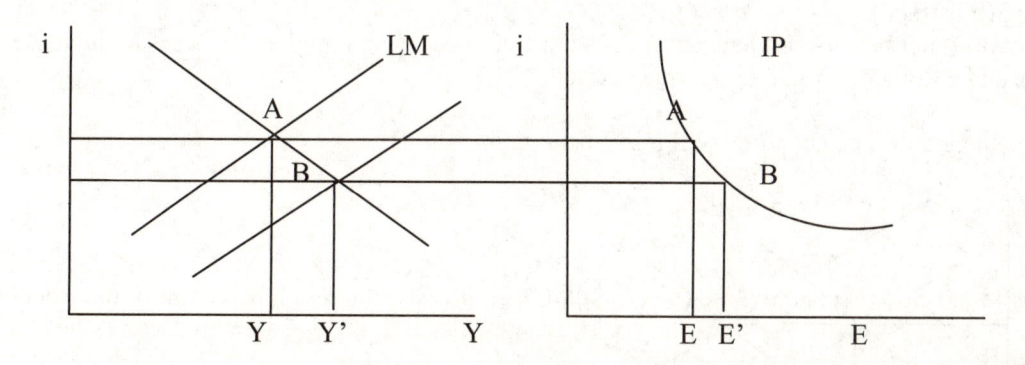

b. To maintain equilibrium in financial markets, i will fall. As i falls, the currency will depreciate (E increases). The depreciation causes NX to increase. As i falls, I increases. The increase in NX and I causes Y to increase to Y'.
c. Same old story! E will increase as investors move away from domestic bonds. This increase in E is also required to maintain the interest parity condition.
d. The increase in E, given E^e, will reduce the size of any expected depreciation. The drop in i causes a reduction in the expected return on the foreign bond.
e. C increases as Y increases. I increases as i falls and as Y increases.
f. Again, ambiguous. The higher Y caused by the increase in I will cause an increase in Q. The depreciation will cause an increase in NX.

10. a. See the graph. The economy will move from point A to B.

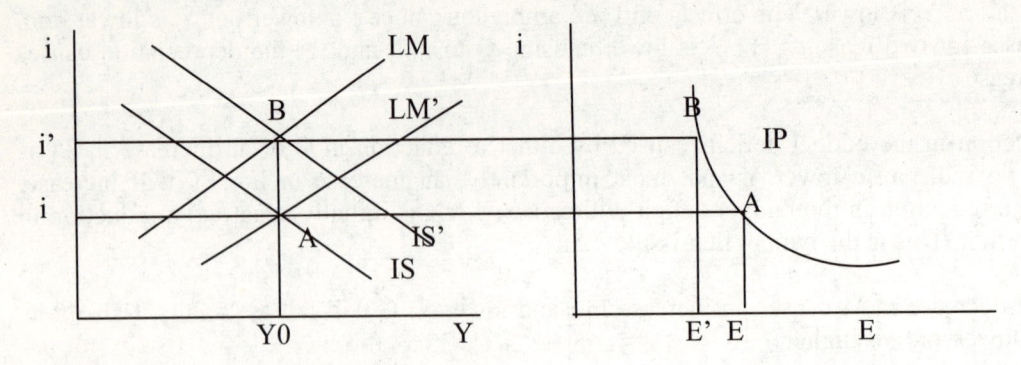

b. To keep Y at Y_0, the central bank will have to pursue contractionary monetary policy to completely offset the effect of the higher G on Y. The LM curve shifts left to LM'. All of the higher G must be offset (see below).
c. I increases and E falls (an appreciation).
d. G is higher. Both I (via I) and NX (via lower E) are lower. In fact, the increase in G is completely offset by the combined reduction in I and NX.

11. a. C is higher as Y rises. I is unambiguously higher since Y is higher. i cannot rise under fixed exchange rates so there is no offsetting effects of higher i under fixed exchange rates.
b. Nothing (it is fixed).
c. It gets worse, not because E changes (it does not), but because the higher Y causes an increase in imports and a further increase in the trade deficit.

12. a. See the graph. The economy will move from point A to B.

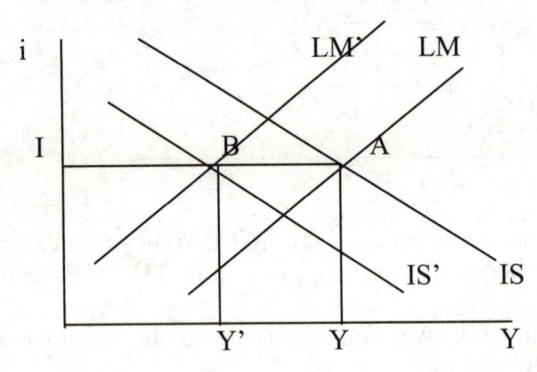

b. The central bank cannot allow i to fall below i* as the IS curve shifts to IS'. The central bank, therefore, reduces the money supply as money demand falls. This causes the LM curve to shift up to LM' leaving i fixed at its original level (which equals the fixed i*).
c. C falls as Y falls. I falls as Y falls.
d. The trade deficit will shrink (not because E has changed, it has not) because Q will fall as Y falls.

13. a. See the graph. Country A will move to point F (as described in #12). Country B will move to point G; i will be allowed to fall in a flexible exchange rate regime causing I and NX to increase and, therefore, partially offsetting the effects of the cut in G on Y.

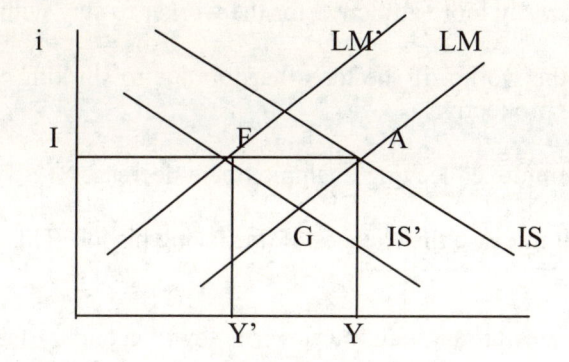

b. The choice matters! Under fixed exchange rates, Y changes more since i and E will not be allowed to change. Under flexible exchange rates, i and E will change partially offsetting the effects of G on A.

14. Under fixed exchange rates, i must equal i*. If i* increases, the central bank will have to pursue policy to raise i. The central bank will, therefore, have to reduce M, causing the LM curve to shift up and raise i. This will cause I to fall and Y to fall. The IS curve does not shift here.

15. Central banks stand by to keep the value of their currency against a key currency of their choice within a band (range). This system is different from a fixed exchange rate system in that unlike the latter central banks have a fair amount of flexibility.

16. Y and i will not change. The central bank sale of bonds will cause M to fall and i to increase above i*. The demand for the dollar will increase since domestic bonds are more attractive The central bank will be forced to "sell" dollars and buy foreign exchange to prevent the appreciation. It will continue to do this as long as i > i*. As it buys foreign currency with domestic currency, the monetary base and money supply increase causing I to fall back to i*. There will be no change in Y. The central bank has reduced its holdings of domestic bonds and increased its holding of foreign currency.

17. Yes. Investors will not respond as quickly to the higher i (described in #15). As long as i is above i*, investment will fall causing Y to fall.

MULTIPLE CHOICE QUESTIONS

1. C 2. B 3. B 4. A 5. B 6. B 7. A 8. A 9. A 10. D 11. B 12. A 13. A 14. A 15. C 16. D 17. A 18. B

CHAPTER 9

REVIEW PROBLEMS

1. a. 15 + 1 = 16
b. 25 - 16 = 9
c. 16/25 = .64 = 64%
d. 1/16 = .62 = 6.2%
e. 15/25 = .6 = 60%

2. a. An increase in the wage makes it financially more attractive for the worker to stay with the firm, thus reducing quits.
b. A higher wage makes it more costly to the worker if she loses her job due to shirking. The worker will, therefore, shirk less and be more productive.

3. It will increase if the proportion of the unemployed leaving unemployment decreases.

4. An increase in the unemployment rate will increase the chances of one losing his job. This will cause the separation rate to increase.

5. Primary labour market: jobs are good, wages are high and turnover is low. Secondary labour market: jobs are poor, wages are low and turnover is high.

6. a. The nominal wage is set based on the expected price level since workers care about the real wage. A reduction in the expected price level will cause a proportionate reduction in W.
b. This increases bargaining power. As bargaining power increases, W will increase.
c. The prospects of being unemployed are more distressing. Workers will be willing to accept lower wages, so W falls.

7. a. The markup increases. Given W, P will increase.
b. The markup decreases. Given W, P will fall.
c. Since firms set P as a markup over cost, a reduction in W will cause a reduction in P.

8. a. As u falls, workers have more bargaining power thus increasing W. Given P, W/P will increase.
b. See explanation in part a! A reduction in u causes an increase in W/P.
c. The prospects of being unemployed are more distressing. Workers will be willing to accept lower wages so W falls. Given P, W/P will fall. So, at each u, W/P is lower. This represents a shift down in the WS relation.
d. At a given u, the chances of getting a job are higher as structural change increases, u is less of a threat to workers so bargaining power increases. This increases W; given P, W/P increases. So, at each u, W/P is higher. This represents a shift up in the WS relation.
e. An increase in P will cause a proportionate increase in W. The WS relation does NOT shift.

9. a. Simply plug the numbers into the equation $W/P = 1/(1 + \mu)$: .91, .83, .77 and .71.
b. It increases.
c. As the markup increases, firms set P even further above W. Given W, this higher P causes the real wage to fall.

10. a. In perfectly competitive markets, firms set prices equal to costs. So, the markup is 0.
b. Since P = W when the markup is 0, W/P = 1.

11. a. As described above, this causes the WS relation to shift down. This will cause an increase in the natural unemployment rate and no change in W/P.
b. As described above, this will cause an increase in W/P in the WS relation. The WS relation shifts up causing the natural unemployment rate to increase with no change in W/P.
c. This will raise the markup of price over cost. Firms will raise P given W. This will reduce W/P in the PS relation. The PS relation shifts down causing an increase in the natural rate of unemployment and a reduction in the real wage.
d. This will cause the WS relation to shift up, the natural rate of unemployment to increase and no change in the real wage.

12. a. Since u_n increased, N and Y will both fall.
   b. Since u_n increased, N and Y will both fall.
   c. Since u_n increased, N and Y will both fall.
   d. Since u_n increased, N and Y will both fall.
   Note: if u_n falls, both N and Y will increase.

13. When WS curve is expressed in terms of N and not u it will be similar to the labour supply curve. This is so because an increase in employment will cause a reduction in the unemployment rate, and this will cause an increase in bargaining power, and hence in W. Given P, the rise in W will cause an increase in W/P.
PS when expressed in N will be similar to the labour demand curve. A horizontal PS in terms of N will change into a downward sloping PS curve when the productivity, A, is subject to diminishing returns.

MULTIPLE CHOICE QUESTIONS

1. B 2. B 3. D 4. A 5. A 6. E 7. B 8. B 9. B 10. A 11. B 12. C 13. D 14. D 15. A 16. B 17. A 18. B 19. C 20. C 21. A

CHAPTER 10

REVIEW PROBLEMS

1. a. The nominal wage will increase by 5%, and firms will increase P by 5%.
   b. The nominal wage will fall by 2% and firms will reduce P by 2%.
   c. Firms will increase the markup over cost. Given W, this indicates that P will increase.
   d. Firms will reduce the markup over cost. Given W, this indicates that P will fall.
   e. An increase in Y corresponds to an increase in employment and reduction in u. As u falls, bargaining power increases causing W to increase. As W increases, firms increase P.
   f. A reduction in Y corresponds to a reduction in employment and increase in u. As u increases, bargaining power falls causing W to fall. As W falls, firms reduce P.

2. An increase in Y corresponds to an increase in employment and reduction in u. As u falls, bargaining power increases causing W to increase. As W increases, firms increase P. Therefore, an increase in Y corresponds to an increase in P. The AS curve is upward sloping.

3. The lower P has no effect on M. As P falls, however, M/P increases causing the LM curve to shift down. As the LM curve shifts down, i falls. The reduction in i causes an increase in I and an increase in Y. We move from point A to point B.

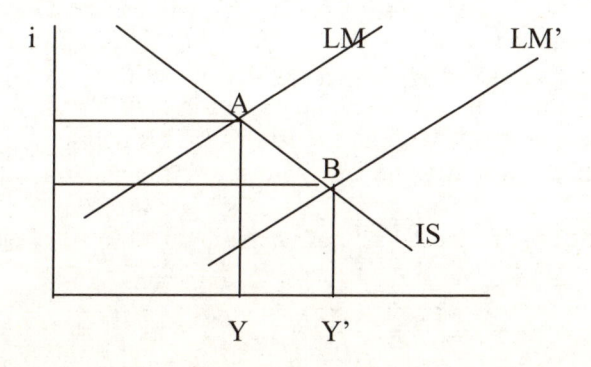

4. A reduction in P causes an increase in M/P. The increase in M/P causes the LM curve to shift down. This shift in the LM curve causes i to fall. As i falls, I increases and Y increases (we move along the IS curve). Therefore, a reduction in P causes an increase in Y in the goods market; the AD curve is downward sloping.

5. Note: if the curve is not listed, it does not shift.
a. IS to right and AD to right
b. IS to left and AD to left
c. LM down and AD to right
d. LM up and AD to left
e. IS to right and AD to right
f. IS to left and AD to left
g. IS to left and AD to left
h. IS to right and AD to right
i. LM up and the AD curve does NOT shift (move along it)
j. LM down and the AD curve does NOT shift (move along it)

6. a. u is below u_n, N above N_n and P above P^e.
b. The expected price level will increase.
c. The nominal wage will increase (because of b)
d. The AS curve will shift up

7. a. u is above u_n, N below N_n and P below P^e.
b. The expected price level will fall.
c. The nominal wage will fall (because of b)
d. The AS curve will shift down

8. a. As the AS curve shifts up, the price level will increase. The higher P has no effect on M. M/P will fall. As M/P falls, i increases causing I to fall. As I falls, Y falls. This describes the movement along the AD curve.
b. As the AS curve shifts down, the price level will fall. The lower P has no effect on M. M/P will rise. As M/P rises, i falls causing I to increase. As I increases, Y increases. This describes the movement along the AD curve.

9. a. The economy goes from A to B to C and, after several more adjustments, to the final equilibrium, D.

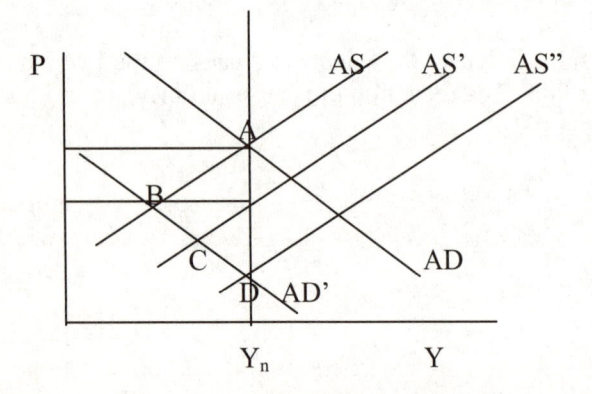

b. The initial effects are: (1) P falls; (2) M/P falls (M falls more than P initially); (3) I increases; (4) I falls; and (5) Y falls.

c. Initially, u increases above u_n and Y falls below Y_n. During the adjustment, u and Y return to their natural levels. In the medium run, u and Y equal their natural levels.
d. The AS curve shifts down as the expected price level falls.
e. P falls; M/P increases; i falls; I increases; I increases; and Y increases.
f. P falls proportionately so that M/P does not change in the medium run. i, I and Y return to their initial levels.
g. Yes. P will equal P^e in the medium run.

10. a. 6%.
b. No.
c. The nominal wage will fall by 6% leaving the real wage unchanged in the medium run.

11. a. The economy goes from A to B to C and, after several more adjustments, to the final equilibrium, D.

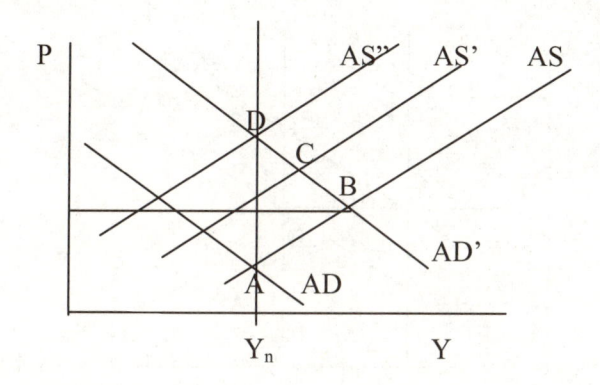

b. P is higher; M/P falls; i increases; effects on I are ambiguous (Y is higher and i is higher); and Y increases.
c. Short-run: u is below u_n, Y is above Y_n. Dynamic adjustment: u returns to u_n, Y returns to Y_n. Medium run: u and Y return to their natural levels.
d. AS shifts up because the expected price level increases.
e. P increases; M/P falls; i increases; I now falls; Y falls.
f. P is higher; M/P is permanently lower; i is permanently higher; I is permanently lower; and Y returns to original. NOTE: the change in G equals the size of the reduction in I.
g. Yes. P will equal P^e in the medium run.

12. Yes. i was higher and I was lower. The IS curve has shifted to the right while the LM curve has shifted up. All of the increase in G is completely offset by the reduction in I.

13. a. The higher price level causes the M/P to fall and the LM curve to shift up. As the interest rate increases output falls. The graph should include an upward shift in the LM curve with no shift in the IS curve.
b. C falls because Y is lower. I falls because i is higher AND because Y is lower.

14. The drop in the price of oil will cause a reduction in the markup over cost. This will cause the PS relation to shift up to PS'; the economy moves from point A to point B. As this happens, the real wage will increase and u will fall.

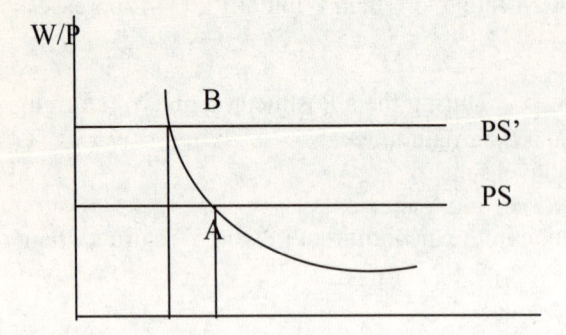

[Graph: W/P vertical axis, with curve from B down to A, horizontal lines PS' (upper) and PS (lower)]

15. The higher price of oil causes a reduction in the natural level of output. This causes the AS curve to shift up (the horizontal distance between AS and AS' is the drop in the natural level of output to Y_n'). The final equilibrium occurs at point D. In the short run: P increases; Y falls, i increases; I fall (i is higher and Y is lower); the real wage is lower; and u is higher. In the medium run: P is higher, Y is lower, i is higher; I is lower; W/P is lower; and u is higher.

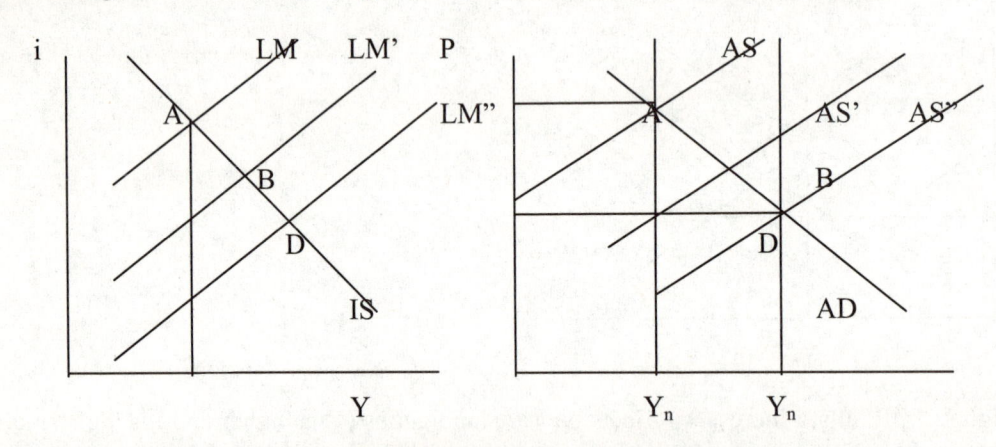

[Two graphs: left is IS-LM diagram with curves LM, LM', LM" and IS, showing points A, B, D; right is AS-AD diagram with AS, AS', AS" and AD, showing points A, B, D with Y_n and Y_n' on horizontal axis]

16. The reduction in unemployment benefits represents a reduction in z. The WS relation shifts down causing a reduction in u_n. The real wage will not change here because the PS relation does not shift. The effects on the IS-LM and AS-AD graphs are the exact opposite of that in #15. Y increases, P falls, I falls, I increases and u falls. Note: the IS and AD curves do not shift here.

MULTIPLE CHOICE QUESTIONS

1. D 2. C 3. B 4. C 5. B 6. C 7. D 8. B 9. D 10. A 11. B 12. D 13. E 14. B 15. B 16. C 17. D 18. E 19. A

CHAPTER 11

REVIEW PROBLEMS

1. a. A reduction in expected inflation will cause a reduction in inflation. Why? As expected inflation falls, wage growth falls. Since firms base price increases as a markup over costs, if wage growth declines, the increase in prices (inflation) will decline.

b. A reduction in the markup over costs will cause firms to reduce the size of any increase in prices. This will cause inflation to fall.
c. Any factor which reduces wages will, given the markup, allow firms to decrease the size of any price increase. This will reduce the inflation rate.

2. a. Any policy which reduces u will increase the bargaining power of workers and cause wages to increase. The increase in wages will cause a higher rate of inflation.
b. u must increase. As u increases, bargaining power falls and wages fall. As wages fall, inflation will fall.

3. a. Plug in the numbers and you get: (in %) 4, 6, 8, 10.
b. Expected inflation is higher, because individuals expect a greater portion of last period's inflation to persist.

4. Note: actual and expected inflation must be equal for u to be equal to the natural rate.
a. $u_n = .10/2 = .05$.
b. $u_n = .10/2 = .05$.
c. How expectations are formed will not affect the natural rate of unemployment.

5. a. Simply plug in the numbers: 7%.
b. 3%. Inflation falls by 4%. As unemployment increases, wage growth declines causing inflation to decline.
c. Nothing. Expected inflation in t is based on last period's inflation rate.

6. The following equation is used to calculate inflation in period t: $\pi_t = \pi_{t-1} - 1.5(u_t - u_n)$.
a. Plug in the numbers and we get .025 = 2.5% inflation. Inflation in t is less than inflation in t-1 (4%). You should know this by simply comparing unemployment in t with the natural rate of unemployment.
b. Plugging in the numbers yields: 1%, -0.5% and -2%.
c. Each 1% increase in unemployment causes the inflation rate to fall by 1.5%.
d. As u falls, the inflation rate is falling.

7. a. Using the equation included in the answer to #6, we obtain a 5.5% inflation rate. It is greater than the inflation rate in the previous period. This should not be surprising since u this period is below the natural rate.
b. We get (in %): 7, 8.5 and 10.
c. Each 1% drop in u causes the inflation rate to increase by 1.5%.
d. As u falls, the inflation rate increases.

8. This should be an easy question!
a. Since u is at the natural rate, we know that the inflation rate will neither increase or decrease. So, inflation in t will be the same as it was in t-1 which was 4%.
b. If inflation in t-1 was 3%, it will be 3% in period t. If inflation in t-1 was 6%, it will be 6% in period t.
c. When u is at the natural rate, inflation will not change; consequently, inflation in t will equal inflation in t-1.

9. a. If inflation is rising, u must be below the natural rate. When u is below the natural rate, there is pressure for wages to increase. As wages increase, inflation will increase above expected.
b. If inflation is falling, u must be above the natural rate. When u is above the natural rate, there is pressure for wages to decrease. As wages decrease, inflation will decrease below expected.
c. When inflation is constant, we know that u is at the natural rate. The labour market is in equilibrium.

10. a. Without information about the natural rates of unemployment in the two countries, we can say nothing about what will happen to the inflation rate in the two countries. The extent to which the inflation rate will change depends on a comparison of u with the natural rate.
b. If the inflation rate in A is falling, this implies that u is above the natural rate in A.
c. If the inflation rate in B is rising, this implies that u is below the natural rate in B.

11. If u is kept below the natural rate, inflation will increase over time.
b. If u is kept above the natural rate, inflation will fall over time.

12. A given reduction in the unemployment rate will now have a smaller effect on inflation in that period. When u falls below the natural rate, inflation falls. If some contracts are indexed, wages will fall within the period in response to the drop in inflation. As wages fall, firms reduce prices even further. If there are fewer contracts that are indexed, the indexation-induced reduction in inflation will be that much smaller. The drop in inflation will be smaller.

13. The unemployment rate for skilled workers is relatively lower than for other workers; the wage is relatively higher causing lower separation rates for skilled workers. As the proportion of skilled workers increases, the natural rate of unemployment will fall.

MULTIPLE CHOICE QUESTIONS

1. D 2. C 3. B 4. C 5. B 6. D 7. C 8. C 9. C 10. A 11. C 12. B 13. B 14. B 15. A 16. B 17. A 18. C

CHAPTER 12

REVIEW PROBLEMS

1. a. Output growth must be (in %): 2, 3, 4, and 5.
b. The normal growth rate must increase. As the labour force grows more quickly, employment will rise at a faster rate. To keep u constant, output will have to grow at a faster rate too.
c. Output growth must be (in %): 1, 2, 3, and 4.
d. If the labour force is more productive, output growth will have to increase to keep u constant.

2. a. (all in %): -.4, -.8, and -1.2. Each 1% increase in output growth causes u to fall by .4 percentage points.
b. (all in %): +.4, +.8, and +1.2. Each 1% decrease in output growth causes u to increase by .4 percentage points.
c. Unemployment does not change. Output growth must be 3% to keep u constant.

3. As output growth falls, there are two reasons why u will increase by less than 1%. First, firms will hoard labour (work them less intensively), rather than lay them off). Second, the prospects for employment are less favourable. Consequently, some workers leave the labour force. The 1% drop in output growth will cause u to increase by less than 1%.

4. Yes. A given deviation of output growth from the normal rate will now have a greater effect on the change in u.

5. a. (all in %) 4, 2, 0, and -2. The growth rate falls.
b. (all in %) 0, 2, and 4. Output growth increases.

6. a. Output growth will be 2% and u will equal 6%. In the medium run, we know that u must be constant. For u to be constant, output growth must equal the normal rate. We also know that inflation must be constant. If inflation is constant, we know that u must be at the natural level.
b. In the medium run, the rate of inflation and the adjusted money growth will be the same: 5% = 7% - 2%.

7. a. Money growth is neutral in the medium run; it will have no effect on these two variables.
b. In the medium run, the rate of inflation and the adjusted money growth will be the same: 1% = 3% - 2%.

8. Again, output growth and unemployment will not be affected by this in the medium run. Inflation will increase by 3% in the long run.

9. To calculate this, simply multiply 2 by the number of years: 2, 4, 6, 9, and 10. The number of point-years of excess unemployment increases the longer u remains above the natural level.

10. The number of point-years of excess u will be given by $u - u_n = 8/\alpha$. Plug in the numbers and we get: 5.3, 5.7, 7, and 8.
b. They increase. α tells us how sensitive inflation is to change in u. As this parameter decreases in size, we will need a greater change in u to decrease inflation by 8%.

11. a. Using the equation in the answer to #10 (after replacing 8 with 9), we get: 7.8.
b. The central bank has no control over this. This is determined by the parameter α.
c. Yes: (1) u could be 7.8% above the natural level for just one year; (2) u could be 3.9% above the natural level for two years; and (3) u could be 2.6% above the natural level for three years. There are many other combinations.

12. a. $-2 = =.5(g_{yt} - 2)$. Solving for the growth rate, we get 6%.
b. $-3 = =.5(g_{yt} - 2)$. Solving for the growth rate, we get 8%.

13. a. The sacrifice ratio is the point-years of excess unemployment needed to reduce inflation by 1%. The sacrifice ratio is equal to $1/\alpha$.
b. .67, .77, .87, 1, and 1.1
c. It increases. α tells us how sensitive inflation is to change in u. As this parameter decreases in size, we will need a greater change in u to decrease inflation by 1%.

14. a. $-8 = -1(u_t - 8)$. Solving for unemployment, we get 16%; that is, u must be 8% above the level.
b. $8 = .5(g_{yt} - 3)$. Solving for g_{yt}, we get -13%.

15. Note: all numbers are in percentage terms.
a.

Year	0	1	2	3	4	5	6	7	8
Inflation	18	15	12	9	6	3	3	3	3
Unemployment	6	9	9	9	9	9	6	6	6
Output growth	3	-3	3	3	3	3	9	3	3
Money growth	21	12	15	12	9	6	12	6	6

Note: Money growth in the above table refers to nominal money growth.

b. First, we determine the path of inflation. Once this is specified, we determine from the Phillips curve, what u must be each year to reduce inflation by 3% each year; u must be 4% above the natural level. Once inflation is at the desired level, u can return to the natural level. Once the path of u is determined, we can determine (from Okun's law) what output growth must be each year. First, output growth must fall to cause the increase in u. Once u remains constant at 9%, output growth returns to normal. To reduce u in year 6, output growth must increase. And finally, output growth settles at the normal rate in years 7 and on. The required path of money growth is obtained by adding inflation and output growth for each year. Money growth first must fall to cause a reduction in output growth and increase in u. In year 2, money growth must increase to get output growth back to normal. Money growth then follows the path of inflation to keep output growth constant. Money growth increases in year 6 to push u back to the natural level (via its effects on output growth).

16. Yes!!! By announcing such a policy, expectations can adjust. Individuals will expect lower inflation. Nominal wages will fall as inflation falls. If actual and expected inflation both fall at t same time, there can be a disinflation without any increase in u.

17. The sacrifice ratios for these three years are not consistent with the traditional approach. The sacrifice ratio for the traditional approach is 1; all three in the table exceed 1. The sacrifice ratios for these three years are not consistent with the Lucas critique. The sacrifice ratio for the Lucas critique is zero; all three in the table exceed 1 and, therefore (!), are greater than 0.

MULTIPLE CHOICE QUESTIONS

1. C 2. A 3. B 4. E 5. C 6. A 7. D 8. B 9. D 10. C 11. D 12. A 13. A 14. B 15. A 16. D 17. A 18. D 19. B

CHAPTER 13

REVIEW PROBLEMS

1. a. A reduction in P causes the real exchange rate to increase. This real depreciation will make domestic goods more attractive so NX increases. The demand for goods will increase causing output to increase as well.
   b. A lower P causes only a movement along the Ad curve (the curve DOES not shift).

2. An increase in E^e will cause E and hence ε to rise (real depreciation), which in turn will result in an increase in NX and hence a shift in the AD curve to the right. This increases Y. The impact of an increase in i* is the same as an increase in E^e.

3. Output is to remain at Y_n in the medium run and the actual prices are to equal prices. When inflation rate is equal to zero, the AD curve and the AS curve remain stationary in their position. The nominal and hence the exchange rate remain unchanged. When inflation rate is positive, the AD curve will shift up by the rate of inflation and since expected prices are to equal actual prices, the AS curve will also shift up by the same rate leaving Y at Y_n. The nominal interest rate and the nominal

exchange rate will also rise by the same percentage as the rate of inflation leaving the real interest rate and the real exchange rate unchanged.

4. In the medium run expected inflation and actual inflation rate are equal and $Y = Y_n$. Nominal exchange rate rises at the rate of 10% per year. Therefore, the real rate of exchange and hence NX and Y remain unchanged.

5. An increase in P, will cause a real exchange rate appreciation. This will reduce NX, AD and hence Y. Therefore, P and Y are inversely related.

6. a. A revaluation causes $\overline{E}$ to fall and the real exchange rate to fall. This reduction in the real exchange rate will cause NX to fall.
b. A revaluation causes the AD curve to shift to the left as the demand for goods falls.

7. a. A 5% devaluation will have no long-run effect on output. The price level will increase by 5%, thus completely offsetting the effects of the devaluation on the real exchange rate.
b. There are no long-run effects on NX. Output has not changed and the real exchange rate returns to its original level.
c. Devaluations have no effect on real variables in the long run. They will affect only the price level, leaving the real exchange rate, output, employment, NX etc. unchanged. It is for this reason that devaluations are said to be neutral.

8. See the graph.

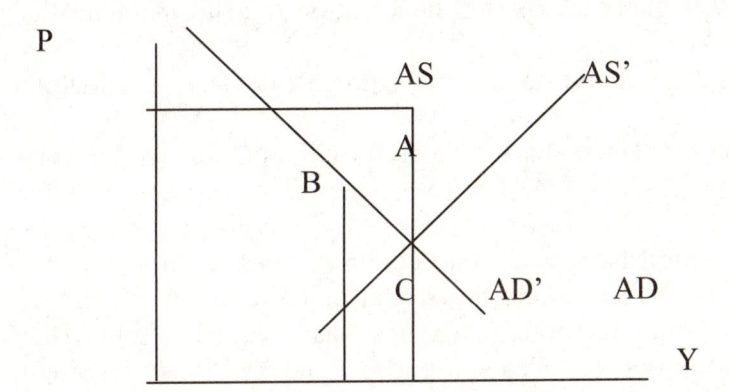

The revaluation will cause the real exchange rate to fall in the short run. This will cause NX and AD to fall; the economy will move to point B. P will fall in the short run, but not enough to prevent the real exchange rate from falling. With Y below the natural level, the AS curve will shift down over time. As this occurs, P falls causing the real exchange rate to increase. Eventually, the economy returns to the natural level at point C. All of the effects of the revaluation have been offset by the lower P. Net exports and Y will return to their original levels.

9. This will increase AD and cause P and Y to increase. As P increases, the real exchange rate falls (i.e., a real appreciation). NX falls in the short run because Y is higher and the real exchange rate has fallen. With Y above Y_n, the AS curve will shift up causing P to rise over time. P will increase and the AS curve will shift up until Y returns to the natural level. At the final equilibrium, Y equals Y_n and G is higher. This increase in G has caused a one-for-one reduction in NX. Why? The permanently higher P causes a real appreciation which causes the reduction in NX.

10. a. P will rise over time as the AS curve shifts up. As P increases, the real exchange rate falls causing NX to fall. As NX falls, Y will also fall.
b. The government would have to reduce AD. To reduce AD (to bring Y back to Y_n), the government would have to revalue the domestic currency. This reduction in $\overline{E}$ would cause a drop in AD and bring Y back to the natural level.

11. a. If you examine this graphically, your graph should be identical to the one included in the answer to #9. In the short-run, Y and P fall. As P falls, the real exchange rate increases causing a real depreciation. As the AS curve shifts down over time, P continues to fall. As P falls, the real exchange rate continues to increase. In the long run, Y returns to the natural level and P is lower. All of the drop in G is completely offset by a real depreciation: NX increases.
b. The lower G permanently reduces the trade deficit through its effects on the real exchange rate.
c. The government should devalue the currency. This will keep AD constant and prevent the drop in Y.

12. a. i must rise to 10% to offset the 5% expected devaluation (and to maintain the interest parity condition).
b. The increase in i will cause a drop in investment. As aggregate demand falls, output will fall.
c. The government must either convince markets that it will not devalue (a very difficult task) or simply devalue.

13. a. The government and the central bank can try to convince markets they have no intention of devaluing.
b. The central bank can increase the interest rate, but by less than needed to satisfy the interest parity equation. This will not however capital outflow and will likely require a foreign exchange intervention.
c. Alternatively the central bank can increase the interest rate enough to satisfy the interest parity equation or to validate the market expectations and devalue.

14. a. The expected devaluation equals .5(0) + .5(10%) = 5%. To maintain interest parity, the monthly interest rate must increase by 5%. The annual rate is 12 x 5% = 60%.
b. The expected devaluation equals .5(0) + .5(20%) = 10%. To maintain interest parity, the monthly interest rate must increase by 10%. The annual rate is 12 x 10% = 120%. It gets larger because the expected devaluation is now greater.

c. The expected devaluation equals .25(0) + .75(10%) = 7.5%. To maintain interest parity, the monthly interest rate must increase by 7.5%. The annual rate is 12 x 7.5% = 90%. It gets larger because the expected devaluation is now greater.
d. It falls because investment falls.

15. a. It decreases. The expected devaluation, given the equal i and i*, causes the expected return on foreign bonds to increase.
b. It must buy its currency to prevent the depreciation as investors sell dollars to buy foreign bonds. It can do this only as long as it has foreign exchange reserves (they will be lost quickly with perfect capital mobility).

16. The higher interest rate depresses aggregate demand and causes Y to fall.

MULTIPLE CHOICE QUESTIONS

1. C 2. D 3. A 4. D 5. A 6. A 7. D 8. B 9. D 10. D 11. E 12. B 13. D 14. C 15. B 16. D 17. B

CHAPTER 14

REVIEW PROBLEMS

1. a. Plug the numbers into the following equation $1000(1 + i)^{40}$ $2388, $1963, $1611 and $1322.
b. The dollar amount drops as i falls.

2. a. $16,362(1 + .017)^{40} = $32,112$.
b. $16,362 (1 + .027)^{40} = $47,496$.
c. The increase in the standard of living drops as the rate of growth declines.

3. The three conclusions are: (1) growth has been strong (i.e., there have been significant increases in the standard of living); (2) growth has slowed since the mid-1970s; and (3) the levels of output per capita have converged over time.

4. The evidence suggests there is a negative relation between the initial level of Y/N and the rate of growth in Y/N. This indicates, all else fixed, that the country with the highest level of Y/N in 1992 (the United States) will experience the slowest growth rate in Y/N while the country with the lowest level of Y/N in 1992 (Italy) will experience the fastest growth rate.

5. a. $14,379(1.03)^{20} = $25,970$.
b. The difference is $8025 - a non-trivial amount!

6. a. $2(4000) + $4(8000) = $40,000
b. (2 pesos times 2000) + (20 pesos times 1000) = 24,000 pesos.
c. (24,000 pesos) times .10 = $2400. Relative consumption is 2400/40000 = .06 (6%).
d. $2(2000) + $4(1000) = $8000. Relative consumption using the purchasing power parity method is 8000/40000 = .20 (20%).
e. The method used can have a significant effect on a comparison of relative consumption and relative standards of living. Simply compare the 6% and 20% figures.

7. a. 141
b. 282. N, K and Y all increase by 100%.
c. 155.6. N, K and Y all increase by 10%.
d. Yes. If you double the inputs, Y also doubles.
e. Easy answer. 2.7%. Why? Constant returns to scale.

8. a. $Y/N = (K^{1/2})(N^{1/2})/N = (K/N)^{1/2}$. Y/N is determined by the level of K/N.
b. $Y/N = (200/100)^{1/2} = 1.41$. K/N = 2.
c. 1.41, 1.73 and 2. Y/N increases at a decreasing rate which is consistent with decreasing returns to capital.
d. Complete the diagram.

9. a. Y/N increases over time in this country.
b. An increase in K/N will cause the curve to shift up. A higher K/N will yield a higher level of Y/N at each point in time.
c. A decrease in K/N will cause the curve to shift down. A lower K/N will yield a lower level of Y/N at each point in time.
d. The slope represents the annual rate of growth in output per worker. It represents the rate of technological progress.
e. The slope would increase if the rate of technological progress increased.
f. Since growth did not occur during this period, the line would be horizontal.

10. a. Country B
b. Country A
c. Country A
d. Country A

MULTIPLE CHOICE QUESTIONS

1. D 2. D 3. E 4. B 5. A 6. B 7. A, C 8. C 9. D 10. B 11. D 12. B 13. C 14. C 15. A 16. C 17. D

CHAPTER 15

REVIEW PROBLEMS

1. Rearrange equation (23.2) to answer this question.
a. 4.4
b. 4.8. The capital stock increases as s increases; there will be more investment as saving increases.
c. 4. The capital stock decreases as δ increases; a greater portion of the capital stock depreciates.

2. Uncertain. Assuming that depreciation occurs, the capital stock will only increase when investment exceeds depreciation. Investment could be positive and the capital stock can fall if I < depreciation.

3. a. If the capital stock is increasing, I must exceed depreciation; therefore, saving per worker must exceed depreciation.

b. If the capital stock is decreasing, I must be less than depreciation; therefore, saving per worker must be less than depreciation.
c. If the capital stock is constant, I must equal depreciation; therefore, saving per worker must equal depreciation.

4. a. Depreciation per worker equals: .2, .3, .4, and .5.
b. Depreciation increases at a constant rate.

5. Note: I have omitted per worker below to save space.
a. AB is depreciation; AC is investment; AD is output; BC is the change in capital; and CD is consumption.
b. Investment exceeds depreciation so K/N will increase. As K/N rises, Y/N will increase as well.
c. No.
d. It is determined by the level of K/N where the investment line intersects the depreciation line.

6. Note: I have omitted per worker below to save space.
a. EF is investment; EG is depreciation; EH is output; FG is the change in capital; and FH is consumption.
b. K/N and Y/N will decrease over time.
c. No.
d. It is determined by the level of K/N where the investment line intersects the depreciation line.

7. a.
b. The lower s causes a reduction in saving and an increase in consumption. It takes one period for the change in saving/investment to affect capital; consequently, K/N and, therefore, Y/N do not change in period t.
c. At the initial K/N, investment is now less than depreciation. K/N and Y/N will fall over time.
d. In the short run, the lower s causes a reduction in Y/N. Hence, the rate of growth in Y/N is negative.
e. Once the new steady state is reached, Y/N remains constant. The lower s has no long-run effect on the growth of Y/N.
f. It permanently reduces the level of Y/N.

8. a. A reduction in δ will reduce the slope of the depreciation line. The line will become flatter.
b. At the initial level of K/N, the decline in the depreciation rate will cause investment to exceed depreciation. This situation will cause K/N and Y/N to increase over time. In short, the drop in the depreciation rate will cause a new steady state level of Y/N and K/N (both increase).

9. a. Increases in the saving rate cause increases in K/N and Y/N. To maximize Y/N, the saving rate must be one (s = 1).
b. Such a policy would cause consumption to be zero. All income would be going to saving to support this high level of K/N. Individuals most likely (!) would not like this since they care about consumption, not production.

10. a. The higher s causes an increase in saving and a reduction in consumption. It takes one period for the change in saving/investment to affect capital; consequently, K/N and Y/N will not change in period t.
b. The higher s will cause K/N and Y/N to increase in the long run. The effects of the higher s on consumption in the long run depend on where the economy is prior to the increase in s. If capital is above the golden rule, the higher s will cause a reduction in consumption. If capital is below the golden rule, the higher s will cause higher consumption (up to a point).

11. a. See answer to part b of #7.
b. The lower s will cause K/N and Y/N to decrease in the long run. The effects of the lower s on consumption in the long run depend on where the economy is prior to the increase in s. If capital is above the golden rule, the lower s will cause an increase in consumption up to a point. If capital is below the golden rule, the lower s will cause lower consumption.

12. a. Plugging in the numbers, we get: 1, 1.41, 1.73, 2, and 2.24.
b. It increases at a decreasing rate.
c. Yes. If you double both N and K, Y will double.

13. Use the following equations to answer this question: $K/N = (s/\delta)^2$; $Y/N = s/\delta$; C/N in the steady state equals $s(1-s)/\delta$.
a. K/N will be: 4, 36, 100, 196 and 324. Y/N will be: 2, 6, 10, 14 and 18.
b. The steady state levels of C/N will be: 1.8, 4.2, 5, 4.2 and 1.8.
c. Capital is below the golden rule and C/N increases.
d. Capital is above the golden rule and C/N falls.
e. K/N is 100; C/N is 5; s is .5.

14. a. The government must raise the saving rate. To do this, it must either reduce the budget deficit or increase the budget surplus.
b. Any increase in s in the short run will reduce C/N.
c. C/N will increase.

15. a. 4.
b. Yes it does. Try doubling K, N and H. Y will also double. Alternatively, Y/N will not change when K, N and H all double.
c. Yes it does. Try increasing K from 400 to 450 to 500. Y will increase at a decreasing rate .
d. Yes it does. Try increasing H from 400 to 450 to 500. Y will increase at a decreasing rate.

16. a. K and H. Increases in K/N will cause increases in Y/N because workers will have more capital with which to produce goods. Increases in H/N will also cause increases in Y/N because workers have a better set of skills to produce goods.
b. The saving rate must increase.
c. Increased education spending or increases in on-the-job training; these will increase H/N.

MULTIPLE CHOICE QUESTIONS

1. C 2. A 3. A 4. C 5. C 6. D 7. A 8. B 9. D 10. B 11. D 12. D 13. B 14. D 15. D 16. B 17. C 18. D 19. B 20. D 21. C 22. C

CHAPTER 16

REVIEW PROBLEMS

1. Patents will have no effect on the fertility of research. Patents will increase the appropriability of research.

2. If patent protection is poor, firms may not be able to profit from their own new products (that are the result of the R&D). Thus, R&D spending will fall and technological progress will likely decrease.

3. a. 100, 110, 120, 130 and 150.
b. NA increases as A increases.

4. a. 100
b. 200. If you double all inputs, output doubles. Yes.
c. Y equals 100, 122.5 and 141.4. Yes. The increase in Y gets smaller with each additional increase in K.
d. Y equals 100, 118.3 and 134.2. Yes. The increase in Y gets smaller with each additional increase in NA.

5. The level of output is determined by K and NA (or N and A). An increase in any two (three) of these variables will cause Y to increase.

6. a. Multiply .15 by each level of I. 15, 16.5, 18 and 19.5.
b. This level of investment increases at a constant rate.

7. a. Multiply .20 by each level of I/NA. 2, 4, 6 and 8.
b. Required investment increases at a constant rate.

8. a. As g_N increases, required investment rises. Since N is growing at a faster rate, more investment will be needed to maintain K/NA.
b. As g_A increases, required investment rises. Since NA (via A) is growing at a faster rate, more investment is needed to maintain K/NA.
c. An increase in δ will cause required investment to increase. Since K is depreciating at a faster rate, more investment will be needed to offset this depreciation.

9. a. 1.5
b. I/NA exceeds the amount needed to keep K/NA constant. K/NA will increase over time.
c. I/NA is less than required investment. K/NA will decrease over time.
d. I/NA must be 1.5 to keep K/NA constant.

10. a. I/NA is greater than the required level. K/NA will increase over time. As K/NA increases, Y/NA will also increase.
b. I/NA is less than the required level. K/NA will fall over time. As K/NA falls, Y/NA will fall.
c. Yes. I/NA equals the required level of investment per NA.

11. a. Since both are constant, the rate of growth is zero!
b. They both grow at 5%.
c. 3%
d. 2%
e. 2%

12. a. The rate of growth of Y in the steady state is determined by the rate of growth in NA. The rate of growth in NA is determined by the rate of growth in the population and rate of technological progress. An increase in either of these will cause the rate of growth in Y to increase.
b. The rate of growth in Y/N equals the rate of technological progress. Increases in the rate of technological progress will cause an increase in the rate of growth in Y/N.

13. a. See the graph.
b. The lower saving rate causes the investment curve to shift down. I/NA is now less than required investment. K/NA and Y/NA will fall over time until the new steady state is reached at point B.
c. Y/NA and K/NA will be permanently lower.
d. Output per worker grew at the rate of growth in technological progress.
e. During the adjustment, the growth rate of Y/N declines.
f. Once the new steady state is reached, Y/N grows at the same long-run rate: the rate of technological progress, g_A.

14. False. As discussed in #13 and in the text, changes in the saving rate only affect the rate of growth of Y/N in the short run. In the long run, Y/N grows at g_A which is independent of the saving rate.

15. Since Y/NA and K/NA are constant. Y and K grow at the same rate as NA ($g_N + g_A$). Y/N and K/N grow at g_A.

16. In the steady state, we know that Y/N grows at g_A. An increase in g_A will, therefore, cause the long-run rate of growth of Y/N to increase permanently.

17. An increase in s will cause K/NA to increase in the short run. Once the new steady state is reached, K/NA will be constant at some permanently higher level. In the short run, Y/NA will increase to some permanently higher level. As Y/NA is rising, Y/N will be growing at a rate about g_A. Once the new steady state is reached, however, Y/N will grow at g_A.

18. a. No. The economy is in steady state when the rate of growth of Y/N equals g_A.
b. This high growth must be caused by capital accumulation.

19. a. No. The economy is in steady state when the rate of growth of Y/N equals g_A.
b. This low growth must be caused by a reduction in capital accumulation.

20. a. Yes. The economy is in steady state when the rate of growth of Y/N equals g_A.
b. The growth in Y/N is caused by balanced growth, the rate of technological progress.

21. The slowdown has been caused by a slowdown in the rate of technological progress. The rate of growth in Y/N has coincided with a decline in the rate of growth in technological progress.

MULTIPLE CHOICE QUESTIONS

1. A 2. B 3. D 4. C 5. D 6. D 7. B 8. C 9. C 10. A 11. A 12. C 13. C 14. E 15. A 16. B 17. D 18. A 19. D 20. D 21. E 22. A 23. C 24. D 25. B 26. A 27. B 28. B,C,D 29. A

CHAPTER 17

REVIEW PROBLEMS

1. The import of technology from the rest of the world is an important part of the growth process as are imports of labour inputs as well as imports of physical and financial capital. Technology can be imported in a number of ways including payments by domestic residents to non residents for the rental of their technology registered in the form of patents and copyrights.

2. We know I = S − NX or, S − I = NX. When I > S, NX will be negative (trade deficit), and therefore the nation will be in a net borrowing position.

3. The steady state of output is such that

   $s.f\left(\frac{K}{N}\right) = \delta\left(\frac{K}{N}\right)$, where s is the saving rate, K/N is the capital labour ratio, and δ is the depreciation rate.

   In an open economy saving need not be equal to investment, but rather S − I = NX = net international borrowing.

4. a. Total hours per year = Average hours per employee x (number of employees/population) x population. Total hours = (38 x 52) x 0.60 x 30 = 35.568 billion hours for the year.
   b. Growth of total hours = Growth of average hours + growth of population. Therefore, growth of total hours = − .5% + 1% = + .5%.

5. a. Population change = change in births − change in deaths + change in immigration − change in emigration = 1708 − 1103 + 1050 − 290 = 1365.

   b. The natural population change = change in births − change in deaths = (1708 − 1103) = 605.

   c. The net immigration change = 1050 − 290 = 760.

6. a. S = Y − C = 500 − 400 = 100.
   b. S − I = 100 − 200 = − 100
   c. S − I = NX. NX = 100 − 200 = − 100 = net borrowing from abroad.

7. a. GDP = C + I + X − Q = 500 + 200 + 100 − 70 = 730.
   b. GNP = rB^f + GDP = 0.05 x 1000 + 730 = 780.
   c. The net lending = GNP − (C + I) = 780 − (700) = 80.

8. a. Foreign assets of Yorktonians = direct investment abroad + portfolio foreign assets + all other assets + official international reserves = 304,366 + 215,328 + 263,421 + 47,801 = 866,916.
    b. Foreign liabilities = Foreign direct investment + portfolio foreign liabilities + all other liabilities. Therefore, foreign direct investment = 1,021,593 − (485,215 + 234,079) = 302,299.
    c. The net international position = net assets − net liabilities = −154,677 (in millions of dollars).

MULTIPLE CHOICE QUESTIONS

1. B 2. A 3. C 4. B 5. D 6. B 7. A 8. A 9. A 10. B 11. B 12. D 13. C 14. B 15. B

CHAPTER 18

REVIEW PROBLEMS

1. Expected inflation = $(P^e_{t+1} - P_t)/P_t$. The exact definition of the real rate is $[(1+i)/1+\pi^e)]-1$. In the answers below, the first number is expected inflation and the second number is r (all in %).
a. 0, 10
b. 3, 6.8
c. 5, 4.8
d. 7, 2.8
e. 10, 0
f. The nominal rate equals the real rate only when expected inflation is 0 (part a).
g. i>r when expected inflation is positive (parts b-d).
h. r=0 when expected inflation equals the nominal interest rate (part e).

2. a. 10 b. 7 c. 5 d. 3 e. 0

3. a. See the answers below.

i	π^e	r^I	r^{II}
2%	0	2%	2%
5%	3%	1.94%	2%
10%	8%	1.85%	2%
15%	13%	1.77%	2%
20%	18%	1.69%	2%
50%	48%	1.35%	2%
100%	98%	1.0%	2%

b. As inflation increases, the approximate definition's ability to measure accurately the real interest rate declines. This is obvious by looking at the numbers.

4. $r = i - \pi^e$, r will increase if I increases, r will increase if, for a given i, π^e falls.

5. Yes. Look at the definition of r in #4. A reduction in i, given expected inflation, would cause r to fall. However, if expected inflation falls more than the reduction in i, the real interest rate will increase.

6. The discount factors are: $1/(1+i)$ for one year and $1/(1+i)^2$ for two years.
a. When the interest rate is zero the discount factors equal 1; we can simply add the sum of future payments. $200,000.
b. $100,000/1.04 + $100,000/1.0816 = #$188,610.
c. $100,000/1.08 + $100,000/1.1664 = $178,327.
d. The higher the interest rates, the lower is the present value. As i increases, the discount factor increases; the weights on the future sums are smaller.

7. a. Individual B receives the larger present value. Each receives a three-year stream of $50,000 payments. However, B receives one today. $1 today is worth more than $1 received a year from now. Since B receives her payments one year sooner than A, the present value is larger.
b. They will be equal only if the interest rate is zero. See the answer to #6, part a.

8. a. $100,000/1.1 = $90,909.
b. $100,000/1.21 = $82,645.
c. $100,000/1.331 = $75,131.
d. As the payment occurs further into the future, the present value falls. The weight gets smaller (the discount factor gets larger).

9. a. Using the (what should now be familiar) equation: present value of the first year payment, $20,000; present value of the second year payment, $20,000; present value of the third year payment, $20,661; present value of the fourth year payment, $21,037.
b. The present value of the 4-year payment option is (add the numbers in a): $81,698. This also represents the highest one-year payment the student should make. If the college's one-year price is below this, you should recommend the one-time payment. If the college's one-year price is above this, you should recommend the four-year payment plan.

10. Use the following equation to obtain the future value of the $100,000: $100,000(1 + i_t) $(1 + i_{t+1})(1+i_{t+2})$.
a. Plugging in the numbers, we get: Case 1, $100,000; Case 2, $184,800; Case 3, $125,928.
b. Case 2 yields the highest future value because the interest rates are higher in this case. Alternatively, with i higher in case 2, you would need to receive a greater future sum to yield a present value of $100,000.

11. a. The opportunity cost of holding money is the nominal interest rate, 9%. All figures are in percentages (%).
b. Real returns on bonds, 9. Real return on money, 0.
c. Real return on bonds ($r = i - \pi^e$): 8, 6, 2, and 0.
Real return on money ($0 - \pi^e$): -1, -3, -7, and -9.
d. Nothing. It remains fixed at 9%.
e. The opportunity cost measured in real terms = real return on bonds - real return on money: 8 - (-1) = 9; 6 - (-3) = 9; 2 - (-7) = 9; and 0 - (-9) = 9. Nothing happens to the opportunity cost of holding money (measured in real terms) as expected inflation increases.
f. Nothing What will determine the opportunity cost of holding money is the nominal interest rate. Changes in expected inflation do not affect the opportunity cost of holding money because they affect the real return on money and bonds equally.

12. a. 10%.
b. The increase in expected inflation will have no effect on money demand (the curve does NOT shift). The real interest rate consistent with financial market equilibrium is 8%.
c. No effect on money demand. The real interest rate consistent with equilibrium falls to 5%.

13. Lets; begin with the medium-run effects of a reduction in money growth. In the medium run, this change in money growth will have no effect on output. That is, Y will return to the natural level of output. The real interest rate will also return to the natural real rate of interest. With output growth unchanged in the medium run, we know that inflation will drop by an amount equal to the reduction in money growth. With inflation lower and the real interest rate unchanged, we know that the nominal interest will fall as well (the Fisher effect also applies when there are reductions in inflation). In the short run, the reduction in money supply growth will cause an increase in the normal interest rate and an increase in the real interest rate. This increase in r will cause a reduction in investment and a reduction in output (Y falls below the natural level). With Y below the natural level, the Phillips curve suggests that expected inflation will fall over time. It is this adjustment in expected inflation that will cause Y or r return to their initial levels and I to fall below is initial level.

14. a. A drop in G will cause a leftward shift in the IS curve. At the initial natural level of output, the real interest rate consistent with goods market equilibrium is lower. Hence, r_n falls.
b. A drop in T will cause a rightward shift in the IS curve. At the initial natural level of output, the real interest rate consistent with goods market equilibrium is higher. Hence, r_n increases.
c. A reduction in the price of oil will cause a reduction in the price level and an increase in the natural level of output. Assuming that the change in the price of oil does not affect the demand for goods, r_n will fall as the economy moves along the fixed the IS curve.

15. a. 2%.
b. See the graph. The drop in expected inflation, given i, causes the equilibrium real interest rate (for the financial market) to increase to 5%. Investment decreases and the IS curve shifts to the left. Note: the vertical distance between the two IS curves represents the reduction in expected inflation. The drop in expected inflation is represented by the distance between points A and B in the graph.

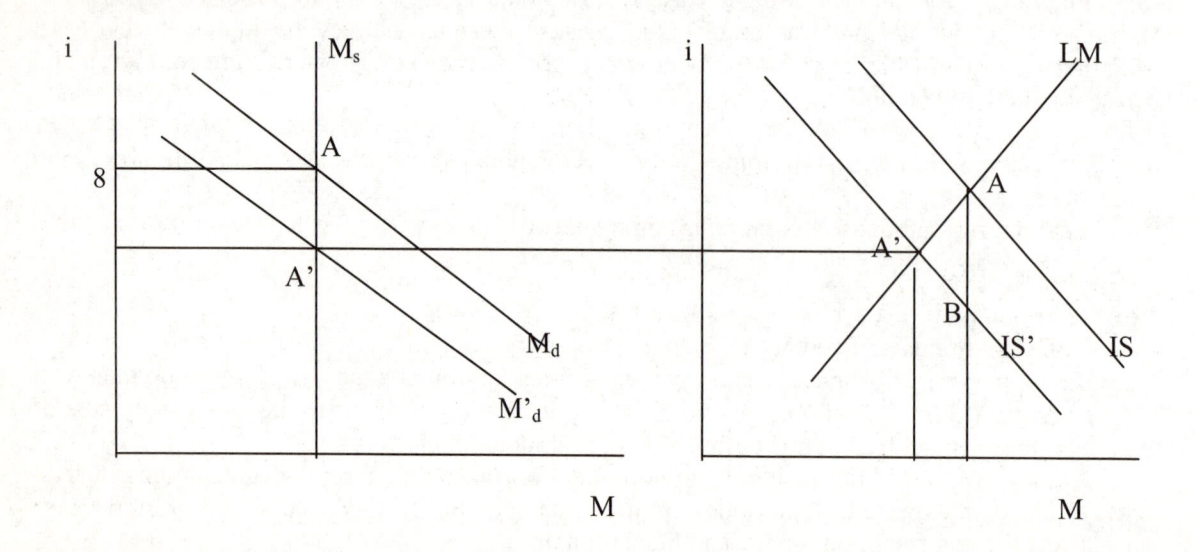

c. The drop in expected inflation causes an initial increases in r. As r increases, I falls causing a reduction in demand and a leftward shift in the IS curve. T will fall causing a reduction in money demand and a reduction in the nominal interest rate. As Y falls, C falls as well.

d. The 3% reduction in expected inflation causes the real interest rate to increase, but by less than 3%. Why? As Y falls, nominal money demand falls, causing the nominal interest rate to fall. So, some of the reduction in expected inflation is offset by a reduction in i. Where would point A' be in the money supply—money demand graph? Money demand falls as Y falls. So, point A' is below A.

MULTIPLE CHOICE QUESTIONS

1. C 2. D 3. B 4. C 5. B 6. C 7. C 8. A 9. C 10. D 11. D 12. C 13. C 14. B 15. C 16. C 17. D 18. B 19. C 20. A 21. D 22. D 23. A 24. B 25. C 26. E

CHAPTER 19

REVIEW PROBLEMS

1. a. 100/1000 = 10%
b. 100/900 = 11.1%

2. As the rating increases, the bond is viewed as less risky (the probability of a default is perceived to be lower). This will cause the risk premium on the bond to fall. As the risk premium falls, the interest rate falls.

3. If a sufficient number of financial market participants believed that the probability of default increased, they might require a (higher) risk premium on bonds issued by the U.S. government. This would have raised the interest rate on these bonds.

4. a. $1000/1.1 = $909.09
b. $1000/[(1.1)(1.08)] = $841.75
c. In one year, this two-year bond is a one-year bond: $1000(1.08) = $925.93

5. a. $1000/1.08 = $925.93
b. $1000[(.108)(1.06)] = $873.52
c. $1000/1.06 = $943.40
In each case, the price of the bonds increases as the interest rates fell. This is what you should expect!!

6. Recall that the two-year rate is (approximately) a simple average of the current one-year rate and expected future one-year rate. Plugging in the numbers, we get:
a. 7% b. 5.5% c. 6%

7. a. It increases by .5% to 7.5%. The yield curve becomes steeper.
b. It falls to 5%. The yield curve becomes steeper (it is still downward sloping).

8. a. 6%. Upward sloping.
b. Two-year rate increases to 6.5%. The two-year rate changes by less than the change in the current one-year rate because the expected future one-year rate did not change.

c. Two-year rate increases to 6.75%. The two-year rate still changes by less than the change in the current one-year rate because the expected future one-year rate changed by less than the current one-year rate.

d. Two-year rate increases to 7%. The two-year rate changes by the same amount as the change in the current one-year rate because the expected future one-year rate also changed by the same amount as the change in the current one-year rate.

e. The two-year rate increased by the same amount as the current one-year rate in the last case where the current and expected future one-year rates increased by the same amount. This is the condition which is needed for the two-year rate to increase by the same amount as the current one-year rate.

9. a. The expected future one-year rate must increase (or, the current one-year rate must fall).
b. The expected future one-year rate must drop so that it equals the current one-year rate (or, the current one-year rate must increase so that it equals the expected future one-year rate).
c. The expected future one-year rate must drop so that it falls below the current one-year rate (or, the current one-year rate must increase so that it increases above the expected future one-year-rate).

10. a. The expected future one-year rate will fall causing the yield curve to become flatter.
b. The expected future one-year rate will fall causing the yield curve to become flatter.
c. The expected future one-year rate will fall causing the yield curve to become flatter.
d. The expected future one-year rate will increase causing the yield curve to become steeper.

11. a. This will cause the expected future interest rate to fall and expected output to increase. The expected increase in Y will raise expectations of future profits. The reduction in the expected future interest rate will increase the present value of future profits. Both of these results will cause stock prices to rise.
b. This will reduce future output. Expectations of future profits will be lower causing stock prices to fall. This answer assumes that expectations of interest rates remain constant.

12. a. No effect. The expectation of the increase in Y is already built into expectations of future profits. Thus, stock prices do not change.
b. No effect. The effects of the expected Bank of Canada's contraction (higher future interest rates and lower future Y) are, again, already built into expectations of future profits. Thus, stock prices do not change.

13. a. This event will raise i^e and cause Y^e to fall. The higher expected interest rate (as described in previous answers) will cause stock prices to fall. The reduction in expected output will (as described in previous answers) cause stock prices to fall. The reduction in expected output will (as described in previous answers) cause stock prices to fall. Therefore, stock prices will fall.

b. This event will cause i^e to fall and cause Y^e to fall. The lower expected interest rate (as described in previous answers) will cause stock prices to rise. The reduction in expected output, however, will (as described in previous answers) cause stock prices to fall. Therefore, the effects of this event on stock prices are ambiguous.

c. This event will cause Y^e to increase with no change in the interest rate. Here, stock prices will increase.

14. a. Unexpected changes in monetary policy will cause: (1) the interest to fall and output to increase; or (2) the interest rate to increase and output to fall. In case 1, both effects cause stock prices to increase. In case 2, both effects cause stock prices to fall. In short, the effects work together here to affect stock prices.
b. Unexpected changes in fiscal policy will cause: (1) the interest to fall and output to fall; or (2) the interest rate to increase and output to increase. In case 1, the lower future i would increase stock prices, while the lower future Y would reduce stock prices. The opposite happens in case 2. Conclusion: we do not know which effect will dominate so the effects are ambiguous.

15. a. As described #14, part b, the effects will be ambiguous.
b. The Bank of Canada acts to keep the interest rate fixed at its original level. To do so, the Bank would have to pursue contractionary monetary policy; reduce the money supply to shift the LM curve up so it intersects the new IS curve at point C.
c. The Bank of Canada acts to keep Y fixed at its original level. To do so, the Bank would have to pursue expansionary monetary policy; increase the money supply to shift the LM curve down so it intersects the new IS curve at point D.
d. Stock prices will fall. The lower output will cause individuals to revise down their expectations of future profits. There is no interest rate here to offset this.
e. Stock prices will increase. The lower interest rate will increase the present value of future profits. There is no output effect to offset this.

16. a. $\varepsilon = \dfrac{\varepsilon^e}{1+(r-r^*)} = 1.4/(1+(.04-.05)) = 1.41$.
b. $\varepsilon = 1.38$

17. a. The current real exchange rate is equal to the expected real rate (=1) since $r = r^*$.
b. Therefore the expected real appreciation or deprecation is equal to zero.

18. Since the real exchange rate is expected to appreciate, $r - r^* = \dfrac{\varepsilon^e}{\varepsilon} - 1$, the right hand side is negative and therefore, the left hand side is negative, i.e., $r < r^*$.

19. $\varepsilon = \dfrac{\varepsilon^e}{1+n(r-r^*)} = 1.16$.

20. The increase in demand for domestic goods, decreases the demand for foreign currency. Therefore, the domestic currency will appreciate in real terms.

MULTIPLE CHOICE QUESTIONS

1. B 2. D 3. C 4. A 5. B 6. D 7. C 8. B 9. C 10. A 11. A 12. B 13. D 14. C 15. C 16. C 17. A 1. D 19. A 20. A 21. D 22. A 23. D 24. B 25. D 26. B

CHAPTER 20

REVIEW PROBLEMS

1. a. $1,600,000
b. Divide total wealth by 40: $30,000.
c. The individual will have to borrow $15,000 to achieve her desired level of consumption: $40,000 - $25,000 (current disposable income) = $15,000.
d. Total wealth will increase by $10,000. Divide this sum by 40 to determine how much consumption can increase each year: $10,000/40 = $250. Or, you could divide her new level of total wealth ($1,610,000) by 40 to get: $40,250.
e. Without knowing the future real interest rates, we cannot calculate the new level of human wealth. We do not know, however, that this permanent increase in income will have a greater effect on total wealth than does the one-time increase in part d. She will, therefore, increase her consumption more as a result of this event than in response to the event in part d.

2. a. This will reduce housing wealth.
b. This will reduce financial wealth.
c. This will reduce current disposable income and reduce human wealth.
d. This will reduce human wealth.

3. a. $10,000/1.05 = $9523.81.
b. $(1-.1)(\$12,000)/(1.05)(1.07) = \$9612.82$.
c. Sum the values in a and b to get: $19,136.6.
d. $10,000/1.06 = $9433.96. $(1-.1)(\$12,000)/(1.06)(1.08) = \$9433.96$.
Adding the two figures yields: $18,867.92.
e. Changing the numbers and using the same approach as that included above yields: $20,890.08.
f. Changing the numbers and using the same approach as that included above yields: $19,350.25.
g. The highest price the firm is willing to pay is the present value of the profits from the machine: in c, $19,136.63; in d, $18,867.92; in e, $20,890.08; and in f, $19,350.25.
h. An increase in r will cause the present value to fall. An increase in expected future profits will increase the present value. A reduction in the rate of depreciation will cause an increase in present value.

4. I will use equation (8.5) to calculate the present values here.
a. Plugging in the numbers yields: $10,000/.15 = $66,666.67. This is also the highest price the firm is willing to pay. The user cost of capital is .15.
b. Plugging in the numbers yields: $10,000/.14 = $71,428.57. This is also the highest price the firm is willing to pay. The user cost of capital is .14; it falls as r falls.
c. Plugging in the numbers yields: $10,000/.17 = $58,823.53. This is also the highest price the firm is willing to pay. The user cost of capital is .17; it increases as the depreciation rate increases.
d. Plugging in the numbers yields: $9,000/.15 = $60,000. This is also the highest price the firm is willing to pay. The user cost of capital does not change when expected profits change.
e. In b, investment will increase; in c, investment will decrease; in d, investment will fall.

5. The rental cost of capital is $r + \delta$. An increase in r and an increase in δ will cause the rental cost of capital to increase. A higher interest rate will reduce the present value of expected profits. Firms will tend to reduce investment when this occurs. When δ increases, the capital wears out more quickly, thus reducing the amount of profits received from each unit of capital over time.

6. a. Firm A is unaffected by this increase in the price of oil, so its investment will not change. As the price of oil increases, profits from oil exploration will rise. The increase in profits represents an increase in cash flows for firm B. With additional cash flows, firm B will likely increase investment in both of its operations.
b. Again, firm A will not be affected by this. If only profitability matters, there is no reason for firm B to increase investment in its steel operation (the profitability of steel has not changed). The profitability of oil has increased so we would likely see an increase in investment for firm B in oil exploration.

7. a. This will decrease profits, decrease profit per unit of capital and, therefore, reduce investment.
b. This will increase sales and increase profits. Profit per unit of capital will increase causing an increase in investment.
c. Given sales, the lower is capital, the higher is profit per unit of capital. Investment will increase.

8. a. To maintain the ratio of capital to sales of 4, this $20 million permanent increase in sales (and output) will cause firms to increase investment by $80 million to achieve the needed increase in investment to maintain the capital to sales ratio. In short, I will increase by $80 million in t. Consumption, on the other hand, will increase at most by $20 million (given the change is perceived to be permanent). If the change in sales/income is believed to be partially temporary, consumption will increase less than $20 million. I changes more than C.
b. The capital stock will increase by $80 million.
c. The initial increase in sales increased profit per unit of capital. As the capital stock increases, however, profit per unit of capital (given the higher sales) will decline to its normal level.

9. Sales will fall. Profit per unit of capital will fall; therefore, investment will fall. The drop in investment will cause the capital stock to fall.

MULTIPLE CHOICE QUESTIONS

1. D 2. B 3. D 4. D 5. B 6. C 7. E 8. D 9. B 10. A 11. B 12. C 13. A 14. D 15. A 16. D 17. C 18. C

CHAPTER 21

REVIEW PROBLEMS

1. Note: If the curve or variable is not listed, it does not change.
a. reduces nonhuman wealth; causes a reduction in consumption; causes a leftward shift in the IS curve.
b. increases the present value of after-tax profits; increases investment; causes a rightward shift in the IS curve.
c. increases human wealth; increases consumption; causes a rightward shift in the IS curve
d. reduces investment; causes a leftward shift in the IS curve.
e. LM shifts down
f. increases nonhuman wealth; increases present value of after-tax profits; increases investment; increases consumption; causes a rightward shift in the IS curve
g. decreases human wealth and, therefore, consumption; decreases expectations of future profits and, therefore, investment; IS shifts to the left
h. IS shifts to the right

2. a. future LM curve shifts up cause Y'^e to fall and r'^e to increase
b. future IS curve shifts to the right causing Y'^e to increase and r'^e to increase
c. future IS curve shifts to the right causing Y'^e to increase and r'^e to increase

3. a. The size of the multiplier depends on the size of the effect of a change in current income on current spending.
b. A change in current income, with expectations of future income unchanged, is unlikely to have a large effect on current spending. This causes a small multiplier to exist.

4. a. The present value of human wealth falls causing a reduction in consumption. Also, the present value of profits falls causing a reduction in investment.
b. Given expectations of future interest rates, changes in the current interest rate are likely to have small effects on the present value of human wealth and small effects on the present value of profits. Thus, the effects of changes in the current interest rate on current spending are likely smaller.

5. a. The IS curve is steeper for two reasons. First, the effects of changes in the current interest rate on consumption and investment are now smaller. Second, given any change in current spending, the multiplier is also smaller. For these reasons, a given reduction in the current interest rate will have a smaller effect on output (the IS curve is steeper).

6. I will not include the graphs here.
a. This event causes C and I to increase resulting in a rightward shift in the IS curve; there is no shift in the LM curve. The shift in the current IS curve causes Y and r to increase.
b. The exact opposite of a.
c. Consumption will increase because of the increase in human wealth. Firms may also increase investment as they revise upwards their expectations of future profits (caused by the increase in Y'^e). The increase in C and I causes a rightward shift in the IS curve. Y and r both increase; the LM curve does not shift.
d. The exact opposite of c.

7. I will not include the graphs here. Hint: you must first examine how each event affects the future r and Y.
a. This will cause r'^e to fall and Y'^e to increase. The lower future r will cause current C and I t increase. The higher future Y will have the same effect. The increase in C and I will cause the IS curve to shift to the right and r and Y will increase.
b. This will cause both r'^e and Y'^e to increase. The higher future Y will cause current C and current I to increase. The increase in C and I will cause the IS curve to shift to the right. However, the higher future r will cause current C and current I to fall. This will tend to cause the IS curve to shift to the left. The effects on the position of the current IS curve are ambiguous. If the combined effects cause the IS curve to shift to the right, Y and r increase. If the combined effects cause the IS curve to shift to the left, Y and r decrease.
c. This is the opposite of b. This event will cause both r'^e and Y'^e to fall. The remainder of the analysis is the exact opposite of that included in b.

8. a. The future IS curve shifts to the right as future G increases. The future r will not change because of the Fed policy. Future output will be higher.
b. The increase in future Y (caused by the increase in G and the Bank of Canada's response) will cause an increase in both current consumption and current investment. This will cause the IS curve to shift to the right (there is no shift in the LM curve), Y to increase and r to increase.

9. a. The future IS curve shifts to the right as future G increases. The Bank of Canada, to keep Y constant, will reduce the future money supply which shifts the LM curve up. The final (future) result: no change in future Y and an increase in the future r.
b. An increase in the future r will cause a reduction in both current C and current I. This causes a leftward shift in the current IS curve (with no shift in the LM curve). Both the current interest rate and current level of output fall.

10. a. The future IS curve shifts to the right as future G increases. There is no central Bank response so the expected future r increases as future Y increases.
b. The results in this case are ambiguous. The increase in future Y would cause an increase in C and I and a rightward shift in the current IS curve. However, the higher future r has the opposite effect. Current output could increase, decrease or remain constant.

11. a. Current output will increase the most in #9 for two reasons: (1) future output increases the most in this case; and (2) there is no (offsetting) increase in the future interest rate in this case.
b. As seen in #8-#10, the effects on current output depend crucially on what individuals expect the Bank of Canada to do. In one case, current output falls; in another case, current output rises; and in the final case, the effects on current Y are ambiguous. The Bank's response can affect future Y and future r, variables that also affect current economic behaviour.

12. a. The increase in future taxes will cause the expected future interest rate to fall. As this occurs, the current long-term interest rate falls, causing the yield curve to become flatter.
b. The increase in future taxes will cause future output to fall. Note: Both the future r and future Y fall. The drop in the future r will cause the current IS curve to shift to the right. The drop in future Y will cause the current IS curve to shift to the left.
c. If the future interest rate effects just offset the future income effects plus the effects of this future tax increase in human wealth, there will no change in current output since the current IS curve does not shift.
d. If the future interest rate effects dominate the future income effects plus the effects of this future tax increase in human wealth, the current IS curve will shift to the right and current Y increases.
e. If the future interest rate effects are less than the future income effects plus the effects of this future tax increase in human wealth, the current IS curve will shift to the left and current Y decreases.

13. a. The increase in current taxes will cause the current IS curve to shift to the left and cause current Y to fall. The expected future tax increase will have (as described in #12) ambiguous effects on current spending and current output.
b. If the expectation of an increase in future taxes would have caused current Y to increase, output will fall even further if financial markets do not expect T to increase in the future. If the expectation of an increase in future taxes would have caused current Y to fall, output will fall less if financial markets do not expect T to increase in the future.

14. a. The increase in future government spending will cause an increase in the expected future interest rate, a reduction in investment, a reduction in capital stock, and, therefore, a reduction in future output.
b. There are three effects that you must consider. The increase in current G will cause the current IS curve to shift right; this would cause current Y to increase. The reduction in future expected income will cause reductions in both current C and I; this would cause the current IS curve to shift left. And finally, the increase in the expected future interest rate IS curve will cause reductions in both current C and I; this would cause the current IS curve to shift left. The final

position of the IS curve depends on the relative magnitude of these three effects (it could shift left, or remain unchanged).
c. Yes, it could be recessionary. If the future r and future Y effects dominate the effects of the increase in current G, the IS curve would shift left causing current output to fall.

15. a. The increase in future government spending will cause an increase in the expected future interest rate, a reduction in investment, no change in the capital stock, and therefore, no change in future output.
b. There are two effects that you must consider. The increase in current G will cause the current IS curve to the shift right; this would cause current Y to increase. The increase in the expected future interest rate IS curve will cause reductions in both current C and I; this would cause the current IS curve to shift left. The final position of the IS curve depends on the relative magnitude of these two effects (it could shift left, or remain unchanged).
c. Yes, it could be necessary. If the future r and Y effects dominate the effects of the increase in current G, the current IS curve would shift left causing current output to fall.

MULTIPLE CHOICE QUESTIONS

1. C 2. A 3. A 4. B 5. D 6. D 7. D 8. A 9. C 10. C 11. C 12. A 13. A 14. E 15. A 16. B 17. D 18. D 19. C 20. A 21. B 22. D 23. A

CHAPTER 22

REVIEW PROBLEMS

1. a. Consumption decreases, the IS curve shifts left, Y falls and r falls. LM does not shift.
b. Consumption decreases, the IS curve shifts left, Y falls and r falls. LM does not shift.
c. Investment decreases, the IS curve shifts left, Y falls and r falls. LM does not shift.
d. The LM curve shifts up, r increases and Y falls. IS does not shift.

2. They expect the price level to fall over time.

3. a. The real interest rate is simply I minus the expected inflation rate. The values of r will be: 2%, 3%, 4%, 5%, 6% and 8%.
b. r increases.
c. r increases.

4. a. The LM curve shifts up by the drop in expected inflation. The IS curve does not shift. r will increase and Y will fall as the demand for goods falls.
b. The expected deflation causes the LM curve to shift up even further since the real rate must be higher. The IS curve does not shift. r will continue to increase and, Y will fall as the demand for goods falls.

5. If individuals no longer expect deflation, the real rate will decrease (the rate which maintains equilibrium in financial markets). The LM curve shifts down by the change in expected inflation. The economy moves from point A to B. r will fall, and Y will increase as the demand for goods increases. The IS curve does not shift. See the graph.

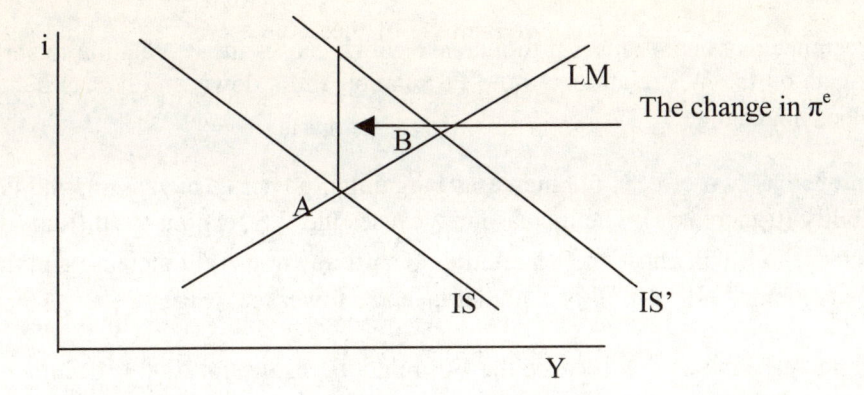

[Figure: IS-LM diagram showing LM curve, IS and IS' curves, with points A and B, and an arrow labeled "The change in π^e"]

6. An increase in the ratio of currency to deposits: (1) has no effect on the monetary base; (2) will cause the money multiplier to fall; (3) will cause the money supply to fall; and (4) will cause the LM curve to shift up.

7. The real money supply is M/P. If M fell and M/P did not change, there must have been a proportionate drop in P.

8. The deflation causes the LM curve to shift up. The reduction in consumer wealth and increase in uncertainty cause the IS curve to shift to the left. The effect on r depend on the size of the shifts in the IS and LM curves. If the new equilibrium occurs at B, r does not change. Given the shift in LM, if the IS curve shifts more, r falls. Given the shift in LM, if the IS curve does not shift as far to the left, r will increase.

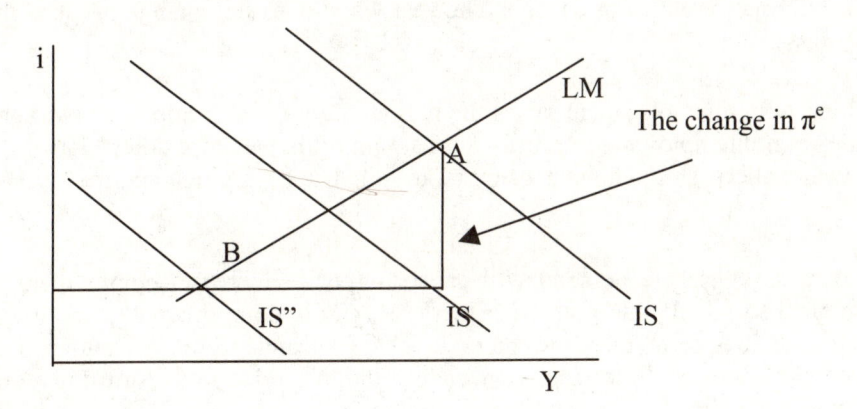

[Figure: IS-LM diagram showing LM curve, IS, IS', and IS'' curves, with points A and B, and an arrow labeled "The change in π^e"]

9. a. Expansionary fiscal policy (via a cut in T and/or an increase in G) would have caused the IS curve to shift to the right. If sufficient, the shift in the IS curve could have prevented the drop in Y.
b. Expansionary monetary policy would have shifted the LM curve down and caused r to fall. This could have prevented the drop in Y.

10. Yes. High growth rates were needed to bring down the high unemployment rate.

11. The deflation caused the real interest rate in financial markets to increase. This caused the LM curve to shift up and raised the real interest rate. The increase in r caused a reduction in the demand for goods.

12. An increase in severance payments causes μ to increase which causes the PS relation to shift down; there are no effects on the WS relation. As the PS relation shifts down, u_n increases and the real wage falls. z does not change.

13. An increase in unions has two effects: (1) increases bargaining power (z increases); and (2) decreases firms' flexibility (μ increases). The increase in z causes the WS relation to shift up (u_n will increase). The increase in μ will cause the PS relation to shift down; u_n will increase and the real wage will fall. The combined effects will be a higher u_n and a lower real wage.

14. This will cause an increase in z and will cause the WS relation to shift up. As this occurs, u_n increases and the real wage does not change. The PS relation and the real wage do not change.

15. This will cause an increase in z and will cause the WS relation to shift up. As this occurs, u_n increases and the real wage does not change. The PS relation and the real wage do not change.

16. a. u_n will fall as all of the above factors have caused an increase in u_n. The real wage will increase.
b. No it is not. The unemployment rate increased during the 1980s.

17. This is an easy answer. If the unemployment is high because u_n is high, there will be no pressure for inflation to fall.

18. A reduction in employment benefits will cause z to fall. As z falls, the WS relation shifts down and u_n falls. The PS relation will not change. The real wage does not change because the PS relation has not changed.

19. The existence of long-term unemployment raises the bargaining power of employed workers. The elimination of long-term unemployment reduces the bargaining power of workers causing z to fall. As z falls, the WS relations shifts down causing u_n to fall. The PS relation and the W/P do not change.

20. Policies which increase aggregate demand will cause output to increase, employment to increase and unemployment to fall. If this policy (to increase AD) is done gradually, the lower unemployment might cause long-term unemployment to decrease and allow governments to reduce employment benefits. Both of these results will cause the WS relation to shift down and cause u_n to fall.

21. Not only did the disinflation policy reduce inflation, it may have caused u_n to increase as well. The higher unemployment (caused by the disinflation policy) could have caused increases in long-term unemployment and increases in employment benefits. Both of these results would have caused the WS relation to shift up and cause u_n to increase. The costs of the disinflation policy would have been greater (as represented by the increase in u_n).

MULTIPLE CHOICE QUESTIONS

1. D 2. B 3. D 4. A 5. A 6. C 7. A 8. D 9. C 10. A 11. A 12. A 13. A 14. A 15. E 16. B 17. A 18. D 19. C 20. A 21. C 22. C

CHAPTER 23

REVIEW PROBLEMS

1. Assume that the price index at the beginning of the first month is 1. The price index at the end of the 12 months will be (1 + monthly rate of inflation)^{12}.
a. $(1 + .001)^{12}$ = 1.012; (1.012 - 1)/1 = .012 -- a 1.2% annual rate.
b. $(1 + .002)^{12}$ = 1.024; (1.024 - 1)/1 = .024 -- a 2.4% annual rate.
c. $(1 + .01)^{12}$ = 1.127; (1.127 - 1)/1 = .127 -- a 12.7% annual rate.
d. $(1 + .09)^{12}$ = 2.813; (2.813 - 1)/1 = 1.813 -- a 181.3% annual rate.
e. $(1 + .20)^{12}$ = 8.916; (8.916 - 1)/1 = 7.916 -- a 791.6% annual rate.
f. $(1 + .40)^{12}$ = 56.694; (56.694 - 1)/1 = 55.694 -- a 5569.4% annual rate.

2. Note: in both cases, the IS curve shifts to the right as G increases.
a. In option 1, we assume that the bonds are bought by individuals other than the central bank. This bond sale by the government, therefore, has no effect on the money supply. The Is curve shifts right and the LM curve does not shift. The interest rate increases, and output increases.
b. In option 2, the central bank buys the bonds causing an increase in the monetary base and an increase in the money supply. The IS curve shifts to the right and the LM curve shifts down because of the debt monetization. Interest rates may not increase at all as a result of this. Output again increases (more than it will in option 1).

3. a. To calculate seignorage, simply multiply money growth and real money balances (which are constant). .01(378) = 3.78 billion; .05(378) = 18.9 billion; and .10(378) = 37.8 billion.
b. Seignorage increases as money growth increases.
c. No. In the long run, the higher money growth will cause higher inflation. The increase in inflation will cause nominal interest rates to increase. As nominal interest rates increase, individuals will reduce their real money balances. That is, M/P will not remain constant at 378 as money growth increases.

4. Use the same approach here as described in #3 to calculate seignorage.
a. When M/P is 800, seignorage is 40. When M/P is 600, seignorage is 30. When M/P is 400, seignorage is 20.
b. Seignorage decreases as real money balances fall. Seignorage is the product of money growth and the level of real money balances. All else fixed, as real money balances fall, seignorage will also fall.

5. a. As Y increases, individuals are making more transactions. To facilitate the purchase of these goods and services, they will demand more money. So, as Y increases, real money balances also increase.
b. As expected inflation increases, given the real interest rate, the nominal interest rate will increase. As nominal interest rates increase, individuals will reduce their real money balances.

6. a. Seignorage will increase. Since M/P is assumed to be constant, any increase in money growth will cause an increase in seignorage since seignorage is the product of money growth and the level of real money balances.
b. From previous chapters, we know that increase in money growth cause a one-for-one increase in expected (and actual) inflation in the medium run. So, an increase in money growth will cause an increase in expected inflation.

c. As expected inflation increases, the nominal interest rate will also increase. As nominal interest rates increase, individuals will reduce their money balances. So, an increase in expected inflation will cause M/P to fall in the medium run.
d. The effects are ambiguous. On the one hand, the higher money growth will tend to cause increases in seignorage. On the other hand, as money growth increases, the higher nominal interest rates (caused by the higher expected inflation) will cause reductions in real money balances. This reduction in real money balances tends to cause seignorage to fall. So, the effects are ambiguous.

7. a. As long as money growth does not exceed 10%, the higher money growth (as shown in the figure in the text and in this study guide) will cause an increase in seignorage. The effects of higher money growth on seignorage offset the effects of the lower real money balances on seignorage.
b. We are past the seignorage-maximizing rate of money growth. Any increases in money growth will cause reductions in seignorage.

8. The inflation tax is simply the inflation rate times the level of real money balances.
a. The inflation tax is .10(500) = 50.
b. Seignorage is money growth times the level of real money balances. The inflation tax and seignorage will be equal only when money growth and inflation are equal.
c. The inflation tax will be greater when inflation exceeds the rate of money growth.
d. The inflation tax will be less than seignorage when money growth exceeds the rate of inflation.

9. a. M/P = 2000[.5 - (.05 + .10)] = 700. To calculate seignorage, simply multiple 700 by each of the rates of money growth: .01(700) = 7; .10(700) = 70; .25(700) = 175; and .30(700) = 210.
b. Seignorage increases as money growth increases.
c. Note: as money growth increases, expected inflation and the nominal interest rate increase. M/P will then decline as money growth increases. When money growth is .01, we have M/P = 2000[.5 - (.05 + .01)] = 880 and seignorage is 8.8 Using a similar approach, when money growth is .10, M/P is 700 and seignorage is 70. When money growth is .25, M/P is 400 and seignorage is 100. When money growth is .30, M/P is 300 and seignorage is 90.
d. Seignorage increases.
e. Seignorage falls. The negative effects of higher money growth on M/P now dominate the positive effects of higher money growth on seignorage.
f. Seignorage always increased in a because we assumed (unrealistically) that M/P would not change as money growth increases. If M/P is constant, higher money growth will always result in higher seignorage. M/P, however, will fall as money growth increases. At some point, seignorage will fall as money growth increases.

10. Orthodox include: a, b and c
Heterodox includes a, b, c, d, and e.

11. In the short run, prior to any adjustment in expectations of inflation, a hyperinflation may cause an increase in economic activity. In the medium run, however, hyperinflations will likely cause economic activity to fall as: (1) the exchange system is less efficient; (2) price signals are less useful; and (3) borrowing at a nominal interest rate is more of a gamble causing investment to fall.

MULTIPLE CHOICE QUESTIONS

1. D 2. D 3. A 4. C 5. A 6. A 7. D 8. B 9. B 10. D 11. B 12. D 13. D 14. A 15. A 16. C 17. C 18. E 19. C 20. D 21. E

CHAPTER 24

REVIEW PROBLEMS

1. a. Firms do not have to worry as much about losses since the transfers from the government will offset the losses. Firms may, therefore, be less concerned about operating as efficiently as possible. In the absence of these transfers, firms would be more concerned about their costs and would produce more efficiently.
b. The transfers will increase the budget deficit.
c. To finance the higher budget deficit, governments may use debt monetization (i.e., money growth will increase as the budget deficit increases).
d. The faster money growth will lead to higher inflation.

2. Reasons: (1) firms had an incentive to overstate production; (2) firms had an incentive to overstate quality improvements; (3) the Soviet Union had an incentive to overstate its aggregate output; (4) prices under central planning do not reflect market prices (some goods were useless); and (5) a different measure of output (net material product) was used.

3. Under central planning, all goods were included in the "official" measure of output. During the transition, these useless goods disappear (both their price and quantity go to zero). Conventional measures of GDP will not include goods that are no longer exchanged, hence they are excluded. In general, those goods that were overpriced under central planning (i.e., the relatively less useful goods) would most likely see the largest drop in production during transition and would receive too large a weight when calculating output.

4. a. Employment equals the distance 0L.
b. The unemployment rate is zero. Why? All of the individuals in the labour force are employed in one of the two sectors: 0B + BL = 0L.
c. SS shifts left (demand for labour in the state sector falls). Given W/P, employment in this sector also falls. Total employment falls by the same amount. With PP the same, the unemployment rate now increases to some positive rate.
d. An increase in PP will cause an increase in employment in the private sector. Total employment will increase by the same amount. This increase in private sector employment, given the labour force, will cause a reduction in the unemployment rate.

5. We have assumed decreasing returns to labour equal increases in employment cause smaller and smaller increases in output. To increase employment, the real wage must now fall. Since each additional worker now produces less output, firms will only hire more workers if the real wage falls.

6. As the transition continues, we would expect increases in output in both the state and private sectors. It is most likely the case that the private sector will grow more quickly than the state sector (thought this does not have to be the case). As output in the two sectors increases, the demand for labour will also increase; SS shift to the right and PP shifts to the left. Assuming the real wage does not change, the final equilibrium will occur where SS and PP intersect at W/P.

Here, unemployment will again be zero (though, you should realize that there will be some unemployment. See point B below.

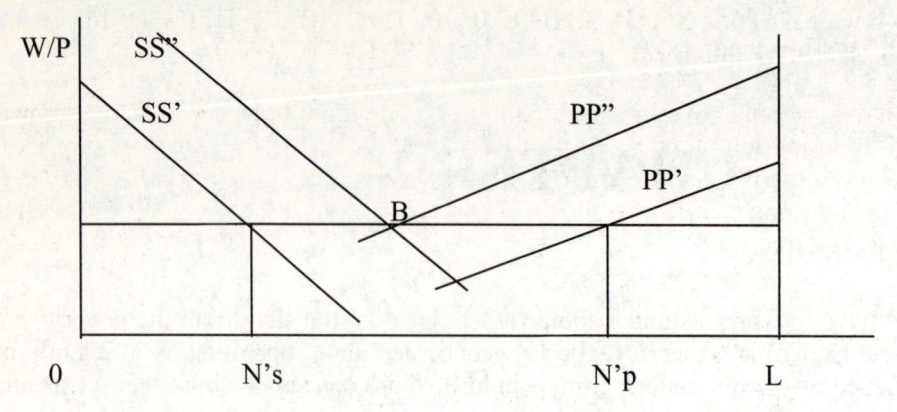

7. Factors: (1) lack of capital; (2) lack of expertise; and (3) lack of credit (loans).

8. Foreign direct investment is the purchase of existing firms or the development of new plants by foreign firms.

9. a. Firms will no longer be able to expect transfers from the government. Firms, most likely, will operate more efficiently.
b. The budget deficit will shrink.
c. Since the budget deficit is smaller, money growth will decrease.
d. As money growth decreases, inflation will decrease as well.

10. First, policy makers can restate their commitment to the pegged value of the currency. If that fails, they can raise interest rats to maintain the interest parity condition and to prevent a depreciation of the currency. If they want to avoid the high interest rates, they can devalue the currency.

11. a. A increase in the budget deficit would cause an increase in the trade deficit (NX would fall).
b. An increase in private saving would cause an increase in NX.
c. An increase in investment would cause a reduction in NX.

12. Answers will vary. Some emphasis should be placed on fundamentals while some emphasis should be placed on self-fulfilling expectations.

MULTIPLE CHOICE QUESTIONS

1. C 2. B 3. D 4. B 5. D 6. D 7. A 8. D 9. B 10. C 11. A 12. D 13. E 14. D 15. D 16. D 17. B 18. A

CHAPTER 25

REVIEW PROBLEMS

1. A change in the money supply will have uncertain effects on output because we do not know: (1) how much short-term and long-term interest rates will change; (2) how much stock prices will change; (3) how long it will take for changes in the above variables to affect investment and consumption; and (4) how long it will take for the J-curve effects to disappear (i.e., for NX to increase in response to a depreciation).

2. Unemployment equals the natural rate of unemployment and the rate of growth of output equals the normal growth rate (i.e., 3%).

3. a. MSG b. LINK c. VAR d. tie: DRI and EPA

4. Self restraint by policy makers represents policy makers who recognize the limitations of macro policy and, therefore, use less active policies. They do this recognizing the more active policies may be harmful to the economy. Restraints on policy makers represent restrictions imposed on policy makers. An example would be a constant-money-growth rule.

5. It is not clear if there are any advantages to such a policy. Because of the uncertainties presented here, it would be virtually impossible for a central bank to achieve this objective. Attempts to achieve this objective would require active monetary policy. Such fine tuning could easily cause greater fluctuations in output and employment.

6. a. This policy reflects the time inconsistency problem. Despite the stated policy, hijackings will likely continue.
b. This is the best of the policies. It would most likely result in the fewest of hijackings.
c. Not a great policy! Actually, such a policy might increase the frequency of hijackings.
d. The stated policy invites hijackings. Once they occur, the government does not negotiate which would increase the costs of the hijackings.

7. a. Recall that Okun's coefficient indicates how much the unemployment rate will change given a growth rate of 1% in excess of normal growth. If Okun's coefficient can taken on values from .3 to .9, more growth (caused by the Bank of Canada's increase in the rate of growth of money) can have significantly different effects on the change in the unemployment rate.
b. Recall that captures the effect of unemployment on inflation. Suppose this increase in money growth causes the unemployment rate to fall by 1% with certainty. Since α can take on a range of values, the effects of the money growth on inflation are unknown. For example, if $\alpha = 2$, the inflation rate rises by 2%. If α is .5, inflation only increases by .5%.
c. If both α and Okun's coefficient can take on a range of values, the final effects on inflation will be even more dispersed (i.e., uncertain).

8. a. Once firms and workers have adjusted their expectations based on this stated policy of the Bank of Canada (zero inflation), the Phillips relation becomes: $\pi = -\alpha(u - u_n)$ since $\pi^e = 0$. Now that wages are set, the Bank can reduce u 1% below the natural rate by accepting just 1% of inflation.
b. The actions described in a would not be consistent with its policy. The Bank of Canada via expansionary monetary policy, has caused inflation of 1% - a result that is inconsistent with its stated policy of zero inflation.

c. The central bank would be lost (or at least reduced).
d. Here is a case where there is an incentive, once the policy has been announced and firms and workers have adjusted their expectations to it, to deviate from the policy.

9. While such a policy/rule would clearly impose restraints on policy makers, it would also prevent monetary policy from being used as a policy instrument. For example, the presence of such a rule would prevent the central bank from responding to a negative shock that causes a severe recession.

10. The table in the chapter indicates that there is a negative relation between central bank independence and average inflation. Since there is a positive relation between money growth and inflation, you should expect a negative relation between central bank independence and average money growth.

11. a. The presence of political business cycles would indicate that policy makers are attempting to (and succeeding!) increase the growth rate prior to an election. This suggests that we should observe the following during the periods prior to an election: (1) higher G; (2) lower T; (3) lower unemployment; and (4) higher growth rate of output.
b. No. This result is not conclusive to support the political business cycles.

12. Again, there are no conclusive results even though one would expect relatively lower money growth during Conservative administrations and faster money growth during Liberal administration.

13. a. The drop in consumer confidence causes a drop in consumption. The lower C causes a leftward shift in the IS curve, a reduction in the demand for goods and a leftward shift in the AD curve. The drop in AD causes a reduction in output and a reduction in tax revenues. The decline in tax revenues causes a budget deficit to occur.
b. To eliminate this budget deficit, policy makers will have to cut G and/or raise T. Note: either of these policies will cause a further reduction in AD.
c. The balanced-budget amendment requires that policy makers pursue contractionary fiscal policy while output is already dropping. This amendment, therefore, worsens the effects of the negative shock to AD. The output effects are greater—the recession worse.
d. This is partly answered in c. Such an amendment would cause fluctuations in output caused by AD shocks to be greater.

MULTIPLE CHOICE QUESTIONS

1. D 2. B 3. C 4. B 5. B 6. C 7. A,B 8. C 9. B 10. D 11. B 12. D

CHAPTER 26

REVIEW PROBLEMS

1. a. Plug in the numbers in the equation in the text. When inflation is 3%: .25(.13739) = .0343 = 3.43%. When inflation is 6%: .25(.2527) = .063 = 6.3%. When inflation is 0%: .25(0) = 0%.
b. The real value of the house does not change cause the nominal value is assumed to increase at the same rate as inflation.
c. When inflation is 0, no tax is owed. Why? Because the value of the house did not change; she sold the house for the same price for which it was bought.
d. The effective tax rate increases as inflation rises.

2. Shoe-leather costs, tax distortions, money illusion and inflation variability.

3. a. Seignorage (and, therefore, lower borrowing or lower taxes), the option of a negative real interest rate, and money illusion which facilitates the adjustment of real wages.
b. The optimal rate of inflation will depend on one's views of the costs and benefits of inflation.

4. No. If i were negative, individuals would not hold any bonds; they would only hold money.

5. a. r = i - the rate of inflation. So, r is: 3%, 2%, 1%, 0%, -1%, -2% and -4%.
b. As inflation increases, the real interest rate falls (given I).
c. As r falls, investment will increase (so will consumption).
d. A negative real interest rate, especially in a recession will stimulate investment and cause an increase in aggregate demand and output.

6. M1B is smaller than M2. Why? M1B is a component of M2. M2 also includes assets not included in M1B.

7. a. Currency in circulation plus chequable deposits.
b. Same as M1 plus personal savings deposits and nonpersonal notice deposits at chartered banks.
c. The sum of M2 plus all deposits at trust and mortgage loan companies, credit unions, etc., plus the value of money market mutual funds and annuities.

8. a. The demand for M1B decreases.
b. The interest rate will fall from i to i'.

9. a. The reduction in the demand for M1 causes a lower interest rate and a shift down in the LM curve, i will fall and Y will increase (Go from point A to C).
b. Aggregate demand increases, the AD curve will shift to the right and the price level will increase.
c. The supply of M1 did NOT change. The higher price was, therefore, not caused by a change in the money supply.

10. a. The demand for both M1 and M2 will fall.
b. As discussed in #9, aggregate demand and the price level will increase.
c. To prevent the increase in AD, the Bank of Canada must prevent i from falling. To keep i constant as the demand for M1 falls, the Bank should reduce the supply of M1. LM' returns to LM and AD does not increase.

11. The analysis suggests that changes in the price level (and inflation) will not always be caused by changes in the money supply. Therefore, the relation between monetary aggregates and inflation will not be perfect.

12. 1935. The Bank has, since 1989, chosen to focus almost exclusively on controlling inflation.

13. a. Open market operations and deposit switching.
b. The former refers to the central bank's purchase and sale of government bonds from and to the public, which increases or decreases the monetary base and money supply, respectively. The latter refers to the Bank of Canada's transfer of the federal government deposits between banks and the Bank of Canada.

14. (1) to send a signal about the Bank's intentions; (2) to serve as a benchmark for judging the Bank's behaviour and (3) to help gain credibility by attaining its preannounced target.

15. a. If inflation is above target, the central will raise the nominal interest rate. If unemployment is above the natural rate, the central bank will reduce the nominal interest rate. When both situations occur simultaneously, the central bank's actions will depend on the relative magnitude of the parameters a and b (in addition to the extent to which inflation and unemployment deviate from target). If a is relatively large, the central bank will raise i. If, however, b is relatively large, the central bank will reduce i.
b. In the extreme, b = 0. Specifically, the central bank will care about only the deviations of inflation from target. Unemployment deviations from target will, in theory, have no effect on the central bank's actions.

MULTIPLE CHOICE QUESTIONS

1. D 2. D 3. A 4. D 5. C 6. A 7. A,B,C 8. C 9. D 10. B 11. D 12. B 13. D 14. E 15. C 16. B 17. B 18. A 19. B 20. B, C ,D 21. B

CHAPTER 27

REVIEW PROBLEMS

1. a. 100 b. 55 c. 10
d. Nothing happens to the primary deficit as i increases. The primary deficit is G - T which is independent of the interest payments (real or nominal).
e. 100 - 55 = 45.
f. B_t = 955; it increases by the size of the correct measure of the deficit.

2. a. G = T which implies that T must equal 200.
b. B_t = 900 to keep the debt constant. Plug in the numbers in equation (29.3): 900 = 945 + 200 - T. T must equal 245.
c. B_t = 0 if the debt is to be repaid in full. Plug in the numbers in equation (29.3): 0 = 945 + 200 - T. T must equal 1145!

3. a. The official measure of the deficit (iB + G - T) does not change as inflation increases. It remains constant at 100.
b. As inflation increases, the real interest rate will drop (since i is fixed). The correct measure (rB + G - T) will be: 72, 64, 46 and 10.
c. Subtract the correct measure from 100: 28, 36, 54 and 90.
d. As inflation increases, the official measure becomes more inaccurate. As inflation increases, the real interest rate falls and the real interest payments decreases. The official measure does not capture this.

4. a. Plug in the numbers into equation (29.3): B_t = 1.05(0) + 400 - 350 = 50.
b. The debt at the end of t+1 will be 0 since the government repaid it! 0 = 1.05(50) + 400 - T implies that T must increase to 452.5—an increase of 52.5.

5. Plug the numbers into equation (29.3) to obtain the debt levels for the end of each period: (1) at the end of period t+1 we have 52.5; at the end of t+2 we have 55.125; and (3) at the end of t+3, the debt will be zero since the government pays it off. Use the same approach to solve for T in t+3, 0 = 1.05(55.125) + 400 - T. T must equal 457.9 in period t+3—an increase of 57.9.

6. a. The size of the future tax increases gets larger. Why? The longer the government waits, the more interest payments have been accumulating on the debt issued when the taxes were cut.
b. The higher interest rate means higher interest payments and larger increases in the debt over time. Again, the tax increase will have to increase.

7. To keep the debt constant, the primary surplus must be equal to the real interest payments. If the primary surplus equals the real interest payments, the inflation-adjusted deficit must be zero to keep the debt from increasing.

8. a. The debt ratio in year t-1 is 1000/2000 = .50. The level of debt in year t is 1150; the debt ratio in year t is 1150/2000 = .575.
b. The debt ratio increased between these two years for two reasons: (1) there were interest payments on the previous level of the debt, and (2) there was a primary deficit in t.

9. The debt ratio increases when r > g (when g = 0). The debt ratio remains constant when r = g (when g = .02). The debt ratio falls when r < g (when g is .04 and .06).

10. See answer to #9. The ratio increases when r is .03 and .04; the ratio is constant when r is .02; and the ratio falls when r is .01.

11. The debt ratio will fall if: (1) g increases; (2) r falls; and (3) primary deficits become primary surpluses.

12. a. Taxes will have to increase by 100(1 + r).
b. Recognizing that future taxes will increase and that human wealth is unaffected by this tax cut, individuals will not increase consumption. Price saving will rise by 100. Total saving does not change. The IS curve does not shift out since consumption has not changed. The interest rate and, therefore, investment does not change. Output does not change since consumption does not increase.
c. It has no effect.

13. a. No effect. b. It increases. c. It will fall. d. No effect.

14. (1) to pass on the burden of the debt; and (2) to reduce tax distortions (smooth taxes).

15. a. A higher r increases the debt ratio since interest payments will be higher.
b. A lower g will also increase the debt ratio since output is not growing as fast.
c. The primary deficit would have to become a primary surplus. To do this, either G must be cut or T increased. Either of these actions will likely cause output growth to slow (g falls).

16. A country could cancel its debt. This would, however, make it very difficult to borrow in future. Who would want to buy bonds from a government that recently canceled its debt? Investors would require a very high risk premium which would cause the interest rate to be high as well.

17. Drastic cuts in expenditure on employment insurance, transfers to provinces, as well as rebuild a responsible social security system. The ultimate objective being balancing the budget.

MULTIPLE CHOICE QUESTIONS

1. B 2. C 3. C 4. D 5. A 6. A,D 7. D 8. C 9. C 10. D 11. A 12. B 13. C 14. C 15. A 16. E 17. A 18. D 19. E 20. E 21. D 22. D

CHAPTER 28

REVIEW PROBLEMS

1. The building blocks introduced by Keynes: (1) the multiplier; (2) the notion of liquidity preference (demand for money); (3) the importance of expectations in affecting consumption and investment; and (4) the idea that expectations can cause changes in demand and output.

2. a. Hicks and Hansen. b. Modigliani and Friedman. c. Tobin and Jorgensen. d. Tobin. e. Solow. f. Lucas, Sargent and Barro. g. Prescott. h. Romer and Lucas.

3. As the IS curve becomes steeper, a given reduction in the interest rate has a smaller effect on demand and, therefore, output. An increase in the money supply causes the LM curve to shift down and the interest rate to fall. The steeper IS curve, therefore, reduces the output effects of a given change in the money supply.

4. Yes, the Bank of Canada should announce it. Why? Under rational expectations, anticipated changes in the money supply do not affect output. If the Bank announces the reduction in the money supply and it is, therefore, anticipated, the lower money supply will not cause output to fall. The price will fall without a recession.

5. a. Here, the money supply increases 2% above expected. With the price level above expected, output will increase above the natural level.
b. Here, all of the 4% increase in the money supply is expected/anticipated. Output, therefore, will not change; it will remain at the natural level of output.
c. Here, the increase in the money supply is 2% less than expected. With the price level below expected, output will fall below the natural level of output.

6. Yes. The work of Fischer and Taylor about the staggering of wage and price decisions explains how output can adjust slowly even in the presence of rational expectations.

7. (1) competitive; and (2) fully flexible wages and prices

8. Output will increase when the state of technology improves (i.e., the economy experiences technological progress). Output will fall if there is technological regress.

9. (1) efficiency wages; (2) nominal rigidities; (3) imperfections in credit markets; (4) menu costs.

10. (1) aggregate demand affects output in the short run; (2) expectations play an important role in determining behaviour in the economy; (3) Y returns to the natural level in the long run; (4) Y is determined by the size of the labour force, capital stock and technology in the long run; (5) monetary policy affects output in the short and medium run and only affects inflation in the long run; (6) fiscal policy affects output in both the short and long run.

MULTIPLE CHOICE QUESTIONS

1. A, B 2. C 3. B 4. C 5. B, C 6. D 7. D 8. F 9. C 10. B 11. B 12. A 13. A 14. C 15. B 16. D 17. C 18. A, B, D 19. C 20. A

SEXUAL POLITICS IN AMERICA

SEXUAL POLITICS IN AMERICA

An Editorials On File Book

Editor: Oliver Trager

Facts On File

SEXUAL POLITICS IN AMERICA

Published by Facts On File, Inc., an Infobase Holdings company
© Copyright 1994 by Facts On File, Inc. an Infobase Holdings company

All rights reserved. No part of this book may be reproduced in any form without permission of the publisher except for reasonably brief extracts used in reviews, which retain their copyrights.

Cataloging-in-Publication Data available on request from Facts On File, Inc., an Infobase Holdings company.

ISBN 0-8160-3024-3

Printed in the United States of America

9 8 7 6 5 4 3 2 1

This book is printed on acid-free paper

CONTENTS

HQ
1421
S48
1994
c. 2
Gill

Preface 1

Part I: Women in America 2
Rape Issues Gain New Importance, Sexual Harassment History Surveyed, Anita Hill Accuses Judge Clarence Thomas of Sexual Harassment, Anita Hill Testifies, William Kennedy Smith Arrested for Rape, William Kennedy Smith Acquitted of Rape, Mike Tyson Convicted of Rape, Clinton Campaign Rocked by Infidelity Charge, Sen. Packwood Accused of Sexual Harassment, Sen. Packwood Ouster Bid Rejected, Navy Secretary Quits in Tailhook Scandal, Tailhook Report Assails Navy, Tailhook Report Details Abuses at Convention, Armed Forces to Allow Women to Serve in Aerial Combat, Canadian Shield Law Narrowed, Canadian Date Rape Law Introduced, Battered Women and Spouse Abuse Issues Debated Nationally, Supreme Court Rules on Sexual Harassment, Breast Implant Sales Halted, FDA Curbs Breast Implants, Women in NFL Locker Rooms Debated, Public Breast-Feeding Law Signed, Women's Issues Surveyed Worldwide, Anglicans Vote to Allow Women Priests

Part II: Gays in America 106
San Francisco AIDS Conference, Male Sex Survey Published, Gays March on D.C., Gays Barred from N.Y.C. St. Patrick's Day Parade, Oregon's Gay Rights Curb Defeated, Colorado Gay-Rights Ban Dealt Setback, Homosexuals in Military Becomes Widely Debated Topic, Clinton Endorses Military Ban on Homosexuals, Homosexual Sailor Reinstated in Navy, Lesbian Loses Custody of Son

Part III: Children, Teenagers & Sexual Issues 156
McMartin Pre-School Child Abuse Trial Ends, Missing N.Y. Girl Found in Hidden Cell, U.S. Comes to Grips with the Sexual Abuse of Children, Teenage Sex and Pregnancy Overview Presented, Michael Jackson Accused of Sexual Abuse, Woody Allen Sues Mia Farrow for Child Custody

Part IV: Sex & The Arts .176
'Obscene' Art Ban Rejected, Bush Opposes Obscene Art Censorship, NEA Rejects Four Grants, Cincinnati Museum Indicted over Mapplethorpe Exhibit, Hollywood X-Rating Replaced by NC-17, Rap Group Acquitted of Obscenity, Madonna Stirs Controversy

Index 204

Preface

In 1991, Anita Hill's charges of sexual harassment against Supreme Court nominee Clarence Thomas ignited a fresh wave of national debate on issues involving sex and sexual politics — debates that continue to rage today.

As the controversies surrounding this important topic increase and affect ever-widening parts of society, a new Editorials On File book, *Sexual Politics in America*, explores the issues surrounding this vital topic and the questions they provoke: Should gays be permitted to serve in the military? What were the issued involved in and what were the consequences of Anita Hill's allegations regarding sexual harassment at the confirmation hearings of Supreme Court nominee Clarence Thomas? What are the current debates surrounding pornography? Should the so-called "Rainbow Curricula" designed to teach children about non-mainstream lifestyles be instituted as national education policy? What was the upshot of the Navy's "Tailhook" scandal? What is the status of women in the workplace? Are rape and sex crimes given the attention they properly deserve? What has accounted for the perceived increase in the sexual abuse of children? How has AIDS affected the sex life of Americans? What are the debates surrounding teenage sex in the U.S.? Should condoms be distributed to high school students?

In *Sexual Politics in America* the nation's leading daily newspaper editorial writers and cartoonists examine the complicated issues informing these emotionally charged subjects.

Part I: Women in America

Conflicts between rights and values pertaining to sex roles appear nowhere in starker relief than in the category of crime. Even with the court-sanctioned removal of abortion from the "crime" list, the lurking violence women often feel commands attention.

The list is dominated by battered women, victims of family violence, even though authorities believe that only a small percentage of this type of violence, politely referred to as "domestic disputes," is actually reported. Major efforts have been made in many communities to establish centers to counsel and shelter battered wives who generally have no choice but to return to homes where they are subject to repeated abuse. Police claim that there is little they can do because the victim is often reluctant to press charges against her husband, is economically dependent on him or is willing to remain in the situation to keep a marriage intact for the sake of children. Statistics show that the problem is perpetuated as children in these families grow up and follow the same patterns.

Judicial decisions have made little change in spouse abuse situations, nor have they altered social customs.

The increasing incidence of reported criminal rape and acquaintance or "date rape," despite intensive efforts aimed at curbing the latter, continues to strike terror in the female heart.

As the number of reported rapes skyrockets, it is not known whether that is attributable to changing mores, which have removed much of the stigma formerly attached to the victim, or to changes in the law, which have made prosecution easier. In addition, highly publicized developments in the "battle of the sexes" have also expanded the definition of sexual harassment.

Studies have shown that many males operate on a set of self-serving assumptions. The men believe that if they are out on a date and spend a certain amount of money, they are entitled to repayment in the form of sex. Moreover, men have often grown up believing that when a women says "no" she really means "yes."

Many misconceptions about date rape are derived from a societal view that male aggression is "normal" and that a woman is somehow responsible for her date's behavior as well as her own.

Sexual harassment, another issue that has garnered significant media attention and legal action in the last several years, is not always included in discussion of violent crimes against women because it does not usually end in physical violence. However, by its very nature, sexual harassment keeps women fearful that it might lead to violence and could also threaten their livelihood.

Sexual harassment can take a variety of forms, including lewd conversation and/or display of lewd pictures; sexual items left on a woman's desk; remarks about her body; requests for sexual favors, sometimes coupled with the promise of promotion or threat of demotion; and touching a woman without her permission, particularly on the breasts or buttocks. Ultimately, there is still no consensus as to what constitutes sexual harassment as liberals and conservatives often split when it comes to establishing a concrete definition.

The military establishment, one of the largest employers in the United States and a bastion of machismo, has long had to attempt to reconcile the need to comply with directives on women's rights with the need to ensure that the physical requirements of military jobs are met. With few exceptions, nowhere have sex roles been so debated and altered as in the military.

Although women have been active during wartime in the military as ferry pilots, nurses and in special services, the actual decision to train them for combat roles was made in 1978 and reinforced in 1993.

It was predicted that sexual fraternization between male and female members of different ranks in the services would present a problem in maintaining discipline, a concern that is still being hotly debated. Basic training of women during pregnancy was another issue which, apparently, has been successfully managed on more than one occasion. The immobility of troops tied down with children was of more than passing interest, and directives were issued for "sole parents," a term which also applied to male soldiers, to make provision for child care.

Rape Issues Gain New Importance

Forcible rape is defined by the Federal Bureau of Investigation as the "carnal knowledge of a female forcibly and against her will." It is estimated that there are over 100,000 forcible rapes in the United States annually, comprising 6% of recorded violent crimes.

Statistics about rape are difficult to generalize from rapes are known to be underreported have remained. Some analysts believe that fewer than 10% of all rapes are reported.

The reasons for underreporting have remained the same for decades: self-blame, psychological trauma and humiliation, the risk of not being believed and recognition by the victim that she will come to be perceived, others as tainted or "damaged goods."

Despite massive efforts by feminist groups to help women understand that rape is not their fault, many victims still feel guilty. They wonder what they could have done to avoid it. In most cases, there is nothing they could have done.

Herald-American
Syracuse, New York, March 25, 1993

The task force on rape and sexual assault at Syracuse University has done some important work on the issue in the three months since it was formed.

Most of the recommendations in its report issued recently are solid. They include: offering more rape education, especially on the link between alcohol consumption and sexual assault; training judicial board members in handling sexual assault and rape cases; creating a permanent university commission to review university handling of rape and sexual assault cases.

However, one aspect of the recommendations is especially troubling. That is the recommendation that rape cases be handled by the university judiciary rather than law-enforcement agencies, if the victim prefers it that way.

We can understand that soon after a rape, the victim must make many choices about how the case is handled. Calling the police, going to the Rape Crisis Center, going to the hospital for a check-up and for evidence gathering, giving statements, maybe looking at a lineup or driving around the neighborhood with officers are all possible courses of action. It is a difficult, upsetting and confusing time.

We fear that when offered the alternative of a secret, on-campus adjudication, some victims will choose it as the path of least resistance. Keeping the whole incident a secret might seem like the easier course when a woman who has just been brutalized is facing the prospect of police questioning and, later on, a public trial.

But there is nothing easy about prosecuting a rape. Evidence is fragile and must be gathered with scientific precision. Investigations — including questioning of potential witnesses and securing crime scenes — have to be done carefully in order to build a case. It seems to us that those things are better left to professionals. We understand that the whole prospect of an investigation would be scary to a victim. So we are troubled by this offer of a seemingly easy alternative.

Because if a victim decides to use student judiciary and then is unhappy with the result, there is no way to go back and start the investigation in those crucial few hours that follow an attack.

Police officers, lawyers and doctors have come a long way in the last 20 years in learning how best to deal with victims of sex crimes. Their professionalism has grown as has the investigative technology they have at their disposal. It has been a long process and it continues. Even with the extra training for judicial board members that the report recommends, they could never approach the level of professionalism that most law-enforcement officers exhibit.

There are other issues as well. The worst punishment a university judicial board could mete out is expulsion from school. That hardly seems like an appropriate punishment for someone who has committed a felony — especially a violent one. And, if it should happen that the suspect is not a student, the board is powerless to do anything.

There is also the issue of public safety. If police and the district attorney's office are not notified of rapes occurring on and around campus, they may not be able to protect others effectively. What if there were a serial rapist that police were attempting to track? Not having access to information about all known cases could handicap their investigations and potentially lead to more assaults.

Members of the Chancellor's Task Force on Student Rights and Responsibilities say they hope that offering victims a secret, campus-based investigation may cause more victims to come forward and participate in some kind of prosecution. And while encouraging more rape victims to come forward is a good goal, there is no point in encouraging unsuccessful prosecutions or trials that a suspect could avoid simply by transferring.

We understand that representatives of the Onondaga County District Attorney's office plan to meet with commission members to express some of these concerns. We hope that happens. And we hope between them, the two organizations can find ways to encourage successful prosecutions of what is certainly one of the most despicable of crimes.

DAYTON DAILY NEWS
Dayton, Ohio, September 11, 1992

In the 1990s, a word that has always been in our vocabularies has re-entered in a new form: stalking, wherein an obsessed man follows a woman relentlessly, disrupting her life, scaring her and, sometimes, worse.

In state after state, anti-stalking laws are being passed. Whether stalking is becoming more common or just more recognized is not clear. But it is amazingly common.

Again and again the story turns out to be this: The man and the woman had a relationship — ranging anywhere from a passing acquaintance to a marriage — that the woman has declared to be over. The guy can't let go.

In Dayton, this week, in a sequence that looked liked some stalking cases, a man killed himself and a young woman whom he was romantically interested in.

What seems to be happening in some cases is the collapse of an extraordinarily weak male ego. A tenuously balanced man puts an enormous emotional investment into one relationship — perhaps prematurely and unrealistically, with little encouragement — and a rebuff is more than he can stand.

Much debate is taking place these days about stalking laws and whether they are too vague to be enforceable or constitutional. Ohio, like California two years ago and Florida this year, has a new stalking law, badly needed by police.

Before anyone gets too wrapped up in the debate about whether some stalking laws are vague, some note should be taking of the underlying problems: There are an awful lot of male explosives walking around. And there are even more guns.

The Pittsburgh PRESS
Pittsburgh, Pennsylvania, February 5, 1992

A long legal battle over the confidentiality of rape counseling sessions and records has ended in a victory for counseling centers. It's a victory that may cause some concern over defendants' rights but, overall, serves the cause of justice for victims of rape.

The 5-1 ruling by the state Supreme Court last week upheld a state law that protects rape-center counselors from testifying in legal proceedings and prevents the disclosure of any written documents resulting from meetings with rape complainants.

The issue had been in contention for at least 12 years and had persuaded the Legislature, in 1981, to grant rape-center workers a privilege against testifying about clients' statements about sexual assaults. Later, after the high court ruled that trial judges could examine counseling records in their chambers to see if they might be useful to defendants, the lawmakers extended immunity to those notes and papers also.

Workers at rape-counseling centers had claimed all along that they deserved the same sort of confidentiality protections as clergy and physicians; that victims would not, in many instances, be willing to come forward if personal matters were to be revealed in subsequent hearings or in a trial.

The court's majority agreed, citing "the very nature of the relationship between a counselor and the victim of such a crime."

Justice Stephen A. Zappala dissented, asserting that the decision would undercut the basic rights of the accused.

It's conceivable, of course, that a defendant's case might be helped on occasion if his lawyer could review what a rape victim discusses with a counselor.

But the therapeutic and intensely private nature of such conversations argue for keeping them confidential, as the Legislature and high court concluded. So does the fact that this will persuade more victims to come forward to help in their own recovery and in finding and punishing their assailants.

THE TAMPA TRIBUNE
Tampa, Florida, February 1, 1992

Government reports tend to be restrained when not obtuse. Not the Board of Regents' report on a University of South Florida scandal. It's a scorcher.

The Regents appointed a team of educators and law-enforcement officials to investigate the way USF officials handled a rape complaint against a star basketball player. Their report minces no words:

"No, good management was not followed, and, no, the students were not treated fairly." The investigators excoriated USF administrators for insisting that they "did nothing wrong, that the matter was handled perfectly, and would be handled in the same way again."

If USF President Francis Borkowski, who has already made some changes, doesn't revamp the way the university handles disciplinary matters, then he'll deserve the Regents', not to mention his students', wrath.

Among the investigators' recommendations, which should be immediately adopted by Borkowski:

■ Make a professional victims' advocate available to students reporting a crime.

■ Appoint a pool of "back-up disciplinary" officers.

■ Change disciplinary rules, which now require administrators to look at only a single event, to allow school officials to "review patterns of previous offenses and [impose] immediate suspension in cases of threat to the community."

■ Verify the criminal records of student applicants.

■ Be open with the public and the press.

■ Help educate students, with special courses, on the dangers of date rape and alcohol.

USF's handling of the incident was staggeringly inept.

A student accused Marvin Taylor, then a star basketball player, of rape in October 1989. An associate dean suspended Taylor, pending an emergency hearing. According to the report, when the alleged victim met with Vice President of Student Affairs Dan Walbolt, she indicated she was "being harassed by members of the basketball team and their girlfriends and other friends of" Taylor and felt she could no longer tolerate the pressure. She asked to withdraw her complaint.

Did Walbolt, who resigned yesterday under pressure, take action to investigate the harassment charges or give the woman reassurance? No, he recommended no action be taken against Taylor since the victim was willing to drop the charge. He inaccurately said the woman had "recanted" her story. He called the athletic director to tell him that Taylor could play basketball again.

Subsequently, three women accused Taylor of harassment. Another accused him of battery. Again, little was done. Taylor kept his scholarship until he missed a curfew, when the scholarship was terminated.

Is it likely Taylor would have received this singular treatment if he had not been a star basketball player? The appearances, at least, are damning.

Walbolt served USF honorably for many years, but his judgment in this case was abominable. His refusal to recognize and acknowledge his mistakes is deeply troubling. Borkowski, too, responded much too lethargically to the scandal. To restore his and the university's credibility, Borkowski must follow through on the promise to reform disciplinary policies. Perhaps his first step should be to require all administrators to undergo a crash course in how to recognize and learn from their mistakes.

But all this may be too late to save Borkowski's job. Education Commissioner Betty Castor, who is a member of the Board of Regents, and several legislators are furious.

Rep. Mary Figg, D-Lutz, is quoted as saying: "I can't tell you the rage I personally feel about this. It is the rage all women feel about this who have been placed in a similar situation, when they've been coerced by a body that's supposed to protect them by not pressing charges.... Either the president didn't know what took place, which means he doesn't know what's going on on this campus, or he did know. I'm assuming he did not know. It's his responsibility to know."

Now the matter is in the hands of state university system Chancellor Charles Reed. It's up to him to recommend to the Board of Regents what action, if any, to take against Borkowski or others at USF. It's a shameful situation, but we urge Reed to give Borkowski the opportunity to respond in detail to the many questions surrounding this ugly case.

LEXINGTON HERALD-LEADER
Lexington, Kentucky, February 6, 1992

Sometimes, a society has to look at itself in the mirror and ask if this is the best that can be done.

It's mirror time here in Kentucky.

If the figures hold up over the last three months of 1991, the number of reported rapes in this state will have risen by more than 80 percent from a year ago.

The numbers are astounding. Kentucky women are being raped at the rate of nearly six a day, seven days a week. Last year, 3.2 women each day were raped in our cities and neighborhoods — a lower number, but still appalling.

It would be nice if there were some way to explain away these figures. Maybe there are just more *reported* rapes, for instance. Maybe the increase is a paper creation.

No way. The numbers are real. "This increase is not just a reporting phenomena," says Carol Jordan, an official with the Cabinet for Human Resources. The fact is, more women are being attacked, more are being hurt. In some areas, the increase dwarfs the statewide statistics. In Somerset, for example, reported rapes have jumped by 141 percent.

Today, we'll learn if the budget of Gov. Brereton Jones provides the money necessary to open new rape crisis centers as well as maintaining the centers we have. We hope the governor sees fit to increase the funding for these vital services. If he doesn't, then the legislature should do the job.

But that is just the beginning. It doesn't touch the real question. It doesn't answer why now — in this past year — so many Kentucky women have become the victims of this crime.

The answer to that question comes from all of us. It's up to us to find out what is going on in our families, churches, schools, communities and workplaces that has led us to such a state.

It is time to look in the mirror.

THE INDIANAPOLIS NEWS
Indianapolis, Indiana, February 3, 1992

Numbers often can be unpleasant.

In the past two years, the number of rapes reported to the Indianapolis Police Department has increased by 41 percent.

That increase is but part of a veritable explosion of violent crime.

Just last year, the number of murders reported to IPD jumped by 64 percent. The number of aggravated assaults climbed 11 percent. Robbery shot up by 20 percent.

All of this took place in a recession economy — at a time when state and local governments were caught in a budget crunch and forced to stretch dollars just to deal with old responsibilities, much less respond to new problems.

Perhaps that is why Marion County Prosecutor Jeffrey Modisett says, simply, "More money would help," when asked if there is a way to aid victims of rape and other violent crimes.

Doubtless money would help, and more money should be found.

At present, a rape victim in Indianapolis can expect to be supported through her trial and trauma by a dedicated but overworked victim's advocate. She is entitled to five free psychiatric counseling sessions.

After those sessions end, if she still needs some therapy — as she likely will — her victim's advocate will scramble to get her funding from the state assistance fund for victims of violent crime. She can draw up to $1,000 — until recently it was $10,000 — from that fund.

That may seem like a lot of money, but it adds up to anywhere from eight to 12 sessions with a therapist in private practice. Medical expenses, of course, can run much higher.

The money often provides just barely enough time to begin the process of healing.

There is a reason for that. The unfortunate truth about rape is that it has an almost singular capacity to bring forth old pain, to reopen old wounds, to reawaken whatever fears may lie sleeping in the psyche.

Most rape victims do not have to simply "get over" a single incident; they have to rebuild their lives.

And this city and state should help them do that, because the reason people band together in communities and form governments is to provide collective security. When a rape or a murder or an assault occurs, it is not just an offense against an individual, it is a crime against the community's security.

Does that mean taxes should be raised to provide more aid and support for victims of violent crime?

No.

Rather, priorities should be rearranged.

A city government that can ante up the money to entice developers to build a Circle-Centre Mall should be able to find the cash to hire more victims' advocates. A state government that can spend the dollars to build new state office buildings should be able to discover a way to provide adequate funds for victims of violent crime.

It is simply a matter of deciding what matters and what doesn't. Who needs help the most and who doesn't.

THE TAMPA TRIBUNE
Tampa, Florida, February 11, 1992

One of the more troubling aspects of the American judicial system is the way a criminal case fades into abstractions as it climbs the ladder of appeals.

It seems to be a legal maxim that oftentimes the facts of a crime count for less and less, the higher the case rises through the courts.

Jurors and trial judges confront the dark, bloody details of a case, gauging the victim's pain, weighing the evidence and rendering a verdict. They fit the law to the circumstances.

But those gritty facts tend to slip into the background as the case slides up the line of appeals. By the time an appeal reaches the Florida Supreme Court, victim and defendant may be nothing more than ciphers. What counts most at that level are procedures, rules, laws, and esoteric arguments about their meaning and intent.

This is not necessarily bad. If the rules and laws are good ones, the system works well. But if they are bad, the justices, and the rest of us, have a problem.

And we do have a problem.

That problem is embodied in one Marcus Edmund Karchesky, formerly of Casselberry, now a resident of New River State Prison near Jacksonville.

Karchesky's victim was the daughter of his live-in girlfriend. In a Sanford courtroom in 1986, the slender, blond-haired girl testified that Karchesky, then 28, sexually assaulted her repeatedly over a two-week period. The first attack occurred just two days after her 12th birthday.

The jury deliberated a little more than an hour before finding Karchesky guilty of three counts of having carnal intercourse with an unmarried person under the age of 18, and seven counts of committing a lewd and lascivious assault upon a child. The judge sentenced him to 60 years in prison as a "mentally disordered sex offender," followed by 60 years probation.

Karchesky appealed. The court found that some of his 10 crimes were actually lesser included offenses, and reversed all but three convictions. That lopped 43 years off his sentence, bringing it down to 17 years plus 15 years probation.

Again he appealed, with disturbing results.

This month the Florida Supreme Court found that Karchesky's trial judge was wrong to add "points" to his sentencing guidelines scoresheet for injury to the victim, because the sentencing rules do not regard penetration by a rapist as "physical trauma" suffered by the victim.

In their decision, the jurists note that "no evidence of any physical injury or trauma to the victim caused by the defendant during the intercourse was present" at the 1986 trial.

It should be noted that not all the justices were so pedantic in their view. Justices Leander Shaw Jr. and Parker Lee McDonald dissented.

Wrote Shaw: "The term 'physical trauma' ... should be read to include sexual contact and penetration."

But the majority of justices said they were bound by the wording of the rules of sentencing guidelines. Karchesky's lawyer said the decision reduces the top range of sentence under the guidelines from 17 years to 5.5 years. Karchesky has already served more than five years in prison.

The sentencing judge can go beyond the guidelines, but he will have to file a written justification for the decision.

The Supreme Court's action has implications far beyond the case of one child molester. The ruling sets a precedent for some other cases involving sexual battery, lewdness and indecent exposure and incest.

This does not mean there will be a wholesale cutback in the sentencing of rapists, because many use a weapon, physically harm their victims, or are repeat offenders; this ruling would not apply to them. But for first offenders who did not "physically" damage their victims, the decision could be a key to the prison gate.

Rape is a crime like no other. Nothing short of murder inflicts such deep and lasting damage to the mind and spirit of the victim. The law should extract a penalty for that harm, even when the victim is not bruised and beaten.

State Rep. Ron Glickman, D-Tampa, has introduced legislation that would alter the sentencing guidelines and restore the penalty for trauma in rape cases, even without physical injury. It deserves prompt attention. The court's unfortunate ruling ought to be nullified quickly.

THE INDIANAPOLIS NEWS
Indianapolis, Indiana, February 3, 1992

Sometime this week — perhaps even while the lawyers at the Mike Tyson trial are arguing back and forth — a man in Richmond will be released from jail.

A little more than a year ago, that man raped and beat his ex-wife while their small children watched. He was tried, convicted and given a 10-year sentence. Eight of those years were suspended. He was given credit for the time — roughly a year — he'd served in jail awaiting trial and then granted parole.

the subject is **RAPE**

Soon he will be back out on the street, another dangerous product of a society and a judicial system that refuse to take rape seriously.

It would be comforting to think that this case in Richmond is an isolated incident — that rape is treated seriously by society and the courts. But that wouldn't necessarily be accurate.

Just last autumn, a Marion County Superior Court jury found Lawrence businessman Paul Stewart guilty of rape. Judge Paula Lopossa's sentence was a hand-slap: a six-year suspended sentence, two years of nights at a work-release center, two years of probation to follow that and a fine of $5,000.

Worse, Lopossa all but abrogated the jury's decision by saying:

"I think it was obvious it was non-consensual sex. But I don't believe it was a violent act, as most people think of rape."

Perhaps the victim in that case — who, by the way, was just a teen-ager — should have undergone a savage beating in order to persuade Judge Lopossa that, by definition, "non-consensual sex" is rape. And rape is a violent act.

In some ways, it's not fair to single out Judge Lopossa or the courts in Richmond for criticism. The truth is that American society has been quite slow to take rape seriously.

Consider the circus atmosphere surrounding the William Kennedy Smith and the Mike Tyson trials. The details that have absorbed this country's attention have not been the ugly realities of rape — the gruesome and vicious violence of the crime, the shattering trauma victims endure and the endless web of hate and mistrust spun by the constant threat of rape.

No, attention in these two celebrated cases has focused itself mostly on trivialities: the lingerie Patricia Bowman was wearing on the night she met William Kennedy Smith, Mike Tyson's bad breath, etc.

Judging from such heavy-breathing analysis of those cases, rape is an issue that could be better handled by Madison Avenue rather than the legal system. More modest underwear and a good breath mint and rape wouldn't be a problem.

Nothing could be further from the truth. The fact is that rape is not trivial; it is life-threatening.

As a story in The News Extra! section and an essay on the opposite page demonstrate, rape uproots and, in many ways, destroys the lives of victims, their families and their friends.

Even if a rape does not produce bruises or broken bones, it can be deadly. Long after the attack ends, the consequences remain, and even multiply.

Rape victims, for example, are high-risk candidates for AIDS. Even if a victim does not contract the deadly virus, the terror of waiting can be overwhelming.

"Every time I went for an AIDS test, I was convinced he had killed me as well as raped me. I couldn't eat. I couldn't sleep. All I could think about was dying. That takes something out of you. And you never get it back," one victim told The News. She weathered the AIDS danger period of six months to a year and no longer is presumed to be at risk from her attack.

Like her, many rape victims complain that society is less than sensitive to their plight. They say that they are victimized afresh when they enter the legal system, that they alone among victims of crime are forced to defend their actions and argue that they did not in some way provoke the attacks upon them.

Their complaints have merit, but solutions are not easy to find.

There is no way to change the way rape cases — most of which boil down to one person's word against another's — are conducted in court without fundamentally undermining presumptions of innocence, one of the foundations of the American legal system.

Furthermore, Indiana and Marion County already have done a great deal to support and accomodate rape victims.

Indiana has a rape shield law — a law preventing defense attorneys from exploring a victim's sexual history in court. There are victims' advocates and funding for victims of violent crime.

More, however, could be done. And that is what the following editorial will explore.

THE DENVER POST
Denver, Colorado, February 17, 1989

THE UNIVERSITY of Colorado's decision to require all CU athletes to attend sex-crime seminars conveys a timely message that ought to be passed on to all students throughout the state.

The lesson is that "date rape" is a serious crime, to be reckoned with and prosecuted as aggressively as violence committed by a stranger. Just because the victim and the perpetrator may be acquainted doesn't mean the behavior should be excused, any more than it would be in an extortion or a case of child abuse.

This important educational effort in Boulder will be undertaken following the arrests of two football players and one former player on charges of sexual assault. But according to coach Bill McCartney, it's been planned since last summer, when Athletic Director Bill Marolt learned a rape-awareness program was available.

Colorado State University took a similar step a year ago after an outbreak of sexual lawlessness among non-athletes. Three dozen fraternity brothers were ordered to take classes in women's studies and write term papers on sexual assault after a midnight panty raid got out of hand and numerous sorority women were manhandled.

It shouldn't take incidents like these, though, to spark preventive action. An explanation of what constitutes rape — and why it's considered a crime of violence, rather than one of passion — should be a part of freshman orientation at every college in the state. It would be wise to add it to high school curricula as well.

San Francisco Chronicle
San Francisco, California, August 18, 1992

CALIFORNIA'S Legislature has successfully rejected the medieval notion that wives are nothing but the personal property of men and overwhelmingly voted to rewrite the law to provide the same possible punishment for all rapists, whether they be husbands or not.

The Senate last week joined the Assembly in approving a bill to subject spousal rapists to the same punishment as other rapists. Currently, the minimum sentence possible for conviction on a spousal rape charge is a year in county jail. Conviction on a non-spousal rape charge carries a minimum three-year prison sentence.

Senator Bill Lockyer, D-San Leandro, who sponsored the measure in the Senate, said the bill is principally designed to levy an appropriate punishment for estranged husbands who return to attack their legal wives.

THE SIGNIFICANT merit in the legislation is its clear statement that the mere existence of a marital relationship is no reason that that status should serve to protect a criminal act.

Sexual Harassment Issues & History Surveyed

Though the topic of sexual harassment was the center of public debate and interest during the Supreme Court confirmation hearings for Judge Clarence Thomas in the fall of 1991, the issue has been the subject of lengthy debate and legislation for decades.

Following is a chronology of key events in the development of U.S. legislative and judicial policy on sexual discrimination and harassment in the work place.

■ *July 2, 1964* – The Civil Rights Act is signed by President Lyndon Johnson. Title VII of the act prohibits employment discrimination. The Equal Employment Opportunity Commission (EEOC) is established to probe complaints of discrimination.

■ *March 24, 1972* – The Equal Employment Opportunity Act, signed by President Richard Nixon, expands the EEOC's jurisdiction and empowers the commission, rather than the Justice Department, to bring suit against employers discriminating in the work place.

■ *June 23, 1972* – President Nixon signs the Education Act Amendment. Title IX of the amendment disqualifies education programs that discriminate on the basis of sex from receiving federal aid.

■ *July 1977* – In *Barnes v. Costle*, the District of Columbia Circuit Court of Appeals rules that, under Title VII of the Civil Rights Act, sexual harassment in the work place constitutes discrimination if it "adversely affects a job condition." The court says a woman forced to have sex to keep her job is discriminated against under Title VII because she would not be victimized "but for her womanhood."

■ *Nov. 15, 1977* – Five female undergraduates at Yale University file the first sexual harassment suit ever under Title IX of the Education Act Amendment.

■ *Oct. 13, 1978* – President Jimmy Carter signs the Civil Service Reform Act, barring discrimination in federal personnel practices. (In 1980 and 1988 surveys, the Merit Systems Protection Board established by the act finds 42% of women employed by the government report having been sexually harassed within the previous two years.)

■ *Dec. 12, 1979* – After a series of hearings investigating allegations of sexual harassment in the federal government, the White House Office of Personnel Management issues a directive to all government offices defining harassment and condemning its practice as impermissible.

■ *April 11, 1980* – The EEOC issues regulations prohibiting sexual harassment in government and private employment. The EEOC regulations state that: "Unwelcome sexual advances, requests for sexual favors, and other verbal or physical conduct of a sexual nature constitute sexual harassment when:

1) submission to such conduct is made either explicitly or implicitly a term or condition of an individual's employment,

2) submission to or rejection of such conduct as the basis for employment decisions . . . or

3) such conduct has the purpose or effect of unreasonably interfering with an individual's work performance or creating an intimidating, hostile or offensive working environment."

■ *June 19, 1985* – The Supreme Court rules in *Meritor Savings Bank v. Vinson*, the first harassment case to come before the high court, that sexual harassment of an employee by a supervisor constitutes sex discrimination under Title VII of the Civil Rights Act. The court's decision upholds the principle that creation of a hostile working environment constitutes harassment, even when no economic harm is suffered by the victim. Catherine McKinnon, a pioneer attorney in the sexual harassment field, helps present the winning case.

■ *Jan. 18, 1991* – In a further extension of the "hostile environment principle," a district court Judge in Florida rules in *Robinson v. Jacksonville Shipyards* that the posting by managers of nude pinups in the work place constitutes sexual harassment of the company's female employees.

Rockford Register Star
Rockford, Illinois, October 9, 1992

One year to the week after the confirmation hearings on Clarence Thomas' nomination to the Supreme Court became a riveting drama involving sexual harassment charges, the nation's high court has done a curious thing: It has effectively ordered a company to rehire a male employee who sexually assaulted a female co-worker. For all the wonders of our system of jurisprudence, justice is not always the end product.

Chrysler's good-faith efforts against sexual misconduct have been thwarted.

One day in 1989 at a Chrysler Corporation facility in Beaver Dam, Wis., a forklift operator named Ronald Gallenbeck was talking on the phone. Suddenly, he put the receiver down and grabbed the breasts of a passing female co-worker. He then picked up the receiver and said to the person on the other end of the line: "Yup, they're real."

Chrysler fired Gallenbeck, but his union took the case to arbitration. Despite evidence of past instances of sexual harassment by the offender, the arbitrator ruled that he should merely have been suspended for 30 days rather than fired. Chrysler appealed the ruling through the courts. The Supreme Court this week let stand a lower court ruling that said the collective bargaining agreement between the union and the company made the arbitrator the final judge in the case.

So, in this instance, Chrysler has been thwarted in its good-faith efforts to discourage sexual harassment in the workplace. Gallenbeck's dismissal would have sent a strong message to any other such goons that sexual assault will not be tolerated. Instead, the message conveyed is that the price to be paid for copping a quick feel is a mere month on the sidelines without pay.

Who can rightly say that justice was done in this case?

The Des Moines Register
Des Moines, Iowa, October 31, 1990

U.S. District Judge Harold Vietor's ruling in the sexual-harassment suit against the University of Iowa is a model of judicial craftsmanship. In 76 prosaic paragraphs, which are excerpted on the opposite page, Vietor presents the story of Dr. Jean Jew's 10-year trial of bigotry, petty jealousy and vicious gossip at the university's College of Medicine.

She was accused by colleagues in the crudest terms of sleeping with her boss, of being a slut, a whore, a bitch. She was the target of nasty rumors, anonymous personal attacks, sexually suggestive cartoons posted in the department and cruel jokes scribbled on the men's room walls. These slurs caused her no end of pain, and retarded her career.

Throughout this shameful ordeal, Jew's superiors ignored the harassment. Even when U of I administrators were put on notice — and urged by a faculty committee to take prompt action — they ignored the advice, dawdled and generally failed to take the situation seriously.

Nowhere in the recitation of these facts or in the subsequent conclusions of law does the judge yield to the temptation to lash out at Jew's colleagues and superiors to say, "Good God! This is a university, and you're acting like a bunch of juvenile thugs." Instead, Vietor let the record speak for itself.

The sordid details make painful reading. One wonders how Jew managed to function at all in such an environment, let alone prevail in her five-year effort to win back her self-respect, her dignity and her professional advancement.

Painful as those details may be, the judge concluded they should be held up for all to see. In addition to awarding her the promotion she was denied, Vietor ordered that the decision be distributed among the Board of Regents, administrators at the University of Iowa and the College of Medicine and be kept on file and accessible to faculty and staff for no less than five years.

Nowhere in the decision does Vietor put in words what prompted him to require the university to face up to this distressing episode. He did not have to.

The university is keeping its options open to appeal Vietor's decision, but an appeal would almost certainly be a waste of time and money, and it would send the message that such behavior could somehow be justified, or excused.

Whatever the cost of accepting this decision, it is a small price compared to what Dr. Jew has paid. It would be an outrage to delay justice in this case a moment longer.

The Honolulu Advertiser
Honolulu, Hawaii, October 29, 1992

The allegations of sexual misconduct made by hair stylist Lenore Kwock against Democratic U.S. Senator Dan Inouye, unfortunately aired in ads by Inouye's opponent, state Senator Rick Reed, have dominated Hawaii political talk for two weeks.

Invariably, the question has turned to: Whom do you believe is telling the truth?

Is it Kwock, who says Inouye sexually molested her in 1975 and fondled her later at her shop? Or Inouye, who denies the charges and says Kwock is lying or imagining things?

In the court of public opinion, the jury returned a mixed verdict, with voters dividing themselves among three camps, according to The Advertiser/Channel 2 News Hawaii Poll. More people tend to believe Kwock (30 percent) than Inouye (24 percent). But nearly half the voters polled either say they don't know — or believe neither side.

Yesterday's report that Kwock had taken and passed a lie detector test on the matter will, of course, add further fuel to the "believability" fire, as people debate the reliability of such tests, which are not normally admissible in court trials.

Most voters seem willing to put the Kwock matter aside and support Inouye over Reed on election day, the poll showed. Inouye's level of support (57 percent) and his margin over Reed haven't changed much since summer.

Finally, there's no confusion among voters on a related point: 83 percent say Reed was wrong to air Kwock's allegations in his campaign ads without her permission. That resounding "no" sends a message that voters here don't buy into sleaze.

THE INDIANAPOLIS STAR
Indianapolis, Indiana, September 26, 1990

Indiana University's Reserve Officers Training Corps students will be faultless victims if the IU Student Senate succeeds in having the university ban the ROTC from all IU campuses by 1995 on grounds the corps discriminates against homosexuals.

Such a ban would be grossly unfair to ROTC students, of which there are 295 on the Bloomington campus alone.

Defense Department policy, which the ROTC is required to follow, says: "Homosexuals are considered unsuitable for military service and are not permitted to serve in the armed forces in any capacity. His or her presence in the military unit would seriously impair discipline, good order, morale and security."

> The critical question is whether defense policy is sound.

The Student Senate resolution, which was passed last week by a 16-3 vote, with five abstentions, said Pentagon policy conflicts with the Code of Student Ethics approved by the IU Board of Trustees last May, said an IU Student Association spokesman.

That code says: "The university does not condone discrimination against members of the university community based on sexual orientation."

The university issued a statement saying that ROTC is a part of its diverse academic opportunities and "Our military services need officers who have a multiplicity of backgrounds."

The statement added that IU has joined other members of the Association of American Universities in asking that all military services bring their policies into conformity with the schools' standards on non-discrimination.

Therefore the future of IU's relationship with ROTC would appear to hinge on the Defense Department's willingness or unwillingness to change its policy. That in turn would depend upon a determination whether the basis of the policy is sound or unsound.

Does the presence of a homosexual in a military unit "seriously impair discipline, good order, morale and security"? What is the source of the Defense Department's contention that it does? What evidence can IU or the other universities adduce that it does not?

If the present policy is based on errors of fact and judgment, the Defense Department and the universities should be able to reach a constructive compromise.

If the present policy is valid, university dissociation from ROTC would be not only grossly unfair to ROTC students but a serious disservice to the armed forces and the nation.

There no doubt are many who disagree with the policy but federal courts have upheld the Defense Department's ban on enlisting known homosexuals in several instances.

THE RICHMOND NEWS LEADER
Richmond, Virginia, March 24, 1989

In politics, an extremist is a person to whom one is losing an argument. In football, the prevent defense was the forerunner of the dreaded vent defense, which eventually gave way to the postvent defense.

This brings us to a word for all seasons: Womanizer. It has been much in the news.

Some say John Tower is a womanizer. Strange. Tower does not exactly possess the looks or the caring personality of Alan Alda — both of which, we are told, appeal mightily to the modern liberated woman.

He doesn't even look like Tom Selleck.

What does the word mean?

Well, to a guy, a womanizer is somebody who stole his ladylove. To a female, a womanizer is somebody who ran off with a new ladylove. It's that simple.

To define man-izer, reverse the above.

The Record
Hackensack, New Jersey, October 14, 1989

Is there anything positive that can come of being handcuffed to a urinal and having your picture taken as your classmates jeer at you? Well, if you are a female midshipman at the United States Naval Academy at Annapolis, maybe there is.

That is the way Gwen Marie Dreyer was humiliated by her male classmates last year, and because of it, some changes are about to be made at the academy. It's a very high price to pay. Ms. Dreyer left the academy after the male midshipmen who harrassed her were disciplined with nothing more than slaps on the wrist. But because Ms. Dreyer had the courage to speak out about what happened, the academy has been publicly embarrassed. Administrators now say sexual harassment will be taken seriously.

Following Ms. Dreyer's resignation from the academy in May, five civilian and military inquiries were begun. Four of those inquiries released their findings this week, and their verdict was unanimous: Sexism is a major problem at the academy, and hostility toward female midshipmen is fairly common.

A committee appointed by the academy's governing body recommended several solutions. It urged that sexual harassment be made a distinct offense under the academy's conduct code, generally punishable by expulsion; that more women officers be appointed to the faculty and administration; and that senior officers who question the role of women in the military be dismissed immediately. The superintendent of the academy said the recommendations will be adopted.

That should help to change the belief, apparently held by many midshipmen and members of the faculty, that women have no business at the academy. That attitude is too bad, because women are at Annapolis to stay. They have been graduating from the academy for a decade and make up 10 percent of its classes.

More important, women in the American military are a given. They are in the sands of Saudi Arabia and on the ships in the Persian Gulf, where they are both taking orders and giving them. Any officer, or future officer, who cannot deal professionally with that fact doesn't belong in uniform.

Richmond Times-Dispatch
Richmond, Virginia, November 3, 1990

Rep. Donald "Buz" Lukens' resignation from the House of Representatives last week was too long in coming. Mr. Lukens was convicted earlier year in Ohio on misdemeanor charges for having sexual relations with a 16-year-old girl. Last Monday, new sex charges were made against Mr. Lukens. A young female elevator operator complained that Mr. Lukens twice made advances on her, fondled her and gave her his card and asked her to call him. Such conduct by anyone, let alone a member of Congress, is disgusting.

This time, fortunately, the congressional leadership acted quickly. The House Ethics Committee announced that it would reopen its investigation of Mr. Lukens' conduct, and Minority Leader Robert Michel told Mr. Lukens, a Republican, to resign or face expulsion from the House, a punishment that would cost him his congressional pension.

The leadership's treatment of Mr. Lukens is quite different from the way it has treated the problem of sexual harassment on Capitol Hill more generally. It was easy to tell Mr. Lukens to resign, since he already was damaged political goods. But the system under which congressional employees must bring harassment complaints discourages reporting all but the most egregious violations of common decency.

Complaints must be brought either to office supervisors or to the Ethics Committee, which in either case biases the process in favor of the officeholder and against the victim. There is no guarantee of protection for the whistle-blower, who might, as a consequence of registering a complaint, expect her (most such harassment is directed at women) career to suffer.

We bid good riddance to Mr. Lukens. But no one should mistake the swift punishment for his latest transgression for congressional intolerance of sexual harassment. On the contrary, sexual harassment on Capitol Hill is too often treated with a wink and a nod. Roll Call, a weekly newspaper that covers Capitol Hill, as long as two years ago reported on sex harassment in other congressional offices, but no one on the Hill has chosen to inquire further. This is a problem that cries out for investigation and institutional reform when Congress reconvenes next January.

THE CHRISTIAN MONITOR SCIENCE
Boston, Massachusetts, October 15, 1990

UNTIL the mid-'70s, the United States armed services academies were all-male clubs. The exclusionary policy spawned attitudes toward women – or, more precisely, women's "place" – similar to those fostered at other bastions of male separatism. If anything, such attitudes were compounded by the machismo that is an accepted, even encouraged, element of martial skills. Then Congress opened the doors of the academies to women.

Some of the academies have adjusted better than others. At West Point, the Army Academy, the corps of cadets last year was commanded by a woman cadet. The Naval Academy at Annapolis, Md., however, has had a tougher time accepting women.

So conclude several reports issued last week by panels investigating sexual harassment at the Naval Academy. The probes were initiated last spring after a woman midshipman resigned, citing harassment by male students.

The two leading reports – one by an internal committee, the other by civilian members of the academy's Board of Visitors – found widespread sentiment among midshipmen, faculty, and staff that women don't belong at Annapolis. The panels confirmed the allegations of Gwen Dreyer, the woman who resigned, that she had been handcuffed to a urinal and jeered at by some of her male peers. The groups further documented a wider and disturbing pattern of harassment against the women midshipmen.

In 1990 – when women soldiers, sailors, and airmen are performing tasks in Saudi Arabia that could involve them in a shooting war – such attitudes and practices are dismayingly atavistic. Fortunately, according to Sen. Barbara Mikulski, the fleet is ahead of the academy in integrating women into operations.

The commanding officers at the Naval Academy should promptly implement the panels' recommendations to improve the environment for women. And the Navy's highest brass and its civilian overseers should closely monitor the progress.

The Des Moines Register
Des Moines, Iowa, November 15, 1990

The University of Iowa is paying an extraordinary price for the sexual harassment of anatomy professor Jean Jew.

The cost goes far beyond the settlement announced this week, which included, among other things, a payment of $176,000 to Jew and $895,000 in legal fees claimed by her lawyer. The university also has seen its reputation tarnished. That may affect everything from recruitment of faculty and students, to raising money from alumni.

It's an expensive lesson not only for the university, but also for every other public and private institution and for every business in the state: Sexual harassment is not just morally and legally wrong; it also can create a huge financial burden.

University officials have acted to ensure that faculty, staff and students have a better understanding of their rights and obligations in regard to sexual harassment. A new set of complaint procedures, noting that "the presence of sexual harassment in this community subverts the mission of the university and will not be tolerated," has been widely distributed. It recognizes that the university has been too lax in explaining policies, procedures and expectations.

That's a notable effort, but much more will be needed to heal the divisions and cynicism that remain, cynicism illustrated by what happened during a recent faculty meeting. As reported by the student-published newspaper, The Daily Iowan, a university vice president, noting changes in procedures dealing with such cases, said, "I would be willing to bet anybody anything that this sort of thing won't happen again."

To which a member of the audience quickly responded, "Do you have a buck?"

The university community still is seeking answers to questions surrounding the case:

• Why did the university so fiercely resist settling the case?

• What action is being taken against the faculty members who harassed Jew and against administrators who, by stonewalling a settlement, perpetuated the injustice? In many businesses, they would be suspended, demoted or fired.

• Was the university involved in any way in the defense of a faculty member who last summer lost a defamation suit filed against him by Jew?

• Are university officials re-examining grievance procedures to ensure prompt and fair resolution of personnel problems?

To his credit, university President Hunter Rawlings has recognized that the settlement doesn't represent the end of the issue, but rather, a renewed challenge for the university to demonstrate that it will not tolerate any form of harassment. The challenge is not just to the university, but also to the Board of Regents, which governs it, to the other regents institutions, and to the entire state.

Minneapolis Star and Tribune
Minneapolis, Minnesota, December 24, 1989

Sexual-harassment charges like those leveled against former Greater Minnesota Corporation President Terry Montgomery involve more than allegations of impropriety. They constitute one of the most serious charges that can be leveled against a public official — abuse of power.

That's why the responses by a number of top state officials were so disappointing. The officials were right not to have prejudged Montgomery. But they should have made clear they will not tolerate attempts to use positions of authority to extract sexual favors. None made that point.

After Montgomery resigned from the GMC following the filing of the charges, Gov. Rudy Perpich praised him for his work at the GMC and as Perpich's chief of staff, and said he was saddened by the resignation. Fair enough. Montgomery has contributed much to the governor and to the state during his public career. GMC officials and legislative leaders echoed Perpich's sentiments.

Missing from their comments, however, was a forceful condemnation of any attempt to use a public position of authority to extract sexual favors.

There was a similar omission in a letter praising Montgomery sent by his close friend, state Planning Commissioner Lani Kawamura, to GMC staff members. Kawamura called Montgomery's resignation "courageous," and, said it "demonstrates his compassion and sincere concern for the future of the GMC." She did not mention the charges or refer to the issue of sexual harassment.

By refusing to acknowledge the charges, and by failing to condemn any behavior under any circumstances, the testimonials showed lack of concern for victims of sexual harassment. However inadvertent the omissions might have been, they are damaging.

Sexual harassment has no place in the workplace. Women have legal tools with which to fight it and should use them. The treatment of working women has improved in recent years, but sexual harassment still occurs. It is illegal. It is cruel. It is simply wrong. Perpich and other state officials should say so, and then they should pledge to eradicate it from state government.

M.G. LORD'S VIEW

[Cartoon: A man on a ladder hanging mistletoe while a woman points at him saying: "PUT THAT MISTLETOE DOWN, MR. ARBUTHNOT! UNLESS YOU WANT TO GET SLAPPED WITH A SUIT FOR SEXUAL HARASSMENT!"]

Thomas Accused of Sexual Harassment; Confirmation Vote Delayed Amid Debate

A former aide to Supreme Court nominee Judge Clarence Thomas Oct. 6, 1991 publicly accused him of sexually harassing her over a period from 1981 to 1983.

The charge sparked an emotional and contentious national debate over the issue of sexual harassment, particularly after the woman, Anita F. Hill, a tenured law professor at the University of Oklahoma, Oct. 7 accused the Senate Judiciary Committee of not fully investigating her complaint. Amidst the growing controversy over the charges and the committee's handling of them, the Senate Oct. 8 agreed to postpone until Oct. 15 the vote on Thomas's confirmation to the Supreme Court. The vote had originally been scheduled for 6:00 p.m., Oct. 8.

The controversy surrounding Hill's charges erupted into a political mudfight as Republican legislators accused Democrats of illegally leaking reports of Hill's charges to the press. A battle of the sexes also developed as female legislators and lobbyists accused their male counterparts of simply not comprehending the seriousness of sexual harassment in the work place.

Until Hill's charges were publicized, Thomas's confirmation had appeared guaranteed. Most Senate Republicans and several Senate Democrats had announced their support for the nominee.

The specifics of Hill's charges were contained in an affidavit submitted to the committee in September, which was later leaked to the press. In the affidavit, Hill charged that beginning in 1981, when she had worked as Thomas's assistant at the Education Department, Thomas had repeatedly asked her out and after she had refused to date him, had begun telling her about his sexual interests. Hill described Thomas's remarks as explicit, saying he had discussed sexual acts he had seen in pornographic movies. She said the comments had stopped for a time and she had moved with Thomas to the Equal Employment Opportunity Commission, where the harassment had begun again. Hill had quit her job at the EEOC in 1983.

According to reports Oct. 6 in New York *Newsday* and on National Public Radio, the Senate Judiciary Committee staff had first heard of Hill's charges the week of Sept. 10. However, the Federal Bureau of Investigation did not begin to investigate the charges until Sept. 23. An FBI report was completed on Sept. 25 and made available to the committee one day before its Sept. 27 tie vote, 7–7, on Thomas's nomination.

Sen. John C. Danforth (R, Mo.), Thomas's main Senate patron, Oct. 6 said Thomas "forcefully denies" Hill's charges. Thomas Oct. 8 released an affidavit that said, "I totally and unequivocally deny Anita Hill's allegations of misconduct of any kind toward her, sexual or otherwise. These allegations are untrue." In the same statement, Thomas asked the Senate to delay the vote on his confirmation to give him a chance to clear his name.

Professor Hill, speaking at a news conference at the University of Oklahoma, Oct. 7 explained her reasons for coming forward with the charges against Thomas and accused the Senate Judiciary Committee of not fully examining the accusations.

Hill denied that her charges had been politically motivated, and she stressed that she had not intended to make public her accusations against Thomas. She did so, she said, only after being contacted by committee staff members in early September. Hill said she had come forward because she believed that Thomas's conduct "reflects his sense of how to carry out his job and that, in effect, he did not feel himself compelled to comply with the guidelines [on sexual harassment] that were established by the EEOC."

Hill said she was frustrated by the way the committee had handled her charges, saying that despite her repeatedly calling the panel and sending her statement by facsimile, certain members had not learned of her account until shortly before the committee vote Sept. 27.

The Star-Ledger

Newark, New Jersey, October 11, 1991

Perhaps more disturbing than the allegation charging Supreme Court nominee Clarence Thomas with sexual harassment of a former employee was the bumbling manner in which the nearly all-male Senate dealt with it. The events leading to the postponement of a confirmation vote did not produce a flattering image of that legislative body.

The delay appears to be more an act of damage control, a furtive effort to contain a growing controversy, than an act of statesmanship. Political pragmatism seemed to play more of a role in the Senate's decision than any sense of conviction.

It was only after senators were deluged with telephone and fax messages from irate female constituents that they opted to put the confirmation vote on hold for a week to investigate the allegation made by University of Oklahoma law professor Anita Hill.

Professor Hill has charged that Judge Thomas made lewd and intimidating comments to her while she worked for him in two different federal jobs in the early 1980s—one at the Equal Employment Opportunity Commission which handles sexual harassment complaints. Judge Thomas has "totally and unequivocally" denied the accusation.

The extra week is not expected to uncork any information that will settle the matter of the nominee's guilt or innocence or Professor Hill's credibility. At best, it will be an opportunity for both parties to respond to direct questioning about the alleged incidents—his word against hers.

Sen. Joseph Biden (D-Del.), who was privy to the charges nearly a month before they became public, said additional hearings are necessary "because we cannot fail to take seriously such a charge." But Sen. Biden, who chairs the Senate Judiciary Committee which grilled the nominee, apparently felt otherwise about the importance of the charge prior to feeling the heat of public opinion.

The committee's action—or inaction—on the allegation seems to lend credence to angry women who charge that the Senate is an exclusive "old boys' club" that chose to wave away what could be a serious charge. Even those who disbelieve Professor Hill's charge are nonetheless appalled at its handling by the Senate committee.

If the senators thought there was insufficient cause to address the allegation—which the Judiciary Committee certainly failed to do—then that should have been clearly stated, and there would have been no need for a delay and additional hearings. But to admit that at this point would mean facing the wrath of angry women who view the Senate as insensitive to their gender, which would be politically unwise.

Whatever the outcome, the Senate has not done itself or the country proud in this matter, and whatever the ultimate decision, the Senate's "advise and consent" role will be tainted by its old boys' blunder.

THE ANN ARBOR NEWS
Ann Arbor, Michigan, October 9, 1991

The U.S. Senate was correct Tuesday in postponing a vote on the Clarence Thomas nomination in the interest of fairness as well as the integrity of the Senate and Supreme Court.

Had a decision been made without having seriously considered the sexual harassment accusations made against the judge, it would been unfair to Thomas and to Anita F. Hill, the law professor who made the charges. It would have ignored the seriousness of the issue and implied that the Senate places expediency above justice. If nominated, it could have cast a permanent shadow over Thomas' effectiveness as a justice and his role on the Supreme Court.

The vote, delayed for a week, gives Thomas a chance to defend himself before the Senate and gives Hill the opportunity to testify under oath. It is the only just way to handle the case.

> If there is a "trial" during these next days of testimony, it will involve the Senate and its capability of handling a sensitive issue in a dignified manner.

At the same time, it should be remembered that the Senate is not a court of law. This is not a trial, and the outcome is to determine Thomas' fitness to serve on the Supreme Court, not his innocence or guilt on sexual harassment charges.

If there is a "trial" during these next days of testimony, it will involve the Senate and its capability of handling a sensitive issue in a dignified manner. So far, in the Hill case, it has not performed well.

Hill has rightfully questioned the way the Judiciary Committee handled her accusations. Thomas ought to be asking similar questions. These charges were serious enough to have delayed the committee's vote to send the nomination to the full floor. No excuses can justify the committee's decision not to give Thomas and Hill full hearings after they received the FBI report on Sept. 25 regarding the professor's charges.

Unfortunately, senators did not find it important to air Hill's charges until the last minute. It signals indifference, ineptitude or rotten politics, all of which are deeply disturbing.

DAILY NEWS
New York City, New York, October 9, 1991

THE SENATE'S REACTION to Anita Hill's explosive allegations against Clarence Thomas has made one thing absolutely clear: There's a distressing degree of confusion and discomfort around the issue of sexual harassment, even at the highest levels of government.

The Equal Employment Opportunity Commission defines sexual harassment as any behavior that has the "purpose or effect of unreasonably interfering with an individual's work performance or creating an intimidating or hostile or offensive environment."

Disturbingly, some members of that mostly men's club, the Senate, have revealed that they didn't know even that basic legal fact. Nor, as Hill correctly contends, did most senators react to the issue at hand. Instead of seriously examining her charges of harassment — and their implications for a prospective Supreme Court justice — the politicians largely saw Hill as an interloper in their confirmation process.

Arguably, the law is uncomfortably vague. Perceptions of a "hostile" or "offensive" environment can vary widely. Still, this incident illustrates why women must move beyond fear and vigorously assert their right not to be verbally assaulted in the workplace. Saying "this offends me and it must stop" is part of the battle. But only part of it.

Most important, men must learn that a supervisor's power is not a tool of seduction, that a "no" (even an unclear one) must be heeded, and that sexual harassment is a serious crime. If nothing else, the Thomas-Hill episode should lead to a more educated population — including the members of the Senate.

The Hutchinson News
Hutchinson, Kansas, October 10, 1991

How much more will the process of selecting a Supreme Court Justice endure?

How many more 11th-hour surprises are in store for Judge Clarence Thomas?

It is not surprising that senators were pressured to postpone their scheduled vote Tuesday on Thomas' confirmation. The charge against him, if true, would make him unsuitable for holding a seat on the nation's highest court.

But how credible is the charge of sexual harassment by Thomas of his former aide, Anita Hill, and why has it been issued so late in the process?

The dilemma pits one honorable reputation against another, a no-win situation, but even more importantly, it delivers a severe blow to the nomination process, a system that already has proven itself less than satisfactory.

Now the issue before the nation is not just the question of who will assume the post to the high court. It has suddenly become broader than that, now including the issue of male insensitivity in matters of sexual harassment.

Surely, Clarence Thomas, who already has been given his day in court on numerous occasions, now will get one more, but this time to defend himself against the charge. Anita Hill, an attorney and a law professor, will also get an opportunity to make her case.

Senator Bob Dole says the postponement of the vote on Thomas and the subsequent hearing will be "a test of (Thomas') character."

That is baloney.

What the nation now faces is a test of the nation's paltry leadership, which plays politics with the nation's future, and special interest opportunists who know when to pounce, having dithered for years without the courage to attempt to fix asserted problems.

Any American ever having contact with Thomas has had dozens of past opportunities to discredit him. He held a high-profile government job before assuming his position on the federal court, both posts highly visible, and one of which was determined by a senate confirmation process.

Judge Thomas' "character" has already been tested under the repetitious and redundant questioning by senators. He has displayed his calm under pressure. He is a decent man who would give service to his country, though the despicable actions of vast numbers of public officials have now ensured that nobody will win this debacle.

FORT WORTH STAR-TELEGRAM
Fort Worth, Texas, October 8, 1991

Allegations that Supreme Court nominee Clarence Thomas was guilty of sexual harassment of a former female aide a decade ago raise sufficient questions to justify a delay in the Senate's confirmation vote, scheduled for later today.

Anita Hill, a law professor at the University of Oklahoma, told Senate committee members in early September that Thomas had harassed her while she was employed as his assistant in the Education Department in 1981 and again after both had transferred to the Equal Employment Opportunities Commission.

According to Hill, Thomas, separated from his first wife at the time, frequently asked her out and, when she refused, described his sexual interests and scenes from pornographic movies. Senate Judiciary Committee Chairman Joseph Biden, D-Del., said he and his fellow committee members knew of Hill's allegations when they voted 7-7 to send Thomas' nomination to the full Senate without recommendation.

Hill has made some troubling accusations, and we are disturbed by the fact that committee members chose not to acknowledge them publicly, thus depriving the full Senate of information it needs to make a sound decision.

The confirmation vote should be delayed long enough for a full investigation. Without it, the allegations will leave a cloud of suspicion over the nominee and, ultimately, the Supreme Court that can do far more damage than a delayed vote could ever do.

THE DENVER POST
Denver, Colorado, October 11, 1991

PUBLIC confidence in the integrity of politicians has never been rated very high, but there are indications that it might be sinking to an all-time low.

The latest New York Times/CBS News poll reports that 83 percent of American adults believe members of Congress intentionally overdrew their House bank accounts because they knew they could get away with it.

The entire environment of national politics — the obscene costs of campaigning, the strong influence of special interests, the isolation of the Washington beltway, the affluent lifestyle of incumbents — is becoming increasingly distasteful to most Americans.

And now, with disclosures of special privileges enjoyed by federal legislators and the question of ethical hypocrisy raised in the Clarence Thomas confirmation process, fuel has been dumped on the flames of voter discontent.

Whether the fire is hot enough to scorch incumbents in next year's election is uncertain, but incumbents have an impressive record of surviving such political infernos in the past. While voters tend to distrust politicians in general, they look more kindly on their own representatives. Consequently, incumbents are seldom defeated even though public sentiment strongly favors throwing the rascals out.

But if we're not yet at the point of a sweeping overhaul of Congress, we clearly are getting closer to it. Just in the past week, several prominent political figures — including Vice President Dan Quayle and conservative columnist George Will — have endorsed the concept of term limitation, restricting the power of incumbency.

This week's spectacle of seven U.S. senators grilling Judge Thomas on issues of morality can do little to improve the overall climate. Several of the seven can't avoid questions of hypocrisy as they sit in judgment of a man accused of moral or ethical peccadilloes.

Meanwhile, the month of October hasn't provided much reassurance to representatives and senators facing re-election one year from now. Their opponents are amassing an arsenal of weapons — supplied by the incumbents themselves.

The Virginian-Pilot
Norfolk, Virginia, October 11, 1991

Once in a while a moment arrives when the nation becomes so focused on an issue that attitudes on it can change overnight. On the issue of sexual harassment, that "defining moment" may come today, when the Senate Judiciary Committee hears Anita Hill's charges against Clarence Thomas.

It's clear that many men — including members of the Judiciary Committee — have not thought much about sexual harassment in the workplace. It's clear that many women have — and resent deeply male ambivalence on the subject. Even women who support Mr. Thomas, such as Sen. Nancy Kassebaum of Kansas, are appalled by the committee's cavalier dismissal of Professor Hill's allegations.

They have reason to be appalled. Ms. Hill is a woman of considerable accomplishment with a reputation for honesty and integrity. Yet the Judiciary Committee simply took her statement (alleging sexual harassment), took his statement (denying the allegation) and called it a draw — not worthy of further examination. In essence, the members of the committee did not think it was a serious complaint.

They do now, of course. Their "consciousness" has been raised by their constituents. That's good for everyone, men and women, who believe sexual harassment deserves to be on the front burner in a time when a majority of women work because they *have* to work — they can't simply quit when their bosses or co-workers treat them as sex objects.

But there is a danger for women in the Hill vs. Thomas confrontation. There are puzzling aspects to Ms. Hill's story. There are questions about why she maintained a personal relationship with Mr. Thomas many years after he allegedly harassed her. So far, other women who worked for or with Mr. Thomas have not come forth to lend credence to her charge.

If, under grilling by the committee and the news media, she is less than convincing, this moment could be a setback for women. Women who have been harassed may not complain — many don't now — because they don't want the hassle. And men who believe the whole issue is much ado about nothing will say: 'I told you so.'

Herald-News
Fall River, Massachusetts, October 10, 1991

Just as the seven women members of the House stormed the Capitol steps Tuesday to the threshold of the Capitol room — demanding to be heard by the male-dominated Senate Democrats on the issue of sexual harassment charges against Supreme Court nominee Clarence Thomas — the women of America are knocking, often unheeded, on the collective consciousness of this country.

And just as these representatives were ignored, the pleas of women and minorities across the nation are repeatedly being pushed aside.

Unjust and digruntling as this may be, reducing the dilemma of sexual harassment to a fight between the sexes will do all of us a disfavor.

For a woman's or man's right to go about business, or schooling or simply life unfettered by matters of a sexual nature is indeed a human issue. Both women and men have a right to be regarded solely as people, aside from their sexual orientation or bulging biceps or the length and shapeliness of their legs.

The photograph of the seven representatives tearing up the Senate steps presents a poignant picture of indignation. It's unfortunate that, whether from ignorance or exclusion, male representatives didn't join the charge alongside their female colleagues, displaying the same outrage.

When a person's worth, however innocently, off-handedly or fleetingly is reduced to a bra-cup size or rumored bedroom prowess, it diminishes all of us.

Not taking seriously charges of sexual harassment is an affront to both genders.

That's why the Senate's failure to act quickly regarding Anita Hill's accusations about Thomas is so disturbing. Thomas supporters seemed more concerned with a slippage of votes for their nominee than the seriousness of the charges against him and the implications for all of us.

And although he should be applauded for his honesty, Massachusetts Sen. John Kerry's question, "How are 98 men going to make a judgment about sexual harassment in the workplace?" is especially telling. How can the 98 men of the Senate fail to make that judgment? It affects men as much as women.

One of the representatives who lobbied the Senate, democratic Rep. Barbara Boxer of California, furthered Kerry's sentiment, commenting, "This is about women, and there's no women over there (the Senate) but two."

But Boxer is wrong. This is about all of us.

THE DENVER POST
Denver, Colorado. October 8, 1991

THE MOST curious aspect of the Clarence Thomas nomination, as columnist Molly Ivins observed on this page a few days ago, is that while he's been judged mainly on his views about abortion — a subject of prime importance to females — those doing the judging have been exclusively male.

This disturbing imbalance has now been underscored by the accusation that Thomas sexually harassed a female employee while serving as chairman of the Equal Employment Opportunity Commission during the Reagan administration.

The members of the Senate Judiciary Committee — all male — apparently knew of the allegations against the Supreme Court nominee last month, but decided they were unfounded before voting to send his name to the floor.

It's possible that the committee would have reached the same conclusion even if some of its members had been women. But the sex-harassment issue would probably have loomed much larger in its deliberations, and might well have led to further inquiries into Thomas's attitudes toward women in general.

Certainly the claim — made by a woman who is now a University of Oklahoma law professor — would not have been summarily dismissed, only to surface at the last minute as an obvious but probably abortive smear tactic.

Now the Senate, which is virtually all male, must presumably pass judgment on Thomas, and by implication, on the importance of these questions to the millions of females who could be affected by his arguments and decisions.

In the long run, the ironies of this process should spur the Democrats and Republicans to work harder to guarantee that women's interests are well-represented in the Senate. The parties have certainly tried to make sure that men's views don't go ignored on the Supreme Court.

THE TENNESSEAN
Nashville, Tennessee, October 11, 1991

IMAGINE this: a male factory supervisor walks up behind a female worker, comments on the tightness of her clothes and invites her for an after-work beer.

Or this: A female secretary works for an elderly executive, who routinely pats all the male workers on the back — and all the female workers on the backend.

Or imagine a 25-year-old female who just graduated from law school and has taken a job with the federal government. Her boss, who is divorced, is attracted to her, and asks her for a date. She turns him down, but in subsequent conversations with her, he tells her graphically his sexual preferences and describes scenes from pornographic films. It is this scenario that Anita Hill, now a tenured law professor, has used to describe her working relationship with Clarence Thomas in the early 1980s.

Sexual harassment? Innocent flirtation? Just joking around? Or as Thomas asserts, a total lie?

If nothing else, the controversy concerning Thomas and Hill has raised the nation's awareness about sexual harassment like nothing else could have.

Although it can take many forms, all cases of sexual harassment share a few elements. The activity must be unwelcomed. It must be sexual. It must have a negative impact on one's working environment. It does not have to involve physical contact, and it does not have to involve a threat to one's job or one's income. Its victims may be men as well as women.

Today, in one of its most highly charged moments, the Senate Judiciary Committee will explore the relationship between Thomas and Hill.

This will be an extremely difficult hearing. When the nature of Hill's FBI report became public this week, the Senate exploded in finger-pointing and blame-laying. Some members seemed more concerned about finding who leaked the information about Hill than they were about getting at the truth about Thomas.

Today, the internal squabbling should be set aside. The committee must focus totally on Thomas and Hill.

Even that won't be easy. Each committee member is already on record on the Thomas nomination. If senators who support Thomas badger Hill about her own personal conduct, they'll look like the worst kind of male chauvinist pigs. If senators who oppose Thomas ask questions that assume his guilt, they'll look like character assassins.

And no one should have to tell the committee members that the public is intensely interested in this matter. If they've never been objective before, the senators must try to be so today. And the hearings should continue until all questions are answered.

Both Hill and Thomas are intelligent, articulate and respected professionals. This week, they have both handled the controversy with considerable grace. Too bad the same can't be said of a few senators, particularly Alan Simpson, R-Wyo. and Dennis DeConcini, D-Ari., whose mean-spirited rantings were demeaning to them and to the body in which they serve.

The U.S. Senate has had an embarrassing lesson in sexual harassment this week. Now that it has learned that it exists, it needs to discover if Clarence Thomas practiced it. ■

SYRACUSE HERALD-JOURNAL
Syracuse, New York, October 10, 1991

Did Supreme Court nominee Clarence Thomas sexually harass his former aide Anita Hill? The Senate rightly has delayed its vote on Thomas to ferret out the truth in renewed hearings. Meanwhile, we're appalled at the Senate Judiciary Committee's shameful handling of the matter.

The committee and the Senate leadership knew of Hill's allegations since September. But they kept them secret and dismissed them without thorough public airing. And they would've allowed their colleagues to remain none the wiser about Hill's charges and vote on Thomas, as they had planned to do Tuesday, had it not been for a news leak.

As Sen. Daniel P. Moynihan, D-N.Y., properly noted while pressing for the vote's postponement early Tuesday: "We cannot have a proceeding where 17 senators know something which, if 83 senators knew, a procedure would not take place."

The leak forced the Senate to do the honorable thing and delay the Thomas vote until next week. That it took an unexpected public revelation of a committee secret to accomplish that is testament to why so many Americans are distrustful, if not fed up, with Congress. One week it's check-bouncing in the House; the next, this fiasco in the Senate.

On Monday, Judiciary Committee Chairman Joseph Biden said he saw no reason to delay the Thomas vote because of the Hill charges. But by Tuesday, Biden was falling all over himself defending the Senate. He announced the FBI would investigate and witnesses would testify. And he declared the hearings must go on "because we cannot fail to take seriously such a charge."

For weeks, Biden and his fellow senators on the panel failed to take the charge seriously. Then, suddenly, they were crusaders, brandishing swords and charging.

What a difference a day can make, especially a 24-hour period during which it became clear that the Hill controversy might cost Thomas the votes needed for his confirmation. Also, a day when, nationally, voices rose in outrage that the Senate, comprised of 98 men and two women, was acting as if sexual-harassment charges were trite.

Could it be the senators slept on the matter and saw sexual-harassment ghosts rising from their own closets? Congresswoman Pat Schroeder of Colorado told the New York Times: "It's a male bonding thing. They (senators) all think of themselves as potential victims, thinking, 'We need to stick together or all these women will come out and make allegations setting us up.'"

Fortunately, the news leak broke the bond in this case. We hope Clarence Thomas' innocence or guilt regarding the sexual-harassment charges now can be determined, once and for all, through a fair and complete presentation by all sides. That's the American way.

Sad is that the U.S. Senate had to be reminded of that.

St. Paul Pioneer Press & Dispatch
St. Paul, Minnesota, October 8, 1991

If a fiction writer set out to plot a movie where cynical politics triumph over governance, it would be difficult to create a tale more symbolic than the Clarence Thomas saga. His nomination for Supreme Court justice heads for an ending bereft of service to the constitutional duties of any branch of the federal government.

Last three days have shown high-impact politics at its worst.

The final scenes are going through a rewrite, thanks to the pre-emptive use of a news leak about Anita Hill's secret testimony to the Senate Judiciary Committee that Mr. Thomas made inappropriate sexual comments to her when she worked for him a half decade ago.

Professor Hill made a reasonable request on Monday. Speaking in Norman, Okla., where she is a law professor at the University of Oklahoma, she asked the full Senate to consider carefully the information she had provided to its committee. That's not likely. The highly politicized nomination and confirmation process surrounding Mr. Thomas intensified immeasurably over the weekend when it was disclosed that Professor Hill's affidavit, submitted to the Judiciary Committee before it voted 7-7 on the Thomas nomination, did not delay or stop the process.

This is not the place to examine the legal merits of Professor Hill's charges. She did not seek a public airing of the case. She has made no formal charge that Mr. Thomas sexually harassed her. Trial by media is as inappropriate as the deceits of politics that have brought the nation to this befuddling confirmation vote day.

Confusion is the common theme of the whole Thomas case. We surrendered to the conventional wisdom early in the hearings, bowing to what seemed inevitable confirmation and the understanding the President Bush could do worse than Mr. Thomas. Yet, the final chapter makes even the most jaded non-Washingtonian marvel that a matter as serious as sexual harassment would be glossed over, even if it did arrive late in the committee's investigation. One is left to conclude that the disparate political agendas on the Thomas nomination had no place for a full examination of a substantive charge made by a credible, legally knowledgeable witness.

One can't help but wonder if there would have been such a grand sweeping under the rug if the Judiciary Committee had a woman member. Could the FBI, part of Mr. Bush's Justice Department, have been pressed harder about Professor Hill's testimony?

In July, the president chose to serve politics above the law when he nominated Mr. Thomas, a beginner on the appeals bench, to the Supreme Court. The senators on the Judiciary Committee failed in confirmation hearings to get straight answers from the nominee. Now in the third branch, the highest court in the land has opened its term ready to receive a justice who comes not with the informed consent of the Senate, but with it abrogation of duty.

The last three days have shown high-impact politics at its worst. This is no atmosphere for the whole Senate to vote on the nomination of a man who could sit on the Supreme Court until two more generations of Americans come of age. But the Clarence Thomas story plot has taken on a life of its own, out past reason and good judgment.

THE SPOKESMAN-REVIEW
Spokane, Washington, October 10, 1991

Another week — even another year — will not yield a conclusive verdict on the sexual harassment allegations against Supreme Court nominee Clarence Thomas.

But if a week's delay in the vote on Thomas' confirmation can begin to restore the Senate's credibility in such matters, then the wait will have served a purpose. That credibility has been eroded in recent years by the increasingly politicized handling of Supreme Court nominations. It has been damaged even more by the indecisive backpedaling over the charges against Thomas.

If Thomas actually made the kind of comments and advances law professor Anita Hill says he did when he was head of the Equal Opportunity Commission a decade ago and she was an aide to him, the Senate is unlikely to do a better job of proving it than the FBI did when it investigated the matter earlier this fall. And if he didn't make them, that defies proof, too.

Will the Senate, which appeared ready to confirm the nominee on Tuesday evening, now change its assessment, based on an unproved accusation? If so it reflects sadly on the attitudes that motivate the Senate.

The Judiciary Committee, with a healthy share of Thomas detractors, knew of the allegations, as well as the FBI's findings, but chose not to make an issue of them during the public confirmation hearings. The reason, some members now say, is not that they considered them immaterial but that they wanted to honor Hill's desire for privacy.

In that case they have to explain why they would place the privacy desires of an individual citizen above the nation's interest in thoroughly examining the qualifications of a prospective Supreme Court justice.

From the beginning, political sideshows have clouded the central issues of the Thomas nomination. President Bush's unblushing assertion that Thomas' race was not a factor in the nomination is but one example. Another is the production by renegade right-wingers of a television ad that purported to support Thomas by assailing the integrity of Judiciary Committee members Ted Kennedy, Joe Biden and Alan Cranston.

And, as the question seemed to be nearing an answer on Tuesday, the House of Representatives wasted most of a day in floor speeches and associated parliamentary entanglements created by members, from both parties, who insisted on sounding off about a decision they have no formal part in.

Now, with a week-long extension during which Hill's allegations will be aired and answered publicly, the Senate will try to redeem itself in the eyes of constituencies that think ignoring charges of this nature looks insensitive.

In the process, unfortunately, not only will Thomas be subject to a grilling but Hill will have to endure cross-examination in the committee room, not to mention in the minds of millions of skeptical Americans. In the end, individual senators ought to make their decisions on the basis of Thomas' qualifications — but in reality the echo of political rhetoric will ring insistently.

In the future, meanwhile, capable Americans who are considered for appointment to important federal office might have second thoughts about exposing themselves to unforeseeable accusations that sprout so vigorously from well-fertilized political turf, and never really die.

For now, the Senate has its hands full finishing work on the Thomas nomination. When that's over, the body should focus its attention on returning dignity and seriousness to the confirmation process.

Lincoln Journal
Lincoln, Nebraska, October 7, 1991

The bombshell allegation of sexual harassment dropped on Clarence Thomas' Supreme Court nomination last month very likely will not keep President Bush's choice from gaining Senate confirmation.

But it should raise serious questions for all who participate in Thomas' elevation from the appellate bench to the highest court, starting with Bush and ending with the senators who vote to confirm.

There is no assertion that Thomas, when he was Anita Hill's boss in the early 1980s, touched her. Rather, he reportedly initiated and laid on sexual descriptions in hopes of dating Hill, currently a University of Oklahoma law professor.

Of the Senate's two female members, Maryland Democrat Barbara Mikulski earlier had announced her opposition to the nomination. With considerable interest, the judgment of Kansas Republican Nancy Kassebaum is now awaited.

Time after time, sexually themed conversation that men deem harmless is offensive, degrading and perhaps even threatening to women — especially economically vulnerable employees.

Not by any objective test did the Thomas nomination need the latest, sensationalized flare to earn a rejection.

Thomas clearly lacks the legal qualifications to hold such a high office for the rest of his life. His well-coached, selective memory performance before the Senate Judiciary Committee was no improvement.

Nebraska Sen. Bob Kerrey does himself and the causes he stands for credit saying he will vote against confirmation.

The Journal wishes Nebraska's senior senator, Jim Exon, would do likewise.

Sexual Politics In America

ANITA HILL'S ALLEGATIONS — 17

"SAME HERE—I'VE NEVER BEEN SEXUALLY HARASSED EITHER"

[Herblock cartoon, ©1991, depicting three senators outside the U.S. Senate reading a newspaper]

TULSA WORLD
Tulsa, Oklahoma, October 11, 1991

WHO'S telling the truth, Judge Thomas or Anita Hill? The question has America buzzing, and members of the Senate Judiciary Committee will attempt to resolve it when they resume hearings Friday on Judge Clarence Thomas' fitness to serve on the U.S. Supreme Court.

Is it possible that each of them is telling the truth?

Anita Hill, now a law professor at the University of Oklahoma, says Thomas made remarks to her nearly 10 years ago, when he was her boss at one federal agency and then another, that constituted sexual harassment. Thomas says no such thing happened.

Based on a number of reactions and comments, both published and on-the-street, many men apparently wonder what the big deal is. Thomas is alleged to have asked Hill for a date and, when she turned him down, attempted to engage in some banter of a sexual nature. If it was so bad, why didn't she say something earlier?

Conversely, many women apparently believe that Hill's accusations merely point up a behavior that women in the workplace have had to face far too often and for far too long. Nor are they bothered by the fact that Hill waited so long to come forward — part of the problem is that despite the law and regulations, there really is little women can do to protect themselves and still preserve their career prospects.

Hill and Thomas both appear to be people of exemplary character — people to be believed. Perhaps the "truth" is that men and women perceive things differently and react to things differently, and that solid definitions of what is sexual harassment remain to be worked out.

The situation has sparked a national debate on what men and women in the workplace can expect of one another, and what is acceptable and unacceptable behavior. In the long run that might be more important than Judge Thomas' fate as a Supreme Court nominee, and the Senate's sorry handling of the confirmation process.

The Gazette
Cedar Rapids, Iowa, October 10, 1991

CLARENCE THOMAS, it is said, "will look the American people in the eye" over the next six days and repeat, frequently we suspect, his "total and unequivocal" denial of allegations that forced the United States Senate to postpone Tuesday's scheduled vote on his suitability to serve on the Supreme Court.

Thomas, of course, is the one with the most at stake, having been accused of sexually harassing a woman a decade ago. Already unpopular with those who disapprove of his silence on the question of reproductive freedom and abortion, Thomas has seen his stock go downhill even more since the allegations by Anita Hill, a University of Oklahoma law professor, were leaked. The next week is intended to give his inquisitors time to determine whether Thomas is guilty, although once again the ideological forces in Congress were quick to pass judgment — one way or the other.

Our sense is that regardless of the ultimate verdict, Thomas is damaged merchandise. Even if he is vindicated, nothing can erase the nagging doubt that surely will surface whenever the issue of sexual harassment crosses his desk, as inevitably it must. If allegations are verified, of course, Thomas need not worry about confirmation. He will remain a jurist in the federal court system, however.

Painful as rejection obviously would be for Thomas at the end of this week of additional probing, we see a potentially bigger loser in this unhappy scenario. If any individual or group is obliged to explain its misdeeds, it is members of the United States Senate in general, and its Judiciary Committee in particular.

From the outset, the examination of Thomas has been marked by pettiness and personal agendas, rather than a thoughtful analysis of attributes most of us find important, indeed essential, qualifications for a member of the United States Supreme Court: education, experience, personality, physical and emotional health, personal background, character. Yes, *character*. Charges brought by a former colleague raise questions about Thomas' moral strength. The Judiciary Committee, too intent on pursuing its political agenda, seems to have swept an important character question under the rug.

We haven't been impressed the last four years with the committee's increasingly hostile attitude toward nominees or the narrowness of its agenda. By giving short-shrift to the Hill accusations, though, the subcommittee has been judged guilty of being insensitive to a concern that is very real to American women. We can't anticipate what will occur next week when the Senate finally votes on the Thomas nomination. Whatever else happens, however, he will have served the nation well if his confirmation hearing was the catalyst that forced an overhaul of this sadly abused hearing process.

Hill Testifies as Nation is Riveted by Harassment Hearings

The country was mesmerized Oct. 11, 1991 as Anita Hill, a tenured law professor at the University of Oklahoma, calmly described what she said were Supreme Court nominee Judge Clarence Thomas's sexually harassing comments and actions over a period from 1981 to 1983. During that period, Hill, who like Thomas, was black, had worked as his assistant at the Department of Education's Office of Civil Rights and then at the Equal Employment Opportunity Commission, where Thomas was chairman.

Thomas, in testimony beginning Oct. 11, emphatically denied ever harassing Hill. He attacked the Judiciary Committee and the confirmation process. He called the process "Kafkaesque" and repeatedly compared it to a "lynching."

Thomas's defense focused on testimonials to his character and attempts to discredit Hill and to paint her accusations as part of a political plot. Some Republicans on the Judiciary Committee and members of panels of witnesses for Thomas attacked Hill's character, her mental stability and her motives.

The hearings, which were broadcast live on television and radio, drew more public attention than any political incident in recent memory. They captured the attention of the country and drew high in television ratings. The Senate was swamped with phone calls and telegrams both for and against Thomas.

A poll conducted Oct. 13 by the *New York Times* and CBS News showed that as the hearings ended, 45% of Americans favored Thomas's confirmation, while 20% opposed it. Asked whom they believed more about the charges of sexual harassment, 58% backed Thomas and 24% backed Hill.

Beginning with his opening statement Oct. 11 and continuing throughout his sworn testimony Oct. 12, Thomas voiced outrage at being questioned on charges he called "lies," "sleaze," "dirt," and "gossip."

Thomas invoked the issues of race and racial hatred during his testimony, saying that the country still had "underlying racial attitudes about black men and their views of sex."

Thomas made his opening statement Oct. 11, before Hill addressed the committee, and then returned Oct. 11 and 12, after she testified, to rebut her allegations. At all times he denied ever having harassed Hill, and he angrily attacked the confirmation process. "This is a circus. It's a national disgrace. From my standpoint as a black American, it is a high-tech lynching for uppity blacks who in any way deign to think for themselves, to do for themselves," Thomas raged at the committee.

Thomas told the committee, "No job is worth what I've been through—no job. No horror in my life has been so debilitating. Confirm me if you want. Don't confirm me if you have been so led. But let this process end. Let me and my family regain our lives."

In an effort to undermine Hill's testimony, Thomas Oct. 12 raised questions about Hill's account of their working relationship. His statements came in response to questions from Utah Republican Orrin G. Hatch, one of Thomas's staunchest defenders on the committee.

Although Hill had denied socializing with Thomas outside the office, Thomas said that while they worked together, he had occasionally driven Hill home after work and that Hill had invited him in for "a Coke or a beer or something."

Hill Oct. 11 had testified under oath before the Senate Judiciary Committee that at the Department of Education in 1981 and extending until she left her job at the EEOC in 1983, Thomas had repeatedly verbally harassed her, asking her out, telling her of his sexual prowess and relating to her sexually explicit scenes he had seen in pornographic movies.

During testimony that lasted for nearly seven hours, Hill was often harshly questioned by committee Republicans. Committee Democrats questioned her more gently.

The Boston Globe
Boston, Massachusetts, October 12, 1991

On her office door at the University of Oklahoma, Anita Hill has placed a poster of Eleanor Roosevelt. It reads: "You gain strength, courage and confidence by every experience in which you really stop to look fear in the face.... You must do the thing that you cannot do."

For Hill, fear was 14 senators, every one of them white and male. Fear was Judge Clarence Thomas, her former employer and alleged harasser. Fear was the embarrassing recollection of verbal humiliation. Fear was the American public tuned in to watch as she sank or swam.

But the power of unadorned truth barreled across the nation as she told her story. After a week of tormenting doubt, all the myths about her allegations of sexual harassment were dispelled one by one.

■ No longer can her view of the situation be dismissed as a misinterpretation of a misstep by Thomas when he was her boss. The harassment she described was far removed from a girlish overreaction to some offhand remark or gesture on his part – an exaggerated response to the equivalent of a casual arm across a subordinate's shoulder.

■ No longer can anyone question whether Hill's allegations constituted genuine sexual harassment. Her youth and strict upbringing were assaulted repeatedly by Thomas' obscene – and singularly cruel – sexual commentary; her intelligence and professional ability were insulted and demeaned.

■ No longer is there any question of the stupidity of the Senate Judiciary Committee for putting Hill's affidavit aside without so much as interviewing her. Members of the committee can decry the leak to the press into eternity. They cannot, however, get away from the hideous prospect that were it not for the leak, Thomas would be sitting on the Supreme Court without having to respond publicly to Hill's charges.

■ No longer can President Bush hide behind a mask of loyalty to his nominee. No longer can he, in good conscience, deride the credibility of Thomas' accuser.

■ No longer can Thomas' cries of victimization be taken seriously. His denial was powerful, but it proved no match for Hill's clarity, her composure, or her pain.

■ No longer, in our view, is there much room for the argument that this was a he-said-she-said standoff, in which the question of who was telling the truth would be to difficult to discern. It seems clear – all too clear. She was.

With every question, Anita Hill became stronger, more courageous, and more confident. She did the thing she could not do.

FORT WORTH STAR-TELEGRAM
Fort Worth, Texas, October 12, 1991

When the Senate Judiciary Committee agreed to hear Professor Anita Hill's tale of sexual harassment at the hands of Judge Clarence Thomas, the ax was poised over Thomas' neck.

When the hearings were televised into millions of American homes and offices, the blade fell.

It is always dangerous to speculate on what a group of senators may find believable or compelling or politically expedient, but the televising of Hill's statement and the committee's questions made the American public the real jury.

It is a far-fetched notion that a young woman of Hill's background — manipulated into coming forth though she may have been — would appear before a Senate committee, on national television, with her octogenarian mother and father in the room, and *invent* the shocking details and graphic descriptions to which she testified.

And it is equally difficult to see how Thomas can be confirmed to the Supreme Court now. Indeed, it may be difficult for him and his sponsors to manage even a graceful withdrawal of Thomas' nomination. There are too many questions that would follow him to the court.

Yesterday's were among the least-orchestrated Senate hearings the public is likely to see. Because the stage was hastily set and the order of business decided on the wing, it was great theater. But it was also honest theater.

Hill, telling her story, was attacking Thomas. Republicans on the committee, by pulling and tugging at Hill's rendition of events, were defending Thomas — but they were really acting as defense counsel for George Bush, whose White House staff somehow failed to detect the bombshell in Thomas' closet, just as the senators seemed to brush it off.

The White House and the Senate, as much as Thomas, need damage control.

If he is not confirmed, Thomas can retreat, for a while at least, to his present appellate court position. He will be remembered as a victim of his president's hit-and-run warfare with a Democratic Congress as well as a victim of alleged character flaws.

Hill can try to resume her relative anonymity. Remember, she is not a guileful, ambitious politician, but a rather private person engaged in teaching law.

The Senate can take a long, embarrassed look at itself, and, with the White House, perhaps begin seeking a more sure-handed and less injurious way of choosing and examining Supreme Court justices.

THE TENNESSEAN
Nashville, Tennessee, October 13, 1991

WHEN seven congresswomen marched to a Senate Democratic caucus room last week to voice concern about Clarence Thomas and sexual harassment, they met a closed door.

Would an delegation of congressmen have received such a cold reception? Only the senators can say. But one thing is clear. Despite years of progress, a closed door still symbolizes the plight of women in government.

And that is embarrassing.

The controversy over Anita Hill and Thomas brought the issue into focus. How can Congress hope to adequately address women's issues when its membership is virtually all men? Representation in Congress is nowhere close to reflecting the nation's population.

Many males in Congress have excellent track records in upholding women's rights. But even the best of those men cannot begin to have the personal understanding of women's issues that women can. That point was brought home painfully by the flap over Thomas and Hill.

The number of American women in high-level elected offices is shameful. Only two U.S. senators are women. Only 29 of the 435 members of the House are women. There are only three female governors.

If half of the Democratic senators in that caucus room last week had been women, there would have been no need for the congresswomen's march up the Capitol steps. And if half the nation's senators were female, the Senate would have known from the beginning that the statements by Anita Hill were extremely serious and could not be ignored.

A Congress that is 95% male deserves the kind of scrutiny it has gotten over the sexual harassment issue.

But the problem goes deeper. Congress has exempted itself from all major civil rights bills, including laws prohibiting discrimination on the basis of sex, race, religion and physical impairment. It claimed the doctrine of separation of powers prohibits any executive branch agency from telling those in the legislative branch what to do.

How horridly ironic! It means that members of Congress — primarily white men — have passed laws that dictate how every other employer acts, but they don't have to answer to anyone. If a congressional employee believes she has been sexually harassed by a congressman, she can't take him to court. She can only take him to the House Ethics Committee — and we all know how that operates.

Women's perspective must be heard on everything — on sexual harassment, on child care, on arms control, on health care, on transportation, on education, on everything. Until the makeup of Congress reflects the nation's sexual, racial and ethnic diversity, its members carry an added responsibility to be totally sensitive and totally receptive to the concerns of all Americans. Last week's event demonstrate painfully how far Congress has to go. ■

The Wichita Eagle-Beacon
Wichita, Kansas, October 15, 1991

Americans have been mesmerized by the Senate Judiciary Committee's hearings into allegations that Supreme Court nominee Clarence Thomas sexually harassed a former colleague.

Most Americans wanted to see a clear-cut resolution, some unequivocal evidence to prove or disprove Professor Anita Hill's allegations. None was forthcoming.

In the Thomas case, there was no third-party witness to support Professor Hill's charges. There was no pattern of harassment shown. That doesn't mean Judge Thomas is guilty or innocent. It means only that the Senate proceedings did not resolve the issue conclusively. It boiled down to his word against hers.

By any measure of fairness it is wrong to destroy Judge Thomas' career and ruin his reputation based on unsubstantiated accusations. In previous appearances before the Senate Judiciary Committee, Judge Thomas proved to be a man of strong moral beliefs, a man who had overcome poverty and racial discrimination, a competent jurist who was qualified to sit on the Supreme Court. It would be tragic for the Senate to refuse to confirm him based solely on unproven sexual harassment allegations.

However, it would also be tragic if the Thomas case were used to disparage the very real problem of sexual harassment in the workplace. Likewise, it would be tragic if women interpreted the Thomas case as evidence that Americans don't take the problem of sexual harassment seriously.

Indeed, Judge Thomas' confirmation process may prove of greater value in making America a more just nation than any decision he may render on the Supreme Court. Reaction to the case has raised the nation's consciousness about sexual harassment. For the past week, the issue has been the No. 1 topic across the country. It's safe to say that the Thomas case has educated millions of Americans about sexual harassment.

Out of that should come a greater awareness of sexual politics in the workplace — of the potential for abuse and unequal power relationships between male bosses and female employees, of the varying senses of propriety men and women bring to the job.

The ultimate goal is mutual respect among professional colleagues, and a work environment where no one faces sexual humiliation, where each person is free from unwanted sexual advances.

Each American has his or her own theory as to why Anita Hill stepped forward and whether Clarence Thomas was convincing. Yet, based on the Senate Judiciary Committee hearing, all is conjecture and personal opinion.

The issue of sexual harassment will continue long past today when the Senate makes its decision on Judge Thomas. There simply was not compelling evidence to disqualify him from the Supreme Court.

THE SUN
Baltimore, Maryland, October 15, 1991

This evening the Senate will vote on Judge Clarence Thomas to be an associate justice of the Supreme Court. On Sept. 22 The Sun recommended his confirmation in what we conceded may have been "a triumph of hope over realistic assessment" of his judicial qualifications. Today we again recommend that he be confirmed, in what we must concede is the hope that he has not been guilty of sexual harassment and of lying about it.

Three days of hearings into the charges against Judge Thomas by a former aide, law professor Anita F. Hill, provided no grounds for a realistic assessment of the charges either way. We predicted that on Oct. 9. Senators are right back where they started. They know more details than they did last week. They have heard more character witnesses for both principals. They have heard witnesses and principals skillfully cross-examined. But they are no surer of the truth.

Even Thomas opponents admit the case against him was not proved. Some argue that nevertheless he should not be confirmed because a Supreme Court justice should not have to labor under a cloud of suspicion and notoriety. Judge Thomas' supporters agree he is under such a cloud. It is perhaps a permanent one, as he himself said.

However, the argument that he therefore be disqualified is revolting. Liberal Democrats and liberal special-interest groups created this cloud (against the expressed wishes of Professor Hill, we would note, resulting in the creation of a cloud of suspected dishonesty over *her*). For these advocates then to suggest that he must be defeated because of the accusation against him is a call for validating a standard operating procedure that encourages character assassins and gives them veto power over nominees.

Ugly as the weekend spectacle was, in some ways Judge Thomas was a more attractive candidate than the first time around. In the first hearings, several senators said they did not find in his bland, evasive, White House-prepared testimony "the real Clarence Thomas." This time, with "no handlers, no advisers," as he put it, a passionate, human Clarence Thomas was on view.

The real Clarence Thomas is still a movement conservative. He is still a black man from a poor, segregated background. He is still young, relatively inexperienced, relatively undistinguished. He is different from the Clarence Thomas we endorsed last month only by having gone through this ordeal. The ordeal may have created a bitter, vindictive personality, which is the last thing a Supreme Court justice should be. It may have created a man with a more acute understanding of the pain of victimization and the horror of invasion of privacy, which would be valuable assets for a justice.

We hope that Judge Thomas has been made stronger and wiser by this weekend. So hoping, we recommend again that the Senate confirm him.

THE DAILY OKLAHOMAN
Oklahoma City, Oklahoma, October 13, 1991

THOSE who watched this weekend's nightmarish Senate Judiciary Committee hearings saw one witness after another counter University of Oklahoma professor Anita Hill's charges against Supreme Court nominee Clarence Thomas. Several called Hill's stability into question, describing her abrupt mood shifts, leading them to discount her testimony.

Back in Oklahoma, Tulsa attorney Larry Shiles, a former student in Hill's legal research classes at Oral Roberts University, says he has submitted to senators a sworn deposition with shocking assertions, the least of which is that she was not respected as a teacher and could not handle her teaching load at the school.

Looking back on his experiences with professor Hill, Shiles described behavior which appears to support charges by other witnesses. At the least, Shiles and others describe Hill in ways that make her sound mercurial. Shiles even described class papers returned to him containing certain extraneous material — an echo of one of Hill's assertions about Thomas. Shiles told *The Oklahoman* he believes Hill is "unreliable" and that he "wouldn't believe a thing she said."

One way or the other, the tribulations of Clarence Thomas and Anita Hill may ease after today's vote in the U.S. Senate. After that, the staffer or senator responsible for the most reprehensible leak in Senate history must be identified and punished.

Wisconsin State Journal
Madison, Wisconsin, October 15, 1991

For those who stayed up late on Sunday night to watch Washington's live soap opera, "As the Worm Turns," one of the most telling episodes came when Sen. Howard Metzenbaum, the doddering disgrace from Ohio, tried to assassinate the character of a Clarence Thomas character witness, John Doggett. Isn't it true, the senator asked, that a woman had just come forth to say that 10 years ago, Doggett kissed her square on the lips on her first day on the job at the firm where both worked?

The Yale law and Harvard business graduate waited until Metzenbaum had fumbled his way through a transcript of an investigator's telephone interview, and then proceeded to dress down the senator in a way that made one wish there were more John Doggetts in the upper house of Congress (and, at least, one less Howard Metzenbaum).

Doggett first explained that he expected that someone would crawl out from under a rock as soon as it became known he would testify against Anita Hill, who has accused Clarence Thomas of sexual harassment, because that's the way Washington works. "I debated with my wife whether to start this process . . . because I knew it would be vicious," but went ahead in hopes of taking "the public process back into the pale of propriety."

Then he demanded to know under what legal rule, what code of fairness, would a member of the Judiciary Committee bring into the record a transcript of unsworn telephone conversations? Chairman Joseph Biden, who had left the room for a few minutes, came back and seemed genuinely stunned by what Metzenbaum had done. He cleared the committee record and ordered that it show there was "no evidence" that Doggett had ever done anything of the kind.

Indeed, there was no such evidence, it smelled of an utter fabrication. But the forces driving the likes of Metzenbaum, not content to destroy the character of Clarence Thomas, had now taken to abusing the rights of ordinary citizens.

The Senate has gone so far beyond its "advise and consent" role in this affair that it may not be possible to repair the damage. The Senate's role was not to substitute its own judgment for that of George Bush, who as president is entitled to send forth a nominee of his choice, but to assess the nominee's basic qualifications for the job.

When it seemed that Thomas would survive the 7-7 "no recommendation" vote of the Judiciary Committee, someone leaked portions of the FBI report involving Anita Hill, and the televised circus began. The very committee that ought to stand for fairness in our legal system became an instrument of raw politics.

Who is telling the truth? Perhaps we'll never know for sure, but there is no more reason to believe Hill than to doubt her. Witnesses on all sides seemed credible. If anything, she comes across as a woman scorned, not sexually, but institutionally.

Even if some version of Hill's story is to be believed, are incidents that took place 10 years ago in a different time and context enough to disqualify Thomas? If purity is now the standard, Washington would be a ghost town.

Thomas has suffered beyond the limits of what a seat on the Supreme Court is worth. Like John Doggett, many Americans are appalled at the actions of the Senate, as much as they abhor the offenses of which Thomas stands accused. Senators may judge the judge based on his judicial experience, background and elements of his character that they know to be true, but not on the basis of a hatchet job.

THE DENVER POST
Denver, Colorado, October 13, 1991

JUDGE Clarence Thomas cannot serve honorably on the Supreme Court of the United States, and his nomination should not be confirmed by the Senate next week.

The accusations against him — which seemingly cannot be proved or disproved — have so tarnished his reputation that he cannot effectively sit in judgment of others on the most important court in this land.

The entire Thomas confirmation process is an American tragedy. Had the Senate Judiciary Committee taken Anita Hill's accusations seriously, it's possible they could have been handled in a more dignified manner. As it occurred, the spectacle not only irreparably damaged the reputations of two people — Thomas and Hill — but further tarnished the institution of the Senate itself.

In her early statement to Senate staff members and the FBI, Miss Hill described persistent, personally offensive behavior by Thomas while she worked for him 10 years ago. But those statements apparently were not considered critical enough by the judiciary committee to merit a role in its deliberations — until they were made public.

Regardless, what has happened has happened. Miss Hill's accusations — denied by Judge Thomas but not clearly refuted by evidence — have indelibly stained the nominee's professional reputation. Although he still enjoys the support and respect of many, he cannot recover the confidence of millions of Americans.

Rightly or wrongly, the hearing has ruined Judge Thomas's distinguished career. This newspaper, which originally endorsed his nomination, recommends that he voluntarily withdraw his name to avoid being rejected by the Senate next Tuesday.

The Atlanta Journal
AND
THE ATLANTA CONSTITUTION
Atlanta, Georgia, October 14, 1991

The U.S. Senate is in the unenviable position of wrestling with a decidedly discomfiting case involving sordid charges of sexual harassment and the diametrically opposed testimony of two compelling figures, Judge Clarence Thomas and law Professor Anita F. Hill.

As powerful as Judge Thomas's denials have been, the greater credibility finally rests in the case presented by Ms. Hill.

Why would Ms. Hill lie? She has nothing to gain by subjecting herself to the intense scrutiny she now faces. Her discomfort discussing explicit sexual language was evident during her testimony, and her reluctance to come forward is clear in the chronology of events leading up to her public appearance.

She has friends who support her testimony. At various times, she spoke to several people about the sexual harassment she endured from her former superior, Clarence Thomas. They recall she spoke of the ordeal reluctantly and in evident distress, reinforcing her account and adding insight about her failure to file formal charges against him.

Judge Thomas has angrily denounced the hearings on the allegations of sexual harassment, charging that groups opposed to his nomination have scoured the countryside to dig up information to smear him. Sadly, the judge is right. Low-road tactics threaten to pervert the entire political process.

But the resort to gutter politics is not confined to groups who oppose him. In fact, it was Judge Thomas's supporters who aired a nasty commercial viciously attacking liberal members of the Senate Judiciary Committee, shortly after the judge was nominated.

At any rate, Ms. Hill is no part of a liberal conspiracy to trash Judge Thomas. She was comfortable working in the Reagan administration and an enthusiastic supporter of the nomination to the Supreme Court of Robert Bork, a doctrinaire conservative.

There were always reasons to doubt Judge Thomas's fitness. When he was nominated, he had only his honorable rise from poverty, his character and his integrity to commend him. He lacks judicial experience.

Nor did the earlier portion of the confirmation hearings shore up a sense of trust in his integrity. He so distanced himself from every strong political position he had taken as to seem to have no beliefs worth defending. When he declared he had never discussed Roe v. Wade, the case that established a woman's right to a legal abortion, he went beyond mere evasiveness to utter implausibility.

Yet, it still seemed possible at the end of the first set of hearings that Judge Thomas could be an asset to the court. Reluctant supporters hoped he might add compassion to political conservatism, and there were indications that he was no rigid ideologue.

But this second set of hearings has shifted the pattern of perceptions of the judge in a different direction. It now seems he lacks the character and the moral compass required to serve on the Supreme Court.

The nation's highest court could survive a justice who has had the poor judgment to ask a subordinate for a date. It might even survive a justice so crude as to view pornographic details as a tactic for seduction. The court ennobles some, such as former Klansman Hugo Black. But the foundations of the court would be rocked by a justice whose veracity cannot be trusted.

Since Judge Thomas has declared that he "would rather die" than withdraw, it is the duty of President Bush to withdraw his name from consideration. The nation deserves a nominee who would bring to the court both the integrity and the experience it demands.

THE BLADE
Toledo, Ohio, October 15, 1991

PRESIDENT Bush is said to have a short list of potential Supreme Court nominees ready should Clarence Thomas be rejected by the Senate in a vote tentatively scheduled for this evening.

But if Judge Thomas is rejected, and the President has to turn to his list, he may find it even shorter than he thought.

For if Clarence Thomas has now decided that a Supreme Court nomination is just not worth the personal pain and sacrifice of a Senate Judiciary Committee "high-tech lynching," it's a safe bet that the men and women on Mr. Bush's replacement list are beginning to wonder the same thing.

No matter what happens in the Senate vote, the real casualty of this whole mess could be the willingness of future prospective nominees to wade into the process. If America now insists that its Supreme Court consists of men and women whose character is as pure as the driven snow, America will have a Supreme Court so out of touch with the real world that its decisions will be meaningless and irrelevant.

Judge Thomas' accuser, Prof. Anita Hill, apparently passed a lie detector test on Sunday, adding yet another bizarre act to an already bizarre theater of the absurd. The pressure grew immediately for Judge Thomas to take a lie detector test of his own, one more glob of mud on a proceeding that is knee-deep in it already.

If Judge Thomas were to pass such a test, nothing would be proven. If he were to fail, the same would be true, yet he would be finished. How fair is that?

Fairness, of course, went out the window when Ms. Hill came forward 10 years after she first claimed Judge Thomas harassed her.

Consequently, one wonders what is going through the minds these days of the individuals most likely to get a long look from Mr. Bush as his new choice, should Judge Thomas fall.

All of the most commonly mentioned prospective nominees are in their 40s and 50s, which means that all of them have actually gone about living their lives, making friends and making enemies and perhaps even entertaining a lustful thought now and then. Can the Republic possibly survive if one of *them* joins the court?

Some members of the Senate will face a difficult political dilemma when they vote up or down on Judge Thomas's confirmation. Those who come from conservative districts may like the judge's philosophical predilections but fret about the fallout of backing a nominee seen by some back home as morally suspect. At the same time, there is no denying that public opinion polls show more support for Judge Thomas than Ms. Hill.

The Senate Judiciary Committee has brought this embarrassment upon itself, and just as Clarence Thomas and Anita Hill are forever scarred by the events of the past few weeks, so is the U.S. Senate.

Arkansas Gazette
Little Rock, Arkansas, October 15, 1991

The awful spectacle that has absorbed them for a week is over, and the relief of Americans is almost palpable. But the mystery over the truth in the Anita Hill-Clarence Thomas saga and the collective misery over its deeply troubling questions will go on, even past the climactic vote this evening on the confirmation of Thomas to the United States Supreme Court.

Most Americans — was there a soul who wasn't transfixed by the television drama? — may now have an opinion on whether Professor Hill or Judge Thomas was being truthful about the ugly sexual incidents that were alleged to have occurred nearly a decade ago when she worked for him in two federal bureaus. But for anyone with any measure of detachment when the saga began even the strongest hunches either way must be afflicted by doubt.

What was both impressive and troubling was the dignity, intelligence, passion and earnestness of these two black Americans whose most intimate experiences were held up for the scrutiny and judgment of a nation. It was troubling because one of them was lying — passionately and convincingly. Like the members of the Senate, everyone is left to judge between them on unsatisfying premises. What would be the motive of each to lie? Judge Thomas' motive is clear — his elevation to one of the majestic jobs in America hangs in the balance — but what could hers be?

The Senate in the end had no choice but to ventilate the charges in the way it did, though it brings further shame to the body and lasting harm to Professor Hill and Judge Thomas, one of whom is undeserving of it.

But the immediate harm is to the confirmation process. The vote on Judge Thomas' confirmation today will be seen as, if it is not in fact, a referendum on the charges that Thomas sexually harassed a female assistant.

It has been our view, and that of many in the Senate, that Judge Thomas should not be confirmed simply because his was a weak appointment with only politics to recommend it. Until he was appointed to the District of Columbia Court of Appeals last year Thomas had had almost no experience in the actual practice or teaching of law. He had never written or spoken with any consequence on important legal doctrines, and such discourse as he had had with the law in political speeches and writings was repudiated or explained away as expedient ramblings when he went before the Senate Judiciary Committee. There was nothing Americans could tie to, except his humble origins and his admirable hard work. He is not asking for a good job, which he may deserve, but the chance to help chart the nation's course for the next half-century.

If Judge Thomas is rejected, it will seem to be confirmation of the harassment charges. But neither should he be confirmed merely to avoid that unfair appearance. The Senate's duty is more solemn than ever. It still rests on the judgment of his qualifications for the Supreme Court. This national trauma must somehow be momentarily forgotten.

THE SAGINAW NEWS
Saginaw, Michigan, October 13, 1991

To hear Clarence Thomas, he is a man so terribly wronged that, had he known what was coming, he would have declined the honor of the nomination to the U.S. Supreme Court.

To hear Anita Hill, she is a woman who suffered "very ugly, very dirty, disgusting" behavior — from the same Clarence Thomas.

In the remarkable national theater in Washington at week's end, all that seemed clear is that one of them was lying.

That is what has made the Senate Judiciary Committee's resumed hearings so fascinating, and also so frustrating.

So much is at stake, with so little to go on, heading into the Senate confirmation vote on Thomas, tentatively rescheduled for Tuesday.

Sen. Joseph Biden, D-Del., started out saying it was not a trial. Oh, but it was, very much so.

Consider the first witness:

Thomas, a judge of the U.S. Court of Appeals, delivered a powerful statement to the Senate panel when it reopened hearings Friday morning.

It was at once a defense of his honor, integrity and reputation, and a scathing indictment of the process that, he said, has put him through an impossible ordeal for 103 days.

"This is not American," declared Thomas. "This is Kafka-esque. This must stop."

What's more, said the black man who raised himself up from Georgia poverty, he would not provide the committee the rope for his own lynching.

No one listening to a phrase so loaded with bitter history and black tragedy could deny the strength of Thomas' feelings, nor the depth of his outrage at the relentless campaign to discredit him enough to keep his conservative views off the court.

He asserted under oath that "I have not done what she has alleged," that he never even asked her for a date.

Then came the second witness: Anita Hill, a professor of law at the University of Oklahoma, and former No. 1 associate to Thomas in a pair of top-level Washington jobs, said she was, indeed, sexually harassed.

What's more, said one of 13 children born to an Oklahoma farmer, she "vividly" recalled the incidents, including repeated requests for dates. And she described what she says Thomas said to her in detailed terms rarely heard in public, never mind network television.

There was an accumulation of incidents, they would certainly offend a reasonable woman, and there was a threat to her career, she said — all telling factors in determining a case of sexual harassment.

Still, this was not a court of law, but of Senate and public opinion. Failing a definitive finding of fact, determining the truth will demand, as Sen. Howell Heflin said, a judgment on character and motivation.

On that, the jury is out.

Aside from what kind of justice he would make, Judge Thomas remains an impressive man. Prof. Hill, so suddenly thrust into the national glare, showed herself a seemingly credible, low-key witness.

More than a dozen of other women who worked with Thomas came forward to vouch for his utterly professional, courteous behavior. Associates of Hill did the same to testify to her lifelong integrity and honesty.

Something is wrong here, besides the confirmation process that Thomas assailed, and even beyond the facts of the alleged harassment. How could either one of these evidently fine people possibly lie under oath, before the world, before their assembled families?

The Senate did not know what to make of it. Neither did the White House. Neither do we.

If Thomas' nomination is destroyed, he says he does not care anymore; he already has a good lifetime job as a federal judge.

Regardless, Prof. Hill's charges have changed the structure of public debate on the subject of harassment in the workplace, and further, on the state of relations between men and women. That much is to the good — unlike the rest of the trial of truth and conscience the country saw and heard last week.

The Houston Post
Houston, Texas, October 15, 1991

AS THE SENATE PREPARES to vote today on Clarence Thomas' nomination to the Supreme Court, the nation is still divided over whether Anita Hill's sexual harassment allegations against the federal appeals judge are true. But public opinion is virtually unanimous that the Senate Judiciary Committee made a mess of the confirmation process.

Three days of riveting televised testimony by Thomas, Hill and their assorted supporters and detractors, with the committee members acting, by turns, as protectors and inquisitors, demonstrated how highly politicized that process has become.

To his credit, Committee Chairman Joseph Biden, D-Del., barred Hill's so-called lie detector test from the hearing record — it purportedly showed she told the truth. Not only are such tests inadmissible in a court of law, but the confirmation process should not be reduced to a polygraph duel.

Yet, some of the nominee's backers on and off the committee resorted to reprehensible tactics to discredit Hill — suggested, without offering any evidence, that she may have fantasized that Thomas made lewd remarks to her when she worked for him at the Department of Education and the Equal Employment Opportunity Commission in the early 1980s.

Other witnesses claimed that she was getting even with Thomas for spurning her and/or that she was the pawn of liberals, feminists and others who would go to any lengths to keep President Bush's black conservative nominee off the high court.

The last-minute leaking of Hill's allegations by one or more Judiciary Committee members or staffers was also a sleazy trick. That information was supposed to have been kept confidential. But had the panel heard her and Thomas privately on the charges, it might have averted the lurid spectacle of the last few days.

Sexual harassment is an ugly offense, difficult to prove because there are frequently no witnesses. Thus, it usually boils down to one person's word against another's and a final judgment about who is telling the truth may well hinge on the reputations of those involved.

Thomas and Hill both had staunch advocates testifying to their good character. Sometimes, the same person praised both.

Yet, barring some bizarre twist of circumstances, one of them is lying. If it is Judge Thomas, who has categorically denied Hill's accusations with convincing eloquence and emotion, he is a hypocrite, unfit not only to serve on the Supreme Court but to hold his present seat on the federal appeals court in Washington, D.C.

If, on the other hand, Hill is deliberately making up her account of recurrent sexual harassment by Thomas to destroy him professionally, it is a contemptible act undeserving of the respect and high esteem accorded her by friends and colleagues.

If the Senate were a court of law, it is doubtful that Hill would have made her case against Thomas. This is not to detract from her air of sincerity — for many she made a highly credible witness. But absent more convincing evidence, the nominee still deserves the benefit of the doubt.

THE DALLAS TIMES HERALD
Dallas, Texas, October 15, 1991

With three days of emotional testimony behind us, and the decision on whether to confirm Clarence Thomas before us, it is the right time to take stock of the collective road we have traveled. There is much we have learned during this weekend journey.

■ The nation is richer for this examination of sexual harassment in the workplace. We have collectively heard testimony, or heard in the media from many victims and experts in the field, of the complexity of sexual harassment. It is widespread. Its victims, by fear of their livlihoods, have no practical way to react other than silent coping. One does not have to subscribe to the veracity of either side to have been enlightened by the dialogue.

■ There is gross insensitivity, predominantly by men, to the victims of sexual harassment. By sweeping Professor Hill's initial charges under the rug in the first round, the 14-man Senate Judiciary Committee gave testimony enough to that. The depth of emotional outrage by many women across the country to that insensitivity secured the case.

■ There is something terribly wrong about the nomination process, which has degenerated as a matter of routine into vicious political free-for-alls that have left mud on the faces of everyone. We should only accept nominees that are among the best and brightest. We should not accept the savaging of the nominee once put forward into a world of screaming professional lobbies and slander by political hacks.

■ Judge Thomas should not be confirmed, but for the right reasons. Even if one would accept the most egregious allegations by one employee against Judge Thomas as fact, it would be unfair to discharge the nominee for this one offense. There appear to be countless other co-workers who have described his conduct as being, at all times, impeccable. Has there been a widespread pattern of sexual harassment in his office? No.

Instead, the criteria in selecting an individual to a life appointment to the highest court of the land should focus on those who have proven themselves on the bench and left behind a wealth of legal decisions for the Senate to properly examine. The Supreme Court needs not the energy of youth, but the wisdom of maturity gained through years of life experience. Judge Thomas does not have that kind of record, but there is no shortage of potential candidates that do.

With more years of seasoning on the appeals court, Judge Thomas may yet build such a record. For today's vote, and for only these reasons, he should not be confirmed.

The Philadelphia Inquirer
Philadelphia, Pennsylvania, October 15, 1991

There are those who blame Clarence Thomas, those who blame Anita Hill and those who blame "the process." That last group may well be the largest. But much as we would like to join in, we are having a hard time finding villains.

The facts are well known. Ms. Hill, after being contacted by a Senate staffer in early September, provided a confidential statement accusing Mr. Thomas of what amounted to sexual harassment. The FBI did a follow-up investigation that was supplied to the Senate Judiciary Committee shortly before it voted on Mr. Thomas' nomination. Then on the weekend before the scheduled vote in the full Senate Ms. Hill's charges were leaked to the press — and the rest, as they say, is history.

So who's to blame? Here is the list of the suspects:

The Judiciary Committee: By failing to fully investigate the charge privately, it set the stage for a public spectacle. In retrospect, chairman Joseph R. Biden Jr. should have postponed the committee vote to delve more deeply into Ms. Hill's eleventh-hour allegations. But that would have set off alarm bells. And once the committee started scouring the country for witnesses, there's little doubt that the sordid details would have leaked out. Ditto if the committee had tried to hold last weekend's hearings behind closed doors.

The leaker: There's no question that whoever leaked the allegations broke Senate rules and, if discovered, will deservedly be punished. But to blame the leaker is to say it would have been better for the confirmation vote to have taken place with an unsatisfactory review of Ms. Hill's charges. We don't believe that's the case.

The press: The motto of the Fourth Estate could well be: Leaks R Us. That's not going to change, nor should it. The media's job is to ferret out information, and this information, as excruciatingly personal as it may be, is relevant to the public debate on Mr. Thomas' fitness to serve on the Supreme Court.

The interest groups: There's little doubt that Mr. Thomas' ideological opponents conducted a full-court press to dig up any dirt that could derail his nomination, and that's unseemly. But those efforts would have failed were it not for the flesh-and-blood reality of Anita Hill. No interest group invented her or her story.

So we're left in a quandary. We hate what happened, but we're not sure how, once Ms. Hill made her charges, that it could have played out in a more satisfactory way. And we don't buy the theory that all future nominees will be similarly accursed.

The Gazette
Cedar Rapids, Iowa, October 12, 1991

DURING THE explosive special hearing Friday on Judge Clarence Thomas' fitness for the Supreme Court, President Bush stayed at the White House, insisting his nominee "will get his good name back."

Maybe Judge Thomas can put his life back together. A tireless worker, he already has accomplished much in his law career. But it is hard to see how he can bounce back and receive the Supreme Court confirmation that, until a week ago, seemed almost certainly his. Accusations aired by his former employee, Law Professor Anita Hill, are simply too devastating. Incidents such as she described — concerning Thomas' supposed preoccupation with his own sexual prowess, his discussion of pornographic films, etc. — aren't the sort of casual confrontations each party tends to partially forget.

Perhaps Thomas is wholly innocent of the alleged sexual harassment. It is, after all, his word against hers. (One or the other is a consummate liar.) And his testimony, in which he denied all, was impressive — even courageous.

The Senate, however, must be concerned with the public's perception of Judge Thomas' character. And after the pyrotechnics in the Senate Judiciary Committee hearing Friday, the Thomas nomination is the stuff from which crude jokes are made. It is enough material to keep The National Enquirer, Tattler, Midnight and Star cooking along merrily for months.

As noted here Thursday, even if Judge Thomas is vindicated, nothing can erase the nagging doubt that will surface whenever a case involving sexual harassment crosses his desk. Thomas' moral strength has been a question most of the way. We thought it curious — and said so Aug. 2 — that more had not been made of the seemingly mean things he had said about his own sister, Emma Mae Martin, a decade ago when she was forced to go on welfare. When the judge answered questions to most inquisitors' satisfaction, we thought the confirmation was in the bag. We, too, were satisfied he was a suitable candidate for a lifetime appointment on the nation's highest court.

Then came the sexual harassment allegations, news of the FBI probe and the leaking of results to the news media. Next, the revelation that Senate Judiciary Committee members had sat on incendiary information concerning alleged sexual harassment. And finally, Friday's unforgettable hearing. Sen. Strom Thurmond said the hearings would be an exceedingly uncomfortable process for all, but "our duty is clear: We must find the truth."

He was right about the discomfort. As for finding truth, the search continues. It proceeds through the wreckage of two lives — Clarence Thomas' and Anita Hills'.

The Seattle Times
Seattle, Washington, October 14, 1991

ONE month ago we said in this space that Clarence Thomas ought to be confirmed to a seat on the U.S. Supreme Court.

Much has changed since we reached that judgment. Today we believe the opposite. When the Senate votes tomorrow, it should reject this nominee.

A Senate vote to reject Thomas would not be a guilty verdict. This is not a judicial proceeding, but an intensely political process requiring elected officials to exercise their judgment about what is best – not for Thomas but for the Supreme Court and for the country.

Unfortunately, the American public may never know whether Thomas sexually harassed Anita Hill. Hour upon hour of testimony and questioning through the weekend failed to discredit either Hill or her allegations against Thomas. Nor have the hearings shaken Thomas from his angry denials or his supporters from their belief that he could not have acted as Hill described.

The dramatic hearing of the Senate Judiciary Committee is over, but a huge cloud of doubt remains: doubt about Thomas' behavior toward a female subordinate in the workplace. That cloud has not been – perhaps cannot be – dispelled.

It should not be seen in isolation from the earlier Thomas confirmation hearing. The culmination of those sessions led to a 7-7 vote by the committee and no recommendation to the Senate.

Even before Hill's allegations became public, Thomas' critics had valid concerns about his lack of judicial experience and his legal views well outside the mainstream.

Thomas' earlier testimony raised questions about his credibility, especially when he said he had never discussed or formed an opinion on one of the most debated legal issues of the time, Roe v. Wade, the 1973 Supreme Court ruling that legalized abortion.

Despite those concerns, many (including The Times' editorial board) felt Thomas would bring an important dimension to the court.

As we said here Sept. 15: "His views are expanding, he refuses to take accepted wisdoms for granted, and in the most profound way he has exhibited an independence of spirit his detractors cannot abide."

But our fragile hope that Thomas would mature into a respected justice with a unique perspective cannot withstand the weight of the doubts now cast upon him.

Rejecting his bid for the Supreme Court would be recognition that still-credible allegations of sexual harassment leave too great a cloud to warrant his ascent to the nation's highest court.

Agonizing as it may be, the Senate is obligated to protect the integrity of the court over the reputation of one man.

Chicago Sun-Times
Chicago, Illinois, October 13, 1991

As the grotesque conflict over the nomination of Clarence Thomas has unfolded, one has to wonder whether, with so much damage done to the way this country selects its Supreme Court justices, the process can ever be repaired.

Certainly, the unprecedented loss of civility leaves one sick in spirit. The mudslinging, the manipulation, the hurtful, damaging leaks and the mean-spirited accusations—all in the name of justice and righteousness—may be unparalleled, even for the political swamps of Washington.

Neither side has a lock on virtue or villainy; both have contributed their share to this spectacle. Perhaps not since the Army-McCarthy hearings have such ghastly attacks on individuals and their character been tolerated in the name of political gain.

But beyond the loss of civility and the appalling personal hurt, this country is faced with damage done to institutions that compose the cornerstone of our democracy.

Who, in his right mind, would be willing to face the kind of keelhauling faced by recent Supreme Court nominees?

Who among us is perfect enough to pass the kind of tests of personal behavior increasingly imposed?

Who, among those of firm and thoughtful convictions, could pass the simultaneous litmus tests required by both sides?

Both sides wear the jacket on this one. The politicization of the selection process by both sides; the cynical nomination of a mediocrity by the president; the attacks on the nominee's religious beliefs by the president's opponents, the refusal to extend to him the time-honored American principle of innocent until proven guilty. The list is too long and depressing to repeat here.

Whether or not the Senate confirms Thomas, whether you believe Thomas or his accusers (indeed, whether you want to believe Thomas or his accusers), it's not too soon for everyone to begin thinking about repairing the damage.

The solution won't be found in new laws or regulations. The solution requires reflecting on the meaning of words such as compromise and consensus.

It has to do with being good losers and good winners. It has to do with remembering that a democracy can only work when everyone accepts that the way to get a free society to adopt your views and policies is not by bludgeoning the other side with invective, but by winning elections.

It has to do with halting the plunge of political discourse in this country into anything-goes venality and mendacity. We, all of us, have allowed that plunge to occur. We, all of us, have to halt it and reverse it.

San Francisco Chronicle
San Francisco, California, October 15, 1991

NOW THE DECISION must be made. After several days of riveting (and occasionally sordid) testimony, members of the U.S. Senate must decide which of two compelling human beings is the most believable: the articulate, intelligent law professor who claims she was sexually harassed some years ago, or the articulate, intelligent U.S. Supreme Court appointee who claims that it all never happened.

Questions of character, competence and politics are involved

No "smoking gun," or definitive fingerprints were produced during the long hours of public scrutiny. Both Anita Hill and Clarence Thomas produced persuasive briefs. A person could stand convinced after one presentation, and then be reduced to uncertainty when rebuttal followed.

So what it will get down to on the Senate floor today will be the familiar crunch of hardball politics, and application of that inner, "gut" sense about who is telling the truth. In a situation as complex — both emotionally and factually — as this one, conscience needs to take precedence over politics.

THERE ARE THOSE who deplore the whole noisy, confused, uncomfortable process. But what better way under the circumstances? Given that leaking of Hill's allegation was reprehensible, once that information was out, what could be more important than to air the festering sore as fully as possible?

Because of this hearing, we have learned much about — and presumably become more sensitive to — the depressing reality of sexual harassment in the workplace, as well as the political perils faced by a high-achieving black man whose views run counter to what is deemed "correct." The Judiciary Committee senators got in their partisan digs, to be sure, but they also tried to be as balanced as possible.

Amidst all the sound and fury, the basic question remains unchanged: Does Clarence Thomas have the stuff of a Supreme Court justice? That's what the senators must decide.

Diario Las Americas
Miami, Florida, October 15, 1991

There are people who logically are concerned with analyzing the last stages in the case of Judge Clarence Thomas before the Senate's Judiciary Committee, from an angle of juridical technique to point out the numerous flaws involved in this spectacle set up against Judge Thomas.

Aside from the fact that there are grounds for this analysis, it would be deviating a little from the essence of the problem to go into a debate of something that basically is subordinate. The important thing in this case is that there exists an ideological persecution against Judge Thomas as there would also be against anyone, notwithstanding his race who upheld the same political philosophy. And all this, of course, under the guise of morality and of "profound social concern regarding the fate of minorities and of the poor"

This is the second case of a candidate to the Supreme Court, with excellent academic credentials and character merits to be judge, as well as with great experience to hold a high post in the judiciary, who is rejected in a more or less noisy fashion because of his ideological convictions that fit perfectly well in the institutional, social and political life of the American nation. In the specific case of Judge Clarence Thomas, though it has reached unimaginable extremes, still the final decision has not been handed down by the Senate, which will debate the case this Tuesday, October 15th. Therefore, it can not be said that there have been two rejections because in Judge Thomas case there has been no final decision. But, why can it be spoken of rejection? Simply because an uproar has started from the extreme liberal currents in the country that are broadly represented in the Legislative Branch of the government, against an individual, against a jurist and a judge whose crime is to have ideas that are compatible with civilization and American traditions and to practice them with civic and professional integrity.

Everything indicates that if the juridical and philosophical mentality of Judge Clarence Thomas were within the lines of American liberal extremism or within a marked liberaloid current, his nomination to the Supreme Court would have encountered no difficulties whatsoever. His credentials as a jurist and a decent individual, even his ethnic origin, should be, nowadays, enough to prevent that his nomination have to go through one hundred and seven days of grilling, of persecution, as if he were a criminal.

It is regrettable that these things should happen in a country of such lofty political culture as the United States of America. The dignity of justice is in jeopardy when a norm is set up that it is necessary to belong to a certain ideological current, not shared by all of the people, to be able to be a Justice of the Supreme Court in this country.

The Courier-Journal
Louisville, Kentucky, October 15, 1991

THE Clarence Thomas nomination to the U.S. Supreme Court has proven to be an embarrassment and a tragedy. To carry through with it would mock the concept of Equal Justice Under Law, the motto of the high court, reproduced above.

Senators Ford and McConnell and their colleagues must reject his nomination for a litany of reasons.

The real villain, of course, is President Bush, whose cynical decision to exploit race is at the bottom of the terrible spectacle this country has witnessed in recent days. President Bush appointed a man:

Who had achieved no real distinction in the law.

Whose record as a steward of the public trust was shabby.

Whose temperament is wrong. He is given to ideological confrontation and excess.

Whose fundamental attitude toward the uses of government in helping victims of discrimination seems cold and arrogant.

Who seems to believe the fiction that self-help is enough — that government need not be prepared to intervene, forcefully, to right wrongs. (Of course, when the shoe is on the other foot he cries, "Victim!")

Then there is Prof. Anita Hill, whose compelling testimony added to the already strong case against Clarence Thomas. What she said certainly suggests that she is not mentally unbalanced, as so many of Judge Thomas's supporters have implied (invoking, predictably, the old hurtful stereotypes about hysterical women). She has no apparent motivation except the one she claims. She has been consistent in those claims for many years. She has been willing to have herself tested in every way. She had nothing to gain by coming forward — and much to lose.

The fact that she is not believed by a majority of Americans tells us how little progress we've made in fostering an understanding of the way in which women are victimized in the workplace, and the way in which that victimization affects them. That is the ultimate tragedy that President Bush's cruel, mean-spirited appointment reveals to us.

On the plus side, the plants and offices of America may be forever changed in positive ways as a result of the Senate Judiciary Committee hearings. The hidden trauma of sexual harassment has been exposed in a dramatic way. The hearings have produced a painful, but useful, dialogue about workplace secrets that long needed airing.

In time, the probing should go even deeper. The issue is not just about sexual harassment. It's not just about women. The debate that needs to occur is about power — how those who have power use it to oppress those who don't. Few who have moved up the ladder of opportunity are guiltless.

William Kennedy Smith Arrested for Rape

William Kennedy Smith, a nephew of Sen. Edward M. Kennedy (D, Mass.), was formally charged May 9, 1991 in connection with the alleged rape of a 29-year-old woman at the Kennedy family's vacation estate in Palm Beach, Fla. in March.

Smith, 30, was charged with one felony count of sexual battery (Florida's legal term for rape) and one misdemeanor count of battery. If convicted on the felony count, he could face a maximum sentence of 15 years in prison, although Florida sentencing guidelines made it more likely that a first offender would receive either probation or a maximum of four and a half years in prison.

In charging Smith, police released a nine-page affidavit detailing the alleged rape. The affidavit quoted the victim as saying that Smith had asked her for a ride home from a nightclub, and later tackled her and raped her near the pool at the estate. Smith allegedly told the woman afterward that "no one would believe her" if she reported that she had been raped. The woman said she had taken a Kennedy family photograph, and that the boyfriend of a friend who came to pick her up had taken an urn, in order to prove that she had been at the estate.

The affidavit noted that detectives in the case reported that the woman had appeared "emotionally frightened, distraught and in shock" after the alleged rape, and that she subsequently passed two lie detector tests.

Smith surrendered to Palm Beach police May 11 and was released after posting a $10,000 bond. He told reporters that the woman's allegations were "an outrageous lie" and that they "represent an attack on me, on my family and on the truth." He added, "I'm very much looking forward to a trial where I can testify and where the truth can come out. I have no question that that will happen."

Palm Beach police May 14 released their entire 1,300 page report on the alleged rape. The report, which included detectives' reports, depositions and transcripts of police interviews, raised questions about the role played by Sen. Kennedy.

Kennedy had repeatedly denied that he knew anything about a rape complaint against Smith until after he had left Palm Beach on April 1, two days after the incident allegedly took place. Kennedy May 10 told reporters in Cambridge, Mass., "I was never, never told that weekend that there would be an alleged charge against Willy Smith." He said the estate's chief of security, William Barry, who had spoken to police officers at the estate, had told him there would be a sexual harassment complaint against Smith. Kennedy said Barry "never used the word 'rape,' never used the word 'rape'—against my nephew William Smith."

Kennedy also said he had "never, never heard her scream," although the woman reported to police that she had screamed repeatedly and wondered "why no one in the house would come out and help her, especially since she knew that Sen. Kennedy was in the house," according to the affidavit.

The police report noted that detectives had gone to the Kennedy estate on March 31 and had asked to interview Kennedy. The report said Barry had told them that Kennedy was "out" and later told them that the senator had left town, even though Kennedy had actually remained in Palm Beach until the next day.

The report also included a deposition from Kennedy in which the senator admitted that he had discussed the allegation in a telephone conversation with Smith on March 31, and that he had referred Smith to a prominent Florida lawyer whom Kennedy himself had already contacted.

Press reports said that police were pursuing an investigation into how Kennedy household members had responded to the police inquiry, in order to determine whether there had been any attempt to obstruct justice.

THE ARIZONA REPUBLIC
Phoenix, Arizona, April 19, 1991

EXCEPT for the involvement of the powerful Kennedy family, it is inconceivable that, nearly three weeks after getting a rape complaint, Palm Beach authorities would still be behaving like so many Barney Fifes, standing first on one foot and then the other.

It also is likely that serious newspapers like *The New York Times* would be pursuing allegations of rough stuff by Kennedy family detectives instead of giving their readers Page One sob stories about Sen. Edward Kennedy struggling to maintain his composure as he dredges up memories of little John-John and Caroline playing hide-and-seek at the Kennedy White House.

These are not the glory days of Camelot, we need to remind ourselves. These are the boozy days of Palm Beach, where a young woman has complained to the police, for all the good it does her, that she joined the Kennedys for drinks after a night on the town and was raped in the Kennedy compound by Sen. Kennedy's nephew William Smith.

The immediate response of the Palm Beach police was to mosey around to the mansion, inquire after Sen. Kennedy and his nephew, and, getting the brushoff by whoever answered the door, return to the squad room without having questioned either the Kennedys or their guests. By the time these sleuths decided that it might be helpful to search the house and grounds for physical evidence of the crime, nearly two weeks had elapsed. Not until last Friday did they even bother to get a Kennedy guest list for the night of the alleged rape.

Incompetence is not unprecedented in the annals of police work, to be sure, and authorities in a resort community such as Palm Beach often are less than eager to batter down the doors of the rich and famous. At the same time, a possible cover-up and clumsy police work are not the only disturbing aspects of this alleged rape. The media, too, have handled the Smith case differently.

Last Tuesday evening, in a notable break with precedent, NBC News announced the name of the complaining witness coast to coast — probably the first time in the history of American broadcasting that an alleged rape victim had been so identified. Many newspapers hastened to follow suit. *The New York Times* even published the next morning a lengthy profile of the woman, disclosing, among other irrelevancies, the number of traffic tickets she had picked up over the past eight years and the birth of her child out of wedlock. (That should make young women think twice about going to the police.)

It is possible that the accuser would have received the same rough handling if her complaint had dealt with someone other than a Kennedy nephew — if the Palm Beach incident had involved, for example, the family of Newt Gingrich or Bob Dole. But when the police are fumbling a criminal investigation this badly and the Kennedys are known to be engaged in high-pressure spin control, it would behoove the American press to behave with a good deal more judgment and restraint than some members of the media are exhibiting.

The Washington Times
Washington, D.C., April 18, 1991

"If you don't have sex with me," William Kennedy Smith told his dream date at the family's Palm Beach manse, "I'm going to get Uncle Ted to drive you home." That's only one joke about the alleged bodice-ripping at the Sunshine State home of the heirs to Old Joe Kennedy's whiskey fortune, where a young lady claims Sen. Ted Kennedy's nephew had his way with her without permission. Now, there's something significant to say about the Kennedy family that has little do with the question of Mr. Smith's guilt or innocence and, if you haven't guessed already, we're going to say it.

First, a few details about the case at hand, which has all the elements of a great Kennedy story — distilled spirits, sex, women and the mob. The senator and his son Patrick, along with young Mr. Smith, were swizzling at a tony saloon known as Au Bar, which is frequented not only by celebrities and Palm Beach ne'er-do-wells but also by at least one transvestite aptly named Neil, which is not to say he has to do with the senator but who does add some atmosphere to the tale.

Not that it needs any. After the three Kennedy boys picked up a few ladies, they returned to the winter White House for a nightcap. Once there, the allegation goes, William the Conqueror took his catch for a stroll on the beach, whereupon he allegedly disrobed. Disgusted either at the thought of having sex with the aspiring doctor or at what she saw (or didn't see), the girl took off for the house. But, so she avers, she couldn't escape the clutches of the aroused and fleet-footed medical student. Tripping her up by the ankle, she says, he raped her, then later tried to tell her it wasn't rape, but simply a command performance of the Kennedy magic.

Back inside, yet another woman says, the evening's entertainment continued. Uncle Ted, clad only in a tailored shirt, was tearing around the house, close on her heels — or should we say ankles. Like the charge against Mr. Smith, this allegation is denied as well, but it doesn't seem out of character with the senator's past antics. At some point, the victim of Mr. Smith's unauthorized and unwelcome amore called a friend, who just happened to be the daughter of one Leonard Mercer, an alleged associate of Philadelphia mobster Nicodemo "Little Nicky" Scarfo.

As it stands now, several stories are floating around that have only one thing in common: Another woman — or women — had an unpleasant brush with the Kennedy men. But what actually happened, if anything at all, is less important than the question of why the Kennedys can't stay out of trouble and the headlines of the kind of newspapers that dwell on the marriages of Madonna and the physical communications of Elvis Presley since his death.

First there was Irish Joe himself, his questionable accumulation of wealth and the fling with Gloria Swanson. Then there was John F., his alleged affair with a Nazi spy, the stolen election, the hootchy-koo at the White House and affairs with gang-moll Judith Exner and sex goddess Marilyn Monroe. Similar charges of a relationship with the tortured actress involve Robert Kennedy as well, which brings us down to the sitting senator: cheating in school, various and sundry traffic violations, rampages through Washington eateries, wild drinking binges and the seemingly endless speculation about what happened to Mary Jo Kopechne. In short, words frequently associated with the Kennedy name include drunkenness, womanizing, law-breaking and general sleaziness. Yet somehow they've gotten away with it, and the family name appears no worse for the wear. Now we have yet another wild party involving not only the senator but also his son and nephew, Mr. Smith. Why?

High-octane testosterone, of which there seems to an abudance, doesn't quite explain it. As one disgusted Kennedy fan told The Washington Post, "It's a dysfunctional family." Dysfunction is one word for it, as far the inability of the old man to instill any character in his sons goes. But a more precise explanation might be that Kennedy men play by different rules. Or should we say they play life's game with no rules at all?

Granted, the Kennedys have been the victims of enough misfortune, including the assassinations of Mr. Kennedy's brothers, to derail Job. But instead of transcending tragedy, it seems as though the power and wealth the family accumulated has given them the idea they are exempt from the moral codes by which the rest of us are expected to abide or else risk public opprobrium and humiliation. Consistent with that self-conferred exemption, the Kennedys have managed to construct a myth of sterling character, mostly built around the cult of compassion and progress that supposedly animated President Kennedy's "Camelot." The myth seems to have been swallowed whole by much of the national news media, and maybe that's one reason some newspapers have almost tearfully observed that the famed Kennedy damage-control experts seem to be sleeping on the job.

The Kennedys were admirable at bamboozling a significant slice of the American population, which may say more about the people who were bamboozled than it does about the Kennedys. But happily the folk humor that has grown up around their exploits may be a sign that most people weren't as naive as the Kennedys thought and many newsmen were (and are). Today, even many who quaffed of the Kennedy bilgewater are finally recognizing that there seems to be something amiss in the Kennedy soul, that there are just too many Kennedys who are low-brow and low-bred, unable to use their tremendous wealth and power for much of anything but their own advancement and, more recently, their own and others' degradation.

We hear that the Palm Beach manor is in a sad state of disrepair. That's a fitting metaphor for the moral character of the Kennedy men themselves, if they ever had any.

Washington, D.C., April 19, 1991

You can't open up a newspaper or turn on the television these days without seeing one media type or another anguishing aloud about whether to disclose the name of a woman allegedly raped at the Kennedy mansion in Palm Beach, Fla. Here was NBC President Michael Gartner on ABC's "Nightline," defending the network's decision to reveal her identity. There was the Miami Herald and other Florida newspapers deciding to withhold her identity. And we can all look forward to more of this self-scrutiny in the next days and weeks.

Interestingly, the media showed less concern over the release of other identities in this case. In the time since that fateful Easter weekend almost everyone, including this newspaper, has reported the fact that William Kennedy Smith is a — if not the — key suspect in the case. The story goes that Mr. Smith raped the woman after she turned down his amour in the dunes of Palm Beach after an evening at a swank watering hole. Mr. Smith has denied being involved in any offense, and to this point neither he nor anyone else has been charged in the case.

Now, as we subtly suggested yesterday, we hold no brief for the personal misdeeds of the Kennedy family. That said, what happens if Mr. Smith is never charged in the case? What if he is charged, but the court acquits him? Who then will stand up to try to remove the tarnish from his reputation?

One retort to this might be that Mr. Smith gives up protections afforded to other suspects because of his celebrity status or at least his relation to celebrity status. He's a public figure, and the media are free to try the case of public figures in the morning newspapers. Very well, but that argument contradicts the claim that the special status of the Kennedys necessarily means special treatment for them. In this case, their status may well work against them.

We don't think newspapers and other media outlets should disclose the names of alleged rape victims. We fear that would discourage their reporting of what is a truly heinous crime, one warranting severe punishment. But we also think it's worth the news media's while to ask whether it's appropriate to report the names of mere suspects, even Kennedy suspects, until law-enforcement officials think they have enough evidence to justify a trial that would change the suspect's life forever, guilty or no. Public figures may or may not deserve that much. But as this case suggests, they shouldn't look forward to it anytime soon.

The Salt Lake Tribune
Salt Lake City, Utah, April 20, 1991

News organizations have given all kinds of excuses for identifying the woman who says she was raped at the Kennedy estate in Palm Beach, Fla., all of them weak.

Alleged rape victims are rarely named in news stories in this country because of the unfair stigma that attaches to the crime. But after NBC Nightly News reported the name of this particular woman, many other news outlets quickly followed suit.

Besides unnecessarily invading the privacy of an individual who may have been forced into the harsh light of public scrutiny, these news accounts may discourage other victims from reporting sex crimes.

One flimsy rationale for the policy exception is the prominence of the Kennedy family. Since when does the identity of the alleged attacker determine the standard of treatment for the accuser, whom the policy is designed to protect? No more in this instance than others.

Even editors of the respected *New York Times* rationalized that other newspapers or broadcast stations took the matter out of their hands by naming the alleged victim. This, added to the intrusive, deprecating description of the woman's private life, is an especially disappointing defense from the publication that often sets the standard for responsible journalism in this country.

Does this mean the *Times* intends to be the follower rather than the leader in matters of journalistic ethics from now on? Haven't *Times* editors learned to "just say no" to outside pressure to compromise their values? Were they trying to discolor the accuser's character before her day in court?

It's true, as some advocacy groups contend, that the stigma will endure as long as society treats rape victims differently than victims of other crimes, and that protecting their identity perpetuates the stigma. The fact remains, however, that victims of sex crimes are brutalized, even in these supposedly enlightened times, by both the attacker and a society that often treats the victims as either damaged goods or willing participants.

If the alleged victim is willing to be named, as was the woman featured in a Pulitzer Prize-winning *Des Moines Register* story last year, fine. Such candor may pave the way for more openness and societal acceptance of sex-crime victims in the future. Meanwhile, victims shouldn't have to suffer the consequences of lingering prejudice and misunderstanding. They deserve to decide for themselves whether this most humiliating of assaults on their privacy should become public knowledge.

Taking that decision out of their hands, as so many news organizations have now done with their lack of restraint in the Kennedy case, is just one more unwarranted, merciless attack on the victims' sense of self-control and self-worth.

The Augusta Chronicle
Augusta, Georgia, April 18, 1991

New York Post editor Jerry Nachman makes a good point about the alleged rape that occurred Easter Saturday at the Kennedy family mansion in Palm Beach. "Isn't it astonishing," he says, "that a week after the alleged incident took place, not one of the three potential suspects (Sen. Ted Kennedy, D-Mass.; Willie Smith, his nephew; and Patrick Kennedy, his son) had been questioned by the police?"

Smith was subsequently fingered as the suspect — and now police complain the Kennedys are making it difficult to interview them. (Perhaps the department is sensitive because it initially gave the Kennedys preferential treatment after a 29-year-old woman aired her rape charge.)

Another thing smacking of cover-up is that the Palm Beach force is a well-staffed, well-funded agency; a spokesmen admitted it had all the expertise and equipment needed to conduct a complex rape investigation. Yet it initially dilly-dallied, claiming it needed help from other agencies. And the department's inability to publicly name Smith as the suspect for *five days* for want of a photograph that turned out to be readily available a few blocks away seems inexcusable.

We can't predict what will happen to Willie. But is it too much to ask that, at some point, Massachusetts voters say "enough is enough" to their senator's penchant for scandal?

Newsday
New York City, April 18, 1991

The New York Times did it Wednesday because NBC News did it Tuesday night. NBC did it because The Globe in Boca Raton, Fla., did it last week. The Globe did it because the London Sunday Mirror did it April 7. What all these news organizations did was to reveal, without her permission, the name of the woman who accused William Kennedy Smith of rape. So much for journalistic ethics.

Pardon us, but we continue to believe that rape survivors are victimized a second time when their names are revealed by the media against their wishes.

Yes, we know that The Des Moines Register won a Pulitzer Prize this year for its courageous story recounting the experience of a rape victim, who was named. But in that case, her name was revealed *at her request*.

Keeping such identities secret is a journalistic tradition (largely followed in the Central Park jogger case, for example) that is being challenged today by a range of critics.

Those who make a case for publicizing rape victims' names make two main points: First, the shame of rape would be lessened if readers were to see the names of the ordinary people who are victims of sexual assaults; secrecy may lead people to infer that there is something unspeakable about rape, or that the victim may have encouraged her assailant. Second, protecting the accuser but naming the accused sets an unfair double standard. In the vernacular, the accused man is hung out to dry while his female accuser gets a free ride.

But if a member of your family were raped, would you want her (or his) name in the headlines, simply to fulfill a journalistic yearning to soften rape's shamefulness? And the double-standard argument doesn't hold up: Rape victims, male or female, deserve privacy; their bodies are the scene of the crime.

These arguments deserve a good airing in journalism seminars — but don't be fooled into thinking that philosophic considerations underlay the decisions of NBC News or The New York Times. NBC's Mike Gartner said, "We are merely reporting what we have learned." And the Times said its editors believed that "NBC's nationwide broadcast took the matter of her privacy out of their hands."

That's not courage, that's expedience.

MILWAUKEE SENTINEL
Milwaukee, Wisconsin, April 15, 1991

Sen. Edward M. Kennedy (D-Mass.) gave an incredible excuse for declining to talk to authorities who had questions about his nephew, William Kennedy Smith, accused of raping a woman at the Kennedy family's estate in Palm Beach, Fla.

Kennedy said he didn't respond to a request for an interview by police because he was "never, never" told that the allegations against Smith involved a rape case.

Kennedy admitted that others at the home told him of at least two police inquiries March 31, but said he thought the case involved sexual harassment, and not rape, and implied that it made a difference.

Compounding this reluctance to cooperate is the fact that, according to an affidavit by a Palm Beach police detective, investigators were told that Kennedy was out of town when he actually was not due to leave until the next day.

Kennedy, it should be noted, is not only a US senator but also an attorney. Shouldn't he have more respect for the legal processes?

Moreover, if he is told police want to question him about a sexual harassment charge against a close family member, shouldn't he at least want to find out what it was all about? After all, Kennedy, his son and Smith were in the bar together when Smith met the woman involved.

One more question. It may be considered below the belt to bring up dirty laundry, but isn't hiding out from the law similar to the judgment used by Kennedy after Chappaquiddick?

The Phoenix Gazette
Phoenix, Arizona, April 20, 1991

The media circus over the alleged rape by a member of the Kennedy family in Palm Beach, Fla., has been fairly effective in eroding what little respect many Americans had for some of the major news organizations.

The decision by NBC News and *The New York Times* to name the woman who allegedly was raped seemed to indicate that long-proclaimed standards designed to protect victims don't mean much when there's a juicy story afoot.

The 29-year-old woman has said William Kennedy Smith, 30, nephew of Sen. Edward Kennedy, raped her at the Kennedy family's estate in Palm Beach. No charges have been filed, pending perhaps the most leisurely investigation in recent years, and the Kennedy family has begun damage-control operations on a number of fronts, including conducting investigations of the woman's past.

Most newspapers, including *The Gazette*, have rules against printing the names of alleged rape victims, in deference to the privacy rights of the women involved. Most, including *The Gazette*, intend to adhere to these rules.

While some women have courageously come forth to publicly speak of their ordeals, there is a substantial difference between identifying a victim who wishes to address the issue publicly and identifying a victim who seeks privacy to avoid the misguided stigma that many people still attach to victims of sex crimes.

If news organizations expect to be believed when they say they have rules to protect victims, they had better be prepared to adhere to these rules, even when competitive pressures tempt them to do otherwise.

Some constitutional law experts and editors say that, by withholding identities, the news organizations perpetuate the stigma of rape. Some say that the crime should be treated like any other, in which both the accused and the accuser are named.

Perhaps this would be the best way for things to evolve, once societal attitudes adjust. But for now, identifying the woman against her will changes the rules in midstream. The public may grow cynical over explanations that the circumstances of this particular case justify ignoring long-standing policies.

In the case of *The Times*, spokesmen said that the decision to print the name was based solely on the fact that NBC broadcast the name. NBC cited the printing of the woman's name in a supermarket tabloid.

Does this mean that the reputable news organizations in this nation make policy based on what the supermarket tabloids do? If so, perhaps news executives should consider the reaction of an editor for the *National Enquirer*, who said that he wasn't so sure his paper would publish the woman's name.

The issue of whether news organizations have the legal right to publish the name is an entirely different matter from whether they *should* do so. It's unfortunate that some have trampled the victim in their haste to jump into the story.

Richmond Times-Dispatch
Richmond, Virginia, April 19, 1991

Michael Gartner is not God. Really. As president of NBC News, he is a powerful man, to be sure, but God he is not.

In deciding to broadcast the name of the woman allegedly raped at the Palm Beach compound of the Kennedy family over the Easter weekend, however, Mr. Gartner acted as if he thinks he's God. His purpose, he said, was to "remove the stigma" of rape by treating it like any other crime.

Now, most respectable and responsible news media, including this newspaper, do not usually publish the names of women who have been sexually assaulted because they know that rape is not like any other crime. Rape can traumatize its victims far more profoundly than other crimes do; the emotional suffering rape victims endure goes far beyond the anger that victims of more impersonal crimes — robbery, for example — might feel. Focusing the spotlight of unwanted publicity on women who have been raped is likely to exacerbate their pain by making them feel they are the victims of voyeurism. If the news media routinely identified rape victims, many women would never report assaults against them to the police. Mr. Gartner can change none of this by waving a peacock feather and saying: "Let there be no more stigma to rape."

Many of Mr. Gartner's journalistic colleagues reacted with dismay to his decision and insisted they would follow their present policy of withholding rape victims' names. Executives of CBS, ABC, CNN, The Washington Post, the New York Post and the New York Daily News took this position. Jerry Nachman, editor of the New York Post, accused Mr. Gartner of "unilaterally making a decision for journalists in this country ... I wonder how much input he got from victims of sex crimes before making a decision" to release the name. The New York Times decided to identify the woman involved in the Palm Beach affair because, it explained, NBC and certain tabloids already had destroyed her privacy. Now The Times is being widely criticized not only for publishing her name but also for delving too deeply into her private life.

Some critics accuse newspapers that withhold the names of rape victims while identifying the alleged rapist of adhering to an unacceptable double standard. Such a policy, they say, is especially unfair to men who are falsely charged, since the accusation itself stigmatizes them. This charge is not without merit. But publicity almost certainly is far more damaging to the victims of rape than to accused rapists.

Committed as they are to the principle that people have the right to be fully informed on public issues, including crimes, most journalists are loath to withhold any information. But they also know that in some instances withholding certain information also can be in the public interest. The names of rape victims, in most cases, fall within that category.

Kennedy Nephew Acquitted of Rape in Florida

William Kennedy Smith, 31, the nephew of Sen. Edward M. Kennedy (D, Mass.), Dec. 11, 1991 was found not guilty of charges that he had raped a woman at his family's Palm Beach, Fla. vacation estate on Easter weekend.

Smith was acquitted on one count of sexual battery (Florida's legal term for rape) and one count of battery. The two-man, four-woman jury deliberated for less than two hours before reaching a verdict.

The 30-year-old alleged victim testified Dec. 4 that she had given Smith a ride home from a popular nightclub, Au Bar, on the night of the attack and had gone for a walk on the beach with him. She said Smith had begun taking his clothes off and asked her if she wanted to go for a swim in the ocean. She said she became concerned about his behavior and began to leave the estate. She said Smith then ran after her and tackled her.

"He had me on the ground and I was trying to get out from underneath of him, 'cause he was crushing me," the woman tearfully testified. "And he had my arm pinned. And I was yelling 'No!' and then 'Stop.' And I tried to arch my back to get him off me, and he slammed me back on the ground, and I got—and then he pushed my dress up and he raped me."

She was cross-examined for more than five hours over a two-day period Dec. 4–5 by lead defense attorney Roy E. Black. Black endeavored to point out inconsistencies in her testimony, including her inability to remember when she had removed her pantyhose. He frequently reduced her to tears with such questions as what position Smith's legs had been in when he tried to penetrate her, whether she had felt him ejaculate and whether she had been sexually aroused. The woman repeatedly refused offers of a brief recess, saying she wished to get the cross-examination over with.

At the end of cross-examination, Black asked her if she had an ulterior motive in accusing Smith of rape. She replied, "I didn't want to live for the rest of my life in fear of that man, and I didn't want to be responsible for him doing it to someone else." At Black's request, the judge, Mary E. Lupo, instructed jurors to disregard the remark.

During nationally televised coverage of the trial, the woman's face was obscured electronically, in accord with a common journalistic policy of protecting the identity of alleged rape victims.

In his testimony Dec. 10, Smith told the court that he had met the woman at Au Bar and that they were "mutually attracted." He said she had offered to drive him back to the Kennedy estate and, once there, went for a walk on the beach with him. He said they began kissing and she "unbuttoned my pants. I took her panties off with her help." After that, Smith said, the woman masturbated him and, after he went for a swim in the ocean, stimulated him into having intercourse with her.

During the act, Smith said, he mistakenly called her "Kathy" (the name of a long-time girlfriend), at which point she "sort of snapped...She got very, very upset, told me to get the hell off of her." He said he had later described her to his cousin Patrick as "a real nut."

Prosecutor Moira K. Lasch was unable to shake Smith's testimony despite four hours of cross-examination and frequent use of sarcasm and ridicule. At one point she asked Smith about his "animal magnetism" and, at another, asked him, "What are you, some kind of sex machine here?" She was admonished several times by Judge Lupo.

FORT WORTH STAR-TELEGRAM
Fort Worth, Texas, December 13, 1991

All over America this week, millions of citizens spent some of their time knotted around television sets, witnessing something important.

And, yes, the William Kennedy Smith rape trial, televised from West Palm Beach, Fla., was a sideshow. It was trivia expanded to national dimensions. Its appeal was to the celebrity-watcher and the peeping Tom. It touched a low, voyeuristic common denominator.

But it was also more than that.

Americans whose notions of the actual workings of criminal trials were probably shaped by *Perry Mason* and *Matlock* got a glimpse of the real thing. They got a taste of how the system really works.

Unlike the slice of senatorial life that was televised in the Clarence Thomas-Anita Hill hearings, what took place in Palm Beach was not decided by partisan politics. This was a real jury, not a committee. This was real life, grubby but important.

Rather than demonstrating the folly of televising courtroom proceedings, the Smith trial — for all its celebrity and checkout-counter-magazine titillation — should make us consider seriously the wisdom of doing it more often.

It is a recent thing that cameras are allowed in courtrooms. Many of us do now get a glimpse of our courts at work on the evening news, which is better than nothing. But cable television makes it possible to occasionally have an extended look at the courts, as in the Smith case.

That is good. It is worth pursuing. Because these are *our* courts. It is *our* justice system. None of it belongs to the judges, or to the lawyers. They merely make their living there, representing us or, more accurately, representing the law.

Federal and state constitutions prescribe the basics of the system, including protections of the rights of defendants. That was a major point in the Smith trial.

The continuous televising of the Smith trial demonstrated the ponderous, often boring process of justice. Rarely, outside the entertainment realm, does a courtroom see a dramatic confession from the witness chair, or see a case suddenly resolved by a resourceful attorney/detective who uncovers the *real* culprit.

We need to know that.

We need to understand the system. We need to realize that it can be difficult to get a conviction without strong and clear-cut evidence. We need to understand that whether it is a Kennedy or a Jones — or a Smith — on trial, the system itself is much too important to be hidden from view or cloaked in mystery.

The Evening Gazette
Worcester, Massachusetts, December 13, 1991

Not one but two date-rape trials were played out in Palm Beach this month:

One proceeded methodically in Judge Mary Lupo's courtroom with scrupulous attention to protecting the rights of accuser and accused. The other was waged outside the courtroom in a shrill, coast-to-coast feeding frenzy of sensation, exploitation and hype.

In Judge Lupo's courtroom, the accuser was given full opportunity to bring the charges of sexual assault and battery. The defendant, presumed innocent until proved guilty, was given full opportunity to confront his accuser and answer the charges.

In the parody of justice played out in the tabloid television and press, accused and accuser both were on trial. In this kangaroo court of hype and glitz, there was little pretense of fairness and decorum and a near-universal presumption that both of the parties involved were guilty until proved innocent.

Whatever one's opinion of the character or actions of the two people involved, members of the jury hardly could have reached a different verdict based on the testimony and forensic evidence placed before them.

There is certainly much to be learned from this case, including lessons about the responsibilities of both parties involved in casual sexual liaisons. Perhaps the publicity given the issue of date rape will raise the consciousness of men and embolden women who have been sexually assaulted to bring charges.

We certainly hope so. It would be a grave and tragic error to interpret the outcome of the Smith trial as a signal that women have no recourse against sexual predation.

The most encouraging aspect of the case is that the proceedings in the courtroom were hardly affected by the circus-like proceedings outside. Nor was, evidently, the impartiality of the jury's deliberations.

No system of justice is perfect, and even the remarkably smooth trial in Judge Lupo's courtroom sprouted a wart or two. But Americans should be heartened to realize that even in the face of sensationalism justice can prevail.

The Globe and Mail
Toronto, Ontario, December 6, 1991

AGAIN we are transfixed. Again it is her word against his, as millions watch, and listen and decide. But this is something new. Anita Hill faced Clarence Thomas at Senate hearings, long open to the prying eyes of television. William K. Smith and his accuser are in a court of law. The charge is rape. And since the trial began on Monday, every minute of it has been carried live from the Palm Beach County Circuit Court: to 4 million American homes on the fledgling Courtroom Television Network, to millions more in the United States and around the world on CNN, with highlights in the evening for those who missed it the first time. By all accounts, the ratings are huge.

Rape trials go on every day all over the country, of course. Given that 44 American states now allow television cameras into the courtroom, a fair number have probably been broadcast. But never before has a criminal trial, and a rape trial at that, been held before such a massive gallery. Explanations for this fascination are not hard to come by. The K is for Kennedy, after all, and not only a Kennedy, but a Kennedy charged with rape: a nice boy, to look at him, from a prominent family. The testimony is as lurid and unsettling as one might expect. The very fact that it is televised adds novelty to its emotive appeal.

Is prurience all there is to it? A Tory MP rose in the Commons yesterday to call on the government to order Newsworld to switch to something more edifying, like the constitutional committee. Many will sympathize, believing it degrading to subject and viewer alike to wallow in such anguished spectacle. More may worry that the law itself is brought low by association with this unwashed medium, its dignity dissolving under the hot glare of the TV lights. Can he get a fair trial? Can she?

This seems a bit dainty. It is a rudiment of common law that the accused has the right to face his accuser in an open court. That is true even in the charged context of a rape trial, though various jurisdictions have seen fit to prohibit publication of the complainant's name. The courtroom has merely been expanded in this case. Someday perhaps we will get over our strange habit of investing television with such totemic powers, as if in common with those tribes who believe the camera steals the soul.

It is good for the people to see the courts at work, to be schooled in the ways of our law. It is especially right when the issue at hand is rape, and best of all now, in these times of fervour and lament at the evil men do. We may better appreciate the complexities that can arise, when real lives are involved and real events are at issue, not just slogans and symbols. We may come to understand why the law's procedures have evolved over centuries as they have, and where perhaps they may need change.

We are not the jury. The screen cannot project the necessary awe, felt only in the actual experience of place: the fault of televised church as much as televised court. But its harrowing intimacy can teach us this: individual men rape individual women, and it is individual men and women who must judge them.

Chicago Tribune
Chicago, Illinois, December 13, 1991

Considering all that could have gone wrong, courtroom television acquitted itself well in the rape trial of William Kennedy Smith.

The high-profile case may have appeared bizarre to some and deadly dull to others among TV-watching masses more accustomed to the fictional dramatics of "L.A. Law" or "Perry Mason."

But by the time the final gavel fell Wednesday, there was no evidence of the intrusive calamities that critics of courtroom cameras had predicted. Lawyers did not grandstand. Witnesses showed no signs of camera shyness. Jurors did not preen or try to wave to their mothers.

Only Judge Mary E. Lupo, of all people, seemed to be preaching to the television congregation as she droned on exhaustively and inexplicably in a post-verdict sermon—when no one but perhaps her own friends and relatives had any reason to care.

But even this moment of spotlight-hogging included unexpected praise for the conduct of news personnel, one of whom the judge had ejected earlier for conspicuous smirking.

On balance and all things considered, the Smith trial became a powerful exhibit in the case for opening courtrooms everywhere to television.

As Steven Brill, founder of the Court TV cable network, observed, the so-called media circus surrounding the Smith trial took place outside the courtroom, not inside.

The worst intrusion may have been the $40,000 paid by the tabloid program "A Current Affair" to prosecution witness Anne Mercer. That transaction became a trial issue when Smith's lawyer, Roy E. Black, used it to discredit her testimony.

Compared to that and other abuses of good taste and good sense committed outside in the name of television journalism, the cameras in the courtroom were quite benign.

Their start-to-finish coverage was more subdued and responsible than was suggested by many of the lurid quotes and sound bites ripped from context for some news reports.

Some 45 states now permit cameras in at least some of their courts. So do some federal civil courts. In the great laboratory that the states provide, the experiment has worked well, although some cautious judges still ban cameras in high-profile cases like New York City's Central Park jogger case last year.

The results have particular importance for Illinois, as it considers whether to allow cameras in its lower courts after having allowed them in appellate courts on an experimental basis.

In an age of small and silent minicams that require no special lighting, there is no reason to limit coverage of trials to second-hand accounts.

Television in courtrooms is but a logical extension of the constitutional principle of public trial.

That principle contemplates not just the protection of the accused, but the enlightenment and education of the public on the operation of the central organs of justice in the society.

When the jury came in in the William Kennedy Smith trial, it also came in for cameras in the courtroom. That verdict? Use them.

The Hartford Courant
Hartford, Connecticut, December 8, 1991

A Kennedy is on trial. The spectacle unfolding on the nation's TV screens has the makings of great melodrama and, fairly or unfairly, has consigned Haitian refugees, a falling-apart Soviet Union, a beginning presidential campaign and the depressed economy to obscurity in the minds of most viewers.

William Kennedy Smith is on trial for rape. The story has all the angles: men vs. women, the family with the fatal flaw dragged yet again into the tabloids, an alleged Jekyll-and-Hyde transformation, an aging senator in his nightshirt, the competing stereotypes of gold-digger-hussy-on-the-make and spoiled-rich-boy-with-the-testosterone-problem.

Serious commentators can bewail, for the umpteenth time, the fact that Americans want to be entertained, not informed. Right-thinking people can express their discomfort with the circus-like atmosphere created in a court of law. It doesn't matter. At night, in front of the tube, the nation is agog. In the bars, in the streets, in the offices and the shops, there is no other subject.

Suddenly the world seems more divided, and the divisions are not simple. There are the Kennedy-lovers and the Kennedy-haters. There are the feminists and the women-haters. There are those who believe Mr. Smith and those who believe his accuser. There are those who think the accuser should be named and her face shown, and those who disagree. There are those who say they aren't interested, and for the most part they're lying.

What makes it all such a compelling saga is that it's not a story about a person; it's about a large, powerful, wealthy and highly visible family, and about one obscure individual who happened to stumble into its periphery. There's something slightly Greek about the story that contributes to its theatrical nature: the lone, anonymous, masked accuser, the chorus of loyal aunts, the fact that what it all revolves around is honor: Has an obscure young woman been wronged, used, hubristically brushed aside? — or has a fine young man been unjustly and vindictively accused, and a great family's name sullied?

It may not be quite right, but nevertheless it's somehow fitting, in this age, that the drama is being played out on television. It is the stuff of American catharsis, in which our complex emotions about money and family and sex and power are engaged communally. We bring our separate concerns to the theater of the courtroom and invest ourselves, together, in the outcome.

The Courier-Journal
Louisville, Kentucky, December 13, 1991

SOME people will say that the acquittal of William Kennedy Smith is yet another example of the raw deal rape victims get in our country's criminal justice system. They're wrong. The proceedings were an aberration in every respect except the most important one — justice was done. Mr. Smith deserved to be found not guilty because the criminal charge against him wasn't proved beyond a reasonable doubt.

It's important to note that the woman's claims were taken seriously. Once Palm Beach authorities overcame their initial inertia, they spared no expense or effort to make the case. Then again they had no choice. Everyone knows that if the principals had been poor Haitian refugees the case would have been handled altogether differently. But he was a Kennedy, and that made all the difference. Had Florida authorities casually dismissed the woman's claims, they'd be lambasted for shielding a member of a powerful family — and rightfully so.

The result, however, was a tawdry circus. It was created by the media but fed by the country's insatiable appetite for titillating tidbits about the Kennedys.

While many onlookers were taking leave of their senses, the jurors held fast to theirs and doing the job they'd been given — weighing the evidence. And there wasn't enough to support conviction. The accusor's case was harmed by some events beyond her control — such as the testimony of her so-called "friend" who sold a version of the salacious happenings at the Kennedy compound to "A Current Affair" for $40,000 and then used the money for a fling in Mexico.

Ultimately, however, the accusor was less credible than the defendant. On the witness stand she came across as strong and unwavering. But skillful cross-examination by the brilliant defense attorney made it clear that there had been numerous gaps and inconsistencies in the various versions of the events that she gave police, lawyers, rape counselors and friends. In contrast, Mr. Kennedy's version never changed. Surely it was that stark contrast that clinched the case.

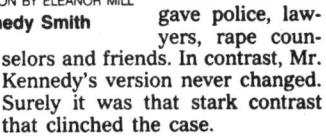

From the promiscuous sex out of which the charges emerged to the gavel-to-gavel television coverage, the case was one of sickening excess.

Most cases are dealt with in obscurity — rarely does an alleged victim have her private life revealed in the press or a courtroom.

As Susan Estrich, the author of *Real Rape*, has noted, too much is read into highly publicized cases. The verdict in the Palm Beach case "does not mean every man will be acquitted, or should be."

ILLUSTRATION BY ELEANOR MILL
William Kennedy Smith

DAYTON DAILY NEWS
Dayton, Ohio, December 13, 1991

Did the television cameras affect the William Kennedy Smith trial?

Well, there's no denying that the participants played to the media. The prosecutors and defense lawyers were adept at putting out information through the media. But much of this jockeying — about Mr. Smith's past encounters with women, and about the accuser's medical and sexual history — took place away from the cameras and, indeed, before the actual trial.

In the trial itself, there were some histrionics, of course. But that happens in court all the time, including in trials in which there are no reporters and no cameras.

Imagine, though, that there had been no cameras, that millions of Americans *didn't* have the opportunity to hear and see the witnesses for themselves.

Wouldn't there now be a lot of cynicism about the verdict? Wouldn't people be saying that the Kennedys own Palm Beach, or that a woman can't get a break?

Because the trial was televised, many people find the jurors' decision understandable. Having watched some or much of the testimony, they can identify with "reasonable doubt."

Some advocates of rape victims are arguing that the trial surely will frighten sexual-assault victims, will scare them away from reporting sexual crimes. Maybe; that definitely would be a shame.

But this trial was unusual. Most rape cases involve anonymous individuals; most rape cases don't attract the public attention that this one received.

Because of the nature of rape, there is no painless way to determine whether an accused person is guilty. But some ordeals are worse than others.

For everybody, this was a particularly difficult case.

Herald News
Fall River, Massachusetts, December 11, 1991

Whether justice was served in the William Kennedy Smith rape trial, which ended in acquittal yesterday, none of us will ever know. We do know that the American judicial process was served and that Smith emerged innocent from charges of raping a 30-year-old woman last Easter weekend.

And yet many thoughout the land are decrying the outcome as a setback for all women. They say the verdict of not guilty will discourage women who have been raped from reporting those rapes. That seeing first-hand our criminal justice system reject the alleged victim's version of the events that night will lead all rape victims to believe their accusations would be similarly treated.

But those who view this trial as a death knell for victim rights base it on the supposition that Kennedy was guilty and simply got away with it. This may be so, but it just as likely may not be so. At least six people felt there was a reasonable doubt. Those who lament the verdict, however, seem to think that because Smith's accuser says he raped her that makes it so. Perhaps even that any man accused of rape is guilty of rape.

The truth is that some women falsely accuse men of rape and some men get away with raping women. Predicting whether women will be dissuaded from reporting rape based on a single case in which only the accused and the accuser really know what happened does a great disservice to both women and men.

* * *

The most important lesson resulting form the Smith trial may be the realization that so-called date rape is a difficult crime to prove and, just maybe, an easier crime to prevent.

Women are not to blame for being raped. But suggesting that women use extreme care when deciding to spend time alone with men they don't know does not amount to blaming those women for whatever men may try to force upon them.

It does mean women should use the examples highlighted in the Smith case as a reminder of situations to avoid. Of course no reasonable person believes that dancing closely with a man nor even accompanying a man home gives him the right to force sex upon a woman. But if women avoid those familiar situations with unfamiliar men, it's less likely the opportunity for rape will occur.

A woman mustn't be held responsible for what a man does, but taking responsibility for using common sense and good judgment are in women's best interests.

The Washington Post
Washington, D.C., December 12, 1991

ONE OF the most disagreeable parts of the William Kennedy Smith trial just concluded could all too easily turn out to be one still to come: the post-mortems. All sorts of commentators are likely to want to be heard. In fact, the most important and safest lesson to be drawn from the tawdry affair, insofar as the legal system is concerned, is probably that there is no single, overriding lesson.

The outcome doesn't prove that people with lots of money to spend on their defense always win (though surely money helps); nor that women in cases such as this are necessarily fated to lose (though they often have an uphill fight); nor even that salacious trials such as this should not be shown on television for fear they will be reduced to national entertainment and soap operas.

Every criminal trial, even every rape trial, is unique, involves a particular accuser, a particular defendant, its own particular circumstances, degrees of credibility and jury. Here the six members of the jury quickly and apparently easily decided that the charges had not been proved beyond the standard of reasonable doubt that the law rightly requires. Mr. Smith is not guilty.

It needs to be added that the victory was hardly unmixed. The whole episode exacted an enormous price. Apart from the criminal trial aspects, the saga of that night in Palm Beach was hardly a reputation enhancer for anyone, and altogether the recounting of it was a degrading experience. But that's a separate matter having to do with things other than the criminal law. Criminal juries are called upon to make very exact decisions, and they're generally pretty good at it. That's what happened here—and that's all that happened. It would be a great mistake to try to read anything more into the verdict than that.

the Charleston Gazette
Charleston, West Virginia, December 13, 1991

THREE conclusions are possible in the Palm Beach spectacle:
(1) The woman is unstable, and William Kennedy Smith told the truth. (2) The woman testified accurately, and Smith crafted lies to undermine her credibility. (3) Both distorted what happened, and the truth lies somewhere between.

We can't fathom which is correct. But it's obvious that the jury reached the right verdict, based on the evidence presented. His guilt wasn't proved beyond a reasonable doubt.

Some puzzles never can be answered with certainty. In such cases, the American jury system is the best method to reach an acceptable decision.

The Oregonian
Portland, Oregon, December 13, 1991

Not guilty.

After deliberating a mere 77 minutes, a Florida jury acquitted William Kennedy Smith of charges that he raped a woman he picked up in a bar only hours earlier.

The temptation is to see this as the archetypal rape case, one whose quick, not-guilty verdict will chill women across the country from reporting rape.

It should do nothing of the kind.

The facts that charges were brought and that a trial was held are evidence that prosecutors will take a rape accusation seriously, even when the encounter occurs after a woman willingly accompanies a man to his home.

In the not-so-distant past, such an allegation would be waved off, under the assumption that a woman's bad judgment to trust a man means that she is entitled to no recourse if he then decides to attack her.

Also noteworthy was the absence of what used to be a fixture in rape trials: a parading of the victim's past sex life, as if that had any relevance to the case. Knowing that they will not have to testify about the most intimate details of their lives should make women more willing to report rape and pursue criminal charges.

The trial did underscore the difficulty of proving rape. Few women need to be reminded of that. Proof becomes even harder to supply when the rape involves an acquaintance — as the vast majority of rapes do.

There is no good remedy for that problem. The U.S. legal system is weighted in the defendant's favor; a crime must be proved beyond a reasonable doubt. That standard protects men — and women — when they are accused of crimes. It should not be changed, but it will always make the prosecution's job difficult when there are no witnesses and the case rests on choosing which of two conflicting accounts to believe.

In the end, this kind of trial comes down to a jury's decision about who is most credible, the man or the woman.

This jury believed William Kennedy Smith. But its verdict says nothing about whose story the jury will believe next time.

Boxer Mike Tyson, Convicted of Rape in Indianapolis

Former world heavyweight boxing champion Mike Tyson was convicted Feb. 10, 1992 of raping Desiree Washington, an 18-year-old Rhode Island woman who competed in the Miss Black America beauty pageant in Indianapolis in 1991.

The nine-man, three-woman jury deliberated for nine-and-a-half hours before convicting Tyson of one count of rape and two criminal counts of deviant conduct (for performing oral sex on Washington and for penetrating her vagina with his fingers). Tyson, 25, faced a maximum sentence of six to 20 years in prison on each of the charges.

(Washington's name was not reported by most U.S. news media during the trial, under a common journalistic policy of protecting the identity of alleged rape victims. The chief exception was NBC. Washington Feb. 13 came forward, however, and identified herself as the accuser in the case.)

The trial had begun on Jan. 27. Washington testified Jan. 30–31. She said she had willingly agreed to go out with Tyson when he telephoned her at about 1:30 a.m. on July 19, 1991, but believed that he intended only to take her for a ride around Indianapolis in his limousine. (The two had met the previous day when Tyson made a promotional appearance at the Indiana Black Expo, of which the beauty pageant formed a part.)

Washington testified that shortly after she joined Tyson in his limousine, he told her he had to make a stop at his hotel. She said she accompanied him to his room, where Tyson overpowered her, fondled her, threw her onto the bed and raped her, causing her excrutiating pain.

"I tried to punch him, but it was like hitting a wall," she testified. (Tyson was 5 feet 11 inches tall and weighed over 200 pounds, while Washington was 5 feet 3 and weighed about 105 pounds.) She testified that after Tyson raped her, he asked her, "'Don't you love me now?'"

Tyson's lead defense attorney, Vincent J. Fuller, insisted that Washington had consented to having sex with Tyson. He accused her of filing the rape charge out of malice, after Tyson refused to accompany her back to her hotel and "she found herself treated to a one-night stand." He also suggested that she hoped to make money out of Tyson by filing a civil lawsuit against him.

Tyson testified Feb. 7–8. He claimed that shortly after he met Washington he had made it clear that he wanted to have sex with her, and that she had replied, "'Sure. Just give me a call.'" In cross-examination Feb. 8, however, lead prosecutor J. Gregory Garrison noted that Tyson had made no such claim in his testimony before a grand jury in September 1991.

Other witnesses included:

- Tyson's hired limousine driver, Virginia Foster, who testified for the prosecution Feb. 1. Foster said that after Washington left Tyson's hotel, "her appearance was like she was in a state of shock. Dazed. Disoriented. She seemed scared."
- Washington's mother, who testified Feb. 4 that the normally outgoing young woman had become a changed person after the rape. "She's reliving this whole nightmare over and over, and I just want my daughter back," she said.
- An emergency-room doctor who said he had found abrasions in Washington's genital area that were consistent with forced sex.
- Sixteen of the 23 beauty pageant contestants. Some testified that Washington had flirted with Tyson and that Tyson had behaved in such a lewd fashion when he met the pageant contestants that it would have been impossible for her not to have known that he was looking for sex.

Rockford Register Star
Rockford, Illinois, February 12, 1992

Prizefighter Mike Tyson, whose own lawyer characterized him in court as a crude and predatory womanizer, has been formally adjudged to be a rapist. This verdict should send a message to victims of acquaintance-rape that not even great wealth, fame, adulation and physical prowess can absolve a sexual thug of his crimes.

Mike Tyson is, indeed, a sexual thug. Barring a reversal of his conviction on appeal, he's going to go to jail — and deservedly so — for what he did to an 18-year-old beauty pageant contestant in Indianapolis one night last summer. Whether he ever boxes in a ring again is irrelevant; the fight game already is so sordid that almost nothing could further tarnish its image.

Also irrelevant are comparisons of the Tyson case with the celebrated rape trial of William Kennedy Smith in Florida last year. As the jurors in Indianapolis have indicated in post-trial interviews, the complainant in this case was credible; her story had no major inconsistencies. The same could not be said of the complainant in the Smith case. The only common factors in these two cases were that both defendants were famous and that rape was the issue. Other than that, the juries, principals, evidence and circumstances were all different.

Nor should racial factors be read into the Tyson verdict. The jurors, black and white alike, agreed that racial considerations played no part in their weighing of the evidence.

Tyson was not railroaded in this case. His personal wealth availed him of expensive legal counsel, and he had more than six months to prepare his defense. The real wonder is that his defense was so self-opprobrious. His lawyers resorted to a calculated depiction of Tyson as a lecher with whom a young woman should have socialized only if she expected to be bedded down. It didn't work. The jury rightly decreed that a badge of conspicuous lechery is not a license to rape.

Again, we hope this verdict encourages bonafide victims of date-rape to file charges against their attackers. But let's not lose sight of the fact that the Tyson trial dealt strictly with the evidence of this isolated case and was not an adjudication of sexual offenses in general.

Justice was done. A former world champion is now just another felon awaiting sentence for having assaulted an innocent young woman.

The Houston Post
Houston, Texas, February 12, 1992

THE JURY THAT convicted former heavyweight boxing champion Mike Tyson was convinced by his accuser's story that she was raped. Tyson said the sex he had with the 18-year-old beauty contestant was consensual — damaging to her, if true. The jurors decided it was not.

Yet they also believed Tyson's defense attorneys when they described him as a relentless, pawing womanizer. And their verdict said, "So?"

Tired old sayings of the "What did she expect?" genre have at long last begun to wear out their welcome in the nation's courtrooms. The Post hopes they will vanish entirely as the emptiness of such arguments becomes increasingly evident. A woman's — or, for that matter, a man's — right to say no to sex is absolute.

Suggestions that Tyson's conviction was racially based are absurd. The racial makeup of the jury roughly mirrored that of the community, and both victim and defendant were black. Racism charges cannot be credibly leveled under such circumstances.

Tyson will appeal. But that will take time, and ultimately he could draw 60 years in prison. At the very least, he will likely serve two to three years — a small sentence indeed for such a crime.

What would be ideal would be for him to serve enough time so that when he emerges from his cell, he will be well over the hill as a fighter. Pro boxing does not need his kind.

Herald News
Fall River, Massachusetts, February 15, 1992

"I didn't do it for fame. It was the right thing to do," said Desiree Washington, the 18-year-old Providence College freshman who a jury decided was raped by boxer Mike Tyson. In the People magazine quote, she was presumably speaking about her decision to proceed with her accusations against the superstar.

That would have been a believable statement until the news Thursday that Desiree chose to go public with her name, as well as revealing photos of herself. By guarding her identity with secrecy befitting a Michael Fox nuptial, but then only days after a guilty verdict for Tyson consenting to a splashy People cover, Washington calls her motives into question and seriously undermines her credibility.

Perhaps her initial decision to report the crime was not done for fame, but what else can we believe about her decision to go public now?

Certainly she has a right to do so. And, at least for the People interview she's not getting paid. But the kind of publicity she'll receive through the and People coverage and an interview with Barbara Walters, money can't buy.

It's disappointing when women like Washington and Patricia Bowman, who accused William Kennedy Smith of raping her, protect their privacy with such fervor and self-righteousness only to turn around and betray that sentiment with celebrity-status interviews. Whatever cathartic, or other, value such after-the-fact confidences promise, they seem discounted by the circus-like forum in which they're presented.

The timing both Washington and Bowman used in going public adds fuel to the argument that rape victims should be named from the onset. Great pains should not be taken to hide the identities of rape victims if they are only going to reveal themselves once the trials are over.

THE TAMPA TRIBUNE
Tampa, Florida, February 13, 1992

An Indianapolis jury didn't knock out Mike Tyson this week. Tyson decked himself.

It is always baffling when an individual who has labored hard for fame and wealth should ruin his prospects by grossly mismanaging his private life. This the former heavyweight champion did, much to the regret of boxing fans who remember his best fights, when he was one of the most ferocious and exciting punchers in the history of the game. Although he has made millions, there were millions more to make, because no contemporary fighter was such a formidable box-office attraction.

Tyson was found guilty of raping a Miss Black America contestant in his hotel room. His defense during the trial was odd. His lawyer argued that the boxer was a crude womanizer and the young woman should have known that his only interest in her was sex. Well, Tyson certainly had a history of trouble with women, but that is anything but a mitigating fact in a rape case.

The former champ grew up poor and angry in Brooklyn, but he was presented with great opportunities to be a historic figure in sports, a lavishly paid hero of the ring. And he reached the top of the mountain and stayed there for a time. He might have regained the championship if he had disciplined himself outside the gym as conscientiously as he did within it.

Mike Tyson will have plenty of time to contemplate his attitude toward women, and what that violent attitude has cost him. And if he blames anyone but himself, he is twice a fool.

The Hutchinson News
Hutchinson, Kansas, February 12, 1992

Mike Tyson's defense essentially was that he was a known, crude womanizer and that those credentials should have been enough for a slug whose other most notable characteristics were, as the jury heard from some of the allegations, that he was both rich and stupid.

The verdict from the Indiana jury should do more than put Mike Tyson in his place (and that should be a jail cell for a few years).

The verdict should also convey some sense of national outrage at all such conduct and the fact that far too many of the nation's overpaid, overcoddled and oversexed athletes not only get away with barbarity, they expect to do so.

The Tyson case was certainly not a rerun of the Clarence Thomas case or even the latest episodes in the Kennedy family's escapades. This time, the victim made a case so convincing, and against a vulgar man with a trail of conduct so contemptible, that few would have expected any other outcome.

Tyson should not be thrown in the slammer longer than any other rapist, just because he is rich and stupid; he most certainly should be shown the inside of a cell as any other rapist should be shown.

The nation has been overly tolerant of conduct by too many of the people on whom it has showered rewards, honors and glory. It is long past time not merely to demand civilized conduct at the very least, even for those who are stupid in their riches.

It is not too difficult to hope that, some day, those who are most honored by a nation for talents and achievements will be expected to set neither lower-than-average nor even average standards of personal conduct, but higher standards of conduct and leadership.

The Hartford Courant
Hartford, Connecticut, February 12, 1992

Mike Tyson's defense didn't do him any favors. His lawyers' strategy at his rape trial was to portray him as such an offensive lout that no woman could be under any illusions about what he wanted. By their logic, any sex with Mr. Tyson would have had to be consensual, since no female would allow herself to be alone with him for any other reason. It didn't work.

Mr. Tyson's accuser was 18 years old, credible and lucky enough to have corroboration from several witnesses and injuries consistent with rape. Rape is a crime usually committed without witnesses and often under circumstances in which guilt is impossible to prove beyond reasonable doubt. It is also a crime in which the victim often goes on trial. Lawyers defending rapists often try to introduce irrelevant issues, such as the victim's sexual history or mode of dress, to prove that in some way the victim was "asking for it."

So Mr. Tyson's accuser accompanied him to his hotel room in the wee hours. Maybe she was stupid. Maybe she was naive. That wouldn't have given Mr. Tyson the right to rape her.

His defense implied, and many people probably still believe, that no 18-year-old female could be naive enough to do this without expecting sex. This is a sad indictment of American society; it says we have become so callous and decadent that no young person could get through adolescence and still maintain her innocence.

They're wrong, of course. There are now and will always be innocent 18-year-olds, both male and female. Fame will always attract some of them, and this puts a special responsibility on the famous. (Magic Johnson, please take note.) It must be a heady cocktail for young men such as Mr. Tyson, coming from deprived, violent backgrounds into riches and renown, and finding, no doubt, that that's enough to get them what they want in most situations. It must make it harder when someone small and young and relatively powerless says the simple word "No."

It's an old theme recast. Some rich people, some famous people, some influential people will always think the rules are not for them. Mr. Tyson's guilty verdict reinforces what women's advocates have been saying all along: Even for you, Mike, no means no.

The Courier-Journal
Louisville, Kentucky, February 12, 1992

From Mike Tyson's sordid concept of a good time with a woman comes a verdict that reflects favorably on the Indianapolis jurors who convicted him.

It was a celebrated case, not only because the man on trial is rich and thinks anything he wants is his for the taking. Mr. Tyson has been in trouble with the law most of his life but rarely paid the price. The defense his lawyer used in the rape trial spoke volumes. Mr. Tyson is lewd and lascivious and any woman should know better than to associate with him, said the lawyer. It was no accident that he called no character witnesses.

By finding the boxer guilty, the jurors did several things that juries often have been reluctant to do. First, they convicted him of rape. Rape charges customarily get dismissed or reduced by the courts. Second, they recognized acquaintance rape as real rape. Acquaintances are implicated in about half of all reported rapes, but many juries have a hard time taking the crime seriously. Third, they believed an African-American victim. Our criminal justice has often refused to acknowledge that the rape of a black woman deserves attention and has been lenient to men accused of assaulting black women.

Mr. Tyson got something that money can't buy. Justice.

THE DENVER POST
Denver, Colorado, February 15, 1992

Donald Trump's suggestion that Mike Tyson be allowed to trade hard cash for hard time should be rejected like a bad check.

Only the rich could call it justice. Tyson, convicted last week of raping a teenage beauty queen, deserves to be put behind bars just like any other violent criminal. As a former world heavyweight boxing champion, he may be better known than most inmates. But that shouldn't entitle him to any special treatment under the law.

More to the point, Tyson clearly poses a threat to society. He's a sex offender who has brutalized a young woman. Incarceration will both protect the public and punish him for his actions.

The Indiana judge who will sentence Tyson next month might well consider imposing an unusually large fine as part of the penalty, for as his wealthy friend Trump said, the boxer has made "millions and millions" of dollars with his fists.

Indeed, it would be appropriate to insist that Tyson make a substantial contribution to a victims' assistance program as part of any community service or probation arrangement.

If Tyson wants to make amends by staging another title fight and donating the proceeds to a good cause, that would be commendable. But for the court to accept a hefty check in lieu of a prison term would invite other wealthy defendants to turn the sentencing process into a bidding game.

Worse, it would mean the poor would continue to go to jail while the rich retained their freedom. That would be as unfair as pitting a fragile young woman against a 215-pound punching machine.

Lincoln Journal
Lincoln, Nebraska, February 12, 1992

Thank God those couple dozen nuts who gathered around the City-County Building in Indianapolis Tuesday to cheer convicted rapist Mike Tyson do not represent the overwhelming thinking in this country.

Imagine shouting "Don't worry about it, Mike!" and "Hang in there, Mike!" to one recently convicted by a jury of three brutal and obnoxious felony charges. What the hell's the matter with those people?

One-time heavyweight boxing champion Tyson is assuredly headed for an extended residence in an Indiana prison. He deserves such punishment.

Bit by bit, putting wayward sports heroes of cosmic dimension (as well as fast-track corporate thieves and jugglers) behind bars for criminal acts helps pound home a welcome social message. Baseball immortal Pete Rose did time. Now Tyson will, too, for raping an 18-year-old.

Asking the jury to believe what happened last July was consensual sex was the only desperation defense Tyson's lawyers could offer. It was, of course, a patently futile defense. He could hardly be seen as falsely accused when his own team admitted Tyson was crude, foul-mouthed and predatory about sex. Any jury would have found the evidence and the testimony of state witnesses easy to agree as the truth.

The last thing we want to hear about this disgraceful episode is that racism bent the jury's verdict against Tyson. The rapist was African-American. The victim was a contestant in the Miss Black America competition. The jury included African-Americans.

The Record
Hackensack, New Jersey, February 12, 1992

WHEN Mike Tyson was called an octopus recently, the description had nothing to do with the swiftness of his punches. This title referred to the boxer's behavior at the Miss Black America beauty pageant in Indianapolis last summer, where he apparently couldn't keep his hands off any woman within grabbing distance.

Mr. Tyson's conviction this week of raping an 18-year-old pageant contestant could end his boxing career. Let's hope it ends his career as a lecher. It should also send a strong message to any other famous man who considers the women he meets as so much fruit ripe for the picking. Mr. Tyson's accuser had worried whether people would believe her word against the word of a man as powerful and as admired as the former heavyweight champion of the world. In this case, the jury believed the woman.

That may have had something to do with Mr. Tyson's defense. The best his lawyers could do was portray him as a crude man, a predator whose accuser must have known he wanted to have sex with her. Witnesses for the defense, 11 other pageant contestants, portrayed Mr. Tyson as lewd and obsessed with sex.

His limousine driver in Indianapolis, a woman, said he grabbed her, too, tried to kiss her, and exposed himself to her — testimony which the judge did not allow the jury to hear but which completes the portrait of a man totally without self-control.

Even if Mr. Tyson had not been convicted of rape, his conduct at the Miss Black America pageant was inexcusable.

Let's hope with this verdict the message goes out that such behavior will not be tolerated, and that women who speak up against it have some chance of being believed.

> The best his lawyers could do was portray him as a predator.

THE SPOKESMAN-REVIEW
Spokane, Washington, February 13, 1992

Why do we care so much about sex scandals? Are we just a nation of prurients? With the Clarence Thomas/Anita Hill, William Kennedy Smith and Mike Tyson cases done, it's time to look at this national mania.

The conviction this week of boxer Tyson will do little to end debate on rape. The discussion is doomed to wobble on and on, never really moving in a straight line, because it revolves around two separate axes — criminal behavior and unwise behavior.

There are the violent, he-leapt-from-the-bushes rapes. And there are acquaintance rapes, instances when social convention is abruptly torn aside. But there also are instances in which a young woman acts in some way that puts her at risk, in a way that her mother or father would have advised against.

Perhaps, as Tyson's victim did, she went to a man's hotel room in the middle of the night. Even if the victim believed Tyson only wanted to make a phone call from his room, the caution that most parents try to teach their children would dictate that going to a relative stranger's hotel room at 2 a.m. is a less than prudent choice.

Does unwise behavior mean that a woman "deserved what she got" or any of the other ways society condemns some rape victims? No. A victim's behavior is never an excuse for a criminal's behavior.

But, in this imperfect world, a victim's behavior can and will put her at risk. The puzzle is that many people tend to blame a victim more for her rash behavior than they blame a rapist for his criminal behavior.

The discussion about rape enters newer territory when we talk about acquaintance rape. A generation ago, there was no such thing. When it happened, women had few resources to turn to. And no legal recourse.

Acquaintance rape is the cloudiest of issues because our society holds that friendship is bound up with a certain caring and respect. No one expects to be assaulted, or sexually assaulted, by a friend.

Enter the next complication: When does a woman's behavior negate her spoken word? Traditional thinking holds that a woman who wears too short a skirt or too tight a sweater is "asking for it." A kiss too many may convince a man that she is "begging for it."

But no Oxford Dictionary explains exactly what a woman's apparel means, and no universal lexicon spells out how to translate body language.

So, the age-old advice still holds for women: Act prudently around men you don't know well. Be clear in your message. When you say no, be sure you mean it.

And for men, some new advice: Don't try to interpret a woman's behavior. Rely on simple English, instead.

Otherwise, the consequences can range from criminal liability to the shattering of a woman's trust to unwanted pregnancy and the spread of AIDS and other disease. The stakes are too high.

Rape won't ever disappear. But a clearer examination of the confusing elements can help educate us all. And that may be the benefit to us all from the recent string of highly publicized sex cases.

San Francisco Chronicle
San Francisco, California, February 13, 1992

THE JURY'S GUILTY verdict in Mike Tyson's trial sends a significant message bearing on all instances of acquaintance rape: A woman has a right to say "no" and she has a right to be believed.

In the Indianapolis rape trial of the former heavyweight boxing champion, the 12 jurors believed the story of an 18-year-old beauty contestant that Tyson overpowered and forced her to have sex despite her pleas to desist.

No matter that she willingly accompanied the rich and famous celebrity to his hotel room at 2 a.m. and perched on his bed. She said "no" to sexual intercourse. She meant it, and the jury agreed.

NOR WILL the conviction of Mike Tyson for rape and two counts of criminal deviate conduct cast an unforgettable shadow over professional boxing and all the other young athletes who have fought their way out of the ghetto and into the prize ring. Other criminals have come and gone in this sport. Boxing has survived.

The Washington Post
Washington, D.C., February 13, 1992

ONE VIEW being heard in the post-mortem examination of Mike Tyson's rape conviction makes it sound as if the Indianapolis jury was sitting in judgment on rich and famous African-American males or the sexual lifestyle of professional athletes. Mike Tyson's trial had nothing to do with race, or his humble origins or the declining fortunes of a boxing hero. The eight-man, four-woman jury was charged with sifting through several days of testimony presented by 49 witnesses and deciding whether Mr. Tyson in fact raped a teenage beauty contestant as charged by the state. They decided he did. So on March 6, it is Mike Tyson, and Mike Tyson alone, who returns to court for sentencing.

Set aside his celebrity status, and Mike Tyson is one more man convicted of committing a sickeningly commonplace offense. Every six minutes, says the Department of Justice, a woman is raped in America. The fighter's defense—that the victim was somehow culpable, that she consented but then changed her mind after the act—is also common in cases where the accused and the victim are acquainted. What makes this trial loom large, however, is not her status as a Miss Black America contestant or the heavyweight crown he once wore. It is the Mike Tyson who was presented to the jury. If in the public's mind, Mike Tyson is a sexual predator who lacks fundamental respect for women or himself, it is precisely because of the way he has behaved and nothing else.

The somewhat sympathetic portrait now being painted of Mike Tyson as "an undereducated, financially unsophisticated gladiator who frittered away much of his earnings on high living, legal entanglements and fees to managers and promoters" (as carried in one story yesterday) may be accurate. But it doesn't go far enough. There is no warrant in law or custom that gave Mike Tyson the prerogative of forcing himself upon a woman without her consent. He chose to ignore a woman's right to call a stop to his assault.

Infidelity Charge Rocks Clinton Presidential Campaign

The presidential campaign of Gov. Bill Clinton (D, Ark.) came under fire Jan. 17–30 as the media reported allegations that the candidate had had an extramarital affair. One newspaper produced tape recordings of telephone conversations purported to be between Clinton and his mistress.

The controversy recalled a similar one that had doomed the 1988 presidential candidacy of former Sen. Gary Hart.

Rumors of adultery had plagued Clinton during his 1990 campaign for governor, and were described by the *Washington Post* as "long-simmering." Clinton had refused to address the rumors on privacy grounds.

At the start of his presidential campaign in the fall of 1991, Clinton and his wife had admitted to the press that they had previously had "difficulties" in their marriage, but said the problems had been resolved.

The new allegations first began to receive prominent attention in the news media Jan. 17, after a weekly supermarket tabloid, the *Star*, alleged that Clinton had had five affairs. The report was based on a 1990 lawsuit by Larry Nichols, a former employee of the Arkansas state government who had been fired for making phone calls at the expense of the state on behalf of the Nicaraguan contra rebels. (Nichols dropped his lawsuit Jan. 26, saying the issue had gotten out of hand.)

The *Star* story was picked up Jan. 17 by the *New York Post*, the New York *Daily News*, the *Boston Herald* and the Fox television network. The following day, the story was carried in most major media outlets, which gave prominent coverage to subsequent developments.

Clinton Jan. 17 ridiculed the sensationalistic nature of the tabloid, saying, "The *Star* says Martians walk on the Earth and people have cow's heads." He called its report "totally bogus."

The issue instantly began to dominate coverage of the presidential campaign Jan. 23 after a follow-up story by the *Star* alleged that Clinton had had a 12-year affair with Gennifer Flowers, a former nightclub singer. The tabloid also announced that it had acquired tape recordings of phone conversations between Clinton and Flowers between December 1990 and mid-January.

Clinton Jan. 23 said, "The story is just not true." He added, "I did call her back every time she called me. She said she was frightened...she felt that her life was being ruined by people harassing her" about rumors of the alleged affair. Clinton said Flowers had previously told him that she was being offered as much as $50,000 to say the two had had an affair.

The *Star* acknowledged that it had paid Flowers for her story, but it would not make public the sum.

Flowers had been hired as a $16,000-a-year administrative assistant by the Arkansas state government in June 1991 after a referral by a member of Clinton's staff. She was fired Jan. 29 for unexcused absences.

The issue Jan. 23 began to dominate Clinton's campaign, as he was questioned about it at every stop. In response, Clinton and his wife, Hillary Rodham Clinton, Jan. 26 appeared in an interview on the CBS television show "60 Minutes."

Clinton, considered the front-runner among the Democratic candidates, denied having had an affair with Flowers. But he said, "You know, I have acknowledged wrongdoing. I have acknowledged causing pain in my marriage. I think most Americans who are watching this tonight, they'll know what we're saying, they'll get it, and they'll feel that we have been more than candid." Clinton accused the press of engaging in a "game of gotcha."

Clinton argued that, in effect, the press was penalizing him for being married, since he would have been subject to little scrutiny had he simply gotten a divorce rather than working out his problems with his wife.

Cuomo rejected Clinton's apology and suggested that Clinton had insulted all minorities.

THE KANSAS CITY STAR
Kansas City, Missouri, January 28, 1992

So far as is known, Adolf Hitler was absolutely faithful to Eva Braun. He also loved his dog, "Blondi." But Hitler did have his faults. No doubt all candidates for president or any other office have theirs. Bill Clinton is imperfect as is everyone else on Earth. Not much room for stone-casters down here.

Marital infidelity is not a negligible failing but it is a human one. The greater question is whether it ought to be an absolute criterion of fitness for public office, and whether the pursuit of gossip and scandal should crowd out rational debate of vital issues.

What measure should candidates be held to? Shall each face a direct inquisition on the Ten Commandments as a requisite of office, and shall each then be investigated to the fullest concerning adultery, stealing, swearing, keeping the sabbath, killing (in war or peace; the scripture does not specify), covetousness, and so on?

What is really important in the selection of a president? The way men and women treat each other obviously is an index of character. But it is not only a matter of sexual fidelity. In how many marriages does one mate publicly humiliate and otherwise inflict mental pain upon the other without a hint of philandering? How does a candidate treat his or her children? Parents? Subordinates?

Other candidates have a responsibility in this area and so do the media. If Clinton's competitors will stand up and denounce, without hypocrisy and embellishment, this sort of prying, that might do wonders.

Bill Clinton acknowledges wrongdoing and having caused pain in his marriage. His wife, Hillary Clinton, says: "You know I'm not sitting here, some little woman standing by my man, like Tammy Wynette. I'm sitting here because I love him and I respect him and I honor what he's been through and what we've been through together. And you know, if that's not enough for people, then heck, don't vote for him."

Prurient curiosity also is a human failing. But does the public need to be distracted from debate over foreign policy, health care, competitiveness and other great questions of the day by this sort of slander?

The regular media must decide whether grimy supermarket tabloids and cheap voyeuristic television will set the standards of what is news. It is possible to take note of a charge without excessive play. It is even possible to ignore the trashiest products of checkbook journalism. To the statement, "It's a dirty job, but somebody's got to do it," there is A.M. Rosenthal's rejoinder: "Not me."

Only two people really know what goes on in a marriage. The Clintons have outlined the proper boundaries between privacy and vicious gossip. Let's leave it at that and lift American elections out of the mud.

The Houston Post
Houston, Texas, January 28, 1992

ARKANSAS GOV. Bill Clinton and his wife, Hillary, may not have helped their political quest any by going on television Sunday to defend their marriage. But in refusing to answer directly the question of infidelity and in effect telling anyone who doesn't like that response to go jump in the lake, they probably did a lot for their own self-respect.

Given the inordinate attention lavished on the claims of Gennifer Flowers (who was paid for her interview) that she'd had an affair with the governor, the Clintons had little choice but to seek to put the matter behind them.

Clinton denied Flowers' claim, but said he would go no further. As a result, we may never know whether he has been absolutely faithful. Voyeurs among us may find that troubling, but it is not nearly as troubling as the idea that a politician must defend his marriage as a true, loving relationship and not just an "arrangement" of political convenience.

Clinton has acknowledged that theirs has not been an ideal marriage, but to conclude that their relationship is anything but loving is absurd. Millions of couples have stormy marriages but continue to love and respect each other. Can't we believe that the Clintons fall in that category?

Hillary Clinton had a right to be insulted by the insinuation. "I'm not sitting here like some little woman, standing by my man like Tammy Wynette," she said. "I'm sitting here because I love him, and I respect him and I honor what he's been through and what we've been through together. And if that's not enough for people, then heck — don't vote for him."

Our sentiments exactly. The public has a right to know about Clinton's public life, about his views on the issues and his commitment to making this a better world. But we don't have a right to know every little detail about his private life. It's time to get out of the mud and get on with the business of choosing a president.

Herald News
Fall River, Massachusetts, January 29, 1992

There's been enough blame bandied about in the Clinton-Flowers controversy to last longer than accuser Gennifer Flowers claims her affair with the presidential candidate did.

The ubiquitous "press" that picked up on the supermarket tabloid's reports of the alleged affair has been one of the chief culprits, probably deservedly so. Amazingly, the Star, which paid Flowers for the story of her alleged 12-year affair with Clinton, has gotten little flak — perhaps because considering that the same edition also claims that Stevie Wonder had a long-time secret lover and Ted Danson's first wife has at last been located — the dubious credibility of such rags is already known among those who purchase them.

Clinton has been blamed for not admitting to the affair, which discounts the possibilty that it never occurred or, if it did, that he may have learned and thus benefitted by it. And Flowers, again with appreciable justification, has been blamed for being a money-grubbing opportunist bent on grapping her 3 minutes of fame at Clinton's considerable expense.

One group that has escaped the whole silly mess virtually unscathed blame-wise, however, is the public. The viewers tuning in to sensational TV programs, the readers rushing to their doorsteps to ingest the latest tidbits, the co-workers debating every lurid detail. They are eating it up.

You could argue that readers and viewers don't decide what makes news and, therefore, shouldn't be held accountable for it. But it's equally true that news organizations know what sells and they serve it up to a willing audience. Then the important question becomes not *whose* fault it is that the Clinton-Flowers entree is on the menu but *why* everyone's ordering it.

In an increasingly complicated world, sex is something people understand. The soaring federal deficit, the ailing health care system, the muddled economy, the failing public school system, the war on drugs, among other important issues, too often confuse folks so profoundly that they give up all attempts to understand.

But who doesn't understand lust? Who hasn't known someone who had an affair, had an affair themselves, thought about having an affair or pronounced that they would never ever have an affair? Infidelity is not hard to understand and it's not hard to form an opinion about it.

It stands to reason that people want to hear about things they can relate to as opposed to things that they can't. They can judge for themselves whether they think Bill Clinton stepped out on his wife much more easily than they can judge whether he knows beans about foreign policy.

That is the real tragedy of this sorry matter. While the question of adultery may speak to a candidate's character, it does not impact upon the myriad of other ingredients that make up a capable and effective leader. And in this complex era we seem less inclined to sort that all out.

The Philadelphia Inquirer
Philadelphia, Pennsylvania, January 26, 1992

By the time you read this, yet another "Smoking Bimbo Story," as our Daily News colleague Sandy Grady calls them, may have hit Bill Clinton, the guy leading the Democratic pack in New Hampshire.

Already, a night-club singer has sold a tale of trysts to the tabs. That's on top of other rumors, most shoveled into the public record by a fired state employee.

Our initial reaction is that, frankly, we don't give a damn.

We'll wait to see if Mr. Clinton gets caught in a Big Lie, or something really crazy pops out of the closet. But for now we're standing by our previous position that a candidate's private life is his (or her) private life, unless there's a clear connection to the candidate's conduct in office.

Mr. Clinton's campaign is just coming into focus, but he seems to have a lot to say about meeting global competition and about retooling big government. He has ideas about ways to give children a healthy start without letting irresponsible parents off the hook. Better yet, he doesn't seem to be reading from cue cards. He seems to be worth, in short, hearing out.

Meanwhile, from where we sit here on the sidelines, the rules of the nomination game seem to be getting ever more irrelevant to the job of governing.

Permit us to explain. If a Gary Hart, with questions about the truthfulness of his resume already dogging him, recklessly shacks up with party girls after challenging the press to tail him, that *does* relate to his judgment. If Clarence Thomas denies harassing a women in his employ in the face of solid corroborating testimony, that *does* raise credibility questions.

But this Clinton business appears different: It involves a long-studied, ostensibly stable political personality. And the infractions (if they in fact occurred) don't involve abuse of office.

Standards for making it to the White House change. Time was when no Catholic need apply. JFK changed that. Ronald "Family Values" Reagan proved divorce was not disqualifying. Today, drug-freeness is a question of current, not past, status.

Sex remains a minefield, however. We don't condone or encourage extramarital sex, but we're less interested in a candidate's personal life than we are in whether he or she can help make the schools work better, move the health debate off dead center, or spark the economy.

If he can do all that — or even a healthy part of it — we're willing to overlook a lot.

The Hutchinson News
Hutchinson, Kansas, January 30, 1992

Is Arkansas Gov. Bill Clinton back on his presidential course or still afloat in the sea of innuendo, rumor and tabloid sex?

We couldn't tell.

His interview with a "60 Minutes" correspondent elicited little new information about the governor's alleged infidelity, although by her own admission Mrs. Clinton is satisfied with her husband's answers and his continuing role as her husband.

Clinton

Every time this sort of titillating allegation arises about a candidate, campaigns stop and issues go by the wayside.

If a presidential campaign is a voyage, such eager allegations are but short excursions to lusty lagoons, where riverbank tabloids sell their naughty wares like odd pots from exotic Chinese ports. They are flimsy tales of tell-all, meant to raise questions, not to deliver definitive answers.

But what the Clintons told all Americans on Sunday night was that if the marriage was strained, it's no one's business but theirs. Presumably this means that if the governor ever was unfaithful to his wife, or vice versa, the husband and wife have worked things out to the satisfaction of both. They smiled when they said it.

Clinton's problems began when the Star, a tabloid newspaper, wrote that the governor had a 12-year affair with Arkansas singer, Gennifer Flowers. The woman sold her story exclusively to the Star, although Ms. Flowers has denied the rumors in the past, which raises the question of whether Ms. Flowers was simply out for an easy buck at the expense of a politician.

Tabloids pay awfully well, so well in fact, it's a wonder half the population hasn't made the same allegations. The problem is that the traditional press is pursuing these tales. What next? Will the Washington Post be sending its correspondent to interview Bigfoot and Elvis, or will it settle for the woman alien who ate a whole town in Wisconisn to stay alive?

Despite any amount of tabloid innuendo, Clinton has few weapons to counter these malicious claims. But he does possess one valuable asset — a smiling Mrs. Clinton by his side. How much more proof do Americans require?

Post-Tribune
Gary, Indiana, January 31, 1992

The public's fascination with who's sleeping with whom is indisputable and, to some extent, understandable.

This prurient interest has been exploited to sell everything from soap to diapers on daytime television. Now, it's being exploited to pick — or at least eliminate — contenders for national political office.

Arkansas Gov. Bill Clinton, arguably the frontrunner for the Democratic Party's presidential nomination, spent the past week refuting charges of marital infidelity that were made public in a supermarket tabloid that lacks journalistic credibility and later self-righteously trumpeted in more respected media.

Our opinion

The repercussions of innuendo-laden, peeking-in-the-bedroom type of journalism go beyond Democratic presidential candidate Bill Clinton.

The attention garnered by Clinton's alleged extra-marital liaisons with a cabaret singer has done little more than detract attention from Clinton's stands on crime, foreign policy and how he would pull the country out of its current economic abyss. Focusing on Clinton's sex life undoubtedly sells more newspapers and soap, but it does nothing to elevate the public discourse on the real issues.

It has been argued that a candidate's character, exemplified by his or her personal behavior, can be used as a barometer for later actions as an elected official. That is true to the extent that their behavior shows a callous disregard for the consequences of their acts, such as in the case of Gary Hart. The 1988 Democratic frontrunner and former Colorado senator dared the media to scrutinize his personal life, and was photographed leaving another woman's townhouse at 3 a.m. two days later.

Hart's actions perhaps hinted at a recklessness of character that one wouldn't want within reach of the nuclear buttons. But who benefits when the charges used to tarnish a candidate and his family arise from unsubstantiated, previously discredited accounts?

Would the country have been better off without the presidencies of Franklin Roosevelt, Dwight Eisenhower, John Kennedy and Lyndon Johnson, all of whom reportedly had extra-marital affairs before and during their terms of office?

The rumors have already taken a toll on Clinton's candidacy: Polls show a double-digit lead has dissipated and left him tied with another candidate in the New Hampshire primary. But the repercussions of this innuendo-laden, peeking-in-the-bedroom type of journalism goes beyond Clinton. It is possible that thousands of men and women who could add much to the country politically will be dissuaded from entering the political arena lest they be subjected to the same type of guttersnipe reporting that threatens to fell Clinton.

Who, besides the sellers of soap and salacious gossip, wins in that case?

The Hartford Courant
Hartford, Connecticut, January 28, 1992

Gov. Bill Clinton's attempt Sunday to put rumors of marital infidelity behind him was gutsy and it may work.

The Arkansas governor and his wife, Hillary Clinton, revealed more about their private life than should be expected of any couple, and Americans may give them credit for that.

And many voters surely think that a candidate's past peccadillos rank far behind the bad economy as an issue. Mr. Clinton, the putative frontrunner for the Democratic presidential nomination — at least until the rumors began — is no Gary Hart. Mr. Hart, the early Democratic favorite four years ago, was undone after denying he was a "womanizer" and daring the news media to follow him around. He was caught in a compromising situation while running for president.

Perhaps Mrs. Clinton put it best when she said that if her husband's soul-bearing Sunday was not enough for people, "then, heck, don't vote for him."

It may not be enough for some voters. Mr. Clinton dropped more than 10 points in the polls in New Hampshire after the rumors became an issue. Although forthcoming about earlier marital problems in his television appearance Sunday, he was nevertheless coy. He admitted to "wrongdoing" and "causing pain in my marriage," but he would not say whether he was ever involved in sexual affairs outside his marriage. He didn't have to deny or confirm that, he said, because Americans will "know what we're saying. They'll get it."

But Mr. Clinton's comments about his personal life were unprecedented in their intimacy. He should have acted sooner. Stories about infidelity have dogged Mr. Clinton for years. He has said that the people of Arkansas are used to the stories. But the rest of the country was not, and it's amazing that his campaign had not given more thought than it apparently had given to coping with such rumors.

Unless credible witnesses come forward to detail a pattern of infidelity that would raise serious questions about his character, Mr. Clinton should be given credit for his painful admissions and the focus of the media and the public should swing back to the issues.

The past few days of titillating rumor have been an unproductive diversion.

THE SPOKESMAN-REVIEW
Spokane, Washington, January 28, 1992

Wasn't this supposed to be the presidential campaign that stuck to the issues? If so, do allegations that Arkansas Gov. Bill Clinton has slept around have any place in the debate?

You bet they do. Voters care about character, and how faithfully one keeps one's marriage vows certainly is a measure of character. However...

Voters also care about a slew of other issues. And while those issues may not be as, well, sexy as a candidate's alleged dalliances, they too warrant a conspicuous place in the debate.

Unfortunately, Clinton's views on education reform or health care would never earn him an appearance on CBS Television's "60 Minutes." For that kind of exposure he had to be defending himself against accusations that he'd had a 12-year affair.

An affair, incidentally, with a woman who was paid handsomely by the Star, the supermarket tabloid that published her story. And a story, incidentally, which was riddled with discrepancies.

Clinton and his wife Hillary convincingly denied the specifics outlined by accuser Gennifer Flowers, but the couple said nothing during Sunday's telecast to reassure voters for whom stories of Clinton's marital infidelity *in general* are a burning concern.

Chances are this issue will follow the Democratic presidential candidate a while longer, even though he's said he's done talking about it.

It will be both ironic and tragic if the infidelity issue is allowed to overshadow all others. Clinton, unlike most candidates at this stage of a campaign, has been remarkably detailed in many of his proposals on such public-policy questions as tax cuts, welfare reform, bureaucratic streamlining, defense cuts and student aid.

Those and other arenas provide ample opportunity for robust debate. How Clinton's and his Democratic rivals' views on them compare deserves to be considered on at least equal footing with whether Clinton's 16-year marriage has suffered its share, or more, of troubles.

News media, candidates and voters all have a responsibility to keep things in perspective during this campaign.

And if fidelity is an issue, a stronger case can be made that Clinton broke faith with his state than with his wife. Arkansas voters elected him to a third term in 1990 after he pledged he'd complete all four years of it. He shattered that promise when he entered the presidential race. Will the Star tackle that one? Will "60 Minutes"?

THE BUFFALO NEWS
Buffalo, New York, January 29, 1992

NO MATTER how Arkansas Gov. Bill Clinton's presidential bid turns out in the wake of a tabloid-induced nightmare, it raises again the question of how much voters really need to know about those who aspire to lead the country.

When it comes to candidates' marital fidelity, the answer should be clear: Not very much, unless it's shown to be relevant.

Obviously, sex that was not consented to by the other party, or sexual intimidation of a subordinate, would disqualify a candidate. But a past infidelity?

Some aspects of a person's purely private life may justifiably be one piece of the puzzle that voters put together. Few — if they knew — would want a president who made a habit of casual flings, with little regard for the impact on a spouse, children or the third parties involved. Such a history would reveal a lack of sensitivity, discretion and seriousness.

On the other hand, when solid evidence of brazenness is lacking — as it certainly is in the Clinton case, but was not when Gary Hart invited media probes — candidates should be able to draw the same curtain around their private lives that others are entitled to.

The fact that the Clintons had marital problems and worked hard to resolve them is clear. That he has not always been faithful has been clearly implied. For those who consider fidelity a litmus test, that is more than enough information. For those who wisely consider it in the context of everything else, it also is more than sufficient.

Other candidates may well refuse to answer even such limited questions as a matter of principle. Any such refusal should be taken for what it is — a refusal, not an admission. The burden then falls on those who would make it an issue to show why it is relevant.

Absent a smoking gun instead of the garbled, incomplete tape produced by supposed lover Gennifer Flowers, the challenge now would seem to be one for the nation as much as for Clinton.

As America goes through puberty, learning to deal with sex rationally now that it is more out in the open, there is evidence that a similar maturation may be occurring in our politics. An ABC News poll showed fewer than 10 percent significantly less likely to vote for Clinton because of allegations of a past, long-running affair. And 80 percent felt it should not be an issue in the campaign.

That still leaves sizable minorities for whom it is an issue. But it is encouraging that most can relegate such titillation to the low rung it merits when considered against plans for dealing with the deficit, education, the underclass and other problems facing the country.

Of course, there's still the likelihood the Star will release more tapes in dribs and drabs to string out the tale and boost circulation. That wouldn't be above the tabloid. Nor would it be above someone who would sell her story to such a publication after first having denied it herself.

At that point, voters who seem now to be giving the story the limited importance it merits will have to decide all over again. If the "evidence" is similar to that already produced, it should be a quick decision. And both voters and the media should focus on the real issues of the campaign.

The Des Moines Register
Des Moines, Iowa, January 28, 1992

Someone asked Gennifer Flowers at her Monday press conference whether Arkansas Gov. Bill Clinton had used a condom during their alleged affair. Is that the level to which political campaigns now have sunk?

The press conference may have indicated that Clinton was overly optimistic in hoping that, during a Sunday night "60 Minutes" broadcast, he had put to rest rumors about alleged marital infidelities.

With months still ahead in the campaign, candidates' staffs will undoubtedly be scouring the Earth and other candidates' closets for new skeletons to haul out and mud to sling. And the front-runners in the race are likely to bear the brunt of it.

Has that become the standard on which candidacies are made? Not on policies or platforms, voting records or demonstrated successes or failures in running governments? Marital problems are commonplace. Is it fair to expect politicians to be immune?

It's not that marital infidelities ought never to be considered in assessing a person's integrity or moral makeup. But it's virtually impossible to know all the variables of a couple's marital life, and therefore extremely dangerous to judge.

An affair could lead a person into unacceptable ethical compromises, such as persistent lies, giving in to blackmail, or using an office to obtain a job or bestow other favors on the lover. A coercive or exploitative relationship also could undermine someone's fitness for office.

But there comes a point at which peering into the candidates' bedroom windows or dissecting every evidence of sexual indiscretion begins to degrade the electoral process. The nation is getting dangerously close to that point.

Clinton and his wife acknowledged on television Sunday that their marriage has had its problems. Few marriages haven't. The governor denied having had a 12-year affair with Flowers, though he refused to issue a blanket denial about ever having had an affair. That is his prerogative. It falls, as Hillary Clinton said, within their marital "zone of privacy." There it should rest.

No judge, jury or ethics board can set the threshold for what constitutes unacceptable personal behavior by a candidate or officeholder. Voters have to do that for themselves.

The allegations against Clinton and his bid to put them to rest are likely to affect his standing at the polls. But it would be far better for voters, instead of scrutinizing the candidate's marriage, to look closer at Clinton's record — and the record of his opponents — on the crucial issues such as taxes, education, health care and the nation's economy.

Sen. Packwood Accused of Sexual Harassment

The *Washington Post* Nov. 22, 1992 reported that 10 women had made allegations of sexual harassment against Sen. Bob Packwood (R, Ore.).

The women, most of whom had been employed by or worked with Packwood, said that he had tried to fondle or kiss them or had propositioned them.

Packwood Nov. 21 released a statement in which he neither denied nor admitted to the behavior. "If any of my comments or actions have indeed been unwelcome or if I have conducted myself in any way that has caused any individual discomfort or embarrassment, for that I am sincerely sorry," he wrote. The *Post* reported that when first asked about the allegations in October, Packwood had denied the allegations.

Packwood, 57, was divorced from his former wife, Georgie.

Many leaders of women's groups expressed dismay at the allegations, since Packwood had been a strong legislative supporter of their agenda, including such causes as family leave, the equal rights amendment and abortion rights.

Packwood became the fourth senator to face charges of sexual misconduct within a year. Sen. Brock Adams (D, Wash.) had denied charges made against him, but had decided not to seek reelection. Sens. Daniel K. Inouye (D, Hawaii) and Dave Durenberger (R, Minn.) also faced allegations.

Packwood Nov. 27 issued a statement in which he pledged to request, and cooperate with, a Senate Ethics Committee investigation of his conduct. The committee Dec. 1 announced that it had begun a preliminary probe, which had also been urged by many women's groups. Packwood also said he had come to realize that he had an alcohol problem, which he said might have been behind the alleged sex-abuse. A spokeswoman for the senator said he had entered an alcohol-treatment program Nov. 29.

The Des Moines Register
Des Moines, Iowa, December 1, 1992

Oregon Senator Robert Packwood has not denied making sexual advances to female members of his Senate staff and to female lobbyists, as was alleged in a Washington Post news story last month. He has issued an apology, as if that would be enough. It isn't.

"If any of my comments or actions have indeed been unwelcome or if I have conducted myself in any way that has caused any individual discomfort or embarrassment, for that I am sincerely sorry. My intentions were never to pressure, to offend, nor to make anyone feel uncomfortable, and I truly regret if that has occurred with anyone either on or off my staff," Packwood said.

The charge is that Packwood wielded his power to gain sexual favors. If that wasn't what was taking place when he grabbed women and kissed them, then what was? And if he can't deny what happened, then he ought to resign. Instead, he has said he will seek professional advice as to whether his actions were connected to his use of alcohol, which seems like an attempt to offer up an excuse, and a flimsy one at that since one of his accusers says Packwood had not been drinking when he assaulted her.

Particularly lamentable about this latest allegation of sexual impropriety against a federal lawmaker is Packwood's previous status as a champion of women's issues. He has favored a federal Equal Rights Amendment. He has supported a woman's right to abortion. He has spoken in favor of legislation requiring employers to provide family leave time for employees. He was one of just two Republicans voting against the confirmation of Clarence Thomas to the U.S. Supreme Court last year.

In response to the Thomas fight and the harassment allegations made against Thomas by a former co-worker, Anita Hill, the Senate set up an office of employment practices to hear complaints raised by Senate employees. But still, the Senate exempts itself from federal law prohibiting sexual harassment.

Iowa Senator Charles Grassley long has argued that Congress should be held to the same laws it applies to everybody else. The allegations against Packwood, and similar ones raised against other senators in the past year, ought to be more than enough to make Grassley take yet another run at the issue.

The Hutchinson News
Hutchinson, Kansas, December 1, 1992

U.S. Sen. Bob Packwood would have you believe that it must have been the booze that led him to the path of uninvited sexual advances to employees.

He fled to an alcohol rehabilitation center over the weekend to avoid discussing the claims further, though during his recent re-election campaign in Oregon, he assured his Oregon constituents that the claims were lies.

He got away with the complaints of the ten former Packwood staff members or lobbyists during the campaign. Oregon voters bought his side of the story, and could be stuck with him unless something else is done to get rid of him.

What will be done will put the nation's attention not only on the Democratic majority in the Senate, but on Kansas' Sen. Bob Dole. Dole, as Republican majority leader for Republican Packwood and the other Republicans, will be a leader in what has to be a serious probe by the Senate Ethics Committee of the sexual-harassment allegations formally posted against Packwood.

My view is the quicker, the better," Dole said on ABC's "This Week With David Brinkley." "Let's get it behind us, maybe before the next Congress convenes."

The Senate should do just that. But the last thing that should be done is to let Packwood hide behind an empty booze bottle with a claim that the booze did it, and that because of that, he's neither accountable nor responsible.

Lying to constituents during a re-election campaign is no capital crime; indeed, it is far too common an event. A later judge will be able to pass judgment on his campaign ethics or his fundamental honesty.

But between now and the ultimate hereafter, a far more important verdict must be rendered after far more than a cursory inquiry into what a drunken senator is doing with his time.

Every American will be interested in seeing just how his senators pursue the charges posted against Packwood, and how those senators approve or set the standards of conduct that are expected in America today. In an ethics inquiry, not only the defendant, but the jurors and audience as well, are on trial.

FORT WORTH STAR-TELEGRAM
Fort Worth, Texas, December 3, 1992

In the wake of last year's nomination hearings for now-Supreme Court Justice Clarence Thomas, women's advocates said — perhaps hopefully — that the attention given Professor Anita Hill's comments about office behavior would change the landscape, that men thereafter would have to take sexual harassment seriously.

Well, Thomas got his appointment, for reasons that had everything to do with politics approaching an election year and not much to do with justice. Partly as a result of the Thomas-Hill hearings, several more women were elected to Congress this year. And now it is clear that sexual harassment *is* being taken seriously, at least in the Senate.

Sen. Bob Packwood, R-Ore., is the latest to learn this. Packwood narrowly won re-election last month, having managed to keep rumors of unwanted sexual advances from dominating the campaign. But then *The Washington Post* quoted 10 women who had worked for Packwood, or with him, about their experiences. It is not a pretty picture.

Long a vocal public supporter of women's rights, Packwood stands accused of forcing his attentions upon those women, trying to kiss or fondle them against their protests. The incidents cover a 20-year period and involved some women who worked for Packwood on Capitol Hill.

A few years ago, this probably would not have been reported. A few years ago, it took a drunken plunge into the Tidal Basin (by then-Rep. Wilbur Mills) to make congressional sexual hijinks public. More recently, in the 1980s and 1990s, nine representatives have been accused of or reprimanded by the House for sexual improprieties ranging from flagrant harassment to homosexual affairs with minors. Three senators have been accused of improper behavior.

Packwood's critics have only one avenue of attack against him, since his constituents in Oregon have honored him with a new six-year term. Several women newly elected to the Senate (plus Sen. Barbara Mikulski, D-Md.) suggested that the Senate Ethics Committee should take up the case, and a preliminary inquiry by that panel has begun.

Yet, if the charges are true, about all the committee, or the Senate, can do under present rules is rap Packwood's knuckles. Congress has exempted itself from laws protecting workers from sexual harassment.

So Sen.-elect Patty Murray, D-Wash., and new Sen. Dianne Feinstein, D-Calif., want new prohibitions. Feinstein suggests extending civil rights laws that already cover sexual harassment in other U.S. workplaces to also cover the Congress of the United States. This is important, not because of what may have happened in the past so much as because of what it would mean to future congressional workers.

It is, after all, *our* Congress, and it should generally follow what is the law of the land for the rest of us. It is certainly time for Congress to specifically apply to itself the laws about civil rights and protection against harassment, and perhaps laws about minimum wage and occupational safety and health regulations while it is at it.

The new sensitivity and openness about sexual harassment might be called the Thomas-Hill phenomenon. Perhaps new laws extending protection from sexual harassment to employees of Congress could be named for Packwood — in recognition of his support for women's rights, among other things.

The Salt Lake Tribune
Salt Lake City, Utah, December 4, 1992

Those commentators who predicted the notorious Anita Hill-Clarence Thomas episode of 1991 would profoundly affect attitudes about sexual harassment were surely correct. Consider the Bob Packwood case.

Aside from the storm Ms. Hill created when she publicly accused U.S. Supreme Court nominee Thomas of improper, on-the-job sexual advances, her willingness to withstand the furor prompted by her Senate hearing disclosures was seen as an exemplary act of courage. Sen. Packwood's startling troubles help measure that influence.

Now the subject of a formal Senate Ethics Committee investigation, the Oregon senator must answer allegations that during his 24 years in the Senate he forced unbidden amorous attention on women who were staff employees, lobbyists or, in the latest allegation, newspaper interviewers. While some of the alleged acts date back decades, the Republican senator has denied nothing, offering, instead, an umbrella apology for behavior he claims he can't recall, insinuating an inability to handle alcohol may explain any act of boorishness.

However, having checked into an alcohol evaluation clinic as an apparent attempt to verify that his flaws where women are concerned can be corrected, the senator makes an acknowledgment that can't help but diminish what's left of his political career, regardless of ethics investigation findings. Whether this means he should resign, as various women's advocacy groups demand, is something he, his party and constituents must decide.

In any event, that as many as 15 women would openly describe the embarrassment a prominent U.S. senator inflicted on them, during instances so deep in the past they might have been considered better forgotten, illustrates a new determination to assign responsibility for causing personal pain and humiliation. It ought to instruct the alert, whether public official or private person, that sexual harassment is an outrageous form of demeaning insult which will no longer be in any manner tolerated. For this instruction, Anita Hill can claim a large share of the credit.

Chicago Tribune
Chicago, Illinois, December 11, 1992

If the case against Sen. Bob Packwood were only that he routinely played the part of a boorish lout, there might not be much debate about whether he should resign from the Senate. The nation, and certainly the Capitol, has plenty of boorish louts.

But while Packwood's behavior toward women triggered all the attention to him, his behavior toward the voters of Oregon deserves as much scrutiny.

On Thursday, more than a month after he was narrowly re-elected to the Senate, Packwood confessed. It wasn't exactly clear to what he was confessing, because he wouldn't talk about the particular allegations made, so far, by 16 women who say he pressured them with unwanted sexual advances. "What I did was not just stupid or boorish," he said. "My actions were just plain wrong, and there is no other better word for it."

Ten women whose allegations were reported last month by the Washington Post, and six others who have come forward since, say Packwood kissed them, fondled them, in some cases tried to remove their clothes. In mitigation, it should be said that Packwood halted his foolish advances when the women made it clear he was succeeding in nothing more than humiliating himself and scaring them.

Packwood insisted he has learned his lesson, but he won't quit the Senate. And if this were just a case of clumsy come-ons, he might ride it out.

But there's another question. It deals with Packwood's honesty and candor. When Packwood was confronted with the allegations less than two weeks before Election Day, he stalled reporters for six days. Then he flatly denied that any of the allegations were true. He tried to discredit some of the women by providing the Post with statements purportedly about their sexual activities and private lives.

Packwood made every effort to stonewall the story until after he had secured another six-year term. He now says he was in a state of self-denial. Ridiculous. He was in a state of political vulnerability.

He won, so now Oregon has to suffer a discredited senator, a legislator whose effectiveness and truthfulness have been thoroughly compromised. Oregon has to await the outcome of a preliminary inquiry begun last week by the Senate Ethics Committee. Oregon voters bargained for none of this when they went to the poll just a month ago.

If Packwood truly wants to put all this behind him, the best road would be to resign his seat and, if he wishes, submit himself to voters in a special election to fill the vacancy. That would allow voters to judge Packwood on a complete record, including those elements he made every effort to keep from them.

DESERET NEWS
Salt Lake City, Utah, December 9, 1992

As Congress reels from allegations that Oregon Republican Sen. Robert Packwood sexually harassed many women on his staff, Washington may finally have to own up to a serious, long-term problem — the practice of Congress routinely excluding itself from regulatory laws it imposes on the rest of the public.

Over the years, lawmakers have cited the constitutional separation of executive and legislative powers in explaining why employment and workplace laws do not apply on Capitol Hill. This weak reasoning won't work any more. It is time Capitol Hill employees had the same rights and protections as everyone else.

With the emphasis on change in the recent congressional elections, and accusations that members of Congress received certain publicized perks that people outside of government don't receive, there are many newly elected members of Congress committed to change.

But there are also many veterans who shudder at such a possibility and say it would violate the Constitution's separation of powers doctrine.

This is ridiculous. On Capitol Hill, where 30,000 employees do everything from drafting legislation to stuffing envelopes to tending the Capitol's rolling lawns, politics instead of business governs the manners of the workplace.

Each congressional office tends to have its own rules and expectations. It has been said that each of the 100 Senate offices is like a small business. The sense of power that grows with such intimacy creates all sorts of opportunities for abuse — from asking employees to fetch dry cleaning to asking them for sexual favors.

There is an immense tradition of deference paid to members of Congress by their staffs, resulting in a feudal environment. It is high time this offensive system was renovated. The people who make the laws cannot be immune to the laws they make. It is just plain wrong, in both a moral and practical sense.

When all the allegations about Packwood first came to the surface, numerous congressional employees could relate to them. Many had come into federal employment in their youth and had either seen such actions or been personally victimized by them. Ironically, many even considered them a "rite of passage."

It is time to put all of that behind us. It is time for a nation founded on principles of equality to speak up for equality in every workplace, including the halls of Congress.

The Hartford Courant
Hartford, Connecticut, December 13, 1992

"I ask for the chance to win back your respect," Sen. Bob Packwood told the people of Oregon last week. There's one way he can do this: resign from the Senate.

Mr. Packwood admitted that many of the accusations of sexual harassment made against him were true and that his conduct was "just plain wrong." The admission means that the senator was re-elected last month under false pretenses. Oregonians didn't know about a side of his character that he had successfully hidden from public view for decades.

Mr. Packwood is not alone. Women in the workforce have learned through sad experience that a man can take ardently feminist positions on public issues — even take political and professional risks on behalf of women — and still be a boor in private life.

To retool one's intellectual and political positions is easy compared with the task of reviewing one's private emotional and sexual habits. The latter is far harder, far more painful.

For Mr. Packwood, the process of unraveling denial has happened, uncomfortably, in public. From outright contradiction of the charges and attempts to smear his accusers, he then progressed through alcohol-as-excuse to last week's mea culpa without specifically admitting much of anything. It seems clear he has decided to tough it out and wait for the outrage to wane.

This is an unworthy course. Mr. Packwood concedes only as much as necessary to keep himself afloat politically. Each new assessment of his responsibility for actions he originally denied makes him seem more cynical, more desperate to hang onto his narrow victory against Les Aucoin, his Democratic opponent.

Mr. Packwood's reputation is too badly compromised for him to be an effective legislator. There is one honorable way for him to repair the bond of trust, as he says he wants to. Resign — and then run again in the ensuing special election.

After looking at all the facts they were denied last fall, the voters in Oregon may still elect him. And that's the only way he'll know he has won back their respect.

THE PLAIN DEALER
Cleveland, Ohio, December 4, 1992

Sexual harassment in the workplace is not an excusable form of boys-will-be-boys bawdiness. When bosses use their position to force unwanted sexual attention on their employees, it's a vicious abuse of power that leaves the victims feeling demeaned and devalued.

The nation got a long-overdue lesson about sexual harassment last year, when Anita Hill told the Senate Judiciary Committee of her allegations that Clarence Thomas had harassed her on the job. Whether they believed Hill or Thomas, voters were educated by the televised hearings about the prevalence of such vile behavior. Now the Senate must pursue another sexual-harassment investigation — this time, involving not a nominee to the Supreme Court, but one of the Senate's own members.

Ten former Capitol Hill staff members have accused Sen. Bob Packwood of Oregon of sexually harassing them during his 24-year Senate career. If the charges against the four-term lawmaker are true — and, in his public apology for the embarrassment he caused, the newly re-elected Packwood did not deny the allegations — then he seems guilty of a serious abuse of his role as a senator. In addition, the Portland Oregonian reported earlier this week that the senator kissed one of its female reporters on the lips following an interview conducted earlier this year. "I considered it totally improper and inappropriate," the reporter said.

The Senate Ethics Committee has rightly begun a preliminary inquiry into Packwood's apparent misconduct, in advance of a full-scale investigation after the new Congress has taken office in January.

It is beside the point for Packwood to claim that his sexual-harassment pattern may have been intensified by alcohol abuse. If Packwood has a drinking problem, in addition to his apparent problem controlling his sexual impulses, then his decision to enter an alcohol-abuse clinic was a sensible first step in confronting his misconduct. But any potential drinking problem is separate from, and no excuse for, his alleged sexual abuses. It would be self-deluding if Packwood tried to use alcohol as a cover for any workplace harassment.

It is premature to call for Packwood's resignation or removal from the Senate. He deserves a fair hearing before the ethics panel, for no one deserves to be condemned just on the strength of allegations. (The Senate committee may also start a probe into a charge against Sen. Daniel Inouye of Hawaii, who has been confronted by one woman's claim that he made an improper sexual overture to her 17 years ago.) The Senate's handling of the harassment question will be a test of Congress' courage and candor. With the Senate about to accept four newly elected women, some of whom were propelled into national politics by the Hill-Thomas episode, Capitol Hill should be even more sensitive to the sexual-harassment issue.

Sexual harassment is not just a question of leering and lechery; it's a question of power, intimidation, domination and compulsion. Although the details of the Packwood and Inouye cases may seem distasteful, it is vital that the Senate pursue these allegations. Beyond the probes of the two lawmakers, the Senate inquiries — like the Hill-Thomas hearings — might help focus the public's concern on the enduring danger of sexual harassment, an intolerable abuse of power in the workplace.

□

While it's at it, the Ethics Committee should also take a look at the sweetheart deal Texas Sen. Phil Gramm received from a savings and loan operator whose companies faced collapse. In 1988 Gramm paid the S&L operator $63,000 for doing $117,000 worth of work on the senator's Maryland vacation home. Not long afterward the S&L owner asked Gramm's office for help in dealing with federal regulators.

Naturally, Gramm has denied any wrongdoing. As to why he used Texas-based laborers to work on a house based in Maryland, Gramm explained he wanted to help the Texas economy and that Maryland contractors and laborers had reputations for being unreliable.

If you find that a bit tough to swallow, join the crowd.

Sexual Politics In America   SEN. PACKWOOD ACCUSED — 45

[Cartoon: A senator at a desk says to his female assistant, "AND DON'T LET ME FORGET THAT ETHICS COMMITTEE MEETING ON BOB PACKWOOD." She replies, "OKAY, SENATOR." In the second panel, he says "THANKS, DOLL."]

ARGUS-LEADER

Sioux Falls, South Dakota, December 14, 1992

Members of Congress who wonder why the federal government is held in such low esteem by many Americans need look only as far as one of their colleagues, Sen. Bob Packwood, for a partial explanation.

Packwood, 60, defiantly proclaimed last week that he would not resign under any circumstances. He apologized at a news conference for sexually mistreating women, but he refused to discuss any allegations in detail.

Despite the apology, his overall attitude reflects big-time arrogance, insensitivity and self-indulgence.

Editorial

The Oregon Republican, who was just re-elected to his fifth term in November, is accused of improperly kissing or fondling 16 former employees and other acquaintances from the 1960s to the 1980s. The divorced senator spent several days recently at a facility that treats people with alcohol problems. He said he would continue to seek counseling, but did not know whether he has a drinking problem.

Regardless of what kind of problem he has — and obviously he has one — Packwood should resign. For the good of the nation, colleagues, including Republican Sen. Larry Pressler of South Dakota, should urge him to step down.

Although Packwood has not been found legally guilty of anything, he has virtually admitted wrongdoing, and the evidence against him is convincing.

There is nothing wrong with holding members of Congress to a higher standard of personal and professional conduct than other Americans. They are, after all, models for the nation. They set standards for others.

The pathetic spectacle of Packwood refusing to quit "under any circumstances" in order to preserve his otherwise distinguished Senate career further erodes public respect for Congress and its work. If Packwood is too self-absorbed to care about the consequences of his actions, members of Congress have a duty to force him out.

The public-interest group Common Cause has urged the Senate Ethics Committee to retain outside counsel to investigate allegations against Packwood. That would be wise, too.

But the Senate and the nation would be better off without him in Congress anymore. His alleged behavior may be forgivable, but it should not be condoned or ignored by the other members of Congress.

Sioux Falls, South Dakota, December 1, 1992

It almost goes without saying that Sen. Bob Packwood should resign.

Accusations of sexual harassment against the Oregon Republican are believable, and he virtually has admitted misconduct.

However, the Packwood affair brings attention to another problem, one that runs deeper than the guilt or innocence of one liberal senator. The case underscores a double standard that, in some ways, makes members of Congress privileged rulers who don't have to worry about laws that apply to others.

Editorial

In Packwood's case, 10 women have reported incidents of unwanted sexual advances from the late 1960s to the early 1980s. Initially, Packwood raised questions about his accusers in a story first reported in *The Washington Post*. But last week he said drinking may partially explain the charges against him.

"I realize I have problems and will seek professional advice in connection with my use of alcohol," he said in a prepared statement. "If I take the proper steps I hope my past conduct is not unforgivable."

His alleged behavior may be forgivable, but it should not be condoned with a light brushoff.

Packwood was elected to his fifth term last month. His constituents have no recourse for six years, when he will be up for re-election again, other than to hope the Senate Ethics Committee reprimands him. And the women Packwood is accused of harassing apparently have no legal recourse because of the legal privilege members of Congress enjoy.

Congress is immune from many laws it imposes on other Americans, including the Civil Rights Act of 1964. The Senate — but not the House — is covered by the Civil Rights Act of 1991, which prohibits sexual harassment in the workplace. However, the 1991 law would not apply to any of Packwood's accusers because the incidents took place before 1991.

Supporters justify Congress' unique legal exemption by arguing that a lawmaking body must be protected from political attack. That's nonsense. The unfairness of such a double standard is obvious. It increases public disrespect for Congress.

Packwood should take some of the critical pressure off his colleagues by doing the right thing: resigning and then getting help. Meanwhile, his colleagues should eliminate the double standard.

Sen. Packwood Ouster Bid Rejected

The Senate Rules Committee May 20, 1993 voted unanimously to dismiss petitions to remove from office Sen. Bob Packwood (R, Ore.) on grounds that he had acted fraudulently to win reelection in 1992. Allegations of sexual harassment against Packwood were currently under investigation by the Senate Ethics Committee.

About 250 Oregon residents had contended that Packwood had deprived them of their right to an informed vote by lying when he denied during his campaign that several female aides and lobbyists had accused him of making unwanted sexual advances toward them. But in a hearing May 10, members of the Senate panel had skeptically received the petitioners' argument that misleading voters during a campaign could constitute election fraud.

Committee members also held that the panel lacked authority to discipline lawmakers for their campaign conduct. They voiced concern that a decision in favor of the Oregon voters would lead to other challenges by voters claiming that they had been misled by candidates' statements made in the heat of election campaigns.

The Virginian-Pilot
Norfolk, Virginia, May 24, 1993

Last week the U.S. Senate Rules Committee rejected a petition by 250 Oregon voters who want Republican Sen. Bob Packwood's victory last November investigated and, they hope, invalidated.

Senator Packwood, these voters charge, won by fraud: He lied, they say, in denying allegations of sexual harassment by some two dozen women over some 20 years. The petitioners also say he intimidated women who made or might have made such allegations and thus delayed news reports of conduct that he later sort of admitted and that would have cost him the election had the voters only known. The media involved dispute that the senator caused delay. The senator disputes them all.

Rules Committee members, Democrat and Republican alike, had real problems with that petition. So do we. Until now, election fraud requiring invalidation has been defined as somehow manipulating voting procedure — stuffing ballot boxes, voting the dead, miscounting ballots — to affect an election outcome. The Constitution permits the Senate (and the House) to accept or refuse a winner; but because the Constitution establishes requirements only as to age, residency and citizenship, Congress has traditionally been loath to deny voters their choice. And should be.

So tradition is one reason the Rules Committee doesn't want to lift the lid on this Pandora's Box. Another is that there would be no end to the allegations of ills — lying, misleading, waffling — that would escape and become grounds for challenging victors. If every campaign misstatement, misjudgment, alteration or (that perennial favorite) clarification is grist for a congressional investigation, a Congress already hard put to complete the nation's business would never get it done.

There is also the very real burden of initially sorting substantive allegations from frivolous. Add, too, the difficulty of establishing a standard of proof for not only the offense but for how the outcome would have changed had the voters known — and for fitting the punishment to the crime. Senator Packwood, for example, won by 78,000 votes, a hefty lead which he has lost in post-election opinion polls — but that's hindsight, which doesn't count in elections; and public-opinion polls are no substitute for elections.

As to punishment, Mr. Packwood's opponents are as convinced that he deserves ouster as they are of his guilt. But sexual harassment has several definitions encompassing several degrees of offense. Lies, like other offenses, come big and small, white and gray. That's why each house of Congress has several levels of penalty it may impose on errant members. And that's why the Rules Committee's demurrer puts the determination of both Mr. Packwood's offense and, if any, his punishment remains now properly where it belongs: with the Senate's ethics committee.

The Washington Post
Washington, D.C., May 24, 1993

THE PETITION challenging the seating of Sen. Bob Packwood, filed in Dec. by 250 Oregonians, was a long shot. Angry that the senator had made it through Election Day before charges of alleged sexual harassment became public, and uncertain that the Ethics Committee now investigating the matter would recommend the ultimate punishment of expulsion or that there were 67 votes to carry out the penalty, the petitioners took an unusual route. They went to the Senate Rules Committee arguing that Sen. Packwood's deception in this matter was the equivalent of election fraud and that he shouldn't be seated. This theory never had many supporters, and on Thursday, the committee unanimously rejected it.

Katherine Meyer, the lead attorney for the petitioners charges that the committee refused to rule in her favor because "[t]he Senate does not think there is anything wrong with lying and cheating and stealing your way into this exclusive club." A more likely explanation is the Pandora's box theory put forward by Sen. Diane Feinstein. If the petitioners had succeeded, charges of election fraud because of lies, evasions, failures to disclose and the like could be raised by challengers at any time. One such application has already been made concerning the alleged failure of Sen. Donald Riegle to reveal information about his savings and loan activities during his 1988 campaign. It would be asking for chaos to establish a precedent that elected officials can be removed from office on a simple majority vote for reasons that are unclear and assumptions about voter reactions that cannot be proved.

The Rules Committee action doesn't clear the senator. Far from it. The Ethics Committee operates in secrecy and does not provide the public with progress reports, but presumably its investigation is proceeding apace. A prompt resolution of the case is important here, not least for the reputation of the committee itself, often guilty of long delays and reluctance to move against peers. The charges are serious. If they are true, there must be a strong response. Undue delay, or any hint that the committee intends to treat this kind of conduct as if it were a prank or an inconsequential, though embarrassing, indiscretion would be a scandal of its own.

The Evening Gazette
Worcester, Massachusetts, May 16, 1993

Sen. Bob Packwood, a Republican from Oregon, has become a major embarrassment to his colleagues.

His admitted sexual misconduct should lead to some form of punishment. However, the accusation that he stole his 1992 re-election by lying to voters is not thus far a convincing argument for denying him his seat on the basis of election fraud.

More than 20 women have come forward in recent months to accuse the senator of making unwanted and often boorish sexual advances. Packwood has apologized. Those incidents — and accusations that he subsequently tried to intimidate the victims — could be the basis for recommending the senator's censure or even expulsion.

The Constitution states: "Each House may determine the rules of its proceedings, punish its members for disorderly behavior, and, with the concurrence of two-thirds, expel a member."

While the Ethics Committee deliberates the harassment issue, the Rules Committee has the task of dealing with the election fraud charges. They stem from petitions by 250 Oregonians asking for a new election on the assertion that Packwood lied in order to delay publication of the harassment charges until after November.

The reasoning is based on a poll indicating that only 34 percent of the electorate would have voted for Packwood had they known about the accusations. He won with 52 percent of the vote.

There are numerous flaws in this reasoning. Polling voters after the fact yields shaky data at best. More important, a dangerous precedent could be established, opening the way for endless post-election challenges based on charges that a candidate promulgated misinformation or intentional disinformation.

Far better that the Rules Committee stick to investigating allegations of balloting improprieties and fraud — as has been its traditional mandate.

Sen. Packwood deserves little sympathy. But he is entitled to a fair and impartial hearing by the Ethics Committee. It already is obvious that his admitted behavior has brought shame on him and his office.

The Hutchinson News
Hutchinson, Kansas, May 24, 1993

It should come as no surprise that the U.S. Senate Rules Committee has decided to dismiss a bid to unseat a fellow senator for lying to the people.

Sen. Bob Packwood, R-Oregon, was accused of defrauding voters during his 1992 campaign by lying about his sexual conduct.

Oregon voters said the senator would have lost the campaign if the public had known of allegations that he sexually harassed female staffers and acquaintances.

In petitions, Packwood's accusers said he successfully schemed to delay news stories about unwanted sexual advances to women until after he was re-elected.

The Oregonians said Packwood lied to the media about his conduct as the election neared and, along with supporters, tried to silence the women by threatening them.

You may remember that after he was safely re-elected, Packwood apologized for his conduct toward women.

What Packwood's fellow senators harrumphed was that they were wary of setting a precedent that elections could be nullified because of misstatements made in the heat of an election battle.

Pardon us if we cover our grins with our hands.

Make misstatements — one of the polite words for lies — a punishable offense in American politics? No, a thousand times, no.

And while that may make us grin, let the word go forth from here that it's good that the effort to unseat Packwood failed.

We, the people, need to understand that politics and government are not exact sciences. They draw charlatans and even pigs.

It is our role to study campaigns carefully, to weigh carefully what is said and done, and to vote for the best man or woman for the job.

Politics is a very serious game with few official rules — especially about free speech. We must carefully keep it that way, even if it causes us to grit our teeth and suspect fraud. How would the rules of political speech be written? Who would make them?

It was embarrassing for the senators to make the ruling they did about a fellow politician, but the Senate did the right thing

The Charlotte Observer
Charlotte, North Carolina, May 24, 1993

If Bob Packwood, R-Ore., were an honorable man, he'd simply resign from the Senate. Months ago, Sen. Packwood acknowledged "unwelcome and offensive" actions against numerous women he worked with during his 24 years in Congress. He called his actions not only "stupid or boorish" but "just plain wrong."

But he has rejected urgings to step down, expecting his apology and promise of good behavior to suffice. With the Senate Rules Committee's dismissal on Thursday of a petition to nullify his election, Sen. Packwood could be tempted to believe that was enough. He would be wrong — as constituents were telling him when they signed the petition saying he committed fraud when he denied to newspapers before the election that he had made improper sexual advances to women.

The rules committee simply decided, according to Sen. Ted Stevens, R-Alaska, that the Senate Ethics Committee was the more appropriate forum to hear the matter. That committee's probe is focusing on allegations that Sen. Packwood made unwanted sexual advances against nearly two dozen women, and that he tried to silence some of them by threatening to expose details of their personal lives. The ethics panel can recommend expulsion by a two-thirds vote of the full Senate.

Much is expected of this panel. In the past, the nearly all-male Senate has had a poor record of disciplining its own, giving only minor chastisements to offenders. But four women were elected senators last year in the aftermath of the furor over the Senate's handling of sexual harassment allegations by Anita Hill against Clarence Thomas, who was confirmed as a Supreme Court justice. Mindful of the bad impression they left viewers of those televised proceedings, the Senate is likely to be very circumspect in handling the charges against Sen. Packwood.

Sen. Packwood, though, continues to minimize the situation. Of the rules committee's action Thursday, he said: "The last thing the Senate wants to do is get into the practice of conducting autopsies ... every two years if the loser claims the winner told a lie."

Despite his early avowal of finally "getting it," Sen. Packwood clearly has not. That he can so cavalierly describe his situation as a political disagreement between winners and losers tells much about the Sen. Packwood that Oregon voters did not know they were electing. The "honorable" senator could have earned that title by following a path many of his fellow politicians have shunned. After acknowledging his wrongdoing, he should have resigned. He still can.

Report Assails Navy In 'Tailhook' Scandal

Navy Acting Secretary Sean C. O'Keefe Sept. 24, 1992 announced the punishment of three admirals in the wake of a sharply worded report on the so-called Tailhook convention sexual-abuse scandal.

At least 26 women—half of them military officers—claimed to have been sexually abused by male aviators at the 1991 convention of the Tailhook Association. The report on the affair, prepared by the Defense Department inspector general, Derek J. Vander Schaaf, criticized top Navy officials for "management failures and personal failures" in their handling of the service's two separate investigations of the Tailhook scandal. One investigation had been conducted by the Naval Investigative Service, the other by the office of the Navy Inspector General. Vander Schaaf had taken over the Tailhook investigation in June, amid public suspicions of a cover-up by the Navy.

Vander Schaaf's report was introduced by O'Keefe at a Pentagon press briefing. A second part of the report, detailing developments at the 1991 convention, was to be issued in late 1992 or early 1993.

O'Keefe announced action against three senior officers prominently cited in the report: Rear Adm. Duvall M. (Mac) Williams Jr., the head of the Naval Investigative Service; Rear Adm. George W. Davis 6th, the Navy's inspector general; and Rear Adm. John E. Gordon, the Navy's judge advocate general.

(The NIS investigated criminal misconduct. The Navy inspector general was the force's watchdog official. The judge advocate general was the Navy's top legal-affairs officer.)

O'Keefe disclosed that Williams and Gordon had been asked to retire. He said that Davis would be relieved of his post and assigned to other duties.

The report contended that the Navy investigations had been flawed by an unwillingness to implicate high-ranking Navy officials in the scandal, by a "gross lack of cooperation" between the NIS and the Navy Inspector General's office, and by the sexist attitudes of some senior male officers involved in the inquiries, including Williams. (Witnesses claimed that Williams had made disparaging remarks about female Navy pilots during the course of the NIS probe.)

Williams, the report maintained, had narrowed the scope of the Naval Investigative Service inquiry in order to shield senior Navy officers from the scandal. (More than 30 admirals had attended the Tailhook convention, but no officer above the rank of lieutenant commander had been questioned by the NIS.) Williams also was said to have rushed the NIS investigation to a premature conclusion.

Williams on several occasions had expressed concern that the Tailhook investigation "could ruin the NIS relationship with the naval-aviation community," the report contended.

Davis, like Williams, had sought to protect fellow admirals from the Tailhook scandal, according to the report. The report said Davis had cautioned his investigators against a "witch hunt" for senior officers who had disregarded objectionable behavior at the convention.

Vander Schaaf chided Gordon, the judge advocate general, for laxity in overseeing the two probes. Gordon, the report stated, had "played no

only complainant in the convention scandal to have made her identity known to the public, went to the White House at the president's invitation.

Coughlin, a 30-year-old helicopter pilot, said that she had been assaulted by 20 to 30 fellow aviators. She described the experience as "the most frightened I've ever been."

Bush's discussion with Coughlin came shortly after the president was briefed on the convention scandal by Defense Secretary Richard B. Cheney.

After briefing the president, Cheney was reported to have telephoned Garrett and told him that Bush—a World War II Navy flier—was upset over the Navy's handling of the scandal. According to the *Washington Post* June 27, Cheney suggested that Garrett step down.

THE SACRAMENTO BEE
Sacramento, California, June 28, 1992

By all accounts, the Navy-sanctioned Tailhook Association convention in Las Vegas last year got way out of hand. Hundreds of retired and active-duty Marine and Navy officers gathered at the association's annual convention to celebrate the Gulf War victory. The celebration turned into a drunken brawl where women were routinely abused and assaulted.

Aircraft squadrons rented "hospitality suites" at the Hilton Hotel, where free liquor flowed, pornographic movies were shown and strippers worked the bars. In one suite liquor spouted from a dispenser shaped like the penis of a rhinoceros. Meanwhile, a gantlet of drunken officers formed along a third-floor corridor of the hotel. Women who ventured onto the floor, some of them officers themselves, were pushed and prodded through the mob. Pawed and fondled as they were passed from man to man down the hall, many had their crotches and breasts grabbed and their clothes torn off.

Reportedly, the gantlet has been a standard feature at Tailhook conventions for years. While the association is a private organization of retired and active-duty Navy and Marine aviators, the Navy spent $190,000 to fly 1,500 officers to the Las Vegas convention.

At least 70 Navy and Marine Corps officers are accused of assaulting or molesting 26 women. Navy Secretary H. Lawrence Garrett, who attended the convention, admits he was on the floor where the hospitality suites were located and where the gantlet formed, but insists he saw nothing. The Navy's first investigation report failed to mention Garrett's presence. A supplemental report issued more than a month later includes an interview with a Marine captain who says Garrett and other senior officers visited one of the hospitality suites.

So far, two internal naval investigations have failed to answer many of the resulting questions, in part because many who were there are refusing to talk. Investigators say a massive cover-up has stymied their probe. The delayed report containing damaging information about Secretary Garrett raises troubling questions about how far up the chain of command the cover-up goes. The Pentagon has initiated an investigation independent of the Navy.

In recent years, amid well publicized charges of sexual harassment at the Naval Academy and elsewhere, the Navy has launched various high-profile initiatives to combat sexism in that branch of the service. The Las Vegas convention suggests that so far the efforts have failed.

The Phoenix Gazette
Phoenix, Arizona, June 27, 1992

There were no admitted homosexuals implicated in the Navy's Tailhook scandal last September, when 26 women were sexually assaulted during a convention of naval pilots.

Homosexuals are not allowed in the military. Oh, they're in all branches of the armed services all right — but not openly. When they are found out, they are dismissed as a security risk.

One security risk, under this logic, is decorated Vietnam veteran and National Guard Col. Margarethe Cammermeyer, a lesbian who has been bounced even though her superiors want to keep her. Col. Cammermeyer hasn't embarrassed the National Guard, far from it.

By contrast, the 70 male officers implicated in the Tailhook investigation have embarrassed the Navy. The (apparently heterosexual) officers, many drunk and out of control, forced female Navy personnel and civilians to walk down a hotel hallway through a gantlet of mauling officers. They assaulted the women, pawing them and tearing their undergarments.

The crude ritual is a "highlight" of the annual symposium for the Tailhook Association, a private group of naval aviators. The Navy is reeling from the scandal, which might end the careers of several admirals ... But it is gays the Pentagon is worried about.

Tailhook was not an isolated incident, not in this man's Navy. Recently a female midshipman at the Naval Academy was chained to a urinal and taunted. In another case, five pilots were accused of raping a woman at a party in Virginia. Yet the security risk, under the Pentagon's logic, lies with gays. The appropriate disciplinary measures must be aimed at homosexuals.

Does this reasoning not fly in the face of the use of female Soviet spies to entrap U.S. Marine Guards in Moscow and penetrate the U.S. embassy there? A security risk is a security risk. Bad conduct is bad conduct. Sexual orientation has nothing to do with it.

Homosexuals in fear of being discovered are no more — or less — disposed toward treason than heterosexuals engaged in illicit love affairs. Indeed, the military ban creates the pressure, not the sexual orientation itself.

What the military is doing to gays is foolish, costly and unfair. We repeat. End the Pentagon ban on gays. Homosexuals weren't on the gantlet at Tailhook.

The Des Moines Register
Des Moines, Iowa, June 30, 1992

There's something ironic about the timing of a rekindled debate about the dangers facing women in combat, triggered by Maj. Rhonda Cornum's accounts of her sexual abuse as a prisoner of war in Iraq last year.

The debate comes amid a continuing scandal involving the sickening sexual assaults on 14 female Navy officers, and a dozen other women, by members of the U.S. Navy and Marines at an aviators' convention last year. It raises the unnerving prospect that the threat of sexual assault to women in uniform comes not just from the enemy, but from men supposedly on their own side.

The events at last September's Tailhook convention in Las Vegas and its aftermath, which led to last Friday's resignation of Navy Secretary H. Lawrence Garrett III, demonstrate the low status of women in the armed forces.

Investigations showed that on each of three nights of the convention, female guests were assaulted by drunken officers in street clothes as the women stepped off a hotel elevator.

The officers, behaving like savage animals, are said to have formed gantlets, shoving women down the line and grabbing at their breasts and genitals and tearing off their clothes as they passed.

Nearly as reprehensible as the conduct itself was the failure of investigators to pursue the matter in a timely and complete fashion. It was a full month before an investigation was launched by the Naval Investigative Service. Later, the Naval Inspector General's office investigated the failure of superior officers at the convention to prevent or halt the assaults.

Many officers refused to cooperate with investigators, and there is still no complete list of the 70 suspects. More recently it was disclosed that the Investigative Service omitted 55 pages from the report it released, including evidence that Garrett himself had stopped by a hotel suite where parties were held in which strippers performed, pornographic movies were shown, and free liquor was served.

The entire episode, from the assaults themselves to the bungled investigations that followed, makes Major Cornum's accounts of being sexually abused by an Iraqi guard almost pale by comparison. Yet the threat of sexual assaults on women has been a major argument advanced to keep women out of combat.

Even as this sort of sexual misconduct is carried out and even tolerated at some levels, the military continues its irrational ban on homosexuals. The ban is based on the unproven fear that gays in the service would prey on heterosexuals. Yet as the Tailhook scandal illustrates, the armed forces have done too little to convey to the ranks an equivalent intolerance for male officers preying sexually on females.

St. Petersburg Times
St. Petersburg, Florida, June 26, 1992

By Navy standards, perhaps, the wheels are turning to bring to justice the officers involved in a grotesque sexual abuse case.

The Navy sought multiple in-house inquiries and reviews of the 1991 Tailhook Association Convention in Las Vegas. It demoted the rear admiral who did not respond seriously to initial complaints by one of the victims. Earlier this month, in attempting to put an end to what it called the "rumor and innuendo of coverup," the Navy even called for a Pentagon investigation.

To the Navy lieutenant whose boss ignored her complaint, however, the wait for some peace of mind to come from the horrible nightmare became understandably intolerable. No longer able to abide by the preference of Navy officials that she keep quiet about her ordeal, Navy Lt. Paula Coughlin spoke to the media.

Her personal account makes the facts even more sickening than reports filtered through naval investigations. Lt. Coughlin relived her terror to a *Washington Post* reporter, telling of the now infamous gantlet of men who forced at least 26 women, more than half of them officers, down a hotel hallway where the women's breasts and buttocks were groped and their clothes ripped.

She recounted how she bit the forearm of one of her attackers, tried to escape and made a plea for help to one man whose response was to shove his hand into her bra. "It was the most frightened I've ever been in my life," she said.

Lt. Coughlin's public disclosure refocuses attention on several particularly troubling aspects of Tailhook. Why was the Navy's initial reaction one of boys will be boys; that's what Navy women should expect? Why is it taking so long to punish the guilty? Why did the Las Vegas Hilton not act to control harmful activities going on under its roof? Why did the city of Las Vegas shirk its duty to investigate the complaints of two victims who just happened to be staying at the same hotel?

To their credit, officials have admitted blame and have taken various steps to show they are committed to preventing the Tailhook shame from recurring. To help dislodge the Navy's entrenched sexist attitude, though, charges against the 70 some men should be resolved swiftly and punishment administered to the deserving. More difficult but even more critical will be ensuring that mandatory training to recognize and prevent sexual harassment is carried from the seminar room to the daily living quarters on base and ship.

Lt. Coughlin says she hopes sharing her experience will help spur a change in the Navy's attitude toward women. In an environment that has for so long sanctioned subtle and blatant discriminatory treatment, that's a tall order.

THE SUN
Baltimore, Maryland, June 30, 1992

Navy attempts to cover its Tailhook are unraveling, much to the embarrassment of big brass who were only too willing to look the other way when they first heard that 26 women, including 14 Navy officers, were manhandled (we use the term advisedly) at a raucous naval aviators convention in Las Vegas last September.

Navy Secretary H. Lawrence Garrett III has resigned, as well he should, both because he was personally nearby, if unawares, when the brawl took place and because he was responsible for an investigation that now looks suspiciously like a cover-up. The Tailhook Association, an organization of retired and active duty Navy pilots, is so named after the mechanism that brings incoming planes to a halt on carrier decks.

What now needs to be halted is a macho culture that considers sexual harassment something that happens to females who ask for it or have no business in the armed forces anyway. Adm. Frank B. Kelso, chief of naval operations, has asserted the Navy has "zero tolerance" for such behavior and warned that those found culpable in the Las Vegas affair will be discharged. He has ordered indoctrination training, under the title "Not in This Navy," throughout the service.

All this smacks of belated damage control — of an official crackdown only because Congress is outraged and one woman shoved through the gantlet of drunken grabbers and squeezers has come forward by name to lay her complaints personally before President Bush, a World War II Navy flier.

Just as the Naval Academy was jolted when a female midshipman was chained to a urinal last year, so the entire Navy deserves to be shocked into a reexamination of its basic attitudes and traditions by the Tailhook outrage. The assaults were civil crimes as well as violations of Navy regulations punishable not only by discharge but by sentences to hard labor. In the end, it should be the brig or Nevada's jails.

The Navy's all-male tradition dies hard, not least among men who resent the exclusion of women from tough combat-ship duty — an exclusion many Navy women have long been fighting.

Last year, under prodding by Rep. Beverly B. Byron, D-Md., Congress removed legal restrictions on women in aerial combat. But Defense Secretary Dick Cheney bucked the emotional issue to a presidential commission due to report Nov. 15 — after the election. In retrospect, this proved to be an unfortunate signal, one from which the brawlers at Tailhook drew all the wrong inferences.

Sexual harassment? Not in this Navy? Oh no?

AKRON BEACON JOURNAL
Akron, Ohio, June 16, 1992

The Navy should continue its investigation of the now-infamous Tailhook Association party last year in Las Vegas, at which about 70 officers either assaulted at least 26 women, including 14 naval officers, or tried to cover up the incidents later, according to the New York Times.

Accounts of the gross sexual harassment in the hotel corridors have made this episode into a major scandal for the Navy, which paid more than $190,000 to fly 1,500 officers to the convention by the private group of retired and active naval aviators. Strong disciplinary action should be taken against those officers involved and those who later winked at the crude and rowdy behavior.

Akron, Ohio, June 30, 1992

The U.S. Navy is creating for itself a crisis of confidence, and it goes beyond the sexual-harassment scandal that has cost Navy Secretary Lawrence Garrett his job. The question is whether the Navy can do a credible job of investigating itself. The Navy has not acquitted itself well in the Tailhook affair in which 26 female naval personnel say they were assaulted at a 1991 convention.

In other high-profile cases in recent memory, the Navy has conducted investigations that raised more questions than they have answered. The result may be public skepticism over the Navy's ability to address internal shortcomings.

Perhaps the most prominent case in point was the Clayton Hartwig incident in which a Navy investigation implied that the 1989 explosion on the battleship USS Iowa was prompted by a Cleveland-area sailor distraught over a failed love affair. However, Hartwig, killed with 46 others, was cleared of blame, and the Navy apologized to his family in October 1991.

In another equally sensational case in 1987, Marine guards Clayton Lonetree and Arnold Bracy were accused of conspiring to allow Soviet agents access to sensitive areas of the U.S. Embassy in Moscow. The espionage case against the guards largely fizzled when Bracy recanted his "confessions," claiming he was pressured into making false statements.

The Tailhook affair makes another example in which the Navy's investigative efforts have been less than credible. When Garrett resigned Friday, he took responsibility for "the leadership failure which allowed the egregious conduct to occur." That's as it should be.

Two investigations by two Navy agencies produced a piecemeal account that tended to minimize the extent of the assault. Damaging details trickled out, giving some credence to charges of a conspiracy of silence and a cavalier attitude toward sexual-harassment issues.

The Navy, to be sure, has made sexual-harassment training a priority, but that comes after the Tailhook affair. The investigation is now in the hands of the Pentagon, and Congress is holding up promotions for several thousand officers and commanders pending a full report.

When this scandal is over, the Navy still has to prove it can do a better job of self-policing.

The Wichita Eagle-Beacon
Wichita, Kansas, June 30, 1992

When a group of Navy and Marine Corps aviators decided to play a macho game at the Tailhook convention in Las Vegas, they unwittingly brought about the end of an era. Many of them were no doubt drunk when they set up a gauntlet in a hotel hallway where women were abused and harassed. What in the past may have been acceptable good-old-boy fun turned into national disgust at the unacceptable treatment of women.

The arrogance of male pilots who believed it was not only OK but a lot of fun to humiliate two dozen or so women was the kind of male chauvinism that once was the stuff of military legend. Big strong men doing what big strong men do. It was never the right stuff, but it was done without much question from society as a whole. And certainly Navy brass never made a big deal out of such guy high jinks.

Now some men involved in that night of terror may be denied promotions or drummed out of the service. The reverberations of what was decidedly not good clean fun has brought down the secretary of the Navy and caught the attention of the commander in chief, President Bush, who met last weekend with the female Navy officer who complained of sexual abuse.

As a result, Adm. Frank Kelso II, the chief of naval operations, has made it clear that the Navy would not give mixed signals about behavior that demeans women — that the harassment and abuse would end.

It's about time. There is no place for sexual harassment or sexual abuse in the U.S. military. The awareness of such acts has increased many-fold since Anita Hill testified against Clarence Thomas. Her courage has emboldened female victims — like the women at Tailhook — to step forward. Authorities are not as quick to dismiss complaints as they once were.

Americans should have zero tolerance for sexual abuse. If that lesson is learned in a traditionally male institution like the Navy, there's hope for all society as well.

Sexual Politics In America   TAILHOOK SCANDAL REVELAED — 51

The San Diego Union
San Diego, California, June 19, 1992

On the sea, it is a time-honored code: Accountability goes hand-in-hand with authority. The captain answers for all that happens on his watch.

So it must be asked: Has Navy Secretary H. Lawrence Garrett been shielded from the sex scandal that has rocked the Navy for months? Why has he remained largely unaccountable for the raunchy events at the Tailhook Association's convention in Las Vegas last September, when at least 26 women, mostly naval officers, were sexually assaulted?

Garrett and scores of high-ranking naval officers were present at the convention, which is an annual affair sponsored by the naval aviators' association named for the hook that enables jets to land on carrier flight decks.

But the Navy's official, 2,000-page report on the incident inexplicably deleted 55 pages of potentially critical information about the actions of Garrett and other top officials. Moreover, during eight months of investigation, the Navy's inspector general never once bothered to question Garrett.

Yesterday, three days after the Navy admitted that information regarding Garrett's attendance at the Tailhook meeting had been omitted from its report, the Navy secretary asked the Defense Department inspector general to conduct an independent probe of the incident.

This is a positive step toward finally carrying out an objective investigation, because the Defense Department inspector general answers only to Congress and the White House.

An independent Pentagon investigation is far preferable to a politically charged, election-year witch hunt on Capitol Hill. And that is the risk entailed in hearings proposed by the congressional women's caucus at the urging of Reps. Barbara Boxer, D-Calif., and Pat Schroeder, D-Colo. Both lawmakers serve on the House Armed Services Committee and are understandably impatient with the Navy's inadequate investigation of the Tailhook scandal.

It is deplorable that the rowdy, macho behavior which the Navy tacitly condoned for so long at Tailhook gatherings escalated to the point of criminal sexual assaults last September.

And it is just as deplorable that the Navy has been so incapable of investigating the misconduct. The foot-dragging has done nothing to restore the credibility of the Naval Investigative Service, which was tarnished by its rush to blame Gunner's Mate Clayton M. Hartwig for the 1989 explosion on the USS Iowa. The Navy later apologized for that misjudgment.

As matters now stand, as many as 70 officers are being investigated for the lewd behavior in the Las Vegas Hilton's third-floor corridors and for the stonewalling that occurred during the course of the investigation. It is only fair to apply the same level of scrutiny to Garrett.

Left to fester for too long, the Tailhook scandal has undermined the Navy's reputation and raised doubts about the fair treatment of women in the military. An independent Defense Department investigation can help restore faith in the Navy's tradition of accountability.

The Hutchinson News
Hutchinson, Kansas, June 28, 1992

Navy Secretary H. Lawrence Garrett III can be classified as a slow learner, though not a hopeless one.

It took him nine months to learn that he as in charge of the Navy and responsible for his actions and those of the crew.

It has been more than nine months since the Sept. 5-7 drunken orgy and well-publicized sex binges, harassment and otherwise contemptible convention of Naval aviators conducted under auspices of the U.S. Navy.

Yet in all those nine months, not a single culprit has been thrown in the brig. Not a single "officer and gentleman" has stepped forward to say his conduct was vulgar and illegal, after an avalanche of complaints made by 26 women, half of whom were Naval officers themselves.

Garrett attended the Las Vegas convention.

Yet he heard and saw nothing. Only last week, he admitted publicly that he had, in fact, been there.

During the long nine months, investigations have been stonewalled. Naval officers have prevented inquiries among the troops, though an inspector general reported in April that the top brass had known for years about the outrageous mistreatment of women at the aviators' raucous annual conventions.

With his resignation, Garrett appears, finally, to have recognized his own accountability. The buck does stop with him in the Navy.

Now, if only his boss, George Bush, could understand accountability.

The collapse of leadership in the Tailhook obscenity is peanuts compared with the nonexistent leadership in the White House, where the management style reflects the notion that when the ship crashes into the lighthouse, it's the lighthouse's fault.

THE PLAIN DEALER
Cleveland, Ohio, June 30, 1992

Edmund Burke, a British statesman and writer, said that without a sense of liberal obedience, a navy is nothing more than a collection of rotten timber. That belief has been confirmed by the raging controversy over the perverse, humiliating way some male Navy officers treated numerous females, including military colleagues, at a gathering last year. It shows the Navy has plenty of deadwood that pays little homage to the department's codes of honor. The resignation of Navy Secretary H. Lawrence Garrett III over this disgraceful episode may mean the Navy is ready to do something other than protect its backside.

Garrett's resignation comes as the Pentagon is to investigate charges that male Navy and Marine Corps pilots sexually manhandled at least 26 women — most of them female officers — in a Las Vegas hotel last September. The incidents occurred during a meeting of the Tailhook Association, a group of active and retired military aviators. The women said when they tried to walk on one floor of the hotel, they were confronted by a "gantlet" of drunken male officers who physically attacked the women, groping and tearing at their skin, clothes and undergarments.

Two Navy investigations have yielded a lame admission that something despicable took place. But the probes were hampered by widespread uncooperativeness by numerous Navy officers. The Navy has shown little stomach for severely disciplining the 70 men believed to have taken part.

The Navy is beginning to pay the price for its self-centered foot-dragging. The Senate Armed Services Committee has delayed promotions for thousands of officers. And yesterday, the House Appropriations Committee vented its anger at the Navy by voting to cut 10,000 administrative and management positions from the department's headquarters.

Garrett's resignation was overdue and necessary, but it's only a first step if the Navy is to cleanse this stain. Too much of the outrage and desire to address this reprehensible incident has been expressed by those outside the Navy, rather than within. The uproar over the Tailhook controversy should not cease until the Navy is forced to acknowledge, and cut away, its rotten timber.

Navy Secretary Quits Amidst Sex-Abuse Furor

Navy Secretary H. Lawrence Garrett 3rd resigned June 26, 1992 amid a controversy over the Navy's handling of accusations of sexual abuse at a rowdy 1991 aviators' convention.

Garrett, 53, had held the post since 1989. He was the only person ever to have risen from the Navy's enlisted ranks to head the service.

The convention in question—held at the Las Vegas (Nev.) Hilton hotel over a weekend in September 1991—had been sponsored by the Tailhook Association, a private organization of active-duty and retired Navy and Marine Corps fliers. According to accounts of the gathering, hospitality suites rented by the association had featured nude exotic dancers, pornographic films and unlimited alcohol.

Separate investigations by the Naval Investigative Service and the Navy's inspector general had concluded that 26 women, including 14 military officers, had been sexually abused at the convention.

The reports, made public in April, held that men at the gathering had subjected the women to sexual or derogatory comments, grabs and fondling. The inquiries stated that some women had been forced to fight off the groping hands of dozens of junior officers who had formed a "gauntlet" in a third-floor corridor.

Garrett, himself a former Navy aviator, had attended the convention. He repeatedly maintained that he had not witnessed any wrongdoing at the gathering.

As of April, only two suspected abusers had been identified by the Navy, and no formal charges had been brought. Since about 5,000 people had attended the convention, the lack of prosecutions led some members of Congress to suspect either a cover-up or bungled investigations by the Navy.

(Only one member of the service had been punished as a direct or indirect result of the allegations. Rear Adm. John W. Snyder Jr. had been relieved of a command in 1991 for ignoring a complaint from a female aide that she had been sexually abused at the convention.)

In response to the suspicions, Garrett June 2 had directed the Navy and the Marine Corps (which came under the Navy's administrative jurisdiction) to begin disciplinary proceedings against at least 70 unidentified officers who had been at the convention. The officers included six men accused of hindering the inquiries, and 57 men suspected of being present at, or of taking part in, the gauntlet or other acts of reported abuse.

The controversy had deepened June 17, when the Naval Investigative Service had released a "supplemental report" that included a statement by a Marine officer that Garrett had visited a hospitality suite during the convention where some of the offensive activities were reported to have taken place. Garrett claimed not to know why the information had been excluded from the original NIS report.

The Defense Department's inspector general took over the scandal investigation June 18 at Garrett's request.

President Bush met with one of the alleged sexual-abuse victims, Navy Lt. Paula Coughlin, June 26, prior to Garrett's resignation. Coughlin, the role in insuring that the Navy investigations were adequate in addressing all relevant issues."

The report also singled out for criticism former Navy Secretary H. Lawrence Garrett 3rd and current Navy Undersecretary J. Daniel Howard.

Vander Schaaf indicated that multiple statements from witnesses "cast doubt on the credibility" of Garrett's repeated insistence that he [Garrett] had not spent any significant time in the convention's rowdy "hospitality suites."

The Chattanooga Times
Chattanooga, Tennessee, September 26, 1992

In this political "Year of the Woman," the U.S. Navy is struggling to recover from the unmasking of its ugly institutional culture of disrespect for and hostility toward women.

The unmasking came after the Tailhook convention of naval aviators last year. The public was rightly outraged by reports of a gantlet of drunken aviators who roughly fondled unsuspecting women, including naval officers, stripping some of their clothes. Among the victims was an admiral's aide who said she feared she would be "gang-raped."

But that incident, as horrible as it was, only marked the beginning of the scandal. It continued as top naval officials pursued an "investigation" which proved to be a farce. Aviators stonewalled to protect themselves and their buddies. Admirals tried to short-circuit the probe and spare the Navy further negative publicity. Their efforts backfired.

The Pentagon inspector general was called in; he issued a scathing report this week. As a result, two admirals are on their way out. Acting Secretary of the Navy Sean O'Keefe forced the early retirement of Rear Adm. Duvall M. Williams Jr., head of the Naval Investigative Service, and Rear Adm. John E. Gordon, the Navy's top legal officer.

The inspector general, however, recommended consideration of termination of *four* top officials. Two got off. Mr. O'Keefe simply reassigned Rear Adm. George W. Davis VI, the Navy inspector general, and took no action against Undersecretary J. Daniel Howard, a civilian, who oversaw the Navy's investigations of the scandal.

Mr. O'Keefe may have gone too easy on the latter officials, but news accounts based on the IG's report make clear that Adms. Williams and Gordon fully deserved termination.

Adm. Gordon, for instance, allowed a junior officer who was a close friend of a pilot under investigation to take part in the probe. Ignoring the conflict of interest was bad enough. The admiral crossed over the line to sabotaging the investigation when he refused to remove the junior officer from the probe even after other investigators said they suspected he was intentionally misleading them.

As for Adm. Williams, he has a clear hostility to women in the Navy. For instance, he faulted one victim for having used profane language to her attackers, saying it showed she "would welcome this type of activity." He also described female naval officers as "hookers" and "topless dancers." A man who would say such things is unfit for any leadership position in the modern Navy.

The sad thing is, the modern Navy is rife with Neanderthal attitudes toward women. Acting Secretary O'Keefe has a Herculean task in trying to redeem the service's reputation.

He has announced a "zero tolerance" policy on sexual harassment and required training on the subject. And his steps this week included not only the forced retirements but a variety of changes to strengthen the independence and integrity of naval investigative services. But there is more to come.

The Pentagon IG is still working on identifying the actual assailants at Tailhook. The Navy's response to that will be seen as an indicator of the seriousness of its commitment to reform.

The Oregonian
Portland, Oregon, September 27, 1992

Now that the Tailhook convention has challenged "Top Gun" as the defining image of military fliers, the armed services should take on a new mission. They should move from providing the worst example of sexual harassment to providing the best example of how to build respect between men and women in the workplace.

A House Armed Services Committee report recommends that the military bring the same techniques that worked well in dealing with widespread racial discrimination and drug abuse to the sexual-harassment problem. The report outlines those basic principles and, in doing so, provides a blueprint for other employers who are truly committed to combating sexual harassment.

Sexual harassment can't be fought effectively if each incident is viewed as an isolated event or as the inescapable consequence of having men and women working together.

Instead, the military branches — and other employers — need to change an internal culture that allows such incidents to take place.

The three steps that worked against racial discrimination and drug abuse and would work against sexual harassment are:

• Total leadership commitment.

• Mandatory career-long training and education for every employee.

• A clear demonstration that harassers will face disciplinary action and engaging in sexual harassment is a career-ending decision.

The military is still a long way from undertaking those steps. Although Navy Adm. Frank B. Kelso II, chief of naval operations, has pledged a zero-tolerance stance on sexual harassment, other military policies still hinge on stereotypes about women. Kelso and other senior military officials feel comfortable basing their objections to integrating women into combat units on their "gut feeling" that women would be unfit rather than on any factual evidence.

And just this week an Air Force training officer was ordered to stop using a sexual-assault questionnaire that presumed women who report sexual assaults were lying and linked the likelihood of their truthfulness to how well they get along with husbands and boyfriends.

Examples in public and private employment abound where supervisors found to be harassing employees sexually are reprimanded or reassigned, but their upwardly mobile career paths are unhurt.

The military is a diverse employer; its ranks include the skilled and unskilled, the highly educated and lesser educated, old and young. Men and women serve together in a variety of workplaces — offices, motor pools, hospital operating rooms.

The Army's successful mantra for drill sergeants is: I don't see black and white, I only see olive drab. The military and other employers should adopt a similar code: I don't see male and female, I only see performance.

Rockford Register Star
Rockford, Illinois, September 28, 1992

At long last, heads are rolling in the Tailhook affair, the U.S. Navy's sexual harassment scandal. We are gratified and encouraged by the no-nonsense posture of acting Navy Secretary Sean O'Keefe in this matter.

Tailhook is the name of the annual convention of Navy aviators. At last year's gathering in Las Vegas, 26 women, some of them Navy officers themselves, allegedly were sexually assaulted by male officers in a hotel corridor. And now the Pentagon says the Navy's initial investigation of the matter was woefully inadequate.

Consequently, two admirals have effectively been cashiered and a third has been conspicuously reassigned. More dominoes are sure to fall as the investigation continues. After all, as many as 200 men are said to have witnessed or participated in the Tailhook assaults, though only two have been identified thus far as primary suspects. After months of dragging its feet, the Navy now seems bent on seeing justice done.

> The sexual harassment scandal is ending a few careers.

One of the brass hats who took the fall last week, Rear Adm. Duvall M. Williams, directed the Navy's initial probe into the Tailhook affair. A Pentagon report raises troubling questions as to why he was assigned the matter in the first place, considering his blatantly sexist attitudes.

The report quotes Williams as saying, "Men simply do not want women in the military." How this macho admiral presumes to speak for all men in the military, we can't say. Well, now he can ponder the fact that the military doesn't want *him*.

Acting Secretary O'Keefe has the right attitude. Says he: "Sexual harassment will not be tolerated. And those who don't get the message will be driven from our ranks."

The Miami Herald
Miami, Florida, September 27, 1992

MISGUIDED Navy admirals made their egregious priorities very clear: Deflect the blame for the sexual attacks at the Tailhook Convention last year, and stay the course. It was a stupid and malicious course, and it finally and rightly led to reassignment and resignation.

The Pentagon finally "got it" and made the *nation's* priorities very clear. With uncharacteristically blunt outrage, its just-released report discloses that Navy brass all but sabotaged the service's investigation into what was a bestial assault on 26 women at a convention of Navy and Marine aviators last year in Las Vegas.

The Pentagon said that investigating officers dragged their feet and possibly lied about their actions. Then, the report said, investigators — each one trying to be more "macho" than the last — arrogantly sought refuge behind the threadbare skirts of a tediously old defense: The women brought it all on themselves.

The nation didn't buy it. Finally the Navy didn't buy it either. Last week two admirals were forced to resign. A third was reassigned. That was a telling, responsible move by the Navy.

Sean O'Keefe, acting Navy secretary, has vowed to change the sexist "culture" that ensured that Tailhook, when exposed, would become a national issue. That culture still impedes women's full acceptance and military careers.

That culture must change. Women should not fear for their safety among colleagues. There will be no sea change in Navy culture until men accept women and behave toward them as peers worthy of respect. Naval officers must exhibit "zero tolerance" of rowdy sexist behavior. That way, the most egregious acts will nevermore materialize.

The new course set by acting Secretary O'Keefe is clear and right, for the Navy and for the nation.

Detroit Free Press
Detroit, Michigan, September 28, 1992

Far later than the Navy should have, it is beginning to address the systemic problems pointed up by the Tailhook sexual harassment scandal. Indications are that more change is needed in its anachronistic culture.

At week's end, acting Navy Secretary Sean O'Keefe waded again into how the Navy conducted its inquiry of the sexual assaults last year on at least 26 Navy women, including 14 officers, at the annual convention of the Tailhook Association in Las Vegas. The group, of present and past Navy pilots, is named for the device used to stop planes as they land on aircraft carriers.

The report, issued by the Defense Department's deputy inspector general, found that senior Navy officers sabotaged the investigation that did not begin until one woman pilot went public, because they wanted to avoid more negative publicity.

The Pentagon report found that the Navy's investigative services refused to cooperate with each other. Both Rear Adm. Duvall M. Williams Jr., commander of the Naval Investigative Service, and Rear Adm. George W. Davis, the Navy's inspector general, dragged their feet about interrogating their fellow admirals who were at the convention. The report said Adm. Davis shielded top officers by not holding them responsible for what had happened.

Secretary O'Keefe announced tough responses. Adm. Williams and Rear Adm. John E. Gordon, the Navy's judge advocate general, are taking early retirement. Adm. Davis is being reassigned. A civilian is being put in charge of the Navy Investigative Service. The rank, and thus power, of the inspector general are being upgraded, and a special assistant to the Navy secretary will coordinate investigations.

But changing the culture of the Navy, which too often remains sexist-and-proud-of-it, will take more.

Many businesses have changed their organizational culture so as to minimize sexual harassment. It begins with top managers recognizing sexist behavior as unacceptable, serious and damaging to individual and collective efficacy, forbidding it, and making violators pay a steep price.

Many employees need to be taught why sexual harassment is wrong and even what it is, often by training that puts the shoe on the other foot.

And so the right lessons will be taught, it is vital to evaluate, assign and promote fairly the women who were victims of the boys who would be boors. Both punishment and reward in the U.S. Navy must become fair and gender-blind.

The San Diego Union-Tribune
San Diego, California, September 25, 1992

CALL IT the Tailhook attitude. Somehow, in some of our institutions the twisted notion has taken hold that protecting those who break the law and deny others their rights is honorable. On the other hand, this philosohpy seems to say, telling the truth, insuring that laws are obeyed and rights protected, is not.

It's an inversion of values evident in police departments in which officers close ranks to protect rogue cops. It's evident in the need for special laws to protect government employees who report wrongdoing. And it was evident in Mayor Griffin's labeling of city workers who cooperated in an FBI probe as "stool pigeons."

In the Navy's Tailhook scandal, that attitude led to a conspiracy of silence that still stymies efforts to punish the guilty and absolve the innocent.

Thursday's retirement of two top Navy officials and the reassignment of a third are appropriate symbolic steps that signal how disgusting the Tailhook scandal really was.

The officers removed were Rear Adm. Duvall M. Williams, head of the Naval Investigative Service, and Rear Adm. John Gordon, the judge advocate general, the Navy's chief legal officer. They were ousted after a report from an outside Pentagon inspector showing that they either tried to halt the Navy's own investigation or did a cursory job, at best.

The sexist attitude that permeates the Navy and that allowed the whole sordid affair to unfold is a cancer. But so is the smug closing of the ranks that followed it. The top brass losing their jobs are getting the right punishment.

Investigators said senior officers tried to stymie the investigation out of a misplaced "concern for the Navy as an institution."

Williams' conduct appeared motivated as well by pure, unvarnished sexism — the same kind manifested during the Tailhook convention at which some two dozen women, some of them Navy officers, were molested by male aviators.

The report cites what probers concluded was Williams' assessment that a lot of Navy female pilots are "go-go dancers, topless dancers or hookers." The report's conclusion that someone with such an attitude should not have been in charge of such an investigation is an understatement. Someone with such an attitude should not have been in charge of anything.

The ousters of Williams and Gordon and the reassignment of the Navy inspector general follow the June resignation of Navy Secretary Lawrence Garrett. The housecleaning at the top is a warning to other senior officials.

There also must be an even more direct signal to the pilots who formed the gauntlet line to grope and fondle scared females in a hotel hallway. This affair will not be over until those officers are punished and until training programs are in place to eradicate bias throughout the Navy's ranks.

Nor will it be over until all the Navy brass take wrongdoing by their officers seriously.

THE CHRISTIAN SCIENCE MONITOR
Boston, Massachusetts, September 29, 1992

ONE of the saddest chapters in recent US naval history, the year-old Tailhook scandal, came closer to a positive conclusion last week. The Pentagon released a major report criticizing the Navy's botched investigation of the incident, which involved the sexual assault on at least 26 women at a convention of aviators. Two admirals who were cited for inept leadership will resign, and a third will be reassigned.

Although a second study is due in several months, this initial report comes as a welcome sign that the Navy, after months of denials and coverups, is acknowledging its errors and promising to change its ways. As acting Navy Secretary Sean O'Keefe told reporters, "I need to emphasize a very important message: We get it."

If that is true, the unfortunate incident and resulting housecleaning will have served an instructive purpose in helping to change a male-dominated naval culture that has for too long remained overtly hostile toward women. Women's place in the military – and in every other career field – is well-established, and along with equal opportunities must come equal respect.

The lessons of Tailhook should not be confined to those in uniform. Corporate executives, too, can use the incident as a reminder that sexual harassment in any form, on the job or off, will not be tolerated.

Not everyone is convinced that newly enlightened attitudes have spread throughout the Navy. One woman involved in the Tailhook assault charged that some military personnel are blaming the victims for bringing notoriety on the service.

Still, the report could mark the beginning of a promising new chapter in naval history. In addition to the personnel shakeup, it calls for broader civilian control in any future investigations. Now it is up to everyone – from young sailors swabbing decks to highly decorated admirals – to prove that Mr. O'Keefe is right and that the Navy does, indeed, "get it."

Portland Press Herald
Portland, Maine, September 26, 1992

"We get it," Acting Navy Secretary Sean O'Keefe assured the nation this week. The Navy, he says, finally understands its serious problems with sexism, problems that contributed to assaults on 26 women, including 14 Navy officers, at a naval aviators' convention last year.

How could it not? A new Pentagon report traces the sclerotic sexism among Navy brass who did much to scuttle their own investigation into the notorious 1991 Tailhook Association convention.

The significance of the report, and O'Keefe's promising reaction to it, goes far beyond a single ham-handed inquiry or the forced retirement of an admiral or two. It suggests strongly that Navy women, no matter how competent, are sexually discounted by superior officers with power to make or break their careers.

Look at the attitudes attributed to Rear Adm. Duvall (Mac) Williams Jr., commander of the Naval Investigative Service charged with pursuing the Tailhook assaults. Williams, the Pentagon report indicates, apparently thinks that women who use the "F-word" welcome sexual groping, manhandling and assault. Female pilots, in his lexicon, become "go-go dancers, topless dancers or hookers."

Williams is one of those being forced out. That's reassuring. More important, however, he is also a product of the Navy command structure itself. The 49-year-old Williams has been a Navy man for 24 years.

To be effective, the effort to eliminate sexism must address that structure, too. It has allowed, if not encouraged, the disdain that sent male pilots jumping to their feet hissing and jeering a woman pilot who asked about flying combat missions last year.

Where did that happen? At the Tailhook Association convention, hours before a mob of drunken male pilots ganged up in a hotel corridor to ambush unsuspecting female pilots and other women.

Initially, the Navy treated the Tailhook assaults as a prank gone wrong, a bit of hanky-panky by junior officers who couldn't hold their liquor. It wasn't. The crime was assault.

A Navy committed to equality can only be led by officers who understand the difference.

THE SPOKESMAN-REVIEW
Spokane, Washington, September 28, 1992

The adage that every generation of parents has imparted to its youngsters — honesty is the best policy — seems to be lost, time and again, on our public institutions.

The U.S. Navy's fumbling attempt to cover up the now-infamous Tailhook scandal is a prime example.

A year ago, the Tailhook Association's annual meeting in Las Vegas had not yet attracted public attention. It was known essentially only to the participants — the retired and active Navy fliers who assembled their traditional gantlet of sexual harrassment in a hotel corridor and the 26 Navy women who later complained of being rudely and vilely accosted as they attempted to pass by it.

Ultimately, the shameful incident exposed not only the archaic sexism that permeated the Tailhook convention but also the Navy's institutional inability to confront embarrassing problems candidly and constructively.

Rear Adm. John W. Snyder Jr. could have been a hero when his aide, Lt. Paula Coughlin, reported to him the lurid mauling to which she'd been subjected. He could have treated her concerns with the seriousness they deserved and insisted that the Navy take steps to protect its honor. Instead, he ignored Coughlin's complaint and ultimately was relieved of his command because he did so.

After the scandal burst into the open last spring, then Navy Secretary H. Lawrence Garrett 3rd resigned. Last week, in the wake of a withering Pentagon report on the Navy's failure to investigate the incident properly, Rear Adms. Duvall Williams Jr., commander of the Naval Investigative Service, and John E. Gordon, the Navy's judge advocate general, announced they would take early retirement. In addition, Rear Adm. George W. Davis, the naval inspector general, was relieved of his duties and reassigned.

Now, even though Navy and Pentagon brass are falling all over themselves to denounce the Tailhook conduct, none of the actual perpetrators has yet been accused. Any action along those lines apparently will have to wait on still another report, this one from the inspector general.

The Navy's embarrassment is deepened by the Pentagon report's mention of a pattern of similar behavior at earlier Tailhook conventions, known to some Navy brass at least as early as 1985.

High-ranking naval officers had recognized and resented the discredit the Tailhook Association's antics brought upon the Navy, yet were not moved to do anything serious about it until public attention forced them into action.

In discussing the Pentagon report, acting Navy Secretary Sean O'Keefe properly focused attention on "the larger . . . cultural problem which has allowed demeaning behavior and attitudes towards women to exist within the Navy."

To correct that underlying problem will require not only a firm resolve to see justice done in this case but also a Pentagon-led determination to bring archaic attitudes into line with 21st century thinking.

THE KANSAS CITY STAR
Kansas City, Missouri, September 26, 1992

The Navy is coming to grips with the Tailhook Association affair and the wider issue of how it views women. Two admirals will be retired early and another reassigned. A Pentagon report also criticized the undersecretary of the Navy. There will be more to come. There should be.

The Las Vegas depredations of the Tailhookers were not just your routine, drunken, boys-will-be-boys affairs. It's difficult to think of a parallel in organized buffoonery in modern times.

In the old days veterans' conventions involved such shenanigans as dropping paper bags of water from hotel rooms. College students have hired strippers for stag shows, and so have business and labor associations. Maybe some bikers' groups have matched the Las Vegas affront to women. But the Tailhook men were in a class by themselves in massive abuse in a public place. Most shamefully of all, some of the victims were women naval officers. Up until now, apparently there had been a halfhearted investigation, coverups, and much looking the other way.

The United States Navy is a fighting force of great efficiency and enormous responsibility. Like most navies, it is permeated with custom and hallowed tradition, some of which is rooted in superstition. Men who pit themselves against the sea with only thin shells and platforms separating them from the depths tend to view themselves as a world apart, and they are.

In that world women have been regarded as aliens, and since they have entered it they often have been treated as such.

A navy resists change for good reason. It's dangerous to take chances at sea. Ships must be taut, disciplined and orderly to the point of excess. Things must go like clockwork, and only the tried and true are seen as really dependable.

All military forces are hidebound for those reasons, and the Navy more so than others. There probably was a reluctance to abandon the oars of triremes. Sail reigned for centuries. The battleship admirals of our times are part of military lore.

But it is exactly that mindset that must be overcome. Women are in the services to stay; they need not interfere with the discipline of survival or the order of battle or the business of engaging an enemy. They won't unless the services continue to treat them as intruders.

Only the military can truly reform itself, and that must be done from top to bottom. At last the U.S. Navy appears to be trying.

Tailhook Report Details Abuses at 1991 Naval Aviators' Convention

A Defense Department report concerning a 1991 convention of naval aviators, released April 23, 1993 found that 90 people had been sexually assaulted at the convention. The report indicated that at least 117 officers could face disciplinary action over the affair.

The report, prepared by acting Pentagon Inspector General Derek J. Vander Schaaf, was the latest in a series of probes relating to the September 1991 convention of the "Tailhook" aviators' group in Las Vegas. (The aviators' group took its name from the apparatus that helped stop planes as they landed on aircraft carriers.) Vander Schaaf found that problems at the convention were "the culmination of a long-term failure of leadership in naval aviation."

The scandal had first come to light in the fall of 1991 with newspaper reports of sexual assaults at the convention. The Navy's initial investigation into the case was criticized by a subsequent probe as inadequate, and a new investigation, resulting in the April 23 report, had been launched.

Vander Schaaf's 300-page report was based on interviews with more than 2,900 people. It had been completed in February, but its release was delayed until the appointment of a new secretary of the Navy. President Clinton April 21 had announced his intention to nominate Texas businessman John H. Dalton to the post.

The inspector general's report cited 23 officers said to have participated directly in indecent assaults at the convention and 23 directly involved in indecent exposure. A total of 117 officers were "implicated in one or more incidents of indecent assault, indecent exposure, conduct unbecoming an officer or failure to act in a proper leadership capacity." Fifty-one people were accused of lying to investigators.

The report added that "the number of individuals involved in all types of misconduct or other inappropriate behavior" at the convention was "more widespread than these figures would suggest." About 4,000 people attended the convention.

Names of the alleged offenders were withheld pending possible disciplinary proceedings by the Navy. Press reports indicated that as many as 175 officers could face charges.

Of the 90 alleged victims of assault, 83 were women and seven were servicemen. Of the women, 49 were civilians, 22 were in the service, six were government employees and six were wives of attendees.

Assaults typically occurred when victims encountered a "gauntlet" of aviators in a hotel hallway, where men would grab the women and tear at their clothes.

Acts of indecent exposure by the aviators included parading about with their genitals exposed and having sex in public. The investigation also found evidence that one naval squadron had sold T-shirts proclaiming "Women Are Property."

The report said problems at the convention stemmed from a traditional belief that the meeting provided "a type of 'free-fire zone' [where aviators] could act indiscriminately and without fear of censure or retribution in matters of sexual conduct and drunkenness." Previous Tailhook conventions had established a pattern of "can you top this" competitiveness, and a triumphant atmosphere resulting from the Persian Gulf war earlier in the year appeared to have exacerbated the improper behavior, the report said.

Vander Schaaf also urged reviews of the cases of 35 Navy, Marine Corps and Navy Reserve "flag officers" (those with rank above captain) who had attended the convention.

President Clinton April 23 said that he wanted "appropriate action taken" in the case, but he added that the report "should not be taken as a general indictment of the United States Navy."

THE SACRAMENTO BEE
Sacramento, California, April 29, 1993

The Pentagon inspector general's report on the 1991 Tailhook Convention reveals, as anticipated, the shocking and shameful details of three days of drunken debauchery that included assaults on at least 83 women and seven men. In all, the report accuses 140 Navy and Marine Corps pilots of sexual misconduct or other misbehavior. But followed by yesterday's announcement that military women will be allowed greater professional opportunities, the report may help close a chapter of shame for the Navy – and by inference the military – and a period of great discomfort for the women who serve in it.

It's clear from the report that because Navy leadership looked the other way for years – in effect condoning offensive behavior that was widely known to take place – the annual convention spiraled into an abusive and macho "free-fire zone." That behavior became such a glorified part of convention culture that it even developed its own vocabulary.

In addition to the now-infamous gauntlet, in which both willing and unwilling women – some of them Navy, some civilian – walked a hotel hallway lined with inebriated gropers, officers engaged in "ballwalking" (exposing genitals for all to see), "belly shots" (slurping tequila from another's navel) and "sharking" (biting another on the buttocks). One squadron of fliers printed special T-shirts for the event with the mottos "Women are Property" and "He-man Women Hater's Club." Pins sporting the phrase "Not in my Squadron," referring to the men's reluctance to fly alongside female pilots, were worn proudly.

The Pentagon's report, and the public outrage stirred by revelations about Tailhook offenses, combine for a clear message: It's no longer acceptable to "let boys be boys." And the message ought to be punctuated, as military leaders promised, by disciplinary action or criminal charges, where appropriate.

Now the Navy and the rest of the military branches face the challenge of transforming themselves into institutions where women, who are playing an increasingly integral and crucial role, are treated with respect. That will require tight adherence to stricter codes about what is acceptable behavior – no more winks and nods at tribal rituals during Navy-subsidized conventions, or anywhere else within the military. And the more women do the same jobs as men, the less room there will be to treat them as anything other than equals.

St. Petersburg Times
St. Petersburg, Florida, April 27, 1993

The new report on the U.S. Navy's 1991 Tailhook Association convention is so replete with ugly incidents that taxpayers aren't really sure what to condemn first: Sexism? Immoral conduct? Outright criminal behavior? There is a bottom line, though. We paid for some of it.

An estimated 4,000 conventioneers attended the annual private gathering, advertised in 1991 as a "professional development" meeting. At least 1,500 of these eager participants, some on active duty and some retired, didn't have to save up frequent flyer miles to get there. Instead, the Navy used government planes to transport them, at a cost reported by one news source as $190,000.

In addition, Pentagon investigators found that administrative personnel devoted time to drumming up business for the meetings, although "by virtually all accounts, large numbers of officers attended for the sole purpose of participating in the 'social' aspects."

C'mon now, fellas. Private debauchery at public expense, on government time, among officers who signed on to defend — not offend — the nation's honor? Once they were caught, literally, with their pants down, many officers questioned during the initial investigation weren't even honorable enough to tell the truth. As a result, taxpayers had to spend more money so that the Pentagon inspector general could unearth the facts.

The Tailhook scandal would be abhorrent as an isolated event, but the Pentagon report suggests a well-established precedent. For instance: "Many attendees viewed the annual conference as a type of 'free-fire zone' wherein they could act indiscriminately and without fear of censure or retribution in matters of sexual conduct and drunkenness."

And further: "Throughout our investigation, officers told us that Tailhook '91 was not significantly different from earlier conventions with respect to outrageous behavior. Most of the officers we spoke to said that excesses seen at Tailhook '91... were accepted by senior officers simply because those things had gone on for years."

The theme of an underlying Navy culture dominates this report. Even the most bizarre behaviors were described as "traditions," passed on from one class of officers to the next. Interviews throughout the document reflect a sense of bewilderment among some participants, who seem genuinely surprised to learn that they had done something "wrong."

"I don't think that anybody saw anything that they felt hadn't happened in the past," one lieutenant told investigators. "And so... if it had been allowed to happen in the past, they'd just let it go."

At least 90 people were assaulted during the Sept. 5-8 bash, all but seven of them women. Sexism is too weak a label here; details of the Pentagon report show that some conventioneers failed to view their victims as full human beings.

The government has enough evidence against at least 140 military officers to warrant further investigation. Disciplinary action, expulsion from the service or jail sentences should follow with deliberate speed. The traditions that led to Tailhook '91 must be permanently unlearned.

THE PLAIN DEALER
Cleveland, Ohio, April 27, 1993

The Navy is the most tradition-bound of America's armed services — and some of its traditions have included an ugly pattern of sexism and sexual harassment.

The Navy has been shamed by last week's disclosures of a shocking breakdown in military discipline: the sexual misconduct by Navy aviators that marred the 1991 convention of its Tailhook Association. As many as 175 officers have been accused of sexual harassment that amounted to "debauchery," according to a long-awaited report by the Pentagon's inspector general. The accounts of the Las Vegas orgy of groping, fondling, exhibitionism and public sex mock the Navy's claim that its members live up to the ideals of "officers and gentlemen."

Tailhook's three-day binge of drunkenness victimized 83 women and seven men, some of whom were forced to run a gantlet of Navy officers whose lecherous lunges amounted to sexual assault. There is no doubt about the episode's misogynist skew: One naval fighter squadron sold a T-shirt declaring, "Women Are Property." The culture of sexism among naval aviators, attributed to "a long-term failure of leadership" within the Navy, included a code of silence that led at least 51 officers to lie to Pentagon investigators about the Tailhook abuses. Hundreds of others turned a blind eye to the outrage.

"What happened at Tailhook '91 was destined to happen sooner or later in the 'can you top this' atmosphere that appeared to increase with each succeeding convention," said the report, which was issued by the Navy's chief of naval operations and the Marine Corps' commandant.

Late and lame, the Pentagon's leadership has finally begun to take seriously the problem of sexual harassment. Last year's outcry over the initial Tailhook disclosures forced the resignation of Secretary of the Navy H. Lawrence Garrett. Meting out discipline will present an early challenge to John H. Dalton, the Naval Academy graduate and former submarine officer who is the Clinton administration's newly nominated secretary of the Navy.

The uniformed services will decide the degree of punishment for 140 lower-ranked officers. But civilian Pentagon officials will weigh the cases of the 35 more senior officers accused of misconduct, including two Marine Corps generals and 33 Navy or Navy Reserve officers above the rank of captain. The pending courts martial — which could include fines, reductions in rank, dismissals or imprisonment — may further damage morale in the armed forces, which are already grumbling about budget cuts and force reductions.

Sexist attitudes and misogynist misconduct must be purged from the armed forces, just as they must be banished from civilian society. The Pentagon must impose the most serious penalties against any officers found guilty of sexual offenses, insisting to the officer corps that it will not tolerate any repetition of Tailhook's orgiastic excesses.

AKRON BEACON JOURNAL
Akron, Ohio, April 27, 1993

It's hard to recall college hijinks of any era that could rival the Navy Tailhook Association's penchant for drunken debauchery, gross sexual harassment and general misconduct.

Made up of active and retired Navy and Marine fighter pilots, Tailhook's now infamous Las Vegas convention in 1991 was at first the object of an apparent cover-up by Navy brass and many of the 4,000 officers who attended.

Last week, however, the Navy released its report of its second and more exhaustive investigation of the Tailhook orgy. It is pleasant reading only for those interested in smut.

Nudity, crude remarks, physical assaults on women and men, strippers, prostitution, extreme drunkenness, public oral sex and sexual intercourse — all were among the activities engaged in by Navy and Marine officers at the Las Vegas Hilton during the three-day Tailhook convention two years ago.

From interviews with more than 2,900 people, the Navy's deputy inspector general reported that 83 women and seven men were assaulted in the hotel's hallways and suites:

"The assaults varied from victims being grabbed on the buttocks to victims being groped, pinched and fondled on their breasts, buttocks and genitals. Some victims were bitten by their assailants, others were knocked to the ground and some had their clothing ripped or removed."

As many of 175 officers now face possible disciplinary action as a result of the new report. The chief of naval operations, Adm. Frank B. Kelso III, said the Tailhook debauch "brought to light the fact that we had an institutional problem in how we treated women. In that regard it was a watershed event that has brought about institutional change."

The lengthy report said the excesses of the Tailhook members had been growing each year, and reflected a failure of senior naval aviation leadership, which had winked at or even encouraged the annual debauchery.

Finally, the Navy with its proud military history has owned up to this problem and promises to correct and eliminate the unmilitary-like and disorderly conduct of so many of its pilots and officers. Remedial action, including strong discipline, can come none too soon.

The State
Columbia, South Carolina, April 27, 1993

THE NAVY scandal concerning sexual harassment at the 1991 Tailhook convention is about to run full circle.

The scandal recently prompted the acting Navy Secretary, Adm. Frank Kelso, to call for an unprecedented relaxation of the rules relating to women's roles in the Navy.

Now, a Pentagon investigator has recommended punitive action against at least 140 Navy and Marine officers who, reportedly, sexually harassed 83 military women and seven men during a Tailhook Association convention in Las Vegas in 1991. Unfortunately, the investigation came only after a massive cover-up that caused the downfall of several top Navy officers.

Belatedly, a few women had the courage to come forward and spill the beans. Soon, that number grew, and the Navy and Marines were forced to launch a full-scale investigation. Then-President Bush was incensed when he heard about the assaults and the attempted cover-up.

Obviously, the complaints were not a set-up. Dozens of women told similar, embarrassing stories about being groped, stripped and worse by male officers during a drunken binge at the Tailhook convention.

After the stories surfaced, the Pentagon's acting inspector general, Derek Vander Shaaf, spent months investigating the complaints. "There's enough stuff there for more than one X-rated movie," he commented after his report was completed.

He has recommended that some of the 140 accused officers be court-martialed and that others receive lesser disciplinary action for their roles in what, by all accounts, was a disgusting, threatening incident. Those found guilty in courts-martial could receive criminal penalties as well as expulsion from military service. Even those who aren't court-martialed will find their careers dead-ended.

Albeit belatedly, the Navy is now leading the way toward cleaning up its act. It's also pushing for an expanded role for women in all naval jobs — including duty on combat ships and in fighter planes. Perhaps this is a *mea culpa* for its earlier chauvinism.

There are many issues to be resolved before the Tailhook episode, as well as the role of women in the military, will be settled. But the objective investigation in the wake of the 1991 Las Vegas scandal is a good beginning.

THE DENVER POST
Denver, Colorado, April 27, 1993

IF THEY GAVE medals for dunderheadedness, the Pentagon would surely win one for its increasingly indefensible approach to the question of homosexuality.

On one hand, a decorated veteran of the Desert Storm campaign, recently named the Sixth Army's "Soldier of the Year," now stands to be discharged after having publicly announced that he is gay — even though his conduct in uniform has been exemplary.

On the other, scores of "straight" officers, whose misconduct in the Tailhook incident has shamed the Navy, are only belatedly being held accountable for their violations of both military law and common decency.

Clearly, the assumption that homosexuals automatically pose a threat to the image or combat readiness of the military services, while heterosexuals don't, has shown itself to be as obsolete as a flintlock rifle.

What counts, as President Clinton recognized in calling for an end to the ban on gays in the military, is not one's sexual orientation, which obviously has little bearing on a person's patriotism or ability to perform a mission. Rather, it is a person's behavior — sexual or otherwise — that determines whether he or she should be honored or disgraced, in the military or in civilian life.

It shouldn't take a march on Washington to demonstrate the moral bankruptcy of the current policy. If the top brass refuse to renounce the belief that homosexuality is "incompatible" with military service, they will be guilty of the same kind of failure of leadership that led to the Tailhook abuses.

THE INDIANAPOLIS NEWS
Indianapolis, Indiana, April 28, 1993

The Tailhook report came out last week.

It is not a pretty story.

Basically, the report said that hundreds of top Navy personnel have no respect for women — or for themselves.

A Pentagon investigation of a 1991 Naval aviator convention in Las Vegas details three nights of sexual misconduct and battery that have scandalized the Navy and shocked this nation.

Not only does the report describe some of the despicable details of the misdeeds — male aviators molesting and abusing their female counterparts in a drunken brawl — it reveals that during the investigation 51 officers lied about what went on those nights in Las Vegas.

Also, according to the report, "several hundred other officers were aware of the misconduct and chose to ignore it."

During the three nights, at least 83 women and seven men were assaulted.

The story is ugly.

It is difficult to imagine how hundreds of officers could stand by while their colleagues participated in such debauchery. Worse yet, they covered up for them after the convention — even lied to protect them from the military wrath that should follow.

It is no wonder that the mind-set of the Navy and of the entire military establishment has come into question following the Tailhook scandal.

Not only must those who have broken the rules of the Navy and of human decency be punished, but the entire military system must be scrutinized. Those who lead this country's armed forces have failed.

When men see women or other men as nothing more than sexual objects or anything less than human, something is terribly wrong. And Tailhook proves that something is terribly wrong.

The training that shapes men and women into warriors should not kill off their humanity. It should not steal that part of their nature that allows them to distinguish right from wrong, in war or in peace. It should not take from them their souls.

Those who have crossed the lines of humanity must answer not only to themselves but to higher military powers. While their actions may have been overlooked, even camouflaged for a while, they are out in the open now.

"Tailhook brought to light the fact that we had an institutional problem in how we treated women," said Adm. Frank Kelso, the chief of naval operations. "I want to ensure that the American people and our officer corps understand the egregious conduct described in this report is not now, never has been and never will be acceptable to Navy leadership."

While the Navy would never openly condone such behavior as took place in Las Vegas, some in the Navy did, and some in the Navy still may believe that what went on was no more than a few good old boys having some fun.

It wasn't fun, for the Navy or this country.

The Navy has acknowledged it has a problem.

Now it and all other branches of the armed forces must rid themselves of the calloused and inhumane attitudes that led to the Tailhook incident and continue to work against women in the military.

The Salt Lake Tribune
Salt Lake City, Utah, April 28, 1993

When the Naval Investigative Service released its report a year ago on the infamous 1991 Tailhook Association convention, its findings were dismissed as a Navy whitewash job. Friday, the nation learned just how much of a whitewash it was.

Tailhook, of course, has become a code word for sexual harassment in the military. It refers to the Tailhook Association convention in Las Vegas in September 1991, when current and retired Navy fliers gathered for what apparently had become an annually escalating orgy of drunken lewdness. Just as Tailhook '91 topped previous conventions for unacceptable behavior, so Friday's Pentagon report topped last year's NIS account in its descriptions of the Vegas fiasco.

The NIS report indicated that 26 women had been molested at Tailhook '91. However, it identified only two suspects and recommended no disciplinary action. The Navy's inspector general simply ran into a stone wall from superiors in his inquiries, thus assuring an incomplete report.

Friday, in the Pentagon inspector general's report, it suddenly wasn't 26 women under assault but a staggering total of 83, plus seven men. And while the NIS report could identify only two suspects, the Pentagon referred the cases of 175 officers for possible disciplinary action, including 33 admirals.

The surprise isn't that the NIS report was so inadequate. That was already addressed last year, when Navy Secretary Lawrence Garrett was forced to resign in June and two admirals who handled the investigation were dismissed. The real stunner is the extensiveness of the Navy pilots' disgraceful behavior within what the Pentagon study called a "general atmosphere of debauchery."

A total of 117 officers were found to have been involved in "one or more incidents of indecent assault, indecent exposure, conduct unbecoming an officer or failure to act in a proper leadership capacity ... " In addition, 51 officers were found to have lied to investigators. One hopes that this isn't stereotypical of the behavior of Navy officers.

The Pentagon report went on to describe the details of the Tailhook '91 activities, and they are nothing to be proud of: a gantlet of 200 men lining a hotel corridor and molesting women who tried to walk down the hall; the shaving of women's legs and pubic areas by pilots; drinking alcohol out of women's navels, and enjoying all of this while wearing T-shirts that say, "Woman Are Property."

What is the matter with these men, these supposed defenders of our freedom? Don't they have mothers or wives or sisters or daughters? Don't they understand each of their victims is somebody's daughter or sister or mother or wife? Don't they think? Well, of course, they don't — which is why drumming them out of the service will be no loss to the national defense.

The Navy has done much in the last year to let its officers know that sexual harassment is unacceptable behavior. It can reinforce that message in the most compelling way by penalizing those who disgraced their uniform at Tailhook '91. And Adm. Frank Kelso, the chief of naval operations who was at the Tailhook convention, could set the ultimate example by resigning himself, once all the penalties have been meted out; he is responsible for the same kind of "leadership failure" that forced Secretary Garrett to resign last June.

In the meantime, the one thing the nation does not need to hear from the Tailhook conventioneers — or from any member of the military that empathizes with their behavior — is their opinion on the gays-in-the-military issue. Anybody in the military who condones what happened at Tailhook '91 has no moral standing to speak on the sexual preferences of gay officers; they've already disqualified themselves from any discussion on sexual relations.

THE TENNESSEAN
Nashville, Tennessee, April 28, 1993

TAILHOOK '91 was bad.

How bad? A Pentagon report issued last week about the sexual abuse at the annual convention was scathing.

As many as 175 officers could face disciplinary action for the events at the Las Vegas convention. Of those, 23 were found to have participated in indecent assaults and another 23 were found to have indecently exposed themselves.

That is more than a few bad men.

Investigators showed that 51 officers had lied in the course of the follow-up investigations.

The investigation team found 83 women and 7 men were assaulted during the three nights of the aviators' convention.

The victims had their clothing ripped off or were fondled repeatedly by drunken aviators.

There were some, including some in the U.S. Navy at first, who dismissed the Tailhook tales as ""boys being boys" or as some exaggerated story, not worthy of attention. The official report ought to sober up everyone.

The party's over. But the Navy's black eye won't heal until the department begins meting out some discipline for the more egregious lapses in behavior.

The report gives the Navy a second chance. The first investigation by the Navy — undertaken only under pressure — resulted in two primary suspects. After that, the officers began to close ranks prompting calls for an independent investigation.

That investigation has now ended, and it's up to the Navy to begin its own inquiries to determine what action should be taken to punish those involved. Those accused deserve fair, impartial hearings. Some incidents may demand court martial proceedings. But the public and the many innocent men and women who serve the U.S. Navy with honor should also expect that justice will be done.

After nearly two years, the Navy should welcome the chance to put this ugly debauchery behind the service.

""The damage suffered by the Navy as a result of Tailhook cannot be fully repaired until the integrity of the Navy is restored, which in turn, depends on the integrity of each of its members," the report concluded. Let the restoration begin. ∎

SYRACUSE HERALD-JOURNAL
Syracuse, New York, April 25, 1993

Disgust. Other reactions rush to mind about the contents of the report issued on the sexual abuse and sexual assaults carried out by the naval aviators who attended the 1991 Tailhook convention, but they come after we heave a deep, deep sigh.

Listen to one of the victims:

"The man ... put both his hands down the front of my tanktop and inside my bra where he grabbed my breast. I dropped to a forward crouch position and placed my hands on the wrists of my attacker in an attempt to remove his hands. ... I sank my teeth into the fleshy part of the man's left forearm, biting hard. I thought I drew blood. ... I then turned and bit the man on the right hand. ... The man removed his hands, and another individual reached up under my skirt and grabbed the crotch of my panties. I kicked one of my attackers. ... I felt as though the group was trying to rape me. I was terrified and had no idea what was going to happen next."

She's a Navy lieutenant who was assaulted by fellow officers. She is one of 83 women and seven men who told stories of abuse, of debauchery, of sick sexual games, of conduct unbecoming any human being, never mind officers — never mind people who are paid to represent some of the best things about this country.

The stories go on and on. There was a "traditional" gauntlet set up in a hotel hallway. Any woman who had to get from one end to the other was pawed, pushed, grabbed, touched and — in some cases — stripped to her waist. When one woman told her boyfriend, a Navy lieutenant, that she'd been assaulted in the hall, his counsel was: Don't tell anyone, they'll think you're a slut.

And that brings us to the biggest shame about this whole sordid mess. When first reports came out about the madness at Tailhook, the Navy closed ranks, tried to bury the truth, tried to blame the women who complained. Officers cast aspersions on the accusers, saying some of them were prostitutes and hangers-on. An internal investigation could find only two officers who had misbehaved — only two.

Now, two years later, after almost 3,000 interviews, an independent committee headed by the Pentagon's inspector general says that 117 officers were implicated in incidents of indecent assault, indecent exposure, conduct unbecoming an officer or failure to act in a proper leadership capacity while at Tailhook. Fifty-one officers are accused of lying to investigators. And Pentagon deputy inspector general Derek Vander Schaaf is recommending that 140 officers' files be turned over to military authorities for legal action.

Good. We hope legal action happens this time. And we hope the legal authorities will go after every person who knew about the abuse and didn't aid in the first investigation. They are as responsible as if they were standing along the gauntlet.

This matter has shaken the Navy to its core. And it's not over yet. Let us hope the misguided attempts to whitewash the whole thing and disparage the victims are over. The wrongdoers should be punished so that all the men and women who wear Navy uniforms know that conduct unbecoming a human being will not be tolerated, not ever.

Armed Forces to Allow Women To Serve in Aerial Combat

Defense Secretary Les Aspin April 28, 1993 removed the Defense Department's restrictions on women's participation in aerial combat. He also said he would seek to allow women to serve in naval combat positions aboard most Navy warships, a policy change that required Congress to repeal an existing ban.

Aspin's decision rejected a presidential panel's recommendation in November 1992 that women continue to be barred from piloting combat aircraft. In 1991, Congress had passed a bill clearing the way for women to fly combat planes once the Pentagon initiated a policy change. Consequently, Aspin's order concerning aviation jobs was effective immediately.

The 1992 panel had also recommended opening up to women combat slots on all naval vessels except for submarines and amphibious assault craft. Adm. Frank B. Kelso, the Navy's top officer and acting Navy secretary, April 28 was given responsibility by Aspin for drafting a legislative proposal to submit to Congress that followed the panel's recommendations and lifted most naval combat restrictions.

Aspin ordered the four armed services—the Army, Navy, Air Force and Marine Corps—to consider whether existing bans on women in other combat jobs, such as artillery and air defense, could be lifted. But he indicated that he would not recommend ending restrictions on women in certain ground combat jobs, such as infantry and armor units. The presidential panel had opposed women participating in all forms of ground combat.

Aspin April 28 said, "The steps we are taking today are historic. The results of all this will be that the services will be able to call upon a much larger pool of talent to perform the vital tasks that our military forces must perform."

Under the new policy, women would be eligible to pilot and serve on fighters and bombers in all four branches of the armed forces. Previously, women had been excluded from all aviation jobs in the Marines, could not fly combat aircraft in the Air Force and were permitted only to pilot transport flights and serve as flight instructors in the Navy and the Army.

In response to Aspin's order, the Air Force planned to begin training female fighter and bomber pilots immediately, many of whom would be assigned to squadrons by early 1994, the *New York Times* reported in an article datelined April 27. The Navy also planned to train carrier-based pilots, and women were expected to be flying helicopter gunships in the Army within a year. No female aviators currently served in the Marines, but that service branch reportedly would open its aviation units to women and commence training them in 1993.

Under existing policy, assignment to combat aviation in all four branches was voluntary for men, a policy that would be extended to women. Land and sea combat appointments currently were compulsory for men, however; Aspin and top military personnel reportedly had not yet agreed whether such appointments initially would be compulsory for women as well.

Aerial and naval combat positions generally emphasized mental and intuitive skills, so women's integration was not expected to affect the units' operations noticeably. However, many ground combat jobs required extensive physical strength and stamina, which might preclude female representation, it was reported.

Many women, both civilians and members of the armed forces, reportedly supported Aspin's policy shift. Many portrayed the further integration of female troops as an equal-rights issue that would have important repercussions in unrelated civilian areas that had resisted women assuming nontraditional roles.

THE SUN
Baltimore, Maryland, April 29, 1993

Secretary of Defense Les Aspin said yesterday that he has ordered the military to drop many restrictions regarding combat assignments. This is a welcome and wise first step, but it is only that. Policy differences among the services remain, and some roles that women could easily assume are still closed to them for the time being. The Army, Navy, Marines and Air Force should have policies as similar as possible, and ultimately all the military services should open all assignments on a non-gender basis.

Opposition to this approach inside the military is widespread. Also heartfelt and honest. Opponents of women in combat should not be demeaned for their views. The Marine Corps commandant recently said this of combat, "It's debasing. It's something I do not want women involved in." An Air Force general said, "I have a very traditional attitude about wives, mothers and daughters being ordered to kill people."

Those views are widely held outside the military as well. Thousands of years of tradition are on their side. But the tide of opinion is running the other way. Seven of 15 members of a presidential commission voted last year to give women aviators more combat chances. The Navy's top leadership favored this idea. The Air Force, meanwhile, was preparing to exclude women from combat tactics training assignments that they have till now been allowed to seek. This divergence no doubt hastened Secretary Aspin's decision to move ahead.

Women in large numbers have demonstrated in previous wars that they have the courage, composure and skills to perform well in some combat environments. Despite this, some of the most prestigious — and most dangerous — combat slots have been denied them. These include many slots in which women could perform as well as men. One obvious example: Flying highly sophisticated aircraft, where intelligence and dexterity rather than physical strength are important. That includes carrier-based aircraft.

One concern is that political pressure might lead to what has been called "gender norming" in combat assignments. Women would be judged by different — lower — standards than men competing for the same jobs. (This is the practice now in competition for some military assignments.) The presidential commission was unanimous in opposing different standards. It should have been. Such a policy would be a serious mistake. It would compromise unit performance. Standards that legitimately relate to combat readiness have to be gender neutral — the same for men and women. Lives are at stake.

Allowing women in combat and applying uniform standards could reduce the number of women in the military overall, but it would at the same time end the second-class status that career women must endure as long as they cannot make the same sorts of career choices that are available to their male counterparts.

The Record
Hackensack, New Jersey, April 30, 1993

FOR ALL THE FANFARE, the Pentagon's announcement that it was lifting its ban on women in air and naval combat roles is nothing more than a matter of basic fairness. For years, women have proven their military ability. To continue to deny them the opportunities afforded to men would have been to continue an injustice.

It's important to note that lifting the combat ban does not entail special treatment for women. It entails equal treatment. Women who want to fly combat missions, for example, will have to meet the same demanding standards as men.

Rep. Pat Schroeder, D-Colo., who led the congressional fight to lift the ban, explains why those standards won't pose a problem. "Women have been flying fighters, dropping bombs, and landing on [aircraft] carriers — and teaching men to do all three — for decades," says Ms. Schroeder. "Clearly they have the skills and strengths to perform in any situation."

What's more, because combat assignments are often a prerequisite to attain senior rank, the Pentagon's order will give women a fairer chance of promotion to the military's upper echelons.

Veterans groups who opposed the lifting of the ban say that the presence of women in combat roles will hurt morale and discipline. Their arguments ring hollow. In the two decades since the military began integrating women into the ranks, concerns over servicewomen's abilities and their effect on morale have declined as their roles have expanded.

•

The Pentagon also announced Wednesday that every branch of the armed services is being asked to justify all jobs that remain off-limits to women, including such ground combat assignments as field artillery and air-defense units. That makes sense as well.

Certainly, there will be instances where total equality won't be feasible. Military experts say, for example, that it would be difficult and costly to build separate quarters for women in the already cramped confines of Navy attack submarines and minesweepers. Those few exceptions, however, should not deter all branches of the armed forces from carrying out the Pentagon's directive as expeditiously as possible.

A Pentagon official said that giving women greater combat roles will make the military look "more like America," but there's more to lifting the ban than that.

During Operation Desert Storm and Operation Desert Shield, 40,000 women were assigned to the Persian Gulf region. Five women were killed in hostile action. Army pilot Maj. Marie Rossi of Oradell died when her Chinook helicopter crashed.

If servicewomen are permitted to risk their lives in battle zones, they should be permitted to fight.

> These women pilots must meet the same tough standards as men.

The Miami Herald
Miami, Florida, April 29, 1993

FORGET, JUST for the moment, about equal opportunity, fair treatment, or social policy. Forget, if possible, the aspirations and dedication of military women. Forget Tailhook. For that matter, leave aside any notion that allowing women to serve in combat is a *women's* issue at all.

Think, for a moment, purely from an employer's point of view. That, after all, is the first role of taxpayers in the U.S. military. All Americans pay the salaries and rely on the labor of the men and women in uniform. As employers — not as social activists — they have good reason to welcome yesterday's order by Defense Secretary Les Aspin to make greater use of women's skills, strength, and patriotism in aerial and naval combat positions. The order clearly paves the way for women's service in ground combat as well. And as well it should.

Mr. Aspin acknowledges physical and logistical requirements that may make some jobs better suited to men than to women. But he wants all such exceptions justified individually. Anything less cheats the military (read: the American people) out of a huge pool of talent and dedication.

Mr. Aspin does not acknowledge — nor should he — any need to shield women more than men from the hardships of war. All troops, male and female, should be kept out of needless combat. But when fighting is necessary, those of either sex who are most willing and gifted should serve first.

It has taken centuries for civilized nations to come to this conclusion. Amazing, isn't it?

The Providence Journal
Providence, Rhode Island, April 30, 1993

Defense Secretary Les Aspin's announcement that women will be permitted to fly combat aircraft, and to serve aboard most warships, was no particular surprise — even if it came a few days early, and before congressional briefings, to plug a leak and to come in under the wire of President Clinton's first 100 days.

This notion has been gathering strength since the Panama invasion, when women soldiers were initially exposed to combat. Meantime, allowing women to serve on warships will require congressional action, and the Defense Secretary has ordered the Chief of Naval Operations to prepare the necessary legislation. Within a year, women might be flying Navy and Air Force fighter jets, and piloting Army attack helicopters. (The Marines have no women flyers trained at this time to switch to combat aircraft.)

Women in the armed forces have been marching toward this day, and it will be interesting to see how they manage in practice, and how the services adapt to this latest revolution in military ranks. It is also worth noting that, while Secretary Aspin has asked the Army and Marines to ponder how women might work in field artillery and air defense combat units, the infantry, armor and cavalry units would still be reserved for male soldiers only. In the words of the Marine Corps commandant: "Direct combat is a role we should limit to men."

This begs a question, and our only reservation: While we're happy to support the cause of women in the military, and will be gratified to learn if they're equal to the challenge, let us hope that the armed forces are not being used as a captive laboratory for social experimentation. Building a military establishment is *not* the same as creating a Cabinet that "looks like America," or recruiting a faculty through set-asides and quotas.

America's armed forces must be second to none, meeting the highest standards and the toughest demands. That is their primary mission. If women can do the job, more power to them. But if they are tested and found wanting, because, after all, they *are* physically different from men, we'll expect an explanation from those who have always regarded the role of women in combat as a social and political, and not a military, issue.

San Francisco Chronicle
San Francisco, California, April 29, 1993

BY DIRECTING the military to drop most restrictions on women in air and naval combat, Defense Secretary Les Aspin has pressed the services closer to reality. What's important in these jobs is capability, and there is no reason to believe that qualified women won't serve with just as much distinction and effectiveness as men.

"We need to recruit the best talent and assign the most qualified person to every job, and right now we're not doing that," the defense secretary declared. "Women have proved they can contribute."

As he lifted the barriers on women flying combat air missions and serving aboard warships, the secretary also ordered the Army and Marines to "examine all possibilities" for women in ground combat, including field artillery and anti-aircraft artillery.

OLD ATTITUDES — particularly those that encrust the military services — need the strengthening that comes from seeing the world as it really is. Here is progress.

Chicago Tribune
Chicago, Illinois, April 29, 1993

At some point, military convenience and custom have to give way to social change. And in the case of many Pentagon restrictions on women in combat, they finally are.

The Defense Department said Wednesday that it will direct the services to open all combat aircraft to women for the first time and will ask Congress to repeal the law barring women from ships assigned to combat missions.

Within a year, the Army says, women could be flying helicopter gunships. The Air Force says it will now start training female fighter and bomber pilots, who could be deployed by February. The Navy and Marine Corps will be close behind.

The U.S. military already relies on women to an extent far greater than traditionalists could have dreamed a generation ago.

They make up 11.5 percent of all military personnel; they attend the service academies; they command troops and they brave the risks of war. But their professional advancement is hindered by their exclusion from combat jobs.

During the showdown with Iraq, 40,000 women were sent to the Persian Gulf, where they served side by side with men in the field. Five women were killed and two were taken prisoner.

Women have already shown that gender is no bar to top performance in the cockpit or at sea. The services have more than 800 female pilots, including some who train males. If women couldn't meet the demands of these missions, no prohibition would be needed, because they would never qualify anyway. The only women affected by the exclusion are those who are perfectly capable of doing the job. Under the new policy, they will get the only thing they ask — the opportunity to rise as far as their abilities will take them.

Secretary of Defense Les Aspin also will ask the services to justify all remaining rules barring women from other jobs. Some of them make sense — particularly when it comes to combat infantry units, where women's physical limitations are an exceptional handicap. A few women could qualify (although when Canada tried it, only one did), but the cost of accommodating them would be too great to justify.

With the odor of the Tailhook scandal still strong, the Pentagon needed to show that its attitude toward women is not dangerously outmoded. Dropping many of the combat barriers is a good start.

ARGUS-LEADER
Sioux Falls, South Dakota, April 19, 1993

Although four years is an awfully long implementation period, the U.S. Navy should be commended for its plan to put women in front-line combat jobs.

The Navy plan would allow women to serve on combat support ships within a matter of months and enter training for more advanced combat jobs.

Approval of the proposal by Defense Secretary Les Aspin would put the Navy in the forefront of an overdue movement. Other branches of the military should follow the Navy's example.

Currently women are barred from flying combat aircraft and from serving on major warships, such as aircraft carriers, destroyers and submarines. Congress has changed laws that, for example, used to ban women from some Air Force aircraft. But military polices remain in place that limit women's roles.

Aspin and the nation's commander in chief, President Clinton, should prod the military into moving faster.

Women have proven themselves. More than 40,000 women served in the Persian Gulf War and performed well. Their opportunities for military careers should not be limited to nursing, clerical and other support jobs.

Women, like black men, used to serve in their own units. Integration of the sexes did not begin on a large scale until the nation went to an all-volunteer army in 1973. Women now make up about 11 percent of the armed forces. They have become a vital part of the military. But for some, combat is a forbidden opportunity and an obstacle on their career path.

A woman's chance of advancing to top military positions is slim because combat is the surest way to promotion. As of last September, only 11 of 1,021 generals or admirals were women.

Physical differences between men and women might prevent some women from holding certain combat positions. But gender, alone, should not be the crucial test.

The United States has welcomed women into the military. Now it should drop what's left of the double standard in the military and give women the same opportunities as men.

The Wichita Eagle-Beacon
Wichita, Kansas, April 30, 1993

Defense Secretary Les Aspin should not hesitate to tell all branches of the U.S. military to start making full use of all available human resources now.

That the military needs his nudge speaks volumes about it and our society. The time is well past when any institution can afford to ignore talent. But the military, like too many other American institutions, clings to invalid and unacceptable excuses for doing just that.

Mr. Aspin's moves of Wednesday to tell the Air Force to use women in combat roles and to ask the Navy to seek repeal of the congressional ban on women aboard combat ships were starts, but only starts. Unfortunately, he continued to sidestep questions about ground combat roles for women. That artificial restriction also should be addressed.

No less than most institutions, the military can set high standards for performance and demand that every person meet the standards. As in professional sports or a successful business, performance is everything; genitals, skin color, sexual orientation and religious belief are irrelevant if performance is there. One can ride a horse or one cannot; one can sell widgets or one cannot; one can carry out a combat role or one cannot.

Males hold no corner on physical strength and courage and discipline, just as they hold no corner on weakness and cowardice and sloth. The military has no apparent problem sorting out which males possess which characteristics in what amounts and, by that process, deciding whether each male is capable of combat or not. It should have no problem making the same evaluation of females or, for that matter, gay males or lesbians.

Change will come slowly. It always does. But once the military begins that process of inclusion, it will become irreversible. It is way past time for that beginning.

The Register-Guard
Eugene, Oregon, April 17, 1993

The U.S. Navy, probably the most tradition-bound of the armed forces, is sailing into a new port: equality. Well, partial equality.

The Navy has announced that it will immediately expand the number of jobs that are open to women on ships and, within four years, allow women to serve in almost any capacity in the Navy — including combat.

That marks a major turnaround for a branch of the U.S. military. All of the armed services have historically limited the role of women, thus depriving about 11 percent of the country's military population of many opportunities for career advancement available to men.

The Navy's enlightened new policy seems to ignore — or deliberately cast aside — recommendations made last year by a presidential commission on the role of women in the military. Among other things, the commission recommended that the current ban on women in combat be retained.

It matters not whether the Navy took the lead in this area as a public relations counterweight to the coming final — and probably scathing — report on the 1991 Tailhook scandal. If the Navy wants to expand gender equity in its ranks to partially atone for the group groping of female naval officers by drunken male aviators, so be it. What's important is the move toward equality.

The other services are less enthusiastic about — perhaps even downright hostile to — the idea of an expanded role for women, especially when it comes to combat duty. However, enlightenment may be forced upon them by the Clinton administration.

In the name of consistency throughout the armed forces, Defense Secretary Les Aspin is preparing a package of initiatives to provide greater job opportunities, including combat positions, to women in the military. Aspin's proposals probably won't go so far as to allow women in ground combat positions, but they should.

Apart from the question of equity, technology is rendering the old notions about women in combat obsolete. Today's high-tech weaponry doesn't separate targets on the basis of gender.

The bottom line is common sense and qualification. If a woman is qualified in all other respects for a job in the military, including combat, there is no reason to prevent her from performing that task. Some women, because of physical limitations, might not make very good combatants. But that's also true of some men.

Women are serving honorably and well all over the United States in a variety of jobs that have military equivalence. As police officers, women capture dangerous criminals, bust drug rings and handle violent or potentially violent situations. As firefighters, they take on fires in residential neighborhoods, urban cores and the nation's forests. They fly commercial jets and serve as prison guards.

Women have proved their mettle in war zones from Libya to Panama and from Grenada to the Persian Gulf. They have earned, and they deserve, the same opportunities as their male counterparts.

If a person is otherwise qualified to fight for his or her country — whether the duty is flying a combat plane or serving in a warship gun crew — that person's gender is no more relevant to the job at hand than is race, religion, political party, marital status or eye color.

The Navy has taken a welcome step, and the secretary of defense seems prepared to bring the other services, even kicking and screaming, along. It's about time.

©1993 Pittsburgh Post-Gazette

Rape Shield Law Narrowed

The Supreme Court of Canada, in a 7 to 2 decision, Aug. 22, 1991 overturned part of a 1983 law that had restricted the circumstances under which a rape victim's sexual history could be introduced as evidence at a trial.

Madam Justice Beverly McLachlin, writing for the majority, said the law could prevent an accused rapist from receiving a fair trial, as guaranteed in the 1982 federal Charter of Rights and Freedoms. "In achieving its purpose—the abolition of the outmoded, sexist-based use of sexual conduct evidence—it overshoots the mark and renders inadmissible evidence which may be essential to the presentation of legitimate defenses and hence to a fair trial."

Specifically, the court struck down section 276 of the Canadian Criminal Code, adopted in 1983, which prevented the introduction of evidence about a rape victim's sexual history, except in a few specific circumstances.

However, the court upheld a companion law, section 277 of the Criminal Code, which prohibited the introduction of evidence about a rape victim's sexual reputation for the purposes of challenging or supporting her credibility.

The court called on Parliament to create new laws "adapted to conform to current reality." The court said such laws should permit evidence of a rape victim's sexual history only at the discretion of the trial judge, in cases where the judge determined that such evidence was crucial to the defendant's guilt or innocence.

The ruling came in response to an appeal by two Ontario men, Steven Seaboyer and Nigel Gayme, both of whom had been charged with rape and whose lawyers argued that the rape shield law would prevent them from obtaining a fair trial. The two would now face trial, but their lawyers would be required to convince a judge that evidence of the victims' sexual conduct was relevant to their clients' guilt or innocence.

The Globe and Mail
Toronto, Ontario, August 23, 1991

IN the early 1980s, Parliament amended the Criminal Code to restrict the questions a defence lawyer can ask an alleged rape victim about her sexual history. Its concern was grounded in centuries of unjust treatment, in which women were grilled about their sexual past, not because the information was relevant to the case but because it played to the bias of the judge and jury: that an "unchaste" woman was more likely to have consented to sleep with the accused, and was more likely to lie about it afterward.

In its ruling yesterday on the 1983 law, the Supreme Court of Canada rightly rejected any link between a complainant's credibility and whether she has had previous sexual experience. It therefore upheld section 277 of the Criminal Code, which prevents the introduction of evidence of sexual reputation "for the purpose of challenging or supporting the credibility of the complainant."

It also rejected the philosophy underpinning the old common-law rules, in which evidence of a woman's sexual activity "was routinely presented (and accepted by judges and juries) as tending to make it more likely that the complainant had consented to the alleged assault. . ." The inference was based on a myth that is "now discredited."

Having made this clear, however, the majority rightly strikes down section 276 of the Code, which prevents the introduction of evidence of a complainant's sexual activity except in three limited circumstances. In seeking to abolish "the outmoded, sexist-based use of sexual-conduct evidence," the court ruled, the law "overshoots the mark and renders inadmissible evidence which may be essential to the presentation of legitimate defences and hence to a fair trial."

The court steers a middle course: It would let the trial judge decide, with the jury out of the room, whether evidence about a complainant's sexual history was admissible; but the judge could not admit the evidence if it was designed solely to question credibility or suggest consent, and he could admit it only if its value as proof of the accused's argument substantially outweighed "the danger of unfair prejudice flowing from the evidence." He would also have to warn the jury against such prejudice. While we are sympathetic to the dissenting judges' concern about the prevalence of sexual stereotypes in the courtroom, as elsewhere in society, the majority's argument for letting the trial judge weigh such concerns, within defined bounds, seems more compelling.

The court cites several past instances in which evidence that would be prohibited by section 276 was necessary to a fair trial. In one disturbing example, a father accused of sexual acts with his daughter sought to show that she had made the accusations out of anger after he stopped her from having sexual relations with her brother.

A judge would weigh such evidence before admitting it; a jury might find it unpersuasive; but to deny the accused the opportunity to present it, where a judge has found it relevant and not an excuse to play on stereotypical views of "good women" and women "who were asking for it," would be to compromise the accused's right to a fair trial.

Winnipeg Free Press
Winnipeg, Manitoba, August 24, 1991

The Supreme Court of Canada has come up with yet another balance-point between the rights of the accused and the rights of the victim in sexual assault trials. It has probably not settled the matter, however: the new rule the court has laid down closes one avenue to injustice while re-opening an old one.

Under the law as it stood before 1983, the lawyer for the man accused of rape could examine the complainant on the witness stand and require explicit evidence about her sexual conduct before the rape of which she complained. This could be done on the pretext of producing evidence that the complainant's previous conduct showed she consented to sexual intercourse and was not raped. But in the course of questioning her on that subject, the defence could hope to give the jurors a low opinion of her so that they would be reluctant to convict the accused on the basis of her evidence.

These courtroom tactics could tend to focus the jury's attention on the character of the victim more than on the events of which she complained. They also turned rape trials into brutal public humiliations of women who reported they were raped so that a rape victim had to think twice about going to the police.

The so-called rape shield law enacted in 1983 forbade questioning the victim about her past sexual conduct. More sexual assault charges have come to trial in the years since 1983, probably because women can complain of rape without being raped all over again, figuratively speaking, on the witness stand.

But the 1983 law went too far, the Supreme Court of Canada found this week. There may be cases where the past relationship between the accused and the complainant or others does throw important light on the events of which the victim complains. False accusations of rape are sometimes made. An accused deserves some chance to produce those facts and prove them.

By the new rule of the Supreme Court of Canada, the judge will decide, after hearing the evidence in a *voir dire* in the absence of the jury, whether the jury should hear the evidence about past sexual conduct. If the judge considers it relevant then the jury can hear it.

This will help ensure that juries will not hear sexual conduct evidence calculated merely to paint the complainant in a bad light. It may also ensure, however, that lawyers defending rape cases can conduct in a *voir dire* the verbal assault upon the victim that they used to conduct in open court. Women complaining of rape will be compelled to detail their sex lives in front of the judge, the accused, the court staff, the teams of lawyers, the press and the spectators but the jury will be excluded. Defence lawyers will be stopped from prejudicing juries against complainants on irrelevant grounds but they will not necessarily be stopped from persecuting the accuser. In those rare cases where the sexual conduct fishing trip does turn up relevant evidence, the complainant will have to provide details of her sex life a first time in the *voir dire* and then repeat the ordeal before the jury.

Parliament may have to act again. If, in applying the supreme court's new rule, trial judges permit pointless humiliation of complainants, then that will have to be explicitly forbidden. Justice is not served when victims of crime are punished for denouncing their attackers.

The Sun
Vancouver, British Columbia, August 23, 1991

OUTRAGE has greeted the Supreme Court of Canada's ruling that overturns the so-called rape shield law. This enlightened measure, adopted into the Criminal Code in 1983 after long and fierce activity by women's groups, was aimed at protecting sexual assault victims from being cross-examined on their sexual history.

Anyone who witnessed a rape trial prior to 1983 knows how vulnerable and wretched is the female rape victim in the witness box. Open season was declared on someone who, allegedly, had suffered the most odious of assaults. Sexual accessibility was equated with promiscuity.

The Supreme Court, in its 7-2 ruling, has sanctioned a return to the bad old days. It says the rape shield law could result in conviction of innocent persons and denies "fundamental justice" and a fair trial guaranteed by the Charter of Rights and Freedoms.

The judgment was written by Madame Justice Beverley McLachlin She declared that the "fishing expeditions" of the past should not be permitted. But in our view that is precisely the reality of this unfortunate ruling. The bulwark of inadmissibility has been removed; in its place, the court extends to individual trial judges the right to decide whether or not a victim's sexual past can be scrutinized.

That's a perogative seen as jeopardy by Justice Claire L'Hereux-Dube, the other woman on the court. Dissenting, she cited myths, sterotypes and discrimination as the reasons the rape shield law existed. She's right. Culpability, not credibility, ought to be tried. Once again, the rape victim is potential plunder. Justice itself is back in the dock.

Times~Colonist
Victoria, British Columbia, August 25, 1991

Suppose Betty tells police she was raped by Ralph.

In the normal legal processing of such a claim, police officers would interview all the witnesses and gather all of the other evidence they could find, provide the Crown prosecutor's office with all of the information — and a Crown attorney would decide whether there was enough evidence to charge Ralph with sexual assault.

Such cases are among the toughest to prosecute because they often involve oath-against-oath situations — basically two people telling contradictory stories.

Suppose the prosecutor believed there was enough evidence to support a charge — and in due course, Betty is called as a witness to describe what happened to her. (Most men can only imagine how traumatic this experience is for women, but it is still an essential part of justice being done, and being seen to be done.)

The prosecutor asks her the questions which will bring before the court the testimony the Crown believes will result in a conviction. But the lawyer defending Ralph has (and deserves) a right to also question Betty. Because Betty might be lying. Maybe she hates Ralph and wants to see him in jail.

Suppose the defence's first question is: "How many men have you had sexual relations with recently?"

If Betty is a prostitute (and many assault cases involve prostitutes), the answer might well prejudice any jury. Some might reason, how can a woman who sells sex ever be raped? But what does that question (and the answer) really have to to do with the specific assault claim before the court? Is a woman's sexual history a fair subject for defence cross-examination — ever?

We suggest it is not — that guilt or innocence should be decided on whatever evidence relates strictly to the incident before the court.

But the Supreme Court of Canada has ruled that a woman's sexual history might be important to a fair defence. A substantial majority (7-2) said the so-called rape-shield provision of the Criminal Code, which has prevented a defence lawyer from delving into the sexual past of an alleged victim, violates the right of an accused to a fair trial.

The Court, however, drew some precise rules regarding what is admissable in this situation and how admissability is determined. If the defence wants to draw out evidence about the victim's sexual past, it must first be cleared by the trial judge, without the jury present. And if the judge agrees to admit the evidence, jury members must be warned they should not read it as an indication that the victim consented to the alleged act or that the victim is not "worthy" of being believed.

As some recent cases have vividly shown, not all judges have the same view of women's language (does "no" mean "maybe"?). And telling any jury what to think about any evidence is a waste of breath once any biases have been awakened by innuendo.

The jury is there to think for itself — based on the evidence it has been shown.

StarPhoenix
Saskatoon, Saskatchewan, August 27, 1991

Even if the federal government drafts a new version of a "rape shield" law, it will not be able to provide the protection to victims that the old law offered. As a result, rape will become an even more under-reported crime than it is now.

In striking down the section of the Criminal Code which restricted the use of trial evidence on a rape victim's sexual history, the Supreme Court offered guidelines for a new law. The guidelines allow a judge the discretion to decide whether the evidence can be admitted.

If it is allowed, the judge must warn the jury the evidence must not be taken to indicate consent by the complainant or that her testimony is less reliable.

This supposes we live in a perfect world where women are truly equal, where there is no need to counterbalance stereotyped attitudes and where there is no double standard that says it is acceptable for men to have sexual experience but not women. That world exists only in the minds of seven Supreme Court judges.

Two of the court's justices have no such delusions.

Writing the dissenting opinion, Madame Justice Claire L'Heureux-Dube said judges have shown they aren't impartial when it comes to women — that's why the shield law was drafted in the first place. She noted society, and therefore the justice system, is still rife with repressive attitudes.

L'Heureux-Dube also said the shield section which was struck down was indeed broad enough to allow relevant evidence of a victim's sexual history. That certainly appears to be the case. The jails are not full of people wrongfully convicted of sexual offences.

Our justice system requires that the proscecution provide sufficient proof of guilt. Some who are charged with sexual offences are acquitted because the case against them cannot be proven. That is as it should be.

It's possible that judges would be extremely careful in their use of new discretionary powers in rape cases. However, that will not change the fact that even more women than before will decide not to report a rape because they don't want to go through the justice mill.

Reporting of sexual assaults increased 127 per cent since 1983, when the old shield law came into effect.

Expect it to decrease drastically.

Calgary Herald
Calgary, Alberta, August 23, 1991

The Supreme Court found a reasonable middle ground in striking down the so-called rape shield law but not returning the old system which tended to put victims instead of accused rapists on trial.

However, in the process, the Court has placed great responsibility on trial judges to determine, on a case-by-case basis, precisely what evidence should be permitted to go before a jury in sexual assault cases.

As both defenders and critics of the shield law agreed, some restrictions on the cross-examination of sexual assault victims are necessary.

The court had to wrestle with the extent of those restrictions.

In its 7-2 ruling the Court rightly decided that the blanket shield law went too far in protecting the rights of witnesses at the expense of the rights of the accused to a fair trial.

The shield law itself, of course, had been put in place to safeguard witnesses against the earlier wide-open practice which made sexual assault victims targets of defendants. Past personal sexual history of a rape victim was too often used as a weapon by defence lawyers to malign the morality of the victim and suggest consent.

This had the doubly negative effect of discouraging women from reporting rapes let alone following through with particularly trying and embarrassing testimony in a court of law.

With its ruling the Court risks permitting this type of defence to once again be mounted by those facing sexual assault charges.

But the ultimate decision regarding the validity of such a defence will be in private by a judge prior to open trial.

Provided that trial judges are sufficiently enlightened as to the nature of the offence of sexual assault then their discretion in the matter of permissible evidence is a reasonable way to deal with a difficult collision of rights.

This approach should work to uphold the right of an accused to a fair trial without sacrificing the right of victims to seek and find justice through the legal system.

The only way to tell is to put this approach to the test and, under Canada's system of justice, there is no better place for that than in a court of law.

San Francisco Chronicle
San Francisco, California, August 30, 1991

AN UNWISE decision by the Supreme Court of Canada may set a dangerous precedent by jeopardizing a woman's willingness to come forward and identify her assailant in a sexual attack.

The court ruled that the past sexual behavior of rape victims may be brought forth by intrusive questioning and offered in evidence, at the trial judge's discretion, where it may serve a useful purpose.

Every state in the United States maintains a "rape shield" law preventing the introduction of evidence about a victim's past sexual history, with certain exceptions, such as previous consensual sex with the defendant. Current interest in the rights of the accused and those of victims has been stimulated by the forthcoming rape trial in Florida of William Kennedy Smith.

THE CANADIAN ruling restores the sexist-based use of sexual conduct evidence and is certain to discourage rape victims from reporting the assaults, and thus inviting the ordeal of prosecutorial questioning in court.

The London Free Press
London, Ontario, August 24, 1991

The Supreme Court of Canada has found a reasonable balance between the rights of persons accused of sexual assault and those of their accusers in striking down the law that prevented the accused from delving into the sexual past of their accusers.

The law — an attempt to protect sexual assault victims from becoming victims all over again in court at the hands of defence lawyers seeking to discredit them and thus to exculpate their clients — prohibited lawyers, except in rare circumstances, from asking victims about their sexual past.

But Justice Beverley McLachlin, who wrote the 7-2 majority decision, said the "rape shield law" is unconstitutional because it could lead to innocent people being convicted.

"In achieving its purpose — the abolition of the outmoded, sexist-based use of sexual conduct evidence — it overshoots the mark and renders inadmissible evidence which may be essential to the presentation of legitimate defences and hence to a fair trial," McLachlin wrote.

But the court clearly did not declare open season on sexual-assault victims for defence lawyers on fishing expeditions, giving power of discretion to trial judges to assess the proposed evidence in the absence of juries to determine its relevance. Quite likely, the exercise of that discretion will be subject to future appeals to higher courts until some general guidelines as to what is appropriate and just is determined.

The two women justices on the court split on the issue. Indeed, Justice Claire l'Heureux-Dube wrote a strongly-worded dissent, arguing that the sexist attitudes of some trial judges remains and make the law still necessary. Those obnoxious attitudes are mercifully being weeded out, but the division between McLachlin and l'Heureux Dube demonstrates that many such controversial issues are not all black and white and need not, indeed should not become ideological battlegrounds.

Finding the appropriate balance between competing rights or social values — in this case, the Canadian Civil Liberties Association supported the challenge to the law against feminist groups which are its usual allies — is an often-daunting task. The Supreme Court has at least pointed the way toward a fairer and just balance.

The Leader Post
Regina, Saskatchewan, August 24, 1991

While traditionally Justice is depicted as blindfolded, in balancing the scales of justice, our judiciary must keep an eye peeled toward societal shifts and sensitivities.

That fact came into play when in 1983 changes to the Criminal Code made it inadmissible to question a sexual assault victim about her past sexual activity. Prior to the code changes, defence lawyers often probed into a victim's background. That left many women uncomfortable and unwilling to pursue sexual assault charges. The 1983 changes to the law were positive in making women more willing to press charges against alleged assailants.

Yet, it's argued that this "rape shield" (section 276 of the Criminal Code) preventing delving into a victim's past and possibly discrediting her testimony, prevented defence lawyers from adequately defending their clients.

This week, a 7-2 Supreme Court of Canada decision ruled the rape shield provision was unconstitutional on grounds that "it overshoots the mark and renders inadmissible evidence which may be essential to the presentation of legitimate defences and hence a fair trial". According to the ruling, Criminal Code section 276 may raise the risk of an innocent person being convicted.

Understandably, the judgment is seen by many women's rights advocates as turning back the clock. Yet it is apparent that the court remains sensitive of the 1983 Criminal Code amendments. The type of evidence precluded under section 276 will be admissible only at the discretion of a judge — something that critics maintain will make judicial personality more important than judicial principle in admission of evidence.

There is no doubt that some judges have been guilty of some Neanderthal statements betraying outdated and unacceptable perceptions of women. However, in recent years, such statements have been swiftly condemned, and there is an increased tendency, through seminars and other means, to sensitize the bench to shifting social trends.

The issues at stake in this Supreme Court decision don't lend themselves to facile judgment and it seems that in searching for justice and fairness for both the victim and the accused, it well may be necessary to further adjust and shift the legal weights.

Edmonton Journal
Edmonton, Alberta, August 23, 1991

The sexual history of a raped woman is nobody's business but her own. Her intimate relationships are irrelevant to the prosecution of a criminal assault.

The Supreme Court of Canada retreated into a darker era on Thursday when it ruled that assault victims can be cross-examined about their unrelated sexual activity. The ruling will only discourage women and children from reporting their allegations to police, and from testifying in court. How many adults, men or women, would be willing to expose their personal lives to such painful scrutiny? And what possible link could there be between a voluntary relationship of pleasure and a separate act of uninvited violence?

The Supreme Court struck down a 1983 provision in the Criminal Code which prohibits defence lawyers from grilling victims about their sexual past. In the court's view, the so-called "rape shield" law could interfere with an accused man's right to a fair trial guaranteed in the Charter of Rights and Freedoms. But hidden in the court's attempt to promote "fundamental justice," is the risk that sexual assault victims will be exposed to far greater injustice.

The Supreme Court justices understand the hazards. They make it clear in their ruling that they do not endorse the "outmoded, sexist-based use of sexual conduct evidence." Madam Justice Beverley McLachlin was careful to note that "the fishing expeditions, which unfortunately did occur in the past, should not be permitted." The court said the trial judge should decide on the value of the testimony with great caution, and warn jurors against using it improperly. But the justices emphasized that a universal prohibition on any type of evidence contradicts the important principle that each case must be tried on its own merits.

In a perfect world, the Supreme Court might be right on this point. In a perfect world, there would be no overzealous defence lawyers ready to exploit a jury's prejudices about unchaste women. And there would be no judges willing to allow such an unwarranted cross-examination in their courtrooms.

We live in an imperfect world, of course. Lawyers and judges and juries are vulnerable to the social prejudices and sexism of their society as much as anyone else. That's why the federal government listened to women's organizations and advocates for children's rights who complained for years that the criminal justice system put victims on trial, rather than sexual offenders. That's why the law was changed to protect the innocent from intrusive questions.

Canadians no longer want to live in a society that regards a sexually experienced woman with contempt. The old-fashioned phrase that marriage "made an honest woman of her" no longer carries the court's sanction. A prostitute's word against her alleged assailant should be considered no less trustworthy than a virgin teenager's testimony. A rape is a rape. It is an act of power and violence, not a sexual union of any description.

Sexual assault trials are fairer to the victim than they once were, but they will always be an ordeal. The private circumstances of the crime are a challenge to both the prosecution and the defence; they protect the true offender but leave the innocent man at great risk of unfair prosecution. Most of all, a trial about an assault that no one witnesses will always be pure torment for the victim.

The rape shield law was sensible and necessary. The Supreme Court's decision leaves sexual assault victims with little shield at all.

Date Rape Law Introduced; Rape Shield Law Reformed

Canadian Justice Minister Kim Campbell Dec. 12, 1991 introduced in the House of Commons legislation designed to create a legal distinction between consensual sexual activity and acquaintance rape.

The proposed law stated that a man could not defend himself against a rape charge by claiming that he had mistakenly thought the woman had agreed to have sex. It said the standard to be used in future trials would be whether a rational and reasonable third person, considering all of the circumstances, would conclude that consent had been given. An accused rapist would have to prove that he had taken "all reasonable steps" to ascertain that the woman had given her consent.

The bill also set out strict limits governing the introduction of evidence about an alleged rape victim's sexual past. The move was in response to a recent Supreme Court decision that had overturned part of a previous Canadian law shielding rape victims from being cross-examined about their sexual history.

In deciding whether to allow such evidence, a judge would have to hold a private hearing. The judge would be required to take into account several factors, including whether the information would pose a risk to the woman's privacy and dignity, and whether it might violate society's interest in encouraging the reporting of sexual offenses.

The proposed law was attacked by many defense lawyers and some Conservative members of Parliament, who argued that it was unconstitutional.

StarPhoenix
Saskatoon, Sakatchewan, December 17, 1991

If Canada's newly proposed rape shield legislation was in place and a case similar to that of William Kennedy Smith's were to occur in a Canadian court, the outcome might well be different.

Smith was acquitted on a rape charge because the jury couldn't find him guilty beyond a reasonable doubt. At issue was whether the woman consented to sexual relations with Smith. Essentially, it was her word against his.

The discussion of consent in Justice Minister Kim Campbell's new bill would prove valuable in sorting out such a dilemma. Consent is defined as "the voluntary agreement of the complainant to engage in the sexual activity in question."

A defendant can't say he believed there was consent it he didn't take all reasonable steps to ascertain the woman was consenting. Also, there's no consent if she expresses disagreement verbally or through her conduct. Consent isn't obtained if the complainant was too drunk to agree or complied because the accused had a position of trust or authority.

The bill limits the circumstances under which a man might claim the honest but mistaken belief that a woman had agreed to sex. The key in a case like the Smith trial would be whether the accused had taken "all reasonable steps" to ascertain consent.

While the bill, at this point, doesn't define reasonable steps, it at least allows a judge or jury to apply the test of community values and expectations to the accused's conduct.

This is not to say the jury's finding in the Smith case was faulty. But with the new law as it is proposed, juries and judges in Canada will have more tools at their disposal to sort through the myths and misconceptions about women and rape.

Campbell has done an admirable job with the new bill. It does not focus only on the issue of consent but also imposes restrictions on the admissability of evidence on the woman's sexual history, even with the accused. It is hoped Parliament supports this initiative.

Winnipeg Free Press
Winnipeg, Manitoba, December 14, 1991

Justice Minister Kim Campbell has done a very good job in balancing the rights of accused and victims in sexual assault cases with respect to past sexual activity. Her bill to replace the rape shield law struck down in August is a good compromise that should satisfy women and legal defenders of men accused of rape. Her effort to define the issue of consent is less even and requires some revision before it becomes law.

Ms. Campbell was right to listen to the pleas of women's groups to draft a new protective law after the Supreme Court of Canada ruling. The court found the almost unlimited prohibition on inquiry into the victim's sexual activity limited the right of an accused to fair trial. It again opened the door to fishing expeditions by defence lawyers that could humiliate and intimidate victims. More importantly, the absence of any shield at all was likely to deter victims from taking part in procedures that left them open to public revictimization.

The new bill requires judges to consider, among other things, the victim's right to personal dignity and privacy. It requires judges to remember society's interest in the reporting of sexual assault cases. It does not require that any victim be a witness in the *voire dire* hearing that must precede any evidence finding its way to a jury or to the public. The fishing expeditions and grilling of victims will no longer be tolerated. It provides a just balance.

On the matter of consent to sexual activity, however, the bill's balance grows tipsy. It would certainly come crashing down if the justice minister agrees to the wishes of women's groups to further amend the bill to remove its gender neutrality.

The minister and her advisers, in fact, have not devised a new definition of consent as the bill was touted to do some weeks ago. They have instead provided a few examples of instances when consent is not given. No clearly means no when it is expressed by words or conduct. Yes can't be given by a partner, parent or friend. Yes can't be presumed by a boss or anyone else in a position of trust or authority. No one should quarrel with those circumstances.

The more troubling examples, however, might have yes meaning no if the victim was drunk or if yes was said repeatedly and then became a last-second no. The bill will require much firmer distinctions between a victim so drunk that consent couldn't granted and a victim whose self-induced tipsiness stirred along thoughts that a yes would be fitting but had second-thoughts along with a morning hangover. The bill would require some virtually impossible distinctions on last-second changes of heart and of glands to judge when passion must take the cold shower of reason. As it stands, it places no onus at all on victims to know their own minds and assume any responsibility.

The gender neutrality of the bill as it's drafted has raised speculation that a man could accuse a woman of sexual assault if he was intoxicated at the time of an encounter. Women's groups would like a change in the preamble to assert that sexual assault is a "gender bias crime"— a crime against women. Neither the bill nor that amendment is a satifactory way to codify the subtleties of human behavior. The minister should welcome other suggestions, and if no better ones surface, delete the troublesome clauses. Only in Canada would candy be dandy but liquor a crime.

THE CHRONICLE-HERALD
Halifax, Nova Scotia, December 16, 1991

WHEN THE Supreme Court of Canada struck down the so-called rape shield provisions of the Criminal Code, the stage was set for an all-out battle over whose rights most need protection in cases of sexual assault — those of victims or those of the accused. Last week Justice Minister Kim Campbell presented a bill which aims to balance the debate.

The proposed legislation attempts to do what the Supreme Court of Canada said that former Criminal Code provisions did not — protect the accused in all cases. In a majority decision in August, the Supreme Court ruled that a blanket ban on evidence pertaining to the complainant's sexual history could sometimes impede the right to a fair trial by making evidence inadmissible.

Critics of the decision rightly argued that past sexual relations usually have little bearing on the two matters most crucial to a rape case — consent and credibility — and that many victims, fearing harassment in court, would refuse to testify without assurances of privacy.

Ms. Campbell's proposed remedy is twofold. First she takes the Supreme Court decision's advice and proposes that the pertinence of a complainant's history be determined during a private hearing. The legislation says judges should only allow such evidence when it is so crucial to a defendant's case that it outweighs society's interest in protecting a complainant's right to privacy and encouraging prosecutions.

Second, in a preamble to the law (the first ever in Canadian history) she emphasizes the need for discretion by stating that past history is "rarely relevant" and that prosecution of such offences must be encouraged. (These explanations are also clearly aimed at quieting concerns over studies, like one based in Nova Scotia, which have presented evidence of some gender bias by the male-dominated judiciary.)

But the legislation goes further, closing loopholes in previous laws by introducing a definition of consent for the first time.

It says consent must be considered the "voluntary agreement of the complainant to engage in the sexual activity in question." It stipulates that such consent is not obtained if the complainant expresses lack of agreement by words or conduct, if the complainant was too drunk to agree, or complied because the accused held a position of trust or authority. It precludes the defendant's intoxication as a defence and states that all "reasonable steps" must be taken to assure consent was acquired previous to the act.

These provisions are sure to spark controversy. Aimed at reinforcing that "no means no", they, sadly, can do little to end the ambiguity which so often accompanies these trials. Key evidence is often "he said, she said" in nature, as was shown in the recent William Kennedy Smith trial in the U.S.

Nonetheless, the proposed legislation is a step forward. It sets standards which meet the tests of fairness and common sense. It speaks to society's need to treat sexual assault as a serious crime. And it attempts to balance scales of justice which (like societal thinking) have often seemed weighted against the victim but which, as the Supreme Court ruling showed, could also impede fair trials for accused.

Lawyers, legislators and concerned citizens will now debate the proposals and amendments may be made. But, in the end, this seemingly sensible approach can only be truly tested in the courts of the land.

The Evening Telegram
St. John's, Newfoundland, December 16, 1991

Last August, when the Supreme Court of Canada struck down the 1982 rape shield law that banned questioning, in sexual assault trials, of a woman's sexual history, Justice Minister Kim Campbell set out to replace it quickly with a law that would strike a balance between the rights of both the accused and complainant. It appears she has succeeded in large measure.

The original law was ruled invalid because, as the court said, its blanket application to all cases violated the Charter of Rights. It was found as well to restrict the rights of the accused to a complete and fair defence.

Ms. Campbell has adequately dealt with this by designing a law that allows for a case-by-case consideration.

A defence lawyer who wishes to question a woman's sexual past must first submit this request in writing to the judge. The judge must then clear the court of the jury and the public, hear the evidence presented, and decide whether it is relevant.

Critics say this still leaves too much discretionary power in the hands of predominantly male judges, but Ms. Campbell's preamble to the new law helps curtail some of this power.

It is the first such preamble to a law in the Criminal Code. In it is a statement of what parliament believes — that a victim's sexual past is "rarely relevant" in rape cases, and this belief carries the same weight as law. Any judge must base his or her decision on this, as well as guidelines set by parliament.

In the space of little more than three months, the minister consulted with women's groups and introduced what many are calling the "no means no" law — one that defines what is and is not consent to sexual intercourse. It limits the circumstances in which a man can claim he misunderstood what the woman said or did, leading to a "mistaken belief" that she did not mean "no."

Under the new law, consent is defined as "the voluntary agreement of the complainant to enage in the sexual actvity in question." Consent is not obtained if the complainant expresses "no" by "words or conduct," if the complainant was too drunk, or if consent was given by a third party. As well, the accused may no longer claim his own drunkeness as a defence.

By focussing on a definition of consent, Ms. Campbell has limited the instances in which a woman's sexual history may be deemed a relevant aspect of the accused's defence.

Women's groups are generally pleased with the new law, saying it is better than the old one. And the two main federal opposition parties say they support the bill in the House of Commons.

Rarely has such an important matter beem dealt with so readily, and with the absence of partisan rancour. Clearly, the political parties are seized of the issue, comprehend it, and are determined to deal with it expeditiously.

It is a rare positive sign that Parliament can function as perhaps it should — when it realizes it has to.

Battered Women Issues Become Focus of National Debate

Wife beating or battering is often cited as the most underreported crime in the nation. Experts estimate that for those who are married the chances of being assaulted by one's spouse are somewhere between one in four and one in three. Most observers believe that estimates of 2,000,000 American women and children battered and beaten by family members are much too low. Not all violence is physical; sometimes it takes the form of ongoing, humiliating assaults on the woman's self-esteem.

With the resurgence of the women's movement during the 1960s. Nevertheless, more than a quarter of a century later the situation of abused women was only slightly improved. Services available to victims had increased, yet individual women faced the same old problems in gaining protection from her spouse or a live-in lover – or from a former spouse or lover.

The popular culture of the 1930s through the 1950s, in movies, comic strips, and radio programs, often featured a man "henpecked" and browbeaten by his wife. The idea was a joke and never reflected the reality of everyday domestic life. When the issue of wife battering came to national attention in the late 1960s and early 1970s, the media – and sometimes feminists – renamed the practice spouse abuse or domestic violence. Other feminists argue that these terms obscure the seriousness of the situation and imply that the behavior is really a two-way street.

There are physical reasons why women are beaten much more often than men. The average woman is physically smaller and has less muscular strength than the average man. Unless a woman attacks a man with a weapon, in a battle, she is the one who is more likely to get hurt. Moreover, a great deal of research has accumulated to establish that women as a group are far less violent than men.

The Des Moines Register
Des Moines, Iowa, February 23, 1993

There's just no telling what's liable to kill a wife these days.

Last week's papers brought stories about the grisly and seemingly freakish deaths of women in two unrelated incidents.

In one — the subject of an Iowa Supreme Court ruling — Brenda Torres of Independence had bled to death from falling on a shard of glass from a lamp her husband had smashed in a fit of rage.

In another, Melissa Wemark of Ridgeway, near Decorah, died of multiple stab wounds from a knife. Her estranged husband, who sits in jail charged with murder, says she accidentally fell on the knife.

Even if that excuse were plausible, and even if Torres' death could not have been foretold in the other case, death can hardly be called accidental when it is the end point of a violent relationship between domestic partners.

In the first case, the Supreme Court narrowly overturned Jimmy Torres Jr.'s conviction for involuntary manslaughter, ruling that he could not have foreseen that his smashing the lamp would result in Brenda's death.

Maybe not. But had he not brutally assaulted her just before that, ripping off her shirt and bra, smacking her face and head with his hands and other objects, according to an autopsy report, and then storming out of the room sweeping the lamp off the table — all when she was drunk — it's unlikely she'd be dead.

Melissa Wemark reportedly suffered a history of violence by her husband, the

> **Workers in the law-enforcement and mental-health communities who see evidence along the way must step in, act to stop it, prosecute to the full extent of the law.**

second of his two wives to do so. The record is filled with evidence of his plans to kill the first wife and kidnap his son. He made good on the latter threat, but all records of his two-year suspended sentence were expunged.

Sooner or later, unchecked violence in the home is likely to lead to tragedy. Those in the law-enforcement and mental-health communities who see evidence along the way must step in, act to stop it, prosecute to the full extent of the law.

A freak death by one judge's definition is, by another's, a death that was waiting to happen.

THE PLAIN DEALER
Cleveland, Ohio, March 3, 1993

As legislators begin the bulky task of scrutinizing the proposed state budget, it might be tempting to trim some smaller items. At least one deserves protection, because Ohio women deserve protection. Lawmakers should leave intact, if not add to, money directed to domestic violence programs.

Not much has been heard about such efforts since 1991, when state officials snuffed one portion of an advertising campaign aimed at reducing domestic violence. In that poster, a frightened woman and child were shown making a telephone call as the shadowy figure of a man loomed in the background. The text read, "Domestic violence is a crime in Ohio. Quit before you hit."

Department of Human Services officials pulled the poster, saying "It was a matter of taste." Gov. George V. Voinovich's administration then scurried to say that scrubbing the poster did not mean the governor would ignore the cause of women victimized by spouses or boyfriends.

That is a necessary view to hold. The demand for services that deal with women fleeing violent situations is growing, said Nancy Neylon, of Templum House in Cleveland. There was a 20% increase in the number of women served by the Templum House's legal advocacy program from 1991 to 1992. The agency is working with about 2,000 women in the suburban court system alone.

To his credit, Voinovich has, indeed, shown some interest in reducing domestic violence. Other initiatives from the state human services department continued after the posters were pulled. Voinovich has proposed increasing the current funding of $259,143 for domestic violence programs by $1.1 million in fiscal year 1995. There would be no increase in fiscal year 1994, which begins this July 1.

The 1995 addition is welcome, but it still leaves Ohio in the bottom third of the country when looking at state population versus the amount of state money for domestic violence programs, Neylon said.

At the very least, legislators should not touch the overall amount Voinovich would direct to these programs in the biennial budget. Ideally, lawmakers should find some way to boost money for shelters and other programs. A legislative proposal that deserves consideration calls for raising the state marriage license fee, which goes for domestic violence programs.

Voinovich and human services officials also should realize that it is domestic violence that is a matter of poor taste. The problem mandates dramatic responses that will catch people's attention long enough to make them think, and, possibly, react responsibly. More money is good. So is more courage to confront an unacceptable problem.

LAS VEGAS REVIEW-JOURNAL
Las Vegas, Nevada, February 2, 1993

Watching the Super Bowl gets men in the mood — to feed their wives knuckle sandwiches. Or so claimed some women's groups last week in advance of the Cowboys-Bills showdown.

It sounded suspiciously like another attempt by radical feminists to nurture distrust of guys for doing guy stuff, and that's precisely what it turned out to be.

The women's groups that weighed in on the issue asserted the Super Bowl, with its mix of stylized violence, cheerleaders in minimalist outfits, beer, and — most heinous of all — male bonding, prompts men to clobber their wives.

Problem was, the whole uproar over the Super Bowl being a field day for wife-beaters was twaddle. The Washington Post checked it out and discovered the activists had cooked the stats to hype their claims.

It brought to mind those rape statistics bandied about by other feminists who are fond of asserting that one out of every three or four women will be raped in her lifetime. But consider the Las Vegas statistics, just released. Granted, some rapes aren't reported, but last year Metro investigated 393 sexual assaults. Even assuming every investigation involved actual and not simply alleged rape, annual assaults on 393 of the Las Vegas area's 400,000 females mean the average woman would have to live to be at least 254 years old to suffer rape, if one out of four is raped in her lifetime.

The late activist Mitch Snyder used to yell about the nation's "3 million homeless" — a bald fiction. The best study of homelessness, by the U.S. Census Bureau in 1990, put the figure at 228,621.

Then there was the kid-snatching scam, perpetrated by well-meaning groups concerned about missing children. These groups in the mid-1980s claimed tens of thousands of children were grabbed off the streets by strangers every year; it caused quite a panic. Problem was, excluding parental custody disputes, the FBI didn't have tens of thousands of such cases on the books — just a handful.

Some argue that problems such as kidnapping, homelessness, rape and wife beating are so severe that gathering accurate statistics is trivial. But it's not. Taxpayers' money and law enforcement and social resources are allocated based on the perceived severity of these problems. Trying to house 3 million homeless people is a waste if there are only 228,000 of them. Focusing energy and resources on Super Bowl wife-beating is idiotic if the phenomenon is a fairy tale.

Let's devote our energies to solving real problems instead of focusing on new ones dreamed up to supercharge some squirrelly political agenda. Worthy causes, such as fighting rape or curtailing spouse abuse, ultimately are undermined when their more hysterical advocates stoop to con artistry.

The Virginian-Pilot
Norfolk, Virginia, February 3, 1993

Do you know who got beat Sunday, besides the Buffalo Bills?

Sound like a joke? It isn't. The answer is: too many women by too many men in too many places.

Could you say, then, as did a spokeswoman for a California women's advocacy group last week, that reports of battered women go up 40 percent on Super Bowl Sunday?

No, you couldn't, not according to authoritative studies or records kept by abuse hot lines. Nor should you conclude, though some women's groups continue to imply, that the Super Bowl causes men to batter women.

Any party situation, say experts on such abuse, can exacerbate the abuse of alcohol and illegal drugs that often triggers a man's battery of a woman. And reports of battery may — or may not — rise in the hometown of a Super Bowl team or in the city where the game is played.

But the battle for power and control that prompts such abuse — typically though not always a man's abuse of a woman — requires no alcohol, no party atmosphere, no smash-and-bash on a TV screen.

Yet again this year some feminist groups perpetuated the Super Bowl-battery myth, even to the extent of misquoting, misrepresenting and misinterpreting studies to bolster it. They do battered women a double disservice:

By singling out Super Bowl Sunday as a "day of dread," they understate the ongoing, constant, daily dread of battered women.

And by forcing authorities to repeatedly debunk the connection as fable, they perpetuate a far more dangerous myth: that the incidence of battery is overstated, that the issue of battered women is just one more weapon feminists wield to wallop men. Worse, they invite the inference that stopping spouse abuse is as simple as stopping football.

The reasons men batter the women in their lives aren't that simple. Neither are the remedies. The reasons women stay with batterers, even return to them, are less simple still. Simple and short-term remedies like shelters help. Distortions never do.

Richmond Times-Dispatch
Richmond, Virginia, February 4, 1993

Fans tuned in to the Super Bowl likely saw a public-service announcement against wife-beating. The segment was the culmination of a media campaign by certain women's rights organizations, which convinced NBC it should give up the pricey air-time because of the harm football causes women.

Earlier in the week, one group declared Super Bowl Sunday "the biggest day of the year for violence against women." *The Boston Globe* reported a 40 percent increase in wife-beatings on past Super Bowl Sundays. And at a Los Angeles news conference, Sheila Kuehl of the California Women's Law Center cited a study by sociologists at Old Dominion University as part of a similar claim. "This game is terrifying for far too many women," she said.

But the claims are false.

When asked by *The Washington Post* about the study, one of the ODU professors involved replied, "That's not what we found at all." The *Globe* reporter said she learned of the study from feminist-leaning Fairness and Accuracy in Reporting (FAIR), which was present at the L.A. news conference. And FAIR's representative said she knew at the time that Sheila Kuehl wasn't telling the truth, but wouldn't say so in front of reporters. So much for fairness and accuracy.

Wife-beaters ought to go to cold jails for long stays. But women's rights activists ought to be able to say so without lying — and without implying that football turns the average Joe into a cretinous goon.

… — BATTERED WOMEN

THE BLADE
Toledo, Ohio, February 4, 1993

FAR more significant than the outcome of this year's Super Bowl was the point made over the weekend that women all too often are victims of post-Super Bowl male violence. It's a point that shouldn't be neglected even though the outcome of this year's game is now history.

Groups concerned about abuse aimed at women said before the Sunday event that battered-women shelters and violence hotlines are flooded with calls during and after the Super Bowl game. Critics, however, countered that no appreciable increase in violence-related complaints was reported.

Watching football, however, often involves drinking large quantities of alcoholic beverages, lending some credence to the conclusions of the committee.

The American sports culture isn't going to change. The Super Bowl will be back in place next year, as always. But just as a slowly changing attitude toward drunk driving, for example, has altered behavior, so too must it become clear that sports-provoked violence directed at family members or anyone else cannot be tolerated.

BOSTON HERALD
Boston, Massachusetts, March 25, 1993

Every 13 days in Massachusetts, on average, a woman is killed by a man who claims to have once loved her.

Domestic violence is an epidemic that is way out of control — here and throughout this country.

What makes a man kill?
Too much violence on TV?
Too much frustration at work?
Not enough money or a decent job?
A family history of violence — a mother, father who abused each other and then their kids?
Jealousy? Despair? Drink? Drugs?
Where have men learned that they can get away with this?

A seemingly unrelated study might shed some light on the whys of domestic violence. Seventeen magazine and Wellesley College, in the first nationwide study of sexual harassment in schools, surveyed 4,200 girls between the ages of 9 and 19. What they discovered is that young boys harass girls regularly — and they get away with it.

Some 89 percent of the girls who responded to the survey reported that they had been the subject of sexual comments, gestures and looks; 83 percent said they had been touched, pinched or grabbed; and more than two-thirds of the girls wrote that the harassment had occurred in the presence of other people.

"I have told teachers about this a number of times; each time nothing was done about it;" wrote a 13-year-old girl from Pennsylvania. "Teachers would act as if I had done something to cause it."

A 12-year old from Michigan said that her principal had had a "little talk" with several boys who sexually harassed her. But "the boys came out laughing cause they got no punishment."

Nan Stein, the study's principal author, believes that when adults do nothing to stop boys from harassing girls, they "get the message that it's permitted."

So on it goes. "The girls begin to sound like battered women," Stein said.

And what we now know is that far too many of them will go on to become battered women.

Boys use words to wound. Men use fists and knives and guns. When a society tolerates the one, it gives license to the other. Respect has to be taught early and disrespect has to be punished. The place to start is the classroom.

THE KANSAS CITY STAR
Kansas City, Missouri, February 5, 1993

In the wake of Super Bowl Sunday, people are reminded that violence permeates society and most of it is painfully serious.

Researchers have looked at professional football as a possible trigger for domestic violence, calling studies to date inconclusive. The sadness is that the crime is epidemic with or without football. A generation ago, battering was mostly considered a private matter, as long as it took place behind the closed doors of the home. The usual victims — wife, young children, frail elderly — were dependent and voiceless.

Statistics gathered by the American Medical Association and the National Coalition Against Domestic Violence are depressing. Every year, more than 2 million women are abused in the U.S. If there's spousal abuse in the home, children are abused at a rate 1,500 percent higher than the national average.

Violence is passed from generation to generation. Violent behavior is learned behavior. Parents, teachers and others can teach ways of resolving conflicts or handling fustrations that don't include hitting, kicking, pushing or taunting other people.

Pro football may require such behavior. Real life doesn't.

THE LINCOLN STAR
Lincoln, Nebraska, Febraury 5, 1993

Activists seized on the Super Bowl to draw awareness to battered women.

The ploy may have backfired.

Linda Mitchell of Fairness & Accuracy in Reporting and Sheila Kuehl of the California Women's Law Center cited a study to claim that violence against women increased as a direct result of men watching the Super Bowl. In response, NBC aired a public service announcement before the Super Bowl that pointed out wife beating could get a man thrown in jail.

The researchers, however, said the study was misused, the results distorted.

Exaggeration and hyperbole may draw headlines and attention, but over time people wise up. Unfortunately, they get cynical and turn off.

Domestic violence scars children, kills women and it happens every day of the year. It is the leading cause of death and injury for American women.

Marcy Metzger, the director of the Lincoln Rape/Spouse Abuse Center, said the local crisis line didn't show a jump in calls after the football game ended.

But "institutionalized days" — New Year's, Big Red football Saturdays, even Thanksgiving — in which large amounts of alcohol are consumed while violent games play on TV traditionally means more calls to crisis lines.

The connection between football — admittedly a hard-hitting, macho kind of sport — and battering women is conjecture. But alcohol is no stranger to domestic disputes.

Irresponsible drinking is a problem of mammoth proportions in our society. Abuse, murder, vehicular homicides and injury accidents, brawls of all sorts, erupt from alcohol.

Still it is easy to blame other factors: financial stress, job loss, drinking, football. Any and all may be precipitators. But the real issues are power and control, and in too many cases sons learned at their father's knee that they could beat and berate the women in their lives.

There's no need to exaggerate. The truth is bad enough.

THE WALL STREET JOURNAL.
New York City, New York, February 5, 1993

It was not unlike Orson Welles's "War of the Worlds"—the radio broadcast whose report of an invasion from another planet produced panic among gulled listeners. But this time it wasn't the public that panicked.

Shortly before Super Bowl Sunday, word went forth from a devoutly progressive media "watchdog" group called Fairness and Accuracy in Reporting (FAIR) that on the big football day wives and girlfriends en masse could expect to be battered and assaulted by the man of the house. And indeed, NBC broadcast a somber public service spot before the game, announcing that "domestic violence is a crime."

Word went forth also that "studies" existed, proving that woman-battering by football-crazed husbands and boyfriends rose by an astounding 40% on Super Bowl Sundays—that battered women's shelters were besieged on this day by calls for help. Thus, FAIR's specter of shelters' staffs grimly awaiting the blood-drenched tides of victims seeking refuge from males run amok during the Bills and Cowboys game.

All these pronouncements were received as sacred writ by an entirely credulous army of journalists. We are talking here, after all, about the toughest investigative battalions. But feed them a story about mass victimization and how the women of the nation have to go into hiding on a certain Sunday of the year, and they have no questions.

In addition to the air time given this myth by NBC, ABC and CBS, the Boston Globe reported, "Domestic violence hot lines light up as game kicks off...." The San Francisco Examiner recorded the reflections of a woman remembering how she walked down a San Francisco street having "this feeling of dread" during a game, because there were sure to be so many battered women that night.

Michael Collier of the Oakland Tribune wrote with evident assurance that the Super Bowl causes "boyfriends, husbands and fathers" who watch the game to "explode like mad linemen leaving girlfriends, wives and children beaten."

A Toronto Star writer instructed readers that "the Super Bowl's most brutal hits will occur in living rooms across Canada and the United States." The list of media believers who embraced the story goes on and on.

The Super Bowl ring, however, goes to an exceedingly anxious Robert Lipsyte of the New York Times: "A big game electrifies the rec-room with violent action and sexy advertising, heightening male-female tensions, creating a climate of aggression.... Someone shut up that kid or someone's going to get pounded."

There was one exception to all this. The Washington Post's Ken Ringle decided to look into the Day of Dread story. He pursued an arcane reporting technique that has apparently slipped from favor: Mr. Ringle called up the source of the original story to ask if it were true.

The basis for the FAIR activists' sensational assertions about Super Bowl Sunday was an Old Dominion University study that, they said, concluded that beatings and hospital admissions rose 40% after Washington Redskins' football victories. "That's not what we found at all," Professor Janet Katz, one of the authors of the study, told Mr. Ringle. There were some "very tentative findings" about women receiving treatment after televised football games, but the study "certainly doesn't support what these women are saying," the professor concluded.

FAIR's publicists, Dobisky Associates, also quoted forensic psychologist Charles Patrick Ewing as having declared Super Bowl Sunday a day when agencies get most reports of domestic battering and violence. Mr. Ewing told the Post: "I never said that." Further, "I don't know that to be true."

David Silber, the chairman of the psychology department at George Washington University and an expert on domestic violence told the Post's reporter: "I know of no study documenting any such link" between domestic violence and football. "And I know the literature very well."

FAIR representative Linda Mitchell said that she recognized during a Super Bowl news conference that an attorney for the California Women's Law Center was misrepresenting the Old Dominion study. But this member of a media watchdog group devoted to "fairness and accuracy" hadn't corrected her colleague's statements, believing that "she has a right to report it as she wants."

There's some fear that this fiasco has hurt the credibility of efforts to curtail the beating of spouses. Not so. It has mainly hurt the relationship between groups like FAIR and reporters whose sympathies get in the way of doing their jobs right.

The Oregonian
Portland, Oregon, February 4, 1993

Not all of the Super Bowl hype was about football. Some inflated claims were made by women's groups alleging that Super Bowl Sundays are the worst day of the year for domestic violence.

Early reports from across the country suggest that wasn't necessarily true of last Sunday, although one Portland crisis line reported three times as many calls as usual. Nor was there any solid evidence that previous Super Bowl Sundays brought dramatic increases in violence against women.

The Washington Post's reporter Ken Ringle blamed the hype on "a network of feminist activists" who he said "orchestrated a national campaign to ask males to stop beating their wives and girlfriends after the Super Bowl."

Advocacy groups that exaggerate their claims risk harming their own causes by undermining their credibility and misdirecting public attention and concern. And there is no need for overblown claims about domestic violence.

It is a deadly serious problem. The American Medical Association cites conservative estimates of 2 million women per year who are assaulted by their domestic partners. Around 30 percent of all women murder victims are killed by husbands or boyfriends.

Among other questionable claims, however, Ringle found that:

• The California Women's Law Center, which called a pre-Super Bowl press conference, admittedly misrepresented research associated with Washington, D.C., pro football games in 1988 and 1989. The center claimed a 40 percent increase in domestic violence after games Washington won, when in fact emergency-room admissions were only "slightly higher." Janet Katz, one of the researchers involved, said even that finding was "very tentative."

• Patrick Ewing, a forensic psychologist who wrote "Battered Women Who Kill," was quoted by a public-relations firm as saying Super Bowl days were among the worst of the year for domestic violence. "I never said that," Ewing retorted. "I don't know that to be true."

• Lenore E. Walker, a Denver psychiatrist, claimed on network television to have compiled a 10-year record of Super Bowl-related violence against women. Another psychiatrist to whom her office referred calls was at a loss to explain her claim.

• "More folklore than fact" is the way such assertions struck George Washington University's David Silber, a nationally recognized scholar on domestic violence. "I know of no study documenting any such link," he said.

One thing the hype did accomplish was getting a public-service announcement about domestic violence on NBC during the Super Bowl broadcast, which reached an estimated 120 million people. If that was the intent of this misguided campaign, the price in lost credibility was too high.

The Oregonian
Portland, Oregon, September 3, 1992

The casual acceptance of preventable death goes against the grain of most doctors. So it is no surprise that the American Medical Association has decided to wage war against violence.

Maybe you can help, too.

It is especially fitting that one of the association's primary targets is domestic violence. A battered woman's death often follows repeated injuries, many of which are treated in emergency rooms or doctor's offices.

How pervasive is the problem of domestic violence?

• One-third of all women murdered in the United States are killed by husbands or boyfriends.

• Nearly a quarter of American women will be abused by a current or former partner at some time in their lives.

• Between one-fourth and one-third of all emergency-room visits by women are the result of battering.

• As many as one quarter of pregnant women seeking prenatal care are victims of abuse.

Surveys show that battered women — and men for that matter, because a small percentage of battering victims are men — are more likely to confide in their doctors about the violence they experience at home than they are to tell police, family members or the clergy. Doctors, however, have been largely unprepared to elicit or deal with those confidences effectively.

The AMA's Physicians' Campaign Against Family Violence hopes to change that. It is aimed at teaching emergency-room physicians, family doctors and specialists how to intercede and help prevent a patient's further injury from domestic violence.

Doctors are encouraged to screen for domestic violence routinely, asking questions about past and present abuse in the same nonjudgmental way they now inquire about substance abuse and sexual activity. They also are encouraged to make sure their hospitals have help available for victims of domestic violence and are hooked up with community shelters and other resources.

The emphasis is on helping a battered woman on the spot, with careful attention to her safety. If a woman chooses not to take that help, the doctor lets her know it will be available to her whenever she decides she needs it.

What is most striking about these suggestions is that they are not already being practiced widely. Domestic violence for too long has been a problem accepted, and largely ignored, by society.

The medical community clearly can play an important role in reducing the number of deaths and injuries caused by domestic violence. But its willingness to take on this challenge must also galvanize others to consider whether they, too, have been guilty of failing to act.

Coworkers and bosses, family members and religious leaders — everyone who may come in contact with the victims of domestic violence — should consider whether they can do more to help. If you'd like to join in, local women's shelters and the Oregon Coalition Against Domestic and Sexual Violence, 239-4486, can tell you what to do.

Tulsa World
Tulsa, Oklahoma, September 9, 1992

DOMESTIC violence is difficult to discuss, much less understand. Tradition has held that what happens at home is private, and that is still true — up to a point.

That point is violence by one member of the family against another — wives battered by husbands, children abused by parents, elderly attacked by their children.

Society's understanding of these family tragedies is put to the test when the abused person strikes back, killing the abuser. Usually, it is a woman, beaten by husband or boyfriend over a period of years, who finally lashes out.

Is it murder or self defense? That is for a jury to decide. However, until last spring in Oklahoma the woman was at a disadvantage. Evidence of domestic abuse and the fact that she was a victim of "battered woman syndrome" was not admissible in court as a defense.

The Legislature passed a law this session allowing the syndrome to be used as a defense. Last week the state Court of Criminal Appeals gave a boost to the law's status when it overturned the state and trial court decisions in the case of an Edmond woman convicted of killing her husband. The appeals court said testimony about the syndrome could have been used in here trial.

The point is an important one. Each case still will be decided on its merits by a jury. However, the jury will be able to hear all the facts about the threats and abuse the woman endured. It also will hear a professional psychologist explain the "battered woman syndrome" and how it applies.

Asking a jury to decide such difficult issues without hearing from all sides left a battered woman at a disadvantage. The appeals court is correct in allowing all the facts to be laid on the table.

The Daily Gazette
Schenectady, New York, September 28, 1992

A repugnant scare campaign with racist overtones may cause Montgomery County to lose a valuable opportunity to assist battered women.

A proposal by the Women's Crisis Resource Center to build a 14-unit shelter for battered women in Canajoharie was abandoned Tuesday night in response to emotional turmoil caused by a flier that contained much misinformation. Rather than fight an angry crowd that had assembled to protest, Judy Markle, the center's executive director, simply withdrew her non-profit organization's agency proposal.

The proposal was to provide shelter for 28 to 50 Montgomery, Fulton and Schoharie county women and their children for six to 18 months.

Yet the unsigned flier showed a picture of a black woman, purportedly from Brentwood, L.I., who "repeatedly squandered her Social Services rent money, was evicted from her apartment ... passed through the Social Services pipeline .. and emerged 4½ years later in a battered woman's shelter in Utica and then in the domestic violence program in Saratoga Springs." The flier, sent to hundreds of village residents, implied that the Canajoharie shelter would become a "low-income housing project" accepting women from all over the state.

In point of fact, the photo was reprinted — without permission — from a Sept. 13 Sunday Gazette story, after being cropped to eliminate a white woman. The accompanying story concerned a worthwhile program aimed at introducing battered women to traditionally male home skills — such as plumbing and carpentry — in an effort to reduce their dependence on abusive mates. It mentioned very little of the pictured woman's background, and nothing in the unflattering terms used in the flier.

The proposal was apparently sound: It was one of only three deemed eligible by the state for a Housing Trust grant ($965,000). And while the Women's Resource and Crisis Center has run into economic difficulties and is seeking to merge with a larger organization, that wouldn't have affected its ability to operate the shelter.

There were indeed some details of the program that hadn't been adequately publicized. (That was the primary purpose of Tuesday's meeting.) And the Village Board's effort to rush through a land annexation plan for the project, without a public hearing, didn't help.

But too many people of Canajoharie — including three of the village board's trustees — decided they didn't want the shelter before they really had a chance to find out what it was all about. If no alternative site can be found soon, and the state rescinds the conditional grant, the region's battered women will be the victims (again).

The Virginian-Pilot
Norfolk, Virginia, October 5, 1992

One million women, more or less, were domestic-violence victims last year, the Senate Judiciary Committee says. The committee believes that statistic understates the horror because it covers *reported* violent attacks — murders, rapes, aggravated and simple assaults. Unreported incidents, the committee conjectures, totaled about 3 million.

Appalling. Though violence involving lovers and spouses more often goes unremarked outside of families and small groups of friends and acquaintances, it is a public-safety nightmare and a public-policy challenge. It also is a public-health plague that boosts the nation's burdensome medical bill by tens of billions of dollars, as well as its onerous multibillion-dollar law-enforcement bill.

Lawmakers have responded slowly. But now several states, including Virginia, have enacted "anti-stalker" bills — to protect women, mainly, but also children and some men menaced by the angry, the obsessed and the vengeful. Federal legislation is but a matter of time.

The Senate Judiciary Committee report was released to improve prospects for enactment of the proposed Violence Against Women Act, which its sponsor, Sen. Joseph Biden, Democrat of Delaware and committee chairman, hopes against hope will pass in the closing days of the current Congress.

The bill should pass. It would permit women to bring civil cases for attacks against them because of their gender; programs to teach peaceful ways to handle domestic conflict, avert violence and seek help when threatened or victimized by violence; and stiffer laws against spouse abuse.

Police and judges are doing more and more to shield women and children from domestic violence. But thousands of women who obtain court orders to protect themselves against violent husbands, ex-husbands and lovers learn to their sorrow that the strictures are flimsy shields.

Governmental intervention in domestic violence is frequently complicated by the emotional or financial dependency of many women upon their abusers, or many women's fears of worse violence if they do. But public attention — more attention than in the past — must be paid to the plague.

The Wichita Eagle-Beacon
Wichita, Kansas, September 5, 1992

Lisa Dunn, said a jury in Topeka last week, is a victim of an abusive relationship with Daniel Remeta. A federal judge said that Ms. Dunn, convicted of murder at a trial nearly eight years ago, was denied access then to the battered-woman syndrome defense. In her new trial, she testified that Mr. Remeta had routinely raped and sodomized her and threatened her with a gun on several occasions.

Terrified that he would kill her, she didn't try to escape his murderous rampage across several states, including Kansas. Her attorneys argued that she had no other recourse but to follow him because of her fear he would kill her. The jury that reversed the conviction apparently agreed what research has revealed: Women subjected to abusive relationships can become so traumatized that they are literally unable to escape from the horrors of repeated beatings, torture, rape and verbal tyranny.

These woman can be any age and in any socioeconomic group. They are of all races, religions, cultures and educational levels. They are also all characterized by low self-esteem and they accept responsibility for their abuser's actions, since they buy into the belief that they deserve to be treated in such punishing ways. They even feel guilty for the constant battering they receive.

Women like Lisa Dunn deny the terror and anger of an abusive relationship. They present a passive face to the world as they manipulate their environments in order to prevent more violence against themselves. They truly believe that no one will be able to help them resolve their predicament. Thus, a woman who has been constantly assaulted by someone she loves, can and does continue to stay with him even though she knows that he may kill her.

Men like Daniel Remeta can belong to any demographic group. They believe in male supremacy and the stereotypical role of a male-dominated household. They are jealous, blame others for their actions, frequently use sex to enhance self-esteem and don't believe that their violent behavior should have negative consequences.

In other words, men who abuse women think it is their inherent right to do so. And the women they hurt accept their role as the abused because they see no recourse for ending the relationship. It is a tragic and much too common occurrence.

No doubt there are men who would never hit anyone no matter what the circumstances and women who would never be passive in the face of violence against themselves, who find the battered-woman syndrome to be curious at best.

In most cases, people should be held responsible for their actions. And the battered-woman defense can be abused by defense attorneys. But the syndrome is real. It does happen. A jury said it happened to Lisa Dunn.

THE LINCOLN STAR
Lincoln, Nebraska, August 13, 1992

Kary Voss of Cheyenne, Wyo., is another statistic in the column of women killed by a husband or boyfriend. Nationally, between 30 percent and 50 percent of women who are murdered die at the hands of a man with whom they have been intimate. Nine of 10 female murder victims are killed by men.

A friend said Voss was in constant fear of her ex-husband, who had broken into her home twice and threatened to kill her. She had complained to police that he harassed her and stalked her.

Her formal complaint against him for the last break-in, when he dragged her to the basement and threatened to hang her, "was in the process through municipal court," police said. Acting a bit quicker than the municipal court, Kary Voss' ex-husband shot her outside her workplace.

A police lieutenant said that Wyoming law doesn't adequately address cases in which a person is being followed, threatened and harassed. "My feelings are that Kary did everything that the system would allow her to do," the officer was quoted as saying.

THE SYSTEM is often inadequate. It can't protect people from every harm.

But, historically, it has turned a deaf ear on the screams of women suffering domestic violence. Until recently, rape wasn't a crime if committed by a husband; domestic assault perpetrators weren't arrested.

Today, women often face murder charges when they kill in self-defense or out of fear of an abuser. In Omaha, a woman faces manslaughter charges in the death of her husband. She had a restraining order against him and had filed for divorce. Her attorney has labeled it a possible battered-wife syndrome case.

Battered-wife syndrome is only now gaining recognition and acceptance as a valid defense.

But this is how reform has come. Piecemeal, spurred by sensational, often tragic cases whose effects resonate across state borders.

THE NEBRASKA Legislature, in its last regular session, passed a bill against stalking. Testimony showed how often such harassment occurs. Police testified they were often helpless to curb it.

Perhaps the Voss case will challenge Wyoming authorities to look at their laws.

The laws that protect women in these cases also protect men; they're gender neutral.

What's neither neutral nor equitable is women's vulnerability to male violence. Author Margaret Atwood relates a telling anecdote. When speaking at college campuses, she informally polls the audiences. Men are asked what they fear most about women, and women are asked what they fear most about men.

The men's response is ridicule, they fear being made fun of. For women the greatest fear is being raped or murdered.

Those fears are not unfounded.

The Evening Gazette
Worcester, Massachusetts, October 13, 1992

In recent years, domestic violence in Massachusetts has become an insidious plague that has resisted efforts to curb it through tougher laws and expanded counseling.

The death rate from domestic violence has risen from one murder every 20 days two years ago, to one every 16 days last year, to one every nine days this year.

"For a long time, this crime was virtually ignored, and women who came forward seeking help were told to go home and be a good wife," Gov. William F. Weld said. "That's an attitude that has to change. Men who batter or stalk or otherwise terrorize their wives or girlfriends must know their violence is a crime just like any other crime and will be treated as such."

Worcester District Court Judge Austin T. Philbin has called domestic violence an epidemic. He angrily decried the lack of trained court personnel to deal with the problem and "a real lack of understanding of what is going on in a violent relationship."

A group of Worcester community leaders has called for a broad coalition to help cope with domestic violence and sexual attacks.

Mounting concern has produced some preventive measures, but more are needed.

The creation of a central computer registry of restraining orders is a welcome measure to fight domestic violence. The registry contains the names on all domestic restraining orders issued by courts throughout the state as well as all warrants issued because of violations of those orders.

Judges are required to do a computer check on domestic violence offenders brought before them. Police — the first line of defense for women against abusive husbands or boyfriends — also have access to the computerized information.

Other recent measures include passage of the Stalking Law with mandatory sentences for persons who engage in a pattern of harassment.

There's a $1.5 million increase in this year's budget for shelters and programs for battered women. In Worcester, the reopening of Daybreak Inc.'s shelter for battered women and their children signals growing concern about the personal safety of women at risk.

The American Medical Association has called on physicians to determine whether injured patients have been victims of domestic violence.

Moreover, there is a need for better enforcement of existing laws. Police must realize that domestic abuse is a vicious crime, not a private affair.

They are empowered to arrest anyone violating a restraining order and arrest a suspect when there is probable cause — even if the victim declines to press charges.

Police also can investigate neglect or abuse of children living in homes where there is domestic violence; confiscate firearms and weapons when someone is arrested for domestic abuse; notify a victim when a defendant is out on bail.

Violence in the home, ignored by society far too long, produces frightening consequences. The crisis begs for continuing attention.

LEXINGTON HERALD-LEADER
Lexington, Kentucky, November 14, 1992

Last week, the nation's Roman Catholic bishops issued a first-ever statement on wife-beating, and it was a powerful message of salvation for beaten women.

The Bible doesn't justify spouse abuse, they said. "Violence in any form — physical, sexual, psychological or verbal — is sinful."

The bishops released a report titled, "When I call for Help: A Pastoral Response to Domestic Violence Against Women." They urged parish priests to help beaten women seeking assistance and to build relationships with police and domestic violence agencies.

The importance of the bishops' statement cannot be overestimated. How many times have beaten women sought counsel from their priests or ministers only to be told that the Bible sanctions abuse and that they should return home? No one can say. No one knows how many women suffered further abuse or died while trying to be faithful to those instructions. But the bishops now wisely recognize the danger in the misguided attitudes of some clergy.

"Abused women say, 'I can't leave this relationship. The Bible says it would be wrong.' Abusive men say, 'The Bible says my wife should be submissive to me.' They take the biblical text and distort it to support their right to batter," the bishops said.

The bishops' message is that violence against women is never justified. Their words no doubt will be a source of comfort to Catholic women, who will know that they do not have to submit to abuse, that they have the right not to be beaten.

The bishops' words should inspire clergy in other denominations to take a similar stand.

The Boston Globe
Boston, Massachusetts, December 8, 1993

What went wrong in the case of Elizabeth McCandless Murray, Boston's latest casualty of domestic violence, is a question that will be on the lips of public officials and battered women's advocates for the next several days. The question must be more than rhetorical.

By all indications, McCandless Murray did all the things women are encouraged to do when they are battered. She left her brutal husband after only six months of marriage – for many women it takes years. She took out restraining orders and filed criminal complaints against him. She went into hiding, taking special care to keep her whereabouts secret. She even left her job.

Her husband, Sean Murray, violated the restraining order more than a dozen times, stalked and harassed his estranged wife at every opportunity and failed to appear at hearings. He traveled to Ireland and back even though his passport had been confiscated by authorities. Yet he never spent time in jail, he was never ordered to meet regularly with his probation officer and he was never required to attend a batterers program.

In other cities, officials have conducted "death reviews" to determine where the system fell short in domestic homicide cases. These sessions bring together the mayor, the governor and all judges and police officers who came in contact with the couple. In this tragedy, the process must include officials from the Immigration and Naturalization Service as well.

Such a session should not take on the tone of a witch hunt; it should be a constructive inquiry into which areas of the system need to be improved. The extensive paper trail in this case is likely to provide valuable clues.

Tragically, McCandless Murray's murder will reinforce many women's fears. Public officials have an obligation to get to the bottom of this tragedy and assure other women that they will receive better protection.

The Courier-Journal
Louisville, Kentucky, October 13, 1993

FOR many police officers, the scariest situation to encounter is a domestic fight. But a loophole in a Kentucky law sometimes makes this part of their job tougher than necessary — and imperils lives.

The law allows police to arrest a suspected abuser in a domestic fight if officers have reason to believe that physical abuse took place and the couple are married, divorced or have a child in common. If the participants don't fit those categories and the physical abuse isn't a possible felony, the victim needs to sign a warrant in order for police to make an arrest.

That requirement sometimes makes police intervention impossible in critical situations. The fear of further injury is just one of many reasons some victims don't sign warrants.

No one will ever know why Tanya Vaughn refused to take out a warrant against Michael Brunner recently. If she had, a tragedy surely would have been averted. Less than an hour after police left her home, officers were again summoned. By that time she and two neighbors had been fatally wounded. Mr. Brunner has been charged with murder.

Similar circumstances precipitated a murder in Mayfield in 1987. Because police couldn't arrest a woman's abusive boyfriend at home, she went to the police station to get a warrant. He followed and murdered her.

Past efforts to persuade legislators to close the loophole have failed. Surely now that three more people have died, they'll act.

DESERET NEWS
Salt Lake City, Utah, January 29, 1989

Family violence, mostly in the form of battered women, is a problem so large and so expensive for society that it is hard to comprehend.

Each year around the nation, police are called to intervene in domestic violence against 1.8 million women. There may be up to 10 times as many cases that go unreported.

Women are statistically more likely to fall victim to physical and sexual assault, and even murder, in the home than they are on the street. Family violence results in medical treatment for women that even ranks ahead of auto accidents.

Where a wife is battered, the children are likely to be abused as well. Even without physical beatings, the emotional trauma for children is enormous. Children from violent families tend grow up to be beaters themselves and to have many social problems — from drugs to violent crime.

As Surgeon General C. Everett Koop said recently, in urging more action to resolve domestic violence: "It is an overwhelming moral, economic, and public health burden that our society can no longer bear."

Utah is not an exception to the problem. While accurate figures are hard to assemble, there is no indication that spouse abuse is any less prevalent than the U.S. generally. For example, in Salt Lake County alone, there are an estimated 6,000 to 8,000 situations a year that require police intervention. Unreported cases are, of course, much greater.

The hopeful side to these numbers is that spouse abuse can often be treated and eliminated with firm police action, followed by intensive counseling. In a demonstration project in West Valley City, the Community Counseling Center reports a success rate of more than 70 percent in getting spouse abusers to change their ways.

Unfortunately, treatment is hard to find. What is needed are more counselors, more police trained in handling such cases, more public awareness, better laws and ways to implement them. In other words — more money.

Two bills have been introduced in the 1989 Utah Legislature. Both have the backing of lawmakers, social service groups, and police.

One, HB15, would amend the 1979 Spouse Abuse Act, which outlines procedures by which battered wives can get protective court orders.

The act is not working well because it is complicated, requires women to go through many bureaucratic steps that may be more than a beaten, fearful woman can handle.

The time frames for serving papers and holding hearings are too brief. If the five-day deadline for serving papers on an abusive husband is not met, for example, the whole process must be started again from scratch. In addition, too few women even know about the law.

HB15 seeks to make it a little easier to get protective orders, but the law itself does not solve domestic violence problems.

The second bill, HB16, would set up a state task force to study the whole issue of domestic violence, to examine what is being done elsewhere, to explore the latest research, and to draft model legislation. The group would include legislators, social workers, lawmen and prosecutors, judges, and even victims of domestic violence.

The hope is that all these diverse groups can learn to work together in handling domestic violence and developing an effective statewide plan — including laws with teeth in them — to deal with this vast problem.

More simply has to be done to protect women from this brutality.

St. Petersburg Times
St. Petersburg, Florida, October 7, 1990

Women in Florida are routinely discriminated against in divorce proceedings. They serve longer prison terms than men who commit the same crimes. Domestic violence is not taken seriously in the state's legal system, and women rarely are given support when they attempt to press charges against their abusers. Women lawyers often are awarded smaller fees in domestic cases than their male colleagues. Prosecutions for prostitution overwhelmingly target women despite the fact that state prostitution statutes are gender neutral and meant to address male clients and pimps.

A historic description of the relationship between women and the law? If only it were. The above statements are an assessment of the way Florida's system of justice treats women now, at the close of the 20th century. These and other unsettling findings are reported by the Florida Supreme Court Commission on Gender Bias, a 27-member panel of judges, lawyers, educators and politicians charged with investigating the state's legal framework for bias based solely on sex. The court also directed the commission to recommend ways to correct or at least minimize the effect of such bias.

The commission met its challenge in an impressive, thorough manner. Two years of work included gathering statewide information from questionnaires, public hearings and case studies from legislators, legal professionals as well as women who had first-hand experience with Florida's legal system.

What makes this study even more significant, however, is that the Supreme Court thinks enough of the report to keep it from the fate of many comprehensive studies, which is to do nothing more than collect dust on a shelf. The court was scheduled this week to appoint another commission whose job it will be to make sure the recommendations are implemented.

The implementation commission will propose new legislation and judiciary codes of conduct to achieve the objectives outlined in the report, including ensuring fairer distribution of marital property in divorce cases, increasing resources and programs for rape victim services, mandating the same alternatives for women and men convicted of similar crimes and creating a new chapter in Florida statutes called "Domestic Violence."

The court decided to form this panel, Justice Gerald Kogan told the *St. Petersburg Times*, because of the impact the report had throughout the judiciary. "Judges are starting to realize that it is not fashionable anymore to discriminate against women in the court system," said Kogan, who led the original gender bias commission.

The gender bias report and the follow-up commission to act upon the report's sweeping recommendations are important steps toward equal justice for women in Florida.

Supreme Court Rules on Sex Harassment in Workplace

In a unanimous decision, the Supreme Court Nov. 9, 1993 ruled that workers did not have to prove that they had suffered serious psychological damage as a result of sexual harassment in the workplace to win discrimination cases against employers. The high court overturned a lower court's ruling in the case, *Harris v. Forklift Systems Inc.*

The case focused on the interpretation of Title VII of the Civil Rights Act of 1964, which prohibited discrimination in the workplace on the basis of race, sex, ethnicity or religion. In 1986, the high court had ruled in *Meritor Savings Bank v. Vinson* that Title VII could extend to sexual harassment, if the harassment caused the victim to view the workplace as an abusive environment.

The language of the *Meritor* decision was so general that several lower courts subsequently attempted to define unacceptable sexual harassment more specifically, ruling in several cases that plaintiffs had to prove that they had suffered "severe psychological damage" before collecting damages.

In the current case, Teresa Harris said that Charles Hardy, president of Forklift Systems of Nashville, Tenn., had repeatedly made lewd suggestions and humiliating sexual innuendoes to her while she worked at the company from April 1985 to October 1987. Harris said that she had asked her employer to stop his behavior and had resigned after Hardy continued to harass her in front of co-workers.

Writing for the court, Justice Sandra Day O'Connor stated that a victim did not have to show evidence of serious mental injury to prove that harassment had taken place. O'Connor added that harassment could not be defined by using a "mathematically precise test." She suggested that courts reviewing harassment cases needed to pay attention to the frequency and extremity of inappropriate conduct, its effects on the victim's ability to work, and whether the mental or physical health of the victim was threatened.

O'Connor directed lower courts to invoke the "reasonable person" standard in determining whether a defendant had acted in a discriminatory manner. Using this standard, a court could rule that an employer's actions were discriminatory if they would have been offensive to any reasonable person. Some women's groups voiced fears about the high court's use of the standard, saying that defense lawyers could use it to discredit a plaintiff.

In a concurring opinion, Justice Antonin Scalia criticized O'Connor's decision for failing to clarify the vague definition of harassment, citing its use of the reasonable person standard and the general wording of the opinion. Scalia also found fault with the ruling for giving juries the power to determine whether particular actions constituted illegal behavior in harassment cases. He concluded, however, that he saw no other way for the court to rule in the case.

Justice Ruth Bader Ginsburg also issued a concurring opinion. She argued that gender-based bias was no different from racial discrimination and should be viewed with the same seriousness. As a lawyer in the 1970s, Ginsburg had unsuccessfully attempted to persuade the high court to approach both types of discrimination in a similar manner.

The high court's ruling instructed the 6th U.S. Circuit Court of Appeals to reexamine Harris's case. The appeals court, in ruling against Harris's claim, had cited the fact that Hardy's comments had not seriously affected her "psychological well-being."

LEXINGTON HERALD-LEADER
Lexington, Kentucky, November 11, 1993

The U.S. Supreme Court's unanimous, commonsense ruling on sexual harassment on the job should send a simple but much-needed message to bosses everywhere: Behavior on the job that demeans women is unacceptable. Writing for the court, Justice Sandra Day O'Connor recognized that no precise formula can prescribe when sexist remarks go too far. But she made clear that when women's job performance or dignity are hurt by their working atmosphere, the law is there to help.

The suit was brought by Teresa Harris against Charles Hardy, her boss and the president of Forklift Systems Inc. of Nashville, Tenn. She claimed that in her work as a manager at the firm, she repeatedly was subjected to treatment by Mr. Hardy that she felt was discriminatory and amounted to harassment. Examples included remarks such as "You're a woman, what do you know?" stated in the presence of other employees, or asking whether she had promised a client sexual favors to make a sale. At other times, Ms. Harris added, Mr. Hardy said, "Let's go to the Holiday Inn to negotiate your raise" and asked her to retrieve coins from the front pocket of his pants. She finally had enough.

Ms. Harris sought relief from such boorish, belittling behavior, but lower courts rejected her claim of harassment because she had not proven she had suffered "severe psychological injury." That threshold, unreasonably strict and unnecessarily vague, was struck down Tuesday by the Supreme Court, which sent the case back for review.

In her opinion, Justice O'Connor stated unequivocally that while behavior that hurts an employee psychologically is against the law, such injury is not the only harm that triggers treatment that violates Title VII of the Civil Rights Act of 1964. "Title VII comes into play before the harassing leads to a nervous breakdown," she added. "A discriminatorily abusive work environment, even one that does not seriously affect employees' psychological well-being, can and often will detract from employees' job performance, discourage employees from remaining on the job, or keep them from advancing in their careers."

In short, Justice O'Connor said, the Supreme Court has laid out "a middle path between making actionable any conduct that is merely offensive and requiring the conduct to cause a tangible psychological injury." With an increasing number of women seeking protection and redress from negative working conditions, that kind of sensible outlook is welcome. No woman — or man — should be forced to suffer silently from such indignities. The court's ruling should mean they won't have to.

The Hartford Courant
Hartford, Connecticut, November 13, 1993

That Teresa Harris was harassed at work is beyond question. That she quit rather than continue working with her sadistic boss is understandable. What is hard to comprehend, however, is why she had to go all the way to the U.S. Supreme Court to get justice.

The high court Tuesday restored a big dose of common sense to sex-harassment law with its ruling on her case. It rejected the lower-court conclusion that Ms. Harris had to suffer severe psychological injury before she could fall under the protection of federal job-discrimination law.

An employee as repeatedly and publicly insulted as Ms. Harris was shouldn't have to wind up on the psychiatrist's couch to prevail in court. The focus in sex-harassment cases shouldn't be on the plaintiff's mental deterioration but on the defendant's behavior.

For two years, Ms. Harris's boss, Charles Hardy, president of Forklift Systems in Nashville, Tenn., taunted her. In front of colleagues, he called her "a dumb-ass woman" and said repeatedly, "You're a woman. What do you know?" and "We need a man as the rental manager." He suggested they go to a motel to negotiate a pay raise, among other lewd proposals. She complained and he promised to stop. When he asked whether she had promised a client sexual favors, she quit and sued under Title VII of the 1964 Civil Rights Act, which prohibits discrimination at the workplace on the basis of gender. The Supreme Court had already ruled that sexual harassment under certain circumstances is a form of discrimination.

A federal district court found and an appeals court affirmed that Mr. Hardy's behavior, although offensive, didn't injure Ms. Harris psychologically enough for her to win damages.

The high court, in its unanimous ruling, set a better standard: "So long as the environment would reasonably be perceived, and is perceived, as hostile or abusive, there is no need for it also to be psychologically injurious," the court said.

That's not as tangible a standard as some lower-court judges might like. The new standard means that judges must take into account all circumstances surrounding a case, not simply a plaintiff's mental state.

But the "reasonable person" standard is fairer for the accuser as well as the accused. It allows employers a fighting chance if other workers testify they were not offended by allegedly offensive workplace behavior.

THE BLADE
Toledo, Ohio, November 12, 1993

THE Supreme Court's decision to broaden what qualifies as sexual harassment is a victory for common sense and equity in the workplace. No longer will individuals who are subjected to such harassment have to prove that they were left on the brink of mental collapse and unable to do their job because of it.

A standard set by several lower courts which required proof of such psychological

> *The psychological-damage test was absurd; it is the perpetrator's conduct which should be judged, not the victim's*

injury was an absurd criterion. By demanding that offensive treatment in the workplace be of such a nature that it would drive an employee to near collapse, the standard was rooted in the psychological strength of the victim. But it is the perpetrator's conduct which should be judged in such instances.

In other words, by applying a psychological damage test, lower courts were saying that sexual harassment only occurred if the victim was timid, compliant, or weak-willed and thus susceptible to psychological injury. Was that supposed to mean that a strong-willed individual better able to withstand the abuse but still resentful of it had not been harassed?

In the case before the Supreme Court, Teresa Harris filed suit against a Nashville, Tenn., company alleging that her boss had, among other things, asked her to take coins from his front pants pocket, go to a motel with him to negotiate a pay raise, and indicate whether she had slept with a client.

It doesn't take a rocket scientist to figure that is harassment of the most egregious kind. And yet two courts, in Nashville and Cincinnati, found that the treatment was not sufficient to meet the standard of psychological damage.

The Supreme Court's rejection of the standard does not mean that Ms. Harris has won her case but sends it back to the appeals court for reconsideration. Nonetheless, the ground rules for harassment have changed, and they are now simpler, easier to understand, and easier to enforce.

In any workplace there is bantering between employees, some of it of a sexual nature. Risque comments happen. Men and women do not lose all sexuality when they cross the threshold of their store, factory, or corporation. But this decision redresses a situation which placed an unfair burden on victims of harassment.

And if it's the boss making the remarks, the recipient of the offensive actions or words naturally fears that his or her job may depend upon the response. That is sexual harassment, by definition, even if the victim does not become a psychological basket case.

By making sexual harassment easier to prove and no longer dependent to any extent on psychological harm, the Supreme Court has helped free the workplace of this scourge. But unfortunately, despite the progress, equality is still an unknown quantity in too many American offices, shops, and assembly lines.

The Philadelphia Inquirer
Philadelphia, Pennsylvania, November 12, 1993

Back when the U.S. Court of Appeals for the Sixth District ruled that the humiliation and sexist behavior a Tennessee woman experienced at work wasn't injurious enough to be called sexual harassment, what was the underlying message?

That to be a victim, you had to act like one. It wasn't enough that Teresa Harris' boss made lewd remarks and degrading demands of his female employees. To claim sexual harassment, the appeals court said, Ms. Harris had to prove she was psychologically damaged and unable to do her job.

Fortunately for the integrity of the American workplace, the U.S. Supreme Court this week broadened the legal definition of sexual harassment. In a unanimous decision, Justice Sandra Day O'Connor defined unlawful harassment as creating a work environment that a reasonable person would find "hostile or abusive." Just because a worker is strong enough to withstand that kind of abuse, the justice implied, doesn't mean that something illegal didn't occur.

At a time when the rules of engagement between the sexes are shifting dramatically, the court drew clear boundaries between right and wrong. "The critical issue," Justice Ruth Bader Ginsburg said in a concurring opinion, "is whether members of one sex are exposed to disadvantageous terms or conditions of employment to which members of the other sex are not exposed."

The court took a refreshingly common-sense approach to an issue that has been tugging at the American consciousness for several years. Those naysayers who cry that it will only encourage meritless claims overlook the fact that it is frustratingly hard to bring a sexual harassment case to fruition. Just ask Teresa Harris — who first filed in 1987 and now has won the right only to have her case heard all over again.

Sexual harassment is not about whether off-color jokes can be told around the soda machine. It's about the improper use of power to hurt or denigrate another person.

And it's about civility, or the lack thereof. There's a simple way for American businesses to deal with the "problem" of sexual harassment: Treat workers, male and female alike, with dignity and respect.

FORT WORTH STAR-TELEGRAM
Fort Worth, Texas, November 12, 1993

In Harris vs. Forklift Systems Inc., a sound sexual harassment case made for a sound judgment.

The U.S. Supreme Court rejected a backward standard adopted by some lower courts requiring that plaintiffs prove that sexual harassment made a working environment so hostile that it resulted in psychological harm or compromised job performance.

The 9-0 ruling — only the second by the court on sexual harassment — acknowledges that the protection of federal law kicks in long before mental damage occurs. It directs courts that interpret civil-rights law to consider every possible consequence of sexual harassment.

A simplified scenario plots the path onto which the flawed standard might have taken many more sexual harassment cases:

"Sure. It was a hostile place to work in," a lawyer for an accused employer might say. "But the plaintiff, my client's former employee, came through it just fine. No change in productivity. Worked like a champ despite it all. And no psychological damage resulted. Proof positive, your Honor, that the workplace wasn't hostile enough for the defendant to pay damages."

Psychological damage and decreased work performance can be one of many byproducts of a work environment made uncomfortable by sexual harassment. But equally hostile environments might not produce the same kind of damage.

"The effect of the employee's psychological well-being is, of course, relevant to determining whether the plaintiff actually found the environment abusive," Justice Sandra Day O'Connor wrote. "But while psychological harm, like any other relevant factor, may be taken into account, no single factor is required."

The court instituted a "reasonable person" rule in determining whether a workplace is hostile. Reasonable people treat other people reasonably.

The Miami Herald
Miami, Florida, November 11, 1993

IN HIGH COURT RULING: Employees now don't have to endure sexual harassment or prove psychic harm. Good!

No, the company lecher doesn't have to drive you nuts before you can claim sexual harassment. That's the reassuring message from the U.S. Supreme Court to working women. Ditto for racists who incessantly deride the race, religion, or origins of others.

The lower courts had not been sympathetic to a Nashville, Tenn., office manager's claim that constant sexual innuendo, jibes about her body, and lewd invitations from her boss constituted a "hostile" working environment. Offensive, yes, said the trial court, about the "jokes" told by Theresa Harris's boss. Ms. Harris couldn't prove that she suffered serious psychological damage, so lower courts rejected her claim of having been harmed by sexual harassment.

It's not necessary to prove such harm if the unwelcome overtures are themselves "severe or pervasive," said Tuesday's unanimous decision. Written by Justice Sandra Day O'Connor, it sought a middle course between mere offense and extreme psychological pressure. This opinion leaves a lot of room for trial courts' interpretation, but harassing behavior doesn't fall into neat boxes.

Of course, occasional stupid wisecracks about sex or race make people uneasy. But employees have a right, underscored by this decision, to call a halt before the wisecracks escalate into a flood of abuse that drives them from their work.

This middle course should give comfort to employers who believe in sense and sensitivity. To employers who believe in neither, it's fair warning.

The State
Columbia, South Carolina, November 1, 1993

THE SHIFT in defining sexual harassment was, surprisingly, recognized by a unanimous U.S. Supreme Court in ruling that an employee doesn't have to be psychologically injured to be entitled to damages for chauvinistic workplace conduct. This case could well set a new standard for what is acceptable conduct.

The case was classic. Teresa Harris, a manager at a Tennessee forklift company, was subjected to boorish conduct by her boss, Charles Hardy. She claimed he humiliated her and made sexually suggestive comments and gestures. When she complained, he promised to do better, then laughed it off and went back to his old ways. She quit — and sued.

In courtroom testimony, he admitted making gross gestures and comments, but said they were just "in fun." Lower courts found against Ms. Harris. In essence, they said that although this was a "close case," she was not so "psychologically damaged" in a "hostile work environment" that she was unable to do her job. Therefore, she was not entitled to damages.

The courts explained that even though her boss' comments "offended her (Ms. Harris) and would offend the reasonable woman, they were not so severe as to be expected to seriously affect her psychological well-being...." In short, she probably had a right to be mad as hell, but not to collect damages for sexual harassment.

Ms. Harris appealed all the way to the U.S. Supreme Court. And that court, with two female justices (Sandra Day O'Connor and Ruth Bader Ginsburg) on the bench, took note of the subtle, not-easily-defined problems of defining sexual harassment.

Justice O'Connor, writing for a unanimous court, said that federal law goes beyond barring harassment that would cause the average person "severe psychological injury." The law, said Justice O'Connor, "is not limited to such conduct" but is extended to include conduct that is "hostile and abusive."

And, she added, such hostile and abusive conduct can only be assessed by "looking at all the circumstances" — for instance, by how severe, threatening, humiliating, frequent or offensive it was. (Testimony in this case showed that Mr. Hardy, among other affronts, asked Ms. Harris to put her hands in his front pants pockets to retrieve pocket change, called her derogatory names and suggested she had used sexual favors to secure contracts for the company.)

As Justice O'Connor so rightly pointed out, it is the aggregate, not any single factor, that must be weighed in determining whether Ms. Harris was sexually harassed. And, in a separate, concurring opinion, Justice Ginsburg took the conclusion a step further. Employees, she said, are entitled to recover damages if they can prove that a *reasonable* person would find the harassing conduct "so altered working conditions as to make it more difficult to do the job."

That's a much tougher standard than the likes of professional lechers are accustomed to dealing with. Ms. Harris still will have to prove she was subjected to unreasonable harassment. But now, at least, she'll get her day in court.

THE BUFFALO NEWS
Buffalo, New York, November 1, 1993

THE SUPREME COURT has responsibly revised the legal standard for determining whether an employee was sexually harassed at work. The revision may be vague, but it is also substantially more just than the narrower standard it replaced.

The case arose when a Tennessee woman quit her job in 1987, then sued her ex-boss, accusing him of sexual harassment. She alleged that he had, among other things, asked her to retrieve coins from his front pants pocket and suggested they negotiate her pay raise at a local motel.

The lower courts tossed out the suit. The woman had not proved, they said, that the actions of her boss caused her "severe psychological injury."

But in a unanimous opinion written by Justice Sandra Day O'Connor, the Supreme Court properly disagreed. It decided that while such psychological injury could prove that anti-discriminatory laws were violated, this was not the sole possible proof. Other standards could apply as well.

"So long as the environment would reasonably be perceived and is perceived as hostile or abusive," O'Connor wrote, "there is no need for it also to be psychologically injurious." Whether that environment can be considered hostile or abusive, she added, "can be determined only by looking at all the circumstances."

That does not provide any faultless answer for courts to rely on in future cases. But the psychological injury test is too confining, and the revision corrects that. It establishes a fairer, more realistic test for determining what constitutes discriminatory behavior within differing conditions and circumstances. Important factors to consider can include the frequency of the allegedly offensive conduct, its severity, whether it is physically threatening or whether it interferes with job performance.

This ruling could well carry an immediate, widening impact in quasi-judicial hearings and courtrooms around the country. The federal Equal Employment Opportunity Commission reports that such sexual harassment complaints jumped by more than 50 percent in the year after Anita Hill leveled sexual harassment accusations against Clarence Thomas in his 1991 Senate hearings for a seat on the high court. Thomas, later confirmed, concurred in this week's decision.

Sexual harassment is an emerging area of law with vast practical and economic consequences in a changing workplace.

With its decision, the high court strikes a welcome blow against bias. Hopefully, in addition to other benefits, the ruling will be a deterrent, helping to prevent heedless acts of workplace bias before they get started.

The Providence Journal
Providence, Rhode Island, November 14, 1993

The Supreme Court has moved quickly and without much ado to ease the standard by which sexual harassment in the work place can be determined to exist.

The justices, in a remarkable 9-0 ruling, found that some lower courts have taken an overly narrow view of sexual harassment and its harms. Specifically, these courts have said that plaintiffs must show that any sexual harassment they allege has damaged them psychologically or made them unable to do their jobs. But Justice Sandra Day O'Connor, in writing the opinion for the high court, sensibly noted that the protections of federal law against work-place discrimination can be sought before the point at which a "nervous breakdown" occurs.

In the case under consideration, a woman who had worked as a manager at a truck leasing company in Nashville sued, asserting that the company's president had repeatedly subjected her to demeaning and suggestive comments because of her sex. The Supreme Court's decision revives her suit.

The high court's unambivalent ruling on this matter comes as a breath of fresh air. The issue of sexual harassment has festered in the national psyche ever since the hearings on Clarence Thomas's confirmation to the Supreme Court, whatever the truth of the allegations and denials in that depressing matter.

A Senate panel that, to many people, appeared blind to the reality and seriousness of sexual harassment prompted many women to run for office or become otherwise involved in politics. The Supreme Court's latest ruling, prompt and to the point, should go far to dispel whatever national tendency there might be toward denial of the problem.

The high court, which has had very little to say about sexual harassment, doubtless will be asked to say more in the future. It possibly will be induced to further articulate differences between harassment and free speech; it could also face the problem of defining offensive conduct. In the latest ruling, the court says that the conduct in question should appear offensive to a "reasonable person." But who is to be considered "reasonable"?

We will be interested in hearing more over the next few years.

But the immediate effect of this latest ruling, which will make it easier to prove harassment, should be to give local standards on the issue a badly needed airing. Such discussions, even if regrettably couched in litigation, could help build a greater national consensus on what sexual harassment is, and on how best to handle it.

Meanwhile, the court's newest justice, Ruth Bader Ginsburg, in writing a brief concurring opinion, sought to move sexual discrimination to a position of concern equal to that of racial discrimination. This could presage some interesting developments in the court — and for the country — over the next few years.

The Wichita Eagle-Beacon
Wichita, Kansas, November 12, 1993

The Supreme Court has made it clear that any judge or jury must look at a wide range of factors in sexual harassment cases. Frequent and severe discrimination, whether physically threatening or humiliating, that "unreasonably interferes" with working conditions constitutes sexual harassment, according to the unanimous decision announced this week.

The court quickly acted on two cases that lower courts refused to hear because judges said that specific sexual harassment behaviors did not result in serious psychological injury to the women who brought complaints. Now the lower courts — one in Michigan and one in Tennessee — have to look at the two cases again with the understanding that there can be significant harm done by sexual misconduct without a resulting psychological breakdown.

Although both men and women are protected by law against harassment, most cases involve women who face these situations when males with whom they work make constant, inappropriate sexual advances and/or comments. No one should have to face each work day with the threat of everything from crude and embarrassing jokes and pats on the posterior to sexual propositions and sexual threats.

Such activity can and does lead to losing one's ability to earn a living — either by being fired for not accepting sexist goings-on or by quitting because the situation becomes intolerable. And it can lead to a nonproductive and uncomfortably stressful job situation that no human being should have to endure.

A definition of sexual harassment may never be so explicit that there is nary a doubt as to what it is in the minds of some people. But the Supreme Court went a long way this week to clarify the situation. It is now a certainty that it isn't acceptable to constantly subject women in the workplace to anti-female obscenities and posters of nude women or for a boss to comment on a female employee's anatomy, to ask her to get coins out of his pants pocket or to call her sexist names — examples of the kind of harassment in the lower court cases in question.

Women who are facing such deplorable working conditions now have a more reasonable opportunity of having their concerns addressed in a favorable way by the courts. And the perpetrators — those who can't seem to comprehend that they don't have a right to manhandle or verbally abuse the women with whom they work — now have the Supreme Court's decision to help them figure it out.

San Francisco Chronicle
San Francisco, California, November 12, 1993

PERHAPS AN all-male U.S. Supreme Court would have reached the same judgment, but it is hard not to believe that the presence of two women on the present court helped assure that reason prevailed in Tuesday's unanimous verdict on sexual harassment.

"Reason" is the key word in the court's finding. It is the ingredient that was most obviously missing from recent lower court rulings that held that a woman, in effect, had to be reduced to a psychological basket case before she could claim sexual discrimination under the 1964 Civil Rights Act.

> *A decision that makes simple common sense*

As should be obvious to any reasonable man or woman, sexually motivated behavior can become unacceptable — even unconstitutional — long before it produces tangible psychological or physical damage to the victim. As Justice Sandra Day O'Connor wrote in the unanimous opinion, the law barring sexual harassment is violated when, for any of a variety of reasons, "the (workplace) environment would reasonably be perceived, and is perceived, as hostile or abusive."

THAT MAY SEEM like simple common sense, but it is significant expansion of the constitutional right to workplace equality in view of prior efforts to define sexual harassment as behavior causing actual, severe damage.

Certainly this sensitive issue has not been resolved forever. The courts will no doubt have to wrestle with questions about who or what constitutes a "reasonable person."

But in striking down the blatantly unreasonable restrictions on what constitutes sexual harassment, the court validated the rights of millions of women to insist on a workplace atmosphere free of sexual hostility.

The Record
Hackensack, New Jersey, November 11, 1993

THE U.S. Supreme Court ruling that makes it easier to prove sexual harassment in the workplace is a victory for women, as well as a victory for common sense.

In its unanimous decision this week, the high court said that employees charging sexual harassment do not have to go to the extreme of proving they were psychologically damaged or rendered unable to do their jobs. Obviously, employees can perform their jobs well and still be made miserable by the unwanted off-color intrusions of a boss or co-worker. As the justices reasoned, workers should not have to be debilitated to obtain relief from harassment.

Writing for the court, Justice Sandra Day O'Connor said that the federal law against job discrimination "comes into play before the harassing conduct leads to a nervous breakdown." The law is violated, Justice O'Connor wrote, when the workplace environment is reasonably perceived as "hostile or abusive." The sweeping decision sends the message that sexual harassment is serious and will not be tolerated under federal law.

The ruling was made in the case of Teresa Harris, a Tennessee woman who sued her former company, charging sexual harassment. Charles Hardy, the president of Forklift Systems Inc., where she was a manager, claimed that he was only treating her as "one of the boys." It's highly unlikely, however, that Mr. Hardy would treat a male co-worker the way he treated Ms. Harris.

His conduct included repeated demeaning and sexist remarks such as "You're a woman, what do you know?" He also suggested that they negotiate her raise at a Holiday Inn, and he once asked her if she had obtained a particular account by having sex with the client.

The Supreme Court's decision overturned lower court rulings that had dismissed Ms. Harris' lawsuit against Forklift because she failed to prove the harassment caused her "severe psychological injury."

> *This makes it clear that sexual harassment won't be tolerated.*

While the Supreme Court's ruling makes perfect sense, we can't help but wonder whether the presence of two women on the high court made a difference. Would nine male justices have been more likely to limit sexual harassment to a stricter definition?

As two of the relatively few women at the top of their profession, Justice O'Connor and the court's newest justice, Ruth Bader Ginsburg, undoubtedly know how difficult it can be to work in a male-dominated profession and how uncomfortable women can be made to feel.

They also understand that sexual harassment is one of the barriers that can keep women from full equity in the workplace and from reaching their full career potential.

Newsday
New York City, New York, November 11, 1993

Until this week, a woman couldn't count on winning a sexual harassment case in federal court unless she could show that her "psychological well-being" had been impaired — and maybe not even then. But on Tuesday the Supreme Court unanimously decided that standard was tougher than Congress intended.

Psychological harm might be taken into account, wrote Justice Sandra Day O'Connor in her opinion for the court, but it wasn't required. The relevant civil rights law "comes into play before the harassing conduct leads to a nervous breakdown," she said. And there's no "mathematically precise test" to determine what ingredients make up the abusive or hostile work environment that constitutes unlawful discrimination. Any number of factors can come into play.

The court decision was not only right but unusually quick, coming down less than four weeks after oral arguments were heard in the case of Harris vs. Forklift Systems Inc. O'Connor specifically tried to steer a middle course between the excessively strict standard of psychological harm and the impermissibly lax one of mere offensiveness.

The other woman on the high court, Ruth Bader Ginsburg, chimed in with a brief concurring opinion that stated the nub of the case incisively. "The critical issue," she wrote, ". . . is whether members of one sex are exposed to disadvantageous terms or conditions of employment to which members of the other sex are not exposed." Teresa Harris, whose employer called her "a dumb-ass woman," met the test with room to spare.

There was one other concurring opinion — from Justice Antonin Scalia, who grumbled that he'd like to see a narrower civil rights law. But even he conceded that O'Connor's opinion was "faithful to the inherently vague statutory language." The other men on the court had the good sense to remain silently supportive.

AKRON BEACON JOURNAL
Akron, Ohio, November 15, 1993

The surprise in last week's U.S. Supreme Court ruling on sexual harassment is not so much that the decision was swift as that the court, with its distinctly conservative leaning, unanimously affirmed easier terms of proving sexual harassment than lower courts have allowed.

The court decided that Teresa Harris, who sued her former boss for persistent, crude, gender-based conduct, didn't have to prove that her boss's conduct drove her to a nervous breakdown or that her work suffered as a result of it.

The court thus hewed to common sense, rejecting both the notion that a worker has to become a virtual basket case to prove harassment and the impulse to make a judicial case out of conduct that is "merely offensive."

There is a wide, gray area, of course, between the merely offensive and truly abusive conduct. Distinguishing conduct that is merely boorish from that which interferes with a worker's ability to do a job is complicated by the range of individual sensitivities. But that's precisely the broad distinction the courts are being asked to define.

While the legal tests for sexual misconduct in the workplace are slowly evolving, the ruling offers a timely reminder of the intent of Title VII of the Civil Rights Act of 1964, which is the basis of the sexual harassment law.

As Justice Ruth Bader Ginsburg writes in her concurring opinion, the central issue is to determine "whether members of one sex are exposed to disadvantageous terms or conditions of employment to which members of the other sex are not exposed." Where such conditions exist, the point of the law is to eliminate them.

The courts are still charting the waters where sexual harassment is concerned. Tuesday's decision makes it easier for victims of harassment to seek redress, but it also raises the potential, by the fuzziness of the nature of the offense, for a slew of lawsuits of dubious merit.

The benefit of that may be to establish quickly firm and clear standards for judging this prickly problem.

Meanwhile, the speed and the single voice with which the court ruled on Tuesday emphasize one principle: that workers and employers observe common courtesy and apply common sense in the workplace.

There's a place for sexual overtures, banter and whatever else between consenting adults, but the workplace is not it.

The Seattle Times
Seattle, Washington, November 11, 1993

THE speed and unanimity of the Supreme Court's decision in a sexual harassment case shows that even the conservative-dominated court will no longer let bad employers off the hook.

Prior to this week's ruling, victims of harassment had to show they suffered nervous breakdowns before they could win under federal anti-discrimination law. That requirement effectively eliminated most harassment complaints before they got to the courthouse steps.

The opinion in Harris v. Forklift Systems, Inc., written by Justice Sandra Day O'Connor, lifts that preposterous burden.

The standard for proving harassment, however, is not necessarily lowered. In order to prevail, workers still must show that work conditions were negatively altered. As O'Connor notes, the standard is met by reviewing all the circumstances — the frequency and severity of the harassment, the degree of humiliation, the actuality of physical threats are all factors to be considered. A trial court would determine whether conduct in any particular case "would reasonably be perceived, and is perceived, as hostile and abusive" so as to violate the law.

Some employer groups argued that workers also should have to prove that their job performance suffered. The court wisely rejected that requirement.

The point, after all, is to stop harassment before it renders workers incapacitated.

Conscientious employers who don't tolerate harassment in the workplace will have no trouble complying with the court's new thinking. They know to stop inappropriate behavior as soon as it starts. Bad bosses, however, will have to start taking complaints seriously.

Until now, only victims who have suffered severe psychological injury could get legal relief. At last, those who manage to put up with abusive conditions will get the same consideration.

The Chattanooga Times
Chattanooga, Tennessee, November 1, 1993

It's official: Women don't have to have a nervous breakdown to prove they've suffered sexual harassment in the workplace. The U.S. Supreme Court cleared that question up in a unanimous ruling on Tuesday. The decision is solidly grounded in common sense as well as the law.

It sends Teresa Harris back to court in her case against Forklift Systems Inc. of Nashville. This time around, her harassment claim will be measured against a reasonable standard.

First time around, lower courts dismissed Ms. Harris' claim because harassment by her boss did not cause her actual psychological injury or keep her from being able to do her job. The Supreme Court said that standard was far too high, and it obviously is.

Civil rights law makes it illegal to discriminate on the basis of gender when it comes either to compensation, or to "terms, conditions or privileges of employment." Clearly, being subjected on the job to a continual barrage of unwanted sexual innuendoes and demeaning references to one's gender constitutes a condition of one's employment. If a woman is subjected to that negative condition while her male colleagues are not, that's discrimination. And that's illegal.

Clarification of the standard of proof in sexual harassment cases is particularly welcome because it shifts the focus of inquiry. The previous standard focused on the victim rather than on the behavior of the harasser, with perverse effect.

It penalized women for being psychologically strong and professionally competent.

To have recourse under the previous interpretation of the law, a woman had to prove she had been broken by her harasser — either psychologically damaged or made unable to perform her job. The harassment itself, no matter how outrageous, was not an issue if the victim had been able to withstand and overcome it.

It is remarkable any court would ever have held to such a view of the law but gratifying that the Supreme Court rejected it so definitively. Not only was this decision unanimous, it was rendered with extraordinary swiftness — less than a month after it was argued before the nine justices.

That sends a strong signal that the high court views sexual harassment as a serious violation of civil rights law. It is a warning to employers that they, too, must take it seriously. The warning is timely. In the last two years, workplace sexual harassment complaints have almost doubled.

Complaints may surge again now, since this ruling lets women know their rights will be reasonably protected under the law. It will be some time before the limits of sexual harassment are fully defined in case law, but the Supreme Court made a big step in the right direction this week.

The Tennessean
Nashville, Tennessee, November 12, 1993

LIKE almost everyone else, the Supreme Court can't specifically define sexual harassment, but justices know it when they see it.

For Nashvillian Teresa Harris, the court's rare unanimous decision Tuesday means she can return to court on charges that her Forklift Systems boss, Charles Hardy, sexually harassed her. For other workers elsewhere, the court helped clear up one issue that has divided lower courts across the nation.

Harris' case was originally dismissed when a federal court ruled that she had not suffered psychological harm. The U.S. Sixth Circuit Court of Appeals, one of three appellate courts which used the psychological well-being standard, upheld the lower court decision throwing out Harris' case.

Justice Sandra Day O'Connor, who wrote the unanimous decision, declared that the federal harassment law, while banning any conduct that might harm a worker psychologically, is not limited to one test.

"Whether an environment is 'hostile' or 'abusive' can be determined only by looking at all the circumstances," O'Connor wrote. "These may include the frequency of the discriminatory conduct; its severity; whether it is physically threatening or humiliating, or a mere offensive utterance; and whether it unreasonably interferes with an employee's work performance."

The court's ruling helps clarify its last word on the subject of sexual harassment in 1986. Then, justices held that sexual harassment is illegal when it is "sufficiently severe or pervasive to alter the conditions of the victim's employment."

But seven years is a long time between rulings on sexual harassment. Lawsuits have piled up in lower courts across the country with varying results. Businesses and workers have grappled with it. Even the nomination of a Supreme Court justice, Clarence Thomas, centered on sexual harassment allegations.

As Justice Antonin Scalia said in his concurring opinion, the ruling "adds little certitude" to the legal debate over harassment. The court has yet to determine, for example, a "reasonable person" standard on what constitutes sexual harassment. But the speed with which they made their decision — just a month after arguments — suggests that justices had little trouble determining that the psychological damage standard was inappropriate.

The ruling unquestionably gives women and men more power to fight back in the courts when they are victims of harassment. For Teresa Harris, the fight has been painful, uncomfortable and lengthy. It took six years, but she has won a major victory for herself and many others who owe her a debt for her persistence on this troubling issue. ■

The Charlotte Observer
Charlotte, North Carolina, November 15, 1993

That the U.S. Supreme Court decision in the sexual harassment case of Teresa Harris actually surprised some people indicates how muddled the issue has become. The court on Tuesday rightly rejected the foolish notion that harassed workers had to prove the offensive behavior left them psychologically damaged or unable to do their jobs. Justice Sandra Day O'Connor, writing the court's opinion, was clear and unequivocal: Protection of the law comes into play *before* the harassing conduct leads to a nervous breakdown.

To most of us, that's just plain common sense. Yet opponents sought to obscure the real question with off-the-point arguments about free speech and feminism. The question before the justices was fairly simple: Can offensive conduct be considered sexual harassment if a worker does not become an emotional basket case? To that, the justices gave the only answer they could: Yes. Otherwise, they would have made the reaction of the victim, not the action of the harasser, the basis for determining sexual harassment. And they would have left workers with just two choices in many harassing situations: grin and bear it, or leave.

Teresa Harris wanted and deserved another choice. With the Supreme Court ruling, lower courts must now reconsider the lawsuit she filed against her boss — a lawsuit dismissed when she failed to prove psychological harm resulted from her boss's actions.

This case should be fairly easy to decide. For 2½ years, the Tennessee woman endured sexual taunting and innuendos almost daily from a boss who refused her repeated requests that he stop. The comments? "Let's go to the Holiday Inn and negotiate your raise." "Don't you think it is about time we started screwing around?" "You're just a dumb-ass woman." "I have a quarter way down there, would you get it out of my (front) pocket?" The boss contends he was just joking. But even the lower court judges found his behavior boorish and offensive. Now the courts should find it illegal as well.

The Supreme Court ruling, of course, has broader implications than the Harris case. It's a victory for all workers, especially those laboring under an oppressive and abusive boss. Men, who are filing sexual harassment complaints in increasing numbers, will benefit as well.

Not all the questions about the boundaries of sexual harassment were answered in this court ruling. But as Marcia Greenberger, co-president of the National Women's Law Center, notes, the court ruling sends "as clear a signal as could be to employers that sexual harassment is a serious violation of the law and that the time for strained legal arguments is over." That's as it should be.

THE KANSAS CITY STAR
Kansas City, Missouri, November 14, 1993

Until the Supreme Court ruled last week, sexual harassment was viewed by some courts and defense lawyers in much the same way as rape has often been viewed.

In rape cases, victims frequently have had to show cuts, bruises, broken bones or battered bodies to prove they have been injured by rape.

In sexual harassment claims, women also have often had to demonstrate that they have an injury, that is, that they have fallen apart psychologically as a result of the gender-based actions of an employer or coworker, and cannot perform their jobs.

The Supreme Court's 1986 ruling — its only other on this issue — made it clear that a supervisor who demanded sexual favors in return for job security or a promotion was guilty of sexual harassment. The court also went further than such overt acts, saying that the presence of a "hostile environment" in the workplace also could be grounds for a successful sexual harassment claim by an employee.

But the court did not define what it meant by "hostile environment." Thus, some judges have applied the strictest interpretation, making it more difficult for women to win cases of sexual harassment unless they can show severe psychological harm.

That has changed with the high court's decision in a Tennessee case last week. A unanimous court — a surprise in itself — said that women didn't have to prove psychological damage or poor mental health in these cases.

Laws are violated when there is intimidation, ridicule, and insult of employees by supervisors or co-workers because of their gender, the court said in the opinion written by Justice Sandra Day O'Connor.

In the Tennessee case, Teresa Harris said she had endured harassment from a supervisor who asked her to retrieve coins from his front pants pocket, who made references to going to a motel to talk about her pay raise, and who asked if she got a sales contract by providing sexual favors.

The justices applied a sort of "reasonable person" standard to follow in determining future sexual harassment cases. O'Connor said that "so long as the environment would reasonably be perceived, and is perceived, as hostile or abusive, there is no need for it also to be psychologically injurious."

The court's word on this case had been anxiously awaited by civil rights and women's groups who saw the decision as crucial to the rights of women in employment.

Many of these groups undoubtedly viewed this as Anita Hill's revenge because if it had not been for her, sexual harassment undoubtedly still would be a torment for many workers who instead now have legal recourse.

They also wondered about the position of Justice Clarence Thomas, who had been accused by Hill of sexual harassment and whose confirmation hearings turned into a national dialogue on the issue. He offered no opinion separate from O'Connor's.

The ruling also is a relief to businesses, many of whom have tried to put in place policies which prohibit harassment and which give employees a procedure to follow for help if it has happened to them. A better definition of what is illegal will assist employers who are serious about eradicating this from their businesses.

The Register-Guard
Eugene, Oregon, November 15, 1993

Sexual harassment is difficult to define for purposes of the law. Most attempts wind up taking in too much or too little.

There is no federal statute outlawing sexual harassment. The "law" against this behavior derives from Title VII of the 1964 Civil Rights Act, which prohibits job discrimination on the basis of sex. In 1986, the Supreme Court interpreted that law as covering sexual harassment.

That ruling was so general that lower courts were not sure how to apply it. Most responded conservatively, requiring that a woman claiming workplace sexual harassment prove that she suffered real psychological damage.

Last week the Supreme Court refined the concept of illegal harassment, easing the nearly medical standard that has been used since 1986.

Speaking for a unanimous court, Justice Sandra Day O'Connor said the law is violated when "the (work) environment would reasonably be perceived, and is perceived, as hostile or abusive." She said this means something more than casual remarks that are "merely offensive" but something less than behavior that would cause a nervous breakdown.

Citing no single factor as a key element, she asked courts to consider a variety of circumstances that can contribute to a hostile or abusive environment: the frequency and severity of harassing behavior, whether it is physically threatening or humiliating, and whether it "unreasonably interferes with a person's work performance."

The new decision does not offer a perfect definition of sexual harassment. While honorably attempting to steer between extremes, it won't remove all uncertainty about whether specific instances of sexually unpleasant-or-worse behavior violate the law.

But the case that served as the vehicle for the court's examination of the problem will help by way of illustration. It involved Charles Hardy, the owner of a small trucking company, who was sued by a female employee, rental manager Teresa Harris. She quit after suffering two years of Hardy's sometimes salacious and sometimes sexually insulting remarks.

Lower courts found the boss "inane" and "vulgar" but not guilty of a law violation. Ironically, the main factor working against Harris' legal claim was her own strength. She didn't fall apart. She did her job well and maintained her composure until she became disgusted enough to quit. The Supreme Court sent the case back for rehearing, accompanied by the significant new standards for determining whether Harris is due any damages.

There are many Charles Hardys and Teresa Harrises in the offices and factories of America. This decision will reduce what the one can get away with as a perverse prerogative of authority and what the other must put up with to keep a job.

Locally, it's good to know that the standards embraced by the court for federal purposes are similar to those that have been employed in Oregon since 1986. The civil rights division of the state Bureau of Labor employs these criteria in evaluating sexual harassment complaints filed with it.

Portland Press Herald
Portland, Maine, November 13, 1993

Working women received powerful legal protection against sexual harassment from the U.S. Supreme Court this week.

In a unanimous opinion, written by Justice Sandra Day O'Connor, the court struck down the offensive idea that a woman must demonstrate "severe psychological injury" or be rendered unable to work in order to win judgment in a sexual harassment case. That dubious standard had developed in lower federal courts. It will apply no longer.

Instead, the court decreed, federal law protecting workers from harassment comes into play much earlier, "before the harassing conduct leads to a nervous breakdown." Sexual harassment can't be measured "by a mathematically precise test," O'Connor wrote. Still, a work environment can be perceived as hostile or abusive depending on "the frequency of the discriminatory conduct; its severity; whether it is physically threatening or humiliating, or a mere offensive utterance; and whether it unreasonably interferes with an employee's work performance."

Those factors add up to the courts' new measuring stick. Together, they draw an important distinction between banter at the water cooler and conduct that makes it difficult for competent employees to do their jobs.

Most large companies have long since established policies prohibiting sexual harassment. The new ruling underscores that individuals bear heavy responsibility for making them work.

Most importantly, the decision elevates discriminatory treatment on the basis of sex to a level of seriousness applied to racial discrimination. Marcia Greenberger of the National Women's Law Center caught the significance well. The court, she said, is sending "as clear a signal as could be to employers that sexual harassment is a serious violation of the law and that the time for strained legal arguments is over."

The New York Times
New York City, New York, November 11, 1993

A victim of sexual harassment need not suffer a nervous breakdown to sue an employer for discrimination. A worker has suffered enough, the Supreme Court asserts, if the employer has so polluted the workplace with sexual improprieties that a reasonable person would find it hostile and abusive, a disagreeable, unpromising place to work.

Seems elementary, doesn't it? Yet since 1986, when the high court held that sexual harassment on the job amounted to job discrimination, several Federal courts have contrived to make it more complicated. Justice Sandra Day O'Connor's plainspoken opinion for a unanimous Court brings a refreshing end to the legalese and resistance to change the lower courts have indulged in.

Those courts have loaded up the simple written law with all sorts of rules and extra burdens of proof that Congress never imagined, such as the requirement that a plaintiff prove that the harassment caused psychological damage.

Teresa Harris, a manager with a Tennessee truck leasing firm, didn't fall apart under the sexual insults of the company's president, Charles Hardy. She simply got mad at his vulgar language, his proposal to discuss her salary at a local motel and his suggestion in front of others that she brought the company some business by having sex with a customer. She left, and sued. Lower courts found Mr. Hardy's behavior offensive but not sufficiently injurious.

By the time the case reached the high court, not even her former employer, Forklift Systems Inc., was willing to defend the reasoning of the lower courts that dismissed her lawsuit. The only question became what standard the justices would ordain for her next round of litigation and for similar suits.

That standard — proof that the employer created or tolerated an environment that the worker perceived, and a reasonable person would perceive, as hostile and abusive — came swiftly, clearly and unanimously once the Court took a cold look. Only a month after hearing arguments, Justice O'Connor delivered a ruling that is faithful to the broad language and purpose of the 1964 Civil Rights Act. As usual, she needed no footnotes.

Justice O'Connor laid down a broad principle for the lower courts to follow. Meanwhile people like Mr. Hardy, the company president, know the new rules of the game: Stop what you've been doing. It's against the law.

copyright © The New York Times 1993

Breast Implant Sales Halted

The Food and Drug Administration Jan. 6, 1992 called for a moratorium on the sale and implantation of silicone-gel breast implants, to give the agency time to review data on the devices' safety. The moratorium was expected to last at least 45 days. An FDA advisory panel had recommended in November 1991 that breast implants remain on the market while further safety studies were done.

FDA Commissioner David A. Kessler told a news conference that he had requested the moratorium because new information had come to light that cast doubt on the implants' safety. "We want surgeons to stop using these implants in patients until this new evidence can be thoroughly evaluated," Kessler said.

The new information included additional reports from rheumatologists who reported seeing a growing number of autoimmune and connective-tissue disorders among implant recipients. In addition, the FDA had obtained access to documents that were currently under court seal in several implant lawsuits. The documents suggested that breast-implant manufacturers had had concerns about the devices' safety dating back to the 1970s.

About two million women had had silicone-gel implants inserted since they first came on the market in the 1960s. Of that total, 80% had received the implants for cosmetic reasons and 20% for reconstruction of a breast following surgery for breast cancer. The FDA had not been given authority to fully regulate breast implants or other medical devices until 1976. In the 1980s, the FDA had ordered manufacturers to conduct studies to prove that implants were safe, but the agency subsequently found that the data submitted by the manufacturers were insufficient.

"We still do not know how often the implants leak and, when they do, we do not know exactly what materials get into the body," Kessler said. "We still do not know how often the implants break, or how long they last."

Manufacturers and plastic surgeons said they would comply with the moratorium, although they insisted that implants were safe.

THE PLAIN DEALER
Cleveland, Ohio, January 12, 1992

The Food and Drug Administration, beset by voices of both panic and righteousness, acted wisely last week in requesting a moratorium on the use of silicone-gel breast implants.

The moratorium is to last until FDA and its advisory panel are satisfied they have enough data to decide whether the implants, used by at least a million women, are safe. That could be awhile. Having raised fears by its moratorium, FDA must resolve the matter speedily.

For now, acrimony over the safety of the implants, used for decades but suspected of causing serious illness in some women, has clouded fact and promoted hysteria. The FDA, entering the fray years' late, is smart to call a halt to the name-calling, and breast-implanting, while more data is gathered and assessed.

The implant manufacturers and plastic surgeons pushing the devices have been lax in doing the systematic studies needed to show whether the silicone implants are safe.

The implants had been used for years when FDA first got jurisdiction over their safety in 1976; the agency failed to require safety data from manufacturers until last year. Meanwhile, complaints about everything from leaks of the silicone gel, with suspected debilitating side effects, to botched surgery, mounted. (FDA also has collected complaints about saline-solution breast implants, but these are not covered by the current moratorium.)

Manufacturers insist there's plenty of evidence to show silicone implants are low-risk. An FDA panel that sifted through volumes of data disagrees: It found last fall that the four manufacturers whose silicone implants were still on the market had not proven their safety.

The halt in silicone implants does not mean FDA now believes the devices are unsafe. It just means the agency cannot ensure they are safe. The general rule of thumb should be that if the implants aren't causing problems, women need not worry. Indeed, silicone implants — sacs of silicone gel used to refashion or reconstruct breasts — have a huge cheering section among women. Satisfied customers appear by far to outweigh ones who have experienced trouble. Plastic surgeons cite fewer than 100 problem cases in the literature.

But the seriousness of some reported side effects — from possible autoimmune disorders to connective-tissue diseases and inability to do normal breast-cancer checks — merit thorough review and consideration.

The breast-implant controversy also illustrates the long-term costs of regulatory and industry lapses. If systematic, credible safety studies had been undertaken from the first year breast implants were used, scientists assessing their risks today would have a solid body of fact, instead of horror-story innuendo and anecdote, upon which to base their decisions.

THE TENNESSEAN
Nashville, Tennessee, January 11, 1992

WHATEVER new information is available on breast implants needs to be made public quickly.

Women who have implants, whether they've had trouble or not, need answers to make intelligent choices with their doctors.

Food and Drug Commissioner David Kessler set off a new debate on silicone breast implants this week when he called on doctors to temporarily stop using them until a panel could review new data about safety concerns.

Under the circumstances, Kessler had little choice, though he's been roundly criticized by both proponents and detractors of the implants.

A series of lawsuits claiming that leaking implants can cause immune disorders sparked much of the drive to get the implants banned permanently. Yet, just two months ago, an FDA advisory panel agreed that the silicone implants should be kept on the market. The American Medical Association and the American Society of Plastic and Reconstructive Surgeons both have vouched for their safety.

While there have been lawsuits filed by women who question the safety, there are testimonials as well from those women who have had no problems.

The sole concern should be those women who elect the surgery. Some scoff at surgical breast enhancement. About 80% of the implants are for cosmetic purposes. But who is to say that a matter of self-esteem for some women is not an important health issue.

About 20% of the implants are for women who lost their breasts to cancer. It's a matter of well-being as well as self-esteem at a difficult period for those women.

Certainly, there are other forms of surgery for enhancement, including a saline implant and reconstruction using other tissues from the body.

Yet, the only answer for women with silicone implants is to provide the information at hand. A 45-day moratorium isn't a ban, but it's a long time to be concerned about one's health.

Having raised the question, the FDA needs to provide the information in as timely and responsible a manner as possible. ■

Pittsburgh Post-Gazette
Pittsburgh, Pennsylvania, January 8, 1992

The U.S. Food and Drug Administration's call for a moratorium on the use of silicone gel breast implants is good for women, and as evidence of the agency's renewed vigor and seriousness of purpose it is good for all Americans.

FDA Commissioner David Kessler said he made the recommendation because the safety of the devices had not been proved, despite being on the market for three decades. More than a million women have had silicone gel breast-implant surgery, about 20 percent of them after losing a breast to cancer.

•

In spite of that extensive experience, Dr. Kessler, at his press conference Monday, recited a long and sorry list of unknowns:

"We still do not know how often the implants leak, and when they do, we do not know exactly what materials get into the body. We still do not know how often the implants break, or how long they last. We still do not know how often women with the implants suffer adverse effects. For example, there are reports that painful hardening of the implant can occur in anywhere from 10 percent to 70 percent of patients.

"We still do not know to what extent the implants interfere with mammography examinations. We still do not know whether the implants can increase a woman's risk of developing cancer. And we still do not know enough about the relationship between these devices and autoimmune and connective tissue diseases."

It was the first time in the history of the agency that such an action was taken against a device so widely used. And the move came despite a recommendation by an FDA advisory committee that the implants remain on the market while more information on safety is gathered.

Dr. Kessler stopped short of a total ban, saying that he would reconvene the advisory panel within 45 days to consider new evidence on problems connected with the implants (including sealed court documents indicating that at least one manufacturer knew of potential problems back in the 1970s and did not alert doctors or patients).

Some critics are unhappy that Dr. Kessler did not issue an outright ban. Others contend that the products are safe and that the moratorium is unjustified. Considering the lack of documentation certifying the safety of the devices and the substantial amount of anecdotal evidence about harmful side effects, Dr. Kessler's action is reasonable, and bodes well for the agency under his leadership.

After a decade marked by Reaganesque antipathy for regulation, threadbare budgets, incapacitated leadership and a demoralized staff, Dr. Kessler has breathed new life and vitality into the FDA with a simple commitment to enforce the law.

In less than a year at the helm, he has taken on half a dozen of the leading food and drug manufacturers for misleading labeling and advertising in an increasingly successful effort to demonstrate that the FDA is back and it means business.

•

The fact that the agency addressed the safety of silicone-gel breast implants now, when concerns about possible harmful side effects were voiced a decade ago, is evidence of the serious new direction of the FDA. (The implants were not subject to FDA evaluation or approval when they first came on the market, but in 1976 Congress mandated regulation of medical devices. In the early 1980s the FDA said that since the implants were permanently inserted into the body, they must be proved safe. No action was taken.)

Considering the condition of the agency when Dr. Kessler took over, and the staffing and budget constraints with which he must contend, the rehabilitation will not be complete for years to come. But, so far, the progress is remarkable.

The State
Columbia, South Carolina, January 11, 1992

DOCTORS should heed the Federal Drug Administration's warning to discontinue using silicone gel breast implants until the final verdict is in on their safety.

The FDA has called for a moratorium on the implants for at least 45 days, when an advisory panel will reconvene to assess reports that the devices can cause serious illnesses and tissue damage. Most of the 1 million women who have received silicone gel implants have suffered no ill effects, but about 3,400 have reported various problems such as implant ruptures, skin rashes, lupus, chronic fatigue, arthritis and allergies.

FDA Commissioner David Kessler said his agency may not have received all the existing data on the safety of the silicone implants. And New York Rep. Ted Weiss, who chairs a House subcommittee on human resources, said one manufacturer, Dow Corning, "falsely claimed that their breast implants were proven safe, when in fact their own research indicated they could be dangerous." If Mr. Weiss is correct, the FDA should have banned the silicone implants until scientific evidence proves they are safe.

Apparently, most local plastic surgeons plan to either postpone breast augmentation and reconstructive surgery or use other devices, such as saline implants or TRAMflaps, which are not included in the FDA moratorium. As a local lawyer who specializes in medical malpractice cases pointed out, that is certainly the prudent course.

SYRACUSE HERALD-JOURNAL
Syracuse, New York, January 8, 1992

If the Food and Drug Administration erred when it advised against the use of silicone-gel breast implants, its error was not in issuing the recommendation, as some groups have charged. If anything, the agency could have taken a tougher stance and called for an outright ban against the implants until further testing has been completed.

The FDA's advisory, issued on Monday, asked surgeons to stop using silicone-gel implants and manufacturers to stop supplying them. The agency has received 3,400 complaints about the implants, and says it has evidence of several implant-related problems. They include ruptures and risk of immunity-system disorders. And some researchers believe the implants may cause cancer or chronic inflammatory disease, although no studies have proven those claims thus far.

The American Medical Association says the breast implants have been used for 30 years with no link to cancer. Some psychotherapists and the group "My Image after Breast Cancer" oppose the FDA recommendation. They say the implants are critical to the esteem of women who have had breasts removed.

While the FDA can sympathize with women who rely on the silicone implants after breast removal, its decisions must be based on health and safety concerns — first and foremost.

Already, the agency has been too lenient with Dow Wright Co., which manufactures silicone-gel breast implants.

The FDA said women who called the company's hot line were told the implants were 100 percent safe. Yet the FDA merely warned Dow for giving out misleading information. That means women might have decided to have the implants based on what they thought was reliable information. If Dow is guilty of misinforming women, a slap on the hand is not sufficient.

Really, the breast implant issue comes down to this: American society is preoccupied with breasts — the bigger the better.

Why do women even get breast implants? Only a small minority do so because they have lost a breast to surgery. The fact is 80 percent — one million women have had implants over the last three decades — got breast implants for cosmetic purposes. They want bigger ones.

Even the women who have medical reasons often use arguments like "self-esteem" and "feeling whole" for getting the implants — as if breasts or breast size define women. Certainly that notion is reinforced in commercial and advertising messages.

No wonder then that so many women opt for this optional surgery — even when its safety has not been assured. What a shame.

If the FDA decides to ban silicone-gel implants, women who want breast reconstruction have other options. Saline breast implants are available, and reconstructive breast surgery is also an alternative for women who have had breasts removed.

But real progress will not be made when the 100 percent safe breast implant is discovered. Real progress will happen when our society stops measuring women according to their breast size.

AKRON BEACON JOURNAL
Akron, Ohio, January, January 8, 1992

Where reasonable doubt exists about the safety of a medical device, it's only prudent to limit or suspend its use until conclusive evidence is obtained. On Monday, the federal Food and Drug Administration urged doctors to halt silicone-gel breast implants and asked manufacturers to suspend sale of the devices pending further investigation of safety concerns.

The call for a voluntary moratorium is well-advised. After extensive hearings last November, an FDA advisory panel concluded that the devices could stay on the market. Since then, the FDA says, other evidence has increased concerns about the health risks of the devices.

Most frequently cited are leaks and ruptures; side effects such as hardening of the implants and area around implants; links to connective-tissue disease, to cancer and to autoimmune disorders; and difficulty with getting accurate mammograms of women with implants.

Of course, manufacturers and plastic surgeons argue the safety of silicone implants. And many witnesses testified to their satisfaction with the devices.

The point, however, is that 30 years and an estimated 2 million implants later, questions of health risks have not been conclusively answered.

The FDA is taking a measured stand: The moratorium acknowledges continuing worries, but the advice to women who have the implants is not to have the devices removed unless they have complaints they think may be related to the implants.

Until the FDA panel evaluates and reaches a conclusion on the available data, that stand seems a reasonable one to take.

The Record
Hackensack, New Jersey, January 14, 1992

DOW CORNING Corp. is sticking to its guns. The company continues to insist that its silicone gel breast implants are safe, even though the Food and Drug Administration says their safety cannot be guaranteed. The FDA has asked for a moratorium on the use of all such implants.

Dow maintains it acted properly in testing a new kind of silicone gel implants before marketing them to plastic surgeons in 1975. But an FDA panel found the company's test data on implants inconclusive, and recently warned Dow to stop giving consumers what the agency termed misleading information about the safety of the implants.

Now charges have been made that the company's history of testing the implants is highly questionable. Reports in The New York Times and The Wall Street Journal this week cite internal memos showing that the implants were placed in women before testing on animals was complete, that testing was inadequate, and that Dow researchers realized this and called for more testing years ago.

To beat the competition, an implant task force was apparently given five months to do two years' worth of research and development. One Dow official wrote in 1976, "We are engulfed in unqualified speculation." Moreover, comprehensive tests were not done during more than a decade of consumer use, even after plastic surgeons began reporting problems with the implants in some of their patients.

One memo said Dow was engaged in "unqualified speculation."

The lack of information from Dow, the largest manufacturer of silicone gel breast implants, led a member of an FDA review panel to conclude recently that no one knows how long silicone gel implants last before they deteriorate or rupture, whether they are associated with cancer or immune disorders as a result of silicone leakage, and whether they interfere with mammograms — information that is particularly important to women who have the implants inserted after surgery for breast cancer.

A Dow researcher who quit in protest over the company's implant testing practices said it has conducted "a massive experiment on women."

That charge will sound familiar to anyone who remembers other cases of risks taken with women's health. Two examples: the Dalkon Shield intrauterine device, an insufficiently tested method of birth control that caused sterility and other serious health problems in many women; and the first birth control pills, which also were inadequately tested and which contained far higher levels of hormones than those on the market today.

In light of the newest evidence of questionable testing practices, it's ironic that a Dow official said recently of his company's silicone gel breast implants, "It is of vast importance that the FDA allow this product to remain on the market for all women. To do anything else would make victims of these women."

Victims, indeed.

Newsday
New York City, New York, January 8, 1992

At last the U.S. Food and Drug Administration is taking seriously the potential hazards of silicone breast implants. After a decade of debate, the FDA has acknowledged that it doesn't know whether the implants are safe. On Monday, it asked doctors to stop using them while the question of safety is investigated. That's good news for women.

What's astonishing is that manufacturers, in 30 years, have never conducted reliable studies showing the risks and benefits of the implants. What percentage of women have painful hardening of the breasts after the surgery? How often do the implants rupture? Do they increase the risk of cancer, or autoimmune diseases such as lupus and arthritis? No reliable data exists — although anecdotal information suggests that 40 percent of women with implants experience complications. Without the data, women cannot make informed decisions about whether the benefits of silicone implants outweigh the risks.

Consider the abundance of information now available on birth control pills. Like the breast implants, the pill was developed in the 1960s. But with the pill, unlike implants, exhaustive studies have been conducted. (That's because drugs were regulated at the time and implants were not, and because more grant money was available for research on birth control than for implants). Today, each package of pills comes with an insert giving women vital information on the risk of heart attack, blood clots and so on. The same kind of information should be available for implants.

When it convenes in the next 45 days, the FDA's advisory panel will review evidence that manufacturers of breast implants covered up negative information. Should the implants ultimately be banned? Finally, we'll be getting some answers.

The Washington Post
Washington, D.C., January 8, 1992

THE FOOD and Drug Administration has taken exactly the right step on the volatile and suddenly visible issue of safety in breast implants, calling for a 45-day moratorium on the use and distribution of the silicon gel devices while the FDA assesses new evidence as to whether they are safe. No one can reasonably accuse FDA commissioner David Kessler of jumping to his conclusion too quickly on this serious matter or of failing to give the implant makers a sufficient hearing; on the contrary, following prolonged and emotional November hearings on the subject, an FDA advisory panel ruled that the devices should continue to be available and that manufacturers should take steps to present evidence—so far, lacking—that they were safe and effective. Dr. Kessler changed the ruling Monday, he said in a press conference, after receiving new information about implants that "increases our concerns about their safety," including, apparently, court papers from two pending lawsuits. He offered a lengthy list of questions on which findings are still unavailable—how long the implants last, whether they are related to incidence of several diseases and whether the percentage of women whose implants harden and become painful is closer to 10 percent or 70 percent.

Why is there so little safety information on breast implants, which have been on the market since 1963 and have been implanted in nearly 2 million women? It's partly accident. Between 1963 and 1976, medical devices were unregulated. In 1976, a safety law was enacted, and existing devices were classified as either needing or not needing a retroactive safety check. A dispute developed over whether breast implants should be ruled "class 3"—which would have required the safety studies now being demanded—or "class 2," which would not. That dispute continued *through 1988*, at which point manufacturers were given an additional 30 months to prepare their case. This brings us to the present, and high time, too.

Much has been heard in this process about the importance of implants to women who want them, both the 20 percent who have reconstruction after breast cancer surgery and the remaining 80 percent whose breasts are healthy but who, for a variety of reasons, want them made larger. Some satisfied patients, and some doctors, complain that the public is overreacting to isolated instances of severe complication, which, while horrific when described, are rare. But that's just the point: Nobody knows for sure how rare they are, and nobody will until someone does the necessary studies. Nor have implant manufacturers responded to this process in a way that inspires great confidence. One, Dow Corning Wright Corp., shut down its telephone hot line last week after the FDA accused it of misleading callers on risk levels; another was quoted as observing that the moratorium would not prevent continued sale of implants abroad. The subject cries out for more study. Women who want implants should be able to have safe ones.

The San Diego Union
San Diego, California, January 10, 1992

The Food and Drug Administration's call for a voluntary moratorium on silicone gel breast implants is a prudent caution which plastic surgeons, manufacturers and women ought to heed.

On the basis of new information suggesting possible adverse side effects from implantation, FDA Commissioner David Kessler has concluded there no longer is sufficient cause to consider the procedure "100 percent safe," as one manufacturer previously claimed. However, it is important to recognize that there still is insufficient evidence that the gel implants pose a significant danger.

Of the more than 10,000 women a month who have been receiving silicone implants, about 80 percent have done so for purely cosmetic reasons. Based on the new information about the potential risks, candidates for cosmetic surgery and their physicians should defer the operation for the time being.

The other 20 percent of implant patients have the operation for reconstructive purposes, usually after breast cancer surgery. While the psychological need for implants must be considered, patients and their doctors would be wise to realize that many safety concerns remain unanswered.

There was a clear need for the FDA's warning. The agency has received about 2,500 reports of illnesses or injuries associated with the implants. Although these reports are anecdotal, they cannot be discounted. Frank B. Vasey, a University of South Florida rheumatologist, has linked implants to a connective-tissue disease which causes pain in the joints, general swelling, fatigue and some respiratory illness.

Kessler announced that the FDA also has obtained internal documents from a Dow Corning Corp. subsidiary, the major manufacturer of implants, which he said raises "substantial concerns" about implant leaks and ruptures. Other studies indicate the implants interfere with mammography exams for breast cancer.

Kessler will reconvene an expert panel on implant safety within 45 days to review the new data. All four manufacturers of silicone implants and leaders in organized medicine have pledged to cooperate with the FDA's review.

Surgeons say the great majority of women who have had breast implants express satisfaction. Kessler noted that if they are not experiencing difficulties, "there is no need to consider removing the implants."

All the same, it makes sense to call a timeout on implants until their safety can be clearly established.

Portland Press Herald
Portland, Maine, January 11, 1992

The Food and Drug Administration's moratorium on silicon breast implants pending further study makes good sense both for women and their surgeons. FDA Commissioner David A. Kessler, himself a doctor, underscored the need for caution when he said his agency "cannot assure the safety of these devices at this time."

Continuing to insert the implants while those 10 words hang over the devices invites potential health problems for women and possible litigation for their doctors.

At the same time, the FDA has a responsibility to conduct its study of silicone implants expeditiously. The devices are more than the stuff of Hollywood starlet jokes. They are an important physical and psychological aid for millions of women, particularly those having reconstructive surgery after breast cancer. Two million women have them now.

In addition, women considering the implants need the FDA's help in reaching fully informed decisions about any risk involved.

Meanwhile, let's be cautious not only about the implants, but about overreacting. So far, doctors suggest that, while silicone implants require regular monitoring, women with no symptoms of silicone leakage or scar tissue need not consider having them removed.

The FDA will reconvene an expert panel to review new data about silicone implants between now and Feb. 20. The sooner the better.

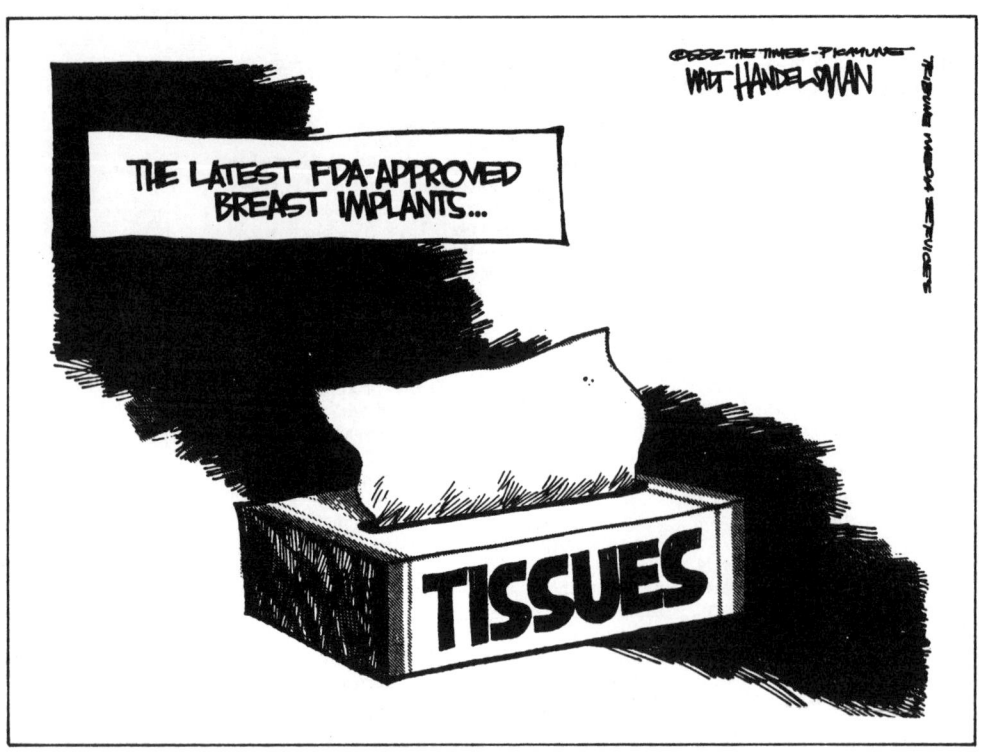

The Seattle Times
Seattle, Washington, January 15, 1992

As more is learned about scientific disagreements among those involved in the manufacture of silicone gel breast implants, the decision last week by Food and Drug Commissioner David Kessler becomes clearer — and wiser.

Kessler ordered a moratorium on use of the implants while the FDA reviews available information, including new data from manufacturer's files, to determine whether they are safe for continued use.

Silicone gel implants have been in use for 30 years. As many as two million American women may have received the implants, 80 percent for nonmedical cosmetic reasons, the remainder for reconstruction after breast removal due to cancer.

Critics of the implants contend the silicone gel can leak and migrate to other parts of the body, causing inflammation or other serious side effects.

A consultant to the FDA said he was astonished by the lack of directly relevant scientific studies of silicone gel breast implants.

Reports this week revealed that implants were inserted in women before they were tested in animals and that subsequent animal testing may not even have been done in breast tissue.

Files of Dow Corning, the major manufacturer of the implants, show that company scientists argued — unsuccessfully — for studies that would assure the safety of implants.

Despite vigorous denials by Dow Corning, one conclusion is inescapable: Market demand, driven by women's desires and aided by willing plastic surgeons, was a far greater influence on company decisions than the nagging of their own cautious scientists.

The FDA moratorium is a welcome, if tardy, intervention on behalf of telling women the truth. It should lead, finally, to putting good science before good marketing.

Las Vegas Review-Journal
Las Vegas, Nevada, January 9, 1992

About 1 million American women have had silicon breast implants, most without complication — the Food and Drug Administration reports it has received only 3,400 complaints about the medical procedure. Yet on Monday, the FDA asked for a voluntary halt to the sale and use of the implants.

The move comes in response to recent information the agency has received about the safety of the devices. FDA chief David A. Kessler refused to label the implants dangerous, but critics claim growing evidence suggests they can rupture and cause auto-immune or connective tissue diseases. The American Medical Association and Dow Corning Wright, the largest manufacturer of the implants, dispute those contentions.

An FDA advisory panel will reconvene to examine allegations against the silicon implants and eventually make a recommendation about the future of the procedure.

While some of Kessler's melodramatic pronouncements needlessly scared thousands of women — "The FDA can not assure women of their safety at this time" — the agency's decision to stop short of an outright ban makes sense. It is the FDA's charge to keep the public informed about medical devices and procedures, and Kessler's announcement accomplished that. But a ban on silicon implants based on anecdotal evidence would amount to an arbitrary and capricious government intrusion.

Chicago Sun-Times
Chicago, Illinois, January 9, 1992

The Food and Drug Administration's request that plastic surgeons stop using silicone gel breast implants has touched off anguish and distress among the 2 million American women who have undergone the surgery.

Coming only two months after the FDA urged that the implants remain on the market pending further study, the reversal stirs fears of new data reflecting on the safety of the implants.

Without specifying the new data, the FDA says the evidence indicates the implants could cause autoimmune or connective tissue disorders.

That being the case, the FDA's call for a voluntary moratorium on these types of implants appears ambivalently weak-kneed.

Any evidence that justifies fanning new fears should have dictated a mandatory order.

Nothing in the FDA's warning casts doubt on the safety of saline-filled implants.

However, while the FDA reconvenes an advisory panel on the issue of silicone gel implants, doctors would be irresponsible not to obey the moratorium on gel implants, especially for the 80 percent that are not related to other medical problems.

The Record
Hackensack, New Jersey, January 7, 1992

THE Food and Drug Administration is right to ask doctors to stop using silicone gel breast implants until all of the information available on their effects has been thoroughly reviewed. The evidence to date suggests that major health risks are involved for some women who have had implants.

Fewer than one-quarter of the women who have the silicone gel implants do so to counter the effects of breast cancer or injuries. Most of the 150,000 implants done each year are done for cosmetic purposes. Women considering such unessential surgery shouldn't mind waiting a while longer until an informed decision can be made by the FDA. The agency has already received about 2,500 reports of illness or injury connected with the implants. About 2 million women have had them.

The new recommendation contradicts an FDA advisory panel that said last fall that the implants should stay on the market, even though their safety could not be guaranteed, because of the overriding public health benefits. That's questionable. There's no overriding public health benefit in having one's breasts enlarged. And women who are having reconstructive surgery after breast cancer have other options. There are implants available that are filled with salt water, instead of the rubbery silicone gel.

When potential risks are involved, there's no harm in waiting for a more definitive answer.

The Phoenix Gazette
Phoenix, Arizona, January 13, 1992

Is it science or bureaucratic paternalism that prompted the U.S. Food and Drug Administration to recommend that doctors stop using silicone gel breast implants until new safety information is assessed?

In November, an FDA advisory panel — the General and Plastic Surgery Devices Committee — recommended that the implants remain on the market while research into their safety continued.

The committee said manufacturers had failed to prove that the devices were safe — but there was nevertheless a compelling public health need to keep them available, particularly for reconstruction after breast cancer surgery.

The FDA should have followed the committee's advice. All that the current directive has done is frighten women who already have the implants and possibly discourage others from having needed cancer surgery because of the fear of disfigurement.

Although the moratorium is voluntary, if FDA Commissioner David Kessler's prediction that "all manufacturers and physicians will abide by it" comes true, the implants will quickly become unobtainable.

Dow Corning Wright, the largest manufacturer of silicone gel breast implants, said it was suspending shipment and sales of the devices. Less satisfactory implants filled with salt water will still be available.

The FDA says it has new concerns about the safety of the products as a result of a California lawsuit over a ruptured silicone implant that resulted in a $7 million federal jury award.

But evidence presented in lawsuits might or might not meet the standard of scientific validity.

About 1 million women in the United States have had implants in the past 30 years. Fewer than 1 percent of them have experienced problems. That's a record that beats many surgical procedures.

Questions abound. The FDA did not recommend a moratorium on silicone penile or testicular implants, joint replacements or insulin syringes that contain silicone materials. The agency's selectivity gives credence to feminists' charge that women are being subjected to a misguided effort to protect them from themselves.

No time limit was put on the moratorium, although Kessler said the agency would move as quickly as possible to settle the issue. Given the FDA's record of handwringing and delay, that is not cause for encouragement.

Until there is scientific evidence that the implants really are unsafe, the decision regarding their use should be left to patients and their physicians.

St. Petersburg Times
St. Petersburg, Florida, January 8, 1992

The Food and Drug Administration (FDA) moved Monday to halt the sale of silicone breast implants and their use by plastic surgeons in cosmetic and prosthetic surgery. The good news is that some 100,000 to 150,000 patients who might otherwise seek the procedure this year will be spared exposure to unknown medical risks. The bad news is that 2-million American women have already opted for a purely elective procedure that may pose serious health threats.

"The FDA cannot assure the safety of these devices at this time," said David Kessler, FDA commissioner. He requested that doctors and manufacturers wait until a panel of experts had studied new data before resuming the use of silicone-filled implants. Implants filled with a saline solution are not affected by the regulatory agency's request.

Kessler's list of belated FDA questions about silicone implants reveals a shocking disregard for product safety. He said the agency doesn't know how often the implants leak, what materials they release into the body, whether they increase the risk of cancer or whether crippling auto-immune and connective tissue diseases may be linked to their use. The FDA can't even say how long the implants should last and under what conditions they might rupture. Polyurethane coverings used on the devices pose another set of questions; again, the FDA has no answers for consumers.

Despite these critical unknowns, silicone implants have been manufactured and profitably marketed for 30 years. Women who trust their doctors — and why shouldn't they? — have been encouraged to accept the devices as a safe cosmetic option or as permanent prostheses after cancer surgery. Only recently have women learned that the presence of implants interferes with mammography, a life-saving tool in breast cancer detection.

Even now, Kessler is considering an ill-conceived proposal to keep implants on the market for women who have a "psychological" need for them. While the need may be real, it is based on women's false assumption that they are making a fully informed, safe choice.

Sadly, this is not the first time that elective health care options for women have been offered as harmless, only to be proved otherwise. The most obvious parallel is the Dalkon Shield, once touted as a highly effective, convenient option for birth control. As with silicone implants, women using the Dalkon Shield reported side effects for years before their complaints were taken seriously. How much damage could have been avoided? The question is destined to be repeated until the medical community and the FDA put the safety of women before the interests of those who profit from inadequately tested health care products.

Breast Implants Curbed by FDA

The Food and Drug Administration April 16, 1992 ended a moratorium on the insertion of silicone-gel breast implants that had been in effect since January. It said limited use of the devices would be permitted for women who agreed to participate in clinical studies on their safety. The action adhered closely to a February recommendation by an FDA advisory panel.

Under the FDA's plan, silicone-gel implants would become available in three stages. In the first stage, women with ruptured or leaking implants would be able to obtain new ones. So would an estimated 9,000 women whose scheduled breast operations were put on hold by the January moratorium.

The second stage would provide implants to women who had an "urgent" physical or psychological need for breast reconstruction. Such patients included burn victims and women who had had surgery for breast cancer.

In the third stage, a few thousand women would be allowed to use implants for breast enlargement. But the number would be far lower than the estimated 100,000 women who had received the implants annually in the late 1980s for cosmetic reasons.

All women who got new implants would have to participate in follow-up studies conducted by both the FDA and manufacturers. In addition, the FDA planned to keep a permanent registry of recipients.

"We know more about the life span of automobile tires than we do about the longevity of breast implants," FDA Commissioner David A. Kessler said at a Washington, D.C. news conference April 16. "The data on failed implants that we've seen so far raises concerns." He added, "No one should think we are resuming business as usual. These are not approved devices, and any woman who wants one will have to be in clinical studies."

Rep. Ted S. Weiss (D, N.Y.), who in 1991 had spearheaded efforts to get the FDA to investigate silicone-gel implants, April 16 called the agency's decision "a reasonable compromise." "Any woman who now chooses implants will understand that she is participating in a massive experiment," he said.

The American Society of Plastic and Reconstructive Surgeons applauded the FDA's move. "This is the first sign that science, logic and compassion are being returned to the review process for these devices," said society president Norman Cole April 16.

Canadian Health Minister Benoit Bouchard April 16 announced a six-month extension of the existing moratorium on the use of silicone breast implants. More than 150,000 Canadian women had received the implants.

Bouchard's announcement came in response to a report by an independent committee set up to study the breast implant controversy, headed by Dr. Cornelia Baines of the University of Toronto. The minister rejected as potentially discriminatory the panel's key recommendation, a compromise that would allow women who needed reconstructive surgery and older women to continue using silicone implants. Of the two million women in North America who had had implants since they first went on the market in the 1960s, 80% had them for cosmetic reasons.

Bouchard announced that the federal Laboratory Centre for Disease Control would conduct a $1-million epidemiological study of the health risks of breast implants. The government also commissioned a survey of women who had had the implants, to determine their experiences with the devices.

Winnipeg Free Press
Winnipeg, Manitoba, April 21, 1992

Health Minister Benoit Bouchard wants a Canadian solution to the nasty problem of breast implants. Nothing could be more Canadian than the thoughts of the committee he asked to think through the dilemma of health vs. well-being. The compromise it suggested — to allow silicone implants for breast reconstruction, but not breast enhancement — is unlikely to be improved upon through another moratorium. It is unfortunate that the health minister could not accept it or the several other good suggestions from Canadian experts.

The compromise solution is akin to the thoughts of a U.S. panel of experts made public in February. It is also the position the U.S. Food and Drug Administration has adopted. As FDA commissioner David Kessler acknowledged, continued disapproval of the gel-filled sacs to create bigger breasts is not a return to business as usual. Restoring approval of silicone breast implants for women who have lost breasts to cancer or other injuries is not risk-free but it is compassionate. It is not, as Mr. Bouchard suggests, unduly discriminatory. The distinction is made on product usage; the distinction is not drawn primarily between women.

The Canadian committee's other suggestion — to limit implants to women over age 40 — is more puzzling and more likely to be the sort of Charter violation that Mr. Bouchard wants to avoid. Physicians have used that age barrier in recommending other procedures, however. The health problems experienced by some women after breast implantation became evident very soon after surgery. Age will not protect women from unfortunate complications; nor should pain and discomfort be less regarded in older women.

The committee's other suggestion should not be hard to implement, but Mr. Bouchard is balking. The committee suggests that a national registry of women who have received breast implants would be helpful. The health minister wonders whether governments can force registration and sort out with provinces the jurisdictional questions. How foolish. How Canadian.

If anything should have been learned from the breast implant fiasco, it was the need to track health problems of people who have unusual devices placed in their bodies. The FDA has proposed that the makers of 35 kinds of devices be required to keep such registries. Instead, Mr. Bouchard will give Canadian women a toll-free telephone number. That's only slightly better than nothing.

The health minister has given himself and his officials another six months to craft a better Canadian policy. The department has badly mishandled the problems of implants for several years running. Mr. Bouchard was wise to appoint an independent committee. He would be wiser to heed its advice.

TULSA WORLD
Tulsa, Oklahoma, April 20, 1992

THE FOOD and Drug Administration faced a controversial question last week: whether to continue to allow silicone breast implants.

The decision and its background presented a classic case of how politics and greedy interests can influence decisions that are supposed to be based on scientific judgment and the public welfare.

The breast implants had been in use for more than a generation with a high percentage of satisfaction. There were, of course, some bad cases that could have been predicted in any extensive surgical procedure.

The decision was forced on the FDA by a publicity blitz backed largely by damage-suit lawyers. After a couple of successful lawsuits involving implants, the attorneys smelled more business if they could stir up controversy on the subject and encourage more claims.

There were a few horror stories of breast operations gone wrong. But thousands of women, fully advised of the risks, were willing to take their chances.

It was a tough one for the FDA. Satisfy the damage-suit hunters and the self-described "consumer" groups. Or satisfy women who wanted to choose for themselves whether to accept the small risk involved.

The FDA ducked. It banned the implants for cosmetic purposes, but allowed them to continue under certain conditions for women whose breasts had been removed or disfigured by accident or surgery.

The compromise doesn't make sense. But what can you expect when a supposedly scientific decision is made on such obvious political grounds?

AUGUSTA HERALD
Augusta, Georgia, April 22, 1992

Federal Food and Drug Administration Commissioner David Kessler finally defined under what conditions American women can have silicone gel breast implants: When they need reconstructive surgery following a serious illness or accident that causes severe deformity; and then only as participants in scientific studies designed to answer questions about safety.

Women can't have it for cosmetic purposes, even if they are fully apprised of the risks and are willing to be a part of the studies. Why not? If the surgery can be made available to some women under the new guidelines, why not to others?

As Augusta plastic surgeon, Dr. Randy Smith says, "If it is a good device, it should be available to all. If it is injurious, it ought not be available to anyone." And isn't it discrimination if it's not?

It seems silicone gel implants are being taken over by proponents of Political Correctness, using the FDA as their instrument of control. Implants for cancer patients are acceptable, but cosmetology patients who want breast augmentation are deemed frivolous, demeaning themselves and their gender.

But that's a social judgment, not a medical decision. Medical decisions should be left to doctors and their patients, not a federal bureaucracy. This is government meddling of the worst sort.

Let's not forget the case against silicone gel is shaky at best. It's been around for several decades and the Augusta area medical community, among many others, has enjoyed great success, with virtually no serious complaints.

This isn't surprising. An enormous body of evidence has built up over the years showing silicone gel implants to be safe, yet the FDA has chosen to respond only to recent anecdotal — not scientific — evidence indicating it might, in some cases, cause health-damaging side effects.

That's a small reed to rest the FDA's takeover of physicians' authority, but at least saline gels are still available for cosmetic breast surgery. But perhaps not for long. The FDA will take a "closer look" at them next year.

The Washington Post
Washington, D.C., April 20, 1992

TO EVALUATE the new Food and Drug Administration guidelines on breast implants, announced last week by FDA head David Kessler, it's important to compare the new formulas with the situation they replace. That situation was not the rosy one of free, fully informed consumer choice and painless, near-universal satisfaction portrayed by many plastic surgeons and implant manufacturers. Instead, women who thought they were in a position of making that free choice were in fact lacking crucial information that manufacturers had repeatedly failed to seek.

Basically, the new guidelines create a process by which every woman with implants becomes part of a comprehensive safety study on their effects. Women who want the devices for medical reasons (to reconstruct a breast they have lost) get priority in the trials over women who want to make their healthy breasts larger. These last were an estimated 80 percent of the previous market. But that may change in light of the case studies and unanswered concerns that have now been aired: whether implants interfere with mammogram detection of breast cancers, whether they leak silicone into the body and cause rheumatoid or autoimmune disease, whether and how often they cause hardness or loss of sensation. Women who already have the implants and have not experienced such problems are advised not to have them removed, but rather to contact a plastic surgeon and join a national registry so their experiences can become part of the data base.

To the criticism that the government is inappropriately interfering with women's freedom to have implants for any reason they like—cosmetic or otherwise—it's important to reiterate that the government is merely giving women the tools to make that calculation in the future. It wouldn't have been necessary if not for the repeated and long-term abrogation of this responsibility by those most directly responsible—manufacturers and doctors.

The FDA notes that fear of liability is a strong force *dissuading* manufacturers from aggressive investigation of possible safety problems such as implant ruptures; so is fear of losing customers. As for the doctors: In March, with the public furor at its peak, Wall Street Journal reporter Jane Berentson asked five plastic surgeons about possible implants. She wrote that "the medical care in these offices is accompanied by a healthy dose of salesmanship" and that, despite the public debate, none mentioned the mammogram or autoimmune concerns the FDA had raised. Many plastic surgeons testified in winter hearings that they are more responsible than that, but they can't and don't regulate their colleagues. In stepping in, the FDA filled a harmful gap.

Debate Over Women in NFL Locker Rooms Intensifies

The alleged harassment of one female reporter in a National Football League locker room Sept. 17, 1990 and the barring of a second on Oct. 1 prompted renewed controversy over access to locker rooms for women journalists seeking interviews.

A federal court in 1978 had ruled that denying women reporters equal access to locker rooms violated the journalists' constitutional rights. The NFL and Major League Baseball had set formal rules in 1985 requiring open locker rooms and equal access, despite the objections of many players.

According to the Association for Women in Sports Media, about 500 of the estimated 10,000 sports reporters and broadcasters in the U.S. were women.

Lisa Olson, a reporter for the *Boston Herald*, charged that she was harassed by several New England Patriots players in their locker room Sept. 17, the day after a game against the Indianapolis Colts. Olson later wrote that "several" naked players "approached me, positioned themselves inches away from my face and dared me to touch their private parts."

Tight end Zeke Mowatt was fined an undisclosed amount for the incident by New England general manager Pat Sullivan. Mowatt later denied wrongdoing. The NFL Sept. 27 said that it would investigate the incident.

Olson was verbally abused by fans at Foxboro (Mass.) Stadium Sept. 30 as she headed for the locker room after a Patriots game. She said Oct. 7 that she had received death threats in the wake of the incident.

NFL Commissioner Paul Tagliabue Oct. 5 fined Cincinnati Bengals coach Sam Wyche one-seventeenth of his salary after Wyche Oct. 1 had barred a female reporter after a loss to the Seattle Seahawks. The reporter, Denise Tom of *USA Today*, was barred even though male reporters were admitted to the locker room.

THE PLAIN DEALER
Cleveland, Ohio, October 4, 1990

When Boston Herald sportswriter Lisa Olson recently charged that a New England Patriots football player exposed himself to her in a locker room while teammates made vulgar remarks, she became a symbol of an uncomfortable fact: The entrenched, shameful practice of men degrading women will not die easily. The controversy has generated widespread, justifiable outrage, especially from media members who stress all sportswriters — male or female — should have equal access and equal opportunity to do their jobs. But the Olson incident suggests the time has come for another practice to die: having sportswriters of any gender in athletic locker rooms.

Olson has said the player exposed himself after angrily saying her presence in the locker room was making players — in various states of undress — uncomfortable. A similar concern was expressed by Cincinnati Bengals coach Sam Wyche in justifying a recent decision not to allow another female reporter into his team's locker room. In both cases, female sportswriters, whose numbers have grown in recent years, became targets of ignorant abuse for merely following an outdated policy.

For decades, the sports media have routinely conducted interviews, especially after events, inside team locker rooms. The traditional reason given for this practice is that access to the dressing quarters allows the press to get the immediate, raw reactions of players and coaches after an event. Such an arrangement was fine in the past, when the number of media covering a team was small, and many writers downplayed the faults — on and off the field — of the athletes they covered. But the increase in recent years of sports media, as well as the scrutiny given to athletes, has made the relationship between writers and sports figures tense. That relationship can worsen as the two sides constantly cross paths in the one area athletes view — rightly or wrongly — as the lone remaining symbol of their privacy: the locker room.

What makes the tradition of locker room interviews even more puzzling is that there is a proven, better way to quiz sports figures after events that gives all media members equal access. It calls for the locker facilities to be closed to the media; athletes are brought to a separate interview room for questioning. That system has been used at various major events — and is the unchallenged policy of womens' golf and tennis organizations — and has had no obvious negative effect on sports reporting. Those sports figures that normally mouth cliches do so whether in a locker room or interview room. Those who are normally colorful remain so wherever they sit.

There is little good news in what apparently happened to Lisa Olson — clearly the fight to open doors for women must continue. A good way to prevent similar incidents from occurring again is to make one door closed to all: the door to the locker room.

The Cincinnati Post
Cincinnati, Ohio, October 6, 1990

Sam Wyche's "Plan A" response to the debate over women reporters in football locker rooms has cost him $30,000.

That's how much NFL commissioner Paul Tagliabue fined him for keeping a woman out of the Bengal's locker room after Monday night's game.

Wyche had it coming. He's been fined once before for closing the media out of his locker room — in violation of NFL rules — and once for knocking a microphone out of a reporter's hand in the dressing room.

This past Monday, he clearly broke the rules again.

But now that Tagliabue has made his point, he should come up with a policy that resolves the locker room dilemma: how to treat male and female sportswriters equally while respecting the sensibilities of those players who, understandably, are uncomfortable standing around naked in front of women they don't know.

Wyche's "Plan B" is a sensible approach. All sportswriters — male and female — would get a set period of time in the locker room before the team undresses.

Wyche proposes 20 minutes for interviews; a few minutes longer would be more reasonable. Whatever the time period, it would be inconvenient for reporters and players — but it would be fair.

Tagliabue should adopt Wyche's plan unless he can come up with something better. Handing out fines is not going to settle the controversy. The league office needs to establish a fair and sensitive policy.

The Dallas Morning News
Dallas, Texas, October 5, 1990

Since last month, a major storm has been growing in the National Football League over the sexual harassment of a female sports reporter from the *Boston Herald* by several members of the New England Patriots in their locker room. Adding to the controversy was the clumsy handling of the incident by Patriot owner Victor Kiam, who was quoted as calling the reporter a "classic bitch." NFL Commissioner Paul Tagliabue has retained a special counsel to investigate the incident, and put the 28 NFL teams on notice that "the longstanding league policies regarding equal access and treatment of all accredited media will continue to be vigorously enforced and that no violations of this policy will be tolerated." Still, the incident and fan reaction to the Boston reporter following the Patriots' loss Sunday remain troubling. The Boston crowd reportedly booed the female reporter, and one heckler jeered that she "got what she deserved." As a result, the question has again been raised: Should female reporters have access to NFL locker rooms?

YES
- Female reporters, like their male counterparts, have deadlines. They can't wait for all the athletes to shower and dress before getting interviews. They must do their job, getting facts and quotes in a timely manner.
- To bar female reporters from the locker room would be outright discrimination. Pure and simple. It would violate all principles of equal rights under the law.
- Why should the NFL be different? Other professional sports allowed such media access to locker rooms before the NFL did and without significant controversy.

NO
- Having female reporters in NFL locker rooms is an invasion of the players' privacy. Pure and simple.
- Female reporters shouldn't have access because the wives of players and coaches don't.
- Locker room interviews in general are unnecessary. Reporters should wait for the players and coaches to come out.
- No professional sports for women has mandatory locker room access, and even if one did, male reporters shouldn't be included.

Our view: some common-sense modifications

Equal access must stand, but with some minor, common-sense modifications. Sports reporters, male and female, should be allowed to conduct their business without having to put up with the kind of harassment endured by *Boston Herald* reporter Lisa Olson.

There can be no question that equal access and treatment must be upheld, as Mr. Tagliabue rightly made known to the NFL teams. His timely appointment of an independent counsel to investigate the Patriot incident was proper. While there is no dispute as to the truth of the incident, having all the facts will provide better guidance as to what punitive measures should be taken.

What is needed now is a cooling-off period. Continued resistance by teams to admitting female reporters to their locker rooms (such as the posting of a security guard by Cincinnati Bengal coach Sam Wyche to keep a female *USA Today* reporter out after the game Monday night) only exacerbates the issue.

What is also needed is a look at how locker room access is actually implemented. According to NFL policy, "after a reasonable waiting period following a game," is defined as no more than seven minutes after the team has entered the locker room. After that time, the home and visiting team locker room areas are supposed to be opened to all accredited media, with immediate access to all players and coaches.

The seven-minute interlude scarcely provides enough time for the coach to congratulate players for a win or deliver a short-and-sweet chewing out for stinking up the field. That's not much time for players to peel off layers of equipment and head for the showers to soak their wounds. Little wonder that when the media is allowed in, bare bodies are everywhere.

Extending the time period before opening the locker room doors, say to a maximum of 15 minutes, would help somewhat. It would be even better if there was an understanding that everyone should be clothed from the waist down.

The league's rules also say that "a club may bring the head coach and selected players to an interview area." But that's generally done only when there is locker room congestion. Why not have a designated interview area as a matter of policy? At present, the Dallas Cowboys organization is the only team with an interview room.

Despite his Monday night resistance to female reporters, coach Wyche said that he would comply with the league's equal access policy, but would instruct his players to stay dressed for 20 minutes following the game. That, too, is a sensible approach.

Admitting female reporters to locker rooms need not be any more disruptive than admitting male reporters to locker rooms if practical procedures can be agreed on and honored by all concerned. If other professional and amateur athletes have managed to do so, surely pro footballers can learn to talk and keep a towel on as well.

The Courier-Journal
Louisville, Kentucky, October 4, 1990

THE Cincinnati Bengals' locker room has been visited by some outdated male chivalry. The would-be knight in shining armor is Coach Sam Wyche, who has vowed to shield his men from their wives' wrath by declaring, "I will not allow women to walk in on 50 naked men." What hooey.

Coach Wyche proposes to keep women sportswriters out of the locker room — a policy that was rejected in federal court years ago. He and Zeke Mowatt of the New England Patriots, who recently harassed a female sportswriter in a locker room, apparently cling to the antiquated idea that women in sports ought to be on the cheerleading squad. Since they appear ignorant of it, here's a recap of that court case: Women won handily; men with dirty minds got zip.

Getting zipped is one sensible way to deal with the situation, if indeed his players' privacy is really the issue. Grabbing towels is another. Or throw all the media folks out of locker rooms — male and female reporters alike.

Coaches looking for a more reasonable solution might also consider using the University of Kentucky approach. Its locker rooms generally stay closed until players shower and dress.

Regardless of what rules prevail, men and women must be treated alike in the locker rooms at both men's and women's events. And bullies who try to drape themselves in an appeal to modesty, in order to keep news professionals from doing their jobs, ought to be sent to the showers.

The Boston Herald
Boston, Massachusetts, October 4, 1990

This is where it starts — in the high school locker room or perhaps the team bus. This is where kids who are gifted athletically learn to play by their own set of rules. This is where they learn that brutality toward those less gifted or physically weaker will bring little or no punishment. This is where they learn that because they are *special* they'll be protected — by coaches, by teachers, by parents, maybe even by local officials, all seduced by the idea that a winning team is worth any price.

In the wake of the sexual harassment of Herald reporter Lisa Olson in the locker room of the New England Patriots, a series which ran this week in the Boston Globe on high school hazing took on new meaning. While we journalistic rivals rarely mention each other by name (Would Filene's send you to Jordan Marsh?) this series, coming when it did, is difficult to ignore.

The articles recounted the following incidents: At Brockton High School 10 members of the track team (many of whom were also members of the football team) allegedly beat and harassed several other members of the team; at a preseason football camp Medford High students harassed and humiliated at least one of their team members; at Watertown High one member of the football team was reportedly put in a duffle bag and kicked around by teammates, and at Lowell High two hockey players suffered serious injuries at the hands of their own teammates.

And these are just high school kids. Imagine what splendid human beings they'll be when they grow up.

So how does it come to pass that big, burly pro football players would find it somehow clever and amusing to taunt with words and to prance naked in front of a 26-year-old woman attempting to conduct an interview? How did these men get to be the way they are today?

They got to be this way because back when *they* were kids it apparently never occurred to anyone to tell them that using their size, their brawn and their clout to intimidate others was wrong.

They got away with it then. They likely thought they could get away with it now. They were wrong.

DESERET NEWS
Salt Lake City, Utah, October 5, 1990

The recent uproar over the treatment of female sports writers in locker rooms of athletic teams raises some serious questions about equal access, decency and the ability of women writers to do their job. Yet these issues can be solved in ways that protect everyone's rights and a basic sense of modesty.

Certainly, the lewd behavior of a New England Patriots football player toward a woman writer is indefensible. Strict action against the offender needs to be taken and an apology issued to the female reporter.

Yet bringing women into a locker room full of men trying to shower and change has all kinds of potential for embarrassing situations — not just for the females, but for everyone else, including male reporters and the players.

Female sports writers need the same access to players for post-game interviews as their male counterparts. But why not arrange it in ways that still meet common standards of modesty for men and women alike?

Chaotic after-game locker rooms can be uncomfortable places for both men and women to conduct interviews. Some standards should be established that would make it easier on everybody.

Sam Wyche, head coach of the Cincinnati Bengals professional football team, may have hit upon a workable solution.

Wyche, who is known for being impulsive and tempestuous, has come up with the level-headed idea that allows male and female journalists equal access but not total access.

After Wyche came under fire for not letting a female reporter into the Bengal locker room last week, he ordered his players to remain dressed for 20 minutes after each game while they field questions from reporters. Journalists would then be excused while the players dress. Follow-up interviews could be scheduled for later.

The "Wyche solution" would keep access fair and would give beat reporters a chance to get the quotes they need and still make deadline.

It's a sane approach to an emotional issue.

THE BUFFALO NEWS
Buffalo, New York, December 15, 1990

ERIE COUNTY Legislator Raymond K. Dusza, D-Cheektowaga, has reconsidered. That's a blessing. His second thoughts were decidedly superior to his first — that county government should legislate fines or even jail terms for reporters entering post-game locker rooms if the team had closed the door.

Mercifully, he has backed away from this vacuous idea.

"I talked with the Buffalo Bills about it," Dusza said, "and they say there isn't a problem here, so maybe we don't need a law at this time." Not now. Not ever.

It's just a shame that Dusza didn't talk with the Bills before, rather than only after, he offered a silly solution to a problem that didn't exist.

All this foolishness evolved from one incident in which several naked New England Patriot football players allegedly harassed a female reporter in their locker room after a game, and from a second incident in which coach Sam Wyche barred a female reporter from entering the Cincinnati Bengals' locker room after a big loss to Seattle.

The NFL and its commissioner, Paul Tagliabue, have launched investigations into the first incident and heavily fined Wyche in the second.

Neither incident in any way touched the Bills. To our knowledge the Bills have suffered no such bonehead lapses. Like several NFL teams, they close the locker room to all reporters for a few minutes after each game and then open it to all reporters. That's fair enough.

It also complies with National Football League rules governing post-game interviews and media relationships.

There's no need for county government, which has plenty else to keep it busy and uncertain jurisdiction in the locker room anyway, to blunder into the middle of this issue. Most professional sports teams and leagues, including the NFL, operate under rules that treat reporters without regard to sex.

Dusza's fifth-down proposal wouldn't have been helpful even if there had been a problem. Sports stars, with their big salaries paid ultimately by fans, have a responsibility to be accessible to reporters trying to do their jobs. Fining or jailing reporters is no way to solve any disputes.

NEW ENGLAND PATRIOTS

DEFENSIVE LINE — **OFFENSIVE LINE**

Mike Keefe '90, The Denver Post

St. Paul Pioneer Press & Dispatch
St. Paul, Minnesota, October 11, 1990

A National Football League brawl on the sports pages has spilled over onto the opinion pages, as you may have noticed. Letter writers and columnists have been going at it over the issue of allowing female sportswriters into men's locker rooms after games. This is far from a new issue; most observers had considered it settled long, long ago — in favor of access to both sexes.

> This football contest, over public opinion, involves very serious matters.

Football may be a game, but this contest over public opinion involves very serious matters: privacy rights, the treatment of women in our society and equal opportunity on the job.

The latest fracas started with accusations that New England Patriot players had lewdly intimidated a sportswriter in their locker room. The league is investigating. The row escalated when the Cincinnati Bengals' coach barred another reporter from his team's locker room after a game because of her sex. The league commissioner fined him $30,000. Many players and their sympathizers are complaining that allowing outsiders of the opposite sex into locker rooms violates players' dignity and privacy.

They're right. But women sportswriters are just as right to demand that they be permitted the same access to professional athletes as men sportswriters get.

The solution has seemed glaringly obvious from the beginning: Ban all outsiders, of all sexes and persuasions and reporting tools, from the locker rooms. Require the professional players, for the sake of promoting their brand of entertainment, to make themselves available in interview areas where they would be clothed.

Of course, by adopting the obvious solution at the start, the league might have clipped the controversy far short of the goal of maximum publicity, and within the bounds of the sports pages.

The Evening Gazette
Worcester, Massachusetts, October 7, 1990

We considered the lewd harassment of the female sportswriter by several Patriots football players inexcusable — and we said so in an editorial last week.

Equally deplorable was the response of owner Victor Kiam, who blamed the victim.

Now, what began as a nasty little incident seems to have gotten out of hand. Advocates, commentators and talk-show hosts of all shades of ideology have all but drowned out appropriate suggestions to avoid repetitions of the incident.

As the battle rages in barrooms and powder rooms across the land, the National Football League has even brought in a former Watergate prosecutor to investigate.

We believe there should be a reasonable solution — before someone suggests United Nations intervention. After all, professional sports from tennis to golf to track and field have systems for interviews that work well for players and sportswriters alike. A bit of tolerance, coupled with common sense, could go a long way.

One aspect of the post-game press coverage that should be reviewed is the amount of time players have to shower and dress before the sportswriters and cameras are ushered in. A few more minutes to allow athletes to get decent might help.

Moving the location of the post-game interviews out of the locker room is another possibility, if there are assurances that the players will be available.

More important than changing post-game procedures is changing some wrongheaded attitudes.

One is the notion that a woman sportswriter may be denied the same opportunity as her male colleagues — as Cincinnati Bengals coach Sam Wyche did when he barred a woman sportswriter from the locker room a few days ago.

Another is that women who choose to compete in a male-dominated profession can be made targets of harassment.

If post-game press procedures are a matter of continuing debate, the underlying principle of fairness is not. Protections against gender discrimination do not stop at the locker room door.

And it should not require an ex-Watergate prosecutor to get that point across.

Public Breast-Feeding Law Signed in Florida

Florida's Gov. Lawton Chiles (D) March 9, 1993 signed into law what was apparently the first state measure to make breast-feeding in public legal. The bill's supporters sought to end the harassment of women breast-feeding in public places.

The Des Moines Register
Des Moines, Iowa, March 8, 1993

In response to reports of women being harassed for breast-feeding their babies in public, the state of Florida has passed a law guaranteeing nursing mothers the right to do so.

The law exempts breast-feeding from statutes on indecent exposure, lewd and lascivious behavior and obscenity. With it, Florida becomes the first state to guarantee that right.

It's an enlightened response to an astounding premise: that breast-feeding a baby — the best form of infant nutrition and bonding — could be obscene. It's especially ironic in a state whose many beaches are peopled by bathers in varied stages of undress.

In fact, one lawmaker cited the ludicrousness of in any way linking breast-feeding with lewd and lascivious behavior, in opposing the legislation. Other opponents, as if to rebut her argument, worried that the law could lead to a relaxation of Florida's public nudity statutes.

State Representative Miguel de Grandy of Miami told The New York Times he introduced the measure after reading about a mother who was harassed by a security guard for nursing her baby in an isolated section of a Miami mall. The story reports that other nursing mothers throughout the United States have complained of similar harassment in bus stations, parks, restaurants and department stores.

The law also endorses breast-feeding as the preferred feeding method for infants, and condemns the attachment of any stigma to it.

Indeed, when a society tacitly condones the parading of sparsely clothed female bodies in beauty pageants, the use of alluring women as a selling technique at car shows, and the annual feature of a leading sports magazine devoted to women in sexy swimsuits, yet questions the propriety of a woman showing part of her breast to feed a child, something has gone astray.

St. Petersburg Times
St. Petersburg, Florida, March 11, 1993

Not too long ago in this country, mothers who were breast-feeding their infants stayed at home.

They might have ventured out to worship, where a nurturing congregation accepted such bonding of mother and child, but for the most part society expected nursing women to keep out of sight. According to a taboo particularly peculiar to American culture, it wasn't considered proper to risk shocking or offending anyone who might be around when a baby gets hungry.

But as women began to realize they didn't have to stay behind closed doors just because they had small children to nourish, they began to go out and take their breast-fed babies with them.

Unfortunately, the odd taboo against nursing infants in public hasn't eased completely with the times. It is still not that difficult to find nursing mothers who have been asked to leave a restaurant or theater or other public place because of the "disruption" caused by placing their babies at their breasts. Even a woman nursing her infant quietly on a bench in a shopping mall unlikely can do so without attracting stares from passers-by.

That's why a new Florida law is so important. The legislation, overwhelmingly approved by the House and the Senate and signed by Gov. Lawton Chiles, ensures that women who breast-feed their babies have the right to do so in public.

The new Florida law amends existing nudity, lewdness and obscenity statutes specifically to exempt and protect breast-feeding women from arrest or other harassment. It also blasts the "outdated moral taboos" that cause mothers to face a "vicious cycle of embarrassment and ignorance" about nursing in public. As Florida becomes the first state to write an endorsement of breast-feeding into its statutes, it officially affirms and encourages a most natural connection between mother and baby.

Such affirmation is needed. Despite breast-feeding's proven health benefits for infants and mothers, only about 25 percent of mothers breast-feed. The lack of societal acceptance for the practice undoubtedly influences the choice of many women and, among those who do breast-feed, the number of months they continue the practice.

It is rare that Florida enjoys the spotlight as a national leader. Other states should be embarrassed not to follow.

The Hartford Courant
Hartford, Connecticut, March 13, 1993

The medical establishment is unanimous on the best way to feed babies. There's no better nourishment than breast milk, which also provides babies with disease-fighting antibodies. Psychologists tout its value in establishing strong bonds between mother and child.

Yet mothers who try to put this advice into practice can find it difficult. Society has not kept up with the doctors, at least when it comes to feeding a baby in a public place. Nursing a child — even discreetly — in a restaurant, a bus or a shopping center can bring stares, rude remarks, and in some cases, outright harassment.

That's why a new law passed this week in Florida is so refreshing. The law states that a mother may breast-feed a baby "in any location, public or private." Passed by an overwhelming majority of the Florida Legislature, the bill provides protection to women who have been told by shopping-mall security guards or waiters in restaurants that they must go elsewhere to nurse their babies. It's the first state law of its kind, and it sets a healthy precedent.

Few women welcome the attention they can attract by breast-feeding a child in a public place. But sometimes they must make a choice between a bit of public discomfort and being confined to their homes. Once a breast-fed baby is out in the world, the child often presents the mother — and those around her — with another choice: a screaming infant or one who is contentedly suckling.

Unfortunately, many people who are happy to see babies feeding on a bottle in any location are uncomfortable with the sight of a mother and child doing it the natural way.

In Connecticut, there is no legal barrier to mothers' breast-feeding in public, but leaders of La Leche League, a group that promotes breast-feeding, say they have heard of women being harassed at shopping centers and restaurants.

Having a state law to back up a woman's right to nurse a baby where she pleases is a step in the right direction.

THE LINCOLN STAR
Lincoln, Nebraska, May 11, 1993

Last year 78 Nebraska women gave birth at home.

Some of the home births were accidents. But many were well-planned events, complete with paid and unpaid helpers.

All of these planned home births were illegal under the current state law. And the people who helped with the birth (including the father) are technically committing a crime, a Class III misdemeanor, punishable by up to three months in jail and/or a $500 fine.

Nebraska's ban on home births (unless a physician is attending) came to public light early this month after a county court judge decided that state law allows lay midwives to practice in Nebraska.

A legislative proposal to clarify state law so that lay midwives are clearly not allowed to practice in the state renewed the home birth controversy.

Sen. Don Wesely's suggestion to study the home birth issue rather than summarily continue the current ban in law is a good idea.

Nebraska doctors have considerable political clout in Nebraska. Thus the legal ban on anyone other than a doctor assisting at home births.

Many other states are less rigid.

Supporters of home birthing with midwives make a compelling case.

Supporters say research shows that home births attended by trained lay midwives can be as safe as hospital births attended by a doctor.

They point out that European countries where many births take place at home have among the world's best infant mortality rates while the U.S. ranks near the bottom among industrialized countries.

In Nebraska giving birth is equated with other surgical procedures under law. There are differences.

You don't hear about a home tonsillectomy or a home bypass surgery.

But babies successfully enter the world in the quiet of their own home.

The Nebraska Legislature should seriously consider allowing home births and creating a system so that people with knowledge and training can assist.

The Gazette
Cedar Rapids, Iowa, May 9, 1993

BEING A MOTHER in the 1990s isn't what it used to be. There are demands on a woman's time — and expectations for her conduct — previous generations did not have to face.

Consider that there are about 70 million women age 15 and older who are mothers (1990 figures), about 69 percent of the women in that age group. A good percentage of those women — 22 million in hard numbers — have children under 18 years old and are in the labor force. For most of those 22 million, career and family compete for time and energy. Many women feel torn between demands of home and office.

It's rough even for the most elite of working moms, according to a Harvard University study described in the May 10 Time magazine. Although 85 percent of the 902 Harvard professionals who responded said they had succeeded at combining career and family, 53 percent said they had changed their jobs or specialties due to family obligations. A quarter of Harvard M.B.A. graduates surveyed said they'd left the workplace completely. Deborah Swiss, a co-author of the study, said one conclusion is "if these women are having a hard time, it's frightening to think of what is happening to working mothers who do not have the advantage of a Harvard education and a senior professional position."

Some Eastern Iowa companies are doing as have others across the nation. As described in today's Life and Leisure section, employers are entering into partnerships to provide child care, giving parents breaks to participate in school activities, making allowances for family illness. They're looking at the long term, and at ways to keep good employees.

But it can add to costs. Other workplaces aren't yet as able to offer the flexibility some parents need. For some, it's like the child who balks at taking bad-tasting medicine: He knows it's good for him, but he can't seem to swallow it.

Motherhood in the 1990s isn't what it used to be. And there's no going back.

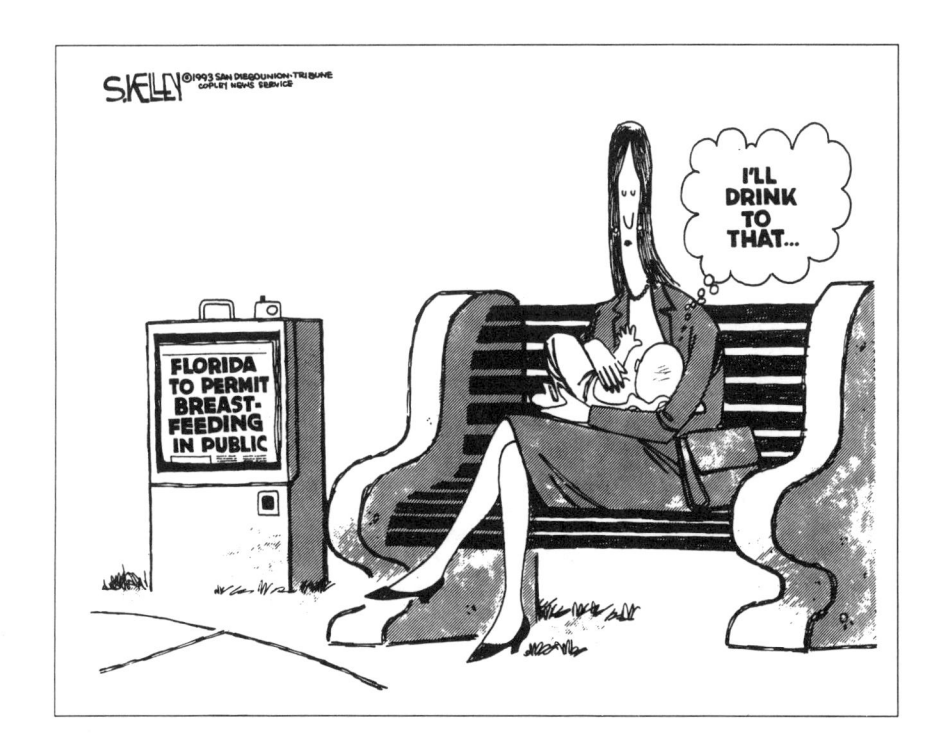

Women's Issues Surveyed Worldwide

Nearly 70 queens and wives of heads of state attended a conference Feb. 25–26, 1991 in Geneva, Switzerland on the plight of rural women in the Third World.

The event was organized by six Third World "first ladies" under the guidance of Belgium's Queen Fabiola. Other attendees included Spain's Queen Sofia, Egypt's Suzanne Mubarak, Nigeria's Maryam Babangida and Colombia's Ana Munoz de Gaviria. Few women from the major industrialized democracies came.

United Nations Secretary General Boutros Boutros-Ghali and Idriss Jazairy, president of the U.N. International Fund for Agricultural Development (IFAD), were also there. IFAD ran the event but did not pay for it. Funding came from governments and private sources.

The aim of the gathering was to reorient development programs to reflect the importance of women in Third World agriculture. Organizers believed that this could by accomplished by getting the influential women to put pressure on their husbands and governments.

According to IFAD, women produced 60% of all food grown in developing countries, and 70% in sub-Saharan Africa. Over the previous 20 years, the number of rural-dwelling women living in poverty in the Third World had risen by over 50%, to 565 million. That growth was faster than the rate for men, who tended to move to cities, leaving women as the head of one in five rural households (excluding China and India). Despite their importance, women accounted for fewer than one in six agricultural advisors in poor nations. Moreover, they were consistently denied access to land, technology, loans, training and government policymaking, according to IFAD.

If we could increase the productivity of rural women by 15%, we could wipe out the food deficit in Africa," said Jazairy. "Unless we can promote the role of women, the goal of eliminating hunger cannot be achieved."

Queen Fabiola decried what she called the way in which sexual discrimination kept Third World women in poverty. "In their millions they end up in prostitution in the big cities of their countries and the Western world. This is a modern form of slavery that must be vigorously condemned," she said.

The Hartford Courant
Hartford, Connecticut, November 14, 1990

Islam's holy book, revealed to the prophet Muhammad in the Seventh Century A.D., does not forbid women from driving automobiles or require them to cover their faces or prohibit them from holding high government positions.

Yet the Saudi dynasty, which is the custodian of Islam's holiest places, has relegated women to an inferior status. Defenders of Saudi Arabia's practices argue otherwise, of course. But the realities cannot be hidden when the eyes of the world are on that country because of the Persian Gulf crisis.

Last week, about 50 Saudi women protested their government's practice of denying driver's licenses to women. The women simply got into cars and drove. It was a peaceful and dignified way to say, "No more second-class citizenship."

But the protesters are being called infidels. Some who worked as professionals have been suspended from their jobs.

Oppression should be denounced, whether practiced by America's friends or foes. When Saudi women are forbidden to leave the house without the escort of a husband or a male relative, that's oppression. When they are denied basic rights, that's not Islam but a perversion of an ancient and noble religion.

Americans should be concerned because by the end of the year some 450,000 U. S. soldiers will be in Saudi Arabia, ostensibly to defend that country and perhaps even to liberate neighboring Kuwait — and protect the Arab world and oil consumers from the likes of Saddam Hussein.

It's wrong to risk the lives of so many Americans but look the other way when the government being protected denies so many of its citizens even the fundamental right of strolling down a boulevard without a chaperon.

The News and Observer
Raleigh, North Carolina, September 23, 1990

In Saudi Arabia, U.S. policy is to do all that conscious effort can do to avoid a clash with Saudi customs, particularly as they relate to women. And on America's side, the emphasis is consciously non-judgmental. No faintest hint is supposed to drift across the sandy line between the two cultures that the Yanks consider our ways better or theirs worse. They're just different.

As columnist Ellen Goodman wrote recently, this policy is quite a lot like what Mr. Rogers tries to teach in the song about how "everybody's special." A venerable and accurate if unfashionable name for this attitude is tolerance, which Webster defines as "sympathy or indulgence for beliefs or practices differing from or conflicting with one's own."

That is a highly useful attitude. It can head off a world of great and small conflicts before they go critical. And maybe it's time to resurrect it at home as well as abroad, to let this nation stop wasting so much of its political and emotional energy on the kind of mutually assured destructiveness that has come to characterize the abortion controversy and that tinges much recent comment about race relations.

The U.S. abortion debate long since ceased to be a debate and became a jihad, a holy war, characterized by the same zealotry and intolerance from both extremes that the most hot-eyed Shi'a Moslem fundamentalist displays in promoting his version of Islam.

When this kind of true-believer fanaticism comes in the door, the prospects for peaceful resolution fly out the window. Small wonder that respect for the other's right to hold his or her own point of view has been, from this melting-pot nation's beginning, one of its foundation stones.

And in America, tolerance has been closely identified with the Golden Rule because of the nation's Judeo-Christian roots. But Christianity has no monopoly on a value that is as opposed as anything could be to the notion of holy war. Plenty of Moslems, Jews, agnostics and atheists realize that a spirit of tolerance is essential to keeping an increasingly crowded world habitable. May it flourish from Riyadh to Raleigh.

Sexual Politics In America

[Cartoon by Chu Haynie, ©1991 The Courier-Journal, showing an angel with a newspaper "The Heavenly Herald" with headlines "SAUDIS DENY RELIGIOUS FREEDOM, WOMEN'S LIB." and "BISHOP DEFENDS MEMBERSHIP IN ALL-WHITE CLUB."]

"Well, gee, I don't know how God feels about all this, but you know, of course, She's black."

St. Paul Pioneer Press & Dispatch
St. Paul, Minnesota, July 6, 1989

If the heat in Minnesota seems intense, consider the political climate in Japan this month as the country moves toward national elections. The ruling Liberal Democratic Party is finding out traumatically how scandal can erode power.

The Hutchinson News
Hutchinson, Kansas, September 30, 1990

One of the more positive results of the American presence in Saudi Arabia could be the influence American women might have on Arab women.

While the various male-dominated Arab factions in the region have heard for years about the vigor of American womanhood, they will now get the opportunity to view it for themselves.

Whether this has an emancipating result for Arab women remains to be seen, but Arab men can't avoid seeing hardy and handsome young American women pulling their weight under the same harsh Middle Eastern sun as the men. It ought to test their cultural and religious beliefs concerning male superiority.

Already, 5,000 Saudi Arabian women are now being used in that nation's civil defense program, a move viewed as extraordinarily progressive for a strict Moslem society that views females as subordinate human beings.

Once these Saudi women experience more fulfilling roles in their own country, coupled with the daily example of American female soldiers, it may be too late — once the present crisis ends — for them to revert to standards that existed before the invasion of Kuwait.

Unfortunately, Iranian woman had a taste of this change under the Shah, but once he was dethroned, strict social standards for women returned, and Iran's female population once again reverted to its second-class status.

Here's hoping Saudi women are more successful. Despite the U.S. military's kowtowing regulations that unfairly restrict the movement of female American soldiers assigned to the Mideast, their presence surely will bolster the hopes of Saudi females who may one day hope to achieve a greater equality in their oppressive and antiquated culture.

A sex scandal has plunged the popularity rating of Prime Minister Sosuke Uno, after just a month in office, to an astonishing 10 percent. The Liberal Democrats took a drubbing — led by outraged women — in Tokyo municipal elections.

The Liberal Democrats could well lose their 35-year hold on power. They are in deep trouble, trying to weather the Recruit bribery scandal, a wildy unpopular consumption tax increase and now a backlash about Mr. Uno's reported sexual liaisons.

So what's new? Japan's upheaval looks familiar from this side of the Pacific Ocean. Watergate, Abscam, Gary Hart, John Tower, the Reagan-era Housing and Urban Development Department. What's new for Japan is that an electorate long satisfied by a government that delivers prosperity has stopped going along automatically with the good old boys.

The easy way out of immediate trouble would be for Mr. Uno, who ironically didn't want the job in the first place, to quit. But that seems unlikely with the Western powers about to meet for their economic summit. There is also the delicate matter of whom the Liberal Democrats could call on to take command of a sinking ship with no real transition time before July 23 elections for the upper house of parliament. The Japan Housewives Association and 51 other women's groups, forming an awesome political alliance, are in no mood to put up with the status quo in political behavior.

Judging from the last few months, who knows where free-wheeling Japanese politics will go? All the governmental and cultural traditions point in an orderly direction. Certainly, things won't go back. There will be no return to winking at the personal indiscretions of politicians. The astonishing new taste of power women are getting won't be easily dismissed.

A parliamentary system like Japan's has more inherent flexibility than does the United States' three-branched, two-party government. So change there has the opportunity to happen more quickly than here and with fewer lasting scars.

With bilateral interests of such critical importance, the United States would be wise now to plan ahead in Japanese-American relations. Foresight could shape mutual security and complex economic interactions.

The Japan Housewives Association could have a lot to do with the price of VCRs in St. Paul and how much Minnesota-grown produce goes to Tokyo.

Anglicans Vote to Allow Women Priests

The governing body of the Church of England Nov. 11, 1992 narrowly voted to allow women to become priests. The action was described as one of the most important since the church broke with the Roman Catholic Church in 1534.

The Church of England was one of 28 national church bodies within the International Anglican Communion. A dozen national Anglican churches, including the U.S. Episcopal Church and the churches in Canada, New Zealand, Kenya and India, already allowed women priests. About 1,000 of the 1,500 Anglican women priests were in the U.S. (Australian Anglicans voted in favor of the ordination of women in late November 1992.)

The English measure, formally the "Priests (Ordination of Women) Measure," needed the approval of two-thirds of members in each of the three houses that made up the church's governing council, the General Synod. The House of Bishops approved the proposal by a vote of 39–13; representatives of the clergy were in support by a margin of 176–74 and the House of Laity backed women priests, 169–82. A change of two votes in the house for lay people would have defeated the measure.

The plan would now be considered by the British Parliament and Queen Elizabeth II, whose approvals were expected. The first women priests would probably not be ordained in England until the late summer of 1994, according to a church spokesman.

The church currently had about 1,350 women deacons, who were able to perform some sacraments, including marriage and baptism. But other functions, including the absolution of sin and the Holy Eucharist (communion), the church's holiest sacrament, could be led only by priests.

Proponents of ordaining women had argued that barring women from the priesthood was discriminatory and undermined the church's moral standing.

The titular head of all Anglicans, Most Rev. George Carey, archbishop of Canterbury, supported ordination of women. In his opening remarks at the debate on the measure at the Church House in London Nov. 11, Carey said, "We must draw on all our available talents if we are to be a credible church engaged in a mission to an increasingly confused and lost world."

While some opponents of women priests claimed scriptural backing for their position, most opponents in the General Synod debate based their appeal on the traditions of the church and on what they said were flaws in the specific legislation in question. (Despite its break with the Roman Catholic Church, the Church of England remained closer to the Vatican than most other churches.)

Archdeacon of Leicester David Silk Nov. 11 argued that change in the church should not be forced by "social and cultural conditioning." He warned that schisms could arise in the church if women were ordained. (Press reports indicated that up to 1,000 priests in England were considering leaving the Anglican Church in protest over women priests.)

In a related development, U.S. Roman Catholic bishops, meeting at the semiannual National Conference of Catholic Bishops in Washington, D.C., voted Nov. 18, 1992 to reject a proposed pastoral letter that reaffirmed traditional roles for women in the church. The meeting took place Nov. 16–19.

The bishops voted, 137 to 110, in support of the letter, but the tally fell 53 votes short of the required two-thirds majority of the active bishops, or 190 votes, for the letter to become an official teaching document. It was the first time that the conference, formed in 1966, had failed to reach a two-thirds majority consensus.

THE KANSAS CITY STAR
Kansas City, Missouri, November 19, 1992

The Church of England's vote to ordain women as priests is a major step forward for women in that church. It also is potential progress for those in other religious denominations.

Although the Roman Catholic Church's Vatican spokesman condemned the change in policy, saying it only created more obstacles for improved relations between the Anglican and Roman Catholic hierarchies, the Lutheran World Federation's general secretary praised the decision as "a positive ecumenical step."

Some within the church itself decried the move by declaring it to be politically motivated rather than spiritual. In truth, the church had seen a decline in attendance at Anglican services over the last two decades. The issue of ordination of women, who now can serve only as deacons, had further split the church. Some bishops, priests and lay members now are expected to leave because of the change of policy. But other leaders believe it will make more women feel at home in and belong to the church.

George Carey, the archbishop of Canterbury and the spiritual leader of the church, said that without using "all of our available talents" the church might not be able to fulfill its mission to an increasingly confused and lost world.

"We are in danger of not being heard if women are exercising leadership in every area of our society's life save the ordained priesthood," he said.

The Church of England is the historic mother church for the 2.5-million member U.S. Episcopal Church, which as one of 28 self-governing Anglican churches worldwide, already permits ordination of women.

Although many other Christian churches ordain women as priests, advances have been slow for women even within those congregations.

The Anglican decision, which is expected to be ratified by Parliament and Queen Elizabeth II, will please many women who have felt shut out not by beliefs, but by gender, from their church. And it provides encouragement for those in other religious denominations who are seeking greater roles in service to God.

The London Free Press
London, Ontario, November 16, 1992

The Church of England's decision to allow women priests should be no big deal.

While Canadian Anglicans have ordained women since 1976, the British branch has just narrowly accepted a move to allow women to become priests. It would take about two years for some of the 1,350 female deacons in England to be elevated to priesthood.

At a time when the demand for priests far outstrips the supply, it's a wise move and one endorsed by Archbishop Michael Peers, leader of Canada's two million Anglicans.

"The ministry of women will allow the Church of England to discover blessings they do not yet know, as all of us in Canada have," Peers notes.

By increasing opportunities for women to serve, the church is giving male and female parishioners a positive message: A calling is not dependent on one's sex, but on one's faith.

Traditionalists might argue Jesus chose 12 men as his disciples and therefore, it should still follow only men are capable of spreading the gospel. During the last two millenia, interpretations of scripture have been altered to suit the times. So why can't the voices telling those stories change as well?

The Anglican Church was formed in the 16th century after the Roman Catholic Church would not allow King Henry VIII an annulment. One Vatican representative said the Anglican decision to elevate women to priesthood was a "grave obstacle" to repairing the split between the two faiths.

On the contrary, the move could prod the Roman Catholic Church — a long-time opponent to women in the priesthood — to reconsider its position. After all, the Catholic Church did reverse its stand on Galileo's views and admit some 350 years later he wasn't a heretic for espousing that the Earth revolves around the sun.

Perhaps the issue of women priests won't take quite so long.

THE SPOKESMAN-REVIEW
Spokane, Washington, November 22, 1992

The church, any church, is tugged in two directions: Be constant enough to stand for enduring values, yet be flexible enough to remain relevant to modern followers' lives.

The magnitude of that dilemma has been evident in the past two weeks as: The Anglican Church approved the ordination of women priests in England; the American Roman Catholic bishops did not; and the Vatican updated a universal catechism that dates back to the Council of Trent in the middle of the 16th Century.

The responses were predictable. Church leaders were either chided for being too timid or condemned for being too bold.

The fact is, none of those decisions — not even the Church of England's decision to ordain women — was all that radical.

Reaction to the ordination decision (which had stronger support among the Anglican clergy than among the laity who participated in it) has indeed been harsh. One retired bishop in London has called for a split in the church, and the Vatican is saying forget about a 22-year-old movement toward reunification between the two faiths.

In fact, though, the Church of England is hardly blazing a new trail within the Anglican Communion. Women already are being ordained in three other countries, including the United States.

Meanwhile, although the American Catholic bishops' view of women in the clergy is unaltered, the seriousness of the debate they devoted to the question has been welcomed by many advocates of change as a sign of real progress.

And there has been a welcoming clarification of the church outlook toward domestic abuse and the inappropriateness of citing scriptural authority to rationalize it. That, too, is evidence of progress.

And if the catechism that the Roman Catholic Church hammered out more than four centuries ago in response to the Protestant Reformation could finally be amended to address such modern concerns as biogenetics and white-collar crime, then perhaps nothing lasts forever, even in church doctrine.

But change within the church ought to be gradual. And in each of the current cases the decisions that have been publicized in the past two weeks have taken years to be worked out.

Theological history is replete with tedious debates over such seemingly trivial issués as how many angels can dance on the head of a pin and whether Adam and Eve had navels. The urgent issues of today demand, and are receiving, the serious study of church leaders.

The church plays a vital role in the lives of church members and in society as a whole. Whichever religion is involved, church teaching provides the core values on which most societies set their expectations and most governments base their laws, even secular governments such as ours.

In the years ahead, as information and technology produce even more rapid change, religious institutions' ability to keep pace without sacrificing lasting principles will be tested as never before.

It's not likely to be another four centuries before the Vatican next updates its universal catechism.

MILWAUKEE SENTINEL
Milwaukee, Wisconsin, November 14, 1992

By voting to ordain women as priests, the Church of England has created a watershed event in one of the major battles of the sexes.

And while some worry that it will create a greater schism than that which occurred when the Anglican church split from Rome more than four and one-half centuries ago, how could the future be more bleak than it is for the church?

Only 10% of British adults regularly attend Sunday services and only one-third of those are Anglicans. If Parliament and Queen Elizabeth assent to the change in rules, the heretofore male sanctuary of the Anglican priesthood would have a vast new reservoir of leadership potential on which to draw.

Ironically, the laity in the church's General Synod, barely gained the two-thirds majority in favor of women priests that was necessary for approval, while 75% of the bishops and 70% of the clergy voted "aye."

One concern is that by allowing women priests, the Anglican church would make reconciliation with the Vatican even less likely.

But that should be secondary to having the church at odds with itself. Twelve of the 28 self-governing provinces in the Church of England already allow ordination of women — most of them in the 2.5 million-member Episcopal Church of the United States.

Of course, there may be those who argue that the concept of freedom of religion makes this matter something for the church, and not outsiders, to decide.

That's true. But the declining standards of morals in the Western world warrant concern by people of all faiths that the traditional religions are no longer meeting their implicit responsibility of establishing the rules of civilized conduct.

Any steps in any nation that allow the clergy to have more in common with the people they serve, be it ordination of women or marriage of priests, bodes well for Western civilization.

Indeed, even the non-believers will be served better if the people who act as the keepers of the Christian conscience include both sexes.

THE ATLANTA CONSTITUTION
Atlanta, Georgia, November 17, 1992

Denomination by denomination, women are transforming organized religion — still among the most sexist of institutions in this last decade of the 20th century.

Last week the Church of England gave its blessing to priesthood for women. If Parliament and Queen Elizabeth II give their expected approval, women in the Anglican tradition can join their American sisters and brothers as equals before the altar of God.

Women have always played an immense role in the life of the church — even in the Middle Ages, when male clerics smugly debated whether women even had souls.

But despite centuries of support and service, there were almost no women in Protestant seminaries even as recently as 20 years ago.

Now women make up 30 percent of students in the almost 300-member Association of Theological Schools in the United States. At prestigious Yale Divinity School, nearly half the students are women; at Harvard Divinity School, 60 percent are women.

The Roman Catholic Church, with its male and celibate clergy, has been most resistant to a larger role for women in the church. In fact, the Vatican greeted the Church of England's decision on women and the priesthood as "a new and grave obstacle to the entire process of reconciliation" between the Roman Catholic and Anglican churches.

American Catholic bishops have struggled for nine years with a pastoral letter on the status of women. That struggle continues this week as bishops meet in Washington, trying to compromise on wording that would reassure Catholic women of their importance in the church while insisting that only men can be priests.

It is an essential contradiction that many cannot accept.

"WHERE ARE ALL THOSE MEN PRIESTS NOW THAT WE NEED THEM?"

St. Louis Review
St. Louis, Missouri, November 20, 1992

This past week saw the three ruling bodies of the Church of England (Anglican) vote to ordain women as priests. Separated from the Roman Catholic Church since the 16th century, the Anglican Church nevertheless feels itself close to the Roman Catholic Church. Discussions toward possible reunification with Rome have gone on for many years. The decision to ordain women priests places one more obstacle in the road to reunification. Vatican officials have publicly voiced their distress over this move.

The Anglican Church is the official church of Great Britain, where in an increasingly secular society very few people (estimated at less than 10 percent) attend church on any sort of a regular basis. Ordaining women as priests has been seen as a valuable way of helping to bridge the gap between formal religion and daily life. Whether it achieves this goal remains to be seen as the move toward women priests caused a large number of Anglican priests and their congregations to threaten a schism if the proposition passed.

All of this has heightened interest in the U.S. bishops' meeting this week in Washington, D.C. For 10 years now the bishops and laypeople have discussed issuing a document that would speak of women's role in the Church. The letter has gone through four drafts, some quite progressive, others more conservative. There are many reasons for saying yes and many for voting no. Some feel the fourth draft goes too far, others that it merely restates the status quo.

In the end the discussions might be seen as a reflection of our own society regarding the roles of men and women. The Church should not be relegated to a passive role in all of this, but should be actively proclaiming the value of all persons in society. We look to the Church for leadership in empowering all persons to use the talents and skills God has given to us.

The Salt Lake Tribune
Salt Lake City, Missouri, November 21, 1992

While they didn't reject the traditional teaching of their faith, a plurality of United States Catholic Church bishops said something distinctive about their female membership this week. Unable to gain a two-thirds vote favoring a pastoral letter proclaiming their group's shared understanding of matters pertaining to women, the bishops reflected a modern sensitivity to those in the congregation moved by anti-discrimination impulses.

Hard on the heels of the Anglican Church's decision to ordain women as priests, the U.S. National Conference of Catholic Bishops convened its annual convention amidst attention generated by the very same question. Sharpening the curiosity was the pending pastoral letter which mentioned, among other matters, the ordination subject.

Although a majority vote, 137-110, approved the letter, that didn't satisfy the two-thirds requirement. Declining, then, to formally reject the notion of ordained women priests, the bishops prevented adverse publicity and, by implication anyway, encouraged those campaigning for full equality of religious opportunity.

The bishops had been developing their statement concerning women's concerns since 1982. After four drafts, clerical ordination still was not at the center of the effort. Yet it became the cause for an unprecedented "rejection" of an intended pastoral statement.

Falling short on the endorsement vote, the prelates successfully adopted a substitute proposal from Chicago's Cardinal Joseph Bernardine, calling for further work by the conference's executive committee on a statement pertaining to women's issues. Since it wasn't blocked, the egalitarian movement gained ground.

That female priesthood was even debated illustrated the U.S. bishops' independent tendencies. Pope John Paul II had decreed that female ordination was not a matter for serious discussion. In fact, no such drastic change can occur other than from the Vatican. Nor should it be based purely on a public relations consideration.

However, numerous observers, inside as well as outside the Catholic Church, agree that the U.S. membership, while part of a universal faith, is nonetheless comfortable trying to influence doctrinal interpretation from the pews, obligating the U.S. ministerial hierarchy to respond as well as inspire. Gender equality has now become part of that procedure and can't be either ignored or short-shrifted.

Obviously, also, it will not soon provoke any profound changes. But the U.S. bishops' actions constituted an acknowledgment, conceding further hearings for the assertion that Catholic Christianity could accommodate female clergy. History discloses that such tolerance can supplant the inertia of tradition with the dynamics of contemporary insistence. If not immediately, then eventually.

The Times-Picayune
New Orleans, Louisiana, November 21, 1992

In voting down a controversial teaching document whose main sticking point was its prohibition against the ordination of women to the priesthood, the nation's Catholic bishops ensured that the issue would continue to be a concern for church leaders and the laity.

Indeed, that the idea of women in the pulpits was discussed at all at such a high level, in view of the Vatican's edict that the question is off-limits, is a strong indication that it not only isn't going to go away but that it has found a place on center stage.

Asked at a news conference if it wasn't unusual for women's ordination to be openly discussed by the bishops when the pope has called it a closed issue, Bishop Joseph Imesch of Joliet, Ill., said, "It's remarkable."

Attacked by both liberals and conservatives for different reasons, the pastoral letter, which affirms women's equal dignity and condemns sexism as a sin, failed to receive the required two-thirds vote for approval. It went through several revisions in its nine-year history.

Following the vote — the result was 137 yes and 110 no — Cardinal Joseph Bernardin of Chicago won passage of a plan for yet more study and dialogue, which he said is needed to show that "our tradition really makes sense."

The bishops' action, which leaders of women's advocacy groups saw as a positive development, follows on the heels of a historic vote by the Church of England to ordain women as priests. Many feared the change would tear the church apart and close the door to closer relations with Rome, which sharply criticized the decision.

The arguments on both sides were similar to those put forward by proponents and opponents of ordaining women that marked deliberations by the American bishops. Church of England members who spoke against the move say it contradicts Scripture and tradition. But the prevailing view, summed up by Archbishop of Canterbury George Carey, was, "The ordination of women to the priesthood alters not a word in the creeds, the Scriptures, or the faith of our church."

Among the Catholic leaders who voted for the pastoral letter was Archbishop Francis B. Schulte of New Orleans, who called it a good document. He said, "It's not a matter of injustice. It's a matter of different callings in the church. Women clearly play a rich variety of roles."

But Bishop Michael Pfeifer of San Angelo, Texas, had a different view. He said the proposed letter failed to live up to its purpose of responding to women's concerns and would have resulted in "more divisiveness and alienation" than ever.

Perhaps the most hopeful view of the bishops' action was offered by Catherine Wessinger, an associate professor of religious studies at Loyola University. "The good thing is the American bishops spent nine years listening to thousands of Roman Catholic women and what they have to say. Certain bishops have learned a lot," she said.

No doubt arguments will continue over whether the pastoral letter was good for the church, but Ms. Wessinger's observation seems particularly apt. Learning is a good thing.

Minneapolis Star and Tribune
Minneapolis, Minnesota, November 20, 1992

However sad or satisfied American Catholics are at their bishops' inability to accept (or press the Vatican to accept) the changed status of women, praise the bishops for their willingness to hear from victims of priestly sexual misconduct. Listening often is difficult for those with great authority, but it is an essential step toward healing. More listening is needed if the church is to come firmly to grips with this unfortunate, life-warping scourge. In the Archdiocese of St. Paul and Minneapolis, a willingness to listen is apparent in policies outlined in a new pastoral, "Understanding Sexual Issues in Ministry."

The new pastoral offers an unequivocal pledge of systematic efforts to prevent future abuse and to minister with care to abuse victims. The need for such policies, and assurance they are firmly enforced in every church, was evident in the confrontation with sexual abuse gently forced on the bishops during their meeting in Washington, D.C. In this year of numerous abuse accusations against former priest James R. Porter, the bishops failed to include the subject on their agenda. That failure didn't stop the victims; nine showed up at the meeting of the National Conference of Catholic Bishops to register protests at their treatment by abusive priests and by church authorities.

The bishops were terrific; rather than being ignored the protesters were invited in to talk. For an hour, one cardinal and two bishops listened and learned from nine people whose trust in their church and its clergy had been violated. Their testimony made a deep impression on Cardinal Roger Mahoney of Los Angeles. "You and I know there are many victims of priestly misconduct," he later told his fellow bishops. "There is no other place for them to come, and I recommend you take seriously all that was said to us." The bishops heard Mahoney, too. On the last day of their meeting, they pledged themselves to a "healing ministry" to abuse victims and adopted a number of policies that closely parallel the new pastoral from the Archdiocese of St. Paul and Minneapolis.

On the issue of women's ordination, voices within the church are discordant. In our view, the refusal to be ministered to by women is the church's great loss. But it also is the church's decision. Sexual misconduct, however, isn't debatable; it's evil. Cardinal Mahoney recommended that the dialogue between bishops and victims continue. It should; nothing is as likely to give power and substance to efforts at preventing abuse and ministering to victims than church leaders' deep first-hand knowledge of the pain suffered by those victims.

Part II: Gays in America

The mere fact that gays and lesbians are a distinct subject indicates how much more varied sex roles are now than in the past. Formerly, gays would have been categorized with men and lesbians with women with little distinction noted between heterosexual and homosexual roles and rights. But in the past two decades, homosexuals have openly declared their pride and demanded recognition.

Whether society-at-large considers homosexuality natural or a perversion, the issue is very much here to stay. Schools, churches and the military have been grappling with the basic issue of whether gays should serve as teachers, ministers and soldiers on the same basis as heterosexuals. The issue has stirred intense feelings and prompted court actions and referendums.

Many gays live together openly, some couples having obtained civil or religious sanctions for their unions. Others have initiated suits contesting bars to same-sex marriages and efforts to adopt children. Some have sought "palimony" at the end of a relationship.

As visibility has increased, public disapproval has apparently decreased and hitherto unheard-of roles for homosexuals have been established – policeman, fireman, etc. – but the debate goes on for teachers and the clergy. Rights and values remain in conflict; knowledge of sexual differences does not necessarily mean acceptance of them. The only certainty is that the word gay will never mean the same thing.

The defining factor in the gay community during the past decade has been AIDS. The controversy surrounding the tragic emergence and rapid spread of AIDS has shaded virtually every aspect of American public and private life. Educational, legal and health-care institutions, insurance companies, broadcasting companies, and the federal government are all faced with new, confusing and frightening questions on how to confront the disease.

The decision by movie star Rock Hudson to reveal his diagnosis of AIDS and his homosexuality not only brought information to a wider audience, but also put into sharper focus the issues of homosexuality and sexual behavior in general in American society.

Though AIDS has changed sexual practices faster than thought possible, persuading individuals to change long-term destructive habits of sexual behavior or drug abuse is extremely difficult. Although recent evidence indicates that carefully designed prevention programs can be effective in the general adult population, many people believe it is equally important to ensure that adolescents, non-English-speaking minorities and drug abusers understand the risk of AIDS and take the necessary protective measures. Controversy has arisen because some people believe that it is inappropriate for government agencies to tell homosexuals or bisexuals how to have "safe sex" or to explain the importance of sterile needles, while others feel that the gravity of the situation warrants such measures.

For many, AIDS poses a severe moral challenge in that promiscuity is a prominent feature of the lifestyles of at least some Americans. The challenge has confronted both those who are not infected with AIDS and those who are. But the question of moral responsibility for individual health is far from settled because, as far as AIDS and sexual promiscuity are concerned, the health risks are not yet known with enough certainty to permit the judgment that promiscuous people are taking *immoral* risks with their health or the health of their partners. Some in the gay community, for instance, regard calls for more "responsible" sexual behavior as an intrusive threat to the community's existence and values, while others argue that it is both prudent and ethical to show restraint in a time of crisis. Regardless of the moral issue, studies have shown that gay men have lowered their risk for AIDS by adopting changes in sexual behavior, such as fewer partners and increasing their use of condoms.

Sixth AIDS Conference Held in San Francisco

The Sixth International AIDS Conference was held in San Francisco, Calif. June 20-23, 1990. The conference was attended by more than 10,000 researchers and public health officials from around the world, who heard a total of 3,000 reports on various medical and social aspects of acquired immune deficiency syndrome.

Few important scientific breakthroughs had been expected to be announced at the conference, and most of the attention was centered around a series of well-organized demonstrations by AIDS activists who were protesting what they regarded as the U.S. government's inadequate response to the AIDS epidemic.

President George Bush had been invited to address the conference, but he declined. Instead, he spent the first day of the conference in North Carolina, raising funds for conservative Sen. Jesse A. Helms (R, N.C.), regarded as an enemy by many AIDS activists. Among other things, Helms had sponsored a controversial 1987 U.S. immigration rule that barred entry to visitors infected with the virus that causes AIDS.

More than 100 groups, including the International Red Cross, Planned Parenthood and the European Community, had urged their researchers to boycott the conference to protest the visa restriction.

On June 19, the eve of the conference, protesters staged the first of a series of demonstrations, each of which was devoted to a specific issue. The June 19 protest was targeted at U.S. immigration policies. Like later protests, it was organized in large part by an activist group called the AIDS Coalition to Unleash Power (ACT-UP). About 500 demonstrators marched through downtown San Francisco to the local office of the U.S. Immigration and Naturalization Service.

Subsequent demonstrations during the course of the conference targeted what protesters viewed as the slow pace of testing and distribution of anti-AIDS drugs and the insufficiency of funds available for AIDS research and treatment. On June 20, ACT-UP held a mock "trial" of five scientists from the AIDS Clinical Trial Group, which conducted drug tests in collaboration with the National Institutes of Health (NIH). The "Gang of Five" were accused of having improper financial relationships with pharmaceutical manufacturers.

Scientists said the demonstrators were being unfair and were targeting their rage at the wrong group. "Activists are mistaken when they assume or at least publicly state that scientists do not care about them," said Anthony S. Fauci, director of AIDS research for the NIH. "This is devastating to a physician or scientist who has devoted years to AIDS research, particularly when they see so many of their young patients suffering and dying."

U.S. Secretary of Health and Human Services Louis W. Sullivan addressed the conference on its closing day, June 24. His 20-minute speech was virtually drowned out by shouts, whistles and horn blasts from some 500 activists (among an audience of 6,000 people) who were angered by federal AIDS policy on immigration and research.

The Evening Gazette

Worcester, Massachusetts,
June 29, 1990

It is tragic that militant AIDS activists chose to alienate the very people who are dedicated to fighting that disease. Members of Aids Coalition to Unleash Power — ACT-UP — turned a recent research conference in San Francisco into a political circus. They altered the agenda, undermined procedures and shouted down Dr. Louis Sullivan, secretary of health and human services.

A couple of weeks ago, screaming Act-Up militants disrupted a ceremony at Boston's Holy Cross Cathedral held to ordain 11 Roman Catholic priests. They chanted slogans and pelted the new priests with condoms. There was profanity in words and acts.

The despair and rage of AIDS sufferers and their friends is understandable; the disease still carries a death sentence. But gay organizations have used political muscle effectively to call attention to the problem and secure help. It is hard to understand, however, what ACT-UP is trying to accomplish.

America has not turned its back on AIDS. Even though it is the 15th leading cause of death in this country — far behind cancer, heart, lung, liver, kidney and other diseases — AIDS receives more than $1 billion a year in federal research money, more than any other illness except cancer. While a major breakthrough in treatment has yet to come, there have been advances.

And while society still tends to isolate AIDS sufferers, Americans are better informed and less prejudiced about the disease than a couple of years ago. Unfortunately, those infected with the AIDS virus find little comfort in slow progress.

Better understanding is needed, along with better education and more money for research and treatment. AIDS victims and their advocates need the public's compassion and support. The tactics of ACT-UP only produce resentment.

Omaha World-Herald

Omaha, Nebraska, June 23, 1990

Activists who rioted and disrupted meetings at an international conference on AIDS this week could give lessons on how to be ineffective in supporting a cause. Screaming at the scientists who are trying to find a cure for AIDS is hardly the way to generate more sympathy for the victims.

The Sixth International Conference on AIDS, held in San Francisco, was attended by 12,000 scientists, policy-makers, drug manufacturers and health-care workers. The focus of the conference was scientific. Demonstrators in the streets seemed intent on making it political.

One of the activists, Larry Kramer, urged others to riot as a protest to what he described as indifference to AIDS. Apparently ignoring the fact that an international conference attended by 12,000 people is not exactly a sign of indifference, Kramer wrote: "We have been lined up in front of a firing squad and it is called AIDS. We must riot!"

To the streets they went, chanting insults at the establishment, battling police and blocking traffic in the area of the conference. One session was interrupted when an activist climbed onto the stage and began haranguing the panel. The panel walked out.

AIDS victims aren't being ignored. Dr. Antonia Novello, who has been picked to succeed Dr. C. Everett Koop as surgeon general, has promised to broaden the fight against AIDS that Dr. Koop began. President Bush has asked Congress for $1.7 billion for AIDS research and prevention in the next fiscal year, which is an increase of $109 million over what is being spent this year.

Developments in AIDS research are being announced with some regularity. The drug AZT has been proved to extend lives. Late last year, doctors announced they had eradicated the deadly virus from a patient's body using a combination of drugs and high technology, including a bone marrow transplant. Experiments are proceeding with a blood-heating technique.

The San Francisco meeting provided opportunities to carry the fight against AIDS forward. Samuel Broder, director of the National Cancer Institute, said: "We still need a forum like this to exchange clinical and scientific information on AIDS." Referring to the demonstrations, he said: "I certainly don't see how violence or disruption can help alleviate death and human suffering, and that is why we are all doing this work, isn't it?"

Frustration and impatience are understandable among AIDS victims, some of whom are additionally embittered by anti-homosexual discrimination. But the pace of research and the level of human understanding aren't likely to be enhanced by disrupting meetings and hurling insults. Indeed, the demonstrators run a serious risk of turning off some of the very people who have been doing the most to solve the problem.

THE SPOKESMAN-REVIEW

Spokane, Washington, June 26, 1990

In Spike Lee's provocative movie, "Do The Right Thing," a character called Buggin' Out tries to arouse residents of a black neighborhood to boycott the local white-owned pizzeria because it has no photos of black heroes on its walls.

"Are you down (for the boycott)?" Buggin' Out asks neighborhood resident, Jade. Her reply: "I'm down for something positive in the community. Are you down for that?"

That's a question that should be put to members of ACT UP, who fully lived up to their acronym in San Francisco this weekend when they threw the Sixth International AIDS Conference into utter disarray.

Protesters organized by ACT UP, the AIDS Coalition to Unleash Power, heckled Health and Human Services Secretary Louis Sullivan, drowning out a speech that he continued to deliver anyway. The day before, members of the group invaded a department store in downtown San Francisco, banners and stickers flying.

To what end? If ACT UP's aim was to generate anger, it did that. If it was to insult, mission accomplished. If it was to obscure the issues involving legitimate debate over the nation's approach to dealing with acquired immune deficiency syndrome, ACT UP can claim victory in that arena, too.

But if what ACT UP intended to do was advance the cause of increasing assistance for people infected with the AIDS virus, it scored a big, fat zero. Acts like these are counterproductive. Belligerence, bullying and bad manners will gain no ground in the fight against AIDS.

Nothing meaningful can occur without dialogue, and meaningful dialogue on such a controversial issue means there will be disagreement.

To act in a manner that puts the two sides in the debate at loggerheads is to become part of the problem rather than part of the solution. To do so when people are dying every day from the fatal disease is inexcusable.

While members of ACT UP were engaged in disruption this weekend, others were trying to make something positive happen. Other activists, researchers and policy makers attending the conference joined in a march through downtown San Francisco to show their unity on a national AIDS agenda focusing on early treatment, improved health care and an end to discrimination against people infected by the virus.

If members of ACT UP don't intend to help, they should step aside so others with a more positive agenda can.

The Atlanta Journal
THE ATLANTA CONSTITUTION

Atlanta, Georgia, June 27, 1990

It wasn't a pretty picture — U.S. Health and Human Services Secretary Louis W. Sullivan getting booed at the sixth International Conference on AIDS. Several hundred protesters shouted, whistled and threw paper wads at Dr. Sullivan as he tried to present information to scientists.

The disruption of what should have been a meaningful exchange among health experts was rude and counterproductive. But before the White House gets too insulted, officials should remember the old saying: what goes around comes around.

For nearly a decade, gay activists have been trying to get the government to treat AIDS as a disease, not a punishment. But during the 1980s, President Reagan and some other conservatives made the virus into a political issue.

No one has been more determined to politicize AIDS than Sen. Jesse Helms (R-N.C.), who sponsored the 1987 law barring people infected with AIDS from entering the country, even though the disease cannot be spread through casual contact. Because of that law, scores of health organizations, including the Red Cross, refused to participate in the conference.

Mr. Helms also pushed Congress into allowing employers to transfer workers with AIDS out of food-handling jobs, although there is not a shred of evidence the virus can be transmitted through food.

So where was President Bush on the conference's opening day? In North Carolina, at a fund-raiser for Mr. Helms.

What kind of signal was Mr. Bush trying to send when he decided to snub the conference, refuse to lift the immigration ban and honor the reactionary most dedicated to stoking congressional homophobia?

While the AIDS activists have plenty of reason to be angry with Mr. Bush, they showed little common sense in picking the target for their noisy protest. If ACT-UP, the radical gay organization, wants to work more closely with the black community to stop the spread of AIDS, they should not be attacking Dr. Sullivan, the dedicated black physician who can help their cause.

ACT-UP leaders are helping the Helms strategy of trying to turn AIDS research into a political football instead of an urgent scientific quest for cures and vaccines.

LAS VEGAS REVIEW-JOURNAL
Las Vegas, Nevada, June 27, 1990

Protests by angry homosexuals have become part and parcel of any scientific conference concerning AIDS. The big international AIDS conference in San Francisco, the heart of AIDS country, was no exception.

The furious homosexuals who constitute the gay pressure group ACT UP (AIDS Coalition to Unleash Power) shouted down U.S. Health and Human Services Secretary Louis Sullivan Sunday as he tried to speak at the close of the conference. The gay protesters pelted the Cabinet secretary with pocket change and wads of paper and shouted "Guilty, guilty, guilty," drowning out his speech.

And of what is Sullivan "guilty"? The United States government pumps more money — $1.7 billion this year — into AIDS research than into any other disease. Because scientists now find it difficult to secure federal grants to do research on non-AIDS-related diseases, AIDS has become, de facto, the nation's No. 1 public health priority. Although AIDS affects far fewer people than heart disease or cancer or Alzheimer's of any number of other maladies, it receives the lion's share of federal dollars.

And for these policies Sullivan is deemed "guilty."

No, the radical homosexual community wants a cure for AIDS and a vaccine right now, immediately, today — ignoring the fact that the people working on that cure are scientists beholden to scientific method, and not miracle workers.

What is the genesis of the gay rage that surfaces at every AIDS conference? You will find a clue to the answer by reading Randy Shilts' book "And the Band Played On."

In that gripping account of the AIDS story, Shilts documents the outrage displayed by many male homosexuals when they learned it was no longer safe to indulge in risky sex with many hundreds — in some cases thousands — of different men in a year. Many homosexuals could not bear to relinquish the unrestrained hedonism that characterized their lifestyle in the days before AIDS. Groups such as ACT UP want the "good old days" back — right now. Anything less just makes them angry.

ST. LOUIS POST-DISPATCH
St. Louis, Missouri, June 29, 1990

An international AIDS conference in San Francisco this week has thrown a spotlight on an overly restrictive and outdated U.S. immigration policy. Current law requires the Immigration and Naturalization Service to take special but unnecessary precautions for anyone entering the United States who declares himself or herself to be a homosexual. The policy should be changed.

Immigration law denies entry to the United States to anyone with a "psychopathic personality, sexual deviation or a mental defect" — language that the U.S. Supreme Court has ruled can be used to bar homosexuals. Normally, the regulation is ignored because immigration officials do not ask those traveling to the United States to state their sexual orientation. But INS officials say they are obligated to enforce the law for any people who declare themselves to be homosexuals. In California, a 1983 court ruling led to INS policy where a Public Health Service doctor must issue a certificate saying someone is a homosexual; that person is then turned over to a judge to determine whether entry to the United States should be barred.

Groups in this country have protested the unfairness of the law, saying that it treats homosexuality as a crime or an illness when it is neither and should not be used as a pretext to prohibit travel.

Homosexuals could evade the law simply by avoiding a declaration of their sexual orientation. But they should not have to be driven underground in that way. The best way to erase such discrimination is to change the regulations, either in Congress or through an emergency administrative order. That way, by 1992, when a similar AIDS conference is scheduled for Boston, no one would be barred by laws that long ago became inappropriate.

THE LINCOLN STAR
Lincoln, Nebraska, June 26, 1990

The frustration and fear expressed by rowdy, disruptive AIDS activists at the Sixth International Conference on AIDS is understandable.

AIDS is a terrible, debilitating affliction to which this nation was slow to respond.

Actions such as the immigration policy that restricts travel by people with AIDS and attacks by conservatives in Congress on funding educational efforts perpetuate the political divisiveness.

On the medical front, access to experimental AIDS drugs is limited and treatment is expensive. Great strides in the treatment of AIDS in the past couple of years, putting medicine within striking distance of an AIDS vaccine, have raised hopes that haven't been met. Faced with dementia and death, often stricken in the prime of life, AIDS patients have a right and a need to vent.

But anarchy is no solution. The protesters did more than cross a few barricades and get themselves arrested.

They shackled free speech by their heckling of Health and Human Services Secretary Louis Sullivan. At least one panel of doctors and researchers was forced off stage by a protester from ACT UP.

More than that, the protesters turned the AIDS symposium into a circus and risked turning off the very people — the doctors, the researchers, the social workers — who have come to help.

ALTHOUGH PROTESTS against the Bush administration are more on target, as one AIDS activist lamented about the Sullivan protest: "It doesn't leave us a lot of maneuvering room."

One doctor who treats AIDS patients said: "How are you supposed to respond? I see their point, but we're here to try to learn so we can help."

We're here to help.

But even before the conference began, concern over the scope of the protests overshadowed the conference. Randy Shilts, reporter with the San Francisco Chronicle and author of a book on AIDS, said that every conversation with AIDS researchers revolved around "What's going to happen?" Shilts called it the "new Era of Bad Feelings" and predicted it would be the beginning of the end of the international AIDS conferences.

As Shilts reported in the San Francisco Chronicle: "One big reason they (researchers, doctors) come to conferences is to get moral support for work that is largely thankless in the larger world.

"Many of these people are saying openly that they will stop coming to these conferences if they turn into mere photo opportunities for protesters to scream at them. If the story of this conference becomes a story about protests, many in the AIDS world believe this will be the last international AIDS conference that scientists want to go to."

WE HAVE learned a great deal about AIDS in the past decade.

The early news reports, eerie for what they didn't say, reported on an unusual number of gay men sick with a rare form of cancer. Since then scientists have identified the virus and its nearly innumerable associative diseases. We have learned how the disease is spread and education on AIDS-associated behaviors has undoubtedly reduced the spread of AIDS through certain populations.

We have learned that AIDS is elusive, mutating its way around treatments such as AZT, and spreading into new groups such as teen-agers and newborns; it has exacerbated other diseases such as tuberculosis in Africa and herpes in this country.

Clearly, for all the progress made there are challenges ahead. It is a pitifully poor time for people essentially on the same side to poke at their differences and destroy the cohesion needed for further progress.

The Phoenix Gazette
Phoenix, Arizona, June 26, 1990

The diagnosis of AIDS is a death sentence more sure than any handed down by a court. So it is understandable that AIDS activists are anxious for quick action to find a cure for the dread disease.

But the sad spectacle activists presented in San Francisco last weekend, disrupting the Sixth International AIDS Conference with an ear-splitting din of shouting and threats, hardly helped do anything but outrage serious scientists who have committed their careers to finding a cure for AIDS.

Members of ACT-UP, the group that sponsored the protest, claimed a victory. But they, in fact, sponsored a defeat. In their frustration, they have begun consuming their natural allies, scientists and public health officials who are doing their best.

Dr. Louis Sullivan, U.S. Secretary of Health and Human Services, spoke stoically through the din, as paper airplanes rained down on him and activists shouted at him.

He told them what they should have known: "We must learn to listen to each other, to learn from each other and to work together. Our frustration must never drive us to close our ears or our hearts."

Jonathan Mann, former head of the World Health Organization's AIDS program, didn't think ACT-UP scored such a victory with its demonstration. "I actually feel we all lost," he said. "The images that will go around the world will be of a man with a noble face speaking quietly and carefully to a sea of wild people."

AIDS is not a war fought among men; it is a race between medical science and death, a race that, incidentally, is costing more than research on the leading killer of humans, cancer. Time will tell what success science has, but it surely will come more quickly if we can hear what public health officials are saying over the din.

THE KANSAS CITY STAR
Kansas City, Missouri, June 24, 1990

If there's one message coming out of an event like the Sixth International Conference on AIDS that ends today, it is that more education is needed about the disease.

Two questions follow: What kind of education, and what makes learning stick? A trial-and-error process to find out continues.

As the head of the National Commission on AIDS told the conference, education is the best vaccine against the disease. But the commission, part of the National Academy of Science, said new groups that were not considered at high risk in the past are showing high rates of AIDS infection.

Contrary to some reports, the commission said, the epidemic is not leveling off. The groups at increased risk include women, adolescents, and users of crack and alcohol.

Additional education programs need to be designed to reach these groups. Current projects must be continued. More evaluation of them is critical if budget decisions are to be cost-effective.

Officials on the academy commission estimated that the $200 million the federal government spends on education needs to be doubled for efforts that might make a difference.

Some people who are uninfected and unaffected by AIDS learn poorly or not at all. They pick the information they want to believe, then couch their hostility toward AIDS patients as protection of their individual rights.

Co-existence between opponents is necessary in an advanced society. The United States is a long way from that, with some communities farther behind than others.

That is probably one reason the issue of laws barring people with the AIDS virus from entering the U.S. dominated the conference. Protesters at the San Francisco conference focused on this as a major symbol of discrimination against people with the condition.

The conference has highlighted both fact and feeling about the state of research, the law and the treatment of people with the AIDS virus. Beneficial as that is to society, it may doom future international forums as scientific exchanges.

St. Petersburg Times
St. Petersburg, Florida, June 28, 1990

The annals of modern public discourse would not be greatly diminished if AIDS activists turned their backs on U.S. Sen. Jesse Helms, R-N.C., every time he attempted to speak on behalf of some piece of scientific ignorance and mean-spirited discrimination, such as his efforts to prevent people infected with the AIDS virus from being employed in food-handling jobs. Nor could AIDS activists be blamed for covering their ears every time Ronald Reagan, whose administration was unconscionably slow to devote resources to AIDS research, attempts to portray himself as a sympathetic advocate for those who have contracted the virus.

However, those hecklers who disrupted Health and Human Resources Secretary Louis Sullivan's closing speech last week at the Sixth International Conference on AIDS were guilty of the same kind of intolerance that often has been directed at them. The Bush administration's record of support for AIDS-related medical research and civil-rights protection is not perfect, but it is a marked improvement over what preceded it. Secretary Sullivan came before the conference as an important ally. The 6,000 people in attendance might not have liked everything that he had to say, but it wouldn't have hurt them to listen.

In fact, the most strident AIDS advocates can only hurt their cause by refusing to listen to Dr. Sullivan and all other officials who are judged to be less than ideologically correct. Several years ago, when well-meaning health officials in the San Francisco area first attempted to regulate the gay bath houses that had become breeding grounds for the AIDS virus, many gay activists, understandably sensitive to the possibility of official discrimination against homosexuals, didn't want to hear the experts' alarms. Their political pressure succeeded in keeping the bath houses open and unregulated for several months after health officials issued their first warnings. Jesse Helms and Ronald Reagan aren't the only people whose poor decisions can be blamed for impeding the government's response to the AIDS epidemic and causing an untold number of people to become unnecessarily exposed to the AIDS virus.

Those errors of the recent past have been largely corrected. Our government now supports more than $1-billion a year in AIDS-related research. The search for a vaccine and cure is agonizingly slow, but not because of inadequate support. The public has a much better understanding of the virus, and the most objectionable forms of discrimination against people with AIDS have been officially repudiated.

That progress is a result of a two-way process of communication and education. Dr. Sullivan went to San Francisco to take part in that process, and a few hundred protesters chose to disrupt it with their whistles, air horns and tossed trash. It's easy to understand the terrible fears and frustrations of those who have faced first-hand the specter of AIDS. It's hard to understand how the closed-minded reception given Secretary Sullivan furthered their cause.

The News Journal
Wilmington, Delaware, June 28, 1990

Some 10,000 researchers, public health officials and others meet in San Francisco today to continue the swirling debate over AIDS. The Sixth International Conference on AIDS is being held as new hopes and new fears about the disease come to light.

Doctors are more optimistic about the chances of developing anti-AIDS vaccines and drugs, and the rate of new cases is slowing. However, reports of AIDS-based discrimination are on the rise, AIDS is shifting from the cities to the heartland and blacks and Hispanics continue to claim a disproportionate percentage of the estimated 136,000 cases in the U.S.

So there is much more work to be done. Rest assured that AIDS' chief allies won't make the San Francisco trip. Apathy, ignorance and indifference will be too busy elsewhere.

ARGUS-LEADER
Sioux Falls, South Dakota, June 26, 1990

The nation's AIDS toll continues to rise at an alarming pace. Projections for the future make the disease an even greater concern.

The frustration of activists who want the slow-moving federal government to do more is understandable. But demonstrators hurt their cause Sunday in San Francisco when they disrupted the Sixth International Conference on AIDS.

Chanting, whistle-blowing protesters drowned out Louis Sullivan, head of the U.S. Health and Human Services Department, as he urged scientists and activists to cooperate. According to news reports, protesters were so loud that, at times, even an interpreter for the deaf standing next to Sullivan could not hear the speech.

"Shame, shame, shame," demonstrators shouted. "No more words. We want action!"

The protest was organized by the group ACT UP, the AIDS Coalition to Unleash Power. The activist group led daily demonstrations outside the convention hall during the five-day meeting. Until Sunday, they had not disrupted sessions inside.

Doctors, scientists, educators and other conference delegates had reason to be upset with Sunday's protesters, who demanded to be heard but silenced the words of others.

There is nothing wrong with peaceful demonstrations, even loud demonstrations. But the First Amendment's right of free expression cuts both ways. Sullivan, a representative of President Bush's administration, also was entitled to be heard. Conference delegates from other countries, especially, might have been interested in what he had to say.

Activists said they are angry with federal efforts for several reasons, including the slow pace at which treatments have been found and made available to people infected with the virus that causes AIDS.

U.S. health officials estimate that about 1 million Americans may be infected with the AIDS virus. Victims who develop the disease become susceptible to infections and cancer. The disease is incurable and fatal.

According to statistics from the federal Centers for Disease Control in Atlanta, 136,204 AIDS cases had been reported as of May 31 and 83,145 people had died.

The agency projects that by the end of 1993, the number of cases will have risen to between 390,000 and 480,000 and the death toll will have increased to somewhere between 285,000 and 340,000.

A health threat of that magnitude demands cooperation.

Activists who disrupted Sullivan succeeded in getting short-term attention focused on themselves. Unfortunately, for the longer term, they may have offended people with the potential to help.

ALBUQUERQUE JOURNAL
Albuquerque, New Mexico, June 24, 1990

Don't be complacent — the epidemic is far from over. That was the main message from the Sixth International AIDS Conference this past week in San Francisco.

AIDS was so bad in its first decade that it's hard to imagine it getting any worse. Whether it's just wishful thinking or a lapse in the public's disease-of-the-moment attention span, we want to believe new cases have leveled off. They haven't.

Instead, the National Academy of Sciences warns that the disease is making inroads into new populations, including women, teen-agers and users of crack cocaine and alcohol. New cases of AIDS even are increasing among young gay men, despite widespread efforts by the gay community — the first and hardest hit by the epidemic — to change risky sexual behavior.

It's not that those efforts didn't work: New cases have slackened among gay men in general. But the implication that a younger generation is reverting to risky behavior means that the commitment to education and prevention can't be abandoned.

And the well-organized gay community has proved to be the *easiest* group to reach. The disease also has ravaged intravenous drug users, hitting minorities especially hard. Getting this population to change risky behavior has proved to be much more difficult.

Conference leaders called for doubling the amount now spent on education efforts, and — equally important — ensuring that the message is delivered in the language of its target group.

This means there's no room for squeamish legislators — why does Sen. Jesse Helms come to mind? — to block funds for educational materials because of "offensive" language or illustrations. Leave it to public health officials to decide what works.

FORT WORTH STAR-TELEGRAM
Fort Worth, Texas, June 26, 1990

Pardon the cliché, but with friends like ACT UP, officials seeking a cure for AIDS don't need enemies.

ACT UP stands for the AIDS Coalition to Unleash Power, and it is composed of AIDS activists who feel that not enough is being done by science and the government to combat the deadly epidemic.

So far, so good. More resources — both human and financial — should be thrown into the battle.

But childish stunts of the type that ACT UP members staged Sunday in trying to prevent the federal government's leading health official from addressing the sixth International Conference on AIDS in San Francisco can do little to garner support for their cause. They can do a great deal to hinder it.

The search for a cure for the virus that causes AIDS is a costly one, and a large amount of tax money will be necessary if it has any chance of success. Rightly or wrongly, the fight against AIDS cannot be conducted solely on the medical front. It must also be waged on the political front.

That means that if researchers are to have access to the funds needed to finance the research that must be conducted, the battle they are waging must have broad public support. Tantrums of the type thrown by ACT UP members inside the conference hall Sunday — not to mention the exhibitionist displays during the Lesbian-Gay Freedom Day Parade in downtown San Francisco at the same time — will not generate such support.

In fact, a majority of Americans are apt to find them so repugnant that the anti-AIDS crusade could have been dealt a serious setback.

Placard-waving ACT UP activists shouted, blew whistles and sounded air horns to prevent conferees from hearing Health and Human Services Secretary Louis Sullivan, who was the last speaker on the final day of the conference. Ironically, Sullivan's speech urged "cooperation, tolerance, understanding and caring," none of which he received from the ill-mannered hecklers.

Neither Sullivan nor the absent President Bush, at whom the insulting demonstration was actually aimed, was hurt by it, but the truly worthwhile and essential fight against AIDS might have been seriously compromised.

AIDS is a killer disease, and a monumental effort by both private and public sectors will be necessary if a cure is to be found before it lays waste to more thousands of Americans. It would be a tragedy if that effort is stalled — even momentarily — by Sunday's ill-advised antics.

USA TODAY
Washington, D.C., June 20, 1990

AIDS discrimination is an infectious disease. It thrives on ignorance, and fear can spread it like wildfire.

Sorry to say, there's no shortage of fear or ignorance.

This week, the American Civil Liberties Union reported on 13,000 AIDS discrimination complaints filed between 1983 and 1988, a number that grew 35% faster than the number of newly diagnosed AIDS cases.

National policies that discriminate against AIDS sufferers are the target of angry demonstrations at this week's Sixth Annual Conference on AIDS in San Francisco.

The discrimination disease infects parents, who think they can protect their families by keeping all AIDS-afflicted youngsters out of school.

The disease infects doctors and dentists, who think they protect themselves by refusing to treat AIDS victims.

The disease infects policymakers, who think they can protect society by keeping out foreigners who are HIV-positive. Now, the only way they can come here is on a temporary, 10-day waiver designed for the AIDS conference.

Discrimination erupts among restaurant owners, who cater to patrons' fears about AIDS-infected food. It erupts among bosses, who fire AIDS victims on flimsy excuses.

Like the writer across the page, defenders of discrimination commit dangerous acts in the name of safety. Acts that will drive AIDS underground.

The best weapons against AIDS are more research and more open minds and hearts.

Compassion can lead AIDS sufferers to seek testing, counseling and treatment. That makes the disease less dangerous to them and safer for the public health.

Education about the real risks of getting AIDS has helped the epidemic's rate of increase level off.

A decade ago, we knew almost nothing about AIDS. We still know too little, but we've learned a lot.

We've learned that AIDS is incredibly difficult to get. It takes sexual contact, contaminated needles, infected blood, or transmission from mother to newborn.

We've learned that handling food, or treating patients, or sharing office space won't transmit the disease.

We've learned that keeping people out of the country does nothing to improve the national health and does a great deal to damage our international reputation.

That policy has been roundly condemned by International Planned Parenthood, the League of Red Cross and Red Crescent Societies, the World Health Organization, and about 100 organizations boycotting the AIDS conference.

Public Health Service officials are convinced that HIV infection should not bar someone from entering the country. They now know the risk of casual transmission is minute, but it will be tough to convince a fear-riddled public.

Exposing myths about AIDS has helped save us from making some dumb political mistakes.

With more education, we can correct some of the dumb mistakes we've already made.

AIDS discrimination must stop. It robs us of resources in the life-and-death battle against the AIDS virus.

The country's call to arms should be: Fight the disease, not the diseased.

The New York Times
New York City, New York, June 26, 1990

No one heard a word of the 15-minute speech given on Sunday by Dr. Louis Sullivan, the Secretary of Health and Human Services, at the San Francisco AIDS conference. Before he had even begun to speak, AIDS activists unfurled a banner saying, "He talks, we die." The secretary's address was drowned out from beginning to end by a roar of shouts and whistles. It's hard to think of a surer way for people with AIDS to alienate their best supporters.

What could have caused such a pointless breakdown in sense and civility? It's not as if society had turned its back on AIDS and those whom it strikes. Gay groups using conventional political methods have persuaded Congress to finance a widespread research effort, now amounting to about $1 billion a year. Though treatments and vaccines are painfully slow in coming, it's not now for want of effort or resources.

The complaints raised by Act-Up, the AIDS Coalition to Unleash Power, were correct. But they were about distinctly secondary issues, like immigration policies and President Bush's decision to pass up the San Francisco conference for a fundraiser for Senator Jesse Helms.

Act-Up's members had no justification for turning a research conference into a political circus. Science and the democratic process may be moving more slowly than all would like, but both are working in their interests, maybe as fast as could reasonably be expected. While Act-Up members were tying up San Francisco's traffic with sit-downs, tens of thousands of people took part peacefully in New York City's Gay and Lesbian Pride March, a diverse parade watched by 120,000 spectators.

Though there is little value in Act-Up's disruptions, it's worth trying to understand the pressures on its members. Many are infected with the AIDS virus, and are desperate for better treatments. Many feel isolated because of society's still-limited acceptance of gays. Many have seen their world collapsing around them as they lose their jobs, housing and health insurance.

Their rage and despair is part of the unmitigated tragedy of AIDS. Act-Up believes it is better to rage than do nothing, and the group's interventions have probably been effective in issues like speeding up the laborious Federal system of drug trials.

But for all their righteous rage, it's important for them to see that shouting down Dr. Sullivan is counterproductive. If Act-Up's members would only keep their faith in education and hard lobbying and put down their bullhorns, they might find their rage surprisingly well understood, and effective when focused in the right way on the right targets.

copyright © The New York Times 1990

The Boston Herald
Boston, Massachusetts, June 26, 1990

AIDS isn't the only disease killing Americans, nor is it the deadliest. According to the National Center for Health Statistics, AIDS is the 15th leading cause of death. Heart disease, cancer, diseases of the lungs, liver, kidneys — even pneumonia and blood poisoning — all kill more people per year than AIDS. And yet, except for cancer, AIDS receives more government research money than any other illness.

Why? Because AIDS activists are communicative, bright, and aggressive, and have organized and worked hard to enlist the public and the government in a fight that in nine years has killed 83,000 Americans. But heart disease kills as many Americans *every six weeks*. Shouldn't more money be going to find a cure for *that* killer?

Because of the work of AIDS activists, America is not a panicked nation but an informed one. People no longer react to the disease as they did nine years ago. The government is heavily involved in AIDS research in large part because the gay community organized and educated the public about the spread of the disease and ways to control it, alleviating public fears in the process.

But now the militant group ACT-UP is threatening to undo all the good that has been done. At the weeklong AIDS conference in San Francisco just ended, daily demonstrations by ACT-UP, not only detracted from but undermined what was going on inside. The group, as it has repeatedly in the past (see Beverly Beckham's column on today's Op-Ed page), acted obnoxiously, screaming, interrupting, obstructing. Their demand is for more government money; but all their foul tactics are accomplishing is the alienation of the public.

In the past, medical strides dominated the news ouf of the annual conference. This year, it was the tactics of the AIDS militants taunting the very people who were meeting to help them.

Activists for most other diseases have reason to complain. Not so AIDS. ACT-UP should shut up.

Birmingham Post-Herald
Birmingham, Alabama, June 26, 1990

Optimism was the novelty at the Sixth International Conference on AIDS in San Francisco, though you might not have noticed amid the demonstrators' hoots and chants.

"He talks, we die," read the large pink banner unfurled as protesters drowned out Secretary of Health and Human Services Louis Sullivan's speech closing the conference. The activists' uncivil methods and misleading message should not obscure the real news of the conference: The giant research effort against the AIDS epidemic is paying off.

After years of little progress, a vaccine is now believed within reach, possibly during this decade. Researchers have succeeded in immunizing monkeys and chimpanzees against the HIV virus, which causes AIDS, a breakdown of the body's immune system. Preliminary safety tests on humans have begun.

A number of questions remain unanswered, notably whether a vaccine developed from one strain of the virus can be used to protect against other strains. Dr. Jonas Salk, creator of the Salk polio vaccine, is among those searching for a vaccine to prevent virus carriers from coming down with full-blown AIDS.

That last would be a boon to the estimated 1 million HIV carriers in the United States and perhaps 8 million worldwide. At present, only one drug, AZT, is approved for routine use to forestall the onset of AIDS and to prolong patients' lives once they have the disease. Its cost — $3,000 to $9,000 a year — is prohibitive for some, especially in the third world countries where the epidemic is most devastating.

Increasing use of AZT probably contributed to another cause of optimism: The epidemic in the United States appears to be leveling off. It has killed over 80,000 people since 1981, but deaths are increasing at a much slower rate than predicted. Public education seems to have discouraged the behavior most sharply associated with transmission of the virus, promiscuous homosexual intercourse and sharing of needles by intravenous drug users.

The San Francisco demonstrators deride the nation's effort against AIDS as utterly inadequate. Yet AIDS research wins more public money than heart disease, the No. 1 killer. Scientific work may be slow to bring results, but they are starting to come in.

MILWAUKEE SENTINEL
Milwaukee, Wisconsin, June 27, 1990

In drowning out a speech by Health and Human Services Secretary Louis W. Sullivan, demonstrators at the sixth International Conference on AIDS managed to get the attention they sought.

But how much public support they will get as a result of their demands for more aggressive government action on finding a cure for AIDS may be another matter.

As a piece of political strategy — and that's what the demonstration was — it was out of date by at least 20 years. Given today's political situation, the mass indulgence in disrespect for the government could backfire.

This reaction is not confined to that segment of society that might derisively be called "flag-wavers."

"I feel like crying," said San Francisco activist Pierre Ludington. "He should be allowed to speak." And Rene Durazzo, spokesman for the San Francisco AIDS Foundation, said he feared that the show of hostility would exhaust sympathy within the administration for AIDS activists.

It is unlikely that President Bush will have any less concern about the problem of AIDS just because the demonstrators would not let the most interested member of his cabinet be heard. But it will make the job of mustering public support for the battle against AIDS more difficult.

An obvious problem is that much of the population connects the disease with the gay lifestyle, with which many "straights" feel uncomfortable. In fact, gays have been identified as a high-risk group for getting AIDS, but the disease afflicts more heterosexuals in some countries.

There also is a feeling that AIDS already is getting special consideration from Congress, which is in the process of allocating billions of dollars specifically to treat that disease. This is a rare occurrence and suggests the AIDS problem is not being minimized.

In addition, except for cancer, AIDS receives more research money than any other disease.

Nonetheless, proponents of more funds for AIDS research make some good arguments. The most significant among them is that fighting AIDS is a matter of stopping an epidemic that could afflict millions more. Cancer and heart disease, the biggest killers, are not in this category.

Critics of new government health rules permitting the reassignment of AIDS sufferers from food-handling jobs also are correct when they say that AIDS cannot be passed on through the handling of food. Sullivan, not incidentally, criticized this proposal in his San Francisco speech, but was not heard.

In any case, drowning out people in a position to help solve this problem is not conducive to the dialog that is necessary if the AIDS problem is to be solved.

The Miami Herald
Miami, Florida, June 21, 1990

AS THE Sixth International Conference on AIDS gets under way today in San Francisco, a pertinent question is whether there ought to be a seventh.

It's not that AIDS has been conquered. Far from it. A cure remains elusive. So does a preventive vaccine. Doctors disagree on several medical treatments commonly used on HIV-infected persons. Worse, epidemiologists say the disease continues to spread, with 300,000 dead in 150 countries.

Research on AIDS thus deserves a high priority and adequate funding. In addition, as long as international conferences can facilitate the sharing of information about AIDS, they ought to continue as well. Whether their format should stay the same is another matter, however.

A key question for this five-day conference is whether the mixing of medical science and political theater is helpful. What raises the question is a trend evident at recent conferences and expected to intensify at this one: their growing use as public forums by persons intent upon making a point on policy questions. Especially unfortunate is the protesters' planned targeting of certain researchers this year.

Granted, some of the protesting groups have legitimate grievances. When AIDS first appeared, for instance, the Reagan Administration was slow to fund research and even slower to condemn an attendant surge in discrimination and hate crimes.

In addition, some of the protesters are themselves HIV-infected or have lost loved ones to AIDS. The more militant among them are thus often inspired by a potent combination of grief, fear, and rage.

Nonetheless, the spectacle of dedicated researchers being heckled or harassed is unacceptable. The proper forum for political protest is Capitol Hill and the other places where policy makers make policy.

What's more, policy makers have a duty to weigh the demands for more AIDS research against other needs. Science funds can't be apportioned solely on the basis of who screams the loudest. Medical problems of women and the elderly have been systematically shortchanged for years.

If there is to be another of these conferences, then, the organizers should try to find a meeting place and to enforce rules conducive to advancing one worthy goal: banishing forever the scourge of AIDS.

The Houston Post
Houston, Texas, June 27, 1990

THE SIXTH INTERNATIONAL AIDS conference, which ended Sunday in San Francisco, on the whole was enlightening and productive. Highlights that come to mind include Dr. Jonas Salk's electrifying and unexpected announcement that he is ready to begin testing on humans a vaccine that he hopes will not only prevent AIDS but treat those already infected with HIV, the virus that leads to the deadly disease.

There was also the conference's success at spotlighting the fact that U.S. immigration policies restrict HIV-infected people from entering the United States. Whether this restriction serves any useful purpose is debatable at best. Certainly it should have been suspended for individuals traveling to this conference.

Given the general tone of the San Francisco meetings, it is a shame that some activists chose to make a mockery of the closing day by drowning out Health and Human Service Secretary Louis Sullivan and pelting him with various objects as he spoke. Among the things they would have heard him say was that he opposes a legal amendment that would allow firing of food-handlers infected with HIV. Sullivan seems to want as badly as anyone to see AIDS wiped out. He deserved better.

ACT UP's chief complaint seems to be that the federal government is not doing enough to fight AIDS. This is an argument that is less persuasive with every passing year. While it is true that Washington was pitifully slow to react to this growing menace, last year federal AIDS spending totaled about $2.2 billion.

That is about 10 percent of the total U.S. Public Health Service budget. It roughly equals what is spent on heart disease or cancer. Also, $2.2 billion looms large when one considers that *all* previous federal spending on AIDS, beginning in 1982, totaled about $3.3 billion.

It is not hard to understand the frustration — indeed, rage — that those involved in the AIDS fight feel in the face of this merciless killer. But heckling people in a position to do the most good is counterproductive. Thank goodness ACT UP, a noisy faction, does not represent the anti-AIDS movement as a whole.

Male Sex Survey Published; Gay Figures Disputed

A survey of male sexuality was published April 15, 1993. Among its most controversial findings, it said the average American male had intercourse once a week, and the number of exclusively homosexual men made up only 1% of the population. Both figures were commonly thought to be higher.

The study appeared in *Family Planning Perspectives*, a journal put out by the Alan Guttmacher Institute, which focused on sexual behavior. It was the work of four demographers at the Battelle Human Affairs Research Centers, who had received a $1.4 million grant from the National Institute of Child Health and Human Development.

The data was obtained in face-to-face interviews with 3,321 men, all between the ages of 20 and 39. The men were selected because census data had shown them to be representative of the American male population in that age bracket.

Among the survey's findings:

■ Only 2.3% of the men interviewed said that they had ever had sex with another man, and just 1.1% reported having had only male partners over the previous 10 years. Those findings indicated that the number of homosexual men was well below the estimated maximum of 10% recorded by sex researcher Alfred Kinsey in his pioneering 1948 survey of male sexuality. That figure had come to be popularly accepted as the percentage of gay men in the country. However, recent studies in both Europe and America had suggested that the lower number was closer to the truth.

■ The median number of female sex partners that each man had had intercourse with was 7.3. (Median meant that half of the men had more than 7.3 partners and half had fewer.) About 23% of the men said that they had had 20 or more partners in their lives, while 28% reported one to three partners. Only 4.6% said they had never had vaginal intercourse.

■ The median age at which white men lost their virginity was 17.2 years. For black men, it was 15.

■ The participants reported having vaginal intercourse an average of about once a week. About 22.5% said they had such sex 10 or more times a week, and 21.9% said they had not had vaginal sex in the four weeks prior to the interview.

■ Seventy-five percent said they had received or performed oral sex at least once.

■ About one-fifth said they had had anal sex at least once.

■ Forty-one percent said they had been tested for the AIDS virus.

■ About 71% believed that the chances of getting AIDS from a single act of intercourse with an infected woman was one in two. (According to doctors, the actual danger was about one in 1,000.)

■ Twenty-seven percent said they had used a condom in the four weeks before the interview. About 75% agreed with the statement that using a condom "shows you are a caring person," while 15% believed it "makes your partner think you have AIDS."

The figures pertaining to the percentage of gay men generated a controversy. Gay advocacy groups had long used Kinsey's figure of 10% in their arguments for equal rights. But if the actual number turned out to be smaller, some feared it would stall the momentum of gay-rights groups.

Gay leaders called the survey flawed. Given the predominant anti-homosexual climate in the U.S., they said, it was only natural that some gays would be reluctant to answer the questions honestly. The leaders also said that the relatively young age-group studied tended to suppress the reporting of homosexuality because some men did not acknowledge their sexual orientation until later in life.

Rev. Lou Sheldon, chairman of the Traditional Values Coalition, which opposed civil rights guarantees for homosexuals, April 15 said that the study would help support the position that homosexuals were "not entitled to special protective status."

The Star-Ledger

Newark, New Jersey, March 10, 1993

American attitudes toward sexual activity have changed somewhat in response to the deadly AIDS virus, but despite that concern, the country appears to be undergoing a second sexual revolution.

That is one of the conclusions of the first major study of the American sexual psyche in four decades. Americans have been enjoying more—and often better and safer—sex since the late 1980s.

"The Janus Report on Sexual Behavior," authored by New Jersey-based Drs. Samuel Janus and his wife, Cynthia Janus, found that most of the nearly 3,000 men and women questioned from 1988 to 1992 said they had more sex than three years previous.

One surprising revelation is that many among those questioned for the study still harbor misconceptions about the AIDS virus. Although more than 80 percent of those surveyed were worried about sexually transmitted diseases, AIDS was considered "primarily a problem of the poor and gay communities."

Most men and women said they had become more cautious about sex, and use of condoms had increased. But the researchers noted, "AIDS never stopped sex. The anxiety made people hesitate, but just as everyone was worried, America seemed to blink."

Mr. Janus noted that the first sexual revolution started in the early 1950s, when the birth control pill gave women more freedom. "Our time is bringing in a second sexual revolution," he said.

But the Janus study added that while sex is back, so is romance. "People are looking for a relationship, somebody to talk to, somebody to hold them," Mr. Janus said.

The report paints a reassuring picture of American sexual attitudes. It seems to indicate that while another sexual revolution may be brewing, it is not the kind that will lead to a new wave of promiscuity, as the earlier one did, and it is accompanied by an awareness of sexually transmitted diseases and a commitment to practicing safe sex.

The Union Leader
Manchester, New Hampshire, April 16, 1992

Where the homosexual controversy is concerned, stated so-called "facts" can be misleading, and especially when the *intent* is to mislead. To cite one of the most blatant examples:

It is certainly true — a fact — that there are homosexuals who lead relatively normal lives involving stable, monogamous relationships. But there are studies that show that very few — one says only 2% — are monogamous or semi-monogamous, the latter meaning they've had 10 or fewer lifetime partners.

Another study found that 43% of white male homosexuals estimated that they had sex with 500 or more different partners, and 28% reported having more than 1,000 lifetime partners.

To call that risky, self-destructive conduct is to understate the case!

On the other hand, an American Psychological Association study said that, by 1984, amid rising fear over the AIDS epidemic, average homosexual promiscuity dropped from 70 to 50 partners per year. That was encouraging. But, tragically, it appears to be rising again.

Yet, the Centers for Disease Control report that nearly two-thirds of all AIDS cases in the United States are directly attributable to homosexual conduct. And even a drop from 70 to 50 partners per year is dismaying in the context of the high rates not only of AIDS but also of syphilis, gonorrhea, genital warts, hepatitis A and hepatitis B among homosexuals.

Editorially, this newspaper hardly ever uses the euphemistic term "gay" to describe those who engage promiscuously in sodomy. It seems strangely out of place. The word tragic seems more appropriate.

Our compassion extends to *them*, but not to their — to use another overworked euphemism — "lifestyle."

THE DAILY OKLAHOMAN
Oklahoma City, Oklahoma, April 16, 1992

IF you've heard it once, you've no doubt heard it a thousand times: one out of every 10 people in the United States is a homosexual. The oft-quoted statistic is apparently a myth. Alfred C. Kinsey, the pioneer sex researcher, came up with the 10 percent figure in the 1940s. Recently, it has been accepted as virtual gospel truth.

Comes now a physician and former medical researcher with convincing evidence that Kinsey's figures on the prevalence of homosexuality are grossly exaggerated. Dr. J. Gordon Muir, who contributed to a 1990 book, "Kinsey, Sex and Fraud," says more recent data suggests that as few as one percent of the population consists of homosexuals.

Writing in the Wall Street Journal, Muir cites recent studies and offers a plausible explanation of how Kinsey's figures were skewed. Muir cites the continuing survey conducted by the census bureau for the Centers for Disease Control. No more than two to three percent of 50,000 men surveyed answered positively to the statement, "you are a man who has had sex with another man at some time since 1977, even one time."

The "even one time" elicits responses even from those who may have experimented with homosexual activity as adolescents, but lead heterosexual lives as adults.

A nationwide 1989 household sample of 1,537 adults conducted by the University of Chicago found only 1.2 percent of both males and females who reported homosexual activity in the year preceding the survey — and only 0.6 to 0.7 percent had homosexual partners exclusively.

The U.S. surveys are virtually identical to surveys in other Western nations including France, Great Britain, Canada, Norway and Denmark.

How did Kinsey go so wrong? In the first place, Muir notes that Kinsey never actually made the 10 percent claim, but did conclude "that 10 percent of men over age 16" had been "more or less exclusively homosexual for periods of up to three years." This figure took in adolescent experimentation, and included behavior that may have occurred only once.

Of importance to note, however, is the fact about 25 percent of Kinsey's 5,300 male subjects were former or present prisoners. Muir said many respondents were recruited from sex lectures where they had gone to solve sex problems.

Muir said at least 200 male prostitutes were among Kinsey's interviewees, and could have amounted to as much as four percent of his sample. Churchgoers, among others, were underrepresented by Kinsey, Muir said, and other segments of the population were missing entirely.

"...The Kinsey 'findings' are based on criminal experiments conducted by pedophiles who stimulated infants (as young as two months) and children against their will, without parental consent (obviously) for up to 24 hours at a time," Muir states.

As politicians pander to the "gay" vote, Muir points out that a national poll showed 2.4 percent of voters in the 1992 presidential election described themselves as homosexuals.

These recent studies definitively debunk the 10 percent fallacy.

The Hartford Courant
Hartford, Connecticut, Septemebr 17, 1990

The Kinsey Institute has come up with another update on the sexual state of the nation. The news is not good.

For example, according to the Kinsey folks, only about 25 percent of all Americans know that the "typical" citizen of this land has intercourse between the age of 16 and 17, or that 30 percent to 40 percent of all married men have an extramarital affair. Kinsey people know. Apparently they even know what typical means.

There is therefore a need, they say, for more sex education. This, even though the low birth rate indicates a widespread comprehension of the fundamentals.

How can the Kinsey Institute be so sure, either of what we know, or of what facts there are to be known? Do all people asked tell the truth about their sexual knowledge or experience when asked by a surveyor? Given the subject, shouldn't the margin of error be more than 3 percentage points?

And though they might have the right solution, do they really know the problem? More sex education makes most sense for babies having babies and to increase understanding of how the AIDS virus is transmitted. But is there any pressing need for high school freshmen to know that up to 40 percent of dads are playing around? What value is served by assuring the teenager that intercourse at age 16 or 17 is typical?

Besides, Kinsey researchers may be wrong. They may have fallen for the biggest pack of locker-room lies in sociological history.

Washington, D.C. March Supports Gay Rights

Hundreds of thousands of homosexuals, bisexuals and their supporters marched in Washington, D.C. April 25, 1993 demanding equal rights and freedom from discrimination.

Organizers said they had reached their goal of one million marchers, a figure that was supported by the office of Mayor Sharon Pratt Kelly (D). But police placed the total at 300,000.

The marchers called for the passage of a civil rights bill and other antidiscrimination measures and for the appropriation of more money for AIDS education, treatment and research. One of the most prominently voiced calls of the day was for the overturning of the ban on homosexuals in the military.

The march was generally peaceful. Police reported only five arrests for disorderly conduct. At one point, hundreds of activists staged a "die-in" to symbolize the death toll caused by AIDS.

Smaller groups of counterdemonstrators lined Pennsylvania Avenue. The Christian Action Network, a conservative religious group opposed to homosexual rights, called the event "a wake-up call to the silent majority of Americans whose individual rights are at stake."

Speakers at rallies on the Washington Mall included civil rights leader Rev. Jesse L. Jackson, Rep. Barney Frank (D, Mass.), who was gay, and Larry Kramer, a playwright and the founder of the AIDS activist group ACT-UP.

President Clinton was out of town during the march, speaking in Boston before a group of publishers. He had decided not to prepare a video or audio presentation, but sent a letter that was read to demonstrators by Rep. Nancy Pelosi (D, Calif.). Some participants were upset that Clinton, who had met with homosexual rights leaders earlier in the month, did not attend the march.

"I stand with you in the struggle for equality for all Americans, including gay men and lesbians," Clinton's letter read. "In this great country, founded on the principle that all people are created equal, we must learn to put aside what divides us and focus on what we share."

In a related development, a survey of male sexuality was published April 15. Among its most controversial findings, it said the average American male had intercourse once a week, and the number of exclusively homosexual men made up only 1% of the population. Both figures were commonly thought to be higher.

The study appeared in *Family Planning Perspectives*, a journal put out by the Alan Guttmacher Institute, which focused on sexual behavior. It was the work of four demographers at the Battelle Human Affairs Research Centers, who had received a $1.4 million grant from the National Institute of Child Health and Human Development.

The data was obtained in face-to-face interviews with 3,321 men, all between the ages of 20 and 39. The men were selected because census data had shown them to be representative of the American male population in that age bracket.

The figures pertaining to the percentage of gay men generated a controversy. Gay advocacy groups had long used sex researcher Alfred Kinsey's figure of 10% – a figure recorded in a pioneering 1948 study of sexuality – in their arguments for equal rights. But if the actual number turned out to be smaller, some feared it would stall the momentum of gay-rights groups.

Gay leaders called the survey flawed. Given the predominantly anti-homosexual climate in the U.S., they said, it was only natural that some gays would be reluctant to answer the questions honestly. The leaders also said that the relatively young age-group studied tended to suppress the reporting of homosexuality because some men did not acknowledge their sexual orientation until later in life.

Rev. Lou Sheldon, chairman of the Traditional Values Coalition, which opposed civil rights guarantees for homosexuals, April 15 said that the study would help support the position that homosexuals were "not entitled to special protective status."

The Register-Guard
Eugene, Oregon, April 21, 1993

The oft-cited claim that 10 percent of the American population is homosexual has grown increasingly threadbare in recent years. Now a new study has revised the percentage sharply downward, concluding that only 1 percent of American men identify themselves as exclusively homosexual. High or low, it's important to avoid assigning too much importance to these figures. The percentages are irrelevant in the superheated debate over gay rights.

The old 10 percent figure came from the 1948 study, "Sexual Behavior in the Human Male," better known as the Kinsey Report. It has long been a suspect figure, partly because of limitations in Kinsey's sampling techniques and partly because it clashes with what people observe in their own families and communities. If one in 10 were gay, America's closets would have to be terribly crowded.

Yet the 10 percent figure has been put to political use by gay rights advocates. The percentage implies that nearly everyone knows someone who is gay. Thus, the argument goes, to discriminate against gay people is to discriminate against co-workers, family members and friends.

A new survey by researchers at the University of Chicago, however, puts the percentage of male homosexuals at 1 percent. An additional 1 percent said they had engaged in homosexual sex but did not consider themselves gay. This survey also has limitations — its validity depends on respondents' willingness to be candid with interviewers and themselves. But the new figure is roughly congruent with similar studies in other nations.

Opponents of gay rights will undoubtedly seize the lower percentage to support their claim that homosexuals deserve no protection against discrimination. American society, they'll argue, is not heavily populated with gay people, and hence the effects of discrimination are not widely felt. The 10 percent figure has presented a problem for opponents of gay rights — it's hard to justify punitive actions toward such a large group. But a smaller minority can more easily be shunned.

Numbers shouldn't matter, however, in debates over rights. Catholics' right to practice their religion, for instance, is no stronger than that of Seventh Day Adventists despite the disparity in the two faiths' memberships. Numerical superiority does not make black people's claim to equal rights more valid than Asians'.

The latest figure on the percentage of gay men in American society is of considerable sociological interest. But even if there were only one gay man in the United States, he would be entitled to full civil rights and protection against discrimination.

The Boston Globe
Boston, Massachusetts, April 26, 1992

Any group of Americans large enough to send hundreds of thousands of representatives to march in Washington in a massive demonstration of common interest has earned a major place in the political equation. As focused as were gay men and lesbians on the issues that plague them with intolerance and worse, the more subtle lesson for all Americans was that any group so large is itself highly diverse.

Americans have tended to stereotype homosexuals, using ostracism, crude jokes and naked aggression as the vehicles for lumping them into a single mass. Homosexuals' fight for equal rights has to some extent reinforced this oversimplification, but the themes of the parades and rallies yesterday illustrated the wide variety of backgrounds, lifestyles and political beliefs that make up the gay community.

While the flamboyant behavior and dress of some participants attracted a lot of attention, the predominating character of the participants was indistinguishable from any other group of randomly selected Americans – it was a good sampling of people from a wide range of backgrounds, lifestyles and ethnic underpinnings.

That range reinforces gays' legitimate claim to equal treatment in law and daily life. The essence of the matter was put well by those who pointed out that many come from ordinary walks of life; they perform useful jobs the same way as those who work with them; they are in general indistinguishable from other "ordinary" Americans.

President Clinton, whose trip to Boston coincided with the massive demonstration, put the issue soundly when he urged that Americans judge each other on the basis of their conduct rather than their orientation.

That it should be necessary for hundreds of thousands to gather in Washington to assert claims to basic rights is a comment on how much remains to be done; that such an event can take place in the open is also a tribute to how much progress has already been made.

The Chattanooga Times
Chattanooga, Tennessee, June 15, 1992

Sunday's Lesbian and Gay Pride March, like the first one in Chattanooga last year, showed that conflicting views on a controversial issue can be strongly expressed without deteriorating into violence. In the process, Chattanooga learned a lot about tolerance — not of the marchers' views, necessarily, but of the right of all Americans to exercise their constitutional freedoms.

Sunday's march ended with a rally at Warner Park, where music and speeches formed a backdrop for minidebates between gays and those who object to their sexual practices. It's doubtful any of the objectors changed the minds of anyone in the rally, but some no doubt made a better impression than others. The same is true of those who participated in the march.

One man, for instance, immediately negated any influence he might have had by carrying a sign which read, "The Circus," with an arrow pointed at the rally participants. Others aimed volleys of random warnings that, not surprisingly, went largely ignored.

And still others distributed a one-page, single-space diatribe which proclaimed that "homosexuals should not be permitted to parade in Chattanooga." Moreover, they also "should not be allowed to live freely in the United States or ... (in) any other nation of the world." Presumably that means they should be targeted for mass execution.

By contrast, some objectors presented their arguments calmly, and no less sincerely, yet with no evident prejudgment. Those discussions seemed to end amicably.

But there was prejudgment on the other side as well. Some rally-goers equated all objections to their practices as bigotry or hatred, which is demonstrably untrue. And others seemed offended by the presence of those who, in furtherance of their beliefs, held up signs expressing those beliefs.

The best way to symbolize Sunday's gathering at Warner Park is with an umbrella — the umbrella of the Constitution, more particularly the First Amendment. It gives all Americans the right to express their views in a variety of ways, excluding violence.

It gave the Gay and Lesbian Pride Committee the right to hold its parade — but only after properly rolling over the City Council's feeble attempt to dictate its format. And it protected the right of others to protest the philosophy that they believed the march exemplified.

The city's granting of a parade permit does not connote official approval of any event, whether it's a gay pride march or the Ku Klux Klan demonstration reportedly scheduled for August.

Moreover, the First Amendment freedom of assembly is not guaranteed only to groups acceptable to the mainstream of society. If that were the case, this would be a sterile and authoritarian society — in short, a contradiction of the intent of our nation's founders.

Those are obvious points, but they are also too easily overlooked, or at least misunderstood, in the heat of debate over this issue. If nothing else, Sunday's march demonstrated the Constitution-based tolerance that can only strengthen Chattanooga.

The Salt Lake Tribune
Salt Lake City, Utah, May 2, 1992

Does anybody remember exactly how many people participated in the civil rights march on Washington or the anti-Vietnam march or the pro-choice march? Probably not. What comes readily to mind is not a number but a powerful statement by a large group of people — the lasting effect of those demonstrations.

This apparently was lost on the organizers of last Sunday's gay and lesbian march on Washington. While the marchers themselves left an image of pride and solidarity, the organizers focused on the numbers, contending that their legions had been undercounted by the U.S. Park Police, on whose grounds the march took place.

The probability is high that officials at the Department of the Interior, which oversees the Park Police, had more pressing things to do last Wednesday, but nonetheless they met with the four co-chairs of the gay and lesbian march to talk numbers. Interior officials said they would review their crowd count from three days earlier and their methodology for reaching it.

Prior to last Sunday's event, march organizers had predicted a turnout of 1 million, and some estimates indicated that projection was reached. But the Park Police estimated only 300,000. One of the march co-chairs said the crowd was underestimated "perhaps by as much as 60 percent." That means the organizers themselves are putting the number at about half a million.

The point is, who cares? Three hundred thousand, half a million, a million, so what? There were a lot of people on Pennsylvania Avenue appealing for their rights, and that is the only image of last Sunday's demonstration that matters. As one of the marchers told *The New York Times,* "It's not the numbers. It's the feeling of brotherhood, of being together."

In fairness, gay and lesbian activists are caught in a numbers game not entirely of their making. The marcher count dispute came only after a wave of April sexual-behavior studies that indicated the population of male homosexuals to be anywhere from 1 to 4.4 percent, well below the 10 percent figure of the 1948 Kinsey report.

Anti-gay conservatives like to use those numbers to dilute the effect of gay demonstrations like last Sunday's. Their not-so-subtle message is, the lower the numbers of the gay and lesbian population, the easier they can be ignored — "as though the right to be treated fairly depended on a head count," *Times* columnist Anna Quindlen appropriately jabbed.

The numbers game — the crowd counts cited by the gays and lesbians and the sexual-behavior surveys cited by their opponents — simply obscures the greater issue of protecting the civil rights of homosexuals. Both sides would do well to drop this numbers nonsense and keep the focus on what matters: the concerns of a minority that feels oppressed. For if even one person's civil rights are abridged, that matters in America.

The Chattanooga Times
Chattanooga, Tennessee, April 27, 1993

To the degree that Americans learned more about the extent of discrimination against homosexuals during Sunday's march in Washington, then the event will have largely achieved its purpose of raising the public consciousness. That is about the best the organizers could hope for at this point.

For all the various agendas published by gay organizations, the prime consideration common to most gays is the desire to enjoy the same rights as other Americans. That's why they focused chiefly on an end to discrimination in, among other things, housing, employment and military service.

Most of the organizers would concede that the march itself will not guarantee successes across the board. Some goals will be achieved with time; others may never be. A recent poll, for instance, reported that nearly two-thirds of Americans surveyed opposed same-sex marriages.

Cornell history professor Joel H. Silbey made an interesting comment to The New York Times, that most progress will come if the gay political movement manages to make the debate one of civil rights.

And he added, "By themselves, demonstrations don't necessarily do anything. But as long as the issue is one of quality of treatment, of civil rights, then I think they will gain. It's when it becomes behavioral that you get stiff opposition."

A related point has been made in the controversy over ending the ban against gays in the military. Opponents of rescinding the ban have raised fears of homosexual soldiers preying on heterosexuals. That is as unacceptable as heterosexual male soldiers hitting on their female counterparts. Both types of behavior should be punished.

The gay rights agenda, for lack of a better term, attracts the criticism that says, essentially, that if we accept certain anti-discrimination goals, that necessarily means approval of the homosexual lifestyle. But that's not true, just as it is untrue to suggest that those who favor ending the ban on gays in the military condone their behavior.

An acceptance of people as they *are* obviously does not automatically connote an acceptance of what they *do*. That point should be kept in mind by religious organizations now busily using the gay issue to raise funds.

Like other countries, the United States has had its problems with discrimination; it took us more than 200 years, for instance, to end the blatant practices that discriminated against blacks.

Americans generally want to be fair; shown evidence of discrimination, most are willing to work at ending it. The claims of discrimination raised by gays are somewhat different, however, because of the behavior factor. And that in turn is tied to the growing debate over whether homosexuality is a choice or a congenital orientation.

Demonizing the gay movement may be effective in fund-raising appeals, but the fact is gays come from all points on the social, racial and economic spectrum. The sooner that recognition infuses the argument for an end to the discrimination many gays endure, the better.

LAS VEGAS REVIEW-JOURNAL
Las Vegas, Nevada, April 18, 1993

Radical homosexuals like to claim gays make up 10 percent of the population. Some lesbian activists double the figure, claiming 10 percent of men are gay and 10 percent of women too, which makes 20 percent. Wrong, it makes 10 percent. But even that number is inflated, as it turns out, by roughly 900 percent.

It is now quite clear that persons who prefer sexual contact with members of the same gender make up only 1 or 2 percent of the population. Comprehensive studies in the United States, Canada, and Europe all serve to debunk the 10 percent theory, advanced in the 1940s by an intellectual charlatan named Alfred C. Kinsey.

For one thing, writes medical researcher and author J. Gordon Muir in the Wall Street Journal, "About 25 percent of Kinsey's 5,300 male subjects were former or present prisoners; a high percentage were sex offenders (and) many respondents were recruited from sex lectures, where they had gone to get the answer to sex problems. ... At least 200 male prostitutes were among his interviewees. ..."

Despite the glaring flaws in the Kinsey study, gay activists seized upon it, and for years trumpeted the fraudulent findings to advance a radical cultural and political agenda.

Now comes the latest study of American sex habits from the Battelle Human Affairs Research Centers in Seattle. Conducting detailed surveys of 3,321 men aged 20 to 39 under a federal grant, they found only 1.1 percent were exclusively homosexual, while just 2.3 percent reported any homosexual activity in the past 10 years.

This is not an isolated finding. Muir cites the 1991-92 French government survey of more than 20,000 citizens which found 1.4 percent of men and 0.4 percent of women to be gay. A nationwide survey of 18,876 adults in Britain turned up 1.4 percent homosexual men. A 1989 U.S. survey by the University of Chicago found 1.2 percent of men and an equal percentage of women had had a homosexual contact in the past year. A nationwide survey in Canada showed 1 percent of the population to be homosexual; in Denmark it was less than 1 percent. And so on.

Homosexuals are a minute minority. Gay groups like to contend there are 85,000 homosexuals in the Las Vegas area. Let's talk maybe 9,000 — not a population the size of North Las Vegas and Carson City combined; closer to the population of Winnemucca.

Why do many homosexual activists continue to assert that there are 25 million homosexuals in the United States, when in reality there are more like 2.5 million? The answers are obvious: To give the impression that they wield great clout at the polls; to consolidate political power; to bolster the demand that their sexual practices be honored as, in all respects, wholesome; to advance a profoundly radical cultural agenda.

It is this agenda, pursued by such groups as Queer Nation, whose elements are so disturbing to many Americans. But for every screeching radical of Queer Nation, there are many gays, including many here in Las Vegas, who live quiet, conventional lives. Their small numbers are, obviously, no excuse for seeking to deprive homosexuals of the fundamental rights all Americans enjoy, nor any excuse for ridiculing or tormenting these citizens.

The Honolulu Advertiser
Honolulu, Hawaii, April 22, 1993

Never mind the dispute over how many. There were enough to put Sunday's March on Washington for Lesbian, Gay and Bi Equal Rights and Liberation in the top three or four such extravaganzas.

What our nation's capital witnessed was a massive outpouring from America's closet.

Only a few counter-protesters showed up, and the marchers were upbeat and mellow, carrying signs, like the one quoted above that makes a powerful point with a smile.

Eighty percent of Americans support equal rights for homosexuals, according to a new USA TODAY/CNN/Gallup poll.

Yet many gays and lesbians are still fighting for what every American should take for granted: To get a job based on ability. To walk down a street without being taunted or beaten up. To rent or buy a place to live. To serve their country.

There is less agreement about some related questions: Should government sanction gay marriage and adoption? What should public schools teach children about homosexuality?

But there is no question about basic rights. They are overdue.

The Union Leader
Manchester, New Hampshire, April 26, 1992

Contrary to the propaganda spouted at Sunday's so-called homosexual pride march in the nation's capital, the protesters are not seeking civil rights.

What they are seeking is legitimization of their perversion.

Despite yesterday's fiery oratory, and the support voiced for "homosexual rights" by a few apparently incurably confused heterosexuals, that fact should not be obscured in the public mind.

What homosexual activists are demanding when they equate their cause with that of the civil rights movement is special privilege.

There are no "Jim Crow" laws on the books against homosexuals as there once were against blacks. There are only laws that prohibit forms of behavior associated with homosexuality, and laws against sodomy are applicable to heterosexuals as well.

And what great economic hardships have homosexuals as a class suffered as a result of discrimination? We are not speaking of the underprivileged here. Indeed, according to surveys conducted by Simmons Market Research Bureau Inc. in 1988, the average household income of the readers of the top eight homosexual newspapers in the country was $55,430, as compared to the average income for all Americans of $32,144.

The key word here is "household." Since, statistically, the average homosexual household has fewer than two people, per capita income among homosexual households is three times that of the general population.

Discrimination? Nearly 60% of the homosexual population have college degrees. Although 15.5% of the general population hold professional or managerial positions, 49% of homosexuals enjoy that advantage.

To equate homosexuality with such immutable characteristics as race or ethnic origin, over which one has no control, is ludicrous. With help, some homosexuals — unfortunately, all too few — are living relatively normal lives with stable, monogamous relationships. Masters and Johnson reports a 79.1% immediate success rate for clients who attempted to discontinue their homosexual practices, and a 71.6% success rate after five years.

But one cannot become a "former" black or a former Hispanic. One much-esteemed black, General Colin Powell, chairman of the Joint Chiefs of Staff, put it this way in opposing the lifting of the ban on homosexuals in the military:

"Skin color is a benign, non-behavioral characteristic. Sexual orientation is perhaps the most profound of human behavioral characteristics. Comparison of the two is a convenient but invalid argument..."

If homosexual conduct is legitimized, what logical argument is there for not legitimizing pedophilic conduct? Granted, not all homosexuals have a preference for or addiction to making children their preferred sexual objects, but according to a recent content analysis of the Advocate, a mainstream homosexual magazine, 58% of the personal ads were for prostitution, many of them openly soliciting boys.

Moreover, there is a strong pedophilic undercurrent of homosexual activists who seek to lower sexual age-of-consent laws for "intergenerational sex."

The Washington Post
Washington, D.C., April 27, 1992

ALTHOUGH THE argument continues over the exact number of participants at Sunday's gay rights march, the figure is really irrelevant. The march—indeed the whole weekend of events—provided a forum for Americans who are homosexual to be heard with reference to their political causes and to be seen as human beings who are only now overcoming the effects of abiding prejudices and disadvantages built into the society and its institutions. The events were exuberant, emotional and almost perfectly peaceful.

It's difficult to say whether the marchers will have an immediate and concrete impact on the government. The question of gays in the military is now being reassessed, and President Clinton's support for change has already brought welcome progress. A thousand gay veterans, some of them in uniform, marched down Pennsylvania Avenue to further the cause. Federal funding for AIDS research, education and treatment is another worthy goal, and considerable progress is being made in that area. But observing the fervor of the gay community where the disease has caused so much pain, and the care given to AIDS victims and to the memory of those who have died should strengthen public determination to meet this challenge. Marchers also were determined to convince others of the justice of according homosexuals the rights accorded to all others in this country and of fighting efforts to discriminate against them, not to mention fighting efforts to make them the object of attacks.

As at most political or group-movement demonstrations, there were the handful of bizarre and ostentatiously gross characters who attempted to take attention from the main event and distort the message the large majority was trying to send. The most indecent offenders among them were on the stage and on national television via C-SPAN, assaulting the good faith of public officials (many of whom are active supporters of gay rights) and seeing how shocking they could be in their sexual exhibitionism before the crowd. The sorry show of these few should not define the event for television viewers across the country. The peaceful power of the demonstration and the truly unexceptional demands of the participants for fair and equal treatment should be the enduring message of the weekend.

The Washington Times
Washington, D.C., April 27, 1992

What do gays and lesbians want? According to the marchers who met on the Mall in Washington this weekend, they simply want what everyone else has in the way of civil and family rights, and most of all they want acceptance. They want to put a human face on homosexuality, to show that they are good Americans, nurses, policemen, military officers, that they are someone's daughters, sons, brothers, sisters, neighbors, colleagues, friends.

That aspect of the march got a big endorsement on the front page of the New York Times Monday: "It was, in fact, a face that seemed rather well-behaved and conventional, and that was the image that Americans saw on the evening news." True enough, that was the image Americans got from the major network evening news. It was clearly the view that the organizers of the march would like projected to the country.

But those who spent the weekend on or around the Mall to observe the event firsthand, the hapless tourists who got trapped there by mistake during their visit to the museums, and those who watched the proceedings on C-SPAN, got an unvetted view that's very different indeed.

What is one to make of men in combat uniforms and high heels or Easter bonnets French kissing in front of the White House? It may not be against the law, but it might strike some ordinary Americans as just a little bizarre. What is one to make of lesbians walking barebreasted down Pennsylvania Avenue? Or bands making obscene gestures on stage in front of the Capitol and performing songs with such titles as "Give Yourself a Breast Exam" and "My Vagina Sings"? What is one to make of the announcer who paid Hillary Rodham Clinton the pretty dubious compliment that finally we have "a first lady who can be f---ed"? In other circumstances, is that the kind of behavior that would be tolerated among Washington's monuments and official institutions?

Organizers and more moderate gays might find these displays distressing and inappropriate, but such behavior was not the exception. In fact, it was very much in tune with the radical "platform" adopted for the march itself, which included federal funding for artificial insemination of lesbian couples, the abolition of the age of consent and homosexuality taught in the nation's schools.

One lesbian activist told The Washington Times that the crowd was fighting a "war of values" in which homosexuals and their supporters represent "traditional American values of democracy and pluralism." One might well agree with the first part of her assertion, but unless public displays of undisciplined and provocative sexual behavior have somehow become traditional American values overnight, one would have to disagree very strongly with the second.

USA TODAY
Washington, D.C., April 26, 1993

Gays and lesbians are still fighting for what most people take for granted: to get and keep a job based on merit; to walk down a street without being taunted or beaten up; to rent an apartment or buy a house; to serve their country.

But these basic rights are so elusive that hundreds of thousands marched on Washington, D.C., Sunday, hoping to make them more certain.

The march itself is a sign of progress. So is 80% support for equal rights for homosexuals in a new USA TODAY/CNN/Gallup poll, a five-year high.

But there's a long way to go.

Anti-gay violence is at a five-year high, up 172% in data collected by the National Gay and Lesbian Task Force.

Only seven states and 42 cities have laws banning discrimination against homosexuals in private employment. Federal civil rights laws do not cover them. Without such legal protection, gays and lesbians can't fight policies like the one that allows Cracker Barrel restaurants to fire any non-heterosexual employee, regardless of job performance.

In some states, gays and lesbians are losing ground. Last year, Colorado passed an initiative to repeal protections against anti-gay discrimination and ban them in the future. Anti-gay groups in a dozen states are working to get similar initiatives on the next ballot.

Only five states protect gays against housing discrimination. Evidence collected by the National Gay and Lesbian Task Force shows homosexuals have persistent problems renting apartments.

And a political battle still rages over allowing gays to serve in the military — something they have been doing honorably but quietly all along.

Other fights brewing are far more controversial. Among them: Should government sanction gay marriages or adoptions, and should school curricula teach tolerance of homosexuality?

Those debates raise more complex issues, with solutions that may vary from community to community.

But on basic rights, there should be no question. They're overdue.

The State
Columbia, South Carolina, April 30, 1993

THE huge group of demonstrators that marched in Washington Sunday were asserting the right to be openly homosexual.

They also had a broader agenda, including legal rights and "mainstreaming." They demanded more legal protection and greater public acceptance for their choice of lifestyles.

We don't see the need for special legal treatment, whether additions to national civil-rights laws or changes in municipal ordinances (which gay rights activists have sought from Columbia City Council). The Constitution and existing civil rights laws do not protect gay relationships (nor, for that matter, many other people with non-traditional lifestyles). In fact, no legislation or demand can force a change in attitudes.

Gay activists like to assert that they are widely represented in all levels of government, the military services, business and society in general. If so, it underscores that those who keep their sex lives to themselves — which most homosexuals as well as heterosexuals do — have no need for special legal protection.

We would oppose any legislation that attempted to force non-discriminatory hiring practices based on sexual orientation on businesses — for example, by requiring the grant of spousal rights to partners of homosexual employees. Or on school children, by requiring that textbooks teach that a child's parents can be two women or two men, and that this is acceptable and normal. These are the types of things that extremists in the movement want.

Gays also marched on Washington for "massive" increases in funding for AIDS education, research and patient care. This is understandable. AIDS is not, exclusively, a disease of homosexuals. But it is predominantly so in Western societies. While increased funding for AIDS may be desirable, this must compete with huge demands for health-care dollars in equally compelling areas of health-care needs, from universal preschool immunization programs to prolonged, life-ending diseases like Alzheimer's.

The demonstration drew a crowd of 300,000, according to the National Park Service estimate. (Organizers said there were many more.) The turnout compared favorably with other notable marches and rallies in Washington, including the civil rights demonstrations of the '60s and two major Vietnam War protest rallies.

One who wasn't there Sunday was President Bill Clinton. He was criticized, but the President owed no special obligation, despite his political support from the openly gay community. He has already been burned for his impetuosity in ordering an end to the ban on gays in the military.

The crowd was mostly peaceful and ordinary, although the kooky element was enough in evidence to reinforce concerns about any broad legislation which would bestow special rights or legitimacy on homosexuality.

The unfettered gathering of so many people underscores gays' ownership of a basic American right, freedom of choice, including the freedom of sexual orientation. Most mainstream Americans are willing to grant this to neighbors and co-workers who are gay. If we know, most of us don't care. If we don't, we usually don't care to know. Most of us have a live-and-let-live attitude that extends to far more than sexual preferences.

THE ATLANTA CONSTITUTION
Atlanta, Georgia, April 20, 1993

With the publication of a new national study on male sexual behavior, a debate is heating up over whether the number of homosexuals has been exaggerated in past years by flawed studies.

Some gay-rights activists stand by the estimate that 10 percent of the population is basically homosexual.

The 10 percent figure has been around since the Kinsey report was published more than four decades ago. But more recent research suggests the figure may be much lower — perhaps 1 percent to 2 percent. The latest studies, released last week by the Alan Guttmacher Institute, found that of 3,321 men between ages 20 and 39, only 1 percent said in face-to-face interviews that they were exclusively homosexual.

This statistic is being used by some right-wing extremists to argue that the gay-rights movement has become disproportionately powerful — that because gays are so few in number, they should not be allowed to press their demands for acceptance in the military or elsewhere. They insist gays represent such a fringe element in society that the remaining 99 percent of the public should ignore them.

Using such statistics to argue against gay rights is ludicrous. Citizens are entitled to basic civil rights whether they are members of the majority or the smallest minority. Should Asian Americans be denied jobs just because they are fewer in number than African-Americans?

The U.S. Constitution is intended to protect all Americans, not just those who belong to a group of some arbitrary size. Gays who cling to the 10 percent figure to bolster arguments for fair treatment in housing and employment are as far off the point as conservatives who tout the 1 percent estimate.

No one knows how much of the population is homosexual because most people are very private about their sexual practices. Few people care to divulge intimate details to strangers with notepads.

The question of numbers may never be settled, but that's just as well. Pursuing gay rights is a matter of justice, not statistics.

The Philadelphia Inquirer
Philadelphia, Pennsylvania, April 24, 1993

Homosexuals are streaming out of the closet and over the ramparts — at least that's how some Bible-thumping conservatives see it. They shrieked that warning, for example, at the Republican convention in Houston last summer. And more recently, they've predicted that the U.S. military would be ruinously transformed if uniformed homosexuals no longer had to hide their sexual orientation.

But this notion of the United States besieged by uncloseted gays seems particularly far-fetched in light of a new estimate that only one out of every 100 American males is gay. That's a far cry from the 10 percent that the Kinsey Report estimated many years ago. Since other recent analyses have put the figure much lower than Kinsey, this new estimate is one more piece of evidence that makes the old 10 percent look way too high.

Ideally, reports that homosexuality isn't nearly so prevalent would cause society's homophobes to relax a little, and the incidence of gay-bashing and other abuses might decline. But don't bet on it. Because the knuckle-heads who beat up homosexuals probably aren't tuned in to demographics.

Gay activists, it should be noted, have been quick to dispute the 1 percent figure, fearful that it will diminish their new-found political clout. But advances have come not through sheer numbers; rather they have resulted from a combination of effective organizing and fund-raising among gays and a growing tolerance of homosexuality among the rest of the population.

Consider what happened in the presidential race last year. The Republicans' efforts to foment an anti-gay backlash help spark an anti-GOP backlash instead. Meanwhile, Bill Clinton paid no political price for supporting equal rights for gays, while pulling in more than $3 million from fund-raising efforts aimed at gays and lesbians.

The subsequent imbroglio over gays in the military and the anti-gay vote in Colorado suggest, however, that the country remains divided over how far and how fast to proceed in recognizing gay rights.

Tomorrow, there will be a march on Washington for gay rights, AIDS funding and other issues important to homosexuals. While the marchers will be seeking specific policy changes, they will also be seeking something more elementary: greater tolerance and respect for millions of Americans who happen to be gay or lesbian. A dignified march by hundreds of thousands — and the right words from the President of the United States — can help to set that tone.

THE SAGINAW NEWS
Saginaw, Michigan, April 27, 1993

Hundreds of thousands of homosexual men and women, and their supporters, marched Sunday in Washington, D.C.

The goal was a show not just of pride and identity, but of power.

March leaders marshaled numbers behind a set of "lesbian, gay, bisexual and transgender" legislative demands, including repeal of all sodomy laws and redefinition of the concept of "family," not quite along the lines envisioned by the American Family Association.

In any case, the march, proclaiming "our time has come," reflected a changing, more open society, whatever the freshly-disputed percentage of exclusively gay Americans.

In terms of increasing acceptance of all people, regardless of other factors, that's for the better.

But the occasion risked provoking rather than promoting, and coming out for the worse; gays are perfectly "normal" politically in sometimes stooping to excess and deliberate outrage.

Some acts Sunday, and some language, dipped into the gutter. What kind of legislation might emerge from the S/M (sado-masochism) leather-fetishist conference, a recognized march-related event Saturday night?

"For Better or for Worse" may, in fact, have done more to create understanding than any number of marchers can.

If you didn't notice, the just-ended story line of the comic strip, carried in The News and some 1,400 other papers, dealt with "Lawrence," a gay teen-ager, and how he and those around him try to cope with his "coming out."

Some papers, as well as readers, were disturbed at such a topic in the "funnies."

But not all comics are meant purely as entertainment. As its title suggests, "Better or Worse" is a reality-based strip that reflects on many difficult subjects affecting our lives.

With her usual fine touch, author Lynn Johnston — who has a gay brother-in-law — handled this story line with grace, sympathy and taste as well as gentle humor. The marchers in Washington can only hope to follow up on their demonstration with a similar style that seeks to educate, not offend.

Like other subscribers, The News could have canceled, or run alternate material. We do understand how some readers would object. We made the choice we did because we believe it's far better to play it — pun intended — straight with all our readers.

THE SUN
Baltimore, Maryland, April 27, 1993

The exact number of marchers at Sunday's gay rights rally in Washington, D.C., is still in dispute, but there is no disagreement about the message: Gays and lesbians are Americans, too. Few issues touch such deep emotions in American life, and many supporters of gay rights had worried that the occasion would give extremists an opportunity to steal the national spotlight and hand conservative anti-gay groups a propaganda bonanza.

Indeed the march did have its share of bizarre characters. But any honest view of the gathering must take into account the diversity of the group, a diversity that makes it impossible to condemn or stigmatize homosexuals.

There were decorated military men and women revealing their sexual orientation for the first time. There were gay parents with signs reading, "I'm gay and in the PTA." There were businessmen and women, bureaucrats and others who lead ordinary, middle-class lives. And there were plenty of non-gay people who came to register their support.

Beyond a few well-publicized issues — removing the ban on military service for gays, increased funding for the fight against AIDS — the political agenda of the gay rights movement is less clearly defined. That in itself can lead to fears that gays are demanding special treatment beyond the protections that should be guaranteed to any American.

In our view, the message all Americans need to hear — and the rights that gays should be able to take for granted — are basic. Chief among them is, of course, the right to life and liberty. The prevalence of gay-bashing is telling evidence that gay Americans cannot take this liberty for granted.

In terms of the broader agenda, too many homosexuals have served honorably in the military for the nation to accept without question the shrill arguments against lifting the ban on gays in the armed services. We also favor a more focused, effective fights against AIDS — although funding for AIDS-related research must also take into account the need for medical advances against other devastating diseases.

Many Americans have a difficult time coming to terms with homosexuality. But those who regard homosexuality as a sin or perversion have to come to terms with the thousands of Americans who insist that their orientation is not a choice, but an innate predisposition. We suspect that the real answer to the demand for gay rights lies not in science or law but in human relations. After all, the American willingness to tolerate diversity is essential to every citizen's freedom.

The Tennessean
Nashville, Tennessee, April 25, 1993

THE hundreds of thousands of people who will march in Washington today for gay rights should symbolize a journey for all Americans.

Our society has lagged woefully on ensuring basic rights for gays and lesbians. The steps of progress are long overdue.

The march should demonstrate that equality for all citizens is a national goal. And that cause should be entrenched in the consciousness of every lawmaker.

On one hand, the cause has much to celebrate. It now has a president, Bill Clinton, who has championed the call for gay rights like no president before him. His leadership has brought hope for an end to discrimination in the federal workplace and in the military. There is hope for a federal civil rights bill. Even a recent meeting between the President and leaders of gay and lesbian groups was an historic event.

And yet, for every step forward there has been frustration. The military issue is far from resolved. Disappointment remains about attention to the AIDS epidemic, and the absence in the administration of an AIDS czar. Only eight states currently ban discrimination against gays. Many states, including this one, still operate under senseless sodomy laws. And for all the attention the President has brought to gay rights issues, he will not attend the march.

It's no wonder some of the activists are asking, "Where's the beef?"

In 1987, about a half-million people participated in a similar march for gay rights in this country. This week, that number is expected to double. The number of gay and lesbian citizens has not doubled since that time, but the recognition of their need for support and protection has. Mr. Clinton's bold leadership on gay rights has been a monumental step for this nation. But there is more to leadership than words and promises. For Mr. Clinton and for society the real proof of commitment will not be in words but in results. ■

The Providence Journal
Providence, Rhode Island, April 27, 1993

Sunday's big march in Washington for gay rights probably did not hurt the cause. But it is also unlikely to have helped it much.

Certainly the throngs of participants emphasized yet again that there are many gay people. No one, of course, knows how many. Is it 10 percent of the population, as Kinsey and many activists have asserted? Or is it closer to 2 percent, as some recent surveys have suggested? Our hunch is that it's somewhere in between. (Many fearful homosexuals, even in anonymous polling, presumably hide their preference.)

Some of the marchers acted in a reasonable, decorous manner, winning some good publicity. Not so some others. The florid participation of leather-bound S & M devotees, of drag queens, and of people barely clad at all, is unlikely to have raised sympathies among many Americans. Indeed, numerous viewers may have gotten the impression that the march included a disturbingly large number of unstable people. Well, it's a free country, up to a point: Americans have the rights to free speech and to demonstrate; and we feel they have very strong implied rights to privacy. But what about the right not to associate with people whose behaviors they dislike? Therein lies a problem with part of the homosexual agenda.

Laws and rules barring entry of avowed gays into the military, and that invade private realms of sexual practices, are wrong, and ought to be repealed. But homosexual activists have yet to come up with a fully credible way of reconciling freedom of association with the demand by some gays for enumerated protections.

In any case, Sunday's march has not shaken our belief that a peaceful tolerance may be the best we can hope from all sides in this issue.

THE SUN
Baltimore, Maryland, April 18, 1993

President Clinton's meeting with gay and lesbian leaders in the White House Friday followed by a day an event that may have as much political impact on homosexuals in America: Publication of a poll done for the Alan Guttmacher Institute concluding only about 2 percent of American men have had homosexual experiences and only 1 percent consider themselves exclusively homosexual.

Most experts in the field of human sexuality have known the homosexual population was about this low. For example, a massive 1988 Census Bureau survey for the Centers for Disease Control found that only between 2 and 3 percent of American men had had even one homosexual experience in the past decade. (A smaller percentage of women is homosexual, according to most surveys.) French, British, Canadian and other national studies have also concluded that only about 2 percent of the populace is homosexual. But the public and political debate on gay rights has been proceeding on the assumption that about one in 10 Americans is gay.

That thinking is likely to change. The polling data is going to be front-page news now whenever homosexual rights are being debated in public, as they will be increasingly. The controversy over gays in the military guarantees that.

We do not know precisely how a changed public perception of the size of the gay population will affect laws and policy, but we suspect it will. On gays in the military, for example, there will be those who say the small percentage means inclusion can't disrupt the services, and there will be those who say that so small a number means too few individuals will benefit to make it worthwhile to risk changing long-standing policy. There will also be politicians who felt inclined to support gay rights when they thought one-tenth of the electorate was gay — but no longer feel the need to now.

The proper point of view by the military, by politicians and other individuals and institutions should be that civil rights are individual. There is no such thing as a minority group that is too small to have its individual members' civil rights respected and protected.

The New York Times
New York City, New York, April 24, 1993

It doesn't really matter whether a million demonstrators show up for tomorrow's rally in Washington in support of gay and lesbian rights, as some planners have predicted. Nor does it matter whether a few marchers are dressed in drag or heavy leather, the better to shock middle-class America and grab TV time. Even President Clinton's absence is only a minor setback. The march will serve a vital purpose if it simply puts a broad and varied human face on a civil rights struggle that is all too often painted in caricatures.

The goals of the gay rights movement are, for the most part, modest and unexceptional: an end to discrimination against gay and lesbian Americans in all realms of life ... repeal of outdated sodomy laws that are routinely violated not only by homosexuals but also by most heterosexuals, including married couples who are pillars of their communities ... the right to serve openly in the military services — and die for their country — without being hounded out of the service for their sexual orientations ... a big boost in funding for AIDS prevention, treatment and research as the disease digs deeper into the American population.

Reasonable people oppose such reasonable goals only if they can somehow demonize gay Americans. So the fiercest opposition comes from those who, wrongly but strongly, twist themselves into viewing homosexuals as alien, weird, immoral, an abomination. That's where tomorrow's parade can be helpful — holding up a mirror for the nation to see its own reflection.

copyright © The New York Times 1993

THE ANN ARBOR NEWS
Ann Arbor, Michigan, April 26, 1993

Sunday's massive march in Washington, D.C., in support of equal rights for homosexual men and women, will leave its mark on America. The issues brought forth make many people uncomfortable, but there has been and will be increased dialogue about homosexuality. Hopefully, it will lead to more awareness of how much discrimination gay men and lesbians face.

Gay men and lesbians often face blatant, verbal acts of prejudice. Name-calling can hurt, but not as much as the other acts of discrimination against homosexual men and women: They can legally be fired for being homosexual. Even the suspicion of homosexuality can prevent them being promoted. They also face housing discrimination and are denied respect granted to other law-abiding, productive citizens.

> That people feel no restraint in taunting gays shows how socially acceptable gay discrimination is.

That people feel no restraint in taunting gays shows how socially acceptable gay discrimination is.

Last summer, for example, two men in Ann Arbor felt free to yell gay slurs at a man walking across the street from the Flame bar, according a News' story that was part of its recent series on discrimination. The two men then proceeded to circle the gay man, blindside him and break his glasses with a punch.

On a popular Detroit radio station last week, a disc jockey and his cohorts joked for several minutes on the air about homosexuality without any fear that someone might be offended.

Daily, people who have not revealed their homosexuality – many on the correct basis that their sexual lives are nobody else's business – sit quietly as colleagues repeat anti-gay jokes.

In The News' survey that accompanied the series "How Separate? How Equal?" homosexuality led the list of groups that respondents said suffer from discrimination. Seven out of 10 Washtenaw County residents interviewed said homosexuals are victims of prejudice. The majority of blacks (84 percent) and whites (68 percent) agreed on this issue.

Some base anti-gay biases on religious beliefs and point to Bible Scripture as justification, often ignoring the principles of love and tolerance within religious teachings. Others have unfounded fears that gays want to impose their sexual lifestyles on others. Still others wrongly believe gays are more likely to abuse children, when statistics clearly show that the most likely persons to molest a child is a male, heterosexual relative.

Prejudice is usually based on fears and misunderstandings, and the best way to fight it is through education.

That was the point of Sunday's march. What the public saw were men and women from all walks of life and of many political beliefs. They marched in unison to tell the world this: They'd like to be able to enjoy the same civil protections the rest of Americans have. They'd like the right to be judged on job performance and not fear losing their jobs solely because of their sexual orientation. They'd like to have the opportunity for economic benefits similar to their heterosexual coworkers, and they'd like the right to settle down in the house of their choice with their loved ones and be respected as are other citizens.

Is that asking too much?

Consider this statement by President Clinton: "I believe when you tell people they can't do certain things in this country that other people can do, there ought to be an overwhelming and compelling reason for it. I just have always had an almost libertarian view that we should try to protect the rights of American individual citizens to live up to the fullest of their capacities, and I'm going to stick right with that."

And then consider the political realities that Clinton faces on his campaign promise to lift the military-service ban. The sea of anti-homosexual sentiment is so strong that the president appears to be ebbing from his support of the rights of individuals. The political price may be too high.

Other polls, like that of The News, show that big majorities say gay men and women should not be subject to discrimination. But doing something about it is another story. Polls also show a lack of support for lifting the military ban or even for laws, like Ann Arbor's, that outlaw discrimination. The contradictions are unfortunate for our society, for when any group is denied the opportunities to contribute to our communities or live up to their potentials, we all lose. Recognizing prejudices is meaningful only if steps are taken to correct them.

ALBUQUERQUE JOURNAL
Albuquerque, New Mexico, April 25, 1993

All the stereotypes will get heavy reinforcement during the events culminating in today's homosexual march on Washington. The nation's video eye will feast on spectacles like the National Lesbutante Ball, the S&M Leather Fetish Kick-Off Party and drag queens strutting their fashions on the mall.

But how long will the cameras dwell on the non-sensational, the downright pedestrian majority of the demonstrators? How long will viewers stay tuned to crowds of people who, except for their cause, look as normal as the woman at the next desk, your accountant or the retired guys that chew over the newspaper together every morning at the coffee shop.

Heterosexuals don't have to get used to flamboyant and flagrantly promiscuous homosexuals, the small minority fringe that has come to loom large in the public perception of gays. But many more need to understand that the reality of the majority of homosexuals has less to do with innumerable partners, cross-dressing and sado-masochism than with the mundane concerns we all share.

Their cause, like that of any other special interest group, needs to be evaluated on its own merits — not by stereotyped notions or judgments about private behavior.

Richmond Times-Dispatch
Richmond, Virginia, April 29, 1993

Sunday's homosexual march on Washington was big (somewhere between 250,000 and 500,000), but was it smart? The parade of characters — and caricatures — did not always do the so-called movement a favor. Homosexuals say they want to stress that except for sexual preference, they resemble regular folks — the couple next door. Yet much that appeared on display on the Mall celebrated not the normal but the *ab*.

Therein lies the difference between the great civil rights marches of the Sixties and the homosexual agitation of today. Civil rights leaders drew attention to condition; Sunday's march drew attention to behavior. Even if genetics plays a role in sexuality, the individual decides for himself how to behave. With the exception of insanity, *all* behavior is a function of choice. The devil can encourage; the devil can tempt. But the devil cannot *make* anyone do it.

Prior to the march, organizers reportedly worried about the political wisdom of projecting images of drag queens and deviates with more than their ears pierced. Yet they could not bring themselves to draw a line, to say, "Sorry, but please stay home."

If the point of the march was to show off, then it succeeded. If the point was to win over the vast tolerant middle, then its own inevitable excesses likely persuaded less than they repelled.

Syndicated columnist William Raspberry describes the difference between arguing, "My sexual orientation and behavior are none of your business," and, "I demand that you acknowledge my sexual choices as the exact equivalent of yours." Sunday stressed the latter. And that was its great mistake.

Chicago Tribune
Chicago, Illinois, April 27, 1993

The march for gay and lesbian rights held in Washington Sunday was important not only for attracting large numbers of people, but for dramatizing the historic gains made by homosexuals in America. No one watching the demonstration could doubt that the movement is here to stay.

That observation may sound quaintly obvious—if you ignore history. The first national rally in the capital was held in 1979, when hostility to homosexual rights—and homosexuals, period—was broad, deep and largely unchallenged. The second, in 1987, was mainly an occasion for mourning those killed by AIDS and demanding more attention to the disease.

Homophobia and AIDS have hardly vanished, but gays as a group have gained ground in spite of them. This march comes in the wake of the election of a president who is committed to homosexual rights and to devoting more funds to the fight against AIDS, a president who unapologetically sought the support of gays and owes his victory partly to them.

Homosexuals may be a small share of the electorate, but they have acquired an influence that exceeds their numbers—because they have gotten organized, because they give lots of money to candidates and causes and because they have a clear agenda.

That doesn't mean they'll always get what they want. The rally featured ample criticism of Bill Clinton, who has frustrated gays by his hesitancy to lift the military's ban on homosexuals, his tardiness in appointing an AIDS czar and his failure to address the marchers. The effort to get laws barring discrimination on the basis of sexual orientation has yielded few successes.

But gays are likely to prevail eventually on the military ban, and AIDS will get more money from Clinton than from George Bush. Clinton is vulnerable to the charge of betrayal only because he made commitments on gay rights that no other president has.

Whatever the political scorecard, it is heartening to note that while gays and lesbians face considerable antagonism, it is easier to be openly homosexual today than ever before. Over the last couple of decades, Americans have realized—and have been compelled to acknowledge—that, as a speaker at the 1979 rally declared, "We are everywhere." Even those who denounce gays on moral grounds no longer expect the government to enforce their view of morality.

It is a testament to the persistence and bravery of gays, and to the American tradition of tolerance, that homosexuals have won a large measure of the acceptance they demand.

AUGUSTA HERALD
Augusta, Georgia, April 27, 1993

What are the signs of a decadent society?

Surely one is when hundreds of thousands of homosexuals and lesbians march to openly flaunt their deviant lifestyle and demand the right to "marry," adopt children and get preferential treatment.

That's what occurred Sunday in Washington, and much of the television coverage we saw obligingly portrayed these deviants as no different from ordinary Americans in their lifestyles and values.

Furthermore, who would have thought, just a few short years ago, that a president of the United States would send a letter to be read praising these people? Or that some Hollywood celebrities would be celebrating such deviancy?

Youngsters who could be influenced by adult homosexual role models should be educated to the fact that "gay" sex is a dangerous activity. It far more hazardous to one's health than smoking, drinking or even drugs.

As the California-based Claremont Institute notes, surveys reveal "male homosexuals in the 1990s, ten years after the onset of the AIDS epidemic, still average between 10 and 100 *different* sex partners per year. And these numbers are down from even higher figures reported in the 1980s and 1970s."

Homosexuals get sick, quite simply, because they are in a high-risk category of disease transmission. No wonder many want to get "free" health care by joining the armed forces!

Of course, if avowed homosexuals are forced onto the U.S. military, then the skids are greased for the rest of the agenda: Legislation making homosexuality a "normal" alternative lifestyle and to stretch the traditional definition of family to include homosexual marriages and the legal rights implied therein.

Despite Sunday's mass rally on the District of Columbia mall, though, the latest surveys show homosexuals comprise only 1 to 2 percent of the U.S. population, not 10 percent as propagandized for decades. This shows that homosexuality is truly aberrant behavior — far removed from anything close to "normal."

Homosexuals deserve the same rights the Constitution guarantees every citizen. But no matter how much Politically Correct hype they generate, we doubt the broad American population will ever stand for affirmative action programs granting them preferential treatment.

San Francisco Chronicle
San Francisco, California, April 27, 1993

IT WAS AN extraordinary demonstration of strength and determination. Hundreds of thousands of gays and lesbians and their supporters filled the capital's streets, and their message was one that should serve to jog the national conscience: We are your brothers and sisters — accept us as full partners in the great social fabric that is America.

The specific figures actually make little difference; whether the throng totaled 300,000 or one million seems irrelevant. Bean counters tend to be niggling and narrow-focused. Besides, there was a spirit out there that may not have translated into numbers but was uplifting in its positive warmth.

The numbers were great and so was the spirit

The point is that here was America in all its diversity. There were entertainers, elected officials, military people and prosaic homebodies. The marchers came in jeans and shorts, Buddhist robes and business suits. Their roots twined into every section of our broad country.

PRESIDENT CLINTON may not have been there in person, but he sounded a thoughtful, supportive note in his statement to the throng: "I stand with you in the struggle for equality for all Americans, including gay men and lesbians." He exhorted the country to "put aside what divides us and focus on what we share."

This may have been one of those defining moments in the national history. Here was a peaceful, positive demonstration by Americans who only ask fairness, acceptance and equal treatment. The great confluence of humanity in Washington's streets gave eloquent expression to long overdue entitlement.

The Salt Lake Tribune
Salt Lake City, Utah, April 16, 1993

As the snow melts in the Rockies and some ball-playing Rockies signal springtime in Denver, early and encouraging returns are in from Colorado's winter tourist season: The boycott is having a minimal impact. That is poetic justice, not only for innocent Coloradans but also for the misguided souls who launched it in the first place.

An economic boycott of the state of Colorado was called by national gay and lesbian groups late last year, after the state's voters approved Amendment 2 on Election Day. That hate-inspired measure, which still has not become law because it is tied up in the courts, would prohibit the state and its municipalities from passing anti-discrimination laws for homosexuals.

The economic protest, organized by a group called Boycott Colorado, was designed to cut a healthy slice from the state's income — specifically, its tourist industry this winter — but it has not succeeded yet. In fact, a season of heavy snowfall translated into a record number of ski lift tickets sold in Colorado this winter.

Colorado still stands to lose several million dollars in convention business in the next few years due to the boycott — an insignificant amount in its total economy — but its tourist industry appears safe. And that is only just, since the ski-resort counties and the cities of Denver and Boulder all voted heavily against Amendment 2 last November and deserve none of the penalties the boycott organizers wished to impose on them.

Boycotts have their legitimate place as a form of protest — witness Rosa Parks and the Montgomery bus boycott in the mid-1950s — but scattergun boycotts like the one in Colorado amount to nothing more than economic terrorism. Their targets are so wide and ill-defined that the innocent cannot avoid being injured.

As if to prove the moral bankruptcy of this boycott, some of its New York leaders tried to intimidate Celestial Seasonings, the Boulder-based tea company that counts New York as a critical market. Although Celestial Seasonings has a progressive hiring record, the boycott leaders still threatened to attack its New York market share if the company did not support the boycott — with dollars. Company founder Mo Siegel felt he was being blackmailed and refused to buckle; for that, he became a state hero.

The only thing the boycott organizers reaped from their tea party was increased venom on the part of Coloradans. In fact, if the point of the boycott was to scare the state's voters into repealing Amendment 2, the case could be made that it is backfiring. Polls this winter showed a hardening of the electorate's position against repeal of the measure. Chalk it up to the simple tenet that people don't like being told what to do by outsiders.

Gay and lesbian rights groups missed that point in Colorado, and they ought to be wary as they plan their strategies against similar amendments being proposed in other Western states. Threatening people with political bludgeons like boycotts only muddles their message and engenders the very acrimony that they are striving to erase. They should stick to the issue of human rights; on that score, they are by far the most persuasive.

The Augusta Chronicle
Augusta, Georgia, April 18, 1993

Last week's acquittal of three Marines charged with assault at a Wilmington, N.C., homosexual bar was the most surprising verdict since the Simi Valley jury set free the Los Angeles cops charged with beating Rodney King.

Anyone who follows the news or watches TV talk shows couldn't have missed Crae Pridgen claiming to be the innocent victim of "gay-bashing." He sure looked the part. His battered and beaten visage testified to the fact that someone bashed him good.

Yet when the case went to trial, it turned out Pridgen wasn't an innocent just minding his own business when he claimed he was "cruelly attacked by a gang of homophobic Marines" on a search-and-destroy mission targeting homosexuals.

In fact, it appears the straight men were defending themselves against homosexual taunts and assaults after they unknowingly walked into the bar.

Whatever happened, the trio somehow found themselves in the middle of an old-fashioned barroom brawl and no one, including other homosexuals who were there, could be certain how it started.

But everyone did agree an aggressive Pridgen was in the middle of it. He took better than he gave. So he tried to transform his whipping into a PR triumph, going public with charges of a "hate crime" and impugning the honored name of the U.S. Marine Corps along the way.

Sadly, the Politically Correct Big Media accepted the homosexual side almost uncritically. Fortunately, the court did not.

We wonder if the truth will ever catch up with Pridgen's hugely publicized scenario.

Rockford Register Star
Rockford, Illinois, April 23, 1993

It has been described as a complex civil-rights march and a simple show of solidarity. It has been called a thank-you to President Clinton and a gesture of anger with him.

In truth, the reasons that hundreds of thousands of people will march in Washington today under the banner of gay rights are as diverse as the marchers themselves. To some, the top priority is AIDS education; to others, it's repealing the ban on homosexuals in the military.

But the marchers, straight as well as gay, are united in something bigger than politics. They come together, as *Detroit News* columnist Deb Price puts it, in a massive demonstration of the "power of love to overcome prejudice and misunderstanding." In that cause we should all unite.

> **Gays and lesbians want what we all do — freedom.**

Too many people in our society treat sexual orientation as the one element that defines the person more than any other. It's a false perception. Just as Martin Luther King pushed us to look beyond skin color to the content of a person's character, we must look beyond gay stereotypes and consider the individual in a deeper context. Is she kind? Is he caring? Would we want any lesser treatment for this person than for a neighbor, a friend, a family member?

We cannot be a moral society if we treat some citizens immorally. We cannot promote family values if we value only some families. We cannot be a decent people if we abhor the differences in others.

Clinton referred to these differences in his inaugural speech, in which he challenged Americans to rededicate themselves to the very idea of America, "an idea enobled by the faith that our nation can summon from its myriad diversity the deepest measure of unity."

In that spirit, we should all join, in hearts if not in hands, with the tens of thousands of Americans marching on the Capitol today.

N.Y. St. Patrick's Day Parade Bars Gay Groups

The annual St. Patrick's Day parade was held in New York City March 17, 1992, the day after a federal judge March 16 had refused to grant a request from an Irish homosexual group that was seeking to march in the parade.

The parade had been a source of controversy since 1990, when the Irish Lesbian and Gay Organization (ILGO) had first sought to participate. Their request had been denied by the private Roman Catholic organization that sponsored the parade, the Ancient Order of Hibernians. The Hibernians argued that they did not wish to include ILGO in the event because the group's presence would be an affront to the Catholic Church's teachings against homosexual acts.

On March 13, an administrative judge for the New York City human rights commission had rejected a request from ILGO, saying that forcing the Hibernians to allow the gay group to march in the parade would violate the Hibernians' First Amendment right to freedom of expression.

In rejecting ILGO's suit, Federal District Court Judge Pierre N. Leval March 16 ruled on narrow, technical grounds that the group had filed its request too close to parade time and that ILGO was not entitled to jump ahead of other groups that were on a waiting list to participate in the parade.

ILGO staged a protest march in New York shortly before the main parade was held. The protest was attended by several local politicians who did not march in the main parade. Mayor David N. Dinkins (D), who was recovering from a blood infection, became the first New York City mayor since 1923 not to march in the St. Patrick's Day parade.

The Hartford Courant
Hartford, Connecticut, March 17, 1993

For more than two centuries, the Irish have marched in New York City to honor St. Patrick on the day of his death. They also marched to demonstrate the solidarity of this harassed, exploited but indomitable group of immigrants. Eventually the marchers welcomed outsiders in an admirable show of good-fellowship. "Everybody is Irish on St. Patrick's Day," the saying now goes.

But that good-fellowship hasn't been extended to the Irish Gay and Lesbian Organization. The group has been shut out from the New York parade on orders from the Ancient Order of Hibernians, the parade organizers, who contend that they do not want marchers who violate the tenets of the religion being celebrated.

New York City leaders fought the exclusion by withholding the parade permit from the Hibernians. But a judge ruled that the parade organizers had a constitutional right to express their tenets however they wanted and to associate with whomever they wanted.

The judge was right. Government shouldn't interfere with peaceful, privately sponsored assemblies, as discriminatory as they may be.

Gay men and lesbians may take part in the New York parade by marching with other groups. Or they may exercise their constitutional right by peacefully protesting the parade.

The Ancient Order of Hibernians, however, blundered in excluding Irish-Americans who have endured their own share of maligning. The show of intolerance is unfortunate on this fine day.

The Boston Globe
Boston, Massachusetts, January 4, 1993

The Allied War Veterans Council of South Boston and an Irish-American gay group are readying for another bruising battle over the content of the St. Patrick's Day Parade.

At issue are competing concepts of rights. Members of the Irish-American Gay, Lesbian and Bisexual Pride Committee were buoyed last March when a Suffolk County Superior Court judge issued a restraining order against the veterans group and ruled that the gay pride group had a constitutional right to march. Now the lawyer for the South Boston veterans is arguing that it is his clients who are being denied the rights of free speech and association.

The issues are complex.

Though the holiday technically marks the anniversary of Evacuation Day, when, on March 17, 1775, the British left Boston, it has long been celebrated as St. Patrick's Day. Because the parade is a privately sponsored event, it could be argued that it is the group seeking the permit that has the right to define the parade's purpose and message.

The gays might counter that since they are expressing pride in their Irish heritage, they fall within the parade's purpose. For a host of reasons this would not be the case if the Ku Klux Klan, for example, asked to join in and show its flag at an NAACP-sponsored march for racial harmony.

South Boston has become a battleground in struggles concerning civil rights and minority groups. The neighborhood underwent school desegregation in the 1970s while nearby suburban school districts remained overwhelmingly white. And now hypocritical observers can stand on the sidelines and point derisively at a working class community caught in yet another struggle.

It is not necessary for the allied veterans group to die on this mountaintop. South Boston is evolving. It is likely that a gay contingent – free of the antics that offend community norms – would be welcomed by many along the parade route. It's a grand parade, and the presence of proud Irish gays hardly compromises the spirit of the day.

City and church leaders should issue strong messages to the unenlightened that threats and thrown objects will not be tolerated on the parade route. Gay activists, too, would do well to ponder the importance of the parade in South Boston.

Many have forgotten that the concept of community is not limited to minority groups. A repeat of last year's provocations by gay activists, such as stuffing condoms into the poor box of a South Boston church, would do great harm.

The Massachusetts Commission Against Discrimination has scheduled a settlement conference for Jan. 14, although the veterans group will probably challenge the commission's authority in a higher court as early as Wednesday of this week.

The veterans group still has time to avoid a divisive legal struggle by remembering the spirit of fair play in South Boston.

In that spirit, parade rest.

The Gazette
Cedar Rapids, Iowa, March 22, 1992

ARE MAINSTREAM Christian churches ready to welcome homosexuals into membership?

Changes could come if church leaders perform a mental exercise touted by Mark Bowman, national coordinator of the Reconciling Congregation Program. Bowman, a Methodist who visited Iowa Methodist churches this week, said the traditionally debated questions have been: Is homosexuality a sin? Can you be a Christian and homosexual?

The questions, said Bowman (who is gay), should be: Can you be a Christian and exclude people from the church? Is it a sin to be homophobic?

Clergy who do not take all Scripture literally probably will agree that excluding homosexuals does not square with Christ's teachings. But inspiring church leaders to rethink doctrine is one thing. Getting the congregation to go along is quite another.

One of Bowman's observations in the May 18 Gazette story was worrisome: He said he believes most Protestant congregations are composed of about 25 percent of people who would welcome gays and lesbians, 25 percent who are vehemently anti-gay and perhaps 50 percent in the middle who have too little information and are steered by "myths and stereotypes." He said it is the middle 50 percent he wants to reach.

But even if that "middle 50 percent" become open-minded toward homosexuals in church membership, what about the 25 percent who are hardcore homophobics?

Who wants to attend a church where 25 percent of the people are unfriendly? A church is a haven — as Edmund Burke put it, "a place where one day's truce ought to be allowed to the dissensions and animosities of mankind."

The inkling here is that the Reconciling Congregation Program has a long way to go. The more liberal churches are receptive. But, then, it was the liberal churches that trailblazed in a number of political causes through American history — opposition to slavery, child labor and (much later) the Vietnam War, support of women's rights, labor unions, civil rights and health care for the indigent.

Among the less liberal congregations, a welcoming handshake for homosexuals will be a tough sell.

The New York Times
New York City, New York, March 2, 1993

The Ancient Order of Hibernians, sponsors of New York's St. Patrick's Day parade, have won the important right to decide who may march with them. A Federal court has upheld what the Dinkins administration refused to acknowledge: that private citizens have a constitutional right to express publicly, in a parade, their own message about their own values without interference by government.

That First Amendment right to decide the content of one's own message includes the right to make a wrong decision — a right the Hibernians seem bent on exercising to the fullest. Celebrating a saintly festival day in their fashion, they have chosen to exclude openly gay Irish from their heritage and religious vision. Many Americans, including many Roman Catholics, are cruelly hurt by that message, even though the Constitution protects the right to deliver it.

After several litigious years, the ruling by Judge Kevin Duffy settles the law so clearly that city officials say they won't appeal. The judge's order covers only this year's parade but his legal reasoning commands respect well into the future: "A parade organized by a private sponsor is the quintessential exercise of the First Amendment right of freedom of expression."

A city may no more determine the marchers, and thus the message, than it may stop a procession of Nazis or force the inclusion of Ku Klux Klansmen in a civil rights demonstration. The city and its Human Rights Commission argued that this parade was a public accommodation open to all who apply. Since Mayor Dinkins will not appeal, his lawyers are no longer free to make that absurd argument.

Now that they've established their right to exhibit their own limited vision, the Hibernians are free also to change their minds and define themselves as magnanimous, tolerant and generous. They could explore ways to let their gay compatriots openly share Fifth Avenue with them on March 17 without denying their own self-image.

If the sponsors insist on their right to exhibit their exclusivity, the public may exercise its right: to ignore the bigoted message, and the march.

copyright © The New York Times 1993

Newsday
New York City, New York, January 3, 1993

Would someone *please* tell New York Mayor David Dinkins that City Hall has higher obligations than ensuring "inclusionary" parades — such as protecting free association and free expression?

Police Commissioner Raymond Kelly issued a permit to the St. Patrick's Day Parade Committee, which would let gay Irish-American groups march in the parade. Fine. But why deny one to the Ancient Order of Hibernians, which has run the parade for more than a century and holds Catholic doctrinal views about homosexuality that Dinkins doesn't like? Should politicians decide which marchers can be included and excluded?

parades and let New Yorkers decide where to march. Politicians can express their opinions, too, but *government* must be neutral in culture wars. Protecting basic rights comes first.

The Constitution says otherwise. So does the American Civil Liberties Union, which no one would accuse of insensitivity to gay rights. It proposes that the city grant permits for two

---

New York City, New York, April 27, 1993

When it comes to protecting human rights, including the civil rights of gays and lesbians, the tristate region hasn't done badly for the most part. Ask the folks who took part in Sunday's historic gay-rights march in Washington. New Jersey and Connecticut have state laws that protect gay men and women from discrimination in jobs, housing and public accommodations. The only tristate spot that hasn't extended antidiscrimination protections to gays and lesbians is the Empire State, where civil rights bills regularly meet their doom in the State Senate.

Now, no one expected to see Sen. Majority Leader Ralph Marino (R-Muttontown) among Sunday's marchers or speakers. Phil Donahue, Jesse Jackson and Cybill Shepherd are not in the crowd he runs with. But many of the gays, lesbians and their supporters *are* Marino's statewide constituents. Gay-rights legislation passed the Assembly earlier this year. Marino ought to back it and release it from the grip of his party caucus so it can go to the floor for a vote.

At least then all of us would find out which senators truly believe in human rights.

Oregon Gay Rights Curb Defeated

Oregon voters Nov. 3, 1992 defeated Measure 9 to limit homosexual rights by a margin of 57% to 43%.

The initiative contained the most controversial language of several proposed homosexual-rights curbs across the nation. It called for "state, regional and local governments" to discourage "homosexuality, pedophilia, sadism and masochism," which the measure called "abnormal, wrong, unnatural and perverse."

The Oregon Citizens Alliance, under founder Lon Mabon, led the campaign for the initiative. Mabon claimed that "homosexuality is not a civil right, but an aberration." While arguing that the measure was designed to curb special-rights protections for gays based on their personal choices, Mabon admitted that the measure would allow discrimination against gays by landlords and employers. The campaign drew much of its support from the evangelical Christian community.

Gay and lesbian groups had fought against the measure, with the backing of the state's political and religious establishment. Oregon Rep. Les AuCoin (D), who unsuccessfully challenged Sen. Bob Packwood (R) in the election, was quoted Sept. 21 as comparing the "pro-9" campaigners to Nazi "brown shirts" who wanted to turn "'family values' into a bludgeon with which they victimize innocent people."

In Colorado, a state measure that would ban localities from enacting gay-rights bills was approved by a margin of 54% to 46%. The measure would override existing gay-rights ordinances in Denver, Aspen and Boulder. Voters in Tampa decided, by a 58% to 42% margin, to repeal a local gay-rights ordinance, but citizens in Portland, Maine rejected a similar repeal by 57% to 43%.

Herald News
Fall River, Massachusetts, November 8, 1992

If you've wondered why Gov. William Weld signed an executive order last February to establish the Commission on Gay and Lesbian Youth, you need only look to Tuesday's election results around the country.

In Colorado, voters approved a ban on anti-discrimination laws that protect homosexuals and repeals of gay rights ordinances in Denver, Aspen and Boulder. In Tampa, a repeal of the gay-rights ordinance was approved.

While it's encouraging that a repeal of the gay-rights ordinance in Portland, Maine, was defeated, and a Oregon measure to declare homosexuality abnormal was likewise rejected, the initiatives that passed illustrate convincingly why the commonwealth's commission is so important.

The commission, whose members are unpaid, serves as an advisory board to combat suicide among homosexual teens, make recommendations to the secretary of health and human services and address anti-violence and discrimination issues.

Homosexual youths are two to three times more likely to attempt suicide than any other group of young people, according to a U.S. Department of Health and Human Services report. It's not so difficult to understand why homosexual teens turn to such desperate tactics when states and cities around the country are attempting to label them as freaks, compounding their confusion and increasing their isolation.

While the commonwealth seems a relatively welcome place for homosexuals — Gov. Weld strongly supports gay rights and the state has a gay rights amendment on the books — intolerance is ever-threatening.

The Commission on Gay and Lesbian Youth will hold its first public hearings this month — on Tuesday, Nov. 17 and Wednesday, Nov. 18 from 2:30 p.m. until 5:30 p.m. in the Gardner Auditorium at the Statehouse. The commission expects to hear from homosexual youths and their parents about their concerns and problems.

Guided by that information, perhaps the commission will be successful in making life a more palatable choice than death for homosexual teens.

The Philadelphia Inquirer
Philadelphia, Pennsylvania, November 7, 1992

Election Day results were decidedly mixed for people concerned about chronic discrimination against gays and lesbians.

Measures protecting homosexuals were wiped off the books in Tampa, Denver and two smaller Colorado communities. The most Neanderthal measure — denouncing homosexuality as "abnormal, wrong, unnatural and perverse" (and requiring schools to teach this attitude) — was, fortunately, rejected in Oregon by 57 percent of the voters.

In the wake of these election returns, it's important to understand what's going on — and to consider what, if anything, government should do about it.

What's going on is that antagonism toward homosexuals — reflected in behavior ranging from crude insults to physical assaults — appears to be on the rise. Studies by the Philadelphia Lesbian and Gay Task Force, as well as by Pennsylvania Attorney General's office, have shown a large, and probably rising, number of anti-homosexual assaults. Recent surveys in other parts of the country have indicated that gay-bashing is outrageously common.

Apparently this behavior has been exacerbated by the threat of AIDS — which has been disproportionately a disease of male homosexuals in this country — as well as by the intolerant blitherings of prominent extremists such as Pat Robertson and Patrick Buchanan.

When people are spared inflammatory rhetoric and they listen calmly to information about how homosexuals are unfairly discriminated against, most come to understand that such discrimination is wrong. That's why Philadelphia has a law, like the ones just removed from the books in Denver and Tampa, that bans discrimination against gays and lesbians in employment, housing and public accommodations.

The person who could do the most to make American society less discriminatory and more tolerant is President-elect Clinton. He promised to issue an executive order ending discrimination against homosexuals in the military. Ideally, he would use the bully pulpit and influence of the presidency to repeat what he has said before: Hate crimes and prejudice against gays and lesbians — or anyone else — are wrong.

The Seattle Times
Seattle, Washington, November 11, 1992

THANKFULLY, Oregon's Measure 9, the intolerant anti-homosexual initiative, was defeated.

But rather than accept the loss and let Oregonians heal from the bitterness of the campaign, backers hope to return with a watered-down proposal in 1994. Sponsors say it is "highly likely" a son of Measure 9 also will be introduced in Washington and perhaps Idaho.

Spare us.

Measure 9 would have classified homosexuality as "abnormal, wrong, unnatural and perverse" and allowed discrimination against homosexuals. It also would have required state officials, particularly teachers, to actively discourage homosexuality.

Stirring up reservoirs of prejudice and malevolence, it created a climate where people sent hate mail to volunteers helping AIDS patients.

Lon Mabon, director of the Oregon Citizens Alliance, which sponsored the initiative, recognizes the proposal has a better chance if he removes some inflammatory language.

In the new version, a passage linking homosexuality with pedophilia, sadism and masochism would be eliminated. So would the requirement that teachers must actively teach that homosexuality is wrong. They would simply be prohibited from teaching homosexuality is normal.

The new measure also would ban use of public funds to promote homosexuality in sensitivity training for government employees.

The debate over special protection for homosexuals is a delicate matter. But Mabon has shown his cards. His ultimate goal is to eliminate homosexuals' legal protection from discrimination in jobs, housing and employment.

The state has already paid a price for a campaign that ripped apart its sense of community and tainted its reputation as a tolerant, progressive place. If Measure 9 had passed, tourists and out-of-state businesses threatened boycotts.

Mabon and company should accept the 57 percent no vote, and leave Washington and Idaho alone.

The Oregonian
Portland, Oregon, November 1, 1992

Ask yourself the following questions. Apply only your own direct experience.

If you can't honestly answer yes, Measure 9 would create a public policy harmful to you, to other Oregonians and to the state:

• Were you ever taught "homosexual behavior" or instructed in "homosexual values" in school?

• Were you or your children ever molested or recruited by a homosexual teacher?

• Is a militant homosexual agenda destroying your own family and its values?

• Has a "special right," quota, subsidy or affirmative action for homosexuals cost you a job, a promotion, a government contract or entry to a public college or community college?

• Have the schools violated your right, if you exercised it, to have your children excused from classes on sex education and sexually transmitted diseases like AIDS? If so, was it clearly part of a homosexual conspiracy?

• Have you filed a complaint that a teacher has violated the state requirement that schools must promote abstinence for school-age youth as the most responsible behavior? If so, again, was the violation clearly part of a homosexual plot?

No Oregon law says that you have to like homosexuals. Nor will there be if you vote no on 9.

Child molesting and sadistic assault are already against Oregon law. A no on 9 won't change that.

Masochism already is regarded as a mental disorder. Voting against 9 won't change that.

The degree to which homosexuality is the result of choice, heredity, hormones or social conditioning is far from settled. Refusing to label homosexuals as abnormal, unnatural and perverse won't change that.

Oregonians insist on fairness for all and no special rights for a few. That's the case now. No on 9 won't change that.

The only real issue on Nov. 3 is whether Oregon will reject a new brand of state-led affirmative action — repression.

Oregonians want their lives to be songs in freedom's cause, not dirges ushering in a new bondage, a new dark age, a new Inquisition. So they will vote no on 9.

The Register-Guard
Eugene, Oregon, November 11, 1992

Last week's election was the worst general election for Oregon ballot measures in more than half a century. Of nine measures on the ballot, only one — Measure 3, limiting legislative and congressional terms — passed. None of the other eight even came close. Oregon hadn't seen a bigger percentage of losing measures since the general election of 1940, when nine proposals appeared on the ballot and all nine were rejected.

The term limits measure passed handily, with 68.9 percent of the vote. The next closest was Measure 1, which would have allowed the state to issue bonds for parks. It received 45.5 percent of the vote. Measure 9, the anti-homosexual initiative, was next with 43.2 percent. Coming in last was Measure 7, the split roll property tax proposal, with only 25 percent.

Over the past 30 years, just over 50 percent of the measures appearing on general election ballots have been approved. In 1984, voters approved seven of nine measures. In 1982, voters approved only one, but there were only six on the ballot. There have been only two general elections in which all the ballot measures were approved — 1904, when three of three won support, and 1902, when voters approved the single measure creating the initiative and referendum process.

It would be premature to make too much of the poor record of ballot measures in this year's election. If a pattern of lower percentages of approval materializes in future years, however, a couple of explanations come to mind. One is that huge amounts of money were mobilized to defeat several of the ballot measures, such as the proposal to ban triple-trailer trucks. Financial power may be gaining an edge over the power citizens express through the initiative.

Another explanation may lie in the nature of the initiative proposals themselves. Measure 9 may have been the most objectionable measure on the ballot since the Ku Klux Klan attempted to impose an anti-Catholic ban on private schools. Measures 5 and 6 proposed the closure of the Trojan Nuclear Plant in Rainier, a question voters had considered and rejected twice before. Having such proposals on the ballot may help guarantee that a high percentage will be defeated.

Measure 6 did slightly better than Measure 5, attracting 43.0 percent of the vote. In 1990 a measure to close Trojan drew 40.3 percent. The first attempt, in 1986, won only 35.7 percent. The pattern suggests a slow increase in support for shutting Oregon's only nuclear power plant. If the current trend holds, a majority of voters will support closure by the end of the century. By then, however, the plant will have been closed for four years.

SYRACUSE HERALD-JOURNAL
Syracuse, New York, November 3, 1992

Americans, like all people who care about justice, are properly alarmed at the rise of neo-Nazis and other violent right-wing groups in the new unified Germany. Some 1,500 attacks this year against non-Germans by members of hate groups provide eerie recollection of the thuggery against Jews in the early 1930s that eventually culminated in the Holocaust.

But before we start feeling morally superior, let us look with shame on the same kind of crimes within our own borders. The presence of an anti-homosexual referendum on the Oregon ballot has given hate-mongers in that state an excuse to loose their violent instincts.

Oregonians today are voting on Ballot Measure 9, which would classify homosexuality as "abnormal, wrong, unnatural and perverse" and would require the state government actively to discourage homosexuality, teaching that it is a moral offense similar to pedophilia, sadism and masochism. People on both sides of the question have acted out their feelings in disgusting ways.

In the last month, Portland churches that support the anti-gay-rights measure as well as churches that are against it have been vandalized, according to a report in the New York Times. Windows have been broken on parked cars with Measure 9 bumper stickers. A lesbian and a gay man were killed in the bombing of an apartment. Police say that Oregon's "skinheads" — a violent right-wing fringe group — have taken the furor over the anti-gay measure as a cue to step up attacks against African-Americans, Jews and other minorities.

Polls indicate that Measure 9 has but small chance of passing, which is good news to anyone who believes that the original American ideal of tolerance still has a place in our culture. Measure 9 is old-fashioned hatred disguised as piety and populism.

You don't have to be gay or an Oregon resident to care about this. Discrimination is everyone's concern — everyone who believes in the freedom to live our personal lives as we see fit. Homophobia, xenophobia — it's all the same sickness. Homosexuals present no more threat to Oregon's non-gay population than Jews presented to Germans 60 years ago. They merely are convenient scapegoats.

Laws can't change what's in people's hearts. But laws can prohibit them from turning their irrational hatred and fear into violence against innocent people. Passage of Measure 9 would lend official authority to the notion that one group of people is inherently inferior to everyone else. That's a scary thought.

Let us hope the people of Oregon have the wisdom to send it down to resounding defeat.

Chicago Tribune
Chicago, Illinois, November 2, 1992

Oregonians have a reputation for jealously guarding their state's assets, even to the point of encouraging outsiders to visit but not stay. The fear is that too many newcomers will spoil a social milieu marked by tolerance and progressive politics.

Yet those fine traits are conspicuously absent from a sweeping anti-homosexual initiative on Tuesday's ballot. If voters approve the proposal, they will have only themselves to blame for degrading Oregon's image.

But image is secondary. Fundamental civil rights, the nature of education in Oregon and government's posture vis-a-vis homosexuality—these are the salient issues in Measure 9, as the ballot initiative is called.

The proposal, illiberal in the extreme, would do nothing less than mandate discrimination against homosexuals. Worse, it could lead to outbreaks of anti-gay violence and vandalism in Oregon and elsewhere.

Where a Colorado ballot initiative would deny minority status based on sexual orientation, the Oregon proposal would go further and also condemn homosexuality. What's more, it would enjoin all levels of government and the schools to "assist in setting a standard for Oregon's youth that recognizes homosexuality, pedophilia, sadism and masochism as abnormal, wrong, unnatural and perverse and that these behaviors are to be discouraged and avoided."

It's not clear how they would do that, but it is not unreasonable to read the injunction as an invitation to intolerance, or worse, against those *presumed* guilty of or disposed to such behavior. Teachers and police officers identified as gay could be fired. Landlords could evict homosexual tenants. Gay and lesbian lawyers and doctors could be denied licenses to practice. Measure 9 opponents also say schools would have to teach that homosexuality is morally wrong and would have to ban books that diverged from that viewpoint.

The Oregon Citizens Alliance, a fundamentalist Christian-backed organization, is the prime mover. The group objects to what it claims homosexuals want: special rights that affirm, in the words of one OCA leader, "that their behavior is good and moral."

Leaving aside that debatable assertion, Measure 9 is pernicious because, in the guise of blocking special rights for gays, it would deprive them of fundamental rights they properly enjoy in common with all citizens.

Also worrisome, it would put the awesome weight of government on one side of an issue about which science and ordinary people learn more each day, an issue that taps wellsprings of ambivalence in society as well as in individuals. This is no place for government.

Fortunately, an impressive collection of political, business, religious, labor and civic leaders are working against Measure 9. They and the majority of voters who say they oppose it are on the right side.

THE DENVER POST
Denver, Colorado, November 6, 1992

THE RELIGIOUS right may have failed in its attempts to put anti-abortion zealots into congressional seats in Colorado, but the movement clearly succeeded in injecting its anti-gay bias into the state's constitution.

Amendment 2, the proposal to outlaw specific civil rights protections for homosexuals, was approved by a vote of about 53 percent to 47 percent. The outcome flatly contradicted pollsters who had predicted just last weekend that it would be defeated by roughly the same margin.

To some extent, the result may have reflected voters' reluctance to reveal to poll-takers their true feelings on this emotional issue. Numerous elections have shown that such prejudices — against oppressed minorities of any kind — are more likely to rear an ugly head in the voting booth than on the front porch or over the telephone.

But another explanation may be that backers of the amendment surged ahead on the basis of a last-minute campaign blitz at some fundamentalist Christian churches last Sunday morning.

Coloradans who don't want anti-gay and other biblical dogmas to be written into law already are planning to challenge the new amendment in court, probably by arguing that it violates the rights of home-rule cities. One provision of the measure will overturn existing gay-rights ordinances in Denver, Boulder and Aspen.

But the advocates of tolerance also should be working out a strategy to counter the "stealth" tactics of the religious right when it makes its next move on this front. Judging from statements made by leaders of Colorado for Family Values, the anti-gay lobby eventually hopes not just to overturn local anti-discrimination laws, but to restrict or prohibit homosexual activity in general.

Such an extreme proposal, akin to the mean-spirited initiative defeated in Oregon this week, would clearly be at odds with Colorado's traditionally liberal approach to social questions. But the ultra-conservative Christians might be able to slip it into the constitution almost unnoticed if their get-out-the-vote forces meet as little resistance as they did this time out.

THE BUFFALO NEWS
Buffalo, New York, November 6, 1992

THE WORST of the anti-gay measures on Tuesday's state ballots around the country was defeated. That's encouraging. But it's too bad voters didn't deal hatred a knockout blow everywhere.

This nation was not the finest hour for a nation still coming to grips with the fact that sexual orientation is no reason for discrimination. Even where open-mindedness won out, the victory margin left room for hatred to grab a foothold.

The defeat of Oregon's Measure 9 — by far the most perverse of the batch — will put a roadblock in front of a movement that would have gained frightening momentum from a victory. Measure 9 would have had state law declare homosexuality "abnormal, wrong, unnatural and perverse" — enshrining both bigotry and ignorance.

Passage of the measure would have meant a wholesale purge of homosexuals from teaching jobs and other government posts and efforts to deny them access to a whole range of activities that "normal" people take for granted.

Substitute some other group for homosexuals, and one can get an idea of how scary such witch hunts can be. The measure lost by a solid 57-43 percent margin. But that tally also means more than a third of Oregonians think such Nazi-style purges are a good idea. Such support can only encourage hate groups everywhere to try again.

In Colorado, the good news is that the ballot proposal was less far-reaching. The bad news is that it passed, 53 to 47 percent. That law prevents localities from enacting measures protecting gay rights. It wipes existing local protections off the books.

In Portland, Maine, citizens stood up to the tide of bigotry by upholding their ordinance protecting gays. But Tampa, Fla., voted to repeal its gay-rights law.

This mixed bag of results reflects the ambivalence of a nation that's never shy about lecturing others on basic human rights, but which moves excruciatingly slowly in guaranteeing the rights of its own citizens.

The attacks — physical, psychological and economic — perpetrated against gays in this country make clear the need for strong legislation affirming the rights of all citizens.

Homosexuals don't need "special rights," but they need need the protection of anti-bias measures that assure equal treatment. Society has a stake in guaranteeing that, not only because gays deserve it as individuals, but also because it promotes the harmonious coexistence of all groups. Any diverse nation must strive for that.

Of course, New York State residents cannot lecture others too strongly, since efforts to get civil rights protections for gays in the Empire State have yet to succeed. Buffalo does have an anti-discrimination measure that covers sexual orientation, but it applies only to employment within city government.

The win by President-elect Bill Clinton, who backs gay rights, might foreshadow something of a change in attitude, here and elsewhere. But the results from elections that dealt directly with gay rights show how far this nation still has to go.

Portland Press Herald
Portland, Maine, November 2, 1992

No, no, no! Not in this city. Not ever. Discrimination has no place in Portland.

On Tuesday citizens should vote "no" on the question of whether to repeal Portland's human rights ordinance.

By doing so, the voters will prevent discrimination in employment, housing, accommodations and credit on the basis of sexual orientation.

Each American deserves equal access to such basic opportunity, and our government is obliged to protect these rights.

Those who oppose the city's human rights ordinance do so out of a misguided sense of priorities. They say the ordinance would deny them the right not to associate with homosexuals.

This right of association, however, does not supersede the right of every American to live and work without fear of discrimination. As with other civil rights issues, tolerance should be the guiding principle here, and our government should stand behind that principle.

Portland should do this out of more than just a sense of justice, though. As a practical matter we don't have a qualified doctor, police officer or teacher to waste.

Some have also argued against the ordinance by saying it is not needed. One need only look at the hate crimes committed in this city to know how vital this protection is.

Remember the Portland man who earlier this year declined to press charges in a gay-bashing incident? He feared he would be fired if his boss knew his sexual preference.

This man gave up his right to justice because he does not have the right to be who he is and still hold a job. We should not allow this.

Let Portland be known as a community of tolerance and respect for human rights. Cast a vote for common dignity and caring. Tell the world that Portland will protect the rights of all of its citizens.

Step into the voting booth and say "no." No to discrimination. No to misguided priorities. No to injustice.

Colorado Gay-Rights Ban Dealt Setback

The Colorado state Supreme Court July 19, 1993 by a 6–1 vote upheld a lower court's injunction against state enforcement of Amendment 2, a measure that prohibited localities from passing laws to protect homosexuals from discrimination.

A state district court judge in January had blocked Amendment 2, ruling that the measure could not go into effect before a challenge to its constitutionality was tried in court. That challenge, a lawsuit brought by nine plaintiffs in Denver, the state capital, was scheduled to be heard in October.

If it took effect, Amendment 2 would overturn ordinances in the cities of Denver, Boulder and Aspen protecting homosexuals from discrimination in employment and housing, and localities and the state would be barred from passing such laws in the future. Proponents of the amendment said such ordinances discriminated in favor of gays and lesbians and gave them "special rights."

In ruling to uphold the injunction, the state Supreme Court held that Amendment 2 would "fence out" homosexuals from civil-rights protections, violating the 14th Amendment's guarantees of equal treatment under the law. "No other identifiable group faces such a burden," the court held. Referring to the referendum process through which the measure had been approved, the court also wrote, "Fundamental rights may not be submitted to a vote; they depend on the outcome of no elections."

The court held that in order for Amendment 2 to take effect, state officials defending the measure in the lower-court case would have to prove a "compelling interest" that would counterbalance its constitutional problems to justify its enforcement.

Legal analysts said that the compelling-interest standard would be very difficult to meet and was likely to lead to a final overturning of the law. But Colorado state Attorney General Gail Norton July 19 said she planned to argue that the upholding of "family values" presented a compelling interest in favor of the amendment.

The Chattanooga Times
Chattanooga, Tennessee, July 30, 1993

In November, 53 percent of Colorado's voters approved an anti-gay law, called Amendment 2, which would prevent state or local governments from passing laws that prohibit discrimination against homosexuals. Amendment 2 also would have invalidated laws in Denver, Boulder and Aspen that forbid such discrimination. Now, it appears, Amendment 2 itself is endangered.

Last week the state's Supreme Court ruled 6-to-1 to uphold a lower court injunction that prevented the law from going into effect. The majority declared it unconstitutional and in effect an attempt to create second-class citizenship for some on the basis of sexual preference.

The court declared that "one's right to life, liberty and property ... and other fundamental rights may not be submitted to vote; they depend on the outcome of no elections." If they were so dependent, the court held, that would "fence out" homosexuals from the political process by prohibiting legal protection of a single group.

The justices continued:

"No other identifiable group faces such a burden. No other group's ability to participate in the political process is restricted and encumbered in a like manner. Such a structuring of the political process is contrary to the notion that the concept of 'we the people' visualizes."

After Amendment 2 passed, the cities of Aspen, Boulder and Denver filed suit to prevent it from taking effect. That lawsuit isn't scheduled to be heard until October, but the Supreme Court's ruling suggest that Amendment 2 is dead. The trial probably will just administer the last rites.

The state justices' ruling could present a major roadblock for similar measures being contemplated in other states, especially if the U.S. Supreme Court declines to hear an appeal from the state of Colorado.

The driving force behind Amendment 2 was Colorado for Family Values, a Colorado Springs organization that argued that ordinances banning discrimination against homosexuals would lead to "special rights" and affirmative-action hiring programs.

Supporters used television advertisements that featured the flamboyant behavior in a San Francisco gay parade, but insisted all the while that they did not support discrimination against homosexuals.

Maybe not, but that's clearly the message that came across on Election Day in Colorado last fall. It's also the not-so-subtle message being used by various groups, including religious ones, to solicit contributions. Homosexuals, judging by some of the fund-raising literature, have apparently replaced communists as the current threat to the nation.

In the face of all that, the Colorado Supreme Court's ruling is a welcome reminder.

The Arizona Republic
Phoenix, Arizona, July 26, 1993

THE Colorado Supreme Court's ruling on the voter-approved anti-gay rights amendment provides the clearest perspective to date on the critical flaw of such propositions: "One's right to life, liberty and property ... and other fundamental rights may not be submitted to vote; they depend on the outcome of no elections."

Fifty-three percent of those voting in the Nov. 4 election in Colorado supported Amendment 2, which bans state and local laws prohibiting discrimination based on sexual orientation and strikes down ordinances already on the books in Aspen, Boulder and Denver. But in last week's 6-1 decision to keep in place a temporary injunction preventing the amendment from taking effect, Colorado's high court said Amendment 2 disrupts the political process in denying a "targeted class" access to established protections from discrimination.

The state's Supreme Court also said the amendment is probably unconstitutional, suggesting that it violates the equal protection clause of the 14th Amendment. The constitutional question will be answered in October when a civil lawsuit challenging the amendment goes to trial, although many legal experts say the upcoming trial is moot because of the signal sent by the Colorado Supreme Court. The amendment's last hope appears to be with the U.S. Supreme Court, where Colorado's governor says he'll appeal his state high court's decision.

Although attempts are strong and many — initiatives similar to Amendment 2 are developing in Arizona, California, Florida, Idaho, Maine, Michigan, Oregon and Washington — the Colorado Supreme Court's ruling is an important lesson on minority rights, a lesson yet unlearned by those with a hankering to impose moral judgments by statutory decree.

Dislike for a group of people, even by a majority, is no grounds to usurp rights guaranteed under the law. The Colorado Supreme Court recognizes this and so does most anyone familiar with the U.S. Constitution.

TULSA WORLD
Tulsa, Oklahoma, July 20, 1993

BACKERS of a a city ordinance prohibiting discrimination based on sexual preference have not made a convincing argument that homosexuals should be singled out for special protection under the law.

As Councilor Robert Nelson points out, there already are plenty of laws and ordinances that prohibit discrimination in general. There is no need to single out homosexuals for further protection.

An ad hoc committee, an offshoot of the Human Rights Commission, reportedly will present a report by October calling for a change in Tulsa's human rights ordinance — which deals with discrimination involving housing, public accomodations and employment — to include homosexuals. Backers of the ordinance cite anecdotal reports of discrimination against homosexuals as justification for a new ordinance.

If sexual preference is indeed a "preference" and a "lifestyle," as we are told, then it is not a fundamental characteristic — like race, gender or religion — that requires special governmental protection. People are discriminated against for all kinds of reasons. Overweight people are discriminated against; so are people whose hair or dress styles don't fit the norm. Government can't be expected to grant special protection to every group that sees itself as a victim.

The problem with too many of those who see sexual orientation as a civil rights issue is that they don't just want equal rights, they want extra rights.

The city will be better off if the council is spared a fight over a homosexual-rights ordinance.

Detroit Free Press
Denver, Colorado, July 20, 1993

The Colorado Supreme Court didn't quite formally kill Colorado's controversial Amendment 2 with its 6-1 ruling Monday. But it denounced the measure as a violation of the equal protection of the laws guaranteed by the U.S. Constitution — a clear sign that it *will* put Amendment 2 out of its legal misery in the fullness of judicial time.

In its most important section, the majority opinion delivered by Chief Justice Luis Rovira specifically ruled that Denver District Judge Jeffrey Bayless was right in saying that the amendment must be judged by "the most exacting standard of review under the Equal Protection Clause" — because it "expressly fences out an independently identifiable group and denies it equal protection in the political process.

"In short, gay men, lesbians and bisexuals are left out of the political process through the denial of having an 'effective voice in the governmental affairs which substantially affect their lives.' . . . They, and they alone, must amend the state constitution in order to seek legislation which is beneficial to them," Rovira said.

That ruling upholds a similar finding by Bayless, who is now free to try Amendment 2 on its merits. But the very discriminatory effect cited by both Bayless and Rovira is an open invitation for Bayless to ultimately rule that Amendment 2 is a violation of the 14th Amendment to the U.S. Constitution. Likewise, having just voted 6-1 to find that Amendment 2 is discriminatory, the high court is virtually certain to uphold Bayless when he does rule that the measure is unconstitutional.

The high court also upheld Bayless on the narrow question of whether Bayless acted properly in issuing a temporary restraining order stopping the state from enforcing Amendment 2 while he determines its constitutionality.

While not unexpected, the high court ruling is notable for the breadth of its margin and the depth of its scholarship. Only Justice William Erickson dissented, and the opinion was delivered by the generally conservative Chief Justice Luis Rovira.

In citing U.S. Supreme Court rulings, Rovira invoked Colorado's favorite legal son, retiring Justice Byron White, who is notably conservative on issues involving homosexuality. In a case out of Akron, Ohio, (Hunter v. Erickson) White noted that the voters of Akron amended their city charter to require any fair housing ordinance to be approved by the voters, whereas other ordinances could be enacted by the city council. Justice White found such a process to be discriminatory, concluding that Akron could "no more disadvantage *any particular group* by making it more difficult to enact legislation in its behalf than it may dilute any person's vote or give any group a smaller representation than another of comparable size."

Commending on White's ruling, Justice Rovira added, "It is significant to note that in support of this proposition, the Court did not rely on any precedent dealing with racial minorities . . . but instead cited *Reynolds v. Sims* and *Avery v. Midland County*, neither of which had anything to do with discrimination against racial, or any other traditionally suspect class of persons."

That is a critical ruling because Amendment 2's backers have insisted that it is fair to single out a group such as homosexuals for special (and unequal) treatment as long as they do not similarly discriminate against racial or religious minorities or women — the usual laundry list of "protected classes." By overwhelmingly rejecting that argument — and buttressing their finding with the conservative credentials of Byron White — the Colorado Supreme Court has foreshadowed the doom of Amendment 2.

To which we can only add: Good riddance to bad law.

San Francisco Chronicle
San Francisco, California, July 21, 1993

THE DECISION in Colorado throwing the legality of the state's anti-gay initiative into extreme doubt has implications extending far beyond that state. It may indicate what the line will be in the legal battle over gays and lesbians in the military.

Ruling that "fundamental rights may not be submitted to a vote," the Colorado Supreme Court upheld an injunction against Proposition 2, the amendment approved by 53 percent of the state's voters last fall. A hearing on the legality of the amendment will be held in a lower court in October, but under the terms set by the Supreme Court, proponents of the initiative must prove "a compelling interest" for barring gays from equal protection.

"No other group's ability to participate in the political process is restricted and encumbered in a like manner," the court ruled.

THE COLORADO COURT provided a preview of what to expect in the challenge of the "don't ask, don't tell" decision President Clinton called "an honorable compromise" in the dispute over gays and lesbians in the armed forces.

If as expected, the case reaches the U.S. Supreme Court, its justices may find that no compromise, honorable or otherwise, is possible.

Homosexuals in Military Becomes Widely Debated Topic

The chaplain of the Marine Corps., Navy Capt. Larry H. Ellis, who was a Southern Baptist minister, had sent to senior officers a position paper characterizing homosexuals in the military as a "physical and psychological threat," according to a *New York Times* story datelined Aug. 25, 1992.

Citing among other factors the deadly disease AIDS, Ellis insisted that "legislators and military leaders" were correct in trying to halt the "spread of homosexual behavior."

Editorials in the Aug. 24 issues of the *Army Times* and *Force Times* newspapers urged a lifting of the ban on homosexuals. The papers, published by a private concern, Army Times Publishing Co., were widely read by members of the armed forces. A third paper, *Navy Times*, in June had called for the gay ban to remain in place but not be enforced.

A Navy board of inquiry July 24 recommended that Lt. (j.g.) Tracy Thorne be dismissed from the service for admitted homosexuality. Thorne, a naval aviator, had revealed his sexual preference during an interview May 19 on the ABC television program "Nightline."

The Washington Post

Washington, D.C., May 25, 1992

SENTIMENT ON Capitol Hill is hardening against President Clinton's intention of removing the ban on gays in the military, and Mr. Clinton must soon decide what to do. Key repeal advocates such as Rep. Barney Frank believe so much ground has been lost since January that Congress probably would enact the current ban into law if a total repeal were attempted. Mr. Frank has offered a compromise proposal; it is meant to be fairer and less inhibiting than a compromise proposal suggested by Sen. Sam Nunn, the leading opponent of removing the ban.

The Nunn proposal, known as "don't ask, don't tell," retains strong features of the current policy of discriminating against men and women in uniform on the basis of their homosexuality. It says that a gay or lesbian soldier who makes no sexual advances on anyone is, by virtue of sexual status, still unfit to associate with heterosexual colleagues. Homosexual status, in other words, under the Nunn proposal, remains an offense and one sufficient to get a gay or lesbian kicked out of the armed services. "Don't ask, don't tell" is only a very slight advance from the original situation, in that it would do away with aggressive investigation and inquiry into the sexuality of presumed homosexual military personnel. It would rest on suppression of information and on subterfuge.

Mr. Frank dislikes the Nunn compromise. But his side is running out of time, and he wants to avoid getting locked into "don't ask, don't tell" or something worse. So he has offered a measure of his own. Under it, military authorities would be instructed not to ask about, investigate or pay attention to a person's sexual orientation or behavior as expressed off base, off duty or out of uniform. Its premise is that homosexual status or conduct is not grounds for expulsion from the military—that is an advance—but that all evidence and profession of it are to be suppressed on the base. Mr. Frank says that this does not include cases in which a military person's homosexual status might become known by happenstance in some casual conversation, and it is plain that given the terms regarding open off-base behavior, that status could be fully known to the military authorities without its leading to expulsion or other punishment.

Does the Frank proposal restrict the freedom of homosexuals to indicate their sexual orientation on the same basis as heterosexuals in uniform? Yes. Does it continue to stigmatize their sexual status? Yes, though in its way it goes a considerable distance from both the original ban and the Nunn proposal toward the ending of this stigmatization. Does it rest on enforced hypocrisy on both sides? Yes. Would it, if enacted into law, represent a substantial advance over the conditions that existed and could still exist under the ban? Also, definitely yes. The question to be decided by Mr. Clinton and his side is whether this is the most and the best that can be accomplished on the Hill.

The Hutchinson News

Hutchinson, Kansas, May 15, 1992

President Bill Clinton has his toe in the legal swamp of sexual preference as an official civil right.

And he's finding plenty of sharks in the swamp for many valid reasons.

Clinton said he would issue an executive order doing away with the ban against homosexuals in the American military. It all seemed simple and straightforward, an issue whose time had come because this nation as a whole is tolerant toward homosexuals.

Enter Democrat Sen. Sam Nunn of Georgia, who has been extremely effective in leading the fight against Clinton.

What's the difference between showering and bunking with a homosexual and showering and bunking with a woman, male servicemen asked the senators.

Open, militant homosexuality would deeply harm morale, Gulf War commander Norman Schwarzkopf told senators. It would leave U.S. troops confused and listless, like the Iraqis "who sat in the deserts of Kuwait" as proud American troops rolled through, Schwarzkopf said.

Suddenly, open homosexuality isn't such a simple matter, even for the tolerant.

There are important and legitimate reasons to keep sexual preference in the military closet.

Yet the firing of heroic gay soldiers for coming out of the closet seems somehow unAmerican. The humiliating question of sexual preference on military enlistment forms seems wrong.

There must be a compromise here somewhere that will allow everyone in the military to keep their jobs and their dignity.

Meanwhile, we should stop kidding ourselves that sexual preference is a simple civil right. It's a legal swamp, and we appear foolish as a nation when we try to shrug our shoulders and act otherwise.

Sexual Politics In America

The Seattle Times
Seattle, Washington, May 17, 1992

REVERSING a 50-year ban on homosexuals serving in the military is emotional and complicated enough, without the chairman of the Senate Armed Services Committee weighing with a feckless suggestion.

Nunn wants the Pentagon and gays to avert their eyes with a silly policy that is summarized as "Don't ask, don't tell."

How about letting the adults make the decision here?

A Pentagon panel is exploring issues about gays serving openly in the military. This is not an easy task. Even those who want to see sexual orientation eliminated as a consideration for serving one's country have to respect the sensitivity of changing a homophobic, macho culture.

Two benchmarks exist: job performance and behavior.

The military's mission is to protect and defend the United States, and gays have served and died for those causes for generations. The strictures of military life on base or aboard ships at sea should have no tolerance for inappropriate sexual activity between or among genders.

Making rules and enforcing them requires the parties to be treated as adults. Nunn's recommendation represents child-like thinking that disagreeable topics can be wished away.

The military exists in society, not isolated and removed from it. Recruits come from the culture at large. They must conform to military standards of discipline, regimen and order, but they should not be expected to deny something as basic as their sexuality.

The Philadelphia Inquirer
Philadelphia, Pennsylvania, May 25, 1992

Activists trying to end the military's ban on homosexuals are appalled. U.S. Rep. Barney Frank (D., Mass.), one of two openly gay members of Congress, has just suggested a compromise: Gays can be out of the closet when out of uniform, but have to keep closeted while on duty. When you're fighting for something as a basic right, ask the activists, how on earth can you compromise?

Emotionally, Mr. Frank's compromise may be hard for supporters of equal rights for gays to accept, but rationally his strategy makes sense.

Like Mr. Frank, we believe that the ban on homosexuals serving in the military is unjustifiable. The fears of a loss of combat cohesion seem overstated, so long as there are strong sanctions against sexual overtures — gay or straight — while on duty. But we also share the congressman's judgment that it's politically impossible to end the military's anti-homosexual policy any time soon, and that it's much better to take a half-step toward nondiscrimination than to end up with nothing at all.

Mr. Frank's proposal is preferable to the so-called "Don't ask, don't tell" compromise offered by the Senate Armed Services Committee chairman, Sam Nunn, which would prevent the military from inquiring about sexual orientation but force homosexuals to hide their sexual orientation at all times. Under Rep. Frank's plan, gays and lesbians could act naturally whenever they're off-duty, off the base and out of uniform. Superiors simply wouldn't show any interest in rumors or reports that so-and-so (in civvies) goes to gay bars, lives with her girlfriend, or what have you. This would greatly reduce the problem of homosexuals being drummed out of the military, as most such cases begin with reports of behavior displayed off the base.

But gays and lesbians still couldn't be open about their sexual orientation while on duty, on a base or in uniform. By their actions and comments, they'd have to keep their sexual orientation to themselves — even while all the macho stud-muffins in the ranks are running off at the mouth. This policy, which is the status quo, is fundamentally hypocritical. But there is no practical way to end it right now.

Indeed, if President Clinton sticks to the letter of his campaign promise and orders an end to the military's disciminatory policy, Congress will almost certainly make the current policy even harder to alter: It will write it into the law.

While some gay-rights activists charge that Mr. Frank gave up too soon, he's really not the kind of guy who retreats under fire. In 1982, after his district was dismantled by gerrymandering, he ran against a Republican incumbent on her home turf and crushed her by a 3-2 margin. And though the House reprimanded him in 1990 for improprieties involving a homosexual lover, he has kept winning re-election.

Mr. Frank's willingness to battle long odds is unquestionable, but he sees no point in pursuing what he calls a "glorious, principled defeat."

MILITARY DEBATE — 137

ARGUS-LEADER
Sioux Falls, South Dakota, May 26, 1992

In principle, striking the ban on homosexuals in the U.S. military would be the right thing to do.

In reality, it might be politically impossible.

A compromise is in order.

Rep. Barney Frank, D-Mass., recently offered the best solution.

Frank, a homosexual, proposed that gays be allowed to serve in the military and do as they please off base when off duty as long as they keep their sexual orientation hidden while on duty.

"It's a policy that says 'don't ask, don't tell and don't listen, and don't investigate,'" he said last week.

Editorial

His proposal goes slightly beyond one offered by Sen. Sam Nunn, D-Ga., who chairs the Senate Armed Services Committee. Nunn wants homosexuals to keep their sexual orientation a secret at all times, not just when they are on duty or on base.

As a candidate for president, Bill Clinton vowed to remove the ban. Since then, he has backed off somewhat, giving Congress time to get involved with hearings and possible legislation.

For the time being, the military has suspended the practice of asking recruits their sexual orientation. That practice should be dropped permanently. So should military investigations aimed solely at weeding out homosexuals.

Sexual orientation should not disqualify a person from serving in the military. That does not mean outrageous sexual behavior should be accepted. Actions that interfere with military performance — whether by heterosexuals or homosexuals — should not be tolerated.

Continuing the ban on homosexuals would serve no purpose, other than lending credibility to fears that letting gays serve legally would destroy military morale. We don't believe that. The military has successfully overcome far greater challenges than dealing with minority lifestyles.

However, in retrospect, it's clear that Clinton has not handled the challenge of removing the ban with the right combination of sensitivity and firmness. He has antagonized a lot of people. His goal of eliminating the gay ban entirely might have slipped out of reach.

The president would be wise to rally around Frank's compromise, a plan not likely to meet with agreement from extremists on either side of the issue.

Eventually, the nation's military leaders will have to accept the reality that homosexuals are part of society. In the meantime, Frank's compromise is a worthwhile stepping stone.

The Atlanta Journal AND THE ATLANTA CONSTITUTION
Atlanta, Georgia, March 27, 1992

President Clinton neatly undercut himself the other day in the debate over ending the ban on gays in the military. He has since shown signs of backing away from saying it might be acceptable to allow gays to serve by relegating them to second-class status, but he really needs to forthrightly repudiate the idea.

Mr. Clinton hurt himself on at least three fronts when he told a press conference he would consider a restricted-assignment policy for gays in uniform, such as limiting them to noncombat roles. First, he virtually conceded the central argument of his opponents, who say lifting the ban will hurt the military's ability to carry out its mission of defending the nation.

Second, he has encouraged further foot-dragging on this issue by the military. His order that the armed services begin preparing for the end of the ban already is being undermined by military leaders who want to continue discriminating against gays. They will see Mr. Clinton's words as a sign that they may win yet.

And, finally, the president has hurt himself among the many Americans who believe he made a principled promise to end the ban. By appearing to backpedal, Mr. Clinton alienates support he desperately needs.

This so-called compromise would please no one, so it has little chance of being implemented. If it were put in place it would add to, rather than solve, the problems already created by the ban.

Military personnel would continue to have an incentive for lying about their sexual orientation. And the services would continue to have an incentive to snoop into the private lives of soldiers suspected of being gay. In fact, the witch hunts likely would intensify, given the appearance of a consensus that keeping such people out of combat is vitally important.

Among the more compelling arguments for ending this outdated and unfair ban are the records of gay men and women who have performed with distinction in all areas of military service, including combat. It would be ludicrous to now open the door to gays and lesbians while denying them the opportunity to serve to the best of their abilities.

Mr. Clinton's press office is emphasizing that the president did not say he favors restricting the assignments of gays in the military or definitely would agree to it if it were proposed. He simply said it is something he would consider if it is proposed.

The president needs to recoup stronger than that from this self-inflicted setback. He should say he considered allowing gays to serve as second-class citizens in the military and decided it is wrong to repay service to the country with discrimination.

Then he should press on with ending the ban . . . period.

> *President Clinton hurt himself when he told a press conference he would consider a restricted-assignment policy for gays in uniform, such as limiting them to noncombat roles.*

Rockford Register Star
Rockford, Illinois, May 18, 1992

A proposal that is gaining support among some federal lawmakers purports to "lift" the ban on homosexuals in the U.S. military in this way: No one will ask recruits if they are gay, but those who are must not discuss their sexual orientation — and they must remain celibate. If they break the rules, they will be barred from military service.

Supporters have dubbed the plan, "Don't ask, don't tell." There is another word for it — discrimination.

It is wrong to condone a plan that forces gay people into a lie of ommission. A person's sexuality is fundamental to who they are. Being forced to lie about it in order to keep a job is no different than a Jew being forced to lie about religious beliefs, a Republican to lie about politics, a young person to lie about the desire to have children.

Clinton should lift the ban on gays by executive order.

To compromise on homosexuals in the military is to discriminate against homosexuals in the military. The only restrictions placed on gays regarding their sexual conduct should be those restrictions that all service personnel sailors have to live by. Anything more is oppressive.

President Clinton made a campaign promise to immediately lift the ban by executive order. But now he seems willing to compromise in the face of opposition from the homophobes in the military who say acknowledged gays would disrupt unit cohesion, undermine discipline, hurt moral.

Stand your ground, Mr President. Lift the ban.

The Washington Times
Washington, D.C., March 12, 1992

Under pressure from the Joint Chiefs of Staff and the members of his own party's high command in Congress, President Clinton has postponed his promised executive order lifting the ban on homosexuals in the armed forces until July 15. In the meantime, we're supposed to think about it, debate it, hold hearings on it. But now it turns out that if you're already in the military, you're not supposed to talk about it, and if you do, you could wind up cleaning latrines in Mogadishu.

This week The Washington Times reported that one of the less politically correct officers of the U.S. Navy, Lt. David Quint, who has let everyone know of his opposition to lifting the ban, has been gagged by order of his superiors. Lt. Quint makes no secret of his views. He has appeared on the Christian Broadcasting Service and a number of conservative radio talk shows to speak against it. He also talks about it while on the job in the Pentagon's central public affairs office. Now he's been told to sit down and shut up.

He's received a memorandum from a superior, Capt. Fred Leeder, deputy chief of information, that reads in part, "Because previous counseling apparently has not been heeded, this letter is directive in nature." In the New Age Navy, you see, that's how they say, "Button it, and that's an order." Hereafter, Lt. Quint may not appear in uniform or identify himself as a naval officer while addressing "the issue," and must be off duty or on a break when he makes arrangements with interest groups about it. "Lt. Quint," says the memo, "was advised that his continued assignment to Chinfo [Chief of Information, in what passes for the English language in the military] could be placed in jeopardy by his continued activities in regard to the media, since his credibility as an unbiased official spokesman for the Navy would be limited." In accordance with his orders, Lt. Quint has not talked to this paper, but friends provided The Times with the memo.

What's particularly rich in the military's gag order on Lt. Quint (and, presumably soon if not already, on other service members opposed to lifting the ban) is that similar gags were never applied to women who favored sending women into combat. As Times reporter Rowan Scarborough reports, Lt. Quint's acquaintances "complained that the Navy took no similar action during the past two years of public debate on women in combat. During that time, female officers in uniform gave numerous press interviews on their opposition to the current combat ban."

OK, so there's a double standard in the Navy, but what's more important is that the muzzle on Lt. Quint points toward a regime of political correctness that will descend once the president actually lifts the ban. As Capt. Leeder wrote, "counseling" — that is, the therapeutic costume assumed by those who disapprove of people disagreeing with them — hasn't "been heeded." In other words, we told you once to keep your mouth shut, and you didn't listen and you didn't learn the wickedness of your ways, so now, because you still disagree, we order you to be quiet. This is precisely the sort of suasion that campus codes of PC use and precisely the reason they have become notorious as a kind of New Age Stalinism.

That's bad enough on campus, but in this case it may be genuinely dangerous. If Mr. Clinton does lift the gay ban, what ensues in the armed forces will be something of an experiment — to see if the military works effectively when gays are free to advertise their sexual orientation. Anyone who thinks the experiment isn't working really should be free to say so and to let his superiors, Congress and the public know about it. If the muzzling of Lt. Quint is any guide, however, they won't be free, and any dangers to the nation's military and our national security that may follow as a result of Mr. Clinton's sociological experiment will remain unknown.

Sexual Politics In America   MILITARY DEBATE — 139

[Editorial cartoon: A military general labeled with stars and medals sits in front of a "CLOSET" door with many hands reaching out from it; a sign on the wall reads "DON'T ASK DON'T TELL." Signed AUTH, 5-25-93 The Philadelphia Inquirer, Universal Press Syndicate.]

THE DAILY OKLAHOMAN
Oklahoma City, Oklahoma, March 5, 1992

HERE is the text of a May 8, 1992, letter which Gen. Colin L. Powell, chairman of the Joint Chiefs of Staff, sent to U.S. Rep. Patricia Schroeder, elaborating his reasons in support of existing policies on known homosexuals in the U.S. military:

"Thank you for your recent letter concerning the position I took before Congress in February concerning homosexuals serving in the Armed Forces. I have given a great deal of thought to my position and continue to hold the view that the presence of homosexuals in the military is prejudicial to good order and discipline.

"This is the policy of the Department of Defense and is supported by all of the Joint Chiefs of Staff. It is also a view held by experts who have studied the sociology of the military for many years. I am including a recent article by Charles Moskos on the subject.

"I am well aware of the attempts to draw parallels between this position and positions used years ago to deny opportunities to African-Americans. I know you are a history major, but I can assure you I need no reminders concerning the history of African-Americans in the defense of their nation and the tribulations they faced. I am a part of that history.

"Skin color is a benign, nonbehavioral characteristic. Sexual orientation is perhaps the most profound of human behavioral characteristics. Comparison of the two is a convenient but invalid argument. I believe the privacy rights of all Americans in uniform have to be considered, especially since those rights are often infringed upon by the conditions of military service.

"As chairman of the Joint Chiefs of Staff, as well as an African-American fully conversant with history, I believe the policy we have adopted is consistent with the necessary standards of good order and discipline required in the Armed Forces."

RAPID CITY JOURNAL—
Rapid City, South Dakota, March 30, 1992

The Senate Armed Services Committee began a series of hearings Monday on ending the ban on gays in the military. One of the issues the committee is attempting to tackle is whether lifting the ban would disrupt military effectiveness.

This question of disruptiveness could be central to a solution.

President Clinton has already ordered armed forces recruiters to stop asking potential recruits about their sexual orientation. And Sen. Sam Nunn, D-Ga., committee chairman, suggested Monday that making that temporary policy permanent may be an alternative to lifting the ban outright.

The Journal's view

Suppose for a moment that this policy continues. People of homosexual orientation, who meet all the other requirements for joining, are allowed to become members of the military. But once they are in, the fears come true: They can't control their sexual urges. They can't keep their hands off others, or they continually make suggestive sexual remarks to their fellow soldiers.

What then? Such behavior certainly cannot and should not be tolerated. Such behavior must be dealt with swiftly and decisively.

Perhaps Nunn is right. Perhaps the military should continue not asking potential recruits about their sexual orientation. But once they're in, if their actions disrupt a unit's effectiveness, it will be up to their superiors to deal with it. Depending on the offense, make the offenders do latrine duty for two weeks, demote them, or throw them in military prison. Or even boot them out if they don't clean up their act.

But then the same goes for anyone else — like members of the military who harass gay men or women, or heterosexual members who can't control their sexual urges.

The military should, and generally does, deal with disruptive behavior. It's difficult to understand why lifting the ban on gays would change that.

The Seattle Times
Seattle, Washington, May 10, 1992

BRAVO to Marine commander Gen. Carl Mundy for his wise and realistic counsel to the members of the U.S. Marine Corps concerned about eventually serving with homosexuals.

Writing in the current issue of "Leatherneck" magazine, Gen. Mundy noted the July 15 deadline for an executive order ending exclusion of homosexuals from the military.

To those who oppose President Clinton on the matter, he wrote, "It is not characteristic of Marines to quit their posts, either under fire or when things are not to their liking." Marines whose "personal moral values run so deep are exactly the ones needed to remain on watch and to provide a steady hand."

Mundy's message to Marines in March should be remembered by Congress in July: "The strict standards on sexual behavior that exist in the military today will continue."

The Tennessean
Nashville, Tennessee, April 10, 1992

THIS should be the Tennessee General Assembly's business:

The state Supreme Court has ruled that Tennessee's system of funding education unfairly discriminates against rural counties.

The state's Medicaid system is in a mess. Lawmakers need to educate themselves on Medicaid so that they can understand the comprehensive, complex reform package which Gov. Ned McWherter has placed on the table.

There are more than a dozen ethics bills floating around the legislature to make lawmakers more accountable to voters.

And there are any number of other bills vitally important to Tennesseans including a bill to get a referendum to end the state's ban on lotteries and other forms of gambling. Another would call a constitutional convention.

What is not the Tennessee lawmaker's business in the issue of gays in the military. In short, Tennessee legislators have a plateful without taking up something that's already dividing national lawmakers. Yet, the House by voice vote registered its displeasure over the matter last week by passing a resolution asking President Clinton to change his mind about allowing gays to serve in the armed services.

It makes absolutely no sense for a legislative body with no responsibility for the military to waste its time in such fashion.

Surely Tennessee's pressing demands eclipse any reason for the Tennessee General Assembly to interfere where members clearly don't belong. Lawmakers supporting the bill even acknowledge the resolution has no legal basis; the resolution simply sent Clinton a message. Those members who felt so strongly should have sent the President a letter instead.

The resolution now goes to the Senate where no official action has been scheduled. Maybe senators realize Tennessee lawmakers have better things to do than meddle in something that is none of their business. ■

The Union Leader
Manchester, New Hampshire, January 4, 1992

It is being suggested that incoming President Bill Clinton is now experiencing painful second thoughts concerning his campaign pledge to terminate the ban on officially allowing homosexuals in the armed services. If so, why?

The nation's top military leaders, even as they pledge their fealty to the commander in chief, are arrayed against lifting the existing rule. But, standing alone, that fact seems not to faze Clinton.

However, when their stance is underscored by the sheer weight and logic of the practical arguments being arrayed against rescinding the ban, it must now seem imperative to Clinton that he back off while at the same time seeking some way to keep at least the spirit of his campaign promise.

Perhaps there could be some compromise that would allow patriotic homosexuals to serve in some capacity that does not directly threaten the general morale and efficiency of the armed services. But, if so, no one has proposed it.

And there remains Clinton's political problem: Homosexual activists will not easily let him off the hook.

Nevertheless, whatever Clinton might say publicly in reiterating his campaign pledge, surely he and his advisers have by now come to realize that lifting the ban on homosexuals is impractical ... because of the very nature of service in the armed forces.

In one of the most persuasive pieces we've seen on the subject, John Luddy, a former U.S. Marine Corps officer who currently serves as defense policy analyst at The Heritage Foundation, cites the basic flaw in the plan:

"Clinton may think the military is the same as any other line of work and that 'sexual orientation' has nothing to do with it. If battles were fought by individuals, this might be true. But success in combat is not based on individual achievement: It depends on like-minded members of a team who have established unity through mutual trust, and thus feel a moral obligation to lay down their lives for one another.

"This kind of camaraderie can thrive only when differences between individuals are kept at a minimum."

This is true, it must be pointed out, even if it were assumed — solely for the sake of argument — that homosexuality constituted normality and heterosexuality abnormality. It is not a question of who is superior or inferior. It *is* a question of who is best suited for military service, where he may be called upon, in Luddy's words, to *"go out into the most unfair, desperately lawless environment on earth — the battlefield — and wrench from it the victories that enable our nation to establish ideals of fairness and equality."*

If references to fairness and equality seem like contradictions here, they really aren't. As Luddy points out, it is *"no reflection on their worth as human beings"* that the armed forces also routinely restrict or deny service to Americans who are too tall, too short, too fat, color blind, flat-footed, or who are mentally or physically handicapped in some way.

Nor is it a question of right or wrong attitudes that might be corrected by "sensitivity training."

Most men, especially those who man our all-volunteer force, Luddy observes from practical experience, *"take strong exception to homosexuality for various reasons. These are gut feelings that will defy any change in Pentagon policy. Men are able to show mutual affection only when there are no sexual implications. Straight men will not 'bond' with homosexuals like they will with each other.... It is a matter of differences so profound as to be incompatible with the nature of the military mission."*

And finally, there is the AIDS problem, of which Luddy says: *"Surely not all homosexuals have AIDS, but their behavior places them at high risk. This is a medical fact, and it begs the question: Should American soldiers be exposed — or think they're being exposed — to a deadly, incurable disease in the name of gay rights?"*

Soldiers in battle do bleed — yes, more than Magic Johnson in a basketball game.

Clinton must find a practical way out of his dilemma.

Sexual Politics In America

MILITARY DEBATE — 141

The News Journal

Wilmington, Delaware, May 20, 1992

WHERE WE STAND

The "Don't ask, don't tell" approach has a chance for approval. The president and Congress should accept this compromise.

WHAT SHOULD BE DONE

Contact Sens. Roth and Biden and Rep. Castle to urge support for the Barney Frank compromise.

U.S. Rep. Barney Frank, a Massachusetts Democrat, is openly homosexual. Not surprisingly, he is a leading advocate for homosexual rights. He is also a canny politician. He understands what the traffic will bear. He is a master of compromise.

This week Rep. Frank acknowledged that President Clinton's proposal to permit homosexuals to serve openly in the military is moribund. It will not pass congressional muster. That, said Mr. Frank, correctly, is political reality.

He does not want the homosexual community nor the leader of his party — to be left with no gains. So he has offered a compromise:

"It's a policy that says, 'Don't ask, don't tell, and don't listen, and don't investigate,'" Mr. Frank explained. "Basically, the policy is 'Don't start, don't get into the whole thing.'"

The Frank proposal is similar to the one offered by Sen. Sam Nunn, the Georgia Democrat who chairs the Senate Armed Services Committee and is the most vocal and powerful opponent of President Clinton's proposal.

Already, Mr. Frank's compromise has drawn fire from some in the homosexual community who appear to want an "all-or-nothing" fight in Congress. That's unfortunate, because they will lose.

Homosexuals have served and continue to serve with distinction in the military. They should be able to do so. The Barney Frank compromise offers a way.

It remains simpler for gay people to refrain from advertising their sexual orientation in situations where it isn't relevant. The "relevancy" issue is a way to solve this complex problem. The whole question of sexual orientation should be ignored. The way to end the official ban on homosexuals in the military is to stop asking people about their sexual preferences and stop treating private, off-duty homosexual behavior as a dischargable offense.

Don't ask, don't tell, don't investigate, don't discharge.

THE SAGINAW NEWS
Saginaw, Michigan, February 4, 1992

As the debate goes on – we refer you to the pro-con discussion on this page – it's evident a lot of critics of the critics of the gays-in-the-military drive are the ones who just don't get it.

That's only natural, since many can cite no personal experience in a boot camp or a barracks. (Dorms don't count.)

Their most common comparison is with the racial discrimination issue of decades ago. That is superficial, if not bogus.

To repeat: Gays can and do serve well in the military. The generals and GIs all know it. As long as gay status does not interfere with duty, usually there's no problem, despite the bigotry that does exist in the ranks. The president was right to stop the costly policy of hunting down gays who have otherwise broken no rules.

Open gayness, however, changes the proposition from human rights to sexual rights. Of course the military has regulations – sometimes poorly enforced – governing behavior. But male and female soldiers, for what used to be obvious reasons, do not live together. Now Bill Clinton wants to integrate third and fourth sexes, and that's a problem.

But a temporary one. The much-derided brass can solve it, given time to work out questions of privacy, assignment, harassment (of any kind).

The real ignorance was in the failure of the gung-ho integrationists to understand that the military is not generally trained in social experimentation, and to allow a period of adjustment.

THE SUN
Baltimore, Maryland, April 11, 1992

Sen. Sam Nunn has thrown himself on the gays-in-the-military grenade and, as one close follower of his committee's hearings has put it, "muffled" the issue. He has done that by bringing before the Senate Armed Services Committee some very scholarly — you might say boring — witnesses to testify about the proposal to lift the Pentagon's ban on homosexuals in the uniformed services.

Also, Chairman Nunn announced that the current temporary policy, worked out between him and the president in January, is "rather a good place to be, [and] it may be a pretty good place to end up." Their compromise has been called "don't ask, don't tell." It says that for now, military commanders won't ask new recruits or veterans about their sexual preferences, and gays in the military won't announce their orientation.

Senator Nunn apparently would accept as permanent a deal that was only meant to be temporary. But real compromise comes after, not before, all the arguments are heard.

Falling on a grenade is not the same thing as disabling one. The explosion hasn't occurred yet, but it is likely to come. One side sees this as *only* a civil rights issue and the other side sees it as *only* a unit-cohesion issue. As long as one side says all that matters is the best interest of an individual, and the other side says all that matters is the best interest of the group, there will be no closure.

The only possibility for a resolution that will not blow up into an acrimonious debate is to maximize individual rights without making it impossible for military units to carry out their missions — and to make it clear to all concerned that that has been done and that every avenue leading to an acceptable compromise has been explored.

It doesn't help to vilify every compromise suggestion offered in good faith — even the very dumb suggestions. President Clinton's assertion that he "wouldn't rule out" limiting some service assignments and units to non-gays was probably dumb, but it hardly justified some of the very harsh denunciations from both sides that followed.

Our own view, stated here before, is that flatly lifting the ban tomorrow probably would not impair the ability of the armed services to defend the nation's interests. But we will wait for all the returns to come in before deciding what we believe the general policy should be.

So should everybody else.

Clinton Endorses Eased Military Ban on Homosexuals

President Clinton July 19, 1993 announced that homosexuals could serve in the armed forces provided that they were discreet about their sexual orientation and did not engage in homosexual acts. Commanders were forbidden to investigate service people for homosexual behavior on suspicion or hearsay alone. However, personnel could be discharged if such behavior were proved. The policy modified an unqualified ban on homosexuals in the military that had stood for 50 years.

The policy, which the administration described as one of "don't ask, don't tell, don't pursue," was contained in a directive issued by Defense Secretary Les Aspin July 19. The directive was sent to the civilian secretaries of the armed services, and to Gen. Colin L. Powell, the chairman of the Joint Chiefs of Staff. The order was to take effect Oct. 1, the date of Powell's retirement.

Speaking to military officers at the National Defense University at Fort McNair, in Washington, D.C., Clinton called the policy an "honorable compromise" that struck a "sensible balance between the rights of the individual and the needs of our military." He admitted, however, that it was not a "perfect solution," nor was it "identical with some of my own goals." Any effort to remove the ban entirely, he said, would have been met with "certain and decisive reversal by the Congress, and the cause for which many have fought for years would be delayed, probably for years." He said, "On grounds of both principle and practicality, this is a major step forward."

With Clinton were Powell and the chiefs of the Army, Navy, Air Force, Marine Corps and Coast Guard. Powell said the heads of the services "fully, fully support" the new policy. Many senior officers, including Marine Corps Commandant Gen. Carl E. Mundy Jr., had opposed easing the ban during the debate about new rules.

Under the policy, applicants for military service would not be asked about their sexuality. A serviceman or servicewoman could associate with homosexuals, frequent gay bars, read gay publications and participate in rallies in civilian dress without fear of investigation or discharge. If challenged, service people who denied, sincerely or not, that they were homosexual would not be dismissed.

Commanders could start investigations into alleged homosexual conduct where there was credible information that homosexual acts had been committed. The initiation of an investigation required "a determination based on articulable facts, not just a belief or suspicion," Defense Department guidelines on the policy said. Homosexual conduct was defined as "a homosexual act, a statement that the member [of the military] is homosexual or bisexual, or a marriage or attempted marriage to someone of the same gender." An accusation by a third party that a service person was a homosexual was not grounds for official action.

Rep. Barney Frank (D, Mass.), an open homosexual who had advocated a total lifting of the military ban, July 19 said that the new measure "falls short of where I thought we would be." Thomas B. Stoddard, coordinator of the Campaign for Military Service, a grouping of homosexual rights organizations, said that Clinton had "acceded, without a fight, to the stereotypes of prejudices he himself had disparaged." Senator Sam Nunn (D, Ga.), chairman of the Senate Armed Services Committee, July 16 said that he would write into the 1993 military authorization bill a competing code on homosexuals in the military. Nunn was opposed to easing the ban.

Aspin and the Joint Chiefs of Staff July 20 appeared before the Senate Armed Services Committee to answer questions on the policy. Potential ambiguities in its interpretation surfaced in an exchange between Aspin and Nunn. Aspin said that a single admission of homosexuality would not be grounds for dismissal, citing a "totality of circumstances" clause in the guidelines.

St. Petersburg Times
St. Petersburg, Florida, July 20, 1993

President Clinton's original unconditional promise to end the ban on homosexuals in the military has become hopelessly bogged down in hypocrisy, political posturing and incomprehensible compromise. Don't ask? Don't tell? Don't pursue? At this point, the most sensible advice to the president and Congress might be: Don't bother.

No two politicians, military officers or judges seem to agree on all of the practical consequences of the policy the president announced Monday. However, they might all concur that the minor changes it would make in the armed services' treatment of homosexuals aren't worth nearly what the president has paid in political capital. Recruits would no longer be asked about their sexual orientation, but active-duty personnel would still find their behavior severely restricted, both on-duty and off-base. That's not what the president proposed last fall.

In any case, there's no reason to bother debating the details of the president's policy. Georgia Sen. Sam Nunn still intends to include a new congressional policy on homosexuals in the military in this year's defense authorization bill, and he has the votes to override the president's plan if necessary. For now, Nunn says he's reserving judgment on whether to mirror the Clinton proposal or replace it with an even more restrictive alternative

It's almost too easy to criticize the errors of timing and strategy that put the president in such an untenable position. He has only himself to blame for forcing this issue onto the national agenda in last year's campaign and in the first days of his presidency. As a result, an inexperienced White House handled the issue ineptly and allowed it to overshadow far more crucial priorities for much of the past six months.

Having created this unnecessary controversy for himself, though, the president could have moved beyond it more quickly and honorably by sticking to his original promise and daring opponents in Congress and the military to buck the commander in chief. Instead, the president comes away looking weak and irresolute on what should have been framed as a question of principle.

Now that so many government institutions have botched the opportunity to resolve this issue, it may finally move to the forum in which it belonged all along. The courts already have rejected most of the armed services' past policies that discriminated against women or ethnic or religious minorities. Homosexuals who wish to serve their country without being forced into a life of fear and subterfuge are sure to turn to the courts now to grant them the rights that the president, Congress and the military leadership continue to deny them.

THE DAILY OKLAHOMAN
Oklahoma City, Oklahoma, July 21, 1993

PRESIDENT Clinton will not be able to put the controversial issue of homosexuals in the military behind him with his "compromise" decision that hardly pleased anyone.

Despite acceptance by military service chiefs of the "don't ask, don't tell, don't pursue" policy, it will not set well with the troops. Gen. Colin Powell, an outspoken critic of lifting the ban on homosexuals in the armed forces, will not have to live with the new policy. He will retire as chairman of the Joint Chiefs Oct. 1, when the plan takes effect.

"Gay rights" groups that Clinton tried to please with his promise to end the ban reacted with predictable anger and scorn. Homosexual and civil liberties activists plan court challenges. Make no mistake: Clinton's policy is the first step in legitimization of homosexuality in the U.S. military.

Congress is likely to be the final arbiter in the dispute. Advocates of a more restrictive policy could overturn the Clinton compromise by writing regulations into law. Sen. Sam Nunn, D-Ga., a leading voice on military affairs, is a key to any legislative showdown.

The politically divisive issue remains unsettled after more than six months of bloodletting that detracted from Clinton's primary goal to improve the economy. The issue strained relations with Congress and deepened military resentment against a Vietnam war draft dodger.

To whatever extent he has damaged his presidency, he brought it all on himself.

AKRON BEACON JOURNAL
Akron, Ohio, July 21, 1993

If gay and lesbian leaders are upset with Bill Clinton and his compromise on homosexuals in the military, they have good reason. In the end, the policy of "don't ask, don't tell, don't pursue" asks gays who serve in the armed services to lie about their sexual status. That's a burden they should not have to carry.

Their real argument, however, is not with the president. He acknowledged that the policy is not "identical with some of my goals." He wanted to lift the ban on gays in the military as cleanly and swiftly as possible.

What gays face is a persistent unwillingness on the part of many military leaders, members of Congress and others to recognize reality, that gays serve now in the military, that they serve bravely and admirably, that gays who serve or wish to serve their country share more in common with their heterosexual colleagues than they do with the Sister Boom-Booms of the world.

The persistence of this denial could be seen in the reaction of Sen. Sam Nunn of Georgia. Following the president's announcement to, significantly enough, an audience of military officers, including the Joints Chiefs of Staff, the senator hinted that he may not be satisfied. At the very least, it would seem, he and his allies should wait to see whether the policy works.

For their part, gay and lesbian leaders, as angry as they may deservedly be, might take a moment to reflect as well. For all the disappointment, the policy does move things forward. Military service will be less onerous for homosexuals.

They will not "be asked or required to reveal their sexual orientation."

Unlike today's witch hunts, in which homosexuals are sought out and dismissed, there would be strict guidelines for pursuing those who engage in specific homosexual conduct. As ominous as that may seem, it also suggests a new zone of privacy for gay soldiers and sailors.

If there is honor in the compromise, it can be seen in Clinton's success in easing the burden, albeit slightly, on gays in the military. He seems to be arguing that while gays may not have achieved acceptance in the eyes of the law or the military code, they will, over time, gain it in actual fact, and that his policy will accelerate the pace of change.

This matter-of-time argument is the best Clinton could have accomplished. The swirl of events surrounding this issue involved far more than gays and the military. Clinton had to deal with his fragile relationship with the Pentagon, as well as with dubious elements of the Democratic Party's past and his own political persona as a "new Democrat."

Playing the many angles tested even the president's well-honed skills as a shaver and rounder of political sharp edges. The result is not satisfactory or fair to gays and lesbians. But neither is it a betrayal. The president grasped realities. Let's hope others can do the same.

San Francisco Chronicle
San Francisco, California, July 20, 1993

IT IS HARD to see where the honor lies in the "honorable compromise" that President Clinton has proclaimed for the gays-in-the-military controversy.

Unless one is willing to engage in semantic games of self-deception, the new policy appears to be little more than the old policy in drag: Homosexuality, per se, is no longer banned in the armed forces, but any outward manifestation of it — including public or even private acknowledgement — is grounds for discharge.

A temporary victory for deception and prejudice

Truth and personal integrity, qualities our society reveres, are henceforth declared to be incompatible with military service — at least for gays and lesbians.

Admittedly, the president found himself in a no-win situation when the Pentagon and its knee-jerk supporters in Congress reacted so hysterically to his original promise to completely lift the ban against gays and lesbians in the armed forces. Given that Congress would likely have over-ruled such an order, Clinton was right to seek a compromise that would temper the Joint Chiefs' anxieties while still respecting the rights of gays to serve their country in uniform.

A MORE GENEROUS version of the basic 'don't ask, don't tell" solution — one that did not infringe upon the private or personal lives of service members — might have met minimal standards of human decency while restricting any forms of behavior that might be disruptive to military life and morale.

Unfortunately, the Pentagon could not raise itself to such minimal standards, and by choosing such a restrictive compromise the president has elected to remain mired in the past with the Joint Chiefs. Better he had stood by his original instincts and risen to the challenge of principle, even if it meant seeing an enlightened policy go down to defeat.

What we have instead is a temporary victory for deception and prejudice — one that the president's own Justice Department will be hard-pressed to defend in the federal courts, where the issue will ultimately be settled.

Herald-American
Syracuse, New York, July 21, 1993

President Clinton is right when he says that his policy on homosexuals in the military, announced this week, "is not a perfect solution." It illustrates the ancient Aesop moral: Try to please everyone and you please no one.

Hardly anyone is happy with what Clinton is calling an "honorable compromise." Homosexuals and their allies don't think it goes far enough. Most members of the military brass and their supporters say it goes too far.

The new policy, which takes effect Oct. 1, orders the military to allow homosexuals to serve as long as they remain silent about their sexuality. It prohibits the military command from asking men and women in the ranks about their sexual orientation. It would make gays subject to discharge for engaging in homosexual activity, from holding hands to kissing and other sexual acts, whether they were on duty or not. But they would not be dismissed for going to gay bars, reading homosexual publications or marching in gay-rights parades.

This is a convoluted mess, but it is an improvement over current policy in one sense: It punishes behavior rather than sexual orientation. Still, the punishment is uneven. Inappropriate sexual behavior of any kind — homosexual or heterosexual — should be proscribed with the same kind of vigor. Private activity between consenting adults should be no one's business but theirs.

The "don't ask, don't tell" policy is as fundamentally hypocritical as what it replaces. It encourages people to lie — or at least not tell the truth — if they want to remain in honorable service of their country. Certainly the services' top commanders, who have lived under the terms of an honor code their whole careers, cannot in their hearts condone the dishonesty this policy inspires.

For Clinton, the compromise is a retreat from an explicit campaign promise to do away with the anti-gay policy. To be sure, he faced enormous political pressure to turn his back on that commitment. Obviously, he concluded that this was not the place to stand and fight, that this was the best deal he could get under the circumstances.

At its worst, the new policy nurtures the lie that homosexuals cannot fight for their country. It lends official credence to old homophobic hatreds and bigotry. Homosexuals have fought and died for their country, of course, at times when a lot of straight men were contriving ways to stay out of harm's way. And homosexuals will fight again, when their country needs them.

The compromise plan was a genuflection to Sam Nunn, the Georgia Democrat who is chairman of the Senate Armed Services Committee and self-anointed protector of morality in the military. It will be interesting to see if Nunn backs away from what appears to be a calculated campaign to embarrass the president or goes ahead with plans to introduce anti-gay legislation in Congress.

This might have been a good place for Clinton to challenge Nunn head-on. The president is not without authoritative allies in the effort to remove the ban on homosexuals in the military. For example, Sen. Barry Goldwater, R-Ariz., whose conservative and military credentials are impeccable, has said the ban should be lifted. So has Sen. Bob Kerrey, D-Neb., who won the Medal of Honor for heroism during the Vietnam war.

The debate over gays in the military will not end with this compromise. It will continue for the foreseeable future, bitterly dividing the country. Of course, that would have been the result no matter what Clinton had decided.

Maybe someday Americans can get over this voyeuristic fascination with what other Americans do in the privacy of their own bedrooms. Maybe someday we'll judge a person's worthiness to do a job solely on the quality of the work they do. Clearly, we're not nearly there yet.

The Birmingham News
Birmingham, Alabama, July 21, 1993

All sound and fury, signifying not a whole lot.

People who react that way to Bill Clinton's faltering attempt to alter military policy toward gays would be correct.

Before it started, gays could not be admitted to the military if they said they were gay. Now, no one will ask. Instead, military personnel will be judged on their actions.

That's a logical step. Every American able to serve the military who will abide by its rules should be given a chance to do so. But this is hardly a policy declaration on the same plane with the Monroe Doctrine.

On another level, the exercise was more revealing. Arkansas columnist Paul Greenberg describes our society as a "condomized culture," in which the belief is that all societal problems, from AIDS to teen pregnancy, can be solved simply with a prophylactic.

The reaction that greeted Clinton's original, fiesty announcement of his more radical change in the status of gays in the military was condom counterculture.

Sure, there were people who objected because of irrational prejudices against gays. But there also were people who genuinely worried how this would impact logistics, military efficiency, corps unity.

Many who opposed it reacted from a gnawing feeling in the gut.

They don't want people discriminated against. Yet to go past that, to say that a gay lifestyle is something their society should not just acknowledge or condone, but approve, was something they were not prepared to do.

As much as the specific issue of gays in the military, it had to do with the general and continuing chipping away at middle-American values by a sort of smirking elitism whose chief answer is: "There, there, you just don't understand."

It is the answer when figures arrive from the census bureau that say one quarter of the nation's single women will become mothers.

It is the answer to statistics that say while America's population has increased by 41 percent since 1960, its violent crime rate has gone up 650 percent.

It is the condescending answer to any number of real, live societal problems which have a real, live moral dimension.

On one level, the backlash was against gays. But on another, it came from people who had a gut reaction to the symbolism involved when their newly elected president dropped a promised middle-class tax cut without a whimper, but vowed to go to the mat on his promise to get gays into the military.

THE PLAIN DEALER
Cleveland, Ohio, July 22, 1993

President Bill Clinton has been teetering on a high wire of indecision ever since he vowed to get rid of the ban on gays in the military. So it's no wonder that when he finally came down the other day, his campaign promise had been shattered by the fall.

Left in its place was a "don't ask, don't tell" policy that gives the illusion of whisking away discrimination without significantly changing the lives of gays and lesbians in the military.

The "don't ask" part is fine: It takes sexual orientation out of the military's purview — at least during the application process. Yet there are other somewhat troubling features.

According to the directive, the military can't open gay service members' closets unless it sees dirty laundry dangling — like evidence of homosexual activity — either on or off the base. The zone of privacy, as Clinton called it, is zilch because gays or lesbians would have to be celibate or lie to keep their jobs.

The policy also approves trips to gay bars and participation in gay parades; however, if you admit you're gay, you must rebut the presumption that you're engaging in homosexual acts. That means more protestations of celibacy, or lying, to avoid discharge.

How did Clinton, who diligently wooed gays into his camp, end up tossing crumbs to his friends? As usual, he didn't look before he walked or talked.

In a case of candidacy-itis, Clinton made the grandest promises to the most constituents, including gays and lesbians. Clinton rashly decided to follow through on his promise to lift the military ban against gays as one of his first acts as president.

He chose an issue considered less important to gays than research and funding on AIDS, yet as crucial to military order as requiring privates to show deference to generals.

Clinton didn't anticipate the furor of the military brass, enlisted ranks and the general public; once opponents pounced on the proposal, he didn't explain his position well.

His administration didn't amplify the tale of Army Col. Margarethe Cammermeyer, a Bronze Star-decorated nurse drummed out because she admitted she is gay, or Jose Zuniga, a decorated Army sergeant dismissed for the same reason.

Cornered by the Joint Chiefs of Staff, who opposed lifting the ban, Clinton accepted a compromise that won't change the status quo. Yet it was probably the best he could do with such tepid political salesmanship.

Ultimately, the issue of gays in the military may be decided by the courts; some have already rendered favorable decisions to gay servicemen and women who have been dismissed.

Congress shouldn't tamper with Clinton's policy. The political reality is that, given the way the president handled the matter, this was the best that could be done.

THE ATLANTA CONSTITUTION
Atlanta, Georgia, July 20, 1993

As a candidate for president, Bill Clinton promised to lift the ban on homosexuals serving in the military. He has since discovered that some things are beyond even the power of the president. He cannot order the Mississippi to return to its banks, and he cannot end the military's ban on homosexuals.

The country is not ready for that change.

The change will happen, in time, as the American people come to understand that judging others by their sexual orientation is just as wrong as judging them by their race, gender or creed. The divisive debate over gays in the military, painful though it is, has helped advance that day.

Meanwhile, President Clinton is trying to salvage something important. The policy announced Monday preserves the gay ban, but it brings some sanity and decency to the method by which the ban is enforced. It discourages the "witch hunts" that have wrecked lives and destroyed careers by requiring that investigations into alleged homosexuality be initiated only by high-ranking officers. In addition, such investigations can begin only after "credible evidence" of homosexuality has surfaced. Rumors alone would not suffice.

The fate of that policy now rests largely with U.S. Sen. Sam Nunn of Georgia. He fought hard to maintain the ban, and he has won that battle. He asked the president to consult carefully with military leaders, and President Clinton followed that advice. Monday's executive order has the input and support of Gen. Colin Powell and the Joint Chiefs of Staff, and is quite close to the "don't ask, don't tell" approach advocated by Mr. Nunn.

It's uncertain, however, whether Mr. Nunn will accept the Clinton attempt to limit investigations of suspected homosexuals. In a speech on the Senate floor last week, Mr. Nunn proposed to allow investigations "based upon any information," a standard that includes rumor and unfounded suspicion.

That's not acceptable. Gay personnel willing to be discreet about their sexual preference deserve the chance to serve their country without being dragged out of the closet against their will.

In promising to end the military ban on homosexuals, Mr. Clinton made a basic commitment to fight for gay Americans. They responded to that commitment with votes, hard work and money. As things have turned out, Mr. Clinton could not keep his promise. It is not within his power. However, he can still honor his commitment to fight.

General Powell calls Mr. Clinton's executive order "an honorable compromise." If the president's opponents try to remove the protection against witch hunts, if they refuse to allow him even that small, face-saving victory, Mr. Clinton has no choice but to fight.

He must be ready to stand with those who stood with him.

-Sen. Sam Nunn

The New York Times
New York City, New York, July 28, 1993

Among the gay-bashing referendums on state and local ballots last fall, Colorado's was one of the most sweeping and punitive. Voters amended the State Constitution to forbid both state and local governments from enacting any laws protecting gay men and lesbians from discrimination. Last week the Colorado Supreme Court, in a creative and thoughtful opinion, struck down the measure as unconstitutional.

The state court, by recognizing that the measure's main vice was a form of disfranchisement for a targeted group of Americans, may have found a constitutional antidote for the political poison of gay-hating campaigners. The decision's reasoning could apply equally well to similar ballot maneuvers afoot in other states.

Colorado's referendum avoided the blatant insults of Oregon's defeated measure, which condemned gay life styles as "abnormal" and "perverse." But it did something worse, as the state court saw clearly: It denied a defined group of citizens — homosexuals — the fundamental right to participate equally in the political process. That right, discernible in a series of U.S. Supreme Court decisions, blends First Amendment rights of political activity and association with the 14th Amendment's guarantee of equal protection.

Identifying this right is useful in two ways. For one, it avoids a tangle over the status of homosexuals, which some argue — and others deny — is so oppressed as to deserve the kind of special constitutional protection blacks enjoy. This ruling simply says that no identifiable group, including homosexuals, may be treated this way by state legal action.

The ruling also identifies the political abuse that would occur if the courts lifted their injunction against the new provision. The measure approved by Colorado voters does much more than deny "special rights" for homosexuals; it repeals the rights they've won politically in cities and towns, and it prevents them from even trying to argue for their interests in state and local legislatures.

In short, homosexuals in Colorado are made political nonpersons. That's an injury far worse than being officially insulted as "perverse" and "abnormal" — since the Colorado provision would prevent homosexuals from trying to achieve fair treatment under the law.

Colorado state officials may petition the U.S. Supreme Court, but the case has not yet been tried and so might not be ripe for review. A sounder official response would be to go to trial. Better still, the state should simply drop the case. Gay people have been on the defensive too long.

copyright © The New York Times 1993

THE SPOKESMAN-REVIEW
Spokane, Washington, July 21, 1993

Well, now that we've determined President Clinton doesn't keep promises, lacks backbone and shrinks from issuing orders his troops dislike, where do we go from here?

His new policy on homosexuals in the military is not, in and of itself, among the nation's most important issues.

But it does tell us something about the president's ability to lead.

Back in the heady days of the campaign, when George Bush and Ross Perot were making Clinton look good by comparison, the president-to-be promised he'd lift the military's ban on homosexuals.

It won him votes among a small section of the electorate. It sounded tolerant, a virtue to a country struggling uncomfortably to coexist with its diversity. It was a clear-cut proposition, requiring nothing more than an order from the commander in chief.

But when Clinton took office, he got the willies.

The military didn't want to change its policy. Congress proved less than enthusiastic as well. And mainstream Americans, uncomfortable with both extremes in the raucous debate over gay rights, fretting over a growing awareness of eroded values, were struggling over how to tolerate a lifestyle of which most disapprove.

What the issue required was leadership. What the nation got was useless mush.

Clinton's new policy permits homosexuals in the military, but only if they keep their orientation secret.

The Joint Chiefs of Staff pronounced themselves pleased. With what? With preventing the president from issuing an order they didn't want to follow?

Whatever the brass hats may think, pity the people further down in the ranks who'd prefer just to get their jobs done but somehow must comply with the pretense and contortions of don't-ask-don't-tell — knowing lawyers lie in wait to second-guess whatever they do.

Indeed, lawyers may be the only ones to profit from the new policy. The courts, heaven help us, now will attempt to settle what Clinton didn't.

The president's policy does gays no favors and it certainly didn't please them.

Its mealy-mouthed mixture of tolerance with intolerance stands no chance of satisfying moral conservatives.

Worse, it made the president of the United States, who has many more difficult and consequential problems to solve, look hopelessly weak. And to think Clinton did all this in an effort to avoid conflict and make people happy! May he discover, soon, the moral courage leadership requires.

The Chattanooga Times
Chattanooga, Tennessee, July 19, 1993

Whatever policy President Clinton unveils this week on gays in the military is likely to be the kind of compromise that will draw attack from all sides. It's also likely to be the first step toward eventual fulfillment of his campaign promise.

The promise, of course, was to eliminate the ban on homosexuals serving in the military. But the tidal wave of controversy that broke over the White House when it appeared Mr. Clinton might actually do that caused the president to back off in January. Since then he's been looking for some way to ease into what will be a radical change in the military culture.

It won't be a radical change in the military itself, because it is now beyond any argument that gays do and have long served admirably in uniform. But that service has been rendered within an institution steeped in hostility toward homosexuals, and that institution is profoundly resistant to abandoning this imbedded prejudice.

Since debate on this issue began in earnest, however, more and more current and former homosexual members of the armed services have come out of the closet. The facts of their lives have disproved the official argument that "homosexuality is incompatible with military service."

That policy language cannot be retained in any compromise worth making. But it's no secret the Pentagon has fought hard to hold on to it, even under a new we-don't-want-to-know-if-you're-gay rule. That simply underscores the difficulty of the adjustment ahead.

Compromise on gay service is being forced upon the military. Opposition to it runs deep, up and down the chain of command. It will be overcome only through a combination of insistent leadership and time.

Whether officers who are themselves opposed to change can rise to the demand for such leadership will be a true test of military discipline. It's one we believe will be met, at least over time.

There was resistance to change when the issue was race, as well, but the U.S. military is now the shining example in this society of a truly integrated institution. It didn't happen in a day.

Neither will discrimination against gays in the military be done away with by the stroke of a presidential pen. Gay rights activists don't like having to accept a compromise solution when they thought they could count on an outright win.

But a properly crafted compromise can be a steppingstone to further progress. Had Mr. Clinton lifted the ban on gays in the military by executive order, it might have been a sweet victory, but it would have been short-lived. Congress would have restored the ban by law, making obstacles to change more formidable than before.

Mr. Clinton was right to seek a workable middle ground, but the search has covered difficult ground, including critical constitutional issues. Such issues account for the delay in Mr. Clinton's announcement of the first step he will take. But he has clearly defined the direction in which it will lead: toward the proper goal of equal treatment for all Americans who desire to serve their nation in uniform.

THE LINCOLN STAR
Lincoln, Nebraska, July 21, 1993

President Clinton's newly announced compromise policy on homosexuals in the military is barely better than the current policy of kicking out all known homosexuals.

(Actually homosexual members of the Armed Forces are less likely to be dismissed in actual war times when there is a greater need for every body in uniform.)

The new policy is an anorexic compromise, thin on reason.

The ban would apparently allow a person in the service to acknowledge his or her sexual orientation, but would not allow them to live that orientation, except deceptively.

Gays and lesbians apparently will be able to go to a gay bar and pick up one-night stands (however discreetly) but not live openly with a long-term, loving partner.

This is a half-measure that gains little. It does not free the homosexual members of the armed services from the fear of dismissal. It does not force the military to deal internally with its stereotypes and homophobia.

THE BEST POLICY is one which acknowledges sexual orientation and treats the sexual activity of both homosexuals and heterosexuals equally.

The most reasonable policy would simply accept everyone (regardless of sexual orientation) who can satisfy the other requirements. It would also require all people in the military to maintain certain standards of behavior that are essential in the workplace.

Neither homosexual nor heterosexual members of the Armed Services should be able to solicit sex by intimidation, sexually harass or rape.

Sen. Bob Kerrey, who early in this debate believed that homosexuals should be allowed in the military but not in combat, has been persuaded to abandon his military mind set.

Kerrey was particularly swayed by the testimony of Col. Fred Peck, a 27-year veteran of the U.S. Marine Corps, who in a presentation before th Armed Services committee talked about the fact that his own son was homosexual. He discovered his son's orientation only a few days earlier.

However Col. Peck said he still believed the ban should remain.

"BUT WHY did he not want his son to be in there?" said Kerrey in explaining his change of heart.

"Was it unit cohesion? Was it the morale of the fighting forces of the U.S. Marine Corps? No. He said he was afraid of his son's life; that maybe he would be beaten up, maybe he would be hurt."

"I must tell you in that moment, I said: 'Time out.' It is time for the military to change. It is one thing to say you are concerned about the fighting spirit of our forces. It is quite another to say that somehow you are afraid that your son might not survive the organization."

Kerrey said he believes the capacity for tolerance inside our armed forces is much higher that we now perceive. He also believes that the quality most important to add to unit cohesion is reliability.

"When the bullets start, will the individual retreat, will they freeze up? Are they someone upon whom you depend? Will they lay down their life for you, if necessary? These are the values that are important."

THE ARIZONA REPUBLIC
Phoenix, Arizona, July 17, 1993

DEFENSE Secretary Les Aspin did his boss no favors when he recommended this week that homosexuals be allowed to serve in the military only if they abstain from making public declarations of their sexual orientation.

Far from being a step forward in resolving the gays-in-the-military flap, this "don't ask, don't tell" approach threatens to perpetuate, rather than dispel, bias and ugly stereotyping. It also promises to only exacerbate President Clinton's political troubles over the issue.

Like the military's existing ban on gays, the proposed policy focuses on labels rather than conduct. In doing so, it suggests a different standard than is applied to any other population.

Clearly, expressions of homosexual conduct should be banned from the military. In fact, expressions of sexual conduct of any kind are inappropriate in a military setting. But the ban should use behavior as its ruler, not whether someone says in public what he thinks about sex. Such a policy would open the door to blackmail of soldiers.

Indeed, the only difference between this policy and the one it would replace is that military brass would be barred from asking soldiers or sailors point-blank about their sexual orientation. The label "homosexual" could still be grounds for discharge, because the issue had somehow come to the attention of the soldier's commanding officer, even if he had an otherwise exemplary military record.

Thus, homosexuals would be permitted in the military only if nobody knew they were homosexuals. Passing this off as progress over the existing ban on gays is like calling day-old grape juice aged wine.

It is possible that word of Aspin's proposal is simply another example of Clinton's unfortunate obsession with government by trial balloon. Variations of this proposal were being leaked yesterday afternoon, along with the word that Clinton was close to announcing the policy. If he pulls back this hat with arrows in it, he may hold off for a while.

It is a dicey issue for the president, to be sure, both substantively and politically. But it is so by his own making. Clinton is the one, after all, who stumped for office on the promise of repealing the military's ban on homosexuals and then, upon being sworn into office, allowed the issue to explode in his face.

The president would be wise to start focusing on a real solution to this problem, rather than on a problem-in-the-making that masquerades as a solution.

The Oregonian
Portland, Oregon, July 21, 1993

President Clinton's new policy on gays in the military is not much different from the "Don't ask, don't tell" policy widely discussed for months.

Ideally, gays and lesbians in the armed forces should be judged on how they do their jobs and how they conduct themselves among their colleagues — not on what they do in private. Clinton's policy falls short of meeting that standard of fairness.

But given congressional and Joint Chiefs of Staff opposition to anything more sweeping, this was probably the best Clinton could do now. He deserves credit for starting the process toward equality after 50 years of military paranoia against homosexuals.

One step forward is that the policy moves away from punishing sexual orientation per se and would punish prohibited homosexual conduct instead. That's a small distinction, but one that heads in the right direction.

The policy also makes commanding officers directly responsible for any decisions to launch investigations of homosexual conduct and sets broad standards for what constitutes reasonable grounds for investigations.

But it wrongly continues to treat gays, lesbians and bisexuals differently from heterosexuals by banning all homosexual acts, private or public, on base or off.

Military recruiters are barred from asking enlistees their sexual orientations, continuing the "Don't ask" policy that has been in effect on an interim basis since Jan. 29.

Homosexual conduct will be punishable by discharge from the service. Among manifestations of prohibited conduct are holding hands with or kissing a member of the same sex or making any statement "that demonstrates a propensity or intent to engage in homosexual acts." That means don't tell.

On the other hand, "association with known homosexuals, presence at a gay bar, possessing or reading homosexual publications or marching in a gay rights rally in civilian clothes will not, in and of themselves, constitute credible information that would provide a basis for initiating an investigation or serve as the basis for an administrative discharge under this policy."

Reasonable observers might consider such activities just different ways of telling.

So making this policy work will depend on clear direction from the top and on the honesty and integrity of commanding officers, who must carry it out fairly and even-handedly. Any commanders who don't should be held fully accountable.

The armed forces did themselves proud when they integrated, reluctantly and under pressure, after 1948. They have done themselves proud in opening up more opportunities for women in recent years. They should do the same for gays and lesbians

The Wichita Eagle-Beacon
Wichita, Kansas, July 21, 1993

To the folks who hate President Clinton's gays-in-the-military order, handed down Monday, either because it doesn't go far enough or because it goes too far: Welcome to democracy.

The order bars the armed services from asking recruits about sexual orientation and from investigating military men and women suspected of being homosexual. And it threatens homosexual military men and women who reveal their sexual orientation with forced discharge.

Critics in the gay and anti-gay communities decry the decision as institutionalized hypocrisy. Both sides have a point — if they insist upon looking at this issue in absolutist terms.

Homophobes believe that the military should continue to leave no stone unturned in pursuit of soldiers, sailors, airmen and Marines who are homosexual or are suspected of having homosexual tendencies. And the gay community believes that homosexual servicemen and women should suffer no penalty should their sexual orientation become public knowledge.

Mr. Clinton's original proposal, of course, was to lift the gay ban entirely. But that stance inspired a fire storm of breast-beating homophobia in the upper echelons of the armed services and in Congress, the result of which likely would have been the codification of the military's anti-gay rules into federal law.

The "don't ask, don't tell" stance that the president ultimately adopted, then, is a compromise between these extreme positions. It's elicited some congressional grumbling, but seems unlikely to trigger a movement to codify the gay ban into law. And while it encourages gay servicemen and women to remain mum about their sexual orientation, it does ensure that they won't be asked improper personal questions when they enlist in the military, and that they won't be harassed by internal investigators once they're on active duty.

Moreover, the order makes good sense from a military-discipline perspective. Sex is a personal matter. Public displays of affection — whether heterosexual or homosexual in nature — are improper in any military setting, as are sexual advances. Mr. Clinton's order ensures that the worst fears about disruption of military discipline won't become a problem.

The order likely will satisfy no one who's taken an interest in this issue. But that's often the way it is in a democracy. To get a deal, everyone has to back away from his or her original position a little bit. This particular deal is a good one, and Mr. Clinton was right to strike it. Now it's time to lay this issue to rest.

Boston Herald
Boston, Massachusetts, July 17, 1993

Safe bet: Whatever President Clinton ultimately decides on the touchy subject of gays in the military, he'll make enemies.

The best he can hope for at this point is that a firm policy decision on his part will at long last put this tangential but emotional issue to rest.

Clinton spent far too much early political capital wrestling with this. That didn't do him, the nation, or those urging an end to the ban on homosexuals any good.

On his desk now is the report he requested from Defense Secretary Les Aspin. It is reported to stake out a compromise along the lines of the "don't ask, don't tell" proposal offered by Senate Armed Services Committee Chairman Sam Nunn earlier this year.

While Clinton has put off until next week any announcement of his final order, the course he should follow is clear:

● Make permanent the policy imposed several months back, which prohibits the military from asking about a recruit's sexual preference.

● Change the Pentagon's policy statement that "homosexuality is incompatible with military services," perhaps replacing it with a more accurate reference to homosexual *conduct*. The honorable service in uniform of any number of homosexual men and women — who only later in their lives identified themselves as such — long ago disproved that phrase.

● Continue to forbid any display of homosexual behavior while on base, or duty, or in uniform.

Gay activists are blasting the Aspin recommendation as discrimination. It is hardly the only kind of discrimination the military imposes, especially on conduct. Ours is a volunteer army; no one is forced to become a soldier. The job can be physically and emotionally demanding. Its efficient operation requires a level of discipline most of us would never tolerate in a civilian setting.

Aspin's report recognizes both that reality and the failures of past policy. It is likely to please few and anger zealots on both sides of the issue. In short, it represents a logical compromise.

Homosexual Sailor Reinstated in Navy

A sailor who had openly admitted to being a homosexual and who had been discharged from the Navy under its ban on gays Nov. 12, 1992 was reinstated in the service. He became the first among the hundreds of gays and lesbians fired from the armed forces each year to reclaim his job.

The sailor, Petty Officer 1st Class Keith Meinhold, was an instructor of airborne submarine detection at Moffet Field Naval Air Station in Mountain View, Calif. His legal odyssey had begun in May, when he disclosed his sexual orientation on the ABC television show "World News Tonight." He was subsequently reassigned as a computer programmer and then honorably discharged in August.

Meinhold, a 12-year veteran, sued for reinstatement in October. His lawyers argued that his discharge had violated the Constitution's guarantee of equal protection.

U.S. District Judge Terry J. Hatter Jr. of Los Angeles Nov. 6 ordered the Navy to give Meinhold his job back until the case was decided. (Experts said the case could be settled in one of three ways: a ruling in Hatter's court, a successful appeal by the Navy to a higher court, or a lifting of the ban on homosexuals, as had been promised by President-elect Bill Clinton.)

"The Navy has shown no rational relationship between the regulation and its purported objective," Hatter said in his ruling. "The Navy will suffer no hardship through reinstatement of Meinhold since he is, by the Navy's own admission, one of their finest airborne sonar analysts."

When Meinhold reported for duty at Moffet Nov. 9, his superiors told him that they were not authorized to reinstate him and made him leave.

The move elicited an angry response from Hatter Nov. 10. He reaffirmed his injunction and threatened to prohibit the Navy from filing further motions in the case if it refused to comply with his order. "This is not a military dictatorship," he said. "It is not the former Soviet socialist republic. Here, the rule of law applies to the military."

The Navy Nov. 10 issued a one-sentence statement saying it would heed the order. Meinhold returned to Moffet Nov. 12, and this time was sworn back in.

Hatter Nov. 16 rejected another legal attempt by the Navy to keep the sailor out. However, in an affidavit filed with the judge the same day, Meinhold said he had not been allowed to resume his post as a sonar analyst.

The Daily Gazette
Schenectady, New York, November 19, 1992

Keeping homosexual men and women out of the armed forces, and expelling those already in, has been something of an obsession with the Pentagon. It spent millions of dollars over the past decade to investigate and dismiss more than 17,000 homosexual servicemen and women.

Bill Clinton has wisely challenged this irrational policy. On his very first public appearance as president-elect on Veteran's Day, Clinton set a reasonable and practical criterion for selecting men and women in uniform. The determining factor, he said, ought to be conduct. Instead of examining the private lives of service personnel, the military should be asking, as Clinton put it, "Has anyone done anything which should disqualify them?"

Precisely. If the military were to base its judgment on sexual conduct instead of sexual orientation, it would begin by disciplining all those Navy officers who mauled their female colleagues at the Tailhook convention earlier this year. On the acid test of conduct, the military should dismiss those officers who abuse their power to demand sexual favors from their subordinates, a practice that is obviously more harmful to the morale of the force than homosexuality in the ranks.

Judging by conduct, the military should be cherishing its homosexual servicemen and women. Most of them are hard-working and law-abiding, and many have distinguished records of bravery on the battlefield.

Although the military's top officials, including Gen. Colin Powell, chairman of the Joint Chiefs of Staff, remain adamantly opposed to the idea of gays wearing uniforms, their objections are unfounded. Indeed, a study commissioned by the Pentagon found that the age-old fear of gays being a bigger security risk is bogus: Gay servicemen were found to be no more susceptible to blackmail by the enemy than their heterosexual counterparts.

The Pentagon's other objections boil down to privacy. The presence of gays, the argument goes, will create problems for others who may feel uncomfortable sharing showers and living quarters with them.

This assumes that gay soldiers won't be able to control their sexual desire for their "straight" colleagues. But evidence from the armed forces of other NATO countries shows that gay soldiers don't behave any less professionally than their heterosexual counterparts when it comes to keeping emotions and work apart. The United States and Britain are the only two members of NATO that bar gays from the military.

Bill Clinton has asked the right question. One hopes that it will soon lead to a military that judges its members by their professional abilities rather than their choice of sexual partners.

The Oregonian
Portland, Oregon, November 21, 1992

President-elect Bill Clinton has pledged to lift the military's ban on homosexuals. So what sense does it make for the Naval Reserve Officers Training Corps to adopt a harsh new policy now against homosexual midshipmen?

The policy requires students in officer-training programs to sign affidavits that say they can be discharged and forced to repay scholarships if they are found to be homosexuals. The average cost to train an ROTC midshipman is about $53,000.

A form used for years by the Army and Air Force asks ROTC students whether they ever have or currently engage in homosexual activity. While the services occasionally demand that a discharged homosexual ROTC student or academy cadet repay a scholarship, legal experts believe none of the armed services has successfully forced repayment.

The Naval policy attempts to make such recoupment easier.

The heart of this problem, of course, lies in the military's 48-year-old ban on homosexuals. That policy is based on inaccurate stereotypes about homosexuals. It should be replaced with rules that instead target sexual misconduct, both homosexual and heterosexual.

The days are numbered for this discriminatory ban. While waiting for Clinton to take office, the Navy should back off this new effort to punish homosexuals.

AKRON BEACON JOURNAL
Akron, Ohio, November 16, 1992

Bill Clinton seems to understand well the difficulty many in the American military will have if, in one of his first steps as president, he lifts the ban on homosexuals in the armed services. None other than Gen. Colin Powell, the chairman of the Joint Chiefs of Staff, has said that removing the ban would be "prejudicial to good order and discipline."

And yet, as sensitive as Clinton is to the concerns of the military, he also appears determined to keep his campaign pledge. And he should be commended. Those who wish to serve their country, professionally and honorably, should not deprived of that opportunity because of their sexual preference.

For many, the change will not be easy, just as it was hard for those in earlier times to accept blacks and then women in the military. But in each of those instances, stereotypes faded, prejudices crumbled, and the armed services flourished.

So is it likely to be the case with gays. Already the Pentagon's own studies have found that homosexuals are no more susceptible to blackmail, and thus, a security risk, than other soldiers. In June, a General Accounting Office study concluded that the ban on homosexuals costs the military $27 million a year in needless investigations, since the policy is unsupported by science or sociology.

Of the NATO countries, only the United States and Great Britain maintain a strict policy of excluding homosexuals from their armed forces.

Gays and lesbians are quick to point out that thousands of homosexuals already serve in the military. And while some may say, fine, but that doesn't mean the ban should be lifted, gays and lesbians rightly respond that they shouldn't have to serve under such a burden, vulnerable to dismissal not because of their performance but because of their sexual orientation.

Frankly, in this age of Madonna, Calvin Klein ads and sundry other examples of sexuality on parade, we join those who wish for a refreshing measure of discretion. At the same time, given the current cultural climate, we find it hard to believe that Americans aren't prepared to accept homosexuals in the military; indeed, polls show that a majority is.

If a homosexual or heterosexual soldier violates the rules, jeopardizing morale and discipline, there should be no reason that he or she shouldn't be tossed out. In the end, however, the Pentagon should have little concern for what is a matter of privacy, a person's sexual preference, as long as it does not interfere with the military's mission.

We suspect that once the controversy passes, the armed services will encounter far less disruption than some expect, and the country will have the benefit of men and women ready to serve, bravely and ably.

THE SPOKESMAN-REVIEW
Spokane, Washington, November 18, 1992

The U.S. military's ban on homosexuals is an exercise in hypocrisy. Everyone in uniform, from Gen. Colin Powell down to the lowliest private, knows it.

Ban or no ban, thousands of gay and lesbian members serve in the armed forces and serve ably. As long as they lie successfully about it, the Pentagon is pleased to make use of their skills. If they have the courage and honesty to identify themselves — as Navy Petty Officer Keith Meinhold and National Guard Col. Margarethe Cammermeyer have done — they sacrifice their careers.

Both Meinhold and Cammermeyer were forced out of the service despite having served honorably. Last spring, the Army insisted that the Washington National Guard discharge Cammermeyer, a decorated senior officer with more than a quarter-century of distinguished service. The Navy discharged Meinhold in August, but he is fighting the order in court.

Between the courts (a federal judge in Los Angeles ordered the Navy to restore Meinhold to duty pending the outcome of his case) and President-elect Bill Clinton (he has said he'll end the ban), it no longer is a case of whether this narrow-minded policy will end, but when. When that does occur, the biggest beneficiary won't be Meinhold or Cammermeyer or any other individual who has suffered similar discrimination. It will be the nation which needs the most capable service members it can get — a nation, by the way, which embraces individual liberty as a core value.

Interestingly, Washington National Guard leaders who knew Cammermeyer and respected her professionalism expressed deep regret at having to carry out the Army's directive to discharge her. In the Pentagon, however, top brass including Powell, chairman of the Joint Chiefs of Staff, cling to the specious argument that a change in current policy would weaken troop morale and violate individual service members' expectations of privacy.

Authorities should deal promptly, firmly and justly with sexual misconduct, whether gay or straight. The military justice system is amply prepared to do so if it has the will (which wasn't altogether clear in the way the Navy handled the shameful Tailhook scandal).

But the focus should be on the behavior, not on the individual's private lifestyle choices.

Under existing policy, the Defense Department is arbitrarily and foolishly depriving itself of the full range of talent it could draw from. The sooner the policy changes, the better served the nation will be.

THE PLAIN DEALER
Cleveland, Ohio, November 16, 1992

Another barrier of social prejudice is about to fall: In early 1993, the Pentagon will be ordered to end its policy of banning homosexuals from serving in uniform. Many traditionalists understandably (if narrow-mindedly) balk at accepting gays and lesbians in the ranks. But last week, both a federal court and the incoming Clinton administration signaled that the armed forces must soon adopt a non-discriminatory personnel policy.

Removing the ban is long overdue, for the anti-gay policy has proven both unworkable and unenforceable. Tens of thousands of homosexuals already serve in uniform, according to the Pentagon, without any apparent shortage of career skills and without causing severe disruption to their comrades' morale. The approximately 1,500 homosexuals who are identified (and then expelled from the ranks) each year are believed to be only a small number of those who are actually enlisted.

Moreover, several independent and Pentagon-sponsored studies have refuted the notion that homosexuals might have a higher risk of undisciplined conduct or vulnerability to blackmail. Indeed, the half-century-old restriction has never applied to civilians in the Pentagon (where the risk of falling prey to espionage may be greatest) but only to uniformed personnel.

Despite traditionalists' complaints, the World War II-era policy seems doomed. Last week, a federal court ordered the reinstatement of Navy petty officer Keith Meinhold, 30, who had been given an honorable discharge after he admitted his homosexuality. In a Veterans Day news conference, President-elect Bill Clinton reiterated his promise to issue an executive order forbidding the use of sexual preference as a criterion for service. Clinton asserts that misconduct, not merely sexual orientation, should be grounds for discharge.

Sensibly, however, Clinton says he will not rush to impose a new policy, preferring to work with military leaders to design a program to ease the transition. That task will not be easy: The armed forces are bound to suffer some morale problems as their culture is challenged.

Just as it took years of training and discipline to help the military break down another barrier of social prejudice — the racial segregation that was enforced in the armed forces until 1948 — it may require a long phase-in period before the Pentagon gets used to the idea of having gays in uniform. But ridding the military of this form of discrimination will help reduce prejudice in other areas, both in civilian and military life, reinforcing a message of social tolerance

The Miami Herald
Miami, Florida, November 17, 1992

THIS PAST Veterans Day was unlike any before, at least in one respect: Gay members of the U.S. armed forces — estimated in the dozens of thousands — received an open and unequivocal pat on the back from their future commander in chief, Bill Clinton.

Forget Mr. Clinton's draft status as a source of controversy. Cast aside, for the moment, his hotly contested plan to reduce Pentagon resources. Mr. Clinton's first, and hottest, controversy in military affairs will surely be his simple proposal to do what's merely fair and honest: permit homosexuals to come out of the barracks' closets and claim credit for the honorable service that they are already rendering.

Whatever your view on this emotionally-charged issue, you have to hand it to Mr. Clinton for addressing it with courage and plainness. He'll open his ears, he pledges, to whatever reservations the top brass hold about it. But he's then determined to issue an executive order lifting the ban that for 50 years has kept gays in a useless and hateful dilemma: either conceal their sexual inclinations or face instant discharge.

Still, Mr. Clinton must be careful not to let his eagerness impede his ability to do right. Recent polls indicate that the military may be intellectually ready to welcome gays. But at the level of morale and emotion, they still need reassurances that the new way of tolerance is better than the old way of prejudice.

In this context, providing reassurance means educating otherwise reasonable people about the proper role of sexuality in military life. For instance, service people need to be wary of sexual harassment both from peers and from superiors. But they should also be aware that sexual harassment is no more prevalent among homosexuals than among heterosexuals.

The question of whether gay and straight members of the military can serve together is moot: They have been doing just that from time out of mind, and with great success. Any social group, though, is wary of change and disinclined to admit its own injustices. The armed forces are no exception. Mr. Clinton's challenge will be to open their eyes, through education and persuasion and not just by decree, to the grave injustice that gay service people have suffered far too long.

Newsday
New York City, New York, November 17, 1992

President-elect Bill Clinton had his priorities exactly right yesterday on his longstanding commitment to lift the ban against gays in the military: He told a news conference he wants "to firmly proceed . . . after consulting with military leaders," but right now he has no timetable for issuing an executive order on the subject.

The message was that the future commander in chief has made a policy decision that he expects to be carried out in due course. But meanwhile there's still time to persuade at least some opponents of the policy change and to work out "a very strict code of conduct" that should meet some of the objections they raise.

Whether acknowledged homosexuals should be able to serve in the military certainly isn't the most critical issue Clinton will face in his first months as president. But he can't afford to back away from his commitment now that Senate Minority Leader Bob Dole (R-Kan.) has warned that Congress might prevent him from carrying it out.

Clinton should consult with Congress, of course — just as he should with the Joint Chiefs of Staff and other top military leaders. He should listen to their advice and take steps to head off some of the problems this change of policy is bound to create. He should carefully weigh the political disadvantages of a move that will inevitably be derided in Republican circles as a sop to a Democratic special-interest constituency.

A new president with a policy he believes in and the power to effect it by executive order mustn't allow himself to be intimidated by congressional opposition. But timing is important. There's no sense in Clinton hitting this issue so hard now that it impairs his ability to push more important legislation through Congress.

The fact is that the problems created by acknowledged gays in the armed forces won't be much different from those raised by women in the armed forces. In both cases the real issue is whether sexual behavior — as opposed to sexual orientation — will be prejudicial to good order and discipline. Experience with women and *un*acknowledged gays powerfully argues that it need not be. Clinton should implement his policy change with all deliberate speed.

The Virginian-Pilot
Norfolk, Virginia, November 29, 1992

The fears which the military, from the brass on down, are expressing about accepting homosexuals in their midst may well be exaggerated. Ten years hence, they may even seem silly. We hope so. Meantime, the straight Americans in the armed forces are due from President-elect Clinton the same reassurance as to strict enforcement and sensitive implementation that he has given homosexuals.

The crux of the Clinton policy — which we support — is that behavior, not sexual orientation, will be the standard of admission to and continued service in the military. And, in truth, if everybody behaves, who's to know whose orientation?

But, in truth, well-publicized heterosexual behavior — at a Tailhook convention, at Oceana, in Rota — isn't reassuring on that point; and well-publicized homosexual behavior in parades, in public parks and private bathhouses, in the promiscuity evidenced by the horrific toll of AIDS in the gay community, isn't either.

Most people *will* behave, as most people do. But those who don't behave could cause excessive trouble if not quickly curbed. Sooner or later the civilian and military authorities will have to sit down and define what behavior is disqualifying, and to what degree. Sooner is better. Gays and straights alike need to know, and ought to know, what the rules and penalties are, and that their superiors will enforce them.

Violence, for example, or physical intimidation is against the rules already. Will the penalties for violating that rule be the same for assaults regardless of gender or provocation? And what will the remedies, the attempts to deter repetition, be?

Sexual activity between different sexes, and between officers and enlisted, is currently banned. Presumably same-sex sexual activity will be likewise verboten. The penalties may be the same. The remedies may have to differ: Sailors of different sexes do not retire to the same bunks.

But short of physical violence and overt sexual activity, what are impermissible behaviors, and what will be the penalties and remedies for them?

Is an unwelcome homosexual advance in the machine shop, the berthing area, the showers a behavioral violation? Assume so. Then what is the penalty and what is the remedy? A reprimand and removal from the machine shop, the berthing area . . . the showers? Or something more? And how many advances, how many penalties before an offender is moved on out of the service?

Those aren't facetious questions. Like gays, straights fear intentional misinterpretations, false accusations, vengeances petty and otherwise, and untold subtle pressures. Some doubt their superiors' ability to withstand political pressure, inside the military and out, not to challenge gays' behavior or acknowledge adverse results lest they be accused of insensitivity or bigotry.

None of the anticipated problems is new, just an added layer upon the old. And though many fears come more from perception than experience, if unallayed they could become self-fulfilling prophecies. The armed forces, like the rest of society, have their gay bashers; they will reveal themselves and should be dealt with summarily. More difficult are those who have genuine misgivings about how dropping the ban against homosexuals will affect their daily lives and the readiness of the armed forces. Their concerns, too, deserve Mr. Clinton's attention.

10% OF THESE MEN WERE HOMOSEXUAL.

THE LINCOLN STAR
Lincoln, Nebraska, November 19, 1992

President-elect Clinton has brought the issue of homosexuals and lesbians in the military out of the closet. He has pledged to end the rule that bars them from serving their country.

This is not the most pressing problem Clinton faces upon assuming office in 1993. Becoming gridlocked with Congress and the joint chiefs would be an unhelpful event. But with a sensible, consultative plan, Clinton should end this unconstructive charade.

The United States doesn't have a person to waste, he said repeatedly in his campaign, calling for national unity on a number of issues.

Certainly there are few more wasteful procedures than the military's gay witch hunts. One Pentagon study said it costs taxpayers about $27 million annually to seek out, discharge and replace personnel. Many of these individuals had long and distinguished service records.

Certainly, there are few less sensible policies.

While it may be a minority of companies that are comfortable with openly gay employees, most workplaces are more concerned about actual behavior than preconceived stereotypes. Disruptive, unproductive individuals find themselves out of work. Few successful companies spend money to discharge otherwise good employees. Why should the military?

The military shouldn't tolerate disruptive behavior. Whether harassment and discrimination is directed at gays or at women, at blacks or at Jews, it is wrong and unacceptable. However, don't blame the victim.

We've seen all this before. President Harry S. Truman fought it in 1948 when he integrated blacks and whites in the armed forces. The argument then, as now, was that people who are different can't work together — differences destroy morale. That notion was wrong then and it's wrong now.

The irony, of course, is that homosexuals and lesbians have always served in the military. If Kinsey and others' statistics for the general population hold true in the military, then 10 to 15 percent are gay. Their jobs should not be in jeopardy for reasons having nothing to do with performance.

An old adage has it that there are no atheists in foxholes. The military may find that under fire, the differences which seemed so paramount among individuals will vanish before the reality that they're all wearing the same uniform.

THE ASHEVILLE CITIZEN
Asheville, North Carolina, November 27, 1992

No matter how much heat President-elect Bill Clinton gets from the military – or anyone else, for that matter – he should stick to his guns and make the military a true equal-opportunity employer.

Homosexuals have officially been excluded from military service for nearly 50 years. It's high time the ban was lifted.

In actuality, homosexuals have always served in the armed forces, most of them honorably and many of them heroically. They just had to keep their sexual preference a secret or get kicked out. And even if the ban is lifted, many will still choose to remain anonymous.

The president-elect's pledge to eliminate the exclusion has the military brass in an uproar. The issue may be the hottest one Clinton will face. Some high-ranking officers are threatening to resign if the barrier falls.

Even Gen. Colin L. Powell, chairman of the Joint Chiefs of Staff, is opposed on the grounds that admitting gays would undermine discipline and morale.

Some field and combat officers worry that having acknowledged homosexuals in a fighting force will complicate the task of training and bonding these units, which often operate in close, intimate conditions. Their concerns can't be dismissed out of hand, but neither can the fact that gays have fought and died for their country down through the years just like their heterosexual companions.

In testimony before Congress, Powell said: "It is difficult in a military setting, where there is no privacy, where you don't get choice of association, where you don't get choice of where you live, to introduce a group of individuals who are proud, brave, loyal, good Americans but who favor a homosexual lifestyle."

Begging the general's pardon, but weren't some of those same arguments put forth by people who opposed racial integration of the military? Of all people, Powell should realize the hypocrisy inherent in that attitude. Had President Harry Truman not rejected such speciousness and ordered an end to segregation in the armed forces, Powell, a black man, might never have had the opportunity to rise to the military's top post.

Powell and others who share his view ought to have more faith in the ability of officers and non-commissioned officers to keep order in the ranks. Every NATO country except the United States and Great Britain allows homosexuals to serve in the military, and they have not experienced a breakdown in discipline or morale.

Homosexuals should be treated just like anyone else in the armed services.

They should be held to the same rules of conduct and competence. If they break the rules governing sexual behavior, they should be disciplined in the same fashion as heterosexuals who ignore the rules – including dismissal. It shouldn't be difficult to establish rules that prohibit homosexual solicitations.

Clinton has said he will be circumspect in changing the policy toward gays. In that, he is wise. The groundwork must be laid first. The reasons for ending the ban must be thoroughly explained to the troops. Mandatory education programs similar to those aimed at ending racial bigotry must be put in place. Tolerance must be emphasized.

Just as the military has overcome prejudices against blacks and women, it can, with the right preparation and education, learn to accept homosexuals.

ST. LOUIS POST-DISPATCH
St. Louis, Missouri, November 15, 1992

At his first press conference as president-elect, Gov. Bill Clinton made an important distinction when he discussed his plan to end the military services' prohibition against homosexuals. The criterion for deciding whether to discharge otherwise qualified people should be behavior, not sexual preference, Mr. Clinton explained. Thus, heterosexuals and homosexuals would be judged on the same terms.

The president-elect made that point tellingly by citing the Tailhook scandal as an example of what he meant. Tailhook involved Navy fliers at a convention who forced women to walk a gauntlet, during which they were grabbed and fondled by the men. That sort of wildly heterosexual behavior is just as debilitating to morale and military discipline as overt homosexual conduct. Both deserve to be punished. What does not deserve punishment or justify discrimination is the fact of being homosexual.

With this distinction, Mr. Clinton will do a lot to promote tolerance in the military and the private sector. The country obviously needs a national leader who will set an example of tolerance and fairness. Oregon recently had a nasty, divisive fight over a ballot proposition that would have made outcasts of gays and lesbians. Fortunately, it was defeated. However, voters in Colorado adopted a measure prohibiting local governments from adopting ordinances that bar discrimination against homosexuals.

It is no coincidence that these two proposals showed up on the ballot when they did. Overt anti-gay action occurs not just when leaders encourage it but when they do nothing to discourage it. For the past 12 years the silence in Washington has sent its own message.

Mr. Clinton also promised to revise the Bush administration's heartless policy toward Haitian refugees, with a view toward softening the arbitrary distinction between political and economic refugees, and he said he would rescind the so-called gag rule, which prohibits workers at federally funded health clinics from mentioning the word abortion. The gag rule not only intrudes on the doctor-patient relationship but seeks to deny women access to information about a perfectly legal procedure.

Mr. Clinton's first post-election press conference was encouraging for several reasons, but none more than the clear message he sent about tolerance and compassion. It has been a long time since the presidency was used to provide strong moral leadership. All Americans have a right to be cheered by the prospect that this will be a kinder, gentler administration in fact as well as rhetoric.

TULSA WORLD
Tulsa, Oklahoma, November 28, 1992

BILL Clinton can be forgiven for temporizing awhile on his promise to remove the ban against gays and lesbians in the armed services.

As a campaign promise, the idea seemed harmless enough. It appealed to a militant special-interest group. No one else paid much attention. It is mindful of George Bush's Read-My-Lips tax promise of 1988 — easy to make at the time but tough to deliver.

The Clinton proposal has the almost unanimous opposition of admirals and generals. The political ramifications go far beyond the Pentagon.

The Wall Street Journal observes that any change favorable to gays will give the Christian Right a new weapon. Homosexual rights were an issue in Tuesday's senate race in Georgia. The Republican challenger, Paul Coverdell, defeated Sen. Wyche Fowler with the help of Pat Robertson's Christian Coalition. Robertson had vowed to distribute a million pamphlets declaring that Fowler was for homosexual rights and Coverdell was opposed.

Colorado voters recently approved, 54 to 46 percent, an amendment that prohibits legal claims of discrimination by homosexuals and rescinds anti-discrimination laws in three cities.

Clinton will probably keep his promise. His best bet is to remove the general ban against homosexuals while emphasizing that overt acts will continue to be outlawed. The standard would be conduct, not preference.

A change in the rules is not likely to change the numbers. The military admits that it already has thousands of homosexuals in its ranks. Under the new rules, they could come out of the closet.

Wisconsin State Journal
Madison, Wisconsin, November 15, 1992

President-elect Bill Clinton pledged last week he would work to end the ban on gays in the military. In a similiar vein, expect Clinton to disregard the recent recommendation that women should be excluded from combat roles in the U.S. armed forces.

Ending both bans is simply the right thing to do. Gay men, and women both straight and gay, have the same right and responsibility to fight for their country that heterosexual men do.

Most of the arguments leveled against allowing gays in any branch of the service and allowing women to serve in combat are old. They are the same arguments Harry Truman heard in the 1940s when he ordered the racial integration of the armed forces: Truman was told that white soldiers would not follow black officers. That white soldiers would refuse to bunk with black soldiers. That there was something inherently wrong with blacks that made them inferior to white soldiers, and that putting black soldiers into white units would cause white soldeirs to die.

Bushwa, said Truman, and the rest is history. Today, the U.S. armed forces are probably the single most successfully integrated institution in American life.

The arguments heard against women in combat sound an awful lot like those heard in the 1970s, when police and fire departments were forced to admit female recruits. Women couldn't handle the physical requirements, opponents said. Male officers and firefighters wouldn't want to be paired with female partners. Women weren't tough enough mentally. And let us not forget the issue of hanky-panky: Put men and women together in a firehouse or squad car and sexual dalliance was sure to erupt.

Just as in the case of the racial integration of the armed forces, none of those fears proved justified. Men and women serve together in police and fire departments all over the country.

There are several objections to having openly gay men and women serving in the military. The first is that they are a security risk. That notion is a holdover from the days when gays hid their sexuality and were thus subject to blackmail. But if a soldier's sexuality is out in the open, the blackmail potential disappears.

The second is the morale issue: that straight men and women will feel sexually threatened by the presence of gays in their living quarters. That notion is based on a deep misunderstanding of the role sexuality plays in the lives of gay men and women.

Gay men and women do not spend every waking minute thinking about sex, or fantasizing about their co-workers. They eat, sleep, brush their teeth, do their jobs, get mad at their bosses, read books, listen to music, watch TV — in short, they do everything that heterosexuals do, with one difference. Those who see that difference as so enormous it should preclude gays from military life are being unrealistic. And if sexual malfeasance occurs, be it between two men or two women, it is a failure of discipline just as if it had occurred between a man and a woman. It should be punished as such.

Change is frightening. Tradition dies hard, especially in the military. Yet because of the extraordinary discipline the military demands of its members, it is also an institution that can break new ground for society. As it did for blacks, so it will, eventually, for gays and women.

The Seattle Times
Seattle, Washington, November 19, 1992

ONE campaign promise President-elect Bill Clinton intends to keep is admitting, and retaining, gays in the military.

He gives every indication he will follow a slow, consultative process, but will order the policy change, tied perhaps to a strict new code of sexual conduct for all service personnel.

Gen. Colin Powell disagrees, but will cooperate. Yesterday he reminded his comrades of the military's place in the chain of command.

"In the final analysis, it's a judgment that will have to be made, and appropriately so in our system, by our civilian political leaders — the president of the United States, Congress," said the chairman of the Joint Chiefs of Staff.

"And the armed forces of the United States will do what we are told to do," Powell said.

Powell is a beneficiary of an executive order that integrated the armed forces and based achievement and advancement in uniform on ability and performance, not race.

Clinton enters a minefield of tradition and emotion with his intent to eliminate homosexuality as a legal barrier to enlistment and retention.

He properly puts the emphasis on behavior, not sexual orientation. Powell is the professional who will accept the order, and challenge, to make it work.

The State
Columbia, South Carolina, November 22, 1992

IT IS a pretty good bet that Bill Clinton will ultimately order the military to keep admitted homosexuals in the ranks. He said during the campaign and repeated in his first post-election press conference that he would take this step as commander in chief, and it will be hard to back away from that pledge.

This matter, which is *the* hot-button issue only for activist homosexuals, has generated the first controversy of his pre-Presidency. Prompted by a court order reinstating a homosexual sailor to duty, Gen. Colin L. Powell, chairman of the Joint Chiefs of Staff, and other members of the military's top brass raised strong objections to lifting the ban on alternate lifestyles in uniform. They were joined by a number of congressmen.

For almost 50 years, the armed forces have discharged homosexuals, whether self-professed or caught in compromising acts. Some 14,000 have been let go in the last decade. The military acknowledges that many remain in the closet and in the service, often, no doubt, serving with distinction.

A major reason given for the ban over the years was that homosexuals pose a greater security risk. It was assumed some would breech security to prevent being revealed as a homosexual. That fear will go by the board if the ban is lifted, since there will be no official stigma attached to the lifestyle.

But General Powell offered another objection. He said he opposes accepting homosexuals, not for moral reasons, but because it would be "prejudicial to good order and discipline."

The African-American general also distinguished this form of discrimination from the racial discrimination in the services until after World War II. The bias then was over skin color. This is over the potential effect on behavior and performance in the highly structured, closely knit military world.

Faced with this opposition, Mr. Clinton hedged a bit: "... And the issue ought to be conduct. Has anybody done anything that would disqualify them, whether it's the Tailhook (heterosexual) scandal or something else. And so what I plan to do in an appropriate fashion, in a prompt fashion, is to put together a group of people and let them advise me about how we might best do this. But I'm not going to change my position on it."

A careful study is appropriate, there being no particular urgency over this. The panel, which we trust will have strong military representation, must consider many factors. Among them:

✓ Does this proposed extension of social justice and civil rights to homosexuals intrude excessively on the rights of service members who, for religious reasons, consider homosexuality to be morally repugnant?

✓ If they are accepted by the services, must "marriage" among homosexuals also be recognized? Would benefits, such as medical care, government housing, pensions, that ordinarily go to military spouses be extended to partners in such marriages?

The major consideration, we expect, was the one mentioned in passing by Mr. Clinton: conduct. The services should not tolerate overt homosexual behavior in the close quarters of barracks life any more than they should tolerate conduct like that of the lechers at the Navy's Tailhook convention. A strict code of conduct strictly enforced will be necessary.

The panel — and Mr. Clinton — must never forget the military mission: to fight our country's battles on land, sea and air. To fight and to win. Nothing done in the name of social justice can be allowed to compromise that mission.

The Hartford Courant
Hartford, Connecticut, November 18, 1992

President-elect Bill Clinton reiterated last week his intention to remove the ban against homosexuals in the military. The president-elect's promise coincided with the reinstatement of a gay sailor in the Navy, pending a final ruling on his court challenge to the half-century ban.

Although it's past time to remove all artificial barriers from joining the armed forces, the issue remains volatile. Last weekend, the chairman of the Senate Armed Services Committee, Sam Nunn, said gays should not be allowed to serve in the military. The Pentagon brass is also opposed to removal of the ban.

Why? Because homosexuality undermines discipline and morale, these defenders of discipline and morality argue. But there have been gays in the military for as long as nations have had armies. And there will continue to be gays in uniform, regardless of the ban.

Most governments don't ban gays from the military. Their armed forces aren't plagued with discipline and morality problems, at least not more than the no-gays-allowed U.S. forces.

Polls show that most Americans favor lifting the ban. The General Accounting Office has determined that the prohibition is not backed up by scientific or sociological evidence, yet the ban costs the Pentagon $27 million yearly in investigations.

Duty to one's country should have nothing to do with sexual orientation, and a soldier shouldn't be prevented from serving simply because he or she might make other soldiers feel uncomfortable, any more than blacks should be banned from the military because they might make some white soldiers uncomfortable.

Rather than worrying about discomfort, military leaders charged with defending the nation's liberties should start thinking about applying the tenets of tolerance within their own ranks.

Lesbian Loses Custody of Son

A circuit court judge in Richmond, Va. Sept. 7, 1993 upheld a juvenile court's decision to award a grandmother custody of her lesbian daughter's son. The grandmother, Kay Bottoms, 42, had sought custody of the two-year-old child, Tyler Doustou, arguing that her daughter's sexual orientation mader her an unfit parent. The daughter, Sharon Bottoms, 23, lived with her female lover, April Wade. Sharon Bottoms contended that her lifestyle had not been detrimental to the child. In handing down his decision, the circuit court judge, Duford M. Parsons Jr., cited a 1985 Virginia Supreme Court ruling that a parent's homosexuality was frounds for having custody of a child taken away because of the state's sodomy laws. Parsons also said Sharon Bottoms's homosexual conduct made her an unfit parent. Gay-rights groups decried the the verdict as discriminatory.

THE DENVER POST
Denver, Colorado, September 10, 1993

Last month it was Baby Jessica, the Michigan toddler whose adoptive parents lost a bitter custody battle when the biological father sought to reclaim the child two years after the mother had given her up.

Now add Baby Tyler to the list of children whose needs were ignored by the courts in bizarre and nationally publicized custody cases. He's the 2-year-old Virginia boy whose mother has been denied the right to raise him because she's a lesbian.

Judging from the news accounts of this messy affair, the 23-year-old mom and her homosexual lover might not have been ideal parents, at least by any conventional definitions. But they hardly appeared to be any less fit for the role than the boy's maternal grandmother, who was given custody despite her daughter's claims that she'd been sexually abused for years by her mom's live-in boyfriend.

What really seemed absurd, though, was the Richmond judge's assertion that the younger woman couldn't be trusted to take good care of the kid because she'd engaged in oral sex, which happens to be a felony in Virginia. If this "immoral" act disqualifies a person for parenthood, then millions of heterosexual Americans — not just gays — would have to be deemed bad parental risks.

Clearly, it would be foolish for a judge to disregard a man or woman's sexual orientation entirely in making a custody decision, since like other personal traits it could affect his or her suitability as a role model for a child.

But it's even more wrong to base such a ruling on sexual conduct alone, or to treat it as a determining factor, as seems to have been done in the Virginia case.

Maturity, stability, responsibility, commitment, selflessness — these are the qualities that make people successful as parents. To focus instead on what may or may not go on in the bedroom demeans the legal process and distorts the real needs of the children involved.

The Detroit News
Detroit, Michigan, September 10, 1993

A Virginia judge on Wednesday declared a lesbian mother unfit, awarding custody of her young son to the boy's grandmother, who had sued for it.

That the judge was merely following a state Supreme Court ruling that regards homosexuality as a legitimate reason to suspend parental rights is, to say the least, disconcerting. That the courts so readily allowed a third party to petition for custody should send shivers down all parents' spines.

The custody battle over Tyler Doustou, 7, was instigated by his maternal grandmother Kay Bottoms, who argued that her daughter was an unfit parent for violating Virginia's sodomy laws. Tyler, the grandmother also claimed, would be irreparably harmed by his mother's lesbian lifestyle. Despite expert testimony that the boy was unaffected by his mother's homosexuality, Henrico County Circuit Judge Buford Parsons Jr. upheld a juvenile court ruling denying Sharon Bottoms custody of her own son. Judge Parsons allowed her visitation two days a week outside her home. The decision likely will be appealed.

Clearly, Kay Bottoms remains unreconciled to her daughter's "lifestyle." But that alone should not earn her legal standing for custody. Imagine the mayhem that would follow if every disgruntled grandparent, aunt, uncle or family friend simply filed a lawsuit challenging parental fitness. Various judges across the country would fast become the unchecked arbiters of who does and doesn't deserve to raise children. Mothers and fathers would fast lose any parental authority; their every decision vulnerable to legal scrutiny.

All custody cases are fraught with their own set of thorny issues, of course. Unflattering testimony about both Kay Bottoms and Sharon Bottoms reportedly emerged during the trial. But Judge Parsons cited a 1985 ruling by the Virginia Supreme Court that homosexuality alone was grounds for denial of custody based on violation of the state's sodomy law.

Whether homosexuals are fit to raise children is only as much a dilemma as whether most heterosexuals make good parents. Research is sparse and inconclusive, with more recent investigations conflicting with older, ill-designed studies that assumed a psychological disadvantage. A definitive study following the adjustment of many children over many decades has not been undertaken.

A good many parents have violated a host of laws, yet retain custody of their children. So it is not violation of a law that has cost Sharon Bottoms her son, but the alleged violation of Virginia's sodomy law. Such moral pronouncements from the bench could easily apply to sodomistic sex acts between heterosexual couples, which, by the strict letter of the law, are just as illegal.

Barring evidence of real and identifiable harm to a child, there is no justification for such judicial overreach. Government already wields an unsettling degree of influence about what constitutes the psychological, economic and moral "fitness" of parents. Such intrusion has proved time and again to be far more destructive to families than simply allowing mothers and fathers to run their own families.

The Evening Gazette
Worcester, Massachusetts, September 20, 1993

A decision by a Virginia judge to take a 2-year-old boy away from his lesbian mother and give him to his grandmother to raise may have been based on state law — but it was wrong.

The case involved Sharon Bottoms, who lived with her child and her female companion. The grandmother — Bottom's mother — argued that the boy would be harmed if he was raised by his mother.

Testimony was presented that the couple sometimes kissed in front of the child, and the mother was described as somewhat immature and undisciplined. However, by all accounts, she was a loving mother. And there was no evidence the boy was abused or neglected.

Nonetheless, in Virginia certain sexual acts between members of the same sex constitute a felony. The judge ruled the mother's conduct was illegal and immoral and made her an unfit parent.

The decision is troubling. The homosexual lifestyle may make some Americans uncomfortable. But it is not sufficient reason to shatter the bond between a mother and child.

The right to privacy is one of the most basic rights held by Americans. U.S. courts have long protected the rights of biological parents to raise their children. Virginia should not interfere in a family in which there is no sign of abuse or neglect.

Numerous studies have found that growing up in a lesbian family does not affect a child's self-concept, intelligence or moral judgment. In addition, the child is no more or less likely to become a gay adult.

It's good to know that the Virginia ruling could not have been made in Massachusetts.

An old statute makes sodomy illegal here, but the Supreme Judicial Court has ruled the law should not be enforced. Legislation was recently introduced to strike it from the law books.

The only reason a child in Massachusetts can be seized from his mother is because of neglect or abuse. The court has ruled that sexual preference alone does not make a woman an unfit mother.

Virginia should take note.

THE SPOKESMAN-REVIEW
Spokane, Washington, September 9, 1993

Just when we had begun to think gay people in America were becoming too politically paranoid for their own good, along comes a Virgina judge to prove their point about feeling harassed because they are who they are.

Judge Buford Parsons ruled that a lesbian is unfit to be a mother, which allowed the lesbian's mother to retain custody of her homosexual daughter's 2-year-old son.

The grandmother, Kay Bottoms, had argued that the little boy could grow up not knowing the difference bewtween men and women if he was returned to Sharon Bottoms, his mother, and her lover, April Wade, also a woman.

Say what? In a world filled with dysfunctional but legally upheld motherhood? In a world struggling to teach care and compassion for all?

Judge Parsons said Sharon Bottoms' homosexual relationship with her live-in partner rendered her "an unfit parent."

The judge also noted that Sharon Bottoms admitted to engaging in oral sex, which is still a felony in Virginia. "In the opinion of this court," the judge ruled, "her conduct is immoral."

What a sad and silly banging of the gavel this turned out to be.

Liz Hendrickson, executive director of the National Center for Lesbian Rights in San Francisco, called the ruling "clearly a decison just based on bigotry."

There's no other logical excuse.

Americans have said repeatedly in almost every way possible that we despise the kind of bigotry that can hurt people, and we just want to be logical about such issues.

Hate in your own living room and it's all right with us.

Harbor ill feelings in your own heart, and be our guest if you want to waste all that energy on something stupid.

But we continue to try to fight bigotry that officially hurts people in some public way just because of who they are. Such bigotry is unfair and unAmerican.

We must become logical without going overboard as a nation on this issue of living and letting live with those of different sexual preference. It's outrageous behavior to snatch a child from his loving mother because of one small part of her lifestyle.

As for oral sex still being against the law in Virginia, the judge has to know the law would have to jail most of New York and a good bit of Kansas if it were to really make a dent in such American behavior.

The child should be given back, by law. Swift and sure.

Chicago Tribune
Chicago, Illinois, September 10, 1993

From now on, travelers arriving at Virginia airports may be advised to set their watches back 20 years. A judge's decision to take a child away from his natural mother simply because she is a lesbian is an outrageous application of obsolete laws and social attitudes.

The decision stems from a suit brought by Kay Bottoms, whose daughter Sharon is raising her own 2-year-old son in a home they share with her lover, April Wade.

Kay Bottoms argued that Sharon was an unfit mother because of her sexual conduct, and that young Tyler would be harmed if brought up by a lesbian couple. Testifying that he calls April Wade "da-da," the grandmother said she fears the boy will grow up not knowing the difference between men and women.

State circuit court Judge Buford Parsons Jr. agreed, giving custody of Tyler to his grandmother and tightly restricting Sharon Bottoms' visitation rights. He based his decision mainly on a state law that makes oral sex a felony, a 1985 state supreme court ruling that homosexuals are inherently unfit parents and his own view that Sharon's conduct is "immoral."

Well. The state sodomy law applies to sex not only between homosexuals, but also between heterosexuals, even if they are married. So if violating that archaic law renders a parent unfit, there probably are precious few Virginians who can pass muster.

Kay Bottoms presumably is not one of those few, having raised Sharon with the help of a live-in boyfriend—one who Sharon says sexually abused her.

A lesbian relationship may be "immoral," but so are plenty of heterosexual relationships. And come puberty, if not sooner, it's safe to assume that Tyler will come to understand the distinctions between men and women.

The 1985 state supreme court ruling didn't mandate this outcome, since it came in the context of a custody fight between a mother and father. In this case, the judge took the child away from his mother to put him in the custody of his grandmother.

It is one thing to say that everything else being equal, children are better off with a heterosexual parent than a homosexual one. It is quite another to say, as this decision did, that no homosexual can be a fit parent.

That is a ridiculous claim. Worse, it led to a cruel result—the sacrifice of a child's welfare to buttress an outmoded prejudice.

Virginians should not be proud of the light this verdict casts on their state, and they should take prompt steps to prevent it from being repeated.

Part III: Children, Teenagers & Sexual Issues

The sexual abuse of children has many dimensions. Though we often think of child abuse in terms of physical violence, various forms of psychological manipulation – coercion, sexual exploitation and even application of folk medicine – can also produce serious and long-lasting damage.

The rapid increase in public awareness of child abuse has led many people to conclude that it is a new phenomenon that has increased in epidemic proportions in the last few years. However, child abuse is not new. Throughout the history of Western civilization, children have been subjected to unspeakable cruelties.

Beginning in the mid-1980s, many social scientists and law enforcement experts were guided by the theory that sex offenders ought to be given mental health treatment instead of simply being imprisoned. Many therapists adopted the view that abusers have disorders called paraphilias which lead to compulsive behavior that some offenders can learn to control through behavioral and chemical therapy and long-term supervision.

Nevertheless, treatment of offenders who sexually abuse children is done only on a limited basis in the United States. That is partially because sex offenders are considered difficult to treat, even though many experts believe that highly motivated offenders can benefit from treatment. But motivation is not always easy to determine.

Children differ in their reactions to sexual abuse. Clinical and empirical studies indicate that sexually victimized children are more likely to be fearful, anxious, depressed, angry and hostile. Anywhere from 20% to 40% of these children show signs of significant emotional disturbance following the abuse. Child victims sometimes exhibit inappropriate sexual behavior as a result of the abuse. Excessive sexual curiosity, open masturbation and exposure of the genitals are frequently observed in young victims. Older children and adolescents are at a greater risk of delinquency, and may engage in self-destructive promiscuity or display inappropriately seductive behavior toward adults. Young girls and older boys seem to be most likely to fall into such patterns.

Children often feel extremely guilty about being sexually abused. Even in cases where there has been a brutal assault, a child may feel that she or he was in some way responsible for or deserving of the abuse. Guilt feelings are almost universal among incest victims who may feel responsible for the breakup of their parents' marriage.

Sexual abuse during childhood often continues to affect the lives of the victims long after the abuse has ended. Women with a history of childhood sexual victimization have higher levels of depression, anxiety, substance abuse and self-destructive behavior. They are also likely to feel isolated and stigmatized and to experience some type of sexual dysfunction or avoidance.

Abuse at the hands of an adult male, which is the most common form of abuse, appears to be more disturbing than that perpetrated by females or adolescents. Abusive fathers and stepfathers are reported to have the most psychologically damaging effects.

The use of force is related to the seriousness and duration of the trauma experienced. Nor surprisingly, abuse over a long period of time is associated with more traumatic and longer-lasting reactions.

Public controversy over issues of teenage sex has exploded in recent decades. Since the 1960s, issues as diverse as the population explosion, the generation gap, abortion, poverty, crime, divorce, working mothers, day care, gay rights, and spouse and child abuse have been the subjects of controversy.

Directly related to these topics is the issue of teen pregnancy. It is well documented that a considerable number of young people are in serious economic trouble throughout the U.S. because of an unplanned or unwanted pregnancy. Of all the issues facing adolescents, teen pregnancy is perhaps the most devastating, to the individual and society alike. It has added to the increasing number of high school dropouts and consigned many young people to a non-productive future and tested society's ability and desire to support them.

According to *Risking the Future*, a report released in 1991 by the National Research Council of the National Academy of Sciences, "Regardless of one's political philosophy or moral perspective, the basic facts are disturbing: more than one million teenage girls in the U.S. become pregnant each year, just over 400,000 teenagers obtain abortions, and nearly 470,000 give birth."

Social critics argue that we cannot afford to ignore the negative impact of untimely parenting on the education and future of both young women and young men. Nor, they point out, can society afford to ignore the well-being of the babies, many of them high-risk, born to teen mothers each year. They also criticize conservatives' ire over increased teenaged pregnancies and their seemingly hypocritical refusal to condone sex education or abortions to counter the rise.

Experts assert that there are no simple solutions to the problems facing today's families. This is not the first generation of Americans to worry about a loosening of family bonds or to complain that parents are growing more selfish and irresponsible or that children are becoming more defiant of adult authority. American families have been through periods of crisis before and, despite recurrent fears of the impending demise of the family, the institution as such has not disappeared. Still, the magnitude of the changes now underway is unprecedented.

McMartin Pre-School Child Abuse Trial Ends

The longest and costliest criminal trial in U.S. history ended Jan. 18, 1990 with the acquittal of the defendants on 52 counts of child molestation and conspiracy. The jury declared itself deadlocked on the remaining 14 charges against Peggy McMartin Buckey, 63, the former director of the McMartin Pre-School in Manhattan Beach, Calif., and her son, Raymond, 31, who had been a teacher's aide at the school.

The case, which had touched off a nationwide wave of concern about child abuse, had begun in 1983, when the mother of a two-and-a-half-year-old boy called local police and claimed that her son had been molested by Raymond Buckey at the McMartin School.

At the suggestion of police, 400 children were interviewed by counselors from a child-therapy center, Children's Institute International. Based on those interviews, a grand jury in March 1984 charged the Buckeys and five others from the school with 115 counts of child molestation.

The charges against the other five defendants, including Virginia McMartin (the founder of the school and the mother of Peggy McMartin Buckey), had been dropped in January 1986 for insufficient evidence.

The Buckeys had been charged with performing lewd and lascivious acts on 11 children who had attended the school between 1978 and 1984. Both Buckeys strongly denied the charges.

The trial, which eventually ran 33 months, opened in July 1987 and featured 14 witnesses, 800 exhibits, and 60,000 pages of transcript. Overall, the case cost the state about $15 million.

In its final weeks, the Buckey case was on the verge of a mistrial, because six of the original 18 jurors and alternates had dropped out for reasons of health or finance, leaving the minimum 12 jurors required by state law.

The final jury of eight men and four women acquitted the Buckeys of 52 of the 66 charges. The remaining 14 counts included 12 molestation charges against Raymond Buckey and one conspiracy charge against him and his mother. Judge William Pounders Jan. 18 declared a mistrial on the charges against Raymond Buckey and dismissed the conspiracy charge against Peggy McMartin Buckey.

The Register-Guard
Eugene, Oregon, January 23, 1990

The trial of Raymond and Peggy McMartin Buckey on charges of child molestation was the longest and most expensive criminal trial in history. It also ranks as having one of the least satisfactory outcomes. The case was painful and frustrating, but the difficulty of such cases should not deter prosecutors.

In the Buckeys' case, everyone lost. Raymond Buckey and his mother were acquitted on 52 counts of child molestation at their preschool in Manhattan Beach, Calif., but their reputations and livelihoods are ruined. Parents of the children the Buckeys and other preschool employees were alleged to have molested believe the courts cheated them of a just verdict by releasing their children's tormentors without punishment. The 30-month trial cost taxpayers an estimated $15 million.

The children were the biggest losers. The arrests came in March of 1984, and the trial began three years later. The children involved have literally grown up with this case. The prosecution's effort to prove its charges against the Buckeys rested almost entirely on children's testimony, but in the end nothing was gained from keeping fresh whatever wounds the children suffered.

Such a process cannot be said to have yielded justice for either the accused or their alleged victims. Yet the failure of this particular case cannot be allowed to deter prosecutions in other cases of child molestation. Some of the problems that plagued the California case can be avoided — indeed, during the course of the trial, notions of how to conduct such proceedings have advanced, particularly in the area of eliciting credible testimony from child witnesses.

Even if future cases threaten to be as difficult as the one just concluded, however, there is no choice but to proceed. Child molestation must be punished when guilt can be established. And people who are wrongly accused deserve a chance to clear their names. These are the hardest trials, but they are also among the most important.

The Salt Lake Tribune
Salt Lake City, Utah, January 21, 1990

As in most child molestation trials, no one won the McMartin Preschool case. This one, though, produced an unprecedented number of losers:

— The 41 children who endured 78 months of trial, on top of many months of investigative interrogation and, possibly, traumatizing sexual exploitation.

— Californians, who spent at least $15 million to have the case investigated and tried and may still be liable for civil damages to the preschool operators, Raymond Buckey and his mother, Peggy McMartin Buckey.

— The Buckeys, who claim to have lost everything, including reputations as competent child-care providers, despite being acquitted of 52 sex-abuse charges.

— The millions of sexually abused children across the country whose stories will be treated more skeptically than ever, impeding public efforts to deter and stop sex abuse of children.

The only apparent benefits are that the case attracted national attention to child molestation problems as early as 1983 and has now emphasized the need to enact and enforce laws in ways that protect the children without violating the constitutional rights of the accused.

Utah, like many other states, continues efforts to balance those frequently competing interests.

Some of Utah's high-profile, child abuse trials presented some of the same problems that bothered the McMartin case jury. Child psychologists were accused of leading the child witnesses into claims that couldn't be convincingly corroborated. Utah's Supreme Court has overturned a number of convictions the past year wherein witness testimony was ruled deficient.

Meanwhile, state social service officials have reported a pronounced increase in the number of substantiated cases of sexual abuse. The number grew from 1,022 to 1,316 cases between 1986 and 1989. Researchers estimate only about 6 percent of the cases are ever reported, meaning the number of abused children is substantial, indeed.

A State Task force on Child Sexual Abuse has been working on methods of improving Utah laws and prosecution policies so that evidence will hold up in court, child witnesses can be treated with sensitivity and accused abusers will more readily admit their actions and submit to treatment.

That's a responsible approach to insidious crimes against children. Letting colossal tragedies like the McMartin case slow Utah's progress would only compound the injustice and anguish so many child victims of sex abuse already suffer.

The Washington Post
Washington, D.C., January 17, 1990

IT IS NATURAL to want to protect children not only from abuse but from the possible trauma that may result if a young victim has to face the alleged abuser in court. It is perhaps less instinctive to care about the rights of an adult accused of a horrendous crime against an innocent youngster. That's why the Constitution so emphatically mandates the protections that must be accorded a defendant in a criminal trial—not just trial by jury and right to counsel but the right "to be confronted with the witnesses against him." When those witnesses are vulnerable children, how far can the courts go to protect them without infringing on the rights of the accused?

About half the states have tried to deal with this dilemma by allowing young witnesses to testify on closed-circuit television that is broadcast into the courtroom. This technique was used in a celebrated child molestation case in Howard County three years ago. Sandra Craig, who operated a preschool center, was convicted of six counts of physical and sexual abuse on the testimony of four children under seven years of age. Mrs. Craig did not "confront" the children, because their testimony was taken in the judge's chambers, but she was able to see them on a television screen and consult her attorney by telephone. The Maryland Court of Appeals reversed her conviction because the trial judge had not questioned the children in her presence to see whether they would in fact have been overwhelmed by presenting their testimony in open court. But the statute authorizing closed-circuit testimony was not overturned. On Tuesday, the U.S. Supreme Court agreed to review the case.

Since child abuse charges involving the McMartin Day Care Center in California surfaced six years ago, similar accusations have been made in dozens of communities around the country. In every case the testimony of young children is critical and the reputation and the liberty of the accused are at stake. In the single case decided by the Supreme Court involving special arrangements for young witnesses, the court in 1988 reversed the conviction of a man who had been surrounded by a one-way viewing screen when his accusers gave evidence. But Justice O'Connor, who concurred in that decision, made clear that other arrangements, such as videotaped testimony or closed-circuit television, might be sustained in a future case. Now the court has an opportunity to provide more comprehensive guidance to legislators who want to protect children in stressful trial situations. The present uncertainty is unfair not only to those on trial but to children and their families whose courtroom ordeals may have to be repeated if the rules are not clear.

THE SACRAMENTO BEE
Sacramento, California, January 20, 1990

There is only one certainty emerging from the McMartin case: that, as Judge William R. Pounders put it, everyone connected with this 2½-year trial, children and parents, defendants, prosecutors, the media, has been "poisoned" by it. And while the two defendants have been acquitted on most of the counts against them — the jury hung on a few others — nothing really has been resolved.

Even the jurors who voted to acquit seemed to believe that children had been molested — there was concrete medical evidence for it, though not enough evidence to convict these defendants. If that's true, the children become victims once again — victims of the abuse, victims of more than six years of investigation and trial, victims of a verdict that declares that what they said, and what many of them surely believed, was not believed by the jury. At the same time both defendants and teachers at McMartin, some of whom were held in jail for years before charges against them were dismissed, will spend the rest of their lives under a cloud of suspicion that few of them may deserve.

There will be books and seminars and conferences galore analyzing what went wrong in the McMartin case — and certainly there will be no end of candidates for blame. Even under the best of circumstances, it's often difficult to render justice in cases where the only witness, other than the defendant, may be a very young child. In the McMartin case, the combination of investigative errors arising from professional incompetence, political ambition, ethical violations and public hysteria fanned by sensationalized pack journalism made it impossible. If this verdict does not seem satisfactory, neither would any other.

Fortunately, the investigative process in child molest cases — in part because of such failures — has become considerably more sophisticated since the McMartin case began nearly seven years ago. Prosecutors, social workers and counselors have learned to work together more effectively, using videotape to reduce the number of times a child is forced to tell the same story. Also fortunately, such cases — cases lending themselves to mass hysteria — are rare. Far and away most child molestation takes place not in schools or playgrounds, but at home, where the perpetrator is not a stranger, but a stepfather, an uncle, a mother's boyfriend. Despite the pressure on children not to report, despite false reports and despite reluctance, particularly in rural courts, to recognize the ugly underside of local life, in these cases the system often works.

The McMartin case has done no end of damage to countless people, not least in reinforcing the false belief that most reports of child molestation are either exaggerated or that there's nothing that realistically can be done about them. An increasing number of molesters are being convicted and a growing part of the work done on their cases is efficient and professional. McMartin, fortunately, was typical of little except its calamitous self.

MILWAUKEE SENTINEL
Milwaukee, Wisconsin, January 20, 1990

The indecision that prevented a jury from convicting a mother and son accused of molesting children in their California preschool places yet another hurdle in front of parents and others who seek to protect children from abuse by adults in whose care they are placed.

While the evidence supporting some of the charges was short of that necessary for conviction, there were split votes on 13 of the 65 counts. And the telling flaw in the tales told by the kids seemed to be that they were too bizarre to believe.

In the words of one juror, it seemed to be a case of: "The more fantastic story (some children) could come up with, the better."

There also were questions about whether the children were led on by individuals from a private agency dealing with child abuse who questioned the youngsters in taped interviews. But such suspicions also can be based on incredible answers to questions dealing with shocking subject matter.

Healthy skepticism, of course, can make for a more responsible juror. But so does awareness that we live in a world where things occur, and people are driven by urges, that so-called decent people can't comprehend.

Here in Wisconsin, it might be recalled, a supervisor at an area technical college who was involved in a counseling program for bedwetters also was part of a so-called "diaper pail" club whose members traded pictures of diaper-clad juvenile boys.

And, if the truth were told, police blotters across the country are rife with similarly disgusting stories, such as the recent case in Milwaukee involving the murder and sexual assault of a 17-month-old child.

As syndicated columnist Ellen Goodman suggested in an article related to the Virginia McMartin preschool case, ways must be found to establish the credibility and get at the truth in cases involving testimony by children.

But sheltered adults should be disabused of the suggestion that runaway imaginations can go further than real life.

Los Angeles Times
Los Angeles, California, January 20, 1990

The McMartin Pre-School case was a trial without victors, only survivors. It was a case that lasted 78 months, cost $15 million just in court expenses, and at times turned the Southland upside down. It is hard to say that we are all better for the experience. It is safe to say that it is an unhappy and upsetting one in almost every respect.

Raymond Buckey, 31, and his mother, Peggy McMartin Buckey, 63, have been judged innocent on 52 counts, but they will never be entirely free of stigma. Many parents of the 41 children involved in the case will never accept the verdict. And Superior Judge William Pounders, who presided over the 2½ years of actual trial, said the case "poisoned everyone who had contact with it"—children, parents, witnesses, litigants, judicial officers. As David Shaw writes elsewhere in The Times today, radio, television and the print press belonged on the list.

How could investigators, even onlookers, miss the many warning signals on the trail along which this case plunged like some wayward tank? A disaffected prosecutor called the case "junk" months ago. And Judy Johnson, mother of the McMartin child who made the original charge, later added the astonishing claim that an AWOL Marine sodomized her family's dog. Nobody paid attention to the flashing lights that said that this was at best a bizarre case.

Another question is whether there is anything in the record of the trial could make even a sliver of the squandering of time and reputations worthwhile?

Answers to the first question must be largely conjecture. When the McMartin allegations surfaced, Americans were only dimly aware that such things ever happened; then the hysteria helped make it seem that they happened everywhere all of the time. From one extreme to the other.

The media's lessons already are sinking in. One is that skepticism is never more important than when government officials make things so sensational as to be irresistible. This is not the end of this case, perhaps. But if this terrible ordeal is to have any lasting value, it should make everybody be better prepared to handle the next terrible case of alleged child molestation.

The other question is easier to deal with. Lael Rubin, chief prosecutor for the final six months of trial, said the McMartin case made clear a need for better techniques of questioning, and understanding the answers of, children who may have been molested. Whatever really happened in the McMartin case, children are, and will be, molested. Surely the longest criminal trial in history will yield the longest list of the right ways and wrong ways to approach such cases so that justice can be done without repeating the grotesqueries of this case. We owe at least that to our children.

DESERET NEWS
Salt Lake City, Utah, January 22, 1990

Few criminal cases cause such wrenching legal, moral and emotional dilemmas as those involving charges of child sexual abuse.

The nation's longest and most expensive trial came to an end last week with acquittal of the defendants — operators of a Los Angeles preschool — on child sex abuse charges. But the verdict did not clearly resolve one of the key legal issues in abuse cases, namely, how to deal with the testimony of child witnesses.

On the one hand is the defendant, guaranteed a fair trial by the U.S. Constitution, including the Sixth Amendment right to be "confronted by the witnesses against him." This is related to the question of whether the child is telling the truth or as been "coached," a charge often raised in such cases.

On the other hand, there is the young victim, perhaps already traumatized by sexual abuse, who is subjected to face-to-face meetings with the adult charged with the abuse — an adult who may have previously threatened the child. The potential psychological trauma is very large and very real.

More than half the states, including Utah, have tried to find ways around the problem, using videotaped testimony by children, closed-circuit TV, and one-way mirrors and screens.

Yet courts have repeatedly overturned such arrangements, including a 1988 U.S. Supreme Court verdict that rejected the conviction of a man who had to sit behind a screen while two 13-year-old girls testified. But that decision left unclear whether there could be exceptions.

The Supreme Court has now agreed to consider two other cases — one from Maryland and one from Idaho — in which the state courts threw out convictions because the defendant was not able to confront his accusers face-to-face.

The right to a fair trial must be jealously guarded. Because children are vulnerable and helpless, the first instinct is to accept their story and protect them, even at the expense of the accused. Yet that instinct must not be allowed to undermine the legal rights of the defendant.

But judges must not get so wrapped up in legal niceties that the consideration of damage to children is simply pushed aside. There ought to be some middle ground. After all, it's not just the defendant who has rights. The victim has rights as well — a principle sometimes overlooked in America's legal system.

It may take greater involvement of judges in deciding on a case-by-case basis whether a child can cope with courtroom appearances, cross examination by the defense, and face-to-face encounters with the accused — or whether videotaped testimony, for example, is acceptable.

If judges insist on a literal interpretation of the accused confronting the witness face-to-face in every instance, it may become nearly impossible to get convictions in molestation or sexual abuse cases.

Many parents may refuse to put the child through such a trauma. And the molester or abuser will walk free. In such eventualities, one can hardly claim that justice will have been served, no matter what the Constitution says.

The Clarion-Ledger

Jackson, Mississippi, Janaury 24, 1990

Rage, frustration, sadness.

The parents of the children — and some of the children themselves — expressed all these emotions when a jury ruled "not guilty" in the McMartin molestation case.

After 6 ½ years, after more than $15 million, after a case that started with 208 counts of molesting 48 children, the longest, costliest trial in U.S. history ended with five women and seven men, 10 of them parents, saying they believed at least 10 preschoolers in Los Angeles had been molested. But they could find no one guilty.

With the acquittal of Raymond Buckey and his mother Peggy McMartin Buckey on 52 counts of child molestation and a mistrial on 13 other allegations, the 16 million Americans who have children in day care must be wondering:

■ What went wrong? Could all the children have made up the allegations? Jurors said they believed children were molested, they just didn't think the prosecution proved who did it.

■ Did our system of justice fail? Anytime children are subjected to a lengthy court battle in which they must repeatedly relive a horrible experience, yes, the system failed.

And the Buckeys were victims, too.

■ Could it happen here? Yes. It could happen anywhere. And the disposition, the length, the cost and the suffering surrounding this case is a chilling reminder.

How do you protect the rights of a defendant who is innocent until proven guilty? How do you protect a child who may have been already brutalized? The McMartin trial may be over, but justice is still undone, those questions remaining like ugly scars on an innocent child.

The Evening Gazette

Worcester, Massachusetts, January 26, 1990

One of the longest and most expensive criminal trials in U.S. history ended in Los Angeles when a daycare center owner and her adult son were acquitted of multiple counts of child molestation.

While the litigation has ended, justice is undone.

We can only imagine the ordeal suffered by the defendants, the children and their families, and that is inexcusable. But compounding the tragedy is the fact that after five years of investigation and litigation, the central question remains: Were the children at the McMartin Preschool indeed molested and, if so, who did it?

Evidently, the trial was doomed to fail before it began. By the time the children's testimony was videotaped for the jury, it was hopelessly tainted by the questioning of parents, police and psychologists and by the confusion of grand jury and lengthy pretrial hearings.

Some children's advocates have expressed fears that the acquittal sends the message that child molesters can get away with their crimes, as juries will believe their testimony rather than that of young victims. That view is refuted by many successful child-molestation prosecutions in Florida and other states, including Massachusetts.

Rather, jurors indicated it was not the youthfulness of the witnesses but the leading questions of the interviewer that undermined the testimony.

Some of the jurors said they believed some of the children might have been molested, but voted acquittal because the prosecution simply failed to present credible, untainted proof.

Strict guidelines are needed for professionals interviewing children who might be victims of abuse.

Psychologists, police and parents all must be aware that influencing a child's testimony, even unintentionally, might prevent a jury from rendering a fair verdict.

Curtailing the length of the process is essential. In the McMartin Preschool case, the sheer duration of the trial might have been enough to make justice nearly impossible. No jury could retain three years of testimony. No witness, regardless of age, could reliably recount events that occurred years earlier.

Neither the public, which footed the $13-million bill, nor those involved were well served by the ordeal, and that's a shame.

THE INDIANAPOLIS STAR

Indianapolis, Indiana, January 22, 1990

Conflict resembling a runaway nuclear reaction burned on as the longest, costliest criminal trial in U.S. history ended in the acquittal of Raymond Buckey and his mother of 52 child molestation charges, spreading a mushroom cloud of anger.

Although the outcome, in many minds, is inconclusive, the trial should teach courts, psychologists, child counselors, the legal profession, lawmakers and the public some valuable lessons.

The case grew from allegations in 1983 of widespread child abuse at the McMartin nursery school at Manhattan Beach. Buckey, now 31, and his mother, Peggy McMartin Buckey, now 63, were charged. He spent nearly five years in jail, she almost two years.

The trial in Los Angeles Superior Court lasted nearly three years and cost $15 million. After deliberating seven weeks the jury, besides returning the acquittals, deadlocked on 12 child abuse charges against Buckey and one conspiracy charge against him and his mother. A hearing to determine whether those charges will be refiled was set for Jan. 31.

Jurors said they did not believe the accounts of nine children who testified because their molestation stories made it appear they had been manipulated by parents' and therapists' suggestions.

Outrage over the verdict was expressed by parents of some children who had been at the school.

Several members of the Buckey and McMartin families prepared to file a federal lawsuit naming the city of Manhattan Beach, Los Angeles County and others as defendants.

The judge, district attorney and prosecutor concur that judicial and probably legislative reforms are needed to prevent such lengthy proceedings in the future. The district attorney, thinking back on the case, said: "Insane is the word that comes to mind."

The word fits. McMartin Pre-School has been ruined. Buckey's and Mrs. Buckey's lives are blighted. Many children may have suffered permanent psychological scars. Many parents are understandably bitter. The public is frustrated because there is no way to be certain what happened at the nursery.

Surfacing of the allegations in 1983 set off a wave of fear and suspicion and brought a rash of sensational stories of mass child sexual abuse in various parts of the country. Most faded away after investigation. But suspicion lingers.

The lessons of the Buckey case stand: Trial length should be limited. Techniques of questioning children in child molestation charge cases need refining that will minimize the risk of coached answers.

Sexual abuse of children is a vile crime. But it is also an emotion-charged subject that can arouse hysteria, delusion and confusion. The law must deal with it intelligently and scientifically in order to deal with it justly.

Missing N.Y. Girl Found in Hidden Cell

A 10-year-old Long Island, N.Y. girl who had been missing for 16 days was found Jan. 13, 1993 in a small underground bunker in the home of a family friend. The girl, Katie Beers, was found after the friend, John Esposito, who had first reported her missing, led police to the cell beneath his Bay Shore home. Esposito, 43, was indicted Jan. 19 on 11 charges, including multiple counts of kidnapping and sexual abuse.

Esposito had originally maintained that he had taken Beers to a video arcade where she disappeared Dec. 28, 1993, two days before her 10th birthday. Police now said that Esposito, who had pleaded guilty to abducting a seven-year-old boy in 1978, had fabricated the incident. It was thought that the pressure of constant police surveillance of his home had caused Esposito, a prime suspect in the case from the beginning, to finally crack and lead police to the bunker.

The elaborately concealed cell in which Beers had been kept measured six-by-seven feet and was located below Esposito's converted garage. Beers said that she was sometimes chained by the neck or kept in a coffinlike loft in the dank bunker. The girl had been able to view police conducting a search of Esposito's home on Dec. 31, 1992 via a closed-circuit television system, but her screams remained unheard outside the sound-proof cell.

Esposito Jan. 14 was initially charged with second-degree kidnapping. Five days later, he was indicted by a Suffolk County grand jury on 11 charges of kidnapping, sexual abuse, endangering the welfare of Beers and making false statements. His lawyer, Sidney Siben, entered not guilty pleas on all the counts in Suffolk County Criminal Court the next day.

Beers, who police said was in good health, was placed in the custody of Suffolk County Child protection workers, who described her mother, Marilyn Beers, as an unfit parent.

The Des Moines Register

Des Moines, Iowa, Febraury 3, 1993

It starts with a phone call. The caller's fear that a child is being abused is routed to Iowa Department of Human Services' investigators, and wheels start to turn. If the abuse is verified, police, juvenile courts, therapists, doctors, foster families and others are likely to become involved. Child abuse so outrages the human sense of compassion and decency that all the stops are pulled, as they should be.

But only 30 percent of the abuse reports check out. That means a lot of unproductive effort — effort that is necessary and justifiable to see that none falls through the cracks. It also means a lot of effort that is not necessary, not justifiable, and which actually gets in the way of professionals trying to help Iowa kids.

Unless the initial complaint is thrown out on obvious grounds — there was no injury, the "victim" was not a child, etc. — every report must involve an interview with and examination of the child, a home visit, and interviews with parents and/or the alleged perpetrator. In the first four days an initial report must be filed with the DHS central registry, the juvenile court and county attorney. By the fifth day, notice must be sent to the parents warning them of the investigation. By the 10th day, a final report must go to parents, the DHS, juvenile court and county attorney.

A finding of abuse, if any, must also go to the parents, perpetrator, the child's attorney and usually the person who filed the original complaint. All must be notified of the right to appeal or request a correction of the report. Included in the process is a 71-item form for the investigator to complete in full and in triplicate, and file. (Not until item No. 54 does the form get into the question of whether abuse took place.)

Obviously, in a good share of cases, an investigator knows where the probe is going before the last bit of the scenario is acted out. Just as obviously, in such cases there should be a way to short-circuit the system at some point to preclude endless wheel-spinning. There isn't. With 70 percent of abuse reports turning out to be groundless, that means a lot of wasted effort. It could be far better spent serving children who have been abused.

The long list of requirements for abuse investigations was adopted out of sincere and understandable intent to minimize the possibility of a complaint getting lost in the system and a case of child abuse continuing unabated. But its effect could be the opposite — binding investigators in so much time-consuming red tape that they must slight the important legwork.

No set of rules can insure conformity with their intent. With 19,000 abuse complaints to check out yearly, investigators must be granted a degree of discretion to do their jobs right.

THE KANSAS CITY STAR

Kansas City, Missouri, February 12, 1993

Shocking data like that recently out of the University of Missouri on fatal child abuse can re-awaken the sleeping watchdog of public anger. But what do we do with it?

For a start, keep it from going back to sleep by emphasizing the links between dysfunctional families and child abuse. Or noting the gap between noble speeches on parental rights and hospitalized toddlers.

It helps to make a connection by tracing the path from protestations of belief in family values to actual homes that mock the concept of family to ongoing domestic violence within them to the lack of state services and, finally, to murdered children.

Society knows how to rewrite the stories. Missouri is trying, but it isn't trying hard enough.

Researcher Bernard Ewigman of the University of Missouri-Columbia School of Medicine believes that more than twice as many children really die of abuse and neglect as are officially reported.

Examining the records of a certain number of children who died of injuries from 1983 through 1986 in Missouri, Ewigman found that 15 percent had been classified as homicides. But by looking further at other evidence such as medical records, fire investigation reports and child protection service reports, Ewigman and his colleagues thought that as many as two-thirds of the children might have been abuse or neglect victims.

The next step was to work with researchers at the U.S. Centers for Disease Control on a national application of the Missouri data. The doubling effect held true on a national basis.

The researchers blamed a violent streak in society and inadeqate social services for the underreporting. But Ewigman, a physician, said it plainly: If he sees a troubled family in his practice, about all he can do is report it. The family gets blamed and labeled, but the child doesn't get help.

Last year Missouri created the Child Fatality Review Project. It investigates child deaths.

The Department of Social Services has its comprehensive Family Preservation Services, an innovative spectrum of services to help families at risk in a timely way. It started in 1989 and by October 1992 was operating in every county in Missouri.

The Children's Trust Fund, set up by the General Assembly in 1983 and dependent on citizens checking off a donation on their state income tax returns, is dedicated to preventing child abuse. Grants are made to local programs that are located all over the state.

The research data indicates that much remains to be done.

THE BUFFALO NEWS
Buffalo, New York, January 16, 1993

HILLARY Clinton has a reputation as an advocate for children. Let's hope she can help because this country surely has to make the welfare, health and protection of children a greater priority. Stories of child abuse and neglect follow one another with depressing regularity.

The latest is the story of Katie Beers, a Long Island girl who spent her 10th birthday chained in a secret underground dungeon. A building contractor who "befriended" Katie and her chaotic family has been charged with second-degree kidnapping, accused of keeping the girl in the well-hidden room beneath his jerry-built garage. There are allegations that the contractor sexually molested the girl and confined her in a tiny box.

It was an outrageous new level of victimization in a life that was already hard. Katie has spent most of her life being shuttled between her unwed mother and a godmother. The two women are tangled in a bitter custody dispute that has seen the godmother's husband arrested on charges he sexually abused Katie and Katie's unemployed mother charged with being an unfit parent.

The godmother has already been on "Donahue" explaining her side of the story. Is a TV movie next?

Katie spent much of her life hanging out on the streets, friendless, skipping school, living on free coffee and food at a laundromat, doing errands for her godmother, wearing ragged clothes and smelling bad. Her mother's home was littered with old trash.

Shortly after Katie was taken from the dungeon, her mother signed over temporary custody of her to Suffolk County authorities, but now she is trying to regain custody.

Meanwhile, local police and the FBI are trying to figure out if the contractor has imprisoned other children in the secret room. He was arrested for abducting a 7-year-old boy in 1978. He pleaded guilty to a reduced charge and got probation. He has a history of befriending children and masquerading as a "big brother." Katie's older brother is saying now that the contractor sexually abused him in the past.

Neighbors say they frequently thought about calling authorities about Katie, but they didn't. School officials reported her absenteeism to welfare authorities, but nothing happened. The father of Katie's brother claims he has long been suspicious of the contractor, but he apparently did nothing. Authorities with the Big Brother/Big Sister program referred the contractor's false ad about being a "big brother" to police, but nothing happened.

What should be done?

Well, if the contractor is found guilty of imprisoning Katie, the maximum sentence of eight to 25 years is too brief. He must have no chance to victimize more children. And why is this "second-degree" kidnapping, anyway?

The dungeon should be destroyed before some other weirdo decides to use it.

And Katie needs to get away from the messy life that adults have dealt her so far. Authorities like to keep families together, but there must be a limit. She needs a new chance.

Finally, authorities and the general public need to be more alert and more caring about children in obvious trouble. How many years does an unwashed, tired-looking child have to roam the streets before somebody does something to help her?

What will the next case look like? Where will it happen?

ALBUQUERQUE JOURNAL
Albuquerque, New Mexico, January 22, 1993

As painful as it is to read about the sad life of little Katie Beers, imagine what it must have been like to *live* it — in a house that neighbors said contained decades of filth, being called "the Cockroach Kid" by classmates.

The 9-year-old girl's unhappy plight finally received the attention it deserved recently, after her short life had taken a particularly horrifying turn. She was found in a underground cell, with a chain around her neck, on property belonging to a "family friend."

All the details of her captivity aren't known yet, but chances are her heartbreaking story will only get sadder once authorities say what happened in that cell. The authorities are finally listening to Katie describe what happened to her. If only someone with the power to help the little girl had listened sooner.

Children belong in families, but children are also part of communities. It's everyone's business if a child appears to be neglected and/or abused. No child should have to shoulder such a terrible burden alone. But Katie Beers did, until she was discovered in the underground cell.

New York authorities must do whatever is necessary to ensure that Katie never has to endure such pain again. But how many more children in America are just as neglected as Katie? The sad ordeal of Katie Beers is a reminder that neighbors, teachers — everyone who deals with children — should keep an eye on the well-being of all children before the youngsters turn up missing, or on a morgue slab.

Richmond Times-Dispatch
Richmond, Virginia, February 7, 1993

The American Civil Liberties Union's frequent lawsuits on behalf of criminals have at least this virtue: They force the government to justify its ways. Now the ACLU has turned its lawyers on the state's Child Protective Services.

Unlike just about any other governmental entity, Child Protective Services can intrude upon a family home and take a child away with no warrant and without so much as a howdy-do from a judge. Protective Services then can keep the child in custody for up to four days, during which it can deny contact between parent and child.

In its lawsuit, the ACLU notes that children who are charged with a crime receive more procedural protection than children who are taken for their own safety.

No one denies the importance of what Protective Services workers do. Yet like cops, they are human; sometimes they can go too far.

Police officers and other law-enforcement agents generally must obtain warrants before making an arrest, and legal authorities can hold detainees for only two days, not four. Reason suggests Protective Services should not have a greater latitude than that — or, if it should, then it should have something else as well: ample justification for its power.

Newsday
New York City, New York, January 5, 1993

The adults in Katie Beers' life let that little girl down — from her mother, whose neglect began when she left the two-month-old Katie with a friend to raise, to child welfare workers who, despite repeated prodding from her teachers and police, failed to protect 10-year-old Katie from that neglect.

Now that she has been rescued from 16 days in subterranean bondage to a family "friend," child welfare officials must end that chain of failure. Suffolk County's Department of Social Services needs to build a solid case on Katie's behalf in the matter of her custody, and it must review where it went wrong and decide how to avoid failing future Katies.

Katie's case may not have set off the usual alarms to social workers. There may have been no burns on her body or drug paraphernalia in the house. But there were plenty of reasons *to act* nonetheless: When she was a toddler, neighbors found her barefoot in the snow. At age 6 she was doing the family wash at the local laundromat — alone. At 9, she stopped going to school after being sent home repeatedly with a case of head lice that her mother failed to treat properly.

And when Child Protective Services workers went to the house, they were chased away. *And* Katie's godmother's husband was charged with sexually abusing Katie. *And* Katie's mother let her go around with a man — John Esposito — who had allegedly molested Katie's half-brother. Esposito now is charged with Katie's kidnaping.

What more evidence could county authorities want? And yet they let Katie live like a slave in a filthy and dangerous home.

The man Katie called "Uncle John" — like other adults in her life — betrayed her trust. He took her by the hand and led her to a pit under his garage. His motivation is unclear. But the responsibility of county authorities is not. As they decide with whom Katie should spend the rest of her childhood, they must, at last, put Katie's best interests first.

U.S. Comes to Grips with the Sexual Abuse of Children

Intrafamilial child sexual abuse is often defined as contact between a child and an adult member of the same household where the objective is sexual stimulation either of the adult instigator or of another person. The critical element in the definition is that the abuser shares a home with the child and fills a parental or quasi-parental role. However, the definition is limited because it overlooks the fact that the person filling the quasi-parental role need not be an adult but often is an older child either a teenager or a preteen. Extrafamilial child sexual abuse involves someone outside the family who may or may not be in some relation of authority to the child, but who is not a relative.

Because of fear and shame, child sexual abuse is probably significantly underreported. Estimates of the incidence of intrafamilial sexual molestation of children are extremely varied depending upon the data used and the sample populations from which the estimates are derived. Construction of estimates is made difficult by the hidden nature of the act.

Research has established that relatives commit more child abuse than strangers. For example, an examination of Massachusetts Department of Social Services records for sexual-abuse offenses referred for prosecution found that 27.5% of the perpetrators were fathers, 16.8% were strangers, 11.6% were boyfriends of the mother, 11.4% were stepfathers, 10.1% were male caretakers, 9.9% were uncles, 6.1% were brothers, and 4.3% were mothers.

Many critics of social-service and welfare departments claim that social workers routinely treat incest as a family illness, when they would treat child molestation as a crime if it were done by a stranger. Even when evidence is forwarded to the criminal justice system for prosecution, many prosecutors dislike bringing child molestation charges because they are difficult to prove.

Herald News
Fall River, Massachusetts, February 21, 1992

If ever good has evolved from bad, then the new sexual abuse procedures developed by the Fall River Diocese are a prime example.

Prompted by the horrific allegations against former priest James R. Porter, the document that has emerged, with notable haste, is sensitive, thorough and unprecedented in this area. Its effect will be felt long after Porter's case becomes a painful memory.

Porter was indicted last year in Bristol County on 46 counts resulting from accusations by adults who said Porter, who was a priest at parishes in Fall River, North Attleboro and New Bedford during the 1960s, sexually abused them when they were young parishioners. On Friday, Chief Justice Robert L. Steadman of the Superior Court refused to dismiss most of indictments.

It was in large part the Porter case, and the adults who have brought the allegations, that provided the impetus for developing guidelines within the Roman Catholic Church for dealing with allegations of sexual misconduct by the clergy. The willingness and urgency of newly installed Fall River Bishop Sean P. O'Malley to deal with the unsavory issue and the perseverence of Porter's alleged victims were the driving forces behind the development of the procedures.

The written guidelines, which, in part, instruct the diocese to report to outside law enforcement any allegations of sexual misconduct with a minor by clergy, will have a profound effect on future generations of young Catholics. Porter's alleged victims should be especially proud of and rightly praised for working toward changes that will not directly help them, but will ensure a safer future for children. Just as surely, without Bishop O'Malley's advocacy and guidance, it's unlikely procedures would have been drafted so quickly, if at all.

Along with shedding light on an area within the Church that has been closeted too long, the adoption of a sexual abuse policy ushers in what seems to be a new partnership between lay people and clergy. If their joint efforts can break down barriers that have been built up for centuries around sexual abuse, there's no telling what lies ahead.

The Charlotte Observer
Charlotte, North Carolina, February 28, 1992

Childhood is not a time of innocence and delight for the children described in staff writer Diane Suchetka's report beginning on Page 1A of today's Observer. It is a time of pain, fear, humiliation and emotional damage that can last a lifetime. It is the story of the sexual abuse of children — by other children.

Nobody knows how vast the problem is, but official statistics are disturbing. From 1988 to 1992 in Mecklenburg County, the number of serious sex crimes charged to children under 16 jumped from seven to 30. Nearly every victim was a child. Last year in North Carolina, mental health officials identified nearly 700 sex offenders who were 17 or younger. That's 50% more than three years earlier.

The damage does not end with the abuse. It is made worse by neglect — neglect by parents and other adults who don't know and perhaps don't want to know about it, by schools where sex education courses evade it, by a state system that lacks the resources to deal effectively with the abused or the abusers. David Hutchinson, an Asheville therapist, describes the problem with a psychological term: The state is "in denial," he says. "We're not even sure we can talk about it."

Child abuse rarely springs from nowhere. There's a strong likelihood that abusers were themselves abused as children. Ken Titus, chief district court judge in Durham County, thinks, "We have to provide intervention if we're going to stop the cycle from repeating itself. What we'll face if we don't deal with this is the possibility of housing that child in prison for the rest of his life."

Some things need to be done by government, and our report today tells you how to help make that happen. But parents and other adults are the first line of defense.

Parents should talk with children about sexual abuse as soon as they're old enough to understand. Tell them they shouldn't let anyone talk them into touching another person's private parts — those covered by a bathing suit. Tell them that no one, not even another child, has a right to touch theirs. Tell them to get away if anyone tries these things, and to tell you about it. Assure them it's not their fault, and nothing bad will happen to them if they tell you. If they tell you something happened, don't dismiss it. Check into it.

Teachers and others who work with children also should be alert to the warning signs described in today's report.

Government resources are stretched thin at every level. But America cannot afford the cost of neglecting its children. Saving them may require cutting other expenditures — welfare for the well-off elderly, tax subsidies for vacation homes, asphalt for every cow path in North Carolina. If that's the choice, wise people should have no trouble making it.

THE TAMPA TRIBUNE
Tampa, Florida, Febraury 10, 1992

There was a time when elementary school teachers and principals were expected to focus their energies on teaching their pupils reading, writing and arithmetic. Unfortunately, that time was long ago.

This sad lesson was driven home last week when it was disclosed that last February in New York City a 9-year-old East Harlem girl had written, in an essay, "I know what it is like to be raped." Asked during the annual observance of Black History Month to compose a paper on a well-known black person, she chose to write about Mike Tyson, the famous boxer who was convicted of rape.

That the girl's essay made headlines was less a function of its dismaying contents — that she was a victim of sexual abuse at the hands of her father — than that the relevant authorities responded so slowly to such a startling disclosure.

Because the school's principal was out of town at the time, the teacher locked the essay away for 10 days. Inexplicably, another 16 days elapsed before the principal passed it along to school health officials.

By then, the girl apparently was desperate to tell someone, so she told her grandmother about the rape. The grandmother in turn confronted the child's father, who acknowledged the rape and was arrested. He was awaiting trial when he died, last June, of AIDS. Fortunately, his daughter tested negative for the virus.

The special commissioner of investigation for New York City's school system said in a report last week that the girl's despair prompted bungling and buck-passing at the school.

"This is a child's cry for help: When a child summons the courage to make that cry, someone has got to be there to hear it," he said.

Child abuse is nothing new. It was happening, if less frequently, back when teachers were instructed to stick to the basics of education and, when it came to abused pupils, to mind their own business. In a very real sense society is the better for the mandated involvement of educators (who better to spot such problems?) in detecting and reporting instances of such abuse.

What's worrisome is that the responsible authorities, and in this case that means at least one teacher and his principal, could be so callously indifferent to such a transparent plea from a person so obviously in peril at home.

We may not adequately teach our teachers to deal effectively with such non-academic matters, but we should be able to expect the exercise of everyday common sense.

The Record
Hackensack, New Jersey, April 4, 1992

MARGARET Kelly Michaels is out of jail, but there is no happy ending to the story of whether she sexually abused children in the Maplewood day care center where she was a teacher almost a decade ago. Her conviction has been overturned but her innocence has not been established.

Ms. Michaels calls the recent ruling by an appellate court a victory. However, it is important to note that while the three-judge panel found fatal flaws in the way prosecutors handled the case, the judges were considering legal and procedural issues and left open the fundamental question of Ms. Michaels' guilt or innocence.

The 1988 trial, and now the ruling that overturned her conviction, call up strong emotions in many people. Those who support Ms. Michaels say she was the victim of a witch hunt. They say hysterical, paranoid parents fueled an investigation and prosecution that spun out of control.

Staff Writer Elliot Pinsley, in an article on the previous page, cites evidence indicating investigators and prosecutors were overly zealous to convict Ms. Michaels. But the piece also points out that many of the young witnesses offered vivid, believable accounts of what happened. In addition, prosecutors are often overly eager to chalk up convictions. The eagerness does not mean there was a witch hunt.

After the conviction was overturned last week, William Kunstler, Ms. Michaels' attorney, said the ruling showed that these kinds of trials can rarely, if ever, be conducted fairly. "It's almost impossible," he said. "You can't trust the children."

Let's hope it's not impossible. It is true that small children can often be swayed and led into saying things they think adults want to hear. They can even be led into believing events took place that did not occur.

But it is also true that sexual abuse of small children does happen, and that the abusers rely on the vulnerability of their victims — on the assumption that no one will believe such things would be done to children, even if the child says it happened. When children say or do things that suggest they may have been abused, responsible parents will follow it up.

The reversal of Ms. Michaels' conviction shows the pitfalls that prosecutors face in such difficult cases, and what must be avoided in similar cases in the future. How does an investigator question small children about embarrassing, frightening things without leading them? How does a prosecutor safeguard a small child who must appear in court as a witness?

In the Michaels case, the children testified on closed-circuit television from the judge's chambers, without having to face their former teacher. But the appellate panel ruled that the judge, by taking the children on his lap or playing with them during testimony, violated his impartiality and may have prejudiced the jury.

In fairness to both defendants and children, the answer would be for investigators and prosecutors to err on the side of caution. Investigators should not manipulate young children into answering questions. Prosecutors should go forward with only the most substantiated charges and the most credible witnesses.

It's true that prosecutors must be concerned about convincing juries and protecting young witnesses. But they must also consider the defendant's rights.

A wrongful conviction is a miscarriage of justice. And a conviction that's reversed on appeal is worth nothing.

> Let's hope that it will not be impossible to convict child molesters.

Teenage Sex and Pregnancy Remain Subjects of Concern

Adolescence is a period of life fraught with upheaval. Hormonal changes prepare a child's body for adulthood, and the society in which the child lives begins to treat him or her in a different way. In Western developed nations, societal pressure moves adolescents constantly in the direction of independence and autonomy. In order to achieve expected autonomy, adolescents must first break away from parental authority.

Sexuality is a particularly sensitive source of controversy. The rules of sexuality have become much more variable and ambiguous. The sexual options or risks include celibacy, intimacy with one or several partners, heterosexual or homosexual contraception, abortion, unmarried parenthood, and sexually transmitted diseases.

AKRON BEACON JOURNAL
Akron, Ohio, March 2, 1993

The pattern of births out of wedlock was no different in 1990 than it has been each decade since the National Center for Health Statistics started keeping records in 1940.

From 3.8 percent of births to unmarried mothers in 1940, the figures have risen steadily, and at bigger percentages: 4 percent in 1950, 5.3 percent in 1960, 10.7 percent in 1970, 18.4 percent in 1980 and 28 percent in 1990. Fully a quarter of America's children in 1990 were born to mothers who were not married.

Increasingly, studies are finding the social costs of births to unmarried mothers to be extensive, linking births out of wedlock to rising childhood poverty, burgeoning welfare rolls and costs and a host of social problems.

For instance, one in four of welfare recipients is likely to stay eight years or longer on public assistance. Single mothers who had babies in their teens and out of wedlock are the most likely to be long-termers.

For the babies, state and federal governments, the effects are far-reaching. A percentage of these single mothers no doubt do support their children adequately, but a large proportion tend to be poorly educated, with little training, few job skills and therefore low earning power.

The current focus on welfare reform is to discourage long-term reliance on public assistance. While privacy and moral concerns make childbirth patterns a touchy subject in welfare reform, the relation of illegitimate births to a range of problems makes a compelling case for reversing the upward trend.

Two aspects of the problem that have received considerable attention are encouraging marriage and delaying childbirth.

With its emphasis on single mothers, the welfare system is frequently criticized for discouraging marriage. Proposals to encourage marriage include allowing mothers who marry to keep more of their benefits without losing aid and eliminating the rule preventing couples on Aid to Families with Dependent Children from working more than 100 hours a month.

Abstention should be promoted as a means for young adults to delay childbirth until they can support themselves and their children. It is a practical goal as compelling for social and economic reasons as it is for what many see as moral reasons.

It is unfortunate that the case for abstention is made almost exclusively in terms of morality vs. degeneracy. The Reagan and Bush administrations, in pursuing an anti-abortion policy, made family planning a dirty word and gave room in some quarters for proposals such as castration and forced use of long-term contraceptives.

As local and federal governments review welfare policies, family planning should be approached as education — on the social and economic benefits of abstention, on the range of effective contraceptions, on adoption services and on legal abortions. Foreclosing on any of the options merely delays a realistic approach to a growing problem.

The Wichita Eagle-Beacon
Wichita, Kansas, April 10, 1993

This week's edition of the top-rated television show "Roseanne" focused on the sexual experiences of the Conner family's teenage daughter.

Whether Darlene actually had sexual intercourse with her boyfriend was somewhat in question at the program's end, but the underlying message of the show was that teenagers are going to have sex and that the best parents can do is to teach them about birth control.

That, in short, was the primary sex education lesson this week for millions of American teenagers. Not surprisingly, many of those same young people are contributing to the national epidemic of teenage pregnancies and cases of sexually transmitted diseases.

America's failure to confront teenager sexuality is destroying what's left of the moral fiber of the younger generation. The most vivid example of that moral collapse came recently in California, where a group of high school boys scored "points" for the number of girls they slept with. Were the boys' parents outraged by this despicable contest? Just the opposite. "Boys will be boys" was one father's comment in a cavalier display of paternal pride.

Meanwhile, the Alan Guttmacher Institute, a non-profit think tank on reproductive issues, reported last week that 12 million sexually transmitted infections occur annually in the United States — two-thirds of them among people under age 25 and one-quarter among teenagers. At that rate, at least one in four Americans will contract an STD at some point in their lives.

The cry immediately goes out for more sex education among young Americans. But as currently taught in many communities, sex education seems to have little impact on teenage sexual practices.

Reviewing research on sex education for Pediatrics magazine, James Stout and Frederick Rivara, of the University of Washington, concluded, "The available evidence indicates that traditional sex education programs in junior and senior high schools have little or no effect either positively or negatively on altering the age of onset or frequency of adolescent sexual activity, on increasing contraceptive use or on preventing unplanned teenage pregnancy."

In other words, people who think current sex education programs are working are woefully deluded.

According to Marion Howard, a professor of obstetrics at Emory University, when 1,000 teenage girls were asked what they most wanted to learn in sex education class, 82 percent answered, "How to say no without hurting the other person's feelings."

Instead of limiting course curriculum to biology and how-to-wear-a-condom lectures, schools should add a section on teaching teenagers to "just say no." Darlene and millions of other teenagers need to learn that maintaining their virginity is far preferable to being just another kid with a kid and/or a sexually transmitted disease.

The Oregonian
Portland, Oregon, April 8, 1993

There's no such thing as "free love. At least not in the corporeal sense, as a report from the respected Alan Guttmacher Institute makes depressingly clear.

The report, "Testing Positive,", astutely points out that public attention has been so focused on the AIDS epidemic that other sexually transmitted diseases have been relegated to the back burner in the collective consciousness, if not the national health profile. Indeed, it says one in five Americans are infected with untreatable sexually transmitted diseases other than AIDS and that 25 percent of all Americans at some time will contract a sexually transmitted disease.

The study, which used data from the Federal Centers for Disease Control and Prevention, hasn't been critically analyzed. But even if the actual number of infected Americans were half the 56 million estimate, it still would be cause for alarm.

Many of the diseases described in the survey could be avoided by the use of condoms. The one-in-five estimate includes viral infections such as herpes, which cannot be cured, unlike the bacterial infections gonorrhea and syphilis that generally respond to antibiotics.

Therefore, it's doubly disturbing when one considers that these numbers also presumably represent the numbers of Americans who have carelessly put themselves at risk for HIV infection.

The study, with reason, faults the government for neglecting efforts to prevent the spread of such illnesses by its reluctance to promote condom use, for example. The study also says the government fails by directing most of its resources to clinics that cater to men, even though women are hardest hit because venereal diseases in women often show no symptoms.

A spokesman for the Centers for Disease Control, while praising the Guttmacher report for turning a spotlight on sexually transmitted diseases, objected to the criticism that women have been neglected.

Whatever disagreements arise over emphasis, however, there can be little dispute that the data underscore the need for continued and expanded sex education, which should include encouraging abstinence. Adults as well as young people need more information on reducing health risks in sexual encounters.

Chicago Defender
Chicago, Illinois, April 5, 1993

Whether or not Americans like it, they are in a war. Not with another country but with a series of illnesses commonly known as sexually transmitted diseases (STDs). A sobering insight into the gravity of the situation can be had by reviewing the data made public recently by the federal government's Center for Disease Control in Atlanta: In 1986, 11,000 STD cases were reported but by 1990, the numbers had zoomed to 35,000.

The troubling statistics should be a source of irritation for the person who contracts the disease but more importantly, it tells women that the STDs can have a horrifying impact on fetuses. Consider, for example, what was said by Tim Hadoc, public relations director for the Chicago's Board of Health: "Because of the increase in sexually transmitted diseases, specifically syphilis and gonorrhea, we have seen a number of newborns affected by the disease. In most cases the infants do not reach their first birthday."

That is one of the most tragic occurrences confronting Chicagoans and it is among the best reasons why human beings, once again, must make special efforts to turn the tide of STDs.

What weapons can be used to lessen the impact of the dreaded diseases? Some things that can greatly reduce the presence of STDs are:

• Education -- A person who is properly informed about how STDs are spread and the several ways by which individuals can avoid catching the diseases is in the best position to protect self and others.

• Lifestyle changes -- Many of the people who contract STDs, particularly those who are repeatedly infected, need to make serious alterations in the way they involve themselves with others. Advice on what changes to make and how to implement them can be acquired from counselors at the board of health, doctors and other medical or health care personel.

• Parental involvement -- Despite the peer pressure which affects the average teenager, mothers and fathers still are some of the biggest influences on the youngsters. By communicating facts about how to avoid catching STDs, parents can help their offspring avoid the sickness, pain and other discomfort that result from the diseases. Most importantly, parents can aid their children in avoiding premature death because one of the most frightening diseases spread through sexual contact is AIDS.

Life is too precious to risk it through cavalier sexual escapades. What should be remembered is that caution should be a key consideration before anyone gets sexually involved.

The New York Times
New York City, New York, April 7, 1993

A country with one of the world's highest standards of living is not a country in which one expects to find a remarkable number of people afflicted with sexually transmitted diseases. But according to a study by the Alan Guttmacher Institute, 56 million Americans are infected with them, and at least one of every four can expect to be.

Such age-old scourges as gonorrhea and syphilis do significant damage, but the widest impact comes from incurable viral diseases, which get far less public health attention. Some 31 million Americans are believed to have genital herpes, while 24 to 40 million are infected with the virus that causes genital warts.

Poverty, ignorance and the attendant lack of medical care are partly responsible for the rising rates of sexually transmitted disease; so is the tragic trade of sex for drugs. But a major reason so many Americans are prey to S.T.D.'s, as they are called, is that they are Americans. Which is to say: They initiate sexual intercourse early, marry late and divorce often. During the periods when they're not married, and sometimes when they are, many will have several sexual partners (adult Americans average seven over a lifetime) and will be inconsistent in their use of condoms.

Although public health programs concentrate on adult males, women and teen-agers are hardest hit. Two-thirds of those who contract S.T.D.'s are under 25; a fourth of them are teen-agers. Women are more susceptible to infection and thus more apt to suffer the consequences — chronic infection, infertility, spontaneous abortions, damaged babies — for life. Condom carelessness is particularly risky for women, to whom these diseases are easy to transmit and in whom they're difficult to diagnose. Just one act of unprotected intercourse with an infected partner, and a woman has a 50 percent likelihood of contracting gonorrhea.

The classic venereal diseases, syphilis and gonorrhea, are most prevalent among the poor, but chlamydia, which infects far more Americans each year, cuts across the economic spectrum. Often it causes pelvic inflammatory disease, which in turn can lead to ectopic pregnancy, infertility and chronic pelvic pain. And if the emotional cost of a venereal disease is high, so is the price of a cure or semi-cure. In 1990 the costs of treating pelvic inflammatory disease and related ectopic pregnancies and infertility added up to $4.2 billion.

Perhaps it is the focus on AIDS that has made Americans forget about their vulnerability to other venereal diseases. But lack of information played a part, too. Because medical emphasis has been on treatment rather than prevention, people may not realize that some of the ailments are literally incurable.

Public health programs need to be redirected — to help women and teen-agers and to target diseases that are currently neglected but afflict millions of Americans. Even more important, the nation needs more prevention and education programs to persuade people to avoid risky sexual encounters and use condoms. To reduce the risk is the most cost-effective way to cut the disease rate. For incurable viral diseases, prevention is the only approach that can work.

Americans, as this country learned too late to prevent many deaths, can't afford to be ignorant about AIDS. They can't afford to be ignorant about other S.T.D.'s either.

copyright © The New York Times 1993

THE INDIANAPOLIS STAR
Indianapolis, Indiana, February 25, 1991

The evidence is inescapable. In 1988, there were more than 3,000 teen-age pregnancies a day. By some estimates, there will be more than 1 million teen-age pregnancies this year, with half of them ending in abortion.

The majority of babies born to teen-age mothers are illegitimate. Most will grow up in low-income, single-parent households. They will have less education and more health problems than average. They will require more public aid and social services. They will be more likely to have illegitimate children and be responsible for more single-parent households. Indiana and especially Indianapolis certainly have such problems.

Given those grim facts, common sense would argue that everything possible should be done to discourage teen-age pregnancy. That means discouraging teen-age sexual activity because the most obvious symptom of sexual activity is pregnancy.

Not everyone agrees. Many individuals and organizations argue that inhibiting sexual activity among the young is a lost cause. Further, that sex and pregnancy don't go together, not if there is plenty of sex education and easy access to contraceptives.

> Is no mention to be allowed of the moral aspects of teen-age sexuality?

The "separatists" are fond of demanding government funding for such things as in-school health clinics that dispense condoms and birth control pills and abortion counseling. They vigorously oppose government programs that discourage premarital sex. In their book, such programs represent an unconstitutional mix of religion and public money.

That is why the 1981 Adolescent Family Life Act is once more under attack. Derided as "the teen chastity law," it funds programs that urge youngsters to abstain from sex until after marriage.

In 1987 a U.S. district judge struck down several key provisions, but the law was subsequently upheld by the Supreme Court. Now the American Civil Liberties Union again is asking that the law be declared unconstitutional.

As evidence it has submitted a pamphlet that, among other advice, urges teen-agers to "pray together and invite God on every date." Horrors!

The ACLU also cited another program that used federal funding to buy books, one of which asks pregnant teen-agers to consider whether giving a child up for adoption is "God's will."

Does constitutionality rest on such fragile and frivolous grounds? Surely not.

It is hard to believe that a few isolated quotations sifted from hundreds of publications can destroy the one government program that dares to see teen sex for what it is: a social abomination.

Given all that has happened in the past 20 years, it is even harder to believe that so many Americans remain convinced that God, moral discipline and religious belief have no place in public discussions of teen-age sexuality.

MILWAUKEE SENTINEL
Milwaukee, Wisconsin, March 6, 1991

Teenage pregnancy is a problem that spins off into long-term generational poverty. That point is well-documented.

So, it is commendable that a legislative committee on teen pregnancy has urged, among other things, mandatory sex education classes in public schools and the opening of three school-related clinics.

But, while there are a few nagging questions about the school-related clinics and the mandatory sex education classes, a red flag goes up with the proposal to distribute free contraceptives. Here's why:

If the committee is counting on contraceptives as a way to reduce alarming teen pregnancy rates, then there is trouble in Legislative Land. Based on previous reports, contraceptives have not been an effective tool in reducing teen pregnancies.

Besides, doesn't offering free contraceptives send a confusing double message: "Don't have sex but, if you do have sex, use contraceptives."

Will teens be told to use contraceptives, such as condoms, to avoid sexually transmitted diseases — such as AIDS — or will somebody just hand them out? Would teen boys use them? Will teen girls remember to take a pill daily?

Other questions also must be answered:

How early should sex education classes begin? Will students be taught to say no to sex and why not, rather than get fully educated about human sexuality? Will they be instructed about the dangers of sexually transmitted diseases?

Are legislators aware that school-related sex clinics have not effectively controlled teen pregnancy?

It is significant to point out that State Rep. Susan B. Vergeront (R-Cedarburg) has said that such centers would provide parents and their teenagers with counseling, mental health and physical health education services and referrals.

She also said the clinics would be modeled after programs such as New Concepts Development Center, directed by June Martin Perry. New Concepts offers a teen mentor program that has shown progress in abating teen pregnancy.

So has Rosalie Manor's program, also based on a mentor concept. These kinds of programs should be replicated at school-related clinics. Otherwise, legislators and the community may not witness any reduction in this rapidly growing problem.

The key is to teach teens to delay sex by giving them a good reason not to engage in sexual activity and other high-risk behavior, such as drugs or alcohol — and not just to hand out birth control pills or condoms in hopes that this will curb the rising teen birth rates.

FORT WORTH STAR-TELEGRAM
Fort Worth, Texas, August 27, 1991

A big cheer and a lot of help and cooperation are due minority community groups and leaders who are currently organizing in Fort Worth to address the problems of teen pregnancy and infant mortality.

In 1989, Fort Worth had the nation's second-highest African-American infant-mortality rate.

The high rate of teen-age pregnancy in minority neighborhoods goes hand in hand with the high rate of infant mortality.

Reducing teen pregnancies through a program to instill self-esteem and a sense of responsibility in those most at risk will help reduce infant mortality.

And while the campaign should eventually be citywide and must address the causes of teen-age pregnancies in all ethnic groups, due credit must be given to those African-Americans who are taking the initiative.

In neighborhoods such as Stop Six and Polytechnic Heights, this campaign is one of self-help, of salvaging families and communities awash in the tragic results of too many children bearing children.

The object is to save lives, both infants and teens, and, by so doing, to prevent wasted lives. The entire city needs to ask what it can do to help.

THE BUFFALO NEWS
Buffalo, New York, August 21, 1991

The state is suffering from a budget crunch, but that's not stopping Gov. Wilson from calling for more money for the Office of Family Planning's birth-control programs.

If budgetary considerations don't give the governor pause on this issue, can we appeal to him on the issues of family rights and choice? Aren't such matters as family size and contraception highly sensitive questions that ought to be decided by families themselves, employing whatever religious or moral calculations they choose? Does the state really have any business trying to shape the way people make such delicate decisions?

Granted, nobody is marching women into state family planning offices, reputed to show a pro-abortion bias, and counseling them by force. But family planning is nonetheless an intrusive role that places the state in an unacceptably presumptuous position. Moreover, the act of raining dollars on the Office of Family Planning means that those dollars — taken by coercion from families that (a) might plan their families better were they permitted to keep more of their own income and that (b) may be morally opposed to abortion — are flowing to clinics that either perform abortions or refer people to abortion clinics.

You don't have to be an abortion opponent to see the injustice in subsidizing such enterprises with public money. Why force taxpayers — many of whom consider the willful destruction of human fetuses to be an act of brutality — to hand over their money for such procedures, or to pay the salaries of people who counsel abortion?

Not only does money go directly or indirectly for abortions, it also assists Planned Parenthood's advertising campaigns to promote abortion and oppose laws to restrict or regulate it. Does the state really have any business subsidizing such a biased organization?

Planned Parenthood has argued that more money for birth control — including abortion — actually saves tax dollars in the long run. Mr. Wilson has echoed the argument, but isn't that really a chilling line of thought? It's based on the assumption that the children who would otherwise be born would cost us too much — that their lives would simply be too great a burden on the public treasury.

Surely that reasoning neglects the contributions those children may make to society over the long run, which are incalculable. Only politicians arrogating to themselves God-like powers would attempt such calculations. Funny enough, such calculations seldom take account of the scientific discoveries, or artistic high notes, or sports achievements that the unborn promise to society. The most hideous calculation of all would be to try to target which families might produce such ultimate resources and to discourage the fecundity of those families deemed unlikely to produce the achievers. Such would be the ultimate political conceit.

Mr. Wilson would raise the allowance of the Family Planning Office. Better that it be disinherited.

The Register
Santa Ana, California, January 20, 1991

HERE'S A SNAPSHOT of the real world. A 14-year-old Buffalo girl, who didn't even know she was pregnant, gave birth to her baby last week. Frightened, alone and ignorant, she left the newborn on a basement table. Police later reported that the new mother said "she saw the baby's head and panicked."

Buffalo now has two more troubled kids. The child mother, who told police she had been raped and who now confronts enormously more demanding adjustments than she had before, and her baby.

This new teen-age mother also becomes part of a statistic that defines grim local reality and shames Buffalo — the highest teen-age pregnancy rate in New York State.

That's right, the highest rate. It is nearly twice the statewide average, significantly higher than for New York City.

Yet the Buffalo public schools confront this emergency with abysmal sex education. Backed by the Victorian fantasies of several board members, sex education programs here actually glorify ignorance.

Children — all of Buffalo's children — must be taught about their own bodies. They must be taught often and well enough so that they understand sexual functioning when their bodies reach sexual maturity. They must be able to talk about it without shame so that they can ask for help from adults when they need it.

Official Buffalo school district policy, which some teachers understandably cannot stomach and try to evade, calls for not even mentioning birth control unless a student brings it up.

That Gothic approach to education is not the one adopted by local Catholic schools.

"Your conscience has to be the deciding factor, but it has to be a well-informed conscience," says Karen Podd, director of campus ministry at Nardin Academy, the Catholic girls' school. "Wanting our kids to be knowledgeable and well-informed, we will tell them about birth control."

So they do, but within the church's own moral context.

The sex education units of city public schools are scant in both time spent on the subject and the material covered. Little wonder, then, that a state inspection team recently criticized the health curriculum.

Buffalo's program rests on the attractive fiction that sex education is the responsibility of parents, not the schools.

The reality is that not all children grow up in wonderfully informed two-parent families. They don't all grow up in families where each parent is articulate and easy in conveying all the right information at the right stages of their children's physical, emotional and mental development.

Paradoxically, there's more to sex education than sex, and lots of parents are not as informed as they might be. So the sad reality of consequence is the 14-year-old mother who gave birth alone, bloody and scared stiff, to the baby she had not even realized she was carrying.

That is the real world of Buffalo for too many teen-agers.

That is the world where ignorance toys with fantasy and denial.

It is the forbidding world that Buffalo School Board members must stop denying. It is the real world that public education here, if it is to truly educate, must address. Comprehensively. Sensitively. Seriously.

THE DALLAS TIMES HERALD
Dallas, Texas, October 31, 1991

Reducing teenage pregnancies doesn't have to be a complicated, expensive process. Girls Inc. of Metropolitan Dallas has been teaching the same message and it works: Sex is not for teenagers and the best way girls can gain control of their future is to abstain.

Some may consider this message too old-fashioned to work. But a recent study called "Truth, Trust and Technology" provided the agency with the data it needed to prove that the method, similar to those tried around the country, helps reduce the rate of teenage pregnancies.

Girls Inc. operates a four-component project for girls ages 9 to 18 that focuses on abstaining as the most effective way to prevent pregnancies. The message is enhanced with focuses on human sexuality and development, building assertiveness, achieving life goals and gaining support from others.

Young girls who participated in the program were more likely to postpone having intercourse. Older girls, who receive lessons on finance, social skills, contraceptives and health care, were less likely to get pregnant than girls who did not attend.

Leslie Linton, Girls Inc. executive director, recommends organizations and parents start early and repeat the message frequently. Girls who attended all segments of the program were more likely to postpone sex and less likely to get pregnant.

Ms. Linton said the program, at a cost of $116 a year per girl, is much cheaper than paying the estimated $8,500 the federal government spends for a pregnant or parenting teenager.

The best news about the Girls Inc. program is that it can be expanded to other youth organizations, such as churches, schools and Girl Scouts. Ms. Linton said they will train facilitators of these organizations so that the programs can be offered at different sites. The next training session is next month.

Girls Inc. offers encouraging news. They're doing a great job helping teenage girls understand that they don't have to bend to peer pressure.

Michael Jackson Accused of Sexual Abuse

Lawyers for pop star Michael Jackson Nov. 15, 1993 said the singer was being treated in an undisclosed location outside of the U.S. for addiction to prescription painkillers. Jackson Nov. 13 had released a taped statement in which he announced that he was canceling his worldwide concert tour to seek treatment for his drug problem. He said his addiction was caused in part by stress over allegations that he had molested a 13-year-old boy. Police were investigating those allegations, which had been made public Aug. 23, but they had not charged the singer. PepsiCo Inc. Nov. 14 said it was terminating its nine-year promotional agreement with Jackson in the wake of his cancellation of the tour, which PepsiCo was sponsoring.

The Wichita Eagle-Beacon
Wichita, Kansas, September 4, 1993

America is obsessed with the saga of Michael Jackson and allegations that he abused a 13-year-old boy. But while the focus has been on the megastar and his trauma in the face of such awful accusations, there is a yet-to-be-told story about the child. Few stargazers seem all that interested in what the young teen's trauma must be like.

And there is still an even larger story — regardless of whether Michael Jackson is innocent or guilty of the charges — about countless victims of child sexual abuse. Just this week in Argentina, cult members — including 60 Americans — were arrested for sexually exploiting their own children. Recent news stories found that computer bulletin boards have been used as a communication link for pedophiles. The list of lost innocence is horrible and unending.

Yet, from coast to coast, attention has been riveted on the singer who has had to work since the age of 5. His homes, private zoo and amusement park are described variously as ways for him to help kids and ways for him to be the child he never was allowed to be. It's as though a case is being built that, if he is guilty, he's the one to be pitied. Poor Michael.

And it has been lamented that Michael Jackson could now lose millions by losing advertising deals with Pepsi and Sony. Poor Michael and poor mega-bucks businesses.

Elizabeth Taylor — proclaiming her devotion to him — headed off to Singapore to see him. His family held a news conference to support him. Poor Liz and poor Jackson family. Curiosity over cited health reasons for canceling concerts on his current world tour has further fueled the Michael-sympathy machine.

But poor Michael shouldn't be the only concern, or even the main one. The 13-year-old child is. If he was not sexually abused, then he is a victim of having a mother who had no more sense than to allow him to have "slumber parties" with a man old enough to be his father. And of having a real father who allegedly used him to get court custody, a film deal, attention, revenge and who knows what else?

If Michael Jackson has been wrongly accused of sexual abuse, that's dreadful. But in the middle of all this mess is a child who may have lost his childhood, too. If not to sexual abuse, then to a value system where running with the rich and famous is more important than loving families and basic good sense.

Poor Michael? Maybe.

Poor young "friend"? Absolutely.

Sadly, the saga of Michael Jackson is just one of many stories about today's children who are victimized by adults. In the case of the rich and famous performer who uses sexually explicit moves for the entertainment of all his fans — including children — it could be that the charge is nothing more than imposing his own retarded emotional growth on minors. Whatever the outcome, it is about time that the world awaken to focusing on children, especially the ones who are sexually exploited.

Poor children.

THE KANSAS CITY STAR
Kansas City, Missouri, August 28, 1993

The investigation into allegations of sexual abuse involving entertainer Michael Jackson reportedly involves at least four young boys. Spokesmen for Jackson say the Los Angeles County investigation will vindicate the singer, who has been on tour in Thailand.

Jackson's camp says the charges, which began with a 13-year-old boy, are false. Jackson's representatives said that private investigators have uncovered an extortion campaign involving this child.

The boy's father, who is in a custody dispute with his ex-wife, says that in July he took his son to a therapist to discuss allegations regarding Jackson. The father reportedly asked his ex-wife to sign a stipulation that their child would have no further contact with Jackson. The official probe of the first claim against Jackson has since expanded to include three other boys.

An unbiased criminal investigation ought to get to the bottom of things. However, due to Jackson's celebrity status, this investigation has gained an inordinate amount of attention. Jackson's name is already tainted, whether the accusations prove to be true or false.

Meanwhile, the international media are in a feeding frenzy. Jackson is used to the paparazzi, whom he dislikes immensely. But the children involved in this case are not so versed in public exposure. Their identities should remain unknown.

That may be unfair to Jackson, who has often been a target of shabby tabloid journalism. But prosecutors who try to put together sexual abuse cases say that fear of public scrutiny often prevents parents from coming forward on behalf of their children. Fortunately, some courtrooms allow videotaped testimony when children are involved.

The Star has a policy generally of not identifying children in criminal proceedings. There are some exceptions, including cases in which a youth is tried as an adult.

The news media should adopt a responsible policy regarding the use of minors' names. Children should not have to be part of a media circus.

THE INDIANAPOLIS NEWS
Indianapolis, Indiana, September 4, 1993

Say it isn't so, Michael.

Last week, a 13-year-old boy told Los Angeles investigators that entertainer Michael Jackson sexually molested him during their recently ended four-month friendship. Jackson, renowned throughout the world for his commitment to children's issues, has denied the boy's accusations.

For the sake of all of the good Jackson has accomplished during his many years as a world-class performer and supporter of charitable causes, we hope the allegations are unfounded.

If they are true, however, not even his good reputation will be able to protect him.

Now in the hands of police, secretly recorded audio tapes reveal plans by the boy's father to blackmail Jackson for $20 million. Alleging Jackson molested his son, the father threatened to go public with the claims unless Jackson compensated him with lucrative movie and writing contracts.

But contradicting the boy's and his father's picture of Jackson as a man who preys on children are other youngsters who are friends with Jackson. They publicly have testified to the singer's relationship to them as a big brother, not a child abuser. One 11-year-old Australian boy told a TV audience he once shared a bed with Jackson, but he said it was a large bed during a slumber-party type event and that nothing improper ever took place between them.

Another boy, a 10-year-old, said he also had shared a bed with Jackson during a visit but that the entertainer never attempted any sexual contact.

Admittedly, bed-sharing between a grown man and a young boy is pretty unusual, even eyebrow-raising. But in itself, it's no proof that sexual abuse ever occurred.

Did it in this particular case?

Since neither physical evidence nor witnesses corroborate the boy suffered abuse, the only ones who really know the truth of the allegations are Jackson and his young accuser — a question of "he said/he said."

How unfortunate for both parties, with emotional scars and humiliation ensured to both, regardless of any eventual verdict.

While there still is a chance that Jackson is guilty of the allegations against him, we hope it isn't so.

During the past decade, Jackson has established himself as a sincere benefactor of children in the global community. He has gained the respect and trust of many.

If Jackson has breached that trust, he will have to pay the consequences. But that would be most tragic, not only for Jackson, but for millions who have admired his talent and interest in children for so many years.

The Hutchinson News
Hutchinson, Kansas, August 31, 1993

Michael Jackson has just run into the downside of fame and fortune.

The allegations against him, true or not, will always linger in some fashion even if he is completely exonerated of the claims of sexual molestation against him.

That is unfair, if untrue. But Jackson, a megastar known worldwide has ridden fame's star into commercial success, riding on the popularity that has been fueled and fed by the enormous publicity machine known as the media.

Famous and rich people are easily victimized, just as they are often forgiven for their actions by an adoring public. Mike Tyson, the professional fighter, is still considered a victim by many of his fans despite his rape conviction. So it is with some of Jackson's fans who have said they will support him whatever the outcome of the allegations against him.

Famous people can't do much about claims against them from others, except hope that law enforcement and the courts work equally as hard for them as those institutions work for the rest of us.

The Union Leader
Manchester, New Hampshire, August 29, 1993

Pop music idol Michael Jackson, an abuser of children?

Well, perhaps not in the way that was alleged last week by the father of a 13-year-old boy. But this very strange fellow and his fawning sponsors are abusing children each and every time he performs his crotch-grabbing routine on stage, videos, films, etc.

Some of Jackson's music is fine. But the cult-like atmosphere that has been fostered for and by this bizarre person is anything but. And those who attempt to portray his pelvic gyrations as choreographic brilliance are not only kidding themselves but countenancing a pretty sick message to our kids.

Make the world a better place, Michael. Clean up your act.

LAS VEGAS SUN
Las Vegas, Nevada, September 7, 1993

IT'S one of those stories we hear too often these days. A child is fondled by an adult, and other inappropriate acts took place between them.

Generally, the investigation of those claims is kept secret until a person is charged with the crime of molesting a child. But not if you're an international megastar. There's no way a probe of Michael Jackson's alleged behavior could be kept under wraps. There are too many people eager to talk; too many people who see this sad situation as a "career builder" or a way to make money.

The investigation even found its way to Las Vegas when police last week searched the rooms at The Mirage where Jackson stays when he's in town. Nothing was found, police said.

Jackson is a super-talented entertainer who may be the most well-known star in the world. He's also renown for his child-like nature, his famous and troubled childhood, and for being just plain "weird."

The father who claims Jackson molested his son is embroiled in a bitter custody dispute. Sadly, more and more charges of molestation are made in custody cases as a way of getting back at the other spouse. It's often difficult to sort out the real cases from the vendettas. Although this adds another emotional twist to the story, the boy's claims should not be taken lightly. He should not be dragged through the media mud because he's making allegations against a superstar.

While the allegations have provided juicy fodder for the tabloids, we must remember that Michael Jackson has not been charged with any crime.

So many details have been printed and aired worldwide that even if he is never charged – or if he is charged and later found innocent – he will be ruined forever.

Whether we should or not, we expect more from our superstars. We put them on a pedestal, and if they fall, we are crushed. In Hollywood's heyday, "indiscretions" of some of the big-name stars were covered up or simply not talked about except in whispers.

No matter who you are or what your status is, child molestation is a heinous crime. It's not something that can be swept under the rug. But a simple accusation is just that, not a criminal conviction. Some news people have apparently forgotten that, and Jackson and the boy will suffer for it.

This is one case that cries out for a fair, extensive (but timely) and thorough investigation conducted by police and other experts – and not talk-show hosts.

Woody Allen Sues Mia Farrow for Child Custody

Filmmaker Woody Allen Aug. 13, 1992 sued his long-time companion, actress Mia Farrow, for custody of their three children. Allen and Farrow had been a couple since 1980 but had never wed or lived together.

Allen, 56, filed the suit in State Supreme Court in the New York City borough of Manhattan for custody of two of the couple's adopted children, Moses Amadeus Farrow, 14, and Dylan O'Sullivan Farrow, seven, and a biological son, Satchel O'Sullivan Farrow, four. (Farrow had a total of 11 children, seven of whom were adopted.)

In the wake of the suit, reports emerged that Allen was having an affair with Soon-Yi Farrow Previn, the adopted daughter of Farrow and her second husband, pianist–conductor Andre Previn. Allen released a statement Aug. 17 acknowledging the romance with Soon-Yi Previn, a college student whose age was most commonly reported as 21. He said reports of their affair were "happily all true."

At a press conference Aug. 18, the usually reclusive Allen denied charges, apparently initiated by the 47-year-old Farrow, that he had sexually abused two of the couple's children. Police officials in Connecticut, where Farrow had a home, Aug. 17 had confirmed that an investigation into possible child abuse had been launched against Allen.

Farrow, who had married 50-year-old singer Frank Sinatra when she was 21, was represented in the case by prominent attorney Alan M. Dershowitz, a Harvard Law School professor who had taken on a number of high-profile cases in recent years.

The Washington Times
Washington, D.C., August 20, 1992

Yesterday was the Republicans' family-values day in Houston. They could not have asked for a better illustration of the importance of keeping that theme before the public than the unholy mess of the Woody Allen-Mia Farrow brawl. Hollywood fiction may be bad when it comes to the American family, but Hollywood reality, it seems, can be infinitely worse.

The plot, of course, does bear a certain resemblance to Mr. Allen's own convoluted movies. One imagines that the resemblance may not be purely coincidental. Mr. Allen and Miss Farrow have for more than a decade enjoyed being known as two of the most "interesting" people in the show biz scene. Their decade-long, non-live-in, not-formalized relationship has been hailed as one of the most creative solutions ever offered to the infinitely complex world of modern men and women — a world in which the solution of marrying and raising a family together seems far too simple-minded. Each had an apartment in Manhattan. He lived alone. She with her 11 children, some the issue of her marriage to conductor Andre Previn, others adopted. One is the biological son of Mr. Allen (the 4½ year-old Satchel) and two others were adopted by her with Mr. Allen, Dylan and Moses. As recently as September, the New York Times Sunday magazine snared an interview with the superstars and enthused over this wonderfully modern arrangement.

As it turned out, Mr. Allen may have progressed to a state of personal liberation that leaves most of his fans way behind, struggling even to comprehend what has happened or indeed to decide what is the most sickening aspect of the whole affair. Is it the news that Mr. Allen for some time has had a relationship with Miss Farrow's 21-year-old adopted daughter, Soon-Yi? She is morally, if not technically, his own step-daughter, not to mention the detail that she is his junior by 35 years. Is it that he took nude pictures of her in his apartment, pictures that revealed the affair when her mother found them in Soon-Yi's room? Or was it his public statement Monday that admitted the affair and raved about the way she "continues to turn my life around in a wonderfully positive way"?

As though this blatant breach of parental trust is not enough, now Miss Farrow, through her lawyer — none other than the redoubtable Alan Derschowitz, who last defended Mike Tyson — has accused Mr. Allen of sexually molesting the couple's 7-year-old adopted daughter, Dylan. Mr. Allen vigorously denied this in a press conference Tuesday and in turn accused Miss Farrow of trying to blackmail him. Someone in Miss Farrow's camp has provided the press with a videotape of her questioning the girl about Mr. Allen's deeds. Police in Connecticut, where her summer home is, are investigating the charges.

Who is telling the truth here remains to be determined, but one thing is certain: The losers in this twisted plot have to be the children, not just Soon-Yi and Dylan, but the others as well, who have to be traumatized by events ripping their lives apart. If this is what happens when traditional family structures break down, when trust and responsibility invested in parents by their children are thrown to the winds, then heaven help us all.

■ **FOOTNOTE**: And, finally, a tidbit for those who somehow missed the fine coverage of the story served up by the New York Post. This is the lead of Post columnist Mike McAlary's sanctimonious musings on the conservative madness of treating family values as a political issue: "In the beginning, there was Murphy Brown, a fictional character giving birth to a fictional baby. Then there was Dan Quayl(e), a national figure of almost fictional proportion, giving us his dreamy vision of the American family. Then there came Bill Clinton, an invention of writers who cannot differentiate fact from fiction, plagerizing [sic] the works of Dan Quayle on family values." O tempora, o mores.

The Hutchinson News
Hutchinson, Kansas, August 21, 1992

But make no mistake, celebrity does not enable participants to transcend the personal invasion of private affairs.

This mess will linger long after the characters in this play begin to run from news conferences, speeches, statements and interviews.

What will remain, of course, is a family of children who look on at the adults leading this public carnival, and they will be left wondering where exactly they might fit in.

The Allen-Farrow ex-couple could have remained tight-lipped about their private lives, but they have chosen to use their own celebrity as a weapon in a burgeoning legal battle.

Perhaps parents of less fame have lives that are less complicated. Even so, the romantic involvements and eruptions for the less-known are no less painful. They simply have a smaller audience.

The Woody Allen-Mia Farrow scandal that is emerging nationwide is as loopy and carnal an affair as we have seen lately.

The dippy comedian, often portrayed as a quiet, unassuming comic genius, is embroiled in a spat of epic proportions, one even he couldn't conjure as one of his glimpses-of-life films for which he is so famous.

Actor-writer Allen, whose cup of tea is the exploration of human angst, now is getting a gut-full of it.

For one thing, the Allen-Farrow dispute is hardly funny. And it is a public debate, which only intensifies the human pain that is already apparent.

The lives of actors are commonly explored in the press by virtue of their fame. But here we have the unfortunate addition of his relationship with Ms. Farrow's adult adopted daughter to complicate the already messy fight.

THE BLADE
Toledo, Ohio, August 22, 1992

THE reaction of much of the civilized world to the reported misdeeds of Woody Allen and his family have largely consisted of expressions of horror and disbelief, but that in part is a reflection of the fact that there's precious little else these days on the cultural front to get upset about.

Granted, the Republicans scored a 9.5 on the horror-and-disbelief scale last week in their war against the alleged moral excesses of network television, but only among Democrats.

The loudest cultural H & D expressions, prior to the Allen blow-up, were prompted by the marital woes that continue to bedevil the British royal family — and, indeed, photos in the London papers last week that reportedly showed a semi-clad Fergie in the company of a man not her husband have sparked renewed outrage in a few circles.

The demise of the Allen-Mia Farrow relationship and the affair that Allen supposedly had with his stepdaughter — not to mention dark accusations of child abuse — all seem to have come from a Woody Allen film, or perhaps the parts that were left on the cutting-room floor before *Manhattan* or *Hannah And Her Sisters* were released. Life, it is often said, imitates art.

However, if Allen weren't a film-maker or the oddball that he appears to be, all of these tidbits might never have leaped off the pages of People magazine to seize the public's imagination.

Certainly the public's horror and disbelief have been aroused in this case. But it might be a better idea to direct it at the widespread suffering that goes in Yugoslavia and Somalia, two current examples of genuine human misery, rather than at the mishaps that afflict one of this nation's most idiosyncratic filmmakers/actors and what's left of his family.

The Hartford Courant
Hartford, Connecticut, August 31, 1992

The Mia Farrow-Woody Allen saga seems to read like a contemporary "Oedipus Rex" with its classic characters and its epic plot: Dynasty has private family trouble, with tragic results.

Yet far less is known about the misalliances in the houses of the movie-screen dynasty of Ms. Farrow and Mr. Allen than about the confusion in the houses of Laius and Jocasta, the ruling dynasty of Thebes. Their son, Oedipus, raised by another king, unwittingly murdered his father and married his mother. There are several million college freshmen who have probed the dynamics of the Greek tragedy, which gave name to the Oedipus complex. The truth of the charges and countercharges in the Farrow-Allen family saga may never be known.

A pox on both the Farrow and Allen houses, however, for the behavior of the adults who head them. When the couple's breakup went public with Mr. Allen's application for custody of the children, and then Ms. Farrow's allegations of child molestation, the former lovers waged open campaigns against each other, employing fax machines and press conferences. Complicating the battle, of course, is Mr. Allen's love affair with Ms. Farrow's adopted 21-year-old daughter, Soon-Yi.

What fascinates Americans about this private drama gone public is that the Farrow-Allen muddle, like the Oedipus cycle, is fundamentally about age-old family dilemmas — who gets included in the definition of the family and what are the rules for the members. Is it taboo to fall in love with a sort-of relative? Is the adopted daughter of a former lover in fact a relative? What makes a man a father figure?

The answers used to be so easy. Now society is groping for a consensus as the definition of the American family changes, and changes again.

THE TAMPA TRIBUNE
Tampa, Florida, August 20, 1992

Woody Allen movies apparently have limited appeal in West Central Florida, perhaps because they are regarded as too "New Yorkerish." The films are shown in only a very few theaters hereabouts and they don't stay around very long. That's too bad because Allen possesses one of the great comic imaginations of our time, and his insistence on brooding about the meaning of life and death is oddly engaging.

Allen's longtime relationship with Mia Farrow, who maintains an apartment across Central Park from his, has always seemed in complete harmony with his eccentric movie scripts. Farrow adopts children and animals in large lots, so her busy domestic life understandably didn't suit the introspective Woody, who likes his peace and quiet.

He will have little peace and quiet anytime soon. In a full-bore domestic squabble that is both bemusing and revolting, Mia and Woody are headed for the courtroom. He wants custody of their biological child and the two children they adopted together. Mia says no. Mia says Woody molested one of their youngsters. And Mia is angry because Woody is having an affair with 21-year-old Soon-Yi Farrow Previn, whom Mia adopted when she was married to conductor Andre Previn. Mia was previously married to Frank Sinatra, who doesn't figure in this story.

Allen, who is 56, is characterized by Mia's 81-year-old mother, the actress Maureen O'Sullivan who played Jane in the old Tarzan movies, as "a desperate and evil man."

Many of us, from time to time, regret our humdrum lives, especially when we observe the glamorous and intensely interesting doings of the rich and famous. But the Mia-Woody saga, along with offering an addendum of sorts to the discourse on family values, makes humdrum look like a heavenly lifestyle.

The Philadelphia Inquirer
Philadelphia, Pennsylvania, August 19, 1992

Like a lot of film buffs, our thoughts upon learning that Woody Allen had taken up with Mia Farrow's 21-year-old adopted daughter turned to the movie *Manhattan*. But not for the obvious reason.

That 1979 movie, which Mr. Allen wrote, directed and starred in, did indeed include a romance between 42-year-old Isaac, the character played by Mr. Allen, and a 17-year-old schoolgirl. But there was an air of innocence about that relationship that is in no way comparable to the real-life situation: a 56-year-old man seducing the daughter of his longtime lover.

Betrayal and moral rot were, however, major themes in *Manhattan*, and Mr. Allen, though never losing his sense of humor, inveighed powerfully against them. In a climactic scene, Isaac confronts his best friend Yale, who has been sleeping with Isaac's girlfriend while deceiving his own wife. The two men are standing in a science classroom with a skeleton hanging between them.

"I'm not a saint, OK?" Yale protests.

"You're too easy on yourself," Isaac counters.

Yale pleads that he's just human while Isaac seems to think he's God. ("I've got to model myself after someone," Isaac replies.) Finally, gesturing to the skeleton, Isaac asks:

"What are future generations going to think of us? Some day we're going to be like him. He was probably one of the beautiful people. He was probably dancing and playing tennis and everything. This is what happens to us. You know, it's very important to have some kind of personal integrity. You know, I'll be hanging in a classroom one day and I want to make sure that when I 'thin out' that I'm well thought of."

Isaac may have been true to those sentiments, but, sadly, Mr. Allen has not.

The Seattle Times
Seattle, Washington, August 24, 1992

A MUCH younger Woody Allen bragged on the "The Ed Sullivan Show" that he grew up in a neighborhood that was so tough the teen-age hoodlums stole hubcaps off moving cars.

A million wisecracks later, Allen, 56 is a celebrated writer and director whose emotional development was apparently arrested along with his juvenile delinquent friends.

Allen is enmeshed in a child custody battle with his companion of 12 years, Mia Farrow. For those dozen years, Allen was the father and father figure for Farrow's 11 biological and adopted children.

Mom is an actress, and Dad is the neurotic alchemist who turns angst into gold. Their bustling household in New York City is spread between separate apartments that face each other across Central Park. Wave at Daddy having toast.

It's the kind of endearingly bizarre arrangement ascribed to wealthy, eccentric show folk, people who move in circles where ignoring conventions is conventional behavior, and the rest of us keep tabs through People magazine.

Still, for all of its Norman Rockwell asymmetry, the Farrow-Allen polyglot was every much a family unit as that statistical anomaly with a working father, stay-at-home mother and 2.3 children. Mutual nurture, support and respect not only sustain, but also define families.

All of which combines to make Allen's love affair with Farrow's 21-year-old daughter as morally repugnant as incest between blood relatives.

For all practical — and perhaps legal — intents he was the woman's father for most of her young life. He has crossed a boundary that cannot be rationalized away with urbane wit or psychological delusion.

In the midst of this personal tragedy, Allen's latest movie with Farrow has opened to a queasy reception from viewers made squeamish by true-life subtext. Allen and Farrow play a husband and wife whose marriage is ending because of the man's affair with a 21-year-old woman.

A generation of movie patrons have worked with Allen on their collective neuroses. This time there are no laughs. Families come in all shapes and sizes, but some values survive the comic's wit and the screen writer's imagination.

THE DENVER POST
Denver, Colorado, August 25, 1992

FROM "Sleeper" to "Radio Days," from "Manhattan" to "Husbands and Wives," Woody Allen's offbeat but delightful visions of life have earned him millions of admirers around the world, as well as the accolades of his peers.

But, even rejecting as untrue the allegations of sexual misconduct made against him by his long-time but now-estranged lover Mia Farrow, there is one aspect of their very public feud that should distress his fans, and that is Allen's self-confessed love for Farrow's adopted daughter, Soon-Yi Previn.

The 56-year-old filmmaker and his 21-year-old consort did not live in the same household, and Previn claims that Allen was not a father figure to her. But the relationship between the two still should have been that of a stepparent and stepchild.

Allen was, after all, the lover of the child's adoptive mother. For Allen to cross into the realm of romance with his de facto stepdaughter was at the least unseemly. This fact is true regardless of whether the child was 18 or 21, as seems to be the dispute in young Previn's case, or whether Allen and Farrow already were on the verge of ending their apparently tumultuous relationship.

Since Allen unquestionably was the adult in the situation, the responsibility must rest on his shoulders. His brilliance on film is no excuse for disreputable stupidity in real life.

Movie-goers may always laugh at Woody Allen's films, but whether they retain personal respect for the man now appears uncertain. People can't always keep themselves from falling in love with someone else, but there ought to be sane limits on all human behavior, and social boundaries are not simply just shadows and fog.

St. Louis Review
St. Louis, Missouri, August 28, 1992

While the Republican Party recently hammered out a platform based on family values, the nation's headlines were focused on the Woody Allen-Mia Farrow breakup and its allegations of incest.

For many, the 11-year-old Allen-Farrow relationship had come to symbolize the nontraditional family. Here were a man and woman who appeared to be happily and successfully challenging the marriage commitment. They lived intimately yet apart and nurtured their biological and adopted children as traditional parents do.

But now Allen has admitted he is having an intimate relationship with one of Farrow's adopted daughters, Soon-Yi, and feels no "great moral dilemma" is involved. And Farrow has accused Allen of sexually molesting the seven-year-old daughter they adopted together.

There are some, including Allen, who question whether incest is involved at all. Allen denies molesting his adopted daughter and says he never assumed the father role with Soon-Yi. But there is evidence that he did, leading many to point to his affair with her as a sign of the moral decay of American society today.

Yet incest has occurred for thousands of years. Paul, in his first letter to the Corinthians, condemned a similar situation. Even earlier, the Ten Commandments were handed down as moral guidelines for all of us as members of families and communities.

What may be more of an indication of our society's moral thinking is the reaction of others to Allen's affair with Soon-Yi. The majority, including many of the more permissive younger generation, have condemned Allen.

In USA Today, columnist Joe Urschel said even an unconventional father has responsibilities to the feelings of the woman he loved, the children he raised with her and the conventions of society. Martha Shirk, in the St. Louis Post-Dispatch, wrote, "That Allen can admit to a relationship with Soon-Yi says there is something wrong with both his judgment and his understanding of the father-daughter bond."

Yet Bruce Howard, a comedy writer and close friend of Allen's, said, "There's a genius built into him, and I think one day people will look back on this and joke about it." Robert Stack said, "Everybody marches to his own drummer . . . It's a bizarre profession with bizarre highs and lows. We deal in a world of fantasy and the cleavage line between talent and strange behavior is very thin."

It would be a serious mistake for us to do as Stack has and write this incident off as something that happens to eccentric celebrities. Incest and other physical and emotional child abuse happen every day in every kind of family, including some traditional families that may appear, from the outside, to be law-abiding, church-going people.

If we become aware of such abuse within our families or among our friends, we have a moral responsibility to reach out to both the children and the abusers, who many times are yesterday's victims. Family values, moral values, are not to be just the subject of political speeches and gossip columns. They are something to be lived.

Sexual Politics In America

WOODY ALLEN

"IT'S MR. ALLEN — HE HAS AN IDEA FOR A MOVIE."

The Gazette
Cedar Rapids, Iowa, August 23, 1992

WHAT ARE fans of comedy writer-actor Woody Allen to make of his suddenly nasty child-custody fight with his former companion, actress Mia Farrow? One week they are quietly sorting out their problems; the next week she is accusing him of child molestation, and her attorney, Alan Dershowitz, is making the talk-show rounds.

First Allen is accused of having an affair with one of Farrow's grown adopted daughters while still being involved with Farrow. Then a supposedly incriminating videotape materializes; it shows the couple's 7-year-old adopted daughter being interviewed by Farrow off camera. Next, two ex-husbands, composer Andre Previn and crooner-actor Frank Sinatra, weigh in with heavy support of Farrow. Previn blasts Allen because it's his adopted daughter Allen allegedly was involved with.

Woody Allen
Charges shatter image

In these liberated times, reports of unsavory conduct don't necessarily hurt a movie star's box office returns. Viewers are concerned mainly with what's on the screen. With Woody Allen, though, infamy could be specially damaging. What's on the screen, especially in the earlier nutty films, is a unique extension of the artist's persona. It has earned Allen the sort of respect once commanded by Charles Chaplin.

When Allen turned 50 in 1985, Lloyd Rose of Atlantic wrote, "He (Allen) knew that although he might look like a nebbish and sometimes act like a nebbish, he was in fact a very smart guy. If he was scared of the world, this was proof of his intelligence. And no matter how much the world might frighten him, nothing could persuade him to take it seriously."

Some commentators feel Allen's later films betray "a loss of artistic moorings." In the tawdry custody lawsuit ahead, Mia Farrow's attorneys probably will make much of those lost moorings. The child-abuse accusations, if they stick, will give Allen's films a retroactive grotesqueness. Viewers may never look at them the same way again.

It is still too early to appraise the damage to Woody Allen's career. But you know your stock is plummeting when Frank Sinatra shows up as a character witness for the other side.

DAYTON DAILY NEWS
Dayton, Ohio, August 21, 1992

Woody Allen's admission about his private life is not going to enhance his reputation. He is having an affair with a woman who is apparently — nobody is quite sure — 21 years old and is the adopted daughter of his former lover and her former husband.

Sort it all out, and it's not incest. It's not child abuse. It's behavior that some will defend as harmless and none of the public's business, anyway.

Woody Allen

Still, the preference of some successful, aging men for women who are not matches for them — and who can be expected to treat them with more awe than anybody should be treated — is not an endearing characteristic.

Would, however, that this were the only issue in Mr. Allen's bitter split with Mia Farrow.

Either he is a child-abusing monster, or she is a monster bent on the destruction of an innocent man. Or, there is one heck of a misunderstanding.

It's all so sad. Millions of middle-aged Americans have — quite simply — loved "Woody" since they were in college. They enjoyed so much of his work for so long that they developed the habit of forgiving him for doing much that was self-indulgent and boring, that seemed to go over the same material over and over.

They have had no difficulty whatsoever in tolerating his choice of a private life that would irritate the Houston Republicans. He ignored the institution of marriage for years, keeping an apartment separate from his loved ones. Such idiosyncratic behavior seemed entirely appropriate for Woody.

What, after all, was he supposed to do — settle in the suburbs and take up gardening? *That* would have been unforgivable.

Woody seemed to be living a life that would make a good Woody Allen comedy.

But now it has changed into a Woody Allen tragedy. And a lot of people are saddened who don't live in Manhattan.

Part IV: The Arts & Sex

A war over culture is being waged in the United States. With the clergy, irate taxpayers and outraged parents on one side, and painters, gallery owners and performance artists on the other, the place of the arts in society and what role government should assume in supporting them is quickly reaching a flash point. As old-fashioned moralists collide with the avant-garde, many issues are being raised for the first time. Who is to judge what art is worthy and what is not? How are conflicts between decency and free expression to be sorted out? What role should the government assume in supporting the arts?

When the National Endowment for the Arts (NEA) was established in 1965 these questions were not much cause for concern. But in recent yars a furor has arisen over the NEA and its grants to a handful of controversial artists. Disputes over morals and free expression, the First Amendment and the Ten Commandments are spilling onto a broad cultural terrain. Everything from the homoerotic works of the late photographer Robert Mapplethorpe to the onstage antics of performance artists such as Karen Finley to the burning of the American flag seems likely to bring out strong opposition.

Certainly the recent sense of purge that the artistic community is experiencing is nothing new in the U.S. During the 1930s, the House Un-American Activities Committee (HUAC) closed the Federal Theatre Project, staffed with the likes of Orson Welles and John Houseman, charging that it was filled with subversives. After World War II, HUAC focused much of its work on Hollywood, resulting in the blackballing of dozens of actors, directors and others for their alleged communist affiliations.

"You've got a fight going on today that is just as emotional as the fight that took place then," said Rep. Sidney Yates (D, Ill.), a 20-term House veteran and defender of the arts. "Except communism isn't the bogeyman. This time it's pornography and obscenity."

Supporters of the arts argue that by current standards, the work of Mapplethorpe and Finley is not obscene. It does, however, disgust many ordinary Americans all the same. Detractors of these and other artists and performers charge that those who delight in shocking conventional people have no right to cry foul when these people kick back.

A Gallup poll released in July 1990 suggests that the art crowd has more public backing than its detractors might want to admit. Though the poll showed that 71% of Americans believed obscenity has increased in the arts and that 78% think parents should do more to protect their children from it, it also showed that 75% don't want anyone imposing laws on what they can see or hear. In addition, the fact that more people now go to arts events than to live sports events indicates that the arts should be able to put up a good fight.

Perhaps their main opponent in this aesthetic and ideological tussle is Sen. Jesse Helms (R, N.C.), Capitol Hill's point man against obscenity. Insisting that he is not a censor, Helms has been bent on preventing the NEA from spending tax money on art that might offend God-fearing Americans. "If America persists in the way it's going, and the Lord doesn't strike us down," he says, "we ought to apologize to Sodom and Gomorrah."

The Mapplethorpe photos have been a boon for Helms's direct-mail fund-raising operation. By suggesting that "perverted art" is just a half-step away from a homosexual takeover, he raised several million dollars in mostly small donations from across the country.

But on Capitol Hill, Helms is often a strike force of one as he harangues his colleagues and threatens to portray them as pro-obscenity. In turn, the Democrats question whether Helms can make Mapplethorpe a metaphor for discontent about cultural values. They point out that though people might be concerned about the state of American morality, it may be Hollywood rather than the NEA that is the focus of their concern.

To make matters even thornier, the NEA is caught in a cross-fire between political opponents such as Helms and detractors from its own ranks. These detractors are members of the artistic community who, though they have no problem with the work of Mapplethorpe, Finley or their ilk, fault the Endowment's coziness with big museums and the power brokers of the New York/Los Angeles art establishment as well as the cronyism that periodically afflicts the peer-review panels who authorize grants.

Censorship is nothing new and is not confined to the arts. All modes of expression whether defined as "art," "news" or "pornography" have been subject to scrutiny for centuries. The tug-of-war that ranges the arts and media against the political, religious, social and business interests that attempt to regulate their dissemination has continued into the late 20th century.

One of the masterworks of modern fiction, James Joyce's *Ulysses*, was banned in the U.S. for years following its publication in France in 1922. But the battle has not ended there. J.D. Salinger's books, most notably *Catcher in the Rye*, are still subject to periodic legal challenge. Most recently, Sen. Jesse Helms has caused heated debate by seeking to limit the nature of the grants awarded by the NEA.

The current test for obscenity, as set down by the U.S. Supreme Court, derives from the case of *Miller v. California* (1973). It requires that all these conditions be satisfied: the "average person," taking contemporary community standards would find a work, taken as a whole, appealing to prurient (sexually arousing) interests; the work depicts or describes sexual conduct in a patently offensive manner; the work taken as a whole, lacks serious literary, artistic, political or scientific value. The general effect of such definitions is for obscenity cases to be limited to allegedly hard-core pornography. State laws generally ban all trafficking in obscene materials, but the compulsion under *Miller* to define such materials by a specific test has forced some states to reenact old laws or create new ones for their own use.

'Obscene' Art Ban Threatened; Compromise Reached

The Senate July 26, 1989 voted to accept the House's $45,000 cut in funding for the National Endowment for the Arts (NEA) and approved additional restrictions that would prohibit any federal funding of "obscene or indecent" art works.

The budget cut and restrictions were contained in an amendment to the Interior Department appropriation, which was passed by a voice vote. The amendment had been proposed by Sen. Jesse A. Helms (R, N.C.)

It specifically barred the NEA from using federal funds to "promote, disseminate or produce obscene or indecent materials, including but not limited to depictions of sadomasochism, homoeroticism, the exploitation of children, or individuals engaged in sex acts; or materials that denigrate the objects or beliefs of the adherents of a particular religion or nonreligion; or material which denigrates, debases, or reviles a person, group, or class of citizens on the basis of race, creed, sex, handicap, age or national origin.

The Senate also voted to cut off all federal grants for the next five years to two institutions that had sponsored controversial exhibits – the Institute for Contemporary Art at the University of Pennsylvania (which had sponsored a retrospective of photographs by Robert Mapplethorpe) and the Southeastern Center for Contemporary Art in Winston-Salem, N.C. (which had supported an exhibit by photographer Andres Serrano).

In addition, the Senate measure called for a cut of $400,000 in the endowment's grants to visual artists and increases of $200,000, respectively, in its budget to local projects and folk art.

A House and Senate conference committee Sept. 29 rejected the amendment.

Instead, the committee unanimously approved a series of compromise measures that had been passed earlier in the day by the Senate. The strongest of the proposals would bar the NEA from funding art work that was obscene as defined by the standards of the Supreme Court's 1973 *Miller v. California* decision. Under the *Miller* ruling, a work was judged to be obscene if it appealed to prurient interest, contained patently offensive portrayals of specific sexual conduct and lacked serious literary or artistic value. The NEA would decide for itself whether a particular work met the definition.

In addition, the compromise allocated $250,000 to establish a 12-member commission that would review the NEA's grant-making procedures and decide whether those procedures should be revised. The measure also cut the agency's total budget by $45,000 – the amount the NEA had spent to support two controversial photography exhibits by Mapplethorpe and Serrano.

The committee dropped the Senate proposal that had called for a five-year ban on federal funding for the Institute on Contemporary Art at the University of Pennsylvania and the Southeastern Center for Contemporary Art in Winston-Salem, N.C. Instead, the committee adopted a compromise that would put both organizations on probation for a year and would require the NEA to "notify" Congress if it wished to provide grant money to either group.

Lastly, the compromise reinstated $400,000 that the Senate had shifted from the NEA's visual arts program to other projects.

The adoption of the compromise followed a Sept. 28 vote in which the Senate had reversed its previous position and voted down the original Helms amendment, 62-35. The Senate then voted Sept. 29 to adopt a revised version of the amendment, by a vote of 65-31, and the revision was sent to the conference committee.

The Washington Post
Washington, D.C., July 30, 1989

THE SENATE, like the House, has been struggling to decide whether to restrict the sort of art the federal government should be allowed to fund and, if so, how. Now comes Sen. Jesse Helms (R-N.C.) to provide guidance. No federal money, the senator proposed, should be used to "promote or disseminate: 1) obscene or indecent materials, including but not limited to depictions of sadomasochism, homoeroticism, the exploitation of children, or individuals engaged in sex acts; or 2) any "material which denigrates the objects or beliefs of the adherents of a particular religion or non-religion; or 3) material which denigrates, debases, or reviles a person, group, or class of citizens on the basis of race, creed, sex, handicap, age, or national origin."

To this array of injunctions upon the content of future artwork the government might fund—not only in the visual arts, where recent controversy has arisen but also in publicly supported plays, poetry readings, films and TV documentaries—the Senate responded unequivocally. It passed the Helms amendment by voice vote.

The two barely cloaked assumptions underlying the vote are that the amendment is unlikely to survive to the final bill and that nobody could be expected actually to *oppose* a measure that proclaims such high sentiments. A bare handful of lawmakers—among them Sens. Howard Metzenbaum (D-Ohio) and John Chafee (R-R.I.)—did express misgivings over whether this kind of proscription would really advance the National Arts Endowment's stated mission of fostering the arts, let alone, as the authorizing legislation puts it, the "encouragement of free inquiry and expression."

Freedom of expression, artistic or otherwise, is not, we stress, censored or suppressed by this sort of legislation. The government as arts patron is within its rights to fund or refuse to fund anything it chooses. But whether it is exercising this right in a way that makes any sense is a different question, and in this case it is not.

The Helms amendment was proposed to a near-empty chamber with little or no advance warning, and with no examination of its implications for the existing peer review system of awarding grants. There was no scrutiny of what previously funded artworks the newly expansive language would cover. Would it have ruled out support for the National Gallery's Gauguin show? For Rodin's sculpture "The Kiss"? For a community Shakespeare series that included "The Merchant of Venice"? On such a matter the senators' hasty, cross-your-fingers-and-look-the-other-way acquiescence to the Helms amendment does not make sense except as a flight from responsibility. The way to debate issues of congressional arts funding is to debate them. The conference committee should delete the Helms amendment, not just for the arts' sake but for the sake of its own dignity.

THE ARIZONA REPUBLIC
Phoenix, Arizona, July 14, 1989

IN a mild rebuke of public subsidies for questionable "art," the House of Representatives this week trimmed $45,000 from its appropriation for the National Endowment for the Arts. This was out of a total budget of $171 million. And though some were heard to gasp "censorship," such modest pruning seems unlikely to touch off the Dark Ages.

What it does do — or so we may hope — is send a warning to those who suppose that the taxpayers are required by the Constitution to dig into their pockets so that kinky "artists" may flaunt their indecencies.

With few exceptions, House members were offended by two government grants in particular. One went to the Southeastern Center for Contemporary Art in North Carolina, which paid Andres Serrano $15,000 to submerge a crucifix in a jar of urine. The other provided $30,000 to the Philadelphia Institute of Contemporary Art, which used the money to exhibit the "homoerotic" photographs of the late Robert Mapplethorpe, who died of AIDS last March.

"The Mapplethorpe show," *The New York Times* reported delicately, "was criticized by many for its sexual content." In fact, the photographs were grossly pornographic. *Washington Post* ombudsman Richard Harwood revealed their character in response to a reader's facetious suggestion that the photographs be published.

"There is not the slightest possibility that this newspaper today or on any other day in the 20th century would publish any of the photographs in question," he wrote. "The storm created would make life in the newsroom difficult and likely would cause certain vacancies in the executive ranks."

If private organizations wish to patronize such "artists" at their own expense, that is their business. But it is indefensible for the government to use its coercive authority to extract money from the public for such purposes.

The law has to be considered as well. Under a 1985 statute, the National Endowment for the Arts is specifically prohibited from funding grossly offensive projects — a category that, by even the most permissive standards, would include the works of Messrs. Mapplethorpe and Serrano. The National Endowment, which nevertheless authorized the funding of these projects, ought to have been flogged much more severely than the House could bring itself to authorize.

Even so, the message may have gotten through. Though it may howl about censorship, what really concerns the art establishment is money. The chances are reasonably good that when the next starving "artist" turns up with a crucifix to dunk, he will be advised to go soak his head.

THE PLAIN DEALER
Cleveland, Ohio, July 30, 1989

Politicians make lousy art critics, but that hasn't stopped meddlesome moralists in Congress from injecting politics into the process of aiding America's cultural institutions. With a series of mean-spirited swipes at the National Endowment for the Arts, Congress has overstepped its oversight role and endangered the NEA's rightful independence in making artistic judgments. By trying to condemn points of view it finds offensive, Congress intrudes intolerably in the freedom of expression.

It was bad enough when the House last week slapped the NEA on the wrist, cutting $45,000 from its budget as punishment for granting money to two controversial recent exhibitions. That cut would offset $45,000 in grants to two groups—the Southeastern Center for Contemporary Art in Winston-Salem, N.C., and the Institute of Contemporary Art at the University of Pennsylvania—that mounted artworks by Robert Mapplethorpe and Andres Serrano.

Those artists' works may indeed be shocking, manipulative and outrageous. We don't presume to pre-empt each viewer's right to judge their artistic merit; neither should Congress. Those works were chosen through the long-standing NEA grantmaking policy of "peer review," designed to insulate artists from the very type of pressure Congress now exerts.

The Senate this week compounded the error, cutting the NEA budget and imposing a punitive, five-year ban on all NEA grants to the Winston-Salem and Philadelphia institutes. But that didn't appease the Senate's self-appointed scourge, Jesse Helms of North Carolina. The Senate approved his amendment to ban all grants for "obscene or indecent materials"—offering a broad-brush denunciation of many topics that are central to great art.

If the Bible Belt bluenose would ban any denigration of religion, presumably the NEA would bar any aid for groups that include Shylock in Shakespeare's "Merchant of Venice." Forbidding any offense to the handicapped, congressional censors would demand that the hunchbacked king in "Richard III" be bowdlerized; if ageism is taboo, there'll be no more grants to depict the addled "King Lear." To avoid any explicit depiction of sex, perhaps the NEA would deny aid to colleges that study classic paintings like "The Rape of the Sabine Women," the erotic poetry of Sappho or bawdy novels like Vladimir Nabokov's "Lolita."

Congress should remove its appalling gag order on art, which reflects a narrow-minded attack on free inquiry and "highbrow" culture. America's commitment to supporting the arts requires sensitivity to the creative process and imaginative viewpoints—a standard that this Congress apparently holds in contempt.

THE COMMERCIAL APPEAL
Memphis, Tennessee, July 18, 1989

ART may be in the eye of the beholder, but most citizens can recognize trash when they see it. And it's a sure thing they don't want their tax dollars used to subsidize it.

The U.S. House of Representatives acted appropriately the other day when it rebuked the National Endowment for the Arts for contributing $45,000 to help finance two exceedingly distasteful photographic productions palmed off as art.

One is a photograph by Andres Serrano of a crucifix submerged in a container of the photographer's urine. This piece of filth was subsidized to the tune of $15,000 by the Southeastern Center for Contemporary Art in Winston-Salem, N.C., which gets federal money from the NEA.

The other is a collection of photographs by Robert Mapplethorpe that have a homosexual and sadomasochistic orientation. Mapplethorpe, an acknowledged homosexual, died recently of complications from AIDS. The NEA provided $30,000 to the Philadelphia Institute of Contemporary Art for a traveling exhibit of his work.

There was some sentiment in the House to give the NEA a very heavy whack. Rep. Dick Armey (R-Texas) wanted to cut the agency's $171 million by 10 percent. A few who don't believe in government subsidization of the arts would like to wipe out the entire budget.

In the end, the House voted 361 to 65 to cut NEA funding by $45,000, the amount the agency gave to the two controversial exhibits.

Rep. Charles Stenholm (D-Texas), who introduced the compromise measure, called it a "shot across the bow" that sends an "appropriate message without shooting everything in sight."

Some arts supporters complained of censorship and said the action sets a disturbing precedent for congressional interference in the NEA's grant procedure. That's hogwash.

Members of Congress are sent to Washington to represent the people, and in this instance the House undoubtedly did. This wasn't censorship of art. The Serranos and Mapplethorpes of the world can photograph whatever they want.

The House simply passed notice, as Armey said, that the taxpayers shouldn't be called on "to fund whatever outrage or trash some artists dream up."

The Register-Guard
Eugene, Oregon, July 31, 1989

We don't expect Sen. Jesse Helms to know any better, but other members of Congress should. Lawmakers have no business deciding what is or isn't art, or who is or isn't an artist.

But that's just what the Senate and House are trying to do in the legislative backlash to a couple of artistic exhibitions that some senators and representatives found objectionable.

At the center of the hubbub were photographic exhibitions by Andres Serrano and the late Robert Mapplethorpe. Both exhibits were supported by arts groups that received funds from the National Endowment for the Arts. The works of both artists are highly controversial, being variously described in terms ranging from "bold" to "disgustingly obscene." The politicians responded because some $45,000 of the NEA's annual $171 million (congressionally approved) budget found its way to the Serrano and Mapplethorpe exhibitions.

While the endowment can be second-guessed for its financial decision, its artistic judgment is specifically designed to be screened from political interference. Congress itself approved a peer-review process by which members of the arts community pass on grant applications in their respective fields. The process is designed to prevent precisely the kind of meddling now going on in the Senate and House.

The two chambers expressed their unhappiness with the NEA in different ways. Neither is acceptable, but the House's approach is far preferable to the Senate's. The House opted for a slap on the wrist; the Senate — led by Helms' righteously indignant harrumphs — chose a firing squad. The House simply cut the NEA's budget by $45,000 — the amount of endowment money that went to the Serrano and Mapplethorpe exhibitions — but the chamber placed no restrictions on the rest of the NEA budget.

In the Senate, Helms obtained voice-vote approval of an amendment to 1) prohibit for five years any NEA grants to the two regional arts groups — one in Pennsylvania, the other in North Carolina — that helped fund the Serrano/Mapplethorpe exhibits; 2) prohibit the use of federal funds to promote, produce or dissiminate "obscene or indecent" art works, and 3) prohibit federal funds for works that denigrate "the objects or beliefs of the adherents of a particular religion or non-religion."

Helms' definitions would cast a wide net — wider even than the South Carolina senator might prefer. But as columnist Tom Wicker points out on the opposite page, Helms' main intent probably was less to pass restrictive legislation than to send a message to the arts world that Congress has become the country's arts arbiter and will quickly jerk the NEA's tether if the agency's grants offend congressional sensitivities.

We suspect that Wicker is right about Helms' intent. If so, the message is chilling indeed, for it could lead the NEA to turn down grant applications for art works that some politician might consider controversial. That in turn could have a stifling effect on artists dependent upon NEA largess. That mustn't be allowed to happen, for as The New York Times says, it would drain art of creativity, controversy — and life.

Art, by definition, involves the artist's imagination and perception, and is inherently a *personal* statement. The NEA's mission, through the peer-review process, is to help visual and performing artists reach the full extent of their potential and, in the process, to help elevate not only the beauty but the spirit of the nation. The peer-review process works in the pursuit of that mission. Congressional interference won't.

The Atlanta Journal and THE ATLANTA CONSTITUTION
Atlanta, Georgia, September 15, 1989

Push is coming to shove in Congress over federal arts funding as House and Senate conference-committee representatives prepare to work out milewide differences in the bills passed by the two chambers. Actually, no legislation at all is called for, but Congress has let itself become embroiled in the flap over a handful of controversial photographs.

The result in the House was legislation giving a slight financial rap to the National Endowment for the Arts, certainly the most that can be justified by the incidents. The Senate, however, suckered for a Jesse Helms bill that would rip major funding away from the two respected art institutions that exhibited the work and would bar federal aid for work that is obscene or indecent, or, for that matter, simply cheeky.

Note the two words. "Obscene" has specific legal standing. Works falling within the definition are illegal, and any congressional prohibition against their funding is thus unnecessary.

"Indecent," however, has no legal meaning. Its adoption in law would allow every on-the-make politician, crusading bluenose or free-form demagogue in the country to raise the charge against even garden-variety nude paintings or plays with salty language. Enactment of the legislation would set legitimate art up for harassment and would have a deeply chilling effect on artists.

Nor is that the end of it. The Helms law also bans funding for art that "denigrates the objects or beliefs of ... a particular religion or non-religion or denigrates, debases or reviles a person, group or class of citizens on the basis of race, creed, sex, handicap or national origin." That would effectively bar aided art from any social controversy, even from unpleasant if apt commentary.

The South in particular has an interest in keeping the prudish Helms cloak from being dropped over arts support.

Traditionally starved for major private funding for the arts, the region has seen a remarkable burst of creativity, especially in drama but in the visual arts as well, as a result of even the relatively modest amount of federal support that has become available. Even small grants have gone a long way n this region. The South's landscape artists and the playwrights of historical givens would have no trouble with the Senate's legislation, but then, such work never wants. The artistic yeastiness of recent years would be flattened.

Presumably the conference committee will have a difficult time rejecting the Helms law. Members fear that a vote against it will set them up for re-election challenges claiming they are thus in favor of obscenity. Already, cynically, Republican candidates have used that charge in some special elections.

Is it too much to ask, however, that for once the members simply do what is right? Or has Congress lost the knack altogether?

The Washington Post
Washington, D.C., September 16, 1989

OPPONENTS OF Sen. Jesse Helms's amendment to restrict federal arts funding had feared that a recorded vote in Congress would be hard to win. The senator's allies, they believed, would depict any vote against the measure as a declaration in favor of pornography, and that would be hard to explain at home. This is exactly the tactic used when the question came up on the House floor Wednesday, but members of Congress refused to be intimidated and said no to the Helms amendment by a recorded vote of 264-153.

The amendment rose on the wave of controversy generated by two photography exhibits—including the work of Andres Serrano and Robert Mapplethorpe—funded by the National Endowment for the Arts. As passed by the Senate on voice (unrecorded) vote in July, it would prohibit spending to produce or disseminate material that is "obscene" or "denigrates" any religion "or nonreligion," or "reviles" anyone on the basis of race, creed, sex, handicap, age or national origin. The difficulty of defining such suggestive terms as "obscene" and "nonreligion" in a way that would leave the First Amendment intact is apparent at a glance. The sweep of the proposal, which applies, for example, to all museums that receive federal funds, is enormous. It would radically rewrite the necessarily uncertain and wary relationship between government and the arts.

In the House last Wednesday, Rep. Dana Rohrabacher (R-Calif.) asked that House conferees on the Interior appropriations bill, which includes the NEA, be directed to accept the Helms provision. He and his supporters repeated his earlier threat to characterize a vote on the procedural question of whether to take up his motion as a vote on pornography. Such an assertion is, of course, absurd. The issue was not whether to embrace pornography but whether to alter a procedure for subsidizing the arts that seems reasonable to most people and that has served both the government's interest in deciding what it should pay for and the arts' interest in maintaining a seemly independence.

The House, in turning down the Helms amendment, directed its conferees to address the issue of NEA grant-making. But House members, who over the summer had heard not only from Helms partisans but from home-town supporters of the current NEA system, did not see reason to order the peremptory replacement of peer review with a set of congressionally mandated standards—a dubious set at that. It's well that the Senate will have a chance in the currently calmer atmosphere to review its cave-in to intimidation and extremism of last July.

The Philadelphia Inquirer
Philadelphia, Pennsylvania,
September 15, 1989

By a wide margin, House members have torn up Sen. Jesse Helms' invitation to attend the gala opening of his punitive campaign against public funding for nasty artwork. The preliminary vote this week on an appropriations bill for the National Endowment for the Arts looks like the death knell for Mr. Helms' demagogic attempt to impose a broad-based ban on federal funding for artwork judged obscene, indecent or denigrating to a religion or ethnic group. As Democratic Rep. Sidney R. Yates of Illinois said, the vote was "a resounding vote against censorship." Glad to say, most Philadelphia-area representatives joined Mr. Yates.

There's still bad news, however, in that the legislation as it now stands would ban federal funding for the University of Pennsylvania's Institute of Contemporary Art for five years. It was the ICA that organized one of the two exhibits that started the ruckus — a showing of photos of Robert Mapplethorpe, including the one of a man urinating into another's mouth. The other exhibit was one by artist Andres Serrano that included a photograph of a crucifix in urine.

It's also unfortunate that one other sanction seems sure to make it into law. That's the provision punishing the NEA with a $45,000 budget cut, an amount equal to the cost of the two controversial exhibits.

Both penalties are blatantly unfair. The photographs of Mapplethorpe and Serrano were cleared by the NEA's peer review process as required by law. No matter what anyone thinks of their taste in art, the institutions involved were playing by the rules. This sort of vindictive political punishment is excessive.

The Helms amendment, which was approved by the Senate in July (but now presumably will be omitted from the NEA legislation by House-Senate conferees), was as unworkable as it was unwarranted. It not would only have stifled NEA arts funding, but also more than 30 other federal agencies where public funds are doled out for artwork.

What's more, members of Congress already have transmitted their displeasure with public funding for this kind of artwork. The NEA has no doubt already gotten the message, and will be most unlikely to use tax dollars for such obviously offensive exhibitions in the future.

The admonitions to the art world are punitive enough, even if too bland for Mr. Helms' tastes.

Bush Opposes Obscene Art Censorship

President George Bush said March 23, 1990 that opposed legislation that would bar the NEA from supporting "obscene" artwork.

In 1989, at the urging of Sen. Jesse Helms, Congress had approved an annual appropriation for the NEA that prohibited the agency from funding artwork that was considered obscene as defined by a 1973 Supreme Court ruling. Subsequently, the NEA had required grant recipients to sign a statement promising that they would not use the funds to create obscene art.

The legislation had been prompted by a controversy over two exhibits sponsored in part by the NEA – a retrospective of photographs by Robert Mapplethorpe, which included scenes of homoeroticism, and a photograph by Andres Serrano that depicted a crucifix in a jar of urine.

Helms had recently introduced an amendment to the NEA's reauthorization legislation for 1990 (the NEA was reauthorized every five years) that would prohibit funding of obscene or indecent art.

Bush said that while he had been "deeply offended by some of the filth that I see into which federal money has gone," nevertheless, he remained opposed to censorship. "I will try to convince those who feel differently in terms of legislation that we will do everything in our power to stop pure blasphemy," Bush pledged.

The Atlanta Journal and THE ATLANTA CONSTITUTION
Atlanta, Georgia, March 23, 1990

It is a scene out of classic melodrama: Little Nell is lashed to the railroad tracks, the locomotive is bearing down and the villain stands to the side, stroking his waxed mustache and chortling at the prospect of Nellburger, when —

When President Bush, to his great credit, comes to the rescue, throws the switch that sends the train fading harmlessly down a spur and the villain, muttering "Curses!" behind his stage mustache, is revealed as Sen. Jesse Helms, the North Carolina Republican, foiled in his attempt to misuse public funding as an excuse for a national witch-hunt against the arts.

But don't applaud too soon. This play isn't over.

The president's sanity will be a huge help, particularly in bucking up the politically faint in Congress, but Mr. Helms very much intends to continue the demagogic campaign he unleashed last year against the National Endowment for the Arts after the flap over NEA funding for a couple of art shows whose sexual content and social commentary stirred controversies.

Mr. Helms tried to bar NEA funding for any art he and his friends would object to. The issue was finessed with a one-year legislative ban on obscene material "including but not limited to, depictions of sadomasochism, homoeroticism, the sexual exploitation of children or individuals engaged in sex acts; and which, taken as a whole, do not have serious literary, artistic, political or scientific value."

Despite its grandstanding language, the law in fact only bars federal aid for material that would be obscene under U.S. Supreme Court guidelines; it is little threat per se. That was the policy already.

Even so, the provision has had a chilling effect in the arts, producing hesitations that numb creativity, and it has provided an excuse for right-wing groups, particularly the religious right, to fly-speck NEA grants even for second-handed association with any project or artist the far right and fundamentalists find untoward. Suddenly, people whose only previous attention to art was the day they bought the day-glo Elvis on black velvet are now scouring art galleries, playbills and esoteric presses.

Mr. Helms has used the law to justify a formal request for the government's General Accounting Office to search for instances of wayward art, and he will be pushing Congress to make his prohibitions — or some more severe version — part of the five-year extension of NEA.

We were late among titularly civilized nations in providing public arts support. NEA was set up just 25 years ago. And we still do far less than most such nations. NEA's $170 million budget is small beer. Even this modest effort has helped to spark remarkable artistic activity, inspiring local-government support, too, and leveraging strong increases in private and corporate funding. And of the 80,000 grants NEA has given, only five have incited controversy.

Mr. Bush and his appointee as NEA chairman, John F. Frohnmayer, have drawn the right line in the sand: It is improper and self-defeating for Congress to start dictating the content of art, and nothing in NEA's responsible stewardship of public funding suggests there is any need for legislative intrusion.

Villain Helms and his black-hat gang ought to be booed off the stage.

LEXINGTON HERALD-LEADER
Lexington, Kentucky, March 27, 1990

The education president? The environmental president? It seems at least as likely that George Bush could well be remembered as the aesthetics president.

The president certainly earned some distinction for refusing to censor the content of federally supported art. That decision bucked the wishes of Sen. Jesse Helms, R-N.C., and others who would like to tell us what's art and what's nasty. The president correctly recognized that the National Endowment for the Arts and its community panels will be better judges of artistic merit than Helms and other self-appointed art cops.

Helms fueled this controversy last year when he proposed legislation to block funding for arts projects that denigrate the beliefs of religion or non-religion, or are found offensive to individuals on the basis of race, creed, sex, handicap, age or national origin. That large legislative fig leaf would have covered just about everything, which was the trouble.

Instead, Congress drew its own line, a softer one. It approved a ban on the use of federal money for one year for works that, in the judgment of the NEA and the National Endowment for the Humanities, "may be considered" obscene and that lack "serious literary, artistic, political or scientific value." That was more vague, but no more sensible.

When Congress began debating the NEA's future again last week, Bush made his stance clear. He is "deeply offended by some of the filth" that passes for art. But he is opposed to censorship and will oppose legislative restrictions on the content of federally funded art.

The president's message to the endowments is simple. Carry on. Let the process work. Let the panels that represent different regions of the country and community attitudes help award the art grants. Keep the politics out of the decisions.

And above all, leave the artists free to show us ourselves and the world around us in ways that are sometimes delightful, sometimes surprising, and sometimes shocking.

THE ARIZONA REPUBLIC
Phoenix, Arizona, March 25, 1990

SEEMINGLY unaware of what the National Endowment for the Arts has been doing with public money since the celebrated Robert Mapplethorpe exhibit of erotica, President Bush last week proposed giving the NEA carte blanche to fund whatever it likes.

Among the projects recently liked was porn queen Annie Sprinkle's New York stage show, which included an exhibit of autoeroticism, followed by "hands on" audience participation. It is hard to believe that Mr. Bush would have approved.

After last week's NEA proposal, the White House switchboard was "deluged" with protests, according to *The New York Times*, and NEA Director John Frohnmayer was shoved into the breach. "I will be diligent that obscenity will not be funded by the endowment," he declared in a prepared statement that did little to quiet the ruckus.

In fact, such guarantees from Mr. Frohnmayer are meaningless. He was equally reassuring last October, when Congress urged the NEA to avoid obscene and sacrilegious exhibits. Within 30 days an NEA-supported project distributed a catalog damning St. Patrick's Cathedral in New York as "that house of swastikas" (evidently because of John Cardinal O'Connor's stand on homosexuality) and fantasizing about setting Sen. Jesse Helms's "putrid a-- on fire" (deletion ours).

Mr. Frohnmayer briefly yanked the project's $10,000 grant, but a few weeks later yielded to cries of "censorship" and restored the money, on condition that the "too political" catalog be withdrawn.

The NEA and its defenders are entirely correct when they point out that the arts kitty is used for other purposes than to bankroll outrageous and salacious peep shows. But it is not enough to demonstrate that some of the public's money, or even most of it, is spent on worthwhile projects. The public is entitled to know that none of its money is being misspent. This is an assurance the NEA cannot truthfully provide.

Most Americans, to be sure, probably would look with disfavor on the appointment of Sen. Helms as keeper of the public morals. At the same time, probably an overwhelming majority also would be appalled to know how NEA funds are being squandered, and not simply on homoerotic exhibits. Here is a short list of NEA grants, as compiled by *Reader's Digest* writer Randy Fitzgerald.

- $10,000 to study thoroughbred racetracks.
- $8,000 to explore and map Newark, N.J.
- $10,000 to investigate "public uses of abandoned Atlas missile silos."
- $36,000 to examine whether the "urban baseball park" can endure past the 20th century.

The battle over NEA funding is not, as some like to pretend, a clash between the high-minded and the small-minded, freedom and censorship. The fundamental question is whether the people, acting through their elected representatives, have a right to determine how their money will be spent, or whether they are obliged, willy-nilly, to fund any project — however offensive or witless — once the NEA proclaims it "art."

The Washington Post
Washington, D.C., March 29, 1990

THE SENATE begins hearings today on the issue that was last summer's longest-running sensation: the matter of what restrictions, if any, should be placed on federally funded art. But the script so far has unfolded with one major difference—an explicit stance by the White House against any legislation that would impose such restrictions through Congress.

The president's budget first telegraphed this position when it offered no proposed restrictions—and a small budget increase—in its five-year reauthorization of the National Endowment for the Arts, which became the target of fierce attacks last summer for grants to artists Andres Serrano and Robert Mapplethorpe. When asked about the issue at a press conference last Friday, the president went further. He answered that he was "deeply offended by some of the filth that I see into which federal money has gone . . . but I would prefer to have this matter handled by a very sensitive, knowledgeable man of the arts, [NEA head] John Frohnmayer, than risk censorship or getting the federal government into telling every artist what he or she can paint or how she or he might express themselves."

This, together with the budget, stakes out a clear and measured position: to object to certain uses to which NEA money has gone, and to accept the government's right to make such objections, and also to believe that Congress is the wrong body and broad legislation the wrong vehicle through which to make them. There are better ways to make such distinctions, ways that do not threaten whole categories of subject area or drastically narrow artists' scope. The arts endowment's chairman, John Frohnmayer, has testified before a House subcommittee on ways in which the endowment itself can become more public and responsive in its decisions, including opening the deliberations of some selection panels to the public; several state councils do this already.

When the Senate last summer overwhelmingly supported a proposal by Sen. Jesse Helms (R-N.C.) to impose sweeping restrictions on federally funded art, passing it by voice vote without debate in a near-empty chamber, many lawmakers later said they had acted out of fear that any attempt to protect the endowment would be used to label them pro-pornography in attack ads at home. What they and their House counterparts lacked was credible political cover for voting their convictions, and that protection is what President Bush has now given them by his carefully modulated statement.

The Hutchinson News
Hutchinson, Kansas, March 25, 1990

The Bush folks have decided to surrender to the hoity-toity "arts" crowd, after all.

The spokesman for the National Endowment for the Arts, John Frohmeyer, went before a congressional committee last week to announce that the Bush administration would oppose any restrictions placed on the taxpayers' money handed over to the arts crowd.

Federal arts subsidies were intended "to be free of political or cultural or content-based restrictions," Frohmeyer said as he suggested that restrictions against "sadomasochism, homoeroticism, or sexual exploitation of children engaged in sex acts" be removed from today's rules.

The modest restrictions were placed in the rule book last year, after two particularly obscene "arts" projects were revealed in Washington. One of the "arts" programs financed by taxpayer money was a crucifix immersed in urine and passed off as great art by the hoity-toity modern-art crowd.

The Bush folks and the NEA may try to hide behind a virtuous cloak of anti-censorship, but they shouldn't be allowed to get away with it.

Nobody is trying to censor those characters who create modern garbage and call it art. They can create as much garbage as muddle-headed buyers will finance.

What needs to be done is to force them to pay for their garbage themselves. They don't have any right to unrestricted handouts from American taxpayers, and the Bush administration is wrong to suggest they do.

Somebody better wave some broccoli at George Bush to get the adrenalin moving so that he'll be strong enough to withstand the selfish screams from the panhandling arts crowd.

THE SACRAMENTO BEE
Sacramento, California,
March 31, 1990

Both the White House and National Endowment for the Arts director John Frohnmayer are getting a lot of heat from social conservatives for failing to back restrictions on the content of federally funded art. The heat is not surprising, but the administration is right, and it should stick to its guns.

The conservative groups complain, correctly, that some federally funded works in the past have verged far enough into the obscene that they would offend the vast majority of those whose taxes helped support them. But writing formal restrictions into law, however worded, opens the door to endless disputes and uncertainty about what fits or doesn't fit the guidelines. One cannot read art like a formula in mechanics or a cookbook recipe. If the committees of artists and critics who evaluate grant requests can't make reasonable choices, they should be replaced.

What's particularly significant about this controversy now is that it marks the first time that George Bush, that most cautious of men, has departed on any significant social issue from the Republican Party's most conservative wing. Many people see that as a test of the party's flexibility and its ability to grow. But it's also a small sign that Bush may be willing to take some risks for the sake of leadership. If he's not turned to stone by the extreme right's protests about dirty pictures, maybe he'll decide he won't be turned to stone by conservative protests on other decisions. The possibilities are breathtaking to contemplate.

THE INDIANAPOLIS NEWS
Indianpolis, Indiana, March 24, 1990

Behind the controversy over offensive art and the National Endowment for the Arts is the issue of whether the federal government ought to be in the business of subsidizing the arts.

The controversy is certainly not going to go away.

On one side, various organizations and artists seem to be itching to see how far they can go to come up with foul and obscene art that is guaranteed to prolong the controversy.

Along with them, some artists and their defenders keep whining about censorship and the First Amendment when the critics want to cut off funding to these offensive projects. Yet the First Amendment says nothing about anyone's right to get a subsidy from other taxpayers.

On the other side, Sen. Jesse Helms, R-N.C., proposed last year to cut off funding to obscene exhibits or art work. Other members of Congress, however, are horrified by his proposal on grounds that it will stifle creativity and threaten free speech.

Rep. Pat Williams, D-Mont., questioned the new NEA chairman, John Frohnmayer, demanding to know whether he thought "offensive" art ought to be funded by the government. Frohnmayer finally said yes in a recent hearing over whether the NEA ought to get a five-year renewal of federal funding.

"For a chairman to answer yes to that question in today's climate shows real determination that the NEA not be used as a censoring agency," Williams declared in triumph.

The issue, though, is not censorship. These artists can go ahead and put their crucifixes in bottles of urine or whatever else they want to call "art." Some of the junk is so bad that USA Today won't accept ads from the American Family Association citing specific art exhibits they don't like. USA Today officials say that the ads are in bad taste, which tells much about federally-funded art projects. Let the artists sell this junk on the open market, not through subsidies through the taxpayers and the federal government.

Philosophy Professor Steven Yates offers an easy way out, and it's so simple that it may not appeal to the bureaucrats in Washington D.C. He suggests just having the government stop the subsidies.

"If federal dollars support certain artists and exhibits, then these artists and exhibits will gain an advantage they would not have had in an open market, in the same way that government-subsidized automobile manufacturers will gain advantages they would not have had otherwise," he writes in The Freeman magazine. "The only satisfactory solution to the problem of censorship in the arts, therefore, is for the government to get out of the art business altogether, and allow people acting under free market conditions to support the kind of art they want."

His proposal makes sense, especially in light of a $150 billion annual federal budget deficit, which threatens the United States in an increasingly competitive world economic environment.

FORT WORTH STAR-TELEGRAM
Fort Worth, Texas, March 24, 1990

Conservative criticism of President Bush for not endorsing legislation to restrict federally funded arts programs is ill-founded.

Bush Wednesday supported National Endowment for the Arts chairman John Frohnmayer, who asked Congress for legislation extending the NEA's life for five years without restrictions on what it may support.

Sen. Jesse Helms and other conservative political and religious leaders have sought strict legislative controls — censorship — over what artistic projects can be supported by the NEA and its public funds.

Such legislation, however, is like using a howitzer to swat flies. NEA's defenders say that it has made more than 85,000 grants, of which fewer than 20 have caused any controversy.

The present squabble arose last year over NEA support of a museum showing of photographs by Robert Mapplethorpe and Andres Serrano. The pictures in question were definitely objectionable to most citizens and to most members of Congress.

That point was made, with soaring rhetoric.

NEA chairman Frohnmayer got the message. Frohnmayer was not appointed to administer obscenity, and he knows it. It comes down to whom you trust and whether Congress needs to be dictating specific standards of artistic merit.

Congress does not. Bush trusts Frohnmayer to keep the NEA's standards up. That should be good enough.

THE INDIANAPOLIS STAR
Indianapolis, Indiana, March 24, 1990

The Bush administration wants nothing to do with controlling the content of art supported by federal tax dollars. In that, the administration is flat out wrong.

It should want nothing to do with using taxes to support art of any kind. But if federal money is going to be handed out in such a fashion, the people have the right not to be insulted, humiliated or outraged by recipients. Not so, says John E. Frohnmayer, chairman of the National Endowment for the Arts.

Frohnmayer told a House subcommittee this week that the administration wants the life of the endowment extended another five years and it wants no restrictions placed on the art that the endowment may support.

That was a kick in the teeth for Sen. Jesse Helms, R-N.C., and other lawmakers who have tried to ban federal support for such artistic obscenities as graphic homosexual photographs and crucifixes in urine and on-stage masturbation.

Maybe administration officials such as Frohnmayer see nothing wrong with subsidizing moral garbage. But every indication is that the average American taxpayer is offended and scandalized when his government uses his money to line the pockets of pretentious phonies and perverts parading as serious artists.

The administration has been bamboozled by a noisy clique that wants public money but no public say-so in how it is used. That is not the way the game is played. In this instance, the game should be called off.

The Seattle Times
Seattle, Washington, D.C, March 22, 1990

TOO much attention has been given to a few smutty pictures financed or displayed by tax dollars from the National Endowment for the Arts.

The NEA needs to clean up its act, but the issue is much more fundamental than a handful of offensive exhibits.

Would-be artists are turning out junk, and expecting Uncle Sam to be the patron of last resort. What truly frightens the arts community is exposure of this much more insidious decline.

Anguished cries against censorship are a smokescreen to distract attention from a vigorous discussion of whether the NEA has been reduced to a mediocre art enterprise.

Sadly, the debate is muddied by excesses on both sides.

Sen. Jesse Helms' legislative sensitivities were so aroused by one erotic display that the North Carolina Republican had a morality oath written into this year's NEA funding.

Legislation to renew the NEA charter for another five years is before Congress, and the Bush administration has decided not to seek extension of Helms' restrictions.

John Frohnmayer, chairman of the arts endowment, has pledged to improve the geographical and cultural representation in NEA grants, and diversify the membership of NEA selection panels.

Don't make the concept of quality a stranger to the review process, either. Why should the taxpayer finance work that would be hooted down by a private gallery or rejected by an art school's admission board? Encouraging excellence is not a totalitarian plot.

If integrity really were a central issue, there'd be a groundswell from the arts community to refuse all government funds, and simply paint, perform or write without fear of contradiction, or Big Brotherly judgment.

Oops, nevermind. This is about money, not censorship.

The Gazette
Cedar Rapids, Iowa, March 31, 1990

DESPITE conservatives' concern over "obscene" and "indecent" art, the Bush administration has urged Congress not to define the types of projects the National Endowment for the Arts (NEA) may support. It is sound advice as far as it goes. Once you specify "no obscenity," you are forced to say which works are "obscene" and which are not. As the courts have found, the definition of "obscenity" is a will-o'-the-wisp.

But while they are mulling NEA funding reauthorization, congressmen should consider asking the arts community to do without the relatively small — $171 million a year — government support.

Initially, the proposal might seem ominous. The national endowment's relatively small role in arts funding has a ripple effect. It probably leverages far more corporate money than might otherwise go to the arts. But if patrons of the arts remain ardent toward their cause, they should have little trouble sustaining a private endowment organization. They are a resourceful, well-heeled group.

With the arts-funding umbilical finally cut, they probably would find it a relief to be free of Jesse Helms-style censorship.

We doubt the NEA will go private. Patrons of the arts are convinced that without federal funding, promising new talents will be stifled. And George Bush, working through NEA Chairman John E. Frohnmayer, does not wish to be the president who put the kibosh to cultural creativity.

A scene we would like to see, though, is that of Bush delivering a charge to the NEA: *"Freedom" and definitions aside, do not underwrite projects that are likely to offend taxpayers. In particular, do not endorse "artistic works" that are antagonistic toward Christ and other religious figures. And never support funding for live performances by porn film stars.*

We are not urging that the president imagine what projects NEA funding might support directly or indirectly. We are asking that he realize how far out NEA backing already has gone — Jesus in drag; a performance by "post-porn modernist" Annie Sprinkle, invoking the spirits of "ancient, sacred prostitutes"; a display of Sen. Helms nailed to a cross (these in addition to the publicized crucifix in artist's urine and the exhibit featuring homoerotic and sadomasochistic behavior).

There is hope. In a discussion with doubting congressmen, Frohnmayer stressed that the reality of pain in the world justifies the reflection of pain in art. "I don't think anybody wants elevator music."

But, said Rep. E. Thomas Coleman, R-Mo., "some people want to cut the elevator cords and record the screams of the people falling — as art."

Frohnmayer said he does not believe such a recording would be art. Nor (he said) would a recent proposal by an artist to show a rat being squeezed between two boards.

That discusssion, passed along by Congressional Quarterly, suggests what the taxpayers would stand for and what they wouldn't in their support of the arts:

Give the world a reflection of humankind's pain — hunger, ignorance, despair. But spare us the crushed rat.

NEA Rejects Four Grants

The National Endownment (NEA) for the Arts June 29, 1990 rejected grant applications from four performance artists who had been recommended by one of the agency's review panels. The move came at a time when the NEA was embroiled in a controversy over funding of artwork that some critics considered to be obscene.

Performance art was a type of live performance in which the artist often addressed unusual subject matter. It often blended elements of other art forms, including theater, dance, storytelling and film.

The four performance artists whose grant requests were rejected were: Karen Finley, who used nudity in dealing with feminist issues; Holly Hughes, who addressed lesbian concerns; John Fleck, who had appeared nude and urinated on stage during his performances; and Tim Miller, whose work concerned homosexuality and AIDS. All four had previously received NEA grants.

Under NEA procedures, grant requests were first submitted to review panels made up of creative artists and arts managers from specific fields. Recommendations from the panels were then passed on to the 26-member National Council on the Arts and to the NEA chairman.

Finley, Hughes, Fleck and Miller had been among a total of 18 artists (out of 95 applicants) whose applications had been approved by the solo-performance review panel. On June 20, however, the National Council on the Arts had voted to recommend to NEA Chairman John E. Frohnmayer that only 14 of the 18 artists receive grant money. Frohnmayer acted on that recommendation June 29 in denying the grants to Finley, Hughes, Fleck and Miller.

Frohnmayer's reversal of the review panel's approval was considered unusual. In 1989, the NEA had calculated that, over the past seven years, the agency's chairman had reversed review panel approvals in only 35 cases out of a total of 33,700 grants.

THE ARIZONA REPUBLIC
Phoenix, Arizona, July 13, 1993

THE controversy in Washington and elsewhere over what is and is not "art" or, more pointedly, what kind of art should be tax-supported, rages on. The largely inept attempts by the chairman of the beleaguered National Endowment for the Arts to mediate the dispute have failed spectacularly.

In fact, if NEA chief John Frohnmayer had deliberately set out to inflame passions on both sides, he could not have done a better job.

It will be recalled that the endowment got itself into hot water in Congress and with the artistically unsophisticated for its funding last year of, among other things, the displays of the scatological homoerotica and kiddie-porn of the late photographer Robert Mapplethorpe and the sacrilegious works of Andres Serrano.

The latest troubles involve 18 grant proposals approved by an NEA peer-review panel. Mr. Frohnmayer's senior deputy, Alvin Felzenberg, thought it might be prudent to review the panel's recommendations, particularly the questionable works of four "performance artists."

When Mr. Felzenberg confirmed to syndicated columnists Rowland Evans and Robert Novak that one of the acts in the running for an NEA grant involved a certain Karen Finley, Mr. Frohnmayer fired him. So much for dedication to truth and freedom of expression at the NEA.

Ms. Finley, it should be noted, does rather unusual things with vegetables. It seems her performance consists of smearing chocolate laced with bean sprouts over her nude anatomy. She then proceeds to put the vegetables into, well, various and unmentionable body orifices. Some, doubtless, regard this as on par with Laurence Olivier's *Hamlet*. Others will be more skeptical.

Another of the four grants the cashiered Mr. Felzenberg flagged for attention was the "artistry" of John Fleck, whose *oeuvre* is urinating on a portrait of Christ painted on the inside of a toilet bowl.

With congressional hearings scheduled for later this month on NEA funding, Mr. Frohnmayer apparently reconsidered his fired deputy's advice, and suspended the approval of the four grants. The esteemed arts panel and the rest of the art world erupted in a predictable frenzy over "government censorship."

The issue, of course, has absolutely nothing to do with censorship. Ms. Finley is perfectly free to do anything she wants with vegetables, except demand that the taxpayers fund her act. The right of free expression, no matter what the arts community would have the rest of us believe, does not depend on public subsidy.

Not to be denied, Ms. Finley, who claims her vegetable performance represents the plight of women in America, says she is "being punished because I am a morally concerned artist." Another of the rejected *artistes*, Holly Hughes, whose act runs along the same line, said she was devastated by the decision. Without the NEA grant, she said, "I have to get a job." Pity.

The Hutchinson News
Hutchinson, Kansas, July 12, 1993

The hoity-toity national arts establishment is simply beside itself again.

Now, the arts crowd is furious at the man who's chairman of the National Endowment for the Arts in Washington.

The poor fellow finally decided that he'd have to step forward and say what he believed was art and what he believed wasn't, before doling out tax money to four, ahem, artists.

In the four cases, John Frohmayer, the chairman, rejected the unanimous recommendation from his (hoity-toity) arts advisory board. Frohmayer decided that the four shows wouldn't meet the anti-obscenity rules for the use of taxpayer money.

One of the artists is known for her performances in covering her nude body with chocolate. Another urinates on stage as part of his, ahem, art.

The arts crowd is horrified. With it hangers-on in the press, the arts crowd is writhing in anguish at the idea that anybody dare question the great talents in these shows or allow untalented and common wretches like us to refuse to pay for the artistic virtues of stage-urinating or chocolate-covered nudes.

A news story in The Washington Post suggests that the arts crowd may be able to force Frohmayer, himself, out of his job.

Heavy drama this NEA flap isn't, no matter what Jesse Helms, John Frohmayer, the arts crowd and the chocolate-smearers may do.

It is, however, high comedy.

Watching a nude chocolate-covered dancer writhe on stage won't do much for anybody. But watching the hoity-toity arts crowd writhe in agony because the peasants don't understand that such high "art" is exhilarating.

DAILY NEWS
New York City, New York, July 5, 1993

WHERE'S SOLOMON when you need him? It's going to take someone with the wisdom of that king of ancient Israel to save the National Endowment for the Arts. The agency is at the center of an obscenity controversy. Some members of Congress want to gut the NEA, or at least place severe restrictions on its operations. Congress should be careful. Mortally wounding the NEA would be needlessly counterproductive.

The firestorm over the NEA started 18 months ago when attention turned to two controversial grants. One went to a Robert Mapplethorpe exhibition that contained several sexually explicit photographs. The other was given to Andres Serrano, whose work includes a photograph of a crucifix submerged in a jar of urine. Is this art offensive? Most certainly. Enough to justify hamstringing the NEA? No.

Those were two grants out of 85,000 the NEA makes every year. The controversial works total about 20 images out of millions the NEA has funded over its 28-year existence. The proposed "punishments" do not fit the "crimes."

THERE'S GENERAL AGREEMENT that the current NEA bill — a five-year, no-strings-attached re-funding — has only a slim chance of passage. President Bush, who originally backed the five-year extension, made a noble attempt at a compromise. His idea is re-funding for one year. But rather than soothe, the Bush idea only angered both sides. A compromise is needed. One that will take the NEA out of the political arena long enough for cooler heads to prevail and for outsiders to monitor the NEA's grant-making process.

A two or three-year extension would do the trick. No restrictions, but lots of observation. An already appointed presidential commission assigned to review the NEA could carry out this mission. And there is good evidence that the NEA can police itself. Agency head John Frohmayer proved that with his recent veto of grants to four performance artists. NEA opponents were impressed. But the art community unwisely bristled at the decision. If the NEA is to retain any independence, artists must get used to this kind of rejection. Government funding isn't a right. It's a privilege — with limits and responsibilities.

The federal government does have a role in supporting the arts. Without its help through the NEA, this nation's cultural life would certainly be much poorer. Oscar and Pulitzer winner "Driving Miss Daisy" might never have been written. Children's dance troupes in Queens and the South Bronx would never have been organized. Oscar Hijuelos might never have written his prize-winning novel on life and music in East Harlem. The list of artistic accomplishments funded by NEA is endless. A few missteps shouldn't put a stop to this agency's good works.

LAS VEGAS REVIEW-JOURNAL
Las Vegas, Nevada, July 3, 1993

Last week the National Endowment for the Arts announced it would not continue to provide fellowship grants to four performance artists, among them New Yorker Karen Finley.

Finley's act includes segments in which she appears on stage naked from the waist up, smeared with chocolate syrup and covered with alfalfa sprouts, which she calls "sperm."

Upon hearing the federal arts agency would not renew her grant, Finley was outraged. "I am being punished because I am a morally concerned artist," Finley said. "We as a nation are now in an era of blacklisting as during the 1950s' McCarthyism. Today begins an era in American history not strong in its cultural diversity but weak in not allowing our cultural diversity a right to speak."

Holly Hughes, another New Yorker whose performance art takes a radical lesbian point of view and who was also denied an NEA grant this year, likened conditions in the United States today to Nazi Germany.

Hughes and Finley are dead wrong. No one would dream of denying their First Amendment right to express themselves through their "art." They have a right to perform as they wish; they do not, however, have a right to feed at the public trough. The NEA is entirely within its rights to deny funding for art of marginal value, or if it finds offensive.

The Seattle Times
Seattle, Washington, July 13, 1993

FEDERAL support for the National Endowment for the Arts should be extended by Congress for five more years, without malicious tampering or restrictions — or a lot of wasted time and debate.

Agitated critics with their well-thumbed examples of objectionable art have failed to make a case that America is headed straight to hell in a salaciously decorated, taxpayer-financed hand basket.

Likewise, the NEA budget ought to be reauthorized despite the self-righteous windbaggery from indignant corners of the nonprofit-arts complex.

The debate is about sponsorship, not censorship. No one has suggested that artists denied federal aid should not be able to display their works in galleries or perform in public.

Both sides use emotional appeals to rally support, and politicians wallow in the demagoguery. Brace yourself for unfettered ranting and raving on the floor of Congress.

NEA's opportunistic foes denounce sexual themes in art with a suspect, transitory relish. Something else will come along.

Meanwhile, the only thing more fun than ferreting out and condemning prurient material is cataloging and describing it over and over again.

Benjamin Benschneider / Seattle Times
Outside the Seattle Opera House, protester Julie Johnson hands out leaflets to people on their way to see the Bolshoi Ballet July 2.

Repetition is not only titillating but necessary. The political-performance artists badgering NEA cannot produce more than a handful of examples to rouse their followers.

After 25 years and 85,000 grants to famous and forgotten artists, plus major and minor chorales, troupes and ensembles around the country, NEA's opponents yammer about maybe two dozen works.

NEA is vulnerable precisely because it goes about its work in a quiet, modest fashion, handing out inconspicuous sums of money to a great number of people and communities.

Seed money and sustenance have been provided for the visual and performing arts, for novelists, poets and playwrights. Federal money has inspired an outpouring of corporate and private donations and matching grants.

The cultural life of this nation has been nurtured and enriched by the NEA through awards to artists and groups in places as diverse as the Big Apple and Yakima, where big apples come from.

Almost three decades of good work must not be destroyed by cynical zealots who will move on to another emotional target when NEA-bashing fails to bring in contributions.

Taxpayers should be proud of their patronage of the arts and NEA's stewardship of their hard-earned dollars.

The Buffalo News
Buffalo, New York, July 9, 1993

NORMALLY, LEGISLATION to renew the National Endowment for the Arts doesn't stir up jumbo controversies on Capitol Hill. But because of last year's fiery dispute over federal funding of an exhibition of photographs that some members of Congress considered obscene, efforts to renew the NEA for another five years could run into obstacles this summer.

The House is expected to open debate on the NEA enabling legislation before the end of this month.

Regrettably, last year's hubbub over the photos of Robert Mapplethorpe also resulted in Congress placing the first limitations ever on grants awarded by the NEA. That was a distressing backward step that puts political and official preferences into the process of deciding artistic values.

The upcoming struggle in Congress will concern new restrictions on NEA grants rather than, primarily, how much money the NEA should get to distribute to artistic works, groups and institutions. In the last quarter-century, the NEA has supported the creative diversity represented in more than 80,000 cultural projects.

To take a local example, Buffalo's outstanding Albright-Knox Art Gallery received a $600,000 challenge grant for its 125th anniversary campaign last year and has received from the NEA other funds for 100 works of art over the last nine years.

Nationally, annual NEA budgets run about $170 million. For the next budget, President Bush recommends $173 million.

The president also wants the NEA enabling legislation renewed without any restrictions clamped over the content of projects applying for and receiving grants.

That's sound judgment. Mistakes will always be made in awarding the grants, of course. Overall, however, the present system under which panels of experts, knowledgeable in their field and independent of government, award the grants to the most promising projects from among all of those that applied offers the surest safeguard against artistic sterility and oppression.

This is a review process that guards against government censorship, or some officially approved government line in art. It's far from ideal. But if artists are to create and experiment and test the limits of human imagination, they must be free to make mistakes — which they surely will — and their peers who judge the worth of the applications must be free to use their best judgment as well.

That's certainly preferable to leaving the job up to some government bureaucrat, or to some member of Congress, who knows little or nothing about the orchestra or novel or series of paintings under review.

The House and Senate committees studying the Bush legislative proposal have not yet recommended, opposed or modified it. In the House, the administration plan is going directly to the floor for open debate.

Once there, efforts to restrict the content of works eligible for federal monies will be vigorous and sustained.

But Congress should follow Bush's lead and resist these temptations to dictate rigid rules on art.

Tulsa World
Tulsa, Oklahoma, July 9, 1990

THE National Education Association has relented in its opposition to allowing professionals who did not follow the traditional education-school route into the classroom.

Reversing earlier opposition, the NEA at its Kansas City convention decided to allow engineers, scientists and others to teach if they are supervised by certified teachers and enroll in teacher accreditation courses.

The change in position is reasonable. One of the main obstacles to attracting prospective teachers has been the lock-step approach toward teacher training that has been formulated over the years by the teaching establishment.

Too often, that approach has put more emphasis on teaching techniques and the cant of education than on mastery of subject matter. This rigid approach is one of the reasons that most teachers today come from the bottom 25 percent of college classes.

Alternative certification of teachers isn't the whole answer for education's problems.

But it can be a part of it. Teachers are going to be in short supply in the future and it opens up a new career path for professionals who might be attracted to the classroom as a second career or as an adjunct to their chosen profession.

NEA delegates were wise in recognizing this.

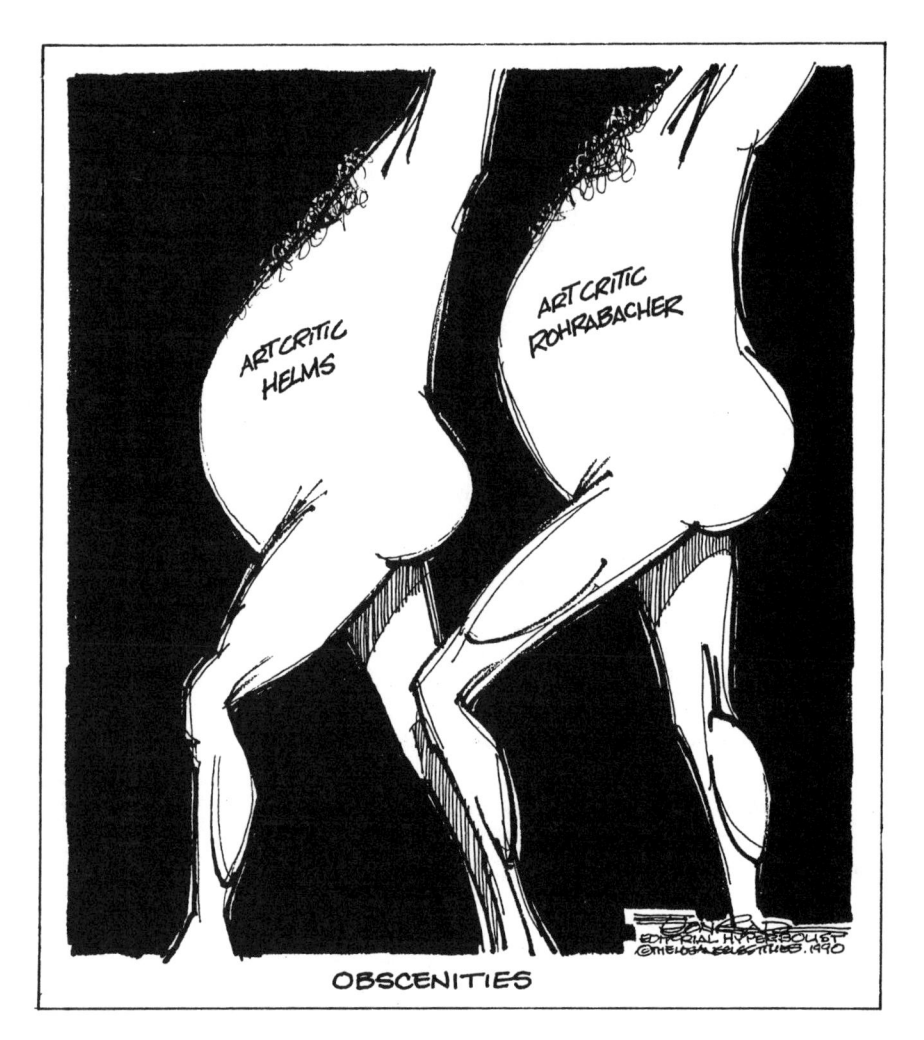

OBSCENITIES

The Philadelphia Inquirer
Philadelphia, Pennsylvania, July 5, 1993

Consider the plight of Joe Kluger, executive director of the Philadelphia Orchestra, as he recently mulled the form he had to send back to the National Endowment for the Arts acknowledging receipt of a major grant.

The form required all grant recipients to promise to obey the NEA's "general terms and conditions," and this year one of the conditions is that none of the funds be used to "promote, disseminate, or produce" obscene materials. Mr. Kluger pondered that for a moment, before deciding to return a letter of protest.

Was the NEA fearful that Maestro Muti might add just a *soupcon* too much sensuality to a rendition of Ravel's *Bolero*? Perhaps it was terrified that the orchestra might choose some works from opera, thereby kindling impure thoughts in the audience's mind of, for example, the lovers living in sin in Puccini's *La Boheme*. It was ridiculous.

And clearly, this ridiculousness has to stop. The NEA deserves support, and the proposed restrictions put forward by Sen. Jesse Helms (R., N.C.) and others are unneeded, demeaning, and, perhaps worst of all, silly.

Even more ludicrous are the calls for abolishing federal funding for the arts. The NEA gets a tiny amount of money, about one one-hundredth of a cent out of every tax dollar. And, with it, it has probably done more good with less money than any other part of the federal government, with the possible exception of the National Park Service. More than 40 different organizations in Philadelphia received a total of more than $2.7 million from the NEA in fiscal 1989. Generally speaking, the money was well spent, greatly enriching the lives of people who attended the concerts, performances and exhibitions of the institutions that received the grants. In fact, out of the thousands of grants the NEA has made, its critics are succeeding in making an amazing amount of hay out of just a few.

We have refrained, however, from getting into too much of a lather over the controversy surrounding such matters as the NEA's support for exhibitions of Robert Mapplethorpe's photographs, some of which are homoerotic, and the work of Andres "Piss Christ" Serrano. The reason we've been holding back is that it has been hard to figure out who, if anyone, was getting unfairly hurt in this brouhaha.

After all, when you have a bunch of artists whose announced goal in life is to shock the ordinary folk, well, it becomes somewhat difficult to feel sorry for such artists when they succeed beyond their wildest imaginings. Wasn't it just a little while ago that we heard lots of whining over how contemporary American society ignores its artists? Now, suddenly, American artists and their work have become front-page news. Attendance is greater than anyone would have dared hope for the Mapplethorpe exhibition. Mr. Serrano, who only months ago seemed likely to live out his life in relative obscurity, has become (for better or worse) a Celebrated Artist.

Moreover, just because an artist is denied federal funds does not mean that his or her art is being suppressed. Consider the rap group 2 Live Crew: Its artistic expressions are even more vulgar than Mr. Serrano's or Mr. Mapplethorpe's, and yet it seems to get along quite well without a penny of federal assistance.

And we think it probably was a lapse in judgment to include, in a federally funded exhibition, pictures of such things as a man with a bullwhip handle stuck up his rear end. That, as the world now knows, is just exactly what our own Institute for Contemporary Art did when it assembled the Mapplethorpe photographs. The ICA has to expect that its subsequent grant applications are going to be greeted with something less than joy unconfined.

But this has all gone far enough now. Sometime after Congress resumes its deliberations after the July Fourth holiday, the saner, more clear-headed members of the House and Senate are going to have to sit down and have a talk with Sen. Helms, along with all the other yahoos and peckerwoods who have been calling for restrictions on, and cuts in, federal aid to the arts. What those wiser members will have to say is something like this:

OK, Jess babes, it's fine for you to be getting all this political mileage, but we're not going to let you turn the U.S. Congress into the laughingstock of the Western world.

The Hartford Courant
Hartford, Connecticut, July 10, 1990

The marriage between government and the arts is necessarily a strained one. In government, the creative impulse usually drives toward an orderly and rational end. In art, one begins with the rules but the drive is toward something chaotic, imaginative and new.

And yet art and power seem to attract one another. Artists have always sought the powerful as patrons, and the powerful have sought out the authenticity of the arts. Had the two been kept separate but equal down through the ages, J.S. Bach would have had to find a day job, and so would Michelangelo.

The rub comes when the patron begins to make demands and suggest restrictions. Here the historical record is clear. The response of the serious artist has been to resist all compromise and to tell the patron that he sponsors the artist not the art.

The patron is then entitled to withdraw support, and the artist must go find another aristocrat or members of the nouveau riche to back him. Or the patron may continue to harass the artist until the artist tells him to get lost and finds another patron. Patrons usually need artists as much as artists need patrons.

The U.S. government, through the National Endowment for the Arts, is playing picky patron these days thanks to the urgings of some members of Congress. The endowment now imposes guidelines with its grants that ask applicants to promise not to "promote, disseminate, or produce obscene or indecent materials, including but not limited to depictions of sadomasochism, homoeroticism, the exploitation of children, or individuals engaged in sex acts, or material which denigrates the objects or beliefs of the adherents of a particular religion or non-religion."

President Bush and the endowment's head dislike the restriction. They have recommended striking the clause from next year's authorizing legislation for the agency. But there has been much pious huffing on the part of both artists and moral majoritarians. The artists say that they are being censored. Sen. Jesse A. Helms, who is the patron of Comstockery, has said that at this rate God will have to apologize to Sodom and Gomorrah. Both claims are bunk.

In this tug of war, the artists must be willing to stand up for themselves, sometimes tell the patrons where to get off, and yes, go hungry. There is no serious possibility of government funding for the arts drying up any time soon. It won't hurt the most provocative artists to look for new patrons. We suspect that gifted actors, composers and painters won't go without for long.

Artists who expect never to struggle, never to make waves and never to be the victims of the controversy they create, are spoiled artists. Government officials who think they can control art — or even judge it — are naive.

Lately, art groups have been saying "no thanks" to the endowment's conditions, notably the theatrical producer Joe Papp and the editor George Plimpton. Others — like the Long Wharf Theatre in New Haven — have said they will take the money but protest the restriction. Still others have said they will do what they want with their grants and fight the government in court if it wants to enforce the tastes of the state. That sounds like the honorable artistic temperament of old.

Cincinnati Museum Indicted Over Mapplethorpe Exhibit

Cincinnati's Contemporary Arts Center and its director, Dennis Barrie, were indicted by a grand jury April 7, 1990 on obscenity charges for displaying an exhibit of photographs by the late Robert Mapplethorpe. The exhibit, which opened at the arts center that day, contained 175 photographs, seven of which were targeted by prosecutors because they depicted naked children or homosexual acts.

The Mapplethorpe exhibit was the same one that had sparked a controversy over federal funding of the arts in 1989, when the Corcoran Gallery of Art in Washington, D.C. canceled a scheduled display, because of fear of a possible congressional backlash. (The exhibit was partially supported by funds from the National Endowment for the Arts.)

Barrie and the museum were each charged with two misdemeanor counts of pandering and illegal use of a minor. If convicted, Barrie faced a fine of up to $1,000 and six months in jail on each count, while the museum could be fined $5,000 on each count.

U.S. District Judge Carl B. Rubin April 8 barred local law enforcement officials from shutting down the exhibit. He told officials from Hamilton County that they could not "remove the photographs or close the exhibit or take action intimidating in nature to prevent the public from seeing the exhibit."

The museum reported that a record 23,000 people attended the exhibit as of April 17. In a poll conducted for the *Cincinnati Post*, 59% of respondents said they believed the museum had a right to display the photographs.

Cincinnati had had a reputation for many years as a city that did not tolerate pornography. The city was home to the National Coalition against Pornography, and local law enforcement officials, headed by Sheriff Simon Leis, had prosecuted numerous obscenity cases, including one against *Hustler* magazine publisher Larry Flynt. As a result, the city was reported to have no adult bookstores, no bars offering nude dancing and no stores in which pornographic magazines or X-rated videotapes could be obtained.

THE BLADE
Toledo, Ohio, April 10, 1990

NOTHING should be more repugnant to citizens of a free society than the image of two dozen Cincinnati police officers storming the Contemporary Arts Center last weekend to shut down the Robert Mapplethorpe photography exhibit.

Members of a Hamilton County grand jury exhibited intolerable ignorance of First Amendment rights and arrogant abuse of the justice system by indicting the center and its director, Dennis Barrie, on obscenity charges in order to close the exhibit. Fortunately, at least one judge had the good sense to allow the show to continue while the court cases proceed.

It is no coincidence that this insult to the Constitution occurred in Cincinnati, which is home to the National Coalition against Pornography and a local group calling itself Citizens for Community Values, which earlier had tried to halt the show's opening.

Certainly these groups have the right to express their objections to the exhibit, which includes a dozen or so sexually explicit photographs, seven of which the grand jury decided to call obscene. But for them to pervert the right of free expression by denying the same rights to the gallery and to the people who paid to see the exhibit is hypocrisy, and it is contemptible.

Equally deserving of contempt are the law-enforcement and other officials who capitulated to the pressures of self-appointed censors by deciding it was a criminal matter and putting the issue before a grand jury.

Of course, we have only to thank GOP Sen. Jesse Helms of North Carolina for catapulting this issue to prominence last summer, when he tried to curtail funding to the National Endowment for the Arts for supporting the exhibition's showing at the Corcoran Gallery in Washington, D.C. The show brought no such outcry in Chicago before the Helms attack, and went on to other cities afterward to be shown with little dissent. It should be noted, too, that the Contemporary Arts Center went out of its way to consider community sensitivity by restricting the 175-photo exhibit to adults.

Toledo Museum of Art Director David Steadman likened treatment of the CAC and the Mapplethorpe showing to the repressions of Nazi Germany and the days of burning books. "Frankly, it has a horrible, chilling effect," he said. "We seem to have really forgotten what happened less than 60 years ago for all of western civilization. I think we'd all better start remembering it."

Mr. Steadman is right. How sad, when the Soviet Union and countries throughout eastern Europe are breathing fresh freedom for the first time in decades, when they restore citizenship to their exiled artists and, in the case of Czechoslovakia, call them to leadership, that some Americans whose rights so much of the world has envied would surrender them to the sheriff of Hamilton County and the Cincinnati police.

AKRON BEACON JOURNAL
Akron, Ohio, April 12, 1990

ON SOME things about art most of us can agree:
- Not everyone likes all art.
- Not everyone can always agree on what is art and what is not.
- A painting or a photograph that seems a masterpiece to some may seem to be junk to others.

However, we each make up our own minds about art, and even whether we want to go and look at it or not.

In Cincinnati, the thought police, in the form of the local sheriff and prosecutor, have decided they should censor art based on their tastes and interfere with the free choice of people to see or not to see photographs by the late Robert Mapplethorpe.

The work is being shown in a current exhibit at Cincinnati's Contemporary Arts Center.

The exhibit contains 175 photos by the artist. There is no controversy over 168 of them. Most people who see those photos, such as Mapplethorpe's glorious photographs of flowers, will generally agree that he was a brilliant photographer.

Seven of the photos, set off in the exhibit from the others, are tough photos of tough subjects. Some call them erotic or homoerotic. The sheriff and the prosecutor contend they are obscene, have indicted the museum and its director and have sought to bar the public from seeing the show.

However, a federal judge has intervened, and it is likely the case will not come to trial until after the show closes.

Instead of criminal charges, why not let people make up their own minds if they even want to see the photos and then if they object to them? The museum is not forcing anyone to look at anything, and one person's definition of obscenity is not always another's.

Freedom is a wonderful thing, but it involves letting others see and read things some may disagree with. The thought police in Cincinnati do not understand freedom, but seek to censor art that they alone have decided others should not view. That is the way a totalitarian society operates.

THE PLAIN DEALER
Cleveland, Ohio, April 11, 1990

The woman with the placard around her neck had it right: "Welcome to Censor-nati!"

A publicity-seeking prosecutor is taking advantage of the Supreme Court's milquetoast waffling on what obscenity is to try to shut down the Robert Mapplethorpe photography exhibit in Cincinnati. The misdemeanor indictments of the Contemporary Arts Center and its director are believed the first criminal counts against a museum merely for choosing to mount a photography display. Even when judged by the high court's ridiculously vague obscenity standards, the charges can't hold up: This is clearly an exhibit with redeeming social value and where the principal motive is not titillation, but illumination. The indictments are based on only seven out of 175 photos.

The artist, who died last year, portrayed flowers and people. Infrequently, he used his lens to capture a part of the spirit of the times — prurient and homoerotic though it was.

So, sure, this exhibit contains some rough stuff. You wouldn't want to take the kids. "Kids" aren't even allowed in. But to have nine grand jurors sneak a peak and then rush back to the grand jury room and indict the arts center and its chief for "pandering obscenity" and using minors in pornography (there are a few pictures of nude or semi-nude children) is pushing it a little far, even if the photos are vulgar or offensive to some. There's no rule that art must be lovely or soothing or socially irrelevent or blind. And where does the pandering come in? In charging admission?

The U.S. Supreme Court in 1973 came up with a three-part "test" for obscenity that included the ambiguous notion of "contemporary community standards." However one arrives at it in a diverse city, that standard appears tough in Cincinnati. The city's anti-obscenity statutes are as legendary as the councilman who paid by check for carnality across the river. Even before the Mapplethorpe exhibit opened at the arts center Saturday, that standard had made itself felt: Harassment against the museum and its principal benefactors was so intense the museum's board chairman resigned and the arts center itself pulled out of a communitywide fund-raiser.

Yet most constitutional scholars, however much they dislike the high court's shrugging off to localities a key part of its obscenity test, feel this case will be no test of that test; it's too obviously "art," not pornography.

Hamilton County Prosecutor Arthur Ney and Sheriff Simon Leis should quit while the quitting is good and leave this exhibit to stand or fall on its own merits, as photography and as a social statement that is often disquieting and, sometimes, disgusting.

But they won't. The free publicity is too great a temptation to politicians who have made careers out of pandering to public gullibility. If, as the court seems to have indicated, obscenity, like beauty, is in the eye of the beholder, then Ney and his fellow bluenoses could use a bucket of eyewash.

The Hartford Courant
Hartford, Connecticut, April 10, 1990

Hartford survived Robert Mapplethorpe's exhibition of photgraphs, which made a 10-week stop at the Wadsworth Atheneum last fall.

In fact, the show came and went with little fuss. There were no daily mass demonstrations, no publicity hounds masquerading as prosecutors, no police chiefs sniffing vice and no grand jurors sneaking a peek to determine if the pictures in the museum violated obscenity laws.

No one was forced to see the exhibition. Visitors had to pay an extra $3 and proceed to a speciallly designated, third-floor gallery. No tax money was involved to bring the exhibit to Hartford.

The people of Connecticut had an opportunity to determine for themselves whether they liked the 150 or so pictures. If they wanted to skip the few homoerotic and sadomasochistic photographs, they could do so easily. The show broke attendance records at the Atheneum.

So what's so different about Cincinnati, where a grand jury indicted the museum and its director on obscenity charges? Are there more bluenoses in the home of Procter & Gamble than in the Insurance City?

Perhaps the head of the Cincinnati Contemporary Arts Center, Dennis Barrie, is a devout student of P.T. Barnum's school of publicity. Mr. Barrie went to court even before the opening to seek a determination whether the exhibition was obscene. A judge predictably refused the request, and the show opened anyway.

Why Mr. Barrie sought to open the door to prior restraint is difficult to understand. In any case, his request further fueled the controversy, and therefore magnified national attention on Cincinnati. It also triggered huge demonstrations in support of First Amendment principles.

But zealots, who are not found only in Iran and Albania, rarely are swayed by arguments about freedom to view, read or write what one pleases. A self-appointed group called the Citizens for Community Values believes that the minds and eyes of Cincinnatians shouldn't be polluted by Mr. Mapplethorpe's pictures. The well organized Community Values brigade has been effective in intimidating public officials. Courage isn't found in abundance among officials faced with controversy.

Any prosecutor worth his law degree could find out that the Bill of Rights, as interpreted by Supreme Court decisions, protects the museum's right to exhibit the Mapplethorpe photographs. The court wisely has set tough tests of what constitutes obscenity. Something may be deemed obscene if, among other standards, "the work taken as a whole lacks serious literary, artistic, political or scientific value," according to the court's Miller vs. California decision of 1973.

Mr. Mapplethorpe's art isn't liked by everyone, or perhaps by most people. But any work that is accepted for exhibition by museums throughout the world can scarcely be regarded as lacking in serious artistic value.

It's sad to see so much energy wasted by people who want to impose their own values on others. If only the protectors of public morals were as determined to fight real crime. Cincinnati's police chief and prosecutor should rest assured that their community will "survive" Mapplethorpe.

The Philadelphia Inquirer
Philadelphia, Pennsylvania, April 11, 1990

When Robert Mapplethorpe's photographs — including the infamous X rated batch — were assembled and hung (without incident) at the University of Pennsylvania's Institute of Contempary Art, who'd have known that they'd soon be almost as familiar to the general public as Ansel Adams' naturescapes. That was in 1988, back before North Carolina's Sen. Jesse Helms popularized the exhibit he sought to punish, back before the late Mr. Mapplethorpe became a *cause celebre* in an art world that had sniffed — at least on occasion — at the photographer's self-promotion and ambitious commercialization.

And, now? If Cincinnati's ham-handed prosecutor gets his way, Mr. Mapplethorpe's occasionally homoerotic work will climb into yet another category — that charmed circle occupied by the repressed works of dissident playwrights, exiled composers and anti-apartheid poets.

Perhaps it doesn't merit such enshrinement — or warrant the surging curiosity that Cincinnati's censors have unwittingly unleashed. (At last count, more than 10,000 viewers had clamored to see the exhibit that Arthur Ney, the local prosecutor, had deemed obscene under local ordinances.) But it surely deserves protection against police with video cameras, gallery-emptying orders by plainclothes sheriff's deputies and all the rest of the jack-booted righteousness involved in this sorry episode.

We take note that a federal judge has already temporarily blocked Cincinnati's art police from interfering further with the exhibit, even under the guise of crowd control. So, we'll moderate the pitch of our protest. Perhaps the prosecutor will take political note of the humiliating rejection of his efforts to defend the public sensibility. Perhaps he'll re-read the Supreme Court's definition of obscenity, which would seem to favor any artwork deemed serious enough to be displayed in a local museum.

And perhaps, he'll recognize the choice available to Ohians who find Mr. Mapplethorpe's imagery offensive: They can just skip the exhibit. Unless the hysteria the prosecutor has whipped up has simply made it impossible to resist.

St. Petersburg Times
St. Petersburg, Florida, April 10, 1990

Thousands of people showed up at the Contemporary Art Center in Cincinnati last weekend to view the exhibit of photographs by the late Robert Mapplethorpe.

That is a point being lost in the midst of the controversy over obscenity that Mapplethorpe's work once again has stirred: People came to the Contemporary Art Center because they chose to see the art work on display.

The freedom to do so is what art is about, just as much as is the freedom of artists to create works that may not have universal appeal. Indeed, some or even all of the 175 Mapplethorpe photographs, most of which depict subjects such as calla lilies and celebrities, are certain to be offensive to some people. The freedom to decide what is offensive should be left to the viewers.

Yet the principle of freedom was lost as sheriff's deputies and police officers converged on the museum Saturday after a grand jury indicted it and its director on charges of obscenity. Officers forced patrons out of the museum while they videotaped as evidence the photographic exhibit that includes seven homoerotic and other sexual images.

That Cincinnati has a reputation for intolerance does not lessen the impact of the indictments. The attitude that pressed for the show's cancellation is indicative of a growing repressive sense toward art in the United States. President Bush may have stated recently that he opposes the extreme requirements approved by Congress last year for artists seeking federal grants, but he still vowed to oppose strongly any federal grants for art he termed obscene.

Fortunately, for the sake of the arts and those who cherish the freedom to enjoy them, the director of the Contemporary Art Center also has remained strong in the face of pressure and legal charges.

It is also fortunate for museum-goers in Cincinnati that a federal district judge has ruled that the Mapplethorpe exhibit cannot be closed to the public before the obscenity trial.

Demonstrators' signs outside the museum last weekend proclaimed "Art is Freedom." The freedom in Cincinnati, however, is guaranteed only until a court attempts to decide what is obscene. That is a distinction history has struggled repeatedly to show is not clear-cut. To struggle over it again in this case is, sadly, to miss the greater implication of art censorship.

The Register-Guard
Eugene, Oregon, April 13, 1990

During his lifetime, which ended a year ago, photographer Robert Mapplethorpe achieved modest fame with his homoerotic and controversial exhibitions. However, his work was relatively unknown to the general population. In death, and for all the wrong reasons, that has changed.

It was a planned Mapplethorpe retrospective exhibit last year in Washington, D.C., that led to an assault on the National Endowment for the Arts by Sen. Jesse Helms, R-S.C., a first-ever congressionally imposed content restriction on NEA grants, the resignation of the director of Washington's prestigious Corcoran Gallery and a mounting threat to the NEA's very existence.

If that wasn't enough, a Cincinnati, Ohio, grand jury has now indicted the director of a local arts center and the center itself on obscenity charges for presenting a Mapplethorpe exhibit. Police even temporarily shut down the Cincinnati exhibit last weekend in the midst of its opening day, so that officers could fan out through the center taking photographs of photographs. And you thought drugs were the No. 1 crime problem.

Threatened with either police closure of the exhibit or seizure of the exhibit's most controversial photographs, the center sought and won a federal court order prohibiting any city, county or law enforcement interference with the exhibit until a trial can be held on the obscenity charges.

While the judge's ruling was a welcome victory for artistic freedom as well as common sense, the indictment and the effort by city and county officials to shut down the exhibit did more to promote it than any advertising campaign ever could. More than 10,000 people — at $4 a pop — already have seen the exhibit and thousands more are expected to see it before it closes on May 26 and heads for Boston. The Mapplethorpe exhibit in Washington, D.C., which turned Helms into an instant art critic, was equally successful.

That's usually the way it turns out for self-appointed censors, be they Ohio prosecutors or U.S. senators. Had Helms and Hamilton (Ohio) County Prosecutor Arthur Ney Jr. simply ignored Mapplethorpe's photographs to concentrate on more important matters, it's likely that a few curious art patrons and some faithful fans would have attended the exhibits, leaving Mapplethorpe to rest in obscure peace.

By their misguided efforts, however, Helms and Ney have turned Mapplethorpe into a kind of folk hero, made themselves look ridiculous and called attention to the very thing they sought to suppress.

The Courier-Journal
Louisville, Kentucky, April 7, 1990

DON'T CONFUSE the Robert Mapplethorpe controversies. Last summer's flap was about public funding for the arts, while the one raging in Cincinnati concerns pure, raw censorship. Law-enforcement officials have indicated that they might keep viewers from the photography exhibition, which has been extremely popular elsewhere, by seizing pictures from the Contemporary Arts Center.

The show, which opens to the public today, represents the center's deliberate attempt to broaden the artistic horizons of a city with a history of caving in to censorship while maintaining its own integrity as an art institution. Director Dennis Barrie arranged for it before the uproar on Capitol Hill, and called it "the most stunning photographic show I'd seen in years."

Most of the 170 photographs are straightforward portraits of men, women and children that are made riveting by their emphasis on form and light as opposed to character. It's the 13 sexually explicit photographs that raised the ire of the Cincinnati posse. Even sophisticated viewers will find their haunting beauty disturbing, because they challenge the assumption that art ought not be overtly sexual. Also, they defy the notion that if one happens to love members of one's own sex, one is supposed to conceal that fact — not advertise it in artwork. This is what makes the pictures especially difficult for some to accept, as critic Ingrid Sischy noted in The New Yorker.

Sometimes what art reveals — be it photography, literature or drama — is difficult, even intolerable, for some persons. But a function of art is to express what otherwise might not be expressed — to stretch our sensibilities.

The controversy in Cincinnati isn't about whether the Mapplethorpe photographs are offensive. It's about the right of the artist to express himself and our right to see his work if we so choose. That right must be protected; otherwise, we will be diminished as individuals and as a nation.

LEXINGTON HERALD-LEADER
Lexington, Kentucky, April 10, 1990

Who decides? That's the question in Cincinnati these days.

The question is being asked because of an exhibition of photographs by Robert Mapplethorpe. A grand jury has decided that seven of the 175 photographs on display at the Contemporary Arts Center are obscene. The grand jury has indicted the center and its director on charges of pandering obscenity and illegal use of a minor in pornographic material.

The indictments are hardly surprising. Even before the exhibit opened, the Hamilton County sheriff and prosecutor were threatening museum officials with criminal charges.

These same pictures had been shown without incident in other cities. But authorities in Cincinnati clearly had decided in advance that citizens there needed to be protected from the pictures.

Why, then, are so many citizens of Cincinnati upset about this protection?

More than 2,000 people have marched in downtown Cincinnati to protest attempts to shut down the show. Thousands of people already have stood in line to see the exhibit. Crowds have been so large that the museum has had to strictly control entry.

Given the shocking nature of some of Mapplethorpe's work, it's not possible that all of these people have liked what they saw at the exhibit. But they all have one common view: They want to decide for themselves about the nature of the work. They don't want to be told what they can and cannot see.

That's the crux of the controversy in Cincinnati. And that's why what happens there is important to the rest of the country.

Mapplethorpe's comparatively few photographs of sadomasochistic and homosexual acts aren't easy to look at. They may not be great art or — to many — not art of any kind.

But in a free society, individuals have the right to make those judgments for themselves. They also have the right not to attend such exhibits, the right to march or picket peacefully, to denounce either orally or in writing.

A society that can take away individuals' rights to make such judgments for themselves can take away the rights to march, to picket, to speak freely. That's why the real issue in Cincinnati is one of freedom. In a free society, individuals can decide for themselves. If residents of Cincinnati can't do that, how free can that city claim to be?

BUFFALO EVENING NEWS
Buffalo, New York, April 11, 1990

LIFE WOULD BE idyllic indeed if it prompted from artists only depictions of searing sunsets, serene seas and children playing ball in the pasture.

Unfortunately, that isn't the totality of human experience. The late artist Robert Mapplethorpe saw more and attempted to depict it — in admittedly graphic detail — in photo exhibits that include images of homosexual acts and nude children.

Now a Cincinnati art center and its director have been indicted for deciding that adults who want to see an exhibit that includes such photographs should have the opportunity to do so.

It is a frightening prospect. Even if that city's Contemporary Arts Center and its administrator are acquitted of all obscenity-related charges, the heavy-handed police action has to make art directors in Cincinnati and elsewhere fearful.

The likely result will be a shrinking from their mission of judging what is artistically significant — whether innocuous or upsetting — and providing the public a forum in which to view such works.

In place of that educated assessment will be a much more stultifying criterion: What can be shown that will not offend the police or the city council? When that becomes the standard, as it already has to some degree following Congress' plunge into the fray last year, this society will be culturally poorer.

The Cincinnati indictments followed a grand jury's viewing of the exhibit, and that will no doubt fuel prosecutors' efforts as they assert that such a panel is an adequate judge of what is acceptable. But using the grand jury as a shield for government regulation of artistic expression is no more defensible than is direct political control.

Art is a distinctly non-democratic medium. Much of its value derives from the fact that it challenges conventions, pokes holes in sacred cows or makes us ponder realities — such as sex and sexual exploitation — that we'd just as soon sweep under the rug.

It may make some uncomfortable, but it is one way change is precipitated. And change is hardly likely when those picked to represent the status quo are set up as arbiters of allowable artistic expression.

Experts at the Cincinnati center and others that have shown the Mapplethorpe exhibit apparently saw a statement in the sexually graphic photos included among images of calla lilies and famous faces.

Should those who are non-expert be allowed to stifle that statement so that no one else gets affected by it? And if the answer to that is "yes," where will it lead?

Not everything that results from letting the art community police itself will be pleasing. Nor should it have to be.

But that system — with patrons and donors setting outer parameters by making their feelings known — is far better than one in which police, prosecutors and grand juries determine which exhibits adults may or may not view.

Los Angeles Times
Los Angeles, California, April 10, 1990

If the wider implications of their actions were not quite so disturbing, it might be possible to muster a small stirring of sympathy for the would-be censors of Cincinnati. Their flinty little campaign to keep their city from seeing seven photographs by the late Robert Mapplethorpe has left the authorities there in a situation something like that of the cat Heine observed chewing its own tail: In the objective sense it was eating, but in the subjective sense it was being eaten.

Until last weekend, the 175 photographs—a few of which depict homoerotic and sadomasochistic images—probably were best known as Exhibit A in the mean-spirited, if politically potent, attack mounted against the National Endowment for the Arts by Sen. Jesse Helms (R-N.C.). Then Cincinnati got into the act. A county grand jury, acting under a local ordinance hailed by anti-pornography crusaders as a national model, indicted the city's Contemporary Arts Museum, where the exhibit is on view, and its director on two counts of pandering and using a minor in material involving nudity.

So far, all the grand jury seems to have accomplished is to give Mapplethorpe's work qualities he could not himself provide. During his life, serious critics frequently took the artist to task for a brittle self-preoccupation and slick technique that borrowed so heavily from the world of commercial advertising that even his self-consciously provocative images seemed like a kind of consumer kink. Thus, by making such art the center of a now unavoidable battle for freedom of expression, the Cincinnati censors have managed to drape the mantle of principle over a set of shoulders that themselves seldom managed more than a shrug of cold disdain. In the process, they also have secured Mapplethorpe's work a public it never found on its own. Openings at the Cincinnati museum usually are free and about 600 people show up. Friday, an estimated 6,000 people stood in line for hours and paid $10 apiece to get in. Thousands more streamed in over the weekend.

This shabby legal exercise is a reminder that what began as a campaign against a handful of vulgar photos has become an attempt to deprive Americans of the right to decide for themselves what kind of art they will enjoy. The events in Cincinnati represent more than tedious yahooism. They are an unacceptable blurring of the distinction between the indispensable right to live according to one's private convictions and the insupportable insistence that others must live by them, too.

OBSCENITY ISSUES:

X Rating Replaced For Films in U.S.

Jack Valenti, the president of the Motion Picture Association of America (MPAA), announced Sept. 26 that the MPAA would eliminate its X rating for films and would replace it with a rating called NC-17, meaning that no children under age 17 would be admitted.

The move came at a time when the X rating was under fire from many filmmakers who charged that it stigmatized films as pornographic. The distributors of such independent films as *Tie Me Up! Tie Me Down!* and *The Cook, The Thief, His Wife and Her Lover* had chosen to release their films without a rating after the MPAA had assigned them an X. Miramax, the distributor of *Tie Me Up!* had appealed the rating in court.

Unlike the old X rating, the new NC-17 rating would be trademarked by the MPAA, meaning that only the MPAA could use it. The lack of trademark for the X rating had led to its use as a promotional gimmick by makers of pornographic films, even though they had not submitted their movies to the MPAA for review. As a result, the X rating had come to be associated with pornographic films, leading many movie theaters to refuse to show films with X ratings.

The first film to be released with an NC-17 rating would be *Henry and June*, directed by Philip Kaufman and released by Universal Pictures. The film, which was scheduled to open on Oct. 5, was the story of the relationship between author Henry Miller, his wife and their mutual lover, writer Anais Nin. The movie included several scenes of lesbian lovemaking and a shot of a Japanese postcard showing a woman embracing an octopus.

Valenti also announced Sept. 26 that the MPAA was revising its R rating, which required anyone under age 17 to be accompanied by a parent or a guardian.

Although the meaning of the rating itself would not change, the MPAA would release a brief statement with each film explaining why it had received an R rating. The move was designed to help parents distinguish between films that had received an R rating for scenes of sex, violence or other reasons.

The Dallas Morning News
Dallas, Texas, September 29, 1990

Twenty-two years ago, the Motion Picture Association of America created a ratings system to guide moviegoers as well as to deter local censorship. For the most part, the system has worked well. The exception has been the X category, which designates films for "mature" viewers — meaning those 17 years old and older.

When the association devised its system, it unfortunately failed to obtain a trademark for its X category. That mistake allowed pornographers to appropriate the rating for themselves. X now has become a promotional lure for porn, and many theaters and newspapers understandably do not play or advertise X films.

As a result, the makers and marketers of serious films — the ones for which the designation was intended — were forced to avoid an X rating at all costs. Some of those movies were re-edited, so that they could be rated R. Others went into theaters without any ratings, thus defeating a major purpose of the system.

The revised movie rating system that was announced by the Motion Picture Association on Wednesday is likely to go a long way toward alleviating the film industry's concerns over self-censorship as well as giving moviegoers a more easily understood symbol for adult-oriented films that have artistic merit.

From now on, such movies will receive an NC-17 designation — that is, no children younger than 17 will be admitted. Having learned from its mistake, the association will obtain a trademark for the new rating, so that pornographers won't be able to steal it. There will be a clear distinction between serious films and porn.

In addition, the Motion Picture Association plans to do better at explaining its R rating, which is given to movies where children younger than 17 must be accompanied by a parent or guardian. Moviegoers now will be told why a particular film was placed in that category — drug use, profanity, sex, violence.

The association is to be congratulated for responding — albeit slowly — to the concerns that have been expressed over the past year about the rating system's shortcomings. Serious movies won't be confused with *Debbie Does Dallas*, and parents will be better able to know what their children may see — or must avoid.

The Hutchinson News
Hutchinson, Kansas, September 29, 1990

The movie industry made a mistake when it caved in to the bellyaching over movie ratings and invented NC-17 (no one under 17 allowed) to replace the fearful X-rating, the designation meant for films deemed pornographic.

Books don't carry ratings, so why should movies or music?

The ratings change is not the result of grand thinking, as much as it is another move by a self-serving industry to cover its own assets.

Members of the Motion Picture Association of America brought this change upon themselves as a result of their inability to judge films on their full merit. Instead, a film that dealt with material of interest to many adults was sent to the gulags of X-dom or was forced to expunge targeted material that was deemed without merit based on the decibel of the complaints hurled against it. These decisions were based on out-of-context reviews, and were often instigated by small but loud segments of society.

Many complaints found an ear from the ratings board, a fact that exposes its members as malleable pushovers unable to bear up under the constant vigilance of special interests eager to cast aspersions on any film they decided was unredeemable.

It is no wonder that Hollywood continues to enrich itself by churning out bland films with just the right levels of violence, sex, foul language and gore, but not enough to suffer the censorship of an extreme rating.

The film industry is populated by hypocrites who give lip service to the creative arts, while hiding behind ratings when deciding the fate of films containing controversial material. The box office should decide the fate of films, just as the reading public decides the fate of books.

The ratings are meaningless — and worse, in a democratic society, they are abominable.

The State
Columbia, South Carolina, September 29, 1990

PRIOR to its release 24 years ago, movie moguls huddled to decide what should be done about sexually explicit words in the film version of Edward Albee's *Who's Afraid of Virginia Woolf*. The group excised "screw" and left in "hump the hostess." The fuss led, in part, to creation of Motion Picture Association of America's Rating System in 1968.

Since then — and until recently — movies were rated G (general audiences, all ages admitted); PG (parental guidance suggested, some material may be unsuitable for children under 17); PG-13 (an alert to parents that material may be unsuitable for children under 13; R (restricted, children must be accompanied by adult); and X (no one under 17 admitted).

This week, in a judicious effort to distinguish adult-theme films from hard-core pornography, the MPAA abolished the X rating for mainstream movies and replaced it with a new one, NC-17. It bars children under 17 from viewing movies judged by the ratings board as adult material.

At the same time, the R rating was clarified to include an explanation as to why a particular film was placed in that category. The explanations could involve such themes as sex, violence, profanity, drug use or suicide.

Over the years, there have been numerous hassles with the ratings, particularly from serious filmmakers unhappy with an X citation that has been completely stigmatized by the porn-movie industry. Many theater chains, for example, won't show X films, and many newspapers and TV stations won't take ads for them.

The current *cause celebre* centered on *Henry & June*, a Universal release directed by Philip Kaufman and originally rated X solely because of sexual explicitness. The movie, a steamy tale based on the autobiographical writings of Anais Nin, details her relationships with the writer Henry Miller and his wife, June. *Henry and June* was the first picture to come out with the new rating.

We have no problem with a system that rates movies so kids can't see them. But there is still something intrinsically wrong with the setup — and with society — when the severing of men's arms in *Total Recall* (rated R) passes, and bare buttocks in *Henry & June* (now NC-17) fail. The changes are an improvement, but the double standard for sex and violence remains a mockery of the ratings system.

The Miami Herald
Miami, Florida, September 30, 1990

WHEN THE Motion Picture Association of America (MPAA) introduced the movie-rating system in 1968, it inadvertently committed two mistakes that since have been a source of much grief for film makers and parents alike.

The first mistake was to choose a titillating label for rating legitimate movies containing adult-only themes. That label was "X," which rhymes with "sex," one of the most attention-grabbing words in the English vocabulary: Ask any advertiser.

The MPAA's second mistake was its failure to trademark the X rating. That legal loophole let the pornographic-movie industry use the rating not as a guide but as a neon-sign appeal to prurient interests.

The gimmick also aroused the ire of indignant groups of parents and religious leaders, who saw little if any difference between an X-rated work of genuine art and the stag-party variety. As XXX establishments began to dot the landscape, these groups banded together successfully to pressure theater chains to ban X-rated films from the neighborhood cinema. Similarly, TV stations and many newspapers refused to carry ads for X-rated films.

Regrettably, this campaign also ended up punishing serious film directors. In order to avoid an X rating, they oftentimes were forced by the major movie studios to censor parts of their work. Earlier this year, independent producers of such fine, artistic films as *Tie Me Up! Time Me Down!*; *Henry: Portrait of a Serial Killer*, and *The Cook, the Thief, His Wife and Her Lover* refused to go along with this policy; they released their films *sans* rating. A fierce public debate about the fairness of the rating system followed.

That debate resulted in the MPAA's welcome decision last week to revise the way that it rates movies intended for adult-viewing only. Henceforth, the X rating will disappear, replaced by an innocuous-sounding rating called NC-17. That's short for "No children under 17 admitted," the group that "X" had sought to protect all along before the porn peddlers swiped it.

Movie buffs throughout the country should rejoice over this change, which is so long in coming. The NC-17 rating upholds artistic freedom while continuing to protect the rights of parents to insulate their children from explicit violence and sex.

THE TENNESSEAN
Nashville, Tennessee, September 30, 1990

OF the 26 letters in the Roman alphabet, surely the most expressive is the letter X.

X can represent the signature of a person who cannot write. It can stand for the word *Christ*, as in Xmas for Christmas. An X on a map indicates a destination.

In Roman numerals, X means 10. In simple arithmetic, X mean multiply. In algebra, X stands for an unknown quantity.

Xs can indicate the degree of fineness of flour or sugar, and the degree of magnification of optical instruction. At the end of a letter, Xs stand for kisses.

Last week, the letter X lost one of its meanings when the Motion Picture Association of American dropped the notorious X rating for movies.

When the rating system was adopted by the Motion Picture Association in 1968, an X rating meant that no one under the age of 17 would be admitted.

But the association failed to protect that X-rating with a trademark, and the pornography industry started to use big, bold Xs on marquees to lure in patrons to lurid movies.

Soon, instead of meaning "no children allowed," most people thought an X rating stood for pornography.

Some movie theaters initiated policies of not showing X-rated movies. Producers of X-rated films couldn't buy advertising in most newspapers or magazines, or on radio and TV stations.

To X-rate movies that were not suitable for children, but not pornographic, X was the kiss of death at the box office.

Last week, the X was dropped totally as a movie rating symbol. Replacing it is NC 17, meaning no children under the age of 17 will be allowed.

The problem with any kind of rating system is that there is little way to account for individual tastes or maturity. A film that one parent may consider inappropriate for a 16-year-old may be deemed by another parent as harmless or thought-provoking.

As rating systems go, the Motion Picture Industry has always had a fairly good one — but swapping the NC for X should be an excellent exchange.

The revamped rating system will give consumers what they want — some kind of rating at the movies to let them know what's in store before they buy their popcorn. ■

THE DENVER POST
Denver, Colorado, September 29, 1990

WHEN THE movie "The Godfather" aired on television, censors blanked out James Caan's line that used the phrase "son of a bitch," yet permitted a scene of Caan's character being blasted by machine guns just a few minutes later.

Such is the twisted way censors have classified sexual and violent behavior in the movies. This distorted thinking has affected how films are rated at the theater.

There have been a number of worthwhile films that have been slapped with an X rating, primarily because they contained sexually suggestive material. Since the X rating had been abused by pornographic filmmakers, audiences assumed that worthwhile X-rated films also were obscene, and so stayed away.

Meantime, the level of explicit violence allowed in R- or PG-13-rated films has been shocking.

Simply put, the rating system isn't doing its job of letting moviegoers know something about a film's content before they buy a ticket and sit down in a theater.

But a new classification proposed by the Motion Picture Association offers some promise that the film industry will at last become more honest in how movies are advertised.

The association plans to abandon the misleading X rating in favor of an NC-17 classification — that is, no children under age 17.

Hopefully, the association will rethink what types of films may be inappropriate for young people, and put the new NC-17 rating on movies that contain explicitly violent material as well as those with sexually suggestive scenes.

To paraphrase another commenter on the same subject, it seems odd that America tolerates films where people are very bad to each other, but prohibits movies showing people being very, very good to one another.

Individual moviegoers may not like films that contain either sex or violence, but the current rating system does not warn them that one or the other may be shown. Hopefully, the new NC-17 classification will lessen the confusion.

THE BLADE
Toledo, Ohio, September 28, 1990

Like the cavalry in a B western, the Motion Picture Association of America has come, at almost the last minute, to the rescue of the controversial film, "Henry & June."

By creating a new NC-17 rating for films at which no one under 17 could be admitted, regardless of whether accompanied by a parent, the MPAA spared director Philip Kaufman a showdown next week over the X rating that initially had been assigned to "Henry & June."

The organization's rating board was scheduled to rule on Kaufman's appeal next Wednesday.

If the X rating stood up it would have obstructed the film's chances to be circulated in reputable theaters.

The NC-17 designation is an attempt to adjust the film industry's 22-year-old rating system to distinguish between raw sleaze and films that have artistic merit but deal with adult themes.

The intensity behind filmmakers' protest against several recent X ratings undercuts the popular assumption that prurient appeal makes for a box office bonanza.

Those who resent explicit sex and violence on the screen might be more reassured, however, if they saw a greater interest by the industry in producing an occasional "G" movie.

ST. LOUIS POST-DISPATCH
St. Louis, Missouri, September 28, 1990

At a time when conservatives seem bound and determined to make art safe and bland, the often stodgy Motion Picture Association of America has made a surprising move. It has decided to ditch its X rating and adopt in its place a new rating, NC-17. (No children under the age of 17 would be admitted to a film rated NC-17.) The new rating is a recognition that films can, in fact, have adult themes or content without being pornographic.

Originally, of course, an X rating did not connote pornography; highly praised films, such as "Midnight Cowboy," were rated X. The MPAA, however, never bothered to copyright its ratings, so the pornographic movie industry appropriated the X — as well as making up XX and even XXX. Once the pornography industry claimed the X, the mainstream movie industry disavowed it. Many movie theaters refused to show X-rated films; many newspapers refused to advertise X-rated films; and contracts with film directors stipulated that they make R-rated, or restricted, films.

This year, however, several controversial, provocative but decidedly non-pornographic films were given X ratings. The NC-17 rating is a belated though welcome admission that an X does not accurately describe the content of these kinds of films. (The new rating, interestingly enough, comes just in time to save a major studio release, a film about Henry Miller and Anais Nin, from an X.)

Unfortunately, though, the new rating still avoids answering serious questions about attitudes toward sexuality and violence. Why, for example, are gory slasher films that revel in violence rated more leniently than films that investigate sexuality? Is nudity really more offensive than the graphic presentation of bodily dismemberment? Why is sexuality considered a not-quite-legitimate topic for cinematic exploration? Why does the movie industry discourage filmmakers with a more sophisticated sensibility than that of the average 14-year-old?

Los Angeles Times
Los Angeles, California, September 22, 1990

There's increasing unhappiness with the movie industry's current system for rating movies.

The problem is that somewhere between R- and X-rated movies are films that are too adult for an R but are hardly in the "Debbie Does Dallas" class. It's probably time for a category between R (Restricted: Under 17 requires accompanying parent or adult guardian) and X (no one under 17 admitted).

The Motion Picture Assn. of America created the ratings system in 1968 to replace the outdated and prudish Hays Code, established in 1924. Though the present system is entirely voluntary, it is a major improvement. However, one unintended result is that exhibitors nationwide are reluctant to show an unrated film.

This forces some directors to cut out footage that technically qualifies the film for an X when in fact "Debbie" actually never really gets much past Cincinnati. Thus a new category—say an AR, for Adult Restricted—would serve the purpose of alerting moviegoers that the film may have gamy scenes without forcing those scenes to be excised or branded with the scarlet letter of an X.

Today, the X rating has become synonymous with pornography; TV and newspapers, including this one, will not take advertising for X-rated films.

Jack Valenti, president of the association and creator of the present ratings system, opposes a new category between R and X. He maintains that the purpose of a rating system is to provide parents with guidance for taking their young children to the movies.

He says that surveys done annually for the last decade indicate nearly three-fourths of parents with young children find the ratings useful. He maintains that a new Adult category would compel the ratings board to make judgments on artistic merit, which it has never done before.

The current system, however, leaves little choice for studios and producers. Since an X-rating today is the kiss of death at the box office, producers typically are contractually bound to edit their films until they qualify for a more acceptable R rating. Indeed, much of the R-rated category consists of films originally intended strictly for adults.

Creating a new category would hardly be unprecedented. In 1984 the MPAA added PG-13 to accommodate Steven Spielberg's "Indiana Jones & the Temple of Doom." It was initially deemed too violent for preteens. An AR-rated film would simply alert adults that the film is for them—and no one else.

THE RICHMOND NEWS LEADER
Richmond, Virginia, September 28, 1990

NC-17 | NO CHILDREN UNDER 17 ADMITTED

The movie industry has come up with the first major change in its 22-year practice of rating flicks — and the thing is wrong, wrong, *wrong*. It amounts to nothing less than a caving-in to forces of the far-out, a collapse before the god of *anything goes*.

The Motion Picture Association of America (MPAA) has made merely a semantic change — dropping the X rating and replacing it with something called NC-17. The new rating means that no children under 17 will be admitted.

That's what the X rating meant, too. But movie producers didn't like the X. They found it inhibiting and intimidating. To avoid the X rating, movies bearing which about half the nation's theaters contracted not to show, producers had to excise steamy sex scenes that they contended (of course) were the essence of their cinematic art.

NC-17 connotes nothing so naughty as the X. So producers will be able to get away with a lot more. In the lingo of jet jockeys, producers will be able to push the envelope — the pornographic envelope — far farther than before.

Los Angeles Times film critic Peter Rainer, who also is chairman of the National Society of Film Critics, let the cat out of the bag. He said:

I think it is good news. By creating a new category that does not have the stigma of the X, it will potentially create a situation where filmmakers are now able to explore adult themes without de facto censorship.

You see the picture: "the stigma of the X." *The X got in the way of "art." It stymied creativity. It shackled true talent. It limited expression.*

We've seen this happen before. *Playboy* began with a bare breast; now it and its magaziny sisters bare gynecological everythings. AIDS began as a consequence of immoral behavior; now practitioners and defenders of that behavior urge (and the public accepts) not a ceasing and desisting but — rather — the use of condoms for "safe sex."

Instead of accepting the norms the X imposed, movie producers have changed the norm. Verily, they have dropped it. Now there is no norm except the norm of *anything goes*. The only limit is the sky — and liberated movie producers are free at last to *create* and *express* through skin-flicks to their hearts' content.

Books are looking better all the time.

San Francisco Chronicle
San Francisco, California, September 28, 1990

BY DROPPING its "X" movie rating and creating a new and more realistic "No Children" category, the Motion Picture Association of America has finally permitted reason to enter a troublesome aspect of film designations. The X denomination had basically become captive to raunch.

By failing to obtain a trademark for the X category, the association allowed makers of pornographic films to appropriate the listing as a promotional lure, thereby forcing the makers and marketers of serious films to shun an X rating at all costs.

In other words, cineastes who dealt frankly, even poetically, with the human sexual component had nowhere to go. An X relegated their fare primarily to the sleaze houses. And editing to avoid the X eroded artistic integrity.

THIS LONG overdue decision is a liberating one.

Newsday
New York City, New York, September 29, 1990

The letter X can go back to more wholesome work (marking the spot and filling tick-tac-toe grids, for example) now that the Motion Picture Association has relieved it of responsibility for warning kids away from adult movies.

Poor old X. Peddlers of porn had pounced upon it and made it a selling device ("Wow! Triple-X Rated") for flicks favored by the dirty-raincoat set. Its meaning was so muddied that you never knew if an X movie would stimulate your intellect or your hormones. Mainstream viewers shunned films marked X.

In its place will be the far more precise NC-17 which sends a very clear message: No Children under 17. That's an important improvement. The first movie to get it is "Henry and June," which tells of the relationship among Henry Miller, wife June and author Anais Nin.

The new rating should be useful to parents and film buffs alike. And it seems unlikely that filmers of pornography will try to exploit it: "Wow! Triple NC-17 Rated" just doesn't sing.

2 Live Crew Rap Group Acquitted of Obscenity

Three members of the black rap music group 2 Live Crew were acquitted of obscenity charges Oct. 20, 1990 by a jury in Fort Lauderdale, Fla.

The three band members – Luther Campbell, Mark Ross and Christopher Wongwon – had been arrested following an adults-only performance at a nightclub in Hollywood, Fla. in June. A fourth band member had not been at the concert and was not charged. During the performance, the band had performed songs from its album *As nasty As They Wanna Be*, which had been declared obscene by a federal district court judge in Fort Lauderdale. The songs featured lyrics in which the singer bragged about his sexual abilities and demanded that women perform oral or anal sex with him.

The band maintained that its lyrics were deliberately exaggerated and were intended as humor or parody. A literature professor from Duke University who testified on behalf of the group, Henry Louis Gates Jr., argued that the songs carried on a black tradition known as "signifying," which involved teasing or insulting rhymes. "It was the way blacks would fight against the oppression of their slave masters," Gates said. "And rapping is a contemporary form of signifying."

In their case against the group, prosecutors relied heavily on a microcasette recording of the concert that had been made by undercover detectives. The tape was of poor quality and difficult to understand, however. Prosecutors' efforts to recite the lyrics in court were frequently met with embarrassment and laughter. At one point, Judge June Johnston told the court that jurors had requested permission to laugh out loud. Noting that "some of them are having physical pain" from holding in their laughter, Johnston Oct. 17 agreed to the request.

The six-member jury took only two hours to reach its verdict. Afterward, jurors said they had found 2 Live Crew's songs to be funny, but not obscene. As for the raunchy lyrics, they noted that "people in everyday society use those words," according to foreman David Garsow, 24, an office clerk and church choir singer.

The Record
Hackensack, New Jersey, October 23, 1990

Once again, a jury that represented a cross-section of middle America has shown better sense than government prosecutors. It took jurors in Broward County, Florida, just two hours to acquit the rap group, the 2 Live Crew, of obscenity charges. The verdict was a sensible end to a farcical case.

The incident offers an interesting parallel with the recent trial of the director of a Cincinnati museum, acquitted on charges stemming from display of sexually explicit photos by Robert Mapplethorpe. Lyrics to the 2 Live Crew's songs, like some of Mr. Mapplethorpe's studies of sexual activities, are definitely not for most of us. Songs by the 2 Live Crew often involve boasting about sexual prowess. The language is earthy, and women are usually portrayed as nothing more than a means of satisfying lust. The groups's album, "As Nasty as They Wanna Be," had been declared obscene by a federal judge, and Broward County sheriff's officers arrested members of the group after a June 10 show in Hollywood, Fla.

But jurors recognized that people who don't want to hear the 2 Live Crew have a perfectly simple remedy. Don't buy their tapes or CDs. And don't go to their concerts. "This is not something I want to see out in the mall," said one of the jurors, Susan Van Hemert, a 42-year-old assistant middle school principal. But Ms. Van Hemert also said that anyone who is 21 is old enough to be sent to fight in the Middle East. And that means, she said, that they should have a right to decide for themselves whether they want to hear the 2 Live Crew perform in a club.

Other jurors, who included a retired hospital administrator, a retired cook, and a diesel mechanic, agreed. One, Beverly Resnick, 65, of Coconut Beach, Fla., put the issue succinctly. "We have the freedom to say what we want in this country, and the minute we don't we're in big trouble."

Jurors also showed they could appreciate the comic aspects of the case. They said they had trouble suppressing laughter at the amateurish, almost incomprehensible tapes of the 2 Live Crew's performance made by sheriff's officers. Ms. Van Hemert said she was intrigued by the idea of having the verdict rendered as a rap song.

In the United States today, any number of performers are testing the limits of public tolerance with songs, photographs, paintings, performance art, and endeavors in other media. Sometimes the results are interesting, sometimes only squalid. Each of us should be free to decide whether we want to be exposed to this material or not. That's what the jury in Fort Lauderdale understood.

The issue wasn't whether the 2 Live Crew's music is good or bad, raunchy or wholesome. The issue was whether people should decide for themselves what music to hear, or have local law enforcement make the decision for them. In a democracy, the people have the right to decide for themselves. Fortunately, the jury in Broward County agreed.

The Des Moines Register
Des Moines, Iowa, October 27, 1990

During the much publicized Florida obscenity trial of the rap group 2 Live Crew last week, the judge issued an unusual ruling. He told jurors it was all right for them to laugh in court.

How appropriate. The very idea of government censorhip of a performance, no matter how offensive the performance may be, is absurd. It only follows that courtroom spectacles surrounding such cases can be equally absurd.

In Fort Lauderdale, the members of the jury had a hard time keeping their faces straight as embarrassed sheriff's deputies struggled to decipher scratchy tape recordings of the coarse and, yes, vile, 2 Live Crew performance. They laughed as attorneys argued and objected over different aspects of the case.

In the end, the jury didn't take the charges seriously. The three band members were found "not guilty" on Saturday. Now the group can be dealt with not by the courts, but in another more appropriate jurisdiction — the public marketplace.

Already, there are signs that 2 Live Crew, after benefiting from publicity surrounding its case, is having trouble selling its message. The Knight-Ridder News Service recently reported that the group's leader, Luther Campbell, went on a road tour and bombed. Some of his shows had to be canceled for lack of interest. The Crew's latest album isn't selling well even where stores display it.

The curious swarmed after the group's "As Nasty As They Wanna Be" album as publicity mounted over the Florida obscenity charges. But now that 2 Live Crew's message has been heard, more and more people are saying they want nothing of it.

The message should be clear: Evaluating artistic expression is best left to the public, not the courts. It is far better that offensive speech is rejected by the public rather than restricted by the government.

St. Petersburg Times
St. Petersburg, Florida, Ocotber 26, 1990

Yo! Guv Martinez and Sheriff Navarro —
Here's free advice that you can borrow:
Governors and sheriffs should spend their time
Protecting us from really serious crime
Like murder, arson or kidnappin'
Instead of hasslin' three black guys rappin'.
Our mamas always told us the American Way
Was to let people say what they have to say.
Lots of rap music's full of sound and fury
But it didn't take long to convince a jury
That even if their lyrics are kinda filthy
2 Live Crew should be found not guilty.
When censorship starts, where does it stop?
Will we bar bebop and ban hip-hop?
How long will it be before you wanna
Throw the handcuffs on Madonna
And haul her sweet @#$%¢ into court
Because her dresses are too short?
Will we turn on the radio one day soon
And get to hear nothing but Pat Boone?
Or Lawrence Welk or, ugh, Slim Whitman?
Some of us won't like that a bit, man.
Our opinion — and we ain't dissin':
If you don't like it, then just don't listen
You tell us it's for our own protection
But we think it's for your re-election.
We'll admit we've heard a few rap lyrics
That leave us all with nasty earaches
But not many songs are as obscene as
Sheriff Nick and Guv Martinez.

The Chattanooga Times
Chattanooga, Tennessee, October 26, 1990

The acquittal of the rap group 2 Live Crew should tell us two things: The broad umbrella of the First Amendment functioned as it should to protect even unsavory speech, and law enforcement resources are better used against something other than misdemeanors with no victims.

As most people know, 2 Live Crew specializes in songs that seem to celebrate abusive sex. They are the musical equivalent of skinheads, using lyrics which severely test the nation's commitment to free speech.

However, if all speech were safe and conventional, there would be no need for the First Amendment's free-speech guarantees. It's a tribute to the genius of the nation's founders that the First Amendment was designed to protect those at the outer edges of society as well as those at its center.

That is important because the vulnerability of free speech increases in direct proportion to its distance outside the limits of what many consider "proper." It is only where unconventional ideas, even anti-social ones, are expressed that prosecution becomes a danger. Some people thought that 2 Live Crew, with its odd fascination with vulgar and abusive themes, seemed to be inviting Broward County (Florida) authorities to file charges.

In a recent related case, another Broward County case resulted in conviction of a record store owner for selling a 2 Live Crew album — which a judge declared this summer was obscene. It's significant that the latest jury, confronted with evidence of the group's performance at an adults-only club, decided not only that the police work had been inept but that the evidence ultimately became "just words." That is, speech.

The jury's ruling underscores both the strength and the weakness of the law's approach to obscenity and free expression. Same community, same group, two juries, two verdicts. Community values, one of the key elements in the U.S. Supreme Court's obscenity test, are not easily categorized.

The problem comes when a community, as the Broward County juries' verdicts illustrate, obviously isn't sure whether a popular work violates the population's values. In that case, the alleged offender should get the benefit of the doubt. Otherwise, would-be censors would prohibit material they don't understand — or simply don't like.

Chicago Tribune
Chicago, Illinois, October 23, 1990

The U.S. Constitution's guarantee of freedom of speech was not intended to protect only inoffensive messages; no one wants to suppress inoffensive messages. The speech that benefits from the 1st Amendment is the kind that shocks and infuriates, because that's the kind that the government would be most likely to ban if the majority had its way.

The offensiveness of a message is not a reason to relax our commitment to freedom, but a reason to strengthen it.

Most Americans would be offended by the rap songs performed by 2 Live Crew, which specializes in graphically glorifying the sexual degradation of women. The Florida jurors who heard the prosecution's obscenity case against three members of the group may have been offended too. Even in an age of ubiquitous vulgarity and violence, 2 Live Crew's lyrics are conspicuously repulsive. Last Saturday, however, the jury concluded that the group's work, whatever its merits, was none of the censor's business.

Luther Campbell, the leader of the group, had said he doubted that a largely white, middle-aged jury could sympathize with a bawdy art form created by defiant young blacks. But the jurors overcame any urge to disown something just because it clashed with their personal tastes.

One of them, a 65-year-old women, said during the deliberations, "You take away one freedom, and pretty soon they're all gone." That insight produced this verdict, just as it led to the recent acquittal of the Cincinnati museum director indicted for exhibiting sexually explicit photographs by Robert Mapplethorpe.

In both cases, prosecutors patronized juries by inviting them to put people in jail for insulting the prevailing mores of the community. The jurors distinguished themselves by insisting that freedom is for all of us.

The Philadelphia Inquirer
Philadelphia, Pennsylvania, October 24, 1990

We can still remember a mild uproar in Chapel Hill, N.C., over what to do about the campus "streakers" who'd been dashing naked through the town's streets. It was 1974 and many a brow was furrowed; many a voice raised. Then, a wise man spoke: "This'll take care of itself when the cold weather hits," he said. And, sure enough, it did.

That's sort of the way we've felt about the fuss over 2 Live Crew, the group that just beat an obscenity rap in Fort Lauderdale, Fla. If the inept — might we say, *stupefyingly* inept — local prosecutor had left the nasty-talking, sex-obsessed rappers to do their thing, they'd have faded from the scene by now. Thus, Lesson No. 1 from this silliness: Those who rush to censor often inflate, rather than suppress, the targets of their wrath.

Lesson 2 is a bit more fundamental. And it took a down-to-earth Florida jury to re-teach it. The lesson is that America is a free country where you can object to, denounce, boycott or tune out one man's filthy lyrics. But you'd better think twice about denying him the right to sing them — or telling his fans they can't listen. (Remember, this was an adults-only club act, not something inflicted on an unsuspecting public.)

We'll note for the record that another Florida jury recently went in the other direction, finding against a Broward County record-store owner who sold one of 2 Live Crew's albums. But the latest verdict, coming so soon after the obscenity acquittal of a Cincinnati arts center director in the Mapplethorpe affair, ought to cool the jets of prosecutors who think they know best what art needs to be banned — and what music can't be sung.

That's one chilling effect that we can wholeheartedly endorse.

ADVANCES IN ETHNIC MUSIC: TWO LIVE CREW IS DECLARED ART, NEW LIVE CREW PLAYS CARNEGIE HALL.

The Phoenix Gazette
Phoenix, Arizona, October 27, 1990

Despite all the rhetoric and posing of law enforcement officials who just happened to be up for re-election, juries in Fort Lauderdale, Fla., and Cincinnati, Ohio, came to the appropriate conclusion in the past week: Law enforcement officers and district attorneys should stick to enforcing laws in the streets and stay out of art galleries and nightclubs.

The Fort Lauderdale jury that acquitted members of 2 Live Crew on obscenity charges and the Cincinnati jury that acquitted art gallery officials for exhibiting photos by the late Robert Mapplethorpe offered a working example of how freedom of speech works. Even unpopular things can be said; even some mighty rough words can be uttered in the course of an artistic performance.

So once again the juries show themselves as more sophisticated in the meaning of America's freedoms than the politicians and county attorneys who have attempted to gain politically by attacking as pornographic that which is unpopular.

One juror was so unimpressed with the prosecution's effort against 2 Live Crew that she toyed with the idea of writing the jury's verdict as a rap number. It's probably a good thing she dispensed with the notion. Rap isn't all that safe in Broward County, Fla., these days.

The Hartford Courant
Hartford, Connecticut, October 23, 1990

If the use of nasty words and sentences were a crime, members of 2 Live Crew should have been convicted. But poor taste is no reason to pronounce the rap group guilty.

Six jurors in Broward County, Fla., grasped the simple but exquisite distinction between what is patently lawless and what is merely offensive. They acquitted the rap group of an obscenity charge on Saturday.

The verdict took most people by surprise. After all, only two weeks ago a Fort Lauderdale record store owner was convicted of obscenity charges for the "crime" of selling the Live Crew's album, "As Nasty as They Wanna Be." Florida is supposed to be a conservative state and its elected prosecutors are among the most zealous in the nation.

But the right to free speech is fundamentally a conservative principle. Government should not be in the business of defining, prohibiting, ordering or decreeing what should be recited in rap. As one juror said after the verdict, "You take away one freedom and pretty soon they're all gone."

Live Crew's leader, Luther Campbell, speculated before his trial that he was likely to be convicted because the jury, which included three women over age 60 and only one black, might be too old, too white and too middle class.

But Mr. Campbell wasn't the only participant at the trial who indulged in cynicism and stereotyping. Pedro Dijols, an assistant prosecutor, suspected the jury from the start, particularly one member, who, he said, "hated me. I could just feel it. She was extremely liberal. She was a sociologist, and I don't like sociologists. They try to reason things out too much."

Mr. Dijols apparently received his education in schools that didn't stress the need to reason out too much. His world is divided between the good and the bad — nothing in the middle that is worth thinking or reasoning deeply about.

Some jurors said they considered Live Crew's rap lyrics to be funny; others saw artistic merit in rap music. Another juror considered writing the verdict in rap language. But whether the rappers engaged in paradoy or artistry is secondary to the underlying issue of freedom of speech.

That issue also was dominant earlier this month in the trial of a museum director in Cincinnati, who was was found not guilty of obscenity charges for exhibiting several sexually explicit photographs by Robert Mapplethorpe.

Thus, two juries selected from mainstream America deserve a national salute for having understood the risky nature of freedom, and for taking seriously America's commitment to individual rights: In a democracy, individuals should make choices about what they want to read, write and listen to.

But freedom's sky is not cloudless in Broward County. While one jury acquitted the creators and performers of the rap songs in "As Nasty as They Wanna Be," another jury convicted the store owner who had sold the album to adults. Justice will be served only if the store owner's conviction is reversed on appeal. Better yet, Florida's lawmakers should give obscenity statutes a long holiday.

Let the people decide, through the power of their purses, whether they want to keep 2 Live Crew and other such groups in business.

THE CHRISTIAN SCIENCE MONITOR
Boston, Massachusetts, October 24, 1990

NOT since David felled Goliath have Philistines suffered such reverses from unexpected sources. At least, that's how the contemporary arts, music, and publishing worlds are regarding two jury verdicts handed down this month in Cincinnati and Fort Lauderdale, Fla.

In the first case, eight Ohio burghers with little interest in art acquitted Cincinnati's Contemporary Arts Center and its director of obscenity charges for including some erotic photographs in an exhibit of works by Robert Mapplethorpe. A few days later, six men and women in Florida acquitted members of the rap group 2 Live Crew on obscenity charges stemming from a performance of lewd songs.

In each case the jurors – defying cultural stereotypes and the apprehensions of the cognoscenti, and relying on the testimony of experts – found artistic merit in the challenged works, which therefore are protected by the First Amendment.

As matters of criminal law and freedom of speech, the two verdicts are a relief. Censorship is anathema to the fundamental American principle of individual liberty and its political and cultural concomitants. Prison bars, even just figuratively, are a crude response to ideas: Prosecutions of words and images, however offensive, evoke the totalitarian's ultimately futile dream, never more than fitfully entertained in this land, that people can be herded into folds of mental conformity.

The American polity has rightly made it exceedingly difficult to criminalize ideas. But law doesn't subsume morality: What's legal isn't necessarily good.

To discuss the works attacked in these trials, the mainstream press has had to sanitize them. Most newspapers and magazines wouldn't reproduce Mapplethorpe's homoerotic photos, and fewer would print the sexually sadistic lyrics of songs from 2 Live Crew's "As Nasty as They Wanna Be" album. As a result, the public debate has been misleadingly abstract. The works in question are, simply stated, vile and grotesque. Far from being liberating, as avant-gardists are wont to proclaim, they are degrading and contribute to imprisoning thought in chains of carnality.

It's one thing that Americans afford such works legal protection. But as a people we must face up to their true nature, and not be morally intimidated by those who curl their lips at the "philistinism" of the "booboisie." If we fail to mount a moral counteroffensive through our families, churches, schools, and other institutions, then we will be abandoning the field of consciousness to those whose idea of freedom of expression seems to begin and end with base observations of the human anatomy.

THE TENNESSEAN
Nashville, Tennessee, October 24, 1990

A jury in Florida declared late last week that the obscenity charges against 2 Live Crew were just a bum rap.

The verdict was quick and clean. It took just two hours for all six jurors to find the group innocent of obscenity. The charges were brought after 2 Live Crew performed its rap music to an all-adult audience in a Fort Lauderdale club.

No doubt about it: 2 Live Crew's rap music is raunchy and sexist. One expert witness who testified in the band's behalf said that the lyrics were a parody. Some of the jurors commented after the trial that they found the lyrics funny and artistic.

But the question before the court was not whether the music was a parody, or funny, or raunchy, or sexist. The question was whether the lyrics were obscene.

The landmark 1973 *Miller v. California* Supreme Court decision set some vague guidelines for obscenity. That decision said that material is obscene if the average person, applying community standards, finds it appealing primarily to prurient interests, patently offensive, and lacking in serious literary, scientific, artistic, or political value.

The jury last week in Fort Lauderdale, applying community standards, declared that 2 Live Crew was not obscene. But another jury in the same county just two weeks ago found a record store owner guilty of an obscenity charge for selling the same group's record, *Nasty as They Wanna Be*.

Same group. Same music. Same lyrics. Same community. Different verdict.

And that will always be the problem with prosecuting material on obscenity charges. What one person in a community finds "primarily prurient," another finds "artistic." Work that one person finds totally offensive, another will find having political merit.

2 Live Crew's music is still the subject of various ordinances, lawsuits, criminal trials and threats of prosecution in several states. That's obscene — but the obscenity is that public tax dollars in those cities are being spent to prevent adults from listening to music that they want to hear.

Some have suggested that the Supreme Court should set more specific guidelines in obscenity cases. That's one answer, but the best answer is to respect the First Amendment. ■

The Washington Post
Washington, D.C., October 28, 1990

A JURY in Florida has acquitted the rap group 2 Live Crew of obscenity charges arising out of a live performance this past spring in Fort Lauderdale. A large number of critics have judged the group's music—which has its fans—to be simplistic, uninteresting and unoriginal. A second, larger group has pronounced it filthy, lewd, disgusting, especially offensive to women and without any artistic merit.

Florida prosecutors were counting on that reaction from a jury they thought demographically favorable. Of the six jurors, five were white and three were women over 60. But the government's strategy backfired. There were mistakes. The tape recording of the performance was indistinct and fuzzy. A key prosecution witness had trouble identifying the offensive language. And a couple of professors testified that repetitious description of sexual acts punctuated by macho fantasy and calls for violence against women was high art. The jurors more or less accepted this evaluation in finding that the material was not obscene. Our guess is that the verdict was less a product of an in-depth search for the meaning of art than it was a much less complicated rejection of the idea that the rappers deserved to go to jail for a year for what they had produced.

An early clue was in a message the jury sent to the judge after the first day of trial. They asked if it was all right to laugh in the jury box. Clearly the case struck some of them as preposterous. After the verdict, members of the panel said they laughed in the van going back to the hotel every evening and that they had made up their own rap parody of the proceedings. They said that their hearing the offensive language time after time during the trial had caused it to lose its shock value for them. That's happening to the entire culture, of course. Why, the jurors wondered, was the government spending so much time and effort prosecuting this case?

The point is that groups like 2 Live Crew are protected by the First Amendment. No one is forced to buy a ticket to a 2 Live Crew performance. Adults can do as they choose, and the government can intervene only under very narrow circumstances. What juries are saying in this case and in the Mapplethorpe case decided in Cincinnati last week is that this society increasingly tolerates controversial material in the arts and narrows the grounds on which the government can justify criminal penalties for speech.

Pop Star Madonna Stirs Controversy

MTV, the cable television music network, had refused to air the latest music video by pop star Madonna, it was reported Nov. 7, 1990. The video, to the song "Justify My Love," showed Madonna and her real-life boyfriend, Tony Ward, having an erotic encounter in a hotel room. The black- and-white video featured scenes of the couple's sexual fantasies, including bisexuality, cross-dressing, multiple partners and mild sado- masochism. The video was scheduled to be sold in record stores beginning in early December.

Madonna's controversial new book, *Sex*, was released Oct. 21, 1992. The book, which sold at $49.95 and was sealed in a special Mylar envelope to prevent bookstore patrons from browsing, contained explicit photographs of the singer enacting sexual fantasies. Shot by photographer Steven Meisel, the images in the book included Madonna, in various stages of undress, practicing sadomasochism and posing suggestively with both men and women of varied races. The text accompanying the photos was written by Madonna. More than one million copies of the book were shipped worldwide, establishing a publishing record for a first printing. Madonna's new dance-pop album, *Erotica*, a came out Oct. 21 to coincide with her book release.

The Houston Post
Houston, Texas, December 26, 1990

QUESTION: WHAT does a sex maniac do? Answer: Sell newspapers.

This old Hollywood film line springs to mind with all the commotion over Madonna's latest rock video. The principle is the same — use sex to sell the product.

People who had hardly heard of either Madonna or *Nightline* were tuned in across America this week to watch the ABC news show air the video in its entirety. And there it was, after Monday Night Football and the local news — Madonna in her traditional black lace doing the sexy things she's so accomplished at — plus segments of voyeurism, homosexuality and a young woman wearing only a pair of thin suspenders from the waist up.

All this interest was generated last week when MTV banned the video. The cable network had planned to premiere it this Saturday. After its executives saw the film clip, they expressed the network's respect for Madonna but said the video is "just not for us." MuchMusic, the major Canadian video music network, has also banned it as "inappropriate for air."

In response, Madonna's record label is releasing the tape as a single. Her representatives vigorously deny that this was planned all along. Maybe not, but all the hype will virtually ensure brisk sales and tidy profits, whether or not the video appears on cable.

Madonna says she is continuing to push the frontiers of what is acceptable TV viewing. Her latest effort seems to have stepped past those limits as far as MTV and some other networks are concerned. In this instance, they exhibited better taste than one of their competitors.

THE RICHMOND NEWS LEADER
Richmond, Virginia, December 6, 1990

Begin, please, with the dismaying fact: Louise Veronica Ciccone is the world's most popular female singer — with 80 million albums sold.

These days the lady Louise goes by another name — Madonna.

For most of her career she has fuzzed the line between pornography and art. Now, at last, MTV (music television) — of all things — thinks it knows where the line is.

Madonna has produced a video she calls "Justify My Love." MTV is more responsible than any other medium for her success, and MTV has said, *Nope*.

She produced one several years ago called "Like a Prayer" — a sewer of blasphemy — and MTV thought it was just fine. But even MTV finds "Justify My Love" too much.

It contains (among other things) bisexualism, voyeurism, transvestism, and sado-masochism.

Wholesome whoring. Delicious deviationism.

MTV announced it won't run the the thing.

Whereupon ABC put her on "Nightline" to complain, and she drew (of course) a record audience.

The vogueish, material Madonna's popularity tells us all we need to know about ourselves — and about our cultural craving for sex. Ms. Madonna acts like anything *but* a virgin. She's into sexual weirdism. That's why people clamor for her "music."

But her latest has stretched her offerings beyond even MTV's elastic lines of prudence and acceptability.

Well, thank Heaven there's a line *somewhere*.

The Chattanooga Times
Chattanooga, Tennessee, October 30, 1992

You think times are bad? Silly you. From his command post at the Excellence in Broadcasting Network on Wednesday, talk show impresario Rush Limbaugh offered proof to the contrary.

Expressing skepticism that Madonna's new book, *Sex*, had sold 500,000 copies worldwide last week alone, Mr. Limbaugh was nonetheless willing to concede that she had sold at least half that number.

And that means? "What recession?" he exclaimed. His point was that the economy's in pretty good shape when 250,000 people are buying Madonna's book at 60 bucks a copy. Who's buying the book? Certainly not rich conservative Republicans, Mr. Limbaugh said. Oh, please. Does anyone believe there are *no* closet Republican Madonnaphiles?

So who's left? Must be all those middle-income Americans, perhaps even some of the unemployed, who are cutting back on their household budgets so they can push *Sex* onto the best-seller lists. Now you know.

Mr. Limbaugh often brags that on his show, he operates with "half my brain tied behind my back." He got that right, at least on the Madonna issue.

THE TENNESSEAN
Nashville, Tennessee, December 6, 1990

REGARDLESS of any debate on whether rock star Madonna's new video is suitable for television, there is no question that she is one smart woman.

Madonna's new video for her song *Justify My Love* has caused a furor since it contains steamy sex scenes and includes images of voyeurism, cross-dressing and mild sadomasochism. The video has been banned by the cable video network MTV.

Instead of whining about MTV's decision, Madonna has used the situation to her advantage. She has decided to sell the video and will likely sell many copies thanks to media attention over it. She wound up with the video airing in its entirety on national television when she appeared on ABC's *Nightline*.

Madonna has displayed a remarkable ability to appeal to a wide audience throughout her career. She has not been afraid to test the limits of artistic expression. Ultimately, Madonna will have to decide for herself what her limits are. If she does go too far, she will lose the audience she has worked so hard to gain. Thus far, she has shown a great capacity for advancing her career.

MTV has its way of doing business. Madonna has hers. To this point, they both have a track record for knowing what they're doing. ■

The Seattle Times
Seattle, Washington, D.C., December 6, 1990

POP singer Madonna wields a bookkeeping pencil that's as sharply pointed as her brassiere cups.

Her latest video, "Justify My Love," is so calculatedly racy that MTV, the music-video channel, decided not to air it. What's a poor entrepreneur to do?

Sell it herself, as she'd probably planned all along.

The ABC program "Nightline" aired the video on its late-night news program, and interviewed Madonna about her artistic license . . . to print money.

What attracted all this lucrative controversy? A short film about the licentious M's sexual fantasies She wears her usual underwear; one or two others don't. Her bustier is nuzzled by a guy who needs to wash his hair. She kisses a woman. Listless onlookers are either recovering from group sex or an all-night bus ride. Hardly a stag reel, but no rock-and-roll fare for the teeny-bopper audience MTV attracts.

MTV made its business decision; Madonna made hers. She told her ABC interviewer she knew the tape pushed the limits, so she had a backup plan: selling the tape herself.

Her "Nightline" host was impressed: She makes money from record sales if MTV airs the tape; she makes money if MTV doesn't.

"Lucky me," was her bottom-line response.

Don't be surprised if "Justify My Love" was originally written as a memo to her tax preparer.

Rockford Register Star
Rockford, Illinois, December 2, 1990

MTV has banned Madonna's new music video and she calls it censorship. Bunk.

The video is purely soft-core pornography, which the pop star insists is her own artistic expression. Fine, but MTV has every right and obligation to express itself by rejecting the video. What's more, Madonna knew "Justify My Love" wouldn't pass the network's standards.

"Half of me thought I was going to be able to get away with it," Madonna said in an interview on ABC's *Nightline* this week.

But the fact that the pop star didn't get away with it is not evidence of a new conservative wave sweeping the nation. Millions of Madonna-lovers will doubtless exercise their rights to buy the video at their local record or video stores.

Which brings up the not-so-pitiful prospect of Madonna making even more money off the video now that the furor's been created. "Yeah. So lucky me," she said.

There's no argument about that.

INDEX

A

ACT-UP—*See AIDS Coalition to Unleash Power*
ADAMS, Sen. Brock (D, Wash.)
    Packwood sex harassment accusation 42–45
AGRICULTURE
    Promotion of women in developing nations 100–101
AIDS (acquired immune deficiency syndrome)
    San Francisco conference 108–115
    NEA grant rejections 186–189
AIDS Coalition to Unleash Power (ACT-UP)
    San Francisco conference 108–115
AIR Force, U.S.
    Women enlarged combat role 60–63
AKRON (Ohio) Beacon-Journal, The (newspaper)
    Tailhook sex-abuse scandal 50
    Tailhook scandal Defense Dept report 57
    Employee sex-harassment Supreme Court ruling 83
    Breast implant moratorium 88
    Gay military ban Clinton compromise 143
    Gay sailor reinstatement 149
    Teenage sex/pregnancy debate 166
    Cincinnati art museum obscenity indictment 190
ALBUQUERQUE (N.M.) Journal (newspaper)
    San Francisco AIDS conference 113
    DC gay rights march 125
    Beers kidnapping, confinement in bunker 163
ALLEN, Woody
    Child custody battle 172–175
AMERICAN Society of Plastic and Reconstructive Surgeons
    FDA breast implant curb 92–93
ANN Arbor (Mich.) News, The (newspaper)
    Thomas sex harassment accusation 13
    DC gay rights march 125

ARGUS-Leader (Sioux Falls, S.D. newspaper)
    Packwood sex harassment accusation 45
    Women's combat duties expansion 62
    San Francisco AIDS conference 112
    Gay military ban debate 137
ARIZONA Republic, The (Phoenix newspaper)
    William Kennedy Smith rape arrest 26
    Colorado gay rights ban reversal 134
    Gay military ban Clinton compromise 146
    NEA obscene art ban debate 179
    Bush arts censorship opposition 183
    NEA grant rejections 186
ARKANSAS Gazette (Little Rock newspaper)
    Hill congressional testimony 22
ARMY, U.S.
    Women armed services debate 60–63
    Gay military ban debate 136–141
    Gay military ban Clinton compromise 142–147
ARTS & Culture
    Michael Jackson sex abuse accusation 170–171
    NEA obscene art ban debate 178–181
    Bush arts censorship opposition 182–185
    NEA grant rejections 186–189
    Cincinnati art museum obscenity indictment 190–193
    Film ratings debate 194–197
    2 Live Crew obscenity acquittal 198–201
    Madonna video, book controversy 202–203
ASHEVILLE (N.C.) Citizen, The (newspaper)
    Gay sailor reinstatement 151
AS Nasty As They Wanna Be (recording)
    2 Live Crew obscenity acquittal 198–201

ASPIN, Les
    Women's combat duties expansion 60–63
ASSOCIATION for Women in Sports Media
    Locker room access debate 94–97
ATLANTA (Ga.) Journal & Constitution, The (newspaper)
    Hill congressional testimony 21
    Women clergy debate 104
    San Francisco AIDS conference 109
    DC gay rights march 122
    Gay military ban debate 138
    Gay military ban Clinton compromise 145
    NEA obscene art ban debate 181
    Bush arts censorship opposition 182
AuCOIN, Rep. Les (D, Ore.)
    Gay rights curb defeat 130–133
AUGUSTA (Ga.) Chronicle and Herald (newspaper)
    William Kennedy Smith rape arrest 28
    FDA breast implant curb 93
    DC gay rights march 126–127

B

BALTIMORE (Md.) Sun, The
    Hill congressional testimony 20
    Tailhook sex-abuse scandal 50
    Women's combat duties expansion 60
    DC gay rights march 123–124
    Gay military ban debate 141
BARRIE, Dennis
    Cincinnati art museum obscenity indictment 190–193
BARRY, William
    William Kennedy Smith rape arrest 26–29
BASEBALL
    Women reporters locker room access debate 94–97
BATTELLE Human Affairs Research Centers
    Male sex survey 116–117
    DC gay rights march 118–127

BEERS, Katie
     Kidnapping, confinement in bunker 162–163
BIRMINGHAM (Ala.) News, The (newspaper)
     Gay military ban Clinton compromise 144
BIRMINGHAM (Ala.) Post-Herald (newspaper)
     San Francisco AIDS conference 114
BLACK, Roy E.
     William Kennedy Smith rape acquittal 30–33
BLACK Americans
     Thomas sex harassment accusation 12–17
     Hill congressional testimony 18–25
     Tyson rape conviction 34–37
BLADE, The (Toledo, Ohio newspaper)
     Hill congressional testimony 21
     Battered women/spouse abuse issues 72
     Employee sex-harassment Supreme Court ruling 79
     Allen/Farrow child custody battle 173
     Cincinnati art museum obscenity indictment 190
     Film ratings debate 196
BLUDWORTH, David
     William Kennedy Smith rape arrest 26–29
BOSTON (Mass.) Globe, The (newspaper)
     Hill congressional testimony 18
     William Kennedy Smith rape arrest 26–29
     Battered women/spouse abuse issues 76
     DC gay rights march 119
     NYC St Patrick's day parade gay ban 128
BOSTON (Mass.) Herald, The (newspaper)
     Battered women/spouse abuse issues 72
     Women sports reporters locker room access debate 94–97
     San Francisco AIDS conference 114
     Gay military ban Clinton compromise 147
BOTTOMS, Kay
     Lesbian child custody denial 154–155
BOTTOMS, Sharon
     Lesbian child custody denial 154–155

BOUCHARD, Benoit
     Canadian breast implant curb 92–93
BOXING
     Tyson rape conviction 34–37
BUCKEY, Peggy McMartin
     California pre-school child abuse trial 158–161
BUCKEY, Raymond
     California pre-school child abuse trial 158–161
BUFFALO (N.Y.) Evening News (newspaper)
     Clinton '92 campaign infidelity charges 41
     Employee sex-harassment Supreme Court ruling 81
     Women sports reporters locker room access debate 97
     Oregon gay rights curb defeat 133
     Beers kidnapping, confinement in bunker 163
     Teenage sex/pregnancy debate 169
     NEA grant rejections 188
     Cincinnati art museum obscenity indictment 193
BUSH, George Herbert Walker (U.S. president, 1989-93; Republican)
     San Francisco AIDS conference 108–115
     Art censorship opposition 182–185

C

CALGARY (Alberta) Herald, The (Canadian newspaper)
     Canada rape shield law narrowing 66
CALIFORNIA
     Manhattan Beach pre-school child abuse trial 158–161
CAMPAIGN for Military Service
     Gay military ban Clinton compromise 142–147
CAMPBELL, Luther
     2 Live Crew obscenity acquittal 198–201
CAMPBELL, Nancy Duff
     Women's combat duties expansion 60–63
CANADA
     Rape shield law narrowing 64–67
     Date rape law introduction 68–69
     FDA breast implant curb 92–93
     Women clergy debate 102–105

CAREY, Rev. George
     Women clergy debate 102–105
CARTOONS
     Tony Auth
          Gay military ban debate 139
     Paul Conrad
          Women clergy debate 104
          Gay sailor reinstatement 151
          California pre-school child abuse trial 160
          NEA grant rejections 188
     Bill Day
          NEA obscene art ban debate 180
     Walt Handelsman
          Breast implant moratorium 90
     Hugh Haynie
          Promotion of women in developing nations 100
     Herblock
          Thomas sex harassment accusation 17
     Lee Judge
          Madonna video, book controversy 203
     Mike Keefe
          Women sports reporters locker room access debate 96
     S. Kelley
          Packwood sex harassment accusation 45
     M.G. Lord
          Sex harassment issues survey 11
          Film ratings debate 196
     Pat Oliphant
          Allen/Farrow child custody battle 175
          2 Live Crew obscenity acquittal 200
     Rogers
          Women's combat duties expansion 62
     Don Wright
          William Kennedy Smith rape arrest 28
          San Francisco AIDS conference 110
CHARLESTON (W. Va.) Gazette (newspaper)
     Thomas sex harassment accusation 17
     Hill congressional testimony 24
     William Kennedy Smith rape acquittal 33
CHARLOTTE (N.C.) Observer, The (newspaper)
     Packwood ouster bid rejection 47
     Employee sex-harassment Supreme Court ruling 84
CHATTANOOGA (Tenn.) Times, The (newspaper)
     Tailhook report 52

Employee sex-harassment Supreme Court ruling 83
DC gay rights march 119–120
Colorado gay rights ban reversal 134
Gay military ban Clinton compromise 146
2 Live Crew obscenity acquittal 199
Madonna video, book controversy 202

CHENEY, Richard B.
Tailhook sex-abuse scandal 48–51

CHICAGO (Ill.) Defender (newspaper)
Child sex abuse survey 164
Teenage sex/pregnancy debate 167

CHICAGO (Ill.) Sun-Times (newspaper)
Hill congressional testimony 24
Breast implant moratorium 90

CHICAGO (Ill.) Tribune (newspaper)
William Kennedy Smith rape acquittal 31
Packwood sex harassment accusation 43
Women's combat duties expansion 62
DC gay rights march 126
Oregon gay rights curb defeat 131
Lesbian child custody denial 155
2 Live Crew obscenity acquittal 199

CHILDREN
Public breast-feeding debate 98–99
DC gay rights march 118–127
Lesbian custody denial 154–155
McMartin abuse trial 158–161
Beers kidnapping, confinement in bunker 162–163
Sex abuse survey 164–165
Teenage sex/pregnancy debate 166–169
Allen/Farrow custody battle 172–175

CHILDREN'S Institute International
California pre-school child abuse trial 158–161

CHILES, Gov. Lawton (D, Fla.)
Public breast-feeding debate 98–99

CHRISTIAN Action Network
DC gay rights march 118–127

CHRISTIAN Science Monitor (newspaper)
Sex harassment issues survey 10
Tailhook report 54
2 Live Crew obscenity acquittal 201

CHRONICLE-Herald, The (Halifax, Canada newspaper)
Canada date rape law introduction 69

CHURCH of England
Women clergy debate 102–105

CINCINNATI (Ohio) Post, The (newspaper)
Women sports reporters locker room access debate 94

CLARION-Ledger, The/Jackson Daily News (Miss. newspaper)
California pre-school child abuse trial 161

CLEVELAND (Ohio) Plain Dealer, The (newspaper)
Packwood sex harassment accusation 44
Tailhook sex-abuse scandal 51
Tailhook scandal Defense Dept report 57
Battered women/spouse abuse issues 70
Breast implant moratorium 86
Women sports reporters locker room access debate 94
Gay military ban Clinton compromise 144
Gay sailor reinstatement 149
NEA obscene art ban debate 179
Cincinnati art museum obscenity indictment 191

CLINTON, Bill (William Jefferson) (U.S. president, 1993- ; Democrat)
'92 campaign infidelity charges 38–41
Tailhook scandal Defense Dept report 56–59
DC gay rights march 118–127
Oregon gay rights curb defeat 130–133
Gay military ban compromise 142–147
Gay sailor reinstatement 148–153

CLINTON, Hillary Rodham
Clinton '92 campaign infidelity charges 38–41

COLORADO
Gay rights curb voter approval 130–133
Gay rights ban legal reversal 134–135

COMMERCIAL Appeal, The (Memphis, Tenn. newspaper)
NEA obscene art ban debate 179

CONGRESS, U.S.
Thomas sex harassment accusation 12–17
Hill sex harassment testimony 18–25

Packwood sex harassment accusation 42–45
Packwood ouster bid rejection 46–47
Gay military ban Clinton compromise 142–147
NEA obscene art ban debate 178–181
Bush arts censorship opposition 182–185

CONTEMPORARY Arts Center (Cincinnati, Ohio)
Indictment on obscenity charges 190–193

CRIME—See also RAPE; SEXUAL Harassment
Battered women/spouse abuse issues 70–77
California pre-school child abuse trial 158–161
Beers kidnapping, confinement in bunker 162–163
Child sex abuse survey 164–165
2 Live Crew obscenity acquittal 198–201

D

DAILY Gazette, The (Schenectady, N.Y. newspaper)
Battered women/spouse abuse issues 74
Gay sailor reinstatement 148

DAILY News (New York City newspaper)
Thomas sex harassment accusation 13
NEA grant rejections 187

DAILY Oklahoman, The (Oklahoma City newspaper)
Hill congressional testimony 20
Male sex survey 117
Gay military ban debate 139
Gay military ban Clinton compromise 143

DALLAS (Tex.) Morning News, The (newspaper)
Women sports reporters locker room access debate 95
Film ratings debate 194

DALLAS (Tex.) Times Herald, The newspaper
Hill congressional testimony 23
Teenage sex/pregnancy debate 169

DANFORTH, Sen. John C. (R, Mo.)
Thomas sex harassment accusation 12–17

206

DAVIS 6th, Rear Adm. George W.
Tailhook report 52–55
DAYTON (Ohio) Daily News (newspaper)
Rape issues survey 4
William Kennedy Smith rape acquittal 32
Allen/Farrow child custody battle 175
DEFENSE, U.S. Department of
Tailhook scandal final report 56–59
DEFENSE & Armed Forces—See also specific branch (e.g., NAVY, U.S.)
Women's combat duties expansion 60–63
Gay military ban debate 136–141
Gay military ban Clinton compromise 142–147
DENVER (Colo.) Post, The (newspaper)
Rape issues survey 7
Thomas sex harassment accusation 14–15
Hill congressional testimony 21
Tyson rape conviction 36
Tailhook scandal Defense Dept report 58
Oregon gay rights curb defeat 133
Colorado gay rights ban reversal 135
Lesbian child custody denial 154
Allen/Farrow child custody battle 174
Film ratings debate 196
DESERET News (Salt Lake City, Utah newspaper)
Packwood sex harassment accusation 44
Battered women/spouse abuse issues 77
Women sports reporters locker room access debate 97
California pre-school child abuse trial 160
DES Moines (Iowa) Register, The (newspaper)
Sex harassment issues survey 9, 11
Clinton '92 campaign infidelity charges 41
Packwood sex harassment accusation 42
Tailhook sex-abuse scandal 49
Battered women/spouse abuse issues 70
Public breast-feeding debate 98
Beers kidnapping, confinement in bunker 162
2 Live Crew obscenity acquittal 198

DETROIT (Mich.) Free Press (newspaper)
Tailhook report 54
DETROIT (Mich.) News (newspaper)
Lesbian child custody denial 154
DIARIO Las Americas (Miami, Fla. newspaper)
Hill congressional testimony 25
DINKINS, David N. (New York City mayor, 1990-94)
St Patrick's day parade gay ban 128–129
DOUTSOU, Tyler
Lesbian child custody denial 154–155
DURENBERGER, Sen. Dave (R, Minn.)
Packwood sex harassment accusation 42–45

E

EDMONTON (Alberta) Journal (Canadian newspaper)
Canada rape shield law narrowing 67
EDUCATION
Sex harassment issues survey 8–11
Teenage sex/pregnancy debate 166–169
EDUCATION, U.S. Department of
Thomas sex harassment accusation 12–17
EEOC—See EQUAL Employment Opportunity Commission
ELLIS, Capt. Larry H.
Gay military ban debate 136–141
ELLISON v. Brady (1991)
Sex harassment issues survey 8–11
EPISCOPAL Church, Protestant
Women clergy debate 102–105
EQUAL Employment Opportunity Commission (EEOC)
Sex harassment issues survey 8–11
Thomas sex harassment accusation 12–17
Hill congressional testimony 18–25
EROTICA (recording)
Madonna video, book controversy 202–203
ESPOSITO, John
Beers kidnapping, confinement in bunker 162–163

EUROPEAN Community (EC)
San Francisco AIDS conference 108–115
EVENING Gazette, The (Worcester, Mass. newspaper)
William Kennedy Smith rape acquittal 31
Packwood ouster bid rejection 47
Battered women/spouse abuse issues 76
Women sports reporters locker room access debate 96
San Francisco AIDS conference 108
Lesbian child custody denial 155
California pre-school child abuse trial 161
EVENING Telegram, The (St. John's, Canada newspaper)
Canada date rape law introduction 69

F

FARROW, Mia
Child custody battle 172–175
FAUCI, Anthony S.
San Francisco AIDS conference 108–115
FBI—See FEDERAL Bureau of Investigation
FDA—See FOOD and Drug Administration
FEDERAL Bureau of Investigation (FBI)
Rape issues survey 4–7
Thomas sex harassment accusation 12–17
FILMS—See ARTS & CULTURE
FINLEY, Karen
NEA grant rejections 186–189
FLECK, John
NEA grant rejections 186–189
FLORIDA
William Kennedy Smith rape arrest, acquittal 26–33
Public breast-feeding debate 98–99
Tampa gay rights curb vote 130–133
2 Live Crew obscenity acquittal 198–201
FLOWERS, Gennifer
Clinton '92 campaign infidelity charges 38–41
FLYNT, Larry
Cincinnati art museum obscenity indictment 190–193

FOOD and Drug Administration (FDA)
  Breast implant moratorium 86–91
  Breast implant curb 92–93
FOOTBALL
  Women reporters locker room access debate 94–97
FORT Worth (Tex.) Star-Telegram (newspaper)
  Thomas sex harassment accusation 13
  Hill congressional testimony 19
  William Kennedy Smith rape acquittal 30
  Packwood sex harassment accusation 43
  Employee sex-harassment Supreme Court ruling 80
  San Francisco AIDS conference 113
  Teenage sex/pregnancy debate 168
  Bush arts censorship opposition 184
FOSTER, Virginia
  Tyson rape conviction 34–37
FRANK, Rep. Barney (D, Mass.)
  DC gay rights march 118–127
  Gay military ban Clinton compromise 142–147
FROHNMAYER, John E.
  Bush arts censorship opposition 182–185
  NEA grant rejections 186–189
FULLER, Vincent T.
  Tyson rape conviction 34–37

G

GARRETT 3rd, H. Lawrence
  Tailhook sex-abuse scandal 48–51
  Tailhook report 52–55
GARRISON, J. Gregory
  Tyson rape conviction 34–37
GARY (Ind.) Post-Tribune (newspaper)
  Clinton '92 campaign infidelity charges 40
GATES Jr., Henry Louis
  2 Live Crew obscenity acquittal 198–201
GAYME, Nigel
  Canada rape shield law narrowing 64–67
GAZETTE, The (Cedar Rapids, Iowa newspaper)
  Public breast-feeding debate 99

Allen/Farrow child custody battle 175
Bush arts censorship opposition 185
GIFFORD, Judge Patricia J.
  Tyson rape conviction 34–37
GLOBE (tabloid)
  William Kennedy Smith rape arrest 26–29
GLOBE and Mail, The (Toronto, Canada newspaper)
  William Kennedy Smith rape acquittal 31
  Canada rape shield law narrowing 64
GORDON, Rear Adm. John E.
  Tailhook report 52–55
GREAT Britain & Northern Ireland, United Kingdom of
  Women clergy debate 102–105
GUTTMACHER Institute, Alan
  Male sex survey 116–117
  DC gay rights march 118–127

H

HARDY, Charles
  Employee sex-harassment Supreme Court ruling 78–85
HARRIS, Teresa
  Employee sex-harassment Supreme Court ruling 78–85
HARRIS v. Forklift Inc. (1993)
  Employee sex-harassment Supreme Court ruling 78–85
HARTFORD (Conn.) Courant, The (newspaper)
  William Kennedy Smith rape acquittal 32
  Tyson rape conviction 36
  Clinton '92 campaign infidelity charges 40
  Packwood sex harassment accusation 44
  Employee sex-harassment Supreme Court ruling 79
  Public breast-feeding debate 98
  Promotion of women in developing nations 100
  Male sex survey 117
  NYC St Patrick's day parade gay ban 128
  Gay sailor reinstatement 153
  Allen/Farrow child custody battle 173
  NEA grant rejections 189
  Cincinnati art museum obscenity indictment 191

2 Live Crew obscenity acquittal 200
HATCH, Sen. Orrin G. (R, Utah)
  Hill congressional testimony 18–25
HATTER Jr., Judge Terry J.
  Gay sailor reinstatement 148–153
HEALTH & Human Services, U.S. Department of (HHS)
  San Francisco AIDS conference 108–115
HELMS, Sen. Jesse A. (R, N.C.)
  San Francisco AIDS conference 108–115
  NEA obscene art ban debate 178–181
  Bush arts censorship opposition 182–185
HERALD News (Fall River, Mass. newspaper)
  Thomas sex harassment accusation 14
  William Kennedy Smith rape acquittal 33
  Tyson rape conviction 35
  Clinton '92 campaign infidelity charges 39
  Oregon gay rights curb defeat 130
  Child sex abuse survey 164
HILL, Anita F.
  Thomas sex harassment accusation 12–17
  Congressional testimony 18–25
HILL, Gen. Clarence A. Mark (ret.)
  Women's combat duties expansion 60–63
HOMOSEXUALITY
  San Francisco AIDS conference 108–115
  Male sex survey 116–117
  DC rights march 118–127
  NYC St Patrick's day parade ban 128–129
  Colorado rights curb voter approval/Oregon defeat 130–133
  Colorado rights ban reversal 134–135
  Military ban debate 136–141
  Clinton military ban compromise 142–147
  Gay sailor reinstatement 148–153
  Lesbian child custody denial 154–155
  Bush arts censorship opposition 182–185
  NEA grant rejections 186–189
HONOLULU (Hawaii) Advertiser, The (newspaper)
  Sex harassment issues survey 9
  DC gay rights march 120

HOUSTON (Tex.) Post, The (newspaper)
  Hill congressional testimony 23
  Tyson rape conviction 35
  Clinton '92 campaign infidelity charges 39
  San Francisco AIDS conference 115
  Madonna video, book controversy 202
HUGHES, Holly
  NEA grant rejections 186–189
HUTCHINSON (Kan.) News, The (newspaper)
  Thomas sex harassment accusation 13
  Tyson rape conviction 35
  Clinton '92 campaign infidelity charges 40
  Packwood sex harassment accusation 42
  Packwood ouster bid rejection 47
  Tailhook sex-abuse scandal 51
  Promotion of women in developing nations 100
  Gay military ban debate 136
  Michael Jackson sex abuse accusation 171
  Allen/Farrow child custody battle 172
  Bush arts censorship opposition 183
  NEA grant rejections 186
  Film ratings debate 194

I

ILGO—*See IRISH Lesbian and Gay Organization*
IMMIGRATION and Naturalization Service (INS)
  San Francisco AIDS conference 108–115
INDIA, Republic of
  Women clergy debate 102–105
INDIANA
  Tyson rape conviction 34–37
INDIANAPOLIS (Ind.) News, The (newspaper)
  Rape issues survey 6–7
  Tailhook scandal Defense Dept report 58
  Michael Jackson sex abuse accusation 171
  Bush arts censorship opposition 184
INDIANAPOLIS (Ind.) Star, The (newspaper)
  Sex harassment issues survey 9

California pre-school child abuse trial 161
  Teenage sex/pregnancy debate 168
  Bush arts censorship opposition 185
INOUYE, Sen. Daniel K. (D, Hawaii)
  Packwood sex harassment accusation 42–45
INS—*See IMMIGRATION & Naturalization Service*
INTERIOR, U.S. Department of the
  NEA obscene art ban debate 178–181
INTERNAL Revenue Service (IRS)
  Sex harassment issues survey 8–11
IRISH Lesbian and Gay Organization (ILGO)
  NYC St Patrick's day parade ban 128–129
IRS—*See INTERNAL Revenue Service*

J

JACKSON, Michael
  Sex abuse accusation 170–171
JACKSON, Rev. Jesse L.
  DC gay rights march 118–127
JUSTIFY My Love (music video)
  Madonna controversy 202–203

K

KANSAS City (Mo.) Star, The (newspaper)
  Clinton '92 campaign infidelity charges 38
  Tailhook report 55
  Battered women/spouse abuse issues 72
  Employee sex-harassment Supreme Court ruling 84
  Women clergy debate 102
  San Francisco AIDS conference 111
  Beers kidnapping, confinement in bunker 162
  Michael Jackson sex abuse accusation 170
KELLY, Sharon Pratt (Washington, D.C. mayor, 1991-)
  Gay rights march 118–127

KENNEDY, Sen. Edward M. (D, Mass.)
  Nephew rape arrest, acquittal 26–33
KENYA, Republic of
  Women clergy debate 102–105
KESSLER, Dr. David A.
  Breast implant moratorium 86–91
KINSEY, Alfred (1894-1956)
  Male sex survey 116–117
KRAMER, Larry
  DC gay rights march 118–127

L

LABOR & Employment
  Employee sex-harassment Supreme Court ruling 78–85
  Oregon gay rights curb defeat 130–133
LASCH, Moira K.
  William Kennedy Smith rape acquittal 30–33
LAS Vegas (Nev.) Review-Journal (newspaper)
  Battered women/spouse abuse issues 71
  Breast implant moratorium 90
  San Francisco AIDS conference 110
  DC gay rights march 120
  NEA grant rejections 187
LAS Vegas (Nev.) Sun (newspaper)
  Michael Jackson sex abuse accusation 171
LEADER Post, The (Regina, Canada newspaper)
  Canada rape shield law narrowing 67
LESBIANS—*See HOMOSEXUALITY*
LEVAL, Judge Pierre N.
  NYC St Patrick's day parade gay ban 128–129
LEXINGTON (Ky.) Herald-Leader (newspaper)
  Rape issues survey 5
  Battered women/spouse abuse issues 76
  Employee sex-harassment Supreme Court ruling 78
  Bush arts censorship opposition 182
  Cincinnati art museum obscenity indictment 193

LINCOLN (Neb.) Journal (newspaper)
  Thomas sex harassment accusation 16
  Tyson rape conviction 36
  Battered women/spouse abuse issues 75
LINCOLN (Neb.) Star, The (newspaper)
  Battered women/spouse abuse issues 72
  Public breast-feeding debate 99
  San Francisco AIDS conference 111
  Gay military ban Clinton compromise 146
  Gay sailor reinstatement 151
LONDON (Ontario) Free Press, The (Canadian newspaper)
  Canada rape shield law narrowing 66
  Women clergy debate 103
LOS Angeles (Calif.) Times (newspaper)
  California pre-school child abuse trial 160
  Cincinnati art museum obscenity indictment 193
  Film ratings debate 197
LOUISVILLE (Ky.) Courier-Journal (newspaper)
  Hill congressional testimony 25
  William Kennedy Smith rape acquittal 32
  Tyson rape conviction 36
  Battered women/spouse abuse issues 77
  Women sports reporters locker room access debate 95
  Cincinnati art museum obscenity indictment 192
LUPO, Judge Mary E.
  William Kennedy Smith rape acquittal 30–33

M

MADONNA (Madonna Louise Ciccone)
  Pop star controversy 202–203
MAPPLETHORPE, Robert (1946-89)
  NEA obscene art ban debate 178–181
  Bush arts censorship opposition 182–185
  Cincinnati art museum obscenity indictment 190–193

MARINE Corps, U.S.—See DEFENSE & Armed Forces
McLACHLIN, Madam Justice Beverly
  Canada rape shield law narrowing 64–67
McMARTIN Pre-School (Manhattan Beach, Calif.) (defunct)
  Child abuse trial 158–161
McPEAK, Gen. Merrill A.
  Women's combat duties expansion 60–63
MEDIA—See PRESS & Broadcasting
MEDICINE & Health
  Breast implant moratorium 86–91
  FDA breast implant curb 92–93
  San Francisco AIDS conference 108–115
  Teenage sex/pregnancy debate 166–169
MEINHOLD, Keith
  Reinstatement in Navy 148–153
MEISEL, Stephen
  Madonna video, book controversy 202–203
MERCER, Anne
  William Kennedy Smith rape acquittal 30–33
MIAMI (Fla.) Herald, The (newspaper)
  Tailhook report 53
  Women's combat duties expansion 61
  Employee sex-harassment Supreme Court ruling 80
  San Francisco AIDS conference 115
  Gay sailor reinstatement 150
  Film ratings debate 195
MILLER, Tim
  NEA grant rejections 186–189
MILWAUKEE (Wis.) Sentinel (newspaper)
  William Kennedy Smith rape arrest 29
  Women clergy debate 103
  San Francisco AIDS conference 115
  California pre-school child abuse trial 159
  Teenage sex/pregnancy debate 168
MINNEAPOLIS (Minn.) Star and Tribune (newspaper)
  Sex harassment issues survey 11
  Women clergy debate 105
MOTION Picture Association of America (MPAA)
  Film ratings debate 194–197

MOVIES—See ARTS & CULTURE
MOWATT, Zeke
  Women sports reporters locker room access debate 94–97
MPAA—See MOTION Picture Association of America
MUSIC—See ARTS & Culture

N

NATIONAL Association of Women and the Law
  Canada rape shield law narrowing 64–67
NATIONAL Coalition Against Pornography
  Cincinnati art museum obscenity indictment 190–193
NATIONAL Conference of Catholic Bishops
  Women clergy debate 102–105
NATIONAL Council on the Arts
  NEA grant rejections 186–189
NATIONAL Endowment for the Arts (NEA)
  Obscene art ban debate 178–181
  Grant rejections 186–189
  Cincinnati art museum obscenity indictment 190–193
NATIONAL Football League (NFL)
  Women in locker rooms debate 94–97
NATIONAL Gay & Lesbian Task Force
  Oregon Gay rights curb defeat 130–133
NATIONAL Institute of Child Health and Human Development
  DC gay rights march 118–127
NATIONAL Women's Law Center
  Women's combat duties expansion 60–63
NAVY, U.S.
  Tailhook sex-abuse scandal 48–51
  Tailhook preliminary/final reports 52–59
  Women's combat duties expansion 60–63
  Gay sailor reinstatement 148–153
NEA—See NATIONAL Endowment for the Arts
NEWSDAY (New York City newspaper)
  William Kennedy Smith rape arrest 28
  Employee sex-harassment Supreme Court ruling 82

Breast implant moratorium 88
NYC St Patrick's day parade gay ban 129
Gay sailor reinstatement 150
Beers kidnapping, confinement in bunker 163
Film ratings debate 197

NEWS Journal, The (Wilmington, Del. newspaper)
San Francisco AIDS conference 112
Gay military ban debate 141

NEW York Times, The (newspaper)
William Kennedy Smith rape arrest 26–29
Employee sex-harassment Supreme Court ruling 85
San Francisco AIDS conference 114
DC gay rights march 124
NYC St Patrick's day parade gay ban 129
Gay military ban Clinton compromise 145
Teenage sex/pregnancy debate 167

NEW Zealand, Dominion of
Women clergy debate 102–105

NFL—See NATIONAL Football League

NICHOLS, Larry
Clinton '92 campaign infidelity charges 38–41

NUNN, Sen. Sam (D, Ga.)
Gay military ban Clinton compromise 142–147

O

OBSCENITY—See PORNOGRAPHY

O'KEEFE, Sean C.
Tailhook report 52–55

OLSON, Lisa
Women sports reporters locker room access debate 94–97

OMAHA (Neb.) World-Herald (newspaper)
San Francisco AIDS conference 109

ORANGE County Register, The (Santa Ana, Calif. newspaper)
Teenage sex/pregnancy debate 169

OREGON
Gay rights curb defeat 130–133

OREGONIAN, The (Portland newspaper)
William Kennedy Smith rape acquittal 33
Tailhook report 53
Battered women/spouse abuse issues 73–74
Oregon gay rights curb defeat 132
Gay military ban Clinton compromise 147
Gay sailor reinstatement 148
Teenage sex/pregnancy debate 167

P

PACKWOOD, Sen. Bob (R, Ore.)
Sex harassment accusation 42–45
Ouster bid rejection 46–47

PARSONS Jr., Judge Duford M.
Lesbian child custody denial 154–155

PENNSYLVANIA, University of (Philadelphia)
NEA obscene art ban debate 178–181

PEPSICO Inc.
Michael Jackson sex abuse accusation 170–171

PERKINS, Will
Colorado gay rights ban reversal 134–135

PHILADELPHIA (Pa.) Inquirer, The (newspaper)
Hill congressional testimony 23
Clinton '92 campaign infidelity charges 39
Employee sex-harassment Supreme Court ruling 79
DC gay rights march 123
Oregon gay rights curb defeat 130
Gay military ban debate 137
Allen/Farrow child custody battle 173
NEA obscene art ban debate 181
NEA grant rejections 189
Cincinnati art museum obscenity indictment 191
2 Live Crew obscenity acquittal 199

PHOENIX (Ariz.) Gazette, The (newspaper)
William Kennedy Smith rape arrest 29
Tailhook sex-abuse scandal 49
Breast implant moratorium 91
San Francisco AIDS conference 111
2 Live Crew obscenity acquittal 200

PHOTOGRAPHY—See ARTS & CULTURE

PITTSBURGH (Pa.) Post-Gazette (newspaper)
Breast implant moratorium 87

PITTSBURGH (Pa.) Press, The (newspaper)
Rape issues survey 5

PLANNED Parenthood Federation of America
San Francisco AIDS conference 108–115

POLITICS
Thomas sex harassment accusation 12–17
Hill congressional testimony 18–25
Clinton '92 campaign infidelity charges 38–41
Packwood sex harassment accusation 42–45
Packwood ouster bid rejection 46–47
NYC St Patrick's day parade gay ban 128–129
Oregon gay rights curb defeat 130–133
NEA obscene art ban debate 178–181
Bush arts censorship opposition 182–185
NEA grant rejections 186–189
Cincinnati art museum obscenity indictment 190–193
2 Live Crew obscenity acquittal 198–201

PORNOGRAPHY
NEA obscene art ban debate 178–181
Bush arts censorship opposition 182–185
NEA grant rejections 186–189
Cincinnati art museum indictment 190–193
Film ratings debate 194–197

PORTLAND (Me.) Press-Herald (newspaper)
Tailhook report 55
Employee sex-harassment Supreme Court ruling 85
Breast implant moratorium 89
Oregon gay rights curb defeat 133

POWELL, Gen. Colin L.
Gay military ban Clinton compromise 142–147

PRESS & Broadcasting
Clinton '92 campaign infidelity charges 38–41
Women sports reporters locker room access debate 94–97

PREVIN, Soon-Yi
   Allen/Farrow child custody battle 172–175
PROVIDENCE (R.I.) Journal, The (newspaper)
   Women's combat duties expansion 61
   Employee sex-harassment Supreme Court ruling 81
   DC gay rights march 124

R

RACE & Racism
   2 Live Crew obscenity acquittal 198–201
RADIO—See PRESS & Broadcasting
RALEIGH (N.C.) News & Observer (newspaper)
   Promotion of women in developing nations 100
RAPE
   Survey of issues 4–7
   William Kennedy Smith arrest, acquittal 26–33
   Canada shield law narrowing 64–67
   Canada date rape law introduction 68–69
RAPID City (S.D.) Journal (newspaper)
   Gay military ban debate 139
RAP Music—See ARTS & Culture
RECORD, The (Hackensack, N.J. newspaper)
   Sex harassment issues survey 10
   Tyson rape conviction 37
   Women's combat duties expansion 61
   Employee sex-harassment Supreme Court ruling 82
   Breast implant moratorium 88, 91
   Child sex abuse survey 165
   2 Live Crew obscenity acquittal 198
RED Cross, International
   San Francisco AIDS conference 108–115
REGISTER-Guard, The (Eugene, Ore. newspaper)
   Women's combat duties expansion 62
   Employee sex-harassment Supreme Court ruling 85
   DC gay rights march 118
   Oregon gay rights curb defeat 131
   California pre-school child abuse trial 158
   NEA obscene art ban debate 180
   Cincinnati art museum obscenity indictment 192
RELIGION
   Women clergy debate 102–105
   Male sex survey 116–117
   NEA obscene art ban debate 178–181
RICHMOND (Va.) News-Leader, The (newspaper)
   Sex harassment issues survey 10
   Film ratings debate 197
   Madonna video, book controversy 202
RICHMOND (Va.) Times-Dispatch (newspaper)
   William Kennedy Smith rape arrest 29
   Battered women/spouse abuse issues 71
   DC gay rights march 125
   Beers kidnapping, confinement in bunker 163
ROBINSON v. Jacksonville Shipyards (1991)
   Sex harassment issues survey 8–11
ROCKFORD (Ill.) Register Star (newspaper)
   Sex harassment issues survey 8
   Tyson rape conviction 34
   Tailhook report 53
   DC gay rights march 127
   Gay military ban debate 138
   Madonna video, book controversy 203
ROMAN Catholic Church
   Women clergy debate 102–105
   NYC St Patrick's day parade gay ban 128–129
ROSS, Mark
   2 Live Crew obscenity acquittal 198–201

S

SACRAMENTO (Calif.) Bee, The (newspaper)
   Tailhook sex-abuse scandal 48
   Tailhook scandal Defense Dept report 56
   California pre-school child abuse trial 159
   Bush arts censorship opposition 184
SAGINAW (Mich.) News, The (newspaper)
   Hill congressional testimony 22
   DC gay rights march 123
   Gay military ban debate 141
St. LOUIS (Mo.) Post-Dispatch (newspaper)
   Gay sailor reinstatement 152
   Film ratings debate 196
St. LOUIS (Mo.) Review (newspaper)
   Women clergy debate 104
   Allen/Farrow child custody battle 174
St. PAUL (Minn.) Pioneer Press & Dispatch (newspaper)
   Thomas sex harassment accusation 16
   Women sports reporters locker room access debate 96
   Promotion of women in developing nations 100
St. PETERSBURG (Fla.) Times (newspaper)
   Tailhook sex-abuse scandal 49
   Tailhook scandal Defense Dept report 57
   Battered women/spouse abuse issues 77
   Breast implant moratorium 91
   Public breast-feeding debate 98
   San Francisco AIDS conference 112
   Gay military ban Clinton compromise 142
   Cincinnati art museum obscenity indictment 192
   2 Live Crew obscenity acquittal 199
SALT Lake (Utah) Tribune, The (newspaper)
   William Kennedy Smith rape arrest 27
   Packwood sex harassment accusation 43
   Tailhook scandal Defense Dept report 59
   Women clergy debate 105
   DC gay rights march 119, 127
   California pre-school child abuse trial 158
SAN Diego (Calif.) Union-Tribune, The (newspaper)
   Tailhook sex-abuse scandal 51
   Tailhook report 54
   Breast implant moratorium 89
SAN Francisco (Calif.) Chronicle (newspaper)
   Rape issues survey 7
   Hill congressional testimony 25
   Tyson rape conviction 37
   Women's combat duties expansion 62
   Canada rape shield law narrowing 66

Employee sex-harassment
Supreme Court ruling 82
DC gay rights march 126
Colorado gay rights ban reversal 135
Gay military ban Clinton compromise 143
Film ratings debate 197
SASKATOON (Saskatchewan) Star-Phoenix (Canadian newspaper)
Canada rape shield law narrowing 65
Canada date rape law introduction 68
SCHROEDER, Rep. Patricia (D, Colo.)
Women's combat duties expansion 60–63
SEABOYER, Steven
Canada rape shield law narrowing 64–67
SEATTLE (Wash.) Times, The (newspaper)
Hill congressional testimony 24
Employee sex-harassment Supreme Court ruling 83
Breast implant moratorium 90
Oregon gay rights curb defeat 132
Gay military ban debate 137, 140
Gay sailor reinstatement 153
Allen/Farrow child custody battle 174
Bush arts censorship opposition 185
NEA grant rejections 187
Madonna video, book controversy 203
SERRANO, Andres
Bush arts censorship opposition 182–185
SEX (book)
Madonna controversy 202–203
SEX & Sexuality—*See also* CHILDREN; HOMOSEXUALITY; WOMEN
Male behavior survey 116–117
SEXUAL Harassment
Survey of issues 8–11
Thomas accusation 12–17
Hill congressional testimony 18–25
Packwood accusation 42–45
Packwood ouster bid rejection 46–47
Navy Tailhook scandal 48–51
Tailhook preliminary/final reports 52–59
SHELDON, Rev. Lou
Male sex survey 116–117
SMITH, William Kennedy
Rape arrest, acquittal 26–33

Canada date rape law introduction 68–69
SOUTHEASTERN Center for Contemporary Art (Winston-Salem, N.C.)
NEA obscene art ban debate 178–181
SPOKESMAN-Review, The (Spokane, Wash. newspaper)
Thomas sex harassment accusation 16
Tyson rape conviction 37
Clinton '92 campaign infidelity charges 41
Tailhook report 55
Women clergy debate 103
San Francisco AIDS conference 109
Gay military ban Clinton compromise 145
Gay sailor reinstatement 149
Lesbian child custody denial 155
SPORTS—*See also specific sport (e.g., BOXING)*
Women reporters locker room access debate 94–97
STAR (tabloid)
Clinton '92 campaign infidelity charges 38–41
STAR-Ledger, The (Newark, N.J. newspaper)
Thomas sex harassment accusation 12
Male sex survey 116
STATE, The (Columbia, S.C. newspaper)
Tailhook scandal Defense Dept report 58
Employee sex-harassment Supreme Court ruling 80
Breast implant moratorium 87
DC gay rights march 122
Gay sailor reinstatement 153
Film ratings debate 195
STODDARD, Thomas B.
Gay military ban Clinton compromise 142–147
SULLIVAN, Dr. Louis W.
San Francisco AIDS conference 108–115
SUN, The (Vancouver, Canada newspaper)
Canada rape shield law narrowing 65
SUPREME Court, U.S.
Sex harassment issues survey 8–11
Thomas sex harassment accusation 12–17
Employee sex-harassment ruling 78–85

NEA obscene art ban debate 178–181
SYRACUSE (N.Y.) Herald-Journal (newspaper)
Rape issues survey 4
Thomas sex harassment accusation 15
Tailhook scandal Defense Dept report 59
Breast implant moratorium 87
Oregon gay rights curb defeat 131
Gay military ban Clinton compromise 144

T

TAGLIABUE, Paul
Women sports reporters locker room access debate 94–97
TAILHOOK Association
Sex-abuse scandal 48–51
Scandal preliminary/final reports 52–59
TAMPA, Florida
Gay rights curb vote 130–133
TAMPA (Fla.) Tribune, The (newspaper)
Rape issues survey 5–6
Tyson rape conviction 35
Child sex abuse survey 165
Allen/Farrow child custody battle 173
TEENAGERS—*See* CHILDREN
TELEVISION—*See* PRESS & *Broadcasting*
TENNESSEAN, The (Nashville newspaper)
Thomas sex harassment accusation 15
Hill congressional testimony 19
Tailhook scandal Defense Dept report 59
Employee sex-harassment Supreme Court ruling 84
Breast implant moratorium 86
DC gay rights march 124
Gay military ban debate 140
Film ratings debate 195
2 Live Crew obscenity acquittal 201
Madonna video, book controversy 203
THIRD World
Promotion of women in agriculture 100
THOMAS, Clarence (U.S. Supreme Court justice, 1991-)
Sex harassment issues survey 8–11

Sex harassment accusation 12–17
Hill congressional testimony 18–25
THORNE, Lt. Tracy
Gay military ban debate 136–141
TIMES-Colonist (Victoria, Canada newspaper)
Canada rape shield law narrowing 65
TIMES-Picayune, The (New Orleans, La. newspaper)
Women clergy debate 105
TOM, Denise
Women sports reporters locker room access debate 94–97
TRADITIONAL Values Coalition
Male sex survey 116–117
TULSA (Okla.) World (newspaper)
Thomas sex harassment accusation 17
Battered women/spouse abuse issues 74
FDA breast implant curb 93
Colorado gay rights ban reversal 135
Gay sailor reinstatement 152
NEA grant rejections 188
TYSON, Mike
Rape conviction 34–37

U

UNION Leader, The (Manchester, N.H. newspaper)
Male sex survey 117
DC gay rights march 121
Gay military ban debate 140
Michael Jackson sex abuse accusation 171
USA Today (Washington, D.C. newspaper)
San Francisco AIDS conference 113
DC gay rights march 122

V

VALENTI, Jack
Film ratings debate 194–197

Vander SCHAAF, Gen. Derek J.
Tailhook scandal Defense Dept report 56–59
VIRGINIAN-Pilot, The (Norfolk newspaper)
Thomas sex harassment accusation 14
Packwood ouster bid rejection 46
Battered women/spouse abuse issues 71, 75
Gay sailor reinstatement 150

W

WALL Street Journal, The (newspaper)
Battered women/spouse abuse issues 73
WASHINGTON, Desiree
Tyson rape conviction 34–37
WASHINGTON Post, The (newspaper)
William Kennedy Smith rape acquittal 33
Tyson rape conviction 37
Clinton '92 campaign infidelity charges 38–41
Packwood ouster bid rejection 46
Breast implant moratorium 89
FDA breast implant curb 93
DC gay rights march 121
Gay military ban debate 136
California pre-school child abuse trial 159
NEA obscene art ban debate 178, 181
Bush arts censorship opposition 183
2 Live Crew obscenity acquittal 201
WASHINGTON Times, The (newspaper)
William Kennedy Smith rape arrest 27
DC gay rights march 121
Gay military ban debate 138
Allen/Farrow child custody battle 172
WEISS, Ted (1927-92) (U.S. representative from N.Y., 1977-92; Democrat)
FDA breast implant curb 92–93

WICHITA (Kan.) Eagle-Beacon, The (newspaper)
Hill congressional testimony 19
Tailhook sex-abuse scandal 50
Women's combat duties expansion 62
Battered women/spouse abuse issues 75
Employee sex-harassment Supreme Court ruling 81
Gay military ban Clinton compromise 147
Teenage sex/pregnancy debate 166
Michael Jackson sex abuse accusation 170
WILLIAMS Jr., Rear Adm. Duvall M.
Tailhook report 52–55
WINNIPEG (Manitoba) Free Press (Canadian newspaper)
Canada rape shield law narrowing 64
Canada date rape law introduction 68
FDA breast implant curb 92
WISCONSIN State Journal (Madison newspaper)
Hill congressional testimony 20
Gay sailor reinstatement 152
WOMEN—See also HOMOSEXUALITY; RAPE; SEXUAL Harassment
Combat duties expansion 60–63
Battering, spouse abuse issues 70–77
Breast implant moratorium 86–91
FDA breast implant curb 92–93
Sports reporters locker room access debate 94–97
Public breast-feeding debate 98–9
Promotion of role in developing nations 100–101
WONGWON, Christopher
2 Live Crew obscenity acquittal 198–201
WYCHE, Sam
Women sports reporters locker room access debate 94–97